Length of Stay by Operation

Western Region, 2004

ISBN: 1-57372-338-X
ISSN: 0895-9862

Statistics reported in the 2004 edition are drawn from individual patient discharge records for the time period October 1, 2002, through September 30, 2003. This volume is one of the books in the *Length of Stay by Diagnosis and Operation* series:

Length of Stay by Diagnosis and Operation, United States
ISSN 0895-9824

Length of Stay by Diagnosis and Operation, Northeastern Region
ISSN 0895-9838

Length of Stay by Diagnosis and Operation, North Central Region
ISSN 0895-9846

Length of Stay by Diagnosis and Operation, Southern Region
ISSN 0895-9854

Length of Stay by Diagnosis and Operation, Western Region
ISSN 0895-9862

Pediatric Length of Stay by Diagnosis and Operation, United States
ISSN 0891-1223

Solucient, LLC
1007 Church Street, Suite 700
Evanston, Illinois 60201
(800) 568-3282

Length of Stay by Diagnosis and Operation, Western Region, 2004

Publications Return Policy
Printed books may be returned, in good condition, for a full refund (minus a $50 handling fee) within 10 **business** days of receipt. Electronic files (i.e., CDs, tapes, diskettes) are not refundable but are guaranteed against physical defects. If your publication arrives damaged, or you need to return it for another reason, please call Solucient Customer Service immediately at (800) 568-3282.

Hard Copy Price: $499

ISSN 0895-9862
ISBN 1-57372-338-X

CONTENTS

INTRODUCTION

Solucient's *Length of Stay* Series: Real Patient Data for Powerful Decision Making

Today's health care professionals are challenged to reduce unnecessary stays and services without sacrificing quality of care. As a result, medical management continues to move toward a more aggressive style of managing inpatient care. This approach makes it essential to establish *Length of Stay* targets that are not only realistic, but based on real benchmark data that reflect the complexity of your patient population.

Solucient's *Length of Stay* (LOS) series is unique. It is the only resource based solely on objective, quantitative data that are consistent and complete across the United States. This methodology ensures that the focus is on statistical rather than anecdotal evidence. Solucient provides empirical data based on millions of discharges, enabling you to identify true utilization and achieve benchmark performance.

Solucient's *Length of Stay* series was created to help you provide quality care while reducing health care costs—by efficiently managing inpatient cases. With LOS percentiles and demographic breakdowns, Solucient's product is the industry's most powerful tool to determine stays by any sizable patient population—from the lowest realistic level to median stays, and stays at the highest outlier levels. While Solucient's percentiles are based on real data from actual inpatient records, other products' panel-determined goals are based on subjective analysis.

Each patient is unique, and Solucient's *Length of Stay* series allows you to factor in those differences. Solucient LOS standards address the illness complexity and age of your patients by providing norms for both simple and more complex patients. Unlike some panel-determined goals, which address only the simple uncomplicated patient, Solucient LOS provides figures for multiple diagnosis patients who have had a significant procedure performed and those who have not.

Designed for Easy Use

Solucient designed the *Length of Stay by Diagnosis and Operation* series to be user-friendly. The front section of each book includes information on practical applications of the data, a step-by-step guide to using the tables, and a description of the data source. The LOS tables themselves include data organized by ICD-9-CM code and represent every diagnosis and procedure group. The tables examine average, median, and percentile length of stay for patients in five age groups, with single and multiple diagnoses or procedures, and according to whether the patient's stay included a significant procedure.

The appendices include counts of U.S. hospitals by bed size, region, census division, setting (rural or urban), and teaching intensity; a list of the states included in each LOS comparative region; and a table showing operative status of every procedure code included in the book. The glossary defines all of the terms used in the tables. An alphabetical index of diagnoses and procedures grouped according to classification categories can assist users who do not know the ICD-9-CM code for a particular diagnosis.

Length of Stay Data for a Variety of Needs

There are 7 different editions of *Length of Stay*, making it easy to find the information you need. Each book in the series is updated annually.

Length of Stay by Diagnosis and Operation provides data representing every ICD-9-CM diagnosis and procedure group.

- National and regional (Northeastern, North Central, Southern, and Western) editions
- National Pediatric edition, with data for patients 19 years old and younger

Psychiatric Length of Stay by Diagnosis catalogs diagnoses unique to psychiatric and substance abuse treatment.

- National—available in electronic format only

Each title is available electronically for efficient analysis. The files load easily onto virtually any system, and give you the convenience to review, set LOS targets, and plan your utilization management quickly. With these files, you can generate custom reports and incorporate the data into your own decision support systems. Call Solucient at 800-568-3282 or send an email to pubs@solucient.com for details.

About Solucient, LLC

Solucient® is an information products company serving the healthcare industry. It is the market leader in providing tools and vital insights that healthcare managers use to improve the performance of their organizations.

By integrating, standardizing and enhancing healthcare information, Solucient provides comparative measurements of cost, quality and market performance. Solucient's expertise and proven solutions enable providers, payers and pharmaceutical companies to drive business growth, manage costs and deliver high quality care. For more information, visit www.solucient.com

DESCRIPTION OF THE DATABASE

Solucient LOS standards are based on all-payer data gathered from nearly 18 million actual inpatient records, representing one of every two discharges from U.S. hospitals annually. This detail-rich database is Solucient's Projected Inpatient Database (PIDB), which is the largest all-payer inpatient database available in the marketplace. The PIDB supports publications, products and custom studies whose results are applicable to all short-term, general, non-federal (STGNF) hospitals in the United States. This exclusive database combines data from both public and proprietary state data as well as individual and group hospital contracts. Updated quarterly, the PIDB is used to create the Length of Stay series, Normative Health Care Measures, the National Link Study, and many other Solucient methodologies and products.

Methodology

The PIDB is created as an external, stable, consolidated database to enable users to make accurate evaluations about the entire universe of U.S. short-term, general, nonfederal (STGNF) hospitals. To make this possible, Solucient projects the data in the PIDB so that it accurately represents the universe. First, the data are standardized from all sources to create a consolidated patient record database. Then each discharge is assigned a projection factor (or weight) to indicate the number of discharges it represents. In this way, Solucient projects the data to represent the universe of all inpatient episodes.

To create the projection factors, Solucient uses the National Hospital Discharge Survey (NHDS) for creating the universe and other sources such as the Medicare Provider Analysis and Review File (MedPAR) to validate its projections. NHDS is a nationally representative survey produced and published by the National Center for Health Statistics (NCHS) that describes the entire universe of non-Federal, general (medical or surgical) or children's general, short stay hospitals in the United States. MedPAR, produced by the Centers for Medicare & Medicaid Services (CMS), contains a complete census of all Medicare inpatient discharges.

The universe of inpatients discharged from all short-term, general, non-federal U.S. hospitals is defined using NHDS. The hospital characteristics are defined according to the American Hospital Association criteria:

Short-Term: The average length of stay for all patients at the facility is less than 30 days, or more than 50 percent of all patients are admitted to units in which the average length of stay is less than 30 days.

General: The primary function of the institution is to provide patient services, diagnostic and therapeutic, for a variety of medical conditions.

Nonfederal: The facility is controlled by a state, county, city, city-county, hospital district authority, or church.

U.S. hospitals include those in the 50 states and the District of Columbia. Data from long-term specialty institutions, e.g., long-term psychiatric or rehabilitation facilities, are also excluded. For the Length of Stay publications, several exclusions are applied to the average length of stay data to eliminate discharge records that do not represent a typical short-term inpatient stay. These exclusions include: admission from other short-term hospital; discharge to other short-term hospital; discharge against medical advice; and death.

Data Quality and Validation

Data from all sources in the PIDB are standardized and run through a set of standard edit screens to ensure their quality. Examples of discrepancies detected by the audit include records with invalid diagnosis or procedure codes, invalid or unrecorded principal diagnosis, sex- or age-specific diagnosis or procedure inconsistencies, and incalculable age or length of stay. All records from hospitals with more than 5 percent of discharges failing any screen are deleted from the database.

The projection methodology ensures that the PIDB will be representative of the inpatient universe defined by NHDS. Using data that were not used to create the projection factors, representativeness of the PIDB has been demonstrated at the ICD-9-CM diagnosis and procedure level as well as by DRG.

To perform a comparison between PIDB data and NHDS the weighted discharges in the PIDB were grouped within ICD-9-CM diagnosis and procedure chapters, as were the discharges in NHDS. PIDB patients were compared to the NHDS for the same age range. The diagnosis and procedure chapter distributions of the PIDB were found to be highly representative of NHDS.

Concordance between DRG-specific Medicare estimates from the PIDB and the actual Medicare counts as found in MedPAR were compared. The correlation between the PIDB and MedPAR counts is 99.9%. Since the PIDB projection methodology accounts for payer, the representativeness of the PIDB is not limited to the Medicare population, but rather is applicable across all payer types.

BENEFITS AND APPLICATIONS

Solucient's *Length of Stay* series is an invaluable standard reference for health care professionals who want to measure inpatient utilization. Using the hospital stay data found in this series, you can compare regional and national norms to an individual institution or a special population. Specifically, the *Length of Stay* series allows you to:

- establish baselines (benchmarking);
- pre-authorize procedures;
- identify candidates for utilization review;
- project extended stay reviews;
- develop forecasts;
- and report lengths of stay versus benchmarks.

Patient severity, managed care market presence, and varying practice patterns all have significant impact on actual LOS statistics. As technological advances and financial pressures reduce inpatient days and increase outpatient volumes, only the most severely ill patients are left in the hospitals. Consequently, health care professionals must have detailed measurement criteria to make truly accurate, patient-focused assessments of appropriate lengths of stay.

Because Solucient's *Length of Stay* series is based on real patient data, you can tailor your LOS analyses to a particular patient age group, or compare the norms for patients with single or multiple diagnoses. You may also study regional variations, as well as specialized groups including pediatric and psychiatric patient populations. And the 10th, 25th, 50th, 75th, 95th, and 99th percentile groups enhance the average length of stay data by allowing you to pick a realistic goal for an individual patient. Solucient's LOS data can help pinpoint whether patients are being cared for efficiently, targeting areas that may need further clinical analysis.

The recent proliferation of new laws regulating utilization management procedures—in part, by requiring the disclosure of criteria used—is fueling the demand for high quality data. To comply with these new legal stipulations and to track fluctuating LOS trends, utilization managers must have reliable, industry-accepted criteria sets. Because Solucient updates the *Length of Stay* series annually with millions of new patient records, it provides extremely useful trend information—including significant developments from one year to the next and over even longer periods of time. Compiled from Solucient's exclusive Projected Inpatient Database (PIDB), the largest all-payor inpatient database available in the marketplace, this series is the most comprehensive, current source for length of stay data available.

HOW TO USE THE TABLES

The data in each Solucient *Length of Stay* volume are organized numerically by the International Classification of Diseases, 9th Revision, Clinical Modification (ICD-9-CM) coding system. Each Diagnosis volume contains every diagnosis chapter (three-digit code), including both summary and valid detail codes, and the nearly 1,200 four- and five-digit codes highest in projected volume. Each Operation volume contains every procedure chapter (two-digit code) including both summary codes and valid detail codes, and the nearly 850 four-digit codes highest in projected volume.

Data are categorized by number of observed patients, average length of stay, variance, and distribution percentiles. In addition, two subtotals and a grand total are included. All data elements except the number of observed patients are calculated using the projection methodology described in the "Description of the Database" section.

Determining length of stay would be easy if all patients were identical, but they are not. Illness, complexity, age, and region of the country will cause some variation in the LOS of patients admitted with the same diagnosis or procedure. Solucient recognizes those differences and our data tables let you to do the same. Solucient's *Length of Stay* series gives you detailed length of stay breakdowns—by individual ICD-9-CM code—listed by age groups, single versus multiple diagnosis patient, and operated versus non-operated status. You can find specific length of stay norms by taking the following steps:

Step 1: Find the desired ICD-9-CM code in the tables in one of the *Length of Stay* volumes. If you do not know a patient's ICD-9-CM code, refer to the index, which provides an alphabetical listing of the descriptive titles for all codes included in the book.

The **Observed Patients** column gives you the number of patients in the stratified group as reported in Solucient's projected inpatient database. "Observed" means that this data element, unlike the other elements in the LOS tables, is not projected. Patients with stays longer than 99 days (indicated as ">99") are not included.

Step 2: For each diagnosis code, patients are stratified by single or multiple diagnoses, operated or not operated status, and age. For each procedure code, patients are stratified by single or multiple diagnoses and age. Find the appropriate portion of the table for review by using the following patient information:

- Number of diagnoses
- Operated status
- Age

Single or Multiple Diagnoses

More than 80 percent of all admissions are complicated (have more than one diagnosis). The data tables include rows for patients with single and multiple diagnoses. This enables you to identify stays that are realistic and on-target with the patient's unique characteristics.

Patients are classified in the multiple diagnoses category if they had at least one valid secondary diagnosis in addition to the principal one. The following codes are not considered valid secondary diagnoses for purposes of this classification:

1. Manifestation codes (conditions that evolved from underlying diseases [etiology] and are in italics in ICD-9-CM, Volume 1)
2. Codes V27.0-V27.9 (outcome of delivery)
3. E Codes (external causes of injury and poisoning)

Operated or Not Operated

In the diagnosis tables, operated patients are those who had at least one procedure that is classified by CMS as an operating room procedure. CMS physician panels classify every ICD-9-CM procedure code according to whether the procedure would in most hospitals be performed in the operating room. This classification system differs slightly from that used in *Length of Stay* publications published before 1995, in which patients were categorized as "operated" if any of their procedures were labeled as Uniform Hospital Discharge Data Set (UHDDS) Class 1. Appendix C contains a list of procedure codes included in this series and their CMS-defined operative status.

Patient's Age

The data tables illustrate the impact of age by providing five age group breakouts. These ages are from the day of the patient's admission.

For diagnosis codes V30-V39, which pertain exclusively to newborns, age is replaced by birth weight in grams. Newborns with unrecorded birth weights with secondary diagnosis codes in the 764.01-764.99 and 765.01-765.19 ranges have been assigned to the appropriate birth weight category on the basis of the fifth digit of these codes. (Data for patients whose birth weights cannot be determined by using this method are included only in the Subtotal and Total rows of the table.)

Step 3: Choose from the average stay or the 10th, 25th, 50th, 75th, 95th, and 99th percentile columns to find the appropriate length of stay for your patient. Solucient LOS standards document the statistical range of stays for each patient group. These ranges are represented as percentiles, so that you can determine a more aggressive (benchmark) or less aggressive (norm) LOS for your patient, depending on individual variables, and are all backed by actual patient data.

Average Length of Stay

The average length of stay is calculated from the admission and discharge dates by counting the day of admission as the first day; the day of discharge is not included. The average is figured by adding the lengths of stay for each patient and then dividing by the total number of patients. Patients discharged on the day of admission are counted as staying one day. Patients with stays over 99 days (>99) are excluded from this calculation.

Median and Percentiles

A statistical range of stays are presented for each patient group. These ranges are represented as percentiles, so that you can determine a more aggressive or less aggressive LOS for your patient, depending on individual variables such as illness complications, age, etc. A length of stay percentile for a stratified group of patients is determined by arranging the individual patient stays from low to high. Counting up from the lowest stay to the point where one-half of the patients have been counted yields the value of the 50th percentile. Counting one-tenth of the total patients gives the 10th percentile, and so on.

The 10th, 25th, 50th, 75th, 90th, 95th, and 99th percentiles of stay are displayed in days. If, for example, the 10th percentile for a group of patients is four, then 10 percent of the patients stayed four days or fewer. The 50th percentile is the median. Any percentile with a value of 100 days or more is listed as >99. Patients who were hospitalized more than 99 days (>99) are not included in the total patients, average stay, and variance categories. The percentiles, however, do include these patients.

Step 4: Consult the total patient sample (**Observed Patients** column) and variance to consider the homogeneity of the data (i.e., to what extent length of stay averages are clustered or spread out within a particular patient group).

The **Total** row represents a subtotal for each of the patient age groups. The **Grand Total** row represents the total number of patients in the specified diagnosis or procedure category.

The **variance** is a measure of the spread of the data (from the lowest to the highest value) around the average. As such, it shows how much individual patient stays ranged around the average. The smallest variance is zero, indicating that all lengths of stay are equal. In tables in which there is a large variance and the patient group size is relatively small, the average stay may appear high. This sometimes occurs when one or two patients with long hospitalizations fall into the group.

FEATURES OF A DIAGNOSIS TABLE

ICD-9-CM diagnosis code and title

008.8: VIRAL ENTERITIS NOS

Type of Patients	Observed Patients	Avg. Stay	Vari-ance	Percentiles 10th	25th	50th	75th	90th	95th	99th
1. SINGLE DX										
A. Not Operated										
0–19 Years	1346	1.9	2	1	1	2	2	3	4	5
20–34	416	1.7	<1	1	1	2	2	3	3	5
35–49	213	2.3	3	1	1	2	3	3	5	10
50–64	89	2.0	3	1	1	1	3	3	4	12
65+	55	2.8	3	1	2	2	3	6	6	9
B. Operated										
0–19 Years	24	2.5	1	1	2	2	3	4	5	6
20–34	21	2.6	<1	1	2	3	3	3	3	4
35–49	6	4.2	2	2	4	5	5	5	5	6
50–64	1	2.0	0	2	2	2	2	2	2	2
65+	0									
2. MULTIPLE DX										
A. Not Operated										
0–19 Years	5020	2.3	5	1	1	2	3	4	5	8
20–34	1625	2.2	3	1	1	2	3	4	5	7
35–49	1453	2.7	3	1	1	2	3	5	6	9
50–64	1301	2.9	3	1	2	2	4	5	6	9
65+	2964	3.6	7	1	2	3	4	7	9	13
B. Operated										
0–19 Years	35	4.3	9	2	2	4	4	8	9	13
20–34	32	3.8	9	1	2	3	4	8	12	12
35–49	23	5.7	20	1	3	4	8	11	20	20
50–64	10	8.0	50	3	4	6	7	25	25	28
65+	27	14.0	92	4	7	10	18	30	31	43
SUBTOTALS:										
1. SINGLE DX										
A. Not Operated	2119	1.9	2	1	1	2	2	3	4	7
B. Operated	52	2.9	1	1	2	3	3	5	5	6
2. MULTIPLE DX										
A. Not Operated	12363	2.7	5	1	1	2	3	5	6	10
B. Operated	127	6.7	46	2	3	4	8	15	20	31
1. SINGLE DX	**2171**	**2.0**	**2**	**1**	**1**	**2**	**2**	**3**	**4**	**7**
2. MULTIPLE DX	**12490**	**2.7**	**6**	**1**	**1**	**2**	**3**	**5**	**7**	**10**
A. NOT OPERATED	**14482**	**2.6**	**5**	**1**	**1**	**2**	**3**	**5**	**6**	**9**
B. OPERATED	**179**	**5.2**	**31**	**2**	**2**	**3**	**5**	**10**	**15**	**30**
TOTAL										
0–19 Years	6425	2.3	4	1	1	2	3	4	5	8
20–34	2094	2.1	3	1	1	2	3	4	4	7
35–49	1695	2.7	4	1	1	2	3	5	6	10
50–64	1401	2.8	4	1	2	2	3	5	6	9
65+	3046	3.7	8	1	2	3	5	7	9	15
GRAND TOTAL	**14661**	**2.6**	**5**	**1**	**1**	**2**	**3**	**5**	**6**	**10**

Because each patient is unique, we stratify patients by single or multiple diagnoses, operated or not operated, status, and age.

Length of stay (in days) by percentile document the statistical range of stays for each patient group, so you can determine the right length of stay for your patient.

Total number of patients

Observed Patients is the actual number of patient discharges. Solucient derives length of stay figures from real patient data projected to represent the inpatient universe. See "Description of the Database" for further explanation.

The variance shows how much the individual patient lengths of stay ranged around the average.

Average length of stay, in days, calculated from the admission and discharge dates

FEATURES OF AN OPERATION TABLE

ICD-9-CM procedure code and title

01.1: SKULL/BRAIN DX PROCEDURE

Type of Patients	Observed Patients	Avg. Stay	Vari-ance	Percentiles						
				10th	25th	50th	75th	90th	95th	99th
1. SINGLE DX										
0–19 Years	78	4.4	20	1	1	3	6	11	11	28
20–34	62	2.6	8	1	1	1	3	5	7	14
35–49	82	4.1	21	1	1	4	4	7	10	18
50–64	92	3.5	17	1	1	2	4	7	9	26
65+	68	5.6	32	1	1	2	10	15	15	17
2. MULTIPLE DX										
0–19 Years	425	15.6	236	2	4	11	21	38	56	71
20–34	429	14.1	238	1	3	7	19	42	49	71
35–49	471	11.0	137	1	3	6	15	29	35	>99
50–64	471	8.5	77	1	3	5	9	21	31	37
65+	665	10.8	120	1	3	7	14	25	33	48
TOTAL SINGLE DX	**382**	**4.1**	**21**	**1**	**1**	**2**	**5**	**10**	**15**	**18**
TOTAL MULTIPLE DX	**2,337**	**11.7**	**159**	**1**	**3**	**7**	**16**	**29**	**40**	**62**
TOTAL										
0–19 Years	503	14.1	222	1	3	9	21	34	56	71
20–34	409	12.6	223	1	2	7	17	39	49	67
35–49	511	9.6	121	1	2	6	14	27	31	77
50–64	563	7.7	71	1	2	5	9	18	28	37
65+	733	10.4	115	1	3	7	14	25	30	48
GRAND TOTAL	**2,719**	**10.7**	**147**	**1**	**2**	**7**	**14**	**28**	**37**	**59**

Because each patient is unique, we stratify patients by single or multiple diagnoses and age.

Total number of patients

Length of stay (in days) by percentile document the statistical range of stays for each patient group, so you can determine the right length of stay for your patient.

Observed Patients is the actual number of patient discharges. Solucient derives length of stay figures from real patient data projected to represent the inpatient universe. See "Description of the Database" for further explanation.

The variance shows how much individual patient lengths of stay ranged around the average.

Average length of stay, in days, calculated from the admission and discharge dates

LENGTH OF STAY TABLES
OPERATION CODES

SUMMARY OF ALL PATIENTS IN OPERATION CODES

Type of Patients	Observed Patients	Avg. Stay	Vari-ance	Percentiles						
				10th	25th	50th	75th	90th	95th	99th
1. SINGLE DX										
0–19 Years	117,460	2.0	2	1	1	2	2	3	4	7
20–34	190,435	2.0	2	1	1	2	2	3	4	6
35–49	47,350	2.3	6	1	1	2	3	4	5	10
50–64	28,458	2.5	6	1	1	2	3	4	6	10
65+	14,470	2.6	4	1	1	2	3	5	6	9
2. MULTIPLE DX										
0–19 Years	263,759	4.5	56	1	2	2	4	9	15	42
20–34	465,948	3.1	13	1	2	2	3	5	7	18
35–49	375,599	4.1	24	1	2	3	4	8	12	25
50–64	414,686	4.9	30	1	2	3	6	10	14	27
65+	690,821	5.5	28	1	2	4	7	11	15	26
TOTAL SINGLE DX	**398,173**	**2.1**	**3**	**1**	**1**	**2**	**2**	**3**	**4**	**7**
TOTAL MULTIPLE DX	**2,210,813**	**4.5**	**29**	**1**	**2**	**3**	**5**	**9**	**14**	**27**
TOTAL										
0–19 Years	381,219	3.7	41	1	1	2	3	7	12	34
20–34	656,383	2.8	10	1	1	2	3	4	6	15
35–49	422,949	3.9	22	1	2	3	4	8	11	24
50–64	443,144	4.7	29	1	2	3	6	10	14	27
65+	705,291	5.4	28	1	2	4	7	11	15	26
GRAND TOTAL	**2,608,986**	**4.2**	**26**	**1**	**2**	**3**	**5**	**8**	**13**	**25**

00.0: THERAPEUTIC ULTRASOUND

Type of Patients	Observed Patients	Avg. Stay	Vari-ance	Percentiles						
				10th	25th	50th	75th	90th	95th	99th
1. SINGLE DX										
0–19 Years	0									
20–34	0									
35–49	0									
50–64	0									
65+	0									
2. MULTIPLE DX										
0–19 Years	0									
20–34	0									
35–49	0									
50–64	2	10.3	40	3	3	14	14	14	14	14
65+	1	4.0	0	4	4	4	4	4	4	4
TOTAL SINGLE DX	**0**									
TOTAL MULTIPLE DX	**3**	**8.5**	**36**	**3**	**4**	**4**	**14**	**14**	**14**	**14**
TOTAL										
0–19 Years	0									
20–34	0									
35–49	0									
50–64	2	10.3	40	3	3	14	14	14	14	14
65+	1	4.0	0	4	4	4	4	4	4	4
GRAND TOTAL	**3**	**8.5**	**36**	**3**	**4**	**4**	**14**	**14**	**14**	**14**

00.1: PHARMACEUTICALS

Type of Patients	Observed Patients	Avg. Stay	Vari-ance	Percentiles						
				10th	25th	50th	75th	90th	95th	99th
1. SINGLE DX										
0–19 Years	0									
20–34	0									
35–49	1	2.0	0	2	2	2	2	2	2	2
50–64	3	1.7	1	1	1	1	3	3	3	3
65+	0									
2. MULTIPLE DX										
0–19 Years	7	15.1	60	7	8	12	19	28	28	28
20–34	15	9.3	38	4	5	7	13	17	26	26
35–49	42	11.5	66	4	6	8	15	22	29	39
50–64	86	10.7	97	2	4	7	15	23	27	40
65+	269	7.3	32	2	4	6	9	14	17	27
TOTAL SINGLE DX	**4**	**1.7**	**<1**	**1**	**1**	**1**	**3**	**3**	**3**	**3**
TOTAL MULTIPLE DX	**419**	**8.7**	**54**	**3**	**4**	**6**	**11**	**18**	**23**	**38**
TOTAL										
0–19 Years	7	15.1	60	7	8	12	19	28	28	28
20–34	15	9.3	38	4	5	7	13	17	26	26
35–49	43	11.4	67	4	6	8	15	22	29	39
50–64	89	10.5	96	2	4	7	15	23	27	40
65+	269	7.3	32	2	4	6	9	14	17	27
GRAND TOTAL	**423**	**8.7**	**54**	**2**	**4**	**6**	**11**	**17**	**23**	**38**

00.11: INFUSE DROTRECOGIN ALFA

Type of Patients	Observed Patients	Avg. Stay	Vari-ance	Percentiles						
				10th	25th	50th	75th	90th	95th	99th
1. SINGLE DX										
0–19 Years	0									
20–34	0									
35–49	0									
50–64	0									
65+	0									
2. MULTIPLE DX										
0–19 Years	7	15.1	60	7	8	12	19	28	28	28
20–34	9	12.5	36	6	7	12	14	26	26	26
35–49	30	13.5	63	6	8	12	17	27	29	39
50–64	32	17.5	125	6	11	15	23	31	40	64
65+	35	13.7	79	6	6	11	18	27	27	40
TOTAL SINGLE DX	**0**									
TOTAL MULTIPLE DX	**113**	**14.7**	**85**	**6**	**8**	**12**	**19**	**27**	**31**	**40**
TOTAL										
0–19 Years	7	15.1	60	7	8	12	19	28	28	28
20–34	9	12.5	36	6	7	12	14	26	26	26
35–49	30	13.5	63	6	8	12	17	27	29	39
50–64	32	17.5	125	6	11	15	23	31	40	64
65+	35	13.7	79	6	6	11	18	27	27	40
GRAND TOTAL	**113**	**14.7**	**85**	**6**	**8**	**12**	**19**	**27**	**31**	**40**

00.13: INJECT NESIRITIDE

Type of Patients	Observed Patients	Avg. Stay	Vari-ance	Percentiles						
				10th	25th	50th	75th	90th	95th	99th
1. SINGLE DX										
0–19 Years	0									
20–34	0									
35–49	0									
50–64	0									
65+	0									
2. MULTIPLE DX										
0–19 Years	0									
20–34	3	4.0	<1	3	3	4	5	5	5	5
35–49	5	4.8	6	1	4	4	7	7	7	7
50–64	45	6.3	26	2	3	5	7	13	17	26
65+	222	6.2	14	2	3	5	8	11	14	17
TOTAL SINGLE DX	**0**									
TOTAL MULTIPLE DX	**275**	**6.1**	**16**	**2**	**3**	**5**	**8**	**11**	**14**	**21**
TOTAL										
0–19 Years	0									
20–34	3	4.0	<1	3	3	4	5	5	5	5
35–49	5	4.8	6	1	4	4	7	7	7	7
50–64	45	6.3	26	2	3	5	7	13	17	26
65+	222	6.2	14	2	3	5	8	11	14	17
GRAND TOTAL	**275**	**6.1**	**16**	**2**	**3**	**5**	**8**	**11**	**14**	**21**

00.5: OTH CARDIOVASCULAR PX

Type of Patients	Observed Patients	Avg. Stay	Vari-ance	Percentiles						
				10th	25th	50th	75th	90th	95th	99th
1. SINGLE DX										
0–19 Years	0									
20–34	1	1.0	0	1	1	1	1	1	1	1
35–49	1	2.0	0	2	2	2	2	2	2	2
50–64	4	2.0	5	1	1	1	1	6	6	6
65+	6	1.3	<1	1	1	1	2	2	2	2
2. MULTIPLE DX										
0–19 Years	8	3.7	19	1	1	2	3	13	13	13
20–34	18	8.4	48	1	1	7	15	15	15	27
35–49	81	4.4	45	1	1	1	6	9	15	45
50–64	402	3.8	23	1	1	1	4	10	17	19
65+	1,499	4.0	27	1	1	2	5	10	13	25
TOTAL SINGLE DX	**12**	**1.4**	**1**	**1**	**1**	**1**	**1**	**2**	**2**	**6**
TOTAL MULTIPLE DX	**2,008**	**4.0**	**28**	**1**	**1**	**2**	**5**	**10**	**14**	**24**
TOTAL										
0–19 Years	8	3.7	19	1	1	2	3	13	13	13
20–34	19	7.4	48	1	1	6	15	15	15	27
35–49	82	4.4	45	1	1	1	6	9	15	45
50–64	406	3.8	23	1	1	1	4	10	17	19
65+	1,505	4.0	27	1	1	2	5	10	13	25
GRAND TOTAL	**2,020**	**4.0**	**27**	**1**	**1**	**2**	**5**	**10**	**14**	**24**

00.50: IMPL CRT-P TOTAL SYSTEM

Type of Patients	Observed Patients	Avg. Stay	Vari-ance	Percentiles						
				10th	25th	50th	75th	90th	95th	99th
1. SINGLE DX										
0–19 Years	0									
20–34	0									
35–49	0									
50–64	1	1.0	0	1	1	1	1	1	1	1
65+	1	1.0	0	1	1	1	1	1	1	1
2. MULTIPLE DX										
0–19 Years	4	5.3	23	2	2	3	13	13	13	13
20–34	2	4.9	6	1	6	6	6	6	6	6
35–49	16	3.0	5	1	1	3	4	7	7	7
50–64	77	2.8	10	1	1	1	3	6	10	14
65+	397	3.6	16	1	1	2	5	9	12	22
TOTAL SINGLE DX	**2**	**1.0**	**0**	**1**	**1**	**1**	**1**	**1**	**1**	**1**
TOTAL MULTIPLE DX	**496**	**3.5**	**15**	**1**	**1**	**2**	**5**	**9**	**12**	**19**
TOTAL										
0–19 Years	4	5.3	23	2	2	3	13	13	13	13
20–34	2	4.9	6	1	6	6	6	6	6	6
35–49	16	3.0	5	1	1	3	4	7	7	7
50–64	78	2.8	10	1	1	1	3	6	10	14
65+	398	3.6	16	1	1	2	5	9	12	22
GRAND TOTAL	**498**	**3.4**	**15**	**1**	**1**	**2**	**5**	**9**	**12**	**19**

00.51: IMPL CRT-D TOTAL SYSTEM

Type of Patients	Observed Patients	Avg. Stay	Vari-ance	Percentiles						
				10th	25th	50th	75th	90th	95th	99th
1. SINGLE DX										
0–19 Years	0									
20–34	1	1.0	0	1	1	1	1	1	1	1
35–49	0									
50–64	2	1.0	0	1	1	1	1	1	1	1
65+	2	1.3	<1	1	1	1	2	2	2	2
2. MULTIPLE DX										
0–19 Years	0									
20–34	14	8.5	55	1	1	10	15	15	27	27
35–49	58	4.7	53	1	1	1	6	10	16	45
50–64	267	4.0	25	1	1	2	5	11	18	19
65+	847	4.4	34	1	1	2	6	11	14	25
TOTAL SINGLE DX	**5**	**1.1**	**<1**	**1**	**1**	**1**	**1**	**2**	**2**	**2**
TOTAL MULTIPLE DX	**1,186**	**4.3**	**34**	**1**	**1**	**2**	**6**	**11**	**15**	**25**
TOTAL										
0–19 Years	0									
20–34	15	7.1	53	1	1	3	12	15	15	27
35–49	58	4.7	53	1	1	1	6	10	16	45
50–64	269	4.0	25	1	1	2	5	11	18	19
65+	849	4.3	34	1	1	2	6	11	14	25
GRAND TOTAL	**1,191**	**4.3**	**34**	**1**	**1**	**2**	**6**	**11**	**15**	**25**

00.52: IMPL LEAD COR VEN SYSTEM

Type of Patients	Observed Patients	Avg. Stay	Vari-ance	Percentiles						
				10th	25th	50th	75th	90th	95th	99th
1. SINGLE DX										
0–19 Years	0									
20–34	0									
35–49	1	2.0	0	2	2	2	2	2	2	2
50–64	1	6.0	0	6	6	6	6	6	6	6
65+	3	1.3	<1	1	1	1	2	2	2	2
2. MULTIPLE DX										
0–19 Years	2	1.0	0	1	1	1	1	1	1	1
20–34	2	11.3	48	1	1	15	15	15	15	15
35–49	6	4.8	66	1	1	1	4	22	22	22
50–64	42	3.8	24	1	1	1	4	10	19	19
65+	194	3.5	19	1	1	2	4	8	12	26
TOTAL SINGLE DX	**5**	**1.8**	**2**	**1**	**1**	**1**	**2**	**2**	**6**	**6**
TOTAL MULTIPLE DX	**246**	**3.7**	**22**	**1**	**1**	**2**	**4**	**10**	**15**	**25**
TOTAL										
0–19 Years	2	1.0	0	1	1	1	1	1	1	1
20–34	2	11.3	48	1	1	15	15	15	15	15
35–49	7	4.5	57	1	1	1	4	22	22	22
50–64	43	3.9	24	1	1	1	5	10	19	19
65+	197	3.5	19	1	1	2	4	8	12	26
GRAND TOTAL	**251**	**3.6**	**21**	**1**	**1**	**2**	**4**	**10**	**15**	**25**

01.0: CRANIAL PUNCTURE

Type of Patients	Observed Patients	Avg. Stay	Vari- ance	Percentiles						
				10th	25th	50th	75th	90th	95th	99th
1. SINGLE DX										
0–19 Years	1	1.0	0	1	1	1	1	1	1	1
20–34	1	3.0	0	3	3	3	3	3	3	3
35–49	2	2.3	<1	2	2	2	3	3	3	3
50–64	1	1.0	0	1	1	1	1	1	1	1
65+	1	3.0	0	3	3	3	3	3	3	3
2. MULTIPLE DX										
0–19 Years	138	4.6	47	1	1	3	6	8	11	27
20–34	37	6.6	50	1	2	5	11	14	18	38
35–49	39	8.8	101	1	2	5	12	33	33	33
50–64	31	6.4	18	2	3	5	11	11	15	17
65+	50	7.1	52	2	3	5	8	11	23	39
TOTAL SINGLE DX	**6**	**2.2**	**<1**	**1**	**1**	**2**	**3**	**3**	**3**	**3**
TOTAL MULTIPLE DX	**295**	**5.7**	**53**	**1**	**2**	**4**	**7**	**11**	**20**	**33**
TOTAL										
0–19 Years	139	4.6	47	1	1	3	6	8	11	27
20–34	38	6.5	49	1	2	5	11	14	18	38
35–49	41	8.4	98	1	2	4	10	33	33	33
50–64	32	6.2	18	2	2	5	11	11	15	17
65+	51	7.0	52	2	3	5	8	11	23	39
GRAND TOTAL	**301**	**5.6**	**53**	**1**	**2**	**4**	**6**	**11**	**20**	**33**

01.02: VENTRICULOPUNCT VIA CATH

Type of Patients	Observed Patients	Avg. Stay	Vari- ance	Percentiles						
				10th	25th	50th	75th	90th	95th	99th
1. SINGLE DX										
0–19 Years	0									
20–34	0									
35–49	0									
50–64	1	1.0	0	1	1	1	1	1	1	1
65+	0									
2. MULTIPLE DX										
0–19 Years	112	3.5	14	1	1	2	4	7	9	27
20–34	33	6.6	54	1	2	4	11	15	18	38
35–49	23	9.8	134	1	2	5	10	33	33	33
50–64	12	6.7	18	1	3	5	11	11	15	15
65+	22	5.8	12	2	4	5	7	11	11	18
TOTAL SINGLE DX	**1**	**1.0**	**0**	**1**	**1**	**1**	**1**	**1**	**1**	**1**
TOTAL MULTIPLE DX	**202**	**4.7**	**33**	**1**	**1**	**3**	**5**	**10**	**15**	**33**
TOTAL										
0–19 Years	112	3.5	14	1	1	2	4	7	9	27
20–34	33	6.6	54	1	2	4	11	15	18	38
35–49	23	9.8	134	1	2	5	10	33	33	33
50–64	13	6.3	19	1	3	5	11	11	15	15
65+	22	5.8	12	2	4	5	7	11	11	18
GRAND TOTAL	**203**	**4.7**	**33**	**1**	**1**	**3**	**5**	**10**	**15**	**33**

01.1: DXTIC PX ON SKULL/BRAIN

Type of Patients	Observed Patients	Avg. Stay	Vari- ance	Percentiles						
				10th	25th	50th	75th	90th	95th	99th
1. SINGLE DX										
0–19 Years	13	2.8	5	1	1	2	4	7	7	7
20–34	18	2.4	8	1	1	1	2	3	10	12
35–49	23	2.5	6	1	1	2	2	7	9	10
50–64	30	1.8	2	1	1	1	2	3	5	8
65+	14	1.4	<1	1	1	1	1	3	3	4
2. MULTIPLE DX										
0–19 Years	163	10.3	114	1	3	6	14	24	30	57
20–34	138	9.8	144	1	2	6	13	26	48	>99
35–49	163	7.0	86	1	1	4	8	15	23	50
50–64	283	7.1	85	1	1	4	9	18	24	46
65+	285	6.1	38	1	1	4	9	13	16	28
TOTAL SINGLE DX	**98**	**2.1**	**4**	**1**	**1**	**1**	**2**	**4**	**7**	**10**
TOTAL MULTIPLE DX	**1,032**	**7.7**	**86**	**1**	**1**	**5**	**10**	**18**	**26**	**50**
TOTAL										
0–19 Years	176	9.8	111	1	3	6	14	23	30	47
20–34	156	9.0	134	1	2	6	12	25	37	>99
35–49	186	6.4	78	1	1	4	8	13	19	50
50–64	313	6.6	79	1	1	3	8	17	24	46
65+	299	5.8	37	1	1	4	9	13	15	28
GRAND TOTAL	**1,130**	**7.2**	**82**	**1**	**1**	**4**	**10**	**17**	**25**	**48**

01.13: CLOSED BRAIN BIOPSY

Type of Patients	Observed Patients	Avg. Stay	Vari- ance	Percentiles						
				10th	25th	50th	75th	90th	95th	99th
1. SINGLE DX										
0–19 Years	3	1.9	2	1	1	1	4	4	4	4
20–34	9	1.2	<1	1	1	1	1	2	2	2
35–49	14	2.3	5	1	1	2	2	7	9	9
50–64	23	1.4	2	1	1	1	1	2	3	8
65+	12	1.3	<1	1	1	1	1	3	3	4
2. MULTIPLE DX										
0–19 Years	16	5.0	30	1	1	4	5	14	14	27
20–34	44	8.3	271	1	1	1	6	24	62	62
35–49	67	4.5	40	1	1	4	6	8	12	14
50–64	169	5.5	59	1	1	2	7	12	22	43
65+	184	5.4	27	1	1	4	8	12	14	22
TOTAL SINGLE DX	**61**	**1.6**	**2**	**1**	**1**	**1**	**1**	**3**	**4**	**9**
TOTAL MULTIPLE DX	**480**	**5.5**	**59**	**1**	**1**	**3**	**7**	**12**	**14**	**43**
TOTAL										
0–19 Years	19	4.7	28	1	1	3	5	9	14	27
20–34	53	7.2	235	1	1	1	4	20	62	62
35–49	81	4.1	35	1	1	2	5	8	11	14
50–64	192	5.0	54	1	1	2	6	11	22	43
65+	196	5.1	26	1	1	4	8	12	14	22
GRAND TOTAL	**541**	**5.1**	**54**	**1**	**1**	**2**	**7**	**11**	**14**	**43**

01.14: OPEN BIOPSY OF BRAIN

Type of Patients	Observed Patients	Avg. Stay	Vari-ance	Percentiles 10th	25th	50th	75th	90th	95th	99th
1. SINGLE DX										
0–19 Years	3	5.0	4	3	3	6	6	7	7	7
20–34	6	2.6	8	1	1	2	2	10	10	10
35–49	8	3.2	11	1	1	2	3	10	10	10
50–64	5	2.7	2	1	2	2	3	5	5	5
65+	2	2.5	<1	2	2	3	3	3	3	3
2. MULTIPLE DX										
0–19 Years	34	7.9	66	2	3	5	9	24	25	41
20–34	26	7.0	52	2	2	3	9	20	26	26
35–49	48	5.5	32	1	2	4	6	13	17	34
50–64	77	9.0	101	1	2	6	11	20	32	46
65+	66	6.1	17	2	3	5	9	12	13	18
TOTAL SINGLE DX	24	3.1	7	1	1	2	3	7	10	10
TOTAL MULTIPLE DX	251	7.2	56	1	2	5	9	15	24	41
TOTAL										
0–19 Years	37	7.7	62	2	3	5	9	24	25	41
20–34	32	6.2	46	1	2	3	8	17	26	26
35–49	56	5.2	30	1	2	4	6	10	13	34
50–64	82	8.6	97	1	2	5	11	20	31	46
65+	68	6.0	17	2	3	5	9	12	13	18
GRAND TOTAL	275	6.8	53	1	2	4	9	13	22	41

01.18: DXTIC PX BRAIN/CEREB NEC

Type of Patients	Observed Patients	Avg. Stay	Vari-ance	Percentiles 10th	25th	50th	75th	90th	95th	99th
1. SINGLE DX										
0–19 Years	5	2.8	4	1	2	2	3	7	7	7
20–34	3	5.4	28	2	2	3	12	12	12	12
35–49	1	2.0	0	2	2	2	2	2	2	2
50–64	1	3.0	0	3	3	3	3	3	3	3
65+	0									
2. MULTIPLE DX										
0–19 Years	109	12.3	136	1	4	10	17	27	30	57
20–34	67	12.1	102	2	6	10	18	33	52	>99
35–49	45	12.8	185	1	3	11	19	32	35	78
50–64	20	14.3	218	2	6	8	18	36	39	64
65+	18	16.4	122	4	11	14	26	28	46	46
TOTAL SINGLE DX	10	3.2	6	2	2	3	3	7	12	12
TOTAL MULTIPLE DX	259	12.8	139	1	4	10	17	28	37	>99
TOTAL										
0–19 Years	114	12.0	134	1	3	10	17	26	30	57
20–34	70	11.8	101	2	6	10	17	29	52	>99
35–49	46	12.2	181	1	3	10	16	28	35	78
50–64	21	12.2	197	2	3	7	17	36	39	64
65+	18	16.4	122	4	11	14	26	28	46	46
GRAND TOTAL	269	12.4	137	1	4	10	17	28	37	78

01.2: CRANIOTOMY & CRANIECTOMY

Type of Patients	Observed Patients	Avg. Stay	Vari-ance	Percentiles 10th	25th	50th	75th	90th	95th	99th
1. SINGLE DX										
0–19 Years	86	3.2	2	2	2	3	4	5	6	9
20–34	40	4.6	21	2	3	3	4	6	16	29
35–49	26	3.3	4	1	2	3	4	6	6	8
50–64	25	2.9	2	1	2	3	4	5	5	5
65+	9	6.9	49	2	3	5	6	26	26	26
2. MULTIPLE DX										
0–19 Years	278	7.2	73	2	3	5	8	15	23	59
20–34	187	7.8	43	3	4	5	10	17	24	32
35–49	202	8.4	71	2	3	6	11	16	24	31
50–64	272	8.1	48	2	4	6	10	17	27	30
65+	323	7.9	34	3	4	6	10	16	19	28
TOTAL SINGLE DX	186	3.6	8	2	2	3	4	5	8	16
TOTAL MULTIPLE DX	1,262	7.8	54	2	3	6	9	16	22	33
TOTAL										
0–19 Years	364	6.3	59	2	3	4	7	13	19	36
20–34	227	7.2	40	2	3	5	9	16	23	32
35–49	228	7.9	67	2	3	6	9	16	24	31
50–64	297	7.8	47	2	3	6	9	16	26	30
65+	332	7.9	34	3	4	6	10	16	19	26
GRAND TOTAL	1,448	7.3	50	2	3	5	9	16	20	31

01.23: REOPEN CRANIOTOMY SITE

Type of Patients	Observed Patients	Avg. Stay	Vari-ance	Percentiles 10th	25th	50th	75th	90th	95th	99th
1. SINGLE DX										
0–19 Years	0									
20–34	1	3.0	0	3	3	3	3	3	3	3
35–49	2	3.0	2	2	2	2	4	4	4	4
50–64	0									
65+	0									
2. MULTIPLE DX										
0–19 Years	9	12.3	70	3	5	7	23	23	23	23
20–34	17	5.9	33	2	3	5	6	8	10	30
35–49	14	6.5	21	2	3	4	11	12	15	15
50–64	25	5.8	7	1	4	6	8	10	10	10
65+	27	7.8	68	1	4	5	9	17	19	48
TOTAL SINGLE DX	3	3.0	<1	2	2	3	4	4	4	4
TOTAL MULTIPLE DX	92	7.7	46	2	4	6	9	17	23	30
TOTAL										
0–19 Years	9	12.3	70	3	5	7	23	23	23	23
20–34	18	5.8	32	2	3	5	6	8	10	30
35–49	16	6.1	20	2	3	4	11	12	15	15
50–64	25	5.8	7	1	4	6	8	10	10	10
65+	27	7.8	68	1	4	5	9	17	19	48
GRAND TOTAL	95	7.6	45	2	4	6	9	17	23	30

01.24: CRANIOTOMY NEC

Type of Patients	Observed Patients	Avg. Stay	Vari-ance	Percentiles						
				10th	25th	50th	75th	90th	95th	99th
1. SINGLE DX										
0–19 Years	67	3.2	3	2	2	3	4	5	6	9
20–34	26	5.6	32	2	3	4	5	12	16	29
35–49	20	3.2	4	1	1	3	5	6	6	8
50–64	14	2.8	1	2	2	3	3	5	5	5
65+	8	7.1	53	2	3	5	6	26	26	26
2. MULTIPLE DX										
0–19 Years	226	6.8	53	2	3	5	8	14	19	36
20–34	141	8.7	49	3	4	6	11	20	25	34
35–49	141	9.7	90	2	4	7	14	18	27	56
50–64	188	9.2	58	3	4	6	13	20	28	31
65+	256	8.1	29	3	4	6	11	15	18	28
TOTAL SINGLE DX	**135**	**3.7**	**11**	**2**	**2**	**3**	**4**	**6**	**8**	**26**
TOTAL MULTIPLE DX	**952**	**8.2**	**53**	**2**	**4**	**6**	**10**	**17**	**23**	**33**
TOTAL										
0–19 Years	293	6.0	44	2	3	4	7	12	18	35
20–34	167	8.2	48	3	4	5	10	19	25	34
35–49	161	9.0	85	2	4	7	13	17	27	56
50–64	202	8.9	57	2	4	6	13	19	28	31
65+	264	8.1	30	3	4	6	11	15	19	26
GRAND TOTAL	**1,087**	**7.7**	**50**	**2**	**3**	**5**	**9**	**16**	**21**	**32**

01.25: CRANIECTOMY NEC

Type of Patients	Observed Patients	Avg. Stay	Vari-ance	Percentiles						
				10th	25th	50th	75th	90th	95th	99th
1. SINGLE DX										
0–19 Years	19	3.4	1	2	3	3	4	5	5	5
20–34	12	3.4	1	2	3	3	4	5	6	6
35–49	4	4.1	2	2	4	4	4	6	6	6
50–64	11	2.9	3	1	1	3	5	5	5	5
65+	1	4.0	0	4	4	4	4	4	4	4
2. MULTIPLE DX										
0–19 Years	43	8.0	191	2	3	4	5	15	28	65
20–34	28	5.4	13	2	3	5	6	12	12	16
35–49	45	5.1	17	2	3	4	6	9	11	24
50–64	44	6.2	25	2	3	5	8	13	16	27
65+	25	6.8	34	1	3	4	8	19	21	21
TOTAL SINGLE DX	**47**	**3.3**	**1**	**2**	**3**	**3**	**4**	**5**	**5**	**6**
TOTAL MULTIPLE DX	**185**	**6.3**	**60**	**2**	**3**	**4**	**7**	**12**	**18**	**65**
TOTAL										
0–19 Years	62	6.2	122	2	3	4	5	7	18	65
20–34	40	4.8	10	2	3	4	6	8	12	16
35–49	49	5.1	16	2	3	4	6	9	11	24
50–64	55	5.7	22	1	3	4	7	10	15	27
65+	26	6.7	34	1	3	4	8	17	21	21
GRAND TOTAL	**232**	**5.7**	**49**	**2**	**3**	**4**	**6**	**10**	**16**	**28**

01.3: INC BRAIN/CEREB MENINGES

Type of Patients	Observed Patients	Avg. Stay	Vari-ance	Percentiles						
				10th	25th	50th	75th	90th	95th	99th
1. SINGLE DX										
0–19 Years	19	5.1	6	2	4	5	7	8	10	10
20–34	26	5.2	12	1	3	4	6	8	16	16
35–49	17	4.1	8	2	2	3	5	11	11	12
50–64	47	5.2	28	2	3	3	6	12	12	29
65+	29	5.3	29	2	3	4	6	7	16	29
2. MULTIPLE DX										
0–19 Years	127	11.2	127	2	4	7	15	23	41	47
20–34	140	11.3	119	3	4	8	14	24	31	49
35–49	298	11.0	91	3	4	9	14	22	33	44
50–64	583	9.3	65	3	4	7	12	20	27	45
65+	1,560	9.0	42	3	5	7	11	18	22	33
TOTAL SINGLE DX	**138**	**5.1**	**18**	**2**	**3**	**4**	**6**	**8**	**12**	**29**
TOTAL MULTIPLE DX	**2,708**	**9.5**	**62**	**3**	**4**	**7**	**12**	**19**	**24**	**41**
TOTAL										
0–19 Years	146	10.4	116	2	4	6	13	23	29	47
20–34	166	10.5	109	2	4	7	14	22	31	49
35–49	315	10.7	89	3	4	8	14	22	30	44
50–64	630	9.1	64	3	4	6	12	20	27	39
65+	1,589	9.0	42	3	5	7	11	18	22	33
GRAND TOTAL	**2,846**	**9.3**	**60**	**3**	**4**	**7**	**12**	**19**	**24**	**40**

01.31: INC CEREBRAL MENINGES

Type of Patients	Observed Patients	Avg. Stay	Vari-ance	Percentiles						
				10th	25th	50th	75th	90th	95th	99th
1. SINGLE DX										
0–19 Years	14	5.1	6	2	5	5	7	8	10	10
20–34	18	4.3	3	2	3	4	6	6	8	8
35–49	15	3.8	5	2	2	3	5	6	11	11
50–64	40	4.6	17	2	3	3	5	9	12	26
65+	27	4.9	26	2	2	4	5	7	8	29
2. MULTIPLE DX										
0–19 Years	88	10.9	100	2	4	8	15	24	29	42
20–34	101	12.6	148	3	5	9	15	30	31	81
35–49	212	10.7	93	3	4	8	14	21	30	48
50–64	438	8.3	58	2	4	6	10	17	26	39
65+	1,360	8.7	40	3	5	7	11	17	21	33
TOTAL SINGLE DX	**114**	**4.7**	**13**	**2**	**3**	**4**	**5**	**7**	**10**	**26**
TOTAL MULTIPLE DX	**2,199**	**9.1**	**56**	**3**	**4**	**7**	**11**	**18**	**24**	**40**
TOTAL										
0–19 Years	102	10.1	91	2	4	6	13	23	29	42
20–34	119	11.5	137	3	4	8	14	28	31	49
35–49	227	10.3	91	3	4	7	14	21	29	48
50–64	478	8.1	56	2	4	5	10	17	24	39
65+	1,387	8.7	40	3	5	7	11	17	21	33
GRAND TOTAL	**2,313**	**8.9**	**55**	**3**	**4**	**7**	**11**	**18**	**23**	**39**

01.39: BRAIN INCISION NEC

Type of Patients	Observed Patients	Avg. Stay	Vari-ance	10th	25th	50th	75th	90th	95th	99th
1. SINGLE DX										
0–19 Years	5	5.2	6	2	3	6	7	8	8	8
20–34	7	7.3	34	1	1	7	8	16	16	16
35–49	2	6.7	45	2	2	2	12	12	12	12
50–64	7	8.3	88	1	3	4	12	29	29	29
65+	2	10.7	47	5	5	16	16	16	16	16
2. MULTIPLE DX										
0–19 Years	31	12.1	189	2	3	10	15	23	42	84
20–34	35	8.0	42	1	4	5	10	19	22	22
35–49	85	11.8	84	4	6	10	14	24	35	41
50–64	143	12.8	72	4	6	12	17	24	28	45
65+	200	11.0	58	3	5	9	16	23	26	32
TOTAL SINGLE DX	**23**	**7.3**	**41**	**1**	**3**	**6**	**8**	**16**	**16**	**29**
TOTAL MULTIPLE DX	**494**	**11.5**	**77**	**3**	**5**	**9**	**16**	**23**	**28**	**41**
TOTAL										
0–19 Years	36	11.4	176	2	3	7	13	23	42	84
20–34	42	7.9	40	1	4	5	10	19	22	22
35–49	87	11.8	83	3	6	9	14	24	35	41
50–64	150	12.6	73	3	6	12	17	24	28	45
65+	202	11.0	58	3	5	9	16	23	26	32
GRAND TOTAL	**517**	**11.3**	**76**	**3**	**5**	**9**	**16**	**23**	**28**	**41**

01.4: THALAMUS/GLOBUS PALL OPS

Type of Patients	Observed Patients	Avg. Stay	Vari-ance	10th	25th	50th	75th	90th	95th	99th
1. SINGLE DX										
0–19 Years	0									
20–34	0									
35–49	0									
50–64	4	1.8	1	1	1	1	3	3	3	3
65+	7	1.0	0	1	1	1	1	1	1	1
2. MULTIPLE DX										
0–19 Years	1	3.0	0	3	3	3	3	3	3	3
20–34	1	1.0	0	1	1	1	1	1	1	1
35–49	2	1.0	0	1	1	1	1	1	1	1
50–64	7	1.6	4	1	1	1	1	1	8	8
65+	17	1.2	<1	1	1	1	1	1	3	4
TOTAL SINGLE DX	**11**	**1.1**	**<1**	**1**	**1**	**1**	**1**	**1**	**1**	**3**
TOTAL MULTIPLE DX	**28**	**1.3**	**1**	**1**	**1**	**1**	**1**	**1**	**3**	**8**
TOTAL										
0–19 Years	1	3.0	0	3	3	3	3	3	3	3
20–34	1	1.0	0	1	1	1	1	1	1	1
35–49	2	1.0	0	1	1	1	1	1	1	1
50–64	11	1.6	3	1	1	1	1	3	8	8
65+	24	1.1	<1	1	1	1	1	1	1	4
GRAND TOTAL	**39**	**1.2**	**<1**	**1**	**1**	**1**	**1**	**1**	**3**	**8**

01.5: EXC/DESTR BRAIN/MENINGES

Type of Patients	Observed Patients	Avg. Stay	Vari-ance	10th	25th	50th	75th	90th	95th	99th
1. SINGLE DX										
0–19 Years	106	4.3	7	2	2	4	5	7	7	13
20–34	139	4.4	10	2	3	3	5	7	9	19
35–49	167	3.8	4	2	2	3	5	7	8	11
50–64	178	4.2	7	2	2	3	5	7	9	12
65+	34	4.1	5	2	2	3	5	7	10	11
2. MULTIPLE DX										
0–19 Years	464	9.6	95	3	4	7	11	20	28	53
20–34	479	6.6	62	2	3	4	7	12	18	56
35–49	897	6.1	26	2	3	4	8	12	16	28
50–64	1,610	6.3	27	2	3	5	8	12	17	26
65+	1,119	7.3	30	2	3	6	9	15	18	26
TOTAL SINGLE DX	**624**	**4.2**	**7**	**2**	**2**	**3**	**5**	**7**	**8**	**14**
TOTAL MULTIPLE DX	**4,569**	**7.0**	**41**	**2**	**3**	**5**	**8**	**14**	**18**	**32**
TOTAL										
0–19 Years	570	8.5	81	2	4	6	10	16	25	50
20–34	618	6.1	51	2	3	4	7	11	17	42
35–49	1,064	5.8	24	2	3	4	7	11	15	25
50–64	1,788	6.1	25	2	3	5	7	11	16	25
65+	1,153	7.2	30	2	3	6	9	14	18	26
GRAND TOTAL	**5,193**	**6.6**	**38**	**2**	**3**	**5**	**8**	**13**	**18**	**30**

01.51: EXC CEREB MENINGEAL LES

Type of Patients	Observed Patients	Avg. Stay	Vari-ance	10th	25th	50th	75th	90th	95th	99th
1. SINGLE DX										
0–19 Years	5	3.7	1	2	4	4	4	5	5	5
20–34	20	3.2	2	1	3	3	4	4	6	7
35–49	53	3.8	3	2	3	3	5	7	8	10
50–64	48	3.8	5	2	2	3	5	8	8	11
65+	10	3.3	1	2	2	3	4	5	5	5
2. MULTIPLE DX										
0–19 Years	18	9.7	89	3	6	7	8	26	41	41
20–34	57	5.7	22	2	3	4	7	11	17	23
35–49	208	5.6	19	2	3	5	6	10	16	28
50–64	380	5.6	24	2	3	4	7	10	15	24
65+	302	7.5	38	2	3	5	9	16	22	26
TOTAL SINGLE DX	**136**	**3.7**	**4**	**2**	**2**	**3**	**5**	**6**	**8**	**10**
TOTAL MULTIPLE DX	**965**	**6.4**	**31**	**2**	**3**	**5**	**7**	**13**	**18**	**27**
TOTAL										
0–19 Years	23	8.5	77	3	4	6	8	26	27	41
20–34	77	5.0	18	2	3	4	6	9	13	23
35–49	261	5.3	17	2	3	4	6	9	14	28
50–64	428	5.4	22	2	3	4	6	10	13	23
65+	312	7.3	37	2	3	5	9	15	22	26
GRAND TOTAL	**1,101**	**6.1**	**28**	**2**	**3**	**4**	**7**	**12**	**16**	**26**

01.53: BRAIN LOBECTOMY

Type of Patients	Observed Patients	Avg. Stay	Vari-ance	Percentiles 10th	25th	50th	75th	90th	95th	99th
1. SINGLE DX										
0–19 Years	1	3.0	0	3	3	3	3	3	3	3
20–34	13	4.2	7	2	2	3	5	10	10	11
35–49	4	3.9	<1	3	3	4	4	5	5	5
50–64	4	4.3	1	2	3	5	5	5	5	5
65+	2	6.7	24	2	2	10	10	10	10	10
2. MULTIPLE DX										
0–19 Years	10	6.7	12	3	4	7	8	14	14	15
20–34	33	7.5	55	3	3	4	9	22	24	33
35–49	31	7.0	33	3	3	5	8	12	20	30
50–64	46	7.8	37	3	4	6	11	12	18	37
65+	24	8.7	24	3	5	9	10	15	21	24
TOTAL SINGLE DX	**24**	**4.3**	**6**	**2**	**3**	**4**	**5**	**10**	**10**	**11**
TOTAL MULTIPLE DX	**144**	**7.7**	**35**	**3**	**4**	**6**	**10**	**14**	**20**	**33**
TOTAL										
0–19 Years	11	6.5	12	3	4	5	8	14	14	15
20–34	46	6.5	43	2	3	4	6	15	22	33
35–49	35	6.6	31	3	3	5	7	12	20	30
50–64	50	7.4	34	2	4	6	10	12	18	37
65+	26	8.6	24	3	5	9	10	15	21	24
GRAND TOTAL	**168**	**7.2**	**32**	**3**	**3**	**5**	**9**	**12**	**19**	**33**

01.59: EXC/DESTR BRAIN LES NEC

Type of Patients	Observed Patients	Avg. Stay	Vari-ance	Percentiles 10th	25th	50th	75th	90th	95th	99th
1. SINGLE DX										
0–19 Years	99	4.3	7	2	2	4	5	7	7	11
20–34	106	4.6	11	2	3	4	6	7	9	19
35–49	110	3.8	5	2	2	3	4	7	8	14
50–64	126	4.4	8	2	3	4	6	8	10	13
65+	22	4.3	6	2	3	4	5	7	8	11
2. MULTIPLE DX										
0–19 Years	431	9.6	93	3	4	7	11	20	28	53
20–34	389	6.6	68	2	3	4	7	12	17	63
35–49	658	6.3	28	2	3	4	8	13	16	29
50–64	1,183	6.4	27	2	3	5	8	13	17	26
65+	792	7.2	27	2	3	6	9	14	17	25
TOTAL SINGLE DX	**463**	**4.3**	**8**	**2**	**2**	**4**	**5**	**7**	**8**	**17**
TOTAL MULTIPLE DX	**3,453**	**7.1**	**43**	**2**	**3**	**5**	**9**	**15**	**18**	**33**
TOTAL										
0–19 Years	530	8.5	80	2	4	6	10	16	25	50
20–34	495	6.2	56	2	3	4	7	10	17	56
35–49	768	5.9	26	2	3	4	8	12	15	25
50–64	1,309	6.3	25	2	3	5	8	12	17	26
65+	814	7.1	27	2	3	6	9	14	17	25
GRAND TOTAL	**3,916**	**6.8**	**40**	**2**	**3**	**5**	**8**	**14**	**18**	**32**

01.6: EXCISION OF SKULL LESION

Type of Patients	Observed Patients	Avg. Stay	Vari-ance	Percentiles 10th	25th	50th	75th	90th	95th	99th
1. SINGLE DX										
0–19 Years	24	1.5	1	1	1	1	1	4	5	5
20–34	15	1.9	<1	1	1	2	2	3	4	4
35–49	13	3.3	10	1	1	2	5	9	10	10
50–64	13	1.4	1	1	1	1	1	2	3	6
65+	2	1.0	0	1	1	1	1	1	1	1
2. MULTIPLE DX										
0–19 Years	21	3.0	5	1	2	2	4	5	5	12
20–34	16	2.7	9	1	1	1	3	6	6	14
35–49	37	3.9	10	1	1	3	5	8	10	15
50–64	46	5.5	34	1	2	4	6	14	16	33
65+	37	6.8	35	1	2	5	10	18	18	19
TOTAL SINGLE DX	**67**	**1.8**	**3**	**1**	**1**	**1**	**2**	**4**	**5**	**10**
TOTAL MULTIPLE DX	**157**	**4.7**	**22**	**1**	**2**	**3**	**6**	**11**	**16**	**19**
TOTAL										
0–19 Years	45	2.4	4	1	1	2	3	5	5	12
20–34	31	2.4	5	1	1	2	3	5	6	14
35–49	50	3.8	10	1	1	2	5	9	10	15
50–64	59	4.3	28	1	1	2	5	10	16	33
65+	39	6.5	35	1	2	5	8	18	18	19
GRAND TOTAL	**224**	**3.9**	**18**	**1**	**1**	**2**	**5**	**9**	**14**	**19**

02.0: CRANIOPLASTY

Type of Patients	Observed Patients	Avg. Stay	Vari-ance	Percentiles 10th	25th	50th	75th	90th	95th	99th
1. SINGLE DX										
0–19 Years	242	2.6	1	1	2	3	3	4	5	5
20–34	23	2.1	4	1	1	2	3	3	3	11
35–49	21	2.1	3	1	1	2	3	3	3	9
50–64	34	2.7	3	1	2	2	3	5	5	8
65+	4	2.9	2	1	1	4	4	4	4	4
2. MULTIPLE DX										
0–19 Years	328	3.9	14	1	2	3	4	6	9	25
20–34	225	6.0	45	1	2	4	7	13	20	28
35–49	185	4.8	21	1	2	3	6	10	14	21
50–64	156	5.5	43	1	2	3	6	17	18	54
65+	45	6.2	41	1	2	4	8	17	19	35
TOTAL SINGLE DX	**324**	**2.6**	**2**	**1**	**2**	**2**	**3**	**4**	**5**	**5**
TOTAL MULTIPLE DX	**939**	**4.8**	**27**	**1**	**2**	**3**	**5**	**10**	**16**	**28**
TOTAL										
0–19 Years	570	3.3	9	1	2	3	4	5	6	17
20–34	248	5.7	43	1	2	3	7	13	20	28
35–49	206	4.6	20	1	2	3	6	10	13	21
50–64	190	5.0	38	1	2	3	6	13	17	28
65+	49	5.9	38	1	2	4	7	15	19	35
GRAND TOTAL	**1,263**	**4.1**	**20**	**1**	**2**	**3**	**4**	**8**	**13**	**24**

02.01: OPENING CRANIAL SUTURE

Type of Patients	Observed Patients	Avg. Stay	Vari-ance	Percentiles 10th	25th	50th	75th	90th	95th	99th
1. SINGLE DX										
0–19 Years	87	2.4	<1	1	2	2	3	4	4	5
20–34	0									
35–49	0									
50–64	4	2.8	<1	2	2	3	3	4	4	4
65+	0									
2. MULTIPLE DX										
0–19 Years	50	3.3	2	2	2	3	4	5	6	7
20–34	1	3.0	0	3	3	3	3	3	3	3
35–49	1	6.0	0	6	6	6	6	6	6	6
50–64	0									
65+	1	4.0	0	4	4	4	4	4	4	4
TOTAL SINGLE DX	**91**	**2.4**	**<1**	**1**	**2**	**2**	**3**	**4**	**4**	**5**
TOTAL MULTIPLE DX	**53**	**3.3**	**2**	**2**	**2**	**3**	**4**	**5**	**6**	**7**
TOTAL										
0–19 Years	137	2.7	1	1	2	3	3	4	5	7
20–34	1	3.0	0	3	3	3	3	3	3	3
35–49	1	6.0	0	6	6	6	6	6	6	6
50–64	4	2.8	<1	2	2	3	3	4	4	4
65+	1	4.0	0	4	4	4	4	4	4	4
GRAND TOTAL	**144**	**2.7**	**1**	**1**	**2**	**3**	**3**	**4**	**5**	**7**

02.02: ELEVATION SKULL FX FRAG

Type of Patients	Observed Patients	Avg. Stay	Vari-ance	Percentiles 10th	25th	50th	75th	90th	95th	99th
1. SINGLE DX										
0–19 Years	35	2.5	2	1	1	2	4	4	4	6
20–34	9	3.3	8	1	2	3	3	11	11	11
35–49	2	5.6	15	3	3	3	9	9	9	9
50–64	3	3.4	8	1	1	3	7	7	7	7
65+	0									
2. MULTIPLE DX										
0–19 Years	76	7.1	40	2	3	5	9	17	18	30
20–34	120	8.0	57	2	3	5	11	20	22	30
35–49	59	6.3	27	1	2	5	9	12	15	33
50–64	29	9.1	94	1	3	5	12	18	28	>99
65+	12	10.2	33	4	4	10	15	18	19	19
TOTAL SINGLE DX	**49**	**2.7**	**3**	**1**	**1**	**2**	**4**	**4**	**6**	**11**
TOTAL MULTIPLE DX	**296**	**7.6**	**50**	**2**	**3**	**5**	**10**	**17**	**20**	**33**
TOTAL										
0–19 Years	111	5.4	31	1	2	4	6	14	17	28
20–34	129	7.7	55	2	3	5	10	19	22	30
35–49	61	6.2	27	1	2	5	9	12	14	33
50–64	32	8.7	90	1	3	5	10	18	28	>99
65+	12	10.2	33	4	4	10	15	18	19	19
GRAND TOTAL	**345**	**6.8**	**46**	**1**	**2**	**4**	**9**	**16**	**20**	**30**

02.03: CRAN BONE FLAP FORMATION

Type of Patients	Observed Patients	Avg. Stay	Vari-ance	Percentiles 10th	25th	50th	75th	90th	95th	99th
1. SINGLE DX										
0–19 Years	19	3.3	<1	2	3	3	4	4	5	5
20–34	1	1.0	0	1	1	1	1	1	1	1
35–49	4	2.0	1	1	1	1	3	3	3	3
50–64	6	1.9	<1	1	1	2	3	3	3	3
65+	0									
2. MULTIPLE DX										
0–19 Years	29	4.9	36	2	3	4	6	8	55	>99
20–34	14	3.6	8	1	2	3	4	10	11	11
35–49	15	5.3	56	2	2	3	5	10	35	35
50–64	14	4.5	16	2	2	3	5	9	18	18
65+	5	7.9	70	1	2	5	19	19	19	19
TOTAL SINGLE DX	**30**	**2.9**	**1**	**1**	**2**	**3**	**4**	**4**	**5**	**5**
TOTAL MULTIPLE DX	**77**	**4.9**	**34**	**2**	**2**	**4**	**6**	**9**	**19**	**>99**
TOTAL										
0–19 Years	48	4.3	25	2	3	4	5	6	9	>99
20–34	15	3.4	8	1	2	2	4	10	11	11
35–49	19	4.7	47	1	2	3	3	9	10	35
50–64	20	3.9	14	1	2	3	4	6	9	18
65+	5	7.9	70	1	2	5	19	19	19	19
GRAND TOTAL	**107**	**4.4**	**26**	**1**	**2**	**3**	**5**	**6**	**10**	**>99**

02.06: CRANIAL OSTEOPLASTY NEC

Type of Patients	Observed Patients	Avg. Stay	Vari-ance	Percentiles 10th	25th	50th	75th	90th	95th	99th
1. SINGLE DX										
0–19 Years	85	2.9	1	1	2	3	4	4	5	5
20–34	10	1.3	<1	1	1	1	2	2	2	2
35–49	10	1.3	<1	1	1	1	1	2	3	3
50–64	14	2.8	2	1	2	2	3	5	5	5
65+	4	2.9	2	1	1	4	4	4	4	4
2. MULTIPLE DX										
0–19 Years	145	2.8	2	1	2	3	4	5	5	9
20–34	53	3.0	24	1	1	2	3	5	7	45
35–49	74	3.4	6	1	2	3	5	7	8	12
50–64	64	5.0	38	1	2	2	5	17	19	24
65+	17	3.1	5	1	1	2	4	6	10	10
TOTAL SINGLE DX	**123**	**2.8**	**2**	**1**	**2**	**3**	**4**	**4**	**5**	**5**
TOTAL MULTIPLE DX	**353**	**3.3**	**11**	**1**	**2**	**2**	**4**	**6**	**8**	**17**
TOTAL										
0–19 Years	230	2.9	2	1	2	3	4	5	5	6
20–34	63	2.8	22	1	1	2	3	4	7	45
35–49	84	3.2	6	1	1	2	5	7	8	10
50–64	78	4.6	32	1	2	2	4	13	17	24
65+	21	3.0	5	1	1	3	4	5	6	10
GRAND TOTAL	**476**	**3.1**	**9**	**1**	**2**	**3**	**4**	**5**	**6**	**17**

02.1: CEREBRAL MENINGES REPAIR

Type of Patients	Observed Patients	Avg. Stay	Vari-ance	Percentiles						
				10th	25th	50th	75th	90th	95th	99th
1. SINGLE DX										
0–19 Years	13	3.0	7	1	1	1	5	7	9	9
20–34	12	3.3	4	2	2	3	3	5	10	10
35–49	13	3.1	1	2	3	3	4	4	5	5
50–64	10	5.8	14	1	2	6	10	10	10	10
65+	1	1.0	0	1	1	1	1	1	1	1
2. MULTIPLE DX										
0–19 Years	57	7.4	53	2	3	4	8	19	28	28
20–34	43	6.8	37	2	3	5	7	16	17	32
35–49	66	5.9	18	2	3	5	7	11	13	22
50–64	82	7.2	45	2	3	5	9	15	19	27
65+	43	7.7	62	1	3	5	10	18	22	41
TOTAL SINGLE DX	**49**	**3.6**	**7**	**1**	**2**	**3**	**4**	**9**	**10**	**10**
TOTAL MULTIPLE DX	**291**	**7.0**	**43**	**2**	**3**	**5**	**8**	**15**	**22**	**31**
TOTAL										
0–19 Years	70	6.7	49	1	3	4	8	17	28	28
20–34	55	6.0	31	2	3	4	7	15	16	32
35–49	79	5.4	16	2	3	4	7	10	13	22
50–64	92	7.0	42	2	3	5	9	14	17	27
65+	44	7.7	62	1	3	5	8	18	22	41
GRAND TOTAL	**340**	**6.5**	**39**	**2**	**3**	**4**	**7**	**14**	**19**	**28**

02.12: REP CEREBRAL MENING NEC

Type of Patients	Observed Patients	Avg. Stay	Vari-ance	Percentiles						
				10th	25th	50th	75th	90th	95th	99th
1. SINGLE DX										
0–19 Years	13	3.0	7	1	1	1	5	7	9	9
20–34	11	3.3	5	2	2	3	3	5	10	10
35–49	13	3.1	1	2	3	3	4	4	5	5
50–64	10	5.8	14	1	2	6	10	10	10	10
65+	1	1.0	0	1	1	1	1	1	1	1
2. MULTIPLE DX										
0–19 Years	52	6.6	46	2	3	4	8	15	28	28
20–34	38	6.7	38	2	3	5	7	16	16	32
35–49	63	5.7	19	2	3	4	7	11	13	22
50–64	81	7.1	46	2	3	5	9	15	19	27
65+	40	7.7	65	1	3	5	8	18	22	41
TOTAL SINGLE DX	**48**	**3.7**	**7**	**1**	**2**	**3**	**4**	**9**	**10**	**10**
TOTAL MULTIPLE DX	**274**	**6.7**	**42**	**2**	**3**	**4**	**8**	**15**	**20**	**31**
TOTAL										
0–19 Years	65	6.1	42	1	3	4	6	14	28	28
20–34	49	6.0	32	2	3	4	7	15	16	32
35–49	76	5.3	17	2	3	4	7	10	13	22
50–64	91	6.9	42	2	3	5	9	15	17	27
65+	41	7.7	65	1	3	5	8	18	22	41
GRAND TOTAL	**322**	**6.3**	**38**	**1**	**3**	**4**	**7**	**14**	**19**	**28**

02.2: VENTRICULOSTOMY

Type of Patients	Observed Patients	Avg. Stay	Vari-ance	Percentiles						
				10th	25th	50th	75th	90th	95th	99th
1. SINGLE DX										
0–19 Years	17	3.5	14	1	1	3	4	8	9	17
20–34	8	4.2	11	1	1	4	7	7	9	9
35–49	5	3.9	16	1	1	2	5	11	11	11
50–64	12	4.6	13	1	1	3	7	7	14	14
65+	6	2.4	3	1	1	1	5	5	5	5
2. MULTIPLE DX										
0–19 Years	148	14.9	303	1	4	8	20	38	60	90
20–34	96	13.8	171	2	5	11	19	32	41	94
35–49	121	13.9	140	2	4	12	19	32	38	49
50–64	226	12.6	111	1	4	10	19	28	33	47
65+	129	13.5	137	2	5	11	18	32	34	38
TOTAL SINGLE DX	**48**	**3.8**	**12**	**1**	**1**	**3**	**7**	**7**	**9**	**17**
TOTAL MULTIPLE DX	**720**	**13.7**	**181**	**1**	**4**	**10**	**19**	**31**	**38**	**77**
TOTAL										
0–19 Years	165	14.0	289	1	3	8	19	33	56	90
20–34	104	13.0	165	2	5	9	17	30	38	94
35–49	126	13.6	139	2	4	11	19	32	38	49
50–64	238	12.0	108	1	3	10	18	26	32	46
65+	135	13.0	136	1	5	11	18	32	34	38
GRAND TOTAL	**768**	**13.1**	**176**	**1**	**4**	**9**	**18**	**30**	**38**	**77**

02.3: EXTRACRANIAL VENT SHUNT

Type of Patients	Observed Patients	Avg. Stay	Vari-ance	Percentiles						
				10th	25th	50th	75th	90th	95th	99th
1. SINGLE DX										
0–19 Years	95	2.4	5	1	1	2	3	4	6	14
20–34	15	3.6	13	1	1	2	4	9	9	15
35–49	11	2.8	3	1	1	2	4	5	5	5
50–64	8	2.7	4	1	1	2	4	7	7	7
65+	34	1.9	1	1	1	2	2	3	5	5
2. MULTIPLE DX										
0–19 Years	362	7.5	131	1	2	3	9	20	28	>99
20–34	122	8.3	84	1	2	5	12	20	32	43
35–49	138	7.7	106	1	2	4	9	20	27	32
50–64	235	7.5	103	1	2	3	9	20	28	57
65+	542	5.6	48	1	2	3	6	13	18	44
TOTAL SINGLE DX	**163**	**2.4**	**5**	**1**	**1**	**2**	**3**	**4**	**6**	**10**
TOTAL MULTIPLE DX	**1,399**	**6.9**	**93**	**1**	**2**	**3**	**8**	**17**	**25**	**62**
TOTAL										
0–19 Years	457	6.4	109	1	1	3	6	18	27	99
20–34	137	7.8	78	1	2	5	11	18	27	43
35–49	149	7.4	101	1	2	4	9	19	25	32
50–64	243	7.3	101	1	2	3	8	20	28	57
65+	576	5.4	46	1	2	3	6	13	18	44
GRAND TOTAL	**1,562**	**6.3**	**84**	**1**	**2**	**3**	**7**	**16**	**24**	**62**

02.34: VENT SHUNT TO ABD CAVITY

Type of Patients	Observed Patients	Avg. Stay	Vari-ance	Percentiles						
				10th	25th	50th	75th	90th	95th	99th
1. SINGLE DX										
0–19 Years	90	2.3	4	1	1	2	3	4	4	10
20–34	14	3.6	14	1	1	2	5	9	15	15
35–49	9	2.8	3	1	1	2	4	5	5	5
50–64	8	2.7	4	1	1	2	4	7	7	7
65+	33	1.9	1	1	1	2	2	3	5	5
2. MULTIPLE DX										
0–19 Years	320	6.0	83	1	1	3	6	16	25	>99
20–34	95	7.5	85	1	2	4	8	16	32	43
35–49	122	7.2	108	1	2	4	9	16	27	32
50–64	224	7.3	103	1	2	3	8	20	28	57
65+	520	5.6	49	1	2	3	6	13	18	44
TOTAL SINGLE DX	**154**	**2.3**	**4**	**1**	**1**	**2**	**3**	**4**	**5**	**10**
TOTAL MULTIPLE DX	**1,281**	**6.2**	**75**	**1**	**2**	**3**	**7**	**15**	**23**	**52**
TOTAL										
0–19 Years	410	5.2	68	1	1	3	5	14	21	75
20–34	109	7.0	78	1	2	3	8	15	32	43
35–49	131	7.0	103	1	2	4	9	16	25	32
50–64	232	7.1	101	1	2	3	8	19	27	57
65+	553	5.3	46	1	2	3	6	13	18	44
GRAND TOTAL	**1,435**	**5.7**	**68**	**1**	**2**	**3**	**6**	**14**	**22**	**52**

02.4: VENT SHUNT REV/RMVL

Type of Patients	Observed Patients	Avg. Stay	Vari-ance	Percentiles						
				10th	25th	50th	75th	90th	95th	99th
1. SINGLE DX										
0–19 Years	46	1.6	2	1	1	1	2	2	3	10
20–34	3	2.3	<1	2	2	2	3	3	3	3
35–49	3	1.0	0	1	1	1	1	1	1	1
50–64	4	1.6	4	1	1	1	1	7	7	7
65+	1	1.0	0	1	1	1	1	1	1	1
2. MULTIPLE DX										
0–19 Years	874	5.1	61	1	1	2	4	13	21	42
20–34	245	5.4	42	1	2	3	6	13	19	31
35–49	180	7.3	83	1	2	4	9	17	30	50
50–64	129	8.6	97	1	2	4	13	24	30	43
65+	178	6.8	63	1	2	3	9	16	29	>99
TOTAL SINGLE DX	**57**	**1.6**	**2**	**1**	**1**	**1**	**2**	**2**	**3**	**7**
TOTAL MULTIPLE DX	**1,606**	**5.7**	**64**	**1**	**1**	**3**	**6**	**14**	**23**	**42**
TOTAL										
0–19 Years	920	4.9	59	1	1	2	4	13	20	42
20–34	248	5.4	41	1	2	3	6	13	19	31
35–49	183	7.2	82	1	2	4	9	16	30	50
50–64	133	8.2	95	1	2	4	12	24	28	43
65+	179	6.7	62	1	2	3	9	16	29	>99
GRAND TOTAL	**1,663**	**5.5**	**63**	**1**	**1**	**2**	**6**	**14**	**22**	**42**

02.42: REPL VENTRICLULAR SHUNT

Type of Patients	Observed Patients	Avg. Stay	Vari-ance	Percentiles						
				10th	25th	50th	75th	90th	95th	99th
1. SINGLE DX										
0–19 Years	42	1.7	2	1	1	1	2	3	4	10
20–34	3	2.3	<1	2	2	2	3	3	3	3
35–49	3	1.0	0	1	1	1	1	1	1	1
50–64	3	1.7	4	1	1	1	1	7	7	7
65+	1	1.0	0	1	1	1	1	1	1	1
2. MULTIPLE DX										
0–19 Years	762	4.1	47	1	1	2	4	9	15	42
20–34	207	4.9	38	1	2	3	5	11	16	30
35–49	131	6.2	62	1	2	3	7	16	29	37
50–64	93	6.2	43	1	2	4	9	15	19	26
65+	141	5.5	35	1	1	3	8	15	18	>99
TOTAL SINGLE DX	**52**	**1.6**	**2**	**1**	**1**	**1**	**2**	**3**	**4**	**10**
TOTAL MULTIPLE DX	**1,334**	**4.6**	**47**	**1**	**1**	**2**	**4**	**11**	**17**	**37**
TOTAL										
0–19 Years	804	4.0	45	1	1	2	4	9	15	42
20–34	210	4.9	37	1	2	3	5	11	16	30
35–49	134	6.0	61	1	1	3	7	16	25	33
50–64	96	5.9	42	1	1	3	9	14	19	26
65+	142	5.5	35	1	1	3	8	15	18	>99
GRAND TOTAL	**1,386**	**4.5**	**45**	**1**	**1**	**2**	**4**	**11**	**16**	**37**

02.43: RMVL VENTRICLULAR SHUNT

Type of Patients	Observed Patients	Avg. Stay	Vari-ance	Percentiles						
				10th	25th	50th	75th	90th	95th	99th
1. SINGLE DX										
0–19 Years	4	1.0	0	1	1	1	1	1	1	1
20–34	0									
35–49	0									
50–64	1	1.0	0	1	1	1	1	1	1	1
65+	0									
2. MULTIPLE DX										
0–19 Years	101	12.6	116	1	4	10	18	30	34	47
20–34	33	9.0	60	1	3	7	13	20	31	32
35–49	44	11.4	139	3	5	7	12	28	50	59
50–64	32	16.1	188	1	3	14	25	30	43	56
65+	37	10.9	131	1	2	7	12	38	38	39
TOTAL SINGLE DX	**5**	**1.0**	**0**	**1**	**1**	**1**	**1**	**1**	**1**	**1**
TOTAL MULTIPLE DX	**247**	**12.2**	**126**	**1**	**4**	**8**	**17**	**30**	**38**	**50**
TOTAL										
0–19 Years	105	12.0	117	1	3	9	18	26	34	47
20–34	33	9.0	60	1	3	7	13	20	31	32
35–49	44	11.4	139	3	5	7	12	28	50	59
50–64	33	15.8	189	1	3	14	25	30	43	56
65+	37	10.9	131	1	2	7	12	38	38	39
GRAND TOTAL	**252**	**11.9**	**126**	**1**	**3**	**8**	**16**	**30**	**36**	**50**

02.9: SKULL & BRAIN OPS NEC

Type of Patients	Observed Patients	Avg. Stay	Vari-ance	Percentiles 10th	25th	50th	75th	90th	95th	99th
1. SINGLE DX										
0–19 Years	16	4.9	15	1	2	4	6	10	14	14
20–34	32	7.5	22	1	4	7	13	14	14	17
35–49	36	3.8	17	1	1	3	4	8	9	22
50–64	76	3.1	13	1	1	2	3	6	8	26
65+	54	2.1	2	1	1	2	3	3	5	9
2. MULTIPLE DX										
0–19 Years	64	8.0	95	1	2	5	10	13	27	46
20–34	122	6.9	27	1	3	5	10	14	16	25
35–49	156	7.2	49	2	3	5	10	15	19	46
50–64	252	5.5	59	1	1	3	6	11	21	43
65+	312	4.6	19	1	1	3	7	9	13	18
TOTAL SINGLE DX	**214**	**3.7**	**15**	**1**	**1**	**2**	**4**	**9**	**13**	**19**
TOTAL MULTIPLE DX	**906**	**5.8**	**42**	**1**	**2**	**4**	**7**	**12**	**17**	**35**
TOTAL										
0–19 Years	80	7.4	81	1	2	5	10	13	23	46
20–34	154	7.0	26	1	3	6	11	14	16	22
35–49	192	6.6	44	1	2	5	9	14	19	40
50–64	328	5.0	50	1	1	3	6	10	17	36
65+	366	4.2	18	1	1	3	6	9	13	18
GRAND TOTAL	**1,120**	**5.4**	**38**	**1**	**1**	**4**	**7**	**11**	**16**	**27**

02.93: IMPL IC NEUROSTIMULATOR

Type of Patients	Observed Patients	Avg. Stay	Vari-ance	Percentiles 10th	25th	50th	75th	90th	95th	99th
1. SINGLE DX										
0–19 Years	6	6.0	30	1	1	3	10	14	14	14
20–34	16	10.1	20	1	8	11	13	14	14	17
35–49	21	4.0	29	1	1	2	6	9	17	22
50–64	62	2.4	10	1	1	2	3	4	6	26
65+	46	1.9	2	1	1	1	3	3	4	9
2. MULTIPLE DX										
0–19 Years	17	5.4	31	1	1	1	11	11	11	23
20–34	29	8.2	27	1	5	8	11	16	17	19
35–49	44	5.9	20	1	2	5	10	11	14	18
50–64	132	3.0	11	1	1	2	4	7	10	15
65+	186	2.7	7	1	1	2	3	7	9	12
TOTAL SINGLE DX	**151**	**3.5**	**18**	**1**	**1**	**2**	**3**	**10**	**14**	**22**
TOTAL MULTIPLE DX	**408**	**3.6**	**14**	**1**	**1**	**2**	**5**	**9**	**11**	**16**
TOTAL										
0–19 Years	23	5.5	30	1	1	2	11	11	14	23
20–34	45	8.9	25	1	5	9	13	16	17	19
35–49	65	5.4	23	1	1	3	9	11	14	22
50–64	194	2.8	11	1	1	2	3	6	9	15
65+	232	2.5	6	1	1	1	3	7	8	9
GRAND TOTAL	**559**	**3.6**	**15**	**1**	**1**	**2**	**4**	**9**	**11**	**17**

02.94: INSERT/REPL SKULL TONGS

Type of Patients	Observed Patients	Avg. Stay	Vari-ance	Percentiles 10th	25th	50th	75th	90th	95th	99th
1. SINGLE DX										
0–19 Years	6	4.0	9	1	2	3	5	10	10	10
20–34	6	3.0	3	1	1	3	4	5	5	5
35–49	6	2.9	<1	1	3	3	4	4	4	4
50–64	6	7.4	29	3	4	7	8	19	19	19
65+	4	1.8	<1	1	1	2	3	3	3	3
2. MULTIPLE DX										
0–19 Years	34	11.1	151	3	5	6	11	27	46	46
20–34	76	6.8	28	2	3	5	10	14	16	25
35–49	79	8.0	71	2	3	5	11	18	21	46
50–64	88	8.9	117	1	3	6	10	25	25	62
65+	111	7.8	26	3	4	7	10	14	17	24
TOTAL SINGLE DX	**28**	**3.8**	**11**	**1**	**2**	**3**	**4**	**7**	**10**	**19**
TOTAL MULTIPLE DX	**388**	**8.2**	**68**	**2**	**4**	**6**	**10**	**17**	**24**	**46**
TOTAL										
0–19 Years	40	9.9	134	2	3	6	10	27	46	46
20–34	82	6.5	28	1	3	5	9	14	16	25
35–49	85	7.5	67	2	3	4	9	17	21	46
50–64	94	8.9	112	1	3	6	9	25	25	62
65+	115	7.6	26	3	4	6	9	14	17	24
GRAND TOTAL	**416**	**7.9**	**65**	**2**	**3**	**6**	**10**	**16**	**22**	**46**

03.0: SPINAL CANAL EXPLORATION

Type of Patients	Observed Patients	Avg. Stay	Vari-ance	Percentiles 10th	25th	50th	75th	90th	95th	99th
1. SINGLE DX										
0–19 Years	31	4.6	25	1	1	3	6	8	22	22
20–34	126	1.9	2	1	1	1	3	3	5	8
35–49	492	1.9	3	1	1	1	2	3	4	8
50–64	794	1.9	2	1	1	2	2	3	4	6
65+	584	2.2	2	1	1	2	3	4	5	6
2. MULTIPLE DX										
0–19 Years	126	4.9	28	1	2	3	5	10	13	36
20–34	277	4.1	32	1	1	2	4	10	13	33
35–49	1,755	3.2	14	1	1	2	4	6	9	20
50–64	4,259	3.1	12	1	1	2	3	6	8	20
65+	7,520	3.5	11	1	2	3	4	7	9	18
TOTAL SINGLE DX	**2,027**	**2.1**	**3**	**1**	**1**	**2**	**3**	**4**	**5**	**7**
TOTAL MULTIPLE DX	**13,937**	**3.4**	**12**	**1**	**1**	**2**	**4**	**6**	**9**	**19**
TOTAL										
0–19 Years	157	4.8	27	1	2	3	5	10	13	30
20–34	403	3.4	24	1	1	2	4	7	12	33
35–49	2,247	2.9	12	1	1	2	3	6	8	16
50–64	5,053	2.9	11	1	1	2	3	5	8	19
65+	8,104	3.4	10	1	2	3	4	6	8	17
GRAND TOTAL	**15,964**	**3.2**	**11**	**1**	**1**	**2**	**4**	**6**	**8**	**18**

03.02: REOPEN LAMINECTOMY SITE

Type of Patients	Observed Patients	Avg. Stay	Vari-ance	Percentiles						
				10th	25th	50th	75th	90th	95th	99th
1. SINGLE DX										
0–19 Years	1	1.0	0	1	1	1	1	1	1	1
20–34	8	1.8	1	1	1	1	3	4	4	4
35–49	16	1.6	1	1	1	1	2	3	3	7
50–64	6	1.9	1	1	1	1	3	3	3	3
65+	5	2.3	2	1	1	2	3	4	4	4
2. MULTIPLE DX										
0–19 Years	2	2.1	8	1	1	1	1	8	8	8
20–34	19	7.0	54	1	3	5	8	12	17	37
35–49	67	4.8	13	1	2	4	7	9	14	16
50–64	93	6.4	46	1	2	4	9	18	23	27
65+	108	7.0	57	1	2	4	8	19	19	31
TOTAL SINGLE DX	**36**	**1.7**	**1**	**1**	**1**	**1**	**2**	**3**	**4**	**7**
TOTAL MULTIPLE DX	**289**	**6.3**	**44**	**1**	**2**	**4**	**7**	**15**	**19**	**27**
TOTAL										
0–19 Years	3	1.7	5	1	1	1	1	8	8	8
20–34	27	5.5	44	1	2	4	6	11	17	37
35–49	83	4.1	12	1	1	3	5	8	14	16
50–64	99	6.1	45	1	2	4	8	15	23	27
65+	113	6.9	56	1	2	4	8	19	19	31
GRAND TOTAL	**325**	**5.8**	**41**	**1**	**2**	**4**	**7**	**15**	**19**	**27**

03.09: SPINAL CANAL EXPL NEC

Type of Patients	Observed Patients	Avg. Stay	Vari-ance	Percentiles						
				10th	25th	50th	75th	90th	95th	99th
1. SINGLE DX										
0–19 Years	29	4.8	26	1	2	3	6	11	22	22
20–34	118	1.9	2	1	1	1	3	3	5	8
35–49	476	1.9	3	1	1	1	2	3	4	8
50–64	788	1.9	2	1	1	2	2	3	4	6
65+	579	2.2	2	1	1	2	3	4	5	6
2. MULTIPLE DX										
0–19 Years	122	4.7	27	1	2	3	5	9	12	36
20–34	255	3.9	30	1	1	2	4	8	13	33
35–49	1,681	3.1	14	1	1	2	4	6	9	20
50–64	4,157	3.0	11	1	1	2	3	5	8	18
65+	7,407	3.4	10	1	2	3	4	6	8	17
TOTAL SINGLE DX	**1,990**	**2.1**	**3**	**1**	**1**	**2**	**3**	**4**	**5**	**7**
TOTAL MULTIPLE DX	**13,622**	**3.3**	**11**	**1**	**1**	**2**	**4**	**6**	**9**	**17**
TOTAL										
0–19 Years	151	4.7	27	1	2	3	5	9	13	36
20–34	373	3.3	22	1	1	2	3	7	10	20
35–49	2,157	2.8	12	1	1	2	3	5	8	17
50–64	4,945	2.8	10	1	1	2	3	5	7	17
65+	7,986	3.3	10	1	2	3	4	6	8	17
GRAND TOTAL	**15,612**	**3.1**	**10**	**1**	**1**	**2**	**4**	**6**	**8**	**17**

03.1: INTRASPIN NERVE ROOT DIV

Type of Patients	Observed Patients	Avg. Stay	Vari-ance	Percentiles						
				10th	25th	50th	75th	90th	95th	99th
1. SINGLE DX										
0–19 Years	4	5.8	20	2	4	4	6	15	15	15
20–34	1	3.0	0	3	3	3	3	3	3	3
35–49	2	2.9	2	2	2	2	4	4	4	4
50–64	1	6.0	0	6	6	6	6	6	6	6
65+	0									
2. MULTIPLE DX										
0–19 Years	18	6.4	20	3	3	6	7	17	17	19
20–34	1	3.0	0	3	3	3	3	3	3	3
35–49	6	4.5	28	1	1	3	4	16	16	16
50–64	2	4.0	4	1	1	5	5	5	5	5
65+	8	7.4	45	1	1	5	11	18	18	18
TOTAL SINGLE DX	**8**	**5.0**	**14**	**2**	**3**	**4**	**6**	**6**	**15**	**15**
TOTAL MULTIPLE DX	**35**	**6.2**	**27**	**1**	**3**	**5**	**7**	**17**	**18**	**19**
TOTAL										
0–19 Years	22	6.3	20	3	3	4	7	15	17	19
20–34	2	3.0	0	3	3	3	3	3	3	3
35–49	8	4.1	21	1	2	3	4	16	16	16
50–64	3	4.3	4	1	5	5	5	6	6	6
65+	8	7.4	45	1	1	5	11	18	18	18
GRAND TOTAL	**43**	**6.0**	**25**	**1**	**3**	**4**	**7**	**17**	**18**	**19**

03.2: CHORDOTOMY

Type of Patients	Observed Patients	Avg. Stay	Vari-ance	Percentiles						
				10th	25th	50th	75th	90th	95th	99th
1. SINGLE DX										
0–19 Years	0									
20–34	0									
35–49	1	4.0	0	4	4	4	4	4	4	4
50–64	0									
65+	0									
2. MULTIPLE DX										
0–19 Years	3	2.4	5	1	1	1	5	5	5	5
20–34	4	3.0	<1	2	3	3	4	4	4	4
35–49	2	12.8	48	9	9	9	22	22	22	22
50–64	8	6.3	37	2	3	3	7	12	22	22
65+	1	8.0	0	8	8	8	8	8	8	8
TOTAL SINGLE DX	**1**	**4.0**	**0**	**4**	**4**	**4**	**4**	**4**	**4**	**4**
TOTAL MULTIPLE DX	**18**	**6.2**	**34**	**1**	**3**	**3**	**8**	**12**	**22**	**22**
TOTAL										
0–19 Years	3	2.4	5	1	1	1	5	5	5	5
20–34	4	3.0	<1	2	3	3	4	4	4	4
35–49	3	10.9	52	4	9	9	9	22	22	22
50–64	8	6.3	37	2	3	3	7	12	22	22
65+	1	8.0	0	8	8	8	8	8	8	8
GRAND TOTAL	**19**	**6.1**	**33**	**1**	**3**	**3**	**8**	**12**	**22**	**22**

03.3: DXTIC PX ON SPINAL CANAL

Type of Patients	Observed Patients	Avg. Stay	Vari-ance	Percentiles						
				10th	25th	50th	75th	90th	95th	99th
1. SINGLE DX										
0–19 Years	4,689	2.5	2	1	2	2	3	4	5	9
20–34	1,075	2.5	2	1	2	2	3	4	5	8
35–49	445	2.9	5	1	2	2	4	5	7	12
50–64	138	3.0	6	1	2	2	4	6	8	12
65+	19	3.8	5	1	2	3	7	7	7	7
2. MULTIPLE DX										
0–19 Years	10,464	3.9	15	1	2	3	4	8	10	18
20–34	3,987	3.9	12	1	2	3	5	7	10	18
35–49	4,582	4.8	23	1	2	4	6	10	13	25
50–64	3,602	5.4	27	1	2	4	7	11	14	26
65+	3,814	6.4	30	2	3	5	8	13	16	24
TOTAL SINGLE DX	**6,366**	**2.5**	**3**	**1**	**2**	**2**	**3**	**4**	**5**	**9**
TOTAL MULTIPLE DX	**26,449**	**4.6**	**20**	**1**	**2**	**3**	**6**	**9**	**13**	**21**
TOTAL										
0–19 Years	15,153	3.5	12	1	2	3	4	7	10	16
20–34	5,062	3.6	11	1	2	3	4	7	9	17
35–49	5,027	4.7	22	1	2	3	6	9	13	24
50–64	3,740	5.4	27	1	2	4	7	11	14	26
65+	3,833	6.4	30	2	3	5	8	13	16	24
GRAND TOTAL	**32,815**	**4.2**	**17**	**1**	**2**	**3**	**5**	**8**	**11**	**20**

03.31: SPINAL TAP

Type of Patients	Observed Patients	Avg. Stay	Vari-ance	Percentiles						
				10th	25th	50th	75th	90th	95th	99th
1. SINGLE DX										
0–19 Years	4,689	2.5	2	1	2	2	3	4	5	9
20–34	1,074	2.5	2	1	2	2	3	4	5	8
35–49	445	2.9	5	1	2	2	4	5	7	12
50–64	136	3.0	6	1	1	2	3	6	8	12
65+	18	3.8	5	1	2	3	7	7	7	7
2. MULTIPLE DX										
0–19 Years	10,460	3.9	15	1	2	3	4	8	10	18
20–34	3,981	3.8	12	1	2	3	5	7	10	18
35–49	4,565	4.8	22	1	2	3	6	10	13	25
50–64	3,566	5.4	27	1	2	4	7	11	14	25
65+	3,766	6.4	30	2	3	5	8	13	16	24
TOTAL SINGLE DX	**6,362**	**2.5**	**3**	**1**	**2**	**2**	**3**	**4**	**5**	**9**
TOTAL MULTIPLE DX	**26,338**	**4.6**	**20**	**1**	**2**	**3**	**6**	**9**	**13**	**21**
TOTAL										
0–19 Years	15,149	3.5	12	1	2	3	4	7	10	16
20–34	5,055	3.6	10	1	2	3	4	7	9	17
35–49	5,010	4.7	21	1	2	3	6	9	13	23
50–64	3,702	5.3	26	1	2	4	7	11	14	25
65+	3,784	6.4	30	2	3	5	8	13	16	24
GRAND TOTAL	**32,700**	**4.2**	**17**	**1**	**2**	**3**	**5**	**8**	**11**	**20**

03.32: SPINAL CORD/MENINGES BX

Type of Patients	Observed Patients	Avg. Stay	Vari-ance	Percentiles						
				10th	25th	50th	75th	90th	95th	99th
1. SINGLE DX										
0–19 Years	0									
20–34	0									
35–49	0									
50–64	2	5.0	2	4	4	6	6	6	6	6
65+	1	2.0	0	2	2	2	2	2	2	2
2. MULTIPLE DX										
0–19 Years	2	8.1	10	6	6	6	11	11	11	11
20–34	1	37.0	0	37	37	37	37	37	37	37
35–49	9	7.2	29	2	3	8	8	11	22	22
50–64	16	7.5	32	1	4	6	8	16	17	21
65+	33	8.8	27	3	5	7	12	18	20	21
TOTAL SINGLE DX	**3**	**4.1**	**4**	**2**	**2**	**4**	**6**	**6**	**6**	**6**
TOTAL MULTIPLE DX	**61**	**8.9**	**44**	**2**	**5**	**7**	**12**	**18**	**21**	**37**
TOTAL										
0–19 Years	2	8.1	10	6	6	6	11	11	11	11
20–34	1	37.0	0	37	37	37	37	37	37	37
35–49	9	7.2	29	2	3	8	8	11	22	22
50–64	18	7.3	30	1	4	6	8	16	17	21
65+	34	8.7	28	3	5	7	12	18	20	21
GRAND TOTAL	**64**	**8.7**	**43**	**2**	**5**	**7**	**12**	**17**	**21**	**37**

03.4: EXC SPINAL CORD LESION

Type of Patients	Observed Patients	Avg. Stay	Vari-ance	Percentiles						
				10th	25th	50th	75th	90th	95th	99th
1. SINGLE DX										
0–19 Years	35	4.2	7	2	3	4	4	7	11	13
20–34	22	3.7	3	2	3	3	4	6	7	8
35–49	59	3.9	7	1	2	3	5	6	9	19
50–64	46	2.9	4	1	2	3	4	5	5	15
65+	22	3.8	6	1	2	3	4	7	8	12
2. MULTIPLE DX										
0–19 Years	104	7.4	173	2	3	4	6	13	19	94
20–34	62	7.7	78	2	3	4	8	20	27	48
35–49	208	6.7	29	2	3	5	8	16	17	24
50–64	328	6.2	45	1	2	4	7	13	18	43
65+	308	6.4	26	2	3	5	8	12	18	26
TOTAL SINGLE DX	**184**	**3.7**	**6**	**1**	**2**	**3**	**4**	**6**	**8**	**13**
TOTAL MULTIPLE DX	**1,010**	**6.6**	**57**	**2**	**3**	**4**	**8**	**13**	**19**	**32**
TOTAL										
0–19 Years	139	6.7	137	2	3	4	6	12	14	94
20–34	84	6.6	61	2	3	4	6	14	26	48
35–49	267	6.0	25	2	3	4	7	14	17	24
50–64	374	5.7	40	1	2	4	7	12	17	29
65+	330	6.2	25	2	3	5	8	12	18	26
GRAND TOTAL	**1,194**	**6.1**	**50**	**2**	**3**	**4**	**7**	**12**	**17**	**29**

03.5: SPINAL CORD PLASTIC OPS

Type of Patients	Observed Patients	Avg. Stay	Vari-ance	Percentiles						
				10th	25th	50th	75th	90th	95th	99th
1. SINGLE DX										
0–19 Years	42	3.0	8	1	1	2	4	5	12	12
20–34	18	3.8	4	2	3	3	5	7	8	9
35–49	22	3.6	5	2	2	3	4	5	8	13
50–64	23	2.5	3	1	1	2	4	5	6	7
65+	38	1.4	1	1	1	1	1	2	5	6
2. MULTIPLE DX										
0–19 Years	274	6.5	36	1	3	5	8	14	18	33
20–34	127	8.0	54	2	4	6	10	15	19	28
35–49	204	7.7	56	1	3	5	10	17	22	37
50–64	247	6.0	45	1	1	4	8	13	16	30
65+	999	4.2	27	1	1	2	6	10	13	25
TOTAL SINGLE DX	143	2.7	5	1	1	2	3	5	7	12
TOTAL MULTIPLE DX	1,851	5.4	37	1	1	3	7	12	16	29
TOTAL										
0–19 Years	316	6.0	34	1	2	4	8	12	18	33
20–34	145	7.4	49	2	3	6	10	14	18	28
35–49	226	7.3	53	1	3	5	9	16	21	37
50–64	270	5.7	43	1	1	4	8	13	16	30
65+	1,037	4.1	26	1	1	2	6	10	13	25
GRAND TOTAL	1,994	5.2	35	1	1	3	7	12	16	28

03.51: SPINAL MENINGOCELE REP

Type of Patients	Observed Patients	Avg. Stay	Vari-ance	Percentiles						
				10th	25th	50th	75th	90th	95th	99th
1. SINGLE DX										
0–19 Years	2	2.0	0	2	2	2	2	2	2	2
20–34	0									
35–49	1	2.0	0	2	2	2	2	2	2	2
50–64	1	3.0	0	3	3	3	3	3	3	3
65+	0									
2. MULTIPLE DX										
0–19 Years	21	8.8	21	1	6	9	12	14	17	17
20–34	5	3.3	12	1	1	1	6	9	9	9
35–49	13	4.9	12	1	2	5	5	12	12	12
50–64	17	4.9	7	2	4	4	6	8	12	12
65+	3	6.6	26	4	4	4	14	14	14	14
TOTAL SINGLE DX	4	2.1	<1	2	2	2	2	3	3	3
TOTAL MULTIPLE DX	59	6.5	19	1	3	5	11	12	14	17
TOTAL										
0–19 Years	23	8.2	23	1	4	9	12	14	17	17
20–34	5	3.3	12	1	1	1	6	9	9	9
35–49	14	4.7	12	1	2	5	5	12	12	12
50–64	18	4.8	7	2	3	4	6	8	8	12
65+	3	6.6	26	4	4	4	14	14	14	14
GRAND TOTAL	63	6.2	19	1	2	5	9	12	14	17

03.53: VERTEBRAL FX REPAIR

Type of Patients	Observed Patients	Avg. Stay	Vari-ance	Percentiles						
				10th	25th	50th	75th	90th	95th	99th
1. SINGLE DX										
0–19 Years	8	7.9	15	4	4	7	12	12	12	12
20–34	9	3.7	5	1	3	3	5	5	9	9
35–49	6	3.4	3	1	2	3	5	5	5	5
50–64	11	2.0	4	1	1	1	2	5	7	7
65+	36	1.3	<1	1	1	1	1	2	3	6
2. MULTIPLE DX										
0–19 Years	37	9.6	37	3	7	8	12	18	23	31
20–34	80	9.4	68	3	4	7	11	18	23	28
35–49	105	9.0	67	1	3	6	12	21	25	37
50–64	137	5.5	60	1	1	2	8	14	18	30
65+	896	4.0	22	1	1	2	5	9	12	25
TOTAL SINGLE DX	70	2.6	8	1	1	1	3	5	12	12
TOTAL MULTIPLE DX	1,255	4.9	35	1	1	3	7	12	16	27
TOTAL										
0–19 Years	45	9.3	33	3	6	8	12	18	18	31
20–34	89	8.9	65	3	4	7	11	17	23	28
35–49	111	8.8	66	1	3	6	12	21	25	37
50–64	148	5.3	57	1	1	2	8	13	17	30
65+	932	3.8	21	1	1	2	5	9	12	25
GRAND TOTAL	1,325	4.8	34	1	1	2	7	11	16	27

03.59: SPINAL STRUCT REPAIR NEC

Type of Patients	Observed Patients	Avg. Stay	Vari-ance	Percentiles						
				10th	25th	50th	75th	90th	95th	99th
1. SINGLE DX										
0–19 Years	29	2.1	1	1	1	2	3	4	4	5
20–34	9	3.9	3	2	3	3	4	7	8	8
35–49	15	3.8	6	2	3	3	4	5	8	13
50–64	11	3.0	2	1	2	3	4	5	6	6
65+	2	5.4	<1	5	5	5	6	6	6	6
2. MULTIPLE DX										
0–19 Years	162	4.0	12	1	2	3	5	7	8	22
20–34	42	5.8	17	2	3	5	8	13	14	17
35–49	86	6.6	47	2	3	4	7	14	21	40
50–64	92	6.9	27	3	3	5	8	14	16	24
65+	100	6.9	75	1	3	5	9	14	16	41
TOTAL SINGLE DX	66	2.8	3	1	2	3	4	5	6	8
TOTAL MULTIPLE DX	482	5.6	33	1	3	4	7	12	16	22
TOTAL										
0–19 Years	191	3.7	10	1	2	3	5	7	8	18
20–34	51	5.4	14	2	3	4	7	12	14	17
35–49	101	6.2	41	2	3	4	7	14	21	40
50–64	103	6.5	26	2	3	5	8	13	16	24
65+	102	6.9	74	1	3	5	8	14	16	41
GRAND TOTAL	548	5.2	30	1	2	4	6	11	15	22

03.6: SPINAL CORD ADHESIOLYSIS

Type of Patients	Observed Patients	Avg. Stay	Vari-ance	Percentiles						
				10th	25th	50th	75th	90th	95th	99th
1. SINGLE DX										
0–19 Years	23	1.0	<1	1	1	1	1	1	1	2
20–34	1	5.0	0	5	5	5	5	5	5	5
35–49	0									
50–64	3	4.3	15	2	2	2	9	9	9	9
65+	1	2.0	0	2	2	2	2	2	2	2
2. MULTIPLE DX										
0–19 Years	112	1.2	<1	1	1	1	1	2	3	6
20–34	11	5.0	34	1	1	2	7	16	17	17
35–49	24	3.5	6	1	2	3	4	6	11	12
50–64	21	4.7	18	1	1	3	6	11	16	16
65+	17	4.6	21	2	2	2	5	11	17	17
TOTAL SINGLE DX	**28**	**1.5**	**2**	**1**	**1**	**1**	**1**	**2**	**5**	**9**
TOTAL MULTIPLE DX	**185**	**2.3**	**9**	**1**	**1**	**1**	**2**	**5**	**9**	**17**
TOTAL										
0–19 Years	135	1.2	<1	1	1	1	1	1	2	5
20–34	12	5.0	30	1	1	2	6	16	17	17
35–49	24	3.5	6	1	2	3	4	6	11	12
50–64	24	4.7	18	1	2	3	6	11	16	16
65+	18	4.5	21	2	2	2	5	11	17	17
GRAND TOTAL	**213**	**2.3**	**8**	**1**	**1**	**1**	**2**	**5**	**9**	**17**

03.7: SPINAL THECAL SHUNT

Type of Patients	Observed Patients	Avg. Stay	Vari-ance	Percentiles						
				10th	25th	50th	75th	90th	95th	99th
1. SINGLE DX										
0–19 Years	3	4.8	2	3	4	6	6	6	6	6
20–34	6	6.1	14	2	3	6	8	8	18	18
35–49	8	2.1	2	1	1	2	3	4	4	4
50–64	2	3.0	0	3	3	3	3	3	3	3
65+	0									
2. MULTIPLE DX										
0–19 Years	18	5.1	11	1	3	4	7	10	10	10
20–34	26	7.8	62	2	3	5	9	20	31	31
35–49	35	4.3	15	1	2	3	5	10	15	15
50–64	24	5.5	35	1	2	3	9	12	13	29
65+	26	5.8	29	1	1	4	8	14	16	21
TOTAL SINGLE DX	**19**	**4.5**	**10**	**1**	**3**	**4**	**6**	**8**	**8**	**18**
TOTAL MULTIPLE DX	**129**	**5.5**	**29**	**1**	**2**	**3**	**7**	**12**	**15**	**29**
TOTAL										
0–19 Years	21	5.0	9	1	3	4	7	10	10	10
20–34	32	7.2	46	2	3	5	8	18	25	31
35–49	43	3.9	14	1	2	3	5	8	15	15
50–64	26	5.3	32	1	2	3	8	12	13	29
65+	26	5.8	29	1	1	4	8	14	16	21
GRAND TOTAL	**148**	**5.4**	**26**	**1**	**2**	**3**	**7**	**11**	**15**	**29**

03.71: SUBARACH-PERITON SHUNT

Type of Patients	Observed Patients	Avg. Stay	Vari-ance	Percentiles						
				10th	25th	50th	75th	90th	95th	99th
1. SINGLE DX										
0–19 Years	2	5.3	1	4	4	6	6	6	6	6
20–34	3	2.9	<1	2	2	3	4	4	4	4
35–49	5	2.3	2	1	1	2	3	4	4	4
50–64	1	3.0	0	3	3	3	3	3	3	3
65+	0									
2. MULTIPLE DX										
0–19 Years	13	4.1	12	1	1	3	9	10	10	10
20–34	17	8.3	85	1	3	4	9	25	31	31
35–49	20	3.3	11	1	2	2	3	7	10	15
50–64	12	4.7	20	1	2	2	5	12	13	13
65+	19	5.1	22	1	1	4	6	14	14	16
TOTAL SINGLE DX	**11**	**3.2**	**2**	**1**	**2**	**3**	**4**	**6**	**6**	**6**
TOTAL MULTIPLE DX	**81**	**5.0**	**31**	**1**	**2**	**3**	**6**	**12**	**15**	**31**
TOTAL										
0–19 Years	15	4.3	10	1	1	3	6	10	10	10
20–34	20	7.1	71	2	3	3	8	25	31	31
35–49	25	3.1	9	1	2	2	3	6	10	15
50–64	13	4.5	18	1	2	3	5	12	13	13
65+	19	5.1	22	1	1	4	6	14	14	16
GRAND TOTAL	**92**	**4.8**	**27**	**1**	**2**	**3**	**5**	**11**	**14**	**31**

03.8: DESTR INJECT-SPINE CANAL

Type of Patients	Observed Patients	Avg. Stay	Vari-ance	Percentiles						
				10th	25th	50th	75th	90th	95th	99th
1. SINGLE DX										
0–19 Years	4	9.3	26	5	7	7	9	18	18	18
20–34	0									
35–49	0									
50–64	0									
65+	0									
2. MULTIPLE DX										
0–19 Years	267	5.8	53	2	2	3	6	13	19	41
20–34	6	5.9	31	2	3	3	5	16	16	16
35–49	11	7.1	35	1	3	7	7	8	19	27
50–64	8	5.0	5	1	4	5	6	9	9	9
65+	5	15.3	110	3	7	25	25	25	25	25
TOTAL SINGLE DX	**4**	**9.3**	**26**	**5**	**7**	**7**	**9**	**18**	**18**	**18**
TOTAL MULTIPLE DX	**297**	**6.0**	**54**	**2**	**2**	**3**	**6**	**13**	**22**	**41**
TOTAL										
0–19 Years	271	5.8	53	2	2	3	6	13	19	41
20–34	6	5.9	31	2	3	3	5	16	16	16
35–49	11	7.1	35	1	3	7	7	8	19	27
50–64	8	5.0	5	1	4	5	6	9	9	9
65+	5	15.3	110	3	7	25	25	25	25	25
GRAND TOTAL	**301**	**6.0**	**54**	**2**	**2**	**3**	**7**	**14**	**22**	**41**

03.9: SPINAL CORD OPS NEC

Type of Patients	Observed Patients	Avg. Stay	Vari-ance	Percentiles						
				10th	25th	50th	75th	90th	95th	99th
1. SINGLE DX										
0–19 Years	74	2.3	2	1	1	2	3	4	4	5
20–34	323	1.8	1	1	1	2	2	3	4	7
35–49	172	2.8	3	1	1	2	4	5	6	9
50–64	110	2.4	3	1	1	2	3	5	6	8
65+	65	2.5	4	1	1	2	3	5	5	14
2. MULTIPLE DX										
0–19 Years	364	4.6	34	1	2	3	5	8	16	30
20–34	915	3.1	14	1	1	2	3	6	9	18
35–49	1,169	4.2	17	1	2	3	5	9	12	22
50–64	1,190	4.9	33	1	2	3	6	10	15	27
65+	2,065	5.3	17	1	3	4	7	10	13	20
TOTAL SINGLE DX	**744**	**2.2**	**2**	**1**	**1**	**2**	**3**	**4**	**5**	**8**
TOTAL MULTIPLE DX	**5,703**	**4.6**	**21**	**1**	**2**	**3**	**6**	**9**	**13**	**22**
TOTAL										
0–19 Years	438	4.2	29	1	2	3	4	7	13	29
20–34	1,238	2.8	11	1	1	2	3	5	7	15
35–49	1,341	4.0	16	1	2	3	5	8	12	22
50–64	1,300	4.7	31	1	2	3	6	9	14	25
65+	2,130	5.2	16	1	2	4	7	10	13	20
GRAND TOTAL	**6,447**	**4.3**	**20**	**1**	**2**	**3**	**5**	**9**	**12**	**22**

03.90: INSERT SPINAL CANAL CATH

Type of Patients	Observed Patients	Avg. Stay	Vari-ance	Percentiles						
				10th	25th	50th	75th	90th	95th	99th
1. SINGLE DX										
0–19 Years	28	2.3	1	1	1	2	3	4	5	5
20–34	166	1.6	<1	1	1	2	2	2	2	4
35–49	39	3.0	5	1	2	2	4	6	8	11
50–64	23	2.9	2	1	2	3	4	5	5	5
65+	13	3.0	2	1	2	3	5	5	5	5
2. MULTIPLE DX										
0–19 Years	47	3.5	6	1	2	2	6	7	9	10
20–34	327	2.7	9	1	1	2	3	4	6	22
35–49	250	3.8	12	1	2	2	5	8	11	18
50–64	294	4.8	24	1	2	3	6	10	12	26
65+	258	5.5	27	1	2	3	7	13	17	21
TOTAL SINGLE DX	**269**	**2.1**	**2**	**1**	**1**	**2**	**2**	**4**	**5**	**8**
TOTAL MULTIPLE DX	**1,176**	**4.1**	**18**	**1**	**2**	**2**	**5**	**9**	**12**	**22**
TOTAL										
0–19 Years	75	3.1	5	1	2	2	4	7	7	9
20–34	493	2.3	7	1	1	2	2	3	5	22
35–49	289	3.7	11	1	2	2	5	8	10	16
50–64	317	4.7	22	1	2	3	6	10	12	26
65+	271	5.4	26	1	2	3	7	13	16	21
GRAND TOTAL	**1,445**	**3.7**	**16**	**1**	**1**	**2**	**4**	**8**	**11**	**21**

03.91: INJECT ANES-SPINAL CANAL

Type of Patients	Observed Patients	Avg. Stay	Vari-ance	Percentiles						
				10th	25th	50th	75th	90th	95th	99th
1. SINGLE DX										
0–19 Years	29	1.8	<1	1	1	2	2	2	3	3
20–34	101	1.7	<1	1	1	2	2	3	3	4
35–49	19	2.3	2	1	1	2	3	4	6	7
50–64	17	2.6	5	1	1	2	3	7	8	8
65+	17	1.9	1	1	1	1	3	4	4	4
2. MULTIPLE DX										
0–19 Years	47	2.8	14	1	2	2	3	3	3	27
20–34	172	2.3	3	1	1	2	3	3	4	11
35–49	159	4.3	12	1	2	3	5	9	13	17
50–64	161	4.9	19	1	2	4	6	10	13	28
65+	427	5.6	14	2	3	5	7	10	12	21
TOTAL SINGLE DX	**183**	**1.8**	**<1**	**1**	**1**	**2**	**2**	**3**	**3**	**7**
TOTAL MULTIPLE DX	**966**	**4.3**	**14**	**1**	**2**	**3**	**6**	**9**	**12**	**19**
TOTAL										
0–19 Years	76	2.5	10	1	2	2	2	3	3	23
20–34	273	2.1	2	1	1	2	2	3	4	8
35–49	178	4.1	12	1	2	3	5	9	12	17
50–64	178	4.7	18	1	2	4	6	9	13	16
65+	444	5.4	14	1	3	5	7	10	12	20
GRAND TOTAL	**1,149**	**3.9**	**12**	**1**	**2**	**3**	**5**	**8**	**11**	**17**

03.92: INJECT SPINAL CANAL NEC

Type of Patients	Observed Patients	Avg. Stay	Vari-ance	Percentiles						
				10th	25th	50th	75th	90th	95th	99th
1. SINGLE DX										
0–19 Years	12	3.2	4	1	1	4	4	5	5	9
20–34	26	3.0	4	1	2	3	4	4	7	12
35–49	55	3.6	2	2	2	3	5	6	6	6
50–64	31	2.5	3	1	1	2	3	5	6	6
65+	18	3.5	10	1	2	2	3	7	13	14
2. MULTIPLE DX										
0–19 Years	222	5.8	48	2	2	3	6	12	22	35
20–34	145	5.6	47	2	3	4	6	11	16	32
35–49	360	5.3	22	1	2	4	6	11	15	26
50–64	439	6.1	54	2	3	4	7	11	17	60
65+	1,176	5.6	14	2	3	5	7	10	12	19
TOTAL SINGLE DX	**142**	**3.2**	**4**	**1**	**2**	**3**	**4**	**6**	**6**	**13**
TOTAL MULTIPLE DX	**2,342**	**5.6**	**28**	**2**	**3**	**4**	**7**	**10**	**14**	**28**
TOTAL										
0–19 Years	234	5.7	46	2	2	3	6	11	22	35
20–34	171	5.2	42	1	2	4	5	10	14	32
35–49	415	5.1	20	1	2	4	6	10	15	26
50–64	470	5.9	52	1	2	4	7	11	16	31
65+	1,194	5.5	14	2	3	5	7	10	12	19
GRAND TOTAL	**2,484**	**5.5**	**27**	**2**	**3**	**4**	**6**	**10**	**14**	**27**

03.93: INSERT SPINAL NEUROSTIM

Type of Patients	Observed Patients	Avg. Stay	Vari-ance	Percentiles 10th	25th	50th	75th	90th	95th	99th
1. SINGLE DX										
0–19 Years	0									
20–34	8	3.1	4	1	1	4	5	5	5	5
35–49	32	2.0	2	1	1	2	3	3	5	5
50–64	29	1.6	3	1	1	1	2	2	3	10
65+	14	1.7	1	1	1	1	3	3	3	4
2. MULTIPLE DX										
0–19 Years	2	19.9	210	5	5	29	29	29	29	29
20–34	37	3.3	14	1	1	2	3	9	14	14
35–49	182	2.9	22	1	1	2	3	4	10	22
50–64	172	2.7	10	1	1	2	3	5	7	18
65+	141	2.5	12	1	1	1	3	5	10	21
TOTAL SINGLE DX	**83**	**1.9**	**2**	**1**	**1**	**1**	**3**	**4**	**5**	**5**
TOTAL MULTIPLE DX	**534**	**2.8**	**16**	**1**	**1**	**2**	**3**	**5**	**10**	**22**
TOTAL										
0–19 Years	2	19.9	210	5	5	29	29	29	29	29
20–34	45	3.3	12	1	1	2	4	8	14	14
35–49	214	2.8	19	1	1	2	3	4	5	22
50–64	201	2.6	10	1	1	2	3	4	7	18
65+	155	2.4	11	1	1	1	3	4	10	19
GRAND TOTAL	**617**	**2.7**	**14**	**1**	**1**	**2**	**3**	**5**	**9**	**22**

03.94: RMVL SPINAL NEUROSTIM

Type of Patients	Observed Patients	Avg. Stay	Vari-ance	Percentiles 10th	25th	50th	75th	90th	95th	99th
1. SINGLE DX										
0–19 Years	0									
20–34	0									
35–49	5	1.1	<1	1	1	1	1	2	2	2
50–64	1	6.0	0	6	6	6	6	6	6	6
65+	0									
2. MULTIPLE DX										
0–19 Years	0									
20–34	5	4.0	6	1	3	4	4	8	8	8
35–49	39	4.0	12	1	2	3	5	12	12	13
50–64	38	3.2	3	1	2	3	4	6	6	8
65+	25	4.6	29	1	1	2	5	15	15	20
TOTAL SINGLE DX	**6**	**1.7**	**3**	**1**	**1**	**1**	**1**	**6**	**6**	**6**
TOTAL MULTIPLE DX	**107**	**3.9**	**14**	**1**	**1**	**3**	**5**	**8**	**13**	**19**
TOTAL										
0–19 Years	0									
20–34	5	4.0	6	1	3	4	4	8	8	8
35–49	44	3.7	11	1	1	2	5	8	12	13
50–64	39	3.2	4	1	2	3	4	6	6	8
65+	25	4.6	29	1	1	2	5	15	15	20
GRAND TOTAL	**113**	**3.8**	**14**	**1**	**1**	**3**	**5**	**8**	**12**	**19**

03.95: SPINAL BLOOD PATCH

Type of Patients	Observed Patients	Avg. Stay	Vari-ance	Percentiles 10th	25th	50th	75th	90th	95th	99th
1. SINGLE DX										
0–19 Years	4	2.0	2	1	1	1	4	4	4	4
20–34	22	2.5	3	1	1	2	3	6	7	7
35–49	19	2.7	3	1	1	3	3	6	8	8
50–64	4	1.8	<1	1	1	2	3	3	3	3
65+	1	3.0	0	3	3	3	3	3	3	3
2. MULTIPLE DX										
0–19 Years	31	2.9	3	1	1	2	4	5	6	6
20–34	200	3.1	5	1	1	2	4	6	8	13
35–49	113	3.3	6	1	1	3	4	6	8	12
50–64	31	3.2	4	1	2	3	4	7	7	8
65+	11	3.0	3	1	2	3	4	6	6	6
TOTAL SINGLE DX	**50**	**2.5**	**3**	**1**	**1**	**2**	**3**	**4**	**7**	**8**
TOTAL MULTIPLE DX	**386**	**3.1**	**5**	**1**	**1**	**2**	**4**	**6**	**7**	**12**
TOTAL										
0–19 Years	35	2.8	3	1	1	2	4	5	6	6
20–34	222	3.0	5	1	1	2	4	6	7	13
35–49	132	3.2	6	1	1	3	4	6	8	12
50–64	35	3.1	4	1	2	3	4	6	7	8
65+	12	3.0	3	1	2	3	4	6	6	6
GRAND TOTAL	**436**	**3.1**	**5**	**1**	**1**	**2**	**4**	**6**	**7**	**12**

03.97: REV SPINAL THECAL SHUNT

Type of Patients	Observed Patients	Avg. Stay	Vari-ance	Percentiles 10th	25th	50th	75th	90th	95th	99th
1. SINGLE DX										
0–19 Years	0									
20–34	0									
35–49	2	1.5	<1	1	1	2	2	2	2	2
50–64	4	1.5	1	1	1	1	1	4	4	4
65+	2	1.9	2	1	1	1	3	3	3	3
2. MULTIPLE DX										
0–19 Years	11	2.1	3	1	1	1	3	5	5	5
20–34	19	3.8	8	1	2	3	5	10	11	11
35–49	31	4.2	27	1	1	2	5	9	12	28
50–64	30	3.7	14	1	2	2	4	10	14	16
65+	10	3.6	6	1	2	2	7	7	7	7
TOTAL SINGLE DX	**8**	**1.6**	**1**	**1**	**1**	**1**	**2**	**4**	**4**	**4**
TOTAL MULTIPLE DX	**101**	**3.6**	**15**	**1**	**1**	**2**	**5**	**7**	**11**	**16**
TOTAL										
0–19 Years	11	2.1	3	1	1	1	3	5	5	5
20–34	19	3.8	8	1	2	3	5	10	11	11
35–49	33	4.0	26	1	1	2	5	9	11	28
50–64	34	3.4	13	1	1	2	4	5	14	16
65+	12	3.5	6	1	2	2	7	7	7	7
GRAND TOTAL	**109**	**3.5**	**14**	**1**	**1**	**2**	**4**	**7**	**11**	**16**

04.0: PERIPH NERVE INC/DIV/EXC

Type of Patients	Observed Patients	Avg. Stay	Vari-ance	10th	25th	50th	75th	90th	95th	99th
1. SINGLE DX										
0–19 Years	7	1.9	<1	1	1	2	2	3	3	4
20–34	22	3.9	3	3	3	3	5	6	7	8
35–49	40	3.8	4	1	2	3	5	7	7	7
50–64	50	2.9	1	1	2	3	3	4	5	7
65+	6	2.6	1	1	2	3	3	4	4	4
2. MULTIPLE DX										
0–19 Years	9	4.5	3	3	3	5	6	6	6	6
20–34	50	3.9	8	1	2	4	5	9	11	15
35–49	125	4.6	13	1	2	4	6	9	12	19
50–64	167	4.1	7	1	3	4	5	7	8	15
65+	65	4.8	24	1	1	4	5	10	13	28
TOTAL SINGLE DX	**125**	**3.1**	**3**	**1**	**2**	**3**	**4**	**5**	**6**	**7**
TOTAL MULTIPLE DX	**416**	**4.4**	**12**	**1**	**2**	**4**	**5**	**8**	**11**	**19**
TOTAL										
0–19 Years	16	3.0	3	1	1	2	4	6	6	6
20–34	72	3.9	6	1	3	3	5	6	10	15
35–49	165	4.4	10	1	2	4	6	8	11	15
50–64	217	3.8	6	1	2	3	4	6	7	15
65+	71	4.6	23	1	1	3	5	10	13	28
GRAND TOTAL	**541**	**4.1**	**10**	**1**	**2**	**3**	**5**	**7**	**10**	**15**

04.01: EXC ACOUSTIC NEUROMA

Type of Patients	Observed Patients	Avg. Stay	Vari-ance	10th	25th	50th	75th	90th	95th	99th
1. SINGLE DX										
0–19 Years	2	3.2	2	2	2	4	4	4	4	4
20–34	11	3.9	2	3	3	3	5	5	8	8
35–49	20	4.5	2	3	3	5	6	6	7	7
50–64	29	3.1	1	2	2	3	4	4	5	7
65+	4	3.4	<1	3	3	3	4	4	4	4
2. MULTIPLE DX										
0–19 Years	4	3.8	<1	3	3	3	5	5	5	5
20–34	21	4.2	6	3	3	4	4	5	6	15
35–49	64	5.4	10	3	4	5	6	10	11	19
50–64	114	4.8	8	3	3	4	5	7	9	15
65+	33	5.9	24	1	3	5	7	11	13	28
TOTAL SINGLE DX	**66**	**3.7**	**2**	**2**	**3**	**3**	**5**	**6**	**6**	**8**
TOTAL MULTIPLE DX	**236**	**5.1**	**11**	**3**	**3**	**4**	**5**	**8**	**11**	**19**
TOTAL										
0–19 Years	6	3.6	<1	3	3	3	4	5	5	5
20–34	32	4.1	4	3	3	4	5	5	8	15
35–49	84	5.2	8	3	3	5	6	8	11	15
50–64	143	4.4	7	2	3	4	5	7	8	15
65+	37	5.7	22	1	3	5	6	11	13	28
GRAND TOTAL	**302**	**4.8**	**9**	**3**	**3**	**4**	**5**	**7**	**10**	**15**

04.07: PERIPH/CRAN NERV EXC NEC

Type of Patients	Observed Patients	Avg. Stay	Vari-ance	10th	25th	50th	75th	90th	95th	99th
1. SINGLE DX										
0–19 Years	3	1.8	<1	1	1	2	2	3	3	3
20–34	10	4.0	4	1	3	4	6	6	7	7
35–49	14	2.3	1	1	2	2	3	4	5	5
50–64	18	2.4	1	1	1	3	3	3	4	5
65+	0									
2. MULTIPLE DX										
0–19 Years	5	4.9	4	1	4	6	6	6	6	6
20–34	22	3.8	11	1	1	3	4	10	11	11
35–49	49	4.0	15	1	1	2	6	9	12	19
50–64	37	2.8	5	1	1	2	4	7	7	8
65+	12	2.2	2	1	1	1	3	4	5	5
TOTAL SINGLE DX	**45**	**2.4**	**2**	**1**	**1**	**2**	**3**	**4**	**5**	**7**
TOTAL MULTIPLE DX	**125**	**3.5**	**10**	**1**	**1**	**2**	**5**	**8**	**10**	**14**
TOTAL										
0–19 Years	8	2.9	4	1	1	2	6	6	6	6
20–34	32	3.9	9	1	1	3	5	9	11	11
35–49	63	3.7	13	1	1	2	5	8	12	19
50–64	55	2.7	4	1	1	2	3	6	7	8
65+	12	2.2	2	1	1	1	3	4	5	5
GRAND TOTAL	**170**	**3.2**	**8**	**1**	**1**	**2**	**4**	**7**	**9**	**12**

04.1: DXTIC PX PERIPH NERV

Type of Patients	Observed Patients	Avg. Stay	Vari-ance	10th	25th	50th	75th	90th	95th	99th
1. SINGLE DX										
0–19 Years	0									
20–34	3	2.3	1	1	1	3	3	3	3	3
35–49	0									
50–64	0									
65+	0									
2. MULTIPLE DX										
0–19 Years	4	2.4	<1	1	1	3	3	3	3	3
20–34	1	17.0	0	17	17	17	17	17	17	17
35–49	7	13.3	156	1	1	9	25	35	35	35
50–64	10	5.8	19	3	3	3	7	15	15	15
65+	17	9.2	29	4	6	7	11	19	19	19
TOTAL SINGLE DX	**3**	**2.3**	**1**	**1**	**1**	**3**	**3**	**3**	**3**	**3**
TOTAL MULTIPLE DX	**39**	**7.0**	**45**	**1**	**3**	**4**	**9**	**18**	**19**	**35**
TOTAL										
0–19 Years	4	2.4	<1	1	1	3	3	3	3	3
20–34	4	5.3	45	1	1	3	3	17	17	17
35–49	7	13.3	156	1	1	9	25	35	35	35
50–64	10	5.8	19	3	3	3	7	15	15	15
65+	17	9.2	29	4	6	7	11	19	19	19
GRAND TOTAL	**42**	**6.7**	**43**	**1**	**3**	**4**	**8**	**18**	**19**	**35**

04.2: DESTR PERIPH/CRAN NERVES

Type of Patients	Observed Patients	Avg. Stay	Variance	10th	25th	50th	75th	90th	95th	99th
1. SINGLE DX										
0–19 Years	0									
20–34	0									
35–49	0									
50–64	0									
65+	3	1.3	<1	1	1	1	2	2	2	2
2. MULTIPLE DX										
0–19 Years	2	1.4	<1	1	1	1	2	2	2	2
20–34	0									
35–49	5	8.7	97	1	1	2	16	23	23	23
50–64	10	3.7	7	1	2	3	7	7	10	10
65+	19	4.5	28	1	1	1	8	11	15	20
TOTAL SINGLE DX	**3**	**1.3**	**<1**	**1**	**1**	**1**	**2**	**2**	**2**	**2**
TOTAL MULTIPLE DX	**36**	**4.5**	**28**	**1**	**1**	**2**	**7**	**11**	**16**	**23**
TOTAL										
0–19 Years	2	1.4	<1	1	1	1	2	2	2	2
20–34	0									
35–49	5	8.7	97	1	1	2	16	23	23	23
50–64	10	3.7	7	1	2	3	7	7	10	10
65+	22	4.2	26	1	1	1	8	11	15	20
GRAND TOTAL	**39**	**4.3**	**27**	**1**	**1**	**2**	**7**	**11**	**16**	**23**

04.3: CRAN/PERIPH NERVE SUTURE

Type of Patients	Observed Patients	Avg. Stay	Variance	10th	25th	50th	75th	90th	95th	99th
1. SINGLE DX										
0–19 Years	4	1.8	2	1	1	1	4	4	4	4
20–34	10	3.8	13	1	1	1	5	10	11	11
35–49	2	1.0	0	1	1	1	1	1	1	1
50–64	1	1.0	0	1	1	1	1	1	1	1
65+	1	1.0	0	1	1	1	1	1	1	1
2. MULTIPLE DX										
0–19 Years	28	2.4	6	1	1	1	2	5	9	11
20–34	86	2.9	6	1	1	2	4	6	8	11
35–49	54	3.3	9	1	1	2	4	8	9	15
50–64	36	1.7	1	1	1	1	2	4	5	5
65+	7	3.0	3	1	1	3	5	5	5	5
TOTAL SINGLE DX	**18**	**2.7**	**9**	**1**	**1**	**1**	**4**	**7**	**10**	**11**
TOTAL MULTIPLE DX	**211**	**2.7**	**6**	**1**	**1**	**2**	**4**	**6**	**8**	**12**
TOTAL										
0–19 Years	32	2.3	5	1	1	1	2	5	9	11
20–34	96	3.0	7	1	1	2	4	6	9	11
35–49	56	3.2	9	1	1	2	4	8	9	15
50–64	37	1.7	1	1	1	1	2	4	4	5
65+	8	2.8	3	1	1	2	5	5	5	5
GRAND TOTAL	**229**	**2.7**	**6**	**1**	**1**	**2**	**4**	**6**	**8**	**12**

04.4: PERIPH NERV ADHESIOLYSIS

Type of Patients	Observed Patients	Avg. Stay	Variance	10th	25th	50th	75th	90th	95th	99th
1. SINGLE DX										
0–19 Years	5	2.9	3	1	2	2	5	5	5	5
20–34	12	1.6	<1	1	1	2	2	2	3	3
35–49	27	2.1	1	1	1	2	3	4	4	4
50–64	45	2.7	2	1	2	2	4	5	5	6
65+	13	3.1	2	2	2	3	4	5	5	5
2. MULTIPLE DX										
0–19 Years	22	4.4	60	1	1	2	5	8	12	49
20–34	75	2.9	8	1	1	2	3	6	9	13
35–49	187	2.8	14	1	1	2	3	5	8	16
50–64	220	2.7	6	1	1	2	3	5	7	10
65+	142	3.2	15	1	1	2	4	6	8	11
TOTAL SINGLE DX	**102**	**2.5**	**2**	**1**	**2**	**2**	**3**	**4**	**5**	**6**
TOTAL MULTIPLE DX	**646**	**3.0**	**13**	**1**	**1**	**2**	**3**	**5**	**8**	**14**
TOTAL										
0–19 Years	27	4.2	52	1	1	2	5	8	12	49
20–34	87	2.8	7	1	1	2	3	6	9	13
35–49	214	2.8	13	1	1	2	3	4	7	14
50–64	265	2.7	5	1	1	2	3	5	6	10
65+	155	3.2	14	1	2	2	4	5	8	11
GRAND TOTAL	**748**	**2.9**	**12**	**1**	**1**	**2**	**3**	**5**	**7**	**13**

04.41: DECOMP TRIGEMINAL ROOT

Type of Patients	Observed Patients	Avg. Stay	Variance	10th	25th	50th	75th	90th	95th	99th
1. SINGLE DX										
0–19 Years	1	5.0	0	5	5	5	5	5	5	5
20–34	5	2.0	<1	1	2	2	2	3	3	3
35–49	7	2.8	<1	2	2	3	3	3	4	4
50–64	26	3.0	1	2	2	3	4	4	4	6
65+	12	2.7	1	2	2	2	3	4	5	5
2. MULTIPLE DX										
0–19 Years	0									
20–34	4	6.1	22	2	2	5	13	13	13	13
35–49	27	3.8	8	2	2	3	4	7	11	16
50–64	53	3.3	3	2	2	3	4	6	7	10
65+	53	3.7	7	2	2	3	5	6	7	21
TOTAL SINGLE DX	**51**	**2.9**	**1**	**2**	**2**	**3**	**4**	**4**	**5**	**6**
TOTAL MULTIPLE DX	**137**	**3.6**	**6**	**2**	**2**	**3**	**4**	**7**	**8**	**16**
TOTAL										
0–19 Years	1	5.0	0	5	5	5	5	5	5	5
20–34	9	3.9	14	1	2	2	5	13	13	13
35–49	34	3.6	7	2	2	3	3	7	7	16
50–64	79	3.2	3	2	2	3	4	5	7	9
65+	65	3.5	6	2	2	3	4	5	7	21
GRAND TOTAL	**188**	**3.4**	**5**	**2**	**2**	**3**	**4**	**5**	**7**	**13**

04.42: CRANIAL NERVE DECOMP NEC

Type of Patients	Observed Patients	Avg. Stay	Vari-ance	Percentiles 10th	25th	50th	75th	90th	95th	99th
1. SINGLE DX										
0–19 Years	1	5.0	0	5	5	5	5	5	5	5
20–34	1	2.0	0	2	2	2	2	2	2	2
35–49	5	2.8	1	1	3	3	3	4	4	4
50–64	7	3.6	3	2	2	3	5	5	6	6
65+	1	5.0	0	5	5	5	5	5	5	5
2. MULTIPLE DX										
0–19 Years	4	7.1	21	1	5	8	12	12	12	12
20–34	7	3.9	6	1	2	3	6	8	8	8
35–49	19	4.8	103	2	2	2	3	5	5	50
50–64	29	3.3	3	1	2	3	4	5	6	8
65+	12	3.8	5	2	3	3	4	9	9	9
TOTAL SINGLE DX	**15**	**3.6**	**2**	**2**	**2**	**4**	**5**	**5**	**5**	**6**
TOTAL MULTIPLE DX	**71**	**4.1**	**28**	**1**	**2**	**3**	**4**	**8**	**9**	**50**
TOTAL										
0–19 Years	5	6.8	18	1	5	5	12	12	12	12
20–34	8	3.7	5	1	2	3	5	8	8	8
35–49	24	4.4	84	1	2	2	3	5	5	50
50–64	36	3.3	3	1	2	3	5	5	6	8
65+	13	4.0	4	2	3	3	5	9	9	9
GRAND TOTAL	**86**	**4.0**	**24**	**2**	**2**	**3**	**5**	**6**	**9**	**12**

04.43: CARPAL TUNNEL RELEASE

Type of Patients	Observed Patients	Avg. Stay	Vari-ance	Percentiles 10th	25th	50th	75th	90th	95th	99th
1. SINGLE DX										
0–19 Years	0									
20–34	0									
35–49	3	2.7	2	1	1	2	4	4	4	4
50–64	3	1.4	<1	1	1	1	2	2	2	2
65+	0									
2. MULTIPLE DX										
0–19 Years	7	6.6	176	1	2	2	5	5	49	49
20–34	37	3.8	11	1	1	3	6	9	11	14
35–49	62	3.3	9	1	1	2	4	9	9	16
50–64	72	2.3	5	1	1	2	2	5	6	13
65+	58	2.8	25	1	1	2	3	5	6	45
TOTAL SINGLE DX	**6**	**2.1**	**2**	**1**	**1**	**2**	**4**	**4**	**4**	**4**
TOTAL MULTIPLE DX	**236**	**3.1**	**19**	**1**	**1**	**2**	**4**	**6**	**9**	**14**
TOTAL										
0–19 Years	7	6.6	176	1	2	2	5	5	49	49
20–34	37	3.8	11	1	1	3	6	9	11	14
35–49	65	3.2	9	1	1	2	4	9	9	16
50–64	75	2.2	5	1	1	2	2	4	6	10
65+	58	2.8	25	1	1	2	3	5	6	45
GRAND TOTAL	**242**	**3.0**	**19**	**1**	**1**	**2**	**4**	**6**	**9**	**14**

04.49: PERIPH NERV ADHESIO NEC

Type of Patients	Observed Patients	Avg. Stay	Vari-ance	Percentiles 10th	25th	50th	75th	90th	95th	99th
1. SINGLE DX										
0–19 Years	3	1.8	<1	1	2	2	2	2	2	2
20–34	6	1.3	<1	1	1	1	2	2	2	2
35–49	10	1.6	<1	1	1	1	2	2	3	3
50–64	8	1.3	<1	1	1	1	1	2	2	2
65+	0									
2. MULTIPLE DX										
0–19 Years	10	2.2	3	1	1	1	5	5	5	5
20–34	24	1.7	<1	1	1	2	2	2	2	3
35–49	73	1.9	2	1	1	2	2	4	4	5
50–64	57	2.6	9	1	1	2	3	6	6	23
65+	14	2.9	10	1	1	2	2	8	11	11
TOTAL SINGLE DX	**27**	**1.5**	**<1**	**1**	**1**	**1**	**2**	**2**	**2**	**3**
TOTAL MULTIPLE DX	**178**	**2.2**	**4**	**1**	**1**	**2**	**2**	**4**	**5**	**11**
TOTAL										
0–19 Years	13	2.2	3	1	1	1	4	5	5	5
20–34	30	1.6	<1	1	1	2	2	2	2	3
35–49	83	1.9	1	1	1	2	2	4	4	5
50–64	65	2.5	8	1	1	2	2	5	6	14
65+	14	2.9	10	1	1	2	2	8	11	11
GRAND TOTAL	**205**	**2.1**	**4**	**1**	**1**	**2**	**2**	**4**	**5**	**9**

04.5: CRAN OR PERIPH NERV GRFT

Type of Patients	Observed Patients	Avg. Stay	Vari-ance	Percentiles 10th	25th	50th	75th	90th	95th	99th
1. SINGLE DX										
0–19 Years	2	1.9	2	1	1	1	3	3	3	3
20–34	0									
35–49	4	2.3	<1	2	2	2	3	3	3	3
50–64	1	1.0	0	1	1	1	1	1	1	1
65+	1	2.0	0	2	2	2	2	2	2	2
2. MULTIPLE DX										
0–19 Years	3	2.2	3	1	1	1	2	5	5	5
20–34	11	1.7	<1	1	1	2	2	2	2	2
35–49	18	3.0	9	1	1	2	3	10	10	10
50–64	6	3.6	8	1	1	2	7	7	7	7
65+	2	1.5	<1	1	1	1	2	2	2	2
TOTAL SINGLE DX	**8**	**2.0**	**<1**	**1**	**2**	**2**	**2**	**3**	**3**	**3**
TOTAL MULTIPLE DX	**40**	**2.6**	**6**	**1**	**1**	**2**	**2**	**7**	**10**	**10**
TOTAL										
0–19 Years	5	2.1	2	1	1	1	3	5	5	5
20–34	11	1.7	<1	1	1	2	2	2	2	2
35–49	22	2.9	8	1	1	2	3	10	10	10
50–64	7	3.3	8	1	1	2	7	7	7	7
65+	3	1.7	<1	1	1	2	2	2	2	2
GRAND TOTAL	**48**	**2.5**	**5**	**1**	**1**	**2**	**2**	**7**	**7**	**10**

04.6: PERIPH NERVES TRANSPOS

Type of Patients	Observed Patients	Avg. Stay	Vari-ance	Percentiles						
				10th	25th	50th	75th	90th	95th	99th
1. SINGLE DX										
0–19 Years	1	1.0	0	1	1	1	1	1	1	1
20–34	5	1.6	<1	1	1	2	2	2	2	2
35–49	1	1.0	0	1	1	1	1	1	1	1
50–64	3	1.3	<1	1	1	1	2	2	2	2
65+	1	1.0	0	1	1	1	1	1	1	1
2. MULTIPLE DX										
0–19 Years	3	1.3	<1	1	1	1	2	2	2	2
20–34	11	2.0	2	1	1	2	2	5	6	6
35–49	21	1.5	<1	1	1	1	2	2	2	2
50–64	15	3.3	10	1	1	2	4	8	13	13
65+	13	1.8	1	1	1	1	2	3	5	5
TOTAL SINGLE DX	**11**	**1.3**	**<1**	**1**	**1**	**1**	**2**	**2**	**2**	**2**
TOTAL MULTIPLE DX	**63**	**2.1**	**4**	**1**	**1**	**2**	**2**	**4**	**6**	**13**
TOTAL										
0–19 Years	4	1.3	<1	1	1	1	2	2	2	2
20–34	16	1.9	1	1	1	2	2	2	5	6
35–49	22	1.5	<1	1	1	1	2	2	2	2
50–64	18	3.0	9	1	1	2	4	8	8	13
65+	14	1.7	1	1	1	1	2	3	5	5
GRAND TOTAL	**74**	**2.0**	**4**	**1**	**1**	**2**	**2**	**4**	**6**	**13**

04.7: OTHER PERIPH NEUROPLASTY

Type of Patients	Observed Patients	Avg. Stay	Vari-ance	Percentiles						
				10th	25th	50th	75th	90th	95th	99th
1. SINGLE DX										
0–19 Years	0									
20–34	4	2.4	1	1	2	2	3	4	4	4
35–49	6	1.5	<1	1	1	1	2	2	2	2
50–64	2	1.0	0	1	1	1	1	1	1	1
65+	0									
2. MULTIPLE DX										
0–19 Years	7	1.6	1	1	1	1	1	4	4	4
20–34	17	3.7	37	1	1	2	3	8	28	28
35–49	19	2.0	3	1	1	1	2	6	6	7
50–64	16	2.2	1	1	1	2	2	4	4	6
65+	7	5.2	13	1	1	6	9	9	9	9
TOTAL SINGLE DX	**12**	**1.7**	**<1**	**1**	**1**	**1**	**2**	**3**	**4**	**4**
TOTAL MULTIPLE DX	**66**	**3.1**	**14**	**1**	**1**	**2**	**4**	**9**	**9**	**28**
TOTAL										
0–19 Years	7	1.6	1	1	1	1	1	4	4	4
20–34	21	3.4	30	1	1	2	3	6	8	28
35–49	25	1.8	2	1	1	1	2	4	6	7
50–64	18	2.0	1	1	1	2	2	4	4	6
65+	7	5.2	13	1	1	6	9	9	9	9
GRAND TOTAL	**78**	**2.9**	**12**	**1**	**1**	**2**	**3**	**8**	**9**	**9**

04.8: PERIPHERAL NERVE INJECT

Type of Patients	Observed Patients	Avg. Stay	Vari-ance	Percentiles						
				10th	25th	50th	75th	90th	95th	99th
1. SINGLE DX										
0–19 Years	3	2.1	<1	1	1	2	3	3	3	3
20–34	5	4.2	2	2	4	4	5	6	6	6
35–49	3	4.7	2	3	3	5	6	6	6	6
50–64	5	3.0	2	1	2	4	4	4	4	4
65+	2	3.0	0	3	3	3	3	3	3	3
2. MULTIPLE DX										
0–19 Years	7	5.4	37	2	2	2	7	10	22	22
20–34	38	5.5	21	2	3	4	7	11	16	25
35–49	64	5.2	20	1	3	4	6	10	13	32
50–64	72	5.5	28	2	2	3	7	15	17	23
65+	123	5.6	21	1	3	4	7	11	14	27
TOTAL SINGLE DX	**18**	**3.5**	**2**	**2**	**2**	**4**	**4**	**6**	**6**	**6**
TOTAL MULTIPLE DX	**304**	**5.5**	**23**	**1**	**2**	**4**	**7**	**12**	**15**	**25**
TOTAL										
0–19 Years	10	4.5	29	1	2	2	7	10	22	22
20–34	43	5.3	19	2	3	4	7	9	12	25
35–49	67	5.2	20	1	3	4	6	10	13	20
50–64	77	5.4	27	2	2	3	7	15	17	23
65+	125	5.6	21	1	3	4	7	11	14	27
GRAND TOTAL	**322**	**5.4**	**22**	**1**	**2**	**4**	**7**	**11**	**15**	**25**

04.81: ANES INJECT PERIPH NERVE

Type of Patients	Observed Patients	Avg. Stay	Vari-ance	Percentiles						
				10th	25th	50th	75th	90th	95th	99th
1. SINGLE DX										
0–19 Years	3	2.1	<1	1	1	2	3	3	3	3
20–34	5	4.2	2	2	4	4	5	6	6	6
35–49	3	4.7	2	3	3	5	6	6	6	6
50–64	3	3.3	1	2	2	4	4	4	4	4
65+	2	3.0	0	3	3	3	3	3	3	3
2. MULTIPLE DX										
0–19 Years	7	5.4	37	2	2	2	7	10	22	22
20–34	38	5.5	21	2	3	4	7	11	16	25
35–49	64	5.2	20	1	3	4	6	10	13	32
50–64	71	5.6	28	2	2	3	8	15	17	23
65+	119	5.7	22	1	3	4	7	11	14	27
TOTAL SINGLE DX	**16**	**3.6**	**2**	**2**	**2**	**4**	**4**	**6**	**6**	**6**
TOTAL MULTIPLE DX	**299**	**5.5**	**23**	**1**	**2**	**4**	**7**	**12**	**15**	**25**
TOTAL										
0–19 Years	10	4.5	29	1	2	2	7	10	22	22
20–34	43	5.3	19	2	3	4	7	9	12	25
35–49	67	5.2	20	1	3	4	6	10	13	20
50–64	74	5.5	27	2	2	3	7	15	17	23
65+	121	5.6	22	1	3	4	7	11	14	27
GRAND TOTAL	**315**	**5.4**	**22**	**2**	**2**	**4**	**7**	**12**	**15**	**25**

04.9: OTH PERIPH NERVE OPS

Type of Patients	Observed Patients	Avg. Stay	Vari-ance	Percentiles						
				10th	25th	50th	75th	90th	95th	99th
1. SINGLE DX										
0–19 Years	27	1.2	<1	1	1	1	1	2	2	2
20–34	19	2.1	10	1	1	1	1	4	14	14
35–49	22	1.6	2	1	1	1	2	2	2	7
50–64	15	1.1	<1	1	1	1	1	2	2	2
65+	1	5.0	0	5	5	5	5	5	5	5
2. MULTIPLE DX										
0–19 Years	72	3.1	106	1	1	1	2	4	7	93
20–34	40	2.5	8	1	1	1	3	5	9	16
35–49	47	2.8	11	1	1	1	3	6	9	19
50–64	43	2.3	8	1	1	1	2	5	11	14
65+	25	5.3	30	1	1	2	14	14	14	14
TOTAL SINGLE DX	**84**	**1.5**	**3**	**1**	**1**	**1**	**1**	**2**	**3**	**14**
TOTAL MULTIPLE DX	**227**	**3.1**	**45**	**1**	**1**	**1**	**3**	**6**	**14**	**16**
TOTAL										
0–19 Years	99	2.5	75	1	1	1	2	3	6	43
20–34	59	2.3	8	1	1	1	2	5	9	16
35–49	69	2.5	9	1	1	1	3	6	9	19
50–64	58	2.1	7	1	1	1	2	5	11	14
65+	26	5.3	30	1	1	2	14	14	14	14
GRAND TOTAL	**311**	**2.7**	**35**	**1**	**1**	**1**	**2**	**5**	**11**	**16**

04.92: IMPL PERIPH NEUROSTIM

Type of Patients	Observed Patients	Avg. Stay	Vari-ance	Percentiles						
				10th	25th	50th	75th	90th	95th	99th
1. SINGLE DX										
0–19 Years	27	1.2	<1	1	1	1	1	2	2	2
20–34	19	2.1	10	1	1	1	1	4	14	14
35–49	20	1.6	2	1	1	1	2	2	2	7
50–64	14	1.1	<1	1	1	1	1	2	2	2
65+	1	5.0	0	5	5	5	5	5	5	5
2. MULTIPLE DX										
0–19 Years	62	3.3	136	1	1	1	1	3	7	93
20–34	30	2.1	8	1	1	1	2	5	5	16
35–49	38	2.7	10	1	1	1	3	5	9	19
50–64	35	2.2	9	1	1	1	1	5	11	14
65+	20	5.6	33	1	1	2	14	14	14	14
TOTAL SINGLE DX	**81**	**1.5**	**3**	**1**	**1**	**1**	**1**	**2**	**3**	**14**
TOTAL MULTIPLE DX	**185**	**3.1**	**54**	**1**	**1**	**1**	**2**	**7**	**14**	**19**
TOTAL										
0–19 Years	89	2.6	89	1	1	1	1	2	6	43
20–34	49	2.1	8	1	1	1	2	4	8	16
35–49	58	2.4	8	1	1	1	2	5	9	19
50–64	49	2.0	7	1	1	1	1	4	11	14
65+	21	5.6	32	1	1	2	14	14	14	14
GRAND TOTAL	**266**	**2.7**	**41**	**1**	**1**	**1**	**2**	**5**	**11**	**16**

05.0: SYMPATH NERVE DIVISION

Type of Patients	Observed Patients	Avg. Stay	Vari-ance	Percentiles						
				10th	25th	50th	75th	90th	95th	99th
1. SINGLE DX										
0–19 Years	0									
20–34	0									
35–49	0									
50–64	0									
65+	0									
2. MULTIPLE DX										
0–19 Years	0									
20–34	0									
35–49	0									
50–64	1	13.0	0	13	13	13	13	13	13	13
65+	0									
TOTAL SINGLE DX	**0**									
TOTAL MULTIPLE DX	**1**	**13.0**	**0**	**13**	**13**	**13**	**13**	**13**	**13**	**13**
TOTAL										
0–19 Years	0									
20–34	0									
35–49	0									
50–64	1	13.0	0	13	13	13	13	13	13	13
65+	0									
GRAND TOTAL	**1**	**13.0**	**0**	**13**	**13**	**13**	**13**	**13**	**13**	**13**

05.1: SYMPATH NERVE DXTIC PX

Type of Patients	Observed Patients	Avg. Stay	Vari-ance	Percentiles						
				10th	25th	50th	75th	90th	95th	99th
1. SINGLE DX										
0–19 Years	0									
20–34	0									
35–49	0									
50–64	0									
65+	0									
2. MULTIPLE DX										
0–19 Years	0									
20–34	0									
35–49	0									
50–64	0									
65+	0									
TOTAL SINGLE DX	**0**									
TOTAL MULTIPLE DX	**0**									
TOTAL										
0–19 Years	0									
20–34	0									
35–49	0									
50–64	0									
65+	0									
GRAND TOTAL	**0**									

05.2: SYMPATHECTOMY

Type of Patients	Observed Patients	Avg. Stay	Vari-ance	Percentiles						
				10th	25th	50th	75th	90th	95th	99th
1. SINGLE DX										
0–19 Years	8	1.2	<1	1	1	1	1	2	2	2
20–34	40	1.3	<1	1	1	1	1	2	2	3
35–49	13	1.3	<1	1	1	1	1	3	3	3
50–64	3	2.2	4	1	1	1	5	5	5	5
65+	4	1.8	<1	1	2	2	2	2	2	2
2. MULTIPLE DX										
0–19 Years	4	1.3	<1	1	1	1	2	2	2	2
20–34	28	2.0	1	1	1	1	3	4	4	5
35–49	29	2.9	10	1	1	2	3	7	14	15
50–64	21	3.3	30	1	1	2	4	4	6	29
65+	15	4.4	8	1	2	4	7	8	8	10
TOTAL SINGLE DX	**68**	**1.4**	**<1**	**1**	**1**	**1**	**2**	**2**	**2**	**5**
TOTAL MULTIPLE DX	**97**	**2.9**	**11**	**1**	**1**	**2**	**3**	**7**	**8**	**15**
TOTAL										
0–19 Years	12	1.2	<1	1	1	1	1	2	2	2
20–34	68	1.6	<1	1	1	1	2	3	4	5
35–49	42	2.5	9	1	1	2	2	4	8	15
50–64	24	3.1	26	1	1	2	4	5	6	29
65+	19	3.5	7	1	2	2	6	8	8	10
GRAND TOTAL	**165**	**2.3**	**7**	**1**	**1**	**1**	**2**	**4**	**7**	**14**

05.29: OTHER SYMPATHECTOMY

Type of Patients	Observed Patients	Avg. Stay	Vari-ance	Percentiles						
				10th	25th	50th	75th	90th	95th	99th
1. SINGLE DX										
0–19 Years	8	1.2	<1	1	1	1	1	2	2	2
20–34	33	1.3	<1	1	1	1	1	2	2	3
35–49	12	1.4	<1	1	1	1	1	3	3	3
50–64	3	2.2	4	1	1	1	5	5	5	5
65+	3	1.7	<1	1	1	2	2	2	2	2
2. MULTIPLE DX										
0–19 Years	4	1.3	<1	1	1	1	2	2	2	2
20–34	22	1.9	1	1	1	1	3	4	4	4
35–49	17	2.4	10	1	1	1	2	3	7	15
50–64	16	3.3	37	1	1	1	4	4	4	29
65+	7	4.2	11	1	1	4	8	8	10	10
TOTAL SINGLE DX	**59**	**1.4**	**<1**	**1**	**1**	**1**	**2**	**2**	**2**	**5**
TOTAL MULTIPLE DX	**66**	**2.6**	**12**	**1**	**1**	**1**	**3**	**4**	**8**	**29**
TOTAL										
0–19 Years	12	1.2	<1	1	1	1	1	2	2	2
20–34	55	1.5	<1	1	1	1	2	3	4	4
35–49	29	2.0	7	1	1	1	2	3	7	15
50–64	19	3.1	32	1	1	1	4	4	5	29
65+	10	3.1	8	1	1	2	4	8	8	10
GRAND TOTAL	**125**	**2.0**	**7**	**1**	**1**	**1**	**2**	**4**	**4**	**15**

05.3: SYMPATH NERVE INJECTION

Type of Patients	Observed Patients	Avg. Stay	Vari-ance	Percentiles						
				10th	25th	50th	75th	90th	95th	99th
1. SINGLE DX										
0–19 Years	6	6.5	28	1	1	6	7	15	15	15
20–34	1	6.0	0	6	6	6	6	6	6	6
35–49	0									
50–64	0									
65+	0									
2. MULTIPLE DX										
0–19 Years	9	4.7	16	1	1	5	8	11	11	11
20–34	19	9.7	35	4	5	7	12	21	21	21
35–49	37	6.1	20	1	2	5	10	13	14	17
50–64	42	6.8	38	1	2	5	8	18	21	27
65+	51	7.6	30	1	3	6	10	18	20	22
TOTAL SINGLE DX	**7**	**6.5**	**26**	**1**	**1**	**6**	**7**	**15**	**15**	**15**
TOTAL MULTIPLE DX	**158**	**7.2**	**31**	**1**	**3**	**6**	**10**	**16**	**20**	**21**
TOTAL										
0–19 Years	15	5.6	22	1	1	5	7	15	15	15
20–34	20	9.5	34	4	5	7	12	21	21	21
35–49	37	6.1	20	1	2	5	10	13	14	17
50–64	42	6.8	38	1	2	5	8	18	21	27
65+	51	7.6	30	1	3	6	10	18	20	22
GRAND TOTAL	**165**	**7.1**	**31**	**1**	**3**	**6**	**10**	**15**	**20**	**21**

05.31: ANES INJECT SYMPATH NERV

Type of Patients	Observed Patients	Avg. Stay	Vari-ance	Percentiles						
				10th	25th	50th	75th	90th	95th	99th
1. SINGLE DX										
0–19 Years	6	6.5	28	1	1	6	7	15	15	15
20–34	1	6.0	0	6	6	6	6	6	6	6
35–49	0									
50–64	0									
65+	0									
2. MULTIPLE DX										
0–19 Years	7	6.1	14	1	2	6	8	11	11	11
20–34	19	9.7	35	4	5	7	12	21	21	21
35–49	34	6.0	20	1	2	4	9	13	14	17
50–64	36	6.5	34	1	2	5	8	14	19	27
65+	48	7.8	31	1	3	7	10	18	20	22
TOTAL SINGLE DX	**7**	**6.5**	**26**	**1**	**1**	**6**	**7**	**15**	**15**	**15**
TOTAL MULTIPLE DX	**144**	**7.3**	**30**	**1**	**3**	**6**	**10**	**16**	**20**	**21**
TOTAL										
0–19 Years	13	6.4	21	1	2	6	8	15	15	15
20–34	20	9.5	34	4	5	7	12	21	21	21
35–49	34	6.0	20	1	2	4	9	13	14	17
50–64	36	6.5	34	1	2	5	8	14	19	27
65+	48	7.8	31	1	3	7	10	18	20	22
GRAND TOTAL	**151**	**7.2**	**30**	**1**	**3**	**6**	**10**	**15**	**20**	**21**

05.8: OTH SYMPATH NERVE OPS

Type of Patients	Observed Patients	Avg. Stay	Vari-ance	Percentiles						
				10th	25th	50th	75th	90th	95th	99th
1. SINGLE DX										
0–19 Years	0									
20–34	0									
35–49	0									
50–64	0									
65+	0									
2. MULTIPLE DX										
0–19 Years	0									
20–34	0									
35–49	1	1.0	0	1	1	1	1	1	1	1
50–64	0									
65+	0									
TOTAL SINGLE DX	**0**									
TOTAL MULTIPLE DX	**1**	**1.0**	**0**	**1**	**1**	**1**	**1**	**1**	**1**	**1**
TOTAL										
0–19 Years	0									
20–34	0									
35–49	1	1.0	0	1	1	1	1	1	1	1
50–64	0									
65+	0									
GRAND TOTAL	**1**	**1.0**	**0**	**1**	**1**	**1**	**1**	**1**	**1**	**1**

05.9: OTHER NERVOUS SYSTEM OPS

Type of Patients	Observed Patients	Avg. Stay	Vari-ance	Percentiles						
				10th	25th	50th	75th	90th	95th	99th
1. SINGLE DX										
0–19 Years	0									
20–34	0									
35–49	0									
50–64	0									
65+	0									
2. MULTIPLE DX										
0–19 Years	0									
20–34	0									
35–49	0									
50–64	0									
65+	0									
TOTAL SINGLE DX	**0**									
TOTAL MULTIPLE DX	**0**									
TOTAL										
0–19 Years	0									
20–34	0									
35–49	0									
50–64	0									
65+	0									
GRAND TOTAL	**0**									

06.0: THYROID FIELD INCISION

Type of Patients	Observed Patients	Avg. Stay	Vari-ance	Percentiles						
				10th	25th	50th	75th	90th	95th	99th
1. SINGLE DX										
0–19 Years	9	2.1	2	1	1	2	4	4	4	4
20–34	5	3.5	5	1	1	3	6	6	6	6
35–49	11	1.2	<1	1	1	1	1	2	2	2
50–64	8	1.9	2	1	1	1	3	4	4	4
65+	2	1.5	<1	1	1	1	2	2	2	2
2. MULTIPLE DX										
0–19 Years	10	3.7	4	1	2	5	5	6	7	7
20–34	23	3.0	6	1	1	2	4	7	8	8
35–49	25	3.5	6	1	2	3	4	9	9	9
50–64	32	6.0	42	1	1	3	8	17	20	20
65+	25	4.4	21	1	1	3	6	9	17	22
TOTAL SINGLE DX	**35**	**2.0**	**2**	**1**	**1**	**1**	**3**	**4**	**6**	**6**
TOTAL MULTIPLE DX	**115**	**4.3**	**20**	**1**	**1**	**3**	**5**	**9**	**17**	**20**
TOTAL										
0–19 Years	19	2.7	3	1	1	2	4	5	6	7
20–34	28	3.1	5	1	1	2	5	7	7	8
35–49	36	2.9	6	1	1	2	4	5	9	9
50–64	40	5.3	37	1	1	3	6	17	20	20
65+	27	4.2	21	1	1	3	6	9	17	22
GRAND TOTAL	**150**	**3.7**	**17**	**1**	**1**	**2**	**5**	**8**	**10**	**20**

06.09: INC THYROID FIELD NEC

Type of Patients	Observed Patients	Avg. Stay	Vari-ance	Percentiles						
				10th	25th	50th	75th	90th	95th	99th
1. SINGLE DX										
0–19 Years	8	2.1	2	1	1	1	4	4	4	4
20–34	4	3.7	5	1	1	3	6	6	6	6
35–49	10	1.2	<1	1	1	1	1	2	2	2
50–64	5	1.4	<1	1	1	1	1	3	3	3
65+	2	1.5	<1	1	1	1	2	2	2	2
2. MULTIPLE DX										
0–19 Years	8	3.2	6	1	1	3	5	7	7	7
20–34	21	3.0	6	1	1	2	5	7	8	8
35–49	21	3.4	7	1	2	2	4	9	9	9
50–64	22	6.6	52	1	1	3	9	20	20	20
65+	13	4.9	37	1	1	2	6	17	22	22
TOTAL SINGLE DX	**29**	**2.0**	**2**	**1**	**1**	**1**	**3**	**4**	**6**	**6**
TOTAL MULTIPLE DX	**85**	**4.3**	**24**	**1**	**1**	**2**	**6**	**9**	**17**	**20**
TOTAL										
0–19 Years	16	2.5	3	1	1	1	4	5	7	7
20–34	25	3.1	6	1	1	2	6	7	8	8
35–49	31	2.8	6	1	1	2	3	9	9	9
50–64	27	5.6	46	1	1	2	8	20	20	20
65+	15	4.5	33	1	1	2	5	17	17	22
GRAND TOTAL	**114**	**3.7**	**19**	**1**	**1**	**2**	**4**	**8**	**16**	**20**

06.1: THYROID/PARATHY DXTIC PX

Type of Patients	Observed Patients	Avg. Stay	Vari-ance	Percentiles						
				10th	25th	50th	75th	90th	95th	99th
1. SINGLE DX										
0–19 Years	1	1.0	0	1	1	1	1	1	1	1
20–34	2	1.4	<1	1	1	1	2	2	2	2
35–49	5	2.1	5	1	1	1	1	6	6	6
50–64	2	1.0	0	1	1	1	1	1	1	1
65+	0									
2. MULTIPLE DX										
0–19 Years	2	1.7	<1	1	1	2	2	2	2	2
20–34	8	4.2	7	1	2	4	5	8	8	8
35–49	30	4.6	18	1	1	3	6	12	12	20
50–64	42	4.9	20	1	2	4	6	11	16	22
65+	133	5.5	22	1	2	4	7	12	16	20
TOTAL SINGLE DX	**10**	**1.6**	**3**	**1**	**1**	**1**	**1**	**6**	**6**	**6**
TOTAL MULTIPLE DX	**215**	**5.2**	**20**	**1**	**2**	**4**	**7**	**12**	**16**	**20**
TOTAL										
0–19 Years	3	1.5	<1	1	1	1	2	2	2	2
20–34	10	3.7	7	1	1	4	5	8	8	8
35–49	35	4.3	17	1	1	2	6	9	12	20
50–64	44	4.7	20	1	2	4	6	11	16	22
65+	133	5.5	22	1	2	4	7	12	16	20
GRAND TOTAL	**225**	**5.1**	**20**	**1**	**2**	**4**	**7**	**12**	**16**	**20**

06.11: CLOSED THYROID BIOPSY

Type of Patients	Observed Patients	Avg. Stay	Vari-ance	Percentiles						
				10th	25th	50th	75th	90th	95th	99th
1. SINGLE DX										
0–19 Years	0									
20–34	1	1.0	0	1	1	1	1	1	1	1
35–49	3	2.7	8	1	1	1	6	6	6	6
50–64	0									
65+	0									
2. MULTIPLE DX										
0–19 Years	0									
20–34	2	7.2	2	5	5	8	8	8	8	8
35–49	12	7.3	24	1	4	7	12	12	20	20
50–64	24	6.9	24	3	4	6	8	16	17	22
65+	98	6.7	22	2	4	5	8	15	16	24
TOTAL SINGLE DX	**4**	**2.2**	**6**	**1**	**1**	**1**	**1**	**6**	**6**	**6**
TOTAL MULTIPLE DX	**136**	**6.8**	**22**	**2**	**4**	**6**	**8**	**14**	**16**	**22**
TOTAL										
0–19 Years	0									
20–34	3	5.5	11	1	1	8	8	8	8	8
35–49	15	6.6	24	1	2	6	9	12	12	20
50–64	24	6.9	24	3	4	6	8	16	17	22
65+	98	6.7	22	2	4	5	8	15	16	24
GRAND TOTAL	**140**	**6.7**	**22**	**2**	**4**	**5**	**8**	**14**	**16**	**22**

06.2: UNILAT THYROID LOBECTOMY

Type of Patients	Observed Patients	Avg. Stay	Vari-ance	Percentiles						
				10th	25th	50th	75th	90th	95th	99th
1. SINGLE DX										
0–19 Years	41	1.3	<1	1	1	1	1	2	2	4
20–34	232	1.2	<1	1	1	1	1	2	2	3
35–49	437	1.2	<1	1	1	1	1	2	2	3
50–64	297	1.2	<1	1	1	1	1	2	2	2
65+	86	1.3	<1	1	1	1	1	2	2	3
2. MULTIPLE DX										
0–19 Years	27	1.4	<1	1	1	1	1	2	3	4
20–34	219	1.4	<1	1	1	1	2	2	3	4
35–49	618	1.5	3	1	1	1	2	2	3	6
50–64	674	1.5	1	1	1	1	2	2	3	6
65+	479	1.7	3	1	1	1	2	3	3	7
TOTAL SINGLE DX	**1,093**	**1.2**	**<1**	**1**	**1**	**1**	**1**	**2**	**2**	**3**
TOTAL MULTIPLE DX	**2,017**	**1.5**	**2**	**1**	**1**	**1**	**2**	**2**	**3**	**7**
TOTAL										
0–19 Years	68	1.3	<1	1	1	1	1	2	2	4
20–34	451	1.3	<1	1	1	1	1	2	2	4
35–49	1,055	1.4	2	1	1	1	1	2	3	5
50–64	971	1.4	1	1	1	1	1	2	3	5
65+	565	1.6	3	1	1	1	2	3	3	7
GRAND TOTAL	**3,110**	**1.4**	**2**	**1**	**1**	**1**	**2**	**2**	**3**	**6**

06.3: OTHER PART THYROIDECTOMY

Type of Patients	Observed Patients	Avg. Stay	Vari-ance	Percentiles						
				10th	25th	50th	75th	90th	95th	99th
1. SINGLE DX										
0–19 Years	14	1.0	<1	1	1	1	1	1	1	2
20–34	76	1.3	<1	1	1	1	1	2	2	4
35–49	146	1.3	<1	1	1	1	1	2	2	4
50–64	114	1.4	<1	1	1	1	2	2	2	3
65+	30	1.1	<1	1	1	1	1	1	2	2
2. MULTIPLE DX										
0–19 Years	9	1.9	2	1	1	1	2	4	5	5
20–34	92	1.6	2	1	1	1	2	3	3	7
35–49	265	1.8	3	1	1	1	2	3	4	10
50–64	267	1.6	2	1	1	1	2	3	3	7
65+	177	2.3	11	1	1	1	2	3	8	16
TOTAL SINGLE DX	**380**	**1.3**	**<1**	**1**	**1**	**1**	**1**	**2**	**2**	**4**
TOTAL MULTIPLE DX	**810**	**1.9**	**5**	**1**	**1**	**1**	**2**	**3**	**4**	**12**
TOTAL										
0–19 Years	23	1.3	<1	1	1	1	1	2	4	5
20–34	168	1.5	1	1	1	1	2	2	3	7
35–49	411	1.6	2	1	1	1	2	2	4	8
50–64	381	1.5	2	1	1	1	2	2	3	7
65+	207	2.1	10	1	1	1	2	3	8	15
GRAND TOTAL	**1,190**	**1.7**	**3**	**1**	**1**	**1**	**2**	**3**	**4**	**10**

06.31: EXCISION THYROID LESION

Type of Patients	Observed Patients	Avg. Stay	Vari-ance	Percentiles						
				10th	25th	50th	75th	90th	95th	99th
1. SINGLE DX										
0–19 Years	4	1.2	<1	1	1	1	1	2	2	2
20–34	9	1.2	<1	1	1	1	1	2	2	2
35–49	14	1.1	<1	1	1	1	1	2	2	2
50–64	7	1.3	<1	1	1	1	2	2	2	2
65+	5	1.0	0	1	1	1	1	1	1	1
2. MULTIPLE DX										
0–19 Years	1	2.0	0	2	2	2	2	2	2	2
20–34	4	1.5	<1	1	1	2	2	2	2	2
35–49	27	1.4	<1	1	1	1	2	2	3	4
50–64	21	2.2	5	1	1	1	2	4	5	11
65+	19	2.5	13	1	1	1	2	8	16	16
TOTAL SINGLE DX	**39**	**1.2**	**<1**	**1**	**1**	**1**	**1**	**2**	**2**	**2**
TOTAL MULTIPLE DX	**72**	**2.0**	**5**	**1**	**1**	**1**	**2**	**3**	**5**	**16**
TOTAL										
0–19 Years	5	1.3	<1	1	1	1	2	2	2	2
20–34	13	1.3	<1	1	1	1	2	2	2	2
35–49	41	1.3	<1	1	1	1	1	2	2	4
50–64	28	2.0	4	1	1	1	2	4	5	11
65+	24	2.3	11	1	1	1	2	3	8	16
GRAND TOTAL	**111**	**1.7**	**4**	**1**	**1**	**1**	**2**	**3**	**4**	**16**

06.39: PART THYROIDECTOMY NEC

Type of Patients	Observed Patients	Avg. Stay	Vari-ance	Percentiles						
				10th	25th	50th	75th	90th	95th	99th
1. SINGLE DX										
0–19 Years	10	1.0	0	1	1	1	1	1	1	1
20–34	67	1.3	<1	1	1	1	1	2	3	4
35–49	132	1.3	<1	1	1	1	2	2	2	4
50–64	107	1.4	<1	1	1	1	2	2	2	3
65+	25	1.1	<1	1	1	1	1	1	2	2
2. MULTIPLE DX										
0–19 Years	8	1.9	2	1	1	1	2	5	5	5
20–34	88	1.6	2	1	1	1	2	3	3	7
35–49	238	1.8	3	1	1	1	2	3	4	10
50–64	246	1.6	2	1	1	1	2	3	3	7
65+	158	2.3	11	1	1	1	2	3	8	15
TOTAL SINGLE DX	**341**	**1.3**	**<1**	**1**	**1**	**1**	**1**	**2**	**2**	**4**
TOTAL MULTIPLE DX	**738**	**1.8**	**5**	**1**	**1**	**1**	**2**	**3**	**4**	**12**
TOTAL										
0–19 Years	18	1.3	<1	1	1	1	1	2	4	5
20–34	155	1.5	2	1	1	1	2	2	3	7
35–49	370	1.7	2	1	1	1	2	3	4	8
50–64	353	1.5	1	1	1	1	2	2	3	6
65+	183	2.1	9	1	1	1	2	3	8	15
GRAND TOTAL	**1,079**	**1.7**	**3**	**1**	**1**	**1**	**2**	**3**	**4**	**10**

06.4: COMPLETE THYROIDECTOMY

Type of Patients	Observed Patients	Avg. Stay	Vari-ance	Percentiles						
				10th	25th	50th	75th	90th	95th	99th
1. SINGLE DX										
0–19 Years	22	1.6	<1	1	1	2	2	2	3	3
20–34	155	1.6	<1	1	1	1	2	3	3	6
35–49	287	1.7	1	1	1	1	2	3	3	7
50–64	192	1.5	<1	1	1	1	2	2	3	5
65+	48	1.6	<1	1	1	1	2	2	3	5
2. MULTIPLE DX										
0–19 Years	35	2.4	3	1	1	2	3	4	5	12
20–34	312	2.3	8	1	1	2	2	4	5	21
35–49	736	2.0	2	1	1	2	2	4	4	8
50–64	746	2.2	5	1	1	2	2	3	6	14
65+	411	2.8	18	1	1	2	3	5	7	17
TOTAL SINGLE DX	**704**	**1.6**	**<1**	**1**	**1**	**1**	**2**	**3**	**3**	**6**
TOTAL MULTIPLE DX	**2,240**	**2.3**	**7**	**1**	**1**	**2**	**2**	**4**	**6**	**14**
TOTAL										
0–19 Years	57	2.1	2	1	1	2	2	3	4	12
20–34	467	2.1	6	1	1	2	2	3	5	11
35–49	1,023	1.9	2	1	1	1	2	3	4	7
50–64	938	2.1	4	1	1	2	2	3	5	13
65+	459	2.7	17	1	1	2	3	5	6	17
GRAND TOTAL	**2,944**	**2.1**	**6**	**1**	**1**	**2**	**2**	**3**	**5**	**13**

06.5: SUBSTERNAL THYROIDECTOMY

Type of Patients	Observed Patients	Avg. Stay	Vari-ance	Percentiles						
				10th	25th	50th	75th	90th	95th	99th
1. SINGLE DX										
0–19 Years	2	2.0	0	2	2	2	2	2	2	2
20–34	11	1.3	<1	1	1	1	1	2	3	3
35–49	33	1.4	<1	1	1	1	2	2	2	3
50–64	16	1.6	<1	1	1	1	2	2	4	4
65+	9	2.1	<1	1	2	2	3	3	3	3
2. MULTIPLE DX										
0–19 Years	5	3.0	1	1	2	4	4	4	4	4
20–34	16	2.6	28	1	1	1	2	4	24	24
35–49	48	2.5	5	1	1	2	3	4	7	13
50–64	46	2.2	4	1	1	2	2	3	5	17
65+	77	4.1	14	1	1	3	6	8	9	21
TOTAL SINGLE DX	**71**	**1.6**	**<1**	**1**	**1**	**1**	**2**	**3**	**3**	**3**
TOTAL MULTIPLE DX	**192**	**3.1**	**10**	**1**	**1**	**2**	**4**	**7**	**8**	**18**
TOTAL										
0–19 Years	7	2.8	1	2	2	2	4	4	4	4
20–34	27	2.0	16	1	1	1	2	2	4	24
35–49	81	2.0	3	1	1	1	2	3	4	10
50–64	62	2.1	4	1	1	2	2	3	4	17
65+	86	3.7	12	1	1	2	5	8	9	21
GRAND TOTAL	**263**	**2.7**	**8**	**1**	**1**	**2**	**3**	**6**	**8**	**18**

06.51: PART SUBSTERN THYROIDECT

Type of Patients	Observed Patients	Avg. Stay	Variance	10th	25th	50th	75th	90th	95th	99th
1. SINGLE DX										
0–19 Years	0									
20–34	2	1.6	<1	1	1	2	2	2	2	2
35–49	10	1.2	<1	1	1	1	1	2	2	2
50–64	6	1.5	<1	1	1	1	2	2	2	2
65+	2	2.0	0	2	2	2	2	2	2	2
2. MULTIPLE DX										
0–19 Years	1	1.0	0	1	1	1	1	1	1	1
20–34	2	1.0	0	1	1	1	1	1	1	1
35–49	9	1.4	<1	1	1	1	2	2	3	3
50–64	15	2.6	12	1	1	2	2	6	6	17
65+	20	4.3	22	1	1	2	6	8	9	21
TOTAL SINGLE DX	20	1.4	<1	1	1	1	2	2	2	2
TOTAL MULTIPLE DX	47	3.1	15	1	1	2	3	8	9	21
TOTAL										
0–19 Years	1	1.0	0	1	1	1	1	1	1	1
20–34	4	1.4	<1	1	1	1	2	2	2	2
35–49	19	1.3	<1	1	1	1	2	2	2	3
50–64	21	2.3	9	1	1	2	2	3	6	17
65+	22	4.1	20	1	2	2	6	8	9	21
GRAND TOTAL	67	2.6	11	1	1	2	2	6	8	21

06.52: TOT SUBSTERN THYROIDECT

Type of Patients	Observed Patients	Avg. Stay	Variance	10th	25th	50th	75th	90th	95th	99th
1. SINGLE DX										
0–19 Years	2	2.0	0	2	2	2	2	2	2	2
20–34	9	1.2	<1	1	1	1	1	2	3	3
35–49	23	1.5	<1	1	1	1	2	2	3	3
50–64	10	1.7	<1	1	1	1	2	2	4	4
65+	7	2.1	<1	1	1	2	3	3	3	3
2. MULTIPLE DX										
0–19 Years	4	3.2	1	2	2	4	4	4	4	4
20–34	14	2.8	32	1	1	1	2	4	24	24
35–49	39	2.7	5	1	1	2	3	4	8	13
50–64	31	2.0	<1	1	1	2	2	3	3	5
65+	56	4.0	11	1	1	3	6	8	9	18
TOTAL SINGLE DX	51	1.7	<1	1	1	2	2	3	3	4
TOTAL MULTIPLE DX	144	3.1	9	1	1	2	4	7	8	18
TOTAL										
0–19 Years	6	2.9	1	2	2	2	4	4	4	4
20–34	23	2.1	18	1	1	1	2	3	4	24
35–49	62	2.3	4	1	1	2	3	3	7	13
50–64	41	1.9	<1	1	1	2	2	3	4	5
65+	63	3.5	9	1	1	3	4	8	8	18
GRAND TOTAL	195	2.7	7	1	1	2	3	6	8	13

06.6: LINGUAL THYROID EXCISION

Type of Patients	Observed Patients	Avg. Stay	Variance	10th	25th	50th	75th	90th	95th	99th
1. SINGLE DX										
0–19 Years	1	1.0	0	1	1	1	1	1	1	1
20–34	1	1.0	0	1	1	1	1	1	1	1
35–49	3	1.2	<1	1	1	1	1	2	2	2
50–64	0									
65+	0									
2. MULTIPLE DX										
0–19 Years	1	3.0	0	3	3	3	3	3	3	3
20–34	1	2.0	0	2	2	2	2	2	2	2
35–49	6	1.7	<1	1	1	2	2	3	3	3
50–64	3	1.0	0	1	1	1	1	1	1	1
65+	2	1.0	0	1	1	1	1	1	1	1
TOTAL SINGLE DX	5	1.2	<1	1	1	1	1	2	2	2
TOTAL MULTIPLE DX	13	1.6	<1	1	1	1	2	3	3	3
TOTAL										
0–19 Years	2	2.2	1	1	1	3	3	3	3	3
20–34	2	1.5	<1	1	1	2	2	2	2	2
35–49	9	1.5	<1	1	1	1	2	2	3	3
50–64	3	1.0	0	1	1	1	1	1	1	1
65+	2	1.0	0	1	1	1	1	1	1	1
GRAND TOTAL	18	1.4	<1	1	1	1	2	3	3	3

06.7: THYROGLOSSAL DUCT EXC

Type of Patients	Observed Patients	Avg. Stay	Variance	10th	25th	50th	75th	90th	95th	99th
1. SINGLE DX										
0–19 Years	66	1.5	2	1	1	1	1	3	5	6
20–34	28	1.3	<1	1	1	1	2	2	3	3
35–49	5	1.0	0	1	1	1	1	1	1	1
50–64	9	1.4	<1	1	1	1	2	3	3	3
65+	5	1.2	<1	1	1	1	1	2	2	2
2. MULTIPLE DX										
0–19 Years	19	1.4	1	1	1	1	1	2	3	8
20–34	10	1.2	<1	1	1	1	1	2	2	2
35–49	17	1.6	1	1	1	1	2	3	3	6
50–64	15	1.2	<1	1	1	1	1	1	2	5
65+	10	2.8	6	1	1	1	6	6	7	7
TOTAL SINGLE DX	113	1.5	1	1	1	1	1	2	5	5
TOTAL MULTIPLE DX	71	1.5	2	1	1	1	1	3	5	7
TOTAL										
0–19 Years	85	1.5	1	1	1	1	1	3	5	6
20–34	38	1.3	<1	1	1	1	1	2	2	3
35–49	22	1.5	1	1	1	1	2	3	3	6
50–64	24	1.3	<1	1	1	1	1	2	3	5
65+	15	2.3	5	1	1	1	2	6	7	7
GRAND TOTAL	184	1.5	1	1	1	1	1	3	5	6

06.8: PARATHYROIDECTOMY

Type of Patients	Observed Patients	Avg. Stay	Vari-ance	10th	25th	50th	75th	90th	95th	99th
1. SINGLE DX										
0–19 Years	1	1.0	0	1	1	1	1	1	1	1
20–34	10	1.6	<1	1	1	1	2	3	3	3
35–49	38	1.2	<1	1	1	1	1	2	2	2
50–64	59	1.3	<1	1	1	1	2	2	2	3
65+	40	1.2	<1	1	1	1	1	2	2	3
2. MULTIPLE DX										
0–19 Years	10	5.5	7	2	3	6	8	9	9	9
20–34	130	3.2	11	1	1	2	4	7	11	15
35–49	439	2.8	11	1	1	2	3	7	10	16
50–64	883	2.1	7	1	1	1	2	4	7	13
65+	837	2.5	15	1	1	1	2	4	10	19
TOTAL SINGLE DX	**148**	**1.3**	**<1**	**1**	**1**	**1**	**2**	**2**	**2**	**3**
TOTAL MULTIPLE DX	**2,299**	**2.5**	**11**	**1**	**1**	**1**	**2**	**5**	**9**	**16**
TOTAL										
0–19 Years	11	5.1	8	2	2	6	8	9	9	9
20–34	140	3.1	10	1	1	2	4	7	11	15
35–49	477	2.7	10	1	1	1	3	6	9	16
50–64	942	2.1	6	1	1	1	2	4	7	13
65+	877	2.4	15	1	1	1	2	4	10	19
GRAND TOTAL	**2,447**	**2.4**	**11**	**1**	**1**	**1**	**2**	**5**	**8**	**16**

06.81: TOTAL PARATHYROIDECTOMY

Type of Patients	Observed Patients	Avg. Stay	Vari-ance	10th	25th	50th	75th	90th	95th	99th
1. SINGLE DX										
0–19 Years	0									
20–34	1	1.0	0	1	1	1	1	1	1	1
35–49	3	1.7	<1	1	1	2	2	2	2	2
50–64	5	1.7	<1	1	1	1	2	3	3	3
65+	7	1.5	<1	1	1	1	2	2	2	2
2. MULTIPLE DX										
0–19 Years	3	6.9	<1	6	6	7	8	8	8	8
20–34	29	4.6	16	1	2	4	5	11	11	21
35–49	90	3.8	13	1	1	2	5	8	10	14
50–64	126	3.2	10	1	1	2	4	7	10	19
65+	120	3.5	35	1	1	1	3	7	14	39
TOTAL SINGLE DX	**16**	**1.6**	**<1**	**1**	**1**	**2**	**2**	**2**	**3**	**3**
TOTAL MULTIPLE DX	**368**	**3.6**	**20**	**1**	**1**	**2**	**4**	**8**	**12**	**21**
TOTAL										
0–19 Years	3	6.9	<1	6	6	7	8	8	8	8
20–34	30	4.4	16	1	2	3	5	9	11	21
35–49	93	3.6	13	1	1	2	4	8	10	14
50–64	131	3.1	9	1	1	2	4	7	10	19
65+	127	3.4	33	1	1	1	3	5	14	39
GRAND TOTAL	**384**	**3.5**	**20**	**1**	**1**	**2**	**4**	**8**	**11**	**21**

06.89: OTHER PARATHYROIDECTOMY

Type of Patients	Observed Patients	Avg. Stay	Vari-ance	10th	25th	50th	75th	90th	95th	99th
1. SINGLE DX										
0–19 Years	1	1.0	0	1	1	1	1	1	1	1
20–34	9	1.7	<1	1	1	1	2	3	3	3
35–49	35	1.2	<1	1	1	1	1	2	2	2
50–64	54	1.3	<1	1	1	1	2	2	2	3
65+	33	1.2	<1	1	1	1	1	2	2	3
2. MULTIPLE DX										
0–19 Years	7	4.8	9	2	2	4	9	9	9	9
20–34	101	2.8	8	1	1	2	3	7	9	14
35–49	349	2.6	10	1	1	1	2	6	8	16
50–64	757	2.0	6	1	1	1	2	4	6	13
65+	717	2.3	12	1	1	1	2	4	9	18
TOTAL SINGLE DX	**132**	**1.3**	**<1**	**1**	**1**	**1**	**1**	**2**	**2**	**3**
TOTAL MULTIPLE DX	**1,931**	**2.3**	**9**	**1**	**1**	**1**	**2**	**5**	**8**	**15**
TOTAL										
0–19 Years	8	4.4	10	1	2	3	7	9	9	9
20–34	110	2.7	8	1	1	2	3	7	8	14
35–49	384	2.5	10	1	1	1	2	6	8	16
50–64	811	2.0	6	1	1	1	2	4	6	12
65+	750	2.3	12	1	1	1	2	4	9	18
GRAND TOTAL	**2,063**	**2.2**	**9**	**1**	**1**	**1**	**2**	**4**	**7**	**15**

06.9: THYROID/PARATHY OPS NEC

Type of Patients	Observed Patients	Avg. Stay	Vari-ance	10th	25th	50th	75th	90th	95th	99th
1. SINGLE DX										
0–19 Years	0									
20–34	1	2.0	0	2	2	2	2	2	2	2
35–49	3	1.0	0	1	1	1	1	1	1	1
50–64	0									
65+	0									
2. MULTIPLE DX										
0–19 Years	0									
20–34	7	4.8	34	1	1	2	8	17	17	17
35–49	12	3.5	5	2	2	3	4	8	8	8
50–64	15	2.7	10	1	1	1	3	8	12	12
65+	10	2.0	1	1	1	2	2	3	5	5
TOTAL SINGLE DX	**4**	**1.2**	**<1**	**1**	**1**	**1**	**1**	**2**	**2**	**2**
TOTAL MULTIPLE DX	**44**	**3.2**	**9**	**1**	**1**	**2**	**3**	**8**	**8**	**17**
TOTAL										
0–19 Years	0									
20–34	8	4.5	30	1	2	2	8	17	17	17
35–49	15	3.2	5	1	2	2	3	8	8	8
50–64	15	2.7	10	1	1	1	3	8	12	12
65+	10	2.0	1	1	1	2	2	3	5	5
GRAND TOTAL	**48**	**3.0**	**8**	**1**	**1**	**2**	**3**	**8**	**8**	**17**

07.0: ADRENAL FIELD EXPL

Type of Patients	Observed Patients	Avg. Stay	Vari-ance	Percentiles						
				10th	25th	50th	75th	90th	95th	99th
1. SINGLE DX										
0–19 Years	0									
20–34	0									
35–49	0									
50–64	0									
65+	0									
2. MULTIPLE DX										
0–19 Years	0									
20–34	0									
35–49	0									
50–64	1	29.0	0	29	29	29	29	29	29	29
65+	0									
TOTAL SINGLE DX	**0**									
TOTAL MULTIPLE DX	**1**	**29.0**	**0**	**29**	**29**	**29**	**29**	**29**	**29**	**29**
TOTAL										
0–19 Years	0									
20–34	0									
35–49	0									
50–64	1	29.0	0	29	29	29	29	29	29	29
65+	0									
GRAND TOTAL	**1**	**29.0**	**0**	**29**	**29**	**29**	**29**	**29**	**29**	**29**

07.1: OTH ENDOCRINE DXTIC PX

Type of Patients	Observed Patients	Avg. Stay	Vari-ance	Percentiles						
				10th	25th	50th	75th	90th	95th	99th
1. SINGLE DX										
0–19 Years	1	3.0	0	3	3	3	3	3	3	3
20–34	0									
35–49	1	4.0	0	4	4	4	4	4	4	4
50–64	1	2.0	0	2	2	2	2	2	2	2
65+	0									
2. MULTIPLE DX										
0–19 Years	10	7.1	19	3	3	6	8	13	16	16
20–34	2	4.4	<1	4	4	4	5	5	5	5
35–49	16	8.0	101	2	3	4	9	17	45	45
50–64	22	5.5	23	1	3	3	8	11	18	25
65+	49	7.1	21	2	4	5	10	12	17	22
TOTAL SINGLE DX	**3**	**3.0**	**<1**	**2**	**2**	**3**	**4**	**4**	**4**	**4**
TOTAL MULTIPLE DX	**99**	**6.8**	**31**	**2**	**3**	**5**	**9**	**12**	**17**	**25**
TOTAL										
0–19 Years	11	6.8	18	3	3	6	8	13	16	16
20–34	2	4.4	<1	4	4	4	5	5	5	5
35–49	17	7.8	97	2	3	4	9	17	45	45
50–64	23	5.4	23	1	3	3	8	11	18	25
65+	49	7.1	21	2	4	5	10	12	17	22
GRAND TOTAL	**102**	**6.7**	**30**	**2**	**3**	**5**	**9**	**12**	**17**	**25**

07.11: CLSD ADRENAL GLAND BX

Type of Patients	Observed Patients	Avg. Stay	Vari-ance	Percentiles						
				10th	25th	50th	75th	90th	95th	99th
1. SINGLE DX										
0–19 Years	0									
20–34	0									
35–49	0									
50–64	0									
65+	0									
2. MULTIPLE DX										
0–19 Years	0									
20–34	0									
35–49	8	5.4	7	2	4	4	9	9	9	9
50–64	21	5.4	24	1	3	3	8	11	18	25
65+	46	7.2	21	2	4	5	10	12	17	22
TOTAL SINGLE DX	**0**									
TOTAL MULTIPLE DX	**75**	**6.5**	**22**	**2**	**3**	**5**	**9**	**11**	**17**	**22**
TOTAL										
0–19 Years	0									
20–34	0									
35–49	8	5.4	7	2	4	4	9	9	9	9
50–64	21	5.4	24	1	3	3	8	11	18	25
65+	46	7.2	21	2	4	5	10	12	17	22
GRAND TOTAL	**75**	**6.5**	**22**	**2**	**3**	**5**	**9**	**11**	**17**	**22**

07.2: PARTIAL ADRENALECTOMY

Type of Patients	Observed Patients	Avg. Stay	Vari-ance	Percentiles						
				10th	25th	50th	75th	90th	95th	99th
1. SINGLE DX										
0–19 Years	8	6.4	4	4	5	6	9	9	10	10
20–34	6	2.7	1	1	2	3	3	4	4	4
35–49	16	2.6	4	1	1	2	4	5	5	9
50–64	11	2.0	2	1	1	1	4	4	4	4
65+	1	1.0	0	1	1	1	1	1	1	1
2. MULTIPLE DX										
0–19 Years	38	7.7	24	3	4	7	10	13	19	26
20–34	40	4.8	18	1	2	4	6	11	14	21
35–49	120	3.9	10	1	2	3	5	7	10	15
50–64	168	4.9	21	1	2	4	6	8	16	23
65+	100	4.7	13	2	2	4	6	9	11	18
TOTAL SINGLE DX	**42**	**3.7**	**7**	**1**	**1**	**3**	**5**	**9**	**9**	**10**
TOTAL MULTIPLE DX	**466**	**4.9**	**18**	**1**	**2**	**4**	**6**	**10**	**13**	**20**
TOTAL										
0–19 Years	46	7.4	20	4	4	6	9	13	17	26
20–34	46	4.6	16	1	2	3	6	8	14	21
35–49	136	3.8	9	1	2	3	5	7	10	14
50–64	179	4.7	20	1	2	3	6	8	16	23
65+	101	4.7	13	1	2	4	6	9	11	18
GRAND TOTAL	**508**	**4.8**	**17**	**1**	**2**	**4**	**6**	**9**	**13**	**20**

07.22: UNILATERAL ADRENALECTOMY

Type of Patients	Observed Patients	Avg. Stay	Vari-ance	Percentiles						
				10th	25th	50th	75th	90th	95th	99th
1. SINGLE DX										
0–19 Years	6	6.5	5	4	4	6	9	9	10	10
20–34	4	2.8	1	1	3	3	4	4	4	4
35–49	15	2.8	4	1	1	2	4	5	9	9
50–64	11	2.0	2	1	1	1	4	4	4	4
65+	1	1.0	0	1	1	1	1	1	1	1
2. MULTIPLE DX										
0–19 Years	26	8.4	29	3	5	7	10	17	19	26
20–34	35	5.0	20	1	2	4	6	11	14	21
35–49	103	3.8	8	1	2	3	5	7	10	14
50–64	156	5.0	22	1	2	4	6	9	16	23
65+	90	4.4	10	1	2	3	6	9	9	16
TOTAL SINGLE DX	**37**	**3.7**	**7**	**1**	**1**	**3**	**5**	**9**	**9**	**10**
TOTAL MULTIPLE DX	**410**	**4.9**	**17**	**1**	**2**	**4**	**6**	**9**	**13**	**20**
TOTAL										
0–19 Years	32	8.0	23	3	5	7	10	13	19	26
20–34	39	4.8	18	1	2	3	6	11	14	21
35–49	118	3.7	7	1	2	3	5	7	9	14
50–64	167	4.8	21	1	2	4	6	8	16	23
65+	91	4.4	10	1	2	3	6	9	9	16
GRAND TOTAL	**447**	**4.8**	**17**	**1**	**2**	**4**	**6**	**9**	**13**	**20**

07.3: BILATERAL ADRENALECTOMY

Type of Patients	Observed Patients	Avg. Stay	Vari-ance	Percentiles						
				10th	25th	50th	75th	90th	95th	99th
1. SINGLE DX										
0–19 Years	0									
20–34	0									
35–49	0									
50–64	1	2.0	0	2	2	2	2	2	2	2
65+	0									
2. MULTIPLE DX										
0–19 Years	3	7.7	34	4	4	6	6	18	18	18
20–34	5	4.6	12	2	3	3	5	11	11	11
35–49	5	3.9	10	2	2	2	3	9	9	9
50–64	6	4.0	3	2	3	3	6	7	7	7
65+	0									
TOTAL SINGLE DX	**1**	**2.0**	**0**	**2**	**2**	**2**	**2**	**2**	**2**	**2**
TOTAL MULTIPLE DX	**19**	**5.0**	**14**	**2**	**3**	**4**	**6**	**9**	**11**	**18**
TOTAL										
0–19 Years	3	7.7	34	4	4	6	6	18	18	18
20–34	5	4.6	12	2	3	3	5	11	11	11
35–49	5	3.9	10	2	2	2	3	9	9	9
50–64	7	3.8	3	2	2	3	5	6	7	7
65+	0									
GRAND TOTAL	**20**	**4.9**	**14**	**2**	**2**	**4**	**6**	**9**	**11**	**18**

07.4: OTHER ADRENAL OPERATIONS

Type of Patients	Observed Patients	Avg. Stay	Vari-ance	Percentiles						
				10th	25th	50th	75th	90th	95th	99th
1. SINGLE DX										
0–19 Years	0									
20–34	0									
35–49	0									
50–64	0									
65+	0									
2. MULTIPLE DX										
0–19 Years	0									
20–34	0									
35–49	1	4.0	0	4	4	4	4	4	4	4
50–64	0									
65+	1	1.0	0	1	1	1	1	1	1	1
TOTAL SINGLE DX	**0**									
TOTAL MULTIPLE DX	**2**	**2.6**	**4**	**1**	**1**	**4**	**4**	**4**	**4**	**4**
TOTAL										
0–19 Years	0									
20–34	0									
35–49	1	4.0	0	4	4	4	4	4	4	4
50–64	0									
65+	1	1.0	0	1	1	1	1	1	1	1
GRAND TOTAL	**2**	**2.6**	**4**	**1**	**1**	**4**	**4**	**4**	**4**	**4**

07.5: PINEAL GLAND OPERATIONS

Type of Patients	Observed Patients	Avg. Stay	Vari-ance	Percentiles						
				10th	25th	50th	75th	90th	95th	99th
1. SINGLE DX										
0–19 Years	0									
20–34	0									
35–49	1	5.0	0	5	5	5	5	5	5	5
50–64	0									
65+	0									
2. MULTIPLE DX										
0–19 Years	4	6.3	8	3	4	6	10	10	10	10
20–34	3	5.0	6	3	3	4	8	8	8	8
35–49	3	8.9	120	3	4	4	4	29	29	29
50–64	3	9.4	16	7	7	7	14	14	14	14
65+	0									
TOTAL SINGLE DX	**1**	**5.0**	**0**	**5**	**5**	**5**	**5**	**5**	**5**	**5**
TOTAL MULTIPLE DX	**13**	**7.4**	**44**	**3**	**4**	**6**	**8**	**14**	**29**	**29**
TOTAL										
0–19 Years	4	6.3	8	3	4	6	10	10	10	10
20–34	3	5.0	6	3	3	4	8	8	8	8
35–49	4	8.4	103	3	4	4	5	29	29	29
50–64	3	9.4	16	7	7	7	14	14	14	14
65+	0									
GRAND TOTAL	**14**	**7.3**	**42**	**3**	**4**	**5**	**8**	**14**	**29**	**29**

07.6: HYPOPHYSECTOMY

Type of Patients	Observed Patients	Avg. Stay	Vari-ance	Percentiles 10th	25th	50th	75th	90th	95th	99th
1. SINGLE DX										
0–19 Years	4	2.6	<1	2	2	3	3	3	3	3
20–34	36	3.1	3	1	1	3	4	5	6	8
35–49	67	3.5	6	1	2	3	4	6	10	15
50–64	48	2.9	2	2	2	2	3	5	6	8
65+	12	3.0	3	1	1	3	5	5	5	5
2. MULTIPLE DX										
0–19 Years	22	6.4	15	2	4	4	8	13	15	15
20–34	144	4.4	9	2	3	4	5	7	11	15
35–49	238	4.4	15	2	3	3	5	7	12	20
50–64	288	4.1	8	2	2	3	5	7	9	14
65+	208	4.8	19	2	3	4	5	10	13	21
TOTAL SINGLE DX	**167**	**3.2**	**4**	**1**	**2**	**3**	**4**	**5**	**6**	**11**
TOTAL MULTIPLE DX	**900**	**4.5**	**13**	**2**	**3**	**4**	**5**	**8**	**12**	**18**
TOTAL										
0–19 Years	26	5.9	15	2	3	4	8	13	13	15
20–34	180	4.2	8	2	3	4	5	7	10	15
35–49	305	4.2	14	2	2	3	5	7	11	20
50–64	336	3.9	7	2	2	3	5	7	9	14
65+	220	4.7	19	2	3	4	5	9	13	21
GRAND TOTAL	**1,067**	**4.3**	**12**	**2**	**2**	**3**	**5**	**7**	**11**	**18**

07.62: EXC PIT LES-TRANSSPHEN

Type of Patients	Observed Patients	Avg. Stay	Vari-ance	Percentiles 10th	25th	50th	75th	90th	95th	99th
1. SINGLE DX										
0–19 Years	3	2.5	<1	2	2	2	3	3	3	3
20–34	26	3.2	4	1	1	3	4	6	6	8
35–49	49	3.6	6	1	2	3	4	6	10	15
50–64	30	2.7	2	2	2	2	3	6	6	6
65+	8	2.7	3	1	1	3	5	5	5	5
2. MULTIPLE DX										
0–19 Years	11	5.4	9	2	3	7	8	10	10	10
20–34	108	3.9	5	2	2	4	4	6	8	13
35–49	179	3.8	6	2	3	3	4	6	8	15
50–64	200	3.9	8	2	2	3	5	7	9	15
65+	155	4.7	16	2	3	4	5	8	13	16
TOTAL SINGLE DX	**116**	**3.1**	**4**	**1**	**2**	**3**	**4**	**6**	**6**	**11**
TOTAL MULTIPLE DX	**653**	**4.1**	**9**	**2**	**2**	**3**	**5**	**7**	**10**	**16**
TOTAL										
0–19 Years	14	4.6	8	2	2	3	7	9	10	10
20–34	134	3.7	5	2	2	3	4	6	8	13
35–49	228	3.8	6	2	2	3	4	6	8	15
50–64	230	3.7	7	2	2	3	4	7	8	15
65+	163	4.6	15	2	3	4	5	7	13	16
GRAND TOTAL	**769**	**4.0**	**9**	**2**	**2**	**3**	**4**	**7**	**9**	**15**

07.65: TOT EXC PIT-TRANSSPHEN

Type of Patients	Observed Patients	Avg. Stay	Vari-ance	Percentiles 10th	25th	50th	75th	90th	95th	99th
1. SINGLE DX										
0–19 Years	1	3.0	0	3	3	3	3	3	3	3
20–34	9	2.8	2	1	1	3	4	4	5	5
35–49	15	3.5	8	1	2	3	4	9	11	11
50–64	13	3.1	1	1	2	3	4	4	5	5
65+	2	2.1	2	1	1	3	3	3	3	3
2. MULTIPLE DX										
0–19 Years	3	4.3	2	4	4	4	4	8	8	8
20–34	21	4.8	9	2	3	4	5	7	15	15
35–49	45	4.1	9	2	2	3	4	8	9	20
50–64	61	3.9	4	2	3	3	5	7	7	11
65+	42	4.9	30	2	2	3	5	10	12	35
TOTAL SINGLE DX	**40**	**3.1**	**4**	**1**	**2**	**3**	**4**	**5**	**5**	**11**
TOTAL MULTIPLE DX	**172**	**4.3**	**12**	**2**	**3**	**3**	**5**	**7**	**9**	**20**
TOTAL										
0–19 Years	4	4.2	2	3	4	4	4	8	8	8
20–34	30	4.1	7	1	3	4	5	7	7	15
35–49	60	4.0	8	2	2	3	4	8	9	20
50–64	74	3.7	3	2	3	3	4	6	7	11
65+	44	4.8	29	2	2	3	5	9	12	35
GRAND TOTAL	**212**	**4.1**	**11**	**2**	**2**	**3**	**4**	**7**	**9**	**18**

07.7: OTHER HYPOPHYSIS OPS

Type of Patients	Observed Patients	Avg. Stay	Vari-ance	Percentiles 10th	25th	50th	75th	90th	95th	99th
1. SINGLE DX										
0–19 Years	0									
20–34	0									
35–49	1	2.0	0	2	2	2	2	2	2	2
50–64	2	4.5	<1	3	5	5	5	5	5	5
65+	1	1.0	0	1	1	1	1	1	1	1
2. MULTIPLE DX										
0–19 Years	4	7.1	22	1	4	7	12	12	12	12
20–34	0									
35–49	5	5.9	12	3	3	3	10	10	10	10
50–64	2	3.7	6	2	2	2	6	6	6	6
65+	3	3.4	1	2	2	4	4	4	4	4
TOTAL SINGLE DX	**4**	**2.4**	**3**	**1**	**1**	**1**	**5**	**5**	**5**	**5**
TOTAL MULTIPLE DX	**14**	**5.6**	**14**	**2**	**3**	**4**	**7**	**12**	**12**	**12**
TOTAL										
0–19 Years	4	7.1	22	1	4	7	12	12	12	12
20–34	0									
35–49	6	5.4	12	2	3	3	10	10	10	10
50–64	4	4.2	2	2	3	5	5	6	6	6
65+	4	1.9	2	1	1	1	4	4	4	4
GRAND TOTAL	**18**	**4.4**	**12**	**1**	**1**	**4**	**6**	**10**	**12**	**12**

07.8: THYMECTOMY

Type of Patients	Observed Patients	Avg. Stay	Vari-ance	Percentiles						
				10th	25th	50th	75th	90th	95th	99th
1. SINGLE DX										
0–19 Years	8	2.9	<1	1	3	3	3	4	4	4
20–34	19	3.2	4	1	2	3	5	5	5	9
35–49	16	2.5	<1	1	2	3	3	3	3	5
50–64	7	3.1	3	1	2	2	4	6	6	6
65+	0									
2. MULTIPLE DX										
0–19 Years	10	4.3	22	1	1	3	5	10	17	17
20–34	46	4.5	11	2	2	3	5	10	12	16
35–49	48	6.1	21	2	3	5	8	12	19	20
50–64	77	5.0	17	2	3	4	6	8	15	30
65+	43	4.9	14	2	3	4	5	8	13	23
TOTAL SINGLE DX	**50**	**2.8**	**2**	**1**	**2**	**3**	**3**	**5**	**5**	**9**
TOTAL MULTIPLE DX	**224**	**5.1**	**17**	**2**	**3**	**4**	**6**	**10**	**14**	**20**
TOTAL										
0–19 Years	18	3.8	16	1	2	3	3	5	17	17
20–34	65	4.1	9	2	2	3	5	9	11	16
35–49	64	5.0	17	2	2	3	6	10	14	20
50–64	84	4.9	16	2	3	4	6	8	15	30
65+	43	4.9	14	2	3	4	5	8	13	23
GRAND TOTAL	**274**	**4.7**	**15**	**2**	**3**	**3**	**5**	**9**	**13**	**19**

07.82: TOTAL EXCISION OF THYMUS

Type of Patients	Observed Patients	Avg. Stay	Vari-ance	Percentiles						
				10th	25th	50th	75th	90th	95th	99th
1. SINGLE DX										
0–19 Years	7	2.9	<1	1	3	3	3	4	4	4
20–34	15	3.7	4	1	2	3	5	5	9	9
35–49	10	2.4	<1	1	2	2	3	3	5	5
50–64	4	2.7	2	1	2	3	4	4	4	4
65+	0									
2. MULTIPLE DX										
0–19 Years	8	4.7	28	1	2	3	3	17	17	17
20–34	33	4.7	11	2	3	3	5	10	12	14
35–49	31	5.6	22	2	3	4	6	11	19	19
50–64	47	5.3	21	2	3	4	6	8	15	30
65+	22	5.6	22	2	3	4	6	13	13	23
TOTAL SINGLE DX	**36**	**3.0**	**2**	**1**	**2**	**3**	**4**	**5**	**5**	**9**
TOTAL MULTIPLE DX	**141**	**5.2**	**20**	**2**	**3**	**4**	**6**	**10**	**15**	**23**
TOTAL										
0–19 Years	15	4.1	19	1	2	3	3	10	17	17
20–34	48	4.4	9	2	2	3	5	9	11	14
35–49	41	4.7	18	2	2	3	5	11	16	19
50–64	51	5.2	21	2	3	4	6	8	15	30
65+	22	5.6	22	2	3	4	6	13	13	23
GRAND TOTAL	**177**	**4.8**	**17**	**2**	**3**	**3**	**5**	**10**	**14**	**23**

07.9: OTHER THYMUS OPERATIONS

Type of Patients	Observed Patients	Avg. Stay	Vari-ance	Percentiles						
				10th	25th	50th	75th	90th	95th	99th
1. SINGLE DX										
0–19 Years	0									
20–34	0									
35–49	0									
50–64	0									
65+	0									
2. MULTIPLE DX										
0–19 Years	0									
20–34	0									
35–49	0									
50–64	0									
65+	0									
TOTAL SINGLE DX	**0**									
TOTAL MULTIPLE DX	**0**									
TOTAL										
0–19 Years	0									
20–34	0									
35–49	0									
50–64	0									
65+	0									
GRAND TOTAL	**0**									

08.0: EYELID INCISION

Type of Patients	Observed Patients	Avg. Stay	Vari-ance	Percentiles						
				10th	25th	50th	75th	90th	95th	99th
1. SINGLE DX										
0–19 Years	5	2.5	1	1	2	2	3	3	5	5
20–34	1	2.0	0	2	2	2	2	2	2	2
35–49	0									
50–64	1	1.0	0	1	1	1	1	1	1	1
65+	0									
2. MULTIPLE DX										
0–19 Years	15	5.9	7	4	4	5	6	10	12	12
20–34	16	2.5	2	1	1	3	3	4	5	6
35–49	17	4.2	7	2	2	4	5	7	8	13
50–64	7	4.5	10	2	3	3	6	11	11	11
65+	10	4.6	9	1	3	3	6	8	11	11
TOTAL SINGLE DX	**7**	**2.2**	**<1**	**1**	**2**	**2**	**2**	**3**	**5**	**5**
TOTAL MULTIPLE DX	**65**	**4.4**	**8**	**1**	**3**	**4**	**5**	**8**	**11**	**13**
TOTAL										
0–19 Years	20	5.2	8	2	4	5	6	10	12	12
20–34	17	2.4	2	1	1	2	3	4	5	6
35–49	17	4.2	7	2	2	4	5	7	8	13
50–64	8	4.0	10	1	2	3	5	11	11	11
65+	10	4.6	9	1	3	3	6	8	11	11
GRAND TOTAL	**72**	**4.1**	**7**	**1**	**2**	**4**	**5**	**7**	**11**	**13**

08.1: DXTIC PX ON EYELID

Type of Patients	Observed Patients	Avg. Stay	Vari-ance	Percentiles						
				10th	25th	50th	75th	90th	95th	99th
1. SINGLE DX										
0–19 Years	0									
20–34	0									
35–49	0									
50–64	0									
65+	0									
2. MULTIPLE DX										
0–19 Years	1	1.0	0	1	1	1	1	1	1	1
20–34	0									
35–49	0									
50–64	1	1.0	0	1	1	1	1	1	1	1
65+	3	6.5	2	5	5	7	8	8	8	8
TOTAL SINGLE DX	**0**									
TOTAL MULTIPLE DX	**5**	**4.4**	**10**	**1**	**1**	**5**	**7**	**8**	**8**	**8**
TOTAL										
0–19 Years	1	1.0	0	1	1	1	1	1	1	1
20–34	0									
35–49	0									
50–64	1	1.0	0	1	1	1	1	1	1	1
65+	3	6.5	2	5	5	7	8	8	8	8
GRAND TOTAL	**5**	**4.4**	**10**	**1**	**1**	**5**	**7**	**8**	**8**	**8**

08.2: EXC/DESTR EYELID LESION

Type of Patients	Observed Patients	Avg. Stay	Vari-ance	Percentiles						
				10th	25th	50th	75th	90th	95th	99th
1. SINGLE DX										
0–19 Years	4	1.0	0	1	1	1	1	1	1	1
20–34	1	1.0	0	1	1	1	1	1	1	1
35–49	2	1.0	0	1	1	1	1	1	1	1
50–64	0									
65+	2	1.0	0	1	1	1	1	1	1	1
2. MULTIPLE DX										
0–19 Years	8	3.0	3	2	2	2	3	6	6	6
20–34	12	3.4	13	1	1	2	6	12	12	12
35–49	9	11.3	54	1	3	16	16	16	16	28
50–64	5	9.8	210	1	1	5	36	>99	>99	>99
65+	16	2.3	3	1	1	1	3	5	6	6
TOTAL SINGLE DX	**9**	**1.0**	**0**	**1**	**1**	**1**	**1**	**1**	**1**	**1**
TOTAL MULTIPLE DX	**50**	**5.8**	**51**	**1**	**1**	**3**	**6**	**16**	**16**	**>99**
TOTAL										
0–19 Years	12	2.0	3	1	1	1	2	6	6	6
20–34	13	3.3	12	1	1	2	4	6	12	12
35–49	11	9.6	60	1	1	11	16	16	16	28
50–64	5	9.8	210	1	1	5	36	>99	>99	>99
65+	18	2.2	3	1	1	1	3	5	5	6
GRAND TOTAL	**59**	**4.7**	**43**	**1**	**1**	**2**	**5**	**16**	**16**	**>99**

08.3: PTOSIS/LID RETRACT REP

Type of Patients	Observed Patients	Avg. Stay	Vari-ance	Percentiles						
				10th	25th	50th	75th	90th	95th	99th
1. SINGLE DX										
0–19 Years	1	1.0	0	1	1	1	1	1	1	1
20–34	0									
35–49	0									
50–64	1	1.0	0	1	1	1	1	1	1	1
65+	0									
2. MULTIPLE DX										
0–19 Years	3	1.3	<1	1	1	1	2	2	2	2
20–34	0									
35–49	1	1.0	0	1	1	1	1	1	1	1
50–64	11	1.0	0	1	1	1	1	1	1	1
65+	8	1.6	2	1	1	1	1	5	5	5
TOTAL SINGLE DX	**2**	**1.0**	**0**	**1**	**1**	**1**	**1**	**1**	**1**	**1**
TOTAL MULTIPLE DX	**23**	**1.2**	**<1**	**1**	**1**	**1**	**1**	**2**	**2**	**5**
TOTAL										
0–19 Years	4	1.2	<1	1	1	1	1	2	2	2
20–34	0									
35–49	1	1.0	0	1	1	1	1	1	1	1
50–64	12	1.0	0	1	1	1	1	1	1	1
65+	8	1.6	2	1	1	1	1	5	5	5
GRAND TOTAL	**25**	**1.2**	**<1**	**1**	**1**	**1**	**1**	**2**	**2**	**5**

08.4: ENTROPION/ECTROPION REP

Type of Patients	Observed Patients	Avg. Stay	Vari-ance	Percentiles						
				10th	25th	50th	75th	90th	95th	99th
1. SINGLE DX										
0–19 Years	1	1.0	0	1	1	1	1	1	1	1
20–34	0									
35–49	0									
50–64	0									
65+	0									
2. MULTIPLE DX										
0–19 Years	1	1.0	0	1	1	1	1	1	1	1
20–34	1	1.0	0	1	1	1	1	1	1	1
35–49	3	2.9	2	1	1	3	4	4	4	4
50–64	5	1.0	0	1	1	1	1	1	1	1
65+	8	2.3	2	1	1	2	3	5	5	5
TOTAL SINGLE DX	**1**	**1.0**	**0**	**1**	**1**	**1**	**1**	**1**	**1**	**1**
TOTAL MULTIPLE DX	**18**	**1.8**	**2**	**1**	**1**	**1**	**3**	**4**	**4**	**5**
TOTAL										
0–19 Years	2	1.0	0	1	1	1	1	1	1	1
20–34	1	1.0	0	1	1	1	1	1	1	1
35–49	3	2.9	2	1	1	3	4	4	4	4
50–64	5	1.0	0	1	1	1	1	1	1	1
65+	8	2.3	2	1	1	2	3	5	5	5
GRAND TOTAL	**19**	**1.8**	**2**	**1**	**1**	**1**	**2**	**4**	**4**	**5**

08.5: OTH ADJUST LID POSITION

Type of Patients	Observed Patients	Avg. Stay	Vari-ance	Percentiles 10th	25th	50th	75th	90th	95th	99th
1. SINGLE DX										
0–19 Years	1	1.0	0	1	1	1	1	1	1	1
20–34	0									
35–49	0									
50–64	0									
65+	1	1.0	0	1	1	1	1	1	1	1
2. MULTIPLE DX										
0–19 Years	21	2.7	8	1	1	1	3	8	8	12
20–34	13	2.8	4	1	1	2	4	5	9	9
35–49	15	4.0	9	1	1	4	6	8	11	11
50–64	16	5.8	19	1	1	5	9	11	15	15
65+	25	3.7	14	1	1	2	5	12	12	13
TOTAL SINGLE DX	**2**	**1.0**	**0**	**1**	**1**	**1**	**1**	**1**	**1**	**1**
TOTAL MULTIPLE DX	**90**	**3.7**	**12**	**1**	**1**	**2**	**5**	**9**	**12**	**15**
TOTAL										
0–19 Years	22	2.6	8	1	1	1	3	8	8	12
20–34	13	2.8	4	1	1	2	4	5	9	9
35–49	15	4.0	9	1	1	4	6	8	11	11
50–64	16	5.8	19	1	1	5	9	11	15	15
65+	26	3.6	14	1	1	2	4	12	12	13
GRAND TOTAL	**92**	**3.6**	**12**	**1**	**1**	**2**	**5**	**9**	**11**	**15**

08.6: EYELID RECONST W GRAFT

Type of Patients	Observed Patients	Avg. Stay	Vari-ance	Percentiles 10th	25th	50th	75th	90th	95th	99th
1. SINGLE DX										
0–19 Years	1	1.0	0	1	1	1	1	1	1	1
20–34	0									
35–49	1	1.0	0	1	1	1	1	1	1	1
50–64	0									
65+	1	2.0	0	2	2	2	2	2	2	2
2. MULTIPLE DX										
0–19 Years	4	1.6	<1	1	1	2	2	2	2	2
20–34	2	5.7	45	1	1	1	11	11	11	11
35–49	7	1.4	1	1	1	1	1	3	3	6
50–64	4	1.7	2	1	1	1	2	4	4	4
65+	9	3.1	10	1	1	1	4	8	10	10
TOTAL SINGLE DX	**3**	**1.2**	**<1**	**1**	**1**	**1**	**1**	**2**	**2**	**2**
TOTAL MULTIPLE DX	**26**	**1.9**	**4**	**1**	**1**	**1**	**2**	**4**	**8**	**11**
TOTAL										
0–19 Years	5	1.4	<1	1	1	1	2	2	2	2
20–34	2	5.7	45	1	1	1	11	11	11	11
35–49	8	1.4	1	1	1	1	1	3	3	6
50–64	4	1.7	2	1	1	1	2	4	4	4
65+	10	3.0	10	1	1	1	4	8	10	10
GRAND TOTAL	**29**	**1.8**	**4**	**1**	**1**	**1**	**2**	**4**	**6**	**11**

08.7: OTHER EYELID RECONST

Type of Patients	Observed Patients	Avg. Stay	Vari-ance	Percentiles 10th	25th	50th	75th	90th	95th	99th
1. SINGLE DX										
0–19 Years	3	1.0	0	1	1	1	1	1	1	1
20–34	1	1.0	0	1	1	1	1	1	1	1
35–49	1	1.0	0	1	1	1	1	1	1	1
50–64	3	1.0	0	1	1	1	1	1	1	1
65+	1	2.0	0	2	2	2	2	2	2	2
2. MULTIPLE DX										
0–19 Years	4	3.0	1	1	3	3	3	5	5	5
20–34	10	1.7	2	1	1	1	1	4	5	5
35–49	9	3.2	4	1	2	3	3	7	7	7
50–64	18	2.0	5	1	1	1	2	6	6	10
65+	7	3.0	4	1	1	4	5	5	5	5
TOTAL SINGLE DX	**9**	**1.1**	**<1**	**1**	**1**	**1**	**1**	**1**	**1**	**2**
TOTAL MULTIPLE DX	**48**	**2.4**	**4**	**1**	**1**	**1**	**3**	**5**	**7**	**10**
TOTAL										
0–19 Years	7	2.1	2	1	1	1	3	3	5	5
20–34	11	1.6	2	1	1	1	1	4	5	5
35–49	10	2.8	4	1	1	3	3	7	7	7
50–64	21	1.8	4	1	1	1	2	3	6	10
65+	8	2.9	3	1	1	4	5	5	5	5
GRAND TOTAL	**57**	**2.1**	**3**	**1**	**1**	**1**	**3**	**5**	**6**	**10**

08.8: OTHER REPAIR OF EYELID

Type of Patients	Observed Patients	Avg. Stay	Vari-ance	Percentiles 10th	25th	50th	75th	90th	95th	99th
1. SINGLE DX										
0–19 Years	17	1.1	<1	1	1	1	1	1	1	3
20–34	9	1.1	<1	1	1	1	1	1	2	2
35–49	5	1.0	0	1	1	1	1	1	1	1
50–64	4	1.3	<1	1	1	1	2	2	2	2
65+	2	1.5	<1	1	1	2	2	2	2	2
2. MULTIPLE DX										
0–19 Years	136	1.9	2	1	1	1	2	4	4	7
20–34	206	2.2	4	1	1	1	3	5	7	11
35–49	204	2.8	7	1	1	2	3	6	9	11
50–64	158	2.6	8	1	1	2	3	5	7	14
65+	349	3.9	17	1	2	3	5	7	12	20
TOTAL SINGLE DX	**37**	**1.1**	**<1**	**1**	**1**	**1**	**1**	**1**	**2**	**3**
TOTAL MULTIPLE DX	**1,053**	**2.7**	**8**	**1**	**1**	**2**	**3**	**5**	**7**	**15**
TOTAL										
0–19 Years	153	1.8	2	1	1	1	2	3	4	6
20–34	215	2.2	4	1	1	1	3	5	7	11
35–49	209	2.7	6	1	1	2	3	6	9	11
50–64	162	2.6	8	1	1	2	3	5	7	14
65+	351	3.9	17	1	2	3	4	7	12	20
GRAND TOTAL	**1,090**	**2.6**	**8**	**1**	**1**	**2**	**3**	**5**	**7**	**15**

08.81: LINEAR REP EYELID LAC

Type of Patients	Observed Patients	Avg. Stay	Vari-ance	Percentiles						
				10th	25th	50th	75th	90th	95th	99th
1. SINGLE DX										
0–19 Years	13	1.1	<1	1	1	1	1	1	3	3
20–34	7	1.1	<1	1	1	1	1	2	2	2
35–49	4	1.0	0	1	1	1	1	1	1	1
50–64	2	1.4	<1	1	1	1	2	2	2	2
65+	2	1.5	<1	1	1	2	2	2	2	2
2. MULTIPLE DX										
0–19 Years	131	1.9	2	1	1	2	2	4	4	7
20–34	201	2.2	4	1	1	1	3	5	7	11
35–49	197	2.8	7	1	1	2	3	6	9	11
50–64	144	2.7	9	1	1	2	3	5	7	14
65+	340	3.9	16	1	2	3	4	7	12	25
TOTAL SINGLE DX	**28**	**1.1**	**<1**	**1**	**1**	**1**	**1**	**1**	**2**	**3**
TOTAL MULTIPLE DX	**1,013**	**2.7**	**8**	**1**	**1**	**2**	**3**	**6**	**7**	**15**
TOTAL										
0–19 Years	144	1.9	2	1	1	1	2	3	4	7
20–34	208	2.2	4	1	1	1	3	5	7	11
35–49	201	2.8	7	1	1	2	3	6	9	11
50–64	146	2.7	9	1	1	2	3	5	7	14
65+	342	3.9	16	1	2	3	4	7	12	25
GRAND TOTAL	**1,041**	**2.7**	**8**	**1**	**1**	**2**	**3**	**5**	**7**	**15**

08.9: OTHER EYELID OPERATIONS

Type of Patients	Observed Patients	Avg. Stay	Vari-ance	Percentiles						
				10th	25th	50th	75th	90th	95th	99th
1. SINGLE DX										
0–19 Years	0									
20–34	0									
35–49	0									
50–64	0									
65+	0									
2. MULTIPLE DX										
0–19 Years	3	1.8	<1	1	2	2	2	2	2	2
20–34	1	19.0	0	19	19	19	19	19	19	19
35–49	1	1.0	0	1	1	1	1	1	1	1
50–64	0									
65+	4	8.9	50	1	3	12	16	16	16	16
TOTAL SINGLE DX	**0**									
TOTAL MULTIPLE DX	**9**	**3.4**	**28**	**1**	**1**	**1**	**2**	**16**	**16**	**19**
TOTAL										
0–19 Years	3	1.8	<1	1	2	2	2	2	2	2
20–34	1	19.0	0	19	19	19	19	19	19	19
35–49	1	1.0	0	1	1	1	1	1	1	1
50–64	0									
65+	4	8.9	50	1	3	12	16	16	16	16
GRAND TOTAL	**9**	**3.4**	**28**	**1**	**1**	**1**	**2**	**16**	**16**	**19**

09.0: LACRIMAL GLAND INCISION

Type of Patients	Observed Patients	Avg. Stay	Vari-ance	Percentiles						
				10th	25th	50th	75th	90th	95th	99th
1. SINGLE DX										
0–19 Years	0									
20–34	0									
35–49	0									
50–64	0									
65+	0									
2. MULTIPLE DX										
0–19 Years	0									
20–34	0									
35–49	0									
50–64	0									
65+	0									
TOTAL SINGLE DX	**0**									
TOTAL MULTIPLE DX	**0**									
TOTAL										
0–19 Years	0									
20–34	0									
35–49	0									
50–64	0									
65+	0									
GRAND TOTAL	**0**									

09.1: LACRIMAL SYSTEM DXTIC PX

Type of Patients	Observed Patients	Avg. Stay	Vari-ance	Percentiles						
				10th	25th	50th	75th	90th	95th	99th
1. SINGLE DX										
0–19 Years	0									
20–34	0									
35–49	0									
50–64	0									
65+	0									
2. MULTIPLE DX										
0–19 Years	0									
20–34	0									
35–49	0									
50–64	0									
65+	1	1.0	0	1	1	1	1	1	1	1
TOTAL SINGLE DX	**0**									
TOTAL MULTIPLE DX	**1**	**1.0**	**0**	**1**	**1**	**1**	**1**	**1**	**1**	**1**
TOTAL										
0–19 Years	0									
20–34	0									
35–49	0									
50–64	0									
65+	1	1.0	0	1	1	1	1	1	1	1
GRAND TOTAL	**1**	**1.0**	**0**	**1**	**1**	**1**	**1**	**1**	**1**	**1**

09.2: LACRIMAL GLAND LES EXC

Type of Patients	Observed Patients	Avg. Stay	Vari-ance	Percentiles						
				10th	25th	50th	75th	90th	95th	99th
1. SINGLE DX										
0–19 Years	0									
20–34	0									
35–49	0									
50–64	0									
65+	0									
2. MULTIPLE DX										
0–19 Years	1	3.0	0	3	3	3	3	3	3	3
20–34	0									
35–49	1	5.0	0	5	5	5	5	5	5	5
50–64	0									
65+	1	1.0	0	1	1	1	1	1	1	1
TOTAL SINGLE DX	**0**									
TOTAL MULTIPLE DX	**3**	**3.3**	**3**	**1**	**1**	**3**	**5**	**5**	**5**	**5**
TOTAL										
0–19 Years	1	3.0	0	3	3	3	3	3	3	3
20–34	0									
35–49	1	5.0	0	5	5	5	5	5	5	5
50–64	0									
65+	1	1.0	0	1	1	1	1	1	1	1
GRAND TOTAL	**3**	**3.3**	**3**	**1**	**1**	**3**	**5**	**5**	**5**	**5**

09.3: OTHER LACRIMAL GLAND OPS

Type of Patients	Observed Patients	Avg. Stay	Vari-ance	Percentiles						
				10th	25th	50th	75th	90th	95th	99th
1. SINGLE DX										
0–19 Years	0									
20–34	0									
35–49	0									
50–64	0									
65+	0									
2. MULTIPLE DX										
0–19 Years	0									
20–34	0									
35–49	0									
50–64	0									
65+	0									
TOTAL SINGLE DX	**0**									
TOTAL MULTIPLE DX	**0**									
TOTAL										
0–19 Years	0									
20–34	0									
35–49	0									
50–64	0									
65+	0									
GRAND TOTAL	**0**									

09.4: LACRIMAL PASSAGE MANIP

Type of Patients	Observed Patients	Avg. Stay	Vari-ance	Percentiles						
				10th	25th	50th	75th	90th	95th	99th
1. SINGLE DX										
0–19 Years	3	1.0	0	1	1	1	1	1	1	1
20–34	1	1.0	0	1	1	1	1	1	1	1
35–49	1	1.0	0	1	1	1	1	1	1	1
50–64	0									
65+	0									
2. MULTIPLE DX										
0–19 Years	30	3.8	7	1	2	3	5	8	8	12
20–34	3	1.6	<1	1	1	2	2	2	2	2
35–49	4	4.1	7	1	3	3	8	8	8	8
50–64	2	1.0	0	1	1	1	1	1	1	1
65+	1	5.0	0	5	5	5	5	5	5	5
TOTAL SINGLE DX	**5**	**1.0**	**0**	**1**	**1**	**1**	**1**	**1**	**1**	**1**
TOTAL MULTIPLE DX	**40**	**3.5**	**7**	**1**	**1**	**3**	**5**	**8**	**8**	**12**
TOTAL										
0–19 Years	33	3.6	7	1	1	3	5	8	8	12
20–34	4	1.5	<1	1	1	1	2	2	2	2
35–49	5	3.8	7	1	1	3	4	8	8	8
50–64	2	1.0	0	1	1	1	1	1	1	1
65+	1	5.0	0	5	5	5	5	5	5	5
GRAND TOTAL	**45**	**3.3**	**7**	**1**	**1**	**2**	**5**	**8**	**8**	**12**

09.5: INC LACRIMAL SAC/PASSG

Type of Patients	Observed Patients	Avg. Stay	Vari-ance	Percentiles						
				10th	25th	50th	75th	90th	95th	99th
1. SINGLE DX										
0–19 Years	2	2.0	1	1	1	3	3	3	3	3
20–34	1	1.0	0	1	1	1	1	1	1	1
35–49	0									
50–64	1	4.0	0	4	4	4	4	4	4	4
65+	0									
2. MULTIPLE DX										
0–19 Years	1	4.0	0	4	4	4	4	4	4	4
20–34	1	5.0	0	5	5	5	5	5	5	5
35–49	0									
50–64	0									
65+	5	2.7	2	1	2	2	4	5	5	5
TOTAL SINGLE DX	**4**	**2.1**	**1**	**1**	**1**	**3**	**3**	**4**	**4**	**4**
TOTAL MULTIPLE DX	**7**	**3.5**	**2**	**1**	**2**	**4**	**4**	**5**	**5**	**5**
TOTAL										
0–19 Years	3	2.7	2	1	1	3	4	4	4	4
20–34	2	3.2	6	1	1	5	5	5	5	5
35–49	0									
50–64	1	4.0	0	4	4	4	4	4	4	4
65+	5	2.7	2	1	2	2	4	5	5	5
GRAND TOTAL	**11**	**2.8**	**2**	**1**	**1**	**3**	**4**	**4**	**5**	**5**

09.6: LACRIMAL SAC/PASSAGE EXC

Type of Patients	Observed Patients	Avg. Stay	Vari-ance	Percentiles						
				10th	25th	50th	75th	90th	95th	99th
1. SINGLE DX										
0–19 Years	0									
20–34	0									
35–49	0									
50–64	0									
65+	0									
2. MULTIPLE DX										
0–19 Years	2	4.3	<1	4	4	4	4	6	6	6
20–34	0									
35–49	0									
50–64	0									
65+	0									
TOTAL SINGLE DX	**0**									
TOTAL MULTIPLE DX	**2**	**4.3**	**<1**	**4**	**4**	**4**	**4**	**6**	**6**	**6**
TOTAL										
0–19 Years	2	4.3	<1	4	4	4	4	6	6	6
20–34	0									
35–49	0									
50–64	0									
65+	0									
GRAND TOTAL	**2**	**4.3**	**<1**	**4**	**4**	**4**	**4**	**6**	**6**	**6**

09.7: CANALICULUS/PUNCTUM REP

Type of Patients	Observed Patients	Avg. Stay	Vari-ance	Percentiles						
				10th	25th	50th	75th	90th	95th	99th
1. SINGLE DX										
0–19 Years	9	1.4	<1	1	1	1	2	2	4	4
20–34	2	1.5	<1	1	1	2	2	2	2	2
35–49	1	1.0	0	1	1	1	1	1	1	1
50–64	0									
65+	0									
2. MULTIPLE DX										
0–19 Years	14	1.6	<1	1	1	1	3	3	3	3
20–34	4	2.0	<1	1	1	2	3	3	3	3
35–49	5	4.7	5	2	3	6	6	7	7	7
50–64	2	1.0	0	1	1	1	1	1	1	1
65+	4	2.9	1	1	3	3	4	4	4	4
TOTAL SINGLE DX	**12**	**1.4**	**<1**	**1**	**1**	**1**	**2**	**2**	**2**	**4**
TOTAL MULTIPLE DX	**29**	**2.0**	**2**	**1**	**1**	**1**	**3**	**3**	**6**	**7**
TOTAL										
0–19 Years	23	1.5	<1	1	1	1	2	3	3	4
20–34	6	1.8	<1	1	1	2	3	3	3	3
35–49	6	4.0	6	1	2	3	6	7	7	7
50–64	2	1.0	0	1	1	1	1	1	1	1
65+	4	2.9	1	1	3	3	4	4	4	4
GRAND TOTAL	**41**	**1.8**	**2**	**1**	**1**	**1**	**3**	**3**	**4**	**7**

09.8: NL FISTULIZATION

Type of Patients	Observed Patients	Avg. Stay	Vari-ance	Percentiles						
				10th	25th	50th	75th	90th	95th	99th
1. SINGLE DX										
0–19 Years	1	1.0	0	1	1	1	1	1	1	1
20–34	0									
35–49	1	2.0	0	2	2	2	2	2	2	2
50–64	0									
65+	0									
2. MULTIPLE DX										
0–19 Years	5	4.8	6	1	2	4	7	7	7	7
20–34	2	2.9	<1	3	3	3	3	3	3	3
35–49	3	1.3	<1	1	1	1	1	1	4	4
50–64	2	9.4	52	3	3	15	15	15	15	15
65+	14	1.6	1	1	1	1	2	2	5	5
TOTAL SINGLE DX	**2**	**1.2**	**<1**	**1**	**1**	**1**	**1**	**2**	**2**	**2**
TOTAL MULTIPLE DX	**26**	**2.9**	**8**	**1**	**1**	**2**	**3**	**7**	**7**	**15**
TOTAL										
0–19 Years	6	3.5	7	1	1	2	7	7	7	7
20–34	2	2.9	<1	3	3	3	3	3	3	3
35–49	4	1.4	<1	1	1	1	1	2	4	4
50–64	2	9.4	52	3	3	15	15	15	15	15
65+	14	1.6	1	1	1	1	2	2	5	5
GRAND TOTAL	**28**	**2.7**	**7**	**1**	**1**	**2**	**3**	**7**	**7**	**15**

09.9: OTH LACRIMAL SYST OPS

Type of Patients	Observed Patients	Avg. Stay	Vari-ance	Percentiles						
				10th	25th	50th	75th	90th	95th	99th
1. SINGLE DX										
0–19 Years	0									
20–34	0									
35–49	0									
50–64	1	1.0	0	1	1	1	1	1	1	1
65+	0									
2. MULTIPLE DX										
0–19 Years	1	4.0	0	4	4	4	4	4	4	4
20–34	0									
35–49	0									
50–64	0									
65+	0									
TOTAL SINGLE DX	**1**	**1.0**	**0**	**1**	**1**	**1**	**1**	**1**	**1**	**1**
TOTAL MULTIPLE DX	**1**	**4.0**	**0**	**4**	**4**	**4**	**4**	**4**	**4**	**4**
TOTAL										
0–19 Years	1	4.0	0	4	4	4	4	4	4	4
20–34	0									
35–49	0									
50–64	1	1.0	0	1	1	1	1	1	1	1
65+	0									
GRAND TOTAL	**2**	**3.4**	**2**	**1**	**4**	**4**	**4**	**4**	**4**	**4**

10.0: INC/RMVL FB-CONJUNCTIVA

Type of Patients	Observed Patients	Avg. Stay	Vari-ance	Percentiles 10th	25th	50th	75th	90th	95th	99th
1. SINGLE DX										
0–19 Years	0									
20–34	0									
35–49	1	1.0	0	1	1	1	1	1	1	1
50–64	0									
65+	0									
2. MULTIPLE DX										
0–19 Years	0									
20–34	1	3.0	0	3	3	3	3	3	3	3
35–49	0									
50–64	1	3.0	0	3	3	3	3	3	3	3
65+	0									
TOTAL SINGLE DX	**1**	**1.0**	**0**	**1**	**1**	**1**	**1**	**1**	**1**	**1**
TOTAL MULTIPLE DX	**2**	**3.0**	**0**	**3**	**3**	**3**	**3**	**3**	**3**	**3**
TOTAL										
0–19 Years	0									
20–34	1	3.0	0	3	3	3	3	3	3	3
35–49	1	1.0	0	1	1	1	1	1	1	1
50–64	1	3.0	0	3	3	3	3	3	3	3
65+	0									
GRAND TOTAL	**3**	**2.5**	**<1**	**1**	**3**	**3**	**3**	**3**	**3**	**3**

10.1: CONJUNCTIVA INCISION NEC

Type of Patients	Observed Patients	Avg. Stay	Vari-ance	Percentiles 10th	25th	50th	75th	90th	95th	99th
1. SINGLE DX										
0–19 Years	1	1.0	0	1	1	1	1	1	1	1
20–34	0									
35–49	0									
50–64	1	1.0	0	1	1	1	1	1	1	1
65+	0									
2. MULTIPLE DX										
0–19 Years	6	1.5	<1	1	1	1	2	2	3	3
20–34	1	1.0	0	1	1	1	1	1	1	1
35–49	0									
50–64	1	3.0	0	3	3	3	3	3	3	3
65+	0									
TOTAL SINGLE DX	**2**	**1.0**	**0**	**1**	**1**	**1**	**1**	**1**	**1**	**1**
TOTAL MULTIPLE DX	**8**	**1.6**	**<1**	**1**	**1**	**1**	**2**	**3**	**3**	**3**
TOTAL										
0–19 Years	7	1.4	<1	1	1	1	2	2	3	3
20–34	1	1.0	0	1	1	1	1	1	1	1
35–49	0									
50–64	2	2.0	1	1	1	3	3	3	3	3
65+	0									
GRAND TOTAL	**10**	**1.4**	**<1**	**1**	**1**	**1**	**2**	**3**	**3**	**3**

10.2: CONJUNCTIVA DXTIC PX

Type of Patients	Observed Patients	Avg. Stay	Vari-ance	Percentiles 10th	25th	50th	75th	90th	95th	99th
1. SINGLE DX										
0–19 Years	0									
20–34	0									
35–49	0									
50–64	0									
65+	0									
2. MULTIPLE DX										
0–19 Years	5	9.7	47	4	5	9	15	22	22	22
20–34	0									
35–49	0									
50–64	0									
65+	0									
TOTAL SINGLE DX	**0**									
TOTAL MULTIPLE DX	**5**	**9.7**	**47**	**4**	**5**	**9**	**15**	**22**	**22**	**22**
TOTAL										
0–19 Years	5	9.7	47	4	5	9	15	22	22	22
20–34	0									
35–49	0									
50–64	0									
65+	0									
GRAND TOTAL	**5**	**9.7**	**47**	**4**	**5**	**9**	**15**	**22**	**22**	**22**

10.3: EXC/DESTR CONJUNCT LES

Type of Patients	Observed Patients	Avg. Stay	Vari-ance	Percentiles 10th	25th	50th	75th	90th	95th	99th
1. SINGLE DX										
0–19 Years	0									
20–34	0									
35–49	0									
50–64	0									
65+	0									
2. MULTIPLE DX										
0–19 Years	0									
20–34	1	1.0	0	1	1	1	1	1	1	1
35–49	1	4.0	0	4	4	4	4	4	4	4
50–64	0									
65+	1	5.0	0	5	5	5	5	5	5	5
TOTAL SINGLE DX	**0**									
TOTAL MULTIPLE DX	**3**	**3.3**	**3**	**1**	**1**	**4**	**4**	**5**	**5**	**5**
TOTAL										
0–19 Years	0									
20–34	1	1.0	0	1	1	1	1	1	1	1
35–49	1	4.0	0	4	4	4	4	4	4	4
50–64	0									
65+	1	5.0	0	5	5	5	5	5	5	5
GRAND TOTAL	**3**	**3.3**	**3**	**1**	**1**	**4**	**4**	**5**	**5**	**5**

10.4: CONJUNCTIVOPLASTY

Type of Patients	Observed Patients	Avg. Stay	Vari-ance	10th	25th	50th	75th	90th	95th	99th
1. SINGLE DX										
0–19 Years	0									
20–34	0									
35–49	0									
50–64	0									
65+	0									
2. MULTIPLE DX										
0–19 Years	1	1.0	0	1	1	1	1	1	1	1
20–34	0									
35–49	0									
50–64	0									
65+	2	4.5	11	2	2	5	7	7	7	7
TOTAL SINGLE DX	**0**									
TOTAL MULTIPLE DX	**3**	**1.6**	**3**	**1**	**1**	**1**	**1**	**2**	**7**	**7**
TOTAL										
0–19 Years	1	1.0	0	1	1	1	1	1	1	1
20–34	0									
35–49	0									
50–64	0									
65+	2	4.5	11	2	2	5	7	7	7	7
GRAND TOTAL	**3**	**1.6**	**3**	**1**	**1**	**1**	**1**	**2**	**7**	**7**

10.5: CONJUNCT/LID ADHESIO

Type of Patients	Observed Patients	Avg. Stay	Vari-ance	10th	25th	50th	75th	90th	95th	99th
1. SINGLE DX										
0–19 Years	0									
20–34	0									
35–49	0									
50–64	0									
65+	0									
2. MULTIPLE DX										
0–19 Years	1	21.0	0	21	21	21	21	21	21	21
20–34	0									
35–49	0									
50–64	0									
65+	0									
TOTAL SINGLE DX	**0**									
TOTAL MULTIPLE DX	**1**	**21.0**	**0**	**21**	**21**	**21**	**21**	**21**	**21**	**21**
TOTAL										
0–19 Years	1	21.0	0	21	21	21	21	21	21	21
20–34	0									
35–49	0									
50–64	0									
65+	0									
GRAND TOTAL	**1**	**21.0**	**0**	**21**	**21**	**21**	**21**	**21**	**21**	**21**

10.6: REPAIR CONJUNCT LAC

Type of Patients	Observed Patients	Avg. Stay	Vari-ance	10th	25th	50th	75th	90th	95th	99th
1. SINGLE DX										
0–19 Years	1	5.0	0	5	5	5	5	5	5	5
20–34	0									
35–49	1	1.0	0	1	1	1	1	1	1	1
50–64	0									
65+	0									
2. MULTIPLE DX										
0–19 Years	1	1.0	0	1	1	1	1	1	1	1
20–34	5	1.9	<1	1	1	2	2	3	3	3
35–49	0									
50–64	4	3.5	2	1	4	4	4	4	6	6
65+	2	1.9	2	1	1	1	3	3	3	3
TOTAL SINGLE DX	**2**	**2.2**	**4**	**1**	**1**	**1**	**5**	**5**	**5**	**5**
TOTAL MULTIPLE DX	**12**	**2.6**	**2**	**1**	**1**	**2**	**4**	**4**	**4**	**6**
TOTAL										
0–19 Years	2	3.6	4	1	1	5	5	5	5	5
20–34	5	1.9	<1	1	1	2	2	3	3	3
35–49	1	1.0	0	1	1	1	1	1	1	1
50–64	4	3.5	2	1	4	4	4	4	6	6
65+	2	1.9	2	1	1	1	3	3	3	3
GRAND TOTAL	**14**	**2.4**	**3**	**1**	**1**	**1**	**4**	**5**	**5**	**6**

10.9: OTHER CONJUNCTIVAL OPS

Type of Patients	Observed Patients	Avg. Stay	Vari-ance	10th	25th	50th	75th	90th	95th	99th
1. SINGLE DX										
0–19 Years	2	2.2	<1	2	2	2	2	3	3	3
20–34	3	1.0	0	1	1	1	1	1	1	1
35–49	0									
50–64	3	1.0	0	1	1	1	1	1	1	1
65+	1	2.0	0	2	2	2	2	2	2	2
2. MULTIPLE DX										
0–19 Years	6	3.8	8	1	1	2	7	7	7	7
20–34	5	1.5	<1	1	1	1	2	3	3	3
35–49	3	4.7	5	2	2	5	7	7	7	7
50–64	5	2.4	1	1	1	2	4	4	4	4
65+	12	2.2	3	1	1	1	3	4	6	6
TOTAL SINGLE DX	**9**	**1.6**	**<1**	**1**	**1**	**1**	**2**	**2**	**3**	**3**
TOTAL MULTIPLE DX	**31**	**2.7**	**4**	**1**	**1**	**2**	**4**	**6**	**7**	**7**
TOTAL										
0–19 Years	8	3.2	6	1	2	2	7	7	7	7
20–34	8	1.3	<1	1	1	1	1	2	3	3
35–49	3	4.7	5	2	2	5	7	7	7	7
50–64	8	2.1	2	1	1	2	4	4	4	4
65+	13	2.1	3	1	1	1	3	4	6	6
GRAND TOTAL	**40**	**2.4**	**3**	**1**	**1**	**2**	**4**	**5**	**7**	**7**

11.0: MAGNET REMOVAL CORNEA FB

Type of Patients	Observed Patients	Avg. Stay	Vari-ance	Percentiles						
				10th	25th	50th	75th	90th	95th	99th
1. SINGLE DX										
0–19 Years	0									
20–34	0									
35–49	0									
50–64	0									
65+	0									
2. MULTIPLE DX										
0–19 Years	0									
20–34	0									
35–49	1	2.0	0	2	2	2	2	2	2	2
50–64	0									
65+	0									
TOTAL SINGLE DX	**0**									
TOTAL MULTIPLE DX	**1**	**2.0**	**0**	**2**	**2**	**2**	**2**	**2**	**2**	**2**
TOTAL										
0–19 Years	0									
20–34	0									
35–49	1	2.0	0	2	2	2	2	2	2	2
50–64	0									
65+	0									
GRAND TOTAL	**1**	**2.0**	**0**	**2**	**2**	**2**	**2**	**2**	**2**	**2**

11.1: CORNEAL INCISION

Type of Patients	Observed Patients	Avg. Stay	Vari-ance	Percentiles						
				10th	25th	50th	75th	90th	95th	99th
1. SINGLE DX										
0–19 Years	0									
20–34	0									
35–49	0									
50–64	0									
65+	0									
2. MULTIPLE DX										
0–19 Years	0									
20–34	1	6.0	0	6	6	6	6	6	6	6
35–49	1	4.0	0	4	4	4	4	4	4	4
50–64	0									
65+	0									
TOTAL SINGLE DX	**0**									
TOTAL MULTIPLE DX	**2**	**4.4**	**<1**	**4**	**4**	**4**	**4**	**6**	**6**	**6**
TOTAL										
0–19 Years	0									
20–34	1	6.0	0	6	6	6	6	6	6	6
35–49	1	4.0	0	4	4	4	4	4	4	4
50–64	0									
65+	0									
GRAND TOTAL	**2**	**4.4**	**<1**	**4**	**4**	**4**	**4**	**6**	**6**	**6**

11.2: DXTIC PX ON CORNEA

Type of Patients	Observed Patients	Avg. Stay	Vari-ance	Percentiles						
				10th	25th	50th	75th	90th	95th	99th
1. SINGLE DX										
0–19 Years	0									
20–34	1	2.0	0	2	2	2	2	2	2	2
35–49	2	9.3	14	7	7	7	13	13	13	13
50–64	0									
65+	0									
2. MULTIPLE DX										
0–19 Years	1	3.0	0	3	3	3	3	3	3	3
20–34	1	4.0	0	4	4	4	4	4	4	4
35–49	3	9.8	108	4	5	5	5	28	28	28
50–64	2	6.7	1	6	6	6	8	8	8	8
65+	1	2.0	0	2	2	2	2	2	2	2
TOTAL SINGLE DX	**3**	**5.8**	**22**	**2**	**2**	**7**	**7**	**13**	**13**	**13**
TOTAL MULTIPLE DX	**8**	**6.9**	**54**	**3**	**4**	**5**	**6**	**8**	**28**	**28**
TOTAL										
0–19 Years	1	3.0	0	3	3	3	3	3	3	3
20–34	2	2.7	1	2	2	2	4	4	4	4
35–49	5	9.7	77	4	5	5	13	28	28	28
50–64	2	6.7	1	6	6	6	8	8	8	8
65+	1	2.0	0	2	2	2	2	2	2	2
GRAND TOTAL	**11**	**6.6**	**45**	**2**	**3**	**5**	**7**	**13**	**28**	**28**

11.3: EXCISION OF PTERYGIUM

Type of Patients	Observed Patients	Avg. Stay	Vari-ance	Percentiles						
				10th	25th	50th	75th	90th	95th	99th
1. SINGLE DX										
0–19 Years	0									
20–34	0									
35–49	0									
50–64	0									
65+	0									
2. MULTIPLE DX										
0–19 Years	0									
20–34	0									
35–49	0									
50–64	1	1.0	0	1	1	1	1	1	1	1
65+	1	1.0	0	1	1	1	1	1	1	1
TOTAL SINGLE DX	**0**									
TOTAL MULTIPLE DX	**2**	**1.0**	**0**	**1**	**1**	**1**	**1**	**1**	**1**	**1**
TOTAL										
0–19 Years	0									
20–34	0									
35–49	0									
50–64	1	1.0	0	1	1	1	1	1	1	1
65+	1	1.0	0	1	1	1	1	1	1	1
GRAND TOTAL	**2**	**1.0**	**0**	**1**	**1**	**1**	**1**	**1**	**1**	**1**

11.4: EXC/DESTR CORNEAL LESION

Type of Patients	Observed Patients	Avg. Stay	Vari-ance	10th	25th	50th	75th	90th	95th	99th
				Percentiles						
1. SINGLE DX										
0–19 Years	0									
20–34	0									
35–49	0									
50–64	0									
65+	0									
2. MULTIPLE DX										
0–19 Years	1	1.0	0	1	1	1	1	1	1	1
20–34	0									
35–49	1	7.0	0	7	7	7	7	7	7	7
50–64	1	9.0	0	9	9	9	9	9	9	9
65+	2	3.3	4	2	2	2	5	5	5	5
TOTAL SINGLE DX	**0**									
TOTAL MULTIPLE DX	**5**	**4.1**	**11**	**1**	**1**	**2**	**7**	**9**	**9**	**9**
TOTAL										
0–19 Years	1	1.0	0	1	1	1	1	1	1	1
20–34	0									
35–49	1	7.0	0	7	7	7	7	7	7	7
50–64	1	9.0	0	9	9	9	9	9	9	9
65+	2	3.3	4	2	2	2	5	5	5	5
GRAND TOTAL	**5**	**4.1**	**11**	**1**	**1**	**2**	**7**	**9**	**9**	**9**

11.5: CORNEAL REPAIR

Type of Patients	Observed Patients	Avg. Stay	Vari-ance	10th	25th	50th	75th	90th	95th	99th
				Percentiles						
1. SINGLE DX										
0–19 Years	27	1.7	<1	1	1	1	3	3	3	4
20–34	25	1.5	<1	1	1	1	2	2	2	3
35–49	13	2.2	1	1	1	2	3	4	4	4
50–64	0									
65+	1	1.0	0	1	1	1	1	1	1	1
2. MULTIPLE DX										
0–19 Years	36	2.1	2	1	1	2	3	3	4	10
20–34	31	2.0	16	1	1	1	2	3	5	33
35–49	20	2.2	5	1	1	1	3	4	7	13
50–64	15	2.4	4	1	1	2	3	6	6	9
65+	21	2.9	8	1	1	2	3	8	8	12
TOTAL SINGLE DX	**66**	**1.7**	**<1**	**1**	**1**	**1**	**2**	**3**	**3**	**4**
TOTAL MULTIPLE DX	**123**	**2.2**	**6**	**1**	**1**	**1**	**3**	**4**	**5**	**12**
TOTAL										
0–19 Years	63	1.9	1	1	1	1	3	3	3	5
20–34	56	1.8	9	1	1	1	2	3	3	6
35–49	33	2.2	4	1	1	1	3	4	4	13
50–64	15	2.4	4	1	1	2	3	6	6	9
65+	22	2.8	8	1	1	2	3	8	8	12
GRAND TOTAL	**189**	**2.0**	**4**	**1**	**1**	**1**	**3**	**3**	**4**	**10**

11.51: SUTURE OF CORNEAL LAC

Type of Patients	Observed Patients	Avg. Stay	Vari-ance	10th	25th	50th	75th	90th	95th	99th
				Percentiles						
1. SINGLE DX										
0–19 Years	25	1.8	<1	1	1	2	3	3	3	4
20–34	21	1.4	<1	1	1	1	2	2	2	3
35–49	12	2.0	<1	1	1	2	3	3	4	4
50–64	0									
65+	1	1.0	0	1	1	1	1	1	1	1
2. MULTIPLE DX										
0–19 Years	34	2.1	2	1	1	2	3	3	3	10
20–34	29	2.0	17	1	1	1	2	3	5	33
35–49	18	2.3	5	1	1	1	3	4	7	13
50–64	11	2.1	2	1	1	2	3	4	6	6
65+	16	2.8	9	1	1	1	3	8	12	12
TOTAL SINGLE DX	**59**	**1.7**	**<1**	**1**	**1**	**1**	**2**	**3**	**3**	**4**
TOTAL MULTIPLE DX	**108**	**2.1**	**7**	**1**	**1**	**1**	**3**	**3**	**4**	**12**
TOTAL										
0–19 Years	59	2.0	1	1	1	2	3	3	3	5
20–34	50	1.8	10	1	1	1	2	3	3	6
35–49	30	2.2	4	1	1	1	3	4	4	13
50–64	11	2.1	2	1	1	2	3	4	6	6
65+	17	2.7	9	1	1	1	3	8	12	12
GRAND TOTAL	**167**	**2.0**	**5**	**1**	**1**	**1**	**3**	**3**	**4**	**10**

11.6: CORNEAL TRANSPLANT

Type of Patients	Observed Patients	Avg. Stay	Vari-ance	10th	25th	50th	75th	90th	95th	99th
				Percentiles						
1. SINGLE DX										
0–19 Years	0									
20–34	0									
35–49	4	3.6	<1	2	4	4	4	4	4	4
50–64	1	2.0	0	2	2	2	2	2	2	2
65+	2	1.5	<1	1	1	1	2	2	2	2
2. MULTIPLE DX										
0–19 Years	4	1.1	<1	1	1	1	1	1	2	2
20–34	2	1.4	<1	1	1	1	2	2	2	2
35–49	4	5.7	7	1	2	7	7	7	8	8
50–64	11	2.4	5	1	1	1	4	4	8	8
65+	25	4.3	22	1	1	2	5	10	12	22
TOTAL SINGLE DX	**7**	**3.2**	**1**	**1**	**2**	**4**	**4**	**4**	**4**	**4**
TOTAL MULTIPLE DX	**46**	**3.3**	**13**	**1**	**1**	**2**	**4**	**7**	**8**	**22**
TOTAL										
0–19 Years	4	1.1	<1	1	1	1	1	1	2	2
20–34	2	1.4	<1	1	1	1	2	2	2	2
35–49	8	4.4	4	2	4	4	7	7	7	8
50–64	12	2.4	5	1	1	1	3	4	8	8
65+	27	4.1	21	1	1	2	5	10	12	22
GRAND TOTAL	**53**	**3.2**	**11**	**1**	**1**	**2**	**4**	**7**	**8**	**22**

11.7: OTHER CORNEA RECONST

Type of Patients	Observed Patients	Avg. Stay	Vari-ance	10th	25th	50th	75th	90th	95th	99th
1. SINGLE DX										
0–19 Years	0									
20–34	0									
35–49	0									
50–64	0									
65+	1	1.0	0	1	1	1	1	1	1	1
2. MULTIPLE DX										
0–19 Years	0									
20–34	2	2.2	5	1	1	1	5	5	5	5
35–49	0									
50–64	0									
65+	0									
TOTAL SINGLE DX	**1**	**1.0**	**0**	**1**	**1**	**1**	**1**	**1**	**1**	**1**
TOTAL MULTIPLE DX	**2**	**2.2**	**5**	**1**	**1**	**1**	**5**	**5**	**5**	**5**
TOTAL										
0–19 Years	0									
20–34	2	2.2	5	1	1	1	5	5	5	5
35–49	0									
50–64	0									
65+	1	1.0	0	1	1	1	1	1	1	1
GRAND TOTAL	**3**	**1.9**	**4**	**1**	**1**	**1**	**1**	**5**	**5**	**5**

11.9: OTHER CORNEAL OPERATIONS

Type of Patients	Observed Patients	Avg. Stay	Vari-ance	10th	25th	50th	75th	90th	95th	99th
1. SINGLE DX										
0–19 Years	0									
20–34	0									
35–49	0									
50–64	0									
65+	0									
2. MULTIPLE DX										
0–19 Years	1	1.0	0	1	1	1	1	1	1	1
20–34	1	2.0	0	2	2	2	2	2	2	2
35–49	0									
50–64	0									
65+	0									
TOTAL SINGLE DX	**0**									
TOTAL MULTIPLE DX	**2**	**1.7**	**<1**	**1**	**1**	**2**	**2**	**2**	**2**	**2**
TOTAL										
0–19 Years	1	1.0	0	1	1	1	1	1	1	1
20–34	1	2.0	0	2	2	2	2	2	2	2
35–49	0									
50–64	0									
65+	0									
GRAND TOTAL	**2**	**1.7**	**<1**	**1**	**1**	**2**	**2**	**2**	**2**	**2**

12.0: RMVL INOC FB ANT SEGMENT

Type of Patients	Observed Patients	Avg. Stay	Vari-ance	10th	25th	50th	75th	90th	95th	99th
1. SINGLE DX										
0–19 Years	0									
20–34	0									
35–49	0									
50–64	0									
65+	0									
2. MULTIPLE DX										
0–19 Years	1	1.0	0	1	1	1	1	1	1	1
20–34	3	2.1	<1	1	2	2	3	3	3	3
35–49	2	1.0	0	1	1	1	1	1	1	1
50–64	1	1.0	0	1	1	1	1	1	1	1
65+	0									
TOTAL SINGLE DX	**0**									
TOTAL MULTIPLE DX	**7**	**1.3**	**<1**	**1**	**1**	**1**	**1**	**2**	**3**	**3**
TOTAL										
0–19 Years	1	1.0	0	1	1	1	1	1	1	1
20–34	3	2.1	<1	1	2	2	3	3	3	3
35–49	2	1.0	0	1	1	1	1	1	1	1
50–64	1	1.0	0	1	1	1	1	1	1	1
65+	0									
GRAND TOTAL	**7**	**1.3**	**<1**	**1**	**1**	**1**	**1**	**2**	**3**	**3**

12.1: IRIDOTOMY/SMP IRIDECTOMY

Type of Patients	Observed Patients	Avg. Stay	Vari-ance	10th	25th	50th	75th	90th	95th	99th
1. SINGLE DX										
0–19 Years	0									
20–34	0									
35–49	1	1.0	0	1	1	1	1	1	1	1
50–64	1	1.0	0	1	1	1	1	1	1	1
65+	0									
2. MULTIPLE DX										
0–19 Years	1	2.0	0	2	2	2	2	2	2	2
20–34	1	1.0	0	1	1	1	1	1	1	1
35–49	0									
50–64	6	4.7	29	1	2	4	4	20	20	20
65+	8	5.9	47	1	1	2	9	20	20	20
TOTAL SINGLE DX	**2**	**1.0**	**0**	**1**	**1**	**1**	**1**	**1**	**1**	**1**
TOTAL MULTIPLE DX	**16**	**4.8**	**33**	**1**	**1**	**3**	**4**	**14**	**20**	**20**
TOTAL										
0–19 Years	1	2.0	0	2	2	2	2	2	2	2
20–34	1	1.0	0	1	1	1	1	1	1	1
35–49	1	1.0	0	1	1	1	1	1	1	1
50–64	7	4.3	28	1	2	4	4	4	20	20
65+	8	5.9	47	1	1	2	9	20	20	20
GRAND TOTAL	**18**	**4.4**	**31**	**1**	**1**	**2**	**4**	**14**	**20**	**20**

12.2: ANTERIOR SEG DXTIC PX

Type of Patients	Observed Patients	Avg. Stay	Vari-ance	Percentiles						
				10th	25th	50th	75th	90th	95th	99th
1. SINGLE DX										
0–19 Years	0									
20–34	0									
35–49	0									
50–64	0									
65+	0									
2. MULTIPLE DX										
0–19 Years	1	5.0	0	5	5	5	5	5	5	5
20–34	0									
35–49	1	16.0	0	16	16	16	16	16	16	16
50–64	1	5.0	0	5	5	5	5	5	5	5
65+	6	3.1	4	1	1	2	4	6	7	7
TOTAL SINGLE DX	**0**									
TOTAL MULTIPLE DX	**9**	**4.1**	**14**	**1**	**1**	**4**	**5**	**7**	**16**	**16**
TOTAL										
0–19 Years	1	5.0	0	5	5	5	5	5	5	5
20–34	0									
35–49	1	16.0	0	16	16	16	16	16	16	16
50–64	1	5.0	0	5	5	5	5	5	5	5
65+	6	3.1	4	1	1	2	4	6	7	7
GRAND TOTAL	**9**	**4.1**	**14**	**1**	**1**	**4**	**5**	**7**	**16**	**16**

12.3: IRIDOPLASTY/COREOPLASTY

Type of Patients	Observed Patients	Avg. Stay	Vari-ance	Percentiles						
				10th	25th	50th	75th	90th	95th	99th
1. SINGLE DX										
0–19 Years	1	2.0	0	2	2	2	2	2	2	2
20–34	0									
35–49	0									
50–64	0									
65+	0									
2. MULTIPLE DX										
0–19 Years	0									
20–34	1	3.0	0	3	3	3	3	3	3	3
35–49	1	1.0	0	1	1	1	1	1	1	1
50–64	0									
65+	0									
TOTAL SINGLE DX	**1**	**2.0**	**0**	**2**	**2**	**2**	**2**	**2**	**2**	**2**
TOTAL MULTIPLE DX	**2**	**1.9**	**2**	**1**	**1**	**1**	**3**	**3**	**3**	**3**
TOTAL										
0–19 Years	1	2.0	0	2	2	2	2	2	2	2
20–34	1	3.0	0	3	3	3	3	3	3	3
35–49	1	1.0	0	1	1	1	1	1	1	1
50–64	0									
65+	0									
GRAND TOTAL	**3**	**2.0**	**<1**	**1**	**2**	**2**	**2**	**3**	**3**	**3**

12.4: DESTR IRIS/CIL BODY LES

Type of Patients	Observed Patients	Avg. Stay	Vari-ance	Percentiles						
				10th	25th	50th	75th	90th	95th	99th
1. SINGLE DX										
0–19 Years	0									
20–34	0									
35–49	0									
50–64	1	1.0	0	1	1	1	1	1	1	1
65+	0									
2. MULTIPLE DX										
0–19 Years	0									
20–34	0									
35–49	0									
50–64	0									
65+	0									
TOTAL SINGLE DX	**1**	**1.0**	**0**	**1**	**1**	**1**	**1**	**1**	**1**	**1**
TOTAL MULTIPLE DX	**0**									
TOTAL										
0–19 Years	0									
20–34	0									
35–49	0									
50–64	1	1.0	0	1	1	1	1	1	1	1
65+	0									
GRAND TOTAL	**1**	**1.0**	**0**	**1**	**1**	**1**	**1**	**1**	**1**	**1**

12.5: INOC CIRCULAT FACILITAT

Type of Patients	Observed Patients	Avg. Stay	Vari-ance	Percentiles						
				10th	25th	50th	75th	90th	95th	99th
1. SINGLE DX										
0–19 Years	2	1.0	0	1	1	1	1	1	1	1
20–34	0									
35–49	0									
50–64	0									
65+	0									
2. MULTIPLE DX										
0–19 Years	3	26.0	392	1	1	40	40	40	40	40
20–34	0									
35–49	0									
50–64	0									
65+	1	1.0	0	1	1	1	1	1	1	1
TOTAL SINGLE DX	**2**	**1.0**	**0**	**1**	**1**	**1**	**1**	**1**	**1**	**1**
TOTAL MULTIPLE DX	**4**	**23.5**	**411**	**1**	**1**	**40**	**40**	**40**	**40**	**40**
TOTAL										
0–19 Years	5	17.3	398	1	1	1	40	40	40	40
20–34	0									
35–49	0									
50–64	0									
65+	1	1.0	0	1	1	1	1	1	1	1
GRAND TOTAL	**6**	**16.2**	**387**	**1**	**1**	**1**	**40**	**40**	**40**	**40**

12.6: SCLERAL FISTULIZATION

Type of Patients	Observed Patients	Avg. Stay	Vari-ance	Percentiles 10th	25th	50th	75th	90th	95th	99th
1. SINGLE DX										
0–19 Years	1	2.0	0	2	2	2	2	2	2	2
20–34	2	1.0	0	1	1	1	1	1	1	1
35–49	1	1.0	0	1	1	1	1	1	1	1
50–64	4	2.8	3	1	1	4	4	4	4	4
65+	2	5.1	34	1	1	1	10	10	10	10
2. MULTIPLE DX										
0–19 Years	11	1.7	2	1	1	1	1	3	6	6
20–34	4	2.2	1	1	2	2	2	4	4	4
35–49	4	6.5	7	1	6	8	8	8	8	8
50–64	18	3.7	17	1	1	2	3	11	13	16
65+	15	1.4	<1	1	1	1	2	3	3	3
TOTAL SINGLE DX	**10**	**2.6**	**7**	**1**	**1**	**1**	**4**	**4**	**10**	**10**
TOTAL MULTIPLE DX	**52**	**2.6**	**9**	**1**	**1**	**1**	**3**	**6**	**10**	**16**
TOTAL										
0–19 Years	12	1.7	2	1	1	1	1	3	6	6
20–34	6	1.8	1	1	1	2	2	4	4	4
35–49	5	5.7	10	1	1	8	8	8	8	8
50–64	22	3.6	15	1	1	2	4	10	13	16
65+	17	1.8	4	1	1	1	2	3	3	10
GRAND TOTAL	**62**	**2.6**	**9**	**1**	**1**	**1**	**3**	**6**	**10**	**13**

12.7: ELEVAT INOC PRESS RELIEF

Type of Patients	Observed Patients	Avg. Stay	Vari-ance	Percentiles 10th	25th	50th	75th	90th	95th	99th
1. SINGLE DX										
0–19 Years	0									
20–34	0									
35–49	0									
50–64	0									
65+	0									
2. MULTIPLE DX										
0–19 Years	2	4.1	36	1	1	1	13	13	13	13
20–34	1	1.0	0	1	1	1	1	1	1	1
35–49	0									
50–64	1	9.0	0	9	9	9	9	9	9	9
65+	0									
TOTAL SINGLE DX	**0**									
TOTAL MULTIPLE DX	**4**	**4.5**	**27**	**1**	**1**	**1**	**9**	**13**	**13**	**13**
TOTAL										
0–19 Years	2	4.1	36	1	1	1	13	13	13	13
20–34	1	1.0	0	1	1	1	1	1	1	1
35–49	0									
50–64	1	9.0	0	9	9	9	9	9	9	9
65+	0									
GRAND TOTAL	**4**	**4.5**	**27**	**1**	**1**	**1**	**9**	**13**	**13**	**13**

12.8: OPERATIONS ON SCLERA

Type of Patients	Observed Patients	Avg. Stay	Vari-ance	Percentiles 10th	25th	50th	75th	90th	95th	99th
1. SINGLE DX										
0–19 Years	1	3.0	0	3	3	3	3	3	3	3
20–34	5	1.8	<1	1	1	2	2	3	3	3
35–49	3	2.0	<1	1	1	2	3	3	3	3
50–64	2	1.0	0	1	1	1	1	1	1	1
65+	2	1.0	0	1	1	1	1	1	1	1
2. MULTIPLE DX										
0–19 Years	6	2.3	3	1	1	2	3	5	5	5
20–34	12	2.6	1	1	1	3	4	4	4	4
35–49	9	2.0	<1	1	1	2	3	3	3	3
50–64	12	2.6	10	1	1	1	2	10	10	10
65+	20	2.1	2	1	1	2	3	4	5	5
TOTAL SINGLE DX	**13**	**2.0**	**<1**	**1**	**1**	**2**	**3**	**3**	**3**	**3**
TOTAL MULTIPLE DX	**59**	**2.3**	**4**	**1**	**1**	**2**	**3**	**4**	**5**	**10**
TOTAL										
0–19 Years	7	2.5	2	1	1	2	3	5	5	5
20–34	17	2.4	1	1	1	2	3	4	4	4
35–49	12	2.0	<1	1	1	2	3	3	3	3
50–64	14	2.4	9	1	1	1	2	10	10	10
65+	22	2.0	2	1	1	1	3	4	5	5
GRAND TOTAL	**72**	**2.3**	**3**	**1**	**1**	**2**	**3**	**4**	**5**	**10**

12.9: OTH ANTERIOR SEGMENT OPS

Type of Patients	Observed Patients	Avg. Stay	Vari-ance	Percentiles 10th	25th	50th	75th	90th	95th	99th
1. SINGLE DX										
0–19 Years	1	1.0	0	1	1	1	1	1	1	1
20–34	1	3.0	0	3	3	3	3	3	3	3
35–49	1	3.0	0	3	3	3	3	3	3	3
50–64	0									
65+	1	1.0	0	1	1	1	1	1	1	1
2. MULTIPLE DX										
0–19 Years	5	4.2	11	1	1	3	8	8	8	8
20–34	2	9.0	37	4	4	9	14	14	14	14
35–49	2	3.6	<1	3	3	4	4	4	4	4
50–64	6	3.9	10	2	2	2	5	10	10	10
65+	7	2.5	2	1	1	3	4	4	4	4
TOTAL SINGLE DX	**4**	**2.0**	**1**	**1**	**1**	**1**	**3**	**3**	**3**	**3**
TOTAL MULTIPLE DX	**22**	**4.0**	**11**	**1**	**2**	**3**	**7**	**8**	**10**	**14**
TOTAL										
0–19 Years	6	3.9	11	1	1	3	8	8	8	8
20–34	3	7.0	32	3	3	4	14	14	14	14
35–49	3	3.4	<1	3	3	3	4	4	4	4
50–64	6	3.9	10	2	2	2	5	10	10	10
65+	8	2.4	2	1	1	2	3	4	4	4
GRAND TOTAL	**26**	**3.8**	**10**	**1**	**2**	**3**	**5**	**8**	**10**	**14**

13.0: REMOVAL FB FROM LENS

Type of Patients	Observed Patients	Avg. Stay	Vari-ance	Percentiles						
				10th	25th	50th	75th	90th	95th	99th
1. SINGLE DX										
0–19 Years	0									
20–34	0									
35–49	0									
50–64	0									
65+	0									
2. MULTIPLE DX										
0–19 Years	0									
20–34	0									
35–49	0									
50–64	1	1.0	0	1	1	1	1	1	1	1
65+	0									
TOTAL SINGLE DX	**0**									
TOTAL MULTIPLE DX	**1**	**1.0**	**0**	**1**	**1**	**1**	**1**	**1**	**1**	**1**
TOTAL										
0–19 Years	0									
20–34	0									
35–49	0									
50–64	1	1.0	0	1	1	1	1	1	1	1
65+	0									
GRAND TOTAL	**1**	**1.0**	**0**	**1**	**1**	**1**	**1**	**1**	**1**	**1**

13.1: INTRACAP LENS EXTRACTION

Type of Patients	Observed Patients	Avg. Stay	Vari-ance	Percentiles						
				10th	25th	50th	75th	90th	95th	99th
1. SINGLE DX										
0–19 Years	1	1.0	0	1	1	1	1	1	1	1
20–34	1	6.0	0	6	6	6	6	6	6	6
35–49	0									
50–64	0									
65+	0									
2. MULTIPLE DX										
0–19 Years	2	3.0	0	3	3	3	3	3	3	3
20–34	1	2.0	0	2	2	2	2	2	2	2
35–49	1	2.0	0	2	2	2	2	2	2	2
50–64	2	1.0	0	1	1	1	1	1	1	1
65+	4	3.8	19	1	1	2	10	10	10	10
TOTAL SINGLE DX	**2**	**1.8**	**4**	**1**	**1**	**1**	**1**	**6**	**6**	**6**
TOTAL MULTIPLE DX	**10**	**2.8**	**5**	**1**	**1**	**3**	**3**	**3**	**10**	**10**
TOTAL										
0–19 Years	3	2.2	1	1	1	3	3	3	3	3
20–34	2	4.1	7	2	2	6	6	6	6	6
35–49	1	2.0	0	2	2	2	2	2	2	2
50–64	2	1.0	0	1	1	1	1	1	1	1
65+	4	3.8	19	1	1	2	10	10	10	10
GRAND TOTAL	**12**	**2.5**	**5**	**1**	**1**	**2**	**3**	**3**	**10**	**10**

13.2: LIN EXTRACAPS LENS EXTR

Type of Patients	Observed Patients	Avg. Stay	Vari-ance	Percentiles						
				10th	25th	50th	75th	90th	95th	99th
1. SINGLE DX										
0–19 Years	0									
20–34	0									
35–49	0									
50–64	0									
65+	0									
2. MULTIPLE DX										
0–19 Years	0									
20–34	0									
35–49	0									
50–64	2	2.0	2	1	1	1	3	3	3	3
65+	0									
TOTAL SINGLE DX	**0**									
TOTAL MULTIPLE DX	**2**	**2.0**	**2**	**1**	**1**	**1**	**3**	**3**	**3**	**3**
TOTAL										
0–19 Years	0									
20–34	0									
35–49	0									
50–64	2	2.0	2	1	1	1	3	3	3	3
65+	0									
GRAND TOTAL	**2**	**2.0**	**2**	**1**	**1**	**1**	**3**	**3**	**3**	**3**

13.3: SIMP ASP LENS EXTRACTION

Type of Patients	Observed Patients	Avg. Stay	Vari-ance	Percentiles						
				10th	25th	50th	75th	90th	95th	99th
1. SINGLE DX										
0–19 Years	0									
20–34	0									
35–49	0									
50–64	0									
65+	0									
2. MULTIPLE DX										
0–19 Years	0									
20–34	0									
35–49	0									
50–64	0									
65+	1	5.0	0	5	5	5	5	5	5	5
TOTAL SINGLE DX	**0**									
TOTAL MULTIPLE DX	**1**	**5.0**	**0**	**5**	**5**	**5**	**5**	**5**	**5**	**5**
TOTAL										
0–19 Years	0									
20–34	0									
35–49	0									
50–64	0									
65+	1	5.0	0	5	5	5	5	5	5	5
GRAND TOTAL	**1**	**5.0**	**0**	**5**	**5**	**5**	**5**	**5**	**5**	**5**

13.4: FRAG-ASP EXTRACAPS LENS

Type of Patients	Observed Patients	Avg. Stay	Vari-ance	Percentiles 10th	25th	50th	75th	90th	95th	99th
1. SINGLE DX										
0–19 Years	2	1.0	0	1	1	1	1	1	1	1
20–34	0									
35–49	1	1.0	0	1	1	1	1	1	1	1
50–64	1	1.0	0	1	1	1	1	1	1	1
65+	2	1.0	0	1	1	1	1	1	1	1
2. MULTIPLE DX										
0–19 Years	4	1.0	0	1	1	1	1	1	1	1
20–34	1	1.0	0	1	1	1	1	1	1	1
35–49	2	6.8	22	3	3	10	10	10	10	10
50–64	21	3.3	45	1	1	1	3	5	6	38
65+	72	2.0	4	1	1	1	2	4	7	10
TOTAL SINGLE DX	**6**	**1.0**	**0**	**1**	**1**	**1**	**1**	**1**	**1**	**1**
TOTAL MULTIPLE DX	**100**	**2.4**	**17**	**1**	**1**	**1**	**2**	**4**	**7**	**38**
TOTAL										
0–19 Years	6	1.0	0	1	1	1	1	1	1	1
20–34	1	1.0	0	1	1	1	1	1	1	1
35–49	3	2.4	10	1	1	1	1	10	10	10
50–64	22	3.3	44	1	1	1	3	5	6	38
65+	74	2.0	4	1	1	1	2	4	7	10
GRAND TOTAL	**106**	**2.3**	**16**	**1**	**1**	**1**	**2**	**4**	**7**	**10**

13.41: CATARACT PHACO & ASP

Type of Patients	Observed Patients	Avg. Stay	Vari-ance	Percentiles 10th	25th	50th	75th	90th	95th	99th
1. SINGLE DX										
0–19 Years	0									
20–34	0									
35–49	1	1.0	0	1	1	1	1	1	1	1
50–64	1	1.0	0	1	1	1	1	1	1	1
65+	2	1.0	0	1	1	1	1	1	1	1
2. MULTIPLE DX										
0–19 Years	2	1.0	0	1	1	1	1	1	1	1
20–34	1	1.0	0	1	1	1	1	1	1	1
35–49	2	6.8	22	3	3	10	10	10	10	10
50–64	21	3.3	45	1	1	1	3	5	6	38
65+	71	2.0	4	1	1	1	2	4	7	10
TOTAL SINGLE DX	**4**	**1.0**	**0**	**1**	**1**	**1**	**1**	**1**	**1**	**1**
TOTAL MULTIPLE DX	**97**	**2.5**	**18**	**1**	**1**	**1**	**3**	**4**	**7**	**38**
TOTAL										
0–19 Years	2	1.0	0	1	1	1	1	1	1	1
20–34	1	1.0	0	1	1	1	1	1	1	1
35–49	3	2.4	10	1	1	1	1	10	10	10
50–64	22	3.3	44	1	1	1	3	5	6	38
65+	73	2.0	4	1	1	1	2	4	7	10
GRAND TOTAL	**101**	**2.4**	**17**	**1**	**1**	**1**	**2**	**4**	**7**	**38**

13.5: OTH EXTRACAPS LENS EXTR

Type of Patients	Observed Patients	Avg. Stay	Vari-ance	Percentiles 10th	25th	50th	75th	90th	95th	99th
1. SINGLE DX										
0–19 Years	1	1.0	0	1	1	1	1	1	1	1
20–34	0									
35–49	1	2.0	0	2	2	2	2	2	2	2
50–64	0									
65+	1	1.0	0	1	1	1	1	1	1	1
2. MULTIPLE DX										
0–19 Years	4	2.0	13	1	1	1	1	1	14	14
20–34	1	1.0	0	1	1	1	1	1	1	1
35–49	0									
50–64	3	1.7	1	1	1	1	3	3	3	3
65+	7	1.3	<1	1	1	1	2	2	2	2
TOTAL SINGLE DX	**3**	**1.2**	**<1**	**1**	**1**	**1**	**1**	**2**	**2**	**2**
TOTAL MULTIPLE DX	**15**	**1.7**	**7**	**1**	**1**	**1**	**1**	**2**	**3**	**14**
TOTAL										
0–19 Years	5	1.7	9	1	1	1	1	1	14	14
20–34	1	1.0	0	1	1	1	1	1	1	1
35–49	1	2.0	0	2	2	2	2	2	2	2
50–64	3	1.7	1	1	1	1	3	3	3	3
65+	8	1.2	<1	1	1	1	1	2	2	2
GRAND TOTAL	**18**	**1.6**	**5**	**1**	**1**	**1**	**1**	**2**	**3**	**14**

13.6: OTH CATARACT EXTRACTION

Type of Patients	Observed Patients	Avg. Stay	Vari-ance	Percentiles 10th	25th	50th	75th	90th	95th	99th
1. SINGLE DX										
0–19 Years	0									
20–34	0									
35–49	0									
50–64	0									
65+	0									
2. MULTIPLE DX										
0–19 Years	2	1.0	0	1	1	1	1	1	1	1
20–34	0									
35–49	0									
50–64	0									
65+	5	3.3	7	1	1	2	4	7	7	7
TOTAL SINGLE DX	**0**									
TOTAL MULTIPLE DX	**7**	**2.5**	**6**	**1**	**1**	**1**	**4**	**7**	**7**	**7**
TOTAL										
0–19 Years	2	1.0	0	1	1	1	1	1	1	1
20–34	0									
35–49	0									
50–64	0									
65+	5	3.3	7	1	1	2	4	7	7	7
GRAND TOTAL	**7**	**2.5**	**6**	**1**	**1**	**1**	**4**	**7**	**7**	**7**

13.7: INSERT PROSTHETIC LENS

Type of Patients	Observed Patients	Avg. Stay	Vari-ance	Percentiles 10th	25th	50th	75th	90th	95th	99th
1. SINGLE DX										
0–19 Years	0									
20–34	1	1.0	0	1	1	1	1	1	1	1
35–49	0									
50–64	0									
65+	0									
2. MULTIPLE DX										
0–19 Years	0									
20–34	0									
35–49	0									
50–64	1	3.0	0	3	3	3	3	3	3	3
65+	4	1.0	0	1	1	1	1	1	1	1
TOTAL SINGLE DX	**1**	**1.0**	**0**	**1**	**1**	**1**	**1**	**1**	**1**	**1**
TOTAL MULTIPLE DX	**5**	**1.4**	**<1**	**1**	**1**	**1**	**1**	**3**	**3**	**3**
TOTAL										
0–19 Years	0									
20–34	1	1.0	0	1	1	1	1	1	1	1
35–49	0									
50–64	1	3.0	0	3	3	3	3	3	3	3
65+	4	1.0	0	1	1	1	1	1	1	1
GRAND TOTAL	**6**	**1.4**	**<1**	**1**	**1**	**1**	**1**	**3**	**3**	**3**

13.8: IMPLANTED LENS REMOVAL

Type of Patients	Observed Patients	Avg. Stay	Vari-ance	Percentiles 10th	25th	50th	75th	90th	95th	99th
1. SINGLE DX										
0–19 Years	0									
20–34	0									
35–49	0									
50–64	0									
65+	1	1.0	0	1	1	1	1	1	1	1
2. MULTIPLE DX										
0–19 Years	0									
20–34	0									
35–49	1	1.0	0	1	1	1	1	1	1	1
50–64	0									
65+	1	2.0	0	2	2	2	2	2	2	2
TOTAL SINGLE DX	**1**	**1.0**	**0**	**1**	**1**	**1**	**1**	**1**	**1**	**1**
TOTAL MULTIPLE DX	**2**	**1.5**	**<1**	**1**	**1**	**1**	**2**	**2**	**2**	**2**
TOTAL										
0–19 Years	0									
20–34	0									
35–49	1	1.0	0	1	1	1	1	1	1	1
50–64	0									
65+	2	1.5	<1	1	1	1	2	2	2	2
GRAND TOTAL	**3**	**1.3**	**<1**	**1**	**1**	**1**	**2**	**2**	**2**	**2**

13.9: OTHER OPERATIONS ON LENS

Type of Patients	Observed Patients	Avg. Stay	Vari-ance	Percentiles 10th	25th	50th	75th	90th	95th	99th
1. SINGLE DX										
0–19 Years	0									
20–34	0									
35–49	0									
50–64	1	1.0	0	1	1	1	1	1	1	1
65+	0									
2. MULTIPLE DX										
0–19 Years	1	2.0	0	2	2	2	2	2	2	2
20–34	0									
35–49	0									
50–64	2	1.0	0	1	1	1	1	1	1	1
65+	2	8.1	53	3	3	3	15	15	15	15
TOTAL SINGLE DX	**1**	**1.0**	**0**	**1**	**1**	**1**	**1**	**1**	**1**	**1**
TOTAL MULTIPLE DX	**5**	**3.3**	**18**	**1**	**2**	**2**	**3**	**15**	**15**	**15**
TOTAL										
0–19 Years	1	2.0	0	2	2	2	2	2	2	2
20–34	0									
35–49	0									
50–64	3	1.0	0	1	1	1	1	1	1	1
65+	2	8.1	53	3	3	3	15	15	15	15
GRAND TOTAL	**6**	**3.0**	**17**	**1**	**1**	**2**	**2**	**3**	**15**	**15**

14.0: RMVL OF POST SEGMENT FB

Type of Patients	Observed Patients	Avg. Stay	Vari-ance	Percentiles 10th	25th	50th	75th	90th	95th	99th
1. SINGLE DX										
0–19 Years	0									
20–34	0									
35–49	0									
50–64	0									
65+	0									
2. MULTIPLE DX										
0–19 Years	1	1.0	0	1	1	1	1	1	1	1
20–34	0									
35–49	1	3.0	0	3	3	3	3	3	3	3
50–64	0									
65+	1	3.0	0	3	3	3	3	3	3	3
TOTAL SINGLE DX	**0**									
TOTAL MULTIPLE DX	**3**	**1.6**	**<1**	**1**	**1**	**1**	**3**	**3**	**3**	**3**
TOTAL										
0–19 Years	1	1.0	0	1	1	1	1	1	1	1
20–34	0									
35–49	1	3.0	0	3	3	3	3	3	3	3
50–64	0									
65+	1	3.0	0	3	3	3	3	3	3	3
GRAND TOTAL	**3**	**1.6**	**<1**	**1**	**1**	**1**	**3**	**3**	**3**	**3**

14.1: DXTIC PX POSTERIOR SEG

Type of Patients	Observed Patients	Avg. Stay	Vari-ance	Percentiles 10th	25th	50th	75th	90th	95th	99th
1. SINGLE DX										
0–19 Years	0									
20–34	0									
35–49	0									
50–64	0									
65+	0									
2. MULTIPLE DX										
0–19 Years	0									
20–34	0									
35–49	0									
50–64	4	8.6	56	1	1	13	16	16	16	16
65+	4	11.3	75	2	6	14	14	23	23	23
TOTAL SINGLE DX	**0**									
TOTAL MULTIPLE DX	**8**	**9.9**	**60**	**1**	**2**	**13**	**16**	**23**	**23**	**23**
TOTAL										
0–19 Years	0									
20–34	0									
35–49	0									
50–64	4	8.6	56	1	1	13	16	16	16	16
65+	4	11.3	75	2	6	14	14	23	23	23
GRAND TOTAL	**8**	**9.9**	**60**	**1**	**2**	**13**	**16**	**23**	**23**	**23**

14.2: RETINA-CHOROID LES DESTR

Type of Patients	Observed Patients	Avg. Stay	Vari-ance	Percentiles 10th	25th	50th	75th	90th	95th	99th
1. SINGLE DX										
0–19 Years	8	1.2	<1	1	1	1	1	2	2	2
20–34	0									
35–49	0									
50–64	5	1.0	0	1	1	1	1	1	1	1
65+	2	1.0	0	1	1	1	1	1	1	1
2. MULTIPLE DX										
0–19 Years	18	13.8	828	1	1	2	76	>99	>99	>99
20–34	3	5.6	23	1	1	6	11	11	11	11
35–49	5	2.6	<1	2	2	2	3	4	4	4
50–64	8	2.7	5	1	1	1	4	6	7	7
65+	5	4.1	11	1	1	4	5	9	9	9
TOTAL SINGLE DX	**15**	**1.1**	**<1**	**1**	**1**	**1**	**1**	**2**	**2**	**2**
TOTAL MULTIPLE DX	**39**	**10.0**	**549**	**1**	**1**	**2**	**8**	**>99**	**>99**	**>99**
TOTAL										
0–19 Years	26	9.3	565	1	1	2	5	>99	>99	>99
20–34	3	5.6	23	1	1	6	11	11	11	11
35–49	5	2.6	<1	2	2	2	3	4	4	4
50–64	13	2.2	4	1	1	1	4	6	7	7
65+	7	3.2	10	1	1	1	5	9	9	9
GRAND TOTAL	**54**	**7.2**	**391**	**1**	**1**	**1**	**4**	**92**	**>99**	**>99**

14.3: REPAIR OF RETINAL TEAR

Type of Patients	Observed Patients	Avg. Stay	Vari-ance	Percentiles 10th	25th	50th	75th	90th	95th	99th
1. SINGLE DX										
0–19 Years	1	1.0	0	1	1	1	1	1	1	1
20–34	0									
35–49	1	1.0	0	1	1	1	1	1	1	1
50–64	0									
65+	0									
2. MULTIPLE DX										
0–19 Years	3	67.6	>999	27	27	93	95	>99	>99	>99
20–34	1	6.0	0	6	6	6	6	6	6	6
35–49	1	2.0	0	2	2	2	2	2	2	2
50–64	1	1.0	0	1	1	1	1	1	1	1
65+	4	1.9	3	1	1	1	1	5	5	5
TOTAL SINGLE DX	**2**	**1.0**	**0**	**1**	**1**	**1**	**1**	**1**	**1**	**1**
TOTAL MULTIPLE DX	**10**	**23.0**	**>999**	**1**	**1**	**5**	**93**	**95**	**>99**	**>99**
TOTAL										
0–19 Years	4	38.7	>999	1	1	27	95	>99	>99	>99
20–34	1	6.0	0	6	6	6	6	6	6	6
35–49	2	1.5	<1	1	1	1	2	2	2	2
50–64	1	1.0	0	1	1	1	1	1	1	1
65+	4	1.9	3	1	1	1	1	5	5	5
GRAND TOTAL	**12**	**17.1**	**>999**	**1**	**1**	**1**	**27**	**95**	**>99**	**>99**

14.4: REP RETINA DETACH/BUCKLE

Type of Patients	Observed Patients	Avg. Stay	Vari-ance	Percentiles 10th	25th	50th	75th	90th	95th	99th
1. SINGLE DX										
0–19 Years	3	1.0	0	1	1	1	1	1	1	1
20–34	26	1.5	<1	1	1	1	2	3	3	3
35–49	13	1.2	<1	1	1	1	1	2	3	3
50–64	25	1.3	<1	1	1	1	2	2	2	2
65+	7	1.1	<1	1	1	1	1	2	2	2
2. MULTIPLE DX										
0–19 Years	12	2.1	3	1	1	1	2	5	6	6
20–34	19	3.5	10	1	1	2	4	9	9	9
35–49	35	1.4	2	1	1	1	1	2	6	6
50–64	74	1.7	8	1	1	1	1	2	3	24
65+	75	2.0	29	1	1	1	1	3	3	48
TOTAL SINGLE DX	**74**	**1.3**	**<1**	**1**	**1**	**1**	**1**	**2**	**2**	**3**
TOTAL MULTIPLE DX	**215**	**2.1**	**13**	**1**	**1**	**1**	**2**	**4**	**7**	**11**
TOTAL										
0–19 Years	15	1.8	2	1	1	1	2	5	5	6
20–34	45	2.8	7	1	1	1	3	9	9	9
35–49	48	1.3	1	1	1	1	1	2	3	6
50–64	99	1.6	6	1	1	1	1	2	2	11
65+	82	1.9	26	1	1	1	1	3	3	48
GRAND TOTAL	**289**	**1.9**	**10**	**1**	**1**	**1**	**2**	**3**	**6**	**9**

14.49: SCLERAL BUCKLING NEC

Type of Patients	Observed Patients	Avg. Stay	Vari-ance	10th	25th	50th	75th	90th	95th	99th
1. SINGLE DX										
0–19 Years	2	1.0	0	1	1	1	1	1	1	1
20–34	25	1.5	<1	1	1	1	2	3	3	3
35–49	12	1.2	<1	1	1	1	1	2	3	3
50–64	21	1.3	<1	1	1	1	2	2	2	2
65+	6	1.2	<1	1	1	1	1	2	2	2
2. MULTIPLE DX										
0–19 Years	10	1.9	3	1	1	1	1	5	6	6
20–34	17	2.0	2	1	1	1	3	3	4	7
35–49	29	1.2	<1	1	1	1	1	1	2	6
50–64	59	1.4	2	1	1	1	1	2	2	11
65+	62	2.1	34	1	1	1	1	3	3	48
TOTAL SINGLE DX	**66**	**1.3**	**<1**	**1**	**1**	**1**	**2**	**2**	**2**	**3**
TOTAL MULTIPLE DX	**177**	**1.7**	**11**	**1**	**1**	**1**	**1**	**3**	**4**	**7**
TOTAL										
0–19 Years	12	1.7	3	1	1	1	1	5	6	6
20–34	42	1.8	1	1	1	1	3	3	3	7
35–49	41	1.2	<1	1	1	1	1	1	2	6
50–64	80	1.4	2	1	1	1	1	2	2	11
65+	68	2.0	32	1	1	1	1	3	3	48
GRAND TOTAL	**243**	**1.6**	**8**	**1**	**1**	**1**	**1**	**3**	**3**	**7**

14.5: OTH REPAIR RETINA DETACH

Type of Patients	Observed Patients	Avg. Stay	Vari-ance	10th	25th	50th	75th	90th	95th	99th
1. SINGLE DX										
0–19 Years	0									
20–34	2	1.0	0	1	1	1	1	1	1	1
35–49	2	1.0	0	1	1	1	1	1	1	1
50–64	12	1.3	<1	1	1	1	1	3	3	3
65+	2	1.4	<1	1	1	1	2	2	2	2
2. MULTIPLE DX										
0–19 Years	15	1.5	<1	1	1	1	2	3	4	4
20–34	3	1.0	0	1	1	1	1	1	1	1
35–49	19	1.9	9	1	1	1	1	5	5	16
50–64	36	2.8	33	1	1	1	1	5	25	25
65+	21	3.1	40	1	1	1	2	5	8	32
TOTAL SINGLE DX	**18**	**1.2**	**<1**	**1**	**1**	**1**	**1**	**2**	**3**	**3**
TOTAL MULTIPLE DX	**94**	**2.3**	**21**	**1**	**1**	**1**	**1**	**4**	**5**	**25**
TOTAL										
0–19 Years	15	1.5	<1	1	1	1	2	3	4	4
20–34	5	1.0	0	1	1	1	1	1	1	1
35–49	21	1.8	8	1	1	1	1	5	5	16
50–64	48	2.4	26	1	1	1	1	3	5	25
65+	23	2.9	37	1	1	1	2	5	8	32
GRAND TOTAL	**112**	**2.1**	**17**	**1**	**1**	**1**	**1**	**3**	**5**	**25**

14.6: RMVL PROSTH MAT POST SEG

Type of Patients	Observed Patients	Avg. Stay	Vari-ance	10th	25th	50th	75th	90th	95th	99th
1. SINGLE DX										
0–19 Years	0									
20–34	0									
35–49	0									
50–64	0									
65+	0									
2. MULTIPLE DX										
0–19 Years	0									
20–34	0									
35–49	1	5.0	0	5	5	5	5	5	5	5
50–64	4	1.6	<1	1	1	2	2	2	2	2
65+	2	5.9	15	3	3	3	9	9	9	9
TOTAL SINGLE DX	**0**									
TOTAL MULTIPLE DX	**7**	**2.6**	**5**	**1**	**1**	**2**	**2**	**5**	**9**	**9**
TOTAL										
0–19 Years	0									
20–34	0									
35–49	1	5.0	0	5	5	5	5	5	5	5
50–64	4	1.6	<1	1	1	2	2	2	2	2
65+	2	5.9	15	3	3	3	9	9	9	9
GRAND TOTAL	**7**	**2.6**	**5**	**1**	**1**	**2**	**2**	**5**	**9**	**9**

14.7: OPERATIONS ON VITREOUS

Type of Patients	Observed Patients	Avg. Stay	Vari-ance	10th	25th	50th	75th	90th	95th	99th
1. SINGLE DX										
0–19 Years	2	1.0	0	1	1	1	1	1	1	1
20–34	3	1.8	<1	1	2	2	2	2	2	2
35–49	2	2.0	2	1	1	2	3	3	3	3
50–64	6	1.0	0	1	1	1	1	1	1	1
65+	7	1.8	2	1	1	1	3	4	4	4
2. MULTIPLE DX										
0–19 Years	15	1.8	12	1	1	1	1	2	3	21
20–34	20	2.4	7	1	1	1	2	8	10	10
35–49	32	3.0	7	1	1	2	3	7	8	12
50–64	100	3.2	21	1	1	1	4	7	8	30
65+	125	2.2	6	1	1	1	2	4	7	13
TOTAL SINGLE DX	**20**	**1.5**	**<1**	**1**	**1**	**1**	**2**	**2**	**3**	**4**
TOTAL MULTIPLE DX	**292**	**2.7**	**13**	**1**	**1**	**1**	**3**	**6**	**8**	**21**
TOTAL										
0–19 Years	17	1.7	10	1	1	1	1	2	3	21
20–34	23	2.2	5	1	1	1	2	5	9	10
35–49	34	2.9	7	1	1	2	3	7	8	12
50–64	106	3.1	20	1	1	1	4	6	8	21
65+	132	2.2	6	1	1	1	3	4	6	13
GRAND TOTAL	**312**	**2.6**	**12**	**1**	**1**	**1**	**3**	**6**	**8**	**21**

14.74: MECH VITRECTOMY NEC

Type of Patients	Observed Patients	Avg. Stay	Vari-ance	Percentiles 10th	25th	50th	75th	90th	95th	99th
1. SINGLE DX										
0–19 Years	1	1.0	0	1	1	1	1	1	1	1
20–34	3	1.8	<1	1	2	2	2	2	2	2
35–49	1	1.0	0	1	1	1	1	1	1	1
50–64	5	1.0	0	1	1	1	1	1	1	1
65+	6	1.3	<1	1	1	1	1	3	3	3
2. MULTIPLE DX										
0–19 Years	7	2.4	27	1	1	1	1	1	21	21
20–34	18	2.2	7	1	1	1	2	5	10	10
35–49	24	2.4	4	1	1	2	3	7	7	7
50–64	85	3.3	23	1	1	1	4	7	10	30
65+	102	2.1	7	1	1	1	2	3	6	13
TOTAL SINGLE DX	**16**	**1.5**	**<1**	**1**	**1**	**1**	**2**	**2**	**2**	**3**
TOTAL MULTIPLE DX	**236**	**2.7**	**15**	**1**	**1**	**1**	**3**	**6**	**8**	**21**
TOTAL										
0–19 Years	8	2.3	25	1	1	1	1	1	21	21
20–34	21	2.1	5	1	1	1	2	4	9	10
35–49	25	2.3	4	1	1	2	3	6	7	7
50–64	90	3.2	22	1	1	1	4	7	8	30
65+	108	2.1	7	1	1	1	2	3	6	13
GRAND TOTAL	**252**	**2.6**	**14**	**1**	**1**	**1**	**2**	**6**	**8**	**21**

14.9: OTHER POST SEGMENT OPS

Type of Patients	Observed Patients	Avg. Stay	Vari-ance	Percentiles 10th	25th	50th	75th	90th	95th	99th
1. SINGLE DX										
0–19 Years	2	1.7	<1	1	1	2	2	2	2	2
20–34	1	3.0	0	3	3	3	3	3	3	3
35–49	0									
50–64	3	1.3	<1	1	1	1	2	2	2	2
65+	4	1.0	0	1	1	1	1	1	1	1
2. MULTIPLE DX										
0–19 Years	2	1.0	0	1	1	1	1	1	1	1
20–34	5	3.4	27	1	1	1	1	13	13	13
35–49	14	1.3	<1	1	1	1	2	2	2	2
50–64	30	1.2	<1	1	1	1	1	2	2	2
65+	23	1.4	<1	1	1	1	1	3	3	5
TOTAL SINGLE DX	**10**	**1.5**	**<1**	**1**	**1**	**1**	**2**	**2**	**3**	**3**
TOTAL MULTIPLE DX	**74**	**1.3**	**2**	**1**	**1**	**1**	**1**	**2**	**2**	**13**
TOTAL										
0–19 Years	4	1.2	<1	1	1	1	1	2	2	2
20–34	6	3.4	23	1	1	1	3	13	13	13
35–49	14	1.3	<1	1	1	1	2	2	2	2
50–64	33	1.2	<1	1	1	1	1	2	2	2
65+	27	1.3	<1	1	1	1	1	2	3	5
GRAND TOTAL	**84**	**1.3**	**2**	**1**	**1**	**1**	**1**	**2**	**2**	**5**

15.0: EXOC MUSC-TEND DXTIC PX

Type of Patients	Observed Patients	Avg. Stay	Vari-ance	Percentiles 10th	25th	50th	75th	90th	95th	99th
1. SINGLE DX										
0–19 Years	0									
20–34	0									
35–49	0									
50–64	0									
65+	0									
2. MULTIPLE DX										
0–19 Years	2	16.8	164	3	3	26	26	26	26	26
20–34	0									
35–49	0									
50–64	1	1.0	0	1	1	1	1	1	1	1
65+	0									
TOTAL SINGLE DX	**0**									
TOTAL MULTIPLE DX	**3**	**13.5**	**172**	**1**	**3**	**3**	**26**	**26**	**26**	**26**
TOTAL										
0–19 Years	2	16.8	164	3	3	26	26	26	26	26
20–34	0									
35–49	0									
50–64	1	1.0	0	1	1	1	1	1	1	1
65+	0									
GRAND TOTAL	**3**	**13.5**	**172**	**1**	**3**	**3**	**26**	**26**	**26**	**26**

15.1: 1 EXOC MUSC OPS W DETACH

Type of Patients	Observed Patients	Avg. Stay	Vari-ance	Percentiles 10th	25th	50th	75th	90th	95th	99th
1. SINGLE DX										
0–19 Years	1	1.0	0	1	1	1	1	1	1	1
20–34	0									
35–49	0									
50–64	0									
65+	0									
2. MULTIPLE DX										
0–19 Years	5	2.2	1	1	1	2	3	4	4	4
20–34	1	3.0	0	3	3	3	3	3	3	3
35–49	0									
50–64	1	1.0	0	1	1	1	1	1	1	1
65+	0									
TOTAL SINGLE DX	**1**	**1.0**	**0**	**1**	**1**	**1**	**1**	**1**	**1**	**1**
TOTAL MULTIPLE DX	**7**	**2.2**	**1**	**1**	**1**	**2**	**3**	**4**	**4**	**4**
TOTAL										
0–19 Years	6	2.0	1	1	1	1	3	4	4	4
20–34	1	3.0	0	3	3	3	3	3	3	3
35–49	0									
50–64	1	1.0	0	1	1	1	1	1	1	1
65+	0									
GRAND TOTAL	**8**	**2.0**	**1**	**1**	**1**	**2**	**3**	**4**	**4**	**4**

15.2: OTH OPS ON 1 EXOC MUSCLE

Type of Patients	Observed Patients	Avg. Stay	Vari-ance	Percentiles						
				10th	25th	50th	75th	90th	95th	99th
1. SINGLE DX										
0–19 Years	0									
20–34	0									
35–49	0									
50–64	0									
65+	0									
2. MULTIPLE DX										
0–19 Years	0									
20–34	0									
35–49	0									
50–64	0									
65+	0									
TOTAL SINGLE DX	**0**									
TOTAL MULTIPLE DX	**0**									
TOTAL										
0–19 Years	0									
20–34	0									
35–49	0									
50–64	0									
65+	0									
GRAND TOTAL	**0**									

15.3: TEMP DETACH >1 EXOC MUSC

Type of Patients	Observed Patients	Avg. Stay	Vari-ance	Percentiles						
				10th	25th	50th	75th	90th	95th	99th
1. SINGLE DX										
0–19 Years	0									
20–34	0									
35–49	1	1.0	0	1	1	1	1	1	1	1
50–64	0									
65+	0									
2. MULTIPLE DX										
0–19 Years	4	1.3	<1	1	1	1	2	2	2	2
20–34	0									
35–49	0									
50–64	2	1.0	0	1	1	1	1	1	1	1
65+	2	1.9	1	1	1	1	3	3	3	3
TOTAL SINGLE DX	**1**	**1.0**	**0**	**1**	**1**	**1**	**1**	**1**	**1**	**1**
TOTAL MULTIPLE DX	**8**	**1.3**	**<1**	**1**	**1**	**1**	**1**	**2**	**2**	**3**
TOTAL										
0–19 Years	4	1.3	<1	1	1	1	2	2	2	2
20–34	0									
35–49	1	1.0	0	1	1	1	1	1	1	1
50–64	2	1.0	0	1	1	1	1	1	1	1
65+	2	1.9	1	1	1	1	3	3	3	3
GRAND TOTAL	**9**	**1.3**	**<1**	**1**	**1**	**1**	**1**	**2**	**2**	**3**

15.4: OTH OPS ON >1 EXOC MUSC

Type of Patients	Observed Patients	Avg. Stay	Vari-ance	Percentiles						
				10th	25th	50th	75th	90th	95th	99th
1. SINGLE DX										
0–19 Years	0									
20–34	0									
35–49	0									
50–64	0									
65+	0									
2. MULTIPLE DX										
0–19 Years	0									
20–34	0									
35–49	0									
50–64	0									
65+	0									
TOTAL SINGLE DX	**0**									
TOTAL MULTIPLE DX	**0**									
TOTAL										
0–19 Years	0									
20–34	0									
35–49	0									
50–64	0									
65+	0									
GRAND TOTAL	**0**									

15.5: EXOC MUSC TRANSPOSITION

Type of Patients	Observed Patients	Avg. Stay	Vari-ance	Percentiles						
				10th	25th	50th	75th	90th	95th	99th
1. SINGLE DX										
0–19 Years	0									
20–34	0									
35–49	0									
50–64	0									
65+	0									
2. MULTIPLE DX										
0–19 Years	0									
20–34	0									
35–49	0									
50–64	0									
65+	0									
TOTAL SINGLE DX	**0**									
TOTAL MULTIPLE DX	**0**									
TOTAL										
0–19 Years	0									
20–34	0									
35–49	0									
50–64	0									
65+	0									
GRAND TOTAL	**0**									

15.6: REV EXOC MUSCLE SURGERY

Type of Patients	Observed Patients	Avg. Stay	Vari-ance	Percentiles						
				10th	25th	50th	75th	90th	95th	99th
1. SINGLE DX										
0–19 Years	0									
20–34	0									
35–49	0									
50–64	0									
65+	0									
2. MULTIPLE DX										
0–19 Years	0									
20–34	0									
35–49	0									
50–64	0									
65+	0									
TOTAL SINGLE DX	**0**									
TOTAL MULTIPLE DX	**0**									
TOTAL										
0–19 Years	0									
20–34	0									
35–49	0									
50–64	0									
65+	0									
GRAND TOTAL	**0**									

15.7: EXOC MUSCLE INJURY REP

Type of Patients	Observed Patients	Avg. Stay	Vari-ance	Percentiles						
				10th	25th	50th	75th	90th	95th	99th
1. SINGLE DX										
0–19 Years	0									
20–34	1	2.0	0	2	2	2	2	2	2	2
35–49	0									
50–64	0									
65+	0									
2. MULTIPLE DX										
0–19 Years	1	1.0	0	1	1	1	1	1	1	1
20–34	3	2.5	7	1	1	1	6	6	6	6
35–49	3	1.0	0	1	1	1	1	1	1	1
50–64	1	1.0	0	1	1	1	1	1	1	1
65+	5	2.2	1	1	1	2	3	4	4	4
TOTAL SINGLE DX	**1**	**2.0**	**0**	**2**	**2**	**2**	**2**	**2**	**2**	**2**
TOTAL MULTIPLE DX	**13**	**1.6**	**2**	**1**	**1**	**1**	**1**	**4**	**6**	**6**
TOTAL										
0–19 Years	1	1.0	0	1	1	1	1	1	1	1
20–34	4	2.4	5	1	1	1	2	6	6	6
35–49	3	1.0	0	1	1	1	1	1	1	1
50–64	1	1.0	0	1	1	1	1	1	1	1
65+	5	2.2	1	1	1	2	3	4	4	4
GRAND TOTAL	**14**	**1.6**	**2**	**1**	**1**	**1**	**2**	**3**	**4**	**6**

15.9: OTH EXOC MUSC-TEND OPS

Type of Patients	Observed Patients	Avg. Stay	Vari-ance	Percentiles						
				10th	25th	50th	75th	90th	95th	99th
1. SINGLE DX										
0–19 Years	0									
20–34	0									
35–49	0									
50–64	0									
65+	0									
2. MULTIPLE DX										
0–19 Years	0									
20–34	0									
35–49	0									
50–64	0									
65+	0									
TOTAL SINGLE DX	**0**									
TOTAL MULTIPLE DX	**0**									
TOTAL										
0–19 Years	0									
20–34	0									
35–49	0									
50–64	0									
65+	0									
GRAND TOTAL	**0**									

16.0: ORBITOTOMY

Type of Patients	Observed Patients	Avg. Stay	Vari-ance	Percentiles						
				10th	25th	50th	75th	90th	95th	99th
1. SINGLE DX										
0–19 Years	4	2.4	3	1	1	1	5	5	5	5
20–34	0									
35–49	4	2.2	4	1	1	1	5	5	5	5
50–64	2	1.0	0	1	1	1	1	1	1	1
65+	0									
2. MULTIPLE DX										
0–19 Years	41	6.7	21	2	3	6	8	12	15	22
20–34	15	3.4	10	1	2	2	4	6	10	15
35–49	31	3.6	8	1	1	3	6	8	9	10
50–64	37	2.8	6	1	1	1	4	5	7	13
65+	23	4.4	55	1	1	2	4	9	16	35
TOTAL SINGLE DX	**10**	**2.1**	**3**	**1**	**1**	**1**	**2**	**5**	**5**	**5**
TOTAL MULTIPLE DX	**147**	**5.0**	**20**	**1**	**2**	**4**	**7**	**11**	**13**	**22**
TOTAL										
0–19 Years	45	6.5	21	2	3	6	8	12	15	22
20–34	15	3.4	10	1	2	2	4	6	10	15
35–49	35	3.4	8	1	1	2	5	7	9	10
50–64	39	2.7	6	1	1	1	4	5	7	13
65+	23	4.4	55	1	1	2	4	9	16	35
GRAND TOTAL	**157**	**4.8**	**20**	**1**	**1**	**4**	**7**	**11**	**13**	**22**

16.09: ORBITOTOMY NEC

Type of Patients	Observed Patients	Avg. Stay	Vari-ance	10th	25th	50th	75th	90th	95th	99th
				Percentiles						
1. SINGLE DX										
0–19 Years	4	2.4	3	1	1	1	5	5	5	5
20–34	0									
35–49	2	1.0	0	1	1	1	1	1	1	1
50–64	2	1.0	0	1	1	1	1	1	1	1
65+	0									
2. MULTIPLE DX										
0–19 Years	37	6.9	20	2	4	6	8	13	15	22
20–34	14	3.4	10	1	2	2	6	6	10	15
35–49	25	3.9	9	1	1	3	7	8	10	10
50–64	31	3.1	7	1	1	2	4	5	10	13
65+	19	5.1	64	1	1	2	4	16	35	35
TOTAL SINGLE DX	**8**	**1.7**	**2**	**1**	**1**	**1**	**2**	**5**	**5**	**5**
TOTAL MULTIPLE DX	**126**	**5.3**	**21**	**1**	**2**	**4**	**7**	**11**	**13**	**22**
TOTAL										
0–19 Years	41	6.7	21	2	3	6	8	12	15	22
20–34	14	3.4	10	1	2	2	6	6	10	15
35–49	27	3.6	9	1	1	3	6	8	10	10
50–64	33	3.0	7	1	1	2	4	5	7	13
65+	19	5.1	64	1	1	2	4	16	35	35
GRAND TOTAL	**134**	**5.2**	**21**	**1**	**2**	**4**	**7**	**11**	**13**	**22**

16.1: RMVL PENETR FB EYE NOS

Type of Patients	Observed Patients	Avg. Stay	Vari-ance	10th	25th	50th	75th	90th	95th	99th
				Percentiles						
1. SINGLE DX										
0–19 Years	1	3.0	0	3	3	3	3	3	3	3
20–34	1	2.0	0	2	2	2	2	2	2	2
35–49	0									
50–64	0									
65+	0									
2. MULTIPLE DX										
0–19 Years	1	3.0	0	3	3	3	3	3	3	3
20–34	4	4.4	3	2	2	5	6	6	6	6
35–49	1	2.0	0	2	2	2	2	2	2	2
50–64	0									
65+	1	1.0	0	1	1	1	1	1	1	1
TOTAL SINGLE DX	**2**	**2.6**	**<1**	**2**	**2**	**3**	**3**	**3**	**3**	**3**
TOTAL MULTIPLE DX	**7**	**3.4**	**3**	**2**	**2**	**3**	**5**	**6**	**6**	**6**
TOTAL										
0–19 Years	2	3.0	0	3	3	3	3	3	3	3
20–34	5	4.0	4	2	2	5	6	6	6	6
35–49	1	2.0	0	2	2	2	2	2	2	2
50–64	0									
65+	1	1.0	0	1	1	1	1	1	1	1
GRAND TOTAL	**9**	**3.3**	**2**	**2**	**2**	**3**	**3**	**6**	**6**	**6**

16.2: ORBIT & EYEBALL DXTIC PX

Type of Patients	Observed Patients	Avg. Stay	Vari-ance	10th	25th	50th	75th	90th	95th	99th
				Percentiles						
1. SINGLE DX										
0–19 Years	0									
20–34	0									
35–49	1	1.0	0	1	1	1	1	1	1	1
50–64	1	5.0	0	5	5	5	5	5	5	5
65+	1	2.0	0	2	2	2	2	2	2	2
2. MULTIPLE DX										
0–19 Years	3	3.4	5	2	2	3	3	8	8	8
20–34	4	2.3	1	1	1	2	3	4	4	4
35–49	7	10.4	127	1	2	8	8	33	33	33
50–64	4	5.3	27	1	1	1	10	11	11	11
65+	6	6.9	26	1	2	4	12	12	12	12
TOTAL SINGLE DX	**3**	**2.5**	**4**	**1**	**1**	**2**	**5**	**5**	**5**	**5**
TOTAL MULTIPLE DX	**24**	**6.7**	**58**	**1**	**2**	**4**	**10**	**12**	**28**	**33**
TOTAL										
0–19 Years	3	3.4	5	2	2	3	3	8	8	8
20–34	4	2.3	1	1	1	2	3	4	4	4
35–49	8	9.5	122	1	2	7	8	33	33	33
50–64	5	5.3	22	1	1	5	10	11	11	11
65+	7	6.4	26	1	2	4	12	12	12	12
GRAND TOTAL	**27**	**6.4**	**55**	**1**	**2**	**3**	**8**	**12**	**28**	**33**

16.3: EVISCERATION OF EYEBALL

Type of Patients	Observed Patients	Avg. Stay	Vari-ance	10th	25th	50th	75th	90th	95th	99th
				Percentiles						
1. SINGLE DX										
0–19 Years	0									
20–34	1	1.0	0	1	1	1	1	1	1	1
35–49	1	3.0	0	3	3	3	3	3	3	3
50–64	1	1.0	0	1	1	1	1	1	1	1
65+	0									
2. MULTIPLE DX										
0–19 Years	1	22.0	0	22	22	22	22	22	22	22
20–34	4	1.0	0	1	1	1	1	1	1	1
35–49	10	2.1	6	1	1	1	2	3	9	10
50–64	7	3.0	16	1	1	1	3	12	12	12
65+	18	4.8	15	1	1	3	8	12	12	12
TOTAL SINGLE DX	**3**	**1.6**	**1**	**1**	**1**	**1**	**3**	**3**	**3**	**3**
TOTAL MULTIPLE DX	**40**	**3.4**	**22**	**1**	**1**	**1**	**3**	**10**	**12**	**22**
TOTAL										
0–19 Years	1	22.0	0	22	22	22	22	22	22	22
20–34	5	1.0	0	1	1	1	1	1	1	1
35–49	11	2.1	6	1	1	1	2	3	9	10
50–64	8	2.8	14	1	1	1	3	12	12	12
65+	18	4.8	15	1	1	3	8	12	12	12
GRAND TOTAL	**43**	**3.3**	**21**	**1**	**1**	**1**	**3**	**10**	**12**	**22**

16.4: ENUCLEATION OF EYEBALL

Type of Patients	Observed Patients	Avg. Stay	Vari-ance	Percentiles						
				10th	25th	50th	75th	90th	95th	99th
1. SINGLE DX										
0–19 Years	7	1.3	<1	1	1	1	1	3	3	3
20–34	1	5.0	0	5	5	5	5	5	5	5
35–49	3	2.0	<1	1	1	2	3	3	3	3
50–64	0									
65+	0									
2. MULTIPLE DX										
0–19 Years	8	1.6	3	1	1	1	1	7	7	7
20–34	9	3.7	6	2	3	3	3	6	10	11
35–49	22	4.0	10	1	1	3	6	7	8	14
50–64	16	2.4	4	1	1	2	3	5	7	9
65+	35	4.3	19	1	1	3	5	11	15	17
TOTAL SINGLE DX	**11**	**1.6**	**1**	**1**	**1**	**1**	**2**	**3**	**5**	**5**
TOTAL MULTIPLE DX	**90**	**3.4**	**10**	**1**	**1**	**2**	**5**	**7**	**9**	**15**
TOTAL										
0–19 Years	15	1.4	2	1	1	1	1	3	7	7
20–34	10	3.9	6	2	3	3	5	6	10	11
35–49	25	3.8	10	1	1	3	6	7	8	14
50–64	16	2.4	4	1	1	2	3	5	7	9
65+	35	4.3	19	1	1	3	5	11	15	17
GRAND TOTAL	**101**	**3.1**	**9**	**1**	**1**	**2**	**4**	**7**	**9**	**15**

16.5: EXENTERATION OF ORBIT

Type of Patients	Observed Patients	Avg. Stay	Vari-ance	Percentiles						
				10th	25th	50th	75th	90th	95th	99th
1. SINGLE DX										
0–19 Years	0									
20–34	0									
35–49	0									
50–64	2	2.0	0	2	2	2	2	2	2	2
65+	0									
2. MULTIPLE DX										
0–19 Years	1	8.0	0	8	8	8	8	8	8	8
20–34	2	2.0	0	2	2	2	2	2	2	2
35–49	5	3.1	4	1	1	2	5	5	5	5
50–64	8	7.5	32	1	3	6	9	19	19	19
65+	9	6.6	41	1	4	4	7	23	23	23
TOTAL SINGLE DX	**2**	**2.0**	**0**	**2**	**2**	**2**	**2**	**2**	**2**	**2**
TOTAL MULTIPLE DX	**25**	**6.1**	**25**	**1**	**2**	**5**	**8**	**12**	**19**	**23**
TOTAL										
0–19 Years	1	8.0	0	8	8	8	8	8	8	8
20–34	2	2.0	0	2	2	2	2	2	2	2
35–49	5	3.1	4	1	1	2	5	5	5	5
50–64	10	5.9	29	1	2	3	9	12	19	19
65+	9	6.6	41	1	4	4	7	23	23	23
GRAND TOTAL	**27**	**5.6**	**24**	**1**	**2**	**5**	**8**	**9**	**19**	**23**

16.6: 2ND PX POST RMVL EYEBALL

Type of Patients	Observed Patients	Avg. Stay	Vari-ance	Percentiles						
				10th	25th	50th	75th	90th	95th	99th
1. SINGLE DX										
0–19 Years	1	1.0	0	1	1	1	1	1	1	1
20–34	1	1.0	0	1	1	1	1	1	1	1
35–49	0									
50–64	0									
65+	0									
2. MULTIPLE DX										
0–19 Years	1	1.0	0	1	1	1	1	1	1	1
20–34	1	2.0	0	2	2	2	2	2	2	2
35–49	2	1.1	<1	1	1	1	1	2	2	2
50–64	6	3.1	5	1	2	3	3	8	8	8
65+	3	1.3	<1	1	1	1	2	2	2	2
TOTAL SINGLE DX	**2**	**1.0**	**0**	**1**	**1**	**1**	**1**	**1**	**1**	**1**
TOTAL MULTIPLE DX	**13**	**2.0**	**3**	**1**	**1**	**1**	**2**	**3**	**8**	**8**
TOTAL										
0–19 Years	2	1.0	0	1	1	1	1	1	1	1
20–34	2	1.5	<1	1	1	2	2	2	2	2
35–49	2	1.1	<1	1	1	1	1	2	2	2
50–64	6	3.1	5	1	2	3	3	8	8	8
65+	3	1.3	<1	1	1	1	2	2	2	2
GRAND TOTAL	**15**	**1.7**	**2**	**1**	**1**	**1**	**2**	**3**	**3**	**8**

16.7: OCULAR/ORBITAL IMPL RMVL

Type of Patients	Observed Patients	Avg. Stay	Vari-ance	Percentiles						
				10th	25th	50th	75th	90th	95th	99th
1. SINGLE DX										
0–19 Years	0									
20–34	1	1.0	0	1	1	1	1	1	1	1
35–49	0									
50–64	0									
65+	0									
2. MULTIPLE DX										
0–19 Years	0									
20–34	1	8.0	0	8	8	8	8	8	8	8
35–49	1	1.0	0	1	1	1	1	1	1	1
50–64	3	7.4	45	2	2	3	14	14	14	14
65+	2	8.2	45	4	4	4	15	15	15	15
TOTAL SINGLE DX	**1**	**1.0**	**0**	**1**	**1**	**1**	**1**	**1**	**1**	**1**
TOTAL MULTIPLE DX	**7**	**7.0**	**31**	**1**	**3**	**4**	**14**	**15**	**15**	**15**
TOTAL										
0–19 Years	0									
20–34	2	4.1	19	1	1	1	8	8	8	8
35–49	1	1.0	0	1	1	1	1	1	1	1
50–64	3	7.4	45	2	2	3	14	14	14	14
65+	2	8.2	45	4	4	4	15	15	15	15
GRAND TOTAL	**8**	**6.1**	**31**	**1**	**1**	**4**	**14**	**15**	**15**	**15**

16.8: EYEBALL/ORBIT INJ REPAIR

Type of Patients	Observed Patients	Avg. Stay	Vari-ance	Percentiles 10th	25th	50th	75th	90th	95th	99th
1. SINGLE DX										
0–19 Years	16	1.9	2	1	1	1	2	4	4	7
20–34	18	1.6	1	1	1	1	3	3	4	4
35–49	9	2.1	<1	1	2	2	2	3	5	5
50–64	3	1.0	0	1	1	1	1	1	1	1
65+	1	4.0	0	4	4	4	4	4	4	4
2. MULTIPLE DX										
0–19 Years	29	2.4	4	1	1	2	3	3	5	16
20–34	31	2.2	12	1	1	1	2	3	5	25
35–49	34	2.3	4	1	1	2	3	4	4	13
50–64	13	3.8	34	1	1	2	4	6	23	23
65+	66	3.6	10	1	2	3	4	7	8	22
TOTAL SINGLE DX	**47**	**1.8**	**1**	**1**	**1**	**1**	**2**	**4**	**4**	**7**
TOTAL MULTIPLE DX	**173**	**2.7**	**10**	**1**	**1**	**2**	**3**	**5**	**7**	**22**
TOTAL										
0–19 Years	45	2.3	4	1	1	2	3	4	5	16
20–34	49	2.0	9	1	1	1	2	3	4	25
35–49	43	2.3	3	1	1	2	3	4	4	13
50–64	16	3.3	29	1	1	1	4	6	23	23
65+	67	3.6	10	1	2	3	4	7	8	22
GRAND TOTAL	**220**	**2.5**	**8**	**1**	**1**	**2**	**3**	**4**	**6**	**16**

16.82: REPAIR EYEBALL RUPTURE

Type of Patients	Observed Patients	Avg. Stay	Vari-ance	Percentiles 10th	25th	50th	75th	90th	95th	99th
1. SINGLE DX										
0–19 Years	11	1.7	2	1	1	1	2	3	4	7
20–34	15	2.0	1	1	1	1	3	4	4	4
35–49	9	2.1	<1	1	2	2	2	3	5	5
50–64	3	1.0	0	1	1	1	1	1	1	1
65+	1	4.0	0	4	4	4	4	4	4	4
2. MULTIPLE DX										
0–19 Years	17	2.5	6	1	2	2	2	5	5	16
20–34	24	2.2	14	1	1	1	2	3	4	25
35–49	22	2.7	5	1	2	2	3	4	4	13
50–64	10	4.1	42	1	1	2	4	4	23	23
65+	50	3.5	12	1	2	3	4	7	8	22
TOTAL SINGLE DX	**39**	**1.9**	**1**	**1**	**1**	**1**	**2**	**4**	**4**	**7**
TOTAL MULTIPLE DX	**123**	**2.8**	**12**	**1**	**1**	**2**	**3**	**5**	**8**	**23**
TOTAL										
0–19 Years	28	2.3	5	1	1	2	2	3	5	16
20–34	39	2.1	11	1	1	1	2	3	4	25
35–49	31	2.4	3	1	2	2	3	4	4	13
50–64	13	3.5	35	1	1	1	3	4	23	23
65+	51	3.5	11	1	2	3	4	7	8	22
GRAND TOTAL	**162**	**2.6**	**10**	**1**	**1**	**2**	**3**	**4**	**6**	**22**

16.9: OTHER EYE & ORBIT OPS

Type of Patients	Observed Patients	Avg. Stay	Vari-ance	Percentiles 10th	25th	50th	75th	90th	95th	99th
1. SINGLE DX										
0–19 Years	4	5.0	23	1	1	1	11	11	11	11
20–34	1	1.0	0	1	1	1	1	1	1	1
35–49	2	2.0	0	2	2	2	2	2	2	2
50–64	6	2.3	2	1	1	1	4	4	4	4
65+	3	1.0	0	1	1	1	1	1	1	1
2. MULTIPLE DX										
0–19 Years	13	2.9	7	1	1	2	4	9	9	>99
20–34	10	3.6	7	1	1	2	6	8	8	8
35–49	15	4.5	16	1	1	3	7	13	13	13
50–64	9	2.2	3	1	1	1	4	5	5	5
65+	12	3.1	11	1	1	2	4	5	13	13
TOTAL SINGLE DX	**16**	**2.5**	**8**	**1**	**1**	**2**	**2**	**4**	**11**	**11**
TOTAL MULTIPLE DX	**59**	**3.3**	**10**	**1**	**1**	**2**	**4**	**9**	**11**	**13**
TOTAL										
0–19 Years	17	3.5	12	1	1	2	4	11	11	>99
20–34	11	2.3	5	1	1	1	2	6	8	8
35–49	17	3.5	11	1	2	2	3	11	13	13
50–64	15	2.2	3	1	1	1	4	5	5	5
65+	15	2.7	9	1	1	1	4	5	13	13
GRAND TOTAL	**75**	**3.1**	**9**	**1**	**1**	**2**	**4**	**9**	**11**	**13**

18.0: EXTERNAL EAR INCISION

Type of Patients	Observed Patients	Avg. Stay	Vari-ance	Percentiles 10th	25th	50th	75th	90th	95th	99th
1. SINGLE DX										
0–19 Years	14	2.1	1	1	1	2	3	3	4	6
20–34	5	2.9	6	1	1	1	4	7	7	7
35–49	3	3.3	4	1	1	4	5	5	5	5
50–64	0									
65+	1	3.0	0	3	3	3	3	3	3	3
2. MULTIPLE DX										
0–19 Years	32	3.7	6	1	1	3	6	6	9	12
20–34	22	5.4	26	1	2	4	7	12	20	20
35–49	19	3.2	2	1	2	4	4	5	6	6
50–64	6	3.8	4	1	4	4	4	8	8	8
65+	5	4.5	6	1	3	3	7	7	7	7
TOTAL SINGLE DX	**23**	**2.3**	**2**	**1**	**1**	**2**	**3**	**4**	**6**	**7**
TOTAL MULTIPLE DX	**84**	**4.0**	**9**	**1**	**2**	**4**	**5**	**7**	**9**	**20**
TOTAL										
0–19 Years	46	3.1	5	1	1	2	5	6	6	9
20–34	27	4.9	22	1	1	3	7	12	12	20
35–49	22	3.2	2	1	1	4	4	5	5	6
50–64	6	3.8	4	1	4	4	4	8	8	8
65+	6	4.3	5	1	3	3	7	7	7	7
GRAND TOTAL	**107**	**3.6**	**8**	**1**	**1**	**3**	**5**	**6**	**9**	**12**

18.09: EXTERNAL EAR INC NEC

Type of Patients	Observed Patients	Avg. Stay	Vari-ance	Percentiles						
				10th	25th	50th	75th	90th	95th	99th
1. SINGLE DX										
0–19 Years	14	2.1	1	1	1	2	3	3	4	6
20–34	5	2.9	6	1	1	1	4	7	7	7
35–49	3	3.3	4	1	1	4	5	5	5	5
50–64	0									
65+	1	3.0	0	3	3	3	3	3	3	3
2. MULTIPLE DX										
0–19 Years	32	3.7	6	1	1	3	6	6	9	12
20–34	21	5.5	27	1	2	4	7	12	20	20
35–49	19	3.2	2	1	2	4	4	5	6	6
50–64	5	4.1	3	1	4	4	4	8	8	8
65+	4	4.7	7	1	3	7	7	7	7	7
TOTAL SINGLE DX	**23**	**2.3**	**2**	**1**	**1**	**2**	**3**	**4**	**6**	**7**
TOTAL MULTIPLE DX	**81**	**4.0**	**10**	**1**	**1**	**4**	**5**	**7**	**9**	**20**
TOTAL										
0–19 Years	46	3.1	5	1	1	2	5	6	6	9
20–34	26	4.9	23	1	1	3	7	12	12	20
35–49	22	3.2	2	1	1	4	4	5	5	6
50–64	5	4.1	3	1	4	4	4	8	8	8
65+	5	4.5	6	1	3	3	7	7	7	7
GRAND TOTAL	**104**	**3.6**	**8**	**1**	**1**	**3**	**5**	**6**	**9**	**12**

18.1: EXTERNAL EAR DXTIC PX

Type of Patients	Observed Patients	Avg. Stay	Vari-ance	Percentiles						
				10th	25th	50th	75th	90th	95th	99th
1. SINGLE DX										
0–19 Years	1	1.0	0	1	1	1	1	1	1	1
20–34	0									
35–49	0									
50–64	0									
65+	0									
2. MULTIPLE DX										
0–19 Years	6	3.0	7	1	2	2	3	9	9	9
20–34	1	3.0	0	3	3	3	3	3	3	3
35–49	2	7.5	5	5	5	9	9	9	9	9
50–64	5	2.8	<1	2	3	3	3	3	3	3
65+	14	6.2	20	2	4	5	7	13	21	21
TOTAL SINGLE DX	**1**	**1.0**	**0**	**1**	**1**	**1**	**1**	**1**	**1**	**1**
TOTAL MULTIPLE DX	**28**	**5.0**	**15**	**2**	**3**	**4**	**6**	**9**	**13**	**21**
TOTAL										
0–19 Years	7	2.6	6	1	1	2	3	9	9	9
20–34	1	3.0	0	3	3	3	3	3	3	3
35–49	2	7.5	5	5	5	9	9	9	9	9
50–64	5	2.8	<1	2	3	3	3	3	3	3
65+	14	6.2	20	2	4	5	7	13	21	21
GRAND TOTAL	**29**	**4.8**	**15**	**1**	**2**	**4**	**5**	**9**	**13**	**21**

18.2: EXC/DESTR EXT EAR LESION

Type of Patients	Observed Patients	Avg. Stay	Vari-ance	Percentiles						
				10th	25th	50th	75th	90th	95th	99th
1. SINGLE DX										
0–19 Years	4	2.2	1	1	1	2	4	4	4	4
20–34	2	3.3	6	1	1	5	5	5	5	5
35–49	0									
50–64	2	3.7	6	2	2	2	6	6	6	6
65+	0									
2. MULTIPLE DX										
0–19 Years	114	2.8	14	1	1	2	3	4	11	23
20–34	11	4.8	9	2	2	3	8	8	8	8
35–49	10	3.2	6	1	1	2	6	6	7	7
50–64	8	9.5	83	1	1	5	21	21	21	21
65+	18	5.2	27	1	1	4	7	13	14	23
TOTAL SINGLE DX	**8**	**2.7**	**3**	**1**	**1**	**2**	**4**	**5**	**6**	**6**
TOTAL MULTIPLE DX	**161**	**3.8**	**21**	**1**	**1**	**2**	**4**	**8**	**14**	**23**
TOTAL										
0–19 Years	118	2.8	13	1	1	2	3	4	8	23
20–34	13	4.7	8	1	2	4	8	8	8	8
35–49	10	3.2	6	1	1	2	6	6	7	7
50–64	10	8.8	76	1	2	5	21	21	21	21
65+	18	5.2	27	1	1	4	7	13	14	23
GRAND TOTAL	**169**	**3.7**	**20**	**1**	**1**	**2**	**4**	**8**	**14**	**23**

18.29: DESTR EXT EAR LES NEC

Type of Patients	Observed Patients	Avg. Stay	Vari-ance	Percentiles						
				10th	25th	50th	75th	90th	95th	99th
1. SINGLE DX										
0–19 Years	1	4.0	0	4	4	4	4	4	4	4
20–34	1	5.0	0	5	5	5	5	5	5	5
35–49	0									
50–64	2	3.7	6	2	2	2	6	6	6	6
65+	0									
2. MULTIPLE DX										
0–19 Years	113	2.9	14	1	1	2	3	4	11	23
20–34	11	4.8	9	2	2	3	8	8	8	8
35–49	9	2.1	4	1	1	1	3	5	7	7
50–64	8	9.5	83	1	1	5	21	21	21	21
65+	18	5.2	27	1	1	4	7	13	14	23
TOTAL SINGLE DX	**4**	**4.2**	**2**	**2**	**4**	**4**	**5**	**6**	**6**	**6**
TOTAL MULTIPLE DX	**159**	**3.8**	**22**	**1**	**1**	**2**	**4**	**8**	**14**	**23**
TOTAL										
0–19 Years	114	2.9	14	1	1	2	3	4	11	23
20–34	12	4.8	8	2	2	4	8	8	8	8
35–49	9	2.1	4	1	1	1	3	5	7	7
50–64	10	8.8	76	1	2	5	21	21	21	21
65+	18	5.2	27	1	1	4	7	13	14	23
GRAND TOTAL	**163**	**3.8**	**21**	**1**	**1**	**2**	**4**	**8**	**14**	**23**

18.3: OTHER EXTERNAL EAR EXC

Type of Patients	Observed Patients	Avg. Stay	Variance	Percentiles 10th	25th	50th	75th	90th	95th	99th
1. SINGLE DX										
0–19 Years	0									
20–34	1	6.0	0	6	6	6	6	6	6	6
35–49	0									
50–64	0									
65+	0									
2. MULTIPLE DX										
0–19 Years	2	1.0	0	1	1	1	1	1	1	1
20–34	0									
35–49	1	1.0	0	1	1	1	1	1	1	1
50–64	3	2.2	1	1	2	2	2	4	4	4
65+	18	4.3	19	1	2	2	5	9	17	18
TOTAL SINGLE DX	**1**	**6.0**	**0**	**6**	**6**	**6**	**6**	**6**	**6**	**6**
TOTAL MULTIPLE DX	**24**	**3.5**	**16**	**1**	**1**	**2**	**4**	**8**	**12**	**18**
TOTAL										
0–19 Years	2	1.0	0	1	1	1	1	1	1	1
20–34	1	6.0	0	6	6	6	6	6	6	6
35–49	1	1.0	0	1	1	1	1	1	1	1
50–64	3	2.2	1	1	2	2	2	4	4	4
65+	18	4.3	19	1	2	2	5	9	17	18
GRAND TOTAL	**25**	**3.6**	**15**	**1**	**1**	**2**	**4**	**8**	**12**	**18**

18.4: SUTURE EXT EAR LAC

Type of Patients	Observed Patients	Avg. Stay	Variance	Percentiles 10th	25th	50th	75th	90th	95th	99th
1. SINGLE DX										
0–19 Years	2	1.0	0	1	1	1	1	1	1	1
20–34	1	1.0	0	1	1	1	1	1	1	1
35–49	0									
50–64	1	1.0	0	1	1	1	1	1	1	1
65+	0									
2. MULTIPLE DX										
0–19 Years	39	1.9	<1	1	1	2	3	3	4	5
20–34	71	2.4	7	1	1	2	2	4	7	14
35–49	47	2.3	4	1	1	2	3	4	5	12
50–64	41	2.7	9	1	1	2	4	5	8	16
65+	42	3.5	9	1	2	2	4	8	10	14
TOTAL SINGLE DX	**4**	**1.0**	**0**	**1**	**1**	**1**	**1**	**1**	**1**	**1**
TOTAL MULTIPLE DX	**240**	**2.6**	**6**	**1**	**1**	**2**	**3**	**5**	**7**	**14**
TOTAL										
0–19 Years	41	1.9	<1	1	1	2	2	3	4	5
20–34	72	2.4	7	1	1	2	2	4	7	14
35–49	47	2.3	4	1	1	2	3	4	5	12
50–64	42	2.7	8	1	1	2	4	5	8	16
65+	42	3.5	9	1	2	2	4	8	10	14
GRAND TOTAL	**244**	**2.5**	**6**	**1**	**1**	**2**	**3**	**5**	**7**	**14**

18.5: CORRECTION PROMINENT EAR

Type of Patients	Observed Patients	Avg. Stay	Variance	Percentiles 10th	25th	50th	75th	90th	95th	99th
1. SINGLE DX										
0–19 Years	2	1.0	0	1	1	1	1	1	1	1
20–34	1	4.0	0	4	4	4	4	4	4	4
35–49	0									
50–64	0									
65+	0									
2. MULTIPLE DX										
0–19 Years	3	1.0	0	1	1	1	1	1	1	1
20–34	1	1.0	0	1	1	1	1	1	1	1
35–49	1	1.0	0	1	1	1	1	1	1	1
50–64	0									
65+	0									
TOTAL SINGLE DX	**3**	**1.5**	**1**	**1**	**1**	**1**	**1**	**4**	**4**	**4**
TOTAL MULTIPLE DX	**5**	**1.0**	**0**	**1**	**1**	**1**	**1**	**1**	**1**	**1**
TOTAL										
0–19 Years	5	1.0	0	1	1	1	1	1	1	1
20–34	2	2.4	4	1	1	1	4	4	4	4
35–49	1	1.0	0	1	1	1	1	1	1	1
50–64	0									
65+	0									
GRAND TOTAL	**8**	**1.2**	**<1**	**1**	**1**	**1**	**1**	**1**	**4**	**4**

18.6: EXT AUDIT CANAL RECONST

Type of Patients	Observed Patients	Avg. Stay	Variance	Percentiles 10th	25th	50th	75th	90th	95th	99th
1. SINGLE DX										
0–19 Years	8	1.4	<1	1	1	1	2	3	3	3
20–34	1	1.0	0	1	1	1	1	1	1	1
35–49	2	3.3	2	1	4	4	4	4	4	4
50–64	2	1.0	0	1	1	1	1	1	1	1
65+	0									
2. MULTIPLE DX										
0–19 Years	12	1.2	<1	1	1	1	1	2	3	3
20–34	4	1.0	0	1	1	1	1	1	1	1
35–49	6	1.5	<1	1	1	1	2	3	3	3
50–64	4	1.1	<1	1	1	1	1	2	2	2
65+	6	1.8	<1	1	1	2	2	4	4	4
TOTAL SINGLE DX	**13**	**1.5**	**<1**	**1**	**1**	**1**	**2**	**3**	**4**	**4**
TOTAL MULTIPLE DX	**32**	**1.3**	**<1**	**1**	**1**	**1**	**2**	**2**	**3**	**4**
TOTAL										
0–19 Years	20	1.3	<1	1	1	1	1	2	3	3
20–34	5	1.0	0	1	1	1	1	1	1	1
35–49	8	2.0	2	1	1	1	3	4	4	4
50–64	6	1.1	<1	1	1	1	1	2	2	2
65+	6	1.8	<1	1	1	2	2	4	4	4
GRAND TOTAL	**45**	**1.4**	**<1**	**1**	**1**	**1**	**2**	**3**	**3**	**4**

18.7: OTH PLASTIC REP EXT EAR

Type of Patients	Observed Patients	Avg. Stay	Vari-ance	10th	25th	50th	75th	90th	95th	99th
1. SINGLE DX										
0–19 Years	76	1.7	<1	1	1	1	2	3	3	6
20–34	5	3.4	2	1	3	3	5	5	5	5
35–49	20	1.6	<1	1	1	1	2	3	3	4
50–64	2	2.4	1	1	1	3	3	3	3	3
65+	3	1.0	0	1	1	1	1	1	1	1
2. MULTIPLE DX										
0–19 Years	66	2.2	2	1	1	2	3	4	5	6
20–34	27	2.3	4	1	1	1	3	5	6	10
35–49	27	3.5	18	1	2	2	3	6	10	24
50–64	15	3.4	9	1	1	2	5	10	11	11
65+	24	4.0	22	1	1	2	3	16	16	18
TOTAL SINGLE DX	106	1.8	1	1	1	1	2	3	4	5
TOTAL MULTIPLE DX	159	2.7	8	1	1	2	3	5	6	16
TOTAL										
0–19 Years	142	2.0	1	1	1	2	2	4	5	6
20–34	32	2.4	4	1	1	1	3	5	6	10
35–49	47	2.9	13	1	1	2	3	6	6	24
50–64	17	3.3	8	1	1	2	4	6	10	11
65+	27	3.8	21	1	1	2	3	9	16	18
GRAND TOTAL	265	2.4	6	1	1	2	3	4	6	16

18.79: PLASTIC REP EXT EAR NEC

Type of Patients	Observed Patients	Avg. Stay	Vari-ance	10th	25th	50th	75th	90th	95th	99th
1. SINGLE DX										
0–19 Years	28	1.7	1	1	1	1	2	3	3	6
20–34	1	3.0	0	3	3	3	3	3	3	3
35–49	5	1.8	2	1	1	1	2	4	4	4
50–64	1	3.0	0	3	3	3	3	3	3	3
65+	3	1.0	0	1	1	1	1	1	1	1
2. MULTIPLE DX										
0–19 Years	35	1.9	2	1	1	1	2	4	6	6
20–34	21	2.1	4	1	1	1	3	6	6	10
35–49	21	3.7	21	1	2	2	3	6	10	24
50–64	9	2.8	6	1	1	2	3	5	10	10
65+	23	4.2	23	1	1	2	5	16	16	18
TOTAL SINGLE DX	38	1.7	1	1	1	1	3	3	3	6
TOTAL MULTIPLE DX	109	2.8	11	1	1	2	3	6	8	18
TOTAL										
0–19 Years	63	1.8	2	1	1	1	2	4	4	6
20–34	22	2.2	4	1	1	1	3	6	6	10
35–49	26	3.5	19	1	1	2	3	6	10	24
50–64	10	2.9	5	1	2	2	3	5	10	10
65+	26	3.9	22	1	1	2	3	16	16	18
GRAND TOTAL	147	2.5	9	1	1	2	3	5	6	16

18.9: OTHER EXT EAR OPERATIONS

Type of Patients	Observed Patients	Avg. Stay	Vari-ance	10th	25th	50th	75th	90th	95th	99th
1. SINGLE DX										
0–19 Years	0									
20–34	0									
35–49	0									
50–64	0									
65+	0									
2. MULTIPLE DX										
0–19 Years	1	2.0	0	2	2	2	2	2	2	2
20–34	0									
35–49	1	1.0	0	1	1	1	1	1	1	1
50–64	0									
65+	0									
TOTAL SINGLE DX	0									
TOTAL MULTIPLE DX	2	1.9	<1	2	2	2	2	2	2	2
TOTAL										
0–19 Years	1	2.0	0	2	2	2	2	2	2	2
20–34	0									
35–49	1	1.0	0	1	1	1	1	1	1	1
50–64	0									
65+	0									
GRAND TOTAL	2	1.9	<1	2	2	2	2	2	2	2

19.0: STAPES MOBILIZATION

Type of Patients	Observed Patients	Avg. Stay	Vari-ance	10th	25th	50th	75th	90th	95th	99th
1. SINGLE DX										
0–19 Years	0									
20–34	0									
35–49	1	1.0	0	1	1	1	1	1	1	1
50–64	0									
65+	0									
2. MULTIPLE DX										
0–19 Years	0									
20–34	0									
35–49	0									
50–64	1	1.0	0	1	1	1	1	1	1	1
65+	0									
TOTAL SINGLE DX	1	1.0	0	1	1	1	1	1	1	1
TOTAL MULTIPLE DX	1	1.0	0	1	1	1	1	1	1	1
TOTAL										
0–19 Years	0									
20–34	0									
35–49	1	1.0	0	1	1	1	1	1	1	1
50–64	1	1.0	0	1	1	1	1	1	1	1
65+	0									
GRAND TOTAL	2	1.0	0	1	1	1	1	1	1	1

19.1: STAPEDECTOMY

Type of Patients	Observed Patients	Avg. Stay	Vari-ance	Percentiles						
				10th	25th	50th	75th	90th	95th	99th
1. SINGLE DX										
0–19 Years	1	1.0	0	1	1	1	1	1	1	1
20–34	3	1.0	0	1	1	1	1	1	1	1
35–49	5	1.7	<1	1	1	1	3	3	3	3
50–64	1	1.0	0	1	1	1	1	1	1	1
65+	0									
2. MULTIPLE DX										
0–19 Years	1	2.0	0	2	2	2	2	2	2	2
20–34	5	2.1	3	1	1	2	2	6	6	6
35–49	19	1.2	<1	1	1	1	1	2	2	2
50–64	12	1.8	1	1	1	1	3	3	4	4
65+	1	2.0	0	2	2	2	2	2	2	2
TOTAL SINGLE DX	**10**	**1.4**	**<1**	**1**	**1**	**1**	**1**	**3**	**3**	**3**
TOTAL MULTIPLE DX	**38**	**1.5**	**<1**	**1**	**1**	**1**	**2**	**2**	**3**	**6**
TOTAL										
0–19 Years	2	1.5	<1	1	1	2	2	2	2	2
20–34	8	1.7	2	1	1	1	2	2	6	6
35–49	24	1.3	<1	1	1	1	1	2	2	3
50–64	13	1.7	1	1	1	1	3	3	4	4
65+	1	2.0	0	2	2	2	2	2	2	2
GRAND TOTAL	**48**	**1.5**	**<1**	**1**	**1**	**1**	**2**	**3**	**3**	**6**

19.2: STAPEDECTOMY REVISION

Type of Patients	Observed Patients	Avg. Stay	Vari-ance	Percentiles						
				10th	25th	50th	75th	90th	95th	99th
1. SINGLE DX										
0–19 Years	0									
20–34	0									
35–49	0									
50–64	0									
65+	0									
2. MULTIPLE DX										
0–19 Years	0									
20–34	1	1.0	0	1	1	1	1	1	1	1
35–49	0									
50–64	4	1.0	0	1	1	1	1	1	1	1
65+	2	1.6	<1	1	1	2	2	2	2	2
TOTAL SINGLE DX	**0**									
TOTAL MULTIPLE DX	**7**	**1.1**	**<1**	**1**	**1**	**1**	**1**	**2**	**2**	**2**
TOTAL										
0–19 Years	0									
20–34	1	1.0	0	1	1	1	1	1	1	1
35–49	0									
50–64	4	1.0	0	1	1	1	1	1	1	1
65+	2	1.6	<1	1	1	2	2	2	2	2
GRAND TOTAL	**7**	**1.1**	**<1**	**1**	**1**	**1**	**1**	**2**	**2**	**2**

19.3: OSSICULAR CHAIN OPS NEC

Type of Patients	Observed Patients	Avg. Stay	Vari-ance	Percentiles						
				10th	25th	50th	75th	90th	95th	99th
1. SINGLE DX										
0–19 Years	0									
20–34	0									
35–49	0									
50–64	0									
65+	0									
2. MULTIPLE DX										
0–19 Years	0									
20–34	0									
35–49	0									
50–64	0									
65+	1	4.0	0	4	4	4	4	4	4	4
TOTAL SINGLE DX	**0**									
TOTAL MULTIPLE DX	**1**	**4.0**	**0**	**4**	**4**	**4**	**4**	**4**	**4**	**4**
TOTAL										
0–19 Years	0									
20–34	0									
35–49	0									
50–64	0									
65+	1	4.0	0	4	4	4	4	4	4	4
GRAND TOTAL	**1**	**4.0**	**0**	**4**	**4**	**4**	**4**	**4**	**4**	**4**

19.4: MYRINGOPLASTY

Type of Patients	Observed Patients	Avg. Stay	Vari-ance	Percentiles						
				10th	25th	50th	75th	90th	95th	99th
1. SINGLE DX										
0–19 Years	4	1.0	0	1	1	1	1	1	1	1
20–34	1	1.0	0	1	1	1	1	1	1	1
35–49	1	1.0	0	1	1	1	1	1	1	1
50–64	3	1.0	0	1	1	1	1	1	1	1
65+	2	1.9	2	1	1	1	3	3	3	3
2. MULTIPLE DX										
0–19 Years	16	1.7	6	1	1	1	2	2	2	15
20–34	4	1.0	0	1	1	1	1	1	1	1
35–49	9	1.8	5	1	1	1	1	8	8	8
50–64	3	2.0	2	1	1	1	4	4	4	4
65+	9	1.6	1	1	1	1	2	2	5	5
TOTAL SINGLE DX	**11**	**1.1**	**<1**	**1**	**1**	**1**	**1**	**1**	**1**	**3**
TOTAL MULTIPLE DX	**41**	**1.7**	**4**	**1**	**1**	**1**	**1**	**2**	**4**	**15**
TOTAL										
0–19 Years	20	1.6	5	1	1	1	1	2	2	15
20–34	5	1.0	0	1	1	1	1	1	1	1
35–49	10	1.4	3	1	1	1	1	1	8	8
50–64	6	1.5	1	1	1	1	1	4	4	4
65+	11	1.6	1	1	1	1	2	3	5	5
GRAND TOTAL	**52**	**1.5**	**3**	**1**	**1**	**1**	**1**	**2**	**4**	**15**

19.5: OTHER TYMPANOPLASTY

Type of Patients	Observed Patients	Avg. Stay	Vari-ance	Percentiles 10th	25th	50th	75th	90th	95th	99th
1. SINGLE DX										
0–19 Years	1	1.0	0	1	1	1	1	1	1	1
20–34	0									
35–49	3	1.0	0	1	1	1	1	1	1	1
50–64	2	1.0	0	1	1	1	1	1	1	1
65+	1	1.0	0	1	1	1	1	1	1	1
2. MULTIPLE DX										
0–19 Years	4	1.0	0	1	1	1	1	1	1	1
20–34	2	1.0	0	1	1	1	1	1	1	1
35–49	6	2.2	6	1	1	1	2	8	8	8
50–64	2	1.0	0	1	1	1	1	1	1	1
65+	4	1.0	0	1	1	1	1	1	1	1
TOTAL SINGLE DX	**7**	**1.0**	**0**	**1**	**1**	**1**	**1**	**1**	**1**	**1**
TOTAL MULTIPLE DX	**18**	**1.4**	**3**	**1**	**1**	**1**	**1**	**2**	**8**	**8**
TOTAL										
0–19 Years	5	1.0	0	1	1	1	1	1	1	1
20–34	2	1.0	0	1	1	1	1	1	1	1
35–49	9	2.0	5	1	1	1	1	8	8	8
50–64	4	1.0	0	1	1	1	1	1	1	1
65+	5	1.0	0	1	1	1	1	1	1	1
GRAND TOTAL	**25**	**1.3**	**2**	**1**	**1**	**1**	**1**	**1**	**2**	**8**

19.6: TYMPANOPLASTY REVISION

Type of Patients	Observed Patients	Avg. Stay	Vari-ance	Percentiles 10th	25th	50th	75th	90th	95th	99th
1. SINGLE DX										
0–19 Years	1	6.0	0	6	6	6	6	6	6	6
20–34	0									
35–49	1	1.0	0	1	1	1	1	1	1	1
50–64	0									
65+	0									
2. MULTIPLE DX										
0–19 Years	1	1.0	0	1	1	1	1	1	1	1
20–34	1	1.0	0	1	1	1	1	1	1	1
35–49	2	1.0	0	1	1	1	1	1	1	1
50–64	3	1.5	<1	1	1	2	2	2	2	2
65+	2	1.0	0	1	1	1	1	1	1	1
TOTAL SINGLE DX	**2**	**3.3**	**7**	**1**	**1**	**1**	**6**	**6**	**6**	**6**
TOTAL MULTIPLE DX	**9**	**1.2**	**<1**	**1**	**1**	**1**	**1**	**2**	**2**	**2**
TOTAL										
0–19 Years	2	5.1	5	1	6	6	6	6	6	6
20–34	1	1.0	0	1	1	1	1	1	1	1
35–49	3	1.0	0	1	1	1	1	1	1	1
50–64	3	1.5	<1	1	1	2	2	2	2	2
65+	2	1.0	0	1	1	1	1	1	1	1
GRAND TOTAL	**11**	**1.9**	**3**	**1**	**1**	**1**	**2**	**6**	**6**	**6**

19.9: MIDDLE EAR REPAIR NEC

Type of Patients	Observed Patients	Avg. Stay	Vari-ance	Percentiles 10th	25th	50th	75th	90th	95th	99th
1. SINGLE DX										
0–19 Years	0									
20–34	0									
35–49	0									
50–64	1	1.0	0	1	1	1	1	1	1	1
65+	0									
2. MULTIPLE DX										
0–19 Years	0									
20–34	0									
35–49	4	2.2	<1	1	2	2	3	3	3	3
50–64	1	9.0	0	9	9	9	9	9	9	9
65+	3	2.5	4	1	1	1	5	5	5	5
TOTAL SINGLE DX	**1**	**1.0**	**0**	**1**	**1**	**1**	**1**	**1**	**1**	**1**
TOTAL MULTIPLE DX	**8**	**3.1**	**7**	**1**	**1**	**2**	**5**	**5**	**9**	**9**
TOTAL										
0–19 Years	0									
20–34	0									
35–49	4	2.2	<1	1	2	2	3	3	3	3
50–64	2	5.9	22	1	1	9	9	9	9	9
65+	3	2.5	4	1	1	1	5	5	5	5
GRAND TOTAL	**9**	**3.0**	**7**	**1**	**1**	**2**	**5**	**5**	**9**	**9**

20.0: MYRINGOTOMY

Type of Patients	Observed Patients	Avg. Stay	Vari-ance	Percentiles 10th	25th	50th	75th	90th	95th	99th
1. SINGLE DX										
0–19 Years	16	2.8	4	1	1	2	4	5	6	9
20–34	0									
35–49	3	3.3	<1	3	3	3	4	4	4	4
50–64	0									
65+	0									
2. MULTIPLE DX										
0–19 Years	633	2.5	17	1	1	1	3	5	7	17
20–34	18	3.5	6	1	1	4	4	6	6	16
35–49	30	5.8	44	1	2	3	6	17	24	24
50–64	34	6.4	42	1	1	4	8	17	23	23
65+	28	7.6	39	3	4	7	8	12	25	32
TOTAL SINGLE DX	**19**	**2.9**	**3**	**1**	**1**	**3**	**4**	**4**	**6**	**9**
TOTAL MULTIPLE DX	**743**	**3.1**	**22**	**1**	**1**	**2**	**3**	**6**	**10**	**24**
TOTAL										
0–19 Years	649	2.5	17	1	1	1	3	5	7	17
20–34	18	3.5	6	1	1	4	4	6	6	16
35–49	33	5.6	41	1	2	3	6	15	24	24
50–64	34	6.4	42	1	1	4	8	17	23	23
65+	28	7.6	39	3	4	7	8	12	25	32
GRAND TOTAL	**762**	**3.1**	**22**	**1**	**1**	**2**	**3**	**6**	**10**	**24**

20.01: MYRINGOTOMY W INTUBATION

Type of Patients	Observed Patients	Avg. Stay	Vari-ance	Percentiles 10th	25th	50th	75th	90th	95th	99th
1. SINGLE DX										
0–19 Years	14	2.4	2	1	1	2	4	4	4	5
20–34	0									
35–49	2	3.0	0	3	3	3	3	3	3	3
50–64	0									
65+	0									
2. MULTIPLE DX										
0–19 Years	625	2.5	17	1	1	1	3	5	7	17
20–34	17	3.3	3	1	1	4	4	6	6	8
35–49	24	6.5	52	1	1	4	8	24	24	24
50–64	31	6.8	45	1	1	5	10	20	23	23
65+	26	8.1	40	3	4	7	10	14	25	32
TOTAL SINGLE DX	**16**	**2.5**	**2**	**1**	**1**	**3**	**4**	**4**	**4**	**5**
TOTAL MULTIPLE DX	**723**	**3.1**	**22**	**1**	**1**	**2**	**3**	**6**	**10**	**24**
TOTAL										
0–19 Years	639	2.5	17	1	1	1	3	5	7	17
20–34	17	3.3	3	1	1	4	4	6	6	8
35–49	26	6.3	49	1	1	4	7	24	24	24
50–64	31	6.8	45	1	1	5	10	20	23	23
65+	26	8.1	40	3	4	7	10	14	25	32
GRAND TOTAL	**739**	**3.1**	**22**	**1**	**1**	**2**	**3**	**6**	**10**	**24**

20.1: TYMPANOSTOMY TUBE RMVL

Type of Patients	Observed Patients	Avg. Stay	Vari-ance	Percentiles 10th	25th	50th	75th	90th	95th	99th
1. SINGLE DX										
0–19 Years	1	1.0	0	1	1	1	1	1	1	1
20–34	0									
35–49	0									
50–64	0									
65+	0									
2. MULTIPLE DX										
0–19 Years	10	3.5	2	2	3	3	4	4	8	8
20–34	1	1.0	0	1	1	1	1	1	1	1
35–49	0									
50–64	0									
65+	0									
TOTAL SINGLE DX	**1**	**1.0**	**0**	**1**	**1**	**1**	**1**	**1**	**1**	**1**
TOTAL MULTIPLE DX	**11**	**3.4**	**2**	**1**	**3**	**3**	**4**	**4**	**8**	**8**
TOTAL										
0–19 Years	11	3.4	2	1	3	3	4	4	8	8
20–34	1	1.0	0	1	1	1	1	1	1	1
35–49	0									
50–64	0									
65+	0									
GRAND TOTAL	**12**	**3.3**	**2**	**1**	**3**	**3**	**4**	**4**	**8**	**8**

20.2: MASTOID & MID EAR INC

Type of Patients	Observed Patients	Avg. Stay	Vari-ance	Percentiles 10th	25th	50th	75th	90th	95th	99th
1. SINGLE DX										
0–19 Years	2	5.0	5	1	6	6	6	6	6	6
20–34	0									
35–49	1	1.0	0	1	1	1	1	1	1	1
50–64	0									
65+	0									
2. MULTIPLE DX										
0–19 Years	6	4.4	7	3	3	4	4	4	15	15
20–34	1	1.0	0	1	1	1	1	1	1	1
35–49	9	1.4	2	1	1	1	1	1	6	6
50–64	7	2.1	5	1	1	1	3	3	9	9
65+	7	4.3	43	1	1	1	4	18	18	18
TOTAL SINGLE DX	**3**	**4.0**	**7**	**1**	**1**	**6**	**6**	**6**	**6**	**6**
TOTAL MULTIPLE DX	**30**	**3.0**	**12**	**1**	**1**	**1**	**4**	**4**	**9**	**18**
TOTAL										
0–19 Years	8	4.5	7	3	3	4	4	6	6	15
20–34	1	1.0	0	1	1	1	1	1	1	1
35–49	10	1.3	2	1	1	1	1	1	6	6
50–64	7	2.1	5	1	1	1	3	3	9	9
65+	7	4.3	43	1	1	1	4	18	18	18
GRAND TOTAL	**33**	**3.1**	**12**	**1**	**1**	**1**	**4**	**6**	**9**	**18**

20.3: MID & INNER EAR DXTIC PX

Type of Patients	Observed Patients	Avg. Stay	Vari-ance	Percentiles 10th	25th	50th	75th	90th	95th	99th
1. SINGLE DX										
0–19 Years	0									
20–34	0									
35–49	0									
50–64	0									
65+	0									
2. MULTIPLE DX										
0–19 Years	0									
20–34	0									
35–49	1	13.0	0	13	13	13	13	13	13	13
50–64	0									
65+	0									
TOTAL SINGLE DX	**0**									
TOTAL MULTIPLE DX	**1**	**13.0**	**0**	**13**	**13**	**13**	**13**	**13**	**13**	**13**
TOTAL										
0–19 Years	0									
20–34	0									
35–49	1	13.0	0	13	13	13	13	13	13	13
50–64	0									
65+	0									
GRAND TOTAL	**1**	**13.0**	**0**	**13**	**13**	**13**	**13**	**13**	**13**	**13**

20.4: MASTOIDECTOMY

Type of Patients	Observed Patients	Avg. Stay	Vari-ance	10th	25th	50th	75th	90th	95th	99th
1. SINGLE DX										
0–19 Years	10	1.9	4	1	1	1	1	5	8	8
20–34	9	1.2	<1	1	1	1	1	2	4	4
35–49	10	1.3	1	1	1	1	1	2	2	7
50–64	6	1.3	<1	1	1	1	2	2	2	2
65+	1	1.0	0	1	1	1	1	1	1	1
2. MULTIPLE DX										
0–19 Years	55	4.8	86	1	1	2	2	11	39	39
20–34	35	2.6	6	1	1	1	3	6	9	10
35–49	51	4.3	24	1	1	2	7	10	18	20
50–64	52	2.9	18	1	1	1	3	7	10	29
65+	63	4.2	48	1	1	1	4	11	11	47
TOTAL SINGLE DX	**36**	**1.5**	**2**	**1**	**1**	**1**	**1**	**2**	**5**	**8**
TOTAL MULTIPLE DX	**256**	**3.9**	**42**	**1**	**1**	**1**	**3**	**10**	**15**	**39**
TOTAL										
0–19 Years	65	4.2	71	1	1	1	2	8	17	39
20–34	44	2.3	5	1	1	1	2	6	8	10
35–49	61	3.7	21	1	1	1	6	10	15	20
50–64	58	2.7	17	1	1	1	2	7	10	20
65+	64	4.1	47	1	1	1	4	11	11	47
GRAND TOTAL	**292**	**3.5**	**37**	**1**	**1**	**1**	**3**	**9**	**11**	**39**

20.42: RADICAL MASTOIDECTOMY

Type of Patients	Observed Patients	Avg. Stay	Vari-ance	10th	25th	50th	75th	90th	95th	99th
1. SINGLE DX										
0–19 Years	2	1.0	0	1	1	1	1	1	1	1
20–34	4	1.0	0	1	1	1	1	1	1	1
35–49	3	1.0	0	1	1	1	1	1	1	1
50–64	2	1.0	0	1	1	1	1	1	1	1
65+	0									
2. MULTIPLE DX										
0–19 Years	21	1.9	3	1	1	1	1	5	7	8
20–34	16	2.5	6	1	1	1	2	7	9	9
35–49	19	5.2	34	1	1	2	10	10	20	20
50–64	21	3.3	30	1	1	1	2	7	20	29
65+	28	4.4	56	1	1	2	5	11	11	47
TOTAL SINGLE DX	**11**	**1.0**	**0**	**1**	**1**	**1**	**1**	**1**	**1**	**1**
TOTAL MULTIPLE DX	**105**	**3.5**	**27**	**1**	**1**	**1**	**3**	**10**	**11**	**20**
TOTAL										
0–19 Years	23	1.8	3	1	1	1	1	5	7	8
20–34	20	2.0	5	1	1	1	2	7	8	9
35–49	22	4.9	32	1	1	1	10	10	20	20
50–64	23	3.2	29	1	1	1	2	7	20	29
65+	28	4.4	56	1	1	2	5	11	11	47
GRAND TOTAL	**116**	**3.2**	**25**	**1**	**1**	**1**	**3**	**10**	**10**	**20**

20.49: MASTOIDECTOMY NEC

Type of Patients	Observed Patients	Avg. Stay	Vari-ance	10th	25th	50th	75th	90th	95th	99th
1. SINGLE DX										
0–19 Years	5	1.0	0	1	1	1	1	1	1	1
20–34	4	2.3	2	1	1	2	4	4	4	4
35–49	7	1.4	2	1	1	1	1	2	2	7
50–64	2	1.4	<1	1	1	1	2	2	2	2
65+	0									
2. MULTIPLE DX										
0–19 Years	21	2.2	10	1	1	2	2	2	2	17
20–34	17	2.2	6	1	1	1	2	5	10	10
35–49	22	3.2	10	1	1	2	6	7	9	15
50–64	24	2.6	7	1	1	1	3	7	10	11
65+	24	3.8	51	1	1	1	2	11	27	31
TOTAL SINGLE DX	**18**	**1.3**	**<1**	**1**	**1**	**1**	**1**	**2**	**2**	**7**
TOTAL MULTIPLE DX	**108**	**2.7**	**14**	**1**	**1**	**1**	**2**	**7**	**10**	**17**
TOTAL										
0–19 Years	26	1.9	7	1	1	1	2	2	2	17
20–34	21	2.2	5	1	1	1	2	5	10	10
35–49	29	2.6	8	1	1	1	3	7	7	15
50–64	26	2.5	7	1	1	1	3	7	10	11
65+	24	3.8	51	1	1	1	2	11	27	31
GRAND TOTAL	**126**	**2.4**	**12**	**1**	**1**	**1**	**2**	**6**	**7**	**17**

20.5: OTH MIDDLE EAR EXCISION

Type of Patients	Observed Patients	Avg. Stay	Vari-ance	10th	25th	50th	75th	90th	95th	99th
1. SINGLE DX										
0–19 Years	0									
20–34	1	1.0	0	1	1	1	1	1	1	1
35–49	1	4.0	0	4	4	4	4	4	4	4
50–64	2	1.0	0	1	1	1	1	1	1	1
65+	0									
2. MULTIPLE DX										
0–19 Years	5	3.1	14	1	1	2	2	11	11	11
20–34	0									
35–49	2	1.6	1	1	1	1	3	3	3	3
50–64	3	6.8	5	4	4	8	8	8	8	8
65+	6	4.0	7	1	2	4	7	7	7	7
TOTAL SINGLE DX	**4**	**1.6**	**2**	**1**	**1**	**1**	**1**	**4**	**4**	**4**
TOTAL MULTIPLE DX	**16**	**4.4**	**11**	**1**	**1**	**3**	**8**	**8**	**11**	**11**
TOTAL										
0–19 Years	5	3.1	14	1	1	2	2	11	11	11
20–34	1	1.0	0	1	1	1	1	1	1	1
35–49	3	2.1	2	1	1	1	3	4	4	4
50–64	5	5.5	10	1	2	8	8	8	8	8
65+	6	4.0	7	1	2	4	7	7	7	7
GRAND TOTAL	**20**	**4.0**	**11**	**1**	**1**	**2**	**8**	**8**	**8**	**11**

20.6: FENESTRATION INNER EAR

Type of Patients	Observed Patients	Avg. Stay	Vari-ance	Percentiles 10th	25th	50th	75th	90th	95th	99th
1. SINGLE DX										
0–19 Years	0									
20–34	0									
35–49	0									
50–64	0									
65+	0									
2. MULTIPLE DX										
0–19 Years	0									
20–34	0									
35–49	1	2.0	0	2	2	2	2	2	2	2
50–64	0									
65+	0									
TOTAL SINGLE DX	**0**									
TOTAL MULTIPLE DX	**1**	**2.0**	**0**	**2**	**2**	**2**	**2**	**2**	**2**	**2**
TOTAL										
0–19 Years	0									
20–34	0									
35–49	1	2.0	0	2	2	2	2	2	2	2
50–64	0									
65+	0									
GRAND TOTAL	**1**	**2.0**	**0**	**2**	**2**	**2**	**2**	**2**	**2**	**2**

20.7: INC/EXC/DESTR INNER EAR

Type of Patients	Observed Patients	Avg. Stay	Vari-ance	Percentiles 10th	25th	50th	75th	90th	95th	99th
1. SINGLE DX										
0–19 Years	0									
20–34	0									
35–49	0									
50–64	1	1.0	0	1	1	1	1	1	1	1
65+	1	4.0	0	4	4	4	4	4	4	4
2. MULTIPLE DX										
0–19 Years	1	3.0	0	3	3	3	3	3	3	3
20–34	4	3.5	4	2	2	2	6	7	7	7
35–49	6	2.6	2	1	2	2	3	5	5	5
50–64	8	2.7	6	1	1	1	4	4	10	10
65+	6	2.7	3	1	1	3	4	5	5	5
TOTAL SINGLE DX	**2**	**2.4**	**4**	**1**	**1**	**1**	**4**	**4**	**4**	**4**
TOTAL MULTIPLE DX	**25**	**2.9**	**4**	**1**	**1**	**2**	**4**	**5**	**7**	**10**
TOTAL										
0–19 Years	1	3.0	0	3	3	3	3	3	3	3
20–34	4	3.5	4	2	2	2	6	7	7	7
35–49	6	2.6	2	1	2	2	3	5	5	5
50–64	9	2.7	6	1	1	1	4	4	10	10
65+	7	2.9	2	1	1	3	4	5	5	5
GRAND TOTAL	**27**	**2.9**	**4**	**1**	**1**	**2**	**4**	**5**	**7**	**10**

20.8: EUSTACHIAN TUBE OPS

Type of Patients	Observed Patients	Avg. Stay	Vari-ance	Percentiles 10th	25th	50th	75th	90th	95th	99th
1. SINGLE DX										
0–19 Years	0									
20–34	0									
35–49	0									
50–64	0									
65+	0									
2. MULTIPLE DX										
0–19 Years	0									
20–34	0									
35–49	1	2.0	0	2	2	2	2	2	2	2
50–64	0									
65+	0									
TOTAL SINGLE DX	**0**									
TOTAL MULTIPLE DX	**1**	**2.0**	**0**	**2**	**2**	**2**	**2**	**2**	**2**	**2**
TOTAL										
0–19 Years	0									
20–34	0									
35–49	1	2.0	0	2	2	2	2	2	2	2
50–64	0									
65+	0									
GRAND TOTAL	**1**	**2.0**	**0**	**2**	**2**	**2**	**2**	**2**	**2**	**2**

20.9: OTHER ME & IE OPS

Type of Patients	Observed Patients	Avg. Stay	Vari-ance	Percentiles 10th	25th	50th	75th	90th	95th	99th
1. SINGLE DX										
0–19 Years	22	1.0	0	1	1	1	1	1	1	1
20–34	3	1.0	0	1	1	1	1	1	1	1
35–49	5	1.0	0	1	1	1	1	1	1	1
50–64	2	1.0	0	1	1	1	1	1	1	1
65+	2	2.0	2	1	1	3	3	3	3	3
2. MULTIPLE DX										
0–19 Years	23	1.4	<1	1	1	1	2	2	2	6
20–34	9	2.7	2	1	1	4	4	4	4	4
35–49	9	2.6	4	1	1	2	3	5	9	9
50–64	21	2.1	5	1	1	1	2	8	8	8
65+	34	2.3	9	1	1	1	2	5	6	17
TOTAL SINGLE DX	**34**	**1.0**	**<1**	**1**	**1**	**1**	**1**	**1**	**1**	**3**
TOTAL MULTIPLE DX	**96**	**2.1**	**5**	**1**	**1**	**1**	**2**	**4**	**6**	**17**
TOTAL										
0–19 Years	45	1.2	<1	1	1	1	1	2	2	6
20–34	12	2.4	2	1	1	1	4	4	4	4
35–49	14	2.1	3	1	1	1	3	5	5	9
50–64	23	2.1	5	1	1	1	2	8	8	8
65+	36	2.3	9	1	1	1	2	5	6	17
GRAND TOTAL	**130**	**1.8**	**4**	**1**	**1**	**1**	**2**	**4**	**5**	**9**

21.0: CONTROL OF EPISTAXIS

Type of Patients	Observed Patients	Avg. Stay	Vari-ance	Percentiles						
				10th	25th	50th	75th	90th	95th	99th
1. SINGLE DX										
0–19 Years	7	1.6	<1	1	1	1	2	3	3	3
20–34	14	3.4	3	2	2	3	5	6	6	6
35–49	24	2.1	2	1	1	2	3	4	5	5
50–64	17	2.2	2	1	1	2	3	5	5	5
65+	20	2.7	2	1	2	2	4	5	5	5
2. MULTIPLE DX										
0–19 Years	47	3.0	3	1	2	3	4	5	6	9
20–34	59	4.3	40	1	2	3	5	7	15	48
35–49	201	3.8	16	1	2	3	5	7	10	32
50–64	402	3.4	10	1	1	3	4	6	9	16
65+	1,165	4.0	18	1	2	3	5	8	10	24
TOTAL SINGLE DX	**82**	**2.5**	**2**	**1**	**1**	**2**	**3**	**5**	**5**	**6**
TOTAL MULTIPLE DX	**1,874**	**3.8**	**17**	**1**	**2**	**3**	**5**	**8**	**10**	**23**
TOTAL										
0–19 Years	54	2.8	3	1	1	3	4	5	6	9
20–34	73	4.1	32	1	2	3	5	7	15	48
35–49	225	3.7	15	1	1	3	4	7	10	19
50–64	419	3.4	10	1	1	3	4	6	9	16
65+	1,185	3.9	18	1	2	3	5	8	10	24
GRAND TOTAL	**1,956**	**3.8**	**16**	**1**	**2**	**3**	**5**	**8**	**10**	**23**

21.01: ANT NAS PACK FOR EPISTX

Type of Patients	Observed Patients	Avg. Stay	Vari-ance	Percentiles						
				10th	25th	50th	75th	90th	95th	99th
1. SINGLE DX										
0–19 Years	2	1.3	<1	1	1	1	2	2	2	2
20–34	5	2.7	2	1	2	3	3	5	5	5
35–49	7	2.2	4	1	1	1	5	5	5	5
50–64	4	1.5	<1	1	1	1	2	2	2	2
65+	3	2.2	<1	1	2	2	3	3	3	3
2. MULTIPLE DX										
0–19 Years	19	2.7	2	1	2	2	4	5	5	6
20–34	25	5.7	78	1	2	3	5	15	18	48
35–49	69	4.1	19	1	2	3	6	8	13	33
50–64	153	3.0	12	1	1	2	4	6	8	16
65+	462	3.7	17	1	1	2	4	8	11	23
TOTAL SINGLE DX	**21**	**2.0**	**2**	**1**	**1**	**2**	**3**	**5**	**5**	**5**
TOTAL MULTIPLE DX	**728**	**3.7**	**18**	**1**	**1**	**2**	**4**	**8**	**10**	**23**
TOTAL										
0–19 Years	21	2.6	2	1	2	2	4	4	5	6
20–34	30	5.2	66	1	2	3	5	7	18	48
35–49	76	4.0	19	1	1	3	5	8	11	33
50–64	157	3.0	12	1	1	2	4	6	8	16
65+	465	3.7	17	1	1	2	4	8	11	23
GRAND TOTAL	**749**	**3.6**	**17**	**1**	**1**	**2**	**4**	**8**	**10**	**23**

21.02: POST NAS PACK FOR EPISTX

Type of Patients	Observed Patients	Avg. Stay	Vari-ance	Percentiles						
				10th	25th	50th	75th	90th	95th	99th
1. SINGLE DX										
0–19 Years	2	2.1	1	1	1	3	3	3	3	3
20–34	5	4.4	2	3	3	4	5	6	6	6
35–49	8	2.3	<1	1	2	2	3	4	4	4
50–64	6	2.6	2	1	2	2	3	5	5	5
65+	9	3.0	2	2	2	2	5	5	5	5
2. MULTIPLE DX										
0–19 Years	3	2.1	<1	1	1	2	3	3	3	3
20–34	14	2.3	2	1	1	2	3	3	6	6
35–49	57	3.5	4	1	2	3	5	5	7	10
50–64	92	3.6	5	1	2	3	5	6	8	10
65+	279	3.5	6	1	2	3	4	6	9	12
TOTAL SINGLE DX	**30**	**2.9**	**2**	**1**	**2**	**2**	**4**	**5**	**5**	**6**
TOTAL MULTIPLE DX	**445**	**3.5**	**5**	**1**	**2**	**3**	**5**	**6**	**8**	**11**
TOTAL										
0–19 Years	5	2.1	<1	1	1	2	3	3	3	3
20–34	19	2.9	2	1	2	3	3	6	6	6
35–49	65	3.3	3	1	2	3	5	5	6	10
50–64	98	3.5	5	1	2	3	5	6	8	10
65+	288	3.5	6	1	2	3	5	6	9	12
GRAND TOTAL	**475**	**3.4**	**5**	**1**	**2**	**3**	**5**	**6**	**8**	**11**

21.03: CAUT TO CNTRL EPISTAXIS

Type of Patients	Observed Patients	Avg. Stay	Vari-ance	Percentiles						
				10th	25th	50th	75th	90th	95th	99th
1. SINGLE DX										
0–19 Years	2	1.5	<1	1	1	1	2	2	2	2
20–34	2	4.4	7	2	2	6	6	6	6	6
35–49	5	1.5	<1	1	1	1	2	3	3	3
50–64	3	1.0	0	1	1	1	1	1	1	1
65+	5	1.6	<1	1	1	1	2	3	3	3
2. MULTIPLE DX										
0–19 Years	19	3.3	3	1	3	3	5	5	6	6
20–34	16	3.9	14	1	1	3	6	7	7	18
35–49	62	3.4	16	1	1	2	4	7	14	19
50–64	115	3.9	12	1	2	3	4	8	12	16
65+	338	4.5	29	1	2	3	5	9	11	34
TOTAL SINGLE DX	**17**	**1.8**	**2**	**1**	**1**	**1**	**2**	**3**	**6**	**6**
TOTAL MULTIPLE DX	**550**	**4.2**	**23**	**1**	**2**	**3**	**5**	**9**	**11**	**31**
TOTAL										
0–19 Years	21	3.2	3	1	1	3	5	5	6	6
20–34	18	3.9	13	1	1	3	6	7	7	18
35–49	67	3.3	15	1	1	2	4	7	14	19
50–64	118	3.8	12	1	2	3	4	8	12	16
65+	343	4.5	29	1	2	3	5	9	11	34
GRAND TOTAL	**567**	**4.2**	**23**	**1**	**2**	**3**	**5**	**8**	**11**	**24**

21.09: EPISTAXIS CONTROL NEC

Type of Patients	Observed Patients	Avg. Stay	Vari-ance	Percentiles 10th	25th	50th	75th	90th	95th	99th
1. SINGLE DX										
0–19 Years	0									
20–34	0									
35–49	1	2.0	0	2	2	2	2	2	2	2
50–64	1	1.0	0	1	1	1	1	1	1	1
65+	3	3.0	5	1	1	1	5	5	5	5
2. MULTIPLE DX										
0–19 Years	2	1.4	<1	1	1	1	2	2	2	2
20–34	3	2.0	<1	1	1	2	3	3	3	3
35–49	8	6.2	112	1	2	2	3	32	32	32
50–64	19	3.4	14	1	1	3	5	6	9	21
65+	55	5.1	18	1	2	3	7	11	16	16
TOTAL SINGLE DX	**5**	**2.5**	**4**	**1**	**1**	**2**	**5**	**5**	**5**	**5**
TOTAL MULTIPLE DX	**87**	**4.6**	**22**	**1**	**2**	**3**	**6**	**9**	**16**	**21**
TOTAL										
0–19 Years	2	1.4	<1	1	1	1	2	2	2	2
20–34	3	2.0	<1	1	1	2	3	3	3	3
35–49	9	5.7	99	1	2	2	3	32	32	32
50–64	20	3.3	14	1	1	3	5	6	9	21
65+	58	5.0	18	1	2	3	7	11	16	16
GRAND TOTAL	**92**	**4.5**	**21**	**1**	**2**	**3**	**5**	**9**	**16**	**21**

21.1: NOSE INCISION

Type of Patients	Observed Patients	Avg. Stay	Vari-ance	Percentiles 10th	25th	50th	75th	90th	95th	99th
1. SINGLE DX										
0–19 Years	5	2.1	1	1	1	2	3	4	4	4
20–34	3	1.5	<1	1	1	2	2	2	2	2
35–49	3	4.3	<1	4	4	4	4	6	6	6
50–64	0									
65+	1	3.0	0	3	3	3	3	3	3	3
2. MULTIPLE DX										
0–19 Years	11	3.7	6	2	2	3	4	6	9	11
20–34	11	4.1	8	2	2	3	6	8	10	10
35–49	20	4.2	10	2	2	3	5	7	8	17
50–64	9	3.8	7	2	3	3	3	5	13	13
65+	3	9.3	114	4	4	4	7	32	32	32
TOTAL SINGLE DX	**12**	**2.8**	**2**	**1**	**2**	**2**	**4**	**4**	**6**	**6**
TOTAL MULTIPLE DX	**54**	**4.3**	**15**	**2**	**2**	**3**	**5**	**8**	**10**	**17**
TOTAL										
0–19 Years	16	3.4	5	1	2	3	4	6	9	11
20–34	14	3.5	7	1	2	2	4	8	10	10
35–49	23	4.2	9	2	2	4	5	7	8	17
50–64	9	3.8	7	2	3	3	3	5	13	13
65+	4	8.5	103	3	4	4	7	32	32	32
GRAND TOTAL	**66**	**4.1**	**13**	**2**	**2**	**3**	**4**	**7**	**9**	**17**

21.2: NASAL DIAGNOSTIC PX

Type of Patients	Observed Patients	Avg. Stay	Vari-ance	Percentiles 10th	25th	50th	75th	90th	95th	99th
1. SINGLE DX										
0–19 Years	1	1.0	0	1	1	1	1	1	1	1
20–34	1	1.0	0	1	1	1	1	1	1	1
35–49	0									
50–64	0									
65+	0									
2. MULTIPLE DX										
0–19 Years	13	4.6	16	1	1	3	7	11	13	13
20–34	6	5.4	22	1	2	3	8	14	14	14
35–49	12	7.8	17	3	6	7	10	14	14	18
50–64	7	2.3	3	1	1	2	2	4	7	7
65+	16	5.6	19	2	2	4	7	10	19	19
TOTAL SINGLE DX	**2**	**1.0**	**0**	**1**	**1**	**1**	**1**	**1**	**1**	**1**
TOTAL MULTIPLE DX	**54**	**5.4**	**18**	**1**	**2**	**4**	**7**	**11**	**14**	**19**
TOTAL										
0–19 Years	14	4.5	16	1	1	3	7	11	13	13
20–34	7	4.8	21	1	1	3	8	14	14	14
35–49	12	7.8	17	3	6	7	10	14	14	18
50–64	7	2.3	3	1	1	2	2	4	7	7
65+	16	5.6	19	2	2	4	7	10	19	19
GRAND TOTAL	**56**	**5.3**	**18**	**1**	**2**	**4**	**7**	**11**	**14**	**19**

21.21: RHINOSCOPY

Type of Patients	Observed Patients	Avg. Stay	Vari-ance	Percentiles 10th	25th	50th	75th	90th	95th	99th
1. SINGLE DX										
0–19 Years	1	1.0	0	1	1	1	1	1	1	1
20–34	1	1.0	0	1	1	1	1	1	1	1
35–49	0									
50–64	0									
65+	0									
2. MULTIPLE DX										
0–19 Years	10	3.2	7	1	1	2	6	7	7	7
20–34	4	4.5	9	1	1	6	6	8	8	8
35–49	9	8.1	18	3	6	7	10	14	14	18
50–64	4	3.4	6	1	2	2	4	7	7	7
65+	10	4.7	9	2	2	6	6	7	12	12
TOTAL SINGLE DX	**2**	**1.0**	**0**	**1**	**1**	**1**	**1**	**1**	**1**	**1**
TOTAL MULTIPLE DX	**37**	**5.1**	**15**	**1**	**2**	**6**	**7**	**10**	**14**	**18**
TOTAL										
0–19 Years	11	3.1	7	1	1	1	6	7	7	7
20–34	5	3.8	9	1	1	3	6	8	8	8
35–49	9	8.1	18	3	6	7	10	14	14	18
50–64	4	3.4	6	1	2	2	4	7	7	7
65+	10	4.7	9	2	2	6	6	7	12	12
GRAND TOTAL	**39**	**5.0**	**15**	**1**	**1**	**5**	**7**	**10**	**14**	**18**

21.3: NASAL LESION DESTR/EXC

Type of Patients	Observed Patients	Avg. Stay	Vari-ance	Percentiles 10th	25th	50th	75th	90th	95th	99th
1. SINGLE DX										
0–19 Years	2	1.7	<1	1	1	2	2	2	2	2
20–34	1	2.0	0	2	2	2	2	2	2	2
35–49	1	1.0	0	1	1	1	1	1	1	1
50–64	3	2.5	3	1	1	2	5	5	5	5
65+	0									
2. MULTIPLE DX										
0–19 Years	7	3.4	3	1	2	3	5	5	5	6
20–34	3	3.4	2	1	4	4	4	4	4	4
35–49	8	1.9	3	1	1	1	2	6	6	6
50–64	13	5.6	39	1	1	2	8	17	19	19
65+	23	3.3	10	1	1	1	4	8	10	10
TOTAL SINGLE DX	**7**	**2.0**	**1**	**1**	**1**	**2**	**2**	**5**	**5**	**5**
TOTAL MULTIPLE DX	**54**	**3.6**	**14**	**1**	**1**	**2**	**5**	**8**	**10**	**19**
TOTAL										
0–19 Years	9	3.2	3	1	2	2	5	5	5	6
20–34	4	3.0	2	1	2	4	4	4	4	4
35–49	9	1.9	3	1	1	1	2	6	6	6
50–64	16	5.1	34	1	1	2	5	17	19	19
65+	23	3.3	10	1	1	1	4	8	10	10
GRAND TOTAL	**61**	**3.4**	**13**	**1**	**1**	**2**	**5**	**8**	**10**	**19**

21.4: RESECTION OF NOSE

Type of Patients	Observed Patients	Avg. Stay	Vari-ance	Percentiles 10th	25th	50th	75th	90th	95th	99th
1. SINGLE DX										
0–19 Years	0									
20–34	0									
35–49	0									
50–64	0									
65+	1	3.0	0	3	3	3	3	3	3	3
2. MULTIPLE DX										
0–19 Years	0									
20–34	0									
35–49	3	6.4	45	3	3	3	5	19	19	19
50–64	4	6.4	28	2	2	5	8	8	20	20
65+	9	2.4	7	1	1	2	2	10	10	10
TOTAL SINGLE DX	**1**	**3.0**	**0**	**3**	**3**	**3**	**3**	**3**	**3**	**3**
TOTAL MULTIPLE DX	**16**	**4.7**	**24**	**1**	**2**	**2**	**8**	**10**	**19**	**20**
TOTAL										
0–19 Years	0									
20–34	0									
35–49	3	6.4	45	3	3	3	5	19	19	19
50–64	4	6.4	28	2	2	5	8	8	20	20
65+	10	2.5	7	1	1	2	2	3	10	10
GRAND TOTAL	**17**	**4.7**	**24**	**1**	**2**	**2**	**8**	**10**	**19**	**20**

21.5: SUBMUC NAS SEPTUM RESECT

Type of Patients	Observed Patients	Avg. Stay	Vari-ance	Percentiles 10th	25th	50th	75th	90th	95th	99th
1. SINGLE DX										
0–19 Years	0									
20–34	1	1.0	0	1	1	1	1	1	1	1
35–49	1	1.0	0	1	1	1	1	1	1	1
50–64	1	3.0	0	3	3	3	3	3	3	3
65+	1	2.0	0	2	2	2	2	2	2	2
2. MULTIPLE DX										
0–19 Years	5	1.1	<1	1	1	1	1	1	2	2
20–34	14	1.8	2	1	1	1	2	3	7	7
35–49	35	1.5	2	1	1	1	2	2	2	9
50–64	23	1.4	<1	1	1	1	2	2	2	3
65+	17	2.5	9	1	1	1	3	4	13	13
TOTAL SINGLE DX	**4**	**1.9**	**<1**	**1**	**1**	**2**	**3**	**3**	**3**	**3**
TOTAL MULTIPLE DX	**94**	**1.6**	**2**	**1**	**1**	**1**	**2**	**2**	**3**	**9**
TOTAL										
0–19 Years	5	1.1	<1	1	1	1	1	1	2	2
20–34	15	1.7	2	1	1	1	2	3	7	7
35–49	36	1.5	2	1	1	1	2	2	2	9
50–64	24	1.5	<1	1	1	1	2	2	3	3
65+	18	2.5	8	1	1	1	3	4	13	13
GRAND TOTAL	**98**	**1.6**	**2**	**1**	**1**	**1**	**2**	**2**	**3**	**9**

21.6: TURBINECTOMY

Type of Patients	Observed Patients	Avg. Stay	Vari-ance	Percentiles 10th	25th	50th	75th	90th	95th	99th
1. SINGLE DX										
0–19 Years	0									
20–34	1	2.0	0	2	2	2	2	2	2	2
35–49	0									
50–64	0									
65+	0									
2. MULTIPLE DX										
0–19 Years	36	2.4	76	1	1	1	2	2	2	68
20–34	10	1.4	<1	1	1	1	2	2	4	4
35–49	14	1.9	5	1	1	1	1	4	6	12
50–64	14	1.7	1	1	1	1	2	4	4	4
65+	10	6.2	112	1	1	2	7	35	35	35
TOTAL SINGLE DX	**1**	**2.0**	**0**	**2**	**2**	**2**	**2**	**2**	**2**	**2**
TOTAL MULTIPLE DX	**84**	**2.4**	**51**	**1**	**1**	**1**	**2**	**2**	**4**	**35**
TOTAL										
0–19 Years	36	2.4	76	1	1	1	2	2	2	68
20–34	11	1.6	<1	1	1	1	2	2	4	4
35–49	14	1.9	5	1	1	1	1	4	6	12
50–64	14	1.7	1	1	1	1	2	4	4	4
65+	10	6.2	112	1	1	2	7	35	35	35
GRAND TOTAL	**85**	**2.4**	**49**	**1**	**1**	**1**	**2**	**2**	**4**	**35**

21.7: NASAL FRACTURE REDUCTION

Type of Patients	Observed Patients	Avg. Stay	Vari-ance	Percentiles						
				10th	25th	50th	75th	90th	95th	99th
1. SINGLE DX										
0–19 Years	7	1.2	<1	1	1	1	1	3	3	3
20–34	7	1.1	<1	1	1	1	1	2	2	2
35–49	8	2.0	5	1	1	1	2	8	8	8
50–64	0									
65+	1	1.0	0	1	1	1	1	1	1	1
2. MULTIPLE DX										
0–19 Years	32	3.5	14	1	1	2	3	12	12	12
20–34	60	2.9	6	1	1	2	4	7	8	9
35–49	50	2.6	4	1	1	2	3	4	5	14
50–64	25	3.9	9	1	2	3	4	8	10	14
65+	33	4.3	5	1	3	4	6	8	9	10
TOTAL SINGLE DX	**23**	**1.5**	**2**	**1**	**1**	**1**	**1**	**3**	**4**	**8**
TOTAL MULTIPLE DX	**200**	**3.3**	**8**	**1**	**1**	**2**	**4**	**7**	**9**	**12**
TOTAL										
0–19 Years	39	3.2	13	1	1	2	3	12	12	12
20–34	67	2.8	6	1	1	2	3	7	8	9
35–49	58	2.5	4	1	1	2	3	4	6	14
50–64	25	3.9	9	1	2	3	4	8	10	14
65+	34	4.2	5	1	3	4	6	8	9	10
GRAND TOTAL	**223**	**3.1**	**8**	**1**	**1**	**2**	**4**	**7**	**9**	**12**

21.71: CLSD REDUCTION NASAL FX

Type of Patients	Observed Patients	Avg. Stay	Vari-ance	Percentiles						
				10th	25th	50th	75th	90th	95th	99th
1. SINGLE DX										
0–19 Years	3	1.4	<1	1	1	1	1	3	3	3
20–34	3	1.0	0	1	1	1	1	1	1	1
35–49	3	1.2	<1	1	1	1	1	2	2	2
50–64	0									
65+	1	1.0	0	1	1	1	1	1	1	1
2. MULTIPLE DX										
0–19 Years	21	4.0	18	1	1	2	5	12	12	12
20–34	38	2.9	5	1	1	2	4	7	7	7
35–49	20	2.2	<1	1	1	2	3	4	4	4
50–64	15	4.6	12	1	2	4	8	8	14	14
65+	18	4.4	5	2	3	4	5	8	9	9
TOTAL SINGLE DX	**10**	**1.2**	**<1**	**1**	**1**	**1**	**1**	**2**	**3**	**3**
TOTAL MULTIPLE DX	**112**	**3.4**	**9**	**1**	**1**	**2**	**4**	**8**	**12**	**12**
TOTAL										
0–19 Years	24	3.8	17	1	1	2	3	12	12	12
20–34	41	2.8	5	1	1	2	3	7	7	7
35–49	23	2.0	<1	1	1	2	3	3	4	4
50–64	15	4.6	12	1	2	4	8	8	14	14
65+	19	4.3	5	2	3	4	5	8	8	9
GRAND TOTAL	**122**	**3.3**	**8**	**1**	**1**	**2**	**4**	**7**	**12**	**12**

21.72: OPEN REDUCTION NASAL FX

Type of Patients	Observed Patients	Avg. Stay	Vari-ance	Percentiles						
				10th	25th	50th	75th	90th	95th	99th
1. SINGLE DX										
0–19 Years	4	1.0	0	1	1	1	1	1	1	1
20–34	4	1.2	<1	1	1	1	1	2	2	2
35–49	5	2.6	8	1	1	1	4	8	8	8
50–64	0									
65+	0									
2. MULTIPLE DX										
0–19 Years	11	2.6	7	1	1	1	3	6	6	12
20–34	22	2.9	8	1	1	2	4	8	9	9
35–49	30	3.0	6	1	2	2	4	5	6	14
50–64	10	2.8	4	1	2	2	3	4	10	10
65+	15	4.1	6	1	2	4	6	6	10	10
TOTAL SINGLE DX	**13**	**1.7**	**4**	**1**	**1**	**1**	**1**	**4**	**8**	**8**
TOTAL MULTIPLE DX	**88**	**3.0**	**7**	**1**	**1**	**2**	**4**	**6**	**9**	**12**
TOTAL										
0–19 Years	15	2.4	6	1	1	1	3	6	6	12
20–34	26	2.7	7	1	1	1	3	8	9	9
35–49	35	2.9	6	1	1	2	4	5	8	14
50–64	10	2.8	4	1	2	2	3	4	10	10
65+	15	4.1	6	1	2	4	6	6	10	10
GRAND TOTAL	**101**	**2.9**	**6**	**1**	**1**	**2**	**4**	**6**	**8**	**12**

21.8: NASAL REP & PLASTIC OPS

Type of Patients	Observed Patients	Avg. Stay	Vari-ance	Percentiles						
				10th	25th	50th	75th	90th	95th	99th
1. SINGLE DX										
0–19 Years	30	1.3	<1	1	1	1	1	3	3	3
20–34	15	1.4	<1	1	1	1	1	3	4	4
35–49	15	1.6	<1	1	1	1	2	3	4	4
50–64	11	1.2	<1	1	1	1	1	2	2	2
65+	7	1.6	1	1	1	1	1	4	4	4
2. MULTIPLE DX										
0–19 Years	150	1.8	4	1	1	1	2	3	5	12
20–34	157	1.9	3	1	1	1	2	3	5	11
35–49	170	1.8	2	1	1	1	2	3	4	9
50–64	146	1.8	3	1	1	1	2	3	5	12
65+	203	2.8	6	1	1	2	4	7	8	11
TOTAL SINGLE DX	**78**	**1.4**	**<1**	**1**	**1**	**1**	**1**	**3**	**3**	**4**
TOTAL MULTIPLE DX	**826**	**2.0**	**4**	**1**	**1**	**1**	**2**	**4**	**6**	**11**
TOTAL										
0–19 Years	180	1.7	4	1	1	1	2	3	4	12
20–34	172	1.8	3	1	1	1	2	3	5	11
35–49	185	1.8	2	1	1	1	2	3	4	9
50–64	157	1.7	2	1	1	1	2	3	5	12
65+	210	2.8	6	1	1	2	4	6	8	9
GRAND TOTAL	**904**	**2.0**	**4**	**1**	**1**	**1**	**2**	**4**	**6**	**11**

21.81: NASAL LACERATION SUTURE

Type of Patients	Observed Patients	Avg. Stay	Vari-ance	Percentiles						
				10th	25th	50th	75th	90th	95th	99th
1. SINGLE DX										
0–19 Years	3	1.0	0	1	1	1	1	1	1	1
20–34	0									
35–49	2	1.0	0	1	1	1	1	1	1	1
50–64	1	1.0	0	1	1	1	1	1	1	1
65+	0									
2. MULTIPLE DX										
0–19 Years	17	1.2	<1	1	1	1	1	2	2	4
20–34	54	2.2	5	1	1	1	3	5	7	14
35–49	49	2.0	2	1	1	1	3	5	5	9
50–64	33	2.5	2	1	1	2	3	5	6	6
65+	80	3.6	6	1	2	3	5	7	9	9
TOTAL SINGLE DX	**6**	**1.0**	**0**	**1**	**1**	**1**	**1**	**1**	**1**	**1**
TOTAL MULTIPLE DX	**233**	**2.6**	**4**	**1**	**1**	**2**	**3**	**6**	**7**	**9**
TOTAL										
0–19 Years	20	1.2	<1	1	1	1	1	2	2	4
20–34	54	2.2	5	1	1	1	3	5	7	14
35–49	51	1.9	2	1	1	1	3	4	5	9
50–64	34	2.5	2	1	1	2	3	5	6	6
65+	80	3.6	6	1	2	3	5	7	9	9
GRAND TOTAL	**239**	**2.5**	**4**	**1**	**1**	**2**	**3**	**5**	**7**	**9**

21.88: SEPTOPLASTY NEC

Type of Patients	Observed Patients	Avg. Stay	Vari-ance	Percentiles						
				10th	25th	50th	75th	90th	95th	99th
1. SINGLE DX										
0–19 Years	0									
20–34	2	1.4	<1	1	1	1	2	2	2	2
35–49	4	1.0	0	1	1	1	1	1	1	1
50–64	0									
65+	2	2.8	3	1	1	4	4	4	4	4
2. MULTIPLE DX										
0–19 Years	24	2.0	11	1	1	1	2	3	5	25
20–34	64	1.6	2	1	1	1	2	3	4	11
35–49	73	1.7	2	1	1	1	2	3	4	6
50–64	81	1.6	3	1	1	1	1	3	4	12
65+	61	2.5	5	1	1	2	3	6	8	8
TOTAL SINGLE DX	**8**	**1.5**	**1**	**1**	**1**	**1**	**1**	**4**	**4**	**4**
TOTAL MULTIPLE DX	**303**	**1.9**	**4**	**1**	**1**	**1**	**2**	**4**	**5**	**12**
TOTAL										
0–19 Years	24	2.0	11	1	1	1	2	3	5	25
20–34	66	1.6	2	1	1	1	2	3	4	11
35–49	77	1.7	2	1	1	1	2	3	4	6
50–64	81	1.6	3	1	1	1	1	3	4	12
65+	63	2.5	5	1	1	2	3	6	8	8
GRAND TOTAL	**311**	**1.8**	**4**	**1**	**1**	**1**	**2**	**4**	**5**	**12**

21.89: NASAL REPAIR NEC

Type of Patients	Observed Patients	Avg. Stay	Vari-ance	Percentiles						
				10th	25th	50th	75th	90th	95th	99th
1. SINGLE DX										
0–19 Years	10	1.9	<1	1	1	1	3	3	3	3
20–34	1	4.0	0	4	4	4	4	4	4	4
35–49	3	1.3	<1	1	1	1	2	2	2	2
50–64	3	1.3	<1	1	1	1	1	2	2	2
65+	3	1.2	<1	1	1	1	1	2	2	2
2. MULTIPLE DX										
0–19 Years	27	3.2	12	1	1	1	4	12	12	12
20–34	13	3.1	8	1	1	2	5	5	11	11
35–49	13	2.4	5	1	1	2	3	3	11	11
50–64	10	1.0	0	1	1	1	1	1	1	1
65+	34	1.8	2	1	1	1	2	3	6	7
TOTAL SINGLE DX	**20**	**1.8**	**1**	**1**	**1**	**1**	**3**	**3**	**3**	**4**
TOTAL MULTIPLE DX	**97**	**2.5**	**7**	**1**	**1**	**1**	**3**	**5**	**11**	**12**
TOTAL										
0–19 Years	37	2.8	9	1	1	1	3	7	12	12
20–34	14	3.2	7	1	1	3	5	5	11	11
35–49	16	2.3	5	1	1	2	3	3	3	11
50–64	13	1.1	<1	1	1	1	1	1	2	2
65+	37	1.8	2	1	1	1	2	3	6	7
GRAND TOTAL	**117**	**2.4**	**6**	**1**	**1**	**1**	**3**	**5**	**7**	**12**

21.9: OTHER NASAL OPERATIONS

Type of Patients	Observed Patients	Avg. Stay	Vari-ance	Percentiles						
				10th	25th	50th	75th	90th	95th	99th
1. SINGLE DX										
0–19 Years	1	4.0	0	4	4	4	4	4	4	4
20–34	0									
35–49	0									
50–64	0									
65+	1	1.0	0	1	1	1	1	1	1	1
2. MULTIPLE DX										
0–19 Years	6	4.8	17	1	1	1	10	10	10	10
20–34	2	6.1	3	5	5	5	8	8	8	8
35–49	1	14.0	0	14	14	14	14	14	14	14
50–64	0									
65+	0									
TOTAL SINGLE DX	**2**	**3.6**	**1**	**1**	**4**	**4**	**4**	**4**	**4**	**4**
TOTAL MULTIPLE DX	**9**	**5.7**	**20**	**1**	**1**	**6**	**10**	**10**	**14**	**14**
TOTAL										
0–19 Years	7	4.6	13	1	1	4	7	10	10	10
20–34	2	6.1	3	5	5	5	8	8	8	8
35–49	1	14.0	0	14	14	14	14	14	14	14
50–64	0									
65+	1	1.0	0	1	1	1	1	1	1	1
GRAND TOTAL	**11**	**5.2**	**17**	**1**	**1**	**4**	**10**	**10**	**14**	**14**

22.0: NASAL SINUS ASP & LAVAGE

Type of Patients	Observed Patients	Avg. Stay	Vari-ance	Percentiles						
				10th	25th	50th	75th	90th	95th	99th
1. SINGLE DX										
0–19 Years	0									
20–34	2	3.3	7	1	1	5	5	5	5	5
35–49	0									
50–64	1	3.0	0	3	3	3	3	3	3	3
65+	0									
2. MULTIPLE DX										
0–19 Years	10	7.2	42	2	2	3	11	19	19	22
20–34	1	7.0	0	7	7	7	7	7	7	7
35–49	3	6.2	20	1	6	6	6	14	14	14
50–64	9	6.1	18	2	3	5	8	10	21	21
65+	5	10.5	28	5	5	14	15	15	15	15
TOTAL SINGLE DX	**3**	**3.2**	**4**	**1**	**1**	**3**	**5**	**5**	**5**	**5**
TOTAL MULTIPLE DX	**28**	**7.4**	**31**	**2**	**2**	**6**	**11**	**15**	**19**	**22**
TOTAL										
0–19 Years	10	7.2	42	2	2	3	11	19	19	22
20–34	3	4.5	8	1	1	5	7	7	7	7
35–49	3	6.2	20	1	6	6	6	14	14	14
50–64	10	5.9	18	2	3	5	8	10	21	21
65+	5	10.5	28	5	5	14	15	15	15	15
GRAND TOTAL	**31**	**7.2**	**31**	**2**	**2**	**5**	**11**	**15**	**19**	**22**

22.1: NASAL SINUS DXTIC PX

Type of Patients	Observed Patients	Avg. Stay	Vari-ance	Percentiles						
				10th	25th	50th	75th	90th	95th	99th
1. SINGLE DX										
0–19 Years	0									
20–34	0									
35–49	1	3.0	0	3	3	3	3	3	3	3
50–64	0									
65+	2	4.0	0	4	4	4	4	4	4	4
2. MULTIPLE DX										
0–19 Years	12	10.9	45	1	3	14	14	20	20	23
20–34	7	4.7	7	2	3	5	5	6	11	11
35–49	14	5.9	20	3	3	5	6	11	11	21
50–64	18	4.0	6	2	3	3	4	7	9	13
65+	19	6.3	41	1	2	3	9	16	16	27
TOTAL SINGLE DX	**3**	**3.7**	**<1**	**3**	**3**	**4**	**4**	**4**	**4**	**4**
TOTAL MULTIPLE DX	**70**	**6.5**	**32**	**1**	**3**	**4**	**10**	**14**	**16**	**23**
TOTAL										
0–19 Years	12	10.9	45	1	3	14	14	20	20	23
20–34	7	4.7	7	2	3	5	5	6	11	11
35–49	15	5.7	19	3	3	5	6	11	11	21
50–64	18	4.0	6	2	3	3	4	7	9	13
65+	21	6.1	37	1	2	4	9	16	16	27
GRAND TOTAL	**73**	**6.4**	**31**	**1**	**3**	**4**	**9**	**14**	**16**	**23**

22.2: INTRANASAL ANTROTOMY

Type of Patients	Observed Patients	Avg. Stay	Vari-ance	Percentiles						
				10th	25th	50th	75th	90th	95th	99th
1. SINGLE DX										
0–19 Years	0									
20–34	0									
35–49	1	1.0	0	1	1	1	1	1	1	1
50–64	1	1.0	0	1	1	1	1	1	1	1
65+	0									
2. MULTIPLE DX										
0–19 Years	10	7.7	60	2	2	2	17	17	17	25
20–34	5	6.4	23	1	1	9	11	11	11	11
35–49	4	3.4	4	1	2	2	5	6	6	6
50–64	6	4.9	35	2	2	2	6	12	22	22
65+	5	2.9	6	1	1	1	5	7	7	7
TOTAL SINGLE DX	**2**	**1.0**	**0**	**1**	**1**	**1**	**1**	**1**	**1**	**1**
TOTAL MULTIPLE DX	**30**	**6.0**	**40**	**1**	**2**	**2**	**11**	**17**	**17**	**25**
TOTAL										
0–19 Years	10	7.7	60	2	2	2	17	17	17	25
20–34	5	6.4	23	1	1	9	11	11	11	11
35–49	5	3.1	4	1	2	2	5	6	6	6
50–64	7	4.6	34	2	2	2	2	12	22	22
65+	5	2.9	6	1	1	1	5	7	7	7
GRAND TOTAL	**32**	**5.9**	**39**	**1**	**2**	**2**	**11**	**17**	**17**	**25**

22.3: EXT MAXILLARY ANTROTOMY

Type of Patients	Observed Patients	Avg. Stay	Vari-ance	Percentiles						
				10th	25th	50th	75th	90th	95th	99th
1. SINGLE DX										
0–19 Years	2	3.5	9	1	1	4	6	6	6	6
20–34	0									
35–49	3	6.3	23	2	2	3	11	11	11	11
50–64	2	1.0	0	1	1	1	1	1	1	1
65+	1	2.0	0	2	2	2	2	2	2	2
2. MULTIPLE DX										
0–19 Years	7	6.6	39	1	2	2	8	14	20	20
20–34	6	1.9	2	1	1	2	2	4	6	6
35–49	13	5.0	25	1	2	4	5	9	23	23
50–64	18	1.9	5	1	1	1	1	4	5	14
65+	12	4.8	66	1	1	2	3	24	27	27
TOTAL SINGLE DX	**8**	**3.9**	**15**	**1**	**1**	**2**	**6**	**11**	**11**	**11**
TOTAL MULTIPLE DX	**56**	**3.2**	**20**	**1**	**1**	**2**	**3**	**6**	**14**	**24**
TOTAL										
0–19 Years	9	5.9	33	1	2	2	8	14	20	20
20–34	6	1.9	2	1	1	2	2	4	6	6
35–49	16	5.2	24	2	2	4	5	11	11	23
50–64	20	1.8	5	1	1	1	1	4	5	14
65+	13	4.6	61	1	1	2	3	24	27	27
GRAND TOTAL	**64**	**3.3**	**20**	**1**	**1**	**2**	**4**	**7**	**11**	**24**

22.4: FRONT SINUSOT & SINUSECT

Type of Patients	Observed Patients	Avg. Stay	Variance	10th	25th	50th	75th	90th	95th	99th
1. SINGLE DX										
0–19 Years	1	10.0	0	10	10	10	10	10	10	10
20–34	4	3.2	2	2	2	2	5	5	5	5
35–49	6	1.4	<1	1	1	1	1	3	3	3
50–64	1	1.0	0	1	1	1	1	1	1	1
65+	3	1.4	<1	1	1	1	2	2	2	2
2. MULTIPLE DX										
0–19 Years	12	5.8	12	1	2	7	7	9	14	14
20–34	17	6.1	26	1	2	5	8	14	18	18
35–49	28	7.1	28	2	3	5	14	15	15	16
50–64	34	4.0	9	1	2	3	6	8	8	14
65+	23	3.7	19	1	2	2	3	8	12	21
TOTAL SINGLE DX	**15**	**3.0**	**10**	**1**	**1**	**1**	**3**	**10**	**10**	**10**
TOTAL MULTIPLE DX	**114**	**5.5**	**22**	**1**	**2**	**3**	**8**	**14**	**15**	**18**
TOTAL										
0–19 Years	13	6.3	12	1	3	7	7	10	14	14
20–34	21	5.8	24	1	2	4	8	14	18	18
35–49	34	6.4	28	1	2	3	14	15	15	16
50–64	35	3.9	9	1	2	3	6	8	8	14
65+	26	3.5	18	1	1	2	3	8	12	21
GRAND TOTAL	**129**	**5.3**	**21**	**1**	**2**	**3**	**8**	**14**	**15**	**18**

22.5: OTHER NASAL SINUSOTOMY

Type of Patients	Observed Patients	Avg. Stay	Variance	10th	25th	50th	75th	90th	95th	99th
1. SINGLE DX										
0–19 Years	0									
20–34	0									
35–49	0									
50–64	0									
65+	0									
2. MULTIPLE DX										
0–19 Years	9	5.9	2	4	6	6	7	7	9	9
20–34	10	7.0	41	1	2	6	11	18	18	18
35–49	14	8.1	41	1	2	5	11	19	19	19
50–64	19	3.5	15	1	1	2	5	7	16	16
65+	14	8.2	48	1	2	7	11	21	21	21
TOTAL SINGLE DX	**0**									
TOTAL MULTIPLE DX	**66**	**6.5**	**31**	**1**	**2**	**5**	**10**	**17**	**19**	**21**
TOTAL										
0–19 Years	9	5.9	2	4	6	6	7	7	9	9
20–34	10	7.0	41	1	2	6	11	18	18	18
35–49	14	8.1	41	1	2	5	11	19	19	19
50–64	19	3.5	15	1	1	2	5	7	16	16
65+	14	8.2	48	1	2	7	11	21	21	21
GRAND TOTAL	**66**	**6.5**	**31**	**1**	**2**	**5**	**10**	**17**	**19**	**21**

22.6: OTHER NASAL SINUSECTOMY

Type of Patients	Observed Patients	Avg. Stay	Variance	10th	25th	50th	75th	90th	95th	99th
1. SINGLE DX										
0–19 Years	6	2.1	2	1	1	1	4	5	5	5
20–34	5	2.7	<1	2	2	3	3	4	4	4
35–49	14	2.7	3	1	1	3	3	6	7	7
50–64	17	2.1	1	1	1	2	2	4	4	5
65+	4	2.4	2	1	2	2	4	4	4	4
2. MULTIPLE DX										
0–19 Years	148	6.6	48	1	2	4	8	15	22	31
20–34	104	3.9	27	1	1	2	5	8	11	27
35–49	146	3.2	25	1	1	1	3	7	13	32
50–64	250	3.8	40	1	1	1	3	8	21	35
65+	198	4.1	32	1	1	2	5	10	13	39
TOTAL SINGLE DX	**46**	**2.3**	**2**	**1**	**1**	**2**	**3**	**4**	**5**	**7**
TOTAL MULTIPLE DX	**846**	**4.4**	**37**	**1**	**1**	**2**	**5**	**12**	**18**	**35**
TOTAL										
0–19 Years	154	6.5	47	1	1	4	7	15	21	31
20–34	109	3.9	27	1	1	2	5	8	11	27
35–49	160	3.1	24	1	1	1	3	7	13	32
50–64	267	3.7	37	1	1	1	3	8	20	35
65+	202	4.1	32	1	1	2	5	10	13	39
GRAND TOTAL	**892**	**4.3**	**36**	**1**	**1**	**2**	**5**	**11**	**16**	**35**

22.62: EXC MAX SINUS LESION NEC

Type of Patients	Observed Patients	Avg. Stay	Variance	10th	25th	50th	75th	90th	95th	99th
1. SINGLE DX										
0–19 Years	0									
20–34	2	2.8	2	2	2	2	4	4	4	4
35–49	6	2.5	1	1	2	3	3	4	4	4
50–64	7	1.8	3	1	1	1	1	5	5	5
65+	2	2.0	0	2	2	2	2	2	2	2
2. MULTIPLE DX										
0–19 Years	49	8.3	75	1	3	4	13	19	25	42
20–34	23	3.2	14	1	1	1	3	9	14	16
35–49	38	4.0	58	1	1	1	2	8	32	35
50–64	68	6.5	80	1	1	2	7	21	35	35
65+	63	6.1	60	1	2	3	8	13	19	39
TOTAL SINGLE DX	**17**	**2.3**	**2**	**1**	**1**	**2**	**3**	**4**	**4**	**5**
TOTAL MULTIPLE DX	**241**	**6.1**	**67**	**1**	**1**	**3**	**7**	**19**	**24**	**39**
TOTAL										
0–19 Years	49	8.3	75	1	3	4	13	19	25	42
20–34	25	3.2	14	1	1	1	3	9	12	16
35–49	44	3.8	51	1	1	2	3	7	19	35
50–64	75	6.2	77	1	1	2	7	21	24	35
65+	65	6.0	59	1	2	3	8	13	19	39
GRAND TOTAL	**258**	**5.9**	**64**	**1**	**1**	**3**	**7**	**18**	**23**	**36**

22.63: ETHMOIDECTOMY

Type of Patients	Observed Patients	Avg. Stay	Vari-ance	Percentiles						
				10th	25th	50th	75th	90th	95th	99th
1. SINGLE DX										
0–19 Years	2	1.5	<1	1	1	2	2	2	2	2
20–34	2	2.4	<1	2	2	2	3	3	3	3
35–49	3	1.5	<1	1	1	1	3	3	3	3
50–64	7	2.3	2	1	1	2	4	4	4	4
65+	2	2.8	4	1	1	4	4	4	4	4
2. MULTIPLE DX										
0–19 Years	90	5.8	32	1	1	4	7	14	18	28
20–34	71	3.9	28	1	1	2	5	8	8	40
35–49	91	2.9	13	1	1	1	3	7	13	13
50–64	150	2.8	22	1	1	1	3	5	8	24
65+	109	2.6	11	1	1	1	2	8	10	18
TOTAL SINGLE DX	**16**	**2.2**	**1**	**1**	**1**	**2**	**3**	**4**	**4**	**4**
TOTAL MULTIPLE DX	**511**	**3.6**	**23**	**1**	**1**	**2**	**4**	**8**	**13**	**24**
TOTAL										
0–19 Years	92	5.7	32	1	1	4	7	14	18	28
20–34	73	3.9	28	1	1	2	5	8	8	40
35–49	94	2.9	13	1	1	1	3	7	13	13
50–64	157	2.8	20	1	1	1	3	5	8	23
65+	111	2.6	11	1	1	1	2	8	10	18
GRAND TOTAL	**527**	**3.6**	**23**	**1**	**1**	**2**	**4**	**8**	**13**	**24**

22.7: NASAL SINUS REPAIR

Type of Patients	Observed Patients	Avg. Stay	Vari-ance	Percentiles						
				10th	25th	50th	75th	90th	95th	99th
1. SINGLE DX										
0–19 Years	0									
20–34	0									
35–49	1	4.0	0	4	4	4	4	4	4	4
50–64	1	2.0	0	2	2	2	2	2	2	2
65+	0									
2. MULTIPLE DX										
0–19 Years	3	1.0	0	1	1	1	1	1	1	1
20–34	2	1.9	1	1	1	1	3	3	3	3
35–49	7	6.4	15	1	3	7	7	14	14	14
50–64	11	3.8	9	1	1	3	8	8	8	8
65+	6	1.8	1	1	1	1	3	4	4	4
TOTAL SINGLE DX	**2**	**3.4**	**1**	**2**	**2**	**4**	**4**	**4**	**4**	**4**
TOTAL MULTIPLE DX	**29**	**4.2**	**12**	**1**	**1**	**3**	**7**	**8**	**10**	**14**
TOTAL										
0–19 Years	3	1.0	0	1	1	1	1	1	1	1
20–34	2	1.9	1	1	1	1	3	3	3	3
35–49	8	6.1	14	1	3	7	7	14	14	14
50–64	12	3.7	9	1	1	3	8	8	8	8
65+	6	1.8	1	1	1	1	3	4	4	4
GRAND TOTAL	**31**	**4.2**	**12**	**1**	**1**	**3**	**7**	**8**	**10**	**14**

22.9: OTHER NASAL SINUS OPS

Type of Patients	Observed Patients	Avg. Stay	Vari-ance	Percentiles						
				10th	25th	50th	75th	90th	95th	99th
1. SINGLE DX										
0–19 Years	0									
20–34	0									
35–49	0									
50–64	0									
65+	0									
2. MULTIPLE DX										
0–19 Years	0									
20–34	3	1.2	<1	1	1	1	1	2	2	2
35–49	2	1.0	0	1	1	1	1	1	1	1
50–64	3	7.8	2	6	7	9	9	9	9	9
65+	3	1.9	4	1	1	1	1	6	6	6
TOTAL SINGLE DX	**0**									
TOTAL MULTIPLE DX	**11**	**2.6**	**8**	**1**	**1**	**1**	**2**	**9**	**9**	**9**
TOTAL										
0–19 Years	0									
20–34	3	1.2	<1	1	1	1	1	2	2	2
35–49	2	1.0	0	1	1	1	1	1	1	1
50–64	3	7.8	2	6	7	9	9	9	9	9
65+	3	1.9	4	1	1	1	1	6	6	6
GRAND TOTAL	**11**	**2.6**	**8**	**1**	**1**	**1**	**2**	**9**	**9**	**9**

23.0: FORCEPS TOOTH EXTRACTION

Type of Patients	Observed Patients	Avg. Stay	Vari-ance	Percentiles						
				10th	25th	50th	75th	90th	95th	99th
1. SINGLE DX										
0–19 Years	5	3.0	3	1	2	3	5	5	5	5
20–34	3	2.0	<1	1	1	2	3	3	3	3
35–49	4	1.4	<1	1	1	1	2	2	2	2
50–64	1	2.0	0	2	2	2	2	2	2	2
65+	0									
2. MULTIPLE DX										
0–19 Years	90	3.2	18	1	1	2	3	7	9	34
20–34	66	6.7	74	1	2	3	8	15	25	50
35–49	63	7.0	78	1	2	4	8	18	25	49
50–64	29	7.1	63	1	2	3	7	23	23	26
65+	36	6.4	50	1	2	6	8	10	14	46
TOTAL SINGLE DX	**13**	**2.2**	**2**	**1**	**1**	**2**	**3**	**5**	**5**	**5**
TOTAL MULTIPLE DX	**284**	**5.6**	**54**	**1**	**2**	**3**	**6**	**12**	**20**	**42**
TOTAL										
0–19 Years	95	3.2	18	1	1	2	3	7	9	34
20–34	69	6.5	72	1	2	3	8	15	20	50
35–49	67	6.7	75	1	2	3	8	18	25	49
50–64	30	7.0	62	1	2	3	7	23	23	26
65+	36	6.4	50	1	2	6	8	10	14	46
GRAND TOTAL	**297**	**5.5**	**53**	**1**	**2**	**3**	**6**	**12**	**20**	**42**

23.09: TOOTH EXTRACTION NEC

Type of Patients	Observed Patients	Avg. Stay	Vari-ance	10th	25th	50th	75th	90th	95th	99th
1. SINGLE DX										
0–19 Years	4	3.6	2	2	3	3	5	5	5	5
20–34	3	2.0	<1	1	1	2	3	3	3	3
35–49	4	1.4	<1	1	1	1	2	2	2	2
50–64	1	2.0	0	2	2	2	2	2	2	2
65+	0									
2. MULTIPLE DX										
0–19 Years	74	3.3	21	1	1	2	3	7	10	34
20–34	66	6.7	74	1	2	3	8	15	25	50
35–49	63	7.0	78	1	2	4	8	18	25	49
50–64	29	7.1	63	1	2	3	7	23	23	26
65+	35	6.4	51	1	2	6	8	10	14	46
TOTAL SINGLE DX	**12**	**2.3**	**2**	**1**	**1**	**2**	**3**	**5**	**5**	**5**
TOTAL MULTIPLE DX	**267**	**5.8**	**56**	**1**	**2**	**3**	**6**	**12**	**20**	**42**
TOTAL										
0–19 Years	78	3.3	20	1	1	2	3	7	9	34
20–34	69	6.5	72	1	2	3	8	15	20	50
35–49	67	6.7	75	1	2	3	8	18	25	49
50–64	30	7.0	62	1	2	3	7	23	23	26
65+	35	6.4	51	1	2	6	8	10	14	46
GRAND TOTAL	**279**	**5.7**	**55**	**1**	**2**	**3**	**6**	**12**	**20**	**42**

23.1: SURG REMOVAL OF TOOTH

Type of Patients	Observed Patients	Avg. Stay	Vari-ance	10th	25th	50th	75th	90th	95th	99th
1. SINGLE DX										
0–19 Years	4	1.6	<1	1	1	1	2	3	3	3
20–34	8	3.0	4	2	2	2	3	8	8	8
35–49	4	2.9	3	1	2	2	4	5	5	5
50–64	0									
65+	0									
2. MULTIPLE DX										
0–19 Years	56	2.5	6	1	1	2	3	5	8	16
20–34	55	3.8	36	1	2	3	4	6	8	43
35–49	45	3.6	29	1	1	2	4	7	9	42
50–64	38	5.1	40	1	1	3	6	10	20	33
65+	42	4.7	46	1	1	3	4	10	17	39
TOTAL SINGLE DX	**16**	**2.5**	**3**	**1**	**1**	**2**	**3**	**5**	**5**	**8**
TOTAL MULTIPLE DX	**236**	**3.8**	**30**	**1**	**1**	**2**	**4**	**7**	**10**	**33**
TOTAL										
0–19 Years	60	2.5	6	1	1	2	3	5	8	16
20–34	63	3.7	33	1	2	3	4	6	8	43
35–49	49	3.6	27	1	1	2	4	6	8	28
50–64	38	5.1	40	1	1	3	6	10	20	33
65+	42	4.7	46	1	1	3	4	10	17	39
GRAND TOTAL	**252**	**3.7**	**29**	**1**	**1**	**2**	**4**	**7**	**10**	**33**

23.19: SURG TOOTH EXTRACT NEC

Type of Patients	Observed Patients	Avg. Stay	Vari-ance	10th	25th	50th	75th	90th	95th	99th
1. SINGLE DX										
0–19 Years	4	1.6	<1	1	1	1	2	3	3	3
20–34	8	3.0	4	2	2	2	3	8	8	8
35–49	4	2.9	3	1	2	2	4	5	5	5
50–64	0									
65+	0									
2. MULTIPLE DX										
0–19 Years	56	2.5	6	1	1	2	3	5	8	16
20–34	53	3.8	39	1	2	2	3	6	8	43
35–49	44	3.7	29	1	1	2	4	7	9	42
50–64	38	5.1	40	1	1	3	6	10	20	33
65+	42	4.7	46	1	1	3	4	10	17	39
TOTAL SINGLE DX	**16**	**2.5**	**3**	**1**	**1**	**2**	**3**	**5**	**5**	**8**
TOTAL MULTIPLE DX	**233**	**3.8**	**30**	**1**	**1**	**2**	**4**	**7**	**10**	**33**
TOTAL										
0–19 Years	60	2.5	6	1	1	2	3	5	8	16
20–34	61	3.7	36	1	2	2	3	6	8	43
35–49	48	3.6	28	1	1	2	4	6	8	42
50–64	38	5.1	40	1	1	3	6	10	20	33
65+	42	4.7	46	1	1	3	4	10	17	39
GRAND TOTAL	**249**	**3.7**	**29**	**1**	**1**	**2**	**4**	**7**	**10**	**33**

23.2: TOOTH RESTOR BY FILLING

Type of Patients	Observed Patients	Avg. Stay	Vari-ance	10th	25th	50th	75th	90th	95th	99th
1. SINGLE DX										
0–19 Years	0									
20–34	0									
35–49	0									
50–64	0									
65+	0									
2. MULTIPLE DX										
0–19 Years	15	3.4	33	1	1	1	2	8	20	20
20–34	6	15.4	392	1	1	10	16	49	49	49
35–49	1	2.0	0	2	2	2	2	2	2	2
50–64	1	2.0	0	2	2	2	2	2	2	2
65+	0									
TOTAL SINGLE DX	**0**									
TOTAL MULTIPLE DX	**23**	**5.3**	**103**	**1**	**1**	**1**	**2**	**20**	**20**	**49**
TOTAL										
0–19 Years	15	3.4	33	1	1	1	2	8	20	20
20–34	6	15.4	392	1	1	10	16	49	49	49
35–49	1	2.0	0	2	2	2	2	2	2	2
50–64	1	2.0	0	2	2	2	2	2	2	2
65+	0									
GRAND TOTAL	**23**	**5.3**	**103**	**1**	**1**	**1**	**2**	**20**	**20**	**49**

23.3: TOOTH RESTOR BY INLAY

Type of Patients	Observed Patients	Avg. Stay	Vari-ance	Percentiles						
				10th	25th	50th	75th	90th	95th	99th
1. SINGLE DX										
0–19 Years	0									
20–34	0									
35–49	0									
50–64	0									
65+	0									
2. MULTIPLE DX										
0–19 Years	0									
20–34	0									
35–49	0									
50–64	0									
65+	0									
TOTAL SINGLE DX	**0**									
TOTAL MULTIPLE DX	**0**									
TOTAL										
0–19 Years	0									
20–34	0									
35–49	0									
50–64	0									
65+	0									
GRAND TOTAL	**0**									

23.4: OTHER DENTAL RESTORATION

Type of Patients	Observed Patients	Avg. Stay	Vari-ance	Percentiles						
				10th	25th	50th	75th	90th	95th	99th
1. SINGLE DX										
0–19 Years	0									
20–34	0									
35–49	0									
50–64	0									
65+	0									
2. MULTIPLE DX										
0–19 Years	20	2.8	9	1	1	2	3	6	7	15
20–34	1	2.0	0	2	2	2	2	2	2	2
35–49	2	1.6	<1	1	1	2	2	2	2	2
50–64	0									
65+	1	1.0	0	1	1	1	1	1	1	1
TOTAL SINGLE DX	**0**									
TOTAL MULTIPLE DX	**24**	**2.6**	**8**	**1**	**1**	**2**	**3**	**6**	**7**	**15**
TOTAL										
0–19 Years	20	2.8	9	1	1	2	3	6	7	15
20–34	1	2.0	0	2	2	2	2	2	2	2
35–49	2	1.6	<1	1	1	2	2	2	2	2
50–64	0									
65+	1	1.0	0	1	1	1	1	1	1	1
GRAND TOTAL	**24**	**2.6**	**8**	**1**	**1**	**2**	**3**	**6**	**7**	**15**

23.5: TOOTH IMPLANTATION

Type of Patients	Observed Patients	Avg. Stay	Vari-ance	Percentiles						
				10th	25th	50th	75th	90th	95th	99th
1. SINGLE DX										
0–19 Years	0									
20–34	0									
35–49	0									
50–64	0									
65+	0									
2. MULTIPLE DX										
0–19 Years	3	1.5	<1	1	1	2	2	2	2	2
20–34	2	1.1	<1	1	1	1	1	2	2	2
35–49	0									
50–64	0									
65+	0									
TOTAL SINGLE DX	**0**									
TOTAL MULTIPLE DX	**5**	**1.3**	**<1**	**1**	**1**	**1**	**2**	**2**	**2**	**2**
TOTAL										
0–19 Years	3	1.5	<1	1	1	2	2	2	2	2
20–34	2	1.1	<1	1	1	1	1	2	2	2
35–49	0									
50–64	0									
65+	0									
GRAND TOTAL	**5**	**1.3**	**<1**	**1**	**1**	**1**	**2**	**2**	**2**	**2**

23.6: PROSTHETIC DENTAL IMPL

Type of Patients	Observed Patients	Avg. Stay	Vari-ance	Percentiles						
				10th	25th	50th	75th	90th	95th	99th
1. SINGLE DX										
0–19 Years	0									
20–34	0									
35–49	0									
50–64	0									
65+	0									
2. MULTIPLE DX										
0–19 Years	0									
20–34	0									
35–49	1	3.0	0	3	3	3	3	3	3	3
50–64	0									
65+	0									
TOTAL SINGLE DX	**0**									
TOTAL MULTIPLE DX	**1**	**3.0**	**0**	**3**	**3**	**3**	**3**	**3**	**3**	**3**
TOTAL										
0–19 Years	0									
20–34	0									
35–49	1	3.0	0	3	3	3	3	3	3	3
50–64	0									
65+	0									
GRAND TOTAL	**1**	**3.0**	**0**	**3**	**3**	**3**	**3**	**3**	**3**	**3**

23.7: ROOT CANAL TX & APICOECT

Type of Patients	Observed Patients	Avg. Stay	Vari-ance	Percentiles						
				10th	25th	50th	75th	90th	95th	99th
1. SINGLE DX										
0–19 Years	0									
20–34	0									
35–49	0									
50–64	0									
65+	0									
2. MULTIPLE DX										
0–19 Years	5	2.4	2	1	2	2	2	5	5	5
20–34	1	16.0	0	16	16	16	16	16	16	16
35–49	0									
50–64	0									
65+	1	1.0	0	1	1	1	1	1	1	1
TOTAL SINGLE DX	**0**									
TOTAL MULTIPLE DX	**7**	**3.3**	**17**	**1**	**1**	**2**	**2**	**5**	**16**	**16**
TOTAL										
0–19 Years	5	2.4	2	1	2	2	2	5	5	5
20–34	1	16.0	0	16	16	16	16	16	16	16
35–49	0									
50–64	0									
65+	1	1.0	0	1	1	1	1	1	1	1
GRAND TOTAL	**7**	**3.3**	**17**	**1**	**1**	**2**	**2**	**5**	**16**	**16**

24.0: GUM OR ALVEOLAR INCISION

Type of Patients	Observed Patients	Avg. Stay	Vari-ance	Percentiles						
				10th	25th	50th	75th	90th	95th	99th
1. SINGLE DX										
0–19 Years	9	2.2	1	1	1	2	3	3	5	5
20–34	9	1.8	<1	1	1	2	2	3	3	4
35–49	5	2.1	2	1	1	1	3	4	4	4
50–64	2	1.7	<1	1	1	2	2	2	2	2
65+	2	2.5	4	1	1	3	4	4	4	4
2. MULTIPLE DX										
0–19 Years	21	3.3	6	1	2	3	3	5	11	11
20–34	27	3.4	7	1	2	2	4	10	10	10
35–49	23	2.4	3	1	1	2	3	4	6	9
50–64	21	3.2	6	1	2	2	4	7	9	9
65+	16	4.0	8	1	2	3	6	8	9	9
TOTAL SINGLE DX	**27**	**2.0**	**1**	**1**	**1**	**2**	**3**	**3**	**4**	**5**
TOTAL MULTIPLE DX	**108**	**3.3**	**6**	**1**	**2**	**2**	**4**	**8**	**10**	**11**
TOTAL										
0–19 Years	30	3.0	5	1	2	2	3	5	9	11
20–34	36	3.0	6	1	2	2	3	6	10	10
35–49	28	2.3	3	1	1	2	3	4	5	9
50–64	23	3.1	5	1	2	2	4	7	9	9
65+	18	3.9	8	1	2	3	6	8	9	9
GRAND TOTAL	**135**	**3.0**	**6**	**1**	**1**	**2**	**3**	**6**	**9**	**11**

24.1: TOOTH & GUM DXTIC PX

Type of Patients	Observed Patients	Avg. Stay	Vari-ance	Percentiles						
				10th	25th	50th	75th	90th	95th	99th
1. SINGLE DX										
0–19 Years	0									
20–34	0									
35–49	0									
50–64	0									
65+	0									
2. MULTIPLE DX										
0–19 Years	0									
20–34	0									
35–49	1	7.0	0	7	7	7	7	7	7	7
50–64	0									
65+	3	4.1	6	1	1	5	6	6	6	6
TOTAL SINGLE DX	**0**									
TOTAL MULTIPLE DX	**4**	**5.1**	**6**	**1**	**5**	**6**	**7**	**7**	**7**	**7**
TOTAL										
0–19 Years	0									
20–34	0									
35–49	1	7.0	0	7	7	7	7	7	7	7
50–64	0									
65+	3	4.1	6	1	1	5	6	6	6	6
GRAND TOTAL	**4**	**5.1**	**6**	**1**	**5**	**6**	**7**	**7**	**7**	**7**

24.2: GINGIVOPLASTY

Type of Patients	Observed Patients	Avg. Stay	Vari-ance	Percentiles						
				10th	25th	50th	75th	90th	95th	99th
1. SINGLE DX										
0–19 Years	0									
20–34	0									
35–49	0									
50–64	0									
65+	0									
2. MULTIPLE DX										
0–19 Years	2	1.3	<1	1	1	1	2	2	2	2
20–34	1	14.0	0	14	14	14	14	14	14	14
35–49	0									
50–64	7	5.8	17	1	2	5	11	11	12	12
65+	1	1.0	0	1	1	1	1	1	1	1
TOTAL SINGLE DX	**0**									
TOTAL MULTIPLE DX	**11**	**4.8**	**21**	**1**	**1**	**2**	**8**	**12**	**14**	**14**
TOTAL										
0–19 Years	2	1.3	<1	1	1	1	2	2	2	2
20–34	1	14.0	0	14	14	14	14	14	14	14
35–49	0									
50–64	7	5.8	17	1	2	5	11	11	12	12
65+	1	1.0	0	1	1	1	1	1	1	1
GRAND TOTAL	**11**	**4.8**	**21**	**1**	**1**	**2**	**8**	**12**	**14**	**14**

24.3: OTHER OPERATIONS ON GUMS

Type of Patients	Observed Patients	Avg. Stay	Vari-ance	10th	25th	50th	75th	90th	95th	99th
1. SINGLE DX										
0–19 Years	0									
20–34	0									
35–49	0									
50–64	0									
65+	1	2.0	0	2	2	2	2	2	2	2
2. MULTIPLE DX										
0–19 Years	7	1.5	<1	1	1	1	2	2	3	3
20–34	5	1.0	0	1	1	1	1	1	1	1
35–49	1	3.0	0	3	3	3	3	3	3	3
50–64	2	4.7	29	1	1	1	9	9	9	9
65+	6	2.1	4	1	1	1	2	6	6	6
TOTAL SINGLE DX	**1**	**2.0**	**0**	**2**	**2**	**2**	**2**	**2**	**2**	**2**
TOTAL MULTIPLE DX	**21**	**1.9**	**3**	**1**	**1**	**1**	**2**	**3**	**6**	**9**
TOTAL										
0–19 Years	7	1.5	<1	1	1	1	2	2	3	3
20–34	5	1.0	0	1	1	1	1	1	1	1
35–49	1	3.0	0	3	3	3	3	3	3	3
50–64	2	4.7	29	1	1	1	9	9	9	9
65+	7	2.1	3	1	1	1	2	6	6	6
GRAND TOTAL	**22**	**1.9**	**3**	**1**	**1**	**1**	**2**	**3**	**6**	**9**

24.4: EXC OF DENTAL LES OF JAW

Type of Patients	Observed Patients	Avg. Stay	Vari-ance	10th	25th	50th	75th	90th	95th	99th
1. SINGLE DX										
0–19 Years	2	1.0	0	1	1	1	1	1	1	1
20–34	1	2.0	0	2	2	2	2	2	2	2
35–49	3	1.3	<1	1	1	1	2	2	2	2
50–64	2	6.0	6	1	7	7	7	7	7	7
65+	0									
2. MULTIPLE DX										
0–19 Years	7	3.5	9	1	2	2	5	11	11	11
20–34	8	4.2	7	1	1	6	6	6	10	10
35–49	10	4.2	26	1	1	2	4	13	20	20
50–64	14	4.0	19	1	1	1	5	10	10	19
65+	14	3.2	6	1	1	2	5	9	9	9
TOTAL SINGLE DX	**8**	**2.2**	**6**	**1**	**1**	**1**	**2**	**7**	**7**	**7**
TOTAL MULTIPLE DX	**53**	**3.8**	**13**	**1**	**1**	**2**	**5**	**9**	**10**	**19**
TOTAL										
0–19 Years	9	2.4	6	1	1	1	3	5	11	11
20–34	9	4.1	7	1	1	6	6	6	6	10
35–49	13	3.4	21	1	1	2	3	6	13	20
50–64	16	4.3	17	1	1	4	7	10	10	19
65+	14	3.2	6	1	1	2	5	9	9	9
GRAND TOTAL	**61**	**3.5**	**12**	**1**	**1**	**2**	**5**	**9**	**10**	**19**

24.5: ALVEOLOPLASTY

Type of Patients	Observed Patients	Avg. Stay	Vari-ance	10th	25th	50th	75th	90th	95th	99th
1. SINGLE DX										
0–19 Years	5	1.1	<1	1	1	1	1	2	2	2
20–34	0									
35–49	0									
50–64	0									
65+	0									
2. MULTIPLE DX										
0–19 Years	24	1.7	<1	1	1	2	2	3	3	3
20–34	10	3.5	12	1	1	1	6	6	7	18
35–49	22	3.9	11	1	2	3	4	10	12	12
50–64	27	4.8	24	1	2	3	6	13	18	22
65+	30	4.5	15	1	2	3	6	11	14	15
TOTAL SINGLE DX	**5**	**1.1**	**<1**	**1**	**1**	**1**	**1**	**2**	**2**	**2**
TOTAL MULTIPLE DX	**113**	**3.6**	**13**	**1**	**1**	**2**	**5**	**7**	**12**	**18**
TOTAL										
0–19 Years	29	1.6	<1	1	1	1	2	3	3	3
20–34	10	3.5	12	1	1	1	6	6	7	18
35–49	22	3.9	11	1	2	3	4	10	12	12
50–64	27	4.8	24	1	2	3	6	13	18	22
65+	30	4.5	15	1	2	3	6	11	14	15
GRAND TOTAL	**118**	**3.5**	**13**	**1**	**1**	**2**	**4**	**7**	**12**	**18**

24.6: EXPOSURE OF TOOTH

Type of Patients	Observed Patients	Avg. Stay	Vari-ance	10th	25th	50th	75th	90th	95th	99th
1. SINGLE DX										
0–19 Years	0									
20–34	0									
35–49	0									
50–64	0									
65+	0									
2. MULTIPLE DX										
0–19 Years	1	3.0	0	3	3	3	3	3	3	3
20–34	0									
35–49	0									
50–64	0									
65+	0									
TOTAL SINGLE DX	**0**									
TOTAL MULTIPLE DX	**1**	**3.0**	**0**	**3**	**3**	**3**	**3**	**3**	**3**	**3**
TOTAL										
0–19 Years	1	3.0	0	3	3	3	3	3	3	3
20–34	0									
35–49	0									
50–64	0									
65+	0									
GRAND TOTAL	**1**	**3.0**	**0**	**3**	**3**	**3**	**3**	**3**	**3**	**3**

24.7: APPL ORTHODONT APPLIANCE

Type of Patients	Observed Patients	Avg. Stay	Vari-ance	10th	25th	50th	75th	90th	95th	99th
1. SINGLE DX										
0–19 Years	1	3.0	0	3	3	3	3	3	3	3
20–34	0									
35–49	0									
50–64	1	2.0	0	2	2	2	2	2	2	2
65+	0									
2. MULTIPLE DX										
0–19 Years	1	1.0	0	1	1	1	1	1	1	1
20–34	1	1.0	0	1	1	1	1	1	1	1
35–49	1	6.0	0	6	6	6	6	6	6	6
50–64	1	3.0	0	3	3	3	3	3	3	3
65+	0									
TOTAL SINGLE DX	**2**	**2.5**	**<1**	**2**	**2**	**2**	**3**	**3**	**3**	**3**
TOTAL MULTIPLE DX	**4**	**2.5**	**5**	**1**	**1**	**1**	**3**	**6**	**6**	**6**
TOTAL										
0–19 Years	2	2.2	2	1	1	3	3	3	3	3
20–34	1	1.0	0	1	1	1	1	1	1	1
35–49	1	6.0	0	6	6	6	6	6	6	6
50–64	2	2.4	<1	2	2	2	3	3	3	3
65+	0									
GRAND TOTAL	**6**	**2.5**	**3**	**1**	**1**	**2**	**3**	**6**	**6**	**6**

24.8: OTHER ORTHODONTIC OP

Type of Patients	Observed Patients	Avg. Stay	Vari-ance	10th	25th	50th	75th	90th	95th	99th
1. SINGLE DX										
0–19 Years	1	1.0	0	1	1	1	1	1	1	1
20–34	0									
35–49	1	4.0	0	4	4	4	4	4	4	4
50–64	0									
65+	0									
2. MULTIPLE DX										
0–19 Years	0									
20–34	0									
35–49	0									
50–64	0									
65+	0									
TOTAL SINGLE DX	**2**	**2.5**	**3**	**1**	**1**	**1**	**4**	**4**	**4**	**4**
TOTAL MULTIPLE DX	**0**									
TOTAL										
0–19 Years	1	1.0	0	1	1	1	1	1	1	1
20–34	0									
35–49	1	4.0	0	4	4	4	4	4	4	4
50–64	0									
65+	0									
GRAND TOTAL	**2**	**2.5**	**3**	**1**	**1**	**1**	**4**	**4**	**4**	**4**

24.9: OTHER DENTAL OPERATION

Type of Patients	Observed Patients	Avg. Stay	Vari-ance	10th	25th	50th	75th	90th	95th	99th
1. SINGLE DX										
0–19 Years	0									
20–34	0									
35–49	1	1.0	0	1	1	1	1	1	1	1
50–64	1	1.0	0	1	1	1	1	1	1	1
65+	0									
2. MULTIPLE DX										
0–19 Years	1	1.0	0	1	1	1	1	1	1	1
20–34	0									
35–49	1	2.0	0	2	2	2	2	2	2	2
50–64	1	1.0	0	1	1	1	1	1	1	1
65+	1	3.0	0	3	3	3	3	3	3	3
TOTAL SINGLE DX	**2**	**1.0**	**0**	**1**	**1**	**1**	**1**	**1**	**1**	**1**
TOTAL MULTIPLE DX	**4**	**1.8**	**<1**	**1**	**1**	**2**	**3**	**3**	**3**	**3**
TOTAL										
0–19 Years	1	1.0	0	1	1	1	1	1	1	1
20–34	0									
35–49	2	1.6	<1	1	1	2	2	2	2	2
50–64	2	1.0	0	1	1	1	1	1	1	1
65+	1	3.0	0	3	3	3	3	3	3	3
GRAND TOTAL	**6**	**1.6**	**<1**	**1**	**1**	**1**	**2**	**3**	**3**	**3**

25.0: DXTIC PX ON TONGUE

Type of Patients	Observed Patients	Avg. Stay	Vari-ance	10th	25th	50th	75th	90th	95th	99th
1. SINGLE DX										
0–19 Years	0									
20–34	1	1.0	0	1	1	1	1	1	1	1
35–49	3	3.5	9	1	1	3	7	7	7	7
50–64	5	1.0	0	1	1	1	1	1	1	1
65+	3	1.6	2	1	1	1	1	4	4	4
2. MULTIPLE DX										
0–19 Years	1	1.0	0	1	1	1	1	1	1	1
20–34	1	16.0	0	16	16	16	16	16	16	16
35–49	14	6.8	21	1	4	5	12	12	16	16
50–64	23	4.1	22	1	1	2	5	9	11	22
65+	24	5.6	50	1	2	3	5	11	28	32
TOTAL SINGLE DX	**12**	**1.5**	**2**	**1**	**1**	**1**	**1**	**4**	**4**	**7**
TOTAL MULTIPLE DX	**63**	**5.4**	**34**	**1**	**1**	**3**	**6**	**12**	**16**	**32**
TOTAL										
0–19 Years	1	1.0	0	1	1	1	1	1	1	1
20–34	2	5.2	61	1	1	1	16	16	16	16
35–49	17	6.3	20	1	2	5	12	12	16	16
50–64	28	3.4	18	1	1	1	3	9	11	22
65+	27	4.9	44	1	1	3	5	9	28	32
GRAND TOTAL	**75**	**4.6**	**30**	**1**	**1**	**3**	**5**	**11**	**16**	**28**

25.1: EXC/DESTR TONGUE LES

Type of Patients	Observed Patients	Avg. Stay	Vari-ance	Percentiles						
				10th	25th	50th	75th	90th	95th	99th
1. SINGLE DX										
0–19 Years	5	1.4	<1	1	1	1	1	3	3	3
20–34	1	1.0	0	1	1	1	1	1	1	1
35–49	2	2.1	2	1	1	3	3	3	3	3
50–64	3	1.0	0	1	1	1	1	1	1	1
65+	2	1.4	<1	1	1	1	2	2	2	2
2. MULTIPLE DX										
0–19 Years	3	1.0	0	1	1	1	1	1	1	1
20–34	3	4.3	5	1	3	6	6	6	6	6
35–49	19	2.4	4	1	1	1	4	5	5	9
50–64	27	3.8	14	1	1	2	7	9	9	16
65+	33	6.4	76	1	1	2	13	13	20	43
TOTAL SINGLE DX	**13**	**1.4**	**<1**	**1**	**1**	**1**	**1**	**3**	**3**	**3**
TOTAL MULTIPLE DX	**85**	**4.6**	**41**	**1**	**1**	**2**	**6**	**13**	**13**	**43**
TOTAL										
0–19 Years	8	1.3	<1	1	1	1	1	3	3	3
20–34	4	3.8	6	1	1	3	6	6	6	6
35–49	21	2.4	4	1	1	1	4	5	5	9
50–64	30	3.6	14	1	1	2	4	9	9	16
65+	35	5.9	72	1	1	2	11	13	13	43
GRAND TOTAL	**98**	**4.1**	**37**	**1**	**1**	**2**	**5**	**13**	**13**	**43**

25.2: PARTIAL GLOSSECTOMY

Type of Patients	Observed Patients	Avg. Stay	Vari-ance	Percentiles						
				10th	25th	50th	75th	90th	95th	99th
1. SINGLE DX										
0–19 Years	1	1.0	0	1	1	1	1	1	1	1
20–34	4	3.6	3	1	3	3	6	6	6	6
35–49	12	2.9	7	1	1	2	4	6	11	11
50–64	12	3.0	5	1	2	3	3	5	10	10
65+	5	3.4	7	1	1	2	7	7	7	7
2. MULTIPLE DX										
0–19 Years	9	4.5	5	2	2	4	6	8	8	8
20–34	2	3.5	<1	3	3	3	4	4	4	4
35–49	41	3.3	11	1	1	2	4	7	9	22
50–64	66	4.4	23	1	1	3	6	9	16	26
65+	100	4.1	13	1	2	3	6	9	11	20
TOTAL SINGLE DX	**34**	**3.1**	**5**	**1**	**1**	**3**	**4**	**6**	**7**	**11**
TOTAL MULTIPLE DX	**218**	**4.0**	**14**	**1**	**1**	**3**	**6**	**9**	**11**	**21**
TOTAL										
0–19 Years	10	4.3	5	1	2	4	6	8	8	8
20–34	6	3.6	2	3	3	3	4	6	6	6
35–49	53	3.2	10	1	1	2	4	7	9	22
50–64	78	4.2	20	1	1	3	5	9	11	26
65+	105	4.1	13	1	2	3	6	9	11	20
GRAND TOTAL	**252**	**3.9**	**14**	**1**	**1**	**3**	**5**	**9**	**11**	**20**

25.3: COMPLETE GLOSSECTOMY

Type of Patients	Observed Patients	Avg. Stay	Vari-ance	Percentiles						
				10th	25th	50th	75th	90th	95th	99th
1. SINGLE DX										
0–19 Years	0									
20–34	0									
35–49	0									
50–64	0									
65+	1	11.0	0	11	11	11	11	11	11	11
2. MULTIPLE DX										
0–19 Years	0									
20–34	0									
35–49	2	7.9	15	3	3	10	10	10	10	10
50–64	4	10.1	13	6	8	12	14	14	14	14
65+	1	12.0	0	12	12	12	12	12	12	12
TOTAL SINGLE DX	**1**	**11.0**	**0**	**11**	**11**	**11**	**11**	**11**	**11**	**11**
TOTAL MULTIPLE DX	**7**	**9.5**	**12**	**3**	**8**	**10**	**12**	**14**	**14**	**14**
TOTAL										
0–19 Years	0									
20–34	0									
35–49	2	7.9	15	3	3	10	10	10	10	10
50–64	4	10.1	13	6	8	12	14	14	14	14
65+	2	11.5	<1	11	11	11	12	12	12	12
GRAND TOTAL	**8**	**9.6**	**11**	**3**	**8**	**10**	**12**	**14**	**14**	**14**

25.4: RADICAL GLOSSECTOMY

Type of Patients	Observed Patients	Avg. Stay	Vari-ance	Percentiles						
				10th	25th	50th	75th	90th	95th	99th
1. SINGLE DX										
0–19 Years	0									
20–34	0									
35–49	0									
50–64	0									
65+	0									
2. MULTIPLE DX										
0–19 Years	0									
20–34	0									
35–49	1	9.0	0	9	9	9	9	9	9	9
50–64	2	14.2	33	10	10	10	19	19	19	19
65+	4	6.3	24	3	3	4	14	14	14	14
TOTAL SINGLE DX	**0**									
TOTAL MULTIPLE DX	**7**	**8.2**	**32**	**3**	**4**	**4**	**14**	**14**	**19**	**19**
TOTAL										
0–19 Years	0									
20–34	0									
35–49	1	9.0	0	9	9	9	9	9	9	9
50–64	2	14.2	33	10	10	10	19	19	19	19
65+	4	6.3	24	3	3	4	14	14	14	14
GRAND TOTAL	**7**	**8.2**	**32**	**3**	**4**	**4**	**14**	**14**	**19**	**19**

25.5: REPAIR OF TONGUE

Type of Patients	Observed Patients	Avg. Stay	Vari-ance	Percentiles						
				10th	25th	50th	75th	90th	95th	99th
1. SINGLE DX										
0–19 Years	7	1.4	<1	1	1	1	2	2	2	2
20–34	1	1.0	0	1	1	1	1	1	1	1
35–49	1	1.0	0	1	1	1	1	1	1	1
50–64	1	1.0	0	1	1	1	1	1	1	1
65+	0									
2. MULTIPLE DX										
0–19 Years	11	1.8	<1	1	1	2	2	2	2	4
20–34	14	3.0	2	1	2	3	4	5	5	6
35–49	22	2.9	4	1	1	3	4	6	6	8
50–64	17	3.0	4	1	1	2	3	7	7	7
65+	12	4.2	20	1	2	2	5	6	17	17
TOTAL SINGLE DX	**10**	**1.4**	**<1**	**1**	**1**	**1**	**2**	**2**	**2**	**2**
TOTAL MULTIPLE DX	**76**	**2.8**	**5**	**1**	**1**	**2**	**3**	**6**	**7**	**17**
TOTAL										
0–19 Years	18	1.6	<1	1	1	2	2	2	2	4
20–34	15	2.9	2	1	2	3	4	5	5	6
35–49	23	2.8	4	1	1	2	4	6	6	8
50–64	18	2.9	4	1	1	2	3	7	7	7
65+	12	4.2	20	1	2	2	5	6	17	17
GRAND TOTAL	**86**	**2.5**	**4**	**1**	**1**	**2**	**3**	**5**	**6**	**8**

25.9: OTHER TONGUE OPERATIONS

Type of Patients	Observed Patients	Avg. Stay	Vari-ance	Percentiles						
				10th	25th	50th	75th	90th	95th	99th
1. SINGLE DX										
0–19 Years	0									
20–34	1	2.0	0	2	2	2	2	2	2	2
35–49	0									
50–64	0									
65+	0									
2. MULTIPLE DX										
0–19 Years	183	3.2	10	1	2	2	3	4	11	17
20–34	1	6.0	0	6	6	6	6	6	6	6
35–49	12	2.7	2	1	1	3	4	5	5	5
50–64	9	3.6	4	1	2	3	6	6	6	6
65+	4	3.4	<1	2	3	4	4	4	4	4
TOTAL SINGLE DX	**1**	**2.0**	**0**	**2**	**2**	**2**	**2**	**2**	**2**	**2**
TOTAL MULTIPLE DX	**209**	**3.2**	**9**	**1**	**2**	**2**	**3**	**5**	**9**	**17**
TOTAL										
0–19 Years	183	3.2	10	1	2	2	3	4	11	17
20–34	2	4.5	6	2	2	6	6	6	6	6
35–49	12	2.7	2	1	1	3	4	5	5	5
50–64	9	3.6	4	1	2	3	6	6	6	6
65+	4	3.4	<1	2	3	4	4	4	4	4
GRAND TOTAL	**210**	**3.2**	**9**	**1**	**2**	**2**	**3**	**5**	**9**	**17**

25.91: LINGUAL FRENOTOMY

Type of Patients	Observed Patients	Avg. Stay	Vari-ance	Percentiles						
				10th	25th	50th	75th	90th	95th	99th
1. SINGLE DX										
0–19 Years	0									
20–34	0									
35–49	0									
50–64	0									
65+	0									
2. MULTIPLE DX										
0–19 Years	136	3.1	11	1	2	2	3	4	10	17
20–34	0									
35–49	0									
50–64	1	2.0	0	2	2	2	2	2	2	2
65+	0									
TOTAL SINGLE DX	**0**									
TOTAL MULTIPLE DX	**137**	**3.1**	**11**	**1**	**2**	**2**	**3**	**4**	**10**	**17**
TOTAL										
0–19 Years	136	3.1	11	1	2	2	3	4	10	17
20–34	0									
35–49	0									
50–64	1	2.0	0	2	2	2	2	2	2	2
65+	0									
GRAND TOTAL	**137**	**3.1**	**11**	**1**	**2**	**2**	**3**	**4**	**10**	**17**

26.0: INC SALIVARY GLAND/DUCT

Type of Patients	Observed Patients	Avg. Stay	Vari-ance	Percentiles						
				10th	25th	50th	75th	90th	95th	99th
1. SINGLE DX										
0–19 Years	5	2.8	<1	2	2	3	3	4	4	4
20–34	0									
35–49	3	2.5	1	1	1	3	3	3	3	3
50–64	3	2.3	1	1	1	3	3	3	3	3
65+	1	1.0	0	1	1	1	1	1	1	1
2. MULTIPLE DX										
0–19 Years	4	4.2	8	2	2	4	8	8	8	8
20–34	4	4.6	8	2	2	7	7	7	7	7
35–49	12	5.8	22	2	3	5	6	9	19	19
50–64	15	3.2	3	1	2	3	4	6	6	7
65+	14	4.3	18	2	2	3	6	8	10	21
TOTAL SINGLE DX	**12**	**2.5**	**<1**	**1**	**2**	**3**	**3**	**4**	**4**	**4**
TOTAL MULTIPLE DX	**49**	**4.3**	**13**	**2**	**2**	**3**	**6**	**8**	**10**	**21**
TOTAL										
0–19 Years	9	3.3	3	2	2	3	4	8	8	8
20–34	4	4.6	8	2	2	7	7	7	7	7
35–49	15	5.1	19	1	3	4	6	9	19	19
50–64	18	3.0	3	1	2	3	4	6	6	7
65+	15	4.2	18	2	2	2	6	8	10	21
GRAND TOTAL	**61**	**3.9**	**11**	**1**	**2**	**3**	**5**	**7**	**9**	**21**

26.1: SALIVARY GLAND DXTIC PX

Type of Patients	Observed Patients	Avg. Stay	Variance	Percentiles 10th	25th	50th	75th	90th	95th	99th
1. SINGLE DX										
0–19 Years	1	6.0	0	6	6	6	6	6	6	6
20–34	0									
35–49	1	2.0	0	2	2	2	2	2	2	2
50–64	0									
65+	0									
2. MULTIPLE DX										
0–19 Years	4	5.9	8	4	4	5	10	10	10	10
20–34	6	4.5	12	1	1	4	8	9	9	9
35–49	12	5.0	29	1	2	4	5	13	13	25
50–64	19	6.9	39	1	2	5	10	15	15	27
65+	32	6.1	17	2	4	6	7	9	11	25
TOTAL SINGLE DX	**2**	**4.6**	**5**	**2**	**2**	**6**	**6**	**6**	**6**	**6**
TOTAL MULTIPLE DX	**73**	**5.9**	**23**	**2**	**3**	**5**	**7**	**10**	**15**	**25**
TOTAL										
0–19 Years	5	5.9	5	4	4	5	6	10	10	10
20–34	6	4.5	12	1	1	4	8	9	9	9
35–49	13	4.8	28	1	2	4	5	9	13	25
50–64	19	6.9	39	1	2	5	10	15	15	27
65+	32	6.1	17	2	4	6	7	9	11	25
GRAND TOTAL	**75**	**5.9**	**22**	**2**	**3**	**5**	**7**	**10**	**15**	**25**

26.2: EXC OF SG LESION

Type of Patients	Observed Patients	Avg. Stay	Variance	Percentiles 10th	25th	50th	75th	90th	95th	99th
1. SINGLE DX										
0–19 Years	9	2.0	1	1	1	2	2	4	5	5
20–34	6	1.4	1	1	1	1	1	4	4	4
35–49	6	1.4	<1	1	1	1	2	2	2	2
50–64	10	1.1	<1	1	1	1	1	2	2	2
65+	1	1.0	0	1	1	1	1	1	1	1
2. MULTIPLE DX										
0–19 Years	3	1.4	<1	1	1	1	1	3	3	3
20–34	4	1.3	<1	1	1	1	1	2	2	2
35–49	19	1.9	2	1	1	2	2	2	2	9
50–64	21	1.4	<1	1	1	1	1	2	3	4
65+	29	2.9	24	1	1	1	2	4	12	25
TOTAL SINGLE DX	**32**	**1.6**	**<1**	**1**	**1**	**1**	**2**	**2**	**4**	**5**
TOTAL MULTIPLE DX	**76**	**2.1**	**11**	**1**	**1**	**1**	**2**	**2**	**4**	**25**
TOTAL										
0–19 Years	12	1.9	1	1	1	2	2	3	4	5
20–34	10	1.3	<1	1	1	1	1	2	4	4
35–49	25	1.7	2	1	1	2	2	2	2	9
50–64	31	1.3	<1	1	1	1	1	2	3	4
65+	30	2.8	23	1	1	1	2	4	12	25
GRAND TOTAL	**108**	**1.9**	**8**	**1**	**1**	**1**	**2**	**2**	**4**	**25**

26.29: SALIVARY LES EXC NEC

Type of Patients	Observed Patients	Avg. Stay	Variance	Percentiles 10th	25th	50th	75th	90th	95th	99th
1. SINGLE DX										
0–19 Years	9	2.0	1	1	1	2	2	4	5	5
20–34	6	1.4	1	1	1	1	1	4	4	4
35–49	6	1.4	<1	1	1	1	2	2	2	2
50–64	10	1.1	<1	1	1	1	1	2	2	2
65+	1	1.0	0	1	1	1	1	1	1	1
2. MULTIPLE DX										
0–19 Years	3	1.4	<1	1	1	1	1	3	3	3
20–34	4	1.3	<1	1	1	1	1	2	2	2
35–49	18	1.6	<1	1	1	2	2	2	2	2
50–64	21	1.4	<1	1	1	1	1	2	3	4
65+	29	2.9	24	1	1	1	2	4	12	25
TOTAL SINGLE DX	**32**	**1.6**	**<1**	**1**	**1**	**1**	**2**	**2**	**4**	**5**
TOTAL MULTIPLE DX	**75**	**2.0**	**11**	**1**	**1**	**1**	**2**	**2**	**4**	**25**
TOTAL										
0–19 Years	12	1.9	1	1	1	2	2	3	4	5
20–34	10	1.3	<1	1	1	1	1	2	4	4
35–49	24	1.5	<1	1	1	2	2	2	2	2
50–64	31	1.3	<1	1	1	1	1	2	3	4
65+	30	2.8	23	1	1	1	2	4	12	25
GRAND TOTAL	**107**	**1.9**	**7**	**1**	**1**	**1**	**2**	**2**	**4**	**25**

26.3: SIALOADENECTOMY

Type of Patients	Observed Patients	Avg. Stay	Variance	Percentiles 10th	25th	50th	75th	90th	95th	99th
1. SINGLE DX										
0–19 Years	21	1.6	3	1	1	1	2	2	3	12
20–34	72	1.4	<1	1	1	1	2	2	3	4
35–49	110	1.3	<1	1	1	1	1	2	2	3
50–64	127	1.3	<1	1	1	1	1	2	2	3
65+	52	1.2	<1	1	1	1	1	2	2	3
2. MULTIPLE DX										
0–19 Years	30	1.9	<1	1	1	2	3	3	4	4
20–34	42	1.5	1	1	1	1	2	2	3	7
35–49	144	1.5	1	1	1	1	2	2	3	7
50–64	302	1.7	4	1	1	1	2	3	4	10
65+	343	2.3	13	1	1	1	2	4	6	24
TOTAL SINGLE DX	**382**	**1.3**	**<1**	**1**	**1**	**1**	**1**	**2**	**2**	**3**
TOTAL MULTIPLE DX	**861**	**1.9**	**7**	**1**	**1**	**1**	**2**	**3**	**4**	**16**
TOTAL										
0–19 Years	51	1.8	2	1	1	1	2	3	4	12
20–34	114	1.4	<1	1	1	1	2	2	3	5
35–49	254	1.4	<1	1	1	1	2	2	3	6
50–64	429	1.6	3	1	1	1	2	3	4	7
65+	395	2.2	11	1	1	1	2	3	5	24
GRAND TOTAL	**1,243**	**1.7**	**5**	**1**	**1**	**1**	**2**	**3**	**4**	**12**

26.30: SIALOADENECTOMY NOS

Type of Patients	Observed Patients	Avg. Stay	Vari-ance	10th	25th	50th	75th	90th	95th	99th
1. SINGLE DX										
0–19 Years	4	1.3	<1	1	1	1	2	2	2	2
20–34	5	1.9	<1	1	1	2	3	3	3	3
35–49	12	1.2	<1	1	1	1	1	1	4	4
50–64	19	1.4	<1	1	1	1	2	2	3	4
65+	5	1.5	<1	1	1	2	2	2	2	2
2. MULTIPLE DX										
0–19 Years	3	1.6	<1	1	1	2	2	2	2	2
20–34	2	1.0	0	1	1	1	1	1	1	1
35–49	14	1.7	1	1	1	1	2	3	3	6
50–64	26	1.9	8	1	1	1	1	3	4	16
65+	28	1.6	2	1	1	1	1	3	4	8
TOTAL SINGLE DX	**45**	**1.4**	**<1**	**1**	**1**	**1**	**2**	**2**	**3**	**4**
TOTAL MULTIPLE DX	**73**	**1.7**	**4**	**1**	**1**	**1**	**2**	**3**	**4**	**16**
TOTAL										
0–19 Years	7	1.4	<1	1	1	1	2	2	2	2
20–34	7	1.7	<1	1	1	1	2	3	3	3
35–49	26	1.5	1	1	1	1	2	3	4	6
50–64	45	1.7	5	1	1	1	1	3	4	16
65+	33	1.6	2	1	1	1	2	3	4	8
GRAND TOTAL	**118**	**1.6**	**2**	**1**	**1**	**1**	**2**	**3**	**3**	**8**

26.31: PARTIAL SIALOADENECTOMY

Type of Patients	Observed Patients	Avg. Stay	Vari-ance	10th	25th	50th	75th	90th	95th	99th
1. SINGLE DX										
0–19 Years	10	2.0	6	1	1	1	2	2	12	12
20–34	38	1.2	<1	1	1	1	1	2	2	3
35–49	64	1.3	<1	1	1	1	1	2	2	3
50–64	70	1.3	<1	1	1	1	1	2	2	3
65+	24	1.1	<1	1	1	1	1	1	2	2
2. MULTIPLE DX										
0–19 Years	10	1.6	<1	1	1	1	2	3	3	3
20–34	23	1.2	<1	1	1	1	1	2	2	3
35–49	84	1.4	<1	1	1	1	2	2	3	3
50–64	153	1.5	3	1	1	1	1	2	4	7
65+	173	2.6	24	1	1	1	2	3	9	24
TOTAL SINGLE DX	**206**	**1.3**	**<1**	**1**	**1**	**1**	**1**	**2**	**2**	**3**
TOTAL MULTIPLE DX	**443**	**1.9**	**11**	**1**	**1**	**1**	**2**	**3**	**4**	**24**
TOTAL										
0–19 Years	20	1.8	3	1	1	1	2	3	3	12
20–34	61	1.2	<1	1	1	1	1	2	2	3
35–49	148	1.3	<1	1	1	1	2	2	3	3
50–64	223	1.5	3	1	1	1	1	2	3	7
65+	197	2.4	21	1	1	1	2	3	7	24
GRAND TOTAL	**649**	**1.7**	**8**	**1**	**1**	**1**	**2**	**2**	**3**	**20**

26.32: COMPLETE SIALOADENECTOMY

Type of Patients	Observed Patients	Avg. Stay	Vari-ance	10th	25th	50th	75th	90th	95th	99th
1. SINGLE DX										
0–19 Years	7	1.3	<1	1	1	1	1	2	3	3
20–34	29	1.5	<1	1	1	1	2	3	3	4
35–49	34	1.3	<1	1	1	1	1	2	2	3
50–64	38	1.2	<1	1	1	1	1	2	2	3
65+	23	1.3	<1	1	1	1	1	2	3	3
2. MULTIPLE DX										
0–19 Years	17	2.2	1	1	1	2	3	4	4	4
20–34	17	2.1	2	1	1	2	2	3	5	7
35–49	46	1.7	3	1	1	1	2	2	4	12
50–64	123	1.8	3	1	1	1	2	3	4	10
65+	142	2.1	2	1	1	1	3	4	5	8
TOTAL SINGLE DX	**131**	**1.3**	**<1**	**1**	**1**	**1**	**1**	**2**	**3**	**3**
TOTAL MULTIPLE DX	**345**	**2.0**	**3**	**1**	**1**	**1**	**2**	**4**	**5**	**8**
TOTAL										
0–19 Years	24	2.0	<1	1	1	2	3	3	4	4
20–34	46	1.7	1	1	1	1	2	3	4	7
35–49	80	1.5	2	1	1	1	2	2	3	7
50–64	161	1.7	3	1	1	1	2	3	4	10
65+	165	2.0	2	1	1	1	3	4	5	8
GRAND TOTAL	**476**	**1.8**	**2**	**1**	**1**	**1**	**2**	**3**	**4**	**8**

26.4: SG & DUCT REPAIR

Type of Patients	Observed Patients	Avg. Stay	Vari-ance	10th	25th	50th	75th	90th	95th	99th
1. SINGLE DX										
0–19 Years	0									
20–34	0									
35–49	0									
50–64	1	1.0	0	1	1	1	1	1	1	1
65+	0									
2. MULTIPLE DX										
0–19 Years	8	2.1	1	1	1	2	2	4	4	4
20–34	1	3.0	0	3	3	3	3	3	3	3
35–49	2	2.0	5	1	1	1	1	6	6	6
50–64	1	2.0	0	2	2	2	2	2	2	2
65+	2	2.4	<1	2	2	2	3	3	3	3
TOTAL SINGLE DX	**1**	**1.0**	**0**	**1**	**1**	**1**	**1**	**1**	**1**	**1**
TOTAL MULTIPLE DX	**14**	**2.1**	**2**	**1**	**1**	**2**	**3**	**4**	**4**	**6**
TOTAL										
0–19 Years	8	2.1	1	1	1	2	2	4	4	4
20–34	1	3.0	0	3	3	3	3	3	3	3
35–49	2	2.0	5	1	1	1	1	6	6	6
50–64	2	1.5	<1	1	1	1	2	2	2	2
65+	2	2.4	<1	2	2	2	3	3	3	3
GRAND TOTAL	**15**	**2.1**	**2**	**1**	**1**	**2**	**2**	**4**	**4**	**6**

26.9: OTH SALIVARY OPERATIONS

Type of Patients	Observed Patients	Avg. Stay	Vari-ance	10th	25th	50th	75th	90th	95th	99th
1. SINGLE DX										
0–19 Years	0									
20–34	0									
35–49	0									
50–64	0									
65+	0									
2. MULTIPLE DX										
0–19 Years	1	1.0	0	1	1	1	1	1	1	1
20–34	0									
35–49	2	3.0	2	2	2	4	4	4	4	4
50–64	3	2.6	1	2	2	2	4	4	4	4
65+	6	7.9	47	1	2	8	8	23	23	23
TOTAL SINGLE DX	**0**									
TOTAL MULTIPLE DX	**12**	**5.3**	**32**	**1**	**2**	**4**	**8**	**8**	**23**	**23**
TOTAL										
0–19 Years	1	1.0	0	1	1	1	1	1	1	1
20–34	0									
35–49	2	3.0	2	2	2	4	4	4	4	4
50–64	3	2.6	1	2	2	2	4	4	4	4
65+	6	7.9	47	1	2	8	8	23	23	23
GRAND TOTAL	**12**	**5.3**	**32**	**1**	**2**	**4**	**8**	**8**	**23**	**23**

Percentiles: 10th–99th

27.0: DRAIN FACE & MOUTH FLOOR

Type of Patients	Observed Patients	Avg. Stay	Vari-ance	10th	25th	50th	75th	90th	95th	99th
1. SINGLE DX										
0–19 Years	35	3.7	4	2	2	3	5	6	8	8
20–34	35	2.5	2	1	2	2	3	4	5	6
35–49	34	2.7	3	1	2	2	3	4	5	10
50–64	9	3.4	12	1	1	2	3	11	11	11
65+	1	2.0	0	2	2	2	2	2	2	2
2. MULTIPLE DX										
0–19 Years	124	3.5	3	2	2	4	4	5	7	9
20–34	227	3.7	4	1	2	4	4	6	8	9
35–49	236	4.5	14	2	2	4	5	9	13	21
50–64	117	4.5	13	1	2	3	6	8	11	20
65+	66	5.1	19	1	2	4	6	11	13	23
TOTAL SINGLE DX	**114**	**3.1**	**4**	**1**	**2**	**2**	**4**	**6**	**8**	**11**
TOTAL MULTIPLE DX	**770**	**4.1**	**9**	**1**	**2**	**4**	**5**	**7**	**10**	**16**
TOTAL										
0–19 Years	159	3.5	3	2	2	4	4	6	7	9
20–34	262	3.5	4	1	2	3	4	6	8	9
35–49	270	4.3	13	1	2	3	5	8	12	21
50–64	126	4.4	13	1	2	3	6	8	11	20
65+	67	5.0	19	1	2	4	6	11	13	23
GRAND TOTAL	**884**	**4.0**	**8**	**1**	**2**	**3**	**5**	**7**	**9**	**16**

Percentiles: 10th–99th

27.1: INCISION OF PALATE

Type of Patients	Observed Patients	Avg. Stay	Vari-ance	10th	25th	50th	75th	90th	95th	99th
1. SINGLE DX										
0–19 Years	1	1.0	0	1	1	1	1	1	1	1
20–34	0									
35–49	0									
50–64	0									
65+	0									
2. MULTIPLE DX										
0–19 Years	0									
20–34	2	2.6	<1	2	2	3	3	3	3	3
35–49	6	3.4	1	2	3	3	4	5	5	5
50–64	2	3.1	10	1	1	1	6	6	6	6
65+	1	6.0	0	6	6	6	6	6	6	6
TOTAL SINGLE DX	**1**	**1.0**	**0**	**1**	**1**	**1**	**1**	**1**	**1**	**1**
TOTAL MULTIPLE DX	**11**	**3.4**	**2**	**2**	**2**	**3**	**4**	**6**	**6**	**6**
TOTAL										
0–19 Years	1	1.0	0	1	1	1	1	1	1	1
20–34	2	2.6	<1	2	2	3	3	3	3	3
35–49	6	3.4	1	2	3	3	4	5	5	5
50–64	2	3.1	10	1	1	1	6	6	6	6
65+	1	6.0	0	6	6	6	6	6	6	6
GRAND TOTAL	**12**	**3.1**	**3**	**1**	**2**	**3**	**4**	**6**	**6**	**6**

Percentiles: 10th–99th

27.2: ORAL CAVITY DXTIC PX

Type of Patients	Observed Patients	Avg. Stay	Vari-ance	10th	25th	50th	75th	90th	95th	99th
1. SINGLE DX										
0–19 Years	0									
20–34	1	4.0	0	4	4	4	4	4	4	4
35–49	0									
50–64	3	1.0	0	1	1	1	1	1	1	1
65+	1	1.0	0	1	1	1	1	1	1	1
2. MULTIPLE DX										
0–19 Years	3	7.3	<1	7	7	7	7	9	9	9
20–34	1	3.0	0	3	3	3	3	3	3	3
35–49	7	7.3	16	1	5	7	10	14	14	14
50–64	12	12.0	104	2	3	11	22	29	29	29
65+	17	8.8	25	3	5	8	12	13	22	22
TOTAL SINGLE DX	**5**	**1.6**	**2**	**1**	**1**	**1**	**1**	**4**	**4**	**4**
TOTAL MULTIPLE DX	**40**	**9.2**	**46**	**3**	**5**	**7**	**11**	**22**	**29**	**29**
TOTAL										
0–19 Years	3	7.3	<1	7	7	7	7	9	9	9
20–34	2	3.4	<1	3	3	3	4	4	4	4
35–49	7	7.3	16	1	5	7	10	14	14	14
50–64	15	10.6	104	1	3	6	16	29	29	29
65+	18	8.5	26	2	5	7	12	13	22	22
GRAND TOTAL	**45**	**8.7**	**47**	**2**	**4**	**7**	**11**	**16**	**29**	**29**

Percentiles: 10th–99th

27.3: EXC BONY PALATE LES/TISS

Type of Patients	Observed Patients	Avg. Stay	Vari-ance	Percentiles 10th	25th	50th	75th	90th	95th	99th
1. SINGLE DX										
0–19 Years	0									
20–34	1	1.0	0	1	1	1	1	1	1	1
35–49	0									
50–64	2	2.3	4	1	1	1	4	4	4	4
65+	3	1.8	1	1	1	1	3	3	3	3
2. MULTIPLE DX										
0–19 Years	0									
20–34	2	1.0	0	1	1	1	1	1	1	1
35–49	4	2.1	<1	2	2	2	2	3	3	3
50–64	12	3.1	9	1	2	2	2	7	13	13
65+	17	3.3	13	1	1	2	5	8	8	16
TOTAL SINGLE DX	6	1.8	2	1	1	1	3	4	4	4
TOTAL MULTIPLE DX	35	3.0	10	1	1	2	3	7	9	16
TOTAL										
0–19 Years	0									
20–34	3	1.0	0	1	1	1	1	1	1	1
35–49	4	2.1	<1	2	2	2	2	3	3	3
50–64	14	3.0	9	1	2	2	2	7	9	13
65+	20	3.2	12	1	1	1	3	8	8	16
GRAND TOTAL	41	2.9	9	1	1	2	3	6	9	16

27.4: OTHER EXCISION OF MOUTH

Type of Patients	Observed Patients	Avg. Stay	Vari-ance	Percentiles 10th	25th	50th	75th	90th	95th	99th
1. SINGLE DX										
0–19 Years	9	1.7	1	1	1	1	2	4	4	4
20–34	5	1.6	<1	1	1	1	2	3	3	3
35–49	7	1.3	<1	1	1	1	1	3	3	3
50–64	13	2.3	4	1	1	2	2	5	8	8
65+	4	3.6	5	1	2	4	6	6	6	6
2. MULTIPLE DX										
0–19 Years	20	2.5	11	1	1	1	3	4	10	18
20–34	14	5.4	15	1	3	5	6	13	13	13
35–49	29	5.2	17	1	2	5	8	9	9	22
50–64	55	5.1	38	1	1	3	7	14	22	34
65+	113	5.6	46	1	1	3	7	10	14	45
TOTAL SINGLE DX	38	2.0	3	1	1	1	2	4	6	8
TOTAL MULTIPLE DX	231	5.1	37	1	1	3	7	10	14	22
TOTAL										
0–19 Years	29	2.3	8	1	1	1	2	4	4	18
20–34	19	4.5	14	1	1	3	6	10	13	13
35–49	36	4.5	16	1	1	3	6	9	9	22
50–64	68	4.6	33	1	1	3	5	8	17	34
65+	117	5.5	45	1	1	3	7	10	14	45
GRAND TOTAL	269	4.8	34	1	1	3	7	10	14	22

27.49: EXCISION OF MOUTH NEC

Type of Patients	Observed Patients	Avg. Stay	Vari-ance	Percentiles 10th	25th	50th	75th	90th	95th	99th
1. SINGLE DX										
0–19 Years	5	2.2	1	1	1	2	2	4	4	4
20–34	4	1.5	<1	1	1	1	1	3	3	3
35–49	5	1.4	<1	1	1	1	1	3	3	3
50–64	10	2.4	5	1	1	2	2	5	8	8
65+	3	3.5	7	1	1	2	6	6	6	6
2. MULTIPLE DX										
0–19 Years	5	3.4	26	1	1	2	3	3	18	18
20–34	5	7.8	24	1	3	10	13	13	13	13
35–49	13	5.4	13	1	1	7	9	9	9	9
50–64	39	6.1	49	1	2	4	7	17	22	34
65+	83	5.4	45	1	1	3	7	10	14	21
TOTAL SINGLE DX	27	2.2	3	1	1	2	2	5	6	8
TOTAL MULTIPLE DX	145	5.5	42	1	1	3	7	10	15	34
TOTAL										
0–19 Years	10	2.9	16	1	1	2	3	4	18	18
20–34	9	5.5	25	1	1	3	10	13	13	13
35–49	18	4.4	13	1	1	3	9	9	9	9
50–64	49	5.4	42	1	1	3	7	16	22	34
65+	86	5.3	44	1	1	3	7	10	14	21
GRAND TOTAL	172	5.1	38	1	1	3	7	10	14	22

27.5: MOUTH PLASTIC REPAIR

Type of Patients	Observed Patients	Avg. Stay	Vari-ance	Percentiles 10th	25th	50th	75th	90th	95th	99th
1. SINGLE DX										
0–19 Years	213	1.1	<1	1	1	1	1	2	2	3
20–34	9	1.1	<1	1	1	1	1	2	2	2
35–49	11	1.1	<1	1	1	1	1	2	2	2
50–64	2	1.5	<1	1	1	2	2	2	2	2
65+	1	1.0	0	1	1	1	1	1	1	1
2. MULTIPLE DX										
0–19 Years	330	1.6	2	1	1	1	2	3	4	7
20–34	189	2.2	8	1	1	1	2	5	6	15
35–49	140	2.3	4	1	1	2	3	5	7	9
50–64	105	4.0	61	1	1	2	4	8	10	25
65+	179	3.4	8	1	1	2	4	6	9	14
TOTAL SINGLE DX	236	1.1	<1	1	1	1	1	2	2	3
TOTAL MULTIPLE DX	943	2.3	10	1	1	1	3	5	7	12
TOTAL										
0–19 Years	543	1.4	1	1	1	1	1	2	3	6
20–34	198	2.2	7	1	1	1	2	4	6	15
35–49	151	2.2	4	1	1	2	3	4	7	9
50–64	107	3.9	60	1	1	2	4	8	10	25
65+	180	3.4	8	1	1	2	4	6	9	14
GRAND TOTAL	1,179	2.0	8	1	1	1	2	4	6	11

27.51: SUTURE OF LIP LACERATION

Type of Patients	Observed Patients	Avg. Stay	Vari-ance	Percentiles						
				10th	25th	50th	75th	90th	95th	99th
1. SINGLE DX										
0–19 Years	4	1.0	0	1	1	1	1	1	1	1
20–34	2	1.0	0	1	1	1	1	1	1	1
35–49	1	2.0	0	2	2	2	2	2	2	2
50–64	0									
65+	0									
2. MULTIPLE DX										
0–19 Years	90	1.6	1	1	1	1	2	3	3	7
20–34	143	2.1	7	1	1	1	2	4	6	8
35–49	101	2.2	3	1	1	2	3	4	6	9
50–64	72	3.9	72	1	2	2	4	7	8	85
65+	153	3.1	6	1	1	2	4	6	8	13
TOTAL SINGLE DX	**7**	**1.1**	**<1**	**1**	**1**	**1**	**1**	**1**	**2**	**2**
TOTAL MULTIPLE DX	**559**	**2.6**	**14**	**1**	**1**	**2**	**3**	**5**	**7**	**12**
TOTAL										
0–19 Years	94	1.5	1	1	1	1	2	3	3	7
20–34	145	2.1	7	1	1	1	2	4	6	8
35–49	102	2.2	3	1	1	2	3	4	6	9
50–64	72	3.9	72	1	2	2	4	7	8	85
65+	153	3.1	6	1	1	2	4	6	8	13
GRAND TOTAL	**566**	**2.5**	**14**	**1**	**1**	**2**	**3**	**5**	**7**	**12**

27.54: REPAIR OF CLEFT LIP

Type of Patients	Observed Patients	Avg. Stay	Vari-ance	Percentiles						
				10th	25th	50th	75th	90th	95th	99th
1. SINGLE DX										
0–19 Years	202	1.1	<1	1	1	1	1	2	2	2
20–34	3	1.0	0	1	1	1	1	1	1	1
35–49	1	1.0	0	1	1	1	1	1	1	1
50–64	0									
65+	0									
2. MULTIPLE DX										
0–19 Years	183	1.5	1	1	1	1	2	2	4	6
20–34	4	1.3	<1	1	1	1	2	2	2	2
35–49	1	2.0	0	2	2	2	2	2	2	2
50–64	1	1.0	0	1	1	1	1	1	1	1
65+	0									
TOTAL SINGLE DX	**206**	**1.1**	**<1**	**1**	**1**	**1**	**1**	**2**	**2**	**2**
TOTAL MULTIPLE DX	**189**	**1.5**	**1**	**1**	**1**	**1**	**2**	**2**	**4**	**6**
TOTAL										
0–19 Years	385	1.3	<1	1	1	1	1	2	3	6
20–34	7	1.1	<1	1	1	1	1	2	2	2
35–49	2	1.6	<1	1	1	2	2	2	2	2
50–64	1	1.0	0	1	1	1	1	1	1	1
65+	0									
GRAND TOTAL	**395**	**1.3**	**<1**	**1**	**1**	**1**	**1**	**2**	**3**	**6**

27.59: MOUTH REPAIR NEC

Type of Patients	Observed Patients	Avg. Stay	Vari-ance	Percentiles						
				10th	25th	50th	75th	90th	95th	99th
1. SINGLE DX										
0–19 Years	1	1.0	0	1	1	1	1	1	1	1
20–34	2	1.0	0	1	1	1	1	1	1	1
35–49	1	1.0	0	1	1	1	1	1	1	1
50–64	1	1.0	0	1	1	1	1	1	1	1
65+	0									
2. MULTIPLE DX										
0–19 Years	36	2.2	4	1	1	1	2	5	8	8
20–34	33	2.9	8	1	1	2	4	7	8	15
35–49	25	2.6	6	1	1	1	4	7	8	9
50–64	18	4.4	20	1	1	2	8	10	16	16
65+	11	6.0	11	2	4	6	9	12	12	12
TOTAL SINGLE DX	**5**	**1.0**	**0**	**1**	**1**	**1**	**1**	**1**	**1**	**1**
TOTAL MULTIPLE DX	**123**	**3.3**	**10**	**1**	**1**	**2**	**4**	**8**	**10**	**15**
TOTAL										
0–19 Years	37	2.2	4	1	1	1	2	5	8	8
20–34	35	2.8	8	1	1	2	3	7	8	15
35–49	26	2.5	6	1	1	1	3	7	8	9
50–64	19	4.2	20	1	1	2	8	10	12	16
65+	11	6.0	11	2	4	6	9	12	12	12
GRAND TOTAL	**128**	**3.2**	**10**	**1**	**1**	**2**	**4**	**8**	**10**	**15**

27.6: PALATOPLASTY

Type of Patients	Observed Patients	Avg. Stay	Vari-ance	Percentiles						
				10th	25th	50th	75th	90th	95th	99th
1. SINGLE DX										
0–19 Years	283	1.4	<1	1	1	1	2	2	3	3
20–34	16	1.5	1	1	1	1	2	2	5	5
35–49	38	1.3	<1	1	1	1	2	2	2	3
50–64	29	1.5	<1	1	1	1	2	3	3	3
65+	4	2.3	<1	1	1	3	3	3	3	3
2. MULTIPLE DX										
0–19 Years	507	1.8	9	1	1	1	2	3	3	6
20–34	166	1.5	1	1	1	1	2	2	4	7
35–49	461	1.6	1	1	1	1	2	3	3	7
50–64	338	1.7	2	1	1	1	2	3	4	7
65+	57	1.7	1	1	1	1	2	2	4	7
TOTAL SINGLE DX	**370**	**1.4**	**<1**	**1**	**1**	**1**	**2**	**2**	**3**	**3**
TOTAL MULTIPLE DX	**1,529**	**1.7**	**5**	**1**	**1**	**1**	**2**	**3**	**4**	**6**
TOTAL										
0–19 Years	790	1.7	6	1	1	1	2	3	3	6
20–34	182	1.5	1	1	1	1	2	2	4	7
35–49	499	1.6	1	1	1	1	2	3	3	7
50–64	367	1.6	1	1	1	1	2	3	4	7
65+	61	1.7	1	1	1	1	2	3	4	7
GRAND TOTAL	**1,899**	**1.6**	**4**	**1**	**1**	**1**	**2**	**3**	**3**	**6**

27.62: CLEFT PALATE CORRECTION

Type of Patients	Observed Patients	Avg. Stay	Vari-ance	Percentiles						
				10th	25th	50th	75th	90th	95th	99th
1. SINGLE DX										
0–19 Years	179	1.5	<1	1	1	1	2	2	3	3
20–34	4	1.0	0	1	1	1	1	1	1	1
35–49	2	1.5	<1	1	1	2	2	2	2	2
50–64	0									
65+	0									
2. MULTIPLE DX										
0–19 Years	294	2.0	13	1	1	2	2	3	4	6
20–34	2	3.0	0	3	3	3	3	3	3	3
35–49	0									
50–64	0									
65+	2	1.5	<1	1	1	2	2	2	2	2
TOTAL SINGLE DX	**185**	**1.5**	**<1**	**1**	**1**	**1**	**2**	**2**	**3**	**3**
TOTAL MULTIPLE DX	**298**	**2.0**	**13**	**1**	**1**	**2**	**2**	**3**	**4**	**6**
TOTAL										
0–19 Years	473	1.8	8	1	1	1	2	3	3	6
20–34	6	1.7	1	1	1	1	3	3	3	3
35–49	2	1.5	<1	1	1	2	2	2	2	2
50–64	0									
65+	2	1.5	<1	1	1	2	2	2	2	2
GRAND TOTAL	**483**	**1.8**	**8**	**1**	**1**	**1**	**2**	**3**	**3**	**6**

27.63: REV CLEFT PALATE REPAIR

Type of Patients	Observed Patients	Avg. Stay	Vari-ance	Percentiles						
				10th	25th	50th	75th	90th	95th	99th
1. SINGLE DX										
0–19 Years	69	1.3	<1	1	1	1	1	2	3	3
20–34	6	2.0	3	1	1	1	2	5	5	5
35–49	1	1.0	0	1	1	1	1	1	1	1
50–64	0									
65+	0									
2. MULTIPLE DX										
0–19 Years	156	1.4	1	1	1	1	1	2	3	4
20–34	2	1.5	<1	1	1	2	2	2	2	2
35–49	1	3.0	0	3	3	3	3	3	3	3
50–64	1	1.0	0	1	1	1	1	1	1	1
65+	0									
TOTAL SINGLE DX	**76**	**1.3**	**<1**	**1**	**1**	**1**	**1**	**2**	**3**	**3**
TOTAL MULTIPLE DX	**160**	**1.4**	**1**	**1**	**1**	**1**	**1**	**2**	**3**	**4**
TOTAL										
0–19 Years	225	1.4	1	1	1	1	1	2	3	3
20–34	8	1.9	2	1	1	1	2	5	5	5
35–49	2	1.4	<1	1	1	1	1	3	3	3
50–64	1	1.0	0	1	1	1	1	1	1	1
65+	0									
GRAND TOTAL	**236**	**1.4**	**1**	**1**	**1**	**1**	**1**	**2**	**3**	**4**

27.69: OTHER PLASTIC REP PALATE

Type of Patients	Observed Patients	Avg. Stay	Vari-ance	Percentiles						
				10th	25th	50th	75th	90th	95th	99th
1. SINGLE DX										
0–19 Years	16	1.2	<1	1	1	1	1	2	2	2
20–34	6	1.3	<1	1	1	1	2	2	2	2
35–49	34	1.4	<1	1	1	1	2	2	3	3
50–64	29	1.5	<1	1	1	1	2	3	3	3
65+	4	2.3	<1	1	1	3	3	3	3	3
2. MULTIPLE DX										
0–19 Years	52	1.5	1	1	1	1	2	3	3	8
20–34	158	1.4	<1	1	1	1	2	2	3	7
35–49	457	1.6	1	1	1	1	2	3	3	7
50–64	337	1.7	2	1	1	1	2	3	4	7
65+	54	1.7	2	1	1	1	2	2	4	7
TOTAL SINGLE DX	**89**	**1.4**	**<1**	**1**	**1**	**1**	**2**	**2**	**3**	**3**
TOTAL MULTIPLE DX	**1,058**	**1.6**	**1**	**1**	**1**	**1**	**2**	**3**	**4**	**7**
TOTAL										
0–19 Years	68	1.4	<1	1	1	1	2	2	3	5
20–34	164	1.4	<1	1	1	1	2	2	3	7
35–49	491	1.6	1	1	1	1	2	3	3	7
50–64	366	1.6	1	1	1	1	2	3	4	7
65+	58	1.7	2	1	1	1	2	3	4	7
GRAND TOTAL	**1,147**	**1.6**	**1**	**1**	**1**	**1**	**2**	**3**	**3**	**7**

27.7: OPERATIONS ON UVULA

Type of Patients	Observed Patients	Avg. Stay	Vari-ance	Percentiles						
				10th	25th	50th	75th	90th	95th	99th
1. SINGLE DX										
0–19 Years	0									
20–34	0									
35–49	1	1.0	0	1	1	1	1	1	1	1
50–64	0									
65+	0									
2. MULTIPLE DX										
0–19 Years	2	1.0	0	1	1	1	1	1	1	1
20–34	5	1.4	<1	1	1	1	1	3	3	3
35–49	11	2.4	5	1	1	2	2	6	8	8
50–64	4	1.0	0	1	1	1	1	1	1	1
65+	3	1.0	0	1	1	1	1	1	1	1
TOTAL SINGLE DX	**1**	**1.0**	**0**	**1**	**1**	**1**	**1**	**1**	**1**	**1**
TOTAL MULTIPLE DX	**25**	**1.6**	**2**	**1**	**1**	**1**	**1**	**2**	**6**	**8**
TOTAL										
0–19 Years	2	1.0	0	1	1	1	1	1	1	1
20–34	5	1.4	<1	1	1	1	1	3	3	3
35–49	12	2.3	5	1	1	2	2	6	8	8
50–64	4	1.0	0	1	1	1	1	1	1	1
65+	3	1.0	0	1	1	1	1	1	1	1
GRAND TOTAL	**26**	**1.6**	**2**	**1**	**1**	**1**	**1**	**2**	**6**	**8**

27.9: OTH OPS ON MOUTH & FACE

Type of Patients	Observed Patients	Avg. Stay	Variance	10th	25th	50th	75th	90th	95th	99th
1. SINGLE DX										
0–19 Years	4	2.2	<1	1	1	3	3	3	3	3
20–34	3	2.2	<1	1	1	2	3	3	3	3
35–49	1	3.0	0	3	3	3	3	3	3	3
50–64	1	2.0	0	2	2	2	2	2	2	2
65+	0									
2. MULTIPLE DX										
0–19 Years	20	3.1	5	1	2	3	3	3	6	13
20–34	9	3.1	2	2	2	3	3	5	6	6
35–49	24	3.6	5	1	2	3	5	7	7	10
50–64	11	2.9	8	1	1	2	3	9	9	9
65+	6	12.1	65	3	3	12	22	22	22	22
TOTAL SINGLE DX	**9**	**2.3**	**<1**	**1**	**1**	**3**	**3**	**3**	**3**	**3**
TOTAL MULTIPLE DX	**70**	**4.0**	**16**	**1**	**2**	**3**	**4**	**7**	**13**	**22**
TOTAL										
0–19 Years	24	2.8	4	1	2	3	3	3	6	13
20–34	12	2.9	2	1	2	3	3	5	6	6
35–49	25	3.5	4	1	2	3	5	7	7	10
50–64	12	2.8	7	1	1	2	3	9	9	9
65+	6	12.1	65	3	3	12	22	22	22	22
GRAND TOTAL	**79**	**3.7**	**13**	**1**	**2**	**3**	**3**	**6**	**11**	**22**

28.0: TONSIL/PERITONSILLAR I&D

Type of Patients	Observed Patients	Avg. Stay	Variance	10th	25th	50th	75th	90th	95th	99th
1. SINGLE DX										
0–19 Years	184	2.0	2	1	1	2	2	4	5	6
20–34	89	1.9	<1	1	1	2	2	3	3	5
35–49	35	2.0	1	1	1	2	3	3	4	6
50–64	14	2.1	2	1	1	2	3	4	5	5
65+	3	2.3	4	1	1	1	5	5	5	5
2. MULTIPLE DX										
0–19 Years	184	3.1	6	1	2	2	4	6	7	11
20–34	184	2.6	6	1	1	2	3	4	7	13
35–49	124	3.2	9	1	1	2	4	6	10	15
50–64	49	4.6	25	1	2	2	6	14	14	20
65+	27	5.7	21	1	3	3	10	11	15	19
TOTAL SINGLE DX	**325**	**2.0**	**1**	**1**	**1**	**2**	**3**	**4**	**5**	**6**
TOTAL MULTIPLE DX	**568**	**3.1**	**9**	**1**	**1**	**2**	**4**	**6**	**8**	**15**
TOTAL										
0–19 Years	368	2.6	4	1	1	2	3	5	6	8
20–34	273	2.4	5	1	1	2	3	4	6	13
35–49	159	2.9	8	1	1	2	3	5	8	15
50–64	63	4.0	21	1	1	2	5	14	14	20
65+	30	5.4	20	1	2	3	8	11	15	19
GRAND TOTAL	**893**	**2.8**	**7**	**1**	**1**	**2**	**3**	**5**	**7**	**15**

28.1: TONSIL&ADENOID DXTIC PX

Type of Patients	Observed Patients	Avg. Stay	Variance	10th	25th	50th	75th	90th	95th	99th
1. SINGLE DX										
0–19 Years	2	1.4	<1	1	1	1	2	2	2	2
20–34	0									
35–49	1	1.0	0	1	1	1	1	1	1	1
50–64	0									
65+	2	1.0	0	1	1	1	1	1	1	1
2. MULTIPLE DX										
0–19 Years	2	2.3	6	1	1	1	6	6	6	6
20–34	0									
35–49	8	4.2	17	1	1	3	7	7	14	14
50–64	8	4.7	24	1	1	2	9	13	13	13
65+	13	4.5	20	1	1	3	6	13	17	17
TOTAL SINGLE DX	**5**	**1.2**	**<1**	**1**	**1**	**1**	**1**	**2**	**2**	**2**
TOTAL MULTIPLE DX	**31**	**4.2**	**18**	**1**	**1**	**2**	**6**	**12**	**13**	**17**
TOTAL										
0–19 Years	4	2.1	4	1	1	1	2	6	6	6
20–34	0									
35–49	9	4.0	16	1	1	2	7	7	14	14
50–64	8	4.7	24	1	1	2	9	13	13	13
65+	15	4.0	19	1	1	2	6	13	17	17
GRAND TOTAL	**36**	**3.9**	**17**	**1**	**1**	**2**	**6**	**12**	**13**	**17**

28.2: TONSILLECTOMY

Type of Patients	Observed Patients	Avg. Stay	Variance	10th	25th	50th	75th	90th	95th	99th
1. SINGLE DX										
0–19 Years	57	1.8	<1	1	1	2	2	3	4	4
20–34	40	1.6	<1	1	1	1	2	3	3	3
35–49	6	1.4	<1	1	1	1	2	2	2	2
50–64	3	2.7	7	1	1	1	6	6	6	6
65+	3	1.0	0	1	1	1	1	1	1	1
2. MULTIPLE DX										
0–19 Years	168	1.8	4	1	1	1	2	3	5	8
20–34	113	1.9	1	1	1	2	2	4	4	6
35–49	86	2.1	5	1	1	2	3	3	5	14
50–64	46	3.4	23	1	1	2	3	8	17	19
65+	10	5.0	22	1	1	1	9	12	12	12
TOTAL SINGLE DX	**109**	**1.7**	**<1**	**1**	**1**	**1**	**2**	**3**	**3**	**5**
TOTAL MULTIPLE DX	**423**	**2.1**	**6**	**1**	**1**	**1**	**2**	**4**	**6**	**14**
TOTAL										
0–19 Years	225	1.8	3	1	1	1	2	3	4	8
20–34	153	1.8	1	1	1	1	2	3	4	6
35–49	92	2.1	4	1	1	1	2	3	4	14
50–64	49	3.4	22	1	1	2	3	8	17	19
65+	13	4.2	21	1	1	1	9	12	12	12
GRAND TOTAL	**532**	**2.0**	**5**	**1**	**1**	**1**	**2**	**3**	**6**	**12**

28.3: T&A

Type of Patients	Observed Patients	Avg. Stay	Vari-ance	10th	25th	50th	75th	90th	95th	99th
1. SINGLE DX										
0–19 Years	151	1.2	<1	1	1	1	1	2	2	4
20–34	3	1.0	0	1	1	1	1	1	1	1
35–49	0									
50–64	0									
65+	2	3.0	8	1	1	1	6	6	6	6
2. MULTIPLE DX										
0–19 Years	1,205	1.9	5	1	1	1	2	4	6	13
20–34	21	2.1	5	1	1	1	2	3	10	10
35–49	9	3.1	8	1	1	2	2	9	9	9
50–64	2	1.0	0	1	1	1	1	1	1	1
65+	8	4.7	16	1	1	4	8	9	11	11
TOTAL SINGLE DX	**156**	**1.3**	**<1**	**1**	**1**	**1**	**1**	**2**	**2**	**4**
TOTAL MULTIPLE DX	**1,245**	**1.9**	**5**	**1**	**1**	**1**	**2**	**4**	**6**	**13**
TOTAL										
0–19 Years	1,356	1.8	5	1	1	1	2	3	5	12
20–34	24	2.0	5	1	1	1	2	3	10	10
35–49	9	3.1	8	1	1	2	2	9	9	9
50–64	2	1.0	0	1	1	1	1	1	1	1
65+	10	4.3	14	1	1	1	7	9	11	11
GRAND TOTAL	**1,401**	**1.8**	**5**	**1**	**1**	**1**	**2**	**3**	**5**	**12**

28.4: EXCISION OF TONSIL TAG

Type of Patients	Observed Patients	Avg. Stay	Vari-ance	10th	25th	50th	75th	90th	95th	99th
1. SINGLE DX										
0–19 Years	0									
20–34	0									
35–49	0									
50–64	0									
65+	0									
2. MULTIPLE DX										
0–19 Years	0									
20–34	0									
35–49	0									
50–64	0									
65+	1	3.0	0	3	3	3	3	3	3	3
TOTAL SINGLE DX	**0**									
TOTAL MULTIPLE DX	**1**	**3.0**	**0**	**3**	**3**	**3**	**3**	**3**	**3**	**3**
TOTAL										
0–19 Years	0									
20–34	0									
35–49	0									
50–64	0									
65+	1	3.0	0	3	3	3	3	3	3	3
GRAND TOTAL	**1**	**3.0**	**0**	**3**	**3**	**3**	**3**	**3**	**3**	**3**

28.5: EXCISION LINGUAL TONSIL

Type of Patients	Observed Patients	Avg. Stay	Vari-ance	10th	25th	50th	75th	90th	95th	99th
1. SINGLE DX										
0–19 Years	1	3.0	0	3	3	3	3	3	3	3
20–34	0									
35–49	0									
50–64	0									
65+	0									
2. MULTIPLE DX										
0–19 Years	1	3.0	0	3	3	3	3	3	3	3
20–34	0									
35–49	2	1.0	0	1	1	1	1	1	1	1
50–64	4	2.2	2	1	2	2	2	2	6	6
65+	0									
TOTAL SINGLE DX	**1**	**3.0**	**0**	**3**	**3**	**3**	**3**	**3**	**3**	**3**
TOTAL MULTIPLE DX	**7**	**1.9**	**1**	**1**	**1**	**2**	**2**	**3**	**6**	**6**
TOTAL										
0–19 Years	2	3.0	0	3	3	3	3	3	3	3
20–34	0									
35–49	2	1.0	0	1	1	1	1	1	1	1
50–64	4	2.2	2	1	2	2	2	2	6	6
65+	0									
GRAND TOTAL	**8**	**2.0**	**1**	**1**	**1**	**2**	**2**	**3**	**3**	**6**

28.6: ADENOIDECTOMY

Type of Patients	Observed Patients	Avg. Stay	Vari-ance	10th	25th	50th	75th	90th	95th	99th
1. SINGLE DX										
0–19 Years	4	1.0	0	1	1	1	1	1	1	1
20–34	1	1.0	0	1	1	1	1	1	1	1
35–49	0									
50–64	0									
65+	0									
2. MULTIPLE DX										
0–19 Years	31	2.1	2	1	1	2	2	3	5	8
20–34	1	3.0	0	3	3	3	3	3	3	3
35–49	1	16.0	0	16	16	16	16	16	16	16
50–64	1	4.0	0	4	4	4	4	4	4	4
65+	0									
TOTAL SINGLE DX	**5**	**1.0**	**0**	**1**	**1**	**1**	**1**	**1**	**1**	**1**
TOTAL MULTIPLE DX	**34**	**2.3**	**4**	**1**	**1**	**2**	**3**	**3**	**6**	**16**
TOTAL										
0–19 Years	35	1.9	2	1	1	2	2	3	5	8
20–34	2	2.0	1	1	1	2	3	3	3	3
35–49	1	16.0	0	16	16	16	16	16	16	16
50–64	1	4.0	0	4	4	4	4	4	4	4
65+	0									
GRAND TOTAL	**39**	**2.1**	**4**	**1**	**1**	**2**	**2**	**3**	**5**	**8**

28.7: HEMOR CONTROL POST T&A

Type of Patients	Observed Patients	Avg. Stay	Vari-ance	Percentiles 10th	25th	50th	75th	90th	95th	99th
1. SINGLE DX										
0–19 Years	197	1.1	<1	1	1	1	1	2	2	2
20–34	79	1.4	<1	1	1	1	1	3	3	3
35–49	38	1.7	<1	1	1	1	3	3	3	3
50–64	3	1.0	0	1	1	1	1	1	1	1
65+	0									
2. MULTIPLE DX										
0–19 Years	96	1.7	2	1	1	1	2	3	4	6
20–34	57	1.6	1	1	1	1	2	3	5	5
35–49	33	2.1	2	1	1	1	3	5	5	6
50–64	7	2.2	3	1	1	1	4	4	6	6
65+	2	3.5	8	1	1	4	6	6	6	6
TOTAL SINGLE DX	**317**	**1.2**	**<1**	**1**	**1**	**1**	**1**	**2**	**3**	**3**
TOTAL MULTIPLE DX	**195**	**1.8**	**2**	**1**	**1**	**1**	**2**	**4**	**5**	**6**
TOTAL										
0–19 Years	293	1.3	<1	1	1	1	1	2	2	5
20–34	136	1.5	<1	1	1	1	2	3	4	5
35–49	71	1.9	2	1	1	1	3	3	5	6
50–64	10	1.9	3	1	1	1	2	4	6	6
65+	2	3.5	8	1	1	4	6	6	6	6
GRAND TOTAL	**512**	**1.5**	**<1**	**1**	**1**	**1**	**2**	**2**	**3**	**5**

28.9: OTHER TONSIL/ADENOID OPS

Type of Patients	Observed Patients	Avg. Stay	Vari-ance	Percentiles 10th	25th	50th	75th	90th	95th	99th
1. SINGLE DX										
0–19 Years	0									
20–34	2	1.0	0	1	1	1	1	1	1	1
35–49	0									
50–64	0									
65+	0									
2. MULTIPLE DX										
0–19 Years	8	2.0	1	1	1	2	2	4	4	4
20–34	1	4.0	0	4	4	4	4	4	4	4
35–49	4	2.2	3	1	1	1	4	5	5	5
50–64	4	11.6	61	3	3	7	16	21	21	21
65+	4	3.9	9	1	1	3	8	8	8	8
TOTAL SINGLE DX	**2**	**1.0**	**0**	**1**	**1**	**1**	**1**	**1**	**1**	**1**
TOTAL MULTIPLE DX	**21**	**3.8**	**21**	**1**	**1**	**2**	**4**	**8**	**16**	**21**
TOTAL										
0–19 Years	8	2.0	1	1	1	2	2	4	4	4
20–34	3	2.1	3	1	1	1	4	4	4	4
35–49	4	2.2	3	1	1	1	4	5	5	5
50–64	4	11.6	61	3	3	7	16	21	21	21
65+	4	3.9	9	1	1	3	8	8	8	8
GRAND TOTAL	**23**	**3.6**	**19**	**1**	**1**	**2**	**4**	**7**	**16**	**21**

29.0: PHARYNGOTOMY

Type of Patients	Observed Patients	Avg. Stay	Vari-ance	Percentiles 10th	25th	50th	75th	90th	95th	99th
1. SINGLE DX										
0–19 Years	5	2.1	2	1	1	2	4	4	4	4
20–34	4	2.2	1	1	1	2	3	4	4	4
35–49	1	1.0	0	1	1	1	1	1	1	1
50–64	2	2.5	<1	1	1	3	3	3	3	3
65+	1	10.0	0	10	10	10	10	10	10	10
2. MULTIPLE DX										
0–19 Years	5	2.7	3	1	2	2	2	6	6	6
20–34	2	1.5	<1	1	1	2	2	2	2	2
35–49	5	3.0	11	1	1	1	5	7	12	12
50–64	2	7.0	0	7	7	7	7	7	7	7
65+	1	1.0	0	1	1	1	1	1	1	1
TOTAL SINGLE DX	**13**	**2.7**	**5**	**1**	**1**	**2**	**3**	**4**	**10**	**10**
TOTAL MULTIPLE DX	**15**	**2.8**	**7**	**1**	**1**	**2**	**2**	**7**	**7**	**12**
TOTAL										
0–19 Years	10	2.4	2	1	1	2	2	4	6	6
20–34	6	1.7	<1	1	1	2	2	2	3	4
35–49	6	2.9	10	1	1	1	5	7	12	12
50–64	4	5.5	5	3	3	7	7	7	7	7
65+	2	3.5	20	1	1	1	10	10	10	10
GRAND TOTAL	**28**	**2.7**	**6**	**1**	**1**	**2**	**3**	**7**	**7**	**12**

29.1: PHARYNGEAL DXTIC PX

Type of Patients	Observed Patients	Avg. Stay	Vari-ance	Percentiles 10th	25th	50th	75th	90th	95th	99th
1. SINGLE DX										
0–19 Years	6	1.5	3	1	1	1	1	2	8	8
20–34	6	1.2	<1	1	1	1	1	2	3	3
35–49	7	1.7	<1	1	1	2	2	2	2	2
50–64	4	2.5	<1	1	1	3	3	3	3	3
65+	0									
2. MULTIPLE DX										
0–19 Years	17	2.4	3	1	1	2	3	4	7	7
20–34	23	3.1	6	1	2	2	4	5	8	14
35–49	32	4.3	13	1	2	4	5	10	12	19
50–64	46	5.8	27	1	2	5	7	12	17	30
65+	83	6.1	34	1	2	4	8	13	20	25
TOTAL SINGLE DX	**23**	**1.6**	**1**	**1**	**1**	**1**	**2**	**3**	**3**	**8**
TOTAL MULTIPLE DX	**201**	**5.0**	**24**	**1**	**2**	**4**	**6**	**11**	**17**	**25**
TOTAL										
0–19 Years	23	2.0	3	1	1	1	2	4	7	8
20–34	29	2.4	5	1	1	2	3	5	6	14
35–49	39	3.9	12	1	2	3	4	9	12	19
50–64	50	5.5	25	1	2	4	7	11	17	30
65+	83	6.1	34	1	2	4	8	13	20	25
GRAND TOTAL	**224**	**4.5**	**22**	**1**	**2**	**3**	**5**	**10**	**14**	**25**

29.11: PHARYNGOSCOPY

Type of Patients	Observed Patients	Avg. Stay	Vari-ance	10th	25th	50th	75th	90th	95th	99th
1. SINGLE DX										
0–19 Years	5	1.1	<1	1	1	1	1	1	2	2
20–34	5	1.1	<1	1	1	1	1	1	3	3
35–49	4	1.7	<1	1	1	2	2	2	2	2
50–64	2	3.0	0	3	3	3	3	3	3	3
65+	0									
2. MULTIPLE DX										
0–19 Years	14	2.3	3	1	1	2	2	4	7	7
20–34	21	2.8	4	1	2	2	3	5	8	9
35–49	25	3.3	4	1	2	3	4	5	6	10
50–64	29	6.3	35	2	2	5	7	17	19	30
65+	58	7.0	40	2	3	5	9	17	25	25
TOTAL SINGLE DX	**16**	**1.4**	**<1**	**1**	**1**	**1**	**2**	**3**	**3**	**3**
TOTAL MULTIPLE DX	**147**	**4.9**	**25**	**1**	**2**	**3**	**6**	**10**	**17**	**25**
TOTAL										
0–19 Years	19	1.7	2	1	1	1	2	4	4	7
20–34	26	2.1	3	1	1	2	2	5	5	9
35–49	29	3.1	4	1	2	2	4	5	6	10
50–64	31	5.9	33	2	3	5	7	17	19	30
65+	58	7.0	40	2	3	5	9	17	25	25
GRAND TOTAL	**163**	**4.3**	**23**	**1**	**2**	**3**	**5**	**9**	**16**	**25**

29.2: EXC BRANCHIAL CLEFT CYST

Type of Patients	Observed Patients	Avg. Stay	Vari-ance	10th	25th	50th	75th	90th	95th	99th
1. SINGLE DX										
0–19 Years	11	1.2	<1	1	1	1	1	2	2	2
20–34	18	1.5	<1	1	1	1	2	3	3	5
35–49	8	1.1	<1	1	1	1	1	2	2	2
50–64	5	1.2	<1	1	1	1	1	2	2	2
65+	1	1.0	0	1	1	1	1	1	1	1
2. MULTIPLE DX										
0–19 Years	7	3.1	2	1	3	4	4	4	4	4
20–34	7	1.4	<1	1	1	1	2	3	3	3
35–49	9	1.5	3	1	1	1	1	1	7	7
50–64	12	1.7	<1	1	1	2	2	2	3	4
65+	5	2.6	2	1	1	2	4	4	4	4
TOTAL SINGLE DX	**43**	**1.4**	**<1**	**1**	**1**	**1**	**2**	**2**	**3**	**5**
TOTAL MULTIPLE DX	**40**	**2.0**	**2**	**1**	**1**	**1**	**3**	**4**	**4**	**7**
TOTAL										
0–19 Years	18	2.1	2	1	1	1	4	4	4	4
20–34	25	1.5	<1	1	1	1	2	3	3	5
35–49	17	1.3	2	1	1	1	1	1	2	7
50–64	17	1.6	<1	1	1	2	2	2	3	4
65+	6	2.3	2	1	1	2	4	4	4	4
GRAND TOTAL	**83**	**1.7**	**1**	**1**	**1**	**1**	**2**	**4**	**4**	**5**

29.3: EXC/DESTR PHARYNGEAL LES

Type of Patients	Observed Patients	Avg. Stay	Vari-ance	10th	25th	50th	75th	90th	95th	99th
1. SINGLE DX										
0–19 Years	3	5.1	5	2	2	6	7	7	7	7
20–34	5	2.8	3	1	1	3	4	5	5	5
35–49	4	1.6	<1	1	1	1	2	3	3	3
50–64	11	2.3	1	1	1	2	3	3	5	5
65+	8	1.3	<1	1	1	1	1	2	2	2
2. MULTIPLE DX										
0–19 Years	11	26.3	747	3	4	7	60	60	60	60
20–34	4	1.6	<1	1	1	2	2	2	2	2
35–49	13	5.2	23	1	1	4	8	11	17	17
50–64	52	4.1	23	1	2	2	4	9	18	20
65+	132	4.6	22	1	1	4	7	8	13	18
TOTAL SINGLE DX	**31**	**2.3**	**2**	**1**	**1**	**2**	**3**	**5**	**6**	**7**
TOTAL MULTIPLE DX	**212**	**6.0**	**103**	**1**	**2**	**3**	**7**	**11**	**17**	**60**
TOTAL										
0–19 Years	14	23.3	695	2	4	7	60	60	60	60
20–34	9	2.3	2	1	1	2	3	5	5	5
35–49	17	4.1	19	1	1	2	7	11	11	17
50–64	63	3.9	20	1	2	2	3	9	17	20
65+	140	4.4	22	1	1	3	6	8	12	18
GRAND TOTAL	**243**	**5.6**	**94**	**1**	**1**	**3**	**6**	**11**	**17**	**60**

29.32: PHAR DIVERTICULECTOMY

Type of Patients	Observed Patients	Avg. Stay	Vari-ance	10th	25th	50th	75th	90th	95th	99th
1. SINGLE DX										
0–19 Years	0									
20–34	0									
35–49	0									
50–64	6	1.7	<1	1	1	2	2	2	2	2
65+	7	1.3	<1	1	1	1	2	2	2	2
2. MULTIPLE DX										
0–19 Years	0									
20–34	0									
35–49	2	5.2	19	1	1	8	8	8	8	8
50–64	18	2.7	4	1	1	2	4	5	5	9
65+	60	4.4	11	1	2	4	6	7	12	16
TOTAL SINGLE DX	**13**	**1.4**	**<1**	**1**	**1**	**1**	**2**	**2**	**2**	**2**
TOTAL MULTIPLE DX	**80**	**4.1**	**10**	**1**	**2**	**4**	**6**	**7**	**12**	**16**
TOTAL										
0–19 Years	0									
20–34	0									
35–49	2	5.2	19	1	1	8	8	8	8	8
50–64	24	2.5	3	1	1	2	3	5	5	9
65+	67	4.2	11	1	2	4	6	7	12	16
GRAND TOTAL	**93**	**3.9**	**10**	**1**	**2**	**3**	**5**	**7**	**9**	**16**

29.4: PLASTIC OP ON PHARYNX

Type of Patients	Observed Patients	Avg. Stay	Vari-ance	Percentiles						
				10th	25th	50th	75th	90th	95th	99th
1. SINGLE DX										
0–19 Years	21	1.2	<1	1	1	1	1	2	2	2
20–34	5	1.8	<1	1	1	2	2	3	3	3
35–49	5	1.1	<1	1	1	1	1	1	2	2
50–64	3	2.0	0	2	2	2	2	2	2	2
65+	0									
2. MULTIPLE DX										
0–19 Years	47	2.5	44	1	1	1	2	3	11	51
20–34	21	2.0	<1	1	1	2	3	3	4	4
35–49	66	1.8	<1	1	1	2	2	3	3	4
50–64	50	1.8	<1	1	1	2	2	2	3	8
65+	7	3.4	14	1	1	1	8	9	9	9
TOTAL SINGLE DX	**34**	**1.3**	**<1**	**1**	**1**	**1**	**2**	**2**	**2**	**3**
TOTAL MULTIPLE DX	**191**	**2.1**	**17**	**1**	**1**	**1**	**2**	**3**	**4**	**11**
TOTAL										
0–19 Years	68	2.2	33	1	1	1	2	2	3	51
20–34	26	1.9	<1	1	1	2	2	3	3	4
35–49	71	1.7	<1	1	1	2	2	3	3	4
50–64	53	1.8	<1	1	1	2	2	2	3	5
65+	7	3.4	14	1	1	1	8	9	9	9
GRAND TOTAL	**225**	**2.0**	**15**	**1**	**1**	**1**	**2**	**3**	**3**	**11**

29.5: OTHER PHARYNGEAL REPAIR

Type of Patients	Observed Patients	Avg. Stay	Vari-ance	Percentiles						
				10th	25th	50th	75th	90th	95th	99th
1. SINGLE DX										
0–19 Years	1	1.0	0	1	1	1	1	1	1	1
20–34	0									
35–49	1	2.0	0	2	2	2	2	2	2	2
50–64	0									
65+	0									
2. MULTIPLE DX										
0–19 Years	3	3.6	9	1	2	2	7	7	7	7
20–34	3	3.5	<1	3	3	3	4	4	4	4
35–49	1	1.0	0	1	1	1	1	1	1	1
50–64	5	7.3	37	1	1	4	14	15	15	15
65+	9	9.5	137	2	3	3	9	33	33	33
TOTAL SINGLE DX	**2**	**1.4**	**<1**	**1**	**1**	**1**	**2**	**2**	**2**	**2**
TOTAL MULTIPLE DX	**21**	**6.5**	**62**	**1**	**2**	**3**	**7**	**15**	**23**	**33**
TOTAL										
0–19 Years	4	2.9	8	1	1	2	7	7	7	7
20–34	3	3.5	<1	3	3	3	4	4	4	4
35–49	2	1.2	<1	1	1	1	1	2	2	2
50–64	5	7.3	37	1	1	4	14	15	15	15
65+	9	9.5	137	2	3	3	9	33	33	33
GRAND TOTAL	**23**	**6.2**	**60**	**1**	**2**	**3**	**7**	**15**	**23**	**33**

29.9: OTHER PHARYNGEAL OPS

Type of Patients	Observed Patients	Avg. Stay	Vari-ance	Percentiles						
				10th	25th	50th	75th	90th	95th	99th
1. SINGLE DX										
0–19 Years	0									
20–34	0									
35–49	0									
50–64	0									
65+	0									
2. MULTIPLE DX										
0–19 Years	2	3.0	0	3	3	3	3	3	3	3
20–34	1	1.0	0	1	1	1	1	1	1	1
35–49	0									
50–64	3	3.3	5	1	1	3	6	6	6	6
65+	1	1.0	0	1	1	1	1	1	1	1
TOTAL SINGLE DX	**0**									
TOTAL MULTIPLE DX	**7**	**2.5**	**3**	**1**	**1**	**3**	**3**	**6**	**6**	**6**
TOTAL										
0–19 Years	2	3.0	0	3	3	3	3	3	3	3
20–34	1	1.0	0	1	1	1	1	1	1	1
35–49	0									
50–64	3	3.3	5	1	1	3	6	6	6	6
65+	1	1.0	0	1	1	1	1	1	1	1
GRAND TOTAL	**7**	**2.5**	**3**	**1**	**1**	**3**	**3**	**6**	**6**	**6**

30.0: EXC/DESTR LES LARYNX

Type of Patients	Observed Patients	Avg. Stay	Vari-ance	Percentiles						
				10th	25th	50th	75th	90th	95th	99th
1. SINGLE DX										
0–19 Years	20	1.5	1	1	1	1	1	3	3	5
20–34	1	1.0	0	1	1	1	1	1	1	1
35–49	2	1.0	0	1	1	1	1	1	1	1
50–64	2	1.0	0	1	1	1	1	1	1	1
65+	5	1.2	<1	1	1	1	1	2	2	2
2. MULTIPLE DX										
0–19 Years	77	4.4	23	1	1	2	7	12	16	18
20–34	12	2.8	7	1	1	2	4	8	9	9
35–49	22	3.5	22	1	1	1	5	10	18	18
50–64	32	3.9	16	1	1	2	5	11	15	15
65+	48	2.7	8	1	1	1	5	7	7	13
TOTAL SINGLE DX	**30**	**1.4**	**<1**	**1**	**1**	**1**	**1**	**3**	**3**	**5**
TOTAL MULTIPLE DX	**191**	**3.8**	**18**	**1**	**1**	**2**	**5**	**9**	**15**	**18**
TOTAL										
0–19 Years	97	3.8	20	1	1	2	5	9	14	18
20–34	13	2.7	7	1	1	2	4	8	9	9
35–49	24	3.4	21	1	1	1	3	10	18	18
50–64	34	3.9	16	1	1	2	5	11	15	15
65+	53	2.5	7	1	1	1	2	7	7	13
GRAND TOTAL	**221**	**3.5**	**16**	**1**	**1**	**2**	**5**	**8**	**14**	**18**

30.09: EXC/DESTR LARYNX LES NEC

Type of Patients	Observed Patients	Avg. Stay	Variance	10th	25th	50th	75th	90th	95th	99th
				Percentiles						
1. SINGLE DX										
0–19 Years	20	1.5	1	1	1	1	1	3	3	5
20–34	1	1.0	0	1	1	1	1	1	1	1
35–49	2	1.0	0	1	1	1	1	1	1	1
50–64	2	1.0	0	1	1	1	1	1	1	1
65+	5	1.2	<1	1	1	1	1	2	2	2
2. MULTIPLE DX										
0–19 Years	74	4.3	23	1	1	2	6	12	16	18
20–34	12	2.8	7	1	1	2	4	8	9	9
35–49	22	3.5	22	1	1	1	5	10	18	18
50–64	32	3.9	16	1	1	2	5	11	15	15
65+	48	2.7	8	1	1	1	5	7	7	13
TOTAL SINGLE DX	**30**	**1.4**	**<1**	**1**	**1**	**1**	**1**	**3**	**3**	**5**
TOTAL MULTIPLE DX	**188**	**3.8**	**18**	**1**	**1**	**2**	**5**	**9**	**15**	**18**
TOTAL										
0–19 Years	94	3.7	19	1	1	2	4	9	14	18
20–34	13	2.7	7	1	1	2	4	8	9	9
35–49	24	3.4	21	1	1	1	3	10	18	18
50–64	34	3.9	16	1	1	2	5	11	15	15
65+	53	2.5	7	1	1	1	2	7	7	13
GRAND TOTAL	**218**	**3.5**	**16**	**1**	**1**	**1**	**5**	**8**	**14**	**18**

30.1: HEMILARYNGECTOMY

Type of Patients	Observed Patients	Avg. Stay	Variance	10th	25th	50th	75th	90th	95th	99th
				Percentiles						
1. SINGLE DX										
0–19 Years	0									
20–34	0									
35–49	0									
50–64	0									
65+	0									
2. MULTIPLE DX										
0–19 Years	0									
20–34	0									
35–49	0									
50–64	1	3.0	0	3	3	3	3	3	3	3
65+	2	6.8	4	5	5	8	8	8	8	8
TOTAL SINGLE DX	**0**									
TOTAL MULTIPLE DX	**3**	**5.4**	**6**	**3**	**3**	**5**	**8**	**8**	**8**	**8**
TOTAL										
0–19 Years	0									
20–34	0									
35–49	0									
50–64	1	3.0	0	3	3	3	3	3	3	3
65+	2	6.8	4	5	5	8	8	8	8	8
GRAND TOTAL	**3**	**5.4**	**6**	**3**	**3**	**5**	**8**	**8**	**8**	**8**

30.2: PARTIAL LARYNGECTOMY NEC

Type of Patients	Observed Patients	Avg. Stay	Variance	10th	25th	50th	75th	90th	95th	99th
				Percentiles						
1. SINGLE DX										
0–19 Years	3	1.0	0	1	1	1	1	1	1	1
20–34	1	1.0	0	1	1	1	1	1	1	1
35–49	1	1.0	0	1	1	1	1	1	1	1
50–64	1	1.0	0	1	1	1	1	1	1	1
65+	0									
2. MULTIPLE DX										
0–19 Years	8	14.1	594	1	1	4	10	70	70	70
20–34	0									
35–49	4	4.3	7	1	1	6	6	7	7	7
50–64	21	5.1	12	1	2	4	9	10	10	10
65+	17	5.6	44	1	1	5	7	10	15	32
TOTAL SINGLE DX	**6**	**1.0**	**0**	**1**	**1**	**1**	**1**	**1**	**1**	**1**
TOTAL MULTIPLE DX	**50**	**6.3**	**98**	**1**	**1**	**4**	**8**	**10**	**10**	**70**
TOTAL										
0–19 Years	11	7.9	347	1	1	1	6	10	70	70
20–34	1	1.0	0	1	1	1	1	1	1	1
35–49	5	3.9	7	1	1	4	6	7	7	7
50–64	22	5.0	12	1	2	4	9	10	10	10
65+	17	5.6	44	1	1	5	7	10	15	32
GRAND TOTAL	**56**	**5.6**	**87**	**1**	**1**	**4**	**7**	**10**	**10**	**70**

30.3: COMPLETE LARYNGECTOMY

Type of Patients	Observed Patients	Avg. Stay	Variance	10th	25th	50th	75th	90th	95th	99th
				Percentiles						
1. SINGLE DX										
0–19 Years	0									
20–34	0									
35–49	0									
50–64	0									
65+	3	5.9	3	3	6	6	6	8	8	8
2. MULTIPLE DX										
0–19 Years	1	4.0	0	4	4	4	4	4	4	4
20–34	1	26.0	0	26	26	26	26	26	26	26
35–49	12	8.3	15	4	6	7	10	13	18	18
50–64	61	11.0	38	5	7	10	13	18	21	39
65+	56	10.3	47	4	6	8	13	18	19	42
TOTAL SINGLE DX	**3**	**5.9**	**3**	**3**	**6**	**6**	**6**	**8**	**8**	**8**
TOTAL MULTIPLE DX	**131**	**10.3**	**41**	**4**	**6**	**9**	**12**	**18**	**20**	**39**
TOTAL										
0–19 Years	1	4.0	0	4	4	4	4	4	4	4
20–34	1	26.0	0	26	26	26	26	26	26	26
35–49	12	8.3	15	4	6	7	10	13	18	18
50–64	61	11.0	38	5	7	10	13	18	21	39
65+	59	10.0	46	4	6	8	13	17	19	42
GRAND TOTAL	**134**	**10.2**	**40**	**4**	**6**	**9**	**12**	**18**	**20**	**39**

30.4: RADICAL LARYNGECTOMY

Type of Patients	Observed Patients	Avg. Stay	Vari-ance	Percentiles						
				10th	25th	50th	75th	90th	95th	99th
1. SINGLE DX										
0–19 Years	0									
20–34	0									
35–49	2	8.5	<1	8	8	9	9	9	9	9
50–64	2	7.3	1	6	6	8	8	8	8	8
65+	0									
2. MULTIPLE DX										
0–19 Years	0									
20–34	2	32.5	125	8	37	37	37	37	37	37
35–49	26	13.0	59	7	8	9	18	23	25	41
50–64	68	11.1	32	7	8	9	13	18	22	36
65+	67	13.8	193	5	8	10	15	23	25	96
TOTAL SINGLE DX	**4**	**7.7**	**1**	**6**	**8**	**8**	**8**	**9**	**9**	**9**
TOTAL MULTIPLE DX	**163**	**12.8**	**100**	**6**	**8**	**10**	**15**	**22**	**28**	**41**
TOTAL										
0–19 Years	0									
20–34	2	32.5	125	8	37	37	37	37	37	37
35–49	28	12.8	58	7	8	9	17	23	25	41
50–64	70	11.0	32	6	7	9	13	18	22	36
65+	67	13.8	193	5	8	10	15	23	25	96
GRAND TOTAL	**167**	**12.7**	**99**	**6**	**8**	**9**	**15**	**22**	**28**	**41**

31.0: LARYNX INJECTION

Type of Patients	Observed Patients	Avg. Stay	Vari-ance	Percentiles						
				10th	25th	50th	75th	90th	95th	99th
1. SINGLE DX										
0–19 Years	1	1.0	0	1	1	1	1	1	1	1
20–34	0									
35–49	0									
50–64	0									
65+	1	1.0	0	1	1	1	1	1	1	1
2. MULTIPLE DX										
0–19 Years	1	1.0	0	1	1	1	1	1	1	1
20–34	0									
35–49	4	3.5	15	1	1	1	6	10	10	10
50–64	9	2.6	18	1	1	1	1	7	10	18
65+	12	10.0	146	1	1	4	27	28	29	29
TOTAL SINGLE DX	**2**	**1.0**	**0**	**1**	**1**	**1**	**1**	**1**	**1**	**1**
TOTAL MULTIPLE DX	**26**	**4.6**	**64**	**1**	**1**	**1**	**4**	**18**	**28**	**29**
TOTAL										
0–19 Years	2	1.0	0	1	1	1	1	1	1	1
20–34	0									
35–49	4	3.5	15	1	1	1	6	10	10	10
50–64	9	2.6	18	1	1	1	1	7	10	18
65+	13	9.4	141	1	1	4	27	28	29	29
GRAND TOTAL	**28**	**4.5**	**62**	**1**	**1**	**1**	**2**	**18**	**28**	**29**

31.1: TEMPORARY TRACHEOSTOMY

Type of Patients	Observed Patients	Avg. Stay	Vari-ance	Percentiles						
				10th	25th	50th	75th	90th	95th	99th
1. SINGLE DX										
0–19 Years	2	2.6	3	1	1	4	4	4	4	4
20–34	8	3.0	9	1	1	1	4	9	9	11
35–49	11	5.7	3	4	5	6	7	7	8	8
50–64	12	7.2	15	1	7	7	11	11	11	15
65+	4	6.4	7	2	7	7	7	9	9	9
2. MULTIPLE DX										
0–19 Years	236	26.3	433	7	13	22	45	97	>99	>99
20–34	460	25.4	290	6	14	23	35	52	73	>99
35–49	775	25.8	313	5	12	23	36	52	64	>99
50–64	1,257	23.8	343	5	9	20	34	52	67	>99
65+	1,622	25.0	257	7	14	22	34	48	59	>99
TOTAL SINGLE DX	**37**	**5.3**	**12**	**1**	**1**	**6**	**7**	**10**	**11**	**15**
TOTAL MULTIPLE DX	**4,350**	**24.9**	**306**	**6**	**12**	**22**	**35**	**51**	**67**	**>99**
TOTAL										
0–19 Years	238	26.1	434	7	13	22	45	97	>99	>99
20–34	468	24.6	297	5	12	23	35	51	70	>99
35–49	786	25.4	314	5	11	23	36	51	64	>99
50–64	1,269	23.6	342	5	9	20	33	52	67	>99
65+	1,626	25.0	257	7	14	22	33	48	59	>99
GRAND TOTAL	**4,387**	**24.7**	**307**	**6**	**11**	**22**	**34**	**51**	**67**	**>99**

31.2: PERMANENT TRACHEOSTOMY

Type of Patients	Observed Patients	Avg. Stay	Vari-ance	Percentiles						
				10th	25th	50th	75th	90th	95th	99th
1. SINGLE DX										
0–19 Years	1	3.0	0	3	3	3	3	3	3	3
20–34	0									
35–49	1	26.0	0	26	26	26	26	26	26	26
50–64	2	10.0	8	8	8	8	12	12	12	12
65+	0									
2. MULTIPLE DX										
0–19 Years	36	20.5	219	8	12	16	29	48	>99	>99
20–34	45	23.5	355	4	8	20	32	52	59	>99
35–49	98	24.2	232	6	14	23	33	48	54	>99
50–64	200	21.4	275	4	8	17	31	47	54	>99
65+	320	22.5	213	6	12	20	29	43	51	75
TOTAL SINGLE DX	**4**	**12.6**	**100**	**3**	**3**	**12**	**26**	**26**	**26**	**26**
TOTAL MULTIPLE DX	**699**	**22.4**	**243**	**5**	**10**	**19**	**30**	**46**	**53**	**>99**
TOTAL										
0–19 Years	37	20.3	220	8	9	16	29	46	>99	>99
20–34	45	23.5	355	4	8	20	32	52	59	>99
35–49	99	24.2	230	6	14	23	33	48	54	>99
50–64	202	21.3	274	4	8	17	31	47	51	>99
65+	320	22.5	213	6	12	20	29	43	51	75
GRAND TOTAL	**703**	**22.3**	**242**	**5**	**10**	**19**	**30**	**46**	**53**	**>99**

31.29: OTHER PERM TRACHEOSTOMY

Type of Patients	Observed Patients	Avg. Stay	Vari-ance	Percentiles 10th	25th	50th	75th	90th	95th	99th
1. SINGLE DX										
0–19 Years	1	3.0	0	3	3	3	3	3	3	3
20–34	0									
35–49	1	26.0	0	26	26	26	26	26	26	26
50–64	1	12.0	0	12	12	12	12	12	12	12
65+	0									
2. MULTIPLE DX										
0–19 Years	36	20.5	219	8	12	16	29	48	>99	>99
20–34	45	23.5	355	4	8	20	32	52	59	>99
35–49	97	24.2	238	6	14	23	33	48	54	>99
50–64	196	21.4	276	4	8	18	32	47	51	>99
65+	312	22.4	201	6	12	20	29	41	50	72
TOTAL SINGLE DX	**3**	**14.0**	**132**	**3**	**3**	**12**	**26**	**26**	**26**	**26**
TOTAL MULTIPLE DX	**686**	**22.3**	**238**	**5**	**10**	**19**	**30**	**45**	**53**	**>99**
TOTAL										
0–19 Years	37	20.3	220	8	9	16	29	46	>99	>99
20–34	45	23.5	355	4	8	20	32	52	59	>99
35–49	98	24.3	236	6	14	23	33	48	54	>99
50–64	197	21.3	275	4	8	17	32	47	51	>99
65+	312	22.4	201	6	12	20	29	41	50	72
GRAND TOTAL	**689**	**22.3**	**238**	**5**	**10**	**19**	**30**	**45**	**53**	**>99**

31.3: INC LARYNX/TRACHEA NEC

Type of Patients	Observed Patients	Avg. Stay	Vari-ance	Percentiles 10th	25th	50th	75th	90th	95th	99th
1. SINGLE DX										
0–19 Years	0									
20–34	0									
35–49	0									
50–64	0									
65+	0									
2. MULTIPLE DX										
0–19 Years	4	5.6	22	1	1	4	8	12	12	12
20–34	2	2.0	0	2	2	2	2	2	2	2
35–49	6	5.5	20	1	1	5	9	9	14	14
50–64	6	4.7	29	1	2	3	3	18	18	18
65+	4	5.1	10	2	3	5	5	11	11	11
TOTAL SINGLE DX	**0**									
TOTAL MULTIPLE DX	**22**	**5.1**	**19**	**1**	**1**	**3**	**9**	**11**	**14**	**18**
TOTAL										
0–19 Years	4	5.6	22	1	1	4	8	12	12	12
20–34	2	2.0	0	2	2	2	2	2	2	2
35–49	6	5.5	20	1	1	5	9	9	14	14
50–64	6	4.7	29	1	2	3	3	18	18	18
65+	4	5.1	10	2	3	5	5	11	11	11
GRAND TOTAL	**22**	**5.1**	**19**	**1**	**1**	**3**	**9**	**11**	**14**	**18**

31.4: LARYNX/TRACHEA DXTIC PX

Type of Patients	Observed Patients	Avg. Stay	Vari-ance	Percentiles 10th	25th	50th	75th	90th	95th	99th
1. SINGLE DX										
0–19 Years	86	1.9	2	1	1	1	2	4	4	6
20–34	28	2.3	<1	1	2	2	3	3	4	4
35–49	33	3.2	34	1	1	2	2	4	26	26
50–64	17	1.8	2	1	1	1	2	4	4	7
65+	5	1.3	<1	1	1	1	2	2	2	2
2. MULTIPLE DX										
0–19 Years	338	4.0	24	1	2	2	4	8	14	29
20–34	108	2.9	13	1	1	2	3	4	6	14
35–49	213	3.6	11	1	2	3	5	8	11	12
50–64	272	4.7	28	1	1	3	6	9	12	27
65+	422	5.5	23	1	2	4	7	12	16	24
TOTAL SINGLE DX	**169**	**2.3**	**9**	**1**	**1**	**2**	**2**	**4**	**4**	**26**
TOTAL MULTIPLE DX	**1,353**	**4.4**	**22**	**1**	**2**	**3**	**5**	**10**	**13**	**25**
TOTAL										
0–19 Years	424	3.6	20	1	1	2	4	7	13	28
20–34	136	2.7	10	1	1	2	3	4	6	14
35–49	246	3.5	15	1	1	2	4	8	11	26
50–64	289	4.5	27	1	1	3	6	9	11	27
65+	427	5.5	23	1	2	4	7	12	16	22
GRAND TOTAL	**1,522**	**4.1**	**21**	**1**	**1**	**3**	**5**	**9**	**12**	**26**

31.42: LARYNGOSCOPY/TRACHEOSCPY

Type of Patients	Observed Patients	Avg. Stay	Vari-ance	Percentiles 10th	25th	50th	75th	90th	95th	99th
1. SINGLE DX										
0–19 Years	85	1.8	1	1	1	1	2	4	4	6
20–34	28	2.3	<1	1	2	2	3	3	4	4
35–49	29	1.8	<1	1	1	2	2	3	4	5
50–64	16	1.9	2	1	1	1	2	4	4	7
65+	3	1.3	<1	1	1	1	2	2	2	2
2. MULTIPLE DX										
0–19 Years	330	4.0	24	1	2	2	4	8	14	29
20–34	106	2.8	13	1	1	2	3	4	6	14
35–49	192	3.5	10	1	2	3	4	7	11	12
50–64	208	4.9	33	1	2	3	6	9	13	30
65+	343	5.7	23	1	2	4	7	12	15	24
TOTAL SINGLE DX	**161**	**1.9**	**1**	**1**	**1**	**2**	**2**	**3**	**4**	**6**
TOTAL MULTIPLE DX	**1,179**	**4.4**	**23**	**1**	**2**	**3**	**5**	**9**	**13**	**27**
TOTAL										
0–19 Years	415	3.6	21	1	1	2	4	7	13	28
20–34	134	2.7	9	1	1	2	3	4	6	14
35–49	221	3.3	9	1	1	2	4	6	10	12
50–64	224	4.7	31	1	1	3	6	9	13	30
65+	346	5.6	23	1	2	4	7	12	15	22
GRAND TOTAL	**1,340**	**4.1**	**20**	**1**	**2**	**3**	**5**	**9**	**12**	**25**

31.43: CLOSED LARYNX BIOPSY

Type of Patients	Observed Patients	Avg. Stay	Vari-ance	Percentiles						
				10th	25th	50th	75th	90th	95th	99th
1. SINGLE DX										
0–19 Years	1	5.0	0	5	5	5	5	5	5	5
20–34	0									
35–49	4	11.6	154	1	1	1	26	26	26	26
50–64	1	1.0	0	1	1	1	1	1	1	1
65+	2	1.5	<1	1	1	1	2	2	2	2
2. MULTIPLE DX										
0–19 Years	4	5.4	11	1	1	7	8	8	8	8
20–34	2	6.6	52	1	1	12	12	12	12	12
35–49	16	4.2	18	1	1	2	11	11	11	11
50–64	52	3.7	11	1	1	3	6	10	10	17
65+	69	4.6	19	1	1	3	7	10	16	17
TOTAL SINGLE DX	**8**	**9.1**	**129**	**1**	**1**	**1**	**26**	**26**	**26**	**26**
TOTAL MULTIPLE DX	**143**	**4.2**	**15**	**1**	**1**	**3**	**6**	**10**	**11**	**17**
TOTAL										
0–19 Years	5	5.4	9	1	1	7	8	8	8	8
20–34	2	6.6	52	1	1	12	12	12	12	12
35–49	20	6.3	64	1	1	2	11	26	26	26
50–64	53	3.7	11	1	1	3	6	10	10	17
65+	71	4.5	19	1	1	3	7	10	16	17
GRAND TOTAL	**151**	**4.5**	**23**	**1**	**1**	**3**	**7**	**10**	**12**	**26**

31.5: LOC EXC/DESTR LARYNX LES

Type of Patients	Observed Patients	Avg. Stay	Vari-ance	Percentiles						
				10th	25th	50th	75th	90th	95th	99th
1. SINGLE DX										
0–19 Years	1	6.0	0	6	6	6	6	6	6	6
20–34	2	2.7	<1	2	2	2	4	4	4	4
35–49	0									
50–64	0									
65+	0									
2. MULTIPLE DX										
0–19 Years	35	4.4	28	1	1	2	6	8	18	28
20–34	6	3.9	9	1	1	3	5	8	8	8
35–49	15	5.4	11	2	2	6	7	7	7	18
50–64	27	4.1	16	1	1	2	7	12	12	13
65+	30	6.4	62	1	2	4	8	12	14	48
TOTAL SINGLE DX	**3**	**2.9**	**2**	**2**	**2**	**2**	**4**	**4**	**6**	**6**
TOTAL MULTIPLE DX	**113**	**5.0**	**29**	**1**	**1**	**3**	**7**	**8**	**13**	**24**
TOTAL										
0–19 Years	36	4.5	27	1	1	2	6	8	18	28
20–34	8	3.0	3	1	2	2	4	5	8	8
35–49	15	5.4	11	2	2	6	7	7	7	18
50–64	27	4.1	16	1	1	2	7	12	12	13
65+	30	6.4	62	1	2	4	8	12	14	48
GRAND TOTAL	**116**	**4.8**	**27**	**1**	**2**	**3**	**7**	**8**	**12**	**24**

31.6: REPAIR OF LARYNX

Type of Patients	Observed Patients	Avg. Stay	Vari-ance	Percentiles						
				10th	25th	50th	75th	90th	95th	99th
1. SINGLE DX										
0–19 Years	7	2.9	5	1	2	2	4	8	8	9
20–34	0									
35–49	3	1.1	<1	1	1	1	1	2	2	2
50–64	6	2.3	2	1	1	1	4	4	4	4
65+	4	1.6	<1	1	1	2	2	2	2	2
2. MULTIPLE DX										
0–19 Years	31	7.6	69	1	2	4	11	19	24	37
20–34	5	3.4	17	1	1	2	2	12	12	12
35–49	23	4.2	20	1	1	3	6	11	11	18
50–64	26	3.8	50	1	1	1	4	5	29	29
65+	31	2.2	9	1	1	1	1	5	12	12
TOTAL SINGLE DX	**20**	**2.2**	**3**	**1**	**1**	**2**	**2**	**4**	**8**	**9**
TOTAL MULTIPLE DX	**116**	**4.6**	**41**	**1**	**1**	**2**	**5**	**12**	**19**	**32**
TOTAL										
0–19 Years	38	6.5	58	1	2	3	8	19	23	37
20–34	5	3.4	17	1	1	2	2	12	12	12
35–49	26	3.8	18	1	1	2	3	11	11	18
50–64	32	3.6	42	1	1	1	4	4	29	29
65+	35	2.1	9	1	1	1	1	5	12	12
GRAND TOTAL	**136**	**4.2**	**36**	**1**	**1**	**2**	**4**	**11**	**18**	**29**

31.69: OTHER LARYNGEAL REPAIR

Type of Patients	Observed Patients	Avg. Stay	Vari-ance	Percentiles						
				10th	25th	50th	75th	90th	95th	99th
1. SINGLE DX										
0–19 Years	7	2.9	5	1	2	2	4	8	8	9
20–34	0									
35–49	3	1.1	<1	1	1	1	1	2	2	2
50–64	6	2.3	2	1	1	1	4	4	4	4
65+	4	1.6	<1	1	1	2	2	2	2	2
2. MULTIPLE DX										
0–19 Years	30	7.1	66	1	2	3	10	20	24	37
20–34	3	1.5	<1	1	1	2	2	2	2	2
35–49	21	4.6	25	1	1	2	7	11	18	18
50–64	24	3.7	51	1	1	1	3	4	29	29
65+	31	2.2	9	1	1	1	1	5	12	12
TOTAL SINGLE DX	**20**	**2.2**	**3**	**1**	**1**	**2**	**2**	**4**	**8**	**9**
TOTAL MULTIPLE DX	**109**	**4.5**	**42**	**1**	**1**	**1**	**4**	**11**	**18**	**32**
TOTAL										
0–19 Years	37	6.1	55	1	2	3	8	15	23	37
20–34	3	1.5	<1	1	1	2	2	2	2	2
35–49	24	4.0	23	1	1	1	6	11	18	18
50–64	30	3.4	43	1	1	1	3	4	29	29
65+	35	2.1	9	1	1	1	1	5	12	12
GRAND TOTAL	**129**	**4.1**	**36**	**1**	**1**	**2**	**4**	**11**	**17**	**32**

31.7: REPAIR OF TRACHEA

Type of Patients	Observed Patients	Avg. Stay	Vari-ance	Percentiles						
				10th	25th	50th	75th	90th	95th	99th
1. SINGLE DX										
0–19 Years	9	1.9	4	1	1	1	1	6	6	6
20–34	1	1.0	0	1	1	1	1	1	1	1
35–49	7	3.2	3	1	1	3	5	5	5	5
50–64	3	1.0	0	1	1	1	1	1	1	1
65+	0									
2. MULTIPLE DX										
0–19 Years	103	14.3	249	1	2	10	23	36	45	95
20–34	20	10.0	59	1	5	6	21	21	21	21
35–49	34	5.6	37	1	1	2	7	17	17	26
50–64	67	7.3	91	1	2	6	8	17	21	73
65+	77	9.0	233	1	2	5	9	21	28	>99
TOTAL SINGLE DX	**20**	**2.2**	**3**	**1**	**1**	**1**	**4**	**5**	**6**	**6**
TOTAL MULTIPLE DX	**301**	**10.2**	**178**	**1**	**2**	**6**	**13**	**26**	**36**	**95**
TOTAL										
0–19 Years	112	13.4	242	1	1	8	20	36	45	95
20–34	21	9.8	60	1	5	6	21	21	21	21
35–49	41	5.3	33	1	1	3	6	17	17	26
50–64	70	7.2	90	1	1	6	8	17	21	73
65+	77	9.0	233	1	2	5	9	21	28	>99
GRAND TOTAL	**321**	**9.8**	**173**	**1**	**2**	**5**	**13**	**26**	**33**	**95**

31.74: REVISION OF TRACHEOSTOMY

Type of Patients	Observed Patients	Avg. Stay	Vari-ance	Percentiles						
				10th	25th	50th	75th	90th	95th	99th
1. SINGLE DX										
0–19 Years	0									
20–34	0									
35–49	4	2.8	4	1	1	4	4	5	5	5
50–64	0									
65+	0									
2. MULTIPLE DX										
0–19 Years	14	14.6	218	1	3	10	18	41	42	42
20–34	10	13.6	67	1	6	14	21	21	21	21
35–49	16	5.4	24	1	2	3	7	13	18	18
50–64	42	7.3	52	1	2	6	9	20	26	29
65+	54	11.0	318	2	3	5	10	23	28	95
TOTAL SINGLE DX	**4**	**2.8**	**4**	**1**	**1**	**4**	**4**	**5**	**5**	**5**
TOTAL MULTIPLE DX	**136**	**9.9**	**165**	**1**	**2**	**6**	**11**	**21**	**29**	**95**
TOTAL										
0–19 Years	14	14.6	218	1	3	10	18	41	42	42
20–34	10	13.6	67	1	6	14	21	21	21	21
35–49	20	4.9	22	1	1	3	6	11	18	18
50–64	42	7.3	52	1	2	6	9	20	26	29
65+	54	11.0	318	2	3	5	10	23	28	95
GRAND TOTAL	**140**	**9.8**	**163**	**1**	**2**	**6**	**11**	**21**	**29**	**95**

31.9: OTHER LARYNX/TRACHEA OPS

Type of Patients	Observed Patients	Avg. Stay	Vari-ance	Percentiles						
				10th	25th	50th	75th	90th	95th	99th
1. SINGLE DX										
0–19 Years	2	1.0	0	1	1	1	1	1	1	1
20–34	2	1.6	<1	1	1	2	2	2	2	2
35–49	0									
50–64	2	1.7	<1	1	1	2	2	2	2	2
65+	1	5.0	0	5	5	5	5	5	5	5
2. MULTIPLE DX										
0–19 Years	28	18.2	744	1	2	5	25	84	84	93
20–34	13	10.3	96	2	2	4	24	24	24	24
35–49	15	2.8	11	1	1	2	3	5	5	16
50–64	27	4.7	23	1	1	2	11	13	13	19
65+	55	4.7	49	1	1	2	5	14	18	47
TOTAL SINGLE DX	**7**	**1.8**	**2**	**1**	**1**	**1**	**2**	**5**	**5**	**5**
TOTAL MULTIPLE DX	**138**	**8.5**	**239**	**1**	**1**	**3**	**8**	**24**	**26**	**84**
TOTAL										
0–19 Years	30	17.5	724	1	1	3	25	84	84	93
20–34	15	9.7	94	2	2	4	24	24	24	24
35–49	15	2.8	11	1	1	2	3	5	5	16
50–64	29	4.6	22	1	1	2	8	11	13	19
65+	56	4.7	48	1	1	2	5	14	18	47
GRAND TOTAL	**145**	**8.2**	**232**	**1**	**1**	**3**	**7**	**24**	**26**	**84**

31.99: TRACHEAL OPERATION NEC

Type of Patients	Observed Patients	Avg. Stay	Vari-ance	Percentiles						
				10th	25th	50th	75th	90th	95th	99th
1. SINGLE DX										
0–19 Years	2	1.0	0	1	1	1	1	1	1	1
20–34	1	2.0	0	2	2	2	2	2	2	2
35–49	0									
50–64	2	1.7	<1	1	1	2	2	2	2	2
65+	1	5.0	0	5	5	5	5	5	5	5
2. MULTIPLE DX										
0–19 Years	8	19.0	>999	1	3	3	5	84	84	84
20–34	10	12.7	98	2	4	6	24	24	24	24
35–49	7	3.4	17	1	1	2	3	5	16	16
50–64	21	4.9	24	1	1	2	11	13	13	19
65+	35	6.0	67	1	1	2	7	18	21	47
TOTAL SINGLE DX	**6**	**1.9**	**2**	**1**	**1**	**2**	**2**	**5**	**5**	**5**
TOTAL MULTIPLE DX	**81**	**8.7**	**232**	**1**	**1**	**3**	**11**	**24**	**24**	**84**
TOTAL										
0–19 Years	10	17.4	963	1	3	3	5	84	84	84
20–34	11	12.2	99	2	4	5	24	24	24	24
35–49	7	3.4	17	1	1	2	3	5	16	16
50–64	23	4.7	23	1	1	2	11	13	13	19
65+	36	5.9	66	1	1	2	7	18	21	47
GRAND TOTAL	**87**	**8.3**	**223**	**1**	**1**	**3**	**11**	**24**	**24**	**84**

32.0: LOC EXC/DESTR BRONCH LES

Type of Patients	Observed Patients	Avg. Stay	Vari-ance	Percentiles						
				10th	25th	50th	75th	90th	95th	99th
1. SINGLE DX										
0–19 Years	1	1.0	0	1	1	1	1	1	1	1
20–34	2	6.5	12	4	4	7	9	9	9	9
35–49	2	2.9	7	1	1	1	5	5	5	5
50–64	1	1.0	0	1	1	1	1	1	1	1
65+	0									
2. MULTIPLE DX										
0–19 Years	7	7.7	22	3	3	5	13	14	14	14
20–34	7	5.5	22	1	1	6	10	12	12	12
35–49	7	8.0	18	3	4	10	11	14	14	14
50–64	23	3.7	17	1	1	3	4	7	14	19
65+	18	6.1	13	2	4	4	10	12	12	12
TOTAL SINGLE DX	**6**	**3.2**	**9**	**1**	**1**	**1**	**5**	**9**	**9**	**9**
TOTAL MULTIPLE DX	**62**	**5.9**	**20**	**1**	**3**	**4**	**10**	**13**	**14**	**19**
TOTAL										
0–19 Years	8	7.4	23	3	3	5	13	14	14	14
20–34	9	5.7	19	1	1	6	10	12	12	12
35–49	9	7.1	20	3	3	5	11	14	14	14
50–64	24	3.6	16	1	1	3	4	7	14	19
65+	18	6.1	13	2	4	4	10	12	12	12
GRAND TOTAL	**68**	**5.7**	**20**	**1**	**2**	**4**	**10**	**13**	**14**	**19**

32.1: BRONCHIAL EXCISION NEC

Type of Patients	Observed Patients	Avg. Stay	Vari-ance	Percentiles						
				10th	25th	50th	75th	90th	95th	99th
1. SINGLE DX										
0–19 Years	0									
20–34	0									
35–49	0									
50–64	0									
65+	0									
2. MULTIPLE DX										
0–19 Years	1	5.0	0	5	5	5	5	5	5	5
20–34	1	10.0	0	10	10	10	10	10	10	10
35–49	0									
50–64	1	10.0	0	10	10	10	10	10	10	10
65+	0									
TOTAL SINGLE DX	**0**									
TOTAL MULTIPLE DX	**3**	**8.2**	**7**	**5**	**5**	**10**	**10**	**10**	**10**	**10**
TOTAL										
0–19 Years	1	5.0	0	5	5	5	5	5	5	5
20–34	1	10.0	0	10	10	10	10	10	10	10
35–49	0									
50–64	1	10.0	0	10	10	10	10	10	10	10
65+	0									
GRAND TOTAL	**3**	**8.2**	**7**	**5**	**5**	**10**	**10**	**10**	**10**	**10**

32.2: LOC EXC/DESTR LUNG LES

Type of Patients	Observed Patients	Avg. Stay	Vari-ance	Percentiles						
				10th	25th	50th	75th	90th	95th	99th
1. SINGLE DX										
0–19 Years	25	3.5	6	1	2	3	4	7	10	11
20–34	31	4.5	6	2	3	4	5	9	9	13
35–49	31	4.1	21	1	2	3	5	6	11	29
50–64	37	3.9	5	1	2	4	5	6	8	11
65+	25	3.2	4	1	2	3	3	7	8	8
2. MULTIPLE DX										
0–19 Years	157	8.2	65	2	3	5	11	16	19	39
20–34	242	7.5	79	2	3	5	9	15	20	52
35–49	350	6.9	76	2	3	5	7	13	19	37
50–64	696	6.1	32	2	3	4	7	14	17	26
65+	972	7.2	41	2	3	5	9	15	21	32
TOTAL SINGLE DX	**149**	**3.8**	**8**	**1**	**2**	**3**	**5**	**7**	**9**	**13**
TOTAL MULTIPLE DX	**2,417**	**7.0**	**49**	**2**	**3**	**5**	**8**	**14**	**19**	**34**
TOTAL										
0–19 Years	182	7.6	60	2	3	5	10	15	19	39
20–34	273	7.2	71	2	3	5	8	14	16	52
35–49	381	6.7	73	2	3	5	7	13	19	37
50–64	733	6.0	30	2	3	4	7	13	17	26
65+	997	7.1	41	2	3	5	8	14	20	31
GRAND TOTAL	**2,566**	**6.8**	**48**	**2**	**3**	**5**	**8**	**14**	**18**	**34**

32.28: ENDO EXC/DESTR LUNG LES

Type of Patients	Observed Patients	Avg. Stay	Vari-ance	Percentiles						
				10th	25th	50th	75th	90th	95th	99th
1. SINGLE DX										
0–19 Years	2	1.0	0	1	1	1	1	1	1	1
20–34	2	4.5	3	3	3	6	6	6	6	6
35–49	2	2.5	<1	2	2	2	3	3	3	3
50–64	0									
65+	4	3.8	7	2	2	3	3	8	8	8
2. MULTIPLE DX										
0–19 Years	10	8.0	50	2	3	4	11	19	19	19
20–34	9	5.5	7	3	4	5	5	11	11	11
35–49	13	5.6	56	1	2	3	5	14	29	29
50–64	26	3.3	4	1	2	3	4	5	7	10
65+	33	6.0	46	1	2	3	8	19	24	24
TOTAL SINGLE DX	**10**	**2.6**	**4**	**1**	**1**	**2**	**3**	**6**	**8**	**8**
TOTAL MULTIPLE DX	**91**	**5.5**	**34**	**1**	**2**	**3**	**6**	**14**	**19**	**24**
TOTAL										
0–19 Years	12	6.3	47	1	1	3	10	19	19	19
20–34	11	5.3	6	3	4	5	6	11	11	11
35–49	15	5.2	50	1	2	3	4	14	29	29
50–64	26	3.3	4	1	2	3	4	5	7	10
65+	37	5.9	44	1	2	3	8	19	24	24
GRAND TOTAL	**101**	**5.2**	**32**	**1**	**2**	**3**	**5**	**11**	**19**	**24**

32.29: LOC EXC LUNG LES NEC

Type of Patients	Observed Patients	Avg. Stay	Vari-ance	Percentiles						
				10th	25th	50th	75th	90th	95th	99th
1. SINGLE DX										
0–19 Years	21	3.4	3	1	3	3	4	5	7	10
20–34	26	4.5	6	2	3	4	5	9	9	13
35–49	29	4.2	23	1	2	3	5	6	11	29
50–64	36	3.8	5	1	2	4	5	6	9	11
65+	21	3.1	3	1	2	3	3	5	8	8
2. MULTIPLE DX										
0–19 Years	139	8.2	67	2	3	5	11	16	20	39
20–34	222	7.7	86	2	3	5	9	15	20	52
35–49	325	7.0	80	2	3	5	7	14	19	37
50–64	645	6.0	27	2	3	4	7	13	17	24
65+	928	7.1	41	2	3	5	9	14	20	32
TOTAL SINGLE DX	**133**	**3.9**	**8**	**1**	**2**	**3**	**5**	**6**	**9**	**13**
TOTAL MULTIPLE DX	**2,259**	**7.0**	**49**	**2**	**3**	**5**	**8**	**14**	**18**	**36**
TOTAL										
0–19 Years	160	7.7	63	2	3	5	9	15	18	39
20–34	248	7.4	78	2	3	5	9	15	18	52
35–49	354	6.8	76	2	3	5	7	13	19	37
50–64	681	5.9	26	2	3	4	7	13	17	24
65+	949	7.0	40	2	3	5	8	14	19	32
GRAND TOTAL	**2,392**	**6.8**	**47**	**2**	**3**	**5**	**8**	**14**	**18**	**34**

32.3: SEGMENTAL LUNG RESECTION

Type of Patients	Observed Patients	Avg. Stay	Vari-ance	Percentiles						
				10th	25th	50th	75th	90th	95th	99th
1. SINGLE DX										
0–19 Years	5	2.7	<1	2	2	3	3	3	3	3
20–34	5	3.4	3	1	2	4	5	5	5	5
35–49	3	4.8	2	3	3	5	6	6	6	6
50–64	9	6.0	60	1	1	4	7	9	30	30
65+	6	4.7	9	1	1	5	7	9	9	9
2. MULTIPLE DX										
0–19 Years	26	7.1	33	3	4	4	9	16	22	22
20–34	19	8.1	47	3	4	5	10	21	23	27
35–49	53	7.2	27	4	4	5	8	14	19	33
50–64	162	7.3	22	3	4	6	9	14	16	23
65+	256	7.8	27	3	5	6	9	15	18	29
TOTAL SINGLE DX	**28**	**4.6**	**24**	**1**	**2**	**3**	**6**	**8**	**9**	**30**
TOTAL MULTIPLE DX	**516**	**7.6**	**27**	**3**	**4**	**6**	**9**	**14**	**18**	**29**
TOTAL										
0–19 Years	31	6.6	31	2	3	4	8	16	22	22
20–34	24	7.3	42	2	4	5	8	21	23	27
35–49	56	7.1	26	4	4	5	7	14	19	33
50–64	171	7.3	24	3	4	6	9	14	16	25
65+	262	7.8	27	3	5	6	9	15	18	29
GRAND TOTAL	**544**	**7.4**	**27**	**3**	**4**	**6**	**9**	**14**	**18**	**29**

32.4: LOBECTOMY OF LUNG

Type of Patients	Observed Patients	Avg. Stay	Vari-ance	Percentiles						
				10th	25th	50th	75th	90th	95th	99th
1. SINGLE DX										
0–19 Years	17	3.0	2	2	2	3	3	5	5	8
20–34	7	7.9	22	4	5	5	14	14	14	14
35–49	17	4.2	2	3	3	4	5	6	8	8
50–64	32	5.5	18	2	3	5	6	8	10	27
65+	30	5.2	5	2	4	5	7	8	9	10
2. MULTIPLE DX										
0–19 Years	38	12.1	93	2	4	9	19	29	29	33
20–34	44	6.6	9	4	5	6	8	10	12	18
35–49	229	8.5	66	4	5	7	10	14	19	31
50–64	958	7.6	26	4	5	6	8	13	17	28
65+	1,863	8.4	33	4	5	7	10	14	18	29
TOTAL SINGLE DX	**103**	**4.9**	**11**	**2**	**3**	**4**	**6**	**8**	**10**	**15**
TOTAL MULTIPLE DX	**3,132**	**8.2**	**35**	**4**	**5**	**7**	**9**	**14**	**18**	**29**
TOTAL										
0–19 Years	55	9.4	83	2	3	5	11	29	29	33
20–34	51	6.8	12	4	5	6	8	14	14	18
35–49	246	8.3	63	4	5	7	10	13	18	31
50–64	990	7.5	26	4	5	6	8	12	17	27
65+	1,893	8.3	33	4	5	7	10	14	18	29
GRAND TOTAL	**3,235**	**8.1**	**34**	**4**	**5**	**7**	**9**	**14**	**18**	**29**

32.5: COMPLETE PNEUMONECTOMY

Type of Patients	Observed Patients	Avg. Stay	Vari-ance	Percentiles						
				10th	25th	50th	75th	90th	95th	99th
1. SINGLE DX										
0–19 Years	1	8.0	0	8	8	8	8	8	8	8
20–34	1	3.0	0	3	3	3	3	3	3	3
35–49	1	4.0	0	4	4	4	4	4	4	4
50–64	1	6.0	0	6	6	6	6	6	6	6
65+	2	12.8	45	6	6	17	17	17	17	17
2. MULTIPLE DX										
0–19 Years	1	1.0	0	1	1	1	1	1	1	1
20–34	9	10.2	28	5	5	10	15	15	20	20
35–49	30	8.3	19	5	6	7	12	20	>99	>99
50–64	118	8.6	41	4	5	7	8	16	22	40
65+	105	10.5	291	4	5	6	9	14	22	98
TOTAL SINGLE DX	**6**	**8.1**	**31**	**3**	**4**	**6**	**8**	**17**	**17**	**17**
TOTAL MULTIPLE DX	**263**	**9.4**	**145**	**4**	**5**	**7**	**9**	**16**	**22**	**>99**
TOTAL										
0–19 Years	2	3.9	20	1	1	1	8	8	8	8
20–34	10	9.7	30	4	5	10	15	15	20	20
35–49	31	8.2	19	5	6	7	12	20	>99	>99
50–64	119	8.6	41	4	5	7	8	16	22	40
65+	107	10.5	287	4	5	6	9	14	22	98
GRAND TOTAL	**269**	**9.4**	**143**	**4**	**5**	**7**	**9**	**17**	**22**	**>99**

32.6: RAD DISSECT THOR STRUCT

Type of Patients	Observed Patients	Avg. Stay	Vari-ance	Percentiles						
				10th	25th	50th	75th	90th	95th	99th
1. SINGLE DX										
0–19 Years	0									
20–34	0									
35–49	0									
50–64	0									
65+	0									
2. MULTIPLE DX										
0–19 Years	0									
20–34	1	4.0	0	4	4	4	4	4	4	4
35–49	2	4.5	4	3	3	3	6	6	6	6
50–64	13	9.9	44	4	6	8	15	21	22	22
65+	8	10.0	22	6	7	7	11	20	20	20
TOTAL SINGLE DX	**0**									
TOTAL MULTIPLE DX	**24**	**9.4**	**34**	**4**	**6**	**7**	**11**	**20**	**21**	**22**
TOTAL										
0–19 Years	0									
20–34	1	4.0	0	4	4	4	4	4	4	4
35–49	2	4.5	4	3	3	3	6	6	6	6
50–64	13	9.9	44	4	6	8	15	21	22	22
65+	8	10.0	22	6	7	7	11	20	20	20
GRAND TOTAL	**24**	**9.4**	**34**	**4**	**6**	**7**	**11**	**20**	**21**	**22**

32.9: LUNG EXCISION NEC

Type of Patients	Observed Patients	Avg. Stay	Vari-ance	Percentiles						
				10th	25th	50th	75th	90th	95th	99th
1. SINGLE DX										
0–19 Years	0									
20–34	0									
35–49	0									
50–64	0									
65+	0									
2. MULTIPLE DX										
0–19 Years	3	2.3	<1	2	2	2	2	5	5	5
20–34	1	10.0	0	10	10	10	10	10	10	10
35–49	0									
50–64	4	9.3	45	3	5	9	18	18	18	18
65+	3	11.0	72	6	6	7	23	23	23	23
TOTAL SINGLE DX	**0**									
TOTAL MULTIPLE DX	**11**	**6.4**	**39**	**2**	**2**	**5**	**7**	**18**	**23**	**23**
TOTAL										
0–19 Years	3	2.3	<1	2	2	2	2	5	5	5
20–34	1	10.0	0	10	10	10	10	10	10	10
35–49	0									
50–64	4	9.3	45	3	5	9	18	18	18	18
65+	3	11.0	72	6	6	7	23	23	23	23
GRAND TOTAL	**11**	**6.4**	**39**	**2**	**2**	**5**	**7**	**18**	**23**	**23**

33.0: BRONCHUS INCISION

Type of Patients	Observed Patients	Avg. Stay	Vari-ance	Percentiles						
				10th	25th	50th	75th	90th	95th	99th
1. SINGLE DX										
0–19 Years	0									
20–34	0									
35–49	0									
50–64	1	5.0	0	5	5	5	5	5	5	5
65+	0									
2. MULTIPLE DX										
0–19 Years	0									
20–34	0									
35–49	2	6.8	2	6	6	6	8	8	8	8
50–64	0									
65+	0									
TOTAL SINGLE DX	**1**	**5.0**	**0**	**5**	**5**	**5**	**5**	**5**	**5**	**5**
TOTAL MULTIPLE DX	**2**	**6.8**	**2**	**6**	**6**	**6**	**8**	**8**	**8**	**8**
TOTAL										
0–19 Years	0									
20–34	0									
35–49	2	6.8	2	6	6	6	8	8	8	8
50–64	1	5.0	0	5	5	5	5	5	5	5
65+	0									
GRAND TOTAL	**3**	**6.2**	**2**	**5**	**5**	**6**	**8**	**8**	**8**	**8**

33.1: LUNG INCISION

Type of Patients	Observed Patients	Avg. Stay	Vari-ance	Percentiles						
				10th	25th	50th	75th	90th	95th	99th
1. SINGLE DX										
0–19 Years	0									
20–34	0									
35–49	0									
50–64	0									
65+	1	8.0	0	8	8	8	8	8	8	8
2. MULTIPLE DX										
0–19 Years	3	10.5	17	6	6	11	15	15	15	15
20–34	3	10.1	<1	9	9	10	11	11	11	11
35–49	5	8.0	30	3	3	7	10	10	22	22
50–64	4	20.4	842	5	7	7	11	73	73	73
65+	12	12.5	73	5	5	8	18	26	31	31
TOTAL SINGLE DX	**1**	**8.0**	**0**	**8**	**8**	**8**	**8**	**8**	**8**	**8**
TOTAL MULTIPLE DX	**27**	**11.9**	**135**	**5**	**5**	**9**	**16**	**22**	**26**	**73**
TOTAL										
0–19 Years	3	10.5	17	6	6	11	15	15	15	15
20–34	3	10.1	<1	9	9	10	11	11	11	11
35–49	5	8.0	30	3	3	7	10	10	22	22
50–64	4	20.4	842	5	7	7	11	73	73	73
65+	13	12.3	70	5	5	8	18	26	31	31
GRAND TOTAL	**28**	**11.8**	**132**	**5**	**5**	**9**	**16**	**22**	**26**	**73**

33.2: BRONCHIAL/LUNG DXTIC PX

Type of Patients	Observed Patients	Avg. Stay	Vari-ance	10th	25th	50th	75th	90th	95th	99th
1. SINGLE DX										
0–19 Years	113	2.0	5	1	1	1	2	4	7	12
20–34	53	4.0	21	1	1	2	5	10	18	20
35–49	69	3.2	9	1	1	2	4	6	9	15
50–64	90	3.2	6	1	1	3	4	7	8	16
65+	49	3.3	6	1	1	3	4	7	7	11
2. MULTIPLE DX										
0–19 Years	693	8.1	118	1	2	5	10	19	28	97
20–34	711	8.3	63	2	4	6	10	16	21	38
35–49	2,057	8.1	51	2	4	6	10	15	22	37
50–64	3,914	7.7	39	2	4	6	10	15	20	30
65+	7,783	8.1	36	2	4	7	11	16	20	29
TOTAL SINGLE DX	**374**	**2.9**	**8**	**1**	**1**	**2**	**4**	**6**	**8**	**15**
TOTAL MULTIPLE DX	**15,158**	**8.0**	**45**	**2**	**4**	**6**	**10**	**16**	**20**	**32**
TOTAL										
0–19 Years	806	7.3	107	1	2	4	9	17	26	91
20–34	764	8.1	62	2	4	6	10	16	20	37
35–49	2,126	8.0	50	2	4	6	10	15	21	37
50–64	4,004	7.6	38	2	3	6	10	15	20	30
65+	7,832	8.1	36	2	4	7	11	16	20	29
GRAND TOTAL	**15,532**	**7.9**	**44**	**2**	**4**	**6**	**10**	**15**	**20**	**32**

33.21: BRONCHOSCOPY THRU STOMA

Type of Patients	Observed Patients	Avg. Stay	Vari-ance	10th	25th	50th	75th	90th	95th	99th
1. SINGLE DX										
0–19 Years	0									
20–34	1	1.0	0	1	1	1	1	1	1	1
35–49	0									
50–64	0									
65+	0									
2. MULTIPLE DX										
0–19 Years	30	3.9	13	1	2	3	4	8	15	16
20–34	11	4.2	5	1	2	4	6	8	8	8
35–49	17	7.7	76	1	2	3	10	27	27	27
50–64	26	7.9	142	1	2	6	8	13	19	76
65+	27	8.2	74	1	2	6	12	17	20	42
TOTAL SINGLE DX	**1**	**1.0**	**0**	**1**	**1**	**1**	**1**	**1**	**1**	**1**
TOTAL MULTIPLE DX	**111**	**6.3**	**65**	**1**	**2**	**4**	**8**	**14**	**19**	**42**
TOTAL										
0–19 Years	30	3.9	13	1	2	3	4	8	15	16
20–34	12	4.1	6	1	2	4	6	8	8	8
35–49	17	7.7	76	1	2	3	10	27	27	27
50–64	26	7.9	142	1	2	6	8	13	19	76
65+	27	8.2	74	1	2	6	12	17	20	42
GRAND TOTAL	**112**	**6.2**	**65**	**1**	**2**	**4**	**8**	**13**	**19**	**42**

33.22: FIBER-OPTIC BRONCHOSCOPY

Type of Patients	Observed Patients	Avg. Stay	Vari-ance	10th	25th	50th	75th	90th	95th	99th
1. SINGLE DX										
0–19 Years	19	1.7	1	1	1	1	3	3	4	4
20–34	13	3.2	27	1	1	1	2	9	20	20
35–49	7	2.3	4	1	1	1	2	6	6	6
50–64	1	2.0	0	2	2	2	2	2	2	2
65+	7	1.5	<1	1	1	1	2	3	3	3
2. MULTIPLE DX										
0–19 Years	105	6.9	114	1	2	4	9	13	17	33
20–34	59	5.9	21	1	3	5	7	14	15	26
35–49	148	6.9	31	2	3	5	9	13	18	30
50–64	218	7.3	31	2	3	6	9	16	18	26
65+	497	8.5	40	2	4	7	11	17	22	28
TOTAL SINGLE DX	**47**	**2.1**	**7**	**1**	**1**	**1**	**2**	**4**	**6**	**20**
TOTAL MULTIPLE DX	**1,027**	**7.7**	**45**	**2**	**3**	**6**	**10**	**16**	**19**	**29**
TOTAL										
0–19 Years	124	6.2	101	1	1	3	8	13	14	33
20–34	72	5.5	22	1	2	4	7	14	15	20
35–49	155	6.6	30	1	3	5	9	13	18	30
50–64	219	7.3	31	2	3	6	9	16	18	26
65+	504	8.4	40	2	4	7	11	17	22	28
GRAND TOTAL	**1,074**	**7.5**	**45**	**1**	**3**	**6**	**10**	**15**	**19**	**28**

33.23: BRONCHOSCOPY NEC

Type of Patients	Observed Patients	Avg. Stay	Vari-ance	10th	25th	50th	75th	90th	95th	99th
1. SINGLE DX										
0–19 Years	58	1.3	1	1	1	1	1	2	3	7
20–34	7	3.0	11	1	1	1	4	10	10	10
35–49	1	1.0	0	1	1	1	1	1	1	1
50–64	5	1.9	3	1	1	1	2	5	5	5
65+	1	1.0	0	1	1	1	1	1	1	1
2. MULTIPLE DX										
0–19 Years	159	5.9	108	1	1	3	7	13	25	91
20–34	38	7.0	54	2	2	5	9	14	26	36
35–49	81	6.7	27	1	3	5	9	13	16	30
50–64	120	8.1	50	2	3	6	11	19	27	38
65+	179	7.2	32	1	3	6	10	15	20	25
TOTAL SINGLE DX	**72**	**1.5**	**2**	**1**	**1**	**1**	**1**	**3**	**4**	**7**
TOTAL MULTIPLE DX	**577**	**6.9**	**61**	**1**	**2**	**5**	**9**	**15**	**21**	**44**
TOTAL										
0–19 Years	217	4.7	82	1	1	2	5	9	18	91
20–34	45	6.5	50	2	2	4	8	13	26	36
35–49	82	6.7	27	1	3	5	9	13	16	30
50–64	125	7.9	49	1	3	6	10	19	23	38
65+	180	7.2	32	1	3	6	10	15	20	25
GRAND TOTAL	**649**	**6.2**	**57**	**1**	**2**	**4**	**8**	**14**	**20**	**38**

33.24: CLOSED BRONCHUS BIOPSY

Type of Patients	Observed Patients	Avg. Stay	Vari-ance	10th	25th	50th	75th	90th	95th	99th
				Percentiles						
1. SINGLE DX										
0–19 Years	23	3.5	11	1	1	2	5	7	11	15
20–34	13	5.1	25	1	1	4	6	11	18	18
35–49	19	3.9	11	1	1	4	4	8	11	15
50–64	19	3.9	14	1	1	3	5	9	16	16
65+	12	4.9	12	1	2	4	7	10	11	11
2. MULTIPLE DX										
0–19 Years	305	8.6	96	1	3	6	11	18	23	52
20–34	347	7.9	27	3	4	6	10	15	17	28
35–49	926	7.9	36	3	4	6	10	14	19	29
50–64	1,439	7.8	32	3	4	6	10	14	19	28
65+	3,197	8.5	36	3	4	7	11	16	20	30
TOTAL SINGLE DX	**86**	**4.0**	**13**	**1**	**1**	**3**	**5**	**10**	**11**	**16**
TOTAL MULTIPLE DX	**6,214**	**8.2**	**39**	**3**	**4**	**7**	**10**	**15**	**20**	**29**
TOTAL										
0–19 Years	328	8.2	91	1	3	5	11	17	23	52
20–34	360	7.8	27	3	4	6	10	15	17	26
35–49	945	7.8	36	2	4	6	10	14	19	29
50–64	1,458	7.7	32	3	4	6	10	14	19	28
65+	3,209	8.5	36	3	4	7	11	16	20	30
GRAND TOTAL	**6,300**	**8.2**	**39**	**3**	**4**	**7**	**10**	**15**	**20**	**29**

33.26: CLOSED LUNG BIOPSY

Type of Patients	Observed Patients	Avg. Stay	Vari-ance	10th	25th	50th	75th	90th	95th	99th
				Percentiles						
1. SINGLE DX										
0–19 Years	0									
20–34	2	3.0	8	1	1	5	5	5	5	5
35–49	3	1.7	1	1	1	1	3	3	3	3
50–64	7	2.7	1	1	1	3	4	4	4	4
65+	9	2.6	2	1	1	3	4	4	4	4
2. MULTIPLE DX										
0–19 Years	9	18.4	559	3	7	12	12	81	81	81
20–34	43	8.9	93	2	4	7	9	20	23	50
35–49	148	6.2	31	2	3	4	7	12	18	32
50–64	548	6.5	25	2	3	5	9	12	16	24
65+	1,351	6.5	23	2	3	5	8	12	15	24
TOTAL SINGLE DX	**21**	**2.6**	**2**	**1**	**1**	**3**	**4**	**4**	**4**	**5**
TOTAL MULTIPLE DX	**2,099**	**6.6**	**30**	**2**	**3**	**5**	**9**	**12**	**16**	**24**
TOTAL										
0–19 Years	9	18.4	559	3	7	12	12	81	81	81
20–34	45	8.7	91	2	4	7	9	20	23	50
35–49	151	6.2	31	2	3	4	7	12	17	32
50–64	555	6.4	25	2	3	5	9	12	16	24
65+	1,360	6.4	23	2	3	5	8	12	15	24
GRAND TOTAL	**2,120**	**6.5**	**30**	**2**	**3**	**5**	**9**	**12**	**16**	**24**

33.27: ENDOSCOPIC LUNG BIOPSY

Type of Patients	Observed Patients	Avg. Stay	Vari-ance	10th	25th	50th	75th	90th	95th	99th
				Percentiles						
1. SINGLE DX										
0–19 Years	4	1.0	0	1	1	1	1	1	1	1
20–34	9	7.8	32	3	4	5	12	19	19	19
35–49	13	3.7	11	1	2	2	4	9	14	14
50–64	13	3.2	5	1	1	3	4	8	8	8
65+	6	5.9	1	4	6	6	7	7	7	7
2. MULTIPLE DX										
0–19 Years	25	14.0	170	3	5	9	17	30	30	53
20–34	146	10.0	83	2	4	8	13	19	24	38
35–49	482	9.0	54	3	4	7	11	18	24	32
50–64	996	8.4	43	3	4	7	10	16	22	32
65+	1,907	8.6	36	3	4	7	11	16	20	31
TOTAL SINGLE DX	**45**	**4.1**	**13**	**1**	**1**	**3**	**6**	**8**	**12**	**19**
TOTAL MULTIPLE DX	**3,556**	**8.7**	**43**	**3**	**4**	**7**	**11**	**16**	**21**	**32**
TOTAL										
0–19 Years	29	12.8	169	2	4	8	15	30	30	53
20–34	155	9.9	81	3	4	8	13	19	24	38
35–49	495	8.8	53	2	4	7	11	18	23	32
50–64	1,009	8.3	43	3	4	7	10	16	22	32
65+	1,913	8.6	35	3	4	7	11	16	20	31
GRAND TOTAL	**3,601**	**8.6**	**43**	**3**	**4**	**7**	**11**	**16**	**21**	**32**

33.28: OPEN BIOPSY OF LUNG

Type of Patients	Observed Patients	Avg. Stay	Vari-ance	10th	25th	50th	75th	90th	95th	99th
				Percentiles						
1. SINGLE DX										
0–19 Years	9	2.2	7	1	1	2	2	2	12	12
20–34	8	2.5	4	1	1	2	3	6	6	6
35–49	26	2.8	7	1	1	2	3	6	7	12
50–64	44	3.1	3	1	2	3	4	7	7	8
65+	14	2.3	2	1	1	2	3	5	5	5
2. MULTIPLE DX										
0–19 Years	59	10.1	146	2	3	5	19	36	>99	>99
20–34	65	10.9	242	2	3	6	11	34	43	94
35–49	253	9.3	122	2	2	5	11	22	37	50
50–64	564	7.4	53	1	2	4	10	18	24	31
65+	619	8.4	60	2	3	5	12	20	24	35
TOTAL SINGLE DX	**101**	**2.8**	**4**	**1**	**1**	**2**	**4**	**6**	**7**	**12**
TOTAL MULTIPLE DX	**1,560**	**8.4**	**79**	**2**	**3**	**5**	**11**	**20**	**27**	**46**
TOTAL										
0–19 Years	68	9.0	134	2	2	5	14	33	>99	>99
20–34	73	9.6	214	1	2	3	10	25	43	94
35–49	279	8.8	116	1	2	4	10	22	37	50
50–64	608	7.1	51	1	2	4	9	17	22	31
65+	633	8.3	59	2	3	5	12	20	24	35
GRAND TOTAL	**1,661**	**8.0**	**76**	**1**	**2**	**5**	**11**	**20**	**26**	**43**

33.3: SURG COLLAPSE OF LUNG

Type of Patients	Observed Patients	Avg. Stay	Vari-ance	Percentiles						
				10th	25th	50th	75th	90th	95th	99th
1. SINGLE DX										
0–19 Years	6	5.1	10	2	4	4	5	11	11	11
20–34	2	2.0	2	1	1	3	3	3	3	3
35–49	3	4.8	20	1	1	3	10	10	10	10
50–64	0									
65+	1	5.0	0	5	5	5	5	5	5	5
2. MULTIPLE DX										
0–19 Years	6	6.1	5	2	4	7	7	9	9	9
20–34	13	6.6	20	2	3	5	9	14	14	14
35–49	16	6.8	22	1	3	8	9	13	19	19
50–64	35	6.6	21	2	4	6	6	13	17	22
65+	33	6.7	14	2	4	6	9	11	16	17
TOTAL SINGLE DX	**12**	**4.6**	**10**	**1**	**3**	**4**	**5**	**11**	**11**	**11**
TOTAL MULTIPLE DX	**103**	**6.7**	**18**	**2**	**4**	**6**	**8**	**13**	**15**	**19**
TOTAL										
0–19 Years	12	5.6	7	2	4	5	7	11	11	11
20–34	15	6.1	20	2	3	4	9	14	14	14
35–49	19	6.6	22	1	3	8	9	12	13	19
50–64	35	6.6	21	2	4	6	6	13	17	22
65+	34	6.7	14	2	4	6	9	11	16	17
GRAND TOTAL	**115**	**6.4**	**17**	**2**	**4**	**6**	**8**	**12**	**15**	**19**

33.4: LUNG & BRONCHUS REPAIR

Type of Patients	Observed Patients	Avg. Stay	Vari-ance	Percentiles						
				10th	25th	50th	75th	90th	95th	99th
1. SINGLE DX										
0–19 Years	1	2.0	0	2	2	2	2	2	2	2
20–34	0									
35–49	0									
50–64	0									
65+	0									
2. MULTIPLE DX										
0–19 Years	3	8.0	6	5	5	9	10	10	10	10
20–34	13	11.1	48	6	8	10	12	16	32	32
35–49	10	7.6	13	4	5	7	10	12	15	15
50–64	5	13.2	265	3	5	6	11	44	44	44
65+	12	11.1	81	3	3	9	12	27	27	37
TOTAL SINGLE DX	**1**	**2.0**	**0**	**2**	**2**	**2**	**2**	**2**	**2**	**2**
TOTAL MULTIPLE DX	**43**	**10.3**	**68**	**3**	**5**	**8**	**12**	**16**	**32**	**44**
TOTAL										
0–19 Years	4	6.6	12	2	5	9	9	10	10	10
20–34	13	11.1	48	6	8	10	12	16	32	32
35–49	10	7.6	13	4	5	7	10	12	15	15
50–64	5	13.2	265	3	5	6	11	44	44	44
65+	12	11.1	81	3	3	9	12	27	27	37
GRAND TOTAL	**44**	**10.2**	**68**	**3**	**5**	**8**	**12**	**16**	**32**	**44**

33.5: LUNG TRANSPLANTATION

Type of Patients	Observed Patients	Avg. Stay	Vari-ance	Percentiles						
				10th	25th	50th	75th	90th	95th	99th
1. SINGLE DX										
0–19 Years	0									
20–34	0									
35–49	2	11.6	2	11	11	11	11	14	14	14
50–64	8	7.7	5	5	5	8	9	11	11	11
65+	0									
2. MULTIPLE DX										
0–19 Years	1	26.0	0	26	26	26	26	26	26	26
20–34	11	10.7	31	3	8	11	13	20	20	24
35–49	12	13.4	15	9	11	14	16	20	20	20
50–64	69	11.0	22	7	8	10	13	16	22	28
65+	6	19.9	116	10	14	17	17	39	39	39
TOTAL SINGLE DX	**10**	**8.7**	**7**	**5**	**7**	**8**	**11**	**11**	**14**	**14**
TOTAL MULTIPLE DX	**99**	**12.1**	**38**	**7**	**8**	**11**	**14**	**18**	**24**	**39**
TOTAL										
0–19 Years	1	26.0	0	26	26	26	26	26	26	26
20–34	11	10.7	31	3	8	11	13	20	20	24
35–49	14	12.9	12	10	11	11	16	16	20	20
50–64	77	10.6	21	7	8	9	12	16	22	28
65+	6	19.9	116	10	14	17	17	39	39	39
GRAND TOTAL	**109**	**11.7**	**36**	**7**	**8**	**10**	**14**	**17**	**23**	**39**

33.6: HEART-LUNG TRANSPLANT

Type of Patients	Observed Patients	Avg. Stay	Vari-ance	Percentiles						
				10th	25th	50th	75th	90th	95th	99th
1. SINGLE DX										
0–19 Years	0									
20–34	0									
35–49	0									
50–64	0									
65+	0									
2. MULTIPLE DX										
0–19 Years	0									
20–34	0									
35–49	1	40.0	0	40	40	40	40	40	40	40
50–64	1	17.0	0	17	17	17	17	17	17	17
65+	0									
TOTAL SINGLE DX	**0**									
TOTAL MULTIPLE DX	**2**	**28.4**	**254**	**17**	**17**	**17**	**40**	**40**	**40**	**40**
TOTAL										
0–19 Years	0									
20–34	0									
35–49	1	40.0	0	40	40	40	40	40	40	40
50–64	1	17.0	0	17	17	17	17	17	17	17
65+	0									
GRAND TOTAL	**2**	**28.4**	**254**	**17**	**17**	**17**	**40**	**40**	**40**	**40**

33.9: OTHER BRONCHIAL LUNG OPS

Type of Patients	Observed Patients	Avg. Stay	Vari-ance	Percentiles						
				10th	25th	50th	75th	90th	95th	99th
1. SINGLE DX										
0–19 Years	0									
20–34	1	2.0	0	2	2	2	2	2	2	2
35–49	1	1.0	0	1	1	1	1	1	1	1
50–64	1	5.0	0	5	5	5	5	5	5	5
65+	0									
2. MULTIPLE DX										
0–19 Years	17	11.0	119	2	3	8	19	29	29	46
20–34	5	5.7	2	3	5	6	6	8	8	8
35–49	26	4.9	34	1	1	2	8	11	20	25
50–64	24	7.8	33	1	3	7	10	12	15	26
65+	30	9.3	97	1	2	6	14	21	39	39
TOTAL SINGLE DX	**3**	**2.7**	**4**	**1**	**1**	**2**	**5**	**5**	**5**	**5**
TOTAL MULTIPLE DX	**102**	**8.0**	**70**	**1**	**2**	**6**	**10**	**20**	**25**	**39**
TOTAL										
0–19 Years	17	11.0	119	2	3	8	19	29	29	46
20–34	6	5.3	3	2	5	6	6	8	8	8
35–49	27	4.7	33	1	1	2	8	11	20	25
50–64	25	7.7	31	1	4	7	10	12	15	26
65+	30	9.3	97	1	2	6	14	21	39	39
GRAND TOTAL	**105**	**7.8**	**69**	**1**	**2**	**6**	**10**	**20**	**25**	**39**

34.0: INC CHEST WALL & PLEURA

Type of Patients	Observed Patients	Avg. Stay	Vari-ance	Percentiles						
				10th	25th	50th	75th	90th	95th	99th
1. SINGLE DX										
0–19 Years	124	3.3	4	2	2	3	4	6	7	9
20–34	275	3.3	5	2	2	3	4	6	7	11
35–49	110	3.0	3	1	2	3	4	5	6	11
50–64	45	3.4	3	2	2	3	4	6	7	10
65+	18	5.4	10	2	2	5	8	10	10	10
2. MULTIPLE DX										
0–19 Years	469	7.4	48	2	3	5	10	14	22	34
20–34	969	5.4	20	2	3	4	6	11	14	21
35–49	1,123	6.6	38	2	3	5	8	13	18	37
50–64	1,459	7.0	35	2	3	6	9	14	18	29
65+	2,260	7.4	28	2	4	6	9	14	18	25
TOTAL SINGLE DX	**572**	**3.3**	**4**	**1**	**2**	**3**	**4**	**6**	**8**	**10**
TOTAL MULTIPLE DX	**6,280**	**6.9**	**32**	**2**	**3**	**5**	**9**	**13**	**18**	**29**
TOTAL										
0–19 Years	593	6.6	42	2	3	4	8	14	18	32
20–34	1,244	4.9	18	2	2	4	6	10	13	20
35–49	1,233	6.3	36	2	3	5	8	13	17	36
50–64	1,504	6.9	35	2	3	5	9	13	18	29
65+	2,278	7.4	27	2	4	6	9	14	18	25
GRAND TOTAL	**6,852**	**6.6**	**31**	**2**	**3**	**5**	**8**	**13**	**17**	**28**

34.01: CHEST WALL INCISION

Type of Patients	Observed Patients	Avg. Stay	Vari-ance	Percentiles						
				10th	25th	50th	75th	90th	95th	99th
1. SINGLE DX										
0–19 Years	0									
20–34	5	1.0	0	1	1	1	1	1	1	1
35–49	2	1.0	0	1	1	1	1	1	1	1
50–64	1	1.0	0	1	1	1	1	1	1	1
65+	1	4.0	0	4	4	4	4	4	4	4
2. MULTIPLE DX										
0–19 Years	13	5.0	27	1	1	2	6	17	17	17
20–34	9	4.6	16	1	1	4	7	8	13	13
35–49	28	5.2	22	1	3	4	7	12	25	>99
50–64	46	5.1	32	1	1	2	7	12	16	29
65+	71	5.1	28	1	2	3	7	15	17	22
TOTAL SINGLE DX	**9**	**1.5**	**1**	**1**	**1**	**1**	**1**	**4**	**4**	**4**
TOTAL MULTIPLE DX	**167**	**5.1**	**27**	**1**	**1**	**3**	**7**	**14**	**17**	**25**
TOTAL										
0–19 Years	13	5.0	27	1	1	2	6	17	17	17
20–34	14	3.4	13	1	1	1	5	8	13	13
35–49	30	4.9	22	1	2	4	7	11	25	>99
50–64	47	5.1	32	1	1	2	7	12	16	29
65+	72	5.1	27	1	2	3	7	15	17	22
GRAND TOTAL	**176**	**4.9**	**27**	**1**	**1**	**3**	**7**	**14**	**17**	**25**

34.02: EXPLORATORY THORACOTOMY

Type of Patients	Observed Patients	Avg. Stay	Vari-ance	Percentiles						
				10th	25th	50th	75th	90th	95th	99th
1. SINGLE DX										
0–19 Years	0									
20–34	0									
35–49	2	6.0	2	5	5	7	7	7	7	7
50–64	1	7.0	0	7	7	7	7	7	7	7
65+	0									
2. MULTIPLE DX										
0–19 Years	3	34.3	653	3	9	54	54	54	54	54
20–34	11	8.0	34	2	3	7	12	13	23	23
35–49	11	22.8	465	4	5	8	47	47	63	63
50–64	25	8.7	41	3	4	7	11	19	23	26
65+	51	8.5	23	4	5	7	12	16	18	20
TOTAL SINGLE DX	**3**	**6.4**	**1**	**5**	**5**	**7**	**7**	**7**	**7**	**7**
TOTAL MULTIPLE DX	**101**	**10.8**	**127**	**4**	**5**	**7**	**12**	**19**	**47**	**54**
TOTAL										
0–19 Years	3	34.3	653	3	9	54	54	54	54	54
20–34	11	8.0	34	2	3	7	12	13	23	23
35–49	13	21.0	441	4	5	8	47	47	63	63
50–64	26	8.7	40	3	4	7	11	19	23	26
65+	51	8.5	23	4	5	7	12	16	18	20
GRAND TOTAL	**104**	**10.8**	**125**	**4**	**5**	**7**	**12**	**19**	**47**	**54**

34.04: INSERT INTERCOSTAL CATH

Type of Patients	Observed Patients	Avg. Stay	Vari-ance	Percentiles						
				10th	25th	50th	75th	90th	95th	99th
1. SINGLE DX										
0–19 Years	101	3.3	3	2	2	3	4	6	8	9
20–34	204	3.3	4	2	2	3	4	6	7	11
35–49	86	2.9	3	1	2	3	4	5	5	11
50–64	30	3.5	4	2	2	3	4	6	8	10
65+	12	6.2	11	1	3	7	10	10	10	10
2. MULTIPLE DX										
0–19 Years	351	7.5	44	2	3	5	10	15	23	32
20–34	742	5.3	16	2	3	4	7	10	13	20
35–49	854	6.3	30	2	3	5	8	13	17	29
50–64	1,078	6.9	28	2	3	6	9	13	17	28
65+	1,647	7.2	25	2	4	6	9	14	17	25
TOTAL SINGLE DX	**433**	**3.3**	**4**	**2**	**2**	**3**	**4**	**6**	**8**	**10**
TOTAL MULTIPLE DX	**4,672**	**6.7**	**27**	**2**	**3**	**5**	**9**	**13**	**17**	**27**
TOTAL										
0–19 Years	452	6.7	39	2	3	5	9	13	19	32
20–34	946	4.9	14	2	2	4	6	10	12	19
35–49	940	6.0	28	2	3	5	7	12	17	28
50–64	1,108	6.8	28	2	3	5	9	13	17	28
65+	1,659	7.2	25	2	4	6	9	14	17	25
GRAND TOTAL	**5,105**	**6.5**	**26**	**2**	**3**	**5**	**8**	**13**	**17**	**26**

34.09: PLEURAL INCISION NEC

Type of Patients	Observed Patients	Avg. Stay	Vari-ance	Percentiles						
				10th	25th	50th	75th	90th	95th	99th
1. SINGLE DX										
0–19 Years	23	3.4	7	1	2	3	4	5	6	15
20–34	66	3.6	6	2	2	3	4	7	9	13
35–49	20	3.0	3	1	2	3	4	6	7	7
50–64	13	3.0	<1	2	3	3	3	4	5	5
65+	5	3.1	3	2	2	2	3	6	6	6
2. MULTIPLE DX										
0–19 Years	100	6.8	25	2	3	5	9	14	16	26
20–34	204	5.3	22	2	2	4	6	10	14	29
35–49	219	7.0	37	2	3	5	9	13	17	37
50–64	275	6.6	23	2	3	5	8	13	17	27
65+	455	7.9	29	3	4	7	10	16	19	25
TOTAL SINGLE DX	**127**	**3.4**	**5**	**1**	**2**	**3**	**4**	**6**	**8**	**13**
TOTAL MULTIPLE DX	**1,253**	**7.0**	**28**	**2**	**3**	**6**	**9**	**14**	**18**	**27**
TOTAL										
0–19 Years	123	6.2	23	2	3	4	8	14	15	26
20–34	270	4.9	19	2	2	4	6	9	12	29
35–49	239	6.7	35	2	3	5	9	13	16	37
50–64	288	6.4	22	2	3	5	8	12	17	27
65+	460	7.9	29	3	4	7	10	15	19	25
GRAND TOTAL	**1,380**	**6.8**	**27**	**2**	**3**	**5**	**9**	**13**	**18**	**27**

34.1: MEDIASTINUM INCISION

Type of Patients	Observed Patients	Avg. Stay	Vari-ance	Percentiles						
				10th	25th	50th	75th	90th	95th	99th
1. SINGLE DX										
0–19 Years	0									
20–34	0									
35–49	1	1.0	0	1	1	1	1	1	1	1
50–64	0									
65+	0									
2. MULTIPLE DX										
0–19 Years	3	5.8	7	3	3	8	8	8	8	8
20–34	10	6.7	42	2	3	3	11	19	19	19
35–49	10	9.0	34	3	5	5	15	15	22	22
50–64	21	12.7	180	1	6	9	12	28	38	65
65+	15	6.0	24	1	3	4	10	13	13	21
TOTAL SINGLE DX	**1**	**1.0**	**0**	**1**	**1**	**1**	**1**	**1**	**1**	**1**
TOTAL MULTIPLE DX	**59**	**8.7**	**79**	**2**	**3**	**6**	**11**	**18**	**21**	**65**
TOTAL										
0–19 Years	3	5.8	7	3	3	8	8	8	8	8
20–34	10	6.7	42	2	3	3	11	19	19	19
35–49	11	8.6	35	2	5	5	15	15	22	22
50–64	21	12.7	180	1	6	9	12	28	38	65
65+	15	6.0	24	1	3	4	10	13	13	21
GRAND TOTAL	**60**	**8.6**	**79**	**2**	**3**	**6**	**11**	**18**	**21**	**65**

34.2: THORAX DXTIC PROCEDURES

Type of Patients	Observed Patients	Avg. Stay	Vari-ance	Percentiles						
				10th	25th	50th	75th	90th	95th	99th
1. SINGLE DX										
0–19 Years	13	4.1	5	1	2	4	6	8	8	9
20–34	22	3.7	18	1	1	2	6	11	13	18
35–49	26	1.9	9	1	1	1	1	3	10	15
50–64	38	2.8	7	1	1	2	4	8	8	12
65+	16	3.0	13	1	1	1	3	6	14	14
2. MULTIPLE DX										
0–19 Years	50	8.1	37	2	4	7	10	15	25	29
20–34	116	6.1	40	1	2	4	9	15	19	29
35–49	231	5.9	28	1	2	4	8	13	18	25
50–64	554	5.9	29	1	2	4	8	13	17	25
65+	957	6.5	38	1	2	5	9	14	19	30
TOTAL SINGLE DX	**115**	**3.0**	**10**	**1**	**1**	**2**	**4**	**8**	**10**	**15**
TOTAL MULTIPLE DX	**1,908**	**6.3**	**35**	**1**	**2**	**5**	**9**	**14**	**18**	**28**
TOTAL										
0–19 Years	63	7.3	33	2	3	6	9	13	19	29
20–34	138	5.7	37	1	1	3	8	14	18	29
35–49	257	5.6	28	1	1	4	8	13	17	24
50–64	592	5.7	28	1	2	4	8	13	16	25
65+	973	6.4	38	1	2	5	9	14	19	30
GRAND TOTAL	**2,023**	**6.1**	**34**	**1**	**2**	**4**	**8**	**13**	**18**	**28**

34.21: TRANSPLEURA THORACOSCOPY

Type of Patients	Observed Patients	Avg. Stay	Vari-ance	Percentiles						
				10th	25th	50th	75th	90th	95th	99th
1. SINGLE DX										
0–19 Years	6	3.7	2	1	3	3	4	6	6	6
20–34	6	6.6	38	1	2	6	13	18	18	18
35–49	1	1.0	0	1	1	1	1	1	1	1
50–64	8	2.5	<1	2	2	2	3	4	4	4
65+	0									
2. MULTIPLE DX										
0–19 Years	25	8.8	32	3	4	9	11	19	19	25
20–34	32	7.8	46	1	3	5	12	19	20	29
35–49	57	7.5	34	2	4	6	9	14	23	28
50–64	142	8.4	42	2	3	6	12	18	21	28
65+	249	8.3	42	2	4	6	10	17	21	31
TOTAL SINGLE DX	**21**	**4.0**	**13**	**1**	**2**	**3**	**4**	**6**	**13**	**18**
TOTAL MULTIPLE DX	**505**	**8.2**	**41**	**2**	**4**	**6**	**11**	**17**	**21**	**28**
TOTAL										
0–19 Years	31	7.7	30	3	4	6	10	12	19	25
20–34	38	7.6	44	1	2	5	12	19	20	29
35–49	58	7.4	34	1	4	6	9	14	23	28
50–64	150	8.1	41	2	3	6	12	17	21	28
65+	249	8.3	42	2	4	6	10	17	21	31
GRAND TOTAL	**526**	**8.1**	**40**	**2**	**3**	**6**	**11**	**17**	**21**	**28**

34.22: MEDIASTINOSCOPY

Type of Patients	Observed Patients	Avg. Stay	Vari-ance	Percentiles						
				10th	25th	50th	75th	90th	95th	99th
1. SINGLE DX										
0–19 Years	0									
20–34	4	1.0	0	1	1	1	1	1	1	1
35–49	12	1.0	0	1	1	1	1	1	1	1
50–64	14	1.4	1	1	1	1	1	4	4	4
65+	4	1.0	0	1	1	1	1	1	1	1
2. MULTIPLE DX										
0–19 Years	1	11.0	0	11	11	11	11	11	11	11
20–34	27	4.3	23	1	1	2	6	11	15	18
35–49	76	4.4	19	1	1	3	6	11	15	18
50–64	197	3.8	16	1	1	2	6	8	12	18
65+	287	4.9	39	1	1	2	7	12	15	30
TOTAL SINGLE DX	**34**	**1.2**	**<1**	**1**	**1**	**1**	**1**	**1**	**4**	**4**
TOTAL MULTIPLE DX	**588**	**4.5**	**29**	**1**	**1**	**2**	**6**	**12**	**14**	**26**
TOTAL										
0–19 Years	1	11.0	0	11	11	11	11	11	11	11
20–34	31	3.9	22	1	1	2	6	11	15	18
35–49	88	3.9	18	1	1	2	6	10	15	18
50–64	211	3.6	16	1	1	1	6	8	11	18
65+	291	4.9	39	1	1	2	7	12	15	30
GRAND TOTAL	**622**	**4.3**	**28**	**1**	**1**	**2**	**6**	**12**	**14**	**26**

34.23: CHEST WALL BIOPSY

Type of Patients	Observed Patients	Avg. Stay	Vari-ance	Percentiles						
				10th	25th	50th	75th	90th	95th	99th
1. SINGLE DX										
0–19 Years	1	8.0	0	8	8	8	8	8	8	8
20–34	0									
35–49	2	1.5	<1	1	1	2	2	2	2	2
50–64	3	4.2	16	1	1	1	8	8	8	8
65+	1	1.0	0	1	1	1	1	1	1	1
2. MULTIPLE DX										
0–19 Years	6	5.9	10	1	5	6	6	12	13	13
20–34	6	5.9	31	1	2	3	12	16	16	16
35–49	9	9.9	59	1	3	10	18	20	20	20
50–64	26	6.2	49	1	2	3	8	18	22	33
65+	57	7.6	47	2	4	5	10	19	20	38
TOTAL SINGLE DX	**7**	**3.9**	**12**	**1**	**1**	**2**	**8**	**8**	**8**	**8**
TOTAL MULTIPLE DX	**104**	**7.2**	**43**	**1**	**3**	**5**	**9**	**18**	**20**	**33**
TOTAL										
0–19 Years	7	6.1	10	1	5	6	6	12	13	13
20–34	6	5.9	31	1	2	3	12	16	16	16
35–49	11	8.4	59	1	2	6	18	20	20	20
50–64	29	6.0	46	1	2	3	8	18	22	33
65+	58	7.6	47	2	4	5	10	19	20	38
GRAND TOTAL	**111**	**7.0**	**42**	**1**	**3**	**5**	**9**	**18**	**20**	**33**

34.24: PLEURAL BIOPSY

Type of Patients	Observed Patients	Avg. Stay	Vari-ance	Percentiles						
				10th	25th	50th	75th	90th	95th	99th
1. SINGLE DX										
0–19 Years	0									
20–34	1	2.0	0	2	2	2	2	2	2	2
35–49	1	1.0	0	1	1	1	1	1	1	1
50–64	7	5.1	17	1	2	3	9	12	12	12
65+	4	3.9	3	2	3	3	5	6	6	6
2. MULTIPLE DX										
0–19 Years	1	7.0	0	7	7	7	7	7	7	7
20–34	2	14.1	17	11	11	17	17	17	17	17
35–49	32	6.9	24	1	4	6	9	13	18	23
50–64	86	6.6	23	2	3	5	9	13	18	24
65+	234	6.7	25	2	3	6	9	12	16	28
TOTAL SINGLE DX	**13**	**4.0**	**10**	**1**	**2**	**2**	**6**	**9**	**12**	**12**
TOTAL MULTIPLE DX	**355**	**6.7**	**25**	**2**	**3**	**6**	**9**	**12**	**17**	**25**
TOTAL										
0–19 Years	1	7.0	0	7	7	7	7	7	7	7
20–34	3	6.9	47	2	2	2	11	17	17	17
35–49	33	6.7	24	1	4	6	9	12	18	23
50–64	93	6.5	23	2	3	5	9	13	18	24
65+	238	6.6	25	2	3	6	9	12	16	28
GRAND TOTAL	**368**	**6.6**	**24**	**2**	**3**	**6**	**9**	**12**	**17**	**25**

34.25: CLOSED MEDIASTINAL BX

Type of Patients	Observed Patients	Avg. Stay	Vari-ance	Percentiles						
				10th	25th	50th	75th	90th	95th	99th
1. SINGLE DX										
0–19 Years	3	2.4	1	1	2	2	4	4	4	4
20–34	2	4.2	15	1	1	7	7	7	7	7
35–49	5	5.7	43	1	1	1	10	15	15	15
50–64	1	5.0	0	5	5	5	5	5	5	5
65+	3	7.6	44	1	1	5	14	14	14	14
2. MULTIPLE DX										
0–19 Years	8	5.9	8	2	3	7	8	9	9	9
20–34	24	6.1	57	1	2	3	7	12	13	37
35–49	27	6.4	40	1	2	4	9	17	20	25
50–64	47	6.1	24	1	3	5	8	13	13	21
65+	58	5.6	20	1	2	5	8	11	17	19
TOTAL SINGLE DX	**14**	**4.7**	**22**	**1**	**1**	**2**	**7**	**14**	**15**	**15**
TOTAL MULTIPLE DX	**164**	**6.0**	**28**	**1**	**2**	**5**	**8**	**13**	**17**	**25**
TOTAL										
0–19 Years	11	4.9	9	1	2	4	8	9	9	9
20–34	26	6.0	54	1	2	3	7	12	13	37
35–49	32	6.3	40	1	1	4	10	16	20	25
50–64	48	6.1	23	1	3	5	8	13	13	21
65+	61	5.7	21	1	2	5	8	11	17	19
GRAND TOTAL	**178**	**5.9**	**27**	**1**	**2**	**5**	**8**	**13**	**17**	**25**

34.26: OPEN MEDIASTINAL BIOPSY

Type of Patients	Observed Patients	Avg. Stay	Vari-ance	Percentiles						
				10th	25th	50th	75th	90th	95th	99th
1. SINGLE DX										
0–19 Years	3	7.1	7	4	4	8	9	9	9	9
20–34	9	3.1	11	1	1	2	3	11	11	11
35–49	5	1.4	<1	1	1	1	1	3	3	3
50–64	5	2.6	5	1	1	2	3	6	6	6
65+	4	1.2	<1	1	1	1	1	2	2	2
2. MULTIPLE DX										
0–19 Years	9	12.1	117	1	3	10	15	29	29	29
20–34	25	5.8	32	1	2	3	10	16	17	19
35–49	25	4.0	7	2	2	3	6	8	10	10
50–64	50	5.3	15	1	2	5	7	10	14	20
65+	64	5.0	33	1	1	3	6	14	19	19
TOTAL SINGLE DX	**26**	**2.7**	**7**	**1**	**1**	**1**	**3**	**8**	**9**	**11**
TOTAL MULTIPLE DX	**173**	**5.4**	**30**	**1**	**2**	**3**	**7**	**13**	**19**	**29**
TOTAL										
0–19 Years	12	11.1	99	1	3	9	15	29	29	29
20–34	34	5.1	28	1	1	3	7	14	17	19
35–49	30	3.5	7	1	2	2	5	8	10	10
50–64	55	5.1	15	1	2	5	7	10	12	20
65+	68	4.8	32	1	1	3	4	14	19	19
GRAND TOTAL	**199**	**5.1**	**28**	**1**	**2**	**3**	**7**	**12**	**16**	**29**

34.3: DESTR MEDIASTINUM LES

Type of Patients	Observed Patients	Avg. Stay	Vari-ance	Percentiles						
				10th	25th	50th	75th	90th	95th	99th
1. SINGLE DX										
0–19 Years	8	3.2	6	1	1	2	4	5	9	9
20–34	14	4.3	14	2	3	3	6	8	17	17
35–49	8	4.4	4	2	3	4	7	7	8	8
50–64	7	2.4	3	1	1	2	5	5	5	5
65+	0									
2. MULTIPLE DX										
0–19 Years	25	7.6	34	3	4	6	7	15	26	26
20–34	25	3.9	7	1	2	3	5	8	9	12
35–49	42	3.9	6	1	2	4	6	7	8	10
50–64	59	5.9	28	2	3	5	6	10	13	39
65+	39	5.6	19	2	3	4	7	12	17	19
TOTAL SINGLE DX	**37**	**3.7**	**9**	**1**	**2**	**3**	**5**	**7**	**9**	**17**
TOTAL MULTIPLE DX	**190**	**5.4**	**21**	**1**	**3**	**4**	**6**	**10**	**14**	**26**
TOTAL										
0–19 Years	33	6.5	31	1	4	5	6	15	16	26
20–34	39	4.1	10	1	3	3	5	8	9	17
35–49	50	4.0	6	1	2	4	6	7	8	10
50–64	66	5.6	27	2	3	5	6	10	13	39
65+	39	5.6	19	2	3	4	7	12	17	19
GRAND TOTAL	**227**	**5.2**	**19**	**1**	**3**	**4**	**6**	**9**	**14**	**26**

34.4: EXC/DESTR CHEST WALL LES

Type of Patients	Observed Patients	Avg. Stay	Vari-ance	Percentiles						
				10th	25th	50th	75th	90th	95th	99th
1. SINGLE DX										
0–19 Years	3	3.2	1	1	3	4	4	4	4	4
20–34	10	4.6	5	3	3	4	6	6	10	10
35–49	6	3.3	3	1	2	4	4	6	6	6
50–64	8	3.3	<1	2	3	3	4	5	5	5
65+	6	2.2	1	1	1	2	3	4	4	4
2. MULTIPLE DX										
0–19 Years	10	3.4	3	2	2	3	4	5	7	8
20–34	12	4.4	8	1	1	6	6	7	10	10
35–49	35	4.6	16	2	3	4	6	8	10	26
50–64	46	5.8	50	1	2	3	6	15	26	33
65+	69	4.8	23	1	1	4	6	9	16	26
TOTAL SINGLE DX	**33**	**3.5**	**3**	**1**	**2**	**4**	**4**	**6**	**6**	**10**
TOTAL MULTIPLE DX	**172**	**4.8**	**24**	**1**	**2**	**4**	**6**	**9**	**15**	**26**
TOTAL										
0–19 Years	13	3.4	2	2	2	3	4	4	7	8
20–34	22	4.5	6	1	3	4	6	7	10	10
35–49	41	4.4	14	1	3	4	5	8	8	26
50–64	54	5.5	44	1	2	3	6	13	26	33
65+	75	4.7	22	1	1	4	6	9	16	26
GRAND TOTAL	**205**	**4.6**	**21**	**1**	**2**	**4**	**6**	**8**	**13**	**26**

34.5: PLEURECTOMY

Type of Patients	Observed Patients	Avg. Stay	Vari-ance	Percentiles 10th	25th	50th	75th	90th	95th	99th
1. SINGLE DX										
0–19 Years	1	5.0	0	5	5	5	5	5	5	5
20–34	6	6.9	15	2	4	5	9	9	15	15
35–49	11	8.0	17	4	4	8	11	14	15	15
50–64	4	4.5	3	2	4	4	5	7	7	7
65+	3	4.7	<1	4	4	5	5	5	5	5
2. MULTIPLE DX										
0–19 Years	123	12.7	76	5	6	10	15	23	31	48
20–34	160	12.1	59	5	7	10	15	26	30	35
35–49	356	12.7	65	5	7	11	15	23	29	47
50–64	537	13.1	89	4	7	11	16	23	28	44
65+	539	11.9	50	4	6	11	15	22	26	35
TOTAL SINGLE DX	**25**	**6.3**	**12**	**3**	**4**	**5**	**9**	**11**	**15**	**15**
TOTAL MULTIPLE DX	**1,715**	**12.5**	**68**	**4**	**7**	**11**	**15**	**23**	**28**	**41**
TOTAL										
0–19 Years	124	12.7	76	5	6	10	15	23	31	48
20–34	166	11.9	59	5	6	10	15	23	30	35
35–49	367	12.6	65	4	7	11	15	23	28	47
50–64	541	13.0	89	4	7	11	16	23	28	44
65+	542	11.8	50	4	6	11	15	21	26	35
GRAND TOTAL	**1,740**	**12.4**	**68**	**4**	**7**	**11**	**15**	**23**	**28**	**41**

34.51: DECORTICATION OF LUNG

Type of Patients	Observed Patients	Avg. Stay	Vari-ance	Percentiles 10th	25th	50th	75th	90th	95th	99th
1. SINGLE DX										
0–19 Years	1	5.0	0	5	5	5	5	5	5	5
20–34	3	9.0	13	3	9	9	9	15	15	15
35–49	8	9.5	14	4	7	9	11	15	15	15
50–64	3	4.9	2	4	4	4	5	7	7	7
65+	2	4.4	<1	4	4	4	5	5	5	5
2. MULTIPLE DX										
0–19 Years	116	13.0	78	5	6	11	15	23	31	48
20–34	149	12.7	60	5	7	11	15	27	31	37
35–49	346	12.8	66	5	7	11	15	23	30	47
50–64	490	13.3	86	5	8	11	17	23	28	42
65+	487	12.2	48	5	7	11	15	22	26	35
TOTAL SINGLE DX	**17**	**7.5**	**13**	**4**	**4**	**7**	**9**	**14**	**15**	**15**
TOTAL MULTIPLE DX	**1,588**	**12.8**	**67**	**5**	**7**	**11**	**16**	**23**	**28**	**41**
TOTAL										
0–19 Years	117	12.9	78	5	6	11	15	23	31	48
20–34	152	12.6	59	5	7	10	15	26	30	37
35–49	354	12.7	65	5	7	11	15	23	30	47
50–64	493	13.3	85	4	7	11	16	23	28	42
65+	489	12.2	48	5	7	11	15	22	26	35
GRAND TOTAL	**1,605**	**12.7**	**66**	**5**	**7**	**11**	**16**	**23**	**28**	**41**

34.59: PLEURAL EXCISION NEC

Type of Patients	Observed Patients	Avg. Stay	Vari-ance	Percentiles 10th	25th	50th	75th	90th	95th	99th
1. SINGLE DX										
0–19 Years	0									
20–34	3	3.8	2	2	2	4	5	5	5	5
35–49	3	3.7	<1	3	3	4	4	4	4	4
50–64	1	2.0	0	2	2	2	2	2	2	2
65+	1	5.0	0	5	5	5	5	5	5	5
2. MULTIPLE DX										
0–19 Years	7	7.8	4	6	6	7	10	10	10	10
20–34	11	5.8	13	2	3	6	7	14	14	14
35–49	10	10.5	56	2	5	9	14	18	27	27
50–64	47	10.3	114	2	4	7	12	20	44	44
65+	52	8.5	57	2	4	6	10	18	21	43
TOTAL SINGLE DX	**8**	**4.1**	**1**	**2**	**4**	**4**	**5**	**5**	**5**	**5**
TOTAL MULTIPLE DX	**127**	**9.0**	**70**	**2**	**4**	**6**	**10**	**18**	**27**	**44**
TOTAL										
0–19 Years	7	7.8	4	6	6	7	10	10	10	10
20–34	14	5.5	12	2	3	5	7	9	14	14
35–49	13	9.6	54	2	4	8	14	18	27	27
50–64	48	10.2	114	2	4	7	12	20	44	44
65+	53	8.3	55	2	4	6	9	18	21	43
GRAND TOTAL	**135**	**8.7**	**67**	**2**	**4**	**6**	**10**	**17**	**27**	**44**

34.6: PLEURAL SCARIFICATION

Type of Patients	Observed Patients	Avg. Stay	Vari-ance	Percentiles 10th	25th	50th	75th	90th	95th	99th
1. SINGLE DX										
0–19 Years	12	4.8	8	2	2	4	6	9	10	10
20–34	11	5.3	17	3	3	3	9	14	14	14
35–49	3	3.7	2	2	2	3	5	5	5	5
50–64	3	5.4	6	3	3	5	8	8	8	8
65+	1	2.0	0	2	2	2	2	2	2	2
2. MULTIPLE DX										
0–19 Years	14	9.8	25	4	5	9	14	17	20	20
20–34	38	7.7	26	3	4	6	9	13	19	25
35–49	44	7.9	28	3	4	6	10	15	19	26
50–64	95	9.6	51	4	5	7	11	18	26	38
65+	146	11.6	56	4	6	10	16	22	27	32
TOTAL SINGLE DX	**30**	**4.9**	**10**	**2**	**3**	**4**	**6**	**9**	**10**	**14**
TOTAL MULTIPLE DX	**337**	**10.1**	**49**	**4**	**5**	**8**	**13**	**20**	**25**	**34**
TOTAL										
0–19 Years	26	7.1	22	2	4	6	9	15	17	20
20–34	49	7.1	25	3	4	5	9	13	19	25
35–49	47	7.7	27	3	4	6	10	15	19	26
50–64	98	9.5	50	4	5	7	11	18	23	38
65+	147	11.5	56	4	6	10	16	22	27	32
GRAND TOTAL	**367**	**9.7**	**47**	**3**	**5**	**7**	**13**	**19**	**24**	**34**

34.7: REPAIR OF CHEST WALL

Type of Patients	Observed Patients	Avg. Stay	Vari-ance	10th	25th	50th	75th	90th	95th	99th
				Percentiles						
1. SINGLE DX										
0–19 Years	138	4.1	2	2	3	4	5	6	6	7
20–34	19	3.0	<1	2	3	3	4	4	4	4
35–49	4	4.0	18	1	1	3	10	10	10	10
50–64	17	3.6	2	2	2	3	5	6	6	6
65+	3	2.2	2	1	1	2	4	4	4	4
2. MULTIPLE DX										
0–19 Years	121	5.0	6	3	4	5	6	7	10	16
20–34	43	4.4	8	1	2	4	7	8	11	12
35–49	34	6.4	70	1	2	3	7	15	35	35
50–64	102	7.1	47	2	3	4	9	16	19	35
65+	86	8.2	53	2	3	5	12	17	25	29
TOTAL SINGLE DX	**181**	**4.0**	**2**	**2**	**3**	**4**	**5**	**6**	**6**	**7**
TOTAL MULTIPLE DX	**386**	**6.4**	**35**	**2**	**3**	**4**	**7**	**14**	**17**	**34**
TOTAL										
0–19 Years	259	4.6	4	2	3	4	5	7	7	12
20–34	62	4.0	6	1	3	4	5	7	9	12
35–49	38	6.2	66	1	1	3	7	15	23	35
50–64	119	6.5	41	2	3	4	8	16	19	35
65+	89	8.0	52	2	3	5	12	17	25	29
GRAND TOTAL	**567**	**5.6**	**26**	**2**	**3**	**4**	**6**	**11**	**16**	**28**

34.74: PECTUS DEFORMITY REPAIR

Type of Patients	Observed Patients	Avg. Stay	Vari-ance	10th	25th	50th	75th	90th	95th	99th
				Percentiles						
1. SINGLE DX										
0–19 Years	136	4.1	2	2	3	4	5	6	6	7
20–34	18	3.2	<1	2	3	3	4	4	4	4
35–49	2	6.6	21	3	3	10	10	10	10	10
50–64	14	3.6	1	2	3	3	4	5	6	6
65+	0									
2. MULTIPLE DX										
0–19 Years	110	4.9	4	3	4	5	5	7	8	12
20–34	26	4.7	4	3	3	4	7	7	9	11
35–49	3	3.7	1	3	3	3	5	5	5	5
50–64	16	3.9	3	2	3	3	5	6	9	9
65+	2	2.6	<1	2	2	3	3	3	3	3
TOTAL SINGLE DX	**170**	**4.0**	**2**	**2**	**3**	**4**	**5**	**6**	**6**	**7**
TOTAL MULTIPLE DX	**157**	**4.7**	**4**	**3**	**3**	**4**	**5**	**7**	**8**	**12**
TOTAL										
0–19 Years	246	4.5	3	3	3	4	5	6	7	11
20–34	44	4.2	3	3	3	4	4	7	8	11
35–49	5	4.9	9	3	3	3	5	10	10	10
50–64	30	3.7	2	2	3	3	5	6	6	9
65+	2	2.6	<1	2	2	3	3	3	3	3
GRAND TOTAL	**327**	**4.4**	**3**	**3**	**3**	**4**	**5**	**6**	**7**	**11**

34.79: CHEST WALL REPAIR NEC

Type of Patients	Observed Patients	Avg. Stay	Vari-ance	10th	25th	50th	75th	90th	95th	99th
				Percentiles						
1. SINGLE DX										
0–19 Years	0									
20–34	0									
35–49	1	1.0	0	1	1	1	1	1	1	1
50–64	3	3.9	4	2	2	4	6	6	6	6
65+	3	2.2	2	1	1	2	4	4	4	4
2. MULTIPLE DX										
0–19 Years	8	7.5	31	1	4	5	16	16	16	16
20–34	3	5.4	30	1	1	2	11	11	11	11
35–49	17	6.6	91	1	2	3	5	15	35	35
50–64	67	6.8	53	1	2	4	8	15	19	42
65+	69	7.9	50	3	3	5	10	16	28	29
TOTAL SINGLE DX	**7**	**3.0**	**4**	**1**	**2**	**2**	**4**	**6**	**6**	**6**
TOTAL MULTIPLE DX	**164**	**7.3**	**54**	**2**	**3**	**4**	**8**	**16**	**27**	**35**
TOTAL										
0–19 Years	8	7.5	31	1	4	5	16	16	16	16
20–34	3	5.4	30	1	1	2	11	11	11	11
35–49	18	6.5	89	1	2	3	5	15	35	35
50–64	70	6.6	50	1	2	4	8	15	19	35
65+	72	7.6	49	2	3	4	9	16	28	29
GRAND TOTAL	**171**	**7.1**	**53**	**2**	**3**	**4**	**8**	**16**	**24**	**35**

34.8: OPERATIONS ON DIAPHRAGM

Type of Patients	Observed Patients	Avg. Stay	Vari-ance	10th	25th	50th	75th	90th	95th	99th
				Percentiles						
1. SINGLE DX										
0–19 Years	4	2.4	<1	1	2	3	3	3	3	3
20–34	1	3.0	0	3	3	3	3	3	3	3
35–49	0									
50–64	1	5.0	0	5	5	5	5	5	5	5
65+	0									
2. MULTIPLE DX										
0–19 Years	34	8.8	59	3	4	7	9	16	32	32
20–34	86	8.6	36	3	4	7	12	19	22	23
35–49	28	8.2	40	3	4	6	12	20	22	24
50–64	19	10.4	40	2	6	10	14	21	21	27
65+	7	7.0	13	5	5	5	6	14	14	14
TOTAL SINGLE DX	**6**	**2.8**	**1**	**2**	**2**	**3**	**3**	**5**	**5**	**5**
TOTAL MULTIPLE DX	**174**	**8.7**	**40**	**3**	**4**	**6**	**12**	**16**	**22**	**32**
TOTAL										
0–19 Years	38	7.7	55	2	3	5	9	16	32	32
20–34	87	8.6	36	3	4	6	12	19	22	23
35–49	28	8.2	40	3	4	6	12	20	22	24
50–64	20	10.1	39	2	6	9	14	16	21	27
65+	7	7.0	13	5	5	5	6	14	14	14
GRAND TOTAL	**180**	**8.4**	**40**	**3**	**4**	**6**	**11**	**16**	**22**	**32**

34.82: SUTURE DIAPHRAGM LAC

Type of Patients	Observed Patients	Avg. Stay	Vari-ance	Percentiles						
				10th	25th	50th	75th	90th	95th	99th
1. SINGLE DX										
0–19 Years	3	1.8	<1	1	2	2	2	2	2	2
20–34	1	3.0	0	3	3	3	3	3	3	3
35–49	0									
50–64	0									
65+	0									
2. MULTIPLE DX										
0–19 Years	28	9.4	67	3	4	7	10	18	32	32
20–34	71	7.9	30	3	4	6	11	14	19	32
35–49	23	9.0	43	3	4	6	13	20	22	24
50–64	13	12.6	42	6	8	13	16	21	27	27
65+	3	9.7	22	5	6	6	14	14	14	14
TOTAL SINGLE DX	**4**	**2.0**	**<1**	**1**	**2**	**2**	**2**	**3**	**3**	**3**
TOTAL MULTIPLE DX	**138**	**8.8**	**41**	**3**	**4**	**7**	**12**	**16**	**22**	**32**
TOTAL										
0–19 Years	31	8.6	65	2	3	6	9	18	32	32
20–34	72	7.8	30	3	4	6	11	14	19	32
35–49	23	9.0	43	3	4	6	13	20	22	24
50–64	13	12.6	42	6	8	13	16	21	27	27
65+	3	9.7	22	5	6	6	14	14	14	14
GRAND TOTAL	**142**	**8.6**	**42**	**3**	**4**	**6**	**12**	**16**	**22**	**32**

34.9: OTHER OPS ON THORAX

Type of Patients	Observed Patients	Avg. Stay	Vari-ance	Percentiles						
				10th	25th	50th	75th	90th	95th	99th
1. SINGLE DX										
0–19 Years	8	3.2	4	2	2	2	4	6	8	8
20–34	13	3.9	6	1	2	4	6	8	8	8
35–49	12	4.0	5	1	2	3	6	7	9	9
50–64	15	3.2	6	1	2	2	4	6	10	10
65+	15	3.3	8	1	2	2	4	6	12	12
2. MULTIPLE DX										
0–19 Years	150	7.5	31	2	3	6	10	16	21	23
20–34	339	8.1	47	2	4	6	10	16	19	30
35–49	1,228	6.9	35	2	3	5	9	13	19	30
50–64	2,752	6.6	33	2	3	5	8	13	17	26
65+	8,389	6.7	25	2	3	5	9	13	16	24
TOTAL SINGLE DX	**63**	**3.5**	**6**	**1**	**2**	**2**	**5**	**7**	**8**	**12**
TOTAL MULTIPLE DX	**12,858**	**6.8**	**28**	**2**	**3**	**5**	**9**	**13**	**17**	**26**
TOTAL										
0–19 Years	158	7.3	31	2	3	6	9	15	21	23
20–34	352	7.9	46	2	4	6	10	16	19	30
35–49	1,240	6.9	35	2	3	5	9	13	19	30
50–64	2,767	6.6	33	2	3	5	8	13	17	26
65+	8,404	6.7	25	2	3	5	9	13	16	24
GRAND TOTAL	**12,921**	**6.8**	**28**	**2**	**3**	**5**	**9**	**13**	**17**	**26**

34.91: THORACENTESIS

Type of Patients	Observed Patients	Avg. Stay	Vari-ance	Percentiles						
				10th	25th	50th	75th	90th	95th	99th
1. SINGLE DX										
0–19 Years	4	2.2	<1	2	2	2	2	4	4	4
20–34	12	3.6	5	1	1	3	5	7	8	8
35–49	11	4.2	5	1	3	4	6	7	9	9
50–64	15	3.2	6	1	2	2	4	6	10	10
65+	14	3.2	8	1	2	2	4	6	12	12
2. MULTIPLE DX										
0–19 Years	140	7.7	32	2	4	6	10	16	21	23
20–34	327	8.0	47	2	4	6	10	16	19	30
35–49	1,175	6.9	35	2	3	5	8	13	19	31
50–64	2,626	6.4	31	2	3	5	8	13	16	26
65+	8,092	6.7	25	2	3	5	9	13	16	24
TOTAL SINGLE DX	**56**	**3.3**	**6**	**1**	**2**	**2**	**4**	**6**	**8**	**12**
TOTAL MULTIPLE DX	**12,360**	**6.7**	**28**	**2**	**3**	**5**	**9**	**13**	**17**	**25**
TOTAL										
0–19 Years	144	7.5	32	2	3	6	10	16	21	23
20–34	339	7.8	46	2	4	6	10	16	19	30
35–49	1,186	6.8	35	2	3	5	8	13	19	31
50–64	2,641	6.4	31	2	3	5	8	13	16	26
65+	8,106	6.7	25	2	3	5	9	13	16	24
GRAND TOTAL	**12,416**	**6.7**	**28**	**2**	**3**	**5**	**9**	**13**	**17**	**25**

34.92: INJECT INTO THOR CAVIT

Type of Patients	Observed Patients	Avg. Stay	Vari-ance	Percentiles						
				10th	25th	50th	75th	90th	95th	99th
1. SINGLE DX										
0–19 Years	4	4.9	6	2	2	4	8	8	8	8
20–34	1	8.0	0	8	8	8	8	8	8	8
35–49	1	2.0	0	2	2	2	2	2	2	2
50–64	0									
65+	1	5.0	0	5	5	5	5	5	5	5
2. MULTIPLE DX										
0–19 Years	5	5.2	9	2	2	4	8	9	9	9
20–34	11	10.3	41	4	5	10	13	23	25	25
35–49	50	8.4	23	3	5	8	10	15	18	30
50–64	121	10.0	57	3	4	8	14	21	26	35
65+	290	8.1	34	3	4	7	10	15	20	26
TOTAL SINGLE DX	**7**	**4.9**	**6**	**2**	**2**	**5**	**8**	**8**	**8**	**8**
TOTAL MULTIPLE DX	**477**	**8.6**	**39**	**3**	**4**	**7**	**11**	**16**	**22**	**28**
TOTAL										
0–19 Years	9	5.1	7	2	2	4	8	9	9	9
20–34	12	10.2	39	4	5	8	13	23	25	25
35–49	51	8.3	23	3	5	8	10	15	18	30
50–64	121	10.0	57	3	4	8	14	21	26	35
65+	291	8.1	34	3	4	7	10	15	20	26
GRAND TOTAL	**484**	**8.6**	**39**	**3**	**4**	**7**	**10**	**16**	**21**	**28**

35.0: CLOSED HEART VALVOTOMY

Type of Patients	Observed Patients	Avg. Stay	Vari-ance	Percentiles						
				10th	25th	50th	75th	90th	95th	99th
1. SINGLE DX										
0–19 Years	0									
20–34	2	1.0	0	1	1	1	1	1	1	1
35–49	1	1.0	0	1	1	1	1	1	1	1
50–64	0									
65+	0									
2. MULTIPLE DX										
0–19 Years	1	17.0	0	17	17	17	17	17	17	17
20–34	2	1.0	0	1	1	1	1	1	1	1
35–49	1	1.0	0	1	1	1	1	1	1	1
50–64	4	2.3	8	1	1	1	1	7	7	7
65+	2	1.0	0	1	1	1	1	1	1	1
TOTAL SINGLE DX	**3**	**1.0**	**0**	**1**	**1**	**1**	**1**	**1**	**1**	**1**
TOTAL MULTIPLE DX	**10**	**3.3**	**28**	**1**	**1**	**1**	**1**	**17**	**17**	**17**
TOTAL										
0–19 Years	1	17.0	0	17	17	17	17	17	17	17
20–34	4	1.0	0	1	1	1	1	1	1	1
35–49	2	1.0	0	1	1	1	1	1	1	1
50–64	4	2.3	8	1	1	1	1	7	7	7
65+	2	1.0	0	1	1	1	1	1	1	1
GRAND TOTAL	**13**	**2.3**	**17**	**1**	**1**	**1**	**1**	**7**	**17**	**17**

35.1: OPEN HEART VALVULOPLASTY

Type of Patients	Observed Patients	Avg. Stay	Vari-ance	Percentiles						
				10th	25th	50th	75th	90th	95th	99th
1. SINGLE DX										
0–19 Years	10	2.7	<1	2	2	3	3	4	4	4
20–34	1	5.0	0	5	5	5	5	5	5	5
35–49	5	4.7	1	3	4	5	5	6	6	6
50–64	10	4.0	<1	3	3	4	5	5	5	5
65+	2	6.3	3	5	5	5	8	8	8	8
2. MULTIPLE DX										
0–19 Years	224	6.7	49	3	3	5	7	13	19	29
20–34	46	7.9	57	3	4	6	9	12	16	45
35–49	130	7.1	21	3	4	6	8	13	15	27
50–64	414	8.3	42	4	5	6	9	14	20	41
65+	544	10.7	64	5	6	8	13	19	25	47
TOTAL SINGLE DX	**28**	**3.8**	**2**	**2**	**3**	**4**	**5**	**5**	**6**	**8**
TOTAL MULTIPLE DX	**1,358**	**8.7**	**53**	**3**	**5**	**7**	**10**	**16**	**21**	**44**
TOTAL										
0–19 Years	234	6.6	48	3	3	4	7	13	19	29
20–34	47	7.9	56	3	4	5	9	12	16	45
35–49	135	7.0	20	3	4	6	8	13	15	27
50–64	424	8.2	42	4	5	6	9	14	20	41
65+	546	10.7	64	5	6	8	12	19	25	47
GRAND TOTAL	**1,386**	**8.6**	**53**	**3**	**5**	**6**	**10**	**16**	**21**	**44**

35.11: OPN AORTIC VALVULOPLASTY

Type of Patients	Observed Patients	Avg. Stay	Vari-ance	Percentiles						
				10th	25th	50th	75th	90th	95th	99th
1. SINGLE DX										
0–19 Years	8	2.5	<1	2	2	2	3	4	4	4
20–34	0									
35–49	0									
50–64	0									
65+	1	5.0	0	5	5	5	5	5	5	5
2. MULTIPLE DX										
0–19 Years	80	6.5	62	2	3	4	6	11	29	52
20–34	6	4.5	4	3	3	4	5	9	9	9
35–49	12	8.2	9	5	6	7	12	13	13	13
50–64	24	15.1	224	5	6	10	12	51	51	51
65+	43	11.3	117	3	6	8	12	23	39	55
TOTAL SINGLE DX	**9**	**2.8**	**1**	**2**	**2**	**2**	**3**	**5**	**5**	**5**
TOTAL MULTIPLE DX	**165**	**8.6**	**99**	**3**	**3**	**5**	**10**	**18**	**29**	**52**
TOTAL										
0–19 Years	88	6.3	59	2	3	4	6	11	25	31
20–34	6	4.5	4	3	3	4	5	9	9	9
35–49	12	8.2	9	5	6	7	12	13	13	13
50–64	24	15.1	224	5	6	10	12	51	51	51
65+	44	11.1	115	3	6	8	12	23	39	55
GRAND TOTAL	**174**	**8.4**	**96**	**2**	**3**	**5**	**9**	**16**	**29**	**52**

35.12: OPN MITRAL VALVULOPLASTY

Type of Patients	Observed Patients	Avg. Stay	Vari-ance	Percentiles						
				10th	25th	50th	75th	90th	95th	99th
1. SINGLE DX										
0–19 Years	1	4.0	0	4	4	4	4	4	4	4
20–34	1	5.0	0	5	5	5	5	5	5	5
35–49	5	4.7	1	3	4	5	5	6	6	6
50–64	10	4.0	<1	3	3	4	5	5	5	5
65+	1	8.0	0	8	8	8	8	8	8	8
2. MULTIPLE DX										
0–19 Years	73	7.1	60	3	4	5	9	13	14	22
20–34	31	6.5	11	3	4	5	9	9	12	17
35–49	108	6.7	18	3	4	6	7	13	15	22
50–64	380	7.7	25	4	5	6	9	14	18	28
65+	485	10.7	58	5	6	8	12	19	24	47
TOTAL SINGLE DX	**18**	**4.4**	**1**	**3**	**4**	**4**	**5**	**6**	**8**	**8**
TOTAL MULTIPLE DX	**1,077**	**8.8**	**46**	**4**	**5**	**7**	**10**	**16**	**21**	**41**
TOTAL										
0–19 Years	74	7.0	59	3	4	5	8	13	14	22
20–34	32	6.5	11	3	4	5	9	9	12	17
35–49	113	6.6	18	3	4	6	7	12	15	22
50–64	390	7.6	25	4	5	6	9	13	18	28
65+	486	10.7	58	5	6	8	12	19	24	47
GRAND TOTAL	**1,095**	**8.8**	**46**	**4**	**5**	**7**	**10**	**16**	**21**	**41**

35.2: HEART VALVE REPLACEMENT

Type of Patients	Observed Patients	Avg. Stay	Vari-ance	Percentiles 10th	25th	50th	75th	90th	95th	99th
1. SINGLE DX										
0–19 Years	12	4.1	2	2	3	4	5	5	8	8
20–34	11	4.3	<1	3	4	4	5	5	5	5
35–49	17	4.6	4	3	3	4	5	6	12	12
50–64	19	4.1	2	3	3	4	5	6	7	7
65+	19	5.0	1	3	4	5	6	6	7	7
2. MULTIPLE DX										
0–19 Years	182	7.0	26	3	4	5	8	15	17	26
20–34	208	9.3	67	4	5	6	11	21	25	30
35–49	693	9.0	62	4	5	7	10	16	20	47
50–64	1,832	9.1	49	4	5	7	10	16	21	41
65+	4,761	9.9	42	5	6	8	12	17	23	36
TOTAL SINGLE DX	**78**	**4.5**	**2**	**3**	**4**	**4**	**5**	**6**	**7**	**8**
TOTAL MULTIPLE DX	**7,676**	**9.6**	**46**	**4**	**6**	**7**	**11**	**17**	**22**	**37**
TOTAL										
0–19 Years	194	6.9	26	3	4	5	8	15	17	26
20–34	219	9.0	64	4	5	6	9	20	25	30
35–49	710	8.9	62	4	5	7	10	16	20	47
50–64	1,851	9.0	49	4	5	7	10	16	21	41
65+	4,780	9.9	42	5	6	8	12	17	23	36
GRAND TOTAL	**7,754**	**9.5**	**45**	**4**	**6**	**7**	**11**	**17**	**22**	**37**

35.21: REPL AORTIC VALVE-TISSUE

Type of Patients	Observed Patients	Avg. Stay	Vari-ance	Percentiles 10th	25th	50th	75th	90th	95th	99th
1. SINGLE DX										
0–19 Years	5	3.1	<1	2	2	3	4	4	4	4
20–34	3	4.0	<1	3	3	4	5	5	5	5
35–49	6	3.6	<1	3	3	4	4	4	4	4
50–64	6	3.7	<1	3	3	4	4	5	5	5
65+	8	4.8	<1	4	4	5	5	6	6	6
2. MULTIPLE DX										
0–19 Years	52	5.9	16	3	4	5	6	9	14	26
20–34	43	9.7	61	4	5	6	11	23	30	30
35–49	119	8.0	32	3	4	6	9	17	19	27
50–64	422	8.1	37	4	5	6	9	14	19	38
65+	2,289	9.5	39	5	6	8	11	16	21	36
TOTAL SINGLE DX	**28**	**3.9**	**1**	**3**	**3**	**4**	**5**	**5**	**6**	**6**
TOTAL MULTIPLE DX	**2,925**	**9.2**	**39**	**4**	**6**	**7**	**11**	**16**	**21**	**36**
TOTAL										
0–19 Years	57	5.7	15	3	4	5	6	9	13	26
20–34	46	9.5	59	4	5	6	9	23	30	30
35–49	125	7.9	31	3	4	6	9	17	19	27
50–64	428	8.1	37	4	5	6	9	14	19	38
65+	2,297	9.5	39	5	6	8	11	16	21	36
GRAND TOTAL	**2,953**	**9.2**	**39**	**4**	**6**	**7**	**11**	**16**	**21**	**36**

35.22: REPL AORTIC VALVE NEC

Type of Patients	Observed Patients	Avg. Stay	Vari-ance	Percentiles 10th	25th	50th	75th	90th	95th	99th
1. SINGLE DX										
0–19 Years	3	5.6	3	4	4	5	8	8	8	8
20–34	6	4.3	<1	3	4	4	5	5	5	5
35–49	10	5.2	7	3	4	5	6	6	12	12
50–64	9	4.7	3	3	4	4	6	7	7	7
65+	10	5.3	2	3	5	6	6	7	7	7
2. MULTIPLE DX										
0–19 Years	26	8.8	25	3	4	8	11	16	18	23
20–34	80	9.5	44	4	5	6	12	21	24	29
35–49	344	7.7	31	4	5	6	8	13	17	40
50–64	880	8.5	46	4	5	7	10	14	19	34
65+	1,543	9.9	45	5	6	8	12	18	23	38
TOTAL SINGLE DX	**38**	**4.9**	**3**	**3**	**4**	**5**	**6**	**7**	**7**	**12**
TOTAL MULTIPLE DX	**2,873**	**9.2**	**44**	**4**	**5**	**7**	**11**	**16**	**21**	**36**
TOTAL										
0–19 Years	29	8.5	24	3	4	8	11	16	18	23
20–34	86	9.1	43	4	5	6	12	21	24	29
35–49	354	7.7	31	4	5	6	8	13	17	30
50–64	889	8.5	45	4	5	7	10	14	19	34
65+	1,553	9.8	45	5	6	8	12	17	23	38
GRAND TOTAL	**2,911**	**9.2**	**44**	**4**	**5**	**7**	**11**	**16**	**21**	**36**

35.23: REPL MITRAL VALVE W TISS

Type of Patients	Observed Patients	Avg. Stay	Vari-ance	Percentiles 10th	25th	50th	75th	90th	95th	99th
1. SINGLE DX										
0–19 Years	0									
20–34	1	4.0	0	4	4	4	4	4	4	4
35–49	0									
50–64	2	3.0	0	3	3	3	3	3	3	3
65+	0									
2. MULTIPLE DX										
0–19 Years	7	8.0	26	4	4	5	8	17	17	17
20–34	9	13.5	70	4	5	13	22	23	25	25
35–49	28	13.8	142	5	6	11	17	25	47	59
50–64	90	11.8	64	5	6	10	15	23	28	53
65+	401	11.6	47	6	7	9	14	20	24	38
TOTAL SINGLE DX	**3**	**3.3**	**<1**	**3**	**3**	**3**	**4**	**4**	**4**	**4**
TOTAL MULTIPLE DX	**535**	**11.7**	**54**	**5**	**7**	**9**	**15**	**21**	**25**	**41**
TOTAL										
0–19 Years	7	8.0	26	4	4	5	8	17	17	17
20–34	10	12.6	71	4	5	13	22	23	25	25
35–49	28	13.8	142	5	6	11	17	25	47	59
50–64	92	11.6	64	4	6	9	15	23	28	53
65+	401	11.6	47	6	7	9	14	20	24	38
GRAND TOTAL	**538**	**11.7**	**55**	**5**	**7**	**9**	**15**	**21**	**25**	**41**

35.24: REPL MITRAL VALVE NEC

Type of Patients	Observed Patients	Avg. Stay	Vari-ance	Percentiles 10th	25th	50th	75th	90th	95th	99th
1. SINGLE DX										
0–19 Years	0									
20–34	1	5.0	0	5	5	5	5	5	5	5
35–49	1	6.0	0	6	6	6	6	6	6	6
50–64	2	3.2	2	2	2	4	4	4	4	4
65+	1	4.0	0	4	4	4	4	4	4	4
2. MULTIPLE DX										
0–19 Years	18	9.4	69	4	5	7	11	19	19	40
20–34	39	10.8	171	5	6	6	10	19	30	80
35–49	178	10.4	76	5	6	8	12	17	22	34
50–64	417	10.3	59	5	6	8	12	18	23	49
65+	504	10.5	37	5	6	9	13	18	23	32
TOTAL SINGLE DX	5	4.3	2	2	4	4	5	6	6	6
TOTAL MULTIPLE DX	1,156	10.4	54	5	6	8	12	18	23	36
TOTAL										
0–19 Years	18	9.4	69	4	5	7	11	19	19	40
20–34	40	10.6	167	5	6	6	10	19	30	80
35–49	179	10.4	76	5	6	8	12	17	22	34
50–64	419	10.3	59	5	6	8	12	18	23	49
65+	505	10.5	37	5	6	9	13	18	23	32
GRAND TOTAL	1,161	10.4	54	5	6	8	12	18	23	36

35.3: TISS ADJ TO HRT VALV OPS

Type of Patients	Observed Patients	Avg. Stay	Vari-ance	Percentiles 10th	25th	50th	75th	90th	95th	99th
1. SINGLE DX										
0–19 Years	2	3.7	<1	2	4	4	4	4	4	4
20–34	3	4.3	<1	4	4	4	5	5	5	5
35–49	3	4.3	12	1	1	4	8	8	8	8
50–64	1	4.0	0	4	4	4	4	4	4	4
65+	0									
2. MULTIPLE DX										
0–19 Years	27	5.4	9	3	3	4	6	10	13	13
20–34	8	5.2	5	3	3	5	6	8	11	11
35–49	39	7.6	26	4	5	6	8	11	15	31
50–64	118	9.3	36	4	5	7	12	17	23	32
65+	233	10.6	51	5	6	9	13	18	29	33
TOTAL SINGLE DX	9	3.9	2	2	4	4	4	5	8	8
TOTAL MULTIPLE DX	425	9.5	44	4	5	7	12	17	23	32
TOTAL										
0–19 Years	29	5.1	8	3	3	4	6	10	10	13
20–34	11	5.1	5	3	3	5	6	8	11	11
35–49	42	7.5	26	4	5	6	8	11	15	31
50–64	119	9.3	36	4	5	7	11	17	23	32
65+	233	10.6	51	5	6	9	13	18	29	33
GRAND TOTAL	434	9.3	43	4	5	7	11	17	23	32

35.33: ANNULOPLASTY

Type of Patients	Observed Patients	Avg. Stay	Vari-ance	Percentiles 10th	25th	50th	75th	90th	95th	99th
1. SINGLE DX										
0–19 Years	0									
20–34	2	4.5	<1	4	4	5	5	5	5	5
35–49	2	6.1	7	4	4	8	8	8	8	8
50–64	1	4.0	0	4	4	4	4	4	4	4
65+	0									
2. MULTIPLE DX										
0–19 Years	15	7.3	10	3	5	6	10	13	13	13
20–34	4	6.2	1	5	5	6	6	8	8	8
35–49	36	7.3	18	4	5	6	8	11	15	29
50–64	113	9.3	36	4	5	7	12	16	23	32
65+	224	10.7	51	5	6	9	13	19	29	39
TOTAL SINGLE DX	5	5.1	3	4	4	4	5	8	8	8
TOTAL MULTIPLE DX	392	9.9	44	5	5	8	12	17	24	32
TOTAL										
0–19 Years	15	7.3	10	3	5	6	10	13	13	13
20–34	6	5.8	1	5	5	6	6	8	8	8
35–49	38	7.3	17	4	5	6	8	11	15	29
50–64	114	9.3	36	4	5	7	12	16	23	32
65+	224	10.7	51	5	6	9	13	19	29	39
GRAND TOTAL	397	9.8	43	5	5	8	12	17	24	32

35.4: SEPTAL DEFECT PRODUCTION

Type of Patients	Observed Patients	Avg. Stay	Vari-ance	Percentiles 10th	25th	50th	75th	90th	95th	99th
1. SINGLE DX										
0–19 Years	1	1.0	0	1	1	1	1	1	1	1
20–34	1	1.0	0	1	1	1	1	1	1	1
35–49	1	1.0	0	1	1	1	1	1	1	1
50–64	0									
65+	0									
2. MULTIPLE DX										
0–19 Years	28	11.7	338	2	3	6	8	17	59	90
20–34	1	8.0	0	8	8	8	8	8	8	8
35–49	1	2.0	0	2	2	2	2	2	2	2
50–64	2	2.8	4	1	1	4	4	4	4	4
65+	0									
TOTAL SINGLE DX	3	1.0	0	1	1	1	1	1	1	1
TOTAL MULTIPLE DX	32	11.3	321	2	3	6	8	17	59	90
TOTAL										
0–19 Years	29	11.5	332	2	3	6	8	17	59	90
20–34	2	4.6	21	1	1	8	8	8	8	8
35–49	2	1.5	<1	1	1	1	2	2	2	2
50–64	2	2.8	4	1	1	4	4	4	4	4
65+	0									
GRAND TOTAL	35	10.7	309	2	3	5	8	14	59	90

35.5: PROSTH REP HEART SEPTA

Type of Patients	Observed Patients	Avg. Stay	Vari-ance	Percentiles						
				10th	25th	50th	75th	90th	95th	99th
1. SINGLE DX										
0–19 Years	81	1.4	<1	1	1	1	2	3	3	5
20–34	12	1.6	2	1	1	1	1	4	5	5
35–49	26	1.3	<1	1	1	1	1	2	4	5
50–64	17	1.2	<1	1	1	1	1	1	5	5
65+	2	1.0	0	1	1	1	1	1	1	1
2. MULTIPLE DX										
0–19 Years	268	7.3	99	1	3	4	7	16	23	75
20–34	23	1.9	3	1	1	1	1	5	5	6
35–49	109	2.0	6	1	1	1	1	5	6	10
50–64	90	1.6	3	1	1	1	1	3	6	9
65+	62	2.6	15	1	1	1	2	7	12	19
TOTAL SINGLE DX	**138**	**1.4**	**<1**	**1**	**1**	**1**	**1**	**2**	**3**	**5**
TOTAL MULTIPLE DX	**552**	**5.3**	**71**	**1**	**1**	**3**	**6**	**14**	**20**	**55**
TOTAL										
0–19 Years	349	6.2	86	1	2	4	7	15	21	75
20–34	35	1.8	2	1	1	1	1	4	5	6
35–49	135	1.9	5	1	1	1	1	4	5	10
50–64	107	1.5	3	1	1	1	1	2	6	9
65+	64	2.5	15	1	1	1	2	7	12	19
GRAND TOTAL	**690**	**4.6**	**61**	**1**	**1**	**2**	**5**	**10**	**16**	**37**

35.52: PROSTH REP ASD CLSD TECH

Type of Patients	Observed Patients	Avg. Stay	Vari-ance	Percentiles						
				10th	25th	50th	75th	90th	95th	99th
1. SINGLE DX										
0–19 Years	62	1.1	<1	1	1	1	1	1	1	1
20–34	10	1.1	<1	1	1	1	1	2	2	2
35–49	22	1.0	0	1	1	1	1	1	1	1
50–64	16	1.0	0	1	1	1	1	1	1	1
65+	2	1.0	0	1	1	1	1	1	1	1
2. MULTIPLE DX										
0–19 Years	48	2.5	14	1	1	1	2	4	14	15
20–34	17	1.2	<1	1	1	1	1	1	1	5
35–49	85	1.2	<1	1	1	1	1	1	2	8
50–64	85	1.3	1	1	1	1	1	2	3	6
65+	57	2.5	15	1	1	1	2	6	11	19
TOTAL SINGLE DX	**112**	**1.0**	**<1**	**1**	**1**	**1**	**1**	**1**	**1**	**2**
TOTAL MULTIPLE DX	**292**	**1.8**	**7**	**1**	**1**	**1**	**1**	**3**	**6**	**15**
TOTAL										
0–19 Years	110	1.7	7	1	1	1	1	3	4	15
20–34	27	1.2	<1	1	1	1	1	1	2	5
35–49	107	1.2	<1	1	1	1	1	1	2	4
50–64	101	1.3	1	1	1	1	1	2	3	6
65+	59	2.4	14	1	1	1	2	6	11	19
GRAND TOTAL	**404**	**1.6**	**6**	**1**	**1**	**1**	**1**	**2**	**4**	**15**

35.53: PROSTH REP VSD

Type of Patients	Observed Patients	Avg. Stay	Vari-ance	Percentiles						
				10th	25th	50th	75th	90th	95th	99th
1. SINGLE DX										
0–19 Years	12	2.5	<1	2	2	2	3	3	4	5
20–34	0									
35–49	1	1.0	0	1	1	1	1	1	1	1
50–64	0									
65+	0									
2. MULTIPLE DX										
0–19 Years	156	8.1	131	2	3	5	7	20	23	75
20–34	1	6.0	0	6	6	6	6	6	6	6
35–49	9	6.7	35	3	4	5	6	22	22	22
50–64	2	7.1	78	1	1	1	14	14	14	14
65+	1	12.0	0	12	12	12	12	12	12	12
TOTAL SINGLE DX	**13**	**2.4**	**<1**	**1**	**2**	**2**	**3**	**3**	**4**	**5**
TOTAL MULTIPLE DX	**169**	**8.1**	**128**	**2**	**3**	**5**	**7**	**20**	**23**	**75**
TOTAL										
0–19 Years	168	7.8	125	2	3	4	7	19	23	75
20–34	1	6.0	0	6	6	6	6	6	6	6
35–49	10	6.1	34	1	3	5	6	22	22	22
50–64	2	7.1	78	1	1	1	14	14	14	14
65+	1	12.0	0	12	12	12	12	12	12	12
GRAND TOTAL	**182**	**7.7**	**122**	**2**	**3**	**5**	**7**	**19**	**23**	**75**

35.6: TISS GRFT REP HRT SEPTA

Type of Patients	Observed Patients	Avg. Stay	Vari-ance	Percentiles						
				10th	25th	50th	75th	90th	95th	99th
1. SINGLE DX										
0–19 Years	46	2.9	2	2	2	3	3	4	5	6
20–34	7	3.3	1	2	3	3	4	5	5	5
35–49	5	4.7	3	2	4	5	5	7	7	7
50–64	0									
65+	0									
2. MULTIPLE DX										
0–19 Years	295	7.1	114	2	3	4	7	12	17	83
20–34	20	5.3	3	3	4	5	7	8	8	9
35–49	40	5.4	10	3	4	4	6	9	10	22
50–64	24	5.6	19	2	3	4	6	12	15	21
65+	6	6.2	8	3	4	6	8	11	11	11
TOTAL SINGLE DX	**58**	**3.0**	**2**	**2**	**2**	**3**	**3**	**5**	**5**	**7**
TOTAL MULTIPLE DX	**385**	**6.9**	**100**	**2**	**3**	**4**	**7**	**11**	**16**	**83**
TOTAL										
0–19 Years	341	6.6	102	2	3	4	6	11	15	83
20–34	27	4.8	3	3	3	4	6	8	8	9
35–49	45	5.3	9	3	4	4	6	9	10	22
50–64	24	5.6	19	2	3	4	6	12	15	21
65+	6	6.2	8	3	4	6	8	11	11	11
GRAND TOTAL	**443**	**6.4**	**90**	**2**	**3**	**4**	**6**	**11**	**15**	**83**

35.61: REPAIR ASD W TISS GRAFT

Type of Patients	Observed Patients	Avg. Stay	Vari-ance	10th	25th	50th	75th	90th	95th	99th
1. SINGLE DX										
0–19 Years	32	2.4	<1	2	2	2	3	3	4	5
20–34	7	3.3	1	2	3	3	4	5	5	5
35–49	4	4.8	3	2	5	5	5	7	7	7
50–64	0									
65+	0									
2. MULTIPLE DX										
0–19 Years	109	3.8	6	2	3	3	4	6	9	15
20–34	19	5.3	4	3	4	5	7	8	8	9
35–49	29	5.3	11	3	4	4	6	9	11	22
50–64	20	4.3	6	2	3	4	5	6	9	13
65+	6	6.2	8	3	4	6	8	11	11	11
TOTAL SINGLE DX	**43**	**2.7**	**1**	**2**	**2**	**2**	**3**	**4**	**5**	**7**
TOTAL MULTIPLE DX	**183**	**4.1**	**6**	**2**	**3**	**3**	**5**	**6**	**9**	**15**
TOTAL										
0–19 Years	141	3.5	5	2	2	3	4	5	6	15
20–34	26	4.8	4	3	3	4	6	8	8	9
35–49	33	5.2	10	3	4	4	6	8	9	22
50–64	20	4.3	6	2	3	4	5	6	9	13
65+	6	6.2	8	3	4	6	8	11	11	11
GRAND TOTAL	**226**	**3.8**	**6**	**2**	**3**	**3**	**4**	**6**	**9**	**15**

35.62: REPAIR VSD W TISS GRAFT

Type of Patients	Observed Patients	Avg. Stay	Vari-ance	10th	25th	50th	75th	90th	95th	99th
1. SINGLE DX										
0–19 Years	13	3.9	4	3	3	3	4	5	6	13
20–34	0									
35–49	1	4.0	0	4	4	4	4	4	4	4
50–64	0									
65+	0									
2. MULTIPLE DX										
0–19 Years	111	9.6	256	3	4	5	8	14	46	83
20–34	0									
35–49	7	5.6	7	4	4	4	9	10	10	10
50–64	4	14.9	21	11	11	12	21	21	21	21
65+	0									
TOTAL SINGLE DX	**14**	**3.9**	**4**	**3**	**3**	**4**	**4**	**5**	**6**	**13**
TOTAL MULTIPLE DX	**122**	**9.6**	**246**	**3**	**4**	**5**	**8**	**15**	**46**	**83**
TOTAL										
0–19 Years	124	9.0	234	3	3	5	7	13	46	83
20–34	0									
35–49	8	5.4	7	4	4	4	9	10	10	10
50–64	4	14.9	21	11	11	12	21	21	21	21
65+	0									
GRAND TOTAL	**136**	**9.0**	**225**	**3**	**3**	**5**	**8**	**14**	**46**	**83**

35.7: HEART SEPTA REPAIR NEC

Type of Patients	Observed Patients	Avg. Stay	Vari-ance	10th	25th	50th	75th	90th	95th	99th
1. SINGLE DX										
0–19 Years	38	2.4	2	1	1	2	3	4	6	6
20–34	6	3.5	1	1	3	4	4	4	4	4
35–49	7	3.8	4	1	3	5	5	6	6	6
50–64	1	1.0	0	1	1	1	1	1	1	1
65+	0									
2. MULTIPLE DX										
0–19 Years	166	5.6	46	2	3	3	6	9	16	27
20–34	31	4.8	6	3	3	4	5	8	10	14
35–49	42	4.9	6	3	4	4	6	7	11	15
50–64	44	6.2	14	1	4	6	7	13	14	15
65+	36	8.2	31	4	5	7	9	15	21	28
TOTAL SINGLE DX	**52**	**2.6**	**2**	**1**	**1**	**3**	**3**	**4**	**6**	**6**
TOTAL MULTIPLE DX	**319**	**5.8**	**37**	**2**	**3**	**4**	**6**	**10**	**15**	**27**
TOTAL										
0–19 Years	204	5.1	40	2	3	3	5	9	14	27
20–34	37	4.6	5	3	3	4	5	8	8	14
35–49	49	4.8	6	2	3	5	6	7	7	15
50–64	45	6.2	14	1	4	6	7	13	14	15
65+	36	8.2	31	4	5	7	9	15	21	28
GRAND TOTAL	**371**	**5.3**	**33**	**2**	**3**	**4**	**6**	**9**	**14**	**27**

35.71: REPAIR ASD NEC & NOS

Type of Patients	Observed Patients	Avg. Stay	Vari-ance	10th	25th	50th	75th	90th	95th	99th
1. SINGLE DX										
0–19 Years	30	2.1	1	1	1	2	3	3	4	6
20–34	3	2.7	2	1	1	3	4	4	4	4
35–49	6	3.3	3	1	1	3	5	5	5	5
50–64	1	1.0	0	1	1	1	1	1	1	1
65+	0									
2. MULTIPLE DX										
0–19 Years	67	5.3	40	2	3	3	4	10	22	35
20–34	27	5.0	6	3	4	4	6	8	10	14
35–49	37	5.0	7	3	3	4	6	7	11	15
50–64	40	6.2	14	1	4	6	7	13	14	15
65+	33	8.0	30	4	5	7	8	15	21	28
TOTAL SINGLE DX	**40**	**2.2**	**1**	**1**	**1**	**2**	**3**	**4**	**5**	**6**
TOTAL MULTIPLE DX	**204**	**5.7**	**28**	**2**	**3**	**4**	**7**	**11**	**15**	**27**
TOTAL										
0–19 Years	97	4.5	32	1	2	3	4	9	12	27
20–34	30	4.8	6	3	4	4	5	8	10	14
35–49	43	4.8	7	2	3	4	6	7	11	15
50–64	41	6.1	15	1	4	6	7	13	14	15
65+	33	8.0	30	4	5	7	8	15	21	28
GRAND TOTAL	**244**	**5.1**	**25**	**2**	**3**	**4**	**6**	**9**	**14**	**27**

35.72: REPAIR VSD NEC & NOS

Type of Patients	Observed Patients	Avg. Stay	Vari-ance	10th	25th	50th	75th	90th	95th	99th
1. SINGLE DX										
0–19 Years	7	3.4	2	2	3	3	4	6	6	6
20–34	3	4.0	0	4	4	4	4	4	4	4
35–49	1	6.0	0	6	6	6	6	6	6	6
50–64	0									
65+	0									
2. MULTIPLE DX										
0–19 Years	84	5.3	21	2	3	4	6	9	13	25
20–34	4	3.3	3	1	3	3	4	6	6	6
35–49	5	4.1	4	1	4	5	5	6	6	6
50–64	4	6.8	14	1	7	7	9	11	11	11
65+	2	14.3	3	13	13	13	16	16	16	16
TOTAL SINGLE DX	**11**	**3.7**	**2**	**2**	**3**	**3**	**4**	**6**	**6**	**6**
TOTAL MULTIPLE DX	**99**	**5.3**	**21**	**2**	**3**	**4**	**6**	**9**	**13**	**25**
TOTAL										
0–19 Years	91	5.1	20	2	3	4	6	9	12	25
20–34	7	3.6	1	3	3	4	4	4	6	6
35–49	6	4.5	4	1	4	5	6	6	6	6
50–64	4	6.8	14	1	7	7	9	11	11	11
65+	2	14.3	3	13	13	13	16	16	16	16
GRAND TOTAL	**110**	**5.2**	**19**	**2**	**3**	**4**	**6**	**9**	**13**	**25**

35.8: TOT REP CONG CARD ANOM

Type of Patients	Observed Patients	Avg. Stay	Vari-ance	10th	25th	50th	75th	90th	95th	99th
1. SINGLE DX										
0–19 Years	7	4.4	2	3	3	4	5	5	8	8
20–34	1	4.0	0	4	4	4	4	4	4	4
35–49	3	7.0	<1	6	6	7	8	8	8	8
50–64	0									
65+	0									
2. MULTIPLE DX										
0–19 Years	192	10.8	132	4	5	7	12	20	29	80
20–34	0									
35–49	14	7.8	19	4	5	7	8	13	20	20
50–64	3	12.5	65	7	7	8	22	22	22	22
65+	0									
TOTAL SINGLE DX	**11**	**4.8**	**2**	**3**	**4**	**5**	**5**	**8**	**8**	**8**
TOTAL MULTIPLE DX	**209**	**10.8**	**128**	**4**	**5**	**7**	**12**	**20**	**29**	**80**
TOTAL										
0–19 Years	199	10.6	129	4	5	7	11	20	29	80
20–34	1	4.0	0	4	4	4	4	4	4	4
35–49	17	7.7	16	4	5	7	8	13	20	20
50–64	3	12.5	65	7	7	8	22	22	22	22
65+	0									
GRAND TOTAL	**220**	**10.5**	**124**	**4**	**5**	**7**	**11**	**20**	**28**	**80**

35.81: TOT REP TETRALOGY FALLOT

Type of Patients	Observed Patients	Avg. Stay	Vari-ance	10th	25th	50th	75th	90th	95th	99th
1. SINGLE DX										
0–19 Years	7	4.4	2	3	3	4	5	5	8	8
20–34	1	4.0	0	4	4	4	4	4	4	4
35–49	3	7.0	<1	6	6	7	8	8	8	8
50–64	0									
65+	0									
2. MULTIPLE DX										
0–19 Years	139	9.0	60	4	5	7	10	17	28	69
20–34	0									
35–49	11	6.2	4	4	4	6	8	8	9	9
50–64	1	7.0	0	7	7	7	7	7	7	7
65+	0									
TOTAL SINGLE DX	**11**	**4.8**	**2**	**3**	**4**	**5**	**5**	**8**	**8**	**8**
TOTAL MULTIPLE DX	**151**	**8.9**	**58**	**4**	**5**	**7**	**9**	**17**	**28**	**34**
TOTAL										
0–19 Years	146	8.8	58	4	5	7	9	17	28	34
20–34	1	4.0	0	4	4	4	4	4	4	4
35–49	14	6.4	3	4	5	7	8	8	9	9
50–64	1	7.0	0	7	7	7	7	7	7	7
65+	0									
GRAND TOTAL	**162**	**8.7**	**55**	**4**	**5**	**7**	**9**	**16**	**28**	**34**

35.9: VALVES & SEPTA OPS NEC

Type of Patients	Observed Patients	Avg. Stay	Vari-ance	10th	25th	50th	75th	90th	95th	99th
1. SINGLE DX										
0–19 Years	34	1.9	3	1	1	1	2	4	6	8
20–34	2	1.0	0	1	1	1	1	1	1	1
35–49	4	1.0	0	1	1	1	1	1	1	1
50–64	5	1.0	0	1	1	1	1	1	1	1
65+	1	1.0	0	1	1	1	1	1	1	1
2. MULTIPLE DX										
0–19 Years	230	9.2	95	1	3	6	11	22	36	>99
20–34	15	5.4	17	1	2	6	7	12	12	12
35–49	20	4.2	24	1	1	2	7	8	16	20
50–64	33	3.0	33	1	1	1	2	6	12	35
65+	56	5.1	28	1	1	2	9	13	15	22
TOTAL SINGLE DX	**46**	**1.7**	**2**	**1**	**1**	**1**	**2**	**4**	**5**	**8**
TOTAL MULTIPLE DX	**354**	**7.9**	**81**	**1**	**2**	**6**	**11**	**19**	**29**	**>99**
TOTAL										
0–19 Years	264	8.4	90	1	2	6	11	21	30	>99
20–34	17	5.0	17	1	1	4	7	12	12	12
35–49	24	3.7	22	1	1	1	5	8	16	20
50–64	38	2.7	29	1	1	1	2	6	10	35
65+	57	5.0	28	1	1	2	9	13	15	22
GRAND TOTAL	**400**	**7.3**	**76**	**1**	**1**	**5**	**10**	**17**	**27**	**>99**

35.94: CREAT CONDUIT ATRIUM-PA

Type of Patients	Observed Patients	Avg. Stay	Vari-ance	Percentiles						
				10th	25th	50th	75th	90th	95th	99th
1. SINGLE DX										
0–19 Years	3	3.1	3	1	1	4	4	4	4	4
20–34	0									
35–49	0									
50–64	0									
65+	0									
2. MULTIPLE DX										
0–19 Years	95	12.1	73	5	6	10	14	24	29	43
20–34	1	12.0	0	12	12	12	12	12	12	12
35–49	3	10.0	25	7	7	7	16	16	16	16
50–64	0									
65+	0									
TOTAL SINGLE DX	**3**	**3.1**	**3**	**1**	**1**	**4**	**4**	**4**	**4**	**4**
TOTAL MULTIPLE DX	**99**	**12.0**	**71**	**5**	**7**	**10**	**14**	**23**	**29**	**43**
TOTAL										
0–19 Years	98	11.9	73	5	6	10	14	23	29	43
20–34	1	12.0	0	12	12	12	12	12	12	12
35–49	3	10.0	25	7	7	7	16	16	16	16
50–64	0									
65+	0									
GRAND TOTAL	**102**	**11.9**	**72**	**5**	**6**	**10**	**14**	**23**	**29**	**43**

35.96: PERC VALVULOPLASTY

Type of Patients	Observed Patients	Avg. Stay	Vari-ance	Percentiles						
				10th	25th	50th	75th	90th	95th	99th
1. SINGLE DX										
0–19 Years	27	1.4	<1	1	1	1	1	3	3	6
20–34	2	1.0	0	1	1	1	1	1	1	1
35–49	4	1.0	0	1	1	1	1	1	1	1
50–64	5	1.0	0	1	1	1	1	1	1	1
65+	1	1.0	0	1	1	1	1	1	1	1
2. MULTIPLE DX										
0–19 Years	54	4.1	70	1	1	2	4	19	>99	>99
20–34	7	2.8	13	1	1	2	2	11	11	11
35–49	12	1.8	3	1	1	1	2	3	8	8
50–64	28	1.5	2	1	1	1	1	2	6	6
65+	51	4.6	24	1	1	1	8	11	15	19
TOTAL SINGLE DX	**39**	**1.3**	**<1**	**1**	**1**	**1**	**1**	**2**	**3**	**6**
TOTAL MULTIPLE DX	**152**	**3.8**	**41**	**1**	**1**	**1**	**4**	**11**	**19**	**>99**
TOTAL										
0–19 Years	81	3.2	50	1	1	1	2	15	57	>99
20–34	9	2.4	10	1	1	1	2	11	11	11
35–49	16	1.7	3	1	1	1	2	3	8	8
50–64	33	1.5	1	1	1	1	1	2	6	6
65+	52	4.6	24	1	1	1	8	11	15	19
GRAND TOTAL	**191**	**3.3**	**34**	**1**	**1**	**1**	**3**	**11**	**17**	**>99**

36.0: RMVL COR ART OBSTR/STENT

Type of Patients	Observed Patients	Avg. Stay	Vari-ance	Percentiles						
				10th	25th	50th	75th	90th	95th	99th
1. SINGLE DX										
0–19 Years	0									
20–34	3	1.3	<1	1	1	1	2	2	2	2
35–49	79	1.5	<1	1	1	1	2	3	3	3
50–64	331	1.4	<1	1	1	1	1	2	3	4
65+	403	1.3	<1	1	1	1	1	2	3	5
2. MULTIPLE DX										
0–19 Years	17	2.9	20	1	1	1	2	11	15	17
20–34	228	3.4	12	1	1	3	4	7	8	22
35–49	5,983	2.5	4	1	1	2	3	4	6	11
50–64	22,460	2.4	5	1	1	2	3	4	6	11
65+	31,311	2.9	9	1	1	2	4	6	8	15
TOTAL SINGLE DX	**816**	**1.3**	**<1**	**1**	**1**	**1**	**1**	**2**	**3**	**5**
TOTAL MULTIPLE DX	**59,999**	**2.7**	**7**	**1**	**1**	**2**	**3**	**5**	**7**	**14**
TOTAL										
0–19 Years	17	2.9	20	1	1	1	2	11	15	17
20–34	231	3.4	12	1	1	3	4	7	8	22
35–49	6,062	2.5	4	1	1	2	3	4	6	10
50–64	22,791	2.4	5	1	1	2	3	4	6	11
65+	31,714	2.8	9	1	1	2	3	6	8	15
GRAND TOTAL	**60,815**	**2.7**	**7**	**1**	**1**	**2**	**3**	**5**	**7**	**14**

36.01: 1 PTCA/ATHERECT W/O TL

Type of Patients	Observed Patients	Avg. Stay	Vari-ance	Percentiles						
				10th	25th	50th	75th	90th	95th	99th
1. SINGLE DX										
0–19 Years	0									
20–34	3	1.3	<1	1	1	1	2	2	2	2
35–49	59	1.5	<1	1	1	1	2	3	3	5
50–64	235	1.4	<1	1	1	1	1	3	3	4
65+	278	1.3	<1	1	1	1	1	2	3	5
2. MULTIPLE DX										
0–19 Years	16	3.0	21	1	1	1	2	11	15	17
20–34	177	3.5	14	1	1	3	4	7	10	22
35–49	4,495	2.5	4	1	1	2	3	4	6	10
50–64	16,508	2.4	5	1	1	2	3	4	6	11
65+	22,705	2.9	9	1	1	2	4	6	8	15
TOTAL SINGLE DX	**575**	**1.4**	**<1**	**1**	**1**	**1**	**1**	**3**	**3**	**5**
TOTAL MULTIPLE DX	**43,901**	**2.7**	**7**	**1**	**1**	**2**	**3**	**5**	**7**	**14**
TOTAL										
0–19 Years	16	3.0	21	1	1	1	2	11	15	17
20–34	180	3.5	14	1	1	3	4	7	10	22
35–49	4,554	2.5	4	1	1	2	3	4	6	10
50–64	16,743	2.4	5	1	1	2	3	4	6	11
65+	22,983	2.8	8	1	1	2	3	6	8	15
GRAND TOTAL	**44,476**	**2.7**	**7**	**1**	**1**	**2**	**3**	**5**	**7**	**13**

36.02: 1 PTCA/ATHERECT W TL

Type of Patients	Observed Patients	Avg. Stay	Vari-ance	Percentiles 10th	25th	50th	75th	90th	95th	99th
1. SINGLE DX										
0–19 Years	0									
20–34	0									
35–49	1	1.0	0	1	1	1	1	1	1	1
50–64	19	1.8	2	1	1	1	3	4	4	6
65+	14	1.6	3	1	1	1	1	3	7	7
2. MULTIPLE DX										
0–19 Years	0									
20–34	14	3.0	2	1	2	3	4	4	4	7
35–49	189	2.8	3	1	2	2	4	5	6	7
50–64	802	2.5	5	1	1	2	3	5	6	11
65+	1,017	3.1	9	1	1	2	4	6	9	16
TOTAL SINGLE DX	**34**	**1.7**	**2**	**1**	**1**	**1**	**2**	**4**	**6**	**7**
TOTAL MULTIPLE DX	**2,022**	**2.8**	**7**	**1**	**1**	**2**	**4**	**5**	**7**	**13**
TOTAL										
0–19 Years	0									
20–34	14	3.0	2	1	2	3	4	4	4	7
35–49	190	2.8	3	1	2	2	4	5	6	7
50–64	821	2.5	5	1	1	2	3	5	6	11
65+	1,031	3.0	9	1	1	2	4	6	9	16
GRAND TOTAL	**2,056**	**2.8**	**7**	**1**	**1**	**2**	**4**	**5**	**7**	**13**

36.05: PTCA/ATHERECT-MULT VESS

Type of Patients	Observed Patients	Avg. Stay	Vari-ance	Percentiles 10th	25th	50th	75th	90th	95th	99th
1. SINGLE DX										
0–19 Years	0									
20–34	0									
35–49	10	1.3	<1	1	1	1	1	3	3	3
50–64	41	1.3	<1	1	1	1	1	2	2	3
65+	57	1.3	1	1	1	1	1	2	3	7
2. MULTIPLE DX										
0–19 Years	1	1.0	0	1	1	1	1	1	1	1
20–34	25	2.9	5	1	2	3	3	5	5	13
35–49	784	2.6	5	1	1	2	3	4	6	11
50–64	3,057	2.4	6	1	1	2	3	4	6	12
65+	4,679	3.0	13	1	1	2	4	6	9	16
TOTAL SINGLE DX	**108**	**1.3**	**<1**	**1**	**1**	**1**	**1**	**2**	**3**	**7**
TOTAL MULTIPLE DX	**8,546**	**2.8**	**10**	**1**	**1**	**2**	**3**	**6**	**8**	**15**
TOTAL										
0–19 Years	1	1.0	0	1	1	1	1	1	1	1
20–34	25	2.9	5	1	2	3	3	5	5	13
35–49	794	2.6	5	1	1	2	3	4	6	11
50–64	3,098	2.4	6	1	1	2	3	4	6	12
65+	4,736	3.0	13	1	1	2	4	6	9	16
GRAND TOTAL	**8,654**	**2.8**	**10**	**1**	**1**	**2**	**3**	**6**	**8**	**15**

36.06: NON-DRUG-ELUT COR STENT

Type of Patients	Observed Patients	Avg. Stay	Vari-ance	Percentiles 10th	25th	50th	75th	90th	95th	99th
1. SINGLE DX										
0–19 Years	0									
20–34	0									
35–49	0									
50–64	3	1.0	0	1	1	1	1	1	1	1
65+	5	1.0	0	1	1	1	1	1	1	1
2. MULTIPLE DX										
0–19 Years	0									
20–34	2	1.5	<1	1	1	1	2	2	2	2
35–49	108	2.2	3	1	1	2	2	3	5	10
50–64	329	2.2	3	1	1	2	3	4	5	8
65+	401	2.9	8	1	1	2	3	6	9	16
TOTAL SINGLE DX	**8**	**1.0**	**0**	**1**	**1**	**1**	**1**	**1**	**1**	**1**
TOTAL MULTIPLE DX	**840**	**2.6**	**6**	**1**	**1**	**2**	**3**	**5**	**7**	**14**
TOTAL										
0–19 Years	0									
20–34	2	1.5	<1	1	1	1	2	2	2	2
35–49	108	2.2	3	1	1	2	2	3	5	10
50–64	332	2.2	3	1	1	2	3	4	5	8
65+	406	2.9	8	1	1	2	3	6	9	16
GRAND TOTAL	**848**	**2.6**	**6**	**1**	**1**	**2**	**3**	**5**	**7**	**14**

36.07: DRUG-ELUTING COR STENT

Type of Patients	Observed Patients	Avg. Stay	Vari-ance	Percentiles 10th	25th	50th	75th	90th	95th	99th
1. SINGLE DX										
0–19 Years	0									
20–34	0									
35–49	9	1.1	<1	1	1	1	1	1	2	2
50–64	33	1.0	<1	1	1	1	1	1	1	2
65+	49	1.2	<1	1	1	1	1	2	2	3
2. MULTIPLE DX										
0–19 Years	0									
20–34	10	1.9	1	1	1	1	3	3	4	4
35–49	399	2.2	3	1	1	2	3	4	5	8
50–64	1,748	2.0	3	1	1	1	2	4	5	10
65+	2,493	2.4	7	1	1	1	3	5	7	16
TOTAL SINGLE DX	**91**	**1.1**	**<1**	**1**	**1**	**1**	**1**	**2**	**2**	**3**
TOTAL MULTIPLE DX	**4,650**	**2.3**	**6**	**1**	**1**	**1**	**3**	**5**	**6**	**13**
TOTAL										
0–19 Years	0									
20–34	10	1.9	1	1	1	1	3	3	4	4
35–49	408	2.2	3	1	1	2	3	4	5	8
50–64	1,781	2.0	3	1	1	1	2	4	5	10
65+	2,542	2.4	7	1	1	1	3	5	7	15
GRAND TOTAL	**4,741**	**2.3**	**5**	**1**	**1**	**1**	**3**	**5**	**6**	**13**

36.1: HRT REVASC BYPASS ANAST

Type of Patients	Observed Patients	Avg. Stay	Vari-ance	Percentiles						
				10th	25th	50th	75th	90th	95th	99th
1. SINGLE DX										
0–19 Years	1	7.0	0	7	7	7	7	7	7	7
20–34	2	5.0	0	5	5	5	5	5	5	5
35–49	3	4.0	3	2	2	4	6	6	6	6
50–64	20	4.8	2	3	4	5	5	6	7	9
65+	17	5.1	4	3	4	5	5	10	10	10
2. MULTIPLE DX										
0–19 Years	1	3.0	0	3	3	3	3	3	3	3
20–34	33	7.8	10	5	6	8	9	11	11	20
35–49	1,438	7.0	13	4	5	6	8	11	14	19
50–64	8,128	7.5	21	4	5	6	9	12	15	25
65+	12,051	8.8	30	4	6	7	10	15	19	30
TOTAL SINGLE DX	**43**	**5.3**	**3**	**3**	**4**	**5**	**7**	**7**	**9**	**10**
TOTAL MULTIPLE DX	**21,651**	**8.2**	**26**	**4**	**5**	**7**	**9**	**13**	**17**	**28**
TOTAL										
0–19 Years	2	6.6	1	7	7	7	7	7	7	7
20–34	35	7.7	10	5	5	8	9	11	11	20
35–49	1,441	7.0	13	4	5	6	8	11	14	19
50–64	8,148	7.5	21	4	5	6	9	12	15	25
65+	12,068	8.8	30	4	6	7	10	14	19	30
GRAND TOTAL	**21,694**	**8.2**	**26**	**4**	**5**	**7**	**9**	**13**	**17**	**28**

36.11: AO-COR BYPASS-1 COR ART

Type of Patients	Observed Patients	Avg. Stay	Vari-ance	Percentiles						
				10th	25th	50th	75th	90th	95th	99th
1. SINGLE DX										
0–19 Years	1	7.0	0	7	7	7	7	7	7	7
20–34	0									
35–49	0									
50–64	1	5.0	0	5	5	5	5	5	5	5
65+	1	3.0	0	3	3	3	3	3	3	3
2. MULTIPLE DX										
0–19 Years	1	3.0	0	3	3	3	3	3	3	3
20–34	6	8.8	23	2	5	10	11	17	17	17
35–49	210	6.4	10	3	4	6	8	10	12	19
50–64	960	7.1	18	4	5	6	8	11	14	28
65+	1,215	8.6	37	4	5	7	9	14	19	34
TOTAL SINGLE DX	**3**	**6.0**	**3**	**3**	**5**	**7**	**7**	**7**	**7**	**7**
TOTAL MULTIPLE DX	**2,392**	**7.8**	**28**	**4**	**5**	**7**	**9**	**12**	**17**	**31**
TOTAL										
0–19 Years	2	6.6	1	7	7	7	7	7	7	7
20–34	6	8.8	23	2	5	10	11	17	17	17
35–49	210	6.4	10	3	4	6	8	10	12	19
50–64	961	7.1	18	4	5	6	8	11	14	28
65+	1,216	8.6	37	4	5	7	9	14	19	34
GRAND TOTAL	**2,395**	**7.8**	**28**	**4**	**5**	**7**	**9**	**12**	**17**	**31**

36.12: AO-COR BYPASS-2 COR ART

Type of Patients	Observed Patients	Avg. Stay	Vari-ance	Percentiles						
				10th	25th	50th	75th	90th	95th	99th
1. SINGLE DX										
0–19 Years	0									
20–34	1	5.0	0	5	5	5	5	5	5	5
35–49	0									
50–64	7	5.0	4	3	4	5	5	9	9	9
65+	5	5.4	5	4	4	5	5	10	10	10
2. MULTIPLE DX										
0–19 Years	0									
20–34	10	6.8	4	5	5	7	8	9	11	11
35–49	369	7.2	12	4	5	6	8	12	14	18
50–64	2,248	7.6	18	4	5	6	9	12	15	25
65+	3,426	8.8	29	4	6	7	10	15	19	28
TOTAL SINGLE DX	**13**	**5.2**	**4**	**4**	**4**	**5**	**5**	**9**	**10**	**10**
TOTAL MULTIPLE DX	**6,053**	**8.3**	**25**	**4**	**5**	**7**	**10**	**14**	**17**	**27**
TOTAL										
0–19 Years	0									
20–34	11	6.7	4	5	5	7	8	9	11	11
35–49	369	7.2	12	4	5	6	8	12	14	18
50–64	2,255	7.6	18	4	5	6	9	12	15	25
65+	3,431	8.8	29	4	6	7	10	15	19	28
GRAND TOTAL	**6,066**	**8.3**	**25**	**4**	**5**	**7**	**10**	**14**	**17**	**27**

36.13: AO-COR BYPASS-3 COR ART

Type of Patients	Observed Patients	Avg. Stay	Vari-ance	Percentiles						
				10th	25th	50th	75th	90th	95th	99th
1. SINGLE DX										
0–19 Years	0									
20–34	0									
35–49	2	4.8	1	4	4	4	6	6	6	6
50–64	5	4.2	<1	4	4	4	4	5	5	5
65+	6	6.1	7	3	4	7	7	10	10	10
2. MULTIPLE DX										
0–19 Years	0									
20–34	5	8.0	2	6	6	9	9	9	9	9
35–49	378	7.4	12	4	5	6	9	12	14	18
50–64	2,244	7.9	28	4	5	7	9	13	16	30
65+	3,587	9.0	28	5	6	8	10	15	19	29
TOTAL SINGLE DX	**13**	**5.4**	**5**	**4**	**4**	**4**	**7**	**10**	**10**	**10**
TOTAL MULTIPLE DX	**6,214**	**8.5**	**28**	**4**	**5**	**7**	**10**	**14**	**17**	**29**
TOTAL										
0–19 Years	0									
20–34	5	8.0	2	6	6	9	9	9	9	9
35–49	380	7.4	12	4	5	6	9	12	14	18
50–64	2,249	7.9	28	4	5	7	9	13	16	30
65+	3,593	9.0	28	5	6	8	10	15	19	29
GRAND TOTAL	**6,227**	**8.5**	**28**	**4**	**5**	**7**	**10**	**14**	**17**	**29**

36.14: AO-COR BYPASS-4+ COR ART

Type of Patients	Observed Patients	Avg. Stay	Vari-ance	Percentiles 10th	25th	50th	75th	90th	95th	99th
1. SINGLE DX										
0–19 Years	0									
20–34	1	5.0	0	5	5	5	5	5	5	5
35–49	0									
50–64	4	4.9	4	3	3	6	6	7	7	7
65+	3	3.8	2	2	2	4	5	5	5	5
2. MULTIPLE DX										
0–19 Years	0									
20–34	4	11.2	33	6	9	10	10	20	20	20
35–49	221	7.1	13	4	5	6	9	11	13	22
50–64	1,310	7.9	20	4	5	7	9	12	16	24
65+	2,059	9.1	31	5	6	8	11	15	20	32
TOTAL SINGLE DX	**8**	**4.5**	**3**	**2**	**3**	**5**	**6**	**7**	**7**	**7**
TOTAL MULTIPLE DX	**3,594**	**8.6**	**27**	**4**	**6**	**7**	**10**	**14**	**18**	**29**
TOTAL										
0–19 Years	0									
20–34	5	10.0	32	5	6	9	10	20	20	20
35–49	221	7.1	13	4	5	6	9	11	13	22
50–64	1,314	7.9	20	4	5	7	9	12	16	24
65+	2,062	9.1	31	5	6	8	11	15	20	32
GRAND TOTAL	**3,602**	**8.6**	**27**	**4**	**6**	**7**	**10**	**14**	**18**	**29**

36.15: 1 INT MAM-COR ART BYPASS

Type of Patients	Observed Patients	Avg. Stay	Vari-ance	Percentiles 10th	25th	50th	75th	90th	95th	99th
1. SINGLE DX										
0–19 Years	0									
20–34	0									
35–49	0									
50–64	3	5.3	<1	5	5	5	6	6	6	6
65+	1	5.0	0	5	5	5	5	5	5	5
2. MULTIPLE DX										
0–19 Years	0									
20–34	7	7.0	3	5	6	8	8	8	8	8
35–49	219	6.6	18	3	4	5	8	10	14	31
50–64	1,186	6.6	20	3	4	6	8	11	13	19
65+	1,631	8.1	28	4	5	7	9	13	18	29
TOTAL SINGLE DX	**4**	**5.1**	**<1**	**5**	**5**	**5**	**5**	**6**	**6**	**6**
TOTAL MULTIPLE DX	**3,043**	**7.4**	**25**	**4**	**5**	**6**	**8**	**12**	**16**	**28**
TOTAL										
0–19 Years	0									
20–34	7	7.0	3	5	6	8	8	8	8	8
35–49	219	6.6	18	3	4	5	8	10	14	31
50–64	1,189	6.6	20	3	4	6	8	11	13	19
65+	1,632	8.1	28	4	5	7	9	13	18	29
GRAND TOTAL	**3,047**	**7.4**	**25**	**4**	**5**	**6**	**8**	**12**	**16**	**28**

36.16: 2 INT MAM-COR ART BYPASS

Type of Patients	Observed Patients	Avg. Stay	Vari-ance	Percentiles 10th	25th	50th	75th	90th	95th	99th
1. SINGLE DX										
0–19 Years	0									
20–34	0									
35–49	1	2.0	0	2	2	2	2	2	2	2
50–64	0									
65+	1	6.0	0	6	6	6	6	6	6	6
2. MULTIPLE DX										
0–19 Years	0									
20–34	1	9.0	0	9	9	9	9	9	9	9
35–49	39	5.7	7	3	4	5	6	9	11	17
50–64	172	6.1	12	4	4	5	7	9	11	16
65+	130	8.0	25	4	5	6	9	14	21	25
TOTAL SINGLE DX	**2**	**4.3**	**6**	**2**	**2**	**6**	**6**	**6**	**6**	**6**
TOTAL MULTIPLE DX	**342**	**6.8**	**18**	**4**	**4**	**6**	**8**	**11**	**15**	**25**
TOTAL										
0–19 Years	0									
20–34	1	9.0	0	9	9	9	9	9	9	9
35–49	40	5.6	7	3	4	5	6	9	11	17
50–64	172	6.1	12	4	4	5	7	9	11	16
65+	131	7.9	25	4	5	6	9	14	21	25
GRAND TOTAL	**344**	**6.8**	**18**	**4**	**4**	**6**	**8**	**11**	**15**	**24**

36.2: ARTERIAL IMPLANT REVASC

Type of Patients	Observed Patients	Avg. Stay	Vari-ance	Percentiles 10th	25th	50th	75th	90th	95th	99th
1. SINGLE DX										
0–19 Years	0									
20–34	0									
35–49	0									
50–64	0									
65+	0									
2. MULTIPLE DX										
0–19 Years	0									
20–34	0									
35–49	0									
50–64	0									
65+	1	11.0	0	11	11	11	11	11	11	11
TOTAL SINGLE DX	**0**									
TOTAL MULTIPLE DX	**1**	**11.0**	**0**	**11**	**11**	**11**	**11**	**11**	**11**	**11**
TOTAL										
0–19 Years	0									
20–34	0									
35–49	0									
50–64	0									
65+	1	11.0	0	11	11	11	11	11	11	11
GRAND TOTAL	**1**	**11.0**	**0**	**11**	**11**	**11**	**11**	**11**	**11**	**11**

36.3: OTHER HEART REVASC

Type of Patients	Observed Patients	Avg. Stay	Vari-ance	Percentiles 10th	25th	50th	75th	90th	95th	99th
1. SINGLE DX										
0–19 Years	0									
20–34	0									
35–49	0									
50–64	0									
65+	0									
2. MULTIPLE DX										
0–19 Years	0									
20–34	2	3.6	15	1	1	1	7	7	7	7
35–49	24	7.3	14	3	4	7	9	11	13	20
50–64	116	7.5	14	4	5	7	9	13	15	21
65+	141	7.8	17	4	5	7	9	13	14	25
TOTAL SINGLE DX	**0**									
TOTAL MULTIPLE DX	**283**	**7.6**	**15**	**4**	**5**	**7**	**9**	**13**	**14**	**21**
TOTAL										
0–19 Years	0									
20–34	2	3.6	15	1	1	1	7	7	7	7
35–49	24	7.3	14	3	4	7	9	11	13	20
50–64	116	7.5	14	4	5	7	9	13	15	21
65+	141	7.8	17	4	5	7	9	13	14	25
GRAND TOTAL	**283**	**7.6**	**15**	**4**	**5**	**7**	**9**	**13**	**14**	**21**

36.31: OPEN TRANSMYO REVASC

Type of Patients	Observed Patients	Avg. Stay	Vari-ance	Percentiles 10th	25th	50th	75th	90th	95th	99th
1. SINGLE DX										
0–19 Years	0									
20–34	0									
35–49	0									
50–64	0									
65+	0									
2. MULTIPLE DX										
0–19 Years	0									
20–34	1	7.0	0	7	7	7	7	7	7	7
35–49	24	7.3	14	3	4	7	9	11	13	20
50–64	112	7.5	14	4	5	7	9	13	15	21
65+	140	7.8	17	4	5	7	9	13	14	25
TOTAL SINGLE DX	**0**									
TOTAL MULTIPLE DX	**277**	**7.6**	**15**	**4**	**5**	**7**	**9**	**13**	**14**	**21**
TOTAL										
0–19 Years	0									
20–34	1	7.0	0	7	7	7	7	7	7	7
35–49	24	7.3	14	3	4	7	9	11	13	20
50–64	112	7.5	14	4	5	7	9	13	15	21
65+	140	7.8	17	4	5	7	9	13	14	25
GRAND TOTAL	**277**	**7.6**	**15**	**4**	**5**	**7**	**9**	**13**	**14**	**21**

36.9: OTHER HEART VESSEL OPS

Type of Patients	Observed Patients	Avg. Stay	Vari-ance	Percentiles 10th	25th	50th	75th	90th	95th	99th
1. SINGLE DX										
0–19 Years	1	3.0	0	3	3	3	3	3	3	3
20–34	0									
35–49	0									
50–64	0									
65+	0									
2. MULTIPLE DX										
0–19 Years	12	6.5	38	3	3	5	5	18	21	23
20–34	1	4.0	0	4	4	4	4	4	4	4
35–49	14	8.3	22	4	4	8	12	13	19	19
50–64	28	6.2	26	1	2	5	8	12	18	23
65+	30	9.3	32	5	6	8	11	12	24	32
TOTAL SINGLE DX	**1**	**3.0**	**0**	**3**	**3**	**3**	**3**	**3**	**3**	**3**
TOTAL MULTIPLE DX	**85**	**7.7**	**31**	**3**	**4**	**6**	**10**	**13**	**19**	**32**
TOTAL										
0–19 Years	13	6.2	35	3	3	4	5	18	21	23
20–34	1	4.0	0	4	4	4	4	4	4	4
35–49	14	8.3	22	4	4	8	12	13	19	19
50–64	28	6.2	26	1	2	5	8	12	18	23
65+	30	9.3	32	5	6	8	11	12	24	32
GRAND TOTAL	**86**	**7.6**	**31**	**3**	**4**	**6**	**10**	**13**	**19**	**32**

37.0: PERICARDIOCENTESIS

Type of Patients	Observed Patients	Avg. Stay	Vari-ance	Percentiles 10th	25th	50th	75th	90th	95th	99th
1. SINGLE DX										
0–19 Years	4	4.6	4	1	5	5	6	6	6	6
20–34	4	3.5	3	1	3	4	5	5	5	5
35–49	5	3.3	1	2	2	4	4	4	4	4
50–64	1	2.0	0	2	2	2	2	2	2	2
65+	1	5.0	0	5	5	5	5	5	5	5
2. MULTIPLE DX										
0–19 Years	30	5.1	12	2	3	5	6	8	14	18
20–34	40	6.1	27	2	3	4	9	11	19	28
35–49	87	6.4	22	1	3	5	9	14	17	20
50–64	179	6.2	23	2	3	4	8	12	19	21
65+	221	6.4	24	2	3	5	8	13	17	23
TOTAL SINGLE DX	**15**	**3.8**	**3**	**1**	**3**	**4**	**5**	**6**	**6**	**6**
TOTAL MULTIPLE DX	**557**	**6.2**	**23**	**2**	**3**	**5**	**8**	**13**	**17**	**22**
TOTAL										
0–19 Years	34	5.0	11	2	3	5	6	8	14	18
20–34	44	5.9	25	2	3	4	9	10	13	28
35–49	92	6.2	21	1	3	4	8	14	14	20
50–64	180	6.1	23	2	3	4	8	12	19	21
65+	222	6.4	23	2	3	5	8	13	17	23
GRAND TOTAL	**572**	**6.1**	**22**	**2**	**3**	**5**	**8**	**13**	**17**	**22**

37.1: CARDIOTOMY & PERICARDIOT

Type of Patients	Observed Patients	Avg. Stay	Vari-ance	10th	25th	50th	75th	90th	95th	99th
				Percentiles						
1. SINGLE DX										
0–19 Years	5	4.0	4	2	3	4	5	8	8	8
20–34	6	5.2	6	3	3	4	7	9	9	9
35–49	4	2.5	2	1	2	2	3	4	4	4
50–64	0									
65+	0									
2. MULTIPLE DX										
0–19 Years	37	9.2	96	3	3	6	12	22	29	46
20–34	55	10.0	56	4	5	7	13	23	26	31
35–49	124	8.0	32	3	4	7	9	15	19	31
50–64	241	8.5	53	3	4	7	11	15	18	35
65+	340	9.3	37	3	5	8	12	17	21	32
TOTAL SINGLE DX	**15**	**4.0**	**5**	**2**	**3**	**3**	**5**	**8**	**9**	**9**
TOTAL MULTIPLE DX	**797**	**8.9**	**45**	**3**	**4**	**7**	**11**	**16**	**21**	**33**
TOTAL										
0–19 Years	42	8.7	90	2	3	6	11	22	29	46
20–34	61	9.7	54	3	5	7	11	23	26	31
35–49	128	7.8	32	3	4	7	9	14	19	31
50–64	241	8.5	53	3	4	7	11	15	18	35
65+	340	9.3	37	3	5	8	12	17	21	32
GRAND TOTAL	**812**	**8.8**	**45**	**3**	**4**	**7**	**11**	**16**	**21**	**33**

37.12: PERICARDIOTOMY

Type of Patients	Observed Patients	Avg. Stay	Vari-ance	10th	25th	50th	75th	90th	95th	99th
				Percentiles						
1. SINGLE DX										
0–19 Years	3	5.4	4	4	4	5	8	8	8	8
20–34	4	5.7	7	3	4	4	7	9	9	9
35–49	4	2.5	2	1	2	2	3	4	4	4
50–64	0									
65+	0									
2. MULTIPLE DX										
0–19 Years	32	10.2	111	3	4	6	13	29	29	46
20–34	53	10.1	57	4	5	7	13	23	26	31
35–49	119	7.9	30	3	5	7	9	14	18	31
50–64	233	8.6	54	3	4	7	11	15	18	35
65+	324	9.2	36	3	5	8	12	17	20	32
TOTAL SINGLE DX	**11**	**4.4**	**6**	**2**	**3**	**4**	**5**	**8**	**9**	**9**
TOTAL MULTIPLE DX	**761**	**8.9**	**46**	**3**	**5**	**7**	**11**	**16**	**21**	**33**
TOTAL										
0–19 Years	35	9.9	106	3	4	6	13	29	29	46
20–34	57	9.9	55	3	5	7	12	23	26	31
35–49	123	7.8	30	3	4	7	9	14	18	31
50–64	233	8.6	54	3	4	7	11	15	18	35
65+	324	9.2	36	3	5	8	12	17	20	32
GRAND TOTAL	**772**	**8.9**	**46**	**3**	**4**	**7**	**11**	**16**	**21**	**33**

37.2: DXTIC PX HRT/PERICARDIUM

Type of Patients	Observed Patients	Avg. Stay	Vari-ance	10th	25th	50th	75th	90th	95th	99th
				Percentiles						
1. SINGLE DX										
0–19 Years	83	1.2	<1	1	1	1	1	2	3	3
20–34	84	1.6	<1	1	1	1	2	3	4	4
35–49	242	1.8	4	1	1	1	2	3	3	18
50–64	255	1.7	2	1	1	1	2	3	4	8
65+	120	1.7	1	1	1	1	2	3	4	6
2. MULTIPLE DX										
0–19 Years	337	3.1	24	1	1	1	3	8	14	22
20–34	775	3.5	11	1	2	3	4	7	10	19
35–49	6,594	3.0	11	1	1	2	4	6	8	16
50–64	16,299	3.2	10	1	1	2	4	6	8	15
65+	21,907	3.9	12	1	2	3	5	8	10	17
TOTAL SINGLE DX	**784**	**1.7**	**2**	**1**	**1**	**1**	**2**	**3**	**4**	**7**
TOTAL MULTIPLE DX	**45,912**	**3.5**	**11**	**1**	**1**	**3**	**4**	**7**	**9**	**17**
TOTAL										
0–19 Years	420	2.8	20	1	1	1	2	7	11	21
20–34	859	3.3	10	1	1	2	4	7	9	17
35–49	6,836	3.0	11	1	1	2	4	6	8	16
50–64	16,554	3.2	9	1	1	2	4	6	8	15
65+	22,027	3.9	12	1	2	3	5	8	10	17
GRAND TOTAL	**46,696**	**3.5**	**11**	**1**	**1**	**3**	**4**	**7**	**9**	**17**

37.21: RT HEART CARDIAC CATH

Type of Patients	Observed Patients	Avg. Stay	Vari-ance	10th	25th	50th	75th	90th	95th	99th
				Percentiles						
1. SINGLE DX										
0–19 Years	7	1.1	<1	1	1	1	1	1	2	2
20–34	1	1.0	0	1	1	1	1	1	1	1
35–49	4	1.0	0	1	1	1	1	1	1	1
50–64	4	1.5	<1	1	1	2	2	2	2	2
65+	0									
2. MULTIPLE DX										
0–19 Years	33	5.3	58	1	1	1	8	16	22	36
20–34	41	6.5	34	2	2	4	9	17	19	22
35–49	111	8.2	158	1	2	5	9	14	29	91
50–64	233	6.9	34	2	3	5	10	15	18	24
65+	270	7.2	39	1	3	6	10	16	19	30
TOTAL SINGLE DX	**16**	**1.1**	**<1**	**1**	**1**	**1**	**1**	**2**	**2**	**2**
TOTAL MULTIPLE DX	**688**	**7.1**	**57**	**1**	**2**	**5**	**9**	**15**	**19**	**33**
TOTAL										
0–19 Years	40	4.7	52	1	1	1	7	11	22	36
20–34	42	6.4	34	1	2	4	9	17	19	22
35–49	115	7.8	152	1	1	5	9	14	24	91
50–64	237	6.9	34	2	3	5	10	15	18	24
65+	270	7.2	39	1	3	6	10	16	19	30
GRAND TOTAL	**704**	**7.0**	**57**	**1**	**2**	**5**	**9**	**15**	**19**	**33**

37.22: LEFT HEART CARDIAC CATH

Type of Patients	Observed Patients	Avg. Stay	Vari-ance	Percentiles 10th	25th	50th	75th	90th	95th	99th
1. SINGLE DX										
0–19 Years	5	1.0	0	1	1	1	1	1	1	1
20–34	52	1.8	1	1	1	1	2	3	4	4
35–49	198	1.9	5	1	1	1	2	3	3	18
50–64	193	1.6	1	1	1	1	2	3	4	5
65+	90	1.8	1	1	1	1	2	4	4	6
2. MULTIPLE DX										
0–19 Years	29	2.6	4	1	1	2	4	5	6	9
20–34	502	2.9	6	1	1	2	3	5	7	13
35–49	5,429	2.6	5	1	1	2	3	5	6	12
50–64	13,545	2.9	7	1	1	2	4	6	7	13
65+	17,159	3.6	9	1	2	3	4	7	9	15
TOTAL SINGLE DX	**538**	**1.8**	**2**	**1**	**1**	**1**	**2**	**3**	**4**	**6**
TOTAL MULTIPLE DX	**36,664**	**3.2**	**8**	**1**	**1**	**2**	**4**	**6**	**8**	**14**
TOTAL										
0–19 Years	34	2.4	3	1	1	1	3	5	6	9
20–34	554	2.8	6	1	1	2	3	5	7	11
35–49	5,627	2.6	5	1	1	2	3	5	6	12
50–64	13,738	2.9	7	1	1	2	4	6	7	13
65+	17,249	3.6	9	1	2	3	4	7	9	15
GRAND TOTAL	**37,202**	**3.2**	**8**	**1**	**1**	**2**	**4**	**6**	**8**	**14**

37.23: RT/LEFT HEART CARD CATH

Type of Patients	Observed Patients	Avg. Stay	Vari-ance	Percentiles 10th	25th	50th	75th	90th	95th	99th
1. SINGLE DX										
0–19 Years	51	1.2	<1	1	1	1	1	2	2	3
20–34	3	1.7	1	1	1	1	3	3	3	3
35–49	18	2.3	2	1	1	2	3	4	5	6
50–64	23	2.4	7	1	1	1	2	7	9	9
65+	10	1.3	<1	1	1	1	2	2	2	2
2. MULTIPLE DX										
0–19 Years	213	2.8	24	1	1	1	2	8	14	21
20–34	147	4.6	13	1	2	4	6	8	11	17
35–49	880	4.7	18	1	2	4	6	9	11	19
50–64	2,046	4.6	15	1	2	4	6	9	12	20
65+	3,807	5.1	18	1	2	4	7	10	13	21
TOTAL SINGLE DX	**105**	**1.6**	**2**	**1**	**1**	**1**	**2**	**3**	**4**	**9**
TOTAL MULTIPLE DX	**7,093**	**4.8**	**17**	**1**	**2**	**4**	**6**	**10**	**13**	**20**
TOTAL										
0–19 Years	264	2.5	20	1	1	1	2	6	10	20
20–34	150	4.5	13	1	2	4	6	8	11	17
35–49	898	4.6	17	1	2	4	6	9	11	19
50–64	2,069	4.6	15	1	2	4	6	9	12	20
65+	3,817	5.1	18	1	2	4	7	10	13	21
GRAND TOTAL	**7,198**	**4.8**	**17**	**1**	**2**	**4**	**6**	**9**	**13**	**20**

37.25: CARDIAC BIOPSY

Type of Patients	Observed Patients	Avg. Stay	Vari-ance	Percentiles 10th	25th	50th	75th	90th	95th	99th
1. SINGLE DX										
0–19 Years	4	2.1	<1	1	2	2	2	3	3	3
20–34	0									
35–49	0									
50–64	0									
65+	0									
2. MULTIPLE DX										
0–19 Years	21	5.6	25	1	1	3	8	14	14	17
20–34	17	4.7	9	1	2	5	7	7	8	14
35–49	28	3.8	17	1	1	2	5	7	16	19
50–64	75	5.5	41	1	2	4	7	11	14	49
65+	27	6.5	26	2	3	5	8	16	21	21
TOTAL SINGLE DX	**4**	**2.1**	**<1**	**1**	**2**	**2**	**2**	**3**	**3**	**3**
TOTAL MULTIPLE DX	**168**	**5.3**	**29**	**1**	**2**	**4**	**7**	**12**	**15**	**21**
TOTAL										
0–19 Years	25	4.9	22	1	1	3	6	12	14	17
20–34	17	4.7	9	1	2	5	7	7	8	14
35–49	28	3.8	17	1	1	2	5	7	16	19
50–64	75	5.5	41	1	2	4	7	11	14	49
65+	27	6.5	26	2	3	5	8	16	21	21
GRAND TOTAL	**172**	**5.2**	**29**	**1**	**2**	**4**	**7**	**11**	**15**	**21**

37.26: CARD EPS/RECORD STUDIES

Type of Patients	Observed Patients	Avg. Stay	Vari-ance	Percentiles 10th	25th	50th	75th	90th	95th	99th
1. SINGLE DX										
0–19 Years	15	1.1	<1	1	1	1	1	1	3	3
20–34	28	1.3	<1	1	1	1	1	2	3	4
35–49	21	1.3	<1	1	1	1	1	2	2	5
50–64	35	1.6	2	1	1	1	2	2	5	8
65+	20	1.4	1	1	1	1	1	4	4	4
2. MULTIPLE DX										
0–19 Years	38	2.3	5	1	1	1	3	6	8	8
20–34	62	3.2	14	1	1	2	4	7	8	23
35–49	134	3.6	14	1	1	2	5	8	14	17
50–64	359	3.6	11	1	1	3	5	7	10	18
65+	620	4.2	13	1	1	3	6	9	10	17
TOTAL SINGLE DX	**119**	**1.4**	**1**	**1**	**1**	**1**	**1**	**2**	**4**	**7**
TOTAL MULTIPLE DX	**1,213**	**3.8**	**13**	**1**	**1**	**3**	**5**	**8**	**10**	**17**
TOTAL										
0–19 Years	53	1.9	4	1	1	1	1	6	7	8
20–34	90	2.6	11	1	1	1	3	5	7	23
35–49	155	3.4	13	1	1	2	4	8	12	17
50–64	394	3.4	10	1	1	2	5	7	9	17
65+	640	4.1	13	1	1	3	6	9	10	17
GRAND TOTAL	**1,332**	**3.6**	**12**	**1**	**1**	**2**	**5**	**8**	**10**	**17**

37.3: PERICARDIECT/EXC HRT LES

Type of Patients	Observed Patients	Avg. Stay	Vari-ance	Percentiles						
				10th	25th	50th	75th	90th	95th	99th
1. SINGLE DX										
0–19 Years	55	1.3	<1	1	1	1	1	2	3	7
20–34	93	1.2	<1	1	1	1	1	1	2	4
35–49	142	1.2	<1	1	1	1	1	1	2	6
50–64	179	1.2	<1	1	1	1	1	2	3	6
65+	79	1.1	<1	1	1	1	1	1	1	6
2. MULTIPLE DX										
0–19 Years	87	2.8	11	1	1	2	3	5	6	22
20–34	181	2.4	9	1	1	1	2	5	8	19
35–49	374	3.1	19	1	1	1	4	6	9	28
50–64	899	3.5	26	1	1	1	4	8	13	21
65+	1,115	3.8	27	1	1	2	5	9	14	20
TOTAL SINGLE DX	**548**	**1.2**	**<1**	**1**	**1**	**1**	**1**	**1**	**2**	**6**
TOTAL MULTIPLE DX	**2,656**	**3.5**	**24**	**1**	**1**	**1**	**4**	**8**	**12**	**21**
TOTAL										
0–19 Years	142	2.3	8	1	1	1	3	5	6	19
20–34	274	2.0	7	1	1	1	2	4	7	14
35–49	516	2.6	14	1	1	1	3	6	8	18
50–64	1,078	3.1	22	1	1	1	3	7	12	21
65+	1,194	3.7	26	1	1	1	5	9	13	20
GRAND TOTAL	**3,204**	**3.1**	**21**	**1**	**1**	**1**	**3**	**7**	**11**	**20**

37.31: PERICARDIECTOMY

Type of Patients	Observed Patients	Avg. Stay	Vari-ance	Percentiles						
				10th	25th	50th	75th	90th	95th	99th
1. SINGLE DX										
0–19 Years	0									
20–34	3	2.6	4	1	1	2	5	5	5	5
35–49	5	3.1	11	1	1	2	3	9	9	9
50–64	0									
65+	0									
2. MULTIPLE DX										
0–19 Years	2	11.1	47	7	7	7	19	19	19	19
20–34	9	8.2	31	3	4	7	13	14	21	21
35–49	33	10.0	97	3	4	6	11	28	35	35
50–64	43	10.0	48	4	5	7	15	20	22	34
65+	35	9.3	34	3	4	8	15	18	21	22
TOTAL SINGLE DX	**8**	**2.9**	**7**	**1**	**1**	**2**	**3**	**9**	**9**	**9**
TOTAL MULTIPLE DX	**122**	**9.7**	**55**	**3**	**5**	**7**	**13**	**20**	**27**	**35**
TOTAL										
0–19 Years	2	11.1	47	7	7	7	19	19	19	19
20–34	12	7.1	30	2	3	7	13	14	21	21
35–49	38	9.3	93	2	3	6	10	27	35	35
50–64	43	10.0	48	4	5	7	15	20	22	34
65+	35	9.3	34	3	4	8	15	18	21	22
GRAND TOTAL	**130**	**9.4**	**55**	**3**	**4**	**7**	**13**	**20**	**22**	**35**

37.32: HEART ANEURYSM EXCISION

Type of Patients	Observed Patients	Avg. Stay	Vari-ance	Percentiles						
				10th	25th	50th	75th	90th	95th	99th
1. SINGLE DX										
0–19 Years	0									
20–34	0									
35–49	0									
50–64	0									
65+	0									
2. MULTIPLE DX										
0–19 Years	1	1.0	0	1	1	1	1	1	1	1
20–34	1	4.0	0	4	4	4	4	4	4	4
35–49	4	6.2	<1	5	6	6	7	7	7	7
50–64	25	10.1	35	5	6	6	14	20	20	22
65+	40	9.5	50	3	6	7	9	20	20	40
TOTAL SINGLE DX	**0**									
TOTAL MULTIPLE DX	**71**	**9.5**	**42**	**4**	**6**	**7**	**12**	**20**	**20**	**40**
TOTAL										
0–19 Years	1	1.0	0	1	1	1	1	1	1	1
20–34	1	4.0	0	4	4	4	4	4	4	4
35–49	4	6.2	<1	5	6	6	7	7	7	7
50–64	25	10.1	35	5	6	6	14	20	20	22
65+	40	9.5	50	3	6	7	9	20	20	40
GRAND TOTAL	**71**	**9.5**	**42**	**4**	**6**	**7**	**12**	**20**	**20**	**40**

37.33: HEART LES EXC/DESTR NEC

Type of Patients	Observed Patients	Avg. Stay	Vari-ance	Percentiles						
				10th	25th	50th	75th	90th	95th	99th
1. SINGLE DX										
0–19 Years	1	4.0	0	4	4	4	4	4	4	4
20–34	3	2.7	2	1	1	3	4	4	4	4
35–49	4	3.8	5	1	3	5	5	6	6	6
50–64	7	3.6	4	1	1	4	6	6	6	6
65+	1	6.0	0	6	6	6	6	6	6	6
2. MULTIPLE DX										
0–19 Years	25	4.1	8	3	3	3	5	5	6	22
20–34	13	5.4	25	1	2	4	8	10	19	19
35–49	32	5.7	9	1	4	5	7	10	11	16
50–64	58	7.5	26	2	4	6	10	16	20	21
65+	81	8.1	24	2	4	7	10	15	19	20
TOTAL SINGLE DX	**16**	**3.7**	**4**	**1**	**3**	**4**	**6**	**6**	**6**	**6**
TOTAL MULTIPLE DX	**209**	**6.7**	**22**	**2**	**3**	**5**	**9**	**14**	**17**	**21**
TOTAL										
0–19 Years	26	4.1	7	3	3	3	5	5	6	22
20–34	16	4.9	22	1	2	4	5	10	19	19
35–49	36	5.5	9	1	4	5	7	10	11	16
50–64	65	7.1	26	2	4	6	9	16	17	21
65+	82	8.0	24	2	4	7	10	15	19	20
GRAND TOTAL	**225**	**6.5**	**21**	**2**	**3**	**5**	**8**	**14**	**17**	**21**

37.34: CATH ABLATION HEART LES

Type of Patients	Observed Patients	Avg. Stay	Variance	10th	25th	50th	75th	90th	95th	99th
1. SINGLE DX										
0–19 Years	54	1.2	<1	1	1	1	1	1	2	7
20–34	87	1.1	<1	1	1	1	1	1	2	3
35–49	133	1.1	<1	1	1	1	1	1	1	3
50–64	172	1.1	<1	1	1	1	1	2	2	3
65+	78	1.0	<1	1	1	1	1	1	1	2
2. MULTIPLE DX										
0–19 Years	59	1.7	8	1	1	1	1	3	3	7
20–34	158	1.8	4	1	1	1	2	3	5	12
35–49	305	2.0	4	1	1	1	3	4	6	9
50–64	772	2.5	18	1	1	1	3	6	8	17
65+	957	3.0	22	1	1	1	3	7	10	17
TOTAL SINGLE DX	**524**	**1.1**	**<1**	**1**	**1**	**1**	**1**	**1**	**2**	**3**
TOTAL MULTIPLE DX	**2,251**	**2.6**	**17**	**1**	**1**	**1**	**3**	**6**	**9**	**17**
TOTAL										
0–19 Years	113	1.5	5	1	1	1	1	2	3	7
20–34	245	1.6	3	1	1	1	1	3	4	8
35–49	438	1.7	3	1	1	1	2	4	5	7
50–64	944	2.3	15	1	1	1	2	5	7	16
65+	1,035	2.9	20	1	1	1	3	7	9	17
GRAND TOTAL	**2,775**	**2.3**	**14**	**1**	**1**	**1**	**2**	**5**	**8**	**16**

37.4: REP HEART & PERICARDIUM

Type of Patients	Observed Patients	Avg. Stay	Variance	10th	25th	50th	75th	90th	95th	99th
1. SINGLE DX										
0–19 Years	0									
20–34	0									
35–49	1	3.0	0	3	3	3	3	3	3	3
50–64	0									
65+	0									
2. MULTIPLE DX										
0–19 Years	9	8.3	161	4	5	6	6	8	8	66
20–34	27	9.1	40	4	5	8	10	13	26	33
35–49	12	9.8	38	4	6	9	10	21	25	25
50–64	19	12.2	42	4	6	10	18	20	20	20
65+	11	9.5	29	6	7	8	9	17	23	23
TOTAL SINGLE DX	**1**	**3.0**	**0**	**3**	**3**	**3**	**3**	**3**	**3**	**3**
TOTAL MULTIPLE DX	**78**	**9.8**	**61**	**4**	**6**	**7**	**11**	**20**	**23**	**33**
TOTAL										
0–19 Years	9	8.3	161	4	5	6	6	8	8	66
20–34	27	9.1	40	4	5	8	10	13	26	33
35–49	13	9.4	38	4	6	9	9	21	25	25
50–64	19	12.2	42	4	6	10	18	20	20	20
65+	11	9.5	29	6	7	8	9	17	23	23
GRAND TOTAL	**79**	**9.8**	**61**	**4**	**6**	**7**	**10**	**20**	**23**	**33**

37.5: HEART TRANSPLANTATION

Type of Patients	Observed Patients	Avg. Stay	Variance	10th	25th	50th	75th	90th	95th	99th
1. SINGLE DX										
0–19 Years	0									
20–34	0									
35–49	0									
50–64	0									
65+	0									
2. MULTIPLE DX										
0–19 Years	26	16.8	139	7	8	12	21	42	42	>99
20–34	12	29.3	351	8	22	28	45	88	>99	>99
35–49	28	20.6	343	9	9	13	21	48	48	86
50–64	84	18.8	254	9	10	13	18	33	66	73
65+	14	16.6	111	7	11	13	17	39	39	39
TOTAL SINGLE DX	**0**									
TOTAL MULTIPLE DX	**164**	**19.4**	**250**	**8**	**10**	**14**	**22**	**42**	**53**	**88**
TOTAL										
0–19 Years	26	16.8	139	7	8	12	21	42	42	>99
20–34	12	29.3	351	8	22	28	45	88	>99	>99
35–49	28	20.6	343	9	9	13	21	48	48	86
50–64	84	18.8	254	9	10	13	18	33	66	73
65+	14	16.6	111	7	11	13	17	39	39	39
GRAND TOTAL	**164**	**19.4**	**250**	**8**	**10**	**14**	**22**	**42**	**53**	**88**

37.6: IMPL HEART ASSIST SYST

Type of Patients	Observed Patients	Avg. Stay	Variance	10th	25th	50th	75th	90th	95th	99th
1. SINGLE DX										
0–19 Years	0									
20–34	0									
35–49	0									
50–64	0									
65+	0									
2. MULTIPLE DX										
0–19 Years	1	3.0	0	3	3	3	3	3	3	3
20–34	12	14.5	297	3	4	7	13	39	57	57
35–49	116	7.7	33	3	4	6	8	14	18	29
50–64	331	7.7	50	2	4	6	9	14	19	40
65+	526	9.9	64	3	5	7	12	19	28	35
TOTAL SINGLE DX	**0**									
TOTAL MULTIPLE DX	**986**	**9.0**	**59**	**3**	**4**	**7**	**11**	**17**	**25**	**38**
TOTAL										
0–19 Years	1	3.0	0	3	3	3	3	3	3	3
20–34	12	14.5	297	3	4	7	13	39	57	57
35–49	116	7.7	33	3	4	6	8	14	18	29
50–64	331	7.7	50	2	4	6	9	14	19	40
65+	526	9.9	64	3	5	7	12	19	28	35
GRAND TOTAL	**986**	**9.0**	**59**	**3**	**4**	**7**	**11**	**17**	**25**	**38**

37.61: PULSATION BALLOON IMPL

Type of Patients	Observed Patients	Avg. Stay	Vari-ance	Percentiles						
				10th	25th	50th	75th	90th	95th	99th
1. SINGLE DX										
0–19 Years	0									
20–34	0									
35–49	0									
50–64	0									
65+	0									
2. MULTIPLE DX										
0–19 Years	0									
20–34	8	5.8	10	3	4	5	7	13	13	13
35–49	111	7.3	26	3	4	6	8	13	16	29
50–64	324	7.1	30	2	4	6	8	13	17	26
65+	517	9.7	55	3	5	7	12	18	28	34
TOTAL SINGLE DX	**0**									
TOTAL MULTIPLE DX	**960**	**8.5**	**45**	**3**	**4**	**7**	**11**	**17**	**23**	**34**
TOTAL										
0–19 Years	0									
20–34	8	5.8	10	3	4	5	7	13	13	13
35–49	111	7.3	26	3	4	6	8	13	16	29
50–64	324	7.1	30	2	4	6	8	13	17	26
65+	517	9.7	55	3	5	7	12	18	28	34
GRAND TOTAL	**960**	**8.5**	**45**	**3**	**4**	**7**	**11**	**17**	**23**	**34**

37.7: CARDIAC PACER LEAD OP

Type of Patients	Observed Patients	Avg. Stay	Vari-ance	Percentiles						
				10th	25th	50th	75th	90th	95th	99th
1. SINGLE DX										
0–19 Years	11	1.7	<1	1	1	1	2	3	4	4
20–34	15	1.4	<1	1	1	1	2	2	3	3
35–49	26	1.7	<1	1	1	1	2	3	4	4
50–64	54	1.4	<1	1	1	1	1	2	4	5
65+	214	1.4	<1	1	1	1	1	3	4	4
2. MULTIPLE DX										
0–19 Years	60	3.7	14	1	1	2	4	11	13	15
20–34	76	3.1	8	1	1	2	4	6	8	12
35–49	266	3.8	19	1	1	2	5	9	12	25
50–64	1,295	4.1	23	1	1	3	5	8	12	27
65+	10,634	4.1	15	1	1	3	5	8	11	19
TOTAL SINGLE DX	**320**	**1.5**	**<1**	**1**	**1**	**1**	**2**	**3**	**4**	**4**
TOTAL MULTIPLE DX	**12,331**	**4.1**	**16**	**1**	**1**	**3**	**5**	**8**	**11**	**20**
TOTAL										
0–19 Years	71	3.4	12	1	1	2	4	11	11	15
20–34	91	2.9	7	1	1	2	4	6	8	12
35–49	292	3.7	18	1	1	2	4	8	11	16
50–64	1,349	4.0	22	1	1	3	5	8	12	26
65+	10,848	4.0	14	1	1	3	5	8	11	19
GRAND TOTAL	**12,651**	**4.0**	**15**	**1**	**1**	**3**	**5**	**8**	**11**	**20**

37.71: INSERT TV LEAD-VENTRICLE

Type of Patients	Observed Patients	Avg. Stay	Vari-ance	Percentiles						
				10th	25th	50th	75th	90th	95th	99th
1. SINGLE DX										
0–19 Years	0									
20–34	0									
35–49	0									
50–64	0									
65+	7	1.0	0	1	1	1	1	1	1	1
2. MULTIPLE DX										
0–19 Years	5	1.5	<1	1	1	1	2	2	2	2
20–34	1	1.0	0	1	1	1	1	1	1	1
35–49	10	4.6	23	1	1	2	7	10	16	16
50–64	32	5.4	23	1	1	5	7	10	12	25
65+	687	5.0	20	1	2	4	7	10	14	22
TOTAL SINGLE DX	**7**	**1.0**	**0**	**1**	**1**	**1**	**1**	**1**	**1**	**1**
TOTAL MULTIPLE DX	**735**	**5.0**	**20**	**1**	**2**	**4**	**7**	**10**	**14**	**22**
TOTAL										
0–19 Years	5	1.5	<1	1	1	1	2	2	2	2
20–34	1	1.0	0	1	1	1	1	1	1	1
35–49	10	4.6	23	1	1	2	7	10	16	16
50–64	32	5.4	23	1	1	5	7	10	12	25
65+	694	5.0	20	1	2	4	7	10	14	22
GRAND TOTAL	**742**	**5.0**	**20**	**1**	**1**	**4**	**7**	**10**	**14**	**22**

37.72: INSERT TV LEAD-ATR&VENT

Type of Patients	Observed Patients	Avg. Stay	Vari-ance	Percentiles						
				10th	25th	50th	75th	90th	95th	99th
1. SINGLE DX										
0–19 Years	8	1.7	<1	1	1	2	2	3	3	3
20–34	15	1.4	<1	1	1	1	2	2	3	3
35–49	24	1.7	<1	1	1	1	2	3	4	4
50–64	46	1.4	<1	1	1	1	1	2	4	5
65+	188	1.5	<1	1	1	1	2	3	4	4
2. MULTIPLE DX										
0–19 Years	22	3.7	18	1	2	2	4	14	14	15
20–34	57	3.2	9	1	1	2	4	6	8	21
35–49	210	3.9	21	1	1	2	4	9	12	25
50–64	1,095	3.9	17	1	1	3	5	8	12	22
65+	8,962	4.0	14	1	1	3	5	8	11	18
TOTAL SINGLE DX	**281**	**1.5**	**<1**	**1**	**1**	**1**	**2**	**3**	**4**	**4**
TOTAL MULTIPLE DX	**10,346**	**4.0**	**14**	**1**	**1**	**3**	**5**	**8**	**11**	**19**
TOTAL										
0–19 Years	30	3.1	14	1	1	2	3	5	14	15
20–34	72	2.9	8	1	1	2	4	6	6	21
35–49	234	3.7	19	1	1	2	4	8	12	25
50–64	1,141	3.8	16	1	1	2	5	8	12	21
65+	9,150	3.9	14	1	1	3	5	8	11	18
GRAND TOTAL	**10,627**	**3.9**	**14**	**1**	**1**	**3**	**5**	**8**	**11**	**19**

37.74: INSERT EPICARDIAL LEAD

Type of Patients	Observed Patients	Avg. Stay	Variance	10th	25th	50th	75th	90th	95th	99th
1. SINGLE DX										
0–19 Years	0									
20–34	0									
35–49	0									
50–64	1	1.0	0	1	1	1	1	1	1	1
65+	0									
2. MULTIPLE DX										
0–19 Years	17	3.0	8	1	2	2	3	6	11	13
20–34	2	5.0	7	3	3	5	7	7	7	7
35–49	8	6.0	8	2	3	6	7	11	11	11
50–64	16	12.5	261	2	3	5	16	52	52	52
65+	77	5.4	18	1	3	4	8	11	14	20
TOTAL SINGLE DX	**1**	**1.0**	**0**	**1**	**1**	**1**	**1**	**1**	**1**	**1**
TOTAL MULTIPLE DX	**120**	**5.9**	**48**	**1**	**2**	**4**	**7**	**11**	**16**	**52**
TOTAL										
0–19 Years	17	3.0	8	1	2	2	3	6	11	13
20–34	2	5.0	7	3	3	5	7	7	7	7
35–49	8	6.0	8	2	3	6	7	11	11	11
50–64	17	11.7	251	1	3	5	16	52	52	52
65+	77	5.4	18	1	3	4	8	11	14	20
GRAND TOTAL	**121**	**5.8**	**48**	**1**	**2**	**4**	**7**	**11**	**14**	**52**

37.75: REVISION PACEMAKER LEAD

Type of Patients	Observed Patients	Avg. Stay	Variance	10th	25th	50th	75th	90th	95th	99th
1. SINGLE DX										
0–19 Years	0									
20–34	0									
35–49	0									
50–64	4	1.2	<1	1	1	1	1	2	2	2
65+	7	1.1	<1	1	1	1	1	1	2	2
2. MULTIPLE DX										
0–19 Years	5	2.0	<1	1	2	2	2	3	3	3
20–34	3	2.1	<1	1	1	2	3	3	3	3
35–49	11	2.2	4	1	1	1	3	7	7	7
50–64	34	1.4	<1	1	1	1	1	2	4	4
65+	235	2.9	11	1	1	2	3	6	8	20
TOTAL SINGLE DX	**11**	**1.1**	**<1**	**1**	**1**	**1**	**1**	**2**	**2**	**2**
TOTAL MULTIPLE DX	**288**	**2.6**	**9**	**1**	**1**	**2**	**3**	**6**	**7**	**20**
TOTAL										
0–19 Years	5	2.0	<1	1	2	2	2	3	3	3
20–34	3	2.1	<1	1	1	2	3	3	3	3
35–49	11	2.2	4	1	1	1	3	7	7	7
50–64	38	1.4	<1	1	1	1	1	2	4	4
65+	242	2.8	10	1	1	2	3	6	8	20
GRAND TOTAL	**299**	**2.6**	**9**	**1**	**1**	**2**	**3**	**6**	**7**	**20**

37.76: REPL TRANSVENOUS LEAD

Type of Patients	Observed Patients	Avg. Stay	Variance	10th	25th	50th	75th	90th	95th	99th
1. SINGLE DX										
0–19 Years	1	1.0	0	1	1	1	1	1	1	1
20–34	0									
35–49	2	1.0	0	1	1	1	1	1	1	1
50–64	3	2.0	3	1	1	1	4	4	4	4
65+	7	1.0	0	1	1	1	1	1	1	1
2. MULTIPLE DX										
0–19 Years	6	3.3	4	1	1	4	5	5	5	5
20–34	7	2.9	7	1	1	3	3	8	8	8
35–49	10	1.3	<1	1	1	1	1	2	5	5
50–64	33	5.4	76	1	1	2	4	12	34	34
65+	269	2.9	14	1	1	1	3	6	10	22
TOTAL SINGLE DX	**13**	**1.2**	**<1**	**1**	**1**	**1**	**1**	**1**	**4**	**4**
TOTAL MULTIPLE DX	**325**	**3.1**	**20**	**1**	**1**	**1**	**3**	**7**	**10**	**29**
TOTAL										
0–19 Years	7	2.9	4	1	1	4	5	5	5	5
20–34	7	2.9	7	1	1	3	3	8	8	8
35–49	12	1.2	<1	1	1	1	1	1	2	5
50–64	36	5.2	72	1	1	2	4	12	34	34
65+	276	2.9	14	1	1	1	3	6	10	22
GRAND TOTAL	**338**	**3.1**	**19**	**1**	**1**	**1**	**3**	**7**	**10**	**29**

37.78: INSERT TEMP TV PACER

Type of Patients	Observed Patients	Avg. Stay	Variance	10th	25th	50th	75th	90th	95th	99th
1. SINGLE DX										
0–19 Years	0									
20–34	0									
35–49	0									
50–64	0									
65+	0									
2. MULTIPLE DX										
0–19 Years	2	9.5	13	2	11	11	11	11	11	11
20–34	5	2.7	6	1	1	1	5	7	7	7
35–49	9	6.0	19	2	3	4	11	11	15	15
50–64	66	6.7	42	2	3	4	6	19	22	22
65+	270	5.9	20	2	3	5	7	11	15	23
TOTAL SINGLE DX	**0**									
TOTAL MULTIPLE DX	**352**	**6.1**	**24**	**2**	**3**	**5**	**7**	**12**	**18**	**23**
TOTAL										
0–19 Years	2	9.5	13	2	11	11	11	11	11	11
20–34	5	2.7	6	1	1	1	5	7	7	7
35–49	9	6.0	19	2	3	4	11	11	15	15
50–64	66	6.7	42	2	3	4	6	19	22	22
65+	270	5.9	20	2	3	5	7	11	15	23
GRAND TOTAL	**352**	**6.1**	**24**	**2**	**3**	**5**	**7**	**12**	**18**	**23**

37.79: REV PACEMAKER POCKET

Type of Patients	Observed Patients	Avg. Stay	Variance	10th	25th	50th	75th	90th	95th	99th
1. SINGLE DX										
0–19 Years	1	4.0	0	4	4	4	4	4	4	4
20–34	0									
35–49	0									
50–64	0									
65+	2	4.1	14	1	1	7	7	7	7	7
2. MULTIPLE DX										
0–19 Years	1	2.0	0	2	2	2	2	2	2	2
20–34	1	1.0	0	1	1	1	1	1	1	1
35–49	6	3.0	2	1	2	3	3	6	6	6
50–64	9	3.9	15	1	1	2	7	12	12	12
65+	72	3.5	10	1	1	2	5	8	9	15
TOTAL SINGLE DX	**3**	**4.1**	**7**	**1**	**1**	**4**	**7**	**7**	**7**	**7**
TOTAL MULTIPLE DX	**89**	**3.5**	**10**	**1**	**1**	**2**	**5**	**8**	**9**	**14**
TOTAL										
0–19 Years	2	3.1	1	2	2	4	4	4	4	4
20–34	1	1.0	0	1	1	1	1	1	1	1
35–49	6	3.0	2	1	2	3	3	6	6	6
50–64	9	3.9	15	1	1	2	7	12	12	12
65+	74	3.5	10	1	1	2	5	8	9	15
GRAND TOTAL	**92**	**3.5**	**10**	**1**	**1**	**2**	**5**	**8**	**9**	**14**

37.8: CARDIAC PACEMAKER DEV OP

Type of Patients	Observed Patients	Avg. Stay	Variance	10th	25th	50th	75th	90th	95th	99th
1. SINGLE DX										
0–19 Years	10	1.2	<1	1	1	1	1	1	3	3
20–34	5	1.2	<1	1	1	1	1	2	2	2
35–49	18	2.1	6	1	1	1	2	8	8	8
50–64	29	1.4	<1	1	1	1	2	2	3	3
65+	158	1.4	1	1	1	1	1	2	4	7
2. MULTIPLE DX										
0–19 Years	74	2.5	10	1	1	1	3	5	7	16
20–34	59	3.4	16	1	1	1	4	9	13	20
35–49	165	3.6	12	1	1	3	5	7	9	20
50–64	750	4.1	19	1	1	3	5	9	12	23
65+	6,984	4.2	20	1	1	3	6	9	12	22
TOTAL SINGLE DX	**220**	**1.4**	**1**	**1**	**1**	**1**	**1**	**2**	**4**	**8**
TOTAL MULTIPLE DX	**8,032**	**4.2**	**20**	**1**	**1**	**3**	**5**	**9**	**12**	**22**
TOTAL										
0–19 Years	84	2.4	9	1	1	1	2	5	6	16
20–34	64	3.3	15	1	1	1	4	9	13	20
35–49	183	3.5	11	1	1	3	4	7	8	20
50–64	779	4.0	19	1	1	2	5	9	12	23
65+	7,142	4.2	20	1	1	3	5	9	12	22
GRAND TOTAL	**8,252**	**4.1**	**19**	**1**	**1**	**3**	**5**	**9**	**12**	**22**

37.80: INSERT PACEMAKER DEV NOS

Type of Patients	Observed Patients	Avg. Stay	Variance	10th	25th	50th	75th	90th	95th	99th
1. SINGLE DX										
0–19 Years	0									
20–34	0									
35–49	1	1.0	0	1	1	1	1	1	1	1
50–64	0									
65+	4	1.5	<1	1	1	2	2	2	2	2
2. MULTIPLE DX										
0–19 Years	1	1.0	0	1	1	1	1	1	1	1
20–34	3	2.0	3	1	1	1	4	4	4	4
35–49	2	2.9	7	1	1	1	5	5	5	5
50–64	20	2.5	6	1	1	1	3	6	9	12
65+	121	5.2	23	1	2	4	7	13	14	22
TOTAL SINGLE DX	**5**	**1.5**	**<1**	**1**	**1**	**1**	**2**	**2**	**2**	**2**
TOTAL MULTIPLE DX	**147**	**4.7**	**21**	**1**	**1**	**3**	**6**	**12**	**14**	**22**
TOTAL										
0–19 Years	1	1.0	0	1	1	1	1	1	1	1
20–34	3	2.0	3	1	1	1	4	4	4	4
35–49	3	2.3	5	1	1	1	5	5	5	5
50–64	20	2.5	6	1	1	1	3	6	9	12
65+	125	5.1	22	1	2	3	7	13	14	22
GRAND TOTAL	**152**	**4.6**	**20**	**1**	**1**	**3**	**6**	**12**	**14**	**19**

37.81: INSERT SINGLE CHAMB DEV

Type of Patients	Observed Patients	Avg. Stay	Variance	10th	25th	50th	75th	90th	95th	99th
1. SINGLE DX										
0–19 Years	0									
20–34	0									
35–49	1	1.0	0	1	1	1	1	1	1	1
50–64	1	1.0	0	1	1	1	1	1	1	1
65+	9	3.1	8	1	1	1	7	7	7	7
2. MULTIPLE DX										
0–19 Years	0									
20–34	4	1.2	<1	1	1	1	1	2	2	2
35–49	10	3.7	8	1	1	3	5	9	9	9
50–64	75	4.8	19	1	2	3	7	10	11	25
65+	952	4.7	22	1	1	4	6	10	13	23
TOTAL SINGLE DX	**11**	**2.7**	**7**	**1**	**1**	**1**	**6**	**7**	**7**	**7**
TOTAL MULTIPLE DX	**1,041**	**4.7**	**22**	**1**	**1**	**3**	**6**	**10**	**13**	**23**
TOTAL										
0–19 Years	0									
20–34	4	1.2	<1	1	1	1	1	2	2	2
35–49	11	3.4	7	1	1	3	5	7	9	9
50–64	76	4.8	19	1	2	3	7	10	11	25
65+	961	4.7	22	1	1	3	6	10	13	23
GRAND TOTAL	**1,052**	**4.7**	**22**	**1**	**1**	**3**	**6**	**10**	**13**	**23**

37.82: INSERT RATE-RESPON DEV

Type of Patients	Observed Patients	Avg. Stay	Vari-ance	Percentiles						
				10th	25th	50th	75th	90th	95th	99th
1. SINGLE DX										
0–19 Years	0									
20–34	0									
35–49	1	2.0	0	2	2	2	2	2	2	2
50–64	4	1.0	0	1	1	1	1	1	1	1
65+	13	1.2	<1	1	1	1	1	1	4	4
2. MULTIPLE DX										
0–19 Years	4	13.6	103	1	8	16	16	27	27	27
20–34	2	8.0	88	1	1	1	15	15	15	15
35–49	7	5.5	21	1	1	6	6	15	15	15
50–64	66	6.0	37	1	1	5	9	16	19	23
65+	1,095	4.9	24	1	1	4	7	10	13	26
TOTAL SINGLE DX	**18**	**1.2**	**<1**	**1**	**1**	**1**	**1**	**2**	**2**	**4**
TOTAL MULTIPLE DX	**1,174**	**5.0**	**26**	**1**	**1**	**4**	**7**	**10**	**14**	**26**
TOTAL										
0–19 Years	4	13.6	103	1	8	16	16	27	27	27
20–34	2	8.0	88	1	1	1	15	15	15	15
35–49	8	4.9	19	1	1	4	6	9	15	15
50–64	70	5.8	36	1	1	3	8	15	19	23
65+	1,108	4.9	24	1	1	4	7	10	13	26
GRAND TOTAL	**1,192**	**5.0**	**26**	**1**	**1**	**4**	**7**	**10**	**14**	**26**

37.83: INSERT DUAL-CHAMBER DEV

Type of Patients	Observed Patients	Avg. Stay	Vari-ance	Percentiles						
				10th	25th	50th	75th	90th	95th	99th
1. SINGLE DX										
0–19 Years	3	1.0	0	1	1	1	1	1	1	1
20–34	4	1.2	<1	1	1	1	1	2	2	2
35–49	7	3.2	9	1	1	1	8	8	8	8
50–64	11	1.7	<1	1	1	2	2	3	3	3
65+	64	1.1	<1	1	1	1	1	2	2	3
2. MULTIPLE DX										
0–19 Years	16	3.5	6	1	1	2	6	7	7	8
20–34	22	4.0	15	1	1	3	5	9	13	15
35–49	91	3.5	5	1	2	3	5	7	8	11
50–64	405	4.3	20	1	1	3	5	9	15	23
65+	3,229	4.4	20	1	2	3	6	9	13	21
TOTAL SINGLE DX	**89**	**1.4**	**2**	**1**	**1**	**1**	**1**	**2**	**3**	**8**
TOTAL MULTIPLE DX	**3,763**	**4.4**	**20**	**1**	**2**	**3**	**6**	**9**	**13**	**21**
TOTAL										
0–19 Years	19	3.2	6	1	1	2	6	7	7	8
20–34	26	3.6	14	1	1	2	4	9	13	15
35–49	98	3.5	6	1	1	3	5	7	8	11
50–64	416	4.2	20	1	1	3	5	9	14	23
65+	3,293	4.4	20	1	1	3	6	9	13	21
GRAND TOTAL	**3,852**	**4.3**	**19**	**1**	**1**	**3**	**6**	**9**	**12**	**21**

37.85: REPL W 1-CHAMBER DEVICE

Type of Patients	Observed Patients	Avg. Stay	Vari-ance	Percentiles						
				10th	25th	50th	75th	90th	95th	99th
1. SINGLE DX										
0–19 Years	2	1.0	0	1	1	1	1	1	1	1
20–34	0									
35–49	0									
50–64	1	1.0	0	1	1	1	1	1	1	1
65+	4	1.0	0	1	1	1	1	1	1	1
2. MULTIPLE DX										
0–19 Years	8	1.4	<1	1	1	1	2	2	3	3
20–34	4	3.1	14	1	1	1	3	10	10	10
35–49	6	2.2	<1	1	1	3	3	3	3	3
50–64	10	2.7	11	1	1	2	3	6	14	14
65+	168	2.6	7	1	1	1	4	6	7	15
TOTAL SINGLE DX	**7**	**1.0**	**0**	**1**	**1**	**1**	**1**	**1**	**1**	**1**
TOTAL MULTIPLE DX	**196**	**2.6**	**7**	**1**	**1**	**1**	**3**	**6**	**7**	**15**
TOTAL										
0–19 Years	10	1.4	<1	1	1	1	2	2	3	3
20–34	4	3.1	14	1	1	1	3	10	10	10
35–49	6	2.2	<1	1	1	3	3	3	3	3
50–64	11	2.6	10	1	1	1	2	6	14	14
65+	172	2.6	7	1	1	1	4	6	7	15
GRAND TOTAL	**203**	**2.5**	**7**	**1**	**1**	**1**	**3**	**6**	**7**	**15**

37.86: REPL W RATE-RESPON DEV

Type of Patients	Observed Patients	Avg. Stay	Vari-ance	Percentiles						
				10th	25th	50th	75th	90th	95th	99th
1. SINGLE DX										
0–19 Years	0									
20–34	0									
35–49	0									
50–64	0									
65+	4	1.0	0	1	1	1	1	1	1	1
2. MULTIPLE DX										
0–19 Years	2	1.0	0	1	1	1	1	1	1	1
20–34	0									
35–49	7	1.3	<1	1	1	1	1	4	4	4
50–64	13	2.2	5	1	1	1	2	4	9	9
65+	176	2.5	8	1	1	1	3	7	10	12
TOTAL SINGLE DX	**4**	**1.0**	**0**	**1**	**1**	**1**	**1**	**1**	**1**	**1**
TOTAL MULTIPLE DX	**198**	**2.4**	**8**	**1**	**1**	**1**	**3**	**6**	**10**	**12**
TOTAL										
0–19 Years	2	1.0	0	1	1	1	1	1	1	1
20–34	0									
35–49	7	1.3	<1	1	1	1	1	4	4	4
50–64	13	2.2	5	1	1	1	2	4	9	9
65+	180	2.4	8	1	1	1	3	6	10	12
GRAND TOTAL	**202**	**2.4**	**7**	**1**	**1**	**1**	**2**	**6**	**10**	**12**

37.87: REPL W DUAL-CHAMB DEVICE

Type of Patients	Observed Patients	Avg. Stay	Vari-ance	10th	25th	50th	75th	90th	95th	99th
1. SINGLE DX										
0–19 Years	5	1.3	<1	1	1	1	1	3	3	3
20–34	1	1.0	0	1	1	1	1	1	1	1
35–49	7	1.0	0	1	1	1	1	1	1	1
50–64	12	1.2	<1	1	1	1	1	3	3	3
65+	58	1.3	<1	1	1	1	1	2	4	7
2. MULTIPLE DX										
0–19 Years	39	2.0	2	1	1	1	2	5	5	5
20–34	20	2.6	18	1	1	1	2	4	6	20
35–49	33	3.4	23	1	1	1	4	7	20	20
50–64	140	2.6	7	1	1	2	3	5	7	18
65+	1,140	2.7	10	1	1	1	3	6	9	15
TOTAL SINGLE DX	**83**	**1.3**	**<1**	**1**	**1**	**1**	**1**	**2**	**3**	**4**
TOTAL MULTIPLE DX	**1,372**	**2.7**	**10**	**1**	**1**	**1**	**3**	**6**	**9**	**17**
TOTAL										
0–19 Years	44	1.9	2	1	1	1	2	5	5	5
20–34	21	2.5	17	1	1	1	2	4	6	20
35–49	40	3.0	20	1	1	1	4	5	17	20
50–64	152	2.5	6	1	1	1	3	5	6	13
65+	1,198	2.6	10	1	1	1	3	6	9	15
GRAND TOTAL	**1,455**	**2.6**	**9**	**1**	**1**	**1**	**3**	**6**	**8**	**17**

37.89: REV/RMVL PACEMAKER DEV

Type of Patients	Observed Patients	Avg. Stay	Vari-ance	10th	25th	50th	75th	90th	95th	99th
1. SINGLE DX										
0–19 Years	0									
20–34	0									
35–49	1	1.0	0	1	1	1	1	1	1	1
50–64	0									
65+	2	2.7	3	1	1	4	4	4	4	4
2. MULTIPLE DX										
0–19 Years	4	1.2	<1	1	1	1	1	2	2	2
20–34	4	5.2	7	1	2	6	6	9	9	9
35–49	9	6.9	53	1	3	3	9	11	26	26
50–64	21	4.9	15	1	2	4	7	8	11	19
65+	103	7.0	33	1	3	6	9	18	18	27
TOTAL SINGLE DX	**3**	**2.2**	**3**	**1**	**1**	**1**	**4**	**4**	**4**	**4**
TOTAL MULTIPLE DX	**141**	**6.4**	**31**	**1**	**3**	**5**	**8**	**14**	**18**	**26**
TOTAL										
0–19 Years	4	1.2	<1	1	1	1	1	2	2	2
20–34	4	5.2	7	1	2	6	6	9	9	9
35–49	10	6.2	51	1	1	3	8	11	26	26
50–64	21	4.9	15	1	2	4	7	8	11	19
65+	105	6.9	33	1	3	5	9	18	18	27
GRAND TOTAL	**144**	**6.4**	**31**	**1**	**3**	**5**	**8**	**13**	**18**	**26**

37.9: HRT/PERICARDIUM OPS NEC

Type of Patients	Observed Patients	Avg. Stay	Vari-ance	10th	25th	50th	75th	90th	95th	99th
1. SINGLE DX										
0–19 Years	10	1.7	3	1	1	1	1	6	6	6
20–34	8	2.0	9	1	1	1	1	3	12	12
35–49	14	1.1	<1	1	1	1	1	1	2	2
50–64	26	1.1	<1	1	1	1	1	2	2	2
65+	33	1.3	<1	1	1	1	1	2	2	5
2. MULTIPLE DX										
0–19 Years	38	4.8	24	1	1	4	6	10	20	28
20–34	92	5.0	19	1	1	4	7	11	13	23
35–49	392	5.9	39	1	1	4	8	14	16	21
50–64	1,484	4.7	31	1	1	2	6	11	15	28
65+	3,246	4.8	28	1	1	3	7	11	15	25
TOTAL SINGLE DX	**91**	**1.3**	**1**	**1**	**1**	**1**	**1**	**2**	**2**	**6**
TOTAL MULTIPLE DX	**5,252**	**4.9**	**30**	**1**	**1**	**3**	**7**	**11**	**15**	**25**
TOTAL										
0–19 Years	48	4.2	21	1	1	3	5	7	11	21
20–34	100	4.7	19	1	1	3	7	11	13	18
35–49	406	5.8	38	1	1	4	8	13	16	21
50–64	1,510	4.6	31	1	1	2	6	11	15	27
65+	3,279	4.8	28	1	1	3	7	11	15	25
GRAND TOTAL	**5,343**	**4.8**	**29**	**1**	**1**	**3**	**7**	**11**	**15**	**25**

37.94: IMPL/REPL AICD TOT SYST

Type of Patients	Observed Patients	Avg. Stay	Vari-ance	10th	25th	50th	75th	90th	95th	99th
1. SINGLE DX										
0–19 Years	10	1.7	3	1	1	1	1	6	6	6
20–34	7	2.1	10	1	1	1	1	3	12	12
35–49	10	1.1	<1	1	1	1	1	1	2	2
50–64	17	1.1	<1	1	1	1	1	1	2	2
65+	24	1.4	<1	1	1	1	2	2	2	5
2. MULTIPLE DX										
0–19 Years	30	4.7	25	1	1	3	6	10	11	28
20–34	72	5.5	21	1	1	5	7	12	13	23
35–49	328	6.3	42	1	2	5	9	14	17	23
50–64	1,256	4.9	33	1	1	3	7	11	16	28
65+	2,678	5.2	29	1	1	3	7	12	15	25
TOTAL SINGLE DX	**68**	**1.4**	**2**	**1**	**1**	**1**	**1**	**2**	**3**	**6**
TOTAL MULTIPLE DX	**4,364**	**5.2**	**31**	**1**	**1**	**3**	**7**	**12**	**16**	**26**
TOTAL										
0–19 Years	40	4.0	21	1	1	2	5	10	10	28
20–34	79	5.1	21	1	1	4	7	12	13	23
35–49	338	6.1	42	1	1	4	9	14	17	21
50–64	1,273	4.8	33	1	1	3	7	11	16	28
65+	2,702	5.1	29	1	1	3	7	12	15	25
GRAND TOTAL	**4,432**	**5.1**	**31**	**1**	**1**	**3**	**7**	**12**	**15**	**26**

37.97: REPLACE AICD LEAD ONLY

Type of Patients	Observed Patients	Avg. Stay	Vari-ance	Percentiles						
				10th	25th	50th	75th	90th	95th	99th
1. SINGLE DX										
0–19 Years	0									
20–34	0									
35–49	0									
50–64	0									
65+	0									
2. MULTIPLE DX										
0–19 Years	1	5.0	0	5	5	5	5	5	5	5
20–34	0									
35–49	8	3.8	10	1	2	2	4	11	11	11
50–64	24	3.0	18	1	1	1	4	5	5	22
65+	42	4.2	41	1	1	2	4	9	27	27
TOTAL SINGLE DX	**0**									
TOTAL MULTIPLE DX	**75**	**4.0**	**30**	**1**	**1**	**2**	**5**	**6**	**14**	**27**
TOTAL										
0–19 Years	1	5.0	0	5	5	5	5	5	5	5
20–34	0									
35–49	8	3.8	10	1	2	2	4	11	11	11
50–64	24	3.0	18	1	1	1	4	5	5	22
65+	42	4.2	41	1	1	2	4	9	27	27
GRAND TOTAL	**75**	**4.0**	**30**	**1**	**1**	**2**	**5**	**6**	**14**	**27**

37.98: REPL AICD GENERATOR ONLY

Type of Patients	Observed Patients	Avg. Stay	Vari-ance	Percentiles						
				10th	25th	50th	75th	90th	95th	99th
1. SINGLE DX										
0–19 Years	0									
20–34	1	1.0	0	1	1	1	1	1	1	1
35–49	2	1.0	0	1	1	1	1	1	1	1
50–64	5	1.5	<1	1	1	1	2	2	2	2
65+	7	1.0	0	1	1	1	1	1	1	1
2. MULTIPLE DX										
0–19 Years	3	2.4	7	1	1	1	6	6	6	6
20–34	9	2.5	3	1	1	2	5	5	5	5
35–49	24	1.9	2	1	1	1	2	3	6	6
50–64	117	2.1	6	1	1	1	2	4	6	14
65+	316	2.3	10	1	1	1	2	5	7	18
TOTAL SINGLE DX	**15**	**1.2**	**<1**	**1**	**1**	**1**	**1**	**2**	**2**	**2**
TOTAL MULTIPLE DX	**469**	**2.2**	**8**	**1**	**1**	**1**	**2**	**5**	**7**	**15**
TOTAL										
0–19 Years	3	2.4	7	1	1	1	6	6	6	6
20–34	10	2.4	3	1	1	2	5	5	5	5
35–49	26	1.8	2	1	1	1	2	3	6	6
50–64	122	2.1	6	1	1	1	2	4	6	14
65+	323	2.3	9	1	1	1	2	5	7	15
GRAND TOTAL	**484**	**2.2**	**8**	**1**	**1**	**1**	**2**	**5**	**7**	**15**

37.99: OTH OPS HRT/PERICARDIUM

Type of Patients	Observed Patients	Avg. Stay	Vari-ance	Percentiles						
				10th	25th	50th	75th	90th	95th	99th
1. SINGLE DX										
0–19 Years	0									
20–34	0									
35–49	2	1.5	<1	1	1	2	2	2	2	2
50–64	3	1.0	0	1	1	1	1	1	1	1
65+	1	1.0	0	1	1	1	1	1	1	1
2. MULTIPLE DX										
0–19 Years	3	1.9	<1	1	1	2	3	3	3	3
20–34	9	3.1	7	1	1	3	4	4	10	10
35–49	27	4.9	12	1	2	5	7	11	11	14
50–64	67	5.1	30	1	1	3	8	13	15	32
65+	165	4.5	27	1	1	2	6	10	17	26
TOTAL SINGLE DX	**6**	**1.2**	**<1**	**1**	**1**	**1**	**1**	**2**	**2**	**2**
TOTAL MULTIPLE DX	**271**	**4.6**	**25**	**1**	**1**	**2**	**6**	**11**	**15**	**26**
TOTAL										
0–19 Years	3	1.9	<1	1	1	2	3	3	3	3
20–34	9	3.1	7	1	1	3	4	4	10	10
35–49	29	4.7	12	1	2	4	7	11	11	14
50–64	70	5.0	30	1	1	3	8	13	15	32
65+	166	4.4	27	1	1	2	6	10	17	26
GRAND TOTAL	**277**	**4.5**	**25**	**1**	**1**	**2**	**6**	**11**	**15**	**26**

38.0: INCISION OF VESSEL

Type of Patients	Observed Patients	Avg. Stay	Vari-ance	Percentiles						
				10th	25th	50th	75th	90th	95th	99th
1. SINGLE DX										
0–19 Years	2	8.5	<1	7	9	9	9	9	9	9
20–34	3	6.4	26	1	1	5	12	12	12	12
35–49	4	7.4	4	6	6	6	9	10	10	10
50–64	4	1.8	<1	1	1	1	3	3	3	3
65+	5	1.3	<1	1	1	1	2	2	2	2
2. MULTIPLE DX										
0–19 Years	15	8.8	75	1	2	5	18	22	29	29
20–34	42	7.8	35	2	3	6	10	15	23	29
35–49	131	7.6	40	2	3	6	10	15	16	24
50–64	268	6.5	32	2	3	5	8	12	17	29
65+	778	7.0	36	2	3	5	9	13	19	28
TOTAL SINGLE DX	**18**	**4.7**	**14**	**1**	**1**	**3**	**9**	**9**	**12**	**12**
TOTAL MULTIPLE DX	**1,234**	**7.0**	**36**	**2**	**3**	**5**	**9**	**14**	**18**	**29**
TOTAL										
0–19 Years	17	8.8	64	1	2	5	11	22	29	29
20–34	45	7.7	35	2	3	6	10	15	17	29
35–49	135	7.6	39	2	4	6	10	15	16	24
50–64	272	6.4	32	2	3	5	8	12	17	29
65+	783	6.9	36	2	3	5	9	13	19	28
GRAND TOTAL	**1,252**	**6.9**	**36**	**2**	**3**	**5**	**9**	**14**	**18**	**29**

38.03: UPPER LIMB VESSEL INC

Type of Patients	Observed Patients	Avg. Stay	Vari-ance	Percentiles 10th	25th	50th	75th	90th	95th	99th
1. SINGLE DX										
0–19 Years	1	7.0	0	7	7	7	7	7	7	7
20–34	1	1.0	0	1	1	1	1	1	1	1
35–49	1	6.0	0	6	6	6	6	6	6	6
50–64	2	1.0	0	1	1	1	1	1	1	1
65+	2	1.5	<1	1	1	1	2	2	2	2
2. MULTIPLE DX										
0–19 Years	4	8.2	97	1	1	5	22	22	22	22
20–34	15	5.3	19	1	2	4	5	13	13	15
35–49	48	5.8	47	1	2	4	7	13	16	45
50–64	69	6.3	22	1	3	5	8	15	17	18
65+	221	5.9	39	1	3	4	6	12	18	25
TOTAL SINGLE DX	7	2.6	6	1	1	1	6	7	7	7
TOTAL MULTIPLE DX	357	5.9	36	1	3	4	7	13	17	24
TOTAL										
0–19 Years	5	8.1	82	1	1	5	22	22	22	22
20–34	16	5.1	19	1	2	4	5	13	13	15
35–49	49	5.8	46	1	2	4	7	13	13	45
50–64	71	6.2	22	1	3	5	7	15	17	18
65+	223	5.8	38	1	3	4	6	12	18	25
GRAND TOTAL	364	5.9	36	1	3	4	7	13	17	24

38.06: ABDOMINAL ART INCISION

Type of Patients	Observed Patients	Avg. Stay	Vari-ance	Percentiles 10th	25th	50th	75th	90th	95th	99th
1. SINGLE DX										
0–19 Years	0									
20–34	0									
35–49	0									
50–64	0									
65+	0									
2. MULTIPLE DX										
0–19 Years	0									
20–34	0									
35–49	8	9.7	22	5	7	7	13	15	21	21
50–64	32	6.7	41	2	4	5	7	13	29	29
65+	47	8.1	53	2	4	6	8	23	24	27
TOTAL SINGLE DX	0									
TOTAL MULTIPLE DX	87	7.9	46	2	4	5	9	23	23	29
TOTAL										
0–19 Years	0									
20–34	0									
35–49	8	9.7	22	5	7	7	13	15	21	21
50–64	32	6.7	41	2	4	5	7	13	29	29
65+	47	8.1	53	2	4	6	8	23	24	27
GRAND TOTAL	87	7.9	46	2	4	5	9	23	23	29

38.08: LOWER LIMB ARTERY INC

Type of Patients	Observed Patients	Avg. Stay	Vari-ance	Percentiles 10th	25th	50th	75th	90th	95th	99th
1. SINGLE DX										
0–19 Years	0									
20–34	1	5.0	0	5	5	5	5	5	5	5
35–49	3	7.9	4	6	6	9	10	10	10	10
50–64	1	3.0	0	3	3	3	3	3	3	3
65+	1	1.0	0	1	1	1	1	1	1	1
2. MULTIPLE DX										
0–19 Years	5	8.8	35	1	5	8	11	18	18	18
20–34	13	7.8	42	2	3	7	8	14	29	29
35–49	47	8.0	43	3	4	6	10	15	18	46
50–64	120	6.6	41	2	3	5	8	11	15	49
65+	444	7.3	31	3	4	6	9	13	17	29
TOTAL SINGLE DX	6	5.3	10	1	3	5	6	10	10	10
TOTAL MULTIPLE DX	629	7.3	34	2	4	6	9	13	17	34
TOTAL										
0–19 Years	5	8.8	35	1	5	8	11	18	18	18
20–34	14	7.6	39	2	4	6	8	14	29	29
35–49	50	8.0	41	3	4	6	10	15	18	46
50–64	121	6.6	41	2	3	5	8	11	15	49
65+	445	7.3	31	2	4	6	9	13	17	29
GRAND TOTAL	635	7.3	34	2	4	6	9	13	17	34

38.1: ENDARTERECTOMY

Type of Patients	Observed Patients	Avg. Stay	Vari-ance	Percentiles 10th	25th	50th	75th	90th	95th	99th
1. SINGLE DX										
0–19 Years	0									
20–34	2	6.5	<1	6	6	7	7	7	7	7
35–49	14	1.9	3	1	1	1	3	3	8	8
50–64	123	1.5	<1	1	1	1	2	2	3	4
65+	382	1.5	<1	1	1	1	2	2	3	5
2. MULTIPLE DX										
0–19 Years	1	3.0	0	3	3	3	3	3	3	3
20–34	6	4.7	31	1	1	2	6	9	19	19
35–49	219	4.0	18	1	1	2	5	9	13	22
50–64	2,649	2.8	11	1	1	2	3	6	9	18
65+	10,445	2.9	12	1	1	2	3	6	9	17
TOTAL SINGLE DX	521	1.5	<1	1	1	1	2	2	3	6
TOTAL MULTIPLE DX	13,320	2.9	12	1	1	2	3	6	9	18
TOTAL										
0–19 Years	1	3.0	0	3	3	3	3	3	3	3
20–34	8	5.0	27	1	1	2	7	9	19	19
35–49	233	3.9	17	1	1	2	5	9	13	21
50–64	2,772	2.7	10	1	1	2	3	5	9	18
65+	10,827	2.9	11	1	1	2	3	6	9	17
GRAND TOTAL	13,841	2.9	11	1	1	2	3	6	9	17

38.12: HEAD/NK ENDARTERECT NEC

Type of Patients	Observed Patients	Avg. Stay	Vari-ance	Percentiles 10th	25th	50th	75th	90th	95th	99th
1. SINGLE DX										
0–19 Years	0									
20–34	0									
35–49	10	1.3	<1	1	1	1	1	3	3	3
50–64	113	1.5	<1	1	1	1	2	2	3	4
65+	366	1.4	<1	1	1	1	2	2	3	4
2. MULTIPLE DX										
0–19 Years	0									
20–34	0									
35–49	141	3.0	12	1	1	2	4	7	9	21
50–64	2,309	2.3	6	1	1	1	2	5	7	13
65+	9,465	2.7	9	1	1	2	3	6	8	15
TOTAL SINGLE DX	**489**	**1.4**	**<1**	**1**	**1**	**1**	**2**	**2**	**3**	**4**
TOTAL MULTIPLE DX	**11,915**	**2.6**	**9**	**1**	**1**	**2**	**3**	**6**	**8**	**15**
TOTAL										
0–19 Years	0									
20–34	0									
35–49	151	2.9	12	1	1	1	4	7	8	21
50–64	2,422	2.3	6	1	1	1	2	4	7	13
65+	9,831	2.6	9	1	1	2	3	6	8	15
GRAND TOTAL	**12,404**	**2.6**	**9**	**1**	**1**	**2**	**3**	**5**	**8**	**15**

38.16: ABDOMINAL ENDARTERECTOMY

Type of Patients	Observed Patients	Avg. Stay	Vari-ance	Percentiles 10th	25th	50th	75th	90th	95th	99th
1. SINGLE DX										
0–19 Years	0									
20–34	0									
35–49	0									
50–64	2	1.3	<1	1	1	1	2	2	2	2
65+	2	5.5	9	3	3	3	8	8	8	8
2. MULTIPLE DX										
0–19 Years	0									
20–34	0									
35–49	14	6.1	9	3	5	5	7	10	16	16
50–64	78	6.9	37	1	2	5	9	14	19	29
65+	217	5.2	20	2	3	4	7	9	12	18
TOTAL SINGLE DX	**4**	**3.3**	**9**	**1**	**1**	**2**	**3**	**8**	**8**	**8**
TOTAL MULTIPLE DX	**309**	**5.7**	**25**	**2**	**3**	**4**	**7**	**11**	**14**	**29**
TOTAL										
0–19 Years	0									
20–34	0									
35–49	14	6.1	9	3	5	5	7	10	16	16
50–64	80	6.7	37	1	2	5	9	14	19	29
65+	219	5.2	20	2	3	4	7	9	12	18
GRAND TOTAL	**313**	**5.7**	**25**	**2**	**3**	**4**	**7**	**11**	**14**	**29**

38.18: LOWER LIMB ENDARTERECT

Type of Patients	Observed Patients	Avg. Stay	Vari-ance	Percentiles 10th	25th	50th	75th	90th	95th	99th
1. SINGLE DX										
0–19 Years	0									
20–34	2	6.5	<1	6	6	7	7	7	7	7
35–49	3	2.7	<1	2	2	3	3	3	3	3
50–64	7	1.6	<1	1	1	2	2	2	3	3
65+	13	2.0	1	1	1	2	2	4	5	5
2. MULTIPLE DX										
0–19 Years	0									
20–34	4	4.4	39	1	1	2	9	19	19	19
35–49	52	5.0	21	1	2	3	6	11	16	23
50–64	220	5.2	31	1	2	3	6	13	19	25
65+	703	5.2	24	1	2	4	7	12	16	22
TOTAL SINGLE DX	**25**	**2.2**	**2**	**1**	**1**	**2**	**2**	**4**	**6**	**7**
TOTAL MULTIPLE DX	**979**	**5.2**	**26**	**1**	**2**	**3**	**6**	**12**	**16**	**23**
TOTAL										
0–19 Years	0									
20–34	6	4.8	32	1	1	2	7	9	19	19
35–49	55	4.9	21	1	2	3	5	11	16	23
50–64	227	5.1	30	1	2	3	6	13	16	25
65+	716	5.2	24	1	2	4	6	11	16	22
GRAND TOTAL	**1,004**	**5.2**	**25**	**1**	**2**	**3**	**6**	**12**	**16**	**23**

38.2: DXTIC BLOOD VESSELS PX

Type of Patients	Observed Patients	Avg. Stay	Vari-ance	Percentiles 10th	25th	50th	75th	90th	95th	99th
1. SINGLE DX										
0–19 Years	0									
20–34	2	1.0	0	1	1	1	1	1	1	1
35–49	1	2.0	0	2	2	2	2	2	2	2
50–64	3	2.8	2	1	1	3	4	4	4	4
65+	4	2.8	2	1	1	4	4	4	4	4
2. MULTIPLE DX										
0–19 Years	1	1.0	0	1	1	1	1	1	1	1
20–34	5	8.9	42	4	5	6	10	20	20	20
35–49	14	5.7	13	3	3	5	6	12	15	15
50–64	106	6.7	23	3	3	5	9	13	16	28
65+	360	6.6	30	2	3	5	9	12	16	30
TOTAL SINGLE DX	**10**	**2.5**	**2**	**1**	**1**	**2**	**4**	**4**	**4**	**4**
TOTAL MULTIPLE DX	**486**	**6.6**	**28**	**2**	**3**	**5**	**9**	**13**	**16**	**29**
TOTAL										
0–19 Years	1	1.0	0	1	1	1	1	1	1	1
20–34	7	6.3	42	1	1	5	10	20	20	20
35–49	15	5.5	13	2	3	5	6	12	15	15
50–64	109	6.7	23	2	3	5	9	13	16	28
65+	364	6.6	30	2	3	5	8	12	16	30
GRAND TOTAL	**496**	**6.6**	**28**	**2**	**3**	**5**	**9**	**13**	**16**	**29**

38.21: BLOOD VESSEL BIOPSY

Type of Patients	Observed Patients	Avg. Stay	Vari- ance	Percentiles						
				10th	25th	50th	75th	90th	95th	99th
1. SINGLE DX										
0–19 Years	0									
20–34	1	1.0	0	1	1	1	1	1	1	1
35–49	1	2.0	0	2	2	2	2	2	2	2
50–64	2	3.6	<1	3	3	4	4	4	4	4
65+	4	2.8	2	1	1	4	4	4	4	4
2. MULTIPLE DX										
0–19 Years	0									
20–34	5	8.9	42	4	5	6	10	20	20	20
35–49	12	5.9	14	3	5	5	6	12	15	15
50–64	103	6.9	23	3	3	5	9	13	16	28
65+	355	6.6	29	2	3	5	9	12	16	30
TOTAL SINGLE DX	**8**	**2.7**	**2**	**1**	**1**	**3**	**4**	**4**	**4**	**4**
TOTAL MULTIPLE DX	**475**	**6.7**	**28**	**2**	**3**	**5**	**9**	**13**	**16**	**29**
TOTAL										
0–19 Years	0									
20–34	6	7.1	44	1	4	5	10	20	20	20
35–49	13	5.6	14	2	3	5	5	12	15	15
50–64	105	6.8	23	3	3	5	9	13	16	28
65+	359	6.6	29	2	3	5	9	12	16	30
GRAND TOTAL	**483**	**6.6**	**28**	**2**	**3**	**5**	**9**	**13**	**16**	**29**

38.3: VESSEL RESECT W ANAST

Type of Patients	Observed Patients	Avg. Stay	Vari- ance	Percentiles						
				10th	25th	50th	75th	90th	95th	99th
1. SINGLE DX										
0–19 Years	1	1.0	0	1	1	1	1	1	1	1
20–34	2	3.0	2	2	2	4	4	4	4	4
35–49	2	2.6	3	1	1	4	4	4	4	4
50–64	1	4.0	0	4	4	4	4	4	4	4
65+	0									
2. MULTIPLE DX										
0–19 Years	102	7.6	68	3	3	5	8	13	26	48
20–34	9	8.4	88	2	2	3	12	26	28	28
35–49	26	5.5	40	1	1	3	6	14	23	24
50–64	54	6.8	28	2	4	6	8	11	16	30
65+	115	7.9	35	2	4	6	10	15	17	28
TOTAL SINGLE DX	**6**	**2.5**	**2**	**1**	**1**	**2**	**4**	**4**	**4**	**4**
TOTAL MULTIPLE DX	**306**	**7.5**	**51**	**2**	**3**	**5**	**9**	**14**	**24**	**33**
TOTAL										
0–19 Years	103	7.5	68	3	3	5	8	13	26	48
20–34	11	7.8	81	2	2	3	12	26	28	28
35–49	28	5.3	38	1	1	3	6	14	23	24
50–64	55	6.8	28	2	4	6	8	11	16	30
65+	115	7.9	35	2	4	6	10	15	17	28
GRAND TOTAL	**312**	**7.4**	**51**	**2**	**3**	**5**	**9**	**14**	**24**	**33**

38.34: AORTA RESECTION W ANAST

Type of Patients	Observed Patients	Avg. Stay	Vari- ance	Percentiles						
				10th	25th	50th	75th	90th	95th	99th
1. SINGLE DX										
0–19 Years	0									
20–34	0									
35–49	0									
50–64	0									
65+	0									
2. MULTIPLE DX										
0–19 Years	97	7.6	67	3	3	5	8	13	26	48
20–34	0									
35–49	2	12.3	174	3	3	3	24	24	24	24
50–64	22	6.8	8	4	5	6	8	11	11	16
65+	68	9.9	37	5	6	8	13	15	21	28
TOTAL SINGLE DX	**0**									
TOTAL MULTIPLE DX	**189**	**8.1**	**56**	**3**	**4**	**6**	**9**	**15**	**26**	**48**
TOTAL										
0–19 Years	97	7.6	67	3	3	5	8	13	26	48
20–34	0									
35–49	2	12.3	174	3	3	3	24	24	24	24
50–64	22	6.8	8	4	5	6	8	11	11	16
65+	68	9.9	37	5	6	8	13	15	21	28
GRAND TOTAL	**189**	**8.1**	**56**	**3**	**4**	**6**	**9**	**15**	**26**	**48**

38.4: VESSEL RESECT W REPL

Type of Patients	Observed Patients	Avg. Stay	Vari- ance	Percentiles						
				10th	25th	50th	75th	90th	95th	99th
1. SINGLE DX										
0–19 Years	1	3.0	0	3	3	3	3	3	3	3
20–34	4	2.9	2	2	2	2	5	5	5	5
35–49	3	3.1	4	1	1	3	5	5	5	5
50–64	9	3.0	3	2	2	3	3	7	7	7
65+	14	4.3	2	3	4	4	5	6	7	7
2. MULTIPLE DX										
0–19 Years	32	9.4	122	3	3	6	9	23	39	61
20–34	38	6.1	29	2	3	5	7	9	13	29
35–49	104	8.5	45	3	4	7	11	15	22	36
50–64	539	7.6	29	3	5	6	9	13	17	29
65+	1,959	9.2	43	4	6	7	10	17	22	37
TOTAL SINGLE DX	**31**	**3.7**	**3**	**2**	**2**	**4**	**5**	**6**	**7**	**7**
TOTAL MULTIPLE DX	**2,672**	**8.9**	**42**	**4**	**5**	**7**	**10**	**16**	**21**	**37**
TOTAL										
0–19 Years	33	9.3	120	3	3	6	9	23	39	61
20–34	42	5.6	26	2	2	5	7	9	13	29
35–49	107	8.4	45	2	4	6	11	15	22	36
50–64	548	7.5	29	3	5	6	9	13	17	29
65+	1,973	9.2	43	4	6	7	10	17	22	37
GRAND TOTAL	**2,703**	**8.8**	**42**	**4**	**5**	**7**	**10**	**16**	**21**	**37**

38.44: ABD AORTA RESECT W REPL

Type of Patients	Observed Patients	Avg. Stay	Vari-ance	10th	25th	50th	75th	90th	95th	99th
1. SINGLE DX										
0–19 Years	0									
20–34	0									
35–49	1	5.0	0	5	5	5	5	5	5	5
50–64	2	3.5	<1	3	3	4	4	4	4	4
65+	8	5.3	2	5	5	5	6	7	7	7
2. MULTIPLE DX										
0–19 Years	1	9.0	0	9	9	9	9	9	9	9
20–34	3	5.3	2	4	4	5	7	7	7	7
35–49	18	7.5	11	4	6	6	9	14	14	16
50–64	346	7.8	21	4	5	6	9	12	17	28
65+	1,545	9.4	40	5	6	8	10	17	22	37
TOTAL SINGLE DX	**11**	**5.0**	**2**	**3**	**5**	**5**	**6**	**6**	**7**	**7**
TOTAL MULTIPLE DX	**1,913**	**9.2**	**37**	**5**	**6**	**7**	**10**	**16**	**21**	**35**
TOTAL										
0–19 Years	1	9.0	0	9	9	9	9	9	9	9
20–34	3	5.3	2	4	4	5	7	7	7	7
35–49	19	7.4	11	4	5	6	9	14	14	16
50–64	348	7.8	21	4	5	6	9	12	17	28
65+	1,553	9.4	40	5	6	8	10	17	22	37
GRAND TOTAL	**1,924**	**9.1**	**37**	**5**	**6**	**7**	**10**	**16**	**21**	**35**

38.45: THOR VESS RESECT W REPL

Type of Patients	Observed Patients	Avg. Stay	Vari-ance	10th	25th	50th	75th	90th	95th	99th
1. SINGLE DX										
0–19 Years	1	3.0	0	3	3	3	3	3	3	3
20–34	1	5.0	0	5	5	5	5	5	5	5
35–49	0									
50–64	1	7.0	0	7	7	7	7	7	7	7
65+	0									
2. MULTIPLE DX										
0–19 Years	26	9.9	136	3	4	6	12	23	39	61
20–34	13	6.4	2	5	5	6	7	7	11	11
35–49	48	10.7	54	5	6	8	12	22	24	43
50–64	80	10.7	63	5	6	8	13	20	22	42
65+	139	11.8	63	4	6	10	14	20	28	44
TOTAL SINGLE DX	**3**	**4.9**	**4**	**3**	**3**	**5**	**7**	**7**	**7**	**7**
TOTAL MULTIPLE DX	**306**	**11.0**	**70**	**4**	**6**	**9**	**13**	**20**	**25**	**44**
TOTAL										
0–19 Years	27	9.8	134	3	4	6	12	23	39	61
20–34	14	6.3	2	5	5	6	7	7	11	11
35–49	48	10.7	54	5	6	8	12	22	24	43
50–64	81	10.7	63	5	6	8	13	20	22	42
65+	139	11.8	63	4	6	10	14	20	28	44
GRAND TOTAL	**309**	**11.0**	**69**	**4**	**6**	**9**	**13**	**20**	**25**	**44**

38.46: ABD ARTERY RESECT W REPL

Type of Patients	Observed Patients	Avg. Stay	Vari-ance	10th	25th	50th	75th	90th	95th	99th
1. SINGLE DX										
0–19 Years	0									
20–34	1	5.0	0	5	5	5	5	5	5	5
35–49	0									
50–64	0									
65+	2	4.0	0	4	4	4	4	4	4	4
2. MULTIPLE DX										
0–19 Years	0									
20–34	0									
35–49	5	4.3	5	3	3	4	4	10	10	10
50–64	24	5.8	10	3	4	5	6	10	14	14
65+	64	9.8	54	4	5	7	11	19	23	35
TOTAL SINGLE DX	**3**	**4.2**	**<1**	**4**	**4**	**4**	**4**	**5**	**5**	**5**
TOTAL MULTIPLE DX	**93**	**8.3**	**43**	**3**	**4**	**6**	**9**	**15**	**20**	**35**
TOTAL										
0–19 Years	0									
20–34	1	5.0	0	5	5	5	5	5	5	5
35–49	5	4.3	5	3	3	4	4	10	10	10
50–64	24	5.8	10	3	4	5	6	10	14	14
65+	66	9.3	53	4	5	7	11	19	23	35
GRAND TOTAL	**96**	**8.0**	**42**	**4**	**4**	**6**	**9**	**15**	**20**	**35**

38.48: LEG ARTERY RESECT W REPL

Type of Patients	Observed Patients	Avg. Stay	Vari-ance	10th	25th	50th	75th	90th	95th	99th
1. SINGLE DX										
0–19 Years	0									
20–34	0									
35–49	0									
50–64	3	2.0	<1	1	1	2	3	3	3	3
65+	4	2.8	1	1	3	3	4	4	4	4
2. MULTIPLE DX										
0–19 Years	2	2.1	2	1	1	3	3	3	3	3
20–34	12	4.9	12	2	2	3	9	9	13	13
35–49	11	10.9	69	2	3	11	15	15	36	36
50–64	56	4.5	16	2	3	3	4	7	13	29
65+	164	6.2	38	2	3	4	7	11	21	32
TOTAL SINGLE DX	**7**	**2.5**	**1**	**1**	**1**	**3**	**3**	**4**	**4**	**4**
TOTAL MULTIPLE DX	**245**	**6.0**	**35**	**2**	**3**	**4**	**7**	**12**	**17**	**32**
TOTAL										
0–19 Years	2	2.1	2	1	1	3	3	3	3	3
20–34	12	4.9	12	2	2	3	9	9	13	13
35–49	11	10.9	69	2	3	11	15	15	36	36
50–64	59	4.4	16	2	3	3	4	7	13	29
65+	168	6.1	37	2	3	4	7	11	21	32
GRAND TOTAL	**252**	**5.9**	**35**	**2**	**3**	**4**	**7**	**12**	**16**	**32**

38.5: LIG&STRIP VARICOSE VEINS

Type of Patients	Observed Patients	Avg. Stay	Variance	Percentiles 10th	25th	50th	75th	90th	95th	99th
1. SINGLE DX										
0–19 Years	0									
20–34	13	1.1	<1	1	1	1	1	1	2	2
35–49	24	1.4	<1	1	1	1	1	2	3	5
50–64	24	1.3	<1	1	1	1	1	2	3	3
65+	9	1.6	1	1	1	1	2	2	5	5
2. MULTIPLE DX										
0–19 Years	0									
20–34	7	1.4	<1	1	1	1	2	3	3	3
35–49	53	2.9	21	1	1	1	2	8	11	25
50–64	79	1.8	3	1	1	1	2	3	6	10
65+	66	3.8	14	1	1	2	6	9	11	17
TOTAL SINGLE DX	**70**	**1.3**	**<1**	**1**	**1**	**1**	**1**	**2**	**3**	**5**
TOTAL MULTIPLE DX	**205**	**2.8**	**12**	**1**	**1**	**1**	**3**	**7**	**9**	**18**
TOTAL										
0–19 Years	0									
20–34	20	1.2	<1	1	1	1	1	2	2	3
35–49	77	2.5	16	1	1	1	2	5	8	25
50–64	103	1.7	3	1	1	1	2	3	5	10
65+	75	3.5	13	1	1	2	5	8	10	17
GRAND TOTAL	**275**	**2.4**	**10**	**1**	**1**	**1**	**2**	**6**	**8**	**18**

38.59: LOWER LIMB VV LIG&STRIP

Type of Patients	Observed Patients	Avg. Stay	Variance	Percentiles 10th	25th	50th	75th	90th	95th	99th
1. SINGLE DX										
0–19 Years	0									
20–34	13	1.1	<1	1	1	1	1	1	2	2
35–49	23	1.4	<1	1	1	1	1	2	3	5
50–64	24	1.3	<1	1	1	1	1	2	3	3
65+	9	1.6	1	1	1	1	2	2	5	5
2. MULTIPLE DX										
0–19 Years	0									
20–34	7	1.4	<1	1	1	1	2	3	3	3
35–49	51	3.0	22	1	1	1	2	8	11	25
50–64	79	1.8	3	1	1	1	2	3	6	10
65+	65	3.6	11	1	1	2	6	8	10	16
TOTAL SINGLE DX	**69**	**1.3**	**<1**	**1**	**1**	**1**	**1**	**2**	**3**	**5**
TOTAL MULTIPLE DX	**202**	**2.7**	**11**	**1**	**1**	**1**	**3**	**7**	**9**	**18**
TOTAL										
0–19 Years	0									
20–34	20	1.2	<1	1	1	1	1	2	2	3
35–49	74	2.5	16	1	1	1	2	5	8	25
50–64	103	1.7	3	1	1	1	2	3	5	10
65+	74	3.3	10	1	1	2	5	8	9	16
GRAND TOTAL	**271**	**2.4**	**9**	**1**	**1**	**1**	**2**	**6**	**8**	**17**

38.6: OTHER VESSEL EXCISION

Type of Patients	Observed Patients	Avg. Stay	Variance	Percentiles 10th	25th	50th	75th	90th	95th	99th
1. SINGLE DX										
0–19 Years	10	3.0	3	1	2	3	3	6	7	7
20–34	4	5.2	44	1	1	3	3	16	16	16
35–49	2	4.0	7	2	2	2	6	6	6	6
50–64	3	2.3	5	1	1	1	5	5	5	5
65+	3	3.2	3	1	1	3	5	5	5	5
2. MULTIPLE DX										
0–19 Years	36	6.3	18	3	4	4	8	13	16	18
20–34	18	9.5	107	2	3	7	9	16	34	44
35–49	55	8.3	66	2	3	6	10	15	25	41
50–64	54	6.5	42	2	2	5	8	13	18	38
65+	103	6.9	33	1	3	5	8	16	20	26
TOTAL SINGLE DX	**22**	**3.4**	**10**	**1**	**1**	**3**	**4**	**6**	**7**	**16**
TOTAL MULTIPLE DX	**266**	**7.1**	**42**	**2**	**3**	**5**	**8**	**15**	**19**	**38**
TOTAL										
0–19 Years	46	5.7	17	2	3	4	6	13	16	18
20–34	22	8.6	95	1	3	7	9	16	34	44
35–49	57	8.2	65	2	3	6	10	15	25	41
50–64	57	6.3	41	2	2	4	8	13	18	38
65+	106	6.8	33	1	3	5	8	16	20	26
GRAND TOTAL	**288**	**6.8**	**41**	**2**	**3**	**5**	**8**	**15**	**18**	**34**

38.63: UP LIMB VESSEL EXC NEC

Type of Patients	Observed Patients	Avg. Stay	Variance	Percentiles 10th	25th	50th	75th	90th	95th	99th
1. SINGLE DX										
0–19 Years	1	1.0	0	1	1	1	1	1	1	1
20–34	0									
35–49	1	6.0	0	6	6	6	6	6	6	6
50–64	0									
65+	0									
2. MULTIPLE DX										
0–19 Years	0									
20–34	11	12.0	173	2	3	8	14	34	44	44
35–49	34	9.7	72	2	4	7	14	20	33	41
50–64	20	7.5	53	1	3	6	10	14	15	38
65+	24	8.5	77	1	1	5	13	23	26	29
TOTAL SINGLE DX	**2**	**3.4**	**11**	**1**	**1**	**1**	**6**	**6**	**6**	**6**
TOTAL MULTIPLE DX	**89**	**9.0**	**79**	**1**	**3**	**6**	**12**	**20**	**29**	**41**
TOTAL										
0–19 Years	1	1.0	0	1	1	1	1	1	1	1
20–34	11	12.0	173	2	3	8	14	34	44	44
35–49	35	9.6	71	2	4	7	14	17	33	41
50–64	20	7.5	53	1	3	6	10	14	15	38
65+	24	8.5	77	1	1	5	13	23	26	29
GRAND TOTAL	**91**	**8.9**	**78**	**1**	**3**	**6**	**11**	**20**	**29**	**41**

38.68: LOW LIMB ARTERY EXC NEC

Type of Patients	Observed Patients	Avg. Stay	Vari-ance	Percentiles 10th	25th	50th	75th	90th	95th	99th
1. SINGLE DX										
0–19 Years	0									
20–34	0									
35–49	0									
50–64	0									
65+	0									
2. MULTIPLE DX										
0–19 Years	0									
20–34	0									
35–49	8	5.6	20	1	2	4	10	12	12	12
50–64	13	4.2	15	2	2	3	5	5	18	18
65+	44	5.6	19	2	3	5	8	10	16	24
TOTAL SINGLE DX	**0**									
TOTAL MULTIPLE DX	**65**	**5.3**	**18**	**2**	**2**	**4**	**7**	**10**	**16**	**24**
TOTAL										
0–19 Years	0									
20–34	0									
35–49	8	5.6	20	1	2	4	10	12	12	12
50–64	13	4.2	15	2	2	3	5	5	18	18
65+	44	5.6	19	2	3	5	8	10	16	24
GRAND TOTAL	**65**	**5.3**	**18**	**2**	**2**	**4**	**7**	**10**	**16**	**24**

38.7: INTERRUPTION VENA CAVA

Type of Patients	Observed Patients	Avg. Stay	Vari-ance	Percentiles 10th	25th	50th	75th	90th	95th	99th
1. SINGLE DX										
0–19 Years	0									
20–34	2	6.0	17	3	3	3	9	9	9	9
35–49	4	4.0	14	1	1	2	6	10	10	10
50–64	6	3.0	3	1	1	4	4	4	6	6
65+	2	2.7	7	1	1	1	6	6	6	6
2. MULTIPLE DX										
0–19 Years	20	11.2	36	6	9	9	14	24	25	>99
20–34	87	9.2	49	2	5	7	11	18	22	31
35–49	370	9.2	73	2	5	7	11	18	22	39
50–64	765	9.5	108	2	4	6	11	20	29	53
65+	2,280	8.7	45	2	4	7	11	18	23	31
TOTAL SINGLE DX	**14**	**3.4**	**7**	**1**	**1**	**3**	**6**	**6**	**9**	**10**
TOTAL MULTIPLE DX	**3,522**	**8.9**	**61**	**2**	**4**	**7**	**11**	**18**	**24**	**40**
TOTAL										
0–19 Years	20	11.2	36	6	9	9	14	24	25	>99
20–34	89	9.1	48	2	5	7	11	18	22	31
35–49	374	9.2	73	2	4	7	11	17	22	39
50–64	771	9.4	107	2	4	6	11	20	29	53
65+	2,282	8.7	45	2	4	7	11	18	23	31
GRAND TOTAL	**3,536**	**8.9**	**61**	**2**	**4**	**7**	**11**	**18**	**24**	**40**

38.8: OTHER SURG VESSEL OCCL

Type of Patients	Observed Patients	Avg. Stay	Vari-ance	Percentiles 10th	25th	50th	75th	90th	95th	99th
1. SINGLE DX										
0–19 Years	49	1.7	2	1	1	1	2	3	6	7
20–34	11	1.7	2	1	1	1	2	5	6	6
35–49	12	1.3	<1	1	1	1	1	3	3	3
50–64	9	1.8	5	1	1	1	1	4	9	9
65+	5	4.3	35	1	1	2	4	16	16	16
2. MULTIPLE DX										
0–19 Years	283	17.3	728	1	2	5	30	99	>99	>99
20–34	114	4.5	38	1	1	2	5	10	13	38
35–49	145	5.5	29	1	2	4	7	13	16	27
50–64	128	6.8	42	1	2	5	9	20	21	26
65+	166	7.9	73	1	3	5	9	17	24	48
TOTAL SINGLE DX	**86**	**1.8**	**3**	**1**	**1**	**1**	**2**	**3**	**6**	**9**
TOTAL MULTIPLE DX	**836**	**11.3**	**382**	**1**	**2**	**5**	**12**	**60**	**99**	**>99**
TOTAL										
0–19 Years	332	14.6	638	1	1	4	20	95	>99	>99
20–34	125	4.2	34	1	1	2	5	9	13	38
35–49	157	5.2	28	1	1	3	7	13	16	27
50–64	137	6.4	40	1	2	4	9	16	21	26
65+	171	7.8	72	1	3	5	9	17	24	48
GRAND TOTAL	**922**	**10.2**	**347**	**1**	**2**	**4**	**10**	**42**	**95**	**>99**

38.82: OCCL HEAD/NECK VESS NEC

Type of Patients	Observed Patients	Avg. Stay	Vari-ance	Percentiles 10th	25th	50th	75th	90th	95th	99th
1. SINGLE DX										
0–19 Years	3	1.3	<1	1	1	1	2	2	2	2
20–34	1	2.0	0	2	2	2	2	2	2	2
35–49	2	1.5	<1	1	1	1	2	2	2	2
50–64	2	4.9	27	1	1	1	9	9	9	9
65+	1	2.0	0	2	2	2	2	2	2	2
2. MULTIPLE DX										
0–19 Years	5	19.2	378	2	4	19	19	54	54	54
20–34	26	3.0	9	1	1	2	3	7	10	15
35–49	27	5.7	27	1	2	4	6	16	16	16
50–64	22	5.2	15	1	2	4	8	10	12	13
65+	25	8.8	201	1	2	3	9	24	57	57
TOTAL SINGLE DX	**9**	**2.2**	**6**	**1**	**1**	**2**	**2**	**2**	**9**	**9**
TOTAL MULTIPLE DX	**105**	**6.7**	**101**	**1**	**2**	**3**	**7**	**16**	**19**	**57**
TOTAL										
0–19 Years	8	13.8	328	1	2	4	19	54	54	54
20–34	27	3.0	9	1	1	2	3	7	10	15
35–49	29	5.4	26	1	2	3	6	16	16	16
50–64	24	5.2	15	1	2	4	8	10	12	13
65+	26	8.6	197	1	2	3	9	24	57	57
GRAND TOTAL	**114**	**6.4**	**95**	**1**	**2**	**3**	**7**	**16**	**19**	**57**

38.83: OCCL UPPER LIMB VESS NEC

Type of Patients	Observed Patients	Avg. Stay	Vari-ance	Percentiles						
				10th	25th	50th	75th	90th	95th	99th
1. SINGLE DX										
0–19 Years	1	2.0	0	2	2	2	2	2	2	2
20–34	2	1.0	0	1	1	1	1	1	1	1
35–49	2	1.0	0	1	1	1	1	1	1	1
50–64	1	1.0	0	1	1	1	1	1	1	1
65+	1	1.0	0	1	1	1	1	1	1	1
2. MULTIPLE DX										
0–19 Years	9	2.0	3	1	1	1	4	4	4	7
20–34	25	1.7	3	1	1	1	2	2	4	10
35–49	24	4.6	27	1	1	2	6	14	18	19
50–64	16	9.2	69	1	3	6	21	21	21	21
65+	30	5.4	29	1	2	4	6	14	17	23
TOTAL SINGLE DX	**7**	**1.1**	**<1**	**1**	**1**	**1**	**1**	**2**	**2**	**2**
TOTAL MULTIPLE DX	**104**	**4.5**	**32**	**1**	**1**	**2**	**5**	**14**	**21**	**21**
TOTAL										
0–19 Years	10	2.0	3	1	1	1	4	4	4	7
20–34	27	1.6	2	1	1	1	2	2	4	10
35–49	26	4.3	26	1	1	2	5	14	18	19
50–64	17	8.9	69	1	3	4	21	21	21	21
65+	31	5.2	29	1	1	3	6	14	17	23
GRAND TOTAL	**111**	**4.3**	**30**	**1**	**1**	**2**	**4**	**13**	**21**	**21**

38.85: OCCL THORACIC VESS NEC

Type of Patients	Observed Patients	Avg. Stay	Vari-ance	Percentiles						
				10th	25th	50th	75th	90th	95th	99th
1. SINGLE DX										
0–19 Years	40	1.7	2	1	1	1	2	3	6	7
20–34	3	3.1	7	1	1	2	6	6	6	6
35–49	2	2.0	2	1	1	1	3	3	3	3
50–64	0									
65+	1	1.0	0	1	1	1	1	1	1	1
2. MULTIPLE DX										
0–19 Years	234	19.8	845	1	2	7	61	>99	>99	>99
20–34	22	4.7	6	1	3	5	6	8	9	11
35–49	18	6.9	37	1	2	6	10	10	16	28
50–64	10	12.4	106	1	3	8	26	26	28	28
65+	15	11.9	164	1	2	4	24	34	34	34
TOTAL SINGLE DX	**46**	**1.7**	**2**	**1**	**1**	**1**	**2**	**3**	**6**	**7**
TOTAL MULTIPLE DX	**299**	**18.1**	**752**	**1**	**2**	**6**	**34**	**>99**	**>99**	**>99**
TOTAL										
0–19 Years	274	16.5	739	1	1	4	28	99	>99	>99
20–34	25	4.6	6	1	3	5	6	8	9	11
35–49	20	6.5	35	1	2	6	9	10	16	28
50–64	10	12.4	106	1	3	8	26	26	28	28
65+	16	11.2	160	1	2	4	24	34	34	34
GRAND TOTAL	**345**	**15.4**	**663**	**1**	**2**	**4**	**23**	**96**	**>99**	**>99**

38.86: SURG OCCL ABD ARTERY NEC

Type of Patients	Observed Patients	Avg. Stay	Vari-ance	Percentiles						
				10th	25th	50th	75th	90th	95th	99th
1. SINGLE DX										
0–19 Years	0									
20–34	0									
35–49	2	1.0	0	1	1	1	1	1	1	1
50–64	4	1.1	<1	1	1	1	1	2	2	2
65+	0									
2. MULTIPLE DX										
0–19 Years	10	5.9	16	3	3	6	7	7	19	19
20–34	22	7.0	57	1	3	4	8	13	14	38
35–49	41	6.3	26	1	2	5	8	13	16	22
50–64	44	6.3	27	1	2	5	8	15	17	22
65+	58	8.1	42	3	4	7	10	15	18	48
TOTAL SINGLE DX	**6**	**1.1**	**<1**	**1**	**1**	**1**	**1**	**1**	**2**	**2**
TOTAL MULTIPLE DX	**175**	**7.2**	**36**	**1**	**4**	**6**	**9**	**14**	**17**	**24**
TOTAL										
0–19 Years	10	5.9	16	3	3	6	7	7	19	19
20–34	22	7.0	57	1	3	4	8	13	14	38
35–49	43	5.8	26	1	1	5	8	13	16	22
50–64	48	5.5	27	1	1	4	8	14	17	22
65+	58	8.1	42	3	4	7	10	15	18	48
GRAND TOTAL	**181**	**6.8**	**36**	**1**	**3**	**5**	**9**	**14**	**17**	**24**

38.9: PUNCTURE OF VESSEL

Type of Patients	Observed Patients	Avg. Stay	Vari-ance	Percentiles						
				10th	25th	50th	75th	90th	95th	99th
1. SINGLE DX										
0–19 Years	231	4.4	11	1	2	4	6	8	11	16
20–34	198	3.9	8	1	2	3	5	8	9	15
35–49	158	3.5	8	1	1	3	4	7	10	13
50–64	87	3.8	10	1	2	3	4	9	10	12
65+	37	4.4	12	1	1	3	6	10	12	12
2. MULTIPLE DX										
0–19 Years	5,090	12.7	195	2	4	8	16	30	42	80
20–34	3,721	7.5	48	2	3	6	9	15	20	38
35–49	8,413	7.3	38	2	4	6	9	14	18	31
50–64	10,612	7.6	38	2	4	6	9	15	19	30
65+	17,086	8.1	37	3	4	7	10	16	20	29
TOTAL SINGLE DX	**711**	**4.0**	**10**	**1**	**2**	**3**	**5**	**8**	**10**	**16**
TOTAL MULTIPLE DX	**44,922**	**8.4**	**60**	**2**	**4**	**6**	**10**	**16**	**22**	**40**
TOTAL										
0–19 Years	5,321	12.3	189	2	4	7	15	29	41	77
20–34	3,919	7.3	47	2	3	5	9	15	20	37
35–49	8,571	7.3	38	2	3	6	9	14	18	31
50–64	10,699	7.5	38	2	4	6	9	15	19	30
65+	17,123	8.1	36	3	4	7	10	16	20	29
GRAND TOTAL	**45,633**	**8.3**	**59**	**2**	**4**	**6**	**10**	**16**	**22**	**40**

38.91: ARTERIAL CATHETERIZATION

Type of Patients	Observed Patients	Avg. Stay	Vari-ance	Percentiles						
				10th	25th	50th	75th	90th	95th	99th
1. SINGLE DX										
0–19 Years	10	3.1	4	1	1	2	4	6	7	7
20–34	2	2.0	0	2	2	2	2	2	2	2
35–49	3	1.5	<1	1	1	2	2	2	2	2
50–64	1	1.0	0	1	1	1	1	1	1	1
65+	2	1.0	0	1	1	1	1	1	1	1
2. MULTIPLE DX										
0–19 Years	1,508	16.5	271	3	5	10	23	40	54	97
20–34	57	8.1	210	2	2	3	7	20	29	99
35–49	138	7.4	93	1	2	5	8	17	24	29
50–64	194	7.0	29	2	3	5	9	15	19	26
65+	294	6.8	36	2	3	5	9	15	19	27
TOTAL SINGLE DX	**18**	**2.3**	**3**	**1**	**1**	**2**	**3**	**6**	**6**	**7**
TOTAL MULTIPLE DX	**2,191**	**13.3**	**219**	**2**	**4**	**8**	**17**	**32**	**45**	**91**
TOTAL										
0–19 Years	1,518	16.4	271	3	5	10	23	40	53	97
20–34	59	8.0	206	2	2	3	7	17	29	99
35–49	141	7.2	91	1	2	5	8	17	24	29
50–64	195	7.0	29	1	3	5	9	15	18	26
65+	296	6.7	36	1	3	5	9	15	19	27
GRAND TOTAL	**2,209**	**13.2**	**218**	**2**	**4**	**8**	**17**	**32**	**45**	**91**

38.92: UMBILICAL VEIN CATH

Type of Patients	Observed Patients	Avg. Stay	Vari-ance	Percentiles						
				10th	25th	50th	75th	90th	95th	99th
1. SINGLE DX										
0–19 Years	3	3.0	<1	2	2	3	4	4	4	4
20–34	0									
35–49	0									
50–64	0									
65+	0									
2. MULTIPLE DX										
0–19 Years	830	14.6	291	2	4	8	18	35	55	83
20–34	0									
35–49	1	10.0	0	10	10	10	10	10	10	10
50–64	0									
65+	1	6.0	0	6	6	6	6	6	6	6
TOTAL SINGLE DX	**3**	**3.0**	**<1**	**2**	**2**	**3**	**4**	**4**	**4**	**4**
TOTAL MULTIPLE DX	**832**	**14.6**	**290**	**2**	**4**	**8**	**18**	**35**	**55**	**83**
TOTAL										
0–19 Years	833	14.5	291	2	4	8	18	35	55	83
20–34	0									
35–49	1	10.0	0	10	10	10	10	10	10	10
50–64	0									
65+	1	6.0	0	6	6	6	6	6	6	6
GRAND TOTAL	**835**	**14.5**	**290**	**2**	**4**	**8**	**18**	**35**	**55**	**83**

38.93: VENOUS CATHETER NEC

Type of Patients	Observed Patients	Avg. Stay	Vari-ance	Percentiles						
				10th	25th	50th	75th	90th	95th	99th
1. SINGLE DX										
0–19 Years	200	4.4	10	1	2	4	6	8	11	16
20–34	178	4.1	8	1	2	4	5	8	9	15
35–49	138	3.8	8	1	2	3	5	8	10	13
50–64	77	4.0	10	1	2	3	5	9	10	12
65+	27	5.1	13	1	2	5	6	12	12	12
2. MULTIPLE DX										
0–19 Years	2,422	11.0	132	2	4	7	14	25	33	59
20–34	3,158	7.7	48	2	3	6	9	15	20	38
35–49	7,052	7.4	37	2	4	6	9	14	18	31
50–64	8,343	7.8	37	2	4	6	10	15	19	30
65+	13,028	8.4	35	3	4	7	11	16	20	29
TOTAL SINGLE DX	**620**	**4.2**	**9**	**1**	**2**	**4**	**6**	**8**	**10**	**16**
TOTAL MULTIPLE DX	**34,003**	**8.2**	**46**	**3**	**4**	**6**	**10**	**16**	**21**	**34**
TOTAL										
0–19 Years	2,622	10.4	125	2	4	7	13	24	32	56
20–34	3,336	7.5	46	2	3	6	9	15	20	38
35–49	7,190	7.4	36	2	4	6	9	14	18	30
50–64	8,420	7.7	37	2	4	6	10	15	19	30
65+	13,055	8.4	35	3	4	7	11	16	20	29
GRAND TOTAL	**34,623**	**8.1**	**46**	**3**	**4**	**6**	**10**	**16**	**20**	**34**

38.94: VENOUS CUTDOWN

Type of Patients	Observed Patients	Avg. Stay	Vari-ance	Percentiles						
				10th	25th	50th	75th	90th	95th	99th
1. SINGLE DX										
0–19 Years	4	9.4	75	1	1	3	18	18	18	18
20–34	0									
35–49	0									
50–64	0									
65+	0									
2. MULTIPLE DX										
0–19 Years	55	12.2	200	2	6	8	14	24	34	93
20–34	11	9.8	67	3	5	7	8	22	34	34
35–49	16	8.0	97	1	4	5	8	15	42	42
50–64	30	10.8	198	1	3	6	16	21	44	78
65+	52	7.5	30	1	5	7	10	12	18	35
TOTAL SINGLE DX	**4**	**9.4**	**75**	**1**	**1**	**3**	**18**	**18**	**18**	**18**
TOTAL MULTIPLE DX	**164**	**10.1**	**135**	**2**	**4**	**7**	**11**	**21**	**34**	**78**
TOTAL										
0–19 Years	59	12.0	190	2	5	8	14	24	34	93
20–34	11	9.8	67	3	5	7	8	22	34	34
35–49	16	8.0	97	1	4	5	8	15	42	42
50–64	30	10.8	198	1	3	6	16	21	44	78
65+	52	7.5	30	1	5	7	10	12	18	35
GRAND TOTAL	**168**	**10.1**	**133**	**2**	**4**	**7**	**11**	**21**	**33**	**78**

38.95: VENOUS CATH FOR RD

Type of Patients	Observed Patients	Avg. Stay	Vari-ance	10th	25th	50th	75th	90th	95th	99th
1. SINGLE DX										
0–19 Years	1	1.0	0	1	1	1	1	1	1	1
20–34	2	3.8	4	2	2	5	5	5	5	5
35–49	5	1.2	<1	1	1	1	1	2	2	2
50–64	6	2.9	5	1	1	3	5	6	6	6
65+	5	1.0	0	1	1	1	1	1	1	1
2. MULTIPLE DX										
0–19 Years	101	7.1	40	1	2	5	11	14	22	30
20–34	425	6.6	32	1	3	5	9	14	18	24
35–49	1,019	7.4	43	1	3	6	10	14	20	32
50–64	1,758	7.2	42	1	3	5	9	15	20	32
65+	3,084	7.8	44	1	3	6	10	16	21	29
TOTAL SINGLE DX	**19**	**1.9**	**3**	**1**	**1**	**1**	**2**	**5**	**6**	**6**
TOTAL MULTIPLE DX	**6,387**	**7.5**	**43**	**1**	**3**	**6**	**10**	**15**	**20**	**30**
TOTAL										
0–19 Years	102	7.0	40	1	2	5	11	14	22	30
20–34	427	6.6	32	1	3	5	9	14	17	24
35–49	1,024	7.3	43	1	3	6	10	14	20	32
50–64	1,764	7.2	42	1	3	5	9	15	20	32
65+	3,089	7.8	44	1	3	6	10	16	21	29
GRAND TOTAL	**6,406**	**7.5**	**43**	**1**	**3**	**6**	**10**	**15**	**20**	**30**

(Percentiles: 10th–99th)

38.98: ARTERIAL PUNCTURE NEC

Type of Patients	Observed Patients	Avg. Stay	Vari-ance	10th	25th	50th	75th	90th	95th	99th
1. SINGLE DX										
0–19 Years	9	2.2	<1	1	2	2	3	3	4	4
20–34	0									
35–49	1	3.0	0	3	3	3	3	3	3	3
50–64	2	2.5	<1	2	2	2	3	3	3	3
65+	3	2.5	1	2	2	2	2	5	5	5
2. MULTIPLE DX										
0–19 Years	143	6.7	49	2	2	4	7	19	24	30
20–34	61	2.8	4	1	2	2	3	4	6	10
35–49	126	3.8	9	1	2	3	5	7	9	14
50–64	221	4.6	9	1	2	4	6	8	11	15
65+	541	4.7	10	2	3	4	6	9	11	16
TOTAL SINGLE DX	**15**	**2.4**	**<1**	**1**	**2**	**2**	**3**	**3**	**4**	**5**
TOTAL MULTIPLE DX	**1,092**	**4.7**	**14**	**2**	**2**	**4**	**6**	**9**	**12**	**21**
TOTAL										
0–19 Years	152	6.4	48	2	2	4	7	19	22	30
20–34	61	2.8	4	1	2	2	3	4	6	10
35–49	127	3.8	9	1	2	3	5	7	9	14
50–64	223	4.6	9	1	2	4	6	8	11	15
65+	544	4.7	10	2	3	4	6	9	11	16
GRAND TOTAL	**1,107**	**4.7**	**14**	**2**	**2**	**4**	**6**	**9**	**12**	**21**

(Percentiles: 10th–99th)

38.99: VENOUS PUNCTURE NEC

Type of Patients	Observed Patients	Avg. Stay	Vari-ance	10th	25th	50th	75th	90th	95th	99th
1. SINGLE DX										
0–19 Years	4	3.4	6	1	1	2	5	7	7	7
20–34	16	1.2	<1	1	1	1	1	2	3	3
35–49	11	1.2	<1	1	1	1	1	1	4	4
50–64	1	1.0	0	1	1	1	1	1	1	1
65+	0									
2. MULTIPLE DX										
0–19 Years	31	5.3	31	1	3	4	7	8	15	37
20–34	9	5.7	22	1	2	3	10	10	14	14
35–49	61	4.4	13	1	2	3	6	9	13	16
50–64	66	4.4	14	1	2	4	6	7	7	19
65+	86	4.4	10	1	2	4	5	7	11	18
TOTAL SINGLE DX	**32**	**1.6**	**2**	**1**	**1**	**1**	**1**	**3**	**5**	**7**
TOTAL MULTIPLE DX	**253**	**4.5**	**15**	**1**	**2**	**4**	**6**	**8**	**12**	**18**
TOTAL										
0–19 Years	35	5.1	28	1	3	4	7	8	13	37
20–34	25	2.9	13	1	1	1	3	10	10	14
35–49	72	4.0	12	1	1	3	5	8	13	16
50–64	67	4.4	14	1	2	4	6	7	7	19
65+	86	4.4	10	1	2	4	5	7	11	18
GRAND TOTAL	**285**	**4.3**	**14**	**1**	**2**	**4**	**5**	**8**	**11**	**18**

(Percentiles: 10th–99th)

39.0: SYSTEMIC TO PA SHUNT

Type of Patients	Observed Patients	Avg. Stay	Vari-ance	10th	25th	50th	75th	90th	95th	99th
1. SINGLE DX										
0–19 Years	1	16.0	0	16	16	16	16	16	16	16
20–34	0									
35–49	0									
50–64	0									
65+	0									
2. MULTIPLE DX										
0–19 Years	66	15.6	388	4	6	10	17	24	83	98
20–34	1	9.0	0	9	9	9	9	9	9	9
35–49	1	13.0	0	13	13	13	13	13	13	13
50–64	2	3.0	2	2	2	4	4	4	4	4
65+	0									
TOTAL SINGLE DX	**1**	**16.0**	**0**	**16**	**16**	**16**	**16**	**16**	**16**	**16**
TOTAL MULTIPLE DX	**70**	**15.3**	**379**	**4**	**6**	**10**	**16**	**24**	**72**	**98**
TOTAL										
0–19 Years	67	15.6	382	4	6	10	17	24	83	98
20–34	1	9.0	0	9	9	9	9	9	9	9
35–49	1	13.0	0	13	13	13	13	13	13	13
50–64	2	3.0	2	2	2	4	4	4	4	4
65+	0									
GRAND TOTAL	**71**	**15.4**	**374**	**4**	**6**	**10**	**16**	**24**	**72**	**98**

(Percentiles: 10th–99th)

39.1: INTRA-ABD VENOUS SHUNT

Type of Patients	Observed Patients	Avg. Stay	Vari-ance	Percentiles						
				10th	25th	50th	75th	90th	95th	99th
1. SINGLE DX										
0–19 Years	1	4.0	0	4	4	4	4	4	4	4
20–34	0									
35–49	1	1.0	0	1	1	1	1	1	1	1
50–64	2	8.3	91	1	1	1	16	16	16	16
65+	2	2.7	8	1	1	1	6	6	6	6
2. MULTIPLE DX										
0–19 Years	8	8.4	23	2	5	6	12	12	18	18
20–34	6	5.5	14	2	2	6	7	12	12	12
35–49	151	8.4	54	1	3	6	11	20	24	38
50–64	260	8.2	70	1	3	5	10	20	23	51
65+	122	8.7	58	1	3	7	12	19	22	34
TOTAL SINGLE DX	**6**	**4.4**	**31**	**1**	**1**	**1**	**6**	**16**	**16**	**16**
TOTAL MULTIPLE DX	**547**	**8.4**	**62**	**1**	**3**	**6**	**12**	**20**	**23**	**39**
TOTAL										
0–19 Years	9	7.9	22	2	4	6	12	12	18	18
20–34	6	5.5	14	2	2	6	7	12	12	12
35–49	152	8.4	54	1	3	6	11	20	24	38
50–64	262	8.2	70	1	3	5	10	20	23	51
65+	124	8.7	58	1	3	7	12	18	22	34
GRAND TOTAL	**553**	**8.3**	**61**	**1**	**3**	**6**	**12**	**19**	**23**	**39**

39.2: OTHER SHUNT/VASC BYPASS

Type of Patients	Observed Patients	Avg. Stay	Vari-ance	Percentiles						
				10th	25th	50th	75th	90th	95th	99th
1. SINGLE DX										
0–19 Years	8	3.7	5	2	2	3	4	8	8	8
20–34	5	2.5	1	2	2	2	3	4	5	5
35–49	22	2.5	2	1	2	2	3	5	5	6
50–64	59	2.8	7	1	1	2	3	5	7	17
65+	81	3.7	8	1	2	3	5	8	10	14
2. MULTIPLE DX										
0–19 Years	153	8.0	84	3	4	5	9	14	24	57
20–34	263	7.2	53	1	2	5	10	14	22	30
35–49	1,010	7.2	54	1	3	5	9	15	19	47
50–64	3,661	6.7	42	2	3	5	8	14	19	32
65+	7,606	7.2	42	2	3	5	9	14	19	31
TOTAL SINGLE DX	**175**	**3.2**	**7**	**1**	**2**	**2**	**4**	**7**	**9**	**14**
TOTAL MULTIPLE DX	**12,693**	**7.1**	**44**	**2**	**3**	**5**	**9**	**14**	**19**	**32**
TOTAL										
0–19 Years	161	7.9	81	3	4	5	9	13	22	57
20–34	268	7.1	52	1	2	5	10	14	22	30
35–49	1,032	7.1	54	1	3	5	9	15	19	45
50–64	3,720	6.7	42	1	3	5	8	14	19	32
65+	7,687	7.1	41	2	3	5	9	14	19	31
GRAND TOTAL	**12,868**	**7.0**	**44**	**2**	**3**	**5**	**9**	**14**	**19**	**32**

39.21: CAVAL-PA ANASTOMOSIS

Type of Patients	Observed Patients	Avg. Stay	Vari-ance	Percentiles						
				10th	25th	50th	75th	90th	95th	99th
1. SINGLE DX										
0–19 Years	2	7.7	<1	7	7	8	8	8	8	8
20–34	0									
35–49	0									
50–64	0									
65+	1	5.0	0	5	5	5	5	5	5	5
2. MULTIPLE DX										
0–19 Years	108	8.4	91	3	4	6	9	14	21	57
20–34	0									
35–49	1	8.0	0	8	8	8	8	8	8	8
50–64	1	7.0	0	7	7	7	7	7	7	7
65+	6	9.8	58	3	4	7	20	20	20	20
TOTAL SINGLE DX	**3**	**6.8**	**2**	**5**	**5**	**7**	**8**	**8**	**8**	**8**
TOTAL MULTIPLE DX	**116**	**8.5**	**89**	**3**	**4**	**6**	**9**	**14**	**21**	**57**
TOTAL										
0–19 Years	110	8.4	90	3	4	6	9	14	21	57
20–34	0									
35–49	1	8.0	0	8	8	8	8	8	8	8
50–64	1	7.0	0	7	7	7	7	7	7	7
65+	7	9.2	52	3	4	5	20	20	20	20
GRAND TOTAL	**119**	**8.4**	**88**	**3**	**4**	**6**	**9**	**14**	**21**	**57**

39.22: AORTA-SCL-CAROTID BYPASS

Type of Patients	Observed Patients	Avg. Stay	Vari-ance	Percentiles						
				10th	25th	50th	75th	90th	95th	99th
1. SINGLE DX										
0–19 Years	0									
20–34	0									
35–49	0									
50–64	2	2.0	0	2	2	2	2	2	2	2
65+	3	1.7	<1	1	1	2	2	2	2	2
2. MULTIPLE DX										
0–19 Years	0									
20–34	1	12.0	0	12	12	12	12	12	12	12
35–49	9	4.5	13	2	3	3	4	11	16	16
50–64	72	3.4	15	1	1	2	3	7	12	23
65+	117	4.2	20	1	1	3	5	10	14	25
TOTAL SINGLE DX	**5**	**1.8**	**<1**	**1**	**2**	**2**	**2**	**2**	**2**	**2**
TOTAL MULTIPLE DX	**199**	**3.9**	**18**	**1**	**1**	**3**	**4**	**9**	**14**	**23**
TOTAL										
0–19 Years	0									
20–34	1	12.0	0	12	12	12	12	12	12	12
35–49	9	4.5	13	2	3	3	4	11	16	16
50–64	74	3.4	15	1	1	2	3	7	12	23
65+	120	4.1	20	1	1	3	5	10	14	25
GRAND TOTAL	**204**	**3.9**	**18**	**1**	**1**	**3**	**4**	**9**	**14**	**23**

39.25: AORTA-ILIAC-FEMORAL BYP

Type of Patients	Observed Patients	Avg. Stay	Vari-ance	Percentiles						
				10th	25th	50th	75th	90th	95th	99th
1. SINGLE DX										
0–19 Years	0									
20–34	0									
35–49	1	3.0	0	3	3	3	3	3	3	3
50–64	10	6.3	21	1	2	6	7	12	17	17
65+	7	6.1	2	5	5	6	7	8	8	8
2. MULTIPLE DX										
0–19 Years	1	5.0	0	5	5	5	5	5	5	5
20–34	8	5.0	19	2	2	3	6	16	16	16
35–49	118	7.7	68	3	4	5	7	16	19	49
50–64	631	7.9	39	4	5	6	9	13	20	32
65+	911	8.9	56	4	5	7	10	15	21	35
TOTAL SINGLE DX	**18**	**6.0**	**11**	**2**	**5**	**6**	**7**	**8**	**12**	**17**
TOTAL MULTIPLE DX	**1,669**	**8.4**	**51**	**4**	**5**	**7**	**9**	**15**	**21**	**37**
TOTAL										
0–19 Years	1	5.0	0	5	5	5	5	5	5	5
20–34	8	5.0	19	2	2	3	6	16	16	16
35–49	119	7.7	67	3	4	5	7	14	19	49
50–64	641	7.9	39	4	5	6	8	13	20	32
65+	918	8.8	56	4	5	7	10	15	21	35
GRAND TOTAL	**1,687**	**8.4**	**51**	**4**	**5**	**7**	**9**	**15**	**21**	**37**

39.27: ARTERIOVENOSTOMY FOR RD

Type of Patients	Observed Patients	Avg. Stay	Vari-ance	Percentiles						
				10th	25th	50th	75th	90th	95th	99th
1. SINGLE DX										
0–19 Years	1	4.0	0	4	4	4	4	4	4	4
20–34	4	2.5	2	1	2	2	2	5	5	5
35–49	11	1.9	2	1	1	1	3	5	5	5
50–64	10	1.3	<1	1	1	1	1	3	4	4
65+	14	1.8	5	1	1	1	1	3	9	9
2. MULTIPLE DX										
0–19 Years	24	4.1	20	1	2	3	5	7	7	22
20–34	222	7.2	48	1	2	5	10	14	22	30
35–49	619	6.8	54	1	2	5	9	13	18	45
50–64	1,253	7.4	55	1	2	5	10	16	20	35
65+	2,023	7.8	59	1	2	6	11	16	21	39
TOTAL SINGLE DX	**40**	**1.8**	**2**	**1**	**1**	**1**	**2**	**4**	**5**	**9**
TOTAL MULTIPLE DX	**4,141**	**7.5**	**56**	**1**	**2**	**6**	**10**	**16**	**21**	**36**
TOTAL										
0–19 Years	25	4.1	19	1	2	3	5	6	7	22
20–34	226	7.1	47	1	2	5	10	14	22	30
35–49	630	6.7	54	1	2	5	9	13	18	38
50–64	1,263	7.3	55	1	2	5	10	16	20	35
65+	2,037	7.8	59	1	2	6	11	16	21	39
GRAND TOTAL	**4,181**	**7.4**	**56**	**1**	**2**	**5**	**10**	**16**	**21**	**36**

39.29: VASC SHUNT & BYPASS NEC

Type of Patients	Observed Patients	Avg. Stay	Vari-ance	Percentiles						
				10th	25th	50th	75th	90th	95th	99th
1. SINGLE DX										
0–19 Years	0									
20–34	1	3.0	0	3	3	3	3	3	3	3
35–49	10	3.0	1	2	2	3	3	5	6	6
50–64	37	2.4	2	1	1	2	3	5	5	5
65+	56	3.7	8	2	2	3	4	10	10	14
2. MULTIPLE DX										
0–19 Years	8	8.6	7	5	9	9	9	11	11	16
20–34	26	6.9	88	1	3	4	8	12	21	50
35–49	240	8.0	50	2	3	6	10	17	22	30
50–64	1,657	5.9	35	2	3	4	7	13	17	29
65+	4,489	6.6	29	2	3	5	8	13	17	27
TOTAL SINGLE DX	**104**	**3.2**	**6**	**1**	**2**	**3**	**3**	**6**	**10**	**14**
TOTAL MULTIPLE DX	**6,420**	**6.5**	**32**	**2**	**3**	**5**	**8**	**13**	**17**	**28**
TOTAL										
0–19 Years	8	8.6	7	5	9	9	9	11	11	16
20–34	27	6.8	86	1	3	4	8	12	21	50
35–49	250	7.7	49	2	3	6	10	17	22	30
50–64	1,694	5.9	34	2	3	4	7	13	17	29
65+	4,545	6.5	29	2	3	5	8	13	17	27
GRAND TOTAL	**6,524**	**6.4**	**31**	**2**	**3**	**5**	**8**	**13**	**17**	**28**

39.3: SUTURE OF VESSEL

Type of Patients	Observed Patients	Avg. Stay	Vari-ance	Percentiles						
				10th	25th	50th	75th	90th	95th	99th
1. SINGLE DX										
0–19 Years	6	1.8	<1	1	1	2	2	4	4	4
20–34	8	3.0	11	1	1	1	2	9	9	9
35–49	7	1.4	<1	1	1	1	2	3	3	3
50–64	5	1.0	0	1	1	1	1	1	1	1
65+	2	1.0	0	1	1	1	1	1	1	1
2. MULTIPLE DX										
0–19 Years	54	3.9	17	1	1	2	5	10	17	19
20–34	183	4.2	60	1	1	2	4	9	14	30
35–49	146	5.0	62	1	1	2	5	12	16	50
50–64	117	6.3	32	1	2	4	8	15	19	25
65+	139	5.4	27	1	2	3	7	13	16	25
TOTAL SINGLE DX	**28**	**1.8**	**4**	**1**	**1**	**1**	**2**	**3**	**9**	**9**
TOTAL MULTIPLE DX	**639**	**5.0**	**44**	**1**	**1**	**3**	**6**	**12**	**15**	**28**
TOTAL										
0–19 Years	60	3.7	16	1	1	2	4	9	12	17
20–34	191	4.1	58	1	1	2	4	9	14	24
35–49	153	4.9	60	1	1	2	5	12	16	50
50–64	122	6.1	32	1	2	4	8	13	19	25
65+	141	5.3	27	1	2	3	7	13	16	25
GRAND TOTAL	**667**	**4.9**	**43**	**1**	**1**	**3**	**6**	**12**	**15**	**28**

39.31: SUTURE OF ARTERY

Type of Patients	Observed Patients	Avg. Stay	Vari-ance	10th	25th	50th	75th	90th	95th	99th
1. SINGLE DX										
0–19 Years	4	1.9	1	1	1	2	2	4	4	4
20–34	7	3.2	12	1	1	2	2	9	9	9
35–49	5	1.2	<1	1	1	1	1	2	2	2
50–64	4	1.0	0	1	1	1	1	1	1	1
65+	1	1.0	0	1	1	1	1	1	1	1
2. MULTIPLE DX										
0–19 Years	46	3.9	17	1	1	3	4	10	17	19
20–34	136	4.4	76	1	1	2	5	9	13	30
35–49	103	4.8	54	1	1	3	5	12	16	37
50–64	85	6.8	36	1	3	5	9	15	22	25
65+	105	5.4	29	1	2	3	7	13	17	25
TOTAL SINGLE DX	**21**	**1.9**	**4**	**1**	**1**	**1**	**2**	**4**	**9**	**9**
TOTAL MULTIPLE DX	**475**	**5.1**	**47**	**1**	**1**	**3**	**6**	**12**	**16**	**28**
TOTAL										
0–19 Years	50	3.7	16	1	1	2	4	9	17	19
20–34	143	4.3	73	1	1	2	5	9	12	30
35–49	108	4.7	52	1	1	3	4	12	16	37
50–64	89	6.5	36	1	2	5	9	15	22	25
65+	106	5.4	29	1	2	3	7	13	17	25
GRAND TOTAL	**496**	**4.9**	**45**	**1**	**1**	**3**	**6**	**12**	**16**	**28**

39.32: SUTURE OF VEIN

Type of Patients	Observed Patients	Avg. Stay	Vari-ance	10th	25th	50th	75th	90th	95th	99th
1. SINGLE DX										
0–19 Years	2	1.5	<1	1	1	2	2	2	2	2
20–34	1	1.0	0	1	1	1	1	1	1	1
35–49	2	1.9	2	1	1	1	3	3	3	3
50–64	0									
65+	1	1.0	0	1	1	1	1	1	1	1
2. MULTIPLE DX										
0–19 Years	7	3.6	17	1	1	1	7	12	12	12
20–34	41	3.7	22	1	1	2	4	9	15	24
35–49	36	5.4	89	1	1	1	5	14	25	50
50–64	27	5.2	20	1	2	4	6	15	16	17
65+	22	6.0	25	2	2	3	10	13	15	16
TOTAL SINGLE DX	**6**	**1.5**	**<1**	**1**	**1**	**1**	**2**	**3**	**3**	**3**
TOTAL MULTIPLE DX	**133**	**4.8**	**40**	**1**	**1**	**3**	**5**	**13**	**15**	**35**
TOTAL										
0–19 Years	9	3.3	15	1	1	1	5	12	12	12
20–34	42	3.7	22	1	1	2	4	9	15	24
35–49	38	5.3	86	1	1	1	5	14	25	50
50–64	27	5.2	20	1	2	4	6	15	16	17
65+	23	5.8	25	1	2	3	10	13	15	16
GRAND TOTAL	**139**	**4.7**	**39**	**1**	**1**	**2**	**5**	**13**	**15**	**35**

39.4: VASCULAR PX REVISION

Type of Patients	Observed Patients	Avg. Stay	Vari-ance	10th	25th	50th	75th	90th	95th	99th
1. SINGLE DX										
0–19 Years	0									
20–34	1	1.0	0	1	1	1	1	1	1	1
35–49	4	3.5	9	1	2	2	4	9	9	9
50–64	9	2.6	6	1	1	1	4	5	8	8
65+	12	2.5	3	1	1	2	5	5	5	5
2. MULTIPLE DX										
0–19 Years	24	8.8	116	1	2	4	11	27	27	45
20–34	256	5.0	25	1	2	3	7	12	15	23
35–49	765	5.6	50	1	2	3	7	14	18	35
50–64	1,809	5.3	38	1	2	3	7	11	16	28
65+	2,959	5.4	34	1	2	3	7	12	16	28
TOTAL SINGLE DX	**26**	**2.6**	**4**	**1**	**1**	**2**	**4**	**5**	**8**	**9**
TOTAL MULTIPLE DX	**5,813**	**5.4**	**37**	**1**	**2**	**3**	**7**	**12**	**16**	**28**
TOTAL										
0–19 Years	24	8.8	116	1	2	4	11	27	27	45
20–34	257	5.0	25	1	1	3	7	12	15	23
35–49	769	5.6	50	1	2	3	7	14	18	35
50–64	1,818	5.3	37	1	2	3	7	11	16	28
65+	2,971	5.4	34	1	2	3	7	12	16	28
GRAND TOTAL	**5,839**	**5.4**	**37**	**1**	**2**	**3**	**7**	**12**	**16**	**28**

39.42: REV AV SHUNT FOR RD

Type of Patients	Observed Patients	Avg. Stay	Vari-ance	10th	25th	50th	75th	90th	95th	99th
1. SINGLE DX										
0–19 Years	0									
20–34	0									
35–49	0									
50–64	1	1.0	0	1	1	1	1	1	1	1
65+	2	1.0	0	1	1	1	1	1	1	1
2. MULTIPLE DX										
0–19 Years	6	15.8	144	2	3	22	27	27	27	27
20–34	110	4.4	17	1	1	3	7	11	13	15
35–49	308	5.0	59	1	1	3	6	11	15	35
50–64	574	4.3	29	1	1	3	5	9	13	29
65+	935	4.6	29	1	1	2	6	11	16	26
TOTAL SINGLE DX	**3**	**1.0**	**0**	**1**	**1**	**1**	**1**	**1**	**1**	**1**
TOTAL MULTIPLE DX	**1,933**	**4.6**	**34**	**1**	**1**	**3**	**5**	**10**	**15**	**28**
TOTAL										
0–19 Years	6	15.8	144	2	3	22	27	27	27	27
20–34	110	4.4	17	1	1	3	7	11	13	15
35–49	308	5.0	59	1	1	3	6	11	15	35
50–64	575	4.3	29	1	1	3	5	9	13	29
65+	937	4.6	29	1	1	2	6	11	16	26
GRAND TOTAL	**1,936**	**4.6**	**34**	**1**	**1**	**3**	**5**	**10**	**15**	**28**

39.43: RMVL AV SHUNT FOR RD

Type of Patients	Observed Patients	Avg. Stay	Variance	Percentiles 10th	25th	50th	75th	90th	95th	99th
1. SINGLE DX										
0–19 Years	0									
20–34	0									
35–49	1	4.0	0	4	4	4	4	4	4	4
50–64	0									
65+	0									
2. MULTIPLE DX										
0–19 Years	1	1.0	0	1	1	1	1	1	1	1
20–34	38	6.2	30	2	3	6	7	11	16	33
35–49	81	7.6	66	1	3	5	9	14	27	44
50–64	116	7.4	33	2	3	6	9	13	20	31
65+	130	6.8	37	1	2	5	9	15	21	30
TOTAL SINGLE DX	**1**	**4.0**	**0**	**4**	**4**	**4**	**4**	**4**	**4**	**4**
TOTAL MULTIPLE DX	**366**	**7.1**	**41**	**1**	**3**	**6**	**9**	**14**	**20**	**31**
TOTAL										
0–19 Years	1	1.0	0	1	1	1	1	1	1	1
20–34	38	6.2	30	2	3	6	7	11	16	33
35–49	82	7.6	65	1	3	5	9	14	27	44
50–64	116	7.4	33	2	3	6	9	13	20	31
65+	130	6.8	37	1	2	5	9	15	21	30
GRAND TOTAL	**367**	**7.1**	**41**	**1**	**3**	**6**	**9**	**14**	**20**	**31**

39.49: VASCULAR PX REVISION NEC

Type of Patients	Observed Patients	Avg. Stay	Variance	Percentiles 10th	25th	50th	75th	90th	95th	99th
1. SINGLE DX										
0–19 Years	0									
20–34	1	1.0	0	1	1	1	1	1	1	1
35–49	3	3.3	11	1	2	2	2	9	9	9
50–64	7	3.0	6	1	1	2	5	8	8	8
65+	10	2.7	3	1	1	2	5	5	5	5
2. MULTIPLE DX										
0–19 Years	17	6.3	82	1	2	4	6	11	15	45
20–34	108	5.3	32	1	1	3	7	14	21	23
35–49	375	5.7	39	1	2	3	7	14	19	33
50–64	1,115	5.6	41	1	2	4	7	12	16	27
65+	1,882	5.7	36	1	2	4	7	12	17	28
TOTAL SINGLE DX	**21**	**2.8**	**5**	**1**	**1**	**2**	**5**	**5**	**8**	**9**
TOTAL MULTIPLE DX	**3,497**	**5.7**	**38**	**1**	**2**	**4**	**7**	**12**	**17**	**28**
TOTAL										
0–19 Years	17	6.3	82	1	2	4	6	11	15	45
20–34	109	5.3	31	1	1	3	7	13	21	23
35–49	378	5.7	39	1	2	3	7	14	19	33
50–64	1,122	5.6	41	1	2	4	7	12	16	27
65+	1,892	5.7	36	1	2	4	7	12	17	28
GRAND TOTAL	**3,518**	**5.6**	**38**	**1**	**2**	**4**	**7**	**12**	**17**	**28**

39.5: OTHER VESSEL REPAIR

Type of Patients	Observed Patients	Avg. Stay	Variance	Percentiles 10th	25th	50th	75th	90th	95th	99th
1. SINGLE DX										
0–19 Years	23	2.0	3	1	1	1	2	5	6	7
20–34	41	5.1	24	1	2	3	6	15	17	19
35–49	52	4.4	14	1	2	3	6	8	15	18
50–64	81	3.3	13	1	1	1	4	7	11	17
65+	107	1.6	4	1	1	1	1	3	5	14
2. MULTIPLE DX										
0–19 Years	186	4.4	73	1	1	2	5	8	10	66
20–34	318	7.0	58	1	2	5	9	17	22	47
35–49	971	7.6	75	1	2	5	10	17	23	44
50–64	2,466	5.5	42	1	1	3	7	13	17	31
65+	5,379	5.0	41	1	1	3	7	12	16	28
TOTAL SINGLE DX	**304**	**2.9**	**11**	**1**	**1**	**1**	**4**	**6**	**11**	**17**
TOTAL MULTIPLE DX	**9,320**	**5.4**	**47**	**1**	**1**	**3**	**7**	**13**	**17**	**31**
TOTAL										
0–19 Years	209	4.2	67	1	1	2	5	7	10	66
20–34	359	6.8	55	1	2	4	8	17	22	47
35–49	1,023	7.4	72	1	2	5	10	17	22	44
50–64	2,547	5.4	41	1	1	3	7	13	17	31
65+	5,486	4.9	40	1	1	2	6	12	16	28
GRAND TOTAL	**9,624**	**5.3**	**46**	**1**	**1**	**3**	**7**	**13**	**17**	**31**

39.50: PTA/ATHERECT OTH VESSEL

Type of Patients	Observed Patients	Avg. Stay	Variance	Percentiles 10th	25th	50th	75th	90th	95th	99th
1. SINGLE DX										
0–19 Years	20	1.8	3	1	1	1	1	5	6	7
20–34	19	3.0	3	1	2	3	5	6	6	6
35–49	17	2.5	4	1	1	1	3	6	8	8
50–64	47	1.9	3	1	1	1	2	4	7	7
65+	94	1.2	<1	1	1	1	1	1	4	5
2. MULTIPLE DX										
0–19 Years	125	4.1	99	1	1	1	4	6	9	71
20–34	181	5.5	28	1	2	4	7	12	17	27
35–49	629	5.6	50	1	2	3	7	13	16	34
50–64	1,809	4.3	27	1	1	2	6	10	14	24
65+	4,445	4.2	35	1	1	2	5	10	14	25
TOTAL SINGLE DX	**197**	**1.7**	**2**	**1**	**1**	**1**	**1**	**4**	**5**	**7**
TOTAL MULTIPLE DX	**7,189**	**4.4**	**36**	**1**	**1**	**2**	**6**	**10**	**14**	**27**
TOTAL										
0–19 Years	145	3.8	88	1	1	1	4	6	9	71
20–34	200	5.3	26	1	2	4	7	12	17	27
35–49	646	5.5	49	1	1	3	7	12	16	34
50–64	1,856	4.2	27	1	1	2	5	10	14	24
65+	4,539	4.2	34	1	1	2	5	10	14	25
GRAND TOTAL	**7,386**	**4.3**	**35**	**1**	**1**	**2**	**5**	**10**	**14**	**27**

39.51: CLIPPING OF ANEURYSM

Type of Patients	Observed Patients	Avg. Stay	Vari-ance	Percentiles						
				10th	25th	50th	75th	90th	95th	99th
1. SINGLE DX										
0–19 Years	1	6.0	0	6	6	6	6	6	6	6
20–34	11	10.9	32	3	6	11	17	17	19	19
35–49	25	6.1	16	3	4	5	6	15	17	18
50–64	27	6.2	18	3	3	4	9	13	15	18
65+	4	9.9	22	4	5	11	14	14	14	14
2. MULTIPLE DX										
0–19 Years	4	7.8	5	5	5	8	9	10	10	10
20–34	37	12.9	71	3	4	13	18	28	28	33
35–49	219	13.3	77	4	7	12	17	23	29	43
50–64	320	11.6	78	3	5	9	16	24	29	37
65+	117	12.9	83	4	6	10	17	27	30	46
TOTAL SINGLE DX	**68**	**7.1**	**22**	**3**	**3**	**5**	**10**	**15**	**17**	**19**
TOTAL MULTIPLE DX	**697**	**12.4**	**79**	**3**	**5**	**10**	**16**	**24**	**29**	**43**
TOTAL										
0–19 Years	5	7.5	4	5	6	8	9	10	10	10
20–34	48	12.4	62	3	6	12	17	22	28	33
35–49	244	12.5	76	4	6	11	16	22	29	43
50–64	347	11.2	76	3	4	9	16	23	27	37
65+	121	12.8	82	4	6	10	17	26	29	46
GRAND TOTAL	**765**	**12.0**	**76**	**3**	**5**	**10**	**16**	**23**	**29**	**43**

39.52: ANEURYSM REPAIR NEC

Type of Patients	Observed Patients	Avg. Stay	Vari-ance	Percentiles						
				10th	25th	50th	75th	90th	95th	99th
1. SINGLE DX										
0–19 Years	1	2.0	0	2	2	2	2	2	2	2
20–34	1	1.0	0	1	1	1	1	1	1	1
35–49	2	7.6	47	3	3	3	14	14	14	14
50–64	2	10.4	32	7	7	7	17	17	17	17
65+	4	2.9	5	1	1	2	6	6	6	6
2. MULTIPLE DX										
0–19 Years	1	9.0	0	9	9	9	9	9	9	9
20–34	10	6.9	43	2	2	4	11	19	20	20
35–49	51	9.1	247	1	2	4	6	18	65	65
50–64	197	6.6	41	2	3	5	8	12	16	32
65+	556	8.4	50	2	4	6	10	17	21	34
TOTAL SINGLE DX	**10**	**5.3**	**26**	**1**	**2**	**3**	**7**	**14**	**17**	**17**
TOTAL MULTIPLE DX	**815**	**8.0**	**59**	**2**	**4**	**6**	**10**	**16**	**20**	**41**
TOTAL										
0–19 Years	2	5.4	22	2	2	2	9	9	9	9
20–34	11	6.3	42	2	2	3	6	19	20	20
35–49	53	9.1	240	2	2	4	6	18	65	65
50–64	199	6.7	41	2	3	6	8	13	16	32
65+	560	8.4	50	2	4	6	10	17	21	34
GRAND TOTAL	**825**	**8.0**	**59**	**2**	**4**	**6**	**10**	**16**	**20**	**41**

39.53: AV FISTULA REPAIR

Type of Patients	Observed Patients	Avg. Stay	Vari-ance	Percentiles						
				10th	25th	50th	75th	90th	95th	99th
1. SINGLE DX										
0–19 Years	0									
20–34	3	2.9	1	1	3	3	4	4	4	4
35–49	4	2.0	<1	1	2	2	2	3	3	3
50–64	4	3.4	17	1	1	2	2	10	10	10
65+	1	3.0	0	3	3	3	3	3	3	3
2. MULTIPLE DX										
0–19 Years	2	2.3	3	1	1	1	4	4	4	4
20–34	12	3.0	4	1	1	3	4	6	6	6
35–49	18	4.0	22	1	1	2	5	11	17	19
50–64	50	3.6	7	1	1	3	5	8	8	11
65+	76	5.6	40	1	1	3	6	15	22	27
TOTAL SINGLE DX	**12**	**2.6**	**4**	**1**	**1**	**2**	**3**	**4**	**10**	**10**
TOTAL MULTIPLE DX	**158**	**4.6**	**26**	**1**	**1**	**3**	**6**	**10**	**16**	**27**
TOTAL										
0–19 Years	2	2.3	3	1	1	1	4	4	4	4
20–34	15	2.9	3	1	1	3	4	6	6	6
35–49	22	3.7	19	1	1	2	5	8	17	19
50–64	54	3.6	7	1	1	3	5	8	8	11
65+	77	5.5	39	1	1	3	6	15	22	27
GRAND TOTAL	**170**	**4.4**	**24**	**1**	**1**	**3**	**5**	**10**	**16**	**25**

39.56: REP VESS W TISS PATCH

Type of Patients	Observed Patients	Avg. Stay	Vari-ance	Percentiles						
				10th	25th	50th	75th	90th	95th	99th
1. SINGLE DX										
0–19 Years	0									
20–34	3	2.3	<1	2	2	2	3	3	3	3
35–49	1	3.0	0	3	3	3	3	3	3	3
50–64	1	1.0	0	1	1	1	1	1	1	1
65+	3	2.8	<1	2	3	3	3	3	3	3
2. MULTIPLE DX										
0–19 Years	27	4.7	11	2	3	4	6	8	13	21
20–34	44	7.3	65	2	3	5	7	10	20	47
35–49	25	8.0	48	1	3	6	12	18	24	27
50–64	28	11.2	159	2	3	6	13	35	44	48
65+	51	6.4	40	1	2	4	9	15	15	31
TOTAL SINGLE DX	**8**	**2.4**	**<1**	**1**	**2**	**2**	**3**	**3**	**3**	**3**
TOTAL MULTIPLE DX	**175**	**6.9**	**54**	**2**	**3**	**4**	**8**	**15**	**21**	**44**
TOTAL										
0–19 Years	27	4.7	11	2	3	4	6	8	13	21
20–34	47	6.8	61	2	3	5	7	10	20	47
35–49	26	7.8	47	1	3	5	12	18	24	27
50–64	29	10.6	156	2	2	6	13	28	44	48
65+	54	6.3	39	1	2	4	8	15	15	31
GRAND TOTAL	**183**	**6.7**	**53**	**2**	**3**	**4**	**8**	**14**	**20**	**44**

39.57: REP VESS W SYNTH PATCH

Type of Patients	Observed Patients	Avg. Stay	Vari-ance	Percentiles						
				10th	25th	50th	75th	90th	95th	99th
1. SINGLE DX										
0–19 Years	0									
20–34	1	1.0	0	1	1	1	1	1	1	1
35–49	0									
50–64	0									
65+	0									
2. MULTIPLE DX										
0–19 Years	9	7.2	17	4	5	6	7	14	17	17
20–34	8	17.4	73	7	13	17	24	31	31	31
35–49	12	5.5	23	1	1	4	8	9	21	21
50–64	40	6.7	45	2	3	5	7	14	16	38
65+	82	6.2	31	1	2	4	8	14	18	24
TOTAL SINGLE DX	**1**	**1.0**	**0**	**1**	**1**	**1**	**1**	**1**	**1**	**1**
TOTAL MULTIPLE DX	**151**	**6.7**	**38**	**1**	**2**	**5**	**8**	**15**	**19**	**31**
TOTAL										
0–19 Years	9	7.2	17	4	5	6	7	14	17	17
20–34	9	15.6	93	1	8	13	24	31	31	31
35–49	12	5.5	23	1	1	4	8	9	21	21
50–64	40	6.7	45	2	3	5	7	14	16	38
65+	82	6.2	31	1	2	4	8	14	18	24
GRAND TOTAL	**152**	**6.7**	**38**	**1**	**2**	**5**	**8**	**15**	**19**	**31**

39.59: REPAIR OF VESSEL NEC

Type of Patients	Observed Patients	Avg. Stay	Vari-ance	Percentiles						
				10th	25th	50th	75th	90th	95th	99th
1. SINGLE DX										
0–19 Years	1	3.0	0	3	3	3	3	3	3	3
20–34	2	3.0	0	3	3	3	3	3	3	3
35–49	2	2.0	0	2	2	2	2	2	2	2
50–64	0									
65+	1	1.0	0	1	1	1	1	1	1	1
2. MULTIPLE DX										
0–19 Years	14	5.4	8	1	4	5	7	10	10	10
20–34	23	7.2	215	1	1	3	6	62	>99	>99
35–49	14	4.0	25	1	1	2	6	9	19	19
50–64	19	5.3	31	1	2	4	8	9	22	22
65+	40	4.5	29	1	1	2	7	11	15	25
TOTAL SINGLE DX	**6**	**2.1**	**<1**	**1**	**1**	**2**	**3**	**3**	**3**	**3**
TOTAL MULTIPLE DX	**110**	**5.1**	**50**	**1**	**1**	**3**	**7**	**10**	**19**	**62**
TOTAL										
0–19 Years	15	5.3	8	1	4	5	7	10	10	10
20–34	25	6.9	200	1	1	3	6	62	>99	>99
35–49	16	3.8	23	1	1	2	3	9	19	19
50–64	19	5.3	31	1	2	4	8	9	22	22
65+	41	4.4	28	1	1	2	6	11	15	25
GRAND TOTAL	**116**	**5.0**	**48**	**1**	**1**	**3**	**6**	**10**	**15**	**62**

39.6: OPEN HEART AUXILIARY PX

Type of Patients	Observed Patients	Avg. Stay	Vari-ance	Percentiles						
				10th	25th	50th	75th	90th	95th	99th
1. SINGLE DX										
0–19 Years	0									
20–34	0									
35–49	0									
50–64	0									
65+	0									
2. MULTIPLE DX										
0–19 Years	6	32.8	127	14	24	39	39	41	41	41
20–34	1	10.0	0	10	10	10	10	10	10	10
35–49	2	6.0	2	5	5	7	7	7	7	7
50–64	2	7.7	1	7	7	7	9	9	9	9
65+	7	10.4	84	4	5	6	19	28	28	28
TOTAL SINGLE DX	**0**									
TOTAL MULTIPLE DX	**18**	**22.8**	**232**	**5**	**7**	**19**	**39**	**41**	**41**	**41**
TOTAL										
0–19 Years	6	32.8	127	14	24	39	39	41	41	41
20–34	1	10.0	0	10	10	10	10	10	10	10
35–49	2	6.0	2	5	5	7	7	7	7	7
50–64	2	7.7	1	7	7	7	9	9	9	9
65+	7	10.4	84	4	5	6	19	28	28	28
GRAND TOTAL	**18**	**22.8**	**232**	**5**	**7**	**19**	**39**	**41**	**41**	**41**

39.7: ENDOVASCULAR VESSEL REP

Type of Patients	Observed Patients	Avg. Stay	Vari-ance	Percentiles						
				10th	25th	50th	75th	90th	95th	99th
1. SINGLE DX										
0–19 Years	15	1.1	<1	1	1	1	1	2	2	2
20–34	34	1.6	<1	1	1	1	2	2	3	5
35–49	46	1.7	2	1	1	1	2	3	4	11
50–64	43	1.7	2	1	1	1	2	3	4	7
65+	44	1.7	2	1	1	1	2	2	3	10
2. MULTIPLE DX										
0–19 Years	50	3.5	11	1	1	2	6	8	9	20
20–34	58	5.5	90	1	2	3	7	12	12	71
35–49	131	5.6	36	1	1	3	8	16	20	24
50–64	412	5.0	38	1	1	2	6	12	17	29
65+	1,410	3.9	20	1	2	2	5	8	11	22
TOTAL SINGLE DX	**182**	**1.6**	**2**	**1**	**1**	**1**	**2**	**2**	**3**	**8**
TOTAL MULTIPLE DX	**2,061**	**4.2**	**26**	**1**	**1**	**2**	**5**	**9**	**13**	**24**
TOTAL										
0–19 Years	65	3.0	10	1	1	2	3	7	9	12
20–34	92	4.3	65	1	1	2	4	9	12	47
35–49	177	4.5	30	1	1	2	5	14	18	22
50–64	455	4.7	36	1	1	2	6	12	16	29
65+	1,454	3.8	20	1	2	2	4	8	11	21
GRAND TOTAL	**2,243**	**4.0**	**25**	**1**	**1**	**2**	**5**	**9**	**13**	**23**

39.71: ENDOVASCULAR GRAFT-AAA

Type of Patients	Observed Patients	Avg. Stay	Vari-ance	10th	25th	50th	75th	90th	95th	99th
1. SINGLE DX										
0–19 Years	1	1.0	0	1	1	1	1	1	1	1
20–34	1	1.0	0	1	1	1	1	1	1	1
35–49	0									
50–64	1	7.0	0	7	7	7	7	7	7	7
65+	22	1.6	<1	1	1	2	2	2	2	3
2. MULTIPLE DX										
0–19 Years	1	1.0	0	1	1	1	1	1	1	1
20–34	1	71.0	0	71	71	71	71	71	71	71
35–49	5	6.3	15	2	3	3	10	10	10	10
50–64	130	3.7	24	1	1	2	5	8	10	17
65+	1,149	3.6	19	1	2	2	4	8	10	21
TOTAL SINGLE DX	**25**	**1.7**	**1**	**1**	**1**	**2**	**2**	**2**	**3**	**7**
TOTAL MULTIPLE DX	**1,286**	**3.7**	**21**	**1**	**2**	**2**	**4**	**8**	**10**	**21**
TOTAL										
0–19 Years	2	1.0	0	1	1	1	1	1	1	1
20–34	2	35.4	>999	1	1	1	71	71	71	71
35–49	5	6.3	15	2	3	3	10	10	10	10
50–64	131	3.8	24	1	1	2	5	8	10	17
65+	1,171	3.6	19	1	2	2	4	8	9	21
GRAND TOTAL	**1,311**	**3.7**	**21**	**1**	**2**	**2**	**4**	**8**	**10**	**21**

39.72: ENDOV REP HN VESSEL

Type of Patients	Observed Patients	Avg. Stay	Vari-ance	10th	25th	50th	75th	90th	95th	99th
1. SINGLE DX										
0–19 Years	8	1.2	<1	1	1	1	1	2	2	2
20–34	30	1.7	<1	1	1	2	2	3	3	5
35–49	37	1.8	3	1	1	1	2	3	5	11
50–64	38	1.6	1	1	1	1	2	3	3	7
65+	13	1.5	<1	1	1	1	2	3	4	4
2. MULTIPLE DX										
0–19 Years	27	3.1	6	1	2	2	4	7	8	10
20–34	36	2.9	7	1	1	2	3	7	8	12
35–49	85	5.4	39	1	1	2	8	17	20	24
50–64	196	5.3	43	1	1	2	7	13	18	36
65+	122	4.9	25	1	1	2	7	12	15	23
TOTAL SINGLE DX	**126**	**1.6**	**2**	**1**	**1**	**1**	**2**	**3**	**4**	**8**
TOTAL MULTIPLE DX	**466**	**4.9**	**33**	**1**	**1**	**2**	**7**	**13**	**17**	**25**
TOTAL										
0–19 Years	35	2.7	5	1	1	2	2	7	7	10
20–34	66	2.4	5	1	1	2	2	5	7	12
35–49	122	4.3	30	1	1	2	4	14	18	24
50–64	234	4.7	38	1	1	2	6	13	17	27
65+	135	4.5	23	1	1	2	6	12	15	23
GRAND TOTAL	**592**	**4.2**	**28**	**1**	**1**	**2**	**5**	**12**	**16**	**24**

39.79: ENDOV REP ANEURYSM NEC

Type of Patients	Observed Patients	Avg. Stay	Vari-ance	10th	25th	50th	75th	90th	95th	99th
1. SINGLE DX										
0–19 Years	6	1.0	0	1	1	1	1	1	1	1
20–34	3	1.0	0	1	1	1	1	1	1	1
35–49	9	1.4	<1	1	1	1	2	2	2	2
50–64	4	1.2	<1	1	1	1	1	2	2	2
65+	9	2.0	6	1	1	1	2	2	10	10
2. MULTIPLE DX										
0–19 Years	22	3.8	15	1	1	2	6	8	12	20
20–34	21	7.8	74	1	3	6	9	12	19	47
35–49	41	5.8	33	1	1	4	8	15	18	21
50–64	86	6.5	46	1	2	4	8	15	23	30
65+	139	5.2	27	1	2	3	8	13	16	24
TOTAL SINGLE DX	**31**	**1.5**	**3**	**1**	**1**	**1**	**1**	**2**	**2**	**10**
TOTAL MULTIPLE DX	**309**	**5.6**	**34**	**1**	**2**	**3**	**8**	**13**	**17**	**24**
TOTAL										
0–19 Years	28	3.4	14	1	1	2	6	8	12	20
20–34	24	7.1	70	1	2	5	9	12	19	47
35–49	50	4.9	30	1	1	2	7	13	18	21
50–64	90	6.3	45	1	2	4	8	15	23	30
65+	148	5.0	26	1	1	2	8	12	16	24
GRAND TOTAL	**340**	**5.2**	**32**	**1**	**1**	**3**	**8**	**13**	**17**	**24**

39.8: VASCULAR BODY OPERATIONS

Type of Patients	Observed Patients	Avg. Stay	Vari-ance	10th	25th	50th	75th	90th	95th	99th
1. SINGLE DX										
0–19 Years	0									
20–34	2	1.4	<1	1	1	1	2	2	2	2
35–49	1	1.0	0	1	1	1	1	1	1	1
50–64	4	3.2	<1	2	2	3	4	4	4	4
65+	2	2.0	2	1	1	1	3	3	3	3
2. MULTIPLE DX										
0–19 Years	0									
20–34	2	2.5	<1	2	2	2	3	3	3	3
35–49	11	2.9	14	1	1	2	2	4	14	14
50–64	22	6.3	39	1	2	3	15	15	16	20
65+	28	2.5	4	1	1	2	3	4	6	11
TOTAL SINGLE DX	**9**	**2.1**	**1**	**1**	**1**	**2**	**3**	**4**	**4**	**4**
TOTAL MULTIPLE DX	**63**	**4.0**	**21**	**1**	**1**	**2**	**4**	**15**	**15**	**20**
TOTAL										
0–19 Years	0									
20–34	4	1.9	<1	1	1	2	2	3	3	3
35–49	12	2.7	13	1	1	2	2	4	14	14
50–64	26	5.9	35	1	2	3	7	15	16	20
65+	30	2.5	4	1	1	2	3	4	6	11
GRAND TOTAL	**72**	**3.8**	**19**	**1**	**1**	**2**	**4**	**14**	**15**	**20**

39.9: OTHER VESSEL OPERATIONS

Type of Patients	Observed Patients	Avg. Stay	Vari-ance	Percentiles						
				10th	25th	50th	75th	90th	95th	99th
1. SINGLE DX										
0–19 Years	8	1.2	<1	1	1	1	1	1	3	3
20–34	26	1.9	4	1	1	1	2	4	8	8
35–49	28	1.9	3	1	1	1	2	3	4	8
50–64	33	1.8	2	1	1	1	2	4	6	7
65+	13	1.5	<1	1	1	1	2	2	4	4
2. MULTIPLE DX										
0–19 Years	228	4.7	26	1	2	3	6	9	13	25
20–34	1,581	3.9	16	1	2	3	5	8	11	19
35–49	4,337	3.9	19	1	1	3	5	8	11	23
50–64	7,759	4.1	17	1	2	3	5	8	11	21
65+	11,734	4.8	18	1	2	4	6	10	13	21
TOTAL SINGLE DX	**108**	**1.8**	**2**	**1**	**1**	**1**	**2**	**3**	**4**	**8**
TOTAL MULTIPLE DX	**25,639**	**4.4**	**18**	**1**	**2**	**3**	**5**	**9**	**12**	**21**
TOTAL										
0–19 Years	236	4.6	26	1	2	3	6	9	13	25
20–34	1,607	3.8	15	1	2	3	5	8	11	19
35–49	4,365	3.9	19	1	1	3	5	8	11	23
50–64	7,792	4.1	17	1	2	3	5	8	11	21
65+	11,747	4.8	18	1	2	4	6	10	13	21
GRAND TOTAL	**25,747**	**4.4**	**18**	**1**	**2**	**3**	**5**	**9**	**12**	**21**

39.90: NON-DRUG NON-COR STENT

Type of Patients	Observed Patients	Avg. Stay	Vari-ance	Percentiles						
				10th	25th	50th	75th	90th	95th	99th
1. SINGLE DX										
0–19 Years	1	1.0	0	1	1	1	1	1	1	1
20–34	0									
35–49	1	2.0	0	2	2	2	2	2	2	2
50–64	3	1.4	<1	1	1	1	2	2	2	2
65+	5	1.5	1	1	1	1	1	4	4	4
2. MULTIPLE DX										
0–19 Years	9	7.8	167	1	1	2	6	38	38	38
20–34	4	2.8	7	1	1	1	4	7	7	7
35–49	7	4.4	31	1	1	3	4	17	17	17
50–64	35	4.1	31	1	1	2	3	12	20	22
65+	60	3.1	11	1	1	2	4	7	11	18
TOTAL SINGLE DX	**10**	**1.5**	**<1**	**1**	**1**	**1**	**2**	**2**	**4**	**4**
TOTAL MULTIPLE DX	**115**	**3.8**	**33**	**1**	**1**	**2**	**4**	**9**	**12**	**38**
TOTAL										
0–19 Years	10	7.5	160	1	1	2	6	38	38	38
20–34	4	2.8	7	1	1	1	4	7	7	7
35–49	8	3.6	21	1	2	2	3	4	17	17
50–64	38	3.8	29	1	1	2	3	11	18	22
65+	65	3.0	10	1	1	2	4	7	11	18
GRAND TOTAL	**125**	**3.7**	**30**	**1**	**1**	**2**	**4**	**8**	**12**	**38**

39.93: INSERT VESS-VESS CANNULA

Type of Patients	Observed Patients	Avg. Stay	Vari-ance	Percentiles						
				10th	25th	50th	75th	90th	95th	99th
1. SINGLE DX										
0–19 Years	1	1.0	0	1	1	1	1	1	1	1
20–34	1	8.0	0	8	8	8	8	8	8	8
35–49	3	2.1	<1	1	1	2	3	3	3	3
50–64	2	1.5	<1	1	1	2	2	2	2	2
65+	2	1.6	<1	1	1	2	2	2	2	2
2. MULTIPLE DX										
0–19 Years	9	7.2	60	1	2	2	11	23	23	23
20–34	20	5.8	10	2	3	6	8	9	13	13
35–49	58	6.7	29	1	2	5	10	14	17	23
50–64	126	8.6	58	1	3	6	12	20	26	32
65+	179	7.4	31	1	4	6	10	13	17	29
TOTAL SINGLE DX	**9**	**3.1**	**8**	**1**	**1**	**2**	**3**	**8**	**8**	**8**
TOTAL MULTIPLE DX	**392**	**7.6**	**39**	**1**	**3**	**6**	**10**	**15**	**21**	**26**
TOTAL										
0–19 Years	10	6.3	56	1	1	2	11	15	23	23
20–34	21	6.0	9	2	3	6	8	9	10	13
35–49	61	6.6	29	1	2	5	10	14	17	23
50–64	128	8.5	58	1	3	6	12	20	26	32
65+	181	7.3	31	1	3	6	10	13	17	29
GRAND TOTAL	**401**	**7.5**	**38**	**1**	**3**	**6**	**10**	**15**	**21**	**26**

39.95: HEMODIALYSIS

Type of Patients	Observed Patients	Avg. Stay	Vari-ance	Percentiles						
				10th	25th	50th	75th	90th	95th	99th
1. SINGLE DX										
0–19 Years	0									
20–34	7	1.9	2	1	1	1	4	4	4	4
35–49	11	2.0	6	1	1	1	2	8	8	8
50–64	18	1.9	2	1	1	1	2	4	7	7
65+	3	1.0	0	1	1	1	1	1	1	1
2. MULTIPLE DX										
0–19 Years	181	4.4	16	1	2	3	6	9	11	25
20–34	1,504	3.8	15	1	2	3	5	8	11	19
35–49	4,195	3.9	19	1	1	3	5	8	10	23
50–64	7,516	4.1	16	1	2	3	5	8	11	19
65+	11,387	4.8	18	1	2	4	6	9	13	21
TOTAL SINGLE DX	**39**	**1.9**	**3**	**1**	**1**	**1**	**2**	**4**	**7**	**8**
TOTAL MULTIPLE DX	**24,783**	**4.4**	**17**	**1**	**2**	**3**	**5**	**9**	**12**	**21**
TOTAL										
0–19 Years	181	4.4	16	1	2	3	6	9	11	25
20–34	1,511	3.8	15	1	2	3	5	8	11	19
35–49	4,206	3.9	19	1	1	3	5	8	10	23
50–64	7,534	4.1	16	1	2	3	5	8	11	19
65+	11,390	4.8	18	1	2	4	6	9	13	21
GRAND TOTAL	**24,822**	**4.4**	**17**	**1**	**2**	**3**	**5**	**9**	**12**	**21**

39.98: HEMORRHAGE CONTROL NOS

Type of Patients	Observed Patients	Avg. Stay	Vari-ance	10th	25th	50th	75th	90th	95th	99th
1. SINGLE DX										
0–19 Years	4	1.3	<1	1	1	1	1	3	3	3
20–34	14	1.2	<1	1	1	1	1	2	2	2
35–49	10	1.7	<1	1	1	2	2	2	3	3
50–64	6	1.7	<1	1	1	1	2	4	4	4
65+	3	1.8	<1	1	2	2	2	2	2	2
2. MULTIPLE DX										
0–19 Years	17	3.8	15	1	1	2	4	9	9	17
20–34	46	4.7	29	1	1	2	4	15	15	25
35–49	65	3.0	10	1	1	2	4	7	9	16
50–64	65	4.4	35	1	1	2	4	11	14	36
65+	78	5.5	34	1	2	4	7	12	17	30
TOTAL SINGLE DX	**37**	**1.5**	**<1**	**1**	**1**	**1**	**2**	**2**	**3**	**4**
TOTAL MULTIPLE DX	**271**	**4.4**	**27**	**1**	**1**	**2**	**5**	**11**	**15**	**26**
TOTAL										
0–19 Years	21	3.3	13	1	1	2	4	9	9	17
20–34	60	3.9	25	1	1	2	3	14	15	25
35–49	75	2.8	9	1	1	2	3	7	8	16
50–64	71	4.1	31	1	1	2	4	11	14	36
65+	81	5.4	33	1	2	3	7	12	17	30
GRAND TOTAL	**308**	**4.1**	**24**	**1**	**1**	**2**	**4**	**9**	**15**	**26**

40.0: INC LYMPHATIC STRUCTURE

Type of Patients	Observed Patients	Avg. Stay	Vari-ance	10th	25th	50th	75th	90th	95th	99th
1. SINGLE DX										
0–19 Years	12	3.5	2	2	3	3	4	6	6	7
20–34	0									
35–49	0									
50–64	0									
65+	0									
2. MULTIPLE DX										
0–19 Years	28	4.8	9	2	2	4	7	8	13	14
20–34	7	3.7	2	2	3	4	4	4	7	7
35–49	7	5.2	12	1	2	5	6	12	12	12
50–64	9	5.5	7	1	3	6	7	9	9	9
65+	8	4.5	10	1	2	5	5	8	12	12
TOTAL SINGLE DX	**12**	**3.5**	**2**	**2**	**3**	**3**	**4**	**6**	**6**	**7**
TOTAL MULTIPLE DX	**59**	**4.8**	**9**	**2**	**2**	**4**	**7**	**8**	**12**	**14**
TOTAL										
0–19 Years	40	4.4	7	2	3	4	6	7	8	14
20–34	7	3.7	2	2	3	4	4	4	7	7
35–49	7	5.2	12	1	2	5	6	12	12	12
50–64	9	5.5	7	1	3	6	7	9	9	9
65+	8	4.5	10	1	2	5	5	8	12	12
GRAND TOTAL	**71**	**4.5**	**7**	**2**	**3**	**4**	**6**	**7**	**9**	**14**

40.1: LYMPHATIC DXTIC PX

Type of Patients	Observed Patients	Avg. Stay	Vari-ance	10th	25th	50th	75th	90th	95th	99th
1. SINGLE DX										
0–19 Years	33	4.5	7	1	2	4	6	9	10	10
20–34	9	3.7	7	1	1	3	6	8	8	8
35–49	22	4.0	13	1	1	3	8	10	11	11
50–64	15	2.2	4	1	1	1	2	5	5	9
65+	7	2.5	2	1	1	3	3	4	5	5
2. MULTIPLE DX										
0–19 Years	116	7.6	31	2	3	6	10	15	16	19
20–34	148	6.7	34	2	3	5	8	14	19	39
35–49	290	8.7	113	1	3	6	10	16	23	61
50–64	470	7.3	47	1	3	6	9	14	20	39
65+	663	8.0	49	2	4	6	10	16	20	30
TOTAL SINGLE DX	**86**	**3.7**	**8**	**1**	**1**	**3**	**5**	**8**	**10**	**11**
TOTAL MULTIPLE DX	**1,687**	**7.8**	**57**	**2**	**3**	**6**	**10**	**15**	**19**	**43**
TOTAL										
0–19 Years	149	6.9	27	2	3	6	9	14	16	19
20–34	157	6.6	33	1	3	5	8	14	19	35
35–49	312	8.4	108	1	3	6	10	16	22	61
50–64	485	7.1	47	1	3	6	9	14	19	39
65+	670	7.9	49	2	4	6	10	16	20	30
GRAND TOTAL	**1,773**	**7.6**	**55**	**2**	**3**	**6**	**10**	**15**	**19**	**42**

40.11: LYMPHATIC STRUCT BIOPSY

Type of Patients	Observed Patients	Avg. Stay	Vari-ance	10th	25th	50th	75th	90th	95th	99th
1. SINGLE DX										
0–19 Years	31	4.5	8	1	2	4	7	9	10	10
20–34	9	3.7	7	1	1	3	6	8	8	8
35–49	22	4.0	13	1	1	3	8	10	11	11
50–64	15	2.2	4	1	1	1	2	5	5	9
65+	7	2.5	2	1	1	3	3	4	5	5
2. MULTIPLE DX										
0–19 Years	112	7.6	31	2	3	6	10	15	17	19
20–34	146	6.7	34	2	3	5	8	14	19	39
35–49	287	8.7	114	1	3	6	10	16	23	61
50–64	463	7.3	48	1	3	6	9	14	20	39
65+	652	8.1	50	2	4	6	10	16	20	30
TOTAL SINGLE DX	**84**	**3.7**	**8**	**1**	**1**	**3**	**5**	**8**	**10**	**11**
TOTAL MULTIPLE DX	**1,660**	**7.8**	**57**	**2**	**3**	**6**	**10**	**15**	**20**	**43**
TOTAL										
0–19 Years	143	6.9	28	2	3	6	9	14	16	19
20–34	155	6.5	33	1	3	5	8	14	19	35
35–49	309	8.4	109	1	3	6	10	16	22	61
50–64	478	7.1	47	1	3	6	9	14	19	39
65+	659	8.0	49	2	4	6	10	16	20	30
GRAND TOTAL	**1,744**	**7.6**	**55**	**2**	**3**	**6**	**10**	**15**	**19**	**42**

40.2: SMP EXC LYMPHATIC STRUCT

Type of Patients	Observed Patients	Avg. Stay	Vari-ance	Percentiles						
				10th	25th	50th	75th	90th	95th	99th
1. SINGLE DX										
0–19 Years	33	2.0	3	1	1	1	2	4	8	8
20–34	23	3.2	6	1	1	3	4	7	8	9
35–49	28	1.6	<1	1	1	2	2	2	3	4
50–64	19	1.9	1	1	1	2	2	4	5	5
65+	15	1.2	<1	1	1	1	1	2	2	3
2. MULTIPLE DX										
0–19 Years	46	5.4	15	1	2	5	7	9	15	18
20–34	83	6.5	41	1	2	4	9	20	21	28
35–49	145	5.0	51	1	1	2	6	12	15	46
50–64	227	4.5	30	1	1	3	6	10	13	17
65+	275	5.4	34	1	1	3	7	13	19	27
TOTAL SINGLE DX	**118**	**2.0**	**3**	**1**	**1**	**1**	**2**	**4**	**6**	**8**
TOTAL MULTIPLE DX	**776**	**5.2**	**35**	**1**	**1**	**3**	**7**	**11**	**16**	**27**
TOTAL										
0–19 Years	79	4.0	13	1	1	3	7	8	12	18
20–34	106	5.8	35	1	2	4	7	16	21	26
35–49	173	4.4	43	1	1	2	5	11	15	46
50–64	246	4.3	29	1	1	2	6	10	13	17
65+	290	5.1	33	1	1	3	7	13	18	27
GRAND TOTAL	**894**	**4.7**	**32**	**1**	**1**	**3**	**6**	**11**	**15**	**27**

40.21: EXC DEEP CERVICAL NODE

Type of Patients	Observed Patients	Avg. Stay	Vari-ance	Percentiles						
				10th	25th	50th	75th	90th	95th	99th
1. SINGLE DX										
0–19 Years	7	1.7	4	1	1	1	1	2	8	8
20–34	3	1.0	0	1	1	1	1	1	1	1
35–49	6	1.7	<1	1	1	2	2	2	2	2
50–64	3	3.0	3	2	2	2	5	5	5	5
65+	0									
2. MULTIPLE DX										
0–19 Years	21	6.3	14	2	4	7	7	12	16	18
20–34	24	9.0	59	1	3	8	17	21	21	21
35–49	28	7.1	142	1	1	2	7	12	46	46
50–64	51	4.1	16	1	1	3	6	11	14	17
65+	57	5.0	28	1	1	3	8	13	15	26
TOTAL SINGLE DX	**19**	**1.8**	**3**	**1**	**1**	**1**	**2**	**2**	**5**	**8**
TOTAL MULTIPLE DX	**181**	**5.8**	**47**	**1**	**1**	**4**	**7**	**12**	**18**	**46**
TOTAL										
0–19 Years	28	4.8	15	1	1	4	7	8	12	18
20–34	27	8.3	59	1	2	4	11	21	21	21
35–49	34	5.8	114	1	1	2	5	12	46	46
50–64	54	4.1	15	1	1	3	6	11	13	17
65+	57	5.0	28	1	1	3	8	13	15	26
GRAND TOTAL	**200**	**5.3**	**43**	**1**	**1**	**3**	**7**	**12**	**17**	**46**

40.23: EXC AXILLARY LYMPH NODE

Type of Patients	Observed Patients	Avg. Stay	Vari-ance	Percentiles						
				10th	25th	50th	75th	90th	95th	99th
1. SINGLE DX										
0–19 Years	2	1.4	<1	1	1	1	1	3	3	3
20–34	3	1.4	<1	1	1	1	2	2	2	2
35–49	4	1.1	<1	1	1	1	1	2	2	2
50–64	8	1.2	<1	1	1	1	1	2	2	2
65+	8	1.0	0	1	1	1	1	1	1	1
2. MULTIPLE DX										
0–19 Years	3	4.1	<1	4	4	4	4	4	6	6
20–34	11	6.4	44	1	1	4	8	17	20	20
35–49	43	3.8	20	1	1	1	6	10	14	19
50–64	70	3.8	17	1	1	2	6	9	14	17
65+	66	4.3	18	1	1	2	6	10	13	21
TOTAL SINGLE DX	**25**	**1.2**	**<1**	**1**	**1**	**1**	**1**	**2**	**2**	**3**
TOTAL MULTIPLE DX	**193**	**4.1**	**18**	**1**	**1**	**2**	**6**	**10**	**14**	**19**
TOTAL										
0–19 Years	5	3.3	2	1	3	4	4	4	4	6
20–34	14	5.1	37	1	1	2	7	17	17	20
35–49	47	3.4	18	1	1	1	5	10	14	19
50–64	78	3.5	16	1	1	1	5	9	14	17
65+	74	4.0	17	1	1	2	6	10	13	19
GRAND TOTAL	**218**	**3.7**	**17**	**1**	**1**	**2**	**6**	**9**	**14**	**19**

40.24: EXC INGUINAL LYMPH NODE

Type of Patients	Observed Patients	Avg. Stay	Vari-ance	Percentiles						
				10th	25th	50th	75th	90th	95th	99th
1. SINGLE DX										
0–19 Years	5	3.7	11	1	1	2	8	8	8	8
20–34	4	3.4	8	1	1	1	6	6	6	6
35–49	3	1.9	<1	1	1	2	3	3	3	3
50–64	3	1.8	<1	1	2	2	2	2	2	2
65+	1	1.0	0	1	1	1	1	1	1	1
2. MULTIPLE DX										
0–19 Years	6	7.1	32	2	2	7	15	15	16	16
20–34	14	5.0	36	1	2	2	5	11	26	26
35–49	27	4.0	17	1	2	2	4	7	16	16
50–64	39	4.3	25	1	2	3	5	7	8	33
65+	64	5.3	32	1	1	3	7	13	19	29
TOTAL SINGLE DX	**16**	**2.4**	**5**	**1**	**1**	**2**	**2**	**6**	**8**	**8**
TOTAL MULTIPLE DX	**150**	**5.0**	**29**	**1**	**2**	**3**	**6**	**12**	**16**	**29**
TOTAL										
0–19 Years	11	6.0	27	1	2	2	8	15	16	16
20–34	18	4.7	30	1	2	2	6	11	11	26
35–49	30	3.8	16	1	2	2	4	7	16	16
50–64	42	4.0	22	1	2	3	5	7	8	33
65+	65	5.0	31	1	1	3	7	13	19	29
GRAND TOTAL	**166**	**4.7**	**26**	**1**	**2**	**3**	**6**	**10**	**16**	**26**

40.29: SMP EXC LYMPHATIC NEC

Type of Patients	Observed Patients	Avg. Stay	Vari- ance	Percentiles 10th	25th	50th	75th	90th	95th	99th
1. SINGLE DX										
0–19 Years	19	2.0	<1	1	1	2	3	3	4	4
20–34	13	4.2	6	1	3	4	7	8	9	9
35–49	13	1.8	<1	1	1	2	2	3	4	4
50–64	5	2.6	3	1	1	2	4	5	5	5
65+	6	1.6	<1	1	1	1	2	3	3	3
2. MULTIPLE DX										
0–19 Years	16	3.5	7	1	1	4	5	8	9	9
20–34	33	5.3	24	1	2	5	6	11	11	28
35–49	47	5.2	22	1	2	4	7	12	15	26
50–64	67	5.5	59	1	2	4	7	10	12	64
65+	87	6.4	51	1	2	4	8	17	27	27
TOTAL SINGLE DX	**56**	**2.4**	**3**	**1**	**1**	**2**	**3**	**4**	**7**	**9**
TOTAL MULTIPLE DX	**250**	**5.6**	**42**	**1**	**2**	**4**	**7**	**11**	**17**	**27**
TOTAL										
0–19 Years	35	2.7	4	1	1	2	4	5	6	9
20–34	46	5.0	19	1	2	4	6	10	11	28
35–49	60	4.4	19	1	2	3	5	11	13	26
50–64	72	5.4	56	1	2	4	7	10	12	64
65+	93	6.2	49	1	2	4	8	17	27	27
GRAND TOTAL	**306**	**5.0**	**36**	**1**	**2**	**3**	**6**	**10**	**13**	**27**

40.3: REGIONAL LYMPH NODE EXC

Type of Patients	Observed Patients	Avg. Stay	Vari- ance	Percentiles 10th	25th	50th	75th	90th	95th	99th
1. SINGLE DX										
0–19 Years	6	1.9	2	1	1	1	3	5	5	5
20–34	10	3.5	4	1	1	4	4	6	8	8
35–49	7	3.1	3	1	1	3	5	5	5	5
50–64	15	1.7	<1	1	1	1	2	3	4	4
65+	9	2.5	1	1	2	2	4	4	4	4
2. MULTIPLE DX										
0–19 Years	10	5.2	13	1	1	5	7	9	13	13
20–34	65	4.0	6	1	2	4	5	7	10	11
35–49	98	3.2	7	1	1	3	4	6	9	12
50–64	205	3.3	14	1	1	2	4	7	8	18
65+	207	3.4	11	1	1	2	5	7	9	17
TOTAL SINGLE DX	**47**	**2.3**	**3**	**1**	**1**	**2**	**4**	**5**	**5**	**8**
TOTAL MULTIPLE DX	**585**	**3.4**	**11**	**1**	**1**	**2**	**5**	**7**	**9**	**17**
TOTAL										
0–19 Years	16	3.4	10	1	1	1	5	7	9	13
20–34	75	3.9	6	1	2	4	5	6	10	11
35–49	105	3.2	7	1	1	3	4	6	9	12
50–64	220	3.1	13	1	1	2	4	6	8	18
65+	216	3.4	11	1	1	2	5	7	9	17
GRAND TOTAL	**632**	**3.3**	**10**	**1**	**1**	**2**	**5**	**7**	**9**	**16**

40.4: RAD EXC CERV LYMPH NODE

Type of Patients	Observed Patients	Avg. Stay	Vari- ance	Percentiles 10th	25th	50th	75th	90th	95th	99th
1. SINGLE DX										
0–19 Years	6	3.5	2	2	2	4	4	6	6	6
20–34	8	1.7	<1	1	1	2	2	3	3	3
35–49	19	2.3	2	1	1	2	3	5	5	6
50–64	35	2.7	5	1	1	2	4	5	7	11
65+	18	2.5	3	1	1	2	4	4	6	6
2. MULTIPLE DX										
0–19 Years	20	3.4	9	1	2	2	4	5	8	15
20–34	55	2.7	4	1	1	2	4	5	5	12
35–49	190	3.5	15	1	2	2	4	6	11	23
50–64	449	3.5	11	1	2	3	4	6	8	19
65+	458	3.9	12	1	2	3	4	7	10	19
TOTAL SINGLE DX	**86**	**2.5**	**3**	**1**	**1**	**2**	**4**	**5**	**6**	**9**
TOTAL MULTIPLE DX	**1,172**	**3.6**	**12**	**1**	**2**	**3**	**4**	**6**	**9**	**19**
TOTAL										
0–19 Years	26	3.4	7	1	2	2	4	6	8	15
20–34	63	2.5	3	1	1	2	3	5	5	12
35–49	209	3.4	14	1	2	2	4	6	9	23
50–64	484	3.4	11	1	2	3	4	6	8	19
65+	476	3.8	11	1	2	3	4	7	10	19
GRAND TOTAL	**1,258**	**3.5**	**11**	**1**	**2**	**3**	**4**	**6**	**8**	**18**

40.41: UNILAT RAD NECK DISSECT

Type of Patients	Observed Patients	Avg. Stay	Vari- ance	Percentiles 10th	25th	50th	75th	90th	95th	99th
1. SINGLE DX										
0–19 Years	5	3.3	2	2	2	3	4	6	6	6
20–34	7	1.9	<1	1	1	2	2	3	3	3
35–49	18	2.4	2	1	1	2	3	5	5	6
50–64	33	2.7	6	1	1	2	4	6	7	11
65+	17	2.3	2	1	1	2	3	4	4	6
2. MULTIPLE DX										
0–19 Years	17	3.5	10	1	2	2	5	8	8	15
20–34	49	2.6	4	1	1	2	4	5	6	12
35–49	175	3.4	14	1	2	3	4	6	8	23
50–64	418	3.4	10	1	2	3	4	6	8	18
65+	423	3.7	11	1	2	3	4	7	9	17
TOTAL SINGLE DX	**80**	**2.5**	**3**	**1**	**1**	**2**	**3**	**5**	**6**	**9**
TOTAL MULTIPLE DX	**1,082**	**3.5**	**11**	**1**	**2**	**3**	**4**	**6**	**8**	**18**
TOTAL										
0–19 Years	22	3.5	8	1	2	2	4	6	8	15
20–34	56	2.5	4	1	1	2	3	5	5	12
35–49	193	3.3	13	1	2	3	4	5	7	23
50–64	451	3.3	10	1	2	3	4	6	8	18
65+	440	3.7	11	1	2	3	4	6	9	17
GRAND TOTAL	**1,162**	**3.4**	**10**	**1**	**2**	**3**	**4**	**6**	**8**	**17**

40.5: OTH RAD NODE DISSECTION

Type of Patients	Observed Patients	Avg. Stay	Vari-ance	Percentiles 10th	25th	50th	75th	90th	95th	99th
1. SINGLE DX										
0–19 Years	2	2.6	<1	2	2	3	3	3	3	3
20–34	10	4.5	1	3	4	5	5	6	6	6
35–49	7	2.8	3	1	2	2	3	4	8	8
50–64	11	2.7	4	1	1	2	4	5	7	7
65+	7	2.2	2	1	1	1	4	4	4	4
2. MULTIPLE DX										
0–19 Years	6	6.5	24	2	4	5	7	12	21	21
20–34	47	4.5	9	1	2	4	5	8	10	19
35–49	86	4.0	7	1	2	4	5	7	8	16
50–64	168	4.4	11	1	2	4	5	8	11	18
65+	128	5.0	17	1	2	4	7	10	13	24
TOTAL SINGLE DX	**37**	**3.0**	**3**	**1**	**2**	**3**	**4**	**5**	**6**	**8**
TOTAL MULTIPLE DX	**435**	**4.6**	**12**	**1**	**2**	**4**	**6**	**9**	**11**	**18**
TOTAL										
0–19 Years	8	4.9	18	2	2	4	7	7	12	21
20–34	57	4.5	8	1	3	4	5	8	10	19
35–49	93	3.9	6	1	2	3	5	7	8	16
50–64	179	4.3	11	1	2	4	5	8	10	18
65+	135	4.9	17	1	2	4	7	10	13	24
GRAND TOTAL	**472**	**4.5**	**12**	**1**	**2**	**4**	**5**	**8**	**11**	**18**

40.53: RAD EXC ILIAC LYMPH NODE

Type of Patients	Observed Patients	Avg. Stay	Vari-ance	Percentiles 10th	25th	50th	75th	90th	95th	99th
1. SINGLE DX										
0–19 Years	0									
20–34	0									
35–49	3	4.4	9	2	2	4	8	8	8	8
50–64	3	5.1	4	3	3	5	7	7	7	7
65+	1	1.0	0	1	1	1	1	1	1	1
2. MULTIPLE DX										
0–19 Years	0									
20–34	6	4.5	3	2	3	5	6	6	6	6
35–49	26	4.0	4	2	2	4	5	6	8	11
50–64	55	5.0	19	2	3	4	6	10	18	20
65+	32	5.5	16	2	3	4	7	10	13	24
TOTAL SINGLE DX	**7**	**4.2**	**6**	**1**	**2**	**4**	**7**	**8**	**8**	**8**
TOTAL MULTIPLE DX	**119**	**5.0**	**15**	**2**	**3**	**4**	**6**	**9**	**13**	**20**
TOTAL										
0–19 Years	0									
20–34	6	4.5	3	2	3	5	6	6	6	6
35–49	29	4.0	4	2	2	4	5	7	8	11
50–64	58	5.0	18	2	3	4	6	10	18	20
65+	33	5.5	17	2	3	4	7	10	13	24
GRAND TOTAL	**126**	**4.9**	**14**	**2**	**3**	**4**	**6**	**9**	**13**	**20**

40.59: RAD EXC LYMPH NODE NEC

Type of Patients	Observed Patients	Avg. Stay	Vari-ance	Percentiles 10th	25th	50th	75th	90th	95th	99th
1. SINGLE DX										
0–19 Years	2	2.6	<1	2	2	3	3	3	3	3
20–34	4	4.7	2	3	4	5	6	6	6	6
35–49	1	3.0	0	3	3	3	3	3	3	3
50–64	2	1.8	2	1	1	1	3	3	3	3
65+	1	4.0	0	4	4	4	4	4	4	4
2. MULTIPLE DX										
0–19 Years	2	16.6	35	12	12	21	21	21	21	21
20–34	24	5.5	11	3	4	5	6	10	10	19
35–49	20	5.2	11	2	3	5	7	8	8	16
50–64	39	4.8	5	2	3	4	6	8	10	10
65+	29	5.4	14	2	3	4	8	9	15	16
TOTAL SINGLE DX	**10**	**3.1**	**2**	**2**	**2**	**3**	**3**	**5**	**6**	**6**
TOTAL MULTIPLE DX	**114**	**5.4**	**12**	**2**	**3**	**4**	**7**	**9**	**12**	**19**
TOTAL										
0–19 Years	4	5.1	36	2	2	3	3	12	21	21
20–34	28	5.4	10	3	4	5	6	10	10	19
35–49	21	5.1	11	2	3	4	7	8	8	16
50–64	41	4.7	5	2	3	4	6	8	9	10
65+	30	5.4	13	2	3	4	8	9	15	16
GRAND TOTAL	**124**	**5.1**	**11**	**2**	**3**	**4**	**6**	**9**	**10**	**19**

40.6: THORACIC DUCT OPERATIONS

Type of Patients	Observed Patients	Avg. Stay	Vari-ance	Percentiles 10th	25th	50th	75th	90th	95th	99th
1. SINGLE DX										
0–19 Years	0									
20–34	0									
35–49	0									
50–64	0									
65+	0									
2. MULTIPLE DX										
0–19 Years	1	7.0	0	7	7	7	7	7	7	7
20–34	2	15.3	276	4	4	4	29	29	29	29
35–49	4	14.9	27	10	11	11	21	21	21	21
50–64	2	4.5	<1	4	4	5	5	5	5	5
65+	4	9.6	31	4	4	10	12	18	18	18
TOTAL SINGLE DX	**0**									
TOTAL MULTIPLE DX	**13**	**10.6**	**49**	**4**	**5**	**10**	**12**	**21**	**29**	**29**
TOTAL										
0–19 Years	1	7.0	0	7	7	7	7	7	7	7
20–34	2	15.3	276	4	4	4	29	29	29	29
35–49	4	14.9	27	10	11	11	21	21	21	21
50–64	2	4.5	<1	4	4	5	5	5	5	5
65+	4	9.6	31	4	4	10	12	18	18	18
GRAND TOTAL	**13**	**10.6**	**49**	**4**	**5**	**10**	**12**	**21**	**29**	**29**

40.9: LYMPHATIC STRUCT OPS NEC

Type of Patients	Observed Patients	Avg. Stay	Vari-ance	10th	25th	50th	75th	90th	95th	99th
1. SINGLE DX										
0–19 Years	2	3.9	14	1	1	1	8	8	8	8
20–34	0									
35–49	0									
50–64	0									
65+	0									
2. MULTIPLE DX										
0–19 Years	7	3.6	2	1	3	4	4	6	6	6
20–34	2	3.0	0	3	3	3	3	3	3	3
35–49	6	3.3	4	1	1	3	4	7	7	7
50–64	9	5.0	15	1	3	3	6	9	15	15
65+	13	4.4	9	1	1	4	7	7	11	11
TOTAL SINGLE DX	**2**	**3.9**	**14**	**1**	**1**	**1**	**8**	**8**	**8**	**8**
TOTAL MULTIPLE DX	**37**	**4.0**	**7**	**1**	**2**	**4**	**6**	**7**	**9**	**15**
TOTAL										
0–19 Years	9	3.6	4	1	2	4	4	6	8	8
20–34	2	3.0	0	3	3	3	3	3	3	3
35–49	6	3.3	4	1	1	3	4	7	7	7
50–64	9	5.0	15	1	3	3	6	9	15	15
65+	13	4.4	9	1	1	4	7	7	11	11
GRAND TOTAL	**39**	**4.0**	**7**	**1**	**2**	**4**	**6**	**7**	**8**	**15**

41.0: BONE MARROW TRANSPLANT

Type of Patients	Observed Patients	Avg. Stay	Vari-ance	10th	25th	50th	75th	90th	95th	99th
1. SINGLE DX										
0–19 Years	6	7.4	67	1	1	5	8	23	23	23
20–34	1	19.0	0	19	19	19	19	19	19	19
35–49	5	8.3	118	1	1	2	16	26	26	26
50–64	13	6.0	45	1	1	1	9	18	19	19
65+	5	5.9	63	1	1	1	5	20	20	20
2. MULTIPLE DX										
0–19 Years	146	31.4	205	19	24	29	40	52	77	>99
20–34	122	24.3	121	16	19	23	28	32	39	71
35–49	223	23.4	181	7	17	22	27	36	46	80
50–64	333	19.6	96	6	15	20	23	29	37	53
65+	62	18.6	198	1	12	18	22	28	67	67
TOTAL SINGLE DX	**30**	**7.0**	**61**	**1**	**1**	**3**	**9**	**20**	**23**	**26**
TOTAL MULTIPLE DX	**886**	**23.6**	**174**	**7**	**17**	**22**	**28**	**40**	**50**	**93**
TOTAL										
0–19 Years	152	30.6	219	16	24	29	40	52	62	>99
20–34	123	24.3	120	16	19	23	28	32	39	71
35–49	228	23.2	183	7	17	22	27	36	46	80
50–64	346	19.1	100	5	14	20	23	28	37	53
65+	67	18.0	199	1	11	18	22	28	32	67
GRAND TOTAL	**916**	**23.1**	**178**	**6**	**17**	**22**	**28**	**40**	**50**	**91**

41.03: ALLO MARROW TRANSPL NEC

Type of Patients	Observed Patients	Avg. Stay	Vari-ance	10th	25th	50th	75th	90th	95th	99th
1. SINGLE DX										
0–19 Years	1	2.0	0	2	2	2	2	2	2	2
20–34	0									
35–49	0									
50–64	0									
65+	0									
2. MULTIPLE DX										
0–19 Years	32	36.6	167	26	29	34	42	62	>99	>99
20–34	9	28.5	79	18	23	29	31	34	49	49
35–49	12	27.2	87	17	22	24	28	44	54	54
50–64	12	16.4	64	6	6	19	21	27	29	29
65+	1	12.0	0	12	12	12	12	12	12	12
TOTAL SINGLE DX	**1**	**2.0**	**0**	**2**	**2**	**2**	**2**	**2**	**2**	**2**
TOTAL MULTIPLE DX	**66**	**30.0**	**191**	**12**	**23**	**29**	**35**	**52**	**62**	**>99**
TOTAL										
0–19 Years	33	35.9	189	26	29	34	42	62	>99	>99
20–34	9	28.5	79	18	23	29	31	34	49	49
35–49	12	27.2	87	17	22	24	28	44	54	54
50–64	12	16.4	64	6	6	19	21	27	29	29
65+	1	12.0	0	12	12	12	12	12	12	12
GRAND TOTAL	**67**	**29.7**	**198**	**12**	**23**	**29**	**35**	**52**	**62**	**>99**

41.04: AUTLOG STEM CELL TRANSPL

Type of Patients	Observed Patients	Avg. Stay	Vari-ance	10th	25th	50th	75th	90th	95th	99th
1. SINGLE DX										
0–19 Years	2	14.0	106	5	5	14	23	23	23	23
20–34	1	19.0	0	19	19	19	19	19	19	19
35–49	2	8.4	88	2	2	2	16	16	16	16
50–64	7	10.6	52	1	7	7	18	19	19	19
65+	1	5.0	0	5	5	5	5	5	5	5
2. MULTIPLE DX										
0–19 Years	49	23.7	108	5	21	24	28	40	40	48
20–34	71	20.8	45	10	18	21	24	28	30	41
35–49	110	20.9	138	7	16	19	24	32	45	58
50–64	194	19.8	85	8	16	20	23	28	34	53
65+	48	21.2	225	3	16	19	22	32	67	67
TOTAL SINGLE DX	**13**	**11.0**	**61**	**2**	**5**	**7**	**19**	**23**	**23**	**23**
TOTAL MULTIPLE DX	**472**	**21.0**	**114**	**7**	**17**	**20**	**25**	**30**	**40**	**67**
TOTAL										
0–19 Years	51	23.4	110	5	21	24	28	40	40	48
20–34	72	20.8	45	14	18	21	24	28	30	41
35–49	112	20.7	139	7	16	19	24	31	45	58
50–64	201	19.6	87	7	15	20	23	28	34	53
65+	49	20.9	225	3	16	19	22	32	67	67
GRAND TOTAL	**485**	**20.8**	**115**	**7**	**16**	**20**	**24**	**30**	**40**	**67**

41.05: ALLO STEM CELL TRANSPL

Type of Patients	Observed Patients	Avg. Stay	Vari-ance	Percentiles 10th	25th	50th	75th	90th	95th	99th
1. SINGLE DX										
0–19 Years	3	3.8	11	1	1	1	6	8	8	8
20–34	0									
35–49	3	8.3	179	1	1	1	26	26	26	26
50–64	6	2.1	9	1	1	1	1	9	9	9
65+	4	6.2	90	1	1	1	20	20	20	20
2. MULTIPLE DX										
0–19 Years	35	37.6	182	26	29	38	41	52	58	93
20–34	32	29.3	240	18	20	24	31	60	71	71
35–49	80	28.0	227	17	21	25	30	43	66	94
50–64	87	21.3	130	3	17	22	27	37	39	>99
65+	7	9.2	116	1	1	1	19	27	27	27
TOTAL SINGLE DX	**16**	**4.3**	**46**	**1**	**1**	**1**	**6**	**20**	**20**	**26**
TOTAL MULTIPLE DX	**241**	**26.9**	**234**	**5**	**20**	**25**	**33**	**43**	**56**	**93**
TOTAL										
0–19 Years	38	35.3	245	18	29	34	41	51	58	93
20–34	32	29.3	240	18	20	24	31	60	71	71
35–49	83	27.5	235	16	21	25	30	43	66	80
50–64	93	19.8	147	1	13	21	26	37	39	56
65+	11	8.7	109	1	1	1	19	27	27	27
GRAND TOTAL	**257**	**25.6**	**251**	**1**	**19**	**24**	**32**	**41**	**55**	**93**

41.1: PUNCTURE OF SPLEEN

Type of Patients	Observed Patients	Avg. Stay	Vari-ance	Percentiles 10th	25th	50th	75th	90th	95th	99th
1. SINGLE DX										
0–19 Years	0									
20–34	1	1.0	0	1	1	1	1	1	1	1
35–49	0									
50–64	0									
65+	1	1.0	0	1	1	1	1	1	1	1
2. MULTIPLE DX										
0–19 Years	2	11.6	120	3	3	3	22	22	22	22
20–34	2	4.4	<1	3	3	5	5	5	5	5
35–49	5	7.0	23	1	3	6	12	12	12	12
50–64	1	1.0	0	1	1	1	1	1	1	1
65+	3	6.7	20	2	2	6	12	12	12	12
TOTAL SINGLE DX	**2**	**1.0**	**0**	**1**	**1**	**1**	**1**	**1**	**1**	**1**
TOTAL MULTIPLE DX	**13**	**6.4**	**29**	**2**	**3**	**5**	**12**	**12**	**22**	**22**
TOTAL										
0–19 Years	2	11.6	120	3	3	3	22	22	22	22
20–34	3	4.0	2	1	3	5	5	5	5	5
35–49	5	7.0	23	1	3	6	12	12	12	12
50–64	1	1.0	0	1	1	1	1	1	1	1
65+	4	5.8	21	1	2	6	12	12	12	12
GRAND TOTAL	**15**	**6.0**	**29**	**1**	**3**	**5**	**6**	**12**	**22**	**22**

41.2: SPLENOTOMY

Type of Patients	Observed Patients	Avg. Stay	Vari-ance	Percentiles 10th	25th	50th	75th	90th	95th	99th
1. SINGLE DX										
0–19 Years	0									
20–34	0									
35–49	0									
50–64	0									
65+	0									
2. MULTIPLE DX										
0–19 Years	0									
20–34	1	7.0	0	7	7	7	7	7	7	7
35–49	0									
50–64	0									
65+	0									
TOTAL SINGLE DX	**0**									
TOTAL MULTIPLE DX	**1**	**7.0**	**0**	**7**	**7**	**7**	**7**	**7**	**7**	**7**
TOTAL										
0–19 Years	0									
20–34	1	7.0	0	7	7	7	7	7	7	7
35–49	0									
50–64	0									
65+	0									
GRAND TOTAL	**1**	**7.0**	**0**	**7**	**7**	**7**	**7**	**7**	**7**	**7**

41.3: MARROW & SPLEEN DXTIC PX

Type of Patients	Observed Patients	Avg. Stay	Vari-ance	Percentiles 10th	25th	50th	75th	90th	95th	99th
1. SINGLE DX										
0–19 Years	87	4.3	12	1	2	3	6	9	10	19
20–34	32	5.3	35	1	2	3	8	9	15	34
35–49	17	7.3	61	1	1	4	9	23	27	27
50–64	22	4.9	41	1	2	3	5	9	13	35
65+	13	3.2	8	1	1	2	4	7	11	11
2. MULTIPLE DX										
0–19 Years	533	9.5	80	2	4	6	12	22	29	39
20–34	314	10.3	115	2	3	6	13	26	33	51
35–49	563	9.2	80	2	4	6	11	22	28	44
50–64	991	9.3	77	2	4	7	11	21	27	46
65+	2,120	7.7	39	2	4	6	9	14	19	31
TOTAL SINGLE DX	**171**	**4.7**	**23**	**1**	**2**	**3**	**6**	**9**	**12**	**27**
TOTAL MULTIPLE DX	**4,521**	**8.6**	**63**	**2**	**4**	**6**	**10**	**18**	**25**	**39**
TOTAL										
0–19 Years	620	8.8	74	2	4	6	11	20	27	38
20–34	346	9.8	110	2	3	6	11	25	32	51
35–49	580	9.2	79	2	4	6	11	22	28	44
50–64	1,013	9.2	76	2	4	6	11	21	27	42
65+	2,133	7.6	39	2	4	6	9	14	19	31
GRAND TOTAL	**4,692**	**8.5**	**62**	**2**	**4**	**6**	**10**	**18**	**25**	**39**

41.31: BONE MARROW BIOPSY

Type of Patients	Observed Patients	Avg. Stay	Vari-ance	Percentiles						
				10th	25th	50th	75th	90th	95th	99th
1. SINGLE DX										
0–19 Years	87	4.3	12	1	2	3	6	9	10	19
20–34	32	5.3	35	1	2	3	8	9	15	34
35–49	17	7.3	61	1	1	4	9	23	27	27
50–64	22	4.9	41	1	2	3	5	9	13	35
65+	13	3.2	8	1	1	2	4	7	11	11
2. MULTIPLE DX										
0–19 Years	533	9.5	80	2	4	6	12	22	29	39
20–34	312	10.2	115	2	3	6	12	26	33	51
35–49	561	9.2	80	2	4	6	11	22	28	44
50–64	985	9.3	77	2	4	7	11	21	27	46
65+	2,111	7.7	39	2	4	6	9	14	19	31
TOTAL SINGLE DX	**171**	**4.7**	**23**	**1**	**2**	**3**	**6**	**9**	**12**	**27**
TOTAL MULTIPLE DX	**4,502**	**8.6**	**63**	**2**	**4**	**6**	**10**	**18**	**25**	**39**
TOTAL										
0–19 Years	620	8.8	74	2	4	6	11	20	27	38
20–34	344	9.7	109	2	3	6	11	25	32	51
35–49	578	9.2	79	2	3	6	11	22	28	44
50–64	1,007	9.2	76	2	4	6	11	21	27	42
65+	2,124	7.6	39	2	4	6	9	14	19	31
GRAND TOTAL	**4,673**	**8.5**	**62**	**2**	**4**	**6**	**10**	**18**	**25**	**39**

41.4: EXC/DESTR SPLENIC TISSUE

Type of Patients	Observed Patients	Avg. Stay	Vari-ance	Percentiles						
				10th	25th	50th	75th	90th	95th	99th
1. SINGLE DX										
0–19 Years	2	1.6	<1	1	1	2	2	2	2	2
20–34	3	4.1	6	1	2	6	6	6	6	6
35–49	2	1.0	0	1	1	1	1	1	1	1
50–64	1	3.0	0	3	3	3	3	3	3	3
65+	0									
2. MULTIPLE DX										
0–19 Years	11	4.4	6	1	4	4	5	8	10	10
20–34	8	4.7	6	2	2	5	8	8	8	8
35–49	3	2.0	<1	1	1	2	3	3	3	3
50–64	5	6.8	15	2	5	7	7	13	13	13
65+	3	5.5	13	1	5	5	5	12	12	12
TOTAL SINGLE DX	**8**	**2.4**	**4**	**1**	**1**	**2**	**3**	**6**	**6**	**6**
TOTAL MULTIPLE DX	**30**	**4.7**	**8**	**1**	**3**	**4**	**5**	**8**	**10**	**13**
TOTAL										
0–19 Years	13	4.0	6	1	2	4	4	8	10	10
20–34	11	4.5	6	2	2	5	6	8	8	8
35–49	5	1.4	<1	1	1	1	2	3	3	3
50–64	6	6.2	15	2	3	7	7	13	13	13
65+	3	5.5	13	1	5	5	5	12	12	12
GRAND TOTAL	**38**	**4.2**	**8**	**1**	**2**	**4**	**5**	**8**	**10**	**13**

41.5: TOTAL SPLENECTOMY

Type of Patients	Observed Patients	Avg. Stay	Vari-ance	Percentiles						
				10th	25th	50th	75th	90th	95th	99th
1. SINGLE DX										
0–19 Years	82	3.1	2	1	2	3	5	5	5	7
20–34	56	3.3	6	1	2	2	5	6	8	14
35–49	38	4.3	11	1	2	4	5	7	9	18
50–64	18	3.3	5	1	2	2	5	7	8	8
65+	10	5.0	3	2	4	6	6	7	7	7
2. MULTIPLE DX										
0–19 Years	170	5.7	16	2	3	5	7	11	14	19
20–34	317	7.7	57	3	4	6	9	15	23	47
35–49	365	7.9	52	3	4	6	9	15	21	46
50–64	366	8.2	73	2	4	6	10	16	21	43
65+	440	8.5	54	2	4	7	10	18	21	41
TOTAL SINGLE DX	**204**	**3.4**	**5**	**1**	**2**	**3**	**5**	**6**	**7**	**9**
TOTAL MULTIPLE DX	**1,658**	**7.8**	**54**	**2**	**4**	**6**	**9**	**16**	**21**	**41**
TOTAL										
0–19 Years	252	4.8	13	1	2	4	5	9	11	19
20–34	373	7.1	52	2	3	5	8	14	22	47
35–49	403	7.6	50	2	4	5	9	15	21	44
50–64	384	8.0	71	2	4	6	10	15	21	43
65+	450	8.4	53	2	4	6	10	18	21	41
GRAND TOTAL	**1,862**	**7.3**	**50**	**2**	**3**	**5**	**8**	**15**	**20**	**40**

41.9: OTH SPLEEN & MARROW OPS

Type of Patients	Observed Patients	Avg. Stay	Vari-ance	Percentiles						
				10th	25th	50th	75th	90th	95th	99th
1. SINGLE DX										
0–19 Years	17	2.3	11	1	1	1	1	4	12	12
20–34	13	1.1	<1	1	1	1	1	2	2	2
35–49	11	1.1	<1	1	1	1	1	2	2	2
50–64	3	1.0	0	1	1	1	1	1	1	1
65+	0									
2. MULTIPLE DX										
0–19 Years	36	6.0	37	1	2	4	8	11	25	25
20–34	48	7.4	35	3	4	6	7	15	23	27
35–49	22	7.8	24	3	5	6	11	15	19	19
50–64	11	8.2	21	2	4	9	9	17	17	17
65+	4	8.3	10	4	5	10	11	11	11	11
TOTAL SINGLE DX	**44**	**1.7**	**6**	**1**	**1**	**1**	**1**	**2**	**12**	**12**
TOTAL MULTIPLE DX	**121**	**7.1**	**32**	**1**	**4**	**6**	**8**	**15**	**20**	**25**
TOTAL										
0–19 Years	53	4.8	31	1	1	2	7	11	16	25
20–34	61	6.2	35	1	3	5	7	14	22	27
35–49	33	5.6	26	1	1	5	7	15	15	19
50–64	14	7.4	23	1	4	9	9	17	17	17
65+	4	8.3	10	4	5	10	11	11	11	11
GRAND TOTAL	**165**	**5.7**	**31**	**1**	**1**	**4**	**7**	**12**	**17**	**25**

42.0: ESOPHAGOTOMY

Type of Patients	Observed Patients	Avg. Stay	Vari-ance	Percentiles 10th	25th	50th	75th	90th	95th	99th
1. SINGLE DX										
0–19 Years	0									
20–34	0									
35–49	0									
50–64	0									
65+	0									
2. MULTIPLE DX										
0–19 Years	1	1.0	0	1	1	1	1	1	1	1
20–34	0									
35–49	1	1.0	0	1	1	1	1	1	1	1
50–64	4	10.3	170	3	3	8	8	43	43	43
65+	7	6.8	19	1	4	7	7	12	18	18
TOTAL SINGLE DX	**0**									
TOTAL MULTIPLE DX	**13**	**7.3**	**73**	**1**	**3**	**7**	**8**	**12**	**18**	**43**
TOTAL										
0–19 Years	1	1.0	0	1	1	1	1	1	1	1
20–34	0									
35–49	1	1.0	0	1	1	1	1	1	1	1
50–64	4	10.3	170	3	3	8	8	43	43	43
65+	7	6.8	19	1	4	7	7	12	18	18
GRAND TOTAL	**13**	**7.3**	**73**	**1**	**3**	**7**	**8**	**12**	**18**	**43**

42.1: ESOPHAGOSTOMY

Type of Patients	Observed Patients	Avg. Stay	Vari-ance	Percentiles 10th	25th	50th	75th	90th	95th	99th
1. SINGLE DX										
0–19 Years	0									
20–34	0									
35–49	0									
50–64	0									
65+	0									
2. MULTIPLE DX										
0–19 Years	1	18.0	0	18	18	18	18	18	18	18
20–34	1	8.0	0	8	8	8	8	8	8	8
35–49	0									
50–64	2	17.2	25	13	13	21	21	21	21	21
65+	2	21.0	0	21	21	21	21	21	21	21
TOTAL SINGLE DX	**0**									
TOTAL MULTIPLE DX	**6**	**18.3**	**22**	**8**	**18**	**21**	**21**	**21**	**21**	**21**
TOTAL										
0–19 Years	1	18.0	0	18	18	18	18	18	18	18
20–34	1	8.0	0	8	8	8	8	8	8	8
35–49	0									
50–64	2	17.2	25	13	13	21	21	21	21	21
65+	2	21.0	0	21	21	21	21	21	21	21
GRAND TOTAL	**6**	**18.3**	**22**	**8**	**18**	**21**	**21**	**21**	**21**	**21**

42.2: ESOPHAGEAL DXTIC PX

Type of Patients	Observed Patients	Avg. Stay	Vari-ance	Percentiles 10th	25th	50th	75th	90th	95th	99th
1. SINGLE DX										
0–19 Years	187	1.3	5	1	1	1	1	1	2	8
20–34	4	1.0	0	1	1	1	1	1	1	1
35–49	9	1.4	2	1	1	1	1	5	5	5
50–64	9	1.6	<1	1	1	2	2	2	3	3
65+	2	2.4	4	1	1	1	4	4	4	4
2. MULTIPLE DX										
0–19 Years	79	2.0	5	1	1	1	2	4	7	11
20–34	27	3.4	30	1	1	1	3	9	16	29
35–49	82	4.2	16	1	2	3	5	8	11	22
50–64	131	5.0	27	1	2	4	6	9	14	28
65+	262	6.3	38	1	2	5	7	13	20	38
TOTAL SINGLE DX	**211**	**1.3**	**4**	**1**	**1**	**1**	**1**	**1**	**2**	**8**
TOTAL MULTIPLE DX	**581**	**4.8**	**28**	**1**	**1**	**3**	**6**	**10**	**15**	**26**
TOTAL										
0–19 Years	266	1.6	5	1	1	1	1	2	4	10
20–34	31	3.1	28	1	1	1	3	6	12	29
35–49	91	4.0	16	1	1	3	5	8	11	22
50–64	140	4.8	26	1	2	3	5	9	14	28
65+	264	6.2	38	1	2	4	7	13	20	38
GRAND TOTAL	**792**	**3.8**	**24**	**1**	**1**	**2**	**5**	**8**	**13**	**26**

42.23: ESOPHAGOSCOPY NEC

Type of Patients	Observed Patients	Avg. Stay	Vari-ance	Percentiles 10th	25th	50th	75th	90th	95th	99th
1. SINGLE DX										
0–19 Years	181	1.2	4	1	1	1	1	1	2	4
20–34	4	1.0	0	1	1	1	1	1	1	1
35–49	9	1.4	2	1	1	1	1	5	5	5
50–64	8	1.5	<1	1	1	1	2	2	2	2
65+	2	2.4	4	1	1	1	4	4	4	4
2. MULTIPLE DX										
0–19 Years	64	1.8	5	1	1	1	2	2	7	11
20–34	22	3.6	35	1	1	1	3	9	16	29
35–49	65	4.2	19	1	1	3	5	8	11	24
50–64	97	4.9	27	1	2	4	6	9	12	28
65+	209	6.1	42	1	2	4	7	13	22	38
TOTAL SINGLE DX	**204**	**1.3**	**4**	**1**	**1**	**1**	**1**	**1**	**2**	**4**
TOTAL MULTIPLE DX	**457**	**4.6**	**30**	**1**	**1**	**3**	**6**	**10**	**15**	**26**
TOTAL										
0–19 Years	245	1.4	5	1	1	1	1	2	2	10
20–34	26	3.3	32	1	1	1	3	9	16	29
35–49	74	3.9	18	1	1	2	5	8	11	22
50–64	105	4.7	26	1	2	4	5	9	12	26
65+	211	6.1	42	1	2	4	7	13	22	38
GRAND TOTAL	**661**	**3.5**	**24**	**1**	**1**	**1**	**4**	**8**	**12**	**26**

42.24: CLOSED ESOPHAGEAL BIOPSY

Type of Patients	Observed Patients	Avg. Stay	Vari-ance	Percentiles						
				10th	25th	50th	75th	90th	95th	99th
1. SINGLE DX										
0–19 Years	2	6.2	13	1	1	8	8	8	8	8
20–34	0									
35–49	0									
50–64	1	3.0	0	3	3	3	3	3	3	3
65+	0									
2. MULTIPLE DX										
0–19 Years	4	4.8	2	4	4	4	4	7	8	8
20–34	4	2.3	2	1	2	2	4	4	4	4
35–49	16	4.2	8	2	2	4	5	7	9	14
50–64	34	5.0	28	1	2	3	6	10	16	28
65+	49	6.5	21	2	3	5	8	11	16	26
TOTAL SINGLE DX	**3**	**5.5**	**11**	**1**	**3**	**8**	**8**	**8**	**8**	**8**
TOTAL MULTIPLE DX	**107**	**5.4**	**21**	**2**	**3**	**4**	**7**	**10**	**15**	**26**
TOTAL										
0–19 Years	6	5.2	5	4	4	4	8	8	8	8
20–34	4	2.3	2	1	2	2	4	4	4	4
35–49	16	4.2	8	2	2	4	5	7	9	14
50–64	35	5.0	28	1	2	3	6	9	16	28
65+	49	6.5	21	2	3	5	8	11	16	26
GRAND TOTAL	**110**	**5.4**	**20**	**2**	**3**	**4**	**7**	**10**	**15**	**26**

42.3: EXC/DESTR ESOPH LES/TISS

Type of Patients	Observed Patients	Avg. Stay	Vari-ance	Percentiles						
				10th	25th	50th	75th	90th	95th	99th
1. SINGLE DX										
0–19 Years	2	2.2	1	1	1	3	3	3	3	3
20–34	2	1.2	<1	1	1	1	1	2	2	2
35–49	3	5.0	8	3	3	4	9	9	9	9
50–64	11	2.1	3	1	1	1	2	6	6	6
65+	14	1.6	<1	1	1	1	2	3	3	4
2. MULTIPLE DX										
0–19 Years	39	6.4	68	1	2	4	8	15	16	54
20–34	148	4.5	18	2	2	3	5	10	13	22
35–49	1,224	4.7	14	2	3	4	6	8	11	21
50–64	1,309	4.7	14	2	3	4	6	8	12	20
65+	1,017	5.1	16	2	2	4	6	10	13	21
TOTAL SINGLE DX	**32**	**1.9**	**2**	**1**	**1**	**1**	**2**	**3**	**6**	**9**
TOTAL MULTIPLE DX	**3,737**	**4.8**	**16**	**2**	**3**	**4**	**6**	**9**	**12**	**21**
TOTAL										
0–19 Years	41	6.2	66	1	2	4	7	15	16	54
20–34	150	4.4	18	2	2	3	5	10	13	22
35–49	1,227	4.7	14	2	3	4	6	8	11	21
50–64	1,320	4.7	14	2	3	4	6	8	12	20
65+	1,031	5.0	16	2	2	4	6	10	13	21
GRAND TOTAL	**3,769**	**4.8**	**16**	**2**	**2**	**4**	**6**	**9**	**12**	**21**

42.31: EXC ESOPH DIVERTICULUM

Type of Patients	Observed Patients	Avg. Stay	Vari-ance	Percentiles						
				10th	25th	50th	75th	90th	95th	99th
1. SINGLE DX										
0–19 Years	0									
20–34	0									
35–49	0									
50–64	4	3.7	5	1	2	3	6	6	6	6
65+	5	2.1	<1	1	2	2	2	3	4	4
2. MULTIPLE DX										
0–19 Years	1	10.0	0	10	10	10	10	10	10	10
20–34	1	4.0	0	4	4	4	4	4	4	4
35–49	4	4.1	10	2	2	2	5	9	9	9
50–64	15	3.6	8	1	1	3	4	8	10	10
65+	64	5.6	23	2	2	4	7	13	16	32
TOTAL SINGLE DX	**9**	**2.6**	**2**	**1**	**2**	**2**	**3**	**6**	**6**	**6**
TOTAL MULTIPLE DX	**85**	**5.3**	**21**	**1**	**2**	**4**	**7**	**10**	**13**	**17**
TOTAL										
0–19 Years	1	10.0	0	10	10	10	10	10	10	10
20–34	1	4.0	0	4	4	4	4	4	4	4
35–49	4	4.1	10	2	2	2	5	9	9	9
50–64	19	3.6	7	1	1	3	4	8	10	10
65+	69	5.3	22	2	2	4	6	12	16	32
GRAND TOTAL	**94**	**5.0**	**20**	**1**	**2**	**4**	**6**	**10**	**13**	**17**

42.33: ENDO EXC/DESTR ESOPH LES

Type of Patients	Observed Patients	Avg. Stay	Vari-ance	Percentiles						
				10th	25th	50th	75th	90th	95th	99th
1. SINGLE DX										
0–19 Years	2	2.2	1	1	1	3	3	3	3	3
20–34	1	1.0	0	1	1	1	1	1	1	1
35–49	3	5.0	8	3	3	4	9	9	9	9
50–64	5	1.0	0	1	1	1	1	1	1	1
65+	9	1.3	<1	1	1	1	1	3	3	3
2. MULTIPLE DX										
0–19 Years	36	5.8	51	1	2	3	7	13	15	54
20–34	145	4.5	19	2	2	3	5	10	13	22
35–49	1,210	4.7	14	2	3	4	6	8	11	21
50–64	1,286	4.7	14	2	3	4	6	8	12	20
65+	946	5.0	16	2	2	4	6	10	13	21
TOTAL SINGLE DX	**20**	**1.6**	**2**	**1**	**1**	**1**	**1**	**3**	**4**	**9**
TOTAL MULTIPLE DX	**3,623**	**4.8**	**15**	**2**	**3**	**4**	**6**	**9**	**12**	**21**
TOTAL										
0–19 Years	38	5.7	49	1	2	3	7	13	15	54
20–34	146	4.4	19	2	2	3	5	10	13	22
35–49	1,213	4.7	14	2	3	4	6	8	11	21
50–64	1,291	4.7	14	2	3	4	6	8	12	20
65+	955	5.0	16	2	2	4	6	10	13	21
GRAND TOTAL	**3,643**	**4.8**	**15**	**2**	**3**	**4**	**6**	**9**	**12**	**21**

42.4: EXCISION OF ESOPHAGUS

Type of Patients	Observed Patients	Avg. Stay	Variance	10th	25th	50th	75th	90th	95th	99th
1. SINGLE DX										
0–19 Years	0									
20–34	0									
35–49	0									
50–64	3	22.7	141	10	10	24	34	34	34	34
65+	0									
2. MULTIPLE DX										
0–19 Years	2	6.8	1	6	6	6	8	8	8	8
20–34	9	16.4	59	9	10	14	27	27	27	27
35–49	34	12.4	30	8	8	10	16	20	21	32
50–64	161	13.1	42	8	9	11	16	21	29	36
65+	162	16.0	148	7	9	12	17	28	35	83
TOTAL SINGLE DX	**3**	**22.7**	**141**	**10**	**10**	**24**	**34**	**34**	**34**	**34**
TOTAL MULTIPLE DX	**368**	**14.5**	**94**	**8**	**9**	**11**	**17**	**26**	**32**	**51**
TOTAL										
0–19 Years	2	6.8	1	6	6	6	8	8	8	8
20–34	9	16.4	59	9	10	14	27	27	27	27
35–49	34	12.4	30	8	8	10	16	20	21	32
50–64	164	13.3	44	8	9	11	16	21	30	36
65+	162	16.0	148	7	9	12	17	28	35	83
GRAND TOTAL	**371**	**14.5**	**95**	**8**	**9**	**11**	**17**	**26**	**32**	**51**

42.41: PARTIAL ESOPHAGECTOMY

Type of Patients	Observed Patients	Avg. Stay	Variance	10th	25th	50th	75th	90th	95th	99th
1. SINGLE DX										
0–19 Years	0									
20–34	0									
35–49	0									
50–64	2	29.0	47	24	24	29	34	34	34	34
65+	0									
2. MULTIPLE DX										
0–19 Years	2	6.8	1	6	6	6	8	8	8	8
20–34	1	27.0	0	27	27	27	27	27	27	27
35–49	25	13.0	34	8	9	11	17	20	25	32
50–64	107	13.4	49	8	9	11	16	21	33	38
65+	117	15.6	173	7	9	12	16	28	36	83
TOTAL SINGLE DX	**2**	**29.0**	**47**	**24**	**24**	**29**	**34**	**34**	**34**	**34**
TOTAL MULTIPLE DX	**252**	**14.4**	**108**	**8**	**9**	**11**	**16**	**26**	**33**	**83**
TOTAL										
0–19 Years	2	6.8	1	6	6	6	8	8	8	8
20–34	1	27.0	0	27	27	27	27	27	27	27
35–49	25	13.0	34	8	9	11	17	20	25	32
50–64	109	13.6	52	8	9	11	16	24	33	38
65+	117	15.6	173	7	9	12	16	28	36	83
GRAND TOTAL	**254**	**14.5**	**108**	**8**	**9**	**11**	**16**	**26**	**33**	**83**

42.42: TOTAL ESOPHAGECTOMY

Type of Patients	Observed Patients	Avg. Stay	Variance	10th	25th	50th	75th	90th	95th	99th
1. SINGLE DX										
0–19 Years	0									
20–34	0									
35–49	0									
50–64	1	10.0	0	10	10	10	10	10	10	10
65+	0									
2. MULTIPLE DX										
0–19 Years	0									
20–34	7	16.3	51	8	11	14	23	27	27	27
35–49	7	12.1	21	8	8	10	17	17	19	19
50–64	53	12.6	27	8	9	11	14	19	25	31
65+	42	16.9	105	7	8	14	26	28	35	51
TOTAL SINGLE DX	**1**	**10.0**	**0**	**10**	**10**	**10**	**10**	**10**	**10**	**10**
TOTAL MULTIPLE DX	**109**	**14.9**	**71**	**8**	**9**	**12**	**18**	**26**	**28**	**51**
TOTAL										
0–19 Years	0									
20–34	7	16.3	51	8	11	14	23	27	27	27
35–49	7	12.1	21	8	8	10	17	17	19	19
50–64	54	12.6	27	8	9	11	14	19	25	31
65+	42	16.9	105	7	8	14	26	28	35	51
GRAND TOTAL	**110**	**14.9**	**71**	**8**	**9**	**12**	**18**	**26**	**28**	**51**

42.5: INTRATHOR ESOPH ANAST

Type of Patients	Observed Patients	Avg. Stay	Variance	10th	25th	50th	75th	90th	95th	99th
1. SINGLE DX										
0–19 Years	0									
20–34	0									
35–49	1	2.0	0	2	2	2	2	2	2	2
50–64	0									
65+	0									
2. MULTIPLE DX										
0–19 Years	9	26.6	546	8	12	17	29	53	91	91
20–34	2	9.4	<1	9	9	9	10	10	10	10
35–49	3	11.5	32	6	8	8	19	19	19	19
50–64	8	15.2	89	8	10	12	16	37	37	37
65+	8	16.2	115	9	9	14	14	43	43	43
TOTAL SINGLE DX	**1**	**2.0**	**0**	**2**	**2**	**2**	**2**	**2**	**2**	**2**
TOTAL MULTIPLE DX	**30**	**17.7**	**238**	**8**	**9**	**14**	**19**	**37**	**43**	**91**
TOTAL										
0–19 Years	9	26.6	546	8	12	17	29	53	91	91
20–34	2	9.4	<1	9	9	9	10	10	10	10
35–49	4	10.3	39	2	8	8	19	19	19	19
50–64	8	15.2	89	8	10	12	16	37	37	37
65+	8	16.2	115	9	9	14	14	43	43	43
GRAND TOTAL	**31**	**17.3**	**238**	**8**	**8**	**13**	**19**	**29**	**43**	**91**

42.6: ANTESTERNAL ESOPH ANAST

Type of Patients	Observed Patients	Avg. Stay	Vari-ance	Percentiles						
				10th	25th	50th	75th	90th	95th	99th
1. SINGLE DX										
0–19 Years	0									
20–34	0									
35–49	0									
50–64	0									
65+	0									
2. MULTIPLE DX										
0–19 Years	0									
20–34	0									
35–49	0									
50–64	0									
65+	1	13.0	0	13	13	13	13	13	13	13
TOTAL SINGLE DX	**0**									
TOTAL MULTIPLE DX	**1**	**13.0**	**0**	**13**	**13**	**13**	**13**	**13**	**13**	**13**
TOTAL										
0–19 Years	0									
20–34	0									
35–49	0									
50–64	0									
65+	1	13.0	0	13	13	13	13	13	13	13
GRAND TOTAL	**1**	**13.0**	**0**	**13**	**13**	**13**	**13**	**13**	**13**	**13**

42.7: ESOPHAGOMYOTOMY

Type of Patients	Observed Patients	Avg. Stay	Vari-ance	Percentiles						
				10th	25th	50th	75th	90th	95th	99th
1. SINGLE DX										
0–19 Years	4	4.0	4	2	2	3	6	6	6	6
20–34	15	3.1	7	1	2	2	3	8	10	10
35–49	22	2.0	<1	1	1	2	2	3	3	6
50–64	17	2.2	<1	1	2	2	2	4	5	5
65+	1	1.0	0	1	1	1	1	1	1	1
2. MULTIPLE DX										
0–19 Years	6	5.5	30	2	2	4	4	16	16	16
20–34	40	2.8	3	1	2	2	3	5	7	9
35–49	79	3.1	9	1	2	2	3	7	8	20
50–64	73	2.9	5	1	1	2	3	6	8	12
65+	42	6.5	26	2	3	4	8	15	15	18
TOTAL SINGLE DX	**59**	**2.4**	**3**	**1**	**2**	**2**	**2**	**5**	**6**	**10**
TOTAL MULTIPLE DX	**240**	**3.9**	**14**	**1**	**2**	**2**	**5**	**8**	**15**	**16**
TOTAL										
0–19 Years	10	5.0	21	2	2	3	6	16	16	16
20–34	55	2.9	4	1	2	2	3	6	8	10
35–49	101	2.8	7	1	2	2	3	5	7	17
50–64	90	2.8	4	1	2	2	3	6	8	12
65+	43	6.4	26	2	3	4	8	15	15	18
GRAND TOTAL	**299**	**3.6**	**12**	**1**	**2**	**2**	**4**	**7**	**15**	**16**

42.8: OTHER ESOPHAGEAL REPAIR

Type of Patients	Observed Patients	Avg. Stay	Vari-ance	Percentiles						
				10th	25th	50th	75th	90th	95th	99th
1. SINGLE DX										
0–19 Years	0									
20–34	2	7.8	47	2	2	13	13	13	13	13
35–49	1	6.0	0	6	6	6	6	6	6	6
50–64	1	14.0	0	14	14	14	14	14	14	14
65+	2	1.0	0	1	1	1	1	1	1	1
2. MULTIPLE DX										
0–19 Years	8	7.9	23	2	4	8	9	15	17	17
20–34	12	10.0	56	4	7	8	9	26	29	29
35–49	25	9.2	101	2	4	5	10	22	37	46
50–64	40	8.9	37	3	4	8	12	19	22	25
65+	103	11.8	122	2	4	9	15	26	33	44
TOTAL SINGLE DX	**6**	**6.1**	**33**	**1**	**1**	**6**	**13**	**14**	**14**	**14**
TOTAL MULTIPLE DX	**188**	**10.7**	**98**	**2**	**4**	**8**	**13**	**23**	**30**	**44**
TOTAL										
0–19 Years	8	7.9	23	2	4	8	9	15	17	17
20–34	14	9.7	53	4	5	8	9	20	29	29
35–49	26	9.1	98	2	4	5	10	22	37	46
50–64	41	9.0	37	3	4	8	12	19	22	25
65+	105	11.7	122	2	4	9	15	26	33	44
GRAND TOTAL	**194**	**10.6**	**96**	**2**	**4**	**8**	**13**	**22**	**30**	**44**

42.81: INSERT PERM TUBE ESOPH

Type of Patients	Observed Patients	Avg. Stay	Vari-ance	Percentiles						
				10th	25th	50th	75th	90th	95th	99th
1. SINGLE DX										
0–19 Years	0									
20–34	0									
35–49	1	6.0	0	6	6	6	6	6	6	6
50–64	0									
65+	1	1.0	0	1	1	1	1	1	1	1
2. MULTIPLE DX										
0–19 Years	1	15.0	0	15	15	15	15	15	15	15
20–34	1	20.0	0	20	20	20	20	20	20	20
35–49	9	5.1	14	1	2	4	10	10	10	10
50–64	18	6.7	20	1	3	7	10	13	13	15
65+	48	6.6	24	2	2	6	10	12	18	19
TOTAL SINGLE DX	**2**	**3.5**	**10**	**1**	**1**	**1**	**6**	**6**	**6**	**6**
TOTAL MULTIPLE DX	**77**	**6.7**	**24**	**1**	**2**	**6**	**10**	**13**	**17**	**20**
TOTAL										
0–19 Years	1	15.0	0	15	15	15	15	15	15	15
20–34	1	20.0	0	20	20	20	20	20	20	20
35–49	10	5.2	13	1	2	4	10	10	10	10
50–64	18	6.7	20	1	3	7	10	13	13	15
65+	49	6.5	24	1	2	6	10	12	18	19
GRAND TOTAL	**79**	**6.6**	**24**	**1**	**2**	**6**	**10**	**13**	**17**	**20**

42.9: OTHER ESOPHAGEAL OPS

Type of Patients	Observed Patients	Avg. Stay	Vari-ance	Percentiles						
				10th	25th	50th	75th	90th	95th	99th
1. SINGLE DX										
0–19 Years	8	1.5	2	1	1	1	1	2	6	6
20–34	3	2.2	1	1	1	3	3	3	3	3
35–49	4	2.6	<1	2	2	2	4	4	4	4
50–64	0									
65+	1	4.0	0	4	4	4	4	4	4	4
2. MULTIPLE DX										
0–19 Years	52	3.5	12	1	1	2	6	7	11	18
20–34	43	4.1	34	1	1	3	4	6	20	32
35–49	132	4.5	22	1	2	3	6	9	17	20
50–64	270	5.2	24	1	2	4	6	11	15	24
65+	876	4.9	15	1	2	4	6	9	12	21
TOTAL SINGLE DX	**16**	**1.9**	**2**	**1**	**1**	**1**	**2**	**4**	**4**	**6**
TOTAL MULTIPLE DX	**1,373**	**4.8**	**18**	**1**	**2**	**4**	**6**	**9**	**13**	**23**
TOTAL										
0–19 Years	60	3.2	11	1	1	2	5	7	11	16
20–34	46	3.9	32	1	1	3	4	6	20	32
35–49	136	4.5	21	1	2	3	5	9	17	20
50–64	270	5.2	24	1	2	4	6	11	15	24
65+	877	4.9	15	1	2	4	6	9	12	21
GRAND TOTAL	**1,389**	**4.8**	**18**	**1**	**2**	**4**	**6**	**9**	**13**	**23**

42.92: ESOPHAGEAL DILATION

Type of Patients	Observed Patients	Avg. Stay	Vari-ance	Percentiles						
				10th	25th	50th	75th	90th	95th	99th
1. SINGLE DX										
0–19 Years	8	1.5	2	1	1	1	1	2	6	6
20–34	3	2.2	1	1	1	3	3	3	3	3
35–49	3	2.7	1	2	2	2	4	4	4	4
50–64	0									
65+	1	4.0	0	4	4	4	4	4	4	4
2. MULTIPLE DX										
0–19 Years	49	3.2	12	1	1	2	5	8	11	18
20–34	42	4.1	35	1	1	3	4	6	20	32
35–49	128	4.5	20	1	2	3	6	9	14	20
50–64	261	5.1	24	1	2	4	6	11	14	24
65+	873	4.9	15	1	2	4	6	9	12	22
TOTAL SINGLE DX	**15**	**1.9**	**2**	**1**	**1**	**1**	**2**	**4**	**4**	**6**
TOTAL MULTIPLE DX	**1,353**	**4.8**	**18**	**1**	**2**	**4**	**6**	**9**	**13**	**23**
TOTAL										
0–19 Years	57	2.9	11	1	1	1	3	7	11	18
20–34	45	4.0	33	1	1	3	4	6	20	32
35–49	131	4.4	20	1	2	3	5	9	14	20
50–64	261	5.1	24	1	2	4	6	11	14	24
65+	874	4.9	15	1	2	4	6	9	12	22
GRAND TOTAL	**1,368**	**4.8**	**17**	**1**	**2**	**4**	**6**	**9**	**13**	**23**

43.0: GASTROTOMY

Type of Patients	Observed Patients	Avg. Stay	Vari-ance	Percentiles						
				10th	25th	50th	75th	90th	95th	99th
1. SINGLE DX										
0–19 Years	3	2.9	<1	2	2	3	3	4	4	4
20–34	1	7.0	0	7	7	7	7	7	7	7
35–49	1	4.0	0	4	4	4	4	4	4	4
50–64	0									
65+	1	4.0	0	4	4	4	4	4	4	4
2. MULTIPLE DX										
0–19 Years	13	7.8	19	3	5	8	10	15	17	17
20–34	14	11.4	320	4	5	7	9	10	74	74
35–49	13	10.6	64	4	5	7	12	22	29	29
50–64	16	14.8	162	5	6	10	20	30	37	53
65+	16	9.2	20	5	6	8	10	17	20	20
TOTAL SINGLE DX	**6**	**3.5**	**2**	**2**	**3**	**3**	**4**	**4**	**7**	**7**
TOTAL MULTIPLE DX	**72**	**10.7**	**111**	**4**	**5**	**8**	**11**	**20**	**29**	**74**
TOTAL										
0–19 Years	16	6.5	19	3	3	5	8	14	15	17
20–34	15	11.1	299	4	6	7	9	10	74	74
35–49	14	10.0	61	4	4	6	12	22	29	29
50–64	16	14.8	162	5	6	10	20	30	37	53
65+	17	8.7	21	4	5	7	10	17	20	20
GRAND TOTAL	**78**	**9.8**	**103**	**3**	**4**	**7**	**10**	**20**	**29**	**74**

43.1: GASTROSTOMY

Type of Patients	Observed Patients	Avg. Stay	Vari-ance	Percentiles						
				10th	25th	50th	75th	90th	95th	99th
1. SINGLE DX										
0–19 Years	15	2.7	3	2	2	2	3	4	4	10
20–34	2	5.3	17	2	2	2	9	9	9	9
35–49	6	2.4	8	1	1	1	1	7	9	9
50–64	10	3.8	9	1	1	3	7	8	9	9
65+	4	1.6	<1	1	1	2	2	2	2	2
2. MULTIPLE DX										
0–19 Years	520	6.8	122	1	2	3	7	19	27	70
20–34	96	10.9	113	2	4	9	16	23	29	>99
35–49	282	11.0	100	3	4	8	15	24	32	54
50–64	873	10.4	87	2	4	8	13	21	28	53
65+	5,763	10.0	43	3	6	9	13	19	22	32
TOTAL SINGLE DX	**37**	**2.8**	**5**	**1**	**2**	**2**	**3**	**4**	**9**	**10**
TOTAL MULTIPLE DX	**7,534**	**9.7**	**61**	**2**	**5**	**8**	**13**	**19**	**23**	**40**
TOTAL										
0–19 Years	535	6.7	117	1	2	3	6	19	25	70
20–34	98	10.7	112	2	3	9	16	23	29	>99
35–49	288	10.7	100	2	4	8	15	24	32	54
50–64	883	10.3	87	2	4	8	13	20	28	50
65+	5,767	10.0	43	3	6	9	13	19	22	32
GRAND TOTAL	**7,571**	**9.7**	**61**	**2**	**5**	**8**	**13**	**19**	**23**	**40**

43.11: PEG

Type of Patients	Observed Patients	Avg. Stay	Vari-ance	10th	25th	50th	75th	90th	95th	99th
1. SINGLE DX										
0–19 Years	9	2.4	<1	2	2	2	3	3	3	4
20–34	1	2.0	0	2	2	2	2	2	2	2
35–49	4	1.7	4	1	1	1	1	7	7	7
50–64	8	3.7	8	1	1	3	4	9	9	9
65+	4	1.6	<1	1	1	2	2	2	2	2
2. MULTIPLE DX										
0–19 Years	304	6.1	94	1	1	2	6	16	24	57
20–34	83	10.9	103	2	5	9	16	23	29	>99
35–49	257	11.0	98	3	4	8	15	24	32	54
50–64	800	10.3	79	2	5	8	13	20	28	49
65+	5,553	10.0	43	3	6	9	13	18	22	33
TOTAL SINGLE DX	**26**	**2.4**	**2**	**1**	**2**	**2**	**3**	**4**	**7**	**9**
TOTAL MULTIPLE DX	**6,997**	**9.8**	**54**	**3**	**5**	**8**	**13**	**19**	**23**	**38**
TOTAL										
0–19 Years	313	5.9	91	1	1	2	6	16	24	54
20–34	84	10.8	103	2	5	9	16	23	29	>99
35–49	261	10.7	98	2	4	8	15	24	32	54
50–64	808	10.2	79	2	5	8	13	20	28	49
65+	5,557	10.0	43	3	6	9	13	18	22	33
GRAND TOTAL	**7,023**	**9.8**	**54**	**2**	**5**	**8**	**13**	**19**	**23**	**38**

43.19: GASTROSTOMY NEC

Type of Patients	Observed Patients	Avg. Stay	Vari-ance	10th	25th	50th	75th	90th	95th	99th
1. SINGLE DX										
0–19 Years	6	3.3	6	2	2	2	3	10	10	10
20–34	1	9.0	0	9	9	9	9	9	9	9
35–49	2	6.6	11	4	4	9	9	9	9	9
50–64	2	4.4	23	1	1	1	8	8	8	8
65+	0									
2. MULTIPLE DX										
0–19 Years	216	7.9	158	1	2	3	7	23	27	83
20–34	13	10.5	185	2	2	3	17	27	27	57
35–49	25	11.3	126	2	5	7	14	21	32	53
50–64	73	11.7	189	2	4	7	13	24	59	59
65+	210	9.7	54	2	4	8	14	20	23	29
TOTAL SINGLE DX	**11**	**3.9**	**8**	**2**	**2**	**2**	**4**	**9**	**10**	**10**
TOTAL MULTIPLE DX	**537**	**8.9**	**130**	**2**	**2**	**4**	**11**	**22**	**27**	**59**
TOTAL										
0–19 Years	222	7.7	153	2	2	3	7	23	27	83
20–34	14	10.4	172	2	2	5	17	27	27	57
35–49	27	11.1	120	2	5	7	13	21	32	53
50–64	75	11.5	187	2	4	7	13	24	59	59
65+	210	9.7	54	2	4	8	14	20	23	29
GRAND TOTAL	**548**	**8.8**	**128**	**2**	**2**	**4**	**11**	**22**	**27**	**59**

43.3: PYLOROMYOTOMY

Type of Patients	Observed Patients	Avg. Stay	Vari-ance	10th	25th	50th	75th	90th	95th	99th
1. SINGLE DX										
0–19 Years	689	2.2	<1	1	2	2	3	3	4	5
20–34	0									
35–49	0									
50–64	0									
65+	0									
2. MULTIPLE DX										
0–19 Years	462	3.5	22	1	2	3	4	5	6	25
20–34	4	8.8	32	2	2	8	10	16	16	16
35–49	3	10.7	184	3	3	5	5	32	32	32
50–64	2	8.0	7	6	6	6	10	10	10	10
65+	5	10.8	56	3	6	6	19	21	21	21
TOTAL SINGLE DX	**689**	**2.2**	**<1**	**1**	**2**	**2**	**3**	**3**	**4**	**5**
TOTAL MULTIPLE DX	**476**	**3.6**	**23**	**1**	**2**	**3**	**4**	**5**	**7**	**25**
TOTAL										
0–19 Years	1,151	2.7	10	1	2	2	3	4	5	10
20–34	4	8.8	32	2	2	8	10	16	16	16
35–49	3	10.7	184	3	3	5	5	32	32	32
50–64	2	8.0	7	6	6	6	10	10	10	10
65+	5	10.8	56	3	6	6	19	21	21	21
GRAND TOTAL	**1,165**	**2.8**	**11**	**1**	**2**	**2**	**3**	**4**	**5**	**14**

43.4: LOC EXC GASTRIC LES

Type of Patients	Observed Patients	Avg. Stay	Vari-ance	10th	25th	50th	75th	90th	95th	99th
1. SINGLE DX										
0–19 Years	2	5.0	0	5	5	5	5	5	5	5
20–34	4	4.1	6	1	2	6	6	6	6	6
35–49	5	4.1	3	3	4	4	5	7	7	7
50–64	10	4.7	3	2	3	6	6	7	7	7
65+	2	3.2	2	2	2	4	4	4	4	4
2. MULTIPLE DX										
0–19 Years	14	4.4	10	2	2	3	6	10	12	12
20–34	29	5.7	43	2	3	4	6	11	16	38
35–49	135	5.0	16	2	3	4	6	9	11	21
50–64	255	5.8	31	2	3	4	7	12	17	27
65+	705	5.8	20	2	3	5	7	11	14	23
TOTAL SINGLE DX	**23**	**4.4**	**3**	**2**	**3**	**5**	**6**	**6**	**7**	**7**
TOTAL MULTIPLE DX	**1,138**	**5.7**	**22**	**2**	**3**	**4**	**7**	**11**	**15**	**26**
TOTAL										
0–19 Years	16	4.5	9	2	2	4	5	10	10	12
20–34	33	5.5	39	2	3	4	6	9	13	38
35–49	140	5.0	16	2	3	4	6	9	11	21
50–64	265	5.7	30	2	3	4	7	11	16	27
65+	707	5.8	20	2	3	5	7	11	14	23
GRAND TOTAL	**1,161**	**5.7**	**22**	**2**	**3**	**4**	**7**	**11**	**14**	**23**

43.41: ENDO EXC GASTRIC LES

Type of Patients	Observed Patients	Avg. Stay	Vari-ance	Percentiles 10th	25th	50th	75th	90th	95th	99th
1. SINGLE DX										
0–19 Years	0									
20–34	1	1.0	0	1	1	1	1	1	1	1
35–49	1	1.0	0	1	1	1	1	1	1	1
50–64	4	2.6	<1	2	2	3	3	3	3	3
65+	1	2.0	0	2	2	2	2	2	2	2
2. MULTIPLE DX										
0–19 Years	4	2.6	3	1	2	2	4	6	6	6
20–34	20	3.9	5	2	3	3	4	8	8	9
35–49	99	4.5	16	1	2	4	5	9	10	28
50–64	196	5.0	24	2	2	3	5	10	18	22
65+	544	4.9	15	2	2	4	6	9	12	19
TOTAL SINGLE DX	**7**	**2.0**	**<1**	**1**	**1**	**2**	**3**	**3**	**3**	**3**
TOTAL MULTIPLE DX	**863**	**4.8**	**17**	**2**	**2**	**4**	**6**	**9**	**12**	**22**
TOTAL										
0–19 Years	4	2.6	3	1	2	2	4	6	6	6
20–34	21	3.8	5	1	2	3	4	8	8	9
35–49	100	4.5	16	1	2	4	5	9	10	28
50–64	200	4.9	24	2	2	3	5	10	18	22
65+	545	4.9	14	2	2	4	6	9	12	19
GRAND TOTAL	**870**	**4.8**	**17**	**2**	**2**	**4**	**6**	**9**	**12**	**22**

43.42: LOC GASTRIC LES EXC NEC

Type of Patients	Observed Patients	Avg. Stay	Vari-ance	Percentiles 10th	25th	50th	75th	90th	95th	99th
1. SINGLE DX										
0–19 Years	2	5.0	0	5	5	5	5	5	5	5
20–34	2	6.0	0	6	6	6	6	6	6	6
35–49	4	4.5	2	3	4	4	5	7	7	7
50–64	6	5.5	2	3	5	6	6	7	7	7
65+	1	4.0	0	4	4	4	4	4	4	4
2. MULTIPLE DX										
0–19 Years	8	6.0	8	3	3	5	8	10	10	10
20–34	9	10.0	116	2	4	5	13	38	38	38
35–49	34	6.3	15	3	4	5	7	11	19	20
50–64	51	8.6	48	4	5	7	11	15	16	47
65+	158	8.6	27	4	6	8	9	15	20	29
TOTAL SINGLE DX	**15**	**5.1**	**1**	**3**	**4**	**5**	**6**	**7**	**7**	**7**
TOTAL MULTIPLE DX	**260**	**8.3**	**32**	**4**	**5**	**7**	**9**	**15**	**18**	**30**
TOTAL										
0–19 Years	10	5.7	6	3	4	5	8	10	10	10
20–34	11	9.1	92	2	5	6	11	16	38	38
35–49	38	6.0	13	3	4	5	7	9	12	20
50–64	57	8.2	43	4	5	6	9	14	16	47
65+	159	8.5	27	4	6	8	9	15	20	29
GRAND TOTAL	**275**	**8.1**	**31**	**4**	**5**	**7**	**9**	**14**	**17**	**30**

43.5: PROXIMAL GASTRECTOMY

Type of Patients	Observed Patients	Avg. Stay	Vari-ance	Percentiles 10th	25th	50th	75th	90th	95th	99th
1. SINGLE DX										
0–19 Years	0									
20–34	0									
35–49	1	9.0	0	9	9	9	9	9	9	9
50–64	1	7.0	0	7	7	7	7	7	7	7
65+	1	11.0	0	11	11	11	11	11	11	11
2. MULTIPLE DX										
0–19 Years	1	25.0	0	25	25	25	25	25	25	25
20–34	4	3.5	6	1	1	3	4	7	7	7
35–49	12	13.1	113	7	9	11	12	26	52	52
50–64	39	12.9	32	6	8	11	17	22	22	25
65+	54	13.9	87	7	8	11	17	32	41	>99
TOTAL SINGLE DX	**3**	**9.0**	**4**	**7**	**7**	**9**	**11**	**11**	**11**	**11**
TOTAL MULTIPLE DX	**110**	**13.1**	**68**	**7**	**8**	**11**	**15**	**22**	**32**	**60**
TOTAL										
0–19 Years	1	25.0	0	25	25	25	25	25	25	25
20–34	4	3.5	6	1	1	3	4	7	7	7
35–49	13	12.9	107	7	9	11	12	14	52	52
50–64	40	12.7	32	6	8	11	17	22	22	25
65+	55	13.9	85	7	8	11	17	28	41	>99
GRAND TOTAL	**113**	**13.0**	**67**	**7**	**8**	**11**	**15**	**22**	**32**	**60**

43.6: DISTAL GASTRECTOMY

Type of Patients	Observed Patients	Avg. Stay	Vari-ance	Percentiles 10th	25th	50th	75th	90th	95th	99th
1. SINGLE DX										
0–19 Years	0									
20–34	2	3.0	0	3	3	3	3	3	3	3
35–49	3	3.4	<1	3	3	3	4	4	4	4
50–64	4	3.5	<1	3	3	3	4	4	4	4
65+	3	4.3	2	3	3	3	6	6	6	6
2. MULTIPLE DX										
0–19 Years	3	7.0	3	6	6	6	7	10	10	10
20–34	20	8.3	53	3	3	4	12	20	29	29
35–49	55	8.1	39	3	4	6	10	14	16	43
50–64	104	7.6	26	3	4	7	9	13	18	26
65+	152	9.6	30	3	6	8	12	17	20	32
TOTAL SINGLE DX	**12**	**3.7**	**1**	**3**	**3**	**3**	**4**	**6**	**6**	**6**
TOTAL MULTIPLE DX	**334**	**8.7**	**32**	**3**	**5**	**8**	**11**	**16**	**19**	**29**
TOTAL										
0–19 Years	3	7.0	3	6	6	6	7	10	10	10
20–34	22	7.8	51	3	3	4	10	20	20	29
35–49	58	8.0	39	3	4	6	10	14	16	43
50–64	108	7.4	26	3	3	7	9	13	18	26
65+	155	9.5	30	3	6	8	12	17	20	32
GRAND TOTAL	**346**	**8.6**	**32**	**3**	**4**	**7**	**11**	**15**	**19**	**29**

43.7: PART GASTRECTOMY W ANAST

Type of Patients	Observed Patients	Avg. Stay	Vari-ance	10th	25th	50th	75th	90th	95th	99th
1. SINGLE DX										
0–19 Years	0									
20–34	2	8.5	81	2	2	15	15	15	15	15
35–49	7	7.2	32	4	4	6	7	22	22	22
50–64	5	10.3	42	4	6	7	13	20	20	20
65+	3	5.0	0	5	5	5	5	5	5	5
2. MULTIPLE DX										
0–19 Years	2	21.0	132	10	10	29	29	29	29	29
20–34	16	9.4	35	2	6	7	12	18	20	24
35–49	117	10.7	47	4	6	9	14	18	22	39
50–64	254	12.3	87	5	7	9	14	26	32	39
65+	447	12.4	47	6	8	11	15	22	25	37
TOTAL SINGLE DX	**17**	**7.7**	**30**	**4**	**4**	**5**	**7**	**20**	**22**	**22**
TOTAL MULTIPLE DX	**836**	**12.1**	**59**	**6**	**7**	**10**	**15**	**22**	**27**	**37**
TOTAL										
0–19 Years	2	21.0	132	10	10	29	29	29	29	29
20–34	18	9.3	36	2	6	7	12	18	20	24
35–49	124	10.5	47	4	6	9	14	18	22	39
50–64	259	12.3	86	5	7	9	14	25	31	39
65+	450	12.4	47	6	8	11	15	22	25	37
GRAND TOTAL	**853**	**12.0**	**59**	**6**	**7**	**10**	**15**	**22**	**27**	**37**

43.8: OTH PARTIAL GASTRECTOMY

Type of Patients	Observed Patients	Avg. Stay	Vari-ance	10th	25th	50th	75th	90th	95th	99th
1. SINGLE DX										
0–19 Years	0									
20–34	2	6.5	<1	6	6	6	7	7	7	7
35–49	3	5.7	1	5	5	5	7	7	7	7
50–64	5	4.5	6	1	3	6	6	7	7	7
65+	2	8.0	13	5	5	5	11	11	11	11
2. MULTIPLE DX										
0–19 Years	4	8.6	33	5	5	6	8	19	19	19
20–34	21	4.9	26	2	2	3	5	8	14	25
35–49	58	6.3	14	3	4	5	8	12	14	22
50–64	87	8.3	31	3	5	7	12	15	17	28
65+	156	9.7	49	4	6	8	11	17	19	37
TOTAL SINGLE DX	**12**	**5.9**	**6**	**3**	**5**	**6**	**7**	**11**	**11**	**11**
TOTAL MULTIPLE DX	**326**	**8.3**	**38**	**3**	**5**	**7**	**10**	**15**	**18**	**29**
TOTAL										
0–19 Years	4	8.6	33	5	5	6	8	19	19	19
20–34	23	5.1	24	2	3	4	6	8	14	25
35–49	61	6.3	14	3	4	5	8	12	14	22
50–64	92	8.1	31	3	4	7	12	15	17	28
65+	158	9.7	48	4	6	8	11	17	19	37
GRAND TOTAL	**338**	**8.3**	**37**	**3**	**5**	**7**	**10**	**15**	**18**	**29**

43.89: PARTIAL GASTRECTOMY NEC

Type of Patients	Observed Patients	Avg. Stay	Vari-ance	10th	25th	50th	75th	90th	95th	99th
1. SINGLE DX										
0–19 Years	0									
20–34	2	6.5	<1	6	6	6	7	7	7	7
35–49	3	5.7	1	5	5	5	7	7	7	7
50–64	5	4.5	6	1	3	6	6	7	7	7
65+	2	8.0	13	5	5	5	11	11	11	11
2. MULTIPLE DX										
0–19 Years	4	8.6	33	5	5	6	8	19	19	19
20–34	21	4.9	26	2	2	3	5	8	14	25
35–49	57	6.3	14	3	4	5	8	12	14	22
50–64	87	8.3	31	3	5	7	12	15	17	28
65+	156	9.7	49	4	6	8	11	17	19	37
TOTAL SINGLE DX	**12**	**5.9**	**6**	**3**	**5**	**6**	**7**	**11**	**11**	**11**
TOTAL MULTIPLE DX	**325**	**8.3**	**38**	**3**	**5**	**7**	**10**	**15**	**18**	**29**
TOTAL										
0–19 Years	4	8.6	33	5	5	6	8	19	19	19
20–34	23	5.1	24	2	3	4	6	8	14	25
35–49	60	6.3	14	3	4	5	8	12	14	22
50–64	92	8.1	31	3	4	7	12	15	17	28
65+	158	9.7	48	4	6	8	11	17	19	37
GRAND TOTAL	**337**	**8.3**	**37**	**3**	**5**	**7**	**10**	**15**	**18**	**29**

43.9: TOTAL GASTRECTOMY

Type of Patients	Observed Patients	Avg. Stay	Vari-ance	10th	25th	50th	75th	90th	95th	99th
1. SINGLE DX										
0–19 Years	0									
20–34	1	4.0	0	4	4	4	4	4	4	4
35–49	2	11.0	6	9	9	13	13	13	13	13
50–64	3	11.4	9	8	8	11	14	14	14	14
65+	1	14.0	0	14	14	14	14	14	14	14
2. MULTIPLE DX										
0–19 Years	0									
20–34	12	16.5	221	7	9	11	14	43	43	63
35–49	52	12.7	36	8	9	11	14	22	24	44
50–64	140	14.1	57	7	9	12	17	25	27	40
65+	213	14.0	58	7	9	12	17	24	29	42
TOTAL SINGLE DX	**7**	**11.0**	**12**	**4**	**9**	**13**	**14**	**14**	**14**	**14**
TOTAL MULTIPLE DX	**417**	**14.0**	**61**	**7**	**9**	**11**	**17**	**24**	**29**	**43**
TOTAL										
0–19 Years	0									
20–34	13	16.0	218	7	7	11	14	43	43	63
35–49	54	12.7	35	8	9	11	14	22	24	44
50–64	143	14.1	56	7	9	12	17	25	27	40
65+	214	14.0	58	7	9	12	17	24	29	42
GRAND TOTAL	**424**	**13.9**	**60**	**7**	**9**	**11**	**17**	**24**	**29**	**43**

43.99: TOTAL GASTRECTOMY NEC

Type of Patients	Observed Patients	Avg. Stay	Vari-ance	10th	25th	50th	75th	90th	95th	99th
				Percentiles						
1. SINGLE DX										
0–19 Years	0									
20–34	1	4.0	0	4	4	4	4	4	4	4
35–49	2	11.0	6	9	9	13	13	13	13	13
50–64	3	11.4	9	8	8	11	14	14	14	14
65+	1	14.0	0	14	14	14	14	14	14	14
2. MULTIPLE DX										
0–19 Years	0									
20–34	10	13.2	162	7	7	11	11	20	63	63
35–49	49	12.8	38	8	9	11	14	22	24	44
50–64	137	14.1	58	7	9	12	17	25	28	40
65+	210	13.9	58	7	9	12	17	24	29	42
TOTAL SINGLE DX	**7**	**11.0**	**12**	**4**	**9**	**13**	**14**	**14**	**14**	**14**
TOTAL MULTIPLE DX	**406**	**13.8**	**59**	**7**	**9**	**11**	**17**	**24**	**29**	**42**
TOTAL										
0–19 Years	0									
20–34	11	12.8	158	4	7	11	11	17	63	63
35–49	51	12.7	37	8	9	11	14	22	24	44
50–64	140	14.0	57	7	9	12	17	25	27	40
65+	211	13.9	58	7	9	12	17	24	29	42
GRAND TOTAL	**413**	**13.8**	**58**	**7**	**9**	**11**	**16**	**24**	**29**	**42**

44.0: VAGOTOMY

Type of Patients	Observed Patients	Avg. Stay	Vari-ance	10th	25th	50th	75th	90th	95th	99th
				Percentiles						
1. SINGLE DX										
0–19 Years	0									
20–34	1	10.0	0	10	10	10	10	10	10	10
35–49	2	5.0	0	5	5	5	5	5	5	5
50–64	4	7.1	6	4	6	6	10	10	10	10
65+	1	10.0	0	10	10	10	10	10	10	10
2. MULTIPLE DX										
0–19 Years	0									
20–34	5	6.3	2	5	5	5	8	8	8	8
35–49	24	9.3	42	5	6	7	10	16	19	37
50–64	34	10.4	37	5	6	10	15	16	18	32
65+	44	11.9	23	7	9	11	13	20	24	25
TOTAL SINGLE DX	**8**	**7.2**	**6**	**5**	**5**	**6**	**10**	**10**	**10**	**10**
TOTAL MULTIPLE DX	**107**	**10.5**	**32**	**5**	**7**	**10**	**12**	**17**	**22**	**32**
TOTAL										
0–19 Years	0									
20–34	6	6.8	4	5	5	8	8	10	10	10
35–49	26	8.9	40	5	6	7	10	16	19	37
50–64	38	10.0	34	5	6	9	13	16	18	32
65+	45	11.9	23	7	9	11	13	19	24	25
GRAND TOTAL	**115**	**10.3**	**31**	**5**	**6**	**10**	**12**	**17**	**20**	**32**

44.1: GASTRIC DXTIC PX

Type of Patients	Observed Patients	Avg. Stay	Vari-ance	10th	25th	50th	75th	90th	95th	99th
				Percentiles						
1. SINGLE DX										
0–19 Years	9	1.1	<1	1	1	1	1	1	2	2
20–34	2	1.0	0	1	1	1	1	1	1	1
35–49	2	1.5	<1	1	1	1	2	2	2	2
50–64	0									
65+	2	2.1	2	1	1	3	3	3	3	3
2. MULTIPLE DX										
0–19 Years	19	3.8	18	1	1	2	4	13	13	15
20–34	32	6.4	22	1	3	5	9	13	13	22
35–49	67	7.0	72	1	2	4	9	20	22	39
50–64	90	5.9	29	2	2	4	8	13	19	22
65+	215	5.7	25	1	2	4	8	11	13	23
TOTAL SINGLE DX	**15**	**1.2**	**<1**	**1**	**1**	**1**	**1**	**2**	**3**	**3**
TOTAL MULTIPLE DX	**423**	**5.9**	**33**	**1**	**2**	**4**	**8**	**13**	**16**	**23**
TOTAL										
0–19 Years	28	2.9	14	1	1	1	3	7	13	15
20–34	34	6.1	23	1	2	5	9	13	13	22
35–49	69	6.9	72	1	2	4	9	20	22	39
50–64	90	5.9	29	2	2	4	8	13	19	22
65+	217	5.7	25	1	2	4	8	11	13	23
GRAND TOTAL	**438**	**5.8**	**33**	**1**	**2**	**4**	**8**	**13**	**16**	**23**

44.13: GASTROSCOPY NEC

Type of Patients	Observed Patients	Avg. Stay	Vari-ance	10th	25th	50th	75th	90th	95th	99th
				Percentiles						
1. SINGLE DX										
0–19 Years	8	1.1	<1	1	1	1	1	1	2	2
20–34	1	1.0	0	1	1	1	1	1	1	1
35–49	2	1.5	<1	1	1	1	2	2	2	2
50–64	0									
65+	1	1.0	0	1	1	1	1	1	1	1
2. MULTIPLE DX										
0–19 Years	12	2.8	12	1	1	1	3	4	13	13
20–34	14	5.6	11	3	3	5	7	10	13	13
35–49	31	4.1	13	1	2	3	5	8	10	21
50–64	36	5.1	25	2	2	3	5	12	19	22
65+	100	5.0	23	1	2	4	7	9	11	19
TOTAL SINGLE DX	**12**	**1.1**	**<1**	**1**	**1**	**1**	**1**	**2**	**2**	**2**
TOTAL MULTIPLE DX	**193**	**4.8**	**21**	**1**	**2**	**4**	**6**	**9**	**13**	**22**
TOTAL										
0–19 Years	20	2.1	8	1	1	1	2	4	13	13
20–34	15	5.2	12	1	3	5	7	10	13	13
35–49	33	4.0	13	1	2	3	5	8	10	21
50–64	36	5.1	25	2	2	3	5	12	19	22
65+	101	5.0	23	1	2	4	7	9	11	19
GRAND TOTAL	**205**	**4.6**	**20**	**1**	**2**	**3**	**6**	**9**	**13**	**22**

44.14: CLOSED GASTRIC BIOPSY

Type of Patients	Observed Patients	Avg. Stay	Vari-ance	Percentiles						
				10th	25th	50th	75th	90th	95th	99th
1. SINGLE DX										
0–19 Years	0									
20–34	1	1.0	0	1	1	1	1	1	1	1
35–49	0									
50–64	0									
65+	0									
2. MULTIPLE DX										
0–19 Years	3	3.7	17	1	1	1	4	11	11	11
20–34	11	6.2	22	1	2	6	13	13	13	13
35–49	29	7.2	41	1	2	6	9	22	22	22
50–64	39	5.9	25	1	2	4	8	13	16	21
65+	88	5.1	17	1	2	3	7	10	13	22
TOTAL SINGLE DX	**1**	**1.0**	**0**	**1**	**1**	**1**	**1**	**1**	**1**	**1**
TOTAL MULTIPLE DX	**170**	**5.7**	**24**	**1**	**2**	**4**	**9**	**13**	**14**	**22**
TOTAL										
0–19 Years	3	3.7	17	1	1	1	4	11	11	11
20–34	12	5.9	22	1	2	4	9	13	13	13
35–49	29	7.2	41	1	2	6	9	22	22	22
50–64	39	5.9	25	1	2	4	8	13	16	21
65+	88	5.1	17	1	2	3	7	10	13	22
GRAND TOTAL	**171**	**5.7**	**24**	**1**	**2**	**4**	**9**	**13**	**14**	**22**

44.2: PYLOROPLASTY

Type of Patients	Observed Patients	Avg. Stay	Vari-ance	Percentiles						
				10th	25th	50th	75th	90th	95th	99th
1. SINGLE DX										
0–19 Years	5	3.8	14	1	1	3	3	12	12	12
20–34	2	3.3	<1	3	3	3	4	4	4	4
35–49	3	4.5	2	1	5	5	5	5	5	5
50–64	8	5.1	2	3	4	6	6	7	7	7
65+	2	4.7	3	3	3	6	6	6	6	6
2. MULTIPLE DX										
0–19 Years	26	5.4	22	2	3	4	6	10	19	24
20–34	60	4.4	20	1	2	3	5	7	11	33
35–49	133	5.4	23	2	2	4	7	11	14	26
50–64	153	6.6	40	1	2	6	8	11	19	37
65+	199	10.2	67	2	4	8	14	20	31	37
TOTAL SINGLE DX	**20**	**4.4**	**5**	**1**	**3**	**4**	**5**	**6**	**7**	**12**
TOTAL MULTIPLE DX	**571**	**7.4**	**49**	**2**	**3**	**6**	**9**	**17**	**22**	**33**
TOTAL										
0–19 Years	31	5.2	21	2	3	4	5	10	12	24
20–34	62	4.3	19	1	2	3	5	7	10	33
35–49	136	5.4	22	2	2	4	7	10	14	26
50–64	161	6.6	39	1	2	6	8	11	19	37
65+	201	10.2	67	2	4	8	14	20	31	37
GRAND TOTAL	**591**	**7.3**	**48**	**2**	**3**	**5**	**9**	**17**	**21**	**33**

44.22: ENDO DILATION PYLORUS

Type of Patients	Observed Patients	Avg. Stay	Vari-ance	Percentiles						
				10th	25th	50th	75th	90th	95th	99th
1. SINGLE DX										
0–19 Years	0									
20–34	1	4.0	0	4	4	4	4	4	4	4
35–49	1	1.0	0	1	1	1	1	1	1	1
50–64	1	3.0	0	3	3	3	3	3	3	3
65+	1	3.0	0	3	3	3	3	3	3	3
2. MULTIPLE DX										
0–19 Years	6	4.2	6	1	4	4	4	9	9	9
20–34	49	3.9	23	1	2	3	4	7	13	33
35–49	83	3.8	10	1	2	3	5	7	10	20
50–64	97	4.6	29	1	2	3	6	8	10	37
65+	98	7.8	59	2	3	5	10	17	31	31
TOTAL SINGLE DX	**4**	**2.8**	**1**	**1**	**3**	**3**	**3**	**4**	**4**	**4**
TOTAL MULTIPLE DX	**333**	**5.5**	**37**	**1**	**2**	**3**	**6**	**11**	**17**	**31**
TOTAL										
0–19 Years	6	4.2	6	1	4	4	4	9	9	9
20–34	50	3.9	23	1	2	3	4	7	13	33
35–49	84	3.8	10	1	2	3	5	7	10	20
50–64	98	4.6	29	1	2	3	6	8	10	37
65+	99	7.8	58	2	3	5	10	17	31	31
GRAND TOTAL	**337**	**5.5**	**37**	**1**	**2**	**3**	**6**	**11**	**17**	**31**

44.29: OTHER PYLOROPLASTY

Type of Patients	Observed Patients	Avg. Stay	Vari-ance	Percentiles						
				10th	25th	50th	75th	90th	95th	99th
1. SINGLE DX										
0–19 Years	4	4.9	16	3	3	3	3	12	12	12
20–34	1	3.0	0	3	3	3	3	3	3	3
35–49	2	5.0	0	5	5	5	5	5	5	5
50–64	7	5.4	2	3	5	6	6	7	7	7
65+	1	6.0	0	6	6	6	6	6	6	6
2. MULTIPLE DX										
0–19 Years	17	5.5	29	3	3	4	5	8	24	24
20–34	11	5.9	5	4	4	6	7	9	9	11
35–49	50	7.7	33	3	4	7	8	12	21	30
50–64	56	10.0	42	5	6	8	11	19	24	40
65+	100	12.9	64	6	7	11	18	23	24	54
TOTAL SINGLE DX	**15**	**4.9**	**4**	**3**	**3**	**5**	**6**	**6**	**7**	**12**
TOTAL MULTIPLE DX	**234**	**10.2**	**53**	**4**	**6**	**8**	**13**	**20**	**24**	**40**
TOTAL										
0–19 Years	21	5.4	26	3	3	4	5	12	19	24
20–34	12	5.6	5	3	4	5	7	9	9	11
35–49	52	7.5	31	3	5	7	8	12	21	30
50–64	63	9.6	40	5	6	8	11	19	21	40
65+	101	12.9	64	6	7	11	18	23	24	54
GRAND TOTAL	**249**	**9.9**	**52**	**3**	**5**	**8**	**12**	**20**	**24**	**40**

44.3: GASTROENTEROSTOMY

Type of Patients	Observed Patients	Avg. Stay	Vari-ance	Percentiles						
				10th	25th	50th	75th	90th	95th	99th
1. SINGLE DX										
0–19 Years	5	2.8	<1	2	3	3	3	3	3	3
20–34	223	2.4	<1	1	2	2	3	4	4	5
35–49	228	2.5	<1	1	2	2	3	3	4	5
50–64	112	2.6	2	1	2	2	3	4	6	8
65+	0									
2. MULTIPLE DX										
0–19 Years	64	6.7	49	2	3	3	10	17	25	>99
20–34	2,335	3.3	9	2	2	3	4	5	6	17
35–49	4,889	3.5	11	2	2	3	4	5	7	18
50–64	4,582	4.1	28	2	2	3	4	6	10	27
65+	556	13.3	164	3	5	10	18	26	33	94
TOTAL SINGLE DX	**568**	**2.5**	**1**	**1**	**2**	**2**	**3**	**3**	**4**	**7**
TOTAL MULTIPLE DX	**12,426**	**4.2**	**29**	**2**	**2**	**3**	**4**	**7**	**11**	**27**
TOTAL										
0–19 Years	69	6.1	44	2	3	3	6	17	23	28
20–34	2,558	3.2	8	2	2	3	4	5	6	14
35–49	5,117	3.5	11	2	2	3	4	5	7	17
50–64	4,694	4.1	27	2	2	3	4	6	9	27
65+	556	13.3	164	3	5	10	18	26	33	94
GRAND TOTAL	**12,994**	**4.1**	**28**	**2**	**2**	**3**	**4**	**6**	**11**	**26**

44.31: HIGH GASTRIC BYPASS

Type of Patients	Observed Patients	Avg. Stay	Vari-ance	Percentiles						
				10th	25th	50th	75th	90th	95th	99th
1. SINGLE DX										
0–19 Years	5	2.8	<1	2	3	3	3	3	3	3
20–34	192	2.4	<1	1	2	2	3	4	4	6
35–49	182	2.4	<1	1	2	2	3	3	4	5
50–64	86	2.3	1	1	2	2	3	3	3	7
65+	0									
2. MULTIPLE DX										
0–19 Years	41	3.3	3	2	2	3	4	5	6	13
20–34	2,083	3.1	4	2	2	3	4	5	6	9
35–49	4,287	3.4	7	2	2	3	4	5	6	14
50–64	3,959	3.6	18	2	2	3	4	5	7	15
65+	97	4.6	31	2	3	3	4	6	16	31
TOTAL SINGLE DX	**465**	**2.4**	**<1**	**1**	**2**	**2**	**3**	**3**	**4**	**5**
TOTAL MULTIPLE DX	**10,467**	**3.4**	**11**	**2**	**2**	**3**	**4**	**5**	**6**	**14**
TOTAL										
0–19 Years	46	3.2	3	2	2	3	4	5	6	13
20–34	2,275	3.0	3	2	2	3	3	4	5	9
35–49	4,469	3.3	7	2	2	3	4	5	6	14
50–64	4,045	3.6	18	2	2	3	4	5	7	15
65+	97	4.6	31	2	3	3	4	6	16	31
GRAND TOTAL	**10,932**	**3.4**	**10**	**2**	**2**	**3**	**4**	**5**	**6**	**13**

44.32: PERC GASTROJEJUNOSTOMY

Type of Patients	Observed Patients	Avg. Stay	Vari-ance	Percentiles						
				10th	25th	50th	75th	90th	95th	99th
1. SINGLE DX										
0–19 Years	0									
20–34	0									
35–49	0									
50–64	0									
65+	0									
2. MULTIPLE DX										
0–19 Years	12	12.6	76	1	3	14	17	25	27	27
20–34	14	14.6	146	2	5	8	24	28	29	44
35–49	33	10.8	59	3	4	10	16	24	28	30
50–64	64	13.1	227	3	4	7	16	24	46	94
65+	212	15.7	270	4	7	10	19	33	43	94
TOTAL SINGLE DX	**0**									
TOTAL MULTIPLE DX	**335**	**14.7**	**230**	**3**	**6**	**10**	**19**	**28**	**42**	**94**
TOTAL										
0–19 Years	12	12.6	76	1	3	14	17	25	27	27
20–34	14	14.6	146	2	5	8	24	28	29	44
35–49	33	10.8	59	3	4	10	16	24	28	30
50–64	64	13.1	227	3	4	7	16	24	46	94
65+	212	15.7	270	4	7	10	19	33	43	94
GRAND TOTAL	**335**	**14.7**	**230**	**3**	**6**	**10**	**19**	**28**	**42**	**94**

44.39: GASTROENTEROSTOMY NEC

Type of Patients	Observed Patients	Avg. Stay	Vari-ance	Percentiles						
				10th	25th	50th	75th	90th	95th	99th
1. SINGLE DX										
0–19 Years	0									
20–34	31	2.3	<1	1	2	2	3	4	4	5
35–49	46	2.5	2	1	2	2	3	5	5	8
50–64	26	3.4	4	2	2	3	4	7	8	9
65+	0									
2. MULTIPLE DX										
0–19 Years	11	9.6	70	3	3	10	16	28	>99	>99
20–34	238	4.1	33	2	2	3	4	7	13	49
35–49	569	4.2	31	2	2	3	4	7	11	26
50–64	559	6.2	51	2	2	3	7	15	21	33
65+	247	14.8	86	6	8	13	19	25	29	58
TOTAL SINGLE DX	**103**	**2.7**	**2**	**2**	**2**	**2**	**3**	**5**	**6**	**8**
TOTAL MULTIPLE DX	**1,624**	**6.5**	**60**	**2**	**2**	**3**	**7**	**17**	**22**	**38**
TOTAL										
0–19 Years	11	9.6	70	3	3	10	16	28	>99	>99
20–34	269	3.9	30	2	2	3	4	5	12	19
35–49	615	4.1	30	2	2	3	4	7	11	26
50–64	585	6.1	50	2	2	3	7	15	21	32
65+	247	14.8	86	6	8	13	19	25	29	58
GRAND TOTAL	**1,727**	**6.3**	**58**	**2**	**2**	**3**	**7**	**16**	**21**	**36**

44.4: CNTRL PEPTIC ULCER HEMOR

Type of Patients	Observed Patients	Avg. Stay	Vari-ance	Percentiles						
				10th	25th	50th	75th	90th	95th	99th
1. SINGLE DX										
0–19 Years	5	3.7	2	1	4	4	4	5	5	5
20–34	21	4.6	2	3	4	5	6	6	6	7
35–49	42	4.2	5	1	2	5	6	7	7	8
50–64	13	5.2	7	2	3	5	7	10	10	10
65+	9	3.8	8	1	1	2	7	7	8	8
2. MULTIPLE DX										
0–19 Years	31	5.7	12	2	4	5	7	9	15	16
20–34	293	5.2	28	2	2	4	6	10	14	27
35–49	882	5.5	29	2	2	4	7	11	15	30
50–64	1,665	5.1	32	2	2	3	6	10	15	26
65+	4,353	5.8	31	2	3	4	7	11	16	28
TOTAL SINGLE DX	**90**	**4.3**	**5**	**1**	**2**	**4**	**6**	**7**	**7**	**10**
TOTAL MULTIPLE DX	**7,224**	**5.6**	**31**	**2**	**3**	**4**	**7**	**11**	**15**	**28**
TOTAL										
0–19 Years	36	5.4	11	2	4	5	7	9	12	16
20–34	314	5.2	26	2	2	4	6	10	13	27
35–49	924	5.4	28	2	2	4	7	10	15	30
50–64	1,678	5.1	32	2	2	3	6	10	14	26
65+	4,362	5.8	31	2	3	4	7	11	16	28
GRAND TOTAL	**7,314**	**5.6**	**31**	**2**	**3**	**4**	**7**	**11**	**15**	**27**

44.41: SUT GASTRIC ULCER SITE

Type of Patients	Observed Patients	Avg. Stay	Vari-ance	Percentiles						
				10th	25th	50th	75th	90th	95th	99th
1. SINGLE DX										
0–19 Years	1	4.0	0	4	4	4	4	4	4	4
20–34	2	6.0	0	6	6	6	6	6	6	6
35–49	5	6.3	<1	5	5	7	7	7	7	7
50–64	2	6.2	2	5	5	7	7	7	7	7
65+	2	5.3	9	3	3	3	8	8	8	8
2. MULTIPLE DX										
0–19 Years	7	6.4	5	4	5	6	7	9	12	12
20–34	43	8.7	51	4	5	6	9	15	27	44
35–49	70	8.4	40	4	5	7	8	15	27	>99
50–64	115	11.7	111	5	6	9	13	21	22	67
65+	185	11.6	69	6	7	9	13	19	24	43
TOTAL SINGLE DX	**12**	**6.0**	**2**	**4**	**5**	**6**	**7**	**7**	**8**	**8**
TOTAL MULTIPLE DX	**420**	**10.7**	**75**	**5**	**6**	**8**	**12**	**19**	**25**	**59**
TOTAL										
0–19 Years	8	6.1	5	4	5	6	6	9	12	12
20–34	45	8.5	49	4	5	6	9	15	27	44
35–49	75	8.2	36	4	5	7	8	14	25	>99
50–64	117	11.6	110	5	6	9	13	21	22	67
65+	187	11.5	68	6	7	9	13	19	24	43
GRAND TOTAL	**432**	**10.6**	**73**	**5**	**6**	**8**	**11**	**19**	**25**	**59**

44.42: SUT DUODENAL ULCER SITE

Type of Patients	Observed Patients	Avg. Stay	Vari-ance	Percentiles						
				10th	25th	50th	75th	90th	95th	99th
1. SINGLE DX										
0–19 Years	3	4.1	<1	3	4	4	5	5	5	5
20–34	14	4.9	1	4	4	5	6	6	6	7
35–49	20	5.3	2	3	4	6	6	7	7	8
50–64	7	7.1	4	5	5	6	10	10	10	10
65+	1	7.0	0	7	7	7	7	7	7	7
2. MULTIPLE DX										
0–19 Years	9	7.5	18	4	4	6	7	15	16	16
20–34	60	8.9	31	4	5	7	10	16	23	31
35–49	144	9.7	58	4	6	8	9	18	28	41
50–64	188	10.6	77	5	6	8	12	22	26	41
65+	397	13.0	84	6	8	10	16	22	27	60
TOTAL SINGLE DX	**45**	**5.4**	**2**	**4**	**4**	**6**	**6**	**7**	**8**	**10**
TOTAL MULTIPLE DX	**798**	**11.6**	**76**	**5**	**6**	**9**	**14**	**22**	**27**	**57**
TOTAL										
0–19 Years	12	6.6	15	4	4	5	7	15	16	16
20–34	74	8.1	28	4	5	6	10	14	23	31
35–49	164	9.2	54	4	6	7	9	15	28	41
50–64	195	10.5	75	5	6	8	12	22	25	41
65+	398	13.0	83	6	7	10	16	22	27	59
GRAND TOTAL	**843**	**11.2**	**74**	**5**	**6**	**9**	**13**	**21**	**26**	**48**

44.43: ENDO CNTRL GASTRIC BLEED

Type of Patients	Observed Patients	Avg. Stay	Vari-ance	Percentiles						
				10th	25th	50th	75th	90th	95th	99th
1. SINGLE DX										
0–19 Years	1	1.0	0	1	1	1	1	1	1	1
20–34	5	2.6	<1	2	2	3	3	3	3	3
35–49	17	1.6	<1	1	1	2	2	2	2	2
50–64	4	2.7	<1	2	2	3	3	3	3	3
65+	6	1.8	2	1	1	1	2	2	5	5
2. MULTIPLE DX										
0–19 Years	14	4.2	8	1	2	4	6	9	9	9
20–34	189	3.1	9	1	2	2	4	5	7	13
35–49	660	4.1	14	2	2	3	4	8	11	22
50–64	1,349	3.8	11	1	2	3	4	7	9	20
65+	3,749	4.8	16	2	3	4	6	9	12	21
TOTAL SINGLE DX	**33**	**1.9**	**<1**	**1**	**1**	**2**	**2**	**3**	**3**	**5**
TOTAL MULTIPLE DX	**5,961**	**4.5**	**15**	**2**	**2**	**3**	**5**	**8**	**11**	**21**
TOTAL										
0–19 Years	15	4.0	8	1	2	3	6	9	9	9
20–34	194	3.1	9	1	2	2	3	5	7	13
35–49	677	4.0	14	2	2	3	4	7	11	22
50–64	1,353	3.8	11	1	2	3	4	7	9	20
65+	3,755	4.8	16	2	3	4	6	9	12	21
GRAND TOTAL	**5,994**	**4.4**	**15**	**2**	**2**	**3**	**5**	**8**	**11**	**21**

44.5: REVISION GASTRIC ANAST

Type of Patients	Observed Patients	Avg. Stay	Vari-ance	10th	25th	50th	75th	90th	95th	99th
1. SINGLE DX										
0–19 Years	0									
20–34	1	6.0	0	6	6	6	6	6	6	6
35–49	0									
50–64	1	4.0	0	4	4	4	4	4	4	4
65+	1	25.0	0	25	25	25	25	25	25	25
2. MULTIPLE DX										
0–19 Years	1	6.0	0	6	6	6	6	6	6	6
20–34	44	7.9	87	2	4	6	8	20	24	65
35–49	104	9.6	85	2	3	6	11	31	33	>99
50–64	128	15.3	301	4	5	8	18	39	48	80
65+	44	14.8	92	5	6	13	22	26	30	57
TOTAL SINGLE DX	**3**	**14.5**	**129**	**4**	**4**	**6**	**25**	**25**	**25**	**25**
TOTAL MULTIPLE DX	**321**	**12.3**	**177**	**3**	**4**	**7**	**16**	**30**	**39**	**80**
TOTAL										
0–19 Years	1	6.0	0	6	6	6	6	6	6	6
20–34	45	7.9	86	2	4	6	8	15	24	65
35–49	104	9.6	85	2	3	6	11	31	33	>99
50–64	129	15.2	299	4	5	8	18	39	48	80
65+	45	15.0	93	5	7	13	22	25	30	57
GRAND TOTAL	**324**	**12.3**	**176**	**3**	**4**	**7**	**16**	**30**	**39**	**80**

44.6: OTHER GASTRIC REPAIR

Type of Patients	Observed Patients	Avg. Stay	Vari-ance	10th	25th	50th	75th	90th	95th	99th
1. SINGLE DX										
0–19 Years	106	1.8	1	1	1	1	2	3	5	6
20–34	106	1.7	1	1	1	1	2	3	3	6
35–49	172	1.9	1	1	1	2	2	3	4	6
50–64	96	1.6	<1	1	1	2	2	2	3	4
65+	16	1.7	<1	1	1	1	2	3	4	4
2. MULTIPLE DX										
0–19 Years	980	7.8	104	1	2	4	8	21	28	61
20–34	517	3.1	23	1	1	2	3	6	9	28
35–49	1,276	2.8	15	1	1	2	3	5	7	26
50–64	1,498	2.8	12	1	1	2	3	5	8	20
65+	937	4.8	29	1	2	3	6	10	14	27
TOTAL SINGLE DX	**496**	**1.8**	**1**	**1**	**1**	**2**	**2**	**3**	**4**	**6**
TOTAL MULTIPLE DX	**5,208**	**4.4**	**44**	**1**	**1**	**2**	**5**	**9**	**16**	**35**
TOTAL										
0–19 Years	1,086	7.2	98	1	2	4	8	20	27	57
20–34	623	2.9	19	1	1	2	3	6	8	22
35–49	1,448	2.7	13	1	1	2	3	5	7	25
50–64	1,594	2.8	12	1	1	2	3	5	7	19
65+	953	4.7	29	1	2	3	6	10	14	27
GRAND TOTAL	**5,704**	**4.2**	**41**	**1**	**1**	**2**	**4**	**9**	**16**	**32**

44.61: SUTURE GASTRIC LAC

Type of Patients	Observed Patients	Avg. Stay	Vari-ance	10th	25th	50th	75th	90th	95th	99th
1. SINGLE DX										
0–19 Years	3	3.4	<1	3	3	3	4	4	4	4
20–34	5	4.3	13	1	2	4	5	11	11	11
35–49	0									
50–64	1	1.0	0	1	1	1	1	1	1	1
65+	0									
2. MULTIPLE DX										
0–19 Years	27	8.2	59	2	4	6	8	24	26	35
20–34	57	9.4	63	4	5	7	10	19	22	56
35–49	31	8.3	28	4	5	6	9	13	21	29
50–64	13	18.5	140	5	6	17	31	31	31	31
65+	26	10.0	76	3	4	7	13	23	31	42
TOTAL SINGLE DX	**9**	**3.6**	**9**	**1**	**2**	**3**	**4**	**11**	**11**	**11**
TOTAL MULTIPLE DX	**154**	**10.0**	**74**	**3**	**5**	**7**	**11**	**23**	**31**	**42**
TOTAL										
0–19 Years	30	7.9	57	2	4	5	8	24	26	35
20–34	62	8.9	61	4	5	7	10	18	21	56
35–49	31	8.3	28	4	5	6	9	13	21	29
50–64	14	17.5	149	4	6	13	31	31	31	31
65+	26	10.0	76	3	4	7	13	23	31	42
GRAND TOTAL	**163**	**9.7**	**73**	**3**	**5**	**7**	**11**	**23**	**31**	**35**

44.63: CLOSE STOM FISTULA NEC

Type of Patients	Observed Patients	Avg. Stay	Vari-ance	10th	25th	50th	75th	90th	95th	99th
1. SINGLE DX										
0–19 Years	6	1.3	<1	1	1	1	2	2	2	2
20–34	0									
35–49	0									
50–64	0									
65+	0									
2. MULTIPLE DX										
0–19 Years	50	3.9	45	1	1	2	2	10	25	25
20–34	4	21.3	506	2	2	2	38	44	44	44
35–49	16	16.8	191	1	7	21	44	>99	>99	>99
50–64	5	5.5	12	2	3	5	7	11	11	11
65+	35	8.1	73	2	4	6	10	16	18	49
TOTAL SINGLE DX	**6**	**1.3**	**<1**	**1**	**1**	**1**	**2**	**2**	**2**	**2**
TOTAL MULTIPLE DX	**110**	**6.8**	**93**	**1**	**1**	**2**	**8**	**25**	**40**	**>99**
TOTAL										
0–19 Years	56	3.6	41	1	1	2	2	7	25	25
20–34	4	21.3	506	2	2	2	38	44	44	44
35–49	16	16.8	191	1	7	21	44	>99	>99	>99
50–64	5	5.5	12	2	3	5	7	11	11	11
65+	35	8.1	73	2	4	6	10	16	18	49
GRAND TOTAL	**116**	**6.4**	**88**	**1**	**1**	**2**	**8**	**25**	**38**	**>99**

44.66: CREAT EG SPHINCT COMPET

Type of Patients	Observed Patients	Avg. Stay	Vari-ance	Percentiles						
				10th	25th	50th	75th	90th	95th	99th
1. SINGLE DX										
0–19 Years	90	1.9	1	1	1	1	2	3	5	6
20–34	87	1.7	<1	1	1	1	2	3	3	6
35–49	152	1.9	1	1	1	2	2	3	4	7
50–64	84	1.6	<1	1	1	2	2	2	3	4
65+	16	1.7	<1	1	1	1	2	3	4	4
2. MULTIPLE DX										
0–19 Years	842	8.2	113	1	2	4	9	21	29	61
20–34	341	2.5	10	1	1	2	3	5	7	13
35–49	991	2.5	6	1	1	2	3	5	6	13
50–64	1,238	2.6	7	1	1	2	3	5	7	12
65+	798	4.0	16	1	2	2	5	9	11	19
TOTAL SINGLE DX	**429**	**1.8**	**1**	**1**	**1**	**2**	**2**	**3**	**4**	**5**
TOTAL MULTIPLE DX	**4,210**	**4.3**	**43**	**1**	**1**	**2**	**4**	**9**	**16**	**33**
TOTAL										
0–19 Years	932	7.7	106	1	2	4	8	20	28	61
20–34	428	2.4	8	1	1	2	2	4	6	12
35–49	1,143	2.4	5	1	1	2	3	4	6	12
50–64	1,322	2.6	7	1	1	2	3	5	7	12
65+	814	3.9	15	1	2	2	5	9	11	19
GRAND TOTAL	**4,639**	**4.1**	**40**	**1**	**1**	**2**	**4**	**8**	**14**	**32**

44.69: GASTRIC REPAIR NEC

Type of Patients	Observed Patients	Avg. Stay	Vari-ance	Percentiles						
				10th	25th	50th	75th	90th	95th	99th
1. SINGLE DX										
0–19 Years	2	1.6	1	1	1	1	3	3	3	3
20–34	13	1.4	<1	1	1	1	1	2	4	4
35–49	19	1.6	2	1	1	1	2	3	4	6
50–64	8	1.3	<1	1	1	1	2	2	2	2
65+	0									
2. MULTIPLE DX										
0–19 Years	30	5.9	19	1	2	6	8	10	11	29
20–34	112	2.4	19	1	1	1	2	4	7	17
35–49	226	2.6	24	1	1	1	2	4	6	26
50–64	227	2.9	20	1	1	1	3	6	13	20
65+	51	9.1	55	1	3	6	16	21	21	30
TOTAL SINGLE DX	**42**	**1.5**	**<1**	**1**	**1**	**1**	**2**	**3**	**4**	**6**
TOTAL MULTIPLE DX	**646**	**3.3**	**27**	**1**	**1**	**1**	**3**	**7**	**13**	**26**
TOTAL										
0–19 Years	32	5.7	19	1	2	5	8	10	11	29
20–34	125	2.3	18	1	1	1	2	4	7	17
35–49	245	2.6	23	1	1	1	2	4	6	26
50–64	235	2.9	19	1	1	1	3	6	13	20
65+	51	9.1	55	1	3	6	16	21	21	30
GRAND TOTAL	**688**	**3.2**	**26**	**1**	**1**	**1**	**3**	**7**	**12**	**26**

44.9: OTHER STOMACH OPERATIONS

Type of Patients	Observed Patients	Avg. Stay	Vari-ance	Percentiles						
				10th	25th	50th	75th	90th	95th	99th
1. SINGLE DX										
0–19 Years	0									
20–34	8	2.1	5	1	1	1	2	7	7	7
35–49	10	1.0	0	1	1	1	1	1	1	1
50–64	2	1.0	0	1	1	1	1	1	1	1
65+	0									
2. MULTIPLE DX										
0–19 Years	4	8.3	111	1	1	3	24	24	24	24
20–34	21	1.8	1	1	1	2	2	3	3	6
35–49	48	3.9	59	1	1	2	4	7	12	54
50–64	56	3.3	15	1	1	2	5	8	10	23
65+	32	4.8	15	1	1	3	8	11	11	14
TOTAL SINGLE DX	**20**	**1.5**	**2**	**1**	**1**	**1**	**1**	**2**	**7**	**7**
TOTAL MULTIPLE DX	**161**	**3.8**	**29**	**1**	**1**	**2**	**4**	**9**	**11**	**24**
TOTAL										
0–19 Years	4	8.3	111	1	1	3	24	24	24	24
20–34	29	1.9	2	1	1	1	2	3	6	7
35–49	58	3.5	51	1	1	1	4	6	9	54
50–64	58	3.3	14	1	1	2	4	8	10	23
65+	32	4.8	15	1	1	3	8	11	11	14
GRAND TOTAL	**181**	**3.5**	**27**	**1**	**1**	**2**	**4**	**8**	**11**	**24**

44.99: GASTRIC OPERATION NEC

Type of Patients	Observed Patients	Avg. Stay	Vari-ance	Percentiles						
				10th	25th	50th	75th	90th	95th	99th
1. SINGLE DX										
0–19 Years	0									
20–34	8	2.1	5	1	1	1	2	7	7	7
35–49	10	1.0	0	1	1	1	1	1	1	1
50–64	2	1.0	0	1	1	1	1	1	1	1
65+	0									
2. MULTIPLE DX										
0–19 Years	4	8.3	111	1	1	3	24	24	24	24
20–34	20	1.8	1	1	1	1	2	3	3	6
35–49	41	3.1	51	1	1	1	3	4	7	54
50–64	53	3.1	14	1	1	2	4	8	10	23
65+	18	2.9	9	1	1	2	3	9	11	11
TOTAL SINGLE DX	**20**	**1.5**	**2**	**1**	**1**	**1**	**1**	**2**	**7**	**7**
TOTAL MULTIPLE DX	**136**	**3.1**	**26**	**1**	**1**	**1**	**3**	**6**	**10**	**24**
TOTAL										
0–19 Years	4	8.3	111	1	1	3	24	24	24	24
20–34	28	1.9	2	1	1	1	2	3	6	7
35–49	51	2.7	43	1	1	1	3	4	5	54
50–64	55	3.1	14	1	1	1	4	8	10	23
65+	18	2.9	9	1	1	2	3	9	11	11
GRAND TOTAL	**156**	**2.9**	**24**	**1**	**1**	**1**	**3**	**6**	**9**	**24**

45.0: ENTEROTOMY

Type of Patients	Observed Patients	Avg. Stay	Variance	10th	25th	50th	75th	90th	95th	99th
1. SINGLE DX										
0–19 Years	2	4.5	<1	4	4	4	5	5	5	5
20–34	3	4.4	7	2	2	6	7	7	7	7
35–49	1	9.0	0	9	9	9	9	9	9	9
50–64	6	4.0	6	1	3	4	5	8	8	8
65+	2	5.1	1	4	4	6	6	6	6	6
2. MULTIPLE DX										
0–19 Years	11	16.7	618	3	5	5	14	84	84	84
20–34	19	8.2	51	4	5	6	7	19	26	32
35–49	30	8.1	23	4	4	7	9	17	17	20
50–64	38	9.5	36	4	5	7	12	19	21	31
65+	64	9.9	25	5	7	9	13	16	19	26
TOTAL SINGLE DX	**14**	**4.8**	**6**	**2**	**3**	**4**	**6**	**8**	**9**	**9**
TOTAL MULTIPLE DX	**162**	**9.8**	**67**	**4**	**5**	**8**	**12**	**18**	**21**	**32**
TOTAL										
0–19 Years	13	15.2	556	3	5	5	13	26	84	84
20–34	22	7.7	47	4	5	6	7	19	26	32
35–49	31	8.1	22	4	4	7	9	17	17	20
50–64	44	9.0	36	4	4	7	11	18	21	31
65+	66	9.8	25	5	7	9	12	16	19	26
GRAND TOTAL	**176**	**9.5**	**64**	**4**	**5**	**7**	**11**	**17**	**20**	**32**

45.02: SM INTEST INCISION NEC

Type of Patients	Observed Patients	Avg. Stay	Variance	10th	25th	50th	75th	90th	95th	99th
1. SINGLE DX										
0–19 Years	0									
20–34	3	4.4	7	2	2	6	7	7	7	7
35–49	1	9.0	0	9	9	9	9	9	9	9
50–64	3	4.0	12	1	1	3	8	8	8	8
65+	0									
2. MULTIPLE DX										
0–19 Years	8	20.7	791	3	5	5	22	84	84	84
20–34	14	8.2	57	4	5	5	7	26	32	32
35–49	12	9.3	31	4	4	8	17	17	17	18
50–64	20	10.4	33	4	7	9	13	21	21	21
65+	33	10.4	19	7	7	9	11	16	19	26
TOTAL SINGLE DX	**7**	**5.0**	**10**	**1**	**2**	**6**	**8**	**9**	**9**	**9**
TOTAL MULTIPLE DX	**87**	**10.7**	**94**	**4**	**6**	**9**	**13**	**19**	**22**	**84**
TOTAL										
0–19 Years	8	20.7	791	3	5	5	22	84	84	84
20–34	17	7.7	52	3	5	5	7	8	26	32
35–49	13	9.2	29	4	4	8	17	17	17	18
50–64	23	9.8	34	3	5	9	13	21	21	21
65+	33	10.4	19	7	7	9	11	16	19	26
GRAND TOTAL	**94**	**10.4**	**91**	**4**	**5**	**9**	**11**	**19**	**21**	**84**

45.1: SMALL INTEST DXTIC PX

Type of Patients	Observed Patients	Avg. Stay	Variance	10th	25th	50th	75th	90th	95th	99th
1. SINGLE DX										
0–19 Years	222	2.3	5	1	1	1	3	5	6	10
20–34	134	2.5	4	1	1	2	3	5	6	8
35–49	125	2.6	4	1	1	2	3	5	6	10
50–64	103	2.6	10	1	1	2	3	4	5	18
65+	64	3.0	6	1	1	2	4	7	8	12
2. MULTIPLE DX										
0–19 Years	1,482	5.0	37	1	2	3	6	10	15	30
20–34	4,370	4.0	19	1	2	3	5	8	11	22
35–49	11,311	4.3	13	1	2	3	5	8	11	18
50–64	15,487	4.7	18	1	2	3	6	9	13	22
65+	36,811	5.0	18	2	2	4	6	10	13	22
TOTAL SINGLE DX	**648**	**2.5**	**5**	**1**	**1**	**2**	**3**	**5**	**6**	**10**
TOTAL MULTIPLE DX	**69,461**	**4.8**	**18**	**1**	**2**	**4**	**6**	**9**	**12**	**22**
TOTAL										
0–19 Years	1,704	4.6	34	1	1	3	5	9	14	30
20–34	4,504	4.0	19	1	2	3	5	8	11	22
35–49	11,436	4.2	13	1	2	3	5	8	11	18
50–64	15,590	4.7	18	1	2	3	6	9	13	22
65+	36,875	5.0	18	2	2	4	6	10	13	22
GRAND TOTAL	**70,109**	**4.7**	**18**	**1**	**2**	**4**	**6**	**9**	**12**	**22**

45.13: SM INTEST ENDOSCOPY NEC

Type of Patients	Observed Patients	Avg. Stay	Variance	10th	25th	50th	75th	90th	95th	99th
1. SINGLE DX										
0–19 Years	115	1.3	<1	1	1	1	1	2	4	4
20–34	68	2.6	6	1	1	2	3	6	7	16
35–49	56	2.5	2	1	1	2	3	5	6	7
50–64	57	2.2	9	1	1	2	2	4	5	27
65+	35	2.6	5	1	1	2	3	6	9	12
2. MULTIPLE DX										
0–19 Years	352	4.2	32	1	1	2	5	9	13	33
20–34	1,736	4.1	25	1	2	3	5	8	10	22
35–49	4,700	4.2	14	1	2	3	5	9	11	19
50–64	6,154	4.8	20	1	2	3	6	10	13	22
65+	14,192	5.1	19	2	2	4	6	10	13	23
TOTAL SINGLE DX	**331**	**1.9**	**4**	**1**	**1**	**1**	**2**	**4**	**5**	**9**
TOTAL MULTIPLE DX	**27,134**	**4.8**	**19**	**1**	**2**	**4**	**6**	**9**	**13**	**22**
TOTAL										
0–19 Years	467	3.5	25	1	1	2	4	7	11	33
20–34	1,804	4.0	24	1	2	3	5	7	10	22
35–49	4,756	4.2	14	1	2	3	5	8	11	19
50–64	6,211	4.7	20	1	2	3	6	10	13	22
65+	14,227	5.1	19	2	2	4	6	10	13	23
GRAND TOTAL	**27,465**	**4.8**	**19**	**1**	**2**	**4**	**6**	**9**	**13**	**22**

45.14: CLOSED SMALL INTEST BX

Type of Patients	Observed Patients	Avg. Stay	Vari-ance	Percentiles						
				10th	25th	50th	75th	90th	95th	99th
1. SINGLE DX										
0–19 Years	1	4.0	0	4	4	4	4	4	4	4
20–34	1	2.0	0	2	2	2	2	2	2	2
35–49	1	3.0	0	3	3	3	3	3	3	3
50–64	3	3.8	<1	3	4	4	4	4	4	4
65+	0									
2. MULTIPLE DX										
0–19 Years	15	12.7	109	3	4	8	23	27	29	36
20–34	23	4.8	15	1	3	4	5	13	13	18
35–49	48	5.0	20	2	2	3	6	11	17	20
50–64	55	4.6	8	1	3	4	6	8	11	15
65+	107	4.9	25	1	2	3	5	11	18	23
TOTAL SINGLE DX	**6**	**3.2**	**<1**	**2**	**2**	**4**	**4**	**4**	**4**	**4**
TOTAL MULTIPLE DX	**248**	**5.5**	**31**	**1**	**2**	**4**	**6**	**11**	**19**	**29**
TOTAL										
0–19 Years	16	12.2	106	3	4	8	23	27	29	36
20–34	24	4.5	14	1	2	4	5	7	13	18
35–49	49	5.0	19	2	2	3	6	11	17	20
50–64	58	4.5	8	2	3	4	6	8	11	15
65+	107	4.9	25	1	2	3	5	11	18	23
GRAND TOTAL	**254**	**5.4**	**30**	**1**	**2**	**4**	**6**	**11**	**18**	**29**

45.16: EGD W CLOSED BIOPSY

Type of Patients	Observed Patients	Avg. Stay	Vari-ance	Percentiles						
				10th	25th	50th	75th	90th	95th	99th
1. SINGLE DX										
0–19 Years	106	3.2	7	1	1	3	4	6	7	10
20–34	63	2.4	2	1	1	2	3	4	6	6
35–49	67	2.7	4	1	1	3	3	5	6	14
50–64	43	3.1	11	1	2	2	3	4	5	18
65+	29	3.3	6	1	1	2	5	7	7	10
2. MULTIPLE DX										
0–19 Years	1,112	5.1	37	1	2	3	6	10	15	30
20–34	2,602	4.0	16	1	2	3	5	8	11	22
35–49	6,535	4.3	13	1	2	3	5	8	11	18
50–64	9,241	4.7	18	1	2	3	6	9	12	21
65+	22,468	5.0	17	2	2	4	6	9	12	21
TOTAL SINGLE DX	**308**	**3.0**	**6**	**1**	**1**	**2**	**4**	**6**	**7**	**14**
TOTAL MULTIPLE DX	**41,958**	**4.8**	**17**	**1**	**2**	**4**	**6**	**9**	**12**	**21**
TOTAL										
0–19 Years	1,218	4.9	35	1	2	3	6	10	14	30
20–34	2,665	4.0	15	1	2	3	5	8	11	22
35–49	6,602	4.2	13	1	2	3	5	8	11	18
50–64	9,284	4.6	18	1	2	3	6	9	12	21
65+	22,497	5.0	17	2	2	4	6	9	12	21
GRAND TOTAL	**42,266**	**4.7**	**17**	**1**	**2**	**4**	**6**	**9**	**12**	**21**

45.2: LG INTESTINE DXTIC PX

Type of Patients	Observed Patients	Avg. Stay	Vari-ance	Percentiles						
				10th	25th	50th	75th	90th	95th	99th
1. SINGLE DX										
0–19 Years	70	4.3	20	1	2	3	4	10	17	21
20–34	180	3.5	7	1	2	3	4	6	9	15
35–49	147	3.2	7	1	2	2	3	6	8	14
50–64	98	2.6	4	1	1	2	3	5	7	9
65+	46	2.7	2	1	1	2	4	4	5	7
2. MULTIPLE DX										
0–19 Years	414	5.3	31	1	2	3	7	12	16	29
20–34	1,742	4.7	22	1	2	3	5	9	13	23
35–49	3,626	5.0	28	1	2	4	6	10	13	24
50–64	5,340	4.7	19	1	2	4	6	9	12	20
65+	14,945	5.1	17	2	2	4	6	10	13	21
TOTAL SINGLE DX	**541**	**3.3**	**8**	**1**	**2**	**3**	**4**	**6**	**9**	**16**
TOTAL MULTIPLE DX	**26,067**	**5.0**	**19**	**2**	**2**	**4**	**6**	**10**	**13**	**21**
TOTAL										
0–19 Years	484	5.1	29	1	2	3	6	12	16	29
20–34	1,922	4.6	21	1	2	3	5	9	13	23
35–49	3,773	4.9	27	1	2	3	6	10	13	23
50–64	5,438	4.7	19	1	2	4	6	9	12	20
65+	14,991	5.0	17	2	2	4	6	10	13	21
GRAND TOTAL	**26,608**	**4.9**	**19**	**2**	**2**	**4**	**6**	**10**	**13**	**21**

45.22: ENDO L-INTEST THRU STOMA

Type of Patients	Observed Patients	Avg. Stay	Vari-ance	Percentiles						
				10th	25th	50th	75th	90th	95th	99th
1. SINGLE DX										
0–19 Years	0									
20–34	0									
35–49	0									
50–64	0									
65+	0									
2. MULTIPLE DX										
0–19 Years	0									
20–34	3	6.9	48	2	2	2	14	14	14	14
35–49	10	4.9	12	2	3	3	6	11	12	12
50–64	30	4.8	13	1	2	4	6	10	11	16
65+	62	6.1	30	1	2	4	8	16	16	24
TOTAL SINGLE DX	**0**									
TOTAL MULTIPLE DX	**105**	**5.7**	**24**	**1**	**2**	**4**	**7**	**15**	**16**	**24**
TOTAL										
0–19 Years	0									
20–34	3	6.9	48	2	2	2	14	14	14	14
35–49	10	4.9	12	2	3	3	6	11	12	12
50–64	30	4.8	13	1	2	4	6	10	11	16
65+	62	6.1	30	1	2	4	8	16	16	24
GRAND TOTAL	**105**	**5.7**	**24**	**1**	**2**	**4**	**7**	**15**	**16**	**24**

45.23: COLONOSCOPY

Type of Patients	Observed Patients	Avg. Stay	Vari-ance	Percentiles 10th	25th	50th	75th	90th	95th	99th
1. SINGLE DX										
0–19 Years	12	4.4	34	1	1	3	4	10	21	21
20–34	41	2.9	5	1	2	2	3	5	7	15
35–49	49	2.4	3	1	1	2	3	4	7	8
50–64	45	2.3	4	1	1	2	2	5	7	11
65+	24	1.8	<1	1	1	1	2	3	4	4
2. MULTIPLE DX										
0–19 Years	64	3.7	12	1	2	3	4	8	11	20
20–34	490	3.9	13	1	2	3	5	8	10	20
35–49	1,385	4.9	38	1	2	3	6	9	12	29
50–64	2,367	4.5	20	1	2	3	5	9	11	19
65+	8,040	4.6	14	2	2	4	6	9	12	19
TOTAL SINGLE DX	**171**	**2.6**	**7**	**1**	**1**	**2**	**3**	**5**	**7**	**15**
TOTAL MULTIPLE DX	**12,346**	**4.6**	**17**	**1**	**2**	**3**	**6**	**9**	**12**	**20**
TOTAL										
0–19 Years	76	3.8	15	1	2	3	4	8	11	21
20–34	531	3.8	13	1	2	3	4	7	10	20
35–49	1,434	4.8	37	1	2	3	5	9	12	29
50–64	2,412	4.4	20	1	2	3	5	9	11	19
65+	8,064	4.6	14	2	2	4	6	9	12	19
GRAND TOTAL	**12,517**	**4.6**	**17**	**1**	**2**	**3**	**6**	**9**	**12**	**20**

45.24: FLEXIBLE SIGMOIDOSCOPY

Type of Patients	Observed Patients	Avg. Stay	Vari-ance	Percentiles 10th	25th	50th	75th	90th	95th	99th
1. SINGLE DX										
0–19 Years	6	5.3	35	1	1	1	10	17	17	17
20–34	12	2.9	3	1	1	2	5	5	6	6
35–49	10	4.1	20	1	1	2	6	6	16	16
50–64	2	1.0	0	1	1	1	1	1	1	1
65+	3	3.7	<1	2	4	4	4	4	4	4
2. MULTIPLE DX										
0–19 Years	25	6.3	40	1	2	4	8	14	24	31
20–34	150	5.0	39	1	2	4	6	9	14	29
35–49	273	4.6	16	1	2	3	6	9	12	19
50–64	322	4.8	17	1	2	3	6	10	13	19
65+	1,065	5.6	23	2	3	5	7	11	14	24
TOTAL SINGLE DX	**33**	**3.7**	**14**	**1**	**1**	**2**	**5**	**10**	**10**	**17**
TOTAL MULTIPLE DX	**1,835**	**5.3**	**22**	**1**	**2**	**4**	**7**	**10**	**14**	**23**
TOTAL										
0–19 Years	31	6.1	39	1	1	4	9	14	17	31
20–34	162	4.9	37	1	2	4	6	9	14	20
35–49	283	4.6	16	1	2	3	6	9	13	19
50–64	324	4.7	17	1	2	3	6	10	13	19
65+	1,068	5.6	23	2	3	5	7	11	14	24
GRAND TOTAL	**1,868**	**5.3**	**22**	**1**	**2**	**4**	**7**	**10**	**14**	**23**

45.25: CLOSED LG INTEST BIOPSY

Type of Patients	Observed Patients	Avg. Stay	Vari-ance	Percentiles 10th	25th	50th	75th	90th	95th	99th
1. SINGLE DX										
0–19 Years	51	4.1	16	1	2	3	4	7	15	17
20–34	124	3.8	8	1	2	3	5	7	9	15
35–49	88	3.5	7	1	2	3	4	7	11	13
50–64	51	2.9	4	1	2	2	3	6	7	9
65+	18	3.3	3	1	2	3	4	5	7	7
2. MULTIPLE DX										
0–19 Years	323	5.4	33	1	2	3	7	12	17	29
20–34	1,095	5.0	23	2	2	3	6	10	14	25
35–49	1,951	5.1	22	1	2	4	6	10	14	21
50–64	2,611	4.9	18	2	2	4	6	9	12	22
65+	5,761	5.5	19	2	3	4	7	10	14	23
TOTAL SINGLE DX	**332**	**3.7**	**9**	**1**	**2**	**3**	**4**	**7**	**9**	**15**
TOTAL MULTIPLE DX	**11,741**	**5.3**	**20**	**2**	**3**	**4**	**6**	**10**	**14**	**23**
TOTAL										
0–19 Years	374	5.3	30	1	2	3	6	12	17	29
20–34	1,219	4.9	22	2	2	3	6	10	13	24
35–49	2,039	5.0	22	1	2	4	6	10	14	21
50–64	2,662	4.8	18	2	2	4	6	9	12	21
65+	5,779	5.5	19	2	3	4	7	10	14	23
GRAND TOTAL	**12,073**	**5.2**	**20**	**2**	**2**	**4**	**6**	**10**	**13**	**23**

45.3: LOC EXC/DESTR SMB LES

Type of Patients	Observed Patients	Avg. Stay	Vari-ance	Percentiles 10th	25th	50th	75th	90th	95th	99th
1. SINGLE DX										
0–19 Years	6	3.4	1	1	3	4	4	4	4	4
20–34	7	3.3	2	1	2	4	4	5	5	5
35–49	2	2.7	3	1	1	4	4	4	4	4
50–64	1	10.0	0	10	10	10	10	10	10	10
65+	0									
2. MULTIPLE DX										
0–19 Years	44	5.7	97	2	2	4	6	8	8	96
20–34	35	5.9	14	2	3	6	8	12	14	16
35–49	62	5.3	17	1	2	5	7	10	11	21
50–64	125	6.0	32	2	3	5	8	13	16	19
65+	212	6.9	34	2	3	5	8	12	18	30
TOTAL SINGLE DX	**16**	**3.7**	**5**	**1**	**3**	**4**	**4**	**5**	**10**	**10**
TOTAL MULTIPLE DX	**478**	**6.2**	**40**	**2**	**3**	**5**	**8**	**11**	**16**	**24**
TOTAL										
0–19 Years	50	5.5	90	2	2	4	6	8	8	21
20–34	42	5.5	13	2	3	5	6	11	13	16
35–49	64	5.2	17	1	2	4	7	10	11	21
50–64	126	6.0	31	2	3	5	8	13	16	19
65+	212	6.9	34	2	3	5	8	12	18	30
GRAND TOTAL	**494**	**6.2**	**39**	**2**	**3**	**5**	**8**	**11**	**16**	**24**

45.30: ENDO EXC/DESTR DUOD LES

Type of Patients	Observed Patients	Avg. Stay	Vari-ance	Percentiles 10th	25th	50th	75th	90th	95th	99th
1. SINGLE DX										
0–19 Years	0									
20–34	0									
35–49	0									
50–64	0									
65+	0									
2. MULTIPLE DX										
0–19 Years	0									
20–34	6	3.6	2	2	2	4	4	6	6	6
35–49	21	4.6	26	1	2	3	5	7	19	21
50–64	44	3.6	7	2	2	3	4	5	7	19
65+	112	5.4	21	2	3	4	6	10	12	29
TOTAL SINGLE DX	**0**									
TOTAL MULTIPLE DX	**183**	**4.9**	**19**	**2**	**3**	**4**	**5**	**9**	**10**	**22**
TOTAL										
0–19 Years	0									
20–34	6	3.6	2	2	2	4	4	6	6	6
35–49	21	4.6	26	1	2	3	5	7	19	21
50–64	44	3.6	7	2	2	3	4	5	7	19
65+	112	5.4	21	2	3	4	6	10	12	29
GRAND TOTAL	**183**	**4.9**	**19**	**2**	**3**	**4**	**5**	**9**	**10**	**22**

45.31: LOC EXC DUOD LES NEC

Type of Patients	Observed Patients	Avg. Stay	Vari-ance	Percentiles 10th	25th	50th	75th	90th	95th	99th
1. SINGLE DX										
0–19 Years	0									
20–34	0									
35–49	0									
50–64	1	10.0	0	10	10	10	10	10	10	10
65+	0									
2. MULTIPLE DX										
0–19 Years	3	10.2	11	8	8	8	10	15	15	15
20–34	4	10.1	15	4	9	9	11	16	16	16
35–49	9	7.4	16	3	5	7	10	11	18	18
50–64	22	9.0	28	4	5	8	13	18	18	18
65+	37	10.4	65	5	6	8	11	21	24	47
TOTAL SINGLE DX	**1**	**10.0**	**0**	**10**	**10**	**10**	**10**	**10**	**10**	**10**
TOTAL MULTIPLE DX	**75**	**9.6**	**44**	**4**	**6**	**8**	**11**	**18**	**21**	**47**
TOTAL										
0–19 Years	3	10.2	11	8	8	8	10	15	15	15
20–34	4	10.1	15	4	9	9	11	16	16	16
35–49	9	7.4	16	3	5	7	10	11	18	18
50–64	23	9.1	27	4	5	8	13	18	18	18
65+	37	10.4	65	5	6	8	11	21	24	47
GRAND TOTAL	**76**	**9.6**	**43**	**4**	**6**	**8**	**11**	**18**	**21**	**47**

45.33: LOC EXC S-INTEST LES NEC

Type of Patients	Observed Patients	Avg. Stay	Vari-ance	Percentiles 10th	25th	50th	75th	90th	95th	99th
1. SINGLE DX										
0–19 Years	6	3.4	1	1	3	4	4	4	4	4
20–34	7	3.3	2	1	2	4	4	5	5	5
35–49	2	2.7	3	1	1	4	4	4	4	4
50–64	0									
65+	0									
2. MULTIPLE DX										
0–19 Years	41	5.5	99	2	2	4	6	8	8	96
20–34	24	5.2	11	1	3	5	6	9	13	14
35–49	28	5.8	10	1	4	6	9	10	10	12
50–64	47	6.6	14	2	4	5	9	13	15	15
65+	42	8.3	31	2	5	7	12	17	18	31
TOTAL SINGLE DX	**15**	**3.2**	**2**	**1**	**2**	**4**	**4**	**4**	**5**	**5**
TOTAL MULTIPLE DX	**182**	**6.3**	**47**	**2**	**3**	**5**	**8**	**12**	**15**	**21**
TOTAL										
0–19 Years	47	5.4	92	2	2	4	6	8	8	96
20–34	31	4.8	9	1	3	4	6	8	13	14
35–49	30	5.6	10	1	2	5	8	10	10	12
50–64	47	6.6	14	2	4	5	9	13	15	15
65+	42	8.3	31	2	5	7	12	17	18	31
GRAND TOTAL	**197**	**6.2**	**45**	**2**	**3**	**5**	**8**	**11**	**15**	**21**

45.4: LOC DESTR LG INTEST LES

Type of Patients	Observed Patients	Avg. Stay	Vari-ance	Percentiles 10th	25th	50th	75th	90th	95th	99th
1. SINGLE DX										
0–19 Years	6	1.3	<1	1	1	1	2	2	2	2
20–34	2	4.0	10	1	1	6	6	6	6	6
35–49	9	2.3	3	1	1	2	3	4	7	7
50–64	15	1.7	<1	1	1	1	2	3	3	4
65+	9	2.1	2	1	1	1	3	4	4	4
2. MULTIPLE DX										
0–19 Years	21	3.8	34	1	1	2	4	6	7	36
20–34	88	4.1	8	1	2	3	5	7	8	16
35–49	435	3.8	10	1	2	3	5	8	9	16
50–64	1,298	4.1	13	1	2	3	5	8	10	18
65+	4,702	4.5	13	1	2	3	6	8	11	18
TOTAL SINGLE DX	**41**	**1.9**	**2**	**1**	**1**	**1**	**3**	**4**	**4**	**7**
TOTAL MULTIPLE DX	**6,544**	**4.4**	**13**	**1**	**2**	**3**	**5**	**8**	**11**	**18**
TOTAL										
0–19 Years	27	3.3	29	1	1	2	4	6	7	36
20–34	90	4.1	8	1	2	3	5	7	8	15
35–49	444	3.8	10	1	2	3	5	8	9	16
50–64	1,313	4.1	13	1	2	3	5	8	10	18
65+	4,711	4.5	13	1	2	3	6	8	11	18
GRAND TOTAL	**6,585**	**4.3**	**13**	**1**	**2**	**3**	**5**	**8**	**11**	**18**

45.41: EXC LG INTEST LESION

Type of Patients	Observed Patients	Avg. Stay	Vari-ance	10th	25th	50th	75th	90th	95th	99th
				Percentiles						
1. SINGLE DX										
0–19 Years	0									
20–34	0									
35–49	3	4.0	7	1	1	4	7	7	7	7
50–64	3	1.9	1	1	1	1	3	3	3	3
65+	3	3.5	<1	3	3	3	4	4	4	4
2. MULTIPLE DX										
0–19 Years	3	9.7	167	4	4	4	5	36	36	36
20–34	4	3.0	4	1	2	3	3	6	6	6
35–49	15	3.7	12	1	2	3	4	7	9	18
50–64	40	4.6	5	3	3	4	6	8	10	11
65+	54	6.2	22	2	4	5	7	10	13	34
TOTAL SINGLE DX	**9**	**2.9**	**3**	**1**	**1**	**3**	**4**	**4**	**7**	**7**
TOTAL MULTIPLE DX	**116**	**5.4**	**21**	**2**	**3**	**5**	**6**	**9**	**11**	**34**
TOTAL										
0–19 Years	3	9.7	167	4	4	4	5	36	36	36
20–34	4	3.0	4	1	2	3	3	6	6	6
35–49	18	3.8	11	1	2	3	4	7	9	18
50–64	43	4.4	5	2	3	4	6	7	10	11
65+	57	6.0	21	2	4	5	7	10	13	34
GRAND TOTAL	**125**	**5.2**	**20**	**2**	**3**	**4**	**6**	**9**	**11**	**34**

45.42: ENDO COLON POLYPECTOMY

Type of Patients	Observed Patients	Avg. Stay	Vari-ance	10th	25th	50th	75th	90th	95th	99th
				Percentiles						
1. SINGLE DX										
0–19 Years	6	1.3	<1	1	1	1	2	2	2	2
20–34	2	4.0	10	1	1	6	6	6	6	6
35–49	2	1.0	0	1	1	1	1	1	1	1
50–64	2	2.9	2	2	2	2	4	4	4	4
65+	2	1.4	<1	1	1	1	2	2	2	2
2. MULTIPLE DX										
0–19 Years	16	3.0	3	1	2	2	3	6	7	7
20–34	63	4.3	8	2	3	3	5	8	9	16
35–49	358	3.9	8	1	2	3	5	8	9	14
50–64	936	4.3	14	1	2	3	5	8	11	19
65+	3,543	4.6	13	1	2	4	6	9	11	18
TOTAL SINGLE DX	**14**	**1.8**	**2**	**1**	**1**	**1**	**2**	**4**	**6**	**6**
TOTAL MULTIPLE DX	**4,916**	**4.5**	**13**	**1**	**2**	**3**	**6**	**8**	**11**	**18**
TOTAL										
0–19 Years	22	2.6	3	1	1	2	3	6	6	7
20–34	65	4.3	7	2	3	3	5	8	9	16
35–49	360	3.9	8	1	2	3	5	8	9	14
50–64	938	4.3	14	1	2	3	5	8	11	19
65+	3,545	4.6	13	1	2	4	6	9	11	18
GRAND TOTAL	**4,930**	**4.5**	**13**	**1**	**2**	**3**	**6**	**8**	**11**	**18**

45.43: ENDO DESTR COLON LES NEC

Type of Patients	Observed Patients	Avg. Stay	Vari-ance	10th	25th	50th	75th	90th	95th	99th
				Percentiles						
1. SINGLE DX										
0–19 Years	0									
20–34	0									
35–49	4	2.1	<1	1	1	3	3	3	3	3
50–64	10	1.4	<1	1	1	1	2	2	2	2
65+	4	1.5	1	1	1	1	1	4	4	4
2. MULTIPLE DX										
0–19 Years	2	1.0	0	1	1	1	1	1	1	1
20–34	20	3.7	8	1	2	3	5	6	7	15
35–49	59	3.4	22	1	1	2	3	6	9	32
50–64	322	3.3	9	1	1	2	4	7	10	14
65+	1,101	4.0	11	1	2	3	5	8	10	16
TOTAL SINGLE DX	**18**	**1.6**	**<1**	**1**	**1**	**1**	**2**	**3**	**3**	**4**
TOTAL MULTIPLE DX	**1,504**	**3.9**	**11**	**1**	**2**	**3**	**5**	**8**	**10**	**16**
TOTAL										
0–19 Years	2	1.0	0	1	1	1	1	1	1	1
20–34	20	3.7	8	1	2	3	5	6	7	15
35–49	63	3.2	20	1	1	2	3	6	9	32
50–64	332	3.2	9	1	1	2	4	6	10	14
65+	1,105	4.0	11	1	2	3	5	8	10	16
GRAND TOTAL	**1,522**	**3.8**	**11**	**1**	**2**	**3**	**5**	**7**	**10**	**16**

45.5: INTESTINAL SEG ISOLATION

Type of Patients	Observed Patients	Avg. Stay	Vari-ance	10th	25th	50th	75th	90th	95th	99th
				Percentiles						
1. SINGLE DX										
0–19 Years	0									
20–34	1	7.0	0	7	7	7	7	7	7	7
35–49	0									
50–64	0									
65+	0									
2. MULTIPLE DX										
0–19 Years	2	7.3	1	6	6	8	8	8	8	8
20–34	5	6.5	1	5	6	7	7	8	8	8
35–49	4	9.6	22	4	5	11	11	17	17	17
50–64	5	12.3	53	2	10	12	22	22	22	22
65+	4	7.3	4	5	5	7	10	10	10	10
TOTAL SINGLE DX	**1**	**7.0**	**0**	**7**	**7**	**7**	**7**	**7**	**7**	**7**
TOTAL MULTIPLE DX	**20**	**8.7**	**19**	**4**	**6**	**8**	**11**	**12**	**17**	**22**
TOTAL										
0–19 Years	2	7.3	1	6	6	8	8	8	8	8
20–34	6	6.6	1	5	6	7	7	8	8	8
35–49	4	9.6	22	4	5	11	11	17	17	17
50–64	5	12.3	53	2	10	12	22	22	22	22
65+	4	7.3	4	5	5	7	10	10	10	10
GRAND TOTAL	**21**	**8.7**	**19**	**5**	**6**	**7**	**11**	**12**	**17**	**22**

45.6: SM INTEST EXCISION NEC

Type of Patients	Observed Patients	Avg. Stay	Vari-ance	10th	25th	50th	75th	90th	95th	99th
1. SINGLE DX										
0–19 Years	23	4.9	7	3	4	5	6	7	8	16
20–34	33	5.1	6	3	3	5	7	7	8	16
35–49	38	5.7	6	3	4	5	7	9	10	13
50–64	28	5.3	7	3	3	5	7	9	12	14
65+	7	4.6	5	3	3	4	6	9	9	9
2. MULTIPLE DX										
0–19 Years	267	13.6	250	5	6	8	15	37	75	>99
20–34	434	9.1	54	4	5	7	11	16	20	39
35–49	804	10.9	65	4	6	8	13	20	26	42
50–64	1,301	10.7	61	4	6	8	13	20	25	41
65+	2,489	12.4	63	5	7	10	15	22	28	43
TOTAL SINGLE DX	**129**	**5.2**	**7**	**3**	**3**	**5**	**6**	**8**	**10**	**16**
TOTAL MULTIPLE DX	**5,295**	**11.6**	**76**	**5**	**6**	**9**	**14**	**22**	**28**	**54**
TOTAL										
0–19 Years	290	12.8	234	4	5	7	14	34	65	>99
20–34	467	8.8	51	4	5	7	10	15	19	39
35–49	842	10.6	63	4	6	8	13	20	25	42
50–64	1,329	10.6	60	4	6	8	13	20	25	41
65+	2,496	12.4	63	5	7	10	15	22	28	43
GRAND TOTAL	**5,424**	**11.5**	**75**	**5**	**6**	**9**	**14**	**21**	**28**	**50**

45.61: MULT SEG S-INTEST RESECT

Type of Patients	Observed Patients	Avg. Stay	Vari-ance	10th	25th	50th	75th	90th	95th	99th
1. SINGLE DX										
0–19 Years	0									
20–34	0									
35–49	0									
50–64	0									
65+	0									
2. MULTIPLE DX										
0–19 Years	5	16.1	89	7	11	16	19	34	34	34
20–34	31	10.6	66	5	7	8	15	17	20	54
35–49	44	12.5	67	5	6	9	19	24	26	35
50–64	61	12.1	103	4	5	9	17	22	29	68
65+	121	15.0	98	6	7	13	20	27	40	40
TOTAL SINGLE DX	**0**									
TOTAL MULTIPLE DX	**262**	**13.5**	**92**	**5**	**7**	**10**	**18**	**24**	**33**	**40**
TOTAL										
0–19 Years	5	16.1	89	7	11	16	19	34	34	34
20–34	31	10.6	66	5	7	8	15	17	20	54
35–49	44	12.5	67	5	6	9	19	24	26	35
50–64	61	12.1	103	4	5	9	17	22	29	68
65+	121	15.0	98	6	7	13	20	27	40	40
GRAND TOTAL	**262**	**13.5**	**92**	**5**	**7**	**10**	**18**	**24**	**33**	**40**

45.62: PART S-INTEST RESECT NEC

Type of Patients	Observed Patients	Avg. Stay	Vari-ance	10th	25th	50th	75th	90th	95th	99th
1. SINGLE DX										
0–19 Years	23	4.9	7	3	4	5	6	7	8	16
20–34	33	5.1	6	3	3	5	7	7	8	16
35–49	38	5.7	6	3	4	5	7	9	10	13
50–64	28	5.3	7	3	3	5	7	9	12	14
65+	6	3.7	1	3	3	3	4	6	6	6
2. MULTIPLE DX										
0–19 Years	260	13.5	248	5	6	8	15	37	75	>99
20–34	399	8.9	52	4	5	7	10	15	20	39
35–49	756	10.8	65	4	6	8	13	20	26	42
50–64	1,233	10.6	59	4	6	8	13	20	25	41
65+	2,361	12.3	61	5	7	10	15	22	27	43
TOTAL SINGLE DX	**128**	**5.2**	**7**	**3**	**3**	**5**	**6**	**8**	**10**	**16**
TOTAL MULTIPLE DX	**5,009**	**11.5**	**75**	**5**	**6**	**9**	**14**	**21**	**28**	**54**
TOTAL										
0–19 Years	283	12.7	232	4	5	7	14	34	63	>99
20–34	432	8.7	50	4	5	7	10	14	19	39
35–49	794	10.5	63	4	6	8	13	19	24	42
50–64	1,261	10.5	59	4	6	8	13	19	25	41
65+	2,367	12.2	61	5	7	10	15	22	27	43
GRAND TOTAL	**5,137**	**11.4**	**74**	**5**	**6**	**9**	**14**	**21**	**28**	**50**

45.7: PART LG INTEST EXCISION

Type of Patients	Observed Patients	Avg. Stay	Vari-ance	10th	25th	50th	75th	90th	95th	99th
1. SINGLE DX										
0–19 Years	38	5.6	7	2	3	5	7	10	10	11
20–34	119	5.1	6	3	4	5	6	8	9	14
35–49	298	5.3	7	3	4	5	6	8	9	16
50–64	368	5.1	5	3	4	5	6	8	10	13
65+	203	5.4	4	4	4	5	6	7	9	13
2. MULTIPLE DX										
0–19 Years	266	13.9	258	4	5	7	12	44	60	74
20–34	844	8.3	38	4	5	7	9	14	19	34
35–49	3,113	8.2	42	4	5	7	9	13	18	34
50–64	6,621	8.4	37	4	5	7	9	15	20	34
65+	13,120	9.7	40	5	6	8	11	17	22	34
TOTAL SINGLE DX	**1,026**	**5.3**	**5**	**3**	**4**	**5**	**6**	**8**	**10**	**14**
TOTAL MULTIPLE DX	**23,964**	**9.2**	**44**	**4**	**5**	**7**	**11**	**16**	**21**	**35**
TOTAL										
0–19 Years	304	12.9	236	4	5	7	11	29	60	74
20–34	963	8.0	35	4	5	6	9	14	18	33
35–49	3,411	8.0	40	4	5	7	9	13	18	32
50–64	6,989	8.2	36	4	5	6	9	14	19	34
65+	13,323	9.6	40	4	6	8	11	17	22	34
GRAND TOTAL	**24,990**	**9.0**	**43**	**4**	**5**	**7**	**10**	**16**	**21**	**35**

45.71: MULT SEG L-INTEST RESECT

Type of Patients	Observed Patients	Avg. Stay	Variance	Percentiles 10th	25th	50th	75th	90th	95th	99th
1. SINGLE DX										
0–19 Years	0									
20–34	0									
35–49	0									
50–64	3	4.3	1	3	3	5	5	5	5	5
65+	0									
2. MULTIPLE DX										
0–19 Years	6	20.5	262	10	15	19	20	20	69	69
20–34	9	8.3	7	6	7	7	12	12	12	12
35–49	16	9.5	15	4	7	9	12	14	16	16
50–64	48	7.9	16	4	5	7	10	12	16	23
65+	84	12.2	50	5	7	10	17	21	26	38
TOTAL SINGLE DX	**3**	**4.3**	**1**	**3**	**3**	**5**	**5**	**5**	**5**	**5**
TOTAL MULTIPLE DX	**163**	**10.9**	**52**	**5**	**6**	**9**	**14**	**19**	**23**	**37**
TOTAL										
0–19 Years	6	20.5	262	10	15	19	20	20	69	69
20–34	9	8.3	7	6	7	7	12	12	12	12
35–49	16	9.5	15	4	7	9	12	14	16	16
50–64	51	7.8	16	4	5	6	9	12	16	23
65+	84	12.2	50	5	7	10	17	21	26	38
GRAND TOTAL	**166**	**10.8**	**52**	**5**	**6**	**9**	**14**	**19**	**23**	**37**

45.72: CECECTOMY

Type of Patients	Observed Patients	Avg. Stay	Variance	Percentiles 10th	25th	50th	75th	90th	95th	99th
1. SINGLE DX										
0–19 Years	13	5.4	5	3	4	5	6	10	11	11
20–34	29	4.7	4	2	3	5	6	7	8	12
35–49	32	4.8	8	3	4	4	5	6	9	19
50–64	18	4.0	2	2	3	4	5	6	6	9
65+	6	5.3	<1	4	4	6	6	6	6	6
2. MULTIPLE DX										
0–19 Years	71	12.6	227	4	5	7	11	25	60	60
20–34	150	7.1	28	4	5	6	8	11	16	20
35–49	230	8.3	119	3	4	6	9	13	19	85
50–64	294	7.9	40	3	4	6	9	14	20	38
65+	426	9.1	45	3	5	7	11	17	23	41
TOTAL SINGLE DX	**98**	**4.8**	**5**	**2**	**4**	**5**	**6**	**6**	**8**	**12**
TOTAL MULTIPLE DX	**1,171**	**8.7**	**71**	**3**	**5**	**7**	**9**	**15**	**21**	**50**
TOTAL										
0–19 Years	84	11.3	196	4	5	7	11	24	60	60
20–34	179	6.6	24	3	5	5	8	10	16	20
35–49	262	7.9	109	3	4	6	8	12	17	85
50–64	312	7.7	39	3	4	6	9	14	20	38
65+	432	9.0	44	3	5	7	11	16	22	39
GRAND TOTAL	**1,269**	**8.3**	**66**	**3**	**5**	**6**	**9**	**15**	**20**	**49**

45.73: RIGHT HEMICOLECTOMY

Type of Patients	Observed Patients	Avg. Stay	Variance	Percentiles 10th	25th	50th	75th	90th	95th	99th
1. SINGLE DX										
0–19 Years	12	5.1	7	2	3	5	7	9	9	9
20–34	30	5.0	10	3	3	4	6	8	8	22
35–49	59	5.3	5	3	4	5	6	9	10	12
50–64	109	5.0	4	3	4	5	6	7	9	12
65+	101	5.4	4	4	4	5	6	7	9	13
2. MULTIPLE DX										
0–19 Years	79	12.8	246	4	5	7	11	31	56	91
20–34	274	7.9	35	4	5	6	8	13	18	36
35–49	714	8.3	28	4	5	7	9	14	19	29
50–64	2,110	8.0	36	4	5	6	9	14	19	35
65+	5,911	9.0	32	4	6	7	11	16	20	30
TOTAL SINGLE DX	**311**	**5.2**	**5**	**3**	**4**	**5**	**6**	**7**	**9**	**13**
TOTAL MULTIPLE DX	**9,088**	**8.8**	**36**	**4**	**5**	**7**	**10**	**15**	**20**	**33**
TOTAL										
0–19 Years	91	11.9	222	4	5	7	10	28	56	91
20–34	304	7.6	34	4	5	6	8	12	18	34
35–49	773	8.1	27	4	5	7	9	13	18	29
50–64	2,219	7.9	35	4	5	6	9	14	19	35
65+	6,012	9.0	32	4	6	7	11	16	20	30
GRAND TOTAL	**9,399**	**8.7**	**35**	**4**	**5**	**7**	**10**	**15**	**20**	**33**

45.74: TRANSVERSE COLON RESECT

Type of Patients	Observed Patients	Avg. Stay	Variance	Percentiles 10th	25th	50th	75th	90th	95th	99th
1. SINGLE DX										
0–19 Years	1	5.0	0	5	5	5	5	5	5	5
20–34	0									
35–49	4	5.3	2	3	5	5	7	7	7	7
50–64	8	4.6	<1	4	4	4	5	6	6	6
65+	6	4.4	1	3	3	5	5	5	6	6
2. MULTIPLE DX										
0–19 Years	9	27.4	423	5	5	30	49	49	49	49
20–34	19	9.9	72	5	6	8	11	14	42	42
35–49	73	8.8	41	5	5	7	10	17	20	43
50–64	195	9.4	64	4	5	7	11	17	24	49
65+	622	9.6	40	5	6	8	11	17	20	33
TOTAL SINGLE DX	**19**	**4.7**	**1**	**3**	**4**	**5**	**5**	**6**	**6**	**7**
TOTAL MULTIPLE DX	**918**	**9.8**	**55**	**5**	**6**	**8**	**11**	**18**	**22**	**49**
TOTAL										
0–19 Years	10	25.3	426	5	5	12	49	49	49	49
20–34	19	9.9	72	5	6	8	11	14	42	42
35–49	77	8.6	40	5	5	7	10	17	20	43
50–64	203	9.2	62	4	5	7	10	17	24	49
65+	628	9.6	39	5	6	8	11	17	20	33
GRAND TOTAL	**937**	**9.7**	**54**	**5**	**6**	**7**	**11**	**18**	**22**	**49**

45.75: LEFT HEMICOLECTOMY

Type of Patients	Observed Patients	Avg. Stay	Vari-ance	10th	25th	50th	75th	90th	95th	99th
1. SINGLE DX										
0–19 Years	2	3.7	3	2	2	5	5	5	5	5
20–34	8	5.1	1	4	4	5	6	7	7	7
35–49	30	6.9	13	4	4	6	9	13	16	17
50–64	42	5.5	5	3	4	5	6	8	10	15
65+	17	5.3	2	2	5	5	6	7	7	8
2. MULTIPLE DX										
0–19 Years	21	12.0	99	6	6	9	11	23	26	54
20–34	66	10.2	36	5	7	8	13	16	24	30
35–49	336	9.8	98	5	6	7	10	16	22	79
50–64	807	9.3	41	4	6	7	11	16	22	37
65+	1,558	11.0	51	5	6	9	13	20	25	36
TOTAL SINGLE DX	**99**	**5.7**	**6**	**3**	**4**	**5**	**7**	**8**	**10**	**16**
TOTAL MULTIPLE DX	**2,788**	**10.4**	**54**	**5**	**6**	**8**	**12**	**19**	**24**	**36**
TOTAL										
0–19 Years	23	11.1	95	5	6	9	11	23	26	54
20–34	74	9.8	35	5	6	8	12	16	22	30
35–49	366	9.6	93	4	6	7	10	15	20	79
50–64	849	9.2	40	4	5	7	10	16	21	34
65+	1,575	11.0	51	5	6	9	13	20	25	36
GRAND TOTAL	**2,887**	**10.3**	**54**	**5**	**6**	**8**	**12**	**19**	**24**	**36**

45.76: SIGMOIDECTOMY

Type of Patients	Observed Patients	Avg. Stay	Vari-ance	10th	25th	50th	75th	90th	95th	99th
1. SINGLE DX										
0–19 Years	5	7.6	7	3	6	7	10	10	10	10
20–34	44	5.6	6	3	4	5	6	9	11	14
35–49	148	5.2	7	3	4	5	6	7	9	15
50–64	161	5.2	5	3	4	5	6	8	10	14
65+	54	5.7	7	4	4	5	6	9	11	19
2. MULTIPLE DX										
0–19 Years	37	16.0	435	3	5	6	13	61	61	74
20–34	233	8.2	21	4	5	7	10	13	16	26
35–49	1,482	7.8	26	4	5	6	9	13	17	31
50–64	2,607	8.3	32	4	5	7	9	14	18	31
65+	3,630	10.0	43	5	6	8	12	18	23	34
TOTAL SINGLE DX	**412**	**5.4**	**6**	**3**	**4**	**5**	**6**	**8**	**10**	**15**
TOTAL MULTIPLE DX	**7,989**	**9.1**	**40**	**4**	**5**	**7**	**10**	**16**	**21**	**33**
TOTAL										
0–19 Years	42	15.2	400	3	5	7	13	61	61	74
20–34	277	7.8	20	4	5	7	9	13	14	26
35–49	1,630	7.6	25	4	5	6	9	13	17	30
50–64	2,768	8.1	31	4	5	7	9	14	18	30
65+	3,684	10.0	42	5	6	8	12	18	22	34
GRAND TOTAL	**8,401**	**8.9**	**39**	**4**	**5**	**7**	**10**	**15**	**21**	**32**

45.79: PART LG INTEST EXC NEC

Type of Patients	Observed Patients	Avg. Stay	Vari-ance	10th	25th	50th	75th	90th	95th	99th
1. SINGLE DX										
0–19 Years	5	6.7	10	3	4	6	11	11	11	11
20–34	8	5.5	3	3	3	6	7	7	7	7
35–49	25	5.2	3	3	4	5	7	7	7	9
50–64	27	4.8	5	3	3	4	6	7	9	13
65+	19	5.8	2	3	5	6	7	8	9	9
2. MULTIPLE DX										
0–19 Years	43	11.9	136	4	6	8	12	25	39	>99
20–34	93	10.6	94	4	5	7	13	22	29	38
35–49	262	8.6	33	4	5	7	10	16	19	26
50–64	560	8.8	51	4	5	7	10	16	23	42
65+	889	10.8	55	5	6	8	13	21	25	39
TOTAL SINGLE DX	**84**	**5.3**	**4**	**3**	**4**	**5**	**7**	**7**	**9**	**11**
TOTAL MULTIPLE DX	**1,847**	**10.0**	**57**	**4**	**6**	**8**	**12**	**19**	**24**	**41**
TOTAL										
0–19 Years	48	11.6	130	4	6	7	12	25	29	>99
20–34	101	10.3	89	4	5	7	12	21	29	38
35–49	287	8.3	31	4	5	7	9	15	19	26
50–64	587	8.6	49	4	5	6	9	16	22	42
65+	908	10.7	54	5	6	8	13	20	25	39
GRAND TOTAL	**1,931**	**9.8**	**55**	**4**	**5**	**7**	**11**	**19**	**24**	**39**

45.8: TOT INTRA-ABD COLECTOMY

Type of Patients	Observed Patients	Avg. Stay	Vari-ance	10th	25th	50th	75th	90th	95th	99th
1. SINGLE DX										
0–19 Years	9	6.7	4	4	5	7	8	9	10	10
20–34	25	6.8	12	4	4	6	7	12	13	19
35–49	18	7.0	5	5	6	6	7	9	13	14
50–64	7	6.6	7	4	5	5	7	12	12	12
65+	5	5.4	2	3	5	6	6	7	7	7
2. MULTIPLE DX										
0–19 Years	48	9.8	27	5	6	9	11	18	21	26
20–34	143	10.1	45	5	6	8	11	20	25	28
35–49	180	11.6	91	5	6	8	15	23	29	52
50–64	250	12.5	97	5	7	9	15	23	30	60
65+	303	14.4	107	6	8	12	17	26	33	73
TOTAL SINGLE DX	**64**	**6.7**	**7**	**4**	**5**	**6**	**7**	**11**	**12**	**19**
TOTAL MULTIPLE DX	**924**	**12.5**	**91**	**5**	**7**	**9**	**15**	**23**	**28**	**52**
TOTAL										
0–19 Years	57	9.1	23	5	6	8	10	16	21	26
20–34	168	9.6	41	4	5	7	11	19	24	27
35–49	198	11.2	85	5	6	8	14	22	29	52
50–64	257	12.3	95	5	7	9	15	23	30	60
65+	308	14.3	107	6	8	12	17	26	33	73
GRAND TOTAL	**988**	**12.2**	**87**	**5**	**7**	**9**	**15**	**23**	**28**	**52**

45.9: INTESTINAL ANASTOMOSIS

Type of Patients	Observed Patients	Avg. Stay	Vari-ance	Percentiles 10th	25th	50th	75th	90th	95th	99th
1. SINGLE DX										
0–19 Years	5	4.8	<1	4	5	5	5	5	5	5
20–34	13	4.6	2	3	4	4	5	7	7	7
35–49	14	4.7	5	2	3	5	5	8	8	12
50–64	8	5.3	4	4	4	4	6	9	9	9
65+	6	6.3	3	4	4	7	7	8	8	8
2. MULTIPLE DX										
0–19 Years	53	13.7	87	5	6	12	20	23	28	63
20–34	79	8.3	55	4	4	6	10	14	18	49
35–49	233	7.8	32	3	4	6	10	15	19	32
50–64	347	10.0	55	4	5	8	13	20	27	44
65+	389	11.1	59	5	6	8	14	21	28	36
TOTAL SINGLE DX	**46**	**5.1**	**3**	**3**	**4**	**5**	**6**	**7**	**8**	**9**
TOTAL MULTIPLE DX	**1,101**	**10.0**	**56**	**4**	**5**	**8**	**13**	**20**	**27**	**36**
TOTAL										
0–19 Years	58	12.1	84	5	5	11	18	21	28	63
20–34	92	7.7	49	4	4	6	8	14	18	49
35–49	247	7.6	31	3	4	6	9	15	19	32
50–64	355	9.9	54	4	5	7	13	20	27	44
65+	395	10.9	58	5	6	8	14	21	28	36
GRAND TOTAL	**1,147**	**9.8**	**54**	**4**	**5**	**7**	**12**	**19**	**26**	**36**

45.91: SM-TO-SM INTEST ANAST

Type of Patients	Observed Patients	Avg. Stay	Vari-ance	Percentiles 10th	25th	50th	75th	90th	95th	99th
1. SINGLE DX										
0–19 Years	0									
20–34	5	3.8	<1	3	3	4	4	4	5	5
35–49	3	2.8	<1	2	2	3	3	3	3	3
50–64	0									
65+	1	4.0	0	4	4	4	4	4	4	4
2. MULTIPLE DX										
0–19 Years	35	16.9	95	6	11	14	21	28	34	63
20–34	47	7.7	75	3	4	5	8	12	15	49
35–49	120	6.8	36	2	3	5	8	16	20	34
50–64	123	9.6	76	3	4	7	13	27	31	>99
65+	93	14.1	93	5	6	11	21	28	30	52
TOTAL SINGLE DX	**9**	**3.5**	**<1**	**3**	**3**	**4**	**4**	**4**	**5**	**5**
TOTAL MULTIPLE DX	**418**	**10.4**	**82**	**3**	**4**	**7**	**14**	**23**	**30**	**52**
TOTAL										
0–19 Years	35	16.9	95	6	11	14	21	28	34	63
20–34	52	7.2	67	3	4	5	7	11	15	49
35–49	123	6.7	36	2	3	5	8	15	20	34
50–64	123	9.6	76	3	4	7	13	27	31	>99
65+	94	14.0	93	5	6	11	21	28	30	52
GRAND TOTAL	**427**	**10.2**	**81**	**3**	**4**	**7**	**14**	**23**	**30**	**52**

45.93: SM-LG INTEST ANAST NEC

Type of Patients	Observed Patients	Avg. Stay	Vari-ance	Percentiles 10th	25th	50th	75th	90th	95th	99th
1. SINGLE DX										
0–19 Years	1	4.0	0	4	4	4	4	4	4	4
20–34	1	3.0	0	3	3	3	3	3	3	3
35–49	1	2.0	0	2	2	2	2	2	2	2
50–64	2	5.2	2	4	4	6	6	6	6	6
65+	1	4.0	0	4	4	4	4	4	4	4
2. MULTIPLE DX										
0–19 Years	5	13.2	56	5	5	20	20	20	20	20
20–34	13	9.3	47	3	5	8	11	18	29	29
35–49	40	11.0	30	5	7	10	14	18	19	32
50–64	81	14.3	60	5	8	14	17	26	29	36
65+	113	12.0	66	5	6	9	15	22	29	42
TOTAL SINGLE DX	**6**	**3.9**	**1**	**2**	**4**	**4**	**4**	**6**	**6**	**6**
TOTAL MULTIPLE DX	**252**	**12.5**	**58**	**5**	**7**	**11**	**16**	**22**	**28**	**36**
TOTAL										
0–19 Years	6	10.7	57	4	4	7	20	20	20	20
20–34	14	9.0	46	3	5	6	11	18	29	29
35–49	41	10.8	31	5	6	8	14	18	19	32
50–64	83	14.1	60	5	8	14	17	26	29	36
65+	114	11.9	66	5	6	9	15	22	27	42
GRAND TOTAL	**258**	**12.3**	**59**	**5**	**6**	**11**	**16**	**22**	**28**	**36**

45.94: LG-TO-LG INTEST ANAST

Type of Patients	Observed Patients	Avg. Stay	Vari-ance	Percentiles 10th	25th	50th	75th	90th	95th	99th
1. SINGLE DX										
0–19 Years	2	5.0	0	5	5	5	5	5	5	5
20–34	2	4.9	2	4	4	4	6	6	6	6
35–49	5	5.4	6	3	5	5	5	12	12	12
50–64	2	4.4	1	4	4	4	4	7	7	7
65+	3	7.1	1	7	7	7	8	8	8	8
2. MULTIPLE DX										
0–19 Years	6	6.8	7	6	6	6	6	12	14	14
20–34	4	6.9	6	5	5	5	8	10	10	10
35–49	40	7.3	14	4	5	6	8	12	13	24
50–64	93	7.7	15	4	5	7	9	11	14	24
65+	146	8.8	25	5	6	8	10	14	17	28
TOTAL SINGLE DX	**14**	**5.6**	**3**	**4**	**5**	**5**	**7**	**8**	**8**	**12**
TOTAL MULTIPLE DX	**289**	**8.1**	**20**	**5**	**6**	**7**	**9**	**13**	**15**	**24**
TOTAL										
0–19 Years	8	6.0	5	5	5	6	6	7	12	14
20–34	6	6.2	5	4	5	5	8	10	10	10
35–49	45	7.1	13	4	5	6	8	12	13	24
50–64	95	7.6	15	4	5	7	9	11	14	24
65+	149	8.7	24	5	6	8	10	13	16	28
GRAND TOTAL	**303**	**7.9**	**19**	**5**	**5**	**7**	**9**	**12**	**15**	**24**

45.95: ANASTOMOSIS TO ANUS

Type of Patients	Observed Patients	Avg. Stay	Vari-ance	10th	25th	50th	75th	90th	95th	99th
1. SINGLE DX										
0–19 Years	2	5.0	0	5	5	5	5	5	5	5
20–34	5	5.9	2	4	5	7	7	7	7	7
35–49	3	5.0	0	5	5	5	5	5	5	5
50–64	4	6.7	6	4	4	5	9	9	9	9
65+	1	4.0	0	4	4	4	4	4	4	4
2. MULTIPLE DX										
0–19 Years	7	6.4	23	2	2	5	8	13	16	16
20–34	12	9.0	13	5	5	9	13	14	14	14
35–49	21	7.7	17	4	5	7	9	13	14	21
50–64	42	7.5	18	4	5	7	8	10	17	25
65+	28	7.5	20	3	4	6	9	14	15	25
TOTAL SINGLE DX	**15**	**5.6**	**2**	**4**	**5**	**5**	**7**	**9**	**9**	**9**
TOTAL MULTIPLE DX	**110**	**7.7**	**18**	**4**	**5**	**7**	**9**	**14**	**15**	**25**
TOTAL										
0–19 Years	9	6.1	17	2	2	5	8	13	16	16
20–34	17	8.3	12	5	5	8	10	14	14	14
35–49	24	7.4	15	4	5	6	8	13	14	21
50–64	46	7.4	17	4	5	7	8	10	17	25
65+	29	7.3	20	3	4	6	9	14	15	25
GRAND TOTAL	**125**	**7.4**	**16**	**4**	**5**	**6**	**9**	**13**	**14**	**25**

46.0: INTEST EXTERIORIZATION

Type of Patients	Observed Patients	Avg. Stay	Vari-ance	10th	25th	50th	75th	90th	95th	99th
1. SINGLE DX										
0–19 Years	0									
20–34	5	7.7	18	3	6	7	8	15	15	15
35–49	9	4.3	3	3	3	3	5	8	8	8
50–64	4	11.4	64	6	6	6	11	24	24	24
65+	5	3.4	5	1	1	3	6	6	6	6
2. MULTIPLE DX										
0–19 Years	26	12.7	221	3	6	8	17	19	28	>99
20–34	54	8.6	56	3	5	7	10	17	27	52
35–49	144	9.4	45	4	5	8	11	17	24	33
50–64	251	10.5	58	4	5	8	14	21	27	38
65+	400	11.0	51	4	6	9	14	21	26	37
TOTAL SINGLE DX	**23**	**5.5**	**19**	**1**	**3**	**5**	**6**	**8**	**15**	**24**
TOTAL MULTIPLE DX	**875**	**10.5**	**60**	**4**	**6**	**8**	**13**	**20**	**26**	**38**
TOTAL										
0–19 Years	26	12.7	221	3	6	8	17	19	28	>99
20–34	59	8.5	53	3	5	7	9	17	27	52
35–49	153	9.0	44	3	5	8	10	16	24	33
50–64	255	10.5	58	4	5	8	14	21	27	38
65+	405	10.9	51	4	6	9	14	21	26	37
GRAND TOTAL	**898**	**10.4**	**60**	**4**	**5**	**8**	**13**	**20**	**26**	**38**

46.01: S-INTEST EXTERIORIZATION

Type of Patients	Observed Patients	Avg. Stay	Vari-ance	10th	25th	50th	75th	90th	95th	99th
1. SINGLE DX										
0–19 Years	0									
20–34	2	11.8	21	8	8	15	15	15	15	15
35–49	5	5.2	5	3	3	5	8	8	8	8
50–64	3	7.7	8	6	6	6	11	11	11	11
65+	1	6.0	0	6	6	6	6	6	6	6
2. MULTIPLE DX										
0–19 Years	9	20.4	563	5	7	18	19	93	>99	>99
20–34	26	7.9	44	2	4	5	8	20	20	28
35–49	57	9.5	56	4	5	7	10	15	26	49
50–64	81	9.4	42	4	6	8	11	15	19	44
65+	118	11.9	62	5	7	10	14	22	26	38
TOTAL SINGLE DX	**11**	**6.9**	**11**	**3**	**5**	**6**	**8**	**11**	**15**	**15**
TOTAL MULTIPLE DX	**291**	**10.7**	**79**	**4**	**5**	**8**	**13**	**20**	**27**	**44**
TOTAL										
0–19 Years	9	20.4	563	5	7	18	19	93	>99	>99
20–34	28	8.1	43	2	4	5	8	20	20	28
35–49	62	9.1	53	4	5	7	10	15	26	49
50–64	84	9.4	41	4	6	8	11	15	19	44
65+	119	11.9	62	5	6	10	14	22	26	38
GRAND TOTAL	**302**	**10.5**	**78**	**4**	**5**	**8**	**13**	**20**	**26**	**44**

46.03: L-INTEST EXTERIORIZATION

Type of Patients	Observed Patients	Avg. Stay	Vari-ance	10th	25th	50th	75th	90th	95th	99th
1. SINGLE DX										
0–19 Years	0									
20–34	1	3.0	0	3	3	3	3	3	3	3
35–49	4	3.4	<1	3	3	3	4	5	5	5
50–64	0									
65+	4	2.9	5	1	1	3	5	6	6	6
2. MULTIPLE DX										
0–19 Years	16	8.9	32	3	6	6	11	17	17	26
20–34	24	10.3	83	4	7	7	11	15	27	52
35–49	83	9.2	40	3	5	8	10	17	24	33
50–64	167	11.0	62	3	5	8	15	24	28	32
65+	262	10.5	46	4	6	9	13	19	26	30
TOTAL SINGLE DX	**9**	**3.2**	**3**	**1**	**3**	**3**	**4**	**5**	**6**	**6**
TOTAL MULTIPLE DX	**552**	**10.4**	**51**	**3**	**5**	**8**	**13**	**20**	**26**	**33**
TOTAL										
0–19 Years	16	8.9	32	3	6	6	11	17	17	26
20–34	25	10.0	82	3	7	7	10	15	27	52
35–49	87	8.9	40	3	5	8	10	17	24	33
50–64	167	11.0	62	3	5	8	15	24	28	32
65+	266	10.3	46	4	6	9	13	19	26	30
GRAND TOTAL	**561**	**10.2**	**51**	**3**	**5**	**8**	**13**	**19**	**26**	**33**

46.1: COLOSTOMY

Type of Patients	Observed Patients	Avg. Stay	Variance	10th	25th	50th	75th	90th	95th	99th
				Percentiles						
1. SINGLE DX										
0–19 Years	6	5.7	10	1	4	6	8	12	12	12
20–34	1	6.0	0	6	6	6	6	6	6	6
35–49	3	5.5	2	4	4	5	7	7	7	7
50–64	3	4.5	9	1	1	5	7	7	7	7
65+	4	4.7	5	4	4	4	4	5	13	13
2. MULTIPLE DX										
0–19 Years	52	13.0	150	3	5	9	15	30	44	59
20–34	35	12.6	187	3	6	7	15	36	36	84
35–49	124	11.0	64	4	6	9	14	19	24	50
50–64	240	11.7	86	3	6	9	16	24	29	34
65+	409	10.8	39	4	6	9	14	19	22	33
TOTAL SINGLE DX	**17**	**5.1**	**6**	**4**	**4**	**4**	**6**	**7**	**12**	**13**
TOTAL MULTIPLE DX	**860**	**11.3**	**69**	**4**	**6**	**9**	**14**	**21**	**27**	**39**
TOTAL										
0–19 Years	58	12.3	141	3	4	8	14	29	31	59
20–34	36	12.5	184	3	6	7	15	36	36	84
35–49	127	10.9	63	4	6	9	14	18	24	50
50–64	243	11.6	86	3	6	9	16	24	29	34
65+	413	10.7	39	4	6	9	14	19	22	31
GRAND TOTAL	**877**	**11.1**	**68**	**4**	**6**	**9**	**14**	**20**	**26**	**39**

46.10: COLOSTOMY NOS

Type of Patients	Observed Patients	Avg. Stay	Variance	10th	25th	50th	75th	90th	95th	99th
				Percentiles						
1. SINGLE DX										
0–19 Years	4	6.1	8	4	4	6	6	12	12	12
20–34	0									
35–49	2	4.6	<1	4	4	5	5	5	5	5
50–64	2	3.1	7	1	1	5	5	5	5	5
65+	1	5.0	0	5	5	5	5	5	5	5
2. MULTIPLE DX										
0–19 Years	16	13.1	254	3	3	8	13	27	59	59
20–34	11	11.6	310	6	6	7	9	16	84	84
35–49	53	11.2	67	4	5	11	15	23	27	50
50–64	83	12.8	137	3	6	10	16	26	29	71
65+	160	11.2	43	5	7	10	14	18	25	36
TOTAL SINGLE DX	**9**	**5.1**	**6**	**4**	**4**	**5**	**6**	**6**	**12**	**12**
TOTAL MULTIPLE DX	**323**	**11.7**	**92**	**4**	**6**	**10**	**14**	**20**	**29**	**55**
TOTAL										
0–19 Years	20	11.8	214	3	4	6	13	27	55	59
20–34	11	11.6	310	6	6	7	9	16	84	84
35–49	55	11.0	66	4	5	9	14	20	27	50
50–64	85	12.6	136	3	6	10	16	26	29	71
65+	161	11.1	43	5	7	10	14	18	25	36
GRAND TOTAL	**332**	**11.6**	**91**	**4**	**6**	**9**	**14**	**19**	**29**	**55**

46.11: TEMPORARY COLOSTOMY

Type of Patients	Observed Patients	Avg. Stay	Variance	10th	25th	50th	75th	90th	95th	99th
				Percentiles						
1. SINGLE DX										
0–19 Years	1	8.0	0	8	8	8	8	8	8	8
20–34	0									
35–49	1	7.0	0	7	7	7	7	7	7	7
50–64	0									
65+	1	13.0	0	13	13	13	13	13	13	13
2. MULTIPLE DX										
0–19 Years	27	14.1	112	4	6	12	17	31	31	45
20–34	17	13.9	158	2	5	10	16	36	36	39
35–49	41	11.5	98	3	6	9	14	21	26	50
50–64	78	11.9	71	3	6	9	16	25	30	33
65+	109	12.0	39	5	7	11	16	20	25	29
TOTAL SINGLE DX	**3**	**8.8**	**8**	**7**	**7**	**8**	**8**	**13**	**13**	**13**
TOTAL MULTIPLE DX	**272**	**12.3**	**73**	**4**	**6**	**10**	**16**	**24**	**30**	**44**
TOTAL										
0–19 Years	28	13.9	110	4	6	11	17	31	31	45
20–34	17	13.9	158	2	5	10	16	36	36	39
35–49	42	11.3	95	3	6	8	13	21	26	50
50–64	78	11.9	71	3	6	9	16	25	30	33
65+	110	12.0	39	5	7	11	16	20	25	29
GRAND TOTAL	**275**	**12.2**	**73**	**4**	**6**	**10**	**16**	**24**	**30**	**44**

46.13: PERMANENT COLOSTOMY

Type of Patients	Observed Patients	Avg. Stay	Variance	10th	25th	50th	75th	90th	95th	99th
				Percentiles						
1. SINGLE DX										
0–19 Years	1	1.0	0	1	1	1	1	1	1	1
20–34	1	6.0	0	6	6	6	6	6	6	6
35–49	0									
50–64	1	7.0	0	7	7	7	7	7	7	7
65+	2	4.0	0	4	4	4	4	4	4	4
2. MULTIPLE DX										
0–19 Years	9	9.3	76	2	3	7	11	30	30	30
20–34	7	9.9	17	4	5	11	14	15	15	15
35–49	30	10.3	22	4	7	9	15	16	16	23
50–64	79	10.1	37	5	6	9	12	18	20	33
65+	139	9.7	31	4	6	8	12	18	22	24
TOTAL SINGLE DX	**5**	**4.1**	**2**	**4**	**4**	**4**	**4**	**6**	**7**	**7**
TOTAL MULTIPLE DX	**264**	**9.9**	**33**	**4**	**6**	**8**	**12**	**18**	**22**	**28**
TOTAL										
0–19 Years	10	8.7	75	2	3	5	11	17	30	30
20–34	8	9.5	17	4	5	9	14	15	15	15
35–49	30	10.3	22	4	7	9	15	16	16	23
50–64	80	10.0	36	5	6	8	12	18	20	33
65+	141	9.4	31	4	5	8	12	18	22	24
GRAND TOTAL	**269**	**9.7**	**33**	**4**	**6**	**8**	**12**	**18**	**22**	**28**

46.2: ILEOSTOMY

Type of Patients	Observed Patients	Avg. Stay	Vari-ance	Percentiles						
				10th	25th	50th	75th	90th	95th	99th
1. SINGLE DX										
0–19 Years	3	13.6	52	3	4	18	18	18	18	18
20–34	0									
35–49	4	6.0	5	4	4	7	7	9	9	9
50–64	1	7.0	0	7	7	7	7	7	7	7
65+	1	8.0	0	8	8	8	8	8	8	8
2. MULTIPLE DX										
0–19 Years	21	20.4	419	5	5	18	27	68	>99	>99
20–34	11	10.6	40	5	6	9	14	19	27	27
35–49	39	12.5	103	4	6	11	13	21	33	57
50–64	62	11.1	68	3	5	9	15	26	27	30
65+	73	14.9	111	5	7	11	19	30	32	43
TOTAL SINGLE DX	**9**	**10.0**	**39**	**4**	**4**	**7**	**18**	**18**	**18**	**18**
TOTAL MULTIPLE DX	**206**	**13.7**	**134**	**4**	**6**	**10**	**19**	**28**	**32**	**95**
TOTAL										
0–19 Years	24	19.3	365	5	5	18	27	68	>99	>99
20–34	11	10.6	40	5	6	9	14	19	27	27
35–49	43	12.0	98	4	6	9	13	20	33	57
50–64	63	11.0	67	3	5	9	15	26	27	30
65+	74	14.8	111	5	7	11	19	30	32	43
GRAND TOTAL	**215**	**13.6**	**131**	**4**	**6**	**10**	**18**	**28**	**32**	**95**

46.23: PERMANENT ILEOSTOMY NEC

Type of Patients	Observed Patients	Avg. Stay	Vari-ance	Percentiles						
				10th	25th	50th	75th	90th	95th	99th
1. SINGLE DX										
0–19 Years	2	15.2	40	3	18	18	18	18	18	18
20–34	0									
35–49	1	4.0	0	4	4	4	4	4	4	4
50–64	0									
65+	0									
2. MULTIPLE DX										
0–19 Years	8	20.6	466	6	15	18	19	21	95	95
20–34	6	9.1	30	4	5	8	14	19	19	19
35–49	11	14.2	60	6	9	11	19	21	33	33
50–64	21	9.6	71	3	3	9	9	17	30	42
65+	30	12.5	47	4	7	10	18	25	25	25
TOTAL SINGLE DX	**3**	**13.1**	**54**	**3**	**4**	**18**	**18**	**18**	**18**	**18**
TOTAL MULTIPLE DX	**76**	**12.8**	**115**	**4**	**6**	**10**	**18**	**24**	**25**	**42**
TOTAL										
0–19 Years	10	19.1	346	5	15	18	18	21	95	95
20–34	6	9.1	30	4	5	8	14	19	19	19
35–49	12	13.5	63	4	7	11	19	21	33	33
50–64	21	9.6	71	3	3	9	9	17	30	42
65+	30	12.5	47	4	7	10	18	25	25	25
GRAND TOTAL	**79**	**12.8**	**111**	**4**	**6**	**10**	**18**	**21**	**25**	**42**

46.3: OTHER ENTEROSTOMY

Type of Patients	Observed Patients	Avg. Stay	Vari-ance	Percentiles						
				10th	25th	50th	75th	90th	95th	99th
1. SINGLE DX										
0–19 Years	0									
20–34	0									
35–49	0									
50–64	1	13.0	0	13	13	13	13	13	13	13
65+	2	2.5	<1	2	2	2	4	4	4	4
2. MULTIPLE DX										
0–19 Years	30	12.1	111	2	3	11	19	31	>99	>99
20–34	35	10.3	63	2	5	8	17	19	19	41
35–49	62	9.8	63	2	4	7	14	26	26	38
50–64	109	12.0	91	3	5	9	17	28	31	38
65+	210	10.2	74	2	5	8	13	19	25	33
TOTAL SINGLE DX	**3**	**3.3**	**9**	**2**	**2**	**2**	**4**	**4**	**13**	**13**
TOTAL MULTIPLE DX	**446**	**10.7**	**80**	**2**	**5**	**8**	**15**	**24**	**28**	**54**
TOTAL										
0–19 Years	30	12.1	111	2	3	11	19	31	>99	>99
20–34	35	10.3	63	2	5	8	17	19	19	41
35–49	62	9.8	63	2	4	7	14	26	26	38
50–64	110	12.0	91	3	5	9	17	28	31	38
65+	212	9.9	73	2	4	8	13	19	25	33
GRAND TOTAL	**449**	**10.6**	**79**	**2**	**4**	**8**	**15**	**24**	**28**	**54**

46.32: PEJ

Type of Patients	Observed Patients	Avg. Stay	Vari-ance	Percentiles						
				10th	25th	50th	75th	90th	95th	99th
1. SINGLE DX										
0–19 Years	0									
20–34	0									
35–49	0									
50–64	0									
65+	0									
2. MULTIPLE DX										
0–19 Years	12	11.0	70	1	3	11	19	21	21	21
20–34	10	8.8	30	5	5	6	12	18	18	21
35–49	17	8.5	36	2	6	7	10	15	18	28
50–64	31	8.6	78	2	3	6	8	22	34	40
65+	87	9.7	37	3	5	8	13	17	23	28
TOTAL SINGLE DX	**0**									
TOTAL MULTIPLE DX	**157**	**9.5**	**46**	**2**	**5**	**7**	**13**	**19**	**22**	**30**
TOTAL										
0–19 Years	12	11.0	70	1	3	11	19	21	21	21
20–34	10	8.8	30	5	5	6	12	18	18	21
35–49	17	8.5	36	2	6	7	10	15	18	28
50–64	31	8.6	78	2	3	6	8	22	34	40
65+	87	9.7	37	3	5	8	13	17	23	28
GRAND TOTAL	**157**	**9.5**	**46**	**2**	**5**	**7**	**13**	**19**	**22**	**30**

46.39: ENTEROSTOMY NEC

Type of Patients	Observed Patients	Avg. Stay	Vari-ance	Percentiles 10th	25th	50th	75th	90th	95th	99th
1. SINGLE DX										
0–19 Years	0									
20–34	0									
35–49	0									
50–64	1	13.0	0	13	13	13	13	13	13	13
65+	2	2.5	<1	2	2	2	4	4	4	4
2. MULTIPLE DX										
0–19 Years	18	13.0	145	2	4	17	22	>99	>99	>99
20–34	25	11.0	77	2	5	9	17	19	19	41
35–49	45	10.3	75	2	4	8	14	26	26	38
50–64	78	13.1	91	3	6	10	21	28	31	38
65+	123	10.5	101	2	4	8	13	23	26	36
TOTAL SINGLE DX	**3**	**3.3**	**9**	**2**	**2**	**2**	**4**	**4**	**13**	**13**
TOTAL MULTIPLE DX	**289**	**11.4**	**97**	**2**	**4**	**9**	**17**	**25**	**31**	**>99**
TOTAL										
0–19 Years	18	13.0	145	2	4	17	22	>99	>99	>99
20–34	25	11.0	77	2	5	9	17	19	19	41
35–49	45	10.3	75	2	4	8	14	26	26	38
50–64	79	13.1	90	3	6	10	21	28	31	38
65+	125	10.0	98	2	4	8	12	20	25	36
GRAND TOTAL	**292**	**11.2**	**96**	**2**	**4**	**9**	**17**	**25**	**30**	**>99**

46.4: INTESTINAL STOMA REV

Type of Patients	Observed Patients	Avg. Stay	Vari-ance	Percentiles 10th	25th	50th	75th	90th	95th	99th
1. SINGLE DX										
0–19 Years	1	2.0	0	2	2	2	2	2	2	2
20–34	4	1.8	<1	1	1	1	3	3	3	3
35–49	7	2.8	4	1	2	2	2	6	6	6
50–64	4	3.0	8	1	1	2	3	8	8	8
65+	8	2.1	3	1	1	2	2	2	8	8
2. MULTIPLE DX										
0–19 Years	21	6.6	22	2	3	5	8	16	16	16
20–34	33	5.6	10	2	3	6	7	9	12	15
35–49	83	5.6	19	1	3	4	7	11	17	25
50–64	143	5.6	24	1	3	5	7	10	15	26
65+	264	5.9	20	1	2	5	8	12	14	20
TOTAL SINGLE DX	**24**	**2.4**	**3**	**1**	**1**	**2**	**2**	**6**	**8**	**8**
TOTAL MULTIPLE DX	**544**	**5.8**	**20**	**1**	**3**	**5**	**7**	**12**	**15**	**23**
TOTAL										
0–19 Years	22	6.4	21	2	3	5	8	16	16	16
20–34	37	5.2	11	1	2	5	7	9	10	15
35–49	90	5.3	18	1	2	4	7	11	17	17
50–64	147	5.6	23	1	3	4	7	10	15	26
65+	272	5.7	20	1	2	4	8	12	14	20
GRAND TOTAL	**568**	**5.6**	**20**	**1**	**2**	**5**	**7**	**11**	**15**	**23**

46.41: SM INTEST STOMA REVISION

Type of Patients	Observed Patients	Avg. Stay	Vari-ance	Percentiles 10th	25th	50th	75th	90th	95th	99th
1. SINGLE DX										
0–19 Years	1	2.0	0	2	2	2	2	2	2	2
20–34	2	1.5	<1	1	1	1	2	2	2	2
35–49	2	1.7	<1	1	1	2	2	2	2	2
50–64	4	3.0	8	1	1	2	3	8	8	8
65+	4	1.4	<1	1	1	1	2	2	2	2
2. MULTIPLE DX										
0–19 Years	9	9.1	33	2	3	8	16	16	16	16
20–34	19	5.4	15	1	2	5	7	10	15	15
35–49	37	5.3	18	2	3	5	6	10	11	25
50–64	52	6.6	32	2	3	5	7	13	23	28
65+	69	6.0	19	2	3	5	9	12	14	20
TOTAL SINGLE DX	**13**	**1.9**	**2**	**1**	**1**	**2**	**2**	**2**	**3**	**8**
TOTAL MULTIPLE DX	**186**	**6.2**	**24**	**2**	**3**	**5**	**7**	**13**	**16**	**25**
TOTAL										
0–19 Years	10	8.5	34	2	3	7	16	16	16	16
20–34	21	5.1	15	1	2	5	6	10	15	15
35–49	39	5.1	18	1	2	4	5	10	11	25
50–64	56	6.4	31	2	3	5	7	13	19	28
65+	73	5.7	19	2	3	4	7	12	14	20
GRAND TOTAL	**199**	**5.9**	**24**	**2**	**2**	**5**	**7**	**12**	**16**	**25**

46.42: PERICOLOSTOMY HERNIA REP

Type of Patients	Observed Patients	Avg. Stay	Vari-ance	Percentiles 10th	25th	50th	75th	90th	95th	99th
1. SINGLE DX										
0–19 Years	0									
20–34	1	3.0	0	3	3	3	3	3	3	3
35–49	3	3.8	7	1	2	6	6	6	6	6
50–64	0									
65+	3	3.7	12	1	1	2	8	8	8	8
2. MULTIPLE DX										
0–19 Years	1	5.0	0	5	5	5	5	5	5	5
20–34	8	5.6	8	2	3	6	9	9	9	9
35–49	19	5.7	15	2	3	4	8	11	11	17
50–64	45	5.3	21	1	3	5	7	7	15	26
65+	128	5.7	14	2	3	4	8	11	13	19
TOTAL SINGLE DX	**7**	**3.7**	**7**	**1**	**2**	**2**	**6**	**8**	**8**	**8**
TOTAL MULTIPLE DX	**201**	**5.6**	**15**	**2**	**3**	**5**	**8**	**11**	**13**	**22**
TOTAL										
0–19 Years	1	5.0	0	5	5	5	5	5	5	5
20–34	9	5.4	8	2	3	6	9	9	9	9
35–49	22	5.4	14	2	2	4	7	11	11	17
50–64	45	5.3	21	1	3	5	7	7	15	26
65+	131	5.6	14	2	3	4	8	11	13	19
GRAND TOTAL	**208**	**5.5**	**15**	**2**	**3**	**5**	**7**	**11**	**13**	**22**

46.43: LG INTEST STOMA REV NEC

Type of Patients	Observed Patients	Avg. Stay	Vari-ance	Percentiles 10th	25th	50th	75th	90th	95th	99th
1. SINGLE DX										
0–19 Years	0									
20–34	1	1.0	0	1	1	1	1	1	1	1
35–49	2	2.8	3	2	2	2	2	6	6	6
50–64	0									
65+	1	2.0	0	2	2	2	2	2	2	2
2. MULTIPLE DX										
0–19 Years	11	4.6	5	2	3	5	6	7	9	9
20–34	4	6.0	3	2	6	7	7	7	7	7
35–49	27	6.0	24	1	3	5	8	17	17	17
50–64	43	4.5	10	1	2	4	6	9	11	17
65+	65	5.9	30	1	2	5	9	12	19	30
TOTAL SINGLE DX	**4**	**2.2**	**1**	**1**	**2**	**2**	**2**	**2**	**6**	**6**
TOTAL MULTIPLE DX	**150**	**5.4**	**20**	**1**	**2**	**5**	**7**	**11**	**15**	**19**
TOTAL										
0–19 Years	11	4.6	5	2	3	5	6	7	9	9
20–34	5	5.3	6	1	2	6	7	7	7	7
35–49	29	5.6	23	1	2	4	7	14	17	17
50–64	43	4.5	10	1	2	4	6	9	11	17
65+	66	5.7	29	1	2	4	9	12	19	30
GRAND TOTAL	**154**	**5.2**	**20**	**1**	**2**	**4**	**7**	**11**	**15**	**19**

46.5: INTESTINAL STOMA CLOSURE

Type of Patients	Observed Patients	Avg. Stay	Vari-ance	Percentiles 10th	25th	50th	75th	90th	95th	99th
1. SINGLE DX										
0–19 Years	35	5.8	4	4	5	5	7	9	10	10
20–34	75	4.1	2	2	3	4	5	6	7	8
35–49	107	4.6	3	3	4	5	6	7	7	9
50–64	73	4.8	4	3	4	4	6	7	8	11
65+	24	5.2	4	3	3	5	6	9	9	9
2. MULTIPLE DX										
0–19 Years	187	6.8	74	3	4	5	6	10	16	30
20–34	233	6.1	17	3	3	5	7	10	14	20
35–49	506	6.0	13	3	4	5	7	10	13	21
50–64	737	6.3	19	3	4	5	7	9	15	29
65+	765	7.2	17	3	5	6	8	12	14	24
TOTAL SINGLE DX	**314**	**4.8**	**3**	**3**	**4**	**5**	**6**	**7**	**8**	**10**
TOTAL MULTIPLE DX	**2,428**	**6.6**	**24**	**3**	**4**	**6**	**7**	**10**	**14**	**27**
TOTAL										
0–19 Years	222	6.6	63	3	4	5	7	10	14	30
20–34	308	5.6	14	2	3	5	7	9	12	18
35–49	613	5.8	12	3	4	5	7	9	12	21
50–64	810	6.2	18	3	4	5	7	9	14	29
65+	789	7.1	17	3	5	6	8	12	14	24
GRAND TOTAL	**2,742**	**6.4**	**22**	**3**	**4**	**5**	**7**	**10**	**13**	**26**

46.51: SM INTEST STOMA CLOSURE

Type of Patients	Observed Patients	Avg. Stay	Vari-ance	Percentiles 10th	25th	50th	75th	90th	95th	99th
1. SINGLE DX										
0–19 Years	11	6.2	4	4	5	6	7	10	10	10
20–34	40	3.6	2	2	3	3	4	5	6	7
35–49	27	3.6	2	2	3	3	5	5	6	7
50–64	13	4.0	4	2	3	3	4	8	8	8
65+	6	3.9	2	3	3	3	4	7	7	7
2. MULTIPLE DX										
0–19 Years	85	8.5	161	2	4	5	7	17	26	81
20–34	115	5.4	24	2	3	4	5	9	14	20
35–49	191	5.5	16	2	3	4	6	10	12	26
50–64	253	5.7	29	2	3	4	6	10	15	29
65+	211	6.8	27	3	4	5	8	12	16	27
TOTAL SINGLE DX	**97**	**4.0**	**3**	**2**	**3**	**4**	**5**	**6**	**7**	**10**
TOTAL MULTIPLE DX	**855**	**6.3**	**44**	**2**	**3**	**5**	**7**	**12**	**16**	**30**
TOTAL										
0–19 Years	96	8.3	146	2	4	5	7	16	26	81
20–34	155	4.9	18	2	3	4	5	9	13	20
35–49	218	5.3	15	2	3	4	6	10	12	26
50–64	266	5.6	27	2	3	4	6	10	15	29
65+	217	6.7	27	3	4	5	8	12	16	27
GRAND TOTAL	**952**	**6.0**	**40**	**2**	**3**	**4**	**6**	**11**	**15**	**29**

46.52: LG INTEST STOMA CLOSURE

Type of Patients	Observed Patients	Avg. Stay	Vari-ance	Percentiles 10th	25th	50th	75th	90th	95th	99th
1. SINGLE DX										
0–19 Years	24	5.6	3	3	5	5	7	8	10	10
20–34	35	5.1	2	3	4	5	6	8	8	9
35–49	80	4.9	2	3	4	5	6	7	7	10
50–64	60	5.0	3	3	4	5	6	7	8	14
65+	18	5.7	4	3	4	5	7	9	9	9
2. MULTIPLE DX										
0–19 Years	102	5.5	7	3	4	5	6	9	11	14
20–34	118	6.7	10	3	4	7	9	11	13	15
35–49	315	6.3	11	3	5	6	7	10	13	21
50–64	484	6.6	15	3	5	6	7	9	13	27
65+	551	7.3	14	4	5	7	8	11	14	24
TOTAL SINGLE DX	**217**	**5.2**	**3**	**3**	**4**	**5**	**6**	**7**	**8**	**10**
TOTAL MULTIPLE DX	**1,570**	**6.7**	**13**	**4**	**5**	**6**	**8**	**10**	**13**	**24**
TOTAL										
0–19 Years	126	5.5	6	3	4	5	6	9	11	14
20–34	153	6.3	9	3	4	6	8	10	12	15
35–49	395	6.0	9	3	4	5	7	9	12	19
50–64	544	6.4	14	3	4	6	7	9	12	27
65+	569	7.3	14	4	5	7	8	11	13	24
GRAND TOTAL	**1,787**	**6.5**	**12**	**3**	**5**	**6**	**7**	**10**	**13**	**23**

46.6: FIXATION OF INTESTINE

Type of Patients	Observed Patients	Avg. Stay	Vari-ance	Percentiles 10th	25th	50th	75th	90th	95th	99th
1. SINGLE DX										
0–19 Years	0									
20–34	0									
35–49	0									
50–64	0									
65+	0									
2. MULTIPLE DX										
0–19 Years	1	1.0	0	1	1	1	1	1	1	1
20–34	4	5.5	30	2	3	3	4	15	15	15
35–49	10	7.2	70	2	3	6	6	29	29	29
50–64	10	4.4	9	1	2	5	6	7	11	11
65+	10	9.1	15	4	5	10	12	12	15	15
TOTAL SINGLE DX	**0**									
TOTAL MULTIPLE DX	**35**	**6.6**	**31**	**2**	**2**	**5**	**9**	**12**	**15**	**29**
TOTAL										
0–19 Years	1	1.0	0	1	1	1	1	1	1	1
20–34	4	5.5	30	2	3	3	4	15	15	15
35–49	10	7.2	70	2	3	6	6	29	29	29
50–64	10	4.4	9	1	2	5	6	7	11	11
65+	10	9.1	15	4	5	10	12	12	15	15
GRAND TOTAL	**35**	**6.6**	**31**	**2**	**2**	**5**	**9**	**12**	**15**	**29**

46.7: OTHER INTESTINAL REPAIR

Type of Patients	Observed Patients	Avg. Stay	Vari-ance	Percentiles 10th	25th	50th	75th	90th	95th	99th
1. SINGLE DX										
0–19 Years	20	4.2	4	1	3	4	6	7	7	7
20–34	18	4.4	5	1	3	4	6	7	8	10
35–49	15	5.1	6	2	3	4	7	8	8	9
50–64	11	5.4	1	4	5	5	6	6	8	8
65+	2	3.6	<1	3	3	4	4	4	4	4
2. MULTIPLE DX										
0–19 Years	156	9.9	118	3	4	7	10	17	29	76
20–34	285	8.4	52	3	4	6	10	17	24	44
35–49	334	10.0	106	3	5	7	11	22	25	72
50–64	398	11.1	110	4	6	8	12	24	31	67
65+	543	10.9	59	4	6	9	14	20	25	43
TOTAL SINGLE DX	**66**	**4.6**	**4**	**2**	**3**	**4**	**6**	**7**	**8**	**10**
TOTAL MULTIPLE DX	**1,716**	**10.3**	**85**	**3**	**5**	**8**	**12**	**20**	**26**	**50**
TOTAL										
0–19 Years	176	9.4	110	3	4	7	10	17	26	76
20–34	303	8.1	49	3	4	6	9	16	22	44
35–49	349	9.7	103	3	4	7	10	22	25	59
50–64	409	11.0	108	4	6	7	12	23	29	67
65+	545	10.9	59	4	6	9	14	20	25	43
GRAND TOTAL	**1,782**	**10.1**	**83**	**3**	**5**	**7**	**12**	**20**	**26**	**49**

46.73: SMALL INTEST SUTURE NEC

Type of Patients	Observed Patients	Avg. Stay	Vari-ance	Percentiles 10th	25th	50th	75th	90th	95th	99th
1. SINGLE DX										
0–19 Years	9	4.6	3	3	3	4	7	7	7	7
20–34	13	4.3	3	3	3	4	5	7	8	8
35–49	7	5.6	3	4	4	6	7	7	9	9
50–64	4	5.9	3	4	5	6	8	8	8	8
65+	0									
2. MULTIPLE DX										
0–19 Years	83	8.2	32	3	4	7	10	17	22	>99
20–34	152	8.1	47	3	4	6	9	17	22	44
35–49	167	10.2	101	3	5	7	12	22	26	72
50–64	174	10.5	80	4	6	7	12	24	28	49
65+	237	11.0	41	4	6	10	15	20	23	31
TOTAL SINGLE DX	**33**	**4.8**	**3**	**3**	**3**	**4**	**6**	**7**	**8**	**9**
TOTAL MULTIPLE DX	**813**	**9.9**	**62**	**3**	**5**	**8**	**13**	**20**	**25**	**45**
TOTAL										
0–19 Years	92	7.9	31	3	4	6	10	17	22	>99
20–34	165	7.7	44	3	4	5	8	17	20	31
35–49	174	10.1	98	3	5	7	11	22	26	72
50–64	178	10.4	79	4	6	7	12	23	27	49
65+	237	11.0	41	4	6	10	15	20	23	31
GRAND TOTAL	**846**	**9.7**	**61**	**3**	**5**	**7**	**12**	**19**	**25**	**44**

46.74: CLOSURE SMB FISTULA NEC

Type of Patients	Observed Patients	Avg. Stay	Vari-ance	Percentiles 10th	25th	50th	75th	90th	95th	99th
1. SINGLE DX										
0–19 Years	3	1.6	<1	1	1	1	2	3	3	3
20–34	0									
35–49	2	2.4	<1	2	2	2	3	3	3	3
50–64	1	5.0	0	5	5	5	5	5	5	5
65+	1	4.0	0	4	4	4	4	4	4	4
2. MULTIPLE DX										
0–19 Years	5	9.9	154	1	1	6	12	40	40	40
20–34	10	9.0	76	4	5	6	10	31	31	31
35–49	28	11.6	176	3	4	6	17	25	25	75
50–64	53	12.8	107	5	5	8	20	29	33	>99
65+	58	11.7	137	3	5	8	15	21	33	78
TOTAL SINGLE DX	**7**	**2.4**	**2**	**1**	**1**	**2**	**3**	**4**	**5**	**5**
TOTAL MULTIPLE DX	**154**	**11.8**	**133**	**3**	**5**	**7**	**15**	**25**	**33**	**78**
TOTAL										
0–19 Years	8	6.5	105	1	1	3	6	12	40	40
20–34	10	9.0	76	4	5	6	10	31	31	31
35–49	30	11.2	171	3	4	6	14	25	25	75
50–64	54	12.7	106	5	5	8	20	29	33	>99
65+	59	11.6	136	3	4	8	15	21	33	78
GRAND TOTAL	**161**	**11.4**	**131**	**3**	**5**	**7**	**15**	**25**	**33**	**75**

46.75: LARGE INTESTINE SUTURE

Type of Patients	Observed Patients	Avg. Stay	Vari-ance	10th	25th	50th	75th	90th	95th	99th
1. SINGLE DX										
0–19 Years	3	4.1	3	3	3	3	6	6	6	6
20–34	2	2.1	5	1	1	1	1	6	6	6
35–49	2	3.4	<1	3	3	3	4	4	4	4
50–64	5	5.2	<1	4	4	6	6	6	6	6
65+	1	3.0	0	3	3	3	3	3	3	3
2. MULTIPLE DX										
0–19 Years	23	11.2	219	4	4	6	10	31	31	76
20–34	83	7.4	30	3	4	6	9	12	21	30
35–49	75	7.7	40	3	4	6	9	16	23	31
50–64	78	7.4	18	4	5	7	8	11	14	31
65+	136	9.4	39	5	6	7	10	17	18	36
TOTAL SINGLE DX	**13**	**3.8**	**4**	**1**	**3**	**4**	**6**	**6**	**6**	**6**
TOTAL MULTIPLE DX	**395**	**8.5**	**48**	**3**	**5**	**7**	**10**	**16**	**19**	**31**
TOTAL										
0–19 Years	26	10.6	205	3	4	6	9	31	31	76
20–34	85	7.1	30	3	4	6	8	12	21	30
35–49	77	7.6	39	3	3	6	9	16	23	31
50–64	83	7.3	18	4	5	7	8	11	14	31
65+	137	9.4	39	5	6	7	10	17	18	36
GRAND TOTAL	**408**	**8.3**	**47**	**3**	**5**	**7**	**10**	**16**	**19**	**31**

46.79: REPAIR OF INTESTINE NEC

Type of Patients	Observed Patients	Avg. Stay	Vari-ance	10th	25th	50th	75th	90th	95th	99th
1. SINGLE DX										
0–19 Years	3	4.7	<1	4	4	4	6	6	6	6
20–34	3	6.4	5	3	6	6	6	10	10	10
35–49	3	6.5	5	3	4	8	8	8	8	8
50–64	1	5.0	0	5	5	5	5	5	5	5
65+	0									
2. MULTIPLE DX										
0–19 Years	31	11.6	190	3	6	8	10	18	29	68
20–34	18	7.3	18	4	4	7	8	15	18	18
35–49	34	9.8	97	3	5	7	9	24	32	59
50–64	63	11.3	51	4	7	10	17	19	22	37
65+	76	11.5	49	5	6	9	16	22	26	38
TOTAL SINGLE DX	**10**	**5.9**	**4**	**3**	**4**	**6**	**8**	**8**	**10**	**10**
TOTAL MULTIPLE DX	**222**	**10.9**	**78**	**4**	**6**	**8**	**14**	**19**	**26**	**59**
TOTAL										
0–19 Years	34	11.0	178	3	5	8	10	18	29	68
20–34	21	7.2	15	3	4	6	8	13	15	18
35–49	37	9.4	87	3	5	7	9	19	25	59
50–64	64	11.3	51	4	7	10	15	19	22	37
65+	76	11.5	49	5	6	9	16	22	26	38
GRAND TOTAL	**232**	**10.6**	**75**	**4**	**6**	**8**	**14**	**19**	**25**	**38**

46.8: BOWEL DILATION & MANIP

Type of Patients	Observed Patients	Avg. Stay	Vari-ance	10th	25th	50th	75th	90th	95th	99th
1. SINGLE DX										
0–19 Years	71	2.9	2	1	2	3	3	5	5	7
20–34	1	2.0	0	2	2	2	2	2	2	2
35–49	5	3.2	<1	3	3	3	3	4	4	4
50–64	8	3.0	3	1	2	3	4	7	7	7
65+	3	7.9	23	1	1	10	11	11	11	11
2. MULTIPLE DX										
0–19 Years	140	6.3	47	2	3	4	7	11	24	33
20–34	45	5.9	27	2	3	4	7	11	20	23
35–49	119	5.5	13	2	3	5	7	10	14	21
50–64	112	8.3	36	3	5	6	11	16	23	30
65+	342	8.7	41	3	4	7	11	16	24	29
TOTAL SINGLE DX	**88**	**3.0**	**3**	**1**	**2**	**3**	**4**	**5**	**7**	**10**
TOTAL MULTIPLE DX	**758**	**7.4**	**39**	**2**	**3**	**6**	**9**	**14**	**21**	**33**
TOTAL										
0–19 Years	211	5.0	32	2	2	3	5	8	14	33
20–34	46	5.9	27	2	3	4	7	11	20	23
35–49	124	5.3	13	2	3	5	7	10	14	21
50–64	120	8.0	36	2	4	6	11	16	20	30
65+	345	8.7	41	3	4	7	11	16	24	29
GRAND TOTAL	**846**	**6.7**	**36**	**2**	**3**	**5**	**8**	**13**	**20**	**32**

46.81: INTRA-ABD S-INTEST MANIP

Type of Patients	Observed Patients	Avg. Stay	Vari-ance	10th	25th	50th	75th	90th	95th	99th
1. SINGLE DX										
0–19 Years	30	3.5	2	2	2	3	4	6	7	8
20–34	0									
35–49	2	3.2	<1	3	3	3	3	4	4	4
50–64	2	1.4	<1	1	1	1	2	2	2	2
65+	0									
2. MULTIPLE DX										
0–19 Years	72	8.1	66	2	4	6	8	21	33	33
20–34	22	7.1	14	3	5	6	9	10	11	20
35–49	38	7.2	21	3	5	6	8	16	16	22
50–64	44	10.9	40	5	6	9	13	17	25	32
65+	83	9.8	41	3	6	8	12	21	24	29
TOTAL SINGLE DX	**34**	**3.4**	**2**	**2**	**2**	**3**	**4**	**5**	**7**	**8**
TOTAL MULTIPLE DX	**259**	**8.8**	**48**	**3**	**5**	**7**	**10**	**19**	**24**	**33**
TOTAL										
0–19 Years	102	6.6	50	2	3	4	7	13	24	33
20–34	22	7.1	14	3	5	6	9	10	11	20
35–49	40	6.8	20	3	4	5	8	14	16	22
50–64	46	10.6	41	5	6	9	13	17	25	32
65+	83	9.8	41	3	6	8	12	21	24	29
GRAND TOTAL	**293**	**7.9**	**44**	**2**	**4**	**6**	**9**	**16**	**24**	**33**

46.82: INTRA-ABD L-INTEST MANIP

Type of Patients	Observed Patients	Avg. Stay	Variance	10th	25th	50th	75th	90th	95th	99th
1. SINGLE DX										
0–19 Years	32	2.4	1	1	2	2	3	4	4	7
20–34	1	2.0	0	2	2	2	2	2	2	2
35–49	2	3.5	<1	3	3	4	4	4	4	4
50–64	5	3.7	3	2	3	3	4	7	7	7
65+	1	11.0	0	11	11	11	11	11	11	11
2. MULTIPLE DX										
0–19 Years	44	3.8	5	2	2	3	4	7	8	11
20–34	4	6.3	31	2	2	4	6	16	16	16
35–49	20	5.1	6	3	3	4	6	7	12	15
50–64	8	6.8	11	4	5	5	6	13	13	13
65+	32	12.3	60	5	6	11	14	24	28	39
TOTAL SINGLE DX	**41**	**2.7**	**3**	**1**	**2**	**3**	**3**	**4**	**5**	**11**
TOTAL MULTIPLE DX	**108**	**6.1**	**30**	**2**	**3**	**4**	**7**	**13**	**16**	**28**
TOTAL										
0–19 Years	76	3.2	4	1	2	3	4	6	7	11
20–34	5	5.4	27	2	2	4	6	16	16	16
35–49	22	5.0	6	3	3	4	6	7	8	15
50–64	13	5.5	10	3	4	5	6	12	13	13
65+	33	12.3	57	5	6	11	14	24	28	39
GRAND TOTAL	**149**	**5.0**	**24**	**2**	**2**	**3**	**6**	**11**	**13**	**26**

46.85: DILATION OF INTESTINE

Type of Patients	Observed Patients	Avg. Stay	Variance	10th	25th	50th	75th	90th	95th	99th
1. SINGLE DX										
0–19 Years	0									
20–34	0									
35–49	1	3.0	0	3	3	3	3	3	3	3
50–64	1	3.0	0	3	3	3	3	3	3	3
65+	2	5.4	32	1	1	1	10	10	10	10
2. MULTIPLE DX										
0–19 Years	5	4.4	7	1	2	3	7	7	7	7
20–34	19	4.8	37	1	2	3	4	7	23	23
35–49	53	4.5	9	1	2	4	6	8	11	16
50–64	60	6.5	28	2	3	5	7	14	19	27
65+	224	7.8	36	2	4	6	10	14	20	29
TOTAL SINGLE DX	**4**	**4.3**	**15**	**1**	**1**	**3**	**10**	**10**	**10**	**10**
TOTAL MULTIPLE DX	**361**	**6.9**	**32**	**2**	**3**	**5**	**9**	**14**	**17**	**29**
TOTAL										
0–19 Years	5	4.4	7	1	2	3	7	7	7	7
20–34	19	4.8	37	1	2	3	4	7	23	23
35–49	54	4.5	9	1	2	4	6	8	11	16
50–64	61	6.5	28	2	3	5	7	13	19	27
65+	226	7.8	36	2	4	6	10	14	20	29
GRAND TOTAL	**365**	**6.8**	**32**	**2**	**3**	**5**	**9**	**14**	**17**	**29**

46.9: OTHER INTESTINAL OPS

Type of Patients	Observed Patients	Avg. Stay	Variance	10th	25th	50th	75th	90th	95th	99th
1. SINGLE DX										
0–19 Years	0									
20–34	2	4.1	2	3	3	5	5	5	5	5
35–49	3	4.2	1	3	3	5	5	5	5	5
50–64	1	13.0	0	13	13	13	13	13	13	13
65+	1	2.0	0	2	2	2	2	2	2	2
2. MULTIPLE DX										
0–19 Years	8	11.6	40	5	6	7	17	20	20	20
20–34	12	8.5	37	4	5	6	9	18	24	24
35–49	38	10.4	80	2	5	8	11	23	36	39
50–64	54	8.8	48	3	4	7	11	19	20	40
65+	41	13.9	43	6	10	12	18	22	32	>99
TOTAL SINGLE DX	**7**	**4.9**	**12**	**2**	**3**	**5**	**5**	**13**	**13**	**13**
TOTAL MULTIPLE DX	**153**	**10.9**	**56**	**3**	**6**	**9**	**15**	**20**	**24**	**39**
TOTAL										
0–19 Years	8	11.6	40	5	6	7	17	20	20	20
20–34	14	8.0	35	3	4	5	9	18	24	24
35–49	41	9.9	77	2	5	7	11	23	36	39
50–64	55	8.9	47	3	4	7	11	19	20	40
65+	42	13.6	45	6	9	12	18	22	22	>99
GRAND TOTAL	**160**	**10.7**	**56**	**3**	**5**	**9**	**14**	**20**	**24**	**39**

47.0: APPENDECTOMY

Type of Patients	Observed Patients	Avg. Stay	Variance	10th	25th	50th	75th	90th	95th	99th
1. SINGLE DX										
0–19 Years	9,777	2.4	3	1	1	2	3	5	6	8
20–34	8,852	1.9	2	1	1	1	2	3	4	6
35–49	4,155	2.0	2	1	1	2	2	4	5	7
50–64	1,572	2.3	3	1	1	2	3	4	6	8
65+	212	2.4	2	1	1	2	3	4	5	8
2. MULTIPLE DX										
0–19 Years	5,384	3.9	12	1	2	3	5	8	10	16
20–34	6,325	2.8	7	1	1	2	3	6	7	13
35–49	5,579	3.2	9	1	1	2	4	6	8	15
50–64	4,065	3.7	12	1	2	3	5	7	9	16
65+	2,390	5.1	18	1	2	4	6	10	13	21
TOTAL SINGLE DX	**24,568**	**2.1**	**2**	**1**	**1**	**2**	**3**	**4**	**5**	**8**
TOTAL MULTIPLE DX	**23,743**	**3.6**	**11**	**1**	**1**	**3**	**5**	**7**	**9**	**16**
TOTAL										
0–19 Years	15,161	2.9	7	1	1	2	4	6	7	13
20–34	15,177	2.3	4	1	1	2	3	4	6	10
35–49	9,734	2.7	6	1	1	2	3	5	7	13
50–64	5,637	3.3	10	1	1	2	4	7	8	15
65+	2,602	4.8	18	1	2	4	6	10	13	21
GRAND TOTAL	**48,311**	**2.9**	**7**	**1**	**1**	**2**	**4**	**6**	**7**	**14**

47.01: LAPSCP APPENDECTOMY

Type of Patients	Observed Patients	Avg. Stay	Vari-ance	Percentiles						
				10th	25th	50th	75th	90th	95th	99th
1. SINGLE DX										
0–19 Years	3,478	2.3	3	1	1	2	3	5	6	8
20–34	3,563	1.6	<1	1	1	1	2	3	3	5
35–49	1,844	1.7	1	1	1	1	2	3	4	6
50–64	652	1.9	2	1	1	1	2	4	5	7
65+	70	2.3	2	1	1	2	3	4	5	7
2. MULTIPLE DX										
0–19 Years	1,815	3.4	10	1	1	2	4	7	10	16
20–34	2,716	2.2	4	1	1	2	3	4	6	11
35–49	2,414	2.6	5	1	1	2	3	5	7	12
50–64	1,593	2.9	7	1	1	2	4	6	8	13
65+	783	3.8	11	1	2	3	5	7	9	18
TOTAL SINGLE DX	**9,607**	**1.9**	**2**	**1**	**1**	**1**	**2**	**4**	**5**	**7**
TOTAL MULTIPLE DX	**9,321**	**2.8**	**7**	**1**	**1**	**2**	**3**	**6**	**8**	**14**
TOTAL										
0–19 Years	5,293	2.7	6	1	1	2	3	5	7	13
20–34	6,279	1.9	2	1	1	1	2	3	5	8
35–49	4,258	2.2	4	1	1	2	3	4	6	10
50–64	2,245	2.6	5	1	1	2	3	5	7	12
65+	853	3.7	10	1	2	3	5	7	9	16
GRAND TOTAL	**18,928**	**2.4**	**5**	**1**	**1**	**2**	**3**	**5**	**6**	**11**

47.09: OTHER APPENDECTOMY

Type of Patients	Observed Patients	Avg. Stay	Vari-ance	Percentiles						
				10th	25th	50th	75th	90th	95th	99th
1. SINGLE DX										
0–19 Years	6,299	2.4	3	1	1	2	3	5	6	8
20–34	5,289	2.0	2	1	1	2	2	4	5	7
35–49	2,311	2.2	2	1	1	2	3	4	5	7
50–64	920	2.5	3	1	1	2	3	5	6	9
65+	142	2.4	2	1	1	2	3	4	5	8
2. MULTIPLE DX										
0–19 Years	3,569	4.2	12	1	2	3	6	8	11	16
20–34	3,609	3.2	10	1	1	2	4	6	8	14
35–49	3,165	3.7	11	1	2	3	5	7	10	16
50–64	2,472	4.3	14	1	2	3	5	8	10	18
65+	1,607	5.6	21	1	3	5	7	11	14	22
TOTAL SINGLE DX	**14,961**	**2.3**	**3**	**1**	**1**	**2**	**3**	**4**	**5**	**8**
TOTAL MULTIPLE DX	**14,422**	**4.1**	**13**	**1**	**2**	**3**	**5**	**8**	**11**	**17**
TOTAL										
0–19 Years	9,868	3.1	7	1	1	2	4	6	8	13
20–34	8,898	2.5	6	1	1	2	3	5	6	11
35–49	5,476	3.1	8	1	1	2	4	6	8	15
50–64	3,392	3.8	12	1	2	3	5	7	9	17
65+	1,749	5.4	20	1	2	4	7	11	14	22
GRAND TOTAL	**29,383**	**3.2**	**9**	**1**	**1**	**2**	**4**	**6**	**8**	**14**

47.1: INCIDENTAL APPENDECTOMY

Type of Patients	Observed Patients	Avg. Stay	Vari-ance	Percentiles						
				10th	25th	50th	75th	90th	95th	99th
1. SINGLE DX										
0–19 Years	17	1.3	<1	1	1	1	2	2	2	2
20–34	17	1.8	<1	1	1	1	2	3	3	4
35–49	9	4.1	15	1	1	2	5	9	13	13
50–64	2	2.3	<1	2	2	2	3	3	3	3
65+	2	2.4	4	1	1	1	4	4	4	4
2. MULTIPLE DX										
0–19 Years	27	5.3	30	1	2	3	7	12	17	22
20–34	75	3.0	7	1	1	3	4	5	7	18
35–49	41	3.0	3	1	2	3	3	5	6	7
50–64	13	5.6	20	2	3	4	11	12	15	15
65+	10	10.3	193	2	3	6	7	44	44	44
TOTAL SINGLE DX	**47**	**2.0**	**4**	**1**	**1**	**1**	**2**	**3**	**5**	**13**
TOTAL MULTIPLE DX	**166**	**4.1**	**25**	**1**	**2**	**3**	**4**	**7**	**15**	**22**
TOTAL										
0–19 Years	44	3.8	22	1	1	2	3	11	17	22
20–34	92	2.8	6	1	1	2	3	5	6	18
35–49	50	3.2	5	1	2	3	4	6	7	13
50–64	15	5.0	18	2	2	3	5	12	15	15
65+	12	9.2	171	1	2	4	7	44	44	44
GRAND TOTAL	**213**	**3.6**	**21**	**1**	**1**	**2**	**4**	**7**	**12**	**22**

47.11: LAPSCP INCIDENTAL APPY

Type of Patients	Observed Patients	Avg. Stay	Vari-ance	Percentiles						
				10th	25th	50th	75th	90th	95th	99th
1. SINGLE DX										
0–19 Years	15	1.3	<1	1	1	1	2	2	2	2
20–34	14	1.8	1	1	1	1	3	3	4	4
35–49	7	4.2	18	1	2	2	5	13	13	13
50–64	1	3.0	0	3	3	3	3	3	3	3
65+	1	1.0	0	1	1	1	1	1	1	1
2. MULTIPLE DX										
0–19 Years	20	3.8	19	1	2	3	3	11	17	17
20–34	58	2.6	4	1	1	2	3	4	5	16
35–49	32	2.9	3	1	2	3	4	6	6	7
50–64	7	5.3	23	1	2	4	5	15	15	15
65+	3	3.2	7	1	1	2	6	6	6	6
TOTAL SINGLE DX	**38**	**1.9**	**4**	**1**	**1**	**1**	**2**	**3**	**5**	**13**
TOTAL MULTIPLE DX	**120**	**3.1**	**8**	**1**	**1**	**3**	**3**	**5**	**7**	**17**
TOTAL										
0–19 Years	35	2.7	12	1	1	2	3	3	12	17
20–34	72	2.5	4	1	1	2	3	4	5	7
35–49	39	3.2	6	1	2	3	4	6	9	13
50–64	8	5.0	21	1	2	4	5	15	15	15
65+	4	2.6	6	1	1	2	6	6	6	6
GRAND TOTAL	**158**	**2.8**	**7**	**1**	**1**	**2**	**3**	**5**	**6**	**17**

47.2: DRAIN APPENDICEAL ABSC

Type of Patients	Observed Patients	Avg. Stay	Vari-ance	10th	25th	50th	75th	90th	95th	99th
1. SINGLE DX										
0–19 Years	30	4.8	6	3	3	4	7	8	9	12
20–34	19	4.8	4	3	3	4	6	7	8	12
35–49	4	3.2	1	2	3	3	3	5	5	5
50–64	10	5.2	7	2	3	4	8	8	9	9
65+	2	3.6	4	2	2	5	5	5	5	5
2. MULTIPLE DX										
0–19 Years	32	7.2	24	3	4	7	8	14	15	27
20–34	11	5.7	6	3	5	5	6	9	10	10
35–49	28	5.5	10	2	3	5	7	8	14	15
50–64	24	7.8	32	3	4	7	8	14	20	27
65+	24	7.0	15	3	4	6	8	15	15	15
TOTAL SINGLE DX	**65**	**4.8**	**5**	**3**	**3**	**4**	**6**	**8**	**9**	**12**
TOTAL MULTIPLE DX	**119**	**6.8**	**20**	**3**	**4**	**6**	**8**	**13**	**15**	**27**
TOTAL										
0–19 Years	62	6.2	17	3	3	5	7	9	14	27
20–34	30	5.1	5	3	3	5	6	8	9	12
35–49	32	5.2	9	2	3	5	6	7	12	15
50–64	34	7.1	27	3	4	6	8	13	20	27
65+	26	6.8	15	3	3	6	8	13	15	15
GRAND TOTAL	**184**	**6.1**	**16**	**3**	**3**	**5**	**7**	**11**	**14**	**23**

47.9: OTHER APPENDICEAL OPS

Type of Patients	Observed Patients	Avg. Stay	Vari-ance	10th	25th	50th	75th	90th	95th	99th
1. SINGLE DX										
0–19 Years	3	2.6	<1	2	2	3	3	3	3	3
20–34	0									
35–49	0									
50–64	1	3.0	0	3	3	3	3	3	3	3
65+	0									
2. MULTIPLE DX										
0–19 Years	31	5.6	14	2	3	5	6	12	14	18
20–34	1	2.0	0	2	2	2	2	2	2	2
35–49	1	5.0	0	5	5	5	5	5	5	5
50–64	0									
65+	1	7.0	0	7	7	7	7	7	7	7
TOTAL SINGLE DX	**4**	**2.7**	**<1**	**2**	**2**	**3**	**3**	**3**	**3**	**3**
TOTAL MULTIPLE DX	**34**	**5.6**	**13**	**2**	**3**	**5**	**6**	**12**	**14**	**18**
TOTAL										
0–19 Years	34	5.3	13	2	3	5	6	8	14	18
20–34	1	2.0	0	2	2	2	2	2	2	2
35–49	1	5.0	0	5	5	5	5	5	5	5
50–64	1	3.0	0	3	3	3	3	3	3	3
65+	1	7.0	0	7	7	7	7	7	7	7
GRAND TOTAL	**38**	**5.2**	**13**	**2**	**3**	**5**	**6**	**8**	**14**	**18**

48.0: PROCTOTOMY

Type of Patients	Observed Patients	Avg. Stay	Vari-ance	10th	25th	50th	75th	90th	95th	99th
1. SINGLE DX										
0–19 Years	5	1.5	<1	1	1	1	2	3	3	3
20–34	10	1.9	<1	1	1	2	3	3	3	3
35–49	11	2.4	2	1	1	2	4	5	5	5
50–64	7	2.6	<1	2	2	3	3	3	3	3
65+	2	2.1	2	1	1	3	3	3	3	3
2. MULTIPLE DX										
0–19 Years	4	3.6	1	1	4	4	4	4	4	4
20–34	14	3.4	11	1	1	2	4	8	13	13
35–49	59	3.8	15	1	1	2	5	8	10	26
50–64	33	3.4	8	1	2	2	4	8	11	12
65+	28	7.0	52	1	1	3	9	19	24	25
TOTAL SINGLE DX	**35**	**2.2**	**1**	**1**	**1**	**2**	**3**	**3**	**5**	**5**
TOTAL MULTIPLE DX	**138**	**4.2**	**20**	**1**	**1**	**2**	**5**	**9**	**13**	**24**
TOTAL										
0–19 Years	9	2.7	2	1	1	3	4	4	4	4
20–34	24	2.9	7	1	1	2	3	7	8	13
35–49	70	3.6	13	1	1	2	5	8	10	17
50–64	40	3.2	6	1	2	2	4	7	10	12
65+	30	6.6	50	1	1	3	9	19	24	25
GRAND TOTAL	**173**	**3.8**	**17**	**1**	**1**	**2**	**4**	**8**	**12**	**24**

48.1: PROCTOSTOMY

Type of Patients	Observed Patients	Avg. Stay	Vari-ance	10th	25th	50th	75th	90th	95th	99th
1. SINGLE DX										
0–19 Years	1	1.0	0	1	1	1	1	1	1	1
20–34	0									
35–49	0									
50–64	0									
65+	0									
2. MULTIPLE DX										
0–19 Years	1	45.0	0	45	45	45	45	45	45	45
20–34	0									
35–49	0									
50–64	2	7.5	<1	7	7	8	8	8	8	8
65+	0									
TOTAL SINGLE DX	**1**	**1.0**	**0**	**1**	**1**	**1**	**1**	**1**	**1**	**1**
TOTAL MULTIPLE DX	**3**	**19.1**	**423**	**7**	**7**	**8**	**45**	**45**	**45**	**45**
TOTAL										
0–19 Years	2	8.5	324	1	1	1	1	45	45	45
20–34	0									
35–49	0									
50–64	2	7.5	<1	7	7	8	8	8	8	8
65+	0									
GRAND TOTAL	**4**	**8.2**	**224**	**1**	**1**	**1**	**8**	**45**	**45**	**45**

48.2: RECTAL/PERIRECT DXTIC PX

Type of Patients	Observed Patients	Avg. Stay	Vari-ance	Percentiles						
				10th	25th	50th	75th	90th	95th	99th
1. SINGLE DX										
0–19 Years	41	3.5	11	1	2	3	4	5	9	18
20–34	23	3.0	7	1	1	2	3	8	8	10
35–49	12	2.0	2	1	1	1	3	5	5	5
50–64	12	1.9	2	1	1	1	3	3	5	5
65+	2	1.5	<1	1	1	2	2	2	2	2
2. MULTIPLE DX										
0–19 Years	109	6.3	53	1	2	3	8	14	20	38
20–34	96	5.1	20	1	2	4	6	11	13	23
35–49	216	4.7	17	1	2	3	6	9	13	23
50–64	273	5.1	20	1	2	4	6	10	14	25
65+	748	5.6	22	2	3	4	7	11	13	22
TOTAL SINGLE DX	**90**	**3.1**	**9**	**1**	**1**	**2**	**4**	**5**	**8**	**18**
TOTAL MULTIPLE DX	**1,442**	**5.4**	**24**	**1**	**2**	**4**	**7**	**11**	**14**	**25**
TOTAL										
0–19 Years	150	5.4	41	1	2	3	6	13	18	38
20–34	119	4.6	18	1	2	3	6	11	13	23
35–49	228	4.5	17	1	2	3	6	9	12	23
50–64	285	5.0	20	1	2	4	6	10	14	25
65+	750	5.6	22	2	3	4	7	11	13	22
GRAND TOTAL	**1,532**	**5.2**	**23**	**1**	**2**	**4**	**7**	**11**	**14**	**24**

48.23: RIG PROCTOSIGMOIDOSCOPY

Type of Patients	Observed Patients	Avg. Stay	Vari-ance	Percentiles						
				10th	25th	50th	75th	90th	95th	99th
1. SINGLE DX										
0–19 Years	8	2.1	5	1	1	1	2	8	8	8
20–34	10	1.5	<1	1	1	1	2	3	3	3
35–49	9	1.8	2	1	1	1	2	5	5	5
50–64	8	1.5	<1	1	1	1	2	3	3	3
65+	0									
2. MULTIPLE DX										
0–19 Years	12	5.5	68	1	1	2	7	18	34	34
20–34	24	3.8	10	1	2	3	4	9	10	13
35–49	46	4.2	21	1	2	3	5	9	19	23
50–64	59	3.5	12	1	1	2	5	8	11	16
65+	126	4.9	14	1	2	4	7	10	12	16
TOTAL SINGLE DX	**35**	**1.8**	**2**	**1**	**1**	**1**	**2**	**3**	**5**	**8**
TOTAL MULTIPLE DX	**267**	**4.5**	**17**	**1**	**2**	**3**	**6**	**9**	**12**	**19**
TOTAL										
0–19 Years	20	4.1	45	1	1	1	4	8	18	34
20–34	34	3.2	8	1	1	2	3	8	10	13
35–49	55	3.9	19	1	1	3	4	7	15	23
50–64	67	3.4	11	1	1	2	5	8	11	16
65+	126	4.9	14	1	2	4	7	10	12	16
GRAND TOTAL	**302**	**4.2**	**17**	**1**	**1**	**3**	**5**	**9**	**12**	**19**

48.24: CLOSED RECTAL BIOPSY

Type of Patients	Observed Patients	Avg. Stay	Vari-ance	Percentiles						
				10th	25th	50th	75th	90th	95th	99th
1. SINGLE DX										
0–19 Years	29	4.0	16	1	2	3	4	7	18	18
20–34	13	3.9	9	1	2	3	6	8	8	10
35–49	2	3.1	2	2	2	4	4	4	4	4
50–64	3	2.9	4	1	1	3	5	5	5	5
65+	2	1.5	<1	1	1	2	2	2	2	2
2. MULTIPLE DX										
0–19 Years	82	6.3	50	1	2	3	8	14	20	38
20–34	70	5.6	23	2	2	4	6	12	15	28
35–49	162	4.6	16	1	2	3	6	9	12	21
50–64	207	5.5	22	2	3	4	7	11	16	26
65+	601	5.6	18	2	3	5	7	11	13	19
TOTAL SINGLE DX	**49**	**3.8**	**13**	**1**	**2**	**3**	**4**	**8**	**10**	**18**
TOTAL MULTIPLE DX	**1,122**	**5.5**	**22**	**2**	**3**	**4**	**7**	**11**	**14**	**24**
TOTAL										
0–19 Years	111	5.7	41	1	2	3	7	13	18	38
20–34	83	5.2	21	1	2	4	6	11	13	28
35–49	164	4.6	16	1	2	3	6	9	12	21
50–64	210	5.5	22	2	3	4	7	11	16	26
65+	603	5.6	18	2	3	5	7	11	13	19
GRAND TOTAL	**1,171**	**5.4**	**22**	**1**	**2**	**4**	**7**	**11**	**14**	**23**

48.3: LOC DESTR RECTAL LESION

Type of Patients	Observed Patients	Avg. Stay	Vari-ance	Percentiles						
				10th	25th	50th	75th	90th	95th	99th
1. SINGLE DX										
0–19 Years	2	1.0	0	1	1	1	1	1	1	1
20–34	4	1.5	<1	1	1	2	2	2	2	2
35–49	11	1.8	1	1	1	1	2	4	4	4
50–64	26	1.8	<1	1	1	2	3	3	3	3
65+	20	2.3	2	1	1	2	3	4	4	5
2. MULTIPLE DX										
0–19 Years	4	1.7	1	1	1	1	3	4	4	4
20–34	25	2.7	5	1	1	2	4	5	5	14
35–49	101	4.3	18	1	2	3	5	10	11	22
50–64	210	3.2	12	1	1	2	4	6	9	20
65+	627	4.3	17	1	2	3	5	9	12	21
TOTAL SINGLE DX	**63**	**1.9**	**1**	**1**	**1**	**2**	**3**	**3**	**4**	**5**
TOTAL MULTIPLE DX	**967**	**4.0**	**16**	**1**	**2**	**3**	**5**	**8**	**12**	**21**
TOTAL										
0–19 Years	6	1.6	1	1	1	1	1	3	4	4
20–34	29	2.6	5	1	1	2	3	5	5	14
35–49	112	4.1	17	1	2	3	5	9	11	22
50–64	236	3.1	11	1	1	2	4	6	8	20
65+	647	4.2	16	1	2	3	5	9	12	21
GRAND TOTAL	**1,030**	**3.9**	**15**	**1**	**2**	**3**	**5**	**8**	**11**	**20**

48.32: ELECTROCOAG RECT LES NEC

Type of Patients	Observed Patients	Avg. Stay	Vari-ance	Percentiles						
				10th	25th	50th	75th	90th	95th	99th
1. SINGLE DX										
0–19 Years	0									
20–34	1	1.0	0	1	1	1	1	1	1	1
35–49	0									
50–64	0									
65+	1	1.0	0	1	1	1	1	1	1	1
2. MULTIPLE DX										
0–19 Years	0									
20–34	1	2.0	0	2	2	2	2	2	2	2
35–49	4	2.2	<1	1	2	2	3	3	3	3
50–64	12	2.5	4	1	1	2	4	4	8	8
65+	43	3.7	22	1	1	2	5	6	11	31
TOTAL SINGLE DX	**2**	**1.0**	**0**	**1**	**1**	**1**	**1**	**1**	**1**	**1**
TOTAL MULTIPLE DX	**60**	**3.4**	**18**	**1**	**1**	**2**	**4**	**6**	**8**	**31**
TOTAL										
0–19 Years	0									
20–34	2	1.6	<1	1	1	2	2	2	2	2
35–49	4	2.2	<1	1	2	2	3	3	3	3
50–64	12	2.5	4	1	1	2	4	4	8	8
65+	44	3.7	22	1	1	2	5	6	11	31
GRAND TOTAL	**62**	**3.4**	**17**	**1**	**1**	**2**	**4**	**6**	**8**	**31**

48.35: LOC EXC RECTAL LES/TISS

Type of Patients	Observed Patients	Avg. Stay	Vari-ance	Percentiles						
				10th	25th	50th	75th	90th	95th	99th
1. SINGLE DX										
0–19 Years	1	1.0	0	1	1	1	1	1	1	1
20–34	3	1.7	<1	1	1	2	2	2	2	2
35–49	10	1.9	1	1	1	2	2	4	4	4
50–64	24	1.8	<1	1	1	2	3	3	3	3
65+	17	2.4	2	1	1	2	3	4	5	5
2. MULTIPLE DX										
0–19 Years	1	1.0	0	1	1	1	1	1	1	1
20–34	5	2.0	2	1	1	1	4	4	4	4
35–49	29	4.3	22	1	1	3	6	8	19	19
50–64	62	2.6	4	1	1	2	3	4	7	12
65+	204	4.0	21	1	1	2	5	8	14	26
TOTAL SINGLE DX	**55**	**2.0**	**1**	**1**	**1**	**2**	**3**	**3**	**4**	**5**
TOTAL MULTIPLE DX	**301**	**3.6**	**17**	**1**	**1**	**2**	**4**	**7**	**12**	**21**
TOTAL										
0–19 Years	2	1.0	0	1	1	1	1	1	1	1
20–34	8	1.9	1	1	1	2	2	4	4	4
35–49	39	3.8	18	1	1	3	4	8	13	19
50–64	86	2.4	4	1	1	2	3	4	7	12
65+	221	3.9	19	1	1	2	4	8	12	26
GRAND TOTAL	**356**	**3.4**	**15**	**1**	**1**	**2**	**4**	**7**	**10**	**20**

48.36: ENDO RECTAL POLYPECTOMY

Type of Patients	Observed Patients	Avg. Stay	Vari-ance	Percentiles						
				10th	25th	50th	75th	90th	95th	99th
1. SINGLE DX										
0–19 Years	1	1.0	0	1	1	1	1	1	1	1
20–34	0									
35–49	1	1.0	0	1	1	1	1	1	1	1
50–64	2	1.6	<1	1	1	2	2	2	2	2
65+	2	1.4	<1	1	1	1	2	2	2	2
2. MULTIPLE DX										
0–19 Years	3	2.1	2	1	1	1	3	4	4	4
20–34	19	3.0	7	1	2	2	4	5	7	14
35–49	67	4.5	18	2	2	3	5	10	11	24
50–64	135	3.7	16	1	1	2	4	7	13	21
65+	376	4.6	14	1	2	4	6	9	12	19
TOTAL SINGLE DX	**6**	**1.4**	**<1**	**1**	**1**	**1**	**2**	**2**	**2**	**2**
TOTAL MULTIPLE DX	**600**	**4.3**	**14**	**1**	**2**	**3**	**5**	**9**	**12**	**20**
TOTAL										
0–19 Years	4	1.9	2	1	1	1	3	4	4	4
20–34	19	3.0	7	1	2	2	4	5	7	14
35–49	68	4.5	17	1	2	3	5	10	11	24
50–64	137	3.7	16	1	1	2	4	7	13	21
65+	378	4.6	14	1	2	4	6	9	12	19
GRAND TOTAL	**606**	**4.3**	**14**	**1**	**2**	**3**	**5**	**9**	**12**	**20**

48.4: PULL-THRU RECT RESECTION

Type of Patients	Observed Patients	Avg. Stay	Vari-ance	Percentiles						
				10th	25th	50th	75th	90th	95th	99th
1. SINGLE DX										
0–19 Years	29	4.1	4	2	3	4	4	8	8	10
20–34	0									
35–49	1	2.0	0	2	2	2	2	2	2	2
50–64	3	8.7	17	3	3	11	11	11	11	11
65+	3	1.0	0	1	1	1	1	1	1	1
2. MULTIPLE DX										
0–19 Years	93	7.7	79	3	3	4	10	18	21	22
20–34	4	6.3	7	3	3	6	8	9	9	9
35–49	13	7.2	19	3	4	7	9	12	20	20
50–64	15	6.7	107	1	2	6	6	8	8	55
65+	82	4.9	10	2	3	4	6	9	10	19
TOTAL SINGLE DX	**36**	**4.0**	**5**	**1**	**3**	**4**	**4**	**8**	**10**	**11**
TOTAL MULTIPLE DX	**207**	**6.8**	**58**	**2**	**3**	**4**	**8**	**15**	**21**	**22**
TOTAL										
0–19 Years	122	6.6	59	3	3	4	8	15	21	22
20–34	4	6.3	7	3	3	6	8	9	9	9
35–49	14	6.8	20	3	3	6	9	12	20	20
50–64	18	7.0	93	1	2	6	7	11	11	55
65+	85	4.6	10	1	2	4	6	9	10	19
GRAND TOTAL	**243**	**6.1**	**47**	**2**	**3**	**4**	**7**	**12**	**19**	**22**

48.49: PULL-THRU RECT RESECT

Type of Patients	Observed Patients	Avg. Stay	Vari-ance	Percentiles						
				10th	25th	50th	75th	90th	95th	99th
1. SINGLE DX										
0–19 Years	18	3.5	1	2	3	4	4	4	4	8
20–34	0									
35–49	1	2.0	0	2	2	2	2	2	2	2
50–64	3	8.7	17	3	3	11	11	11	11	11
65+	3	1.0	0	1	1	1	1	1	1	1
2. MULTIPLE DX										
0–19 Years	61	5.9	30	2	3	4	6	13	21	22
20–34	2	7.1	2	6	6	8	8	8	8	8
35–49	13	7.2	19	3	4	7	9	12	20	20
50–64	15	6.7	107	1	2	6	6	8	8	55
65+	78	4.8	10	2	3	4	6	9	10	19
TOTAL SINGLE DX	**25**	**3.5**	**4**	**1**	**3**	**4**	**4**	**4**	**6**	**11**
TOTAL MULTIPLE DX	**169**	**5.7**	**28**	**2**	**3**	**4**	**6**	**10**	**20**	**22**
TOTAL										
0–19 Years	79	5.2	23	2	3	4	5	10	21	22
20–34	2	7.1	2	6	6	8	8	8	8	8
35–49	14	6.8	20	3	3	6	9	12	20	20
50–64	18	7.0	93	1	2	6	7	11	11	55
65+	81	4.6	10	1	2	4	6	9	10	19
GRAND TOTAL	**194**	**5.2**	**24**	**2**	**3**	**4**	**6**	**10**	**15**	**22**

48.5: ABD-PERINEAL RECT RESECT

Type of Patients	Observed Patients	Avg. Stay	Vari-ance	Percentiles						
				10th	25th	50th	75th	90th	95th	99th
1. SINGLE DX										
0–19 Years	0									
20–34	4	9.2	9	6	6	11	12	12	12	12
35–49	8	6.8	11	3	4	7	8	14	14	14
50–64	14	8.0	6	7	7	7	8	14	14	14
65+	12	7.7	8	4	7	8	10	11	11	11
2. MULTIPLE DX										
0–19 Years	2	17.7	143	9	9	9	31	31	31	31
20–34	24	8.6	24	4	4	8	13	15	18	21
35–49	104	9.3	47	5	6	7	12	15	16	48
50–64	296	8.7	25	5	6	7	10	15	18	31
65+	531	10.4	34	6	7	9	12	17	22	30
TOTAL SINGLE DX	**38**	**8.0**	**8**	**5**	**7**	**7**	**10**	**12**	**14**	**14**
TOTAL MULTIPLE DX	**957**	**9.8**	**33**	**5**	**6**	**8**	**11**	**16**	**20**	**31**
TOTAL										
0–19 Years	2	17.7	143	9	9	9	31	31	31	31
20–34	28	8.8	20	4	6	8	12	15	15	21
35–49	112	9.1	45	5	6	7	12	15	16	48
50–64	310	8.7	24	5	6	7	10	15	17	31
65+	543	10.4	33	6	7	9	12	17	22	30
GRAND TOTAL	**995**	**9.7**	**33**	**5**	**6**	**8**	**11**	**16**	**20**	**31**

48.6: OTHER RECTAL RESECTION

Type of Patients	Observed Patients	Avg. Stay	Vari-ance	Percentiles						
				10th	25th	50th	75th	90th	95th	99th
1. SINGLE DX										
0–19 Years	6	6.9	12	3	3	9	10	10	12	12
20–34	6	3.4	<1	2	3	4	4	4	4	4
35–49	28	4.9	2	4	4	5	5	7	7	10
50–64	62	5.2	2	3	4	5	6	7	7	8
65+	44	5.6	3	3	5	6	7	7	9	9
2. MULTIPLE DX										
0–19 Years	12	8.4	34	4	5	7	10	15	26	26
20–34	62	8.1	53	3	5	7	9	11	15	46
35–49	348	7.2	19	4	5	6	8	10	15	27
50–64	848	7.1	14	4	5	6	8	11	14	23
65+	1,418	8.4	27	4	6	7	10	14	17	28
TOTAL SINGLE DX	**146**	**5.3**	**4**	**3**	**4**	**5**	**6**	**7**	**9**	**10**
TOTAL MULTIPLE DX	**2,688**	**7.9**	**23**	**4**	**5**	**7**	**9**	**13**	**16**	**26**
TOTAL										
0–19 Years	18	7.9	26	3	5	7	10	10	26	26
20–34	68	7.7	50	3	4	7	8	11	14	46
35–49	376	7.0	18	4	5	6	8	10	14	27
50–64	910	7.0	13	4	5	6	8	11	13	23
65+	1,462	8.3	26	4	5	7	9	14	17	28
GRAND TOTAL	**2,834**	**7.8**	**22**	**4**	**5**	**7**	**9**	**13**	**16**	**26**

48.62: ANT RECT RESECT W COLOST

Type of Patients	Observed Patients	Avg. Stay	Vari-ance	Percentiles						
				10th	25th	50th	75th	90th	95th	99th
1. SINGLE DX										
0–19 Years	0									
20–34	0									
35–49	3	7.3	5	5	5	7	10	10	10	10
50–64	5	5.7	1	4	5	6	7	7	7	7
65+	4	5.7	<1	5	5	6	6	6	6	6
2. MULTIPLE DX										
0–19 Years	1	9.0	0	9	9	9	9	9	9	9
20–34	9	9.2	7	5	8	10	10	14	14	14
35–49	29	11.1	91	5	6	8	11	27	38	49
50–64	67	9.3	28	4	6	8	10	14	23	29
65+	164	11.7	64	5	7	10	14	18	23	56
TOTAL SINGLE DX	**12**	**6.0**	**2**	**5**	**5**	**6**	**6**	**7**	**7**	**10**
TOTAL MULTIPLE DX	**270**	**11.0**	**57**	**5**	**7**	**9**	**13**	**18**	**23**	**56**
TOTAL										
0–19 Years	1	9.0	0	9	9	9	9	9	9	9
20–34	9	9.2	7	5	8	10	10	14	14	14
35–49	32	10.8	85	5	6	7	10	15	38	49
50–64	72	9.1	27	4	6	8	10	14	23	29
65+	168	11.5	63	5	7	9	14	18	23	56
GRAND TOTAL	**282**	**10.8**	**55**	**5**	**6**	**9**	**13**	**17**	**23**	**56**

48.63: ANTERIOR RECT RESECT NEC

Type of Patients	Observed Patients	Avg. Stay	Vari-ance	Percentiles						
				10th	25th	50th	75th	90th	95th	99th
1. SINGLE DX										
0–19 Years	0									
20–34	5	3.4	<1	2	3	4	4	4	4	4
35–49	18	4.8	1	4	4	4	6	6	7	8
50–64	52	5.3	2	4	4	6	6	7	7	8
65+	34	6.0	2	4	5	6	7	8	9	9
2. MULTIPLE DX										
0–19 Years	2	7.6	4	6	6	9	9	9	9	9
20–34	31	6.3	4	4	5	7	7	8	11	11
35–49	245	7.0	13	4	5	6	8	10	15	21
50–64	655	7.0	11	4	5	6	8	10	12	19
65+	1,031	8.2	19	5	6	7	9	13	16	26
TOTAL SINGLE DX	**109**	**5.4**	**2**	**4**	**4**	**6**	**6**	**7**	**8**	**9**
TOTAL MULTIPLE DX	**1,964**	**7.6**	**16**	**4**	**5**	**7**	**8**	**12**	**15**	**24**
TOTAL										
0–19 Years	2	7.6	4	6	6	9	9	9	9	9
20–34	36	5.9	4	3	4	6	7	8	8	11
35–49	263	6.8	13	4	5	6	8	10	14	21
50–64	707	6.9	11	4	5	6	8	10	12	19
65+	1,065	8.1	19	5	6	7	9	13	16	26
GRAND TOTAL	**2,073**	**7.5**	**16**	**4**	**5**	**7**	**8**	**11**	**15**	**24**

48.69: RECTAL RESECTION NEC

Type of Patients	Observed Patients	Avg. Stay	Vari-ance	Percentiles						
				10th	25th	50th	75th	90th	95th	99th
1. SINGLE DX										
0–19 Years	1	12.0	0	12	12	12	12	12	12	12
20–34	1	3.0	0	3	3	3	3	3	3	3
35–49	7	4.3	2	4	4	5	5	5	5	5
50–64	5	3.2	2	1	2	4	4	5	5	5
65+	5	2.1	<1	1	2	2	3	3	3	3
2. MULTIPLE DX										
0–19 Years	2	4.5	2	4	4	4	4	7	7	7
20–34	22	10.0	138	2	4	6	9	17	46	46
35–49	73	6.5	10	4	5	6	7	9	10	17
50–64	122	6.9	17	3	4	6	8	13	15	25
65+	215	7.3	21	3	4	6	9	13	16	22
TOTAL SINGLE DX	**19**	**3.7**	**5**	**1**	**2**	**4**	**5**	**5**	**5**	**12**
TOTAL MULTIPLE DX	**434**	**7.1**	**23**	**3**	**4**	**6**	**8**	**13**	**15**	**25**
TOTAL										
0–19 Years	3	5.8	10	4	4	4	7	12	12	12
20–34	23	9.7	135	2	4	6	9	17	46	46
35–49	80	6.4	9	4	5	6	7	9	10	17
50–64	127	6.8	17	3	4	6	8	12	15	25
65+	220	7.2	21	3	4	6	9	13	16	22
GRAND TOTAL	**453**	**7.0**	**22**	**3**	**4**	**6**	**8**	**13**	**15**	**25**

48.7: REPAIR OF RECTUM

Type of Patients	Observed Patients	Avg. Stay	Vari-ance	Percentiles						
				10th	25th	50th	75th	90th	95th	99th
1. SINGLE DX										
0–19 Years	6	3.1	3	1	3	3	3	4	7	7
20–34	3	6.3	8	4	4	4	9	9	9	9
35–49	6	2.5	2	1	1	2	4	5	5	5
50–64	7	2.0	2	1	1	1	3	5	5	5
65+	10	3.1	4	1	1	2	5	6	6	6
2. MULTIPLE DX										
0–19 Years	19	5.2	22	1	2	3	7	13	16	16
20–34	33	6.1	32	1	2	4	7	14	19	25
35–49	103	5.8	29	2	3	4	7	9	21	24
50–64	144	5.2	18	1	3	4	7	9	11	25
65+	229	5.8	18	1	3	5	8	12	14	17
TOTAL SINGLE DX	**32**	**3.1**	**4**	**1**	**1**	**3**	**4**	**6**	**7**	**9**
TOTAL MULTIPLE DX	**528**	**5.6**	**21**	**1**	**3**	**4**	**7**	**11**	**15**	**21**
TOTAL										
0–19 Years	25	4.7	17	1	2	3	6	12	16	16
20–34	36	6.1	29	1	2	4	7	14	19	25
35–49	109	5.6	28	1	3	4	7	9	21	24
50–64	151	5.1	17	1	2	4	7	9	11	25
65+	239	5.7	18	1	3	5	8	12	14	17
GRAND TOTAL	**560**	**5.5**	**20**	**1**	**3**	**4**	**7**	**10**	**14**	**21**

48.75: ABDOMINAL PROCTOPEXY

Type of Patients	Observed Patients	Avg. Stay	Vari-ance	Percentiles						
				10th	25th	50th	75th	90th	95th	99th
1. SINGLE DX										
0–19 Years	1	7.0	0	7	7	7	7	7	7	7
20–34	2	7.3	9	4	4	9	9	9	9	9
35–49	3	3.5	2	2	2	4	5	5	5	5
50–64	2	4.1	2	3	3	5	5	5	5	5
65+	3	4.0	2	2	4	4	5	5	5	5
2. MULTIPLE DX										
0–19 Years	2	5.1	17	2	2	2	9	9	9	9
20–34	8	5.2	2	3	4	5	7	7	7	7
35–49	35	8.7	52	4	5	6	9	21	21	40
50–64	67	6.0	18	3	4	5	7	9	10	37
65+	76	7.6	23	3	4	7	9	14	16	29
TOTAL SINGLE DX	**11**	**4.8**	**5**	**2**	**4**	**4**	**5**	**9**	**9**	**9**
TOTAL MULTIPLE DX	**188**	**7.1**	**26**	**3**	**4**	**6**	**8**	**12**	**16**	**29**
TOTAL										
0–19 Years	3	5.7	12	2	2	7	9	9	9	9
20–34	10	5.6	4	4	4	5	7	9	9	9
35–49	38	8.4	50	4	4	5	9	21	21	40
50–64	69	5.9	17	3	4	5	7	9	10	37
65+	79	7.5	23	3	4	7	9	14	16	29
GRAND TOTAL	**199**	**7.0**	**25**	**3**	**4**	**6**	**8**	**12**	**16**	**29**

48.76: PROCTOPEXY NEC

Type of Patients	Observed Patients	Avg. Stay	Vari-ance	Percentiles						
				10th	25th	50th	75th	90th	95th	99th
1. SINGLE DX										
0–19 Years	3	3.2	<1	3	3	3	3	4	4	4
20–34	1	4.0	0	4	4	4	4	4	4	4
35–49	1	1.0	0	1	1	1	1	1	1	1
50–64	4	1.2	<1	1	1	1	1	2	2	2
65+	5	1.2	<1	1	1	1	1	2	2	2
2. MULTIPLE DX										
0–19 Years	3	2.7	<1	2	2	3	3	3	3	3
20–34	5	3.8	24	1	1	2	3	14	14	14
35–49	39	4.4	7	2	2	4	6	8	8	15
50–64	57	4.5	19	1	2	3	5	11	15	25
65+	123	4.6	12	1	2	3	6	9	11	16
TOTAL SINGLE DX	**14**	**2.2**	**1**	**1**	**1**	**2**	**3**	**4**	**4**	**4**
TOTAL MULTIPLE DX	**227**	**4.5**	**13**	**1**	**2**	**3**	**6**	**9**	**12**	**16**
TOTAL										
0–19 Years	6	3.0	<1	3	3	3	3	4	4	4
20–34	6	3.8	21	1	1	2	4	14	14	14
35–49	40	4.3	7	2	2	4	6	8	8	15
50–64	61	4.4	19	1	1	3	5	11	15	25
65+	128	4.5	12	1	2	3	6	9	11	16
GRAND TOTAL	**241**	**4.4**	**12**	**1**	**2**	**3**	**6**	**9**	**12**	**16**

48.8: PERIRECT TISS INC/EXC

Type of Patients	Observed Patients	Avg. Stay	Vari-ance	Percentiles						
				10th	25th	50th	75th	90th	95th	99th
1. SINGLE DX										
0–19 Years	54	2.5	5	1	1	2	3	4	8	11
20–34	104	1.9	<1	1	1	2	2	3	4	6
35–49	154	2.0	3	1	1	1	2	4	4	11
50–64	62	1.8	2	1	1	1	2	3	4	8
65+	9	2.2	<1	1	1	3	3	3	3	3
2. MULTIPLE DX										
0–19 Years	54	3.5	8	1	1	3	5	7	8	15
20–34	263	3.3	12	1	1	2	4	7	10	16
35–49	443	3.4	12	1	1	2	4	7	10	16
50–64	387	4.9	62	1	1	3	5	10	13	50
65+	208	5.1	16	1	2	4	7	10	12	21
TOTAL SINGLE DX	**383**	**2.0**	**2**	**1**	**1**	**2**	**2**	**3**	**4**	**10**
TOTAL MULTIPLE DX	**1,355**	**4.1**	**27**	**1**	**1**	**3**	**5**	**8**	**11**	**22**
TOTAL										
0–19 Years	108	3.1	7	1	1	2	4	7	8	15
20–34	367	2.9	9	1	1	2	3	6	10	16
35–49	597	3.1	10	1	1	2	4	6	9	14
50–64	449	4.5	56	1	1	2	5	9	13	50
65+	217	5.0	16	1	2	4	7	10	12	21
GRAND TOTAL	**1,738**	**3.6**	**22**	**1**	**1**	**2**	**4**	**8**	**10**	**18**

48.81: PERIRECTAL INCISION

Type of Patients	Observed Patients	Avg. Stay	Vari-ance	Percentiles						
				10th	25th	50th	75th	90th	95th	99th
1. SINGLE DX										
0–19 Years	53	2.5	5	1	1	2	3	4	8	11
20–34	102	1.9	<1	1	1	2	2	3	4	6
35–49	151	2.0	3	1	1	1	2	3	4	11
50–64	61	1.8	2	1	1	1	2	3	4	8
65+	7	2.3	<1	1	1	3	3	3	3	3
2. MULTIPLE DX										
0–19 Years	52	3.4	8	1	1	3	5	7	7	15
20–34	258	3.3	12	1	1	2	4	7	10	18
35–49	435	3.4	12	1	1	2	4	7	10	14
50–64	368	4.9	65	1	1	3	5	10	13	50
65+	198	5.1	17	1	2	4	7	10	12	21
TOTAL SINGLE DX	**374**	**2.0**	**2**	**1**	**1**	**2**	**2**	**3**	**4**	**10**
TOTAL MULTIPLE DX	**1,311**	**4.0**	**27**	**1**	**1**	**3**	**5**	**8**	**11**	**22**
TOTAL										
0–19 Years	105	3.0	7	1	1	2	4	7	8	15
20–34	360	2.9	9	1	1	2	3	6	10	16
35–49	586	3.0	10	1	1	2	4	6	9	13
50–64	429	4.5	57	1	1	2	5	9	13	50
65+	205	5.0	17	1	2	4	7	10	12	21
GRAND TOTAL	**1,685**	**3.6**	**23**	**1**	**1**	**2**	**4**	**8**	**10**	**20**

48.9: OTH RECTAL/PERIRECT OP

Type of Patients	Observed Patients	Avg. Stay	Vari-ance	Percentiles						
				10th	25th	50th	75th	90th	95th	99th
1. SINGLE DX										
0–19 Years	1	4.0	0	4	4	4	4	4	4	4
20–34	2	3.6	<1	3	3	4	4	4	4	4
35–49	0									
50–64	1	9.0	0	9	9	9	9	9	9	9
65+	0									
2. MULTIPLE DX										
0–19 Years	4	3.4	13	1	1	3	3	12	12	12
20–34	7	6.4	30	1	2	3	13	14	14	14
35–49	6	5.7	72	1	3	3	3	9	30	30
50–64	4	2.3	3	1	1	1	3	5	5	5
65+	5	2.6	4	1	1	2	3	6	6	6
TOTAL SINGLE DX	**4**	**4.7**	**5**	**3**	**4**	**4**	**4**	**9**	**9**	**9**
TOTAL MULTIPLE DX	**26**	**4.6**	**31**	**1**	**1**	**3**	**5**	**13**	**14**	**30**
TOTAL										
0–19 Years	5	3.5	11	1	1	3	4	12	12	12
20–34	9	6.0	26	1	3	3	13	14	14	14
35–49	6	5.7	72	1	3	3	3	9	30	30
50–64	5	3.2	9	1	1	1	5	9	9	9
65+	5	2.6	4	1	1	2	3	6	6	6
GRAND TOTAL	**30**	**4.6**	**27**	**1**	**1**	**3**	**4**	**13**	**14**	**30**

49.0: PERIANAL TISS INC/EXC

Type of Patients	Observed Patients	Avg. Stay	Vari-ance	Percentiles						
				10th	25th	50th	75th	90th	95th	99th
1. SINGLE DX										
0–19 Years	26	2.0	1	1	1	2	2	4	4	4
20–34	71	1.9	3	1	1	1	2	3	6	12
35–49	55	1.8	1	1	1	1	2	4	5	5
50–64	27	2.2	2	1	1	2	3	4	5	6
65+	5	1.2	<1	1	1	1	1	2	2	2
2. MULTIPLE DX										
0–19 Years	31	4.0	17	1	2	3	5	6	18	19
20–34	100	3.7	27	1	1	2	4	8	9	20
35–49	233	3.3	9	1	1	3	4	6	9	15
50–64	196	4.3	50	1	2	2	5	8	11	42
65+	88	5.9	46	1	2	5	7	10	16	54
TOTAL SINGLE DX	**184**	**1.9**	**2**	**1**	**1**	**1**	**2**	**3**	**5**	**9**
TOTAL MULTIPLE DX	**648**	**4.1**	**30**	**1**	**1**	**3**	**5**	**8**	**11**	**21**
TOTAL										
0–19 Years	57	3.2	11	1	1	2	4	5	7	19
20–34	171	3.0	18	1	1	2	3	7	9	20
35–49	288	3.0	8	1	1	2	4	6	8	13
50–64	223	4.1	45	1	2	2	5	7	10	42
65+	93	5.6	44	1	2	4	7	10	16	54
GRAND TOTAL	**832**	**3.6**	**25**	**1**	**1**	**2**	**4**	**7**	**10**	**20**

49.01: INC PERIANAL ABSCESS

Type of Patients	Observed Patients	Avg. Stay	Vari-ance	Percentiles						
				10th	25th	50th	75th	90th	95th	99th
1. SINGLE DX										
0–19 Years	25	2.0	1	1	1	2	3	4	4	4
20–34	68	2.0	4	1	1	1	2	3	6	12
35–49	55	1.8	1	1	1	1	2	4	5	5
50–64	25	2.3	2	1	1	2	3	5	5	6
65+	5	1.2	<1	1	1	1	1	2	2	2
2. MULTIPLE DX										
0–19 Years	29	3.7	13	1	1	3	4	6	15	19
20–34	91	3.3	12	1	1	2	4	8	8	20
35–49	208	3.2	9	1	1	3	4	6	8	13
50–64	183	4.4	53	1	2	2	5	8	11	42
65+	78	6.3	50	1	3	5	7	10	17	54
TOTAL SINGLE DX	**178**	**1.9**	**2**	**1**	**1**	**1**	**2**	**4**	**5**	**9**
TOTAL MULTIPLE DX	**589**	**4.1**	**30**	**1**	**1**	**3**	**5**	**8**	**10**	**21**
TOTAL										
0–19 Years	54	3.0	9	1	1	2	4	5	6	19
20–34	159	2.7	9	1	1	2	3	7	8	20
35–49	263	2.9	8	1	1	2	4	5	7	12
50–64	208	4.2	48	1	2	2	5	7	10	42
65+	83	5.9	48	1	2	5	7	10	16	54
GRAND TOTAL	**767**	**3.6**	**24**	**1**	**1**	**2**	**4**	**7**	**9**	**20**

49.1: INC/EXC OF ANAL FISTULA

Type of Patients	Observed Patients	Avg. Stay	Vari-ance	Percentiles						
				10th	25th	50th	75th	90th	95th	99th
1. SINGLE DX										
0–19 Years	3	1.5	<1	1	1	1	2	2	2	2
20–34	14	1.8	2	1	1	1	2	3	6	6
35–49	13	1.7	2	1	1	1	2	3	5	5
50–64	6	1.1	<1	1	1	1	1	2	2	2
65+	0									
2. MULTIPLE DX										
0–19 Years	19	1.8	1	1	1	1	2	4	4	4
20–34	31	2.2	3	1	1	2	3	5	7	7
35–49	69	3.3	11	1	1	2	4	8	12	13
50–64	35	3.0	13	1	1	2	3	7	8	18
65+	33	2.4	4	1	1	2	2	5	8	10
TOTAL SINGLE DX	**36**	**1.6**	**1**	**1**	**1**	**1**	**2**	**3**	**5**	**6**
TOTAL MULTIPLE DX	**187**	**2.7**	**8**	**1**	**1**	**2**	**3**	**7**	**8**	**13**
TOTAL										
0–19 Years	22	1.8	1	1	1	1	2	4	4	4
20–34	45	2.1	3	1	1	1	3	5	6	7
35–49	82	3.1	10	1	1	2	3	8	12	13
50–64	41	2.8	12	1	1	1	3	7	8	18
65+	33	2.4	4	1	1	2	2	5	8	10
GRAND TOTAL	**223**	**2.6**	**7**	**1**	**1**	**2**	**3**	**6**	**8**	**13**

49.11: ANAL FISTULOTOMY

Type of Patients	Observed Patients	Avg. Stay	Vari-ance	Percentiles						
				10th	25th	50th	75th	90th	95th	99th
1. SINGLE DX										
0–19 Years	1	1.0	0	1	1	1	1	1	1	1
20–34	6	2.0	3	1	1	1	2	6	6	6
35–49	6	2.0	3	1	1	1	3	5	5	5
50–64	4	1.2	<1	1	1	1	1	2	2	2
65+	0									
2. MULTIPLE DX										
0–19 Years	11	2.2	2	1	1	2	4	4	4	4
20–34	20	2.1	2	1	1	2	2	4	5	7
35–49	41	3.3	12	1	1	2	4	9	13	14
50–64	15	2.5	5	1	1	1	3	8	8	8
65+	15	3.0	6	1	2	2	3	8	9	10
TOTAL SINGLE DX	**17**	**1.8**	**2**	**1**	**1**	**1**	**2**	**5**	**5**	**6**
TOTAL MULTIPLE DX	**102**	**2.8**	**7**	**1**	**1**	**2**	**3**	**7**	**9**	**13**
TOTAL										
0–19 Years	12	2.2	2	1	1	2	4	4	4	4
20–34	26	2.1	2	1	1	2	2	5	6	7
35–49	47	3.2	11	1	1	2	4	8	11	14
50–64	19	2.2	4	1	1	1	2	6	8	8
65+	15	3.0	6	1	2	2	3	8	9	10
GRAND TOTAL	**119**	**2.7**	**7**	**1**	**1**	**2**	**3**	**6**	**9**	**13**

49.12: ANAL FISTULECTOMY

Type of Patients	Observed Patients	Avg. Stay	Variance	10th	25th	50th	75th	90th	95th	99th
1. SINGLE DX										
0–19 Years	2	1.6	<1	1	1	2	2	2	2	2
20–34	8	1.6	<1	1	1	2	2	3	3	3
35–49	7	1.5	<1	1	1	1	2	3	3	3
50–64	2	1.0	0	1	1	1	1	1	1	1
65+	0									
2. MULTIPLE DX										
0–19 Years	8	1.4	<1	1	1	1	2	3	3	3
20–34	11	2.4	4	1	1	1	3	5	7	7
35–49	28	3.4	11	1	1	2	3	8	12	12
50–64	20	3.5	20	1	1	2	3	7	18	18
65+	18	1.9	2	1	1	1	2	4	4	7
TOTAL SINGLE DX	**19**	**1.5**	**<1**	**1**	**1**	**1**	**2**	**3**	**3**	**3**
TOTAL MULTIPLE DX	**85**	**2.7**	**9**	**1**	**1**	**2**	**3**	**7**	**8**	**18**
TOTAL										
0–19 Years	10	1.4	<1	1	1	1	2	2	3	3
20–34	19	2.1	3	1	1	1	3	4	7	7
35–49	35	3.0	9	1	1	2	3	8	12	12
50–64	22	3.3	18	1	1	1	3	7	18	18
65+	18	1.9	2	1	1	1	2	4	4	7
GRAND TOTAL	**104**	**2.5**	**7**	**1**	**1**	**1**	**3**	**6**	**8**	**18**

49.2: ANAL & PERIANAL DXTIC PX

Type of Patients	Observed Patients	Avg. Stay	Variance	10th	25th	50th	75th	90th	95th	99th
1. SINGLE DX										
0–19 Years	2	1.0	0	1	1	1	1	1	1	1
20–34	1	1.0	0	1	1	1	1	1	1	1
35–49	5	1.2	<1	1	1	1	1	2	2	2
50–64	3	1.0	0	1	1	1	1	1	1	1
65+	0									
2. MULTIPLE DX										
0–19 Years	5	4.2	9	1	3	3	4	9	9	9
20–34	23	2.2	2	1	1	2	3	3	6	7
35–49	27	2.9	7	1	1	1	5	7	7	10
50–64	45	3.4	13	1	1	3	4	5	13	19
65+	96	3.3	10	1	1	2	4	6	8	23
TOTAL SINGLE DX	**11**	**1.1**	**<1**	**1**	**1**	**1**	**1**	**1**	**2**	**2**
TOTAL MULTIPLE DX	**196**	**3.2**	**9**	**1**	**1**	**2**	**4**	**6**	**8**	**19**
TOTAL										
0–19 Years	7	3.4	9	1	1	3	4	9	9	9
20–34	24	2.1	2	1	1	2	3	3	6	7
35–49	32	2.7	6	1	1	1	4	7	7	10
50–64	48	3.2	12	1	1	2	4	5	13	19
65+	96	3.3	10	1	1	2	4	6	8	23
GRAND TOTAL	**207**	**3.1**	**9**	**1**	**1**	**2**	**4**	**6**	**7**	**19**

49.21: ANOSCOPY

Type of Patients	Observed Patients	Avg. Stay	Variance	10th	25th	50th	75th	90th	95th	99th
1. SINGLE DX										
0–19 Years	2	1.0	0	1	1	1	1	1	1	1
20–34	1	1.0	0	1	1	1	1	1	1	1
35–49	5	1.2	<1	1	1	1	1	2	2	2
50–64	2	1.0	0	1	1	1	1	1	1	1
65+	0									
2. MULTIPLE DX										
0–19 Years	4	5.0	8	3	3	4	9	9	9	9
20–34	23	2.2	2	1	1	2	3	3	6	7
35–49	21	2.6	5	1	1	1	4	7	7	7
50–64	38	3.2	12	1	1	2	4	5	7	19
65+	87	2.9	8	1	1	2	4	6	6	23
TOTAL SINGLE DX	**10**	**1.1**	**<1**	**1**	**1**	**1**	**1**	**1**	**2**	**2**
TOTAL MULTIPLE DX	**173**	**2.9**	**8**	**1**	**1**	**2**	**4**	**6**	**7**	**19**
TOTAL										
0–19 Years	6	3.8	9	1	1	3	4	9	9	9
20–34	24	2.1	2	1	1	2	3	3	6	7
35–49	26	2.4	5	1	1	1	3	7	7	7
50–64	40	3.1	12	1	1	2	4	5	7	19
65+	87	2.9	8	1	1	2	4	6	6	23
GRAND TOTAL	**183**	**2.8**	**8**	**1**	**1**	**2**	**4**	**6**	**7**	**19**

49.3: LOC DESTR ANAL LES NEC

Type of Patients	Observed Patients	Avg. Stay	Variance	10th	25th	50th	75th	90th	95th	99th
1. SINGLE DX										
0–19 Years	0									
20–34	5	1.9	<1	1	1	2	2	3	3	3
35–49	12	1.4	<1	1	1	1	2	2	3	3
50–64	4	1.0	0	1	1	1	1	1	1	1
65+	2	1.4	<1	1	1	1	2	2	2	2
2. MULTIPLE DX										
0–19 Years	2	1.4	<1	1	1	1	2	2	2	2
20–34	23	3.6	42	1	1	2	3	5	24	34
35–49	60	3.1	9	1	1	2	3	7	8	19
50–64	49	2.3	3	1	1	2	3	4	6	10
65+	52	2.6	4	1	1	2	4	6	6	8
TOTAL SINGLE DX	**23**	**1.4**	**<1**	**1**	**1**	**1**	**2**	**2**	**3**	**3**
TOTAL MULTIPLE DX	**186**	**2.8**	**10**	**1**	**1**	**2**	**3**	**6**	**7**	**19**
TOTAL										
0–19 Years	2	1.4	<1	1	1	1	2	2	2	2
20–34	28	3.4	36	1	1	2	3	5	10	34
35–49	72	2.8	8	1	1	2	3	6	7	13
50–64	53	2.2	3	1	1	2	3	4	6	10
65+	54	2.6	4	1	1	2	3	6	6	8
GRAND TOTAL	**209**	**2.6**	**9**	**1**	**1**	**2**	**3**	**6**	**7**	**13**

49.39: OTH LOC DESTR ANAL LES

Type of Patients	Observed Patients	Avg. Stay	Vari-ance	Percentiles						
				10th	25th	50th	75th	90th	95th	99th
1. SINGLE DX										
0–19 Years	0									
20–34	5	1.9	<1	1	1	2	2	3	3	3
35–49	12	1.4	<1	1	1	1	2	2	3	3
50–64	3	1.0	0	1	1	1	1	1	1	1
65+	1	2.0	0	2	2	2	2	2	2	2
2. MULTIPLE DX										
0–19 Years	1	1.0	0	1	1	1	1	1	1	1
20–34	22	3.7	42	1	1	2	3	5	24	34
35–49	59	3.1	9	1	1	2	4	7	8	19
50–64	44	2.4	3	1	1	2	3	5	6	10
65+	46	2.5	3	1	1	2	3	6	6	8
TOTAL SINGLE DX	**21**	**1.5**	**<1**	**1**	**1**	**1**	**2**	**2**	**3**	**3**
TOTAL MULTIPLE DX	**172**	**2.8**	**11**	**1**	**1**	**2**	**3**	**6**	**7**	**19**
TOTAL										
0–19 Years	1	1.0	0	1	1	1	1	1	1	1
20–34	27	3.4	37	1	1	2	3	5	10	34
35–49	71	2.8	8	1	1	2	3	6	7	13
50–64	47	2.3	3	1	1	2	3	5	6	10
65+	47	2.5	3	1	1	2	3	6	6	8
GRAND TOTAL	**193**	**2.7**	**10**	**1**	**1**	**2**	**3**	**6**	**6**	**19**

49.4: HEMORRHOID PROCEDURES

Type of Patients	Observed Patients	Avg. Stay	Vari-ance	Percentiles						
				10th	25th	50th	75th	90th	95th	99th
1. SINGLE DX										
0–19 Years	1	1.0	0	1	1	1	1	1	1	1
20–34	16	1.9	2	1	1	1	2	4	5	5
35–49	35	1.4	<1	1	1	1	2	2	3	3
50–64	21	1.7	<1	1	1	1	2	3	4	4
65+	5	1.2	<1	1	1	1	1	2	2	2
2. MULTIPLE DX										
0–19 Years	2	45.7	>999	1	1	73	73	73	73	73
20–34	139	2.3	6	1	1	2	3	4	5	8
35–49	408	2.6	8	1	1	2	3	5	7	15
50–64	347	2.7	6	1	1	2	3	6	8	12
65+	365	3.9	13	1	1	3	5	8	10	18
TOTAL SINGLE DX	**78**	**1.6**	**<1**	**1**	**1**	**1**	**2**	**3**	**3**	**5**
TOTAL MULTIPLE DX	**1,261**	**3.1**	**17**	**1**	**1**	**2**	**4**	**6**	**8**	**16**
TOTAL										
0–19 Years	3	37.1	>999	1	1	73	73	73	73	73
20–34	155	2.3	5	1	1	2	3	4	5	8
35–49	443	2.5	7	1	1	2	3	5	7	14
50–64	368	2.7	6	1	1	2	3	6	8	12
65+	370	3.8	13	1	1	3	5	8	10	18
GRAND TOTAL	**1,339**	**3.0**	**16**	**1**	**1**	**2**	**4**	**6**	**8**	**16**

49.45: HEMORRHOID LIGATION

Type of Patients	Observed Patients	Avg. Stay	Vari-ance	Percentiles						
				10th	25th	50th	75th	90th	95th	99th
1. SINGLE DX										
0–19 Years	0									
20–34	0									
35–49	3	2.0	<1	1	1	2	3	3	3	3
50–64	2	2.0	0	2	2	2	2	2	2	2
65+	1	1.0	0	1	1	1	1	1	1	1
2. MULTIPLE DX										
0–19 Years	1	73.0	0	73	73	73	73	73	73	73
20–34	12	3.0	3	1	2	2	4	5	7	7
35–49	24	3.2	6	1	1	3	4	7	10	10
50–64	32	4.0	19	1	1	3	4	10	14	23
65+	69	5.4	11	2	3	5	7	10	11	18
TOTAL SINGLE DX	**6**	**1.8**	**<1**	**1**	**1**	**2**	**2**	**3**	**3**	**3**
TOTAL MULTIPLE DX	**138**	**5.5**	**80**	**1**	**2**	**4**	**6**	**10**	**12**	**73**
TOTAL										
0–19 Years	1	73.0	0	73	73	73	73	73	73	73
20–34	12	3.0	3	1	2	2	4	5	7	7
35–49	27	3.1	6	1	1	3	4	6	10	10
50–64	34	4.0	19	1	1	3	4	10	14	23
65+	70	5.3	11	2	3	5	7	10	11	18
GRAND TOTAL	**144**	**5.4**	**77**	**1**	**2**	**3**	**6**	**10**	**11**	**73**

49.46: EXC OF HEMORRHOIDS

Type of Patients	Observed Patients	Avg. Stay	Vari-ance	Percentiles						
				10th	25th	50th	75th	90th	95th	99th
1. SINGLE DX										
0–19 Years	1	1.0	0	1	1	1	1	1	1	1
20–34	14	2.0	2	1	1	1	3	4	5	5
35–49	30	1.4	<1	1	1	1	2	2	3	3
50–64	18	1.7	<1	1	1	1	2	3	4	4
65+	2	1.0	0	1	1	1	1	1	1	1
2. MULTIPLE DX										
0–19 Years	1	1.0	0	1	1	1	1	1	1	1
20–34	111	2.4	7	1	1	2	3	5	6	8
35–49	356	2.7	8	1	1	2	3	5	7	15
50–64	298	2.5	4	1	1	2	3	5	7	10
65+	266	3.4	11	1	1	2	5	8	9	18
TOTAL SINGLE DX	**65**	**1.6**	**<1**	**1**	**1**	**1**	**2**	**3**	**3**	**5**
TOTAL MULTIPLE DX	**1,032**	**2.8**	**8**	**1**	**1**	**2**	**3**	**6**	**8**	**13**
TOTAL										
0–19 Years	2	1.0	0	1	1	1	1	1	1	1
20–34	125	2.3	7	1	1	2	3	5	5	8
35–49	386	2.6	8	1	1	2	3	5	7	15
50–64	316	2.5	4	1	1	2	3	5	7	10
65+	268	3.4	11	1	1	2	4	7	9	18
GRAND TOTAL	**1,097**	**2.7**	**8**	**1**	**1**	**2**	**3**	**6**	**7**	**13**

49.5: ANAL SPHINCTER DIVISION

Type of Patients	Observed Patients	Avg. Stay	Vari-ance	10th	25th	50th	75th	90th	95th	99th
1. SINGLE DX										
0–19 Years	0									
20–34	2	1.5	<1	1	1	1	2	2	2	2
35–49	2	1.6	<1	1	1	2	2	2	2	2
50–64	0									
65+	0									
2. MULTIPLE DX										
0–19 Years	1	4.0	0	4	4	4	4	4	4	4
20–34	3	3.2	8	1	1	2	7	7	7	7
35–49	19	3.5	11	1	1	3	4	7	15	15
50–64	16	1.9	<1	1	1	2	2	3	4	5
65+	21	4.9	8	1	3	5	6	9	10	11
TOTAL SINGLE DX	**4**	**1.5**	**<1**	**1**	**1**	**2**	**2**	**2**	**2**	**2**
TOTAL MULTIPLE DX	**60**	**3.6**	**8**	**1**	**2**	**2**	**5**	**8**	**10**	**15**
TOTAL										
0–19 Years	1	4.0	0	4	4	4	4	4	4	4
20–34	5	2.4	5	1	1	2	2	7	7	7
35–49	21	3.3	10	1	1	2	4	7	7	15
50–64	16	1.9	<1	1	1	2	2	3	4	5
65+	21	4.9	8	1	3	5	6	9	10	11
GRAND TOTAL	**64**	**3.5**	**8**	**1**	**2**	**2**	**5**	**8**	**9**	**15**

49.6: EXCISION OF ANUS

Type of Patients	Observed Patients	Avg. Stay	Vari-ance	10th	25th	50th	75th	90th	95th	99th
1. SINGLE DX										
0–19 Years	0									
20–34	0									
35–49	0									
50–64	0									
65+	0									
2. MULTIPLE DX										
0–19 Years	0									
20–34	0									
35–49	3	10.9	88	1	4	4	21	21	21	21
50–64	0									
65+	4	5.6	19	1	3	3	7	12	12	12
TOTAL SINGLE DX	**0**									
TOTAL MULTIPLE DX	**7**	**8.4**	**61**	**1**	**3**	**4**	**12**	**21**	**21**	**21**
TOTAL										
0–19 Years	0									
20–34	0									
35–49	3	10.9	88	1	4	4	21	21	21	21
50–64	0									
65+	4	5.6	19	1	3	3	7	12	12	12
GRAND TOTAL	**7**	**8.4**	**61**	**1**	**3**	**4**	**12**	**21**	**21**	**21**

49.7: REPAIR OF ANUS

Type of Patients	Observed Patients	Avg. Stay	Vari-ance	10th	25th	50th	75th	90th	95th	99th
1. SINGLE DX										
0–19 Years	15	2.1	2	1	1	2	3	3	3	6
20–34	16	2.5	2	1	1	2	3	4	7	7
35–49	19	2.5	1	1	2	3	3	4	4	6
50–64	10	2.7	1	1	2	3	4	4	4	4
65+	5	1.2	<1	1	1	1	1	3	3	3
2. MULTIPLE DX										
0–19 Years	60	4.1	13	1	2	3	5	7	9	26
20–34	43	2.7	4	1	2	2	3	4	5	10
35–49	73	2.7	2	1	2	3	3	4	5	6
50–64	65	3.1	5	1	1	3	4	7	7	12
65+	50	2.5	5	1	1	2	3	5	7	14
TOTAL SINGLE DX	**65**	**2.3**	**2**	**1**	**1**	**2**	**3**	**4**	**4**	**7**
TOTAL MULTIPLE DX	**291**	**3.2**	**7**	**1**	**2**	**3**	**4**	**6**	**7**	**14**
TOTAL										
0–19 Years	75	3.8	11	1	2	3	4	6	8	26
20–34	59	2.6	3	1	1	2	3	4	5	10
35–49	92	2.7	2	1	2	3	3	4	5	6
50–64	75	3.0	4	1	2	3	4	5	7	12
65+	55	2.4	5	1	1	2	3	5	7	14
GRAND TOTAL	**356**	**3.0**	**6**	**1**	**2**	**3**	**4**	**6**	**7**	**14**

49.79: ANAL SPHINCTER REP NEC

Type of Patients	Observed Patients	Avg. Stay	Vari-ance	10th	25th	50th	75th	90th	95th	99th
1. SINGLE DX										
0–19 Years	12	2.2	2	1	1	2	3	3	6	6
20–34	10	3.0	2	1	2	3	3	4	7	7
35–49	14	2.6	1	1	2	3	3	4	4	6
50–64	7	2.9	1	1	2	3	4	4	4	4
65+	4	1.4	<1	1	1	1	1	3	3	3
2. MULTIPLE DX										
0–19 Years	56	4.1	12	1	2	4	5	7	9	26
20–34	32	2.7	4	1	1	2	3	4	10	10
35–49	48	2.9	2	2	2	3	3	4	5	10
50–64	49	3.1	4	1	2	3	3	7	7	12
65+	45	2.6	6	1	1	2	3	6	8	14
TOTAL SINGLE DX	**47**	**2.5**	**2**	**1**	**1**	**3**	**3**	**4**	**4**	**7**
TOTAL MULTIPLE DX	**230**	**3.3**	**7**	**1**	**2**	**3**	**4**	**6**	**8**	**14**
TOTAL										
0–19 Years	68	3.8	11	1	2	3	4	6	8	26
20–34	42	2.8	4	1	2	2	3	4	7	10
35–49	62	2.8	2	2	2	3	3	4	5	10
50–64	56	3.0	4	1	2	3	3	5	7	8
65+	49	2.5	5	1	1	2	3	5	8	14
GRAND TOTAL	**277**	**3.1**	**6**	**1**	**2**	**3**	**4**	**6**	**7**	**14**

49.9: OTH OPERATIONS ON ANUS

Type of Patients	Observed Patients	Avg. Stay	Variance	Percentiles 10th	25th	50th	75th	90th	95th	99th
1. SINGLE DX										
0–19 Years	1	1.0	0	1	1	1	1	1	1	1
20–34	0									
35–49	11	2.9	11	1	1	2	2	5	13	13
50–64	7	2.0	<1	1	1	2	3	3	3	3
65+	2	1.0	0	1	1	1	1	1	1	1
2. MULTIPLE DX										
0–19 Years	4	1.8	3	1	1	1	2	2	7	7
20–34	20	2.9	11	1	1	2	3	6	6	19
35–49	32	3.3	14	1	1	2	4	6	10	21
50–64	34	4.6	26	1	1	2	5	16	16	22
65+	22	2.3	3	1	1	2	2	5	7	8
TOTAL SINGLE DX	**21**	**2.4**	**7**	**1**	**1**	**2**	**3**	**4**	**13**	**13**
TOTAL MULTIPLE DX	**112**	**3.2**	**14**	**1**	**1**	**2**	**3**	**7**	**12**	**21**
TOTAL										
0–19 Years	5	1.7	3	1	1	1	2	2	7	7
20–34	20	2.9	11	1	1	2	3	6	6	19
35–49	43	3.2	13	1	1	2	4	6	13	21
50–64	41	4.3	24	1	1	2	5	12	16	22
65+	24	2.2	3	1	1	2	2	5	7	8
GRAND TOTAL	**133**	**3.1**	**13**	**1**	**1**	**2**	**3**	**6**	**12**	**19**

50.0: HEPATOTOMY

Type of Patients	Observed Patients	Avg. Stay	Variance	Percentiles 10th	25th	50th	75th	90th	95th	99th
1. SINGLE DX										
0–19 Years	1	2.0	0	2	2	2	2	2	2	2
20–34	1	2.0	0	2	2	2	2	2	2	2
35–49	0									
50–64	2	1.0	0	1	1	1	1	1	1	1
65+	0									
2. MULTIPLE DX										
0–19 Years	4	14.6	99	6	6	15	28	28	28	28
20–34	8	12.9	327	1	1	7	7	54	54	54
35–49	10	8.6	41	3	4	5	10	20	20	20
50–64	25	14.0	89	6	7	10	17	29	38	38
65+	33	10.9	50	2	7	10	15	15	17	43
TOTAL SINGLE DX	**4**	**1.6**	**<1**	**1**	**1**	**2**	**2**	**2**	**2**	**2**
TOTAL MULTIPLE DX	**80**	**12.0**	**83**	**3**	**7**	**10**	**15**	**21**	**29**	**43**
TOTAL										
0–19 Years	5	11.6	105	2	6	7	15	28	28	28
20–34	9	11.9	305	1	2	5	7	54	54	54
35–49	10	8.6	41	3	4	5	10	20	20	20
50–64	27	13.5	91	4	7	10	17	29	38	38
65+	33	10.9	50	2	7	10	15	15	17	43
GRAND TOTAL	**84**	**11.7**	**84**	**2**	**6**	**10**	**15**	**21**	**29**	**43**

50.1: HEPATIC DXTIC PX

Type of Patients	Observed Patients	Avg. Stay	Variance	Percentiles 10th	25th	50th	75th	90th	95th	99th
1. SINGLE DX										
0–19 Years	77	2.0	4	1	1	1	2	5	8	8
20–34	15	5.0	12	2	2	5	7	11	13	13
35–49	28	1.8	4	1	1	1	2	3	8	9
50–64	15	2.2	4	1	1	1	3	4	6	10
65+	5	2.8	5	1	1	2	3	7	7	7
2. MULTIPLE DX										
0–19 Years	280	4.7	39	1	1	2	6	11	15	30
20–34	145	6.6	33	1	3	5	8	14	20	23
35–49	523	6.9	39	1	3	5	9	14	18	32
50–64	1,068	6.3	30	1	2	5	8	13	17	28
65+	1,298	7.0	24	2	4	6	9	13	16	26
TOTAL SINGLE DX	**140**	**2.2**	**5**	**1**	**1**	**1**	**2**	**5**	**8**	**10**
TOTAL MULTIPLE DX	**3,314**	**6.5**	**31**	**1**	**3**	**5**	**8**	**13**	**17**	**28**
TOTAL										
0–19 Years	357	4.0	32	1	1	2	5	10	13	24
20–34	160	6.5	32	1	3	5	8	14	20	23
35–49	551	6.7	39	1	3	5	8	13	18	32
50–64	1,083	6.2	30	1	2	5	8	13	17	28
65+	1,303	7.0	24	2	4	6	9	13	16	26
GRAND TOTAL	**3,454**	**6.3**	**30**	**1**	**2**	**5**	**8**	**13**	**17**	**28**

50.11: CLOSED LIVER BIOPSY

Type of Patients	Observed Patients	Avg. Stay	Variance	Percentiles 10th	25th	50th	75th	90th	95th	99th
1. SINGLE DX										
0–19 Years	64	1.5	2	1	1	1	1	3	4	8
20–34	13	5.5	12	2	3	5	7	11	13	13
35–49	28	1.8	4	1	1	1	2	3	8	9
50–64	14	2.4	5	1	1	1	3	4	10	10
65+	5	2.8	5	1	1	2	3	7	7	7
2. MULTIPLE DX										
0–19 Years	241	4.1	33	1	1	2	5	10	14	24
20–34	134	6.3	33	1	3	5	8	14	20	23
35–49	486	6.9	38	1	3	5	9	14	18	32
50–64	973	6.2	30	1	2	5	8	13	16	28
65+	1,178	7.0	22	2	4	6	9	13	16	23
TOTAL SINGLE DX	**124**	**2.0**	**4**	**1**	**1**	**1**	**2**	**4**	**7**	**10**
TOTAL MULTIPLE DX	**3,012**	**6.4**	**29**	**1**	**3**	**5**	**8**	**13**	**17**	**28**
TOTAL										
0–19 Years	305	3.5	27	1	1	1	4	10	12	22
20–34	147	6.3	32	1	3	5	8	14	20	23
35–49	514	6.7	38	1	3	5	9	14	18	32
50–64	987	6.1	29	1	2	5	8	13	16	28
65+	1,183	6.9	22	2	4	6	9	13	16	23
GRAND TOTAL	**3,136**	**6.2**	**29**	**1**	**2**	**5**	**8**	**13**	**16**	**26**

50.12: OPEN BIOPSY OF LIVER

Type of Patients	Observed Patients	Avg. Stay	Vari-ance	10th	25th	50th	75th	90th	95th	99th
				Percentiles						
1. SINGLE DX										
0–19 Years	13	4.2	9	1	1	3	8	8	8	8
20–34	2	2.1	2	1	1	3	3	3	3	3
35–49	0									
50–64	1	1.0	0	1	1	1	1	1	1	1
65+	0									
2. MULTIPLE DX										
0–19 Years	39	8.9	60	2	3	7	11	21	26	39
20–34	11	9.0	26	3	6	9	11	18	20	20
35–49	36	6.1	22	2	3	5	7	10	14	23
50–64	95	7.1	39	1	3	5	8	16	18	29
65+	120	7.7	41	1	4	6	10	15	23	33
TOTAL SINGLE DX	**16**	**3.8**	**8**	**1**	**1**	**3**	**7**	**8**	**8**	**8**
TOTAL MULTIPLE DX	**301**	**7.6**	**41**	**2**	**4**	**6**	**10**	**16**	**23**	**31**
TOTAL										
0–19 Years	52	7.5	50	1	2	7	10	13	24	39
20–34	13	8.1	29	2	4	6	10	18	20	20
35–49	36	6.1	22	2	3	5	7	10	14	23
50–64	96	7.0	39	1	3	5	8	16	18	29
65+	120	7.7	41	1	4	6	10	15	23	33
GRAND TOTAL	**317**	**7.3**	**40**	**1**	**3**	**6**	**10**	**15**	**21**	**31**

50.2: LOC EXC/DESTR LIVER LES

Type of Patients	Observed Patients	Avg. Stay	Vari-ance	10th	25th	50th	75th	90th	95th	99th
				Percentiles						
1. SINGLE DX										
0–19 Years	0									
20–34	13	5.0	4	2	4	6	6	7	7	7
35–49	12	4.1	14	1	2	3	4	10	14	14
50–64	18	3.4	5	1	1	3	5	7	8	8
65+	3	1.3	<1	1	1	1	2	2	2	2
2. MULTIPLE DX										
0–19 Years	13	9.3	31	2	7	8	12	16	23	23
20–34	50	6.3	19	2	4	6	7	9	15	30
35–49	129	5.7	16	2	3	5	7	9	12	31
50–64	352	5.4	18	1	3	5	7	9	12	21
65+	325	5.5	17	1	2	5	7	10	14	19
TOTAL SINGLE DX	**46**	**3.9**	**7**	**1**	**1**	**3**	**6**	**7**	**8**	**14**
TOTAL MULTIPLE DX	**869**	**5.6**	**18**	**1**	**3**	**5**	**7**	**10**	**13**	**21**
TOTAL										
0–19 Years	13	9.3	31	2	7	8	12	16	23	23
20–34	63	6.0	16	2	4	6	7	9	15	30
35–49	141	5.6	16	2	3	5	7	9	12	17
50–64	370	5.4	18	1	3	5	7	9	12	21
65+	328	5.4	17	1	2	5	7	10	14	19
GRAND TOTAL	**915**	**5.5**	**18**	**1**	**3**	**5**	**7**	**10**	**13**	**21**

50.22: PARTIAL HEPATECTOMY

Type of Patients	Observed Patients	Avg. Stay	Vari-ance	10th	25th	50th	75th	90th	95th	99th
				Percentiles						
1. SINGLE DX										
0–19 Years	0									
20–34	9	5.7	2	4	4	6	7	7	7	7
35–49	7	3.8	6	2	3	3	4	10	10	10
50–64	7	5.6	3	3	5	6	7	8	8	8
65+	0									
2. MULTIPLE DX										
0–19 Years	8	12.1	32	2	9	12	14	23	23	23
20–34	31	6.7	21	4	5	6	7	9	16	30
35–49	77	6.9	19	4	4	6	8	12	13	31
50–64	161	7.0	18	4	4	6	8	12	13	23
65+	110	7.6	15	4	5	7	9	12	17	20
TOTAL SINGLE DX	**23**	**5.1**	**4**	**3**	**3**	**5**	**6**	**7**	**8**	**10**
TOTAL MULTIPLE DX	**387**	**7.3**	**18**	**4**	**5**	**6**	**9**	**12**	**16**	**23**
TOTAL										
0–19 Years	8	12.1	32	2	9	12	14	23	23	23
20–34	40	6.5	17	4	5	6	7	8	9	30
35–49	84	6.6	19	3	4	6	8	11	13	31
50–64	168	6.9	17	3	4	6	8	12	13	23
65+	110	7.6	15	4	5	7	9	12	17	20
GRAND TOTAL	**410**	**7.2**	**18**	**4**	**5**	**6**	**8**	**12**	**15**	**23**

50.29: HEPATIC LESION DESTR NEC

Type of Patients	Observed Patients	Avg. Stay	Vari-ance	10th	25th	50th	75th	90th	95th	99th
				Percentiles						
1. SINGLE DX										
0–19 Years	0									
20–34	4	3.8	4	1	2	5	5	6	6	6
35–49	5	4.4	29	1	1	1	5	14	14	14
50–64	9	1.9	2	1	1	1	3	5	5	5
65+	2	1.0	0	1	1	1	1	1	1	1
2. MULTIPLE DX										
0–19 Years	5	6.4	15	1	3	7	7	9	15	15
20–34	18	5.1	10	2	3	5	6	9	10	15
35–49	52	3.9	6	1	2	3	6	7	8	11
50–64	182	3.8	8	1	1	3	5	7	8	15
65+	199	4.4	15	1	2	4	6	8	10	17
TOTAL SINGLE DX	**20**	**2.9**	**9**	**1**	**1**	**1**	**5**	**5**	**6**	**14**
TOTAL MULTIPLE DX	**456**	**4.2**	**12**	**1**	**2**	**4**	**6**	**8**	**10**	**15**
TOTAL										
0–19 Years	5	6.4	15	1	3	7	7	9	15	15
20–34	22	4.8	9	2	2	5	6	9	10	15
35–49	57	4.0	7	1	2	3	6	7	8	14
50–64	191	3.7	8	1	1	3	5	7	8	15
65+	201	4.4	15	1	2	4	6	8	10	17
GRAND TOTAL	**476**	**4.2**	**12**	**1**	**2**	**3**	**6**	**8**	**10**	**15**

50.3: HEPATIC LOBECTOMY

Type of Patients	Observed Patients	Avg. Stay	Vari-ance	Percentiles						
				10th	25th	50th	75th	90th	95th	99th
1. SINGLE DX										
0–19 Years	0									
20–34	5	5.9	1	5	5	6	6	8	8	8
35–49	5	5.2	4	2	6	6	6	7	7	7
50–64	2	8.9	52	3	3	14	14	14	14	14
65+	1	8.0	0	8	8	8	8	8	8	8
2. MULTIPLE DX										
0–19 Years	10	11.7	72	7	7	9	11	31	31	31
20–34	28	10.9	70	5	6	7	11	20	35	42
35–49	49	7.7	15	4	6	7	8	12	17	25
50–64	113	8.4	27	5	6	7	9	13	16	42
65+	96	8.0	16	5	6	7	9	12	18	23
TOTAL SINGLE DX	**13**	**6.2**	**7**	**3**	**5**	**6**	**7**	**8**	**14**	**14**
TOTAL MULTIPLE DX	**296**	**8.5**	**27**	**5**	**6**	**7**	**9**	**13**	**19**	**31**
TOTAL										
0–19 Years	10	11.7	72	7	7	9	11	31	31	31
20–34	33	9.9	61	5	6	7	10	20	22	42
35–49	54	7.5	14	4	6	7	8	12	17	25
50–64	115	8.4	27	5	6	7	9	14	16	42
65+	97	8.0	16	5	6	7	9	12	18	23
GRAND TOTAL	**309**	**8.4**	**26**	**5**	**6**	**7**	**9**	**13**	**19**	**31**

50.4: TOTAL HEPATECTOMY

Type of Patients	Observed Patients	Avg. Stay	Vari-ance	Percentiles						
				10th	25th	50th	75th	90th	95th	99th
1. SINGLE DX										
0–19 Years	0									
20–34	0									
35–49	0									
50–64	0									
65+	0									
2. MULTIPLE DX										
0–19 Years	1	15.0	0	15	15	15	15	15	15	15
20–34	0									
35–49	1	9.0	0	9	9	9	9	9	9	9
50–64	4	14.3	56	5	5	19	21	21	21	21
65+	0									
TOTAL SINGLE DX	**0**									
TOTAL MULTIPLE DX	**6**	**13.1**	**38**	**5**	**9**	**10**	**19**	**21**	**21**	**21**
TOTAL										
0–19 Years	1	15.0	0	15	15	15	15	15	15	15
20–34	0									
35–49	1	9.0	0	9	9	9	9	9	9	9
50–64	4	14.3	56	5	5	19	21	21	21	21
65+	0									
GRAND TOTAL	**6**	**13.1**	**38**	**5**	**9**	**10**	**19**	**21**	**21**	**21**

50.5: LIVER TRANSPLANT

Type of Patients	Observed Patients	Avg. Stay	Vari-ance	Percentiles						
				10th	25th	50th	75th	90th	95th	99th
1. SINGLE DX										
0–19 Years	0									
20–34	1	5.0	0	5	5	5	5	5	5	5
35–49	0									
50–64	0									
65+	0									
2. MULTIPLE DX										
0–19 Years	33	21.1	178	11	14	18	23	28	50	88
20–34	13	14.2	95	8	9	10	13	34	38	38
35–49	113	12.8	72	6	7	10	15	29	31	37
50–64	227	13.5	83	6	8	10	16	26	32	50
65+	25	11.1	40	6	8	9	12	18	18	38
TOTAL SINGLE DX	**1**	**5.0**	**0**	**5**	**5**	**5**	**5**	**5**	**5**	**5**
TOTAL MULTIPLE DX	**411**	**14.2**	**98**	**6**	**8**	**11**	**18**	**27**	**32**	**50**
TOTAL										
0–19 Years	33	21.1	178	11	14	18	23	28	50	88
20–34	14	13.5	93	7	9	10	13	34	38	38
35–49	113	12.8	72	6	7	10	15	29	31	37
50–64	227	13.5	83	6	8	10	16	26	32	50
65+	25	11.1	40	6	8	9	12	18	18	38
GRAND TOTAL	**412**	**14.2**	**98**	**6**	**8**	**11**	**17**	**27**	**32**	**50**

50.59: LIVER TRANSPLANT NEC

Type of Patients	Observed Patients	Avg. Stay	Vari-ance	Percentiles						
				10th	25th	50th	75th	90th	95th	99th
1. SINGLE DX										
0–19 Years	0									
20–34	1	5.0	0	5	5	5	5	5	5	5
35–49	0									
50–64	0									
65+	0									
2. MULTIPLE DX										
0–19 Years	33	21.1	178	11	14	18	23	28	50	88
20–34	13	14.2	95	8	9	10	13	34	38	38
35–49	111	12.7	71	6	7	10	15	29	31	37
50–64	225	13.5	83	6	8	10	16	26	32	50
65+	25	11.1	40	6	8	9	12	18	18	38
TOTAL SINGLE DX	**1**	**5.0**	**0**	**5**	**5**	**5**	**5**	**5**	**5**	**5**
TOTAL MULTIPLE DX	**407**	**14.2**	**98**	**6**	**8**	**11**	**17**	**27**	**32**	**50**
TOTAL										
0–19 Years	33	21.1	178	11	14	18	23	28	50	88
20–34	14	13.5	93	7	9	10	13	34	38	38
35–49	111	12.7	71	6	7	10	15	29	31	37
50–64	225	13.5	83	6	8	10	16	26	32	50
65+	25	11.1	40	6	8	9	12	18	18	38
GRAND TOTAL	**408**	**14.2**	**98**	**6**	**8**	**11**	**17**	**27**	**32**	**50**

50.6: REPAIR OF LIVER

Type of Patients	Observed Patients	Avg. Stay	Vari-ance	10th	25th	50th	75th	90th	95th	99th
1. SINGLE DX										
0–19 Years	1	1.0	0	1	1	1	1	1	1	1
20–34	7	3.4	<1	2	3	3	4	5	5	5
35–49	2	2.5	<1	2	2	2	3	3	3	3
50–64	0									
65+	1	2.0	0	2	2	2	2	2	2	2
2. MULTIPLE DX										
0–19 Years	23	9.4	37	5	6	9	10	16	24	30
20–34	94	9.0	75	3	4	7	10	22	30	42
35–49	43	7.9	27	4	5	6	9	14	20	28
50–64	32	9.9	222	2	4	6	11	14	21	94
65+	16	10.2	28	2	5	12	13	15	21	21
TOTAL SINGLE DX	**11**	**2.9**	**1**	**1**	**2**	**3**	**4**	**4**	**5**	**5**
TOTAL MULTIPLE DX	**208**	**9.0**	**76**	**3**	**4**	**7**	**11**	**18**	**24**	**42**
TOTAL										
0–19 Years	24	9.1	38	5	5	8	10	16	24	30
20–34	101	8.7	72	3	4	6	10	21	27	42
35–49	45	7.7	28	3	4	6	9	14	20	28
50–64	32	9.9	222	2	4	6	11	14	21	94
65+	17	9.7	30	2	4	11	13	15	21	21
GRAND TOTAL	**219**	**8.8**	**74**	**3**	**4**	**6**	**11**	**17**	**23**	**42**

50.61: CLOSURE OF LIVER LAC

Type of Patients	Observed Patients	Avg. Stay	Vari-ance	10th	25th	50th	75th	90th	95th	99th
1. SINGLE DX										
0–19 Years	1	1.0	0	1	1	1	1	1	1	1
20–34	5	3.4	1	2	3	3	4	5	5	5
35–49	2	2.5	<1	2	2	2	3	3	3	3
50–64	0									
65+	1	2.0	0	2	2	2	2	2	2	2
2. MULTIPLE DX										
0–19 Years	19	9.1	38	5	5	9	9	16	24	30
20–34	89	9.1	79	3	4	6	10	22	30	42
35–49	40	8.1	31	4	5	6	9	14	20	28
50–64	27	9.9	257	2	4	6	11	14	21	94
65+	13	10.0	32	2	4	11	12	15	21	21
TOTAL SINGLE DX	**9**	**2.7**	**1**	**1**	**2**	**3**	**3**	**5**	**5**	**5**
TOTAL MULTIPLE DX	**188**	**9.0**	**83**	**3**	**4**	**6**	**11**	**18**	**25**	**42**
TOTAL										
0–19 Years	20	8.7	39	4	5	8	9	16	24	30
20–34	94	8.8	77	3	4	6	10	22	30	42
35–49	42	7.9	31	3	4	6	9	14	20	28
50–64	27	9.9	257	2	4	6	11	14	21	94
65+	14	9.5	34	2	3	11	12	15	21	21
GRAND TOTAL	**197**	**8.8**	**81**	**3**	**4**	**6**	**10**	**17**	**25**	**42**

50.9: OTHER LIVER OPERATIONS

Type of Patients	Observed Patients	Avg. Stay	Vari-ance	10th	25th	50th	75th	90th	95th	99th
1. SINGLE DX										
0–19 Years	1	10.0	0	10	10	10	10	10	10	10
20–34	11	5.7	7	2	3	6	6	10	11	11
35–49	9	5.6	9	2	3	5	9	10	10	10
50–64	2	2.5	4	1	1	1	4	4	4	4
65+	3	5.7	11	1	1	7	8	8	8	8
2. MULTIPLE DX										
0–19 Years	7	9.2	66	2	5	7	10	27	27	27
20–34	50	8.2	24	3	5	6	11	15	18	23
35–49	99	7.7	26	3	4	7	10	15	17	25
50–64	163	7.7	52	2	3	6	9	15	21	49
65+	231	8.2	42	2	3	7	11	16	21	35
TOTAL SINGLE DX	**26**	**5.9**	**9**	**2**	**3**	**6**	**9**	**10**	**10**	**11**
TOTAL MULTIPLE DX	**550**	**8.0**	**41**	**2**	**4**	**6**	**10**	**15**	**21**	**32**
TOTAL										
0–19 Years	8	9.4	51	2	5	7	10	27	27	27
20–34	61	7.8	22	3	5	6	11	15	15	23
35–49	108	7.5	25	2	4	6	10	15	17	25
50–64	165	7.7	52	2	3	6	9	15	21	49
65+	234	8.1	42	2	3	7	11	16	21	35
GRAND TOTAL	**576**	**7.9**	**40**	**2**	**4**	**6**	**10**	**15**	**21**	**32**

50.91: PERC LIVER ASPIRATION

Type of Patients	Observed Patients	Avg. Stay	Vari-ance	10th	25th	50th	75th	90th	95th	99th
1. SINGLE DX										
0–19 Years	1	10.0	0	10	10	10	10	10	10	10
20–34	11	5.7	7	2	3	6	6	10	11	11
35–49	8	6.4	7	3	4	5	9	10	10	10
50–64	2	2.5	4	1	1	1	4	4	4	4
65+	3	5.7	11	1	1	7	8	8	8	8
2. MULTIPLE DX										
0–19 Years	5	11.5	65	5	7	7	13	27	27	27
20–34	46	8.6	25	4	5	7	11	15	18	23
35–49	88	8.2	27	3	5	7	11	16	18	25
50–64	138	8.5	55	2	4	6	11	16	21	49
65+	194	9.2	44	3	4	8	12	17	21	35
TOTAL SINGLE DX	**25**	**6.1**	**9**	**2**	**4**	**6**	**9**	**10**	**10**	**11**
TOTAL MULTIPLE DX	**471**	**8.8**	**43**	**3**	**4**	**7**	**11**	**16**	**21**	**35**
TOTAL										
0–19 Years	6	11.1	47	5	7	10	10	27	27	27
20–34	57	8.1	23	3	5	6	11	15	18	23
35–49	96	8.1	26	3	5	7	11	15	17	25
50–64	140	8.4	55	2	4	6	11	16	21	49
65+	197	9.2	43	3	4	7	11	17	21	35
GRAND TOTAL	**496**	**8.7**	**42**	**3**	**4**	**7**	**11**	**16**	**21**	**34**

50.94: HEPATIC INJECTION NEC

Type of Patients	Observed Patients	Avg. Stay	Vari-ance	Percentiles 10th	25th	50th	75th	90th	95th	99th
1. SINGLE DX										
0–19 Years	0									
20–34	0									
35–49	1	2.0	0	2	2	2	2	2	2	2
50–64	0									
65+	0									
2. MULTIPLE DX										
0–19 Years	2	2.0	0	2	2	2	2	2	2	2
20–34	4	4.8	6	2	2	5	5	9	9	9
35–49	10	3.6	2	2	2	4	4	5	7	7
50–64	23	2.1	2	1	1	2	3	4	4	6
65+	35	3.3	6	1	1	3	6	7	8	10
TOTAL SINGLE DX	**1**	**2.0**	**0**	**2**	**2**	**2**	**2**	**2**	**2**	**2**
TOTAL MULTIPLE DX	**74**	**3.1**	**5**	**1**	**1**	**3**	**4**	**6**	**8**	**9**
TOTAL										
0–19 Years	2	2.0	0	2	2	2	2	2	2	2
20–34	4	4.8	6	2	2	5	5	9	9	9
35–49	11	3.5	2	2	2	4	4	5	7	7
50–64	23	2.1	2	1	1	2	3	4	4	6
65+	35	3.3	6	1	1	3	6	7	8	10
GRAND TOTAL	**75**	**3.1**	**5**	**1**	**1**	**2**	**4**	**6**	**8**	**9**

51.0: GB INC & CHOLECYSTOSTOMY

Type of Patients	Observed Patients	Avg. Stay	Vari-ance	Percentiles 10th	25th	50th	75th	90th	95th	99th
1. SINGLE DX										
0–19 Years	0									
20–34	1	1.0	0	1	1	1	1	1	1	1
35–49	1	3.0	0	3	3	3	3	3	3	3
50–64	3	4.0	3	3	3	3	6	6	6	6
65+	2	4.4	<1	4	4	4	5	5	5	5
2. MULTIPLE DX										
0–19 Years	0									
20–34	9	9.3	34	5	5	7	13	18	19	19
35–49	23	5.9	16	2	3	5	7	11	13	20
50–64	69	8.6	35	2	5	7	11	16	23	27
65+	189	9.1	37	3	5	8	13	15	19	29
TOTAL SINGLE DX	**7**	**3.6**	**2**	**1**	**3**	**3**	**5**	**6**	**6**	**6**
TOTAL MULTIPLE DX	**290**	**8.7**	**35**	**3**	**5**	**7**	**12**	**15**	**19**	**27**
TOTAL										
0–19 Years	0									
20–34	10	8.6	37	1	5	7	13	18	19	19
35–49	24	5.8	16	2	3	5	7	11	11	20
50–64	72	8.4	34	2	5	7	11	16	19	27
65+	191	9.1	37	3	5	8	13	15	19	29
GRAND TOTAL	**297**	**8.6**	**35**	**3**	**5**	**7**	**12**	**15**	**19**	**27**

51.01: PERC ASPIRATION OF GB

Type of Patients	Observed Patients	Avg. Stay	Vari-ance	Percentiles 10th	25th	50th	75th	90th	95th	99th
1. SINGLE DX										
0–19 Years	0									
20–34	1	1.0	0	1	1	1	1	1	1	1
35–49	1	3.0	0	3	3	3	3	3	3	3
50–64	1	6.0	0	6	6	6	6	6	6	6
65+	2	4.4	<1	4	4	4	5	5	5	5
2. MULTIPLE DX										
0–19 Years	0									
20–34	2	11.5	86	5	5	5	19	19	19	19
35–49	14	7.0	19	2	4	6	10	11	20	20
50–64	33	8.0	31	3	5	6	10	16	23	27
65+	109	8.0	30	3	4	7	10	15	16	25
TOTAL SINGLE DX	**5**	**3.9**	**3**	**1**	**3**	**4**	**5**	**6**	**6**	**6**
TOTAL MULTIPLE DX	**158**	**8.0**	**30**	**3**	**4**	**7**	**10**	**15**	**18**	**25**
TOTAL										
0–19 Years	0									
20–34	3	8.0	80	1	1	5	19	19	19	19
35–49	15	6.8	19	2	4	6	10	11	11	20
50–64	34	7.9	30	3	5	6	10	16	23	27
65+	111	8.0	30	3	4	7	10	15	16	25
GRAND TOTAL	**163**	**7.9**	**29**	**3**	**4**	**6**	**10**	**15**	**18**	**25**

51.03: CHOLECYSTOSTOMY NEC

Type of Patients	Observed Patients	Avg. Stay	Vari-ance	Percentiles 10th	25th	50th	75th	90th	95th	99th
1. SINGLE DX										
0–19 Years	0									
20–34	0									
35–49	0									
50–64	2	3.0	0	3	3	3	3	3	3	3
65+	0									
2. MULTIPLE DX										
0–19 Years	0									
20–34	3	8.7	15	5	5	7	13	13	13	13
35–49	3	5.0	2	4	4	4	7	7	7	7
50–64	20	9.8	33	4	5	8	12	16	19	26
65+	41	10.1	34	3	6	9	14	15	19	37
TOTAL SINGLE DX	**2**	**3.0**	**0**	**3**	**3**	**3**	**3**	**3**	**3**	**3**
TOTAL MULTIPLE DX	**67**	**9.6**	**32**	**3**	**5**	**8**	**14**	**16**	**19**	**26**
TOTAL										
0–19 Years	0									
20–34	3	8.7	15	5	5	7	13	13	13	13
35–49	3	5.0	2	4	4	4	7	7	7	7
50–64	22	9.2	34	3	5	8	12	16	19	26
65+	41	10.1	34	3	6	9	14	15	19	37
GRAND TOTAL	**69**	**9.4**	**32**	**3**	**5**	**8**	**14**	**15**	**19**	**26**

51.1: BILIARY TRACT DXTIC PX

Type of Patients	Observed Patients	Avg. Stay	Vari-ance	Percentiles						
				10th	25th	50th	75th	90th	95th	99th
1. SINGLE DX										
0–19 Years	6	2.4	2	1	1	2	3	5	5	5
20–34	45	2.7	4	1	1	2	4	6	7	9
35–49	34	2.9	3	1	2	2	4	5	7	8
50–64	25	2.7	3	1	2	2	4	5	6	6
65+	6	2.4	<1	1	1	3	3	3	3	3
2. MULTIPLE DX										
0–19 Years	50	6.3	54	2	2	3	7	14	28	32
20–34	285	4.6	15	2	2	3	6	9	12	19
35–49	540	5.7	33	2	3	4	6	10	16	33
50–64	760	5.7	21	2	3	4	7	11	15	25
65+	1,328	6.0	21	2	3	5	8	12	14	21
TOTAL SINGLE DX	**116**	**2.7**	**3**	**1**	**1**	**2**	**3**	**5**	**6**	**8**
TOTAL MULTIPLE DX	**2,963**	**5.8**	**23**	**2**	**3**	**5**	**7**	**11**	**14**	**24**
TOTAL										
0–19 Years	56	5.9	51	1	2	3	7	10	28	32
20–34	330	4.3	13	1	2	3	5	8	11	19
35–49	574	5.5	32	2	3	4	6	10	15	33
50–64	785	5.6	21	2	3	4	7	11	15	23
65+	1,334	6.0	21	2	3	5	8	12	14	21
GRAND TOTAL	**3,079**	**5.7**	**23**	**2**	**3**	**4**	**7**	**11**	**14**	**24**

51.10: ERCP

Type of Patients	Observed Patients	Avg. Stay	Vari-ance	Percentiles						
				10th	25th	50th	75th	90th	95th	99th
1. SINGLE DX										
0–19 Years	6	2.4	2	1	1	2	3	5	5	5
20–34	42	2.8	4	1	1	2	4	6	7	9
35–49	30	3.0	3	1	2	2	4	5	7	8
50–64	24	2.7	3	1	2	2	4	5	6	6
65+	5	2.6	<1	1	3	3	3	3	3	3
2. MULTIPLE DX										
0–19 Years	48	6.4	56	2	2	3	7	14	30	32
20–34	276	4.6	14	2	2	3	6	9	12	20
35–49	495	5.7	34	2	3	4	6	10	15	33
50–64	670	5.8	23	2	3	4	7	11	15	26
65+	1,089	6.1	21	2	3	5	8	12	14	21
TOTAL SINGLE DX	**107**	**2.8**	**3**	**1**	**1**	**2**	**4**	**5**	**6**	**8**
TOTAL MULTIPLE DX	**2,578**	**5.8**	**24**	**2**	**3**	**4**	**7**	**11**	**15**	**25**
TOTAL										
0–19 Years	54	6.0	52	1	2	3	6	10	28	32
20–34	318	4.3	13	1	2	3	6	8	11	18
35–49	525	5.6	33	2	3	4	6	10	15	33
50–64	694	5.7	22	2	3	4	7	11	15	26
65+	1,094	6.1	21	2	3	5	8	12	14	21
GRAND TOTAL	**2,685**	**5.7**	**24**	**2**	**3**	**4**	**7**	**11**	**14**	**24**

51.11: ERC

Type of Patients	Observed Patients	Avg. Stay	Vari-ance	Percentiles						
				10th	25th	50th	75th	90th	95th	99th
1. SINGLE DX										
0–19 Years	0									
20–34	3	1.7	<1	1	1	2	2	2	2	2
35–49	1	2.0	0	2	2	2	2	2	2	2
50–64	0									
65+	0									
2. MULTIPLE DX										
0–19 Years	1	2.0	0	2	2	2	2	2	2	2
20–34	7	4.3	29	1	2	2	4	19	19	19
35–49	16	4.7	22	1	2	4	5	11	21	21
50–64	17	5.5	11	2	2	6	7	10	10	14
65+	49	6.1	23	2	2	4	8	12	16	21
TOTAL SINGLE DX	**4**	**1.8**	**<1**	**1**	**1**	**2**	**2**	**2**	**2**	**2**
TOTAL MULTIPLE DX	**90**	**5.6**	**20**	**2**	**2**	**4**	**7**	**12**	**16**	**21**
TOTAL										
0–19 Years	1	2.0	0	2	2	2	2	2	2	2
20–34	10	3.5	21	1	2	2	3	5	19	19
35–49	17	4.5	21	1	2	4	5	11	21	21
50–64	17	5.5	11	2	2	6	7	10	10	14
65+	49	6.1	23	2	2	4	8	12	16	21
GRAND TOTAL	**94**	**5.4**	**20**	**2**	**2**	**4**	**7**	**12**	**16**	**21**

51.14: CLSD BD/SPHINCT ODDI BX

Type of Patients	Observed Patients	Avg. Stay	Vari-ance	Percentiles						
				10th	25th	50th	75th	90th	95th	99th
1. SINGLE DX										
0–19 Years	0									
20–34	0									
35–49	3	2.3	<1	2	2	2	3	3	3	3
50–64	1	2.0	0	2	2	2	2	2	2	2
65+	1	1.0	0	1	1	1	1	1	1	1
2. MULTIPLE DX										
0–19 Years	0									
20–34	2	4.1	8	2	2	6	6	6	6	6
35–49	20	7.1	25	2	3	6	10	16	17	19
50–64	60	5.0	12	2	2	5	6	9	14	18
65+	165	5.4	16	2	3	5	7	11	13	18
TOTAL SINGLE DX	**5**	**1.9**	**<1**	**1**	**1**	**2**	**2**	**3**	**3**	**3**
TOTAL MULTIPLE DX	**247**	**5.4**	**15**	**2**	**2**	**5**	**7**	**11**	**14**	**18**
TOTAL										
0–19 Years	0									
20–34	2	4.1	8	2	2	6	6	6	6	6
35–49	23	6.6	24	2	2	5	10	16	17	19
50–64	61	5.0	12	2	2	4	6	9	14	18
65+	166	5.4	16	2	2	5	7	11	13	18
GRAND TOTAL	**252**	**5.4**	**15**	**2**	**2**	**5**	**7**	**10**	**14**	**18**

51.2: CHOLECYSTECTOMY

Type of Patients	Observed Patients	Avg. Stay	Vari-ance	Percentiles						
				10th	25th	50th	75th	90th	95th	99th
1. SINGLE DX										
0–19 Years	379	2.0	2	1	1	2	2	4	5	7
20–34	3,120	2.1	2	1	1	2	3	4	5	8
35–49	2,314	2.0	2	1	1	2	2	4	5	8
50–64	1,271	2.0	2	1	1	1	3	4	5	8
65+	451	2.2	5	1	1	1	3	5	6	10
2. MULTIPLE DX										
0–19 Years	829	3.5	10	1	2	3	4	6	8	21
20–34	8,121	3.3	8	1	2	3	4	6	8	14
35–49	9,582	3.6	11	1	2	3	4	7	9	16
50–64	10,662	4.1	17	1	2	3	5	8	11	21
65+	14,297	5.6	24	1	2	4	7	11	15	24
TOTAL SINGLE DX	**7,535**	**2.0**	**2**	**1**	**1**	**2**	**2**	**4**	**5**	**8**
TOTAL MULTIPLE DX	**43,491**	**4.4**	**18**	**1**	**2**	**3**	**5**	**9**	**12**	**21**
TOTAL										
0–19 Years	1,208	3.0	8	1	1	2	4	6	7	17
20–34	11,241	2.9	7	1	1	2	4	6	7	13
35–49	11,896	3.3	10	1	1	2	4	6	8	15
50–64	11,933	3.9	16	1	2	3	5	8	11	20
65+	14,748	5.5	24	1	2	4	7	11	15	23
GRAND TOTAL	**51,026**	**4.0**	**16**	**1**	**2**	**3**	**5**	**8**	**11**	**20**

51.22: CHOLECYSTECTOMY NOS

Type of Patients	Observed Patients	Avg. Stay	Vari-ance	Percentiles						
				10th	25th	50th	75th	90th	95th	99th
1. SINGLE DX										
0–19 Years	10	2.8	13	1	1	1	3	7	7	18
20–34	74	4.3	9	1	2	3	6	9	9	14
35–49	76	4.0	6	1	2	4	5	7	9	13
50–64	64	3.9	5	2	2	4	5	6	8	13
65+	30	6.0	19	2	3	5	7	10	18	18
2. MULTIPLE DX										
0–19 Years	61	4.8	4	2	3	5	6	8	8	10
20–34	729	5.6	16	2	3	5	7	9	13	23
35–49	1,305	5.9	23	2	3	5	7	10	13	24
50–64	1,954	6.6	27	3	3	5	8	12	15	30
65+	3,237	8.2	34	3	5	7	10	15	19	29
TOTAL SINGLE DX	**254**	**4.3**	**10**	**1**	**2**	**4**	**6**	**7**	**9**	**18**
TOTAL MULTIPLE DX	**7,286**	**7.1**	**30**	**3**	**4**	**6**	**9**	**13**	**17**	**28**
TOTAL										
0–19 Years	71	4.4	7	1	2	4	6	7	8	10
20–34	803	5.4	16	2	3	5	7	9	13	23
35–49	1,381	5.8	22	2	3	5	7	10	13	24
50–64	2,018	6.5	26	2	3	5	8	11	15	28
65+	3,267	8.2	34	3	5	7	10	15	19	29
GRAND TOTAL	**7,540**	**7.1**	**29**	**3**	**4**	**6**	**8**	**13**	**17**	**28**

51.23: LAPSCP CHOLECYSTECTOMY

Type of Patients	Observed Patients	Avg. Stay	Vari-ance	Percentiles						
				10th	25th	50th	75th	90th	95th	99th
1. SINGLE DX										
0–19 Years	369	2.0	2	1	1	2	2	4	5	7
20–34	3,041	2.0	2	1	1	2	2	4	4	8
35–49	2,234	1.9	2	1	1	1	2	3	4	7
50–64	1,206	1.9	2	1	1	1	2	4	5	8
65+	420	1.9	3	1	1	1	2	4	5	7
2. MULTIPLE DX										
0–19 Years	766	3.4	11	1	2	3	4	6	8	21
20–34	7,376	3.0	6	1	1	2	4	6	7	13
35–49	8,265	3.2	8	1	1	2	4	6	8	14
50–64	8,682	3.5	13	1	1	3	4	7	9	18
65+	11,025	4.8	19	1	2	4	6	10	13	21
TOTAL SINGLE DX	**7,270**	**2.0**	**2**	**1**	**1**	**2**	**2**	**4**	**5**	**7**
TOTAL MULTIPLE DX	**36,114**	**3.8**	**13**	**1**	**2**	**3**	**5**	**7**	**10**	**18**
TOTAL										
0–19 Years	1,135	2.9	8	1	1	2	4	5	7	17
20–34	10,417	2.7	5	1	1	2	3	5	7	12
35–49	10,499	2.9	7	1	1	2	4	6	7	14
50–64	9,888	3.4	12	1	1	2	4	7	9	17
65+	11,445	4.7	18	1	2	4	6	10	13	21
GRAND TOTAL	**43,384**	**3.5**	**12**	**1**	**1**	**2**	**4**	**7**	**9**	**17**

51.3: BILIARY TRACT ANAST

Type of Patients	Observed Patients	Avg. Stay	Vari-ance	Percentiles						
				10th	25th	50th	75th	90th	95th	99th
1. SINGLE DX										
0–19 Years	9	7.7	33	4	5	6	6	22	22	22
20–34	3	5.7	7	3	3	5	9	9	9	9
35–49	0									
50–64	4	9.8	48	5	6	8	8	21	21	21
65+	0									
2. MULTIPLE DX										
0–19 Years	42	11.4	48	5	7	8	17	21	29	30
20–34	25	9.4	21	4	5	9	12	17	17	18
35–49	74	11.1	70	4	6	8	13	23	28	47
50–64	157	10.8	42	5	7	9	13	22	25	30
65+	269	11.7	36	6	7	10	14	19	23	37
TOTAL SINGLE DX	**16**	**7.5**	**30**	**3**	**5**	**6**	**6**	**21**	**22**	**22**
TOTAL MULTIPLE DX	**567**	**11.3**	**42**	**5**	**7**	**9**	**14**	**20**	**24**	**32**
TOTAL										
0–19 Years	51	10.7	47	5	6	7	13	21	29	30
20–34	28	8.8	21	4	4	9	12	17	17	18
35–49	74	11.1	70	4	6	8	13	23	28	47
50–64	161	10.8	42	5	6	9	13	22	25	30
65+	269	11.7	36	6	7	10	14	19	23	37
GRAND TOTAL	**583**	**11.1**	**42**	**5**	**7**	**9**	**14**	**20**	**24**	**32**

51.32: GB-TO-INTESTINE ANAST

Type of Patients	Observed Patients	Avg. Stay	Vari-ance	Percentiles 10th	25th	50th	75th	90th	95th	99th
1. SINGLE DX										
0–19 Years	1	3.0	0	3	3	3	3	3	3	3
20–34	2	4.0	1	3	3	4	5	5	5	5
35–49	0									
50–64	0									
65+	0									
2. MULTIPLE DX										
0–19 Years	6	12.1	35	7	7	9	19	19	24	24
20–34	1	15.0	0	15	15	15	15	15	15	15
35–49	9	12.0	76	3	3	11	18	28	28	28
50–64	28	13.5	46	7	9	12	15	25	27	30
65+	48	11.7	26	6	9	11	13	18	22	32
TOTAL SINGLE DX	3	3.7	1	3	3	3	5	5	5	5
TOTAL MULTIPLE DX	92	12.2	35	6	9	11	15	21	24	30
TOTAL										
0–19 Years	7	11.3	39	6	7	9	19	19	24	24
20–34	3	7.7	31	3	3	5	15	15	15	15
35–49	9	12.0	76	3	3	11	18	28	28	28
50–64	28	13.5	46	7	9	12	15	25	27	30
65+	48	11.7	26	6	9	11	13	18	22	32
GRAND TOTAL	95	11.8	37	5	8	11	14	21	24	30

51.36: CHOLEDOCHOENTEROSTOMY

Type of Patients	Observed Patients	Avg. Stay	Vari-ance	Percentiles 10th	25th	50th	75th	90th	95th	99th
1. SINGLE DX										
0–19 Years	0									
20–34	0									
35–49	0									
50–64	3	6.6	2	5	5	6	8	8	8	8
65+	0									
2. MULTIPLE DX										
0–19 Years	6	9.3	28	5	5	8	13	21	21	21
20–34	13	9.5	29	4	4	9	13	17	18	18
35–49	42	9.6	42	5	6	8	10	20	26	37
50–64	82	10.1	36	5	6	8	12	22	24	26
65+	181	12.0	42	6	8	11	14	20	24	37
TOTAL SINGLE DX	3	6.6	2	5	5	6	8	8	8	8
TOTAL MULTIPLE DX	324	11.2	41	5	7	9	14	20	24	37
TOTAL										
0–19 Years	6	9.3	28	5	5	8	13	21	21	21
20–34	13	9.5	29	4	4	9	13	17	18	18
35–49	42	9.6	42	5	6	8	10	20	26	37
50–64	85	10.0	35	5	6	8	12	22	24	26
65+	181	12.0	42	6	8	11	14	20	24	37
GRAND TOTAL	327	11.1	41	5	7	9	14	20	24	37

51.37: HEPATIC DUCT-GI ANAST

Type of Patients	Observed Patients	Avg. Stay	Vari-ance	Percentiles 10th	25th	50th	75th	90th	95th	99th
1. SINGLE DX										
0–19 Years	7	8.2	35	5	6	6	6	22	22	22
20–34	1	9.0	0	9	9	9	9	9	9	9
35–49	0									
50–64	1	21.0	0	21	21	21	21	21	21	21
65+	0									
2. MULTIPLE DX										
0–19 Years	23	10.4	39	5	7	7	13	18	29	29
20–34	11	8.1	6	4	7	9	9	12	12	12
35–49	20	14.3	133	4	6	10	17	30	47	47
50–64	44	10.8	49	5	6	7	13	19	30	30
65+	35	9.6	18	6	7	9	10	15	21	22
TOTAL SINGLE DX	9	8.8	36	5	6	6	9	22	22	22
TOTAL MULTIPLE DX	133	10.6	46	5	7	8	13	18	29	30
TOTAL										
0–19 Years	30	9.8	39	5	6	7	11	20	22	29
20–34	12	8.3	5	4	7	9	9	12	12	12
35–49	20	14.3	133	4	6	10	17	30	47	47
50–64	45	11.0	50	5	6	9	13	21	30	30
65+	35	9.6	18	6	7	9	10	15	21	22
GRAND TOTAL	142	10.4	45	5	6	8	12	20	28	30

51.4: INC BILE DUCT OBSTR

Type of Patients	Observed Patients	Avg. Stay	Vari-ance	Percentiles 10th	25th	50th	75th	90th	95th	99th
1. SINGLE DX										
0–19 Years	1	9.0	0	9	9	9	9	9	9	9
20–34	2	5.0	0	5	5	5	5	5	5	5
35–49	4	6.6	16	1	1	9	9	9	9	9
50–64	4	6.9	34	2	2	4	7	16	16	16
65+	1	1.0	0	1	1	1	1	1	1	1
2. MULTIPLE DX										
0–19 Years	3	4.7	23	2	2	2	7	14	14	14
20–34	16	7.6	23	3	3	6	10	16	17	17
35–49	32	7.2	45	2	3	5	8	14	28	30
50–64	43	8.8	41	3	5	7	9	15	22	34
65+	123	9.7	63	4	5	7	13	17	24	30
TOTAL SINGLE DX	12	6.1	17	1	2	5	9	9	16	16
TOTAL MULTIPLE DX	217	9.0	54	3	4	7	12	17	22	30
TOTAL										
0–19 Years	4	5.2	22	2	2	2	9	14	14	14
20–34	18	7.3	21	3	4	6	10	16	17	17
35–49	36	7.1	41	2	3	5	8	10	28	30
50–64	47	8.6	41	2	5	7	9	16	22	34
65+	124	9.7	63	4	5	7	13	17	24	30
GRAND TOTAL	229	8.8	53	3	4	7	11	17	22	30

51.43: INSERT CBD-HEP TUBE

Type of Patients	Observed Patients	Avg. Stay	Vari-ance	Percentiles 10th	25th	50th	75th	90th	95th	99th
1. SINGLE DX										
0–19 Years	0									
20–34	0									
35–49	0									
50–64	1	2.0	0	2	2	2	2	2	2	2
65+	1	1.0	0	1	1	1	1	1	1	1
2. MULTIPLE DX										
0–19 Years	1	14.0	0	14	14	14	14	14	14	14
20–34	6	7.1	18	4	5	6	7	16	16	16
35–49	16	6.9	43	2	3	6	7	14	28	28
50–64	25	9.3	38	5	6	7	10	18	22	30
65+	46	9.5	95	4	4	7	13	15	21	87
TOTAL SINGLE DX	**2**	**1.5**	**<1**	**1**	**1**	**1**	**2**	**2**	**2**	**2**
TOTAL MULTIPLE DX	**94**	**9.0**	**70**	**3**	**4**	**7**	**12**	**15**	**21**	**30**
TOTAL										
0–19 Years	1	14.0	0	14	14	14	14	14	14	14
20–34	6	7.1	18	4	5	6	7	16	16	16
35–49	16	6.9	43	2	3	6	7	14	28	28
50–64	26	9.1	38	2	6	7	10	18	22	30
65+	47	9.3	95	4	4	7	13	15	21	87
GRAND TOTAL	**96**	**8.9**	**70**	**3**	**4**	**7**	**12**	**15**	**21**	**30**

51.5: OTHER BILE DUCT INCISION

Type of Patients	Observed Patients	Avg. Stay	Vari-ance	Percentiles 10th	25th	50th	75th	90th	95th	99th
1. SINGLE DX										
0–19 Years	1	2.0	0	2	2	2	2	2	2	2
20–34	2	2.0	2	1	1	3	3	3	3	3
35–49	2	5.0	32	1	1	1	10	10	10	10
50–64	0									
65+	0									
2. MULTIPLE DX										
0–19 Years	4	4.5	<1	3	5	5	5	5	5	5
20–34	10	6.0	8	2	5	6	8	9	13	13
35–49	16	5.1	15	2	3	4	5	9	14	16
50–64	32	6.1	45	1	2	4	8	12	19	40
65+	59	8.7	37	3	5	7	9	19	19	29
TOTAL SINGLE DX	**5**	**3.0**	**10**	**1**	**1**	**2**	**3**	**10**	**10**	**10**
TOTAL MULTIPLE DX	**121**	**7.2**	**35**	**2**	**4**	**6**	**8**	**14**	**19**	**34**
TOTAL										
0–19 Years	5	3.8	2	2	2	5	5	5	5	5
20–34	12	5.5	9	1	3	6	8	9	13	13
35–49	18	5.1	15	1	2	4	7	10	14	16
50–64	32	6.1	45	1	2	4	8	12	19	40
65+	59	8.7	37	3	5	7	9	19	19	29
GRAND TOTAL	**126**	**7.1**	**34**	**2**	**3**	**6**	**8**	**14**	**19**	**34**

51.6: LOC EXC BD & S OF O LES

Type of Patients	Observed Patients	Avg. Stay	Vari-ance	Percentiles 10th	25th	50th	75th	90th	95th	99th
1. SINGLE DX										
0–19 Years	5	6.4	<1	6	6	6	7	7	7	7
20–34	2	2.8	7	1	1	1	5	5	5	5
35–49	4	2.2	2	1	1	2	3	4	4	4
50–64	3	4.2	2	3	3	4	6	6	6	6
65+	1	2.0	0	2	2	2	2	2	2	2
2. MULTIPLE DX										
0–19 Years	11	7.4	10	4	6	7	9	11	11	16
20–34	11	4.9	7	2	3	5	6	7	13	13
35–49	19	6.3	22	2	3	6	8	9	19	20
50–64	31	6.9	29	1	4	6	8	12	21	29
65+	50	7.6	15	4	5	7	9	13	14	23
TOTAL SINGLE DX	**15**	**4.5**	**5**	**1**	**3**	**6**	**6**	**7**	**7**	**7**
TOTAL MULTIPLE DX	**122**	**7.0**	**18**	**2**	**5**	**6**	**9**	**11**	**14**	**23**
TOTAL										
0–19 Years	16	7.1	7	4	6	7	9	11	11	16
20–34	13	4.7	7	1	3	5	5	7	7	13
35–49	23	5.6	21	2	2	5	7	9	19	20
50–64	34	6.7	27	1	4	6	8	12	13	29
65+	51	7.5	15	4	5	7	9	11	14	23
GRAND TOTAL	**137**	**6.7**	**17**	**2**	**4**	**6**	**8**	**11**	**13**	**22**

51.7: REPAIR OF BILE DUCTS

Type of Patients	Observed Patients	Avg. Stay	Vari-ance	Percentiles 10th	25th	50th	75th	90th	95th	99th
1. SINGLE DX										
0–19 Years	0									
20–34	1	4.0	0	4	4	4	4	4	4	4
35–49	2	3.6	3	2	2	5	5	5	5	5
50–64	0									
65+	0									
2. MULTIPLE DX										
0–19 Years	3	7.0	10	4	4	6	11	11	11	11
20–34	13	5.0	5	2	3	5	7	9	10	10
35–49	21	6.0	17	2	3	6	7	9	10	25
50–64	32	11.0	106	3	6	8	12	22	35	53
65+	44	11.2	59	6	7	9	11	25	30	41
TOTAL SINGLE DX	**3**	**3.8**	**2**	**2**	**2**	**4**	**5**	**5**	**5**	**5**
TOTAL MULTIPLE DX	**113**	**9.4**	**62**	**3**	**5**	**8**	**10**	**16**	**27**	**53**
TOTAL										
0–19 Years	3	7.0	10	4	4	6	11	11	11	11
20–34	14	4.9	5	2	3	5	5	9	10	10
35–49	23	5.8	16	2	3	6	7	9	10	25
50–64	32	11.0	106	3	6	8	12	22	35	53
65+	44	11.2	59	6	7	9	11	25	30	41
GRAND TOTAL	**116**	**9.3**	**62**	**3**	**5**	**7**	**10**	**16**	**27**	**53**

51.8: SPHINCTER OF ODDI OP NEC

Type of Patients	Observed Patients	Avg. Stay	Vari-ance	Percentiles						
				10th	25th	50th	75th	90th	95th	99th
1. SINGLE DX										
0–19 Years	16	2.3	2	1	1	2	3	4	6	6
20–34	153	2.6	3	1	2	2	3	4	5	11
35–49	91	2.9	3	1	2	3	3	5	6	11
50–64	83	3.0	7	1	1	2	4	7	8	16
65+	58	2.3	2	1	1	2	3	5	5	7
2. MULTIPLE DX										
0–19 Years	74	6.6	42	2	3	4	7	17	26	28
20–34	764	4.2	13	1	2	3	5	8	11	18
35–49	1,035	4.8	19	2	2	4	6	9	12	23
50–64	1,413	5.2	20	2	2	4	7	10	14	22
65+	3,058	5.5	20	2	3	4	7	10	13	23
TOTAL SINGLE DX	**401**	**2.7**	**4**	**1**	**1**	**2**	**3**	**5**	**6**	**10**
TOTAL MULTIPLE DX	**6,344**	**5.2**	**20**	**2**	**2**	**4**	**6**	**10**	**13**	**23**
TOTAL										
0–19 Years	90	5.9	38	1	2	4	7	15	22	28
20–34	917	4.0	12	1	2	3	5	7	10	18
35–49	1,126	4.7	18	1	2	3	5	9	12	22
50–64	1,496	5.1	19	1	2	4	6	10	14	22
65+	3,116	5.4	20	2	3	4	7	10	13	23
GRAND TOTAL	**6,745**	**5.0**	**19**	**2**	**2**	**4**	**6**	**10**	**13**	**23**

51.84: ENDO AMPULLA & BD DILAT

Type of Patients	Observed Patients	Avg. Stay	Vari-ance	Percentiles						
				10th	25th	50th	75th	90th	95th	99th
1. SINGLE DX										
0–19 Years	0									
20–34	1	2.0	0	2	2	2	2	2	2	2
35–49	1	2.0	0	2	2	2	2	2	2	2
50–64	2	1.6	<1	1	1	2	2	2	2	2
65+	0									
2. MULTIPLE DX										
0–19 Years	1	22.0	0	22	22	22	22	22	22	22
20–34	24	3.5	3	1	2	3	4	6	6	9
35–49	34	3.7	9	1	1	3	5	9	11	12
50–64	79	4.4	12	1	2	3	6	9	12	20
65+	112	4.6	14	1	2	4	6	9	12	22
TOTAL SINGLE DX	**4**	**1.8**	**<1**	**1**	**2**	**2**	**2**	**2**	**2**	**2**
TOTAL MULTIPLE DX	**250**	**4.4**	**13**	**1**	**2**	**3**	**6**	**9**	**12**	**22**
TOTAL										
0–19 Years	1	22.0	0	22	22	22	22	22	22	22
20–34	25	3.5	3	1	2	3	4	6	6	9
35–49	35	3.6	9	1	2	3	5	9	9	12
50–64	81	4.3	12	1	2	3	6	9	12	20
65+	112	4.6	14	1	2	4	6	9	12	22
GRAND TOTAL	**254**	**4.4**	**13**	**1**	**2**	**3**	**6**	**9**	**12**	**22**

51.85: ENDO SPHINCTOT/PAPILLOT

Type of Patients	Observed Patients	Avg. Stay	Vari-ance	Percentiles						
				10th	25th	50th	75th	90th	95th	99th
1. SINGLE DX										
0–19 Years	8	2.3	<1	1	2	2	3	3	4	4
20–34	82	2.8	4	1	2	2	3	5	6	13
35–49	52	2.7	2	1	2	2	3	5	6	10
50–64	45	3.1	6	1	1	2	5	8	8	8
65+	29	2.3	2	1	1	2	3	4	5	5
2. MULTIPLE DX										
0–19 Years	50	5.8	25	2	3	4	7	9	20	28
20–34	460	4.4	14	1	2	3	5	9	12	18
35–49	624	4.6	16	2	2	4	6	9	12	21
50–64	761	5.2	21	2	2	4	6	10	14	28
65+	1,575	5.4	21	2	3	4	7	10	13	24
TOTAL SINGLE DX	**216**	**2.7**	**4**	**1**	**1**	**2**	**3**	**5**	**7**	**10**
TOTAL MULTIPLE DX	**3,470**	**5.1**	**19**	**2**	**2**	**4**	**6**	**10**	**13**	**24**
TOTAL										
0–19 Years	58	5.4	24	2	2	4	7	9	20	28
20–34	542	4.2	13	1	2	3	5	8	11	18
35–49	676	4.5	15	2	2	3	5	8	11	19
50–64	806	5.1	21	1	2	4	6	10	14	27
65+	1,604	5.4	20	2	3	4	7	10	13	24
GRAND TOTAL	**3,686**	**5.0**	**19**	**2**	**2**	**4**	**6**	**9**	**12**	**23**

51.87: ENDO INSERT BD STENT

Type of Patients	Observed Patients	Avg. Stay	Vari-ance	Percentiles						
				10th	25th	50th	75th	90th	95th	99th
1. SINGLE DX										
0–19 Years	4	2.8	5	1	1	1	4	6	6	6
20–34	13	2.9	1	2	2	3	4	5	5	5
35–49	12	3.2	5	1	2	3	3	7	9	9
50–64	11	3.8	20	1	1	2	3	10	16	16
65+	14	2.4	3	1	1	2	3	5	7	7
2. MULTIPLE DX										
0–19 Years	11	9.6	98	2	3	3	17	26	26	26
20–34	104	4.8	15	2	2	4	6	8	13	17
35–49	187	6.0	31	2	3	4	7	11	14	26
50–64	303	5.5	19	2	3	4	7	11	15	21
65+	645	5.8	20	2	3	5	7	11	14	23
TOTAL SINGLE DX	**54**	**3.0**	**6**	**1**	**2**	**2**	**3**	**5**	**7**	**16**
TOTAL MULTIPLE DX	**1,250**	**5.8**	**22**	**2**	**3**	**4**	**7**	**11**	**15**	**26**
TOTAL										
0–19 Years	15	8.4	88	1	3	3	8	26	26	26
20–34	117	4.5	14	2	2	3	5	8	13	17
35–49	199	5.9	30	2	3	4	7	11	14	26
50–64	314	5.5	19	2	3	4	7	11	15	21
65+	659	5.8	19	2	3	4	7	11	14	23
GRAND TOTAL	**1,304**	**5.7**	**22**	**2**	**3**	**4**	**7**	**11**	**14**	**26**

51.88: ENDO RMVL BILIARY STONE

Type of Patients	Observed Patients	Avg. Stay	Vari-ance	10th	25th	50th	75th	90th	95th	99th
1. SINGLE DX										
0–19 Years	4	1.8	2	1	1	1	2	4	4	4
20–34	56	2.3	2	1	2	2	3	4	4	10
35–49	26	3.1	4	1	2	3	4	5	5	11
50–64	24	2.5	3	1	1	2	3	5	7	7
65+	14	1.9	2	1	1	1	3	4	5	5
2. MULTIPLE DX										
0–19 Years	12	5.2	24	1	2	4	5	15	15	15
20–34	163	3.3	7	1	2	3	4	6	8	15
35–49	174	3.9	13	1	2	3	5	7	9	19
50–64	247	4.4	12	1	2	3	6	9	10	14
65+	677	5.0	17	2	2	4	6	9	13	22
TOTAL SINGLE DX	**124**	**2.5**	**3**	**1**	**1**	**2**	**3**	**4**	**5**	**10**
TOTAL MULTIPLE DX	**1,273**	**4.5**	**15**	**1**	**2**	**3**	**6**	**9**	**12**	**20**
TOTAL										
0–19 Years	16	4.4	20	1	1	3	4	15	15	15
20–34	219	3.1	6	1	2	2	4	5	7	15
35–49	200	3.8	12	1	2	3	5	7	9	19
50–64	271	4.3	12	1	2	3	6	8	10	14
65+	691	4.9	17	1	2	4	6	9	13	22
GRAND TOTAL	**1,397**	**4.4**	**14**	**1**	**2**	**3**	**5**	**8**	**11**	**20**

51.9: OTHER BILIARY TRACT OPS

Type of Patients	Observed Patients	Avg. Stay	Vari-ance	10th	25th	50th	75th	90th	95th	99th
1. SINGLE DX										
0–19 Years	0									
20–34	2	4.0	0	4	4	4	4	4	4	4
35–49	2	7.5	49	1	1	12	12	12	12	12
50–64	1	3.0	0	3	3	3	3	3	3	3
65+	2	1.9	2	1	1	1	3	3	3	3
2. MULTIPLE DX										
0–19 Years	8	7.1	43	1	1	3	12	17	17	17
20–34	23	7.0	20	2	4	7	8	15	16	17
35–49	63	7.3	31	2	3	5	10	15	18	24
50–64	129	6.4	32	2	3	5	8	13	16	35
65+	250	7.4	39	2	3	6	9	18	21	26
TOTAL SINGLE DX	**7**	**4.2**	**13**	**1**	**3**	**4**	**4**	**12**	**12**	**12**
TOTAL MULTIPLE DX	**473**	**7.1**	**36**	**2**	**3**	**5**	**9**	**15**	**20**	**25**
TOTAL										
0–19 Years	8	7.1	43	1	1	3	12	17	17	17
20–34	25	6.7	19	2	4	5	8	14	16	17
35–49	65	7.3	31	2	3	5	10	14	18	24
50–64	130	6.4	32	2	3	4	8	13	16	35
65+	252	7.4	39	2	3	5	9	18	21	26
GRAND TOTAL	**480**	**7.1**	**35**	**2**	**3**	**5**	**9**	**15**	**19**	**25**

51.98: PERC OP ON BIL TRACT NEC

Type of Patients	Observed Patients	Avg. Stay	Vari-ance	10th	25th	50th	75th	90th	95th	99th
1. SINGLE DX										
0–19 Years	0									
20–34	1	4.0	0	4	4	4	4	4	4	4
35–49	2	7.5	49	1	1	12	12	12	12	12
50–64	1	3.0	0	3	3	3	3	3	3	3
65+	1	1.0	0	1	1	1	1	1	1	1
2. MULTIPLE DX										
0–19 Years	7	6.3	45	1	1	3	10	17	17	17
20–34	17	7.2	19	3	4	7	8	15	16	17
35–49	47	8.1	35	2	3	7	13	16	19	24
50–64	111	6.5	34	2	3	4	8	13	16	35
65+	210	6.9	32	2	3	5	9	14	19	26
TOTAL SINGLE DX	**5**	**4.5**	**20**	**1**	**1**	**3**	**4**	**12**	**12**	**12**
TOTAL MULTIPLE DX	**392**	**6.9**	**33**	**2**	**3**	**5**	**9**	**15**	**18**	**25**
TOTAL										
0–19 Years	7	6.3	45	1	1	3	10	17	17	17
20–34	18	7.0	19	3	4	7	8	15	16	17
35–49	49	8.1	35	2	3	7	12	16	19	24
50–64	112	6.4	33	2	3	4	8	13	16	35
65+	211	6.9	32	2	3	5	9	14	18	26
GRAND TOTAL	**397**	**6.9**	**33**	**2**	**3**	**5**	**9**	**14**	**18**	**25**

52.0: PANCREATOTOMY

Type of Patients	Observed Patients	Avg. Stay	Vari-ance	10th	25th	50th	75th	90th	95th	99th
1. SINGLE DX										
0–19 Years	2	5.5	4	5	5	5	5	5	12	12
20–34	1	11.0	0	11	11	11	11	11	11	11
35–49	1	9.0	0	9	9	9	9	9	9	9
50–64	3	4.0	12	1	1	3	8	8	8	8
65+	1	7.0	0	7	7	7	7	7	7	7
2 MULTIPLE DX										
0–19 Years	5	32.6	74	22	23	36	36	36	47	47
20–34	34	15.3	225	4	6	8	20	32	43	>99
35–49	66	18.0	304	4	8	12	23	39	39	95
50–64	70	12.2	65	4	7	10	17	22	27	49
65+	43	17.6	249	6	8	12	25	36	60	>99
TOTAL SINGLE DX	**8**	**6.1**	**7**	**3**	**5**	**5**	**7**	**11**	**11**	**12**
TOTAL MULTIPLE DX	**218**	**16.6**	**216**	**4**	**7**	**12**	**22**	**36**	**39**	**95**
TOTAL										
0–19 Years	7	22.0	225	5	5	22	36	36	47	47
20–34	35	15.1	218	4	6	9	20	32	43	>99
35–49	67	17.9	302	4	8	12	23	39	39	95
50–64	73	12.0	66	3	6	10	17	22	27	49
65+	44	17.4	246	6	8	11	25	36	60	>99
GRAND TOTAL	**226**	**16.0**	**211**	**4**	**7**	**12**	**22**	**36**	**39**	**93**

52.01: DRAIN PANC CYST BY CATH

Type of Patients	Observed Patients	Avg. Stay	Vari-ance	Percentiles 10th	25th	50th	75th	90th	95th	99th
1. SINGLE DX										
0–19 Years	2	5.5	4	5	5	5	5	5	12	12
20–34	0									
35–49	0									
50–64	2	4.5	24	1	1	8	8	8	8	8
65+	0									
2. MULTIPLE DX										
0–19 Years	3	31.7	57	22	22	36	36	36	36	36
20–34	24	13.9	115	4	7	8	19	28	38	43
35–49	52	16.4	257	4	7	12	23	32	37	95
50–64	47	12.0	49	3	7	12	17	22	22	37
65+	33	15.9	210	7	8	11	22	28	36	>99
TOTAL SINGLE DX	**4**	**5.4**	**5**	**5**	**5**	**5**	**5**	**8**	**12**	**12**
TOTAL MULTIPLE DX	**159**	**15.7**	**176**	**4**	**8**	**12**	**22**	**32**	**36**	**95**
TOTAL										
0–19 Years	5	20.5	206	5	5	22	36	36	36	36
20–34	24	13.9	115	4	7	8	19	28	38	43
35–49	52	16.4	257	4	7	12	23	32	37	95
50–64	49	11.9	50	3	7	11	17	20	22	37
65+	33	15.9	210	7	8	11	22	28	36	>99
GRAND TOTAL	**163**	**15.2**	**172**	**5**	**7**	**12**	**20**	**32**	**36**	**93**

52.1: PANCREATIC DXTIC PX

Type of Patients	Observed Patients	Avg. Stay	Vari-ance	Percentiles 10th	25th	50th	75th	90th	95th	99th
1. SINGLE DX										
0–19 Years	0									
20–34	1	1.0	0	1	1	1	1	1	1	1
35–49	3	3.1	3	1	3	3	3	6	6	6
50–64	3	10.1	17	7	7	8	15	15	15	15
65+	5	3.8	5	1	2	3	6	6	6	6
2. MULTIPLE DX										
0–19 Years	3	11.1	114	5	5	5	26	26	26	26
20–34	22	5.3	38	1	2	4	6	8	13	31
35–49	59	7.2	54	2	3	5	9	14	19	42
50–64	130	8.8	47	3	4	6	11	19	22	32
65+	253	7.4	48	2	4	6	9	14	18	28
TOTAL SINGLE DX	**12**	**4.8**	**14**	**1**	**2**	**3**	**6**	**8**	**15**	**15**
TOTAL MULTIPLE DX	**467**	**7.7**	**49**	**2**	**4**	**6**	**9**	**15**	**20**	**32**
TOTAL										
0–19 Years	3	11.1	114	5	5	5	26	26	26	26
20–34	23	5.2	37	1	2	4	6	8	13	31
35–49	62	7.0	52	2	3	5	8	14	19	42
50–64	133	8.8	46	3	4	6	12	19	22	32
65+	258	7.4	47	2	4	6	9	14	18	28
GRAND TOTAL	**479**	**7.6**	**48**	**2**	**4**	**6**	**9**	**15**	**20**	**32**

52.11: PANCREAS ASPIRATION BX

Type of Patients	Observed Patients	Avg. Stay	Vari-ance	Percentiles 10th	25th	50th	75th	90th	95th	99th
1. SINGLE DX										
0–19 Years	0									
20–34	0									
35–49	1	6.0	0	6	6	6	6	6	6	6
50–64	2	11.5	28	7	7	15	15	15	15	15
65+	4	4.2	4	2	2	3	6	6	6	6
2. MULTIPLE DX										
0–19 Years	2	14.9	162	5	5	5	26	26	26	26
20–34	10	5.2	72	1	1	2	6	7	31	31
35–49	32	7.0	29	2	3	5	9	16	19	22
50–64	73	7.8	41	2	4	6	9	20	20	29
65+	178	6.8	35	2	4	6	8	13	16	22
TOTAL SINGLE DX	**7**	**6.1**	**17**	**2**	**3**	**6**	**6**	**15**	**15**	**15**
TOTAL MULTIPLE DX	**295**	**7.0**	**38**	**2**	**4**	**6**	**8**	**14**	**19**	**27**
TOTAL										
0–19 Years	2	14.9	162	5	5	5	26	26	26	26
20–34	10	5.2	72	1	1	2	6	7	31	31
35–49	33	7.0	28	2	3	5	9	16	19	22
50–64	75	7.8	41	2	4	7	9	19	20	29
65+	182	6.8	35	2	4	6	8	13	16	22
GRAND TOTAL	**302**	**7.0**	**38**	**2**	**4**	**6**	**8**	**14**	**19**	**27**

52.12: OPEN PANCREATIC BIOPSY

Type of Patients	Observed Patients	Avg. Stay	Vari-ance	Percentiles 10th	25th	50th	75th	90th	95th	99th
1. SINGLE DX										
0–19 Years	0									
20–34	0									
35–49	0									
50–64	1	8.0	0	8	8	8	8	8	8	8
65+	0									
2. MULTIPLE DX										
0–19 Years	0									
20–34	4	6.8	2	5	6	7	8	8	8	8
35–49	8	12.4	228	1	5	7	9	42	42	42
50–64	31	10.5	55	4	5	6	14	19	23	35
65+	32	13.3	167	3	6	10	15	23	37	65
TOTAL SINGLE DX	**1**	**8.0**	**0**	**8**	**8**	**8**	**8**	**8**	**8**	**8**
TOTAL MULTIPLE DX	**75**	**11.5**	**110**	**4**	**5**	**8**	**14**	**22**	**35**	**65**
TOTAL										
0–19 Years	0									
20–34	4	6.8	2	5	6	7	8	8	8	8
35–49	8	12.4	228	1	5	7	9	42	42	42
50–64	32	10.4	54	4	5	6	14	19	23	35
65+	32	13.3	167	3	6	10	15	23	37	65
GRAND TOTAL	**76**	**11.5**	**108**	**4**	**5**	**8**	**14**	**22**	**35**	**65**

52.2: PANC/PANC DUCT LES DESTR

Type of Patients	Observed Patients	Avg. Stay	Vari-ance	Percentiles						
				10th	25th	50th	75th	90th	95th	99th
1. SINGLE DX										
0–19 Years	0									
20–34	2	11.5	204	1	1	1	23	23	23	23
35–49	2	4.5	<1	4	4	4	5	5	5	5
50–64	1	4.0	0	4	4	4	4	4	4	4
65+	0									
2. MULTIPLE DX										
0–19 Years	3	6.5	4	4	7	7	>99	>99	>99	>99
20–34	17	22.7	216	4	13	21	32	46	49	49
35–49	29	19.4	208	5	7	13	36	44	>99	>99
50–64	32	15.8	307	3	6	9	20	53	91	>99
65+	33	19.9	243	4	8	14	24	56	56	>99
TOTAL SINGLE DX	**5**	**7.1**	**71**	**1**	**4**	**4**	**5**	**23**	**23**	**23**
TOTAL MULTIPLE DX	**114**	**18.7**	**247**	**4**	**7**	**14**	**29**	**53**	**56**	**>99**
TOTAL										
0–19 Years	3	6.5	4	4	7	7	>99	>99	>99	>99
20–34	19	21.5	218	3	9	21	32	44	46	49
35–49	31	18.6	208	5	7	13	36	44	>99	>99
50–64	33	15.5	303	3	4	9	20	53	91	>99
65+	33	19.9	243	4	8	14	24	56	56	>99
GRAND TOTAL	**119**	**18.3**	**245**	**4**	**7**	**14**	**29**	**53**	**56**	**>99**

52.22: PANC DUCT LES DESTR NEC

Type of Patients	Observed Patients	Avg. Stay	Vari-ance	Percentiles						
				10th	25th	50th	75th	90th	95th	99th
1. SINGLE DX										
0–19 Years	0									
20–34	1	23.0	0	23	23	23	23	23	23	23
35–49	2	4.5	<1	4	4	4	5	5	5	5
50–64	1	4.0	0	4	4	4	4	4	4	4
65+	0									
2. MULTIPLE DX										
0–19 Years	2	6.1	10	4	4	9	>99	>99	>99	>99
20–34	17	22.7	216	4	13	21	32	46	49	49
35–49	28	19.8	205	5	8	13	36	44	>99	>99
50–64	32	15.8	307	3	6	9	20	53	91	>99
65+	31	20.4	243	4	9	16	27	56	56	>99
TOTAL SINGLE DX	**4**	**8.7**	**79**	**4**	**4**	**4**	**5**	**23**	**23**	**23**
TOTAL MULTIPLE DX	**110**	**19.1**	**248**	**4**	**7**	**14**	**29**	**53**	**56**	**>99**
TOTAL										
0–19 Years	2	6.1	10	4	4	9	>99	>99	>99	>99
20–34	18	22.7	204	4	13	21	32	44	46	49
35–49	30	19.0	206	5	7	13	36	44	>99	>99
50–64	33	15.5	303	3	4	9	20	53	91	>99
65+	31	20.4	243	4	9	16	27	56	56	>99
GRAND TOTAL	**114**	**18.9**	**246**	**4**	**7**	**14**	**29**	**53**	**56**	**>99**

52.3: PANCREATIC CYST MARSUP

Type of Patients	Observed Patients	Avg. Stay	Vari-ance	Percentiles						
				10th	25th	50th	75th	90th	95th	99th
1. SINGLE DX										
0–19 Years	0									
20–34	0									
35–49	0									
50–64	0									
65+	0									
2. MULTIPLE DX										
0–19 Years	0									
20–34	1	1.0	0	1	1	1	1	1	1	1
35–49	3	17.8	125	7	7	14	29	29	29	29
50–64	4	13.5	6	11	11	13	17	17	17	17
65+	3	17.5	252	6	6	15	40	40	40	40
TOTAL SINGLE DX	**0**									
TOTAL MULTIPLE DX	**11**	**14.9**	**128**	**6**	**6**	**13**	**17**	**40**	**40**	**40**
TOTAL										
0–19 Years	0									
20–34	1	1.0	0	1	1	1	1	1	1	1
35–49	3	17.8	125	7	7	14	29	29	29	29
50–64	4	13.5	6	11	11	13	17	17	17	17
65+	3	17.5	252	6	6	15	40	40	40	40
GRAND TOTAL	**11**	**14.9**	**128**	**6**	**6**	**13**	**17**	**40**	**40**	**40**

52.4: INT DRAIN PANC CYST

Type of Patients	Observed Patients	Avg. Stay	Vari-ance	Percentiles						
				10th	25th	50th	75th	90th	95th	99th
1. SINGLE DX										
0–19 Years	0									
20–34	0									
35–49	2	8.5	59	3	3	3	15	15	15	15
50–64	2	5.8	3	4	4	7	7	7	7	7
65+	0									
2. MULTIPLE DX										
0–19 Years	2	11.2	44	6	6	6	17	17	17	17
20–34	14	15.5	294	6	7	7	13	38	77	77
35–49	20	15.1	444	5	5	7	13	22	84	84
50–64	16	11.1	18	6	10	10	15	16	17	21
65+	9	14.4	142	6	7	9	15	41	41	41
TOTAL SINGLE DX	**4**	**7.1**	**24**	**3**	**3**	**7**	**7**	**15**	**15**	**15**
TOTAL MULTIPLE DX	**61**	**13.7**	**208**	**5**	**7**	**10**	**15**	**21**	**41**	**84**
TOTAL										
0–19 Years	2	11.2	44	6	6	6	17	17	17	17
20–34	14	15.5	294	6	7	7	13	38	77	77
35–49	22	14.5	409	4	5	7	15	22	84	84
50–64	18	10.7	19	6	7	10	13	16	17	21
65+	9	14.4	142	6	7	9	15	41	41	41
GRAND TOTAL	**65**	**13.4**	**200**	**5**	**7**	**10**	**15**	**21**	**41**	**84**

52.5: PARTIAL PANCREATECTOMY

Type of Patients	Observed Patients	Avg. Stay	Vari-ance	Percentiles						
				10th	25th	50th	75th	90th	95th	99th
1. SINGLE DX										
0–19 Years	3	6.9	6	5	5	6	10	10	10	10
20–34	3	4.7	3	3	3	5	5	7	7	7
35–49	4	5.9	2	4	4	6	7	7	7	7
50–64	1	6.0	0	6	6	6	6	6	6	6
65+	0									
2. MULTIPLE DX										
0–19 Years	14	13.6	42	6	8	15	15	21	24	29
20–34	28	16.4	288	7	8	10	13	41	41	85
35–49	68	10.6	48	5	6	8	13	22	23	38
50–64	101	11.1	87	5	7	8	12	21	25	54
65+	115	11.7	77	6	7	9	13	21	27	37
TOTAL SINGLE DX	**11**	**5.8**	**4**	**3**	**5**	**6**	**7**	**7**	**10**	**10**
TOTAL MULTIPLE DX	**326**	**11.9**	**91**	**6**	**7**	**9**	**13**	**22**	**27**	**54**
TOTAL										
0–19 Years	17	12.9	42	6	8	10	15	21	24	29
20–34	31	15.2	271	4	7	9	13	41	41	85
35–49	72	10.4	47	4	6	8	13	22	23	38
50–64	102	11.1	86	5	7	8	12	21	25	54
65+	115	11.7	77	6	7	9	13	21	27	37
GRAND TOTAL	**337**	**11.7**	**89**	**5**	**7**	**9**	**13**	**22**	**27**	**54**

52.52: DISTAL PANCREATECTOMY

Type of Patients	Observed Patients	Avg. Stay	Vari-ance	Percentiles						
				10th	25th	50th	75th	90th	95th	99th
1. SINGLE DX										
0–19 Years	2	7.3	9	5	5	5	10	10	10	10
20–34	3	4.7	3	3	3	5	5	7	7	7
35–49	4	5.9	2	4	4	6	7	7	7	7
50–64	1	6.0	0	6	6	6	6	6	6	6
65+	0									
2. MULTIPLE DX										
0–19 Years	11	12.6	26	6	8	15	15	21	21	21
20–34	22	15.4	148	6	9	11	13	41	41	41
35–49	55	10.9	45	5	6	9	13	22	22	38
50–64	80	9.7	52	5	6	7	10	16	22	54
65+	86	10.4	64	6	6	8	12	16	21	68
TOTAL SINGLE DX	**10**	**5.8**	**4**	**3**	**5**	**6**	**7**	**10**	**10**	**10**
TOTAL MULTIPLE DX	**254**	**10.9**	**63**	**5**	**6**	**8**	**13**	**21**	**22**	**41**
TOTAL										
0–19 Years	13	12.1	27	6	8	10	15	21	21	21
20–34	25	14.1	142	4	7	10	13	41	41	41
35–49	59	10.6	44	5	6	8	13	22	22	38
50–64	81	9.7	52	5	6	7	10	16	22	54
65+	86	10.4	64	6	6	8	12	16	21	68
GRAND TOTAL	**264**	**10.8**	**62**	**5**	**6**	**8**	**13**	**21**	**22**	**41**

52.6: TOTAL PANCREATECTOMY

Type of Patients	Observed Patients	Avg. Stay	Vari-ance	Percentiles						
				10th	25th	50th	75th	90th	95th	99th
1. SINGLE DX										
0–19 Years	0									
20–34	0									
35–49	0									
50–64	0									
65+	1	12.0	0	12	12	12	12	12	12	12
2. MULTIPLE DX										
0–19 Years	0									
20–34	2	6.1	22	3	3	3	10	10	10	10
35–49	4	12.0	54	6	9	9	11	25	25	25
50–64	17	12.5	40	6	8	11	15	25	28	28
65+	10	13.6	37	7	8	12	20	20	25	25
TOTAL SINGLE DX	**1**	**12.0**	**0**	**12**	**12**	**12**	**12**	**12**	**12**	**12**
TOTAL MULTIPLE DX	**33**	**12.6**	**40**	**7**	**8**	**10**	**16**	**25**	**25**	**28**
TOTAL										
0–19 Years	0									
20–34	2	6.1	22	3	3	3	10	10	10	10
35–49	4	12.0	54	6	9	9	11	25	25	25
50–64	17	12.5	40	6	8	11	15	25	28	28
65+	11	13.5	35	7	8	12	20	20	25	25
GRAND TOTAL	**34**	**12.5**	**39**	**7**	**8**	**11**	**16**	**25**	**25**	**28**

52.7: RAD PANC/DUODENECTOMY

Type of Patients	Observed Patients	Avg. Stay	Vari-ance	Percentiles						
				10th	25th	50th	75th	90th	95th	99th
1. SINGLE DX										
0–19 Years	0									
20–34	1	11.0	0	11	11	11	11	11	11	11
35–49	2	13.3	4	12	12	12	15	15	15	15
50–64	4	9.7	7	7	7	8	12	12	12	12
65+	0									
2. MULTIPLE DX										
0–19 Years	0									
20–34	10	11.9	46	5	8	9	13	18	29	29
35–49	77	18.0	130	9	10	14	21	34	38	68
50–64	234	16.9	124	8	10	13	20	30	38	60
65+	300	16.2	74	8	10	13	20	27	33	53
TOTAL SINGLE DX	**7**	**11.1**	**7**	**7**	**8**	**12**	**12**	**15**	**15**	**15**
TOTAL MULTIPLE DX	**621**	**16.6**	**97**	**8**	**10**	**14**	**20**	**28**	**37**	**57**
TOTAL										
0–19 Years	0									
20–34	11	11.8	41	5	8	10	13	18	29	29
35–49	79	17.9	127	9	10	14	21	34	38	68
50–64	238	16.8	123	8	10	13	20	30	38	60
65+	300	16.2	74	8	10	13	20	27	33	53
GRAND TOTAL	**628**	**16.6**	**97**	**8**	**10**	**13**	**20**	**28**	**37**	**57**

52.8: TRANSPLANT OF PANCREAS

Type of Patients	Observed Patients	Avg. Stay	Vari-ance	Percentiles 10th	25th	50th	75th	90th	95th	99th
1. SINGLE DX										
0–19 Years	0									
20–34	0									
35–49	1	2.0	0	2	2	2	2	2	2	2
50–64	0									
65+	0									
2. MULTIPLE DX										
0–19 Years	0									
20–34	23	10.1	30	6	7	9	11	15	24	27
35–49	48	11.4	83	5	7	9	13	21	28	57
50–64	16	9.5	30	5	7	8	11	17	26	26
65+	0									
TOTAL SINGLE DX	**1**	**2.0**	**0**	**2**	**2**	**2**	**2**	**2**	**2**	**2**
TOTAL MULTIPLE DX	**87**	**10.8**	**61**	**5**	**7**	**9**	**12**	**17**	**26**	**57**
TOTAL										
0–19 Years	0									
20–34	23	10.1	30	6	7	9	11	15	24	27
35–49	49	11.2	83	4	7	9	13	17	28	57
50–64	16	9.5	30	5	7	8	11	17	26	26
65+	0									
GRAND TOTAL	**88**	**10.7**	**61**	**5**	**7**	**9**	**12**	**17**	**26**	**57**

52.9: OTHER OPS ON PANCREAS

Type of Patients	Observed Patients	Avg. Stay	Vari-ance	Percentiles 10th	25th	50th	75th	90th	95th	99th
1. SINGLE DX										
0–19 Years	1	3.0	0	3	3	3	3	3	3	3
20–34	4	4.1	4	2	3	3	5	7	7	7
35–49	16	5.4	15	2	2	4	8	12	15	15
50–64	2	3.7	16	1	1	1	7	7	7	7
65+	1	4.0	0	4	4	4	4	4	4	4
2. MULTIPLE DX										
0–19 Years	8	9.7	93	2	4	9	12	37	>99	>99
20–34	37	8.3	62	2	3	6	7	21	25	34
35–49	102	8.0	49	2	3	6	10	18	25	31
50–64	98	6.3	29	1	3	5	8	14	20	23
65+	145	7.6	36	2	4	6	9	15	19	29
TOTAL SINGLE DX	**24**	**4.9**	**11**	**2**	**2**	**4**	**7**	**9**	**12**	**15**
TOTAL MULTIPLE DX	**390**	**7.5**	**41**	**2**	**3**	**6**	**9**	**16**	**21**	**31**
TOTAL										
0–19 Years	9	9.2	89	2	3	9	12	37	>99	>99
20–34	41	7.8	57	2	3	6	7	21	23	34
35–49	118	7.7	46	2	3	6	10	18	22	31
50–64	100	6.2	29	1	2	5	8	14	20	23
65+	146	7.6	36	2	4	6	9	15	19	29
GRAND TOTAL	**414**	**7.4**	**40**	**2**	**3**	**6**	**9**	**16**	**21**	**31**

52.93: ENDO INSERT PANC STENT

Type of Patients	Observed Patients	Avg. Stay	Vari-ance	Percentiles 10th	25th	50th	75th	90th	95th	99th
1. SINGLE DX										
0–19 Years	1	3.0	0	3	3	3	3	3	3	3
20–34	2	2.6	<1	2	2	3	3	3	3	3
35–49	5	3.3	10	1	2	2	3	9	9	9
50–64	1	1.0	0	1	1	1	1	1	1	1
65+	1	4.0	0	4	4	4	4	4	4	4
2. MULTIPLE DX										
0–19 Years	3	11.8	287	2	2	2	37	37	37	37
20–34	19	6.6	42	2	2	5	7	21	21	21
35–49	37	6.1	30	2	3	4	8	12	16	29
50–64	47	4.5	12	1	3	4	6	8	12	21
65+	98	6.9	24	2	3	6	8	15	18	19
TOTAL SINGLE DX	**10**	**2.9**	**5**	**1**	**2**	**3**	**3**	**4**	**9**	**9**
TOTAL MULTIPLE DX	**204**	**6.3**	**28**	**2**	**3**	**5**	**7**	**14**	**19**	**28**
TOTAL										
0–19 Years	4	9.9	229	2	2	3	4	37	37	37
20–34	21	6.2	39	2	2	3	7	21	21	21
35–49	42	5.8	28	1	2	3	8	11	16	29
50–64	48	4.5	12	1	2	4	6	8	12	21
65+	99	6.8	24	2	3	6	8	15	18	19
GRAND TOTAL	**214**	**6.1**	**28**	**2**	**3**	**5**	**7**	**14**	**18**	**28**

52.96: PANCREATIC ANASTOMOSIS

Type of Patients	Observed Patients	Avg. Stay	Vari-ance	Percentiles 10th	25th	50th	75th	90th	95th	99th
1. SINGLE DX										
0–19 Years	0									
20–34	2	5.9	2	5	5	5	7	7	7	7
35–49	8	6.7	20	2	4	5	8	15	15	15
50–64	1	7.0	0	7	7	7	7	7	7	7
65+	0									
2. MULTIPLE DX										
0–19 Years	2	11.2	1	10	10	12	12	>99	>99	>99
20–34	10	13.8	105	6	6	7	23	34	34	34
35–49	32	10.5	54	5	6	7	14	25	28	31
50–64	21	10.7	37	6	6	8	16	23	23	24
65+	23	12.1	41	6	8	9	14	24	27	29
TOTAL SINGLE DX	**11**	**6.6**	**14**	**2**	**4**	**5**	**7**	**12**	**15**	**15**
TOTAL MULTIPLE DX	**88**	**11.4**	**49**	**6**	**6**	**9**	**14**	**24**	**28**	**34**
TOTAL										
0–19 Years	2	11.2	1	10	10	12	12	>99	>99	>99
20–34	12	12.5	96	6	6	7	19	25	34	34
35–49	40	9.9	49	4	6	7	13	21	28	31
50–64	22	10.6	36	6	6	8	16	23	23	24
65+	23	12.1	41	6	8	9	14	24	27	29
GRAND TOTAL	**99**	**11.0**	**48**	**5**	**6**	**8**	**14**	**23**	**28**	**34**

53.0: UNILAT IH REPAIR

Type of Patients	Observed Patients	Avg. Stay	Vari- ance	Percentiles						
				10th	25th	50th	75th	90th	95th	99th
1. SINGLE DX										
0–19 Years	151	1.3	<1	1	1	1	1	2	3	6
20–34	134	1.4	<1	1	1	1	1	3	3	5
35–49	128	1.7	1	1	1	1	2	3	4	7
50–64	132	1.7	1	1	1	1	2	3	4	6
65+	108	1.8	1	1	1	1	2	3	4	5
2. MULTIPLE DX										
0–19 Years	182	4.7	186	1	1	1	2	10	47	>99
20–34	155	2.8	16	1	1	2	3	5	7	19
35–49	264	2.9	8	1	1	2	3	6	9	14
50–64	451	3.3	16	1	1	2	4	7	11	20
65+	1,499	3.4	12	1	1	2	4	7	10	18
TOTAL SINGLE DX	**653**	**1.5**	**1**	**1**	**1**	**1**	**2**	**3**	**4**	**6**
TOTAL MULTIPLE DX	**2,551**	**3.4**	**29**	**1**	**1**	**2**	**4**	**7**	**10**	**26**
TOTAL										
0–19 Years	333	3.1	101	1	1	1	1	3	12	>99
20–34	289	2.2	10	1	1	1	2	4	5	19
35–49	392	2.5	7	1	1	2	3	5	7	14
50–64	583	2.9	13	1	1	2	3	6	8	16
65+	1,607	3.3	11	1	1	2	4	7	10	17
GRAND TOTAL	**3,204**	**3.0**	**24**	**1**	**1**	**2**	**3**	**6**	**9**	**21**

53.00: UNILAT IH REPAIR NOS

Type of Patients	Observed Patients	Avg. Stay	Vari- ance	Percentiles						
				10th	25th	50th	75th	90th	95th	99th
1. SINGLE DX										
0–19 Years	63	1.3	<1	1	1	1	1	2	3	4
20–34	7	1.7	2	1	1	1	2	5	5	5
35–49	16	1.4	2	1	1	1	1	2	7	7
50–64	8	2.5	7	1	1	2	2	9	9	9
65+	4	1.3	<1	1	1	1	2	2	2	2
2. MULTIPLE DX										
0–19 Years	80	4.8	266	1	1	1	2	3	47	>99
20–34	12	5.3	126	1	1	2	4	4	44	44
35–49	18	6.0	29	1	3	5	8	11	14	25
50–64	32	5.2	79	1	1	3	5	6	37	40
65+	80	4.3	11	1	1	3	6	9	10	14
TOTAL SINGLE DX	**98**	**1.4**	**1**	**1**	**1**	**1**	**1**	**2**	**3**	**7**
TOTAL MULTIPLE DX	**222**	**4.8**	**134**	**1**	**1**	**2**	**5**	**8**	**13**	**92**
TOTAL										
0–19 Years	143	3.2	151	1	1	1	1	3	5	92
20–34	19	4.0	82	1	1	2	3	4	5	44
35–49	34	4.0	22	1	1	2	5	10	11	25
50–64	40	4.8	67	1	1	2	5	6	37	40
65+	84	4.2	11	1	1	3	6	9	10	14
GRAND TOTAL	**320**	**3.7**	**95**	**1**	**1**	**1**	**3**	**7**	**9**	**90**

53.01: UNILAT REP DIRECT IH

Type of Patients	Observed Patients	Avg. Stay	Vari- ance	Percentiles						
				10th	25th	50th	75th	90th	95th	99th
1. SINGLE DX										
0–19 Years	6	1.0	0	1	1	1	1	1	1	1
20–34	3	2.0	<1	1	1	2	3	3	3	3
35–49	6	2.2	2	1	1	1	4	4	4	4
50–64	5	2.6	3	1	1	2	4	5	5	5
65+	7	2.3	2	1	1	2	3	5	5	5
2. MULTIPLE DX										
0–19 Years	13	1.3	<1	1	1	1	1	2	3	3
20–34	6	8.7	74	2	2	2	19	19	19	19
35–49	11	2.8	8	1	1	2	3	10	10	10
50–64	21	3.0	8	1	1	2	3	7	11	11
65+	106	3.7	10	1	1	3	4	8	10	14
TOTAL SINGLE DX	**27**	**2.0**	**2**	**1**	**1**	**1**	**3**	**4**	**5**	**5**
TOTAL MULTIPLE DX	**157**	**3.5**	**14**	**1**	**1**	**2**	**4**	**8**	**10**	**19**
TOTAL										
0–19 Years	19	1.2	<1	1	1	1	1	2	3	3
20–34	9	7.4	67	1	2	2	19	19	19	19
35–49	17	2.6	6	1	1	2	3	4	10	10
50–64	26	2.9	7	1	1	2	4	7	10	11
65+	113	3.6	10	1	1	3	4	8	9	14
GRAND TOTAL	**184**	**3.3**	**12**	**1**	**1**	**2**	**4**	**8**	**10**	**19**

53.02: UNILAT REP INDIRECT IH

Type of Patients	Observed Patients	Avg. Stay	Vari- ance	Percentiles						
				10th	25th	50th	75th	90th	95th	99th
1. SINGLE DX										
0–19 Years	69	1.3	1	1	1	1	1	2	4	6
20–34	11	1.7	2	1	1	1	2	4	4	4
35–49	12	2.0	1	1	1	2	3	3	5	5
50–64	12	1.9	<1	1	1	2	3	3	4	4
65+	5	1.7	<1	1	1	2	2	3	3	3
2. MULTIPLE DX										
0–19 Years	70	6.2	166	1	1	1	3	36	>99	>99
20–34	19	2.3	2	1	1	2	2	5	5	5
35–49	17	3.1	4	1	1	3	5	6	6	6
50–64	27	5.0	32	1	1	3	7	15	21	24
65+	98	3.5	12	1	1	2	4	7	11	18
TOTAL SINGLE DX	**109**	**1.5**	**1**	**1**	**1**	**1**	**1**	**2**	**4**	**6**
TOTAL MULTIPLE DX	**231**	**4.4**	**63**	**1**	**1**	**2**	**4**	**10**	**24**	**>99**
TOTAL										
0–19 Years	139	3.5	79	1	1	1	2	6	36	>99
20–34	30	2.2	2	1	1	2	2	5	5	5
35–49	29	2.7	3	1	1	2	4	6	6	6
50–64	39	4.2	25	1	1	2	5	8	15	24
65+	103	3.4	12	1	1	2	4	7	11	18
GRAND TOTAL	**340**	**3.4**	**44**	**1**	**1**	**1**	**3**	**6**	**14**	**>99**

53.03: UNILAT REP DIR IH/GRAFT

Type of Patients	Observed Patients	Avg. Stay	Vari-ance	Percentiles						
				10th	25th	50th	75th	90th	95th	99th
1. SINGLE DX										
0–19 Years	0									
20–34	12	1.2	<1	1	1	1	1	2	2	2
35–49	22	1.2	<1	1	1	1	1	2	3	3
50–64	34	1.4	<1	1	1	1	2	2	3	3
65+	37	1.9	1	1	1	1	3	4	4	6
2. MULTIPLE DX										
0–19 Years	2	7.3	46	3	3	3	14	14	14	14
20–34	20	2.3	2	1	1	2	3	4	4	6
35–49	66	2.1	3	1	1	1	3	4	6	7
50–64	117	3.0	11	1	1	2	3	8	13	13
65+	409	3.2	10	1	1	2	4	7	9	16
TOTAL SINGLE DX	**105**	**1.5**	**<1**	**1**	**1**	**1**	**2**	**3**	**3**	**6**
TOTAL MULTIPLE DX	**614**	**3.0**	**10**	**1**	**1**	**2**	**3**	**7**	**9**	**14**
TOTAL										
0–19 Years	2	7.3	46	3	3	3	14	14	14	14
20–34	32	1.9	2	1	1	1	3	3	4	6
35–49	88	1.9	3	1	1	1	2	3	5	7
50–64	151	2.7	9	1	1	1	3	6	12	13
65+	446	3.1	10	1	1	2	4	7	9	16
GRAND TOTAL	**719**	**2.9**	**9**	**1**	**1**	**2**	**3**	**6**	**9**	**14**

53.04: UNILAT INDIRECT IH/GRAFT

Type of Patients	Observed Patients	Avg. Stay	Vari-ance	Percentiles						
				10th	25th	50th	75th	90th	95th	99th
1. SINGLE DX										
0–19 Years	8	1.0	0	1	1	1	1	1	1	1
20–34	63	1.3	<1	1	1	1	1	2	3	3
35–49	37	1.7	1	1	1	1	2	3	4	6
50–64	36	1.4	<1	1	1	1	2	2	3	3
65+	28	1.4	<1	1	1	1	2	2	3	4
2. MULTIPLE DX										
0–19 Years	11	1.6	<1	1	1	1	3	3	3	3
20–34	67	2.2	3	1	1	2	3	5	7	7
35–49	72	3.6	13	1	1	2	4	11	12	14
50–64	137	2.9	10	1	1	2	3	7	9	20
65+	420	3.3	15	1	1	2	4	7	10	22
TOTAL SINGLE DX	**172**	**1.4**	**<1**	**1**	**1**	**1**	**2**	**2**	**3**	**4**
TOTAL MULTIPLE DX	**707**	**3.1**	**13**	**1**	**1**	**2**	**3**	**7**	**10**	**19**
TOTAL										
0–19 Years	19	1.4	<1	1	1	1	1	3	3	3
20–34	130	1.8	2	1	1	1	2	3	5	7
35–49	109	3.0	10	1	1	2	3	8	11	14
50–64	173	2.6	9	1	1	2	3	6	8	14
65+	448	3.2	14	1	1	2	3	7	10	22
GRAND TOTAL	**879**	**2.8**	**11**	**1**	**1**	**2**	**3**	**7**	**9**	**17**

53.05: UNILAT REP IH/GRAFT NOS

Type of Patients	Observed Patients	Avg. Stay	Vari-ance	Percentiles						
				10th	25th	50th	75th	90th	95th	99th
1. SINGLE DX										
0–19 Years	5	1.4	<1	1	1	1	2	2	3	3
20–34	38	1.7	2	1	1	1	2	3	4	8
35–49	35	1.8	1	1	1	1	2	3	4	7
50–64	37	2.0	2	1	1	2	2	4	4	6
65+	27	1.9	1	1	1	2	2	4	4	5
2. MULTIPLE DX										
0–19 Years	6	1.8	1	1	1	1	3	3	3	3
20–34	31	2.1	4	1	1	2	2	4	9	10
35–49	80	2.2	2	1	1	2	3	4	5	7
50–64	117	3.0	5	1	1	2	4	6	7	11
65+	386	3.4	11	1	1	2	4	7	10	17
TOTAL SINGLE DX	**142**	**1.8**	**2**	**1**	**1**	**1**	**2**	**4**	**4**	**7**
TOTAL MULTIPLE DX	**620**	**3.1**	**9**	**1**	**1**	**2**	**4**	**7**	**8**	**16**
TOTAL										
0–19 Years	11	1.6	<1	1	1	1	2	3	3	3
20–34	69	1.9	3	1	1	1	2	4	4	10
35–49	115	2.1	2	1	1	2	3	4	4	7
50–64	154	2.7	5	1	1	2	4	6	7	11
65+	413	3.3	10	1	1	2	4	7	10	17
GRAND TOTAL	**762**	**2.9**	**8**	**1**	**1**	**2**	**4**	**6**	**8**	**16**

53.1: BILAT IH REPAIR

Type of Patients	Observed Patients	Avg. Stay	Vari-ance	Percentiles						
				10th	25th	50th	75th	90th	95th	99th
1. SINGLE DX										
0–19 Years	94	1.1	<1	1	1	1	1	2	2	2
20–34	11	1.1	<1	1	1	1	1	2	2	2
35–49	18	1.6	2	1	1	1	2	5	5	5
50–64	21	1.7	<1	1	1	1	3	3	4	4
65+	21	1.3	<1	1	1	1	2	2	2	2
2. MULTIPLE DX										
0–19 Years	191	8.0	435	1	1	1	2	54	99	>99
20–34	18	2.1	3	1	1	2	2	5	5	9
35–49	45	1.6	2	1	1	1	2	3	4	7
50–64	110	2.1	4	1	1	1	3	3	6	8
65+	225	2.9	10	1	1	2	3	6	9	21
TOTAL SINGLE DX	**165**	**1.2**	**<1**	**1**	**1**	**1**	**1**	**2**	**2**	**5**
TOTAL MULTIPLE DX	**589**	**4.9**	**200**	**1**	**1**	**1**	**3**	**7**	**40**	**>99**
TOTAL										
0–19 Years	285	5.8	307	1	1	1	2	14	77	>99
20–34	29	1.8	2	1	1	1	2	3	5	9
35–49	63	1.6	2	1	1	1	2	3	5	7
50–64	131	2.1	4	1	1	1	3	3	5	8
65+	246	2.8	10	1	1	2	3	6	8	21
GRAND TOTAL	**754**	**4.1**	**158**	**1**	**1**	**1**	**2**	**5**	**18**	**>99**

53.10: BILAT IH REPAIR NOS

Type of Patients	Observed Patients	Avg. Stay	Vari-ance	Percentiles						
				10th	25th	50th	75th	90th	95th	99th
1. SINGLE DX										
0–19 Years	45	1.2	<1	1	1	1	1	2	2	2
20–34	2	1.6	<1	1	1	2	2	2	2	2
35–49	1	5.0	0	5	5	5	5	5	5	5
50–64	0									
65+	1	1.0	0	1	1	1	1	1	1	1
2. MULTIPLE DX										
0–19 Years	82	7.7	334	1	1	1	2	40	76	>99
20–34	0									
35–49	1	1.0	0	1	1	1	1	1	1	1
50–64	6	3.7	24	1	1	2	5	5	18	18
65+	6	10.9	68	3	3	10	21	21	21	21
TOTAL SINGLE DX	**49**	**1.2**	**<1**	**1**	**1**	**1**	**1**	**2**	**2**	**2**
TOTAL MULTIPLE DX	**95**	**7.6**	**309**	**1**	**1**	**1**	**3**	**40**	**67**	**>99**
TOTAL										
0–19 Years	127	5.7	243	1	1	1	2	18	62	>99
20–34	2	1.6	<1	1	1	2	2	2	2	2
35–49	2	3.0	8	1	1	3	5	5	5	5
50–64	6	3.7	24	1	1	2	5	5	18	18
65+	7	9.8	70	1	3	6	21	21	21	21
GRAND TOTAL	**144**	**5.8**	**228**	**1**	**1**	**1**	**2**	**18**	**54**	**>99**

53.12: BILAT INDIRECT IH REPAIR

Type of Patients	Observed Patients	Avg. Stay	Vari-ance	Percentiles						
				10th	25th	50th	75th	90th	95th	99th
1. SINGLE DX										
0–19 Years	45	1.1	<1	1	1	1	1	1	2	5
20–34	1	1.0	0	1	1	1	1	1	1	1
35–49	1	1.0	0	1	1	1	1	1	1	1
50–64	0									
65+	1	2.0	0	2	2	2	2	2	2	2
2. MULTIPLE DX										
0–19 Years	96	8.8	568	1	1	1	2	62	99	>99
20–34	2	2.0	0	2	2	2	2	2	2	2
35–49	1	1.0	0	1	1	1	1	1	1	1
50–64	2	2.5	<1	2	2	3	3	3	3	3
65+	5	2.6	2	1	1	3	4	4	4	4
TOTAL SINGLE DX	**48**	**1.1**	**<1**	**1**	**1**	**1**	**1**	**1**	**2**	**5**
TOTAL MULTIPLE DX	**106**	**8.2**	**524**	**1**	**1**	**1**	**2**	**61**	**99**	**>99**
TOTAL										
0–19 Years	141	6.1	383	1	1	1	1	8	99	>99
20–34	3	1.7	<1	1	1	2	2	2	2	2
35–49	2	1.0	0	1	1	1	1	1	1	1
50–64	2	2.5	<1	2	2	3	3	3	3	3
65+	6	2.5	2	1	1	3	4	4	4	4
GRAND TOTAL	**154**	**5.8**	**358**	**1**	**1**	**1**	**2**	**5**	**88**	**>99**

53.14: BILAT DIRECT IH REP-GRFT

Type of Patients	Observed Patients	Avg. Stay	Vari-ance	Percentiles						
				10th	25th	50th	75th	90th	95th	99th
1. SINGLE DX										
0–19 Years	0									
20–34	1	1.0	0	1	1	1	1	1	1	1
35–49	1	1.0	0	1	1	1	1	1	1	1
50–64	8	1.8	1	1	1	1	3	4	4	4
65+	8	1.1	<1	1	1	1	1	2	2	2
2. MULTIPLE DX										
0–19 Years	0									
20–34	3	1.0	0	1	1	1	1	1	1	1
35–49	16	1.4	<1	1	1	1	2	2	3	3
50–64	43	1.7	2	1	1	1	2	3	5	8
65+	75	2.4	5	1	1	2	2	5	6	13
TOTAL SINGLE DX	**18**	**1.4**	**<1**	**1**	**1**	**1**	**1**	**3**	**4**	**4**
TOTAL MULTIPLE DX	**137**	**2.1**	**4**	**1**	**1**	**1**	**2**	**4**	**6**	**13**
TOTAL										
0–19 Years	0									
20–34	4	1.0	0	1	1	1	1	1	1	1
35–49	17	1.4	<1	1	1	1	2	2	3	3
50–64	51	1.7	2	1	1	1	2	3	5	8
65+	83	2.3	5	1	1	2	2	5	6	13
GRAND TOTAL	**155**	**2.0**	**3**	**1**	**1**	**1**	**2**	**4**	**6**	**13**

53.15: BILAT INDIRECT IH-GRAFT

Type of Patients	Observed Patients	Avg. Stay	Vari-ance	Percentiles						
				10th	25th	50th	75th	90th	95th	99th
1. SINGLE DX										
0–19 Years	1	1.0	0	1	1	1	1	1	1	1
20–34	4	1.0	0	1	1	1	1	1	1	1
35–49	4	1.3	<1	1	1	1	2	2	2	2
50–64	4	2.0	1	1	1	3	3	3	3	3
65+	2	1.5	<1	1	1	1	2	2	2	2
2. MULTIPLE DX										
0–19 Years	0									
20–34	5	3.0	7	1	2	2	5	9	9	9
35–49	9	1.5	2	1	1	1	1	2	7	7
50–64	20	2.3	3	1	1	2	3	3	8	8
65+	42	2.5	5	1	1	2	3	5	6	13
TOTAL SINGLE DX	**15**	**1.4**	**<1**	**1**	**1**	**1**	**2**	**3**	**3**	**3**
TOTAL MULTIPLE DX	**76**	**2.3**	**4**	**1**	**1**	**2**	**3**	**5**	**7**	**10**
TOTAL										
0–19 Years	1	1.0	0	1	1	1	1	1	1	1
20–34	9	2.3	5	1	1	1	2	5	9	9
35–49	13	1.4	2	1	1	1	1	2	2	7
50–64	24	2.3	3	1	1	2	3	3	8	8
65+	44	2.5	5	1	1	2	3	5	6	13
GRAND TOTAL	**91**	**2.2**	**4**	**1**	**1**	**2**	**2**	**4**	**6**	**10**

53.16: DIRECT/INDIRECT IH-GRAFT

Type of Patients	Observed Patients	Avg. Stay	Vari-ance	Percentiles 10th	25th	50th	75th	90th	95th	99th
1. SINGLE DX										
0–19 Years	0									
20–34	0									
35–49	4	1.2	<1	1	1	1	1	2	2	2
50–64	3	1.3	<1	1	1	1	2	2	2	2
65+	3	1.3	<1	1	1	1	2	2	2	2
2. MULTIPLE DX										
0–19 Years	1	2.0	0	2	2	2	2	2	2	2
20–34	4	2.1	3	1	1	1	2	5	5	5
35–49	12	1.8	2	1	1	1	2	3	6	7
50–64	18	2.1	4	1	1	1	3	6	8	8
65+	40	1.9	2	1	1	1	2	4	5	7
TOTAL SINGLE DX	**10**	**1.2**	**<1**	**1**	**1**	**1**	**1**	**2**	**2**	**2**
TOTAL MULTIPLE DX	**75**	**1.9**	**2**	**1**	**1**	**1**	**2**	**4**	**6**	**8**
TOTAL										
0–19 Years	1	2.0	0	2	2	2	2	2	2	2
20–34	4	2.1	3	1	1	1	2	5	5	5
35–49	16	1.7	2	1	1	1	2	3	6	7
50–64	21	2.0	4	1	1	1	2	6	6	8
65+	43	1.9	2	1	1	1	2	4	5	7
GRAND TOTAL	**85**	**1.9**	**2**	**1**	**1**	**1**	**2**	**3**	**6**	**7**

53.17: BILAT IH REP-GRAFT NOS

Type of Patients	Observed Patients	Avg. Stay	Vari-ance	Percentiles 10th	25th	50th	75th	90th	95th	99th
1. SINGLE DX										
0–19 Years	0									
20–34	3	1.0	0	1	1	1	1	1	1	1
35–49	6	1.8	3	1	1	1	1	5	5	5
50–64	5	1.4	<1	1	1	1	1	3	3	3
65+	4	1.3	<1	1	1	1	2	2	2	2
2. MULTIPLE DX										
0–19 Years	1	1.0	0	1	1	1	1	1	1	1
20–34	1	3.0	0	3	3	3	3	3	3	3
35–49	6	2.3	2	1	1	2	3	4	4	4
50–64	19	2.2	3	1	1	2	3	3	7	7
65+	50	3.6	14	1	1	2	4	7	9	21
TOTAL SINGLE DX	**18**	**1.5**	**1**	**1**	**1**	**1**	**1**	**3**	**5**	**5**
TOTAL MULTIPLE DX	**77**	**3.1**	**10**	**1**	**1**	**2**	**4**	**6**	**8**	**21**
TOTAL										
0–19 Years	1	1.0	0	1	1	1	1	1	1	1
20–34	4	1.6	1	1	1	1	3	3	3	3
35–49	12	2.0	2	1	1	1	3	5	5	5
50–64	24	2.0	2	1	1	1	3	3	5	7
65+	54	3.5	13	1	1	2	4	7	9	21
GRAND TOTAL	**95**	**2.8**	**9**	**1**	**1**	**2**	**4**	**6**	**8**	**21**

53.2: UNILAT FH REPAIR

Type of Patients	Observed Patients	Avg. Stay	Vari-ance	Percentiles 10th	25th	50th	75th	90th	95th	99th
1. SINGLE DX										
0–19 Years	1	1.0	0	1	1	1	1	1	1	1
20–34	9	1.4	<1	1	1	1	1	4	4	4
35–49	22	1.3	<1	1	1	1	1	2	3	5
50–64	19	1.5	2	1	1	1	1	2	7	7
65+	24	1.8	<1	1	1	2	2	2	3	6
2. MULTIPLE DX										
0–19 Years	0									
20–34	6	2.6	7	1	1	2	2	8	8	8
35–49	30	2.2	3	1	1	1	3	5	7	8
50–64	40	2.2	6	1	1	1	2	4	6	13
65+	303	4.5	16	1	2	3	6	9	12	21
TOTAL SINGLE DX	**75**	**1.5**	**1**	**1**	**1**	**1**	**2**	**2**	**4**	**7**
TOTAL MULTIPLE DX	**379**	**4.0**	**14**	**1**	**1**	**3**	**5**	**8**	**11**	**21**
TOTAL										
0–19 Years	1	1.0	0	1	1	1	1	1	1	1
20–34	15	1.9	3	1	1	1	2	4	8	8
35–49	52	1.9	2	1	1	1	2	3	5	8
50–64	59	2.0	5	1	1	1	2	4	6	13
65+	327	4.3	15	1	2	3	6	9	11	21
GRAND TOTAL	**454**	**3.6**	**13**	**1**	**1**	**2**	**5**	**8**	**10**	**20**

53.21: UNILAT FH REP W GRAFT

Type of Patients	Observed Patients	Avg. Stay	Vari-ance	Percentiles 10th	25th	50th	75th	90th	95th	99th
1. SINGLE DX										
0–19 Years	0									
20–34	7	1.4	1	1	1	1	1	4	4	4
35–49	17	1.3	<1	1	1	1	1	2	5	5
50–64	14	1.3	2	1	1	1	1	1	2	7
65+	17	1.8	1	1	1	2	2	3	3	6
2. MULTIPLE DX										
0–19 Years	0									
20–34	4	3.7	9	2	2	2	8	8	8	8
35–49	19	1.9	1	1	1	1	3	3	3	5
50–64	24	2.6	9	1	1	1	2	5	13	13
65+	202	4.2	18	1	2	3	5	9	12	23
TOTAL SINGLE DX	**55**	**1.5**	**1**	**1**	**1**	**1**	**2**	**2**	**4**	**7**
TOTAL MULTIPLE DX	**249**	**3.9**	**16**	**1**	**1**	**2**	**5**	**9**	**11**	**21**
TOTAL										
0–19 Years	0									
20–34	11	2.1	4	1	1	1	2	4	8	8
35–49	36	1.6	1	1	1	1	2	3	3	5
50–64	38	2.1	7	1	1	1	2	4	7	13
65+	219	4.0	17	1	2	2	5	9	11	23
GRAND TOTAL	**304**	**3.5**	**14**	**1**	**1**	**2**	**4**	**7**	**9**	**21**

53.29: UNILAT FH REP NEC

Type of Patients	Observed Patients	Avg. Stay	Vari-ance	Percentiles 10th	25th	50th	75th	90th	95th	99th
1. SINGLE DX										
0–19 Years	1	1.0	0	1	1	1	1	1	1	1
20–34	2	1.4	<1	1	1	1	2	2	2	2
35–49	5	1.4	<1	1	1	1	1	3	3	3
50–64	5	2.1	5	1	1	1	2	7	7	7
65+	7	1.8	<1	1	2	2	2	2	2	2
2. MULTIPLE DX										
0–19 Years	0									
20–34	2	1.0	0	1	1	1	1	1	1	1
35–49	11	3.1	7	1	1	2	6	7	8	8
50–64	16	1.7	1	1	1	1	2	3	3	6
65+	101	4.9	11	1	2	4	7	9	10	16
TOTAL SINGLE DX	**20**	**1.7**	**2**	**1**	**1**	**1**	**2**	**2**	**3**	**7**
TOTAL MULTIPLE DX	**130**	**4.3**	**11**	**1**	**2**	**3**	**6**	**8**	**10**	**16**
TOTAL										
0–19 Years	1	1.0	0	1	1	1	1	1	1	1
20–34	4	1.2	<1	1	1	1	1	2	2	2
35–49	16	2.6	6	1	1	1	4	7	8	8
50–64	21	1.7	2	1	1	1	2	3	6	7
65+	108	4.8	11	1	2	4	6	9	10	16
GRAND TOTAL	**150**	**4.0**	**10**	**1**	**1**	**3**	**6**	**8**	**10**	**16**

53.3: BILAT FH REPAIR

Type of Patients	Observed Patients	Avg. Stay	Vari-ance	Percentiles 10th	25th	50th	75th	90th	95th	99th
1. SINGLE DX										
0–19 Years	0									
20–34	0									
35–49	1	1.0	0	1	1	1	1	1	1	1
50–64	0									
65+	1	2.0	0	2	2	2	2	2	2	2
2. MULTIPLE DX										
0–19 Years	0									
20–34	1	2.0	0	2	2	2	2	2	2	2
35–49	1	2.0	0	2	2	2	2	2	2	2
50–64	0									
65+	6	5.7	14	1	2	5	10	10	10	10
TOTAL SINGLE DX	**2**	**1.5**	**<1**	**1**	**1**	**1**	**2**	**2**	**2**	**2**
TOTAL MULTIPLE DX	**8**	**5.0**	**13**	**1**	**2**	**5**	**10**	**10**	**10**	**10**
TOTAL										
0–19 Years	0									
20–34	1	2.0	0	2	2	2	2	2	2	2
35–49	2	1.5	<1	1	1	1	2	2	2	2
50–64	0									
65+	7	5.3	14	1	2	5	10	10	10	10
GRAND TOTAL	**10**	**4.4**	**13**	**1**	**2**	**2**	**8**	**10**	**10**	**10**

53.4: UMBILICAL HERNIA REPAIR

Type of Patients	Observed Patients	Avg. Stay	Vari-ance	Percentiles 10th	25th	50th	75th	90th	95th	99th
1. SINGLE DX										
0–19 Years	18	1.7	<1	1	1	1	2	3	3	5
20–34	40	1.8	2	1	1	1	2	3	4	10
35–49	93	1.6	<1	1	1	1	2	2	3	7
50–64	73	1.6	<1	1	1	1	2	3	3	6
65+	6	2.4	<1	1	2	2	3	4	4	4
2. MULTIPLE DX										
0–19 Years	63	6.0	124	1	1	2	4	17	26	54
20–34	119	2.3	3	1	1	2	2	5	6	9
35–49	357	2.9	8	1	1	2	3	6	9	15
50–64	426	3.2	13	1	1	2	4	6	8	21
65+	422	3.9	20	1	1	3	5	9	11	21
TOTAL SINGLE DX	**230**	**1.7**	**1**	**1**	**1**	**1**	**2**	**3**	**3**	**6**
TOTAL MULTIPLE DX	**1,387**	**3.5**	**22**	**1**	**1**	**2**	**4**	**7**	**10**	**22**
TOTAL										
0–19 Years	81	4.9	96	1	1	1	4	9	23	51
20–34	159	2.1	3	1	1	2	2	4	5	9
35–49	450	2.7	7	1	1	2	3	6	8	15
50–64	499	3.0	12	1	1	2	4	6	8	21
65+	428	3.9	20	1	1	2	5	9	11	21
GRAND TOTAL	**1,617**	**3.2**	**19**	**1**	**1**	**2**	**4**	**7**	**9**	**21**

53.41: UMB HERNIA REPAIR-PROSTH

Type of Patients	Observed Patients	Avg. Stay	Vari-ance	Percentiles 10th	25th	50th	75th	90th	95th	99th
1. SINGLE DX										
0–19 Years	0									
20–34	13	1.8	<1	1	1	2	2	2	5	5
35–49	26	1.4	<1	1	1	1	2	2	2	4
50–64	27	1.7	1	1	1	1	2	3	4	6
65+	0									
2. MULTIPLE DX										
0–19 Years	1	3.0	0	3	3	3	3	3	3	3
20–34	49	2.5	4	1	1	2	3	5	7	10
35–49	142	2.8	6	1	1	2	3	6	9	11
50–64	170	3.2	12	1	1	2	4	6	10	19
65+	170	3.3	13	1	1	2	4	7	9	19
TOTAL SINGLE DX	**66**	**1.6**	**<1**	**1**	**1**	**1**	**2**	**3**	**4**	**6**
TOTAL MULTIPLE DX	**532**	**3.0**	**10**	**1**	**1**	**2**	**4**	**6**	**9**	**17**
TOTAL										
0–19 Years	1	3.0	0	3	3	3	3	3	3	3
20–34	62	2.3	3	1	1	2	2	5	6	10
35–49	168	2.6	6	1	1	2	3	6	7	11
50–64	197	3.0	11	1	1	2	3	6	8	19
65+	170	3.3	13	1	1	2	4	7	9	19
GRAND TOTAL	**598**	**2.9**	**9**	**1**	**1**	**2**	**3**	**6**	**8**	**17**

53.49: UMB HERNIA REPAIR NEC

Type of Patients	Observed Patients	Avg. Stay	Vari- ance	Percentiles 10th	25th	50th	75th	90th	95th	99th
1. SINGLE DX										
0–19 Years	18	1.7	<1	1	1	1	2	3	3	5
20–34	27	1.7	3	1	1	1	2	3	4	10
35–49	67	1.7	1	1	1	1	2	3	3	7
50–64	46	1.5	<1	1	1	1	2	3	3	3
65+	6	2.4	<1	1	2	2	3	4	4	4
2. MULTIPLE DX										
0–19 Years	62	6.1	125	1	1	2	5	17	26	54
20–34	70	2.1	2	1	1	2	2	3	5	9
35–49	215	3.0	10	1	1	2	4	6	9	18
50–64	256	3.3	14	1	1	2	4	6	8	21
65+	252	4.4	23	1	1	3	6	9	12	22
TOTAL SINGLE DX	**164**	**1.7**	**1**	**1**	**1**	**1**	**2**	**3**	**3**	**7**
TOTAL MULTIPLE DX	**855**	**3.8**	**29**	**1**	**1**	**2**	**4**	**8**	**11**	**24**
TOTAL										
0–19 Years	80	4.9	96	1	1	1	4	13	23	51
20–34	97	2.0	3	1	1	1	2	3	5	9
35–49	282	2.7	8	1	1	2	3	6	9	16
50–64	302	3.0	12	1	1	2	4	6	8	21
65+	258	4.3	23	1	1	3	6	9	11	22
GRAND TOTAL	**1,019**	**3.4**	**25**	**1**	**1**	**2**	**4**	**7**	**10**	**23**

53.5: REP OTH ABD WALL HERNIA

Type of Patients	Observed Patients	Avg. Stay	Vari- ance	Percentiles 10th	25th	50th	75th	90th	95th	99th
1. SINGLE DX										
0–19 Years	8	2.5	2	1	1	2	4	4	5	5
20–34	29	1.6	<1	1	1	1	2	3	3	4
35–49	68	2.1	2	1	1	2	3	4	5	7
50–64	52	2.3	3	1	1	2	3	4	5	12
65+	34	1.9	2	1	1	1	2	5	5	6
2. MULTIPLE DX										
0–19 Years	25	5.1	83	1	2	3	40	>99	>99	>99
20–34	100	3.3	5	1	2	2	4	7	8	10
35–49	350	3.4	8	1	1	3	4	6	8	20
50–64	547	4.2	24	1	2	3	5	9	12	22
65+	495	4.6	19	1	2	4	6	9	13	21
TOTAL SINGLE DX	**191**	**2.1**	**2**	**1**	**1**	**2**	**3**	**4**	**5**	**7**
TOTAL MULTIPLE DX	**1,517**	**4.1**	**19**	**1**	**2**	**3**	**5**	**9**	**12**	**30**
TOTAL										
0–19 Years	33	4.4	61	1	1	3	7	>99	>99	>99
20–34	129	2.8	5	1	1	2	4	5	7	10
35–49	418	3.2	8	1	1	2	4	6	7	18
50–64	599	4.1	22	1	2	3	4	8	11	22
65+	529	4.4	18	1	1	3	6	9	12	21
GRAND TOTAL	**1,708**	**3.9**	**17**	**1**	**1**	**3**	**5**	**8**	**11**	**23**

53.51: INCISIONAL HERNIA REPAIR

Type of Patients	Observed Patients	Avg. Stay	Vari- ance	Percentiles 10th	25th	50th	75th	90th	95th	99th
1. SINGLE DX										
0–19 Years	2	1.5	<1	1	1	1	1	3	3	3
20–34	17	1.8	<1	1	1	1	2	3	3	4
35–49	40	2.1	2	1	1	1	3	4	5	7
50–64	34	2.3	2	1	1	2	3	4	6	7
65+	24	1.9	2	1	1	1	2	5	5	5
2. MULTIPLE DX										
0–19 Years	17	2.5	3	1	1	3	>99	>99	>99	>99
20–34	67	3.4	6	1	2	3	4	7	8	13
35–49	222	3.1	4	1	2	3	4	6	7	9
50–64	394	4.2	23	1	2	3	5	8	11	22
65+	329	4.5	16	1	2	4	6	9	13	21
TOTAL SINGLE DX	**117**	**2.0**	**2**	**1**	**1**	**2**	**3**	**4**	**5**	**7**
TOTAL MULTIPLE DX	**1,029**	**4.0**	**15**	**1**	**2**	**3**	**5**	**8**	**11**	**32**
TOTAL										
0–19 Years	19	2.4	3	1	1	3	>99	>99	>99	>99
20–34	84	2.9	5	1	1	2	4	7	7	10
35–49	262	2.9	4	1	1	2	4	6	7	9
50–64	428	4.0	21	1	2	3	4	8	11	22
65+	353	4.3	16	1	1	3	6	9	12	21
GRAND TOTAL	**1,146**	**3.8**	**14**	**1**	**1**	**3**	**5**	**8**	**10**	**23**

53.59: ABD WALL HERNIA REP NEC

Type of Patients	Observed Patients	Avg. Stay	Vari- ance	Percentiles 10th	25th	50th	75th	90th	95th	99th
1. SINGLE DX										
0–19 Years	6	2.9	2	1	1	4	4	4	5	5
20–34	12	1.4	<1	1	1	1	2	2	2	2
35–49	28	2.2	2	1	1	2	2	4	5	6
50–64	18	2.4	4	1	1	2	3	3	4	12
65+	10	1.8	2	1	1	1	2	6	6	6
2. MULTIPLE DX										
0–19 Years	8	12.5	253	1	3	4	10	40	40	40
20–34	33	3.1	5	1	1	2	5	5	9	9
35–49	128	4.0	17	1	1	3	5	8	11	20
50–64	153	4.4	27	1	2	3	5	9	19	42
65+	166	4.9	23	1	2	3	6	10	12	23
TOTAL SINGLE DX	**74**	**2.1**	**2**	**1**	**1**	**2**	**2**	**4**	**4**	**6**
TOTAL MULTIPLE DX	**488**	**4.5**	**26**	**1**	**1**	**3**	**6**	**9**	**15**	**30**
TOTAL										
0–19 Years	14	7.5	141	1	2	4	5	39	40	40
20–34	45	2.6	4	1	1	2	3	5	8	9
35–49	156	3.7	15	1	1	2	5	7	11	20
50–64	171	4.1	25	1	2	3	4	9	19	25
65+	176	4.7	23	1	1	3	6	10	12	23
GRAND TOTAL	**562**	**4.2**	**23**	**1**	**1**	**3**	**5**	**9**	**12**	**25**

53.6: REP OTH ABD HERNIA-GRAFT

Type of Patients	Observed Patients	Avg. Stay	Vari-ance	Percentiles 10th	25th	50th	75th	90th	95th	99th
1. SINGLE DX										
0–19 Years	2	1.8	1	1	1	1	3	3	3	3
20–34	76	2.2	2	1	1	2	3	4	5	8
35–49	285	2.2	2	1	1	2	3	4	5	7
50–64	276	2.3	2	1	1	2	3	5	5	7
65+	139	1.9	1	1	1	2	3	3	4	5
2. MULTIPLE DX										
0–19 Years	13	4.1	6	2	3	4	4	6	7	14
20–34	250	2.8	5	1	1	2	4	5	7	10
35–49	1,380	3.2	16	1	2	3	4	6	7	12
50–64	2,357	3.5	11	1	2	3	4	7	8	18
65+	2,432	3.9	16	1	2	3	5	7	10	18
TOTAL SINGLE DX	**778**	**2.2**	**2**	**1**	**1**	**2**	**3**	**4**	**5**	**7**
TOTAL MULTIPLE DX	**6,432**	**3.6**	**14**	**1**	**2**	**3**	**4**	**7**	**8**	**17**
TOTAL										
0–19 Years	15	3.9	6	1	3	4	4	6	7	14
20–34	326	2.7	4	1	1	2	3	5	7	10
35–49	1,665	3.0	14	1	1	2	4	5	7	11
50–64	2,633	3.4	10	1	2	3	4	6	8	17
65+	2,571	3.8	16	1	2	3	5	7	9	17
GRAND TOTAL	**7,210**	**3.4**	**13**	**1**	**2**	**3**	**4**	**6**	**8**	**16**

53.61: INC HERNIA REPAIR-PROSTH

Type of Patients	Observed Patients	Avg. Stay	Vari-ance	Percentiles 10th	25th	50th	75th	90th	95th	99th
1. SINGLE DX										
0–19 Years	1	3.0	0	3	3	3	3	3	3	3
20–34	57	2.4	3	1	1	2	3	4	5	11
35–49	224	2.2	2	1	1	2	3	4	5	7
50–64	220	2.3	2	1	1	2	3	5	5	7
65+	109	1.9	<1	1	1	2	3	3	4	5
2. MULTIPLE DX										
0–19 Years	8	4.1	7	3	3	4	4	5	14	14
20–34	190	2.9	4	1	2	2	4	5	7	9
35–49	1,146	3.3	17	1	2	3	4	6	7	12
50–64	1,885	3.5	12	1	2	3	4	7	8	18
65+	1,966	3.8	16	1	2	3	5	7	9	18
TOTAL SINGLE DX	**611**	**2.2**	**2**	**1**	**1**	**2**	**3**	**4**	**5**	**7**
TOTAL MULTIPLE DX	**5,195**	**3.6**	**14**	**1**	**2**	**3**	**4**	**7**	**8**	**17**
TOTAL										
0–19 Years	9	4.0	7	3	3	4	4	5	14	14
20–34	247	2.8	4	1	1	2	4	5	7	9
35–49	1,370	3.1	15	1	2	2	4	5	7	12
50–64	2,105	3.4	11	1	2	3	4	6	8	17
65+	2,075	3.7	15	1	2	3	5	7	9	17
GRAND TOTAL	**5,806**	**3.4**	**13**	**1**	**2**	**3**	**4**	**6**	**8**	**16**

53.69: ABD HERNIA REP-GRFT NEC

Type of Patients	Observed Patients	Avg. Stay	Vari-ance	Percentiles 10th	25th	50th	75th	90th	95th	99th
1. SINGLE DX										
0–19 Years	1	1.0	0	1	1	1	1	1	1	1
20–34	19	1.8	1	1	1	1	2	4	4	4
35–49	61	2.2	2	1	1	2	3	4	5	7
50–64	56	2.1	3	1	1	1	2	4	5	10
65+	30	2.0	1	1	1	2	3	3	4	5
2. MULTIPLE DX										
0–19 Years	5	4.2	5	2	2	3	6	7	7	7
20–34	60	2.8	5	1	1	2	3	6	10	10
35–49	234	3.0	14	1	1	2	3	5	7	9
50–64	472	3.3	9	1	2	2	4	6	8	20
65+	466	4.1	18	1	2	3	5	8	12	17
TOTAL SINGLE DX	**167**	**2.1**	**2**	**1**	**1**	**2**	**3**	**4**	**4**	**7**
TOTAL MULTIPLE DX	**1,237**	**3.5**	**14**	**1**	**2**	**3**	**4**	**7**	**9**	**17**
TOTAL										
0–19 Years	6	3.6	6	1	2	3	6	7	7	7
20–34	79	2.5	4	1	1	2	3	4	10	10
35–49	295	2.8	12	1	1	2	3	5	6	9
50–64	528	3.2	9	1	1	2	4	6	8	17
65+	496	4.0	17	1	2	3	5	8	12	17
GRAND TOTAL	**1,404**	**3.4**	**13**	**1**	**1**	**2**	**4**	**7**	**9**	**17**

53.7: ABD REP-DIAPH HERNIA

Type of Patients	Observed Patients	Avg. Stay	Vari-ance	Percentiles 10th	25th	50th	75th	90th	95th	99th
1. SINGLE DX										
0–19 Years	13	2.7	1	1	2	3	3	4	5	5
20–34	2	2.6	4	1	1	4	4	4	4	4
35–49	7	4.9	6	1	3	5	7	8	8	8
50–64	10	2.6	3	1	2	2	4	4	7	7
65+	6	4.1	11	2	2	3	4	12	12	12
2. MULTIPLE DX										
0–19 Years	65	10.2	104	2	4	5	13	24	27	46
20–34	17	4.8	25	1	2	3	5	13	17	18
35–49	77	6.3	45	1	3	5	8	14	15	25
50–64	150	5.8	35	2	3	4	7	10	17	31
65+	300	7.7	40	2	3	6	10	14	20	31
TOTAL SINGLE DX	**38**	**3.3**	**5**	**1**	**2**	**3**	**4**	**7**	**7**	**12**
TOTAL MULTIPLE DX	**609**	**7.4**	**50**	**2**	**3**	**5**	**9**	**15**	**21**	**39**
TOTAL										
0–19 Years	78	9.1	96	2	3	5	13	23	26	46
20–34	19	4.6	24	1	2	3	5	13	17	18
35–49	84	6.2	42	1	3	5	8	13	15	25
50–64	160	5.7	34	2	3	4	7	10	15	31
65+	306	7.6	40	2	3	6	10	14	20	31
GRAND TOTAL	**647**	**7.2**	**48**	**2**	**3**	**5**	**9**	**14**	**20**	**39**

53.8: REPAIR DH THOR APPR

Type of Patients	Observed Patients	Avg. Stay	Variance	10th	25th	50th	75th	90th	95th	99th
1. SINGLE DX										
0–19 Years	3	3.8	3	1	3	5	5	5	5	5
20–34	1	9.0	0	9	9	9	9	9	9	9
35–49	0									
50–64	4	3.5	4	2	2	2	6	7	7	7
65+	0									
2. MULTIPLE DX										
0–19 Years	26	9.5	155	2	3	6	8	20	22	59
20–34	14	5.8	13	3	4	5	7	11	16	16
35–49	19	6.7	98	1	1	4	8	11	14	52
50–64	40	7.5	17	4	5	5	12	14	15	17
65+	50	8.1	67	2	4	6	9	16	25	48
TOTAL SINGLE DX	**8**	**4.0**	**5**	**2**	**2**	**4**	**5**	**7**	**9**	**9**
TOTAL MULTIPLE DX	**149**	**8.0**	**74**	**2**	**4**	**6**	**8**	**15**	**20**	**59**
TOTAL										
0–19 Years	29	9.0	144	2	3	5	8	20	22	59
20–34	15	6.0	13	3	4	5	8	11	16	16
35–49	19	6.7	98	1	1	4	8	11	14	52
50–64	44	7.1	17	2	4	5	8	14	14	17
65+	50	8.1	67	2	4	6	9	16	25	48
GRAND TOTAL	**157**	**7.8**	**71**	**2**	**4**	**5**	**8**	**15**	**20**	**59**

53.80: REPAIR DH THOR APPR NOS

Type of Patients	Observed Patients	Avg. Stay	Variance	10th	25th	50th	75th	90th	95th	99th
1. SINGLE DX										
0–19 Years	2	4.5	<1	3	3	5	5	5	5	5
20–34	1	9.0	0	9	9	9	9	9	9	9
35–49	0									
50–64	3	3.0	4	2	2	2	4	7	7	7
65+	0									
2. MULTIPLE DX										
0–19 Years	16	6.7	32	2	2	5	8	15	21	22
20–34	13	5.9	14	3	3	5	8	11	16	16
35–49	15	6.8	121	1	1	2	8	11	14	52
50–64	30	7.0	16	3	5	5	8	13	15	17
65+	41	7.9	72	2	4	5	9	16	23	48
TOTAL SINGLE DX	**6**	**4.0**	**5**	**2**	**2**	**4**	**5**	**7**	**9**	**9**
TOTAL MULTIPLE DX	**115**	**7.2**	**51**	**2**	**3**	**5**	**8**	**15**	**19**	**48**
TOTAL										
0–19 Years	18	6.5	29	2	3	5	8	15	21	22
20–34	14	6.1	13	3	4	5	8	11	16	16
35–49	15	6.8	121	1	1	2	8	11	14	52
50–64	33	6.5	17	2	4	5	8	13	15	17
65+	41	7.9	72	2	4	5	9	16	23	48
GRAND TOTAL	**121**	**7.0**	**49**	**2**	**3**	**5**	**8**	**15**	**17**	**48**

53.9: OTHER HERNIA REPAIR

Type of Patients	Observed Patients	Avg. Stay	Variance	10th	25th	50th	75th	90th	95th	99th
1. SINGLE DX										
0–19 Years	1	3.0	0	3	3	3	3	3	3	3
20–34	3	1.4	<1	1	1	1	1	3	3	3
35–49	7	2.7	5	1	1	2	3	7	7	7
50–64	0									
65+	3	2.8	2	1	1	3	4	4	4	4
2. MULTIPLE DX										
0–19 Years	7	29.6	701	3	6	20	65	65	65	65
20–34	26	7.7	304	1	1	2	4	9	64	64
35–49	54	5.0	33	1	2	3	6	10	15	41
50–64	50	5.6	32	1	2	5	6	9	11	34
65+	71	7.1	26	2	4	6	9	13	16	30
TOTAL SINGLE DX	**14**	**2.3**	**3**	**1**	**1**	**1**	**3**	**4**	**6**	**7**
TOTAL MULTIPLE DX	**208**	**7.3**	**112**	**1**	**2**	**5**	**7**	**14**	**21**	**65**
TOTAL										
0–19 Years	8	26.9	693	3	6	15	65	65	65	65
20–34	29	6.8	262	1	1	2	4	9	64	64
35–49	61	4.8	31	1	2	3	6	10	14	41
50–64	50	5.6	32	1	2	5	6	9	11	34
65+	74	7.0	26	2	4	6	9	13	16	30
GRAND TOTAL	**222**	**7.0**	**107**	**1**	**2**	**4**	**7**	**13**	**20**	**65**

54.0: ABDOMINAL WALL INCISION

Type of Patients	Observed Patients	Avg. Stay	Variance	10th	25th	50th	75th	90th	95th	99th
1. SINGLE DX										
0–19 Years	26	2.9	3	1	1	3	4	6	6	6
20–34	23	2.6	3	1	1	2	3	6	6	7
35–49	20	1.9	3	1	1	1	2	4	5	8
50–64	10	3.7	5	1	2	3	6	7	7	7
65+	7	4.5	4	1	3	5	6	7	7	7
2. MULTIPLE DX										
0–19 Years	64	4.5	12	1	2	3	6	10	12	17
20–34	129	5.6	22	1	3	4	7	10	15	26
35–49	260	5.8	26	1	3	4	8	12	16	25
50–64	228	6.6	42	1	2	5	9	13	17	37
65+	255	6.6	30	1	3	5	8	13	17	28
TOTAL SINGLE DX	**86**	**2.8**	**3**	**1**	**1**	**2**	**4**	**6**	**6**	**7**
TOTAL MULTIPLE DX	**936**	**6.0**	**29**	**1**	**3**	**4**	**8**	**12**	**16**	**27**
TOTAL										
0–19 Years	90	4.1	10	1	2	3	5	10	11	13
20–34	152	5.1	20	1	2	4	6	9	14	26
35–49	280	5.5	25	1	2	4	7	11	16	25
50–64	238	6.5	41	1	2	5	8	13	16	37
65+	262	6.5	29	1	3	5	8	13	17	28
GRAND TOTAL	**1,022**	**5.8**	**28**	**1**	**2**	**4**	**8**	**12**	**16**	**27**

54.1: LAPAROTOMY

Type of Patients	Observed Patients	Avg. Stay	Vari-ance	Percentiles						
				10th	25th	50th	75th	90th	95th	99th
1. SINGLE DX										
0–19 Years	50	3.9	7	1	2	3	7	8	8	9
20–34	98	3.2	5	1	2	3	4	6	7	11
35–49	65	3.2	4	1	2	3	4	6	7	10
50–64	24	3.6	6	1	1	3	5	6	8	11
65+	13	4.9	24	1	1	4	6	15	18	18
2. MULTIPLE DX										
0–19 Years	259	7.8	66	2	3	6	9	18	24	>99
20–34	574	6.4	46	2	3	4	7	13	19	33
35–49	634	7.7	48	2	4	6	9	15	19	38
50–64	654	9.5	99	2	4	7	12	20	25	52
65+	677	9.7	63	3	4	7	12	19	25	41
TOTAL SINGLE DX	**250**	**3.5**	**7**	**1**	**2**	**3**	**4**	**7**	**8**	**12**
TOTAL MULTIPLE DX	**2,798**	**8.4**	**66**	**2**	**4**	**6**	**11**	**18**	**23**	**44**
TOTAL										
0–19 Years	309	7.2	59	2	3	5	8	16	24	>99
20–34	672	5.9	40	2	3	4	6	12	18	31
35–49	699	7.2	45	2	3	6	9	15	18	35
50–64	678	9.4	97	2	4	6	12	20	25	52
65+	690	9.6	62	3	4	7	12	19	25	41
GRAND TOTAL	**3,048**	**8.0**	**63**	**2**	**3**	**6**	**10**	**17**	**22**	**43**

54.11: EXPLORATORY LAPAROTOMY

Type of Patients	Observed Patients	Avg. Stay	Vari-ance	Percentiles						
				10th	25th	50th	75th	90th	95th	99th
1. SINGLE DX										
0–19 Years	38	3.7	7	1	1	3	7	8	8	9
20–34	78	3.4	5	1	2	3	4	6	7	10
35–49	48	3.2	3	1	2	3	4	4	6	12
50–64	18	4.1	6	1	2	4	5	8	11	11
65+	6	3.6	31	1	1	1	4	18	18	18
2. MULTIPLE DX										
0–19 Years	149	7.4	65	2	3	5	9	18	19	>99
20–34	355	5.9	48	2	3	4	6	13	21	33
35–49	333	7.3	39	2	3	6	9	15	18	35
50–64	376	8.3	47	2	4	6	11	18	22	29
65+	441	9.7	57	3	5	7	13	19	24	41
TOTAL SINGLE DX	**188**	**3.5**	**6**	**1**	**2**	**3**	**4**	**7**	**8**	**12**
TOTAL MULTIPLE DX	**1,654**	**8.0**	**53**	**2**	**3**	**6**	**10**	**17**	**21**	**40**
TOTAL										
0–19 Years	187	6.6	55	1	3	4	8	15	18	>99
20–34	433	5.4	41	2	2	4	5	10	17	33
35–49	381	6.7	36	2	3	5	8	14	18	35
50–64	394	8.2	46	2	4	6	11	18	21	29
65+	447	9.5	57	3	4	7	12	19	24	41
GRAND TOTAL	**1,842**	**7.5**	**50**	**2**	**3**	**5**	**9**	**16**	**21**	**38**

54.12: REOPEN RECENT LAP SITE

Type of Patients	Observed Patients	Avg. Stay	Vari-ance	Percentiles						
				10th	25th	50th	75th	90th	95th	99th
1. SINGLE DX										
0–19 Years	2	6.2	1	5	5	7	7	7	7	7
20–34	8	3.7	13	1	1	2	4	11	11	11
35–49	7	1.6	<1	1	1	1	2	3	3	3
50–64	5	1.4	<1	1	1	1	1	3	3	3
65+	3	6.4	2	5	5	6	8	8	8	8
2. MULTIPLE DX										
0–19 Years	26	6.1	8	3	4	6	7	11	11	17
20–34	57	5.5	12	2	3	5	7	11	14	19
35–49	84	6.5	35	2	4	5	7	11	18	25
50–64	81	9.7	133	1	3	6	13	23	28	78
65+	73	8.0	49	1	4	5	12	17	18	33
TOTAL SINGLE DX	**25**	**3.4**	**8**	**1**	**1**	**2**	**5**	**8**	**8**	**11**
TOTAL MULTIPLE DX	**321**	**7.3**	**52**	**2**	**3**	**5**	**8**	**15**	**19**	**41**
TOTAL										
0–19 Years	28	6.1	8	3	4	6	7	10	11	17
20–34	65	5.4	12	2	3	4	6	11	13	15
35–49	91	6.2	34	1	3	5	7	10	18	25
50–64	86	9.2	129	1	3	5	11	22	28	43
65+	76	7.9	47	1	4	5	12	17	18	33
GRAND TOTAL	**346**	**7.0**	**50**	**1**	**3**	**5**	**8**	**14**	**19**	**37**

54.19: LAPAROTOMY NEC

Type of Patients	Observed Patients	Avg. Stay	Vari-ance	Percentiles						
				10th	25th	50th	75th	90th	95th	99th
1. SINGLE DX										
0–19 Years	10	4.4	6	1	3	5	7	7	7	7
20–34	12	2.4	1	1	2	2	3	3	4	6
35–49	10	4.1	7	2	2	3	6	8	8	10
50–64	1	6.0	0	6	6	6	6	6	6	6
65+	4	6.7	24	3	4	5	5	15	15	15
2. MULTIPLE DX										
0–19 Years	84	9.0	82	2	4	7	11	24	24	86
20–34	162	7.7	51	2	4	6	9	16	19	41
35–49	217	8.7	63	2	4	7	10	17	20	44
50–64	197	11.6	176	3	4	8	14	24	30	90
65+	163	10.8	82	2	5	9	13	21	26	60
TOTAL SINGLE DX	**37**	**3.8**	**7**	**1**	**2**	**3**	**6**	**7**	**8**	**15**
TOTAL MULTIPLE DX	**823**	**9.6**	**95**	**2**	**4**	**7**	**12**	**19**	**25**	**60**
TOTAL										
0–19 Years	94	8.7	78	2	4	7	10	24	24	31
20–34	174	7.2	49	2	3	5	9	16	19	30
35–49	227	8.4	61	2	4	6	10	16	20	44
50–64	198	11.6	175	3	4	8	14	24	30	90
65+	167	10.7	81	2	4	9	13	21	26	60
GRAND TOTAL	**860**	**9.3**	**92**	**2**	**4**	**7**	**12**	**19**	**25**	**60**

54.2: ABD REGION DXTIC PX

Type of Patients	Observed Patients	Avg. Stay	Vari-ance	Percentiles						
				10th	25th	50th	75th	90th	95th	99th
1. SINGLE DX										
0–19 Years	70	1.8	2	1	1	1	2	3	5	10
20–34	163	2.1	3	1	1	1	3	4	5	8
35–49	74	2.2	2	1	1	2	3	5	5	5
50–64	33	2.4	2	1	1	2	3	4	6	7
65+	7	4.4	53	1	1	1	2	19	19	19
2. MULTIPLE DX										
0–19 Years	196	5.6	65	1	2	3	6	15	22	33
20–34	608	3.6	16	1	1	2	4	7	11	22
35–49	496	4.7	20	1	2	3	6	12	14	20
50–64	507	6.4	43	1	2	4	8	14	18	34
65+	679	7.2	41	1	3	5	9	15	19	29
TOTAL SINGLE DX	**347**	**2.1**	**3**	**1**	**1**	**1**	**3**	**4**	**5**	**8**
TOTAL MULTIPLE DX	**2,486**	**5.6**	**36**	**1**	**2**	**4**	**7**	**13**	**17**	**29**
TOTAL										
0–19 Years	266	4.7	52	1	1	3	5	10	21	33
20–34	771	3.3	14	1	1	2	4	7	9	18
35–49	570	4.4	19	1	1	3	5	10	14	20
50–64	540	6.1	41	1	2	4	8	14	18	34
65+	686	7.2	41	1	3	5	9	15	19	29
GRAND TOTAL	**2,833**	**5.2**	**33**	**1**	**2**	**3**	**6**	**12**	**17**	**28**

54.21: LAPAROSCOPY

Type of Patients	Observed Patients	Avg. Stay	Vari-ance	Percentiles						
				10th	25th	50th	75th	90th	95th	99th
1. SINGLE DX										
0–19 Years	63	1.6	<1	1	1	1	2	3	4	5
20–34	153	2.1	2	1	1	1	3	4	5	8
35–49	63	2.3	2	1	1	2	3	5	5	7
50–64	19	2.4	3	1	1	2	3	5	6	7
65+	3	1.3	<1	1	1	1	2	2	2	2
2. MULTIPLE DX										
0–19 Years	153	4.1	50	1	2	3	5	7	10	32
20–34	539	3.3	11	1	1	2	4	7	9	18
35–49	346	4.1	16	1	1	3	5	9	13	20
50–64	231	5.1	31	1	2	3	6	11	15	30
65+	194	7.0	62	1	2	5	9	15	22	44
TOTAL SINGLE DX	**301**	**2.0**	**2**	**1**	**1**	**1**	**3**	**4**	**5**	**7**
TOTAL MULTIPLE DX	**1,463**	**4.4**	**29**	**1**	**1**	**3**	**5**	**9**	**14**	**27**
TOTAL										
0–19 Years	216	3.4	37	1	1	2	4	7	8	21
20–34	692	3.0	10	1	1	2	4	6	8	18
35–49	409	3.8	14	1	1	3	5	8	12	20
50–64	250	4.8	28	1	2	3	6	10	14	30
65+	197	6.9	62	1	2	4	8	15	22	44
GRAND TOTAL	**1,764**	**4.0**	**25**	**1**	**1**	**3**	**5**	**8**	**12**	**26**

54.22: ABD WALL OR UMBILICUS BX

Type of Patients	Observed Patients	Avg. Stay	Vari-ance	Percentiles						
				10th	25th	50th	75th	90th	95th	99th
1. SINGLE DX										
0–19 Years	1	10.0	0	10	10	10	10	10	10	10
20–34	0									
35–49	0									
50–64	0									
65+	0									
2. MULTIPLE DX										
0–19 Years	3	5.6	<1	5	5	6	6	6	6	6
20–34	4	2.3	<1	1	2	2	3	3	3	3
35–49	9	9.5	42	3	4	9	10	23	23	23
50–64	23	8.0	45	4	4	5	10	14	29	29
65+	26	7.1	22	1	3	7	10	15	15	18
TOTAL SINGLE DX	**1**	**10.0**	**0**	**10**	**10**	**10**	**10**	**10**	**10**	**10**
TOTAL MULTIPLE DX	**65**	**7.3**	**32**	**2**	**4**	**5**	**10**	**15**	**18**	**29**
TOTAL										
0–19 Years	4	6.8	5	5	5	6	10	10	10	10
20–34	4	2.3	<1	1	2	2	3	3	3	3
35–49	9	9.5	42	3	4	9	10	23	23	23
50–64	23	8.0	45	4	4	5	10	14	29	29
65+	26	7.1	22	1	3	7	10	15	15	18
GRAND TOTAL	**66**	**7.3**	**32**	**2**	**4**	**6**	**10**	**15**	**18**	**29**

54.23: PERITONEAL BIOPSY

Type of Patients	Observed Patients	Avg. Stay	Vari-ance	Percentiles						
				10th	25th	50th	75th	90th	95th	99th
1. SINGLE DX										
0–19 Years	3	4.1	6	1	1	6	6	6	6	6
20–34	2	1.6	<1	1	1	2	2	2	2	2
35–49	3	1.6	<1	1	1	1	2	3	3	3
50–64	6	2.2	<1	1	2	2	3	3	3	3
65+	1	1.0	0	1	1	1	1	1	1	1
2. MULTIPLE DX										
0–19 Years	23	11.8	101	1	3	7	22	28	28	33
20–34	18	10.0	88	2	3	8	12	17	30	39
35–49	53	6.4	33	1	2	4	10	17	17	20
50–64	119	7.0	42	2	3	5	8	14	15	46
65+	173	8.3	40	2	4	6	10	17	23	29
TOTAL SINGLE DX	**15**	**2.4**	**3**	**1**	**1**	**2**	**3**	**6**	**6**	**6**
TOTAL MULTIPLE DX	**386**	**8.0**	**48**	**2**	**3**	**6**	**11**	**17**	**22**	**33**
TOTAL										
0–19 Years	26	10.8	96	1	3	6	22	22	28	33
20–34	20	8.5	82	2	2	7	11	17	30	39
35–49	56	6.0	32	1	2	4	8	17	17	20
50–64	125	6.8	41	2	3	5	8	14	15	46
65+	174	8.3	40	2	4	6	10	17	23	29
GRAND TOTAL	**401**	**7.8**	**48**	**2**	**3**	**6**	**10**	**17**	**22**	**33**

54.24: CLSD INTRA-ABD MASS BX

Type of Patients	Observed Patients	Avg. Stay	Vari-ance	Percentiles 10th	25th	50th	75th	90th	95th	99th
1. SINGLE DX										
0–19 Years	0									
20–34	2	7.9	87	2	2	2	17	17	17	17
35–49	6	2.0	<1	1	1	2	3	3	3	3
50–64	8	2.5	2	1	2	2	3	6	6	6
65+	3	8.6	109	1	1	1	19	19	19	19
2. MULTIPLE DX										
0–19 Years	7	4.8	11	1	3	4	5	11	11	11
20–34	29	7.4	56	1	2	5	9	18	25	31
35–49	66	6.2	22	1	3	5	7	13	14	20
50–64	125	7.2	48	1	3	5	10	16	18	43
65+	277	6.7	27	2	3	5	9	14	19	27
TOTAL SINGLE DX	**19**	**3.9**	**28**	**1**	**1**	**2**	**3**	**17**	**19**	**19**
TOTAL MULTIPLE DX	**504**	**6.8**	**32**	**1**	**3**	**5**	**9**	**14**	**18**	**27**
TOTAL										
0–19 Years	7	4.8	11	1	3	4	5	11	11	11
20–34	31	7.5	56	1	2	5	10	17	25	31
35–49	72	6.0	22	1	2	5	7	13	14	20
50–64	133	7.0	47	1	2	4	9	16	18	43
65+	280	6.7	27	2	3	5	9	14	19	27
GRAND TOTAL	**523**	**6.7**	**32**	**1**	**3**	**5**	**9**	**14**	**18**	**27**

54.3: EXC/DESTR ABD WALL LES

Type of Patients	Observed Patients	Avg. Stay	Vari-ance	Percentiles 10th	25th	50th	75th	90th	95th	99th
1. SINGLE DX										
0–19 Years	9	1.4	<1	1	1	1	1	3	4	4
20–34	22	2.7	8	1	1	2	3	6	8	15
35–49	21	2.6	4	1	1	2	4	6	6	7
50–64	7	1.8	1	1	1	1	3	4	4	4
65+	2	1.0	0	1	1	1	1	1	1	1
2. MULTIPLE DX										
0–19 Years	30	5.9	37	1	2	4	8	11	23	36
20–34	45	5.0	14	1	2	4	7	11	14	16
35–49	84	6.8	33	1	2	5	10	16	17	26
50–64	152	5.8	21	1	3	4	8	12	15	17
65+	133	5.5	30	1	3	4	6	11	14	27
TOTAL SINGLE DX	**61**	**2.2**	**4**	**1**	**1**	**1**	**3**	**5**	**6**	**8**
TOTAL MULTIPLE DX	**444**	**5.8**	**27**	**1**	**2**	**4**	**8**	**12**	**15**	**25**
TOTAL										
0–19 Years	39	5.0	33	1	1	3	7	10	18	36
20–34	67	4.2	13	1	1	3	5	10	13	16
35–49	105	6.0	30	1	2	4	9	14	17	26
50–64	159	5.5	21	1	2	4	8	12	15	17
65+	135	5.4	30	1	3	4	6	11	14	27
GRAND TOTAL	**505**	**5.4**	**26**	**1**	**2**	**4**	**7**	**12**	**15**	**24**

54.4: EXC/DESTR PERITON TISS

Type of Patients	Observed Patients	Avg. Stay	Vari-ance	Percentiles 10th	25th	50th	75th	90th	95th	99th
1. SINGLE DX										
0–19 Years	32	3.8	7	1	2	3	5	6	10	11
20–34	44	2.7	4	1	2	2	3	4	6	12
35–49	32	3.0	4	1	2	3	4	5	8	10
50–64	37	4.2	5	2	3	4	5	7	9	11
65+	11	4.8	39	2	2	3	5	6	30	30
2. MULTIPLE DX										
0–19 Years	59	5.1	16	2	3	4	6	10	13	26
20–34	133	3.9	14	1	2	3	5	7	11	25
35–49	251	4.6	10	2	2	4	6	9	11	15
50–64	402	6.7	33	2	3	5	8	13	21	28
65+	358	7.7	35	3	4	6	9	15	20	28
TOTAL SINGLE DX	**156**	**3.5**	**8**	**1**	**2**	**3**	**4**	**6**	**9**	**11**
TOTAL MULTIPLE DX	**1,203**	**6.2**	**27**	**2**	**3**	**5**	**7**	**12**	**16**	**28**
TOTAL										
0–19 Years	91	4.7	13	1	2	4	5	10	11	18
20–34	177	3.6	11	1	2	3	4	7	9	16
35–49	283	4.4	10	2	2	4	5	8	11	15
50–64	439	6.5	31	2	3	5	7	12	20	28
65+	369	7.6	35	3	4	6	9	15	20	30
GRAND TOTAL	**1,359**	**5.8**	**26**	**2**	**3**	**4**	**7**	**11**	**15**	**28**

54.5: PERITONEAL ADHESIOLYSIS

Type of Patients	Observed Patients	Avg. Stay	Vari-ance	Percentiles 10th	25th	50th	75th	90th	95th	99th
1. SINGLE DX										
0–19 Years	46	5.1	8	2	4	4	6	9	10	15
20–34	74	3.8	9	1	2	3	5	8	9	14
35–49	123	4.2	8	1	2	4	6	7	9	16
50–64	75	4.8	6	2	3	4	6	8	8	11
65+	26	5.7	9	2	3	5	8	9	9	13
2. MULTIPLE DX										
0–19 Years	323	7.7	50	2	4	6	10	16	22	38
20–34	834	5.3	29	1	2	4	7	10	15	24
35–49	1,928	6.0	30	2	3	5	7	12	16	27
50–64	2,030	8.1	40	2	4	7	10	16	20	31
65+	2,768	10.0	43	3	6	9	13	18	22	33
TOTAL SINGLE DX	**344**	**4.5**	**8**	**1**	**2**	**4**	**6**	**8**	**9**	**14**
TOTAL MULTIPLE DX	**7,883**	**8.0**	**41**	**2**	**4**	**7**	**10**	**16**	**20**	**31**
TOTAL										
0–19 Years	369	7.4	46	2	4	6	9	15	22	38
20–34	908	5.2	27	1	2	4	7	10	14	22
35–49	2,051	5.9	29	2	3	5	7	12	16	27
50–64	2,105	8.0	39	2	4	6	10	16	20	31
65+	2,794	10.0	43	3	6	9	13	18	22	33
GRAND TOTAL	**8,227**	**7.9**	**41**	**2**	**4**	**6**	**10**	**16**	**20**	**30**

54.51: LAPSCP PERITON ADHESIO

Type of Patients	Observed Patients	Avg. Stay	Vari-ance	Percentiles						
				10th	25th	50th	75th	90th	95th	99th
1. SINGLE DX										
0–19 Years	11	2.2	1	1	1	2	3	4	4	4
20–34	29	2.2	2	1	1	1	3	5	6	6
35–49	46	2.8	5	1	1	2	5	6	7	11
50–64	26	3.2	3	1	1	4	4	5	6	8
65+	6	4.4	9	1	1	5	5	9	9	9
2. MULTIPLE DX										
0–19 Years	98	5.7	57	1	2	4	6	12	22	48
20–34	368	3.9	13	1	2	3	5	7	10	21
35–49	595	3.9	19	1	2	3	5	8	11	18
50–64	408	4.5	19	1	2	3	6	9	12	27
65+	343	6.4	34	1	2	4	8	14	17	27
TOTAL SINGLE DX	**118**	**2.7**	**4**	**1**	**1**	**2**	**4**	**5**	**6**	**9**
TOTAL MULTIPLE DX	**1,812**	**4.7**	**24**	**1**	**2**	**3**	**6**	**10**	**14**	**24**
TOTAL										
0–19 Years	109	5.4	53	1	2	4	6	12	21	48
20–34	397	3.8	12	1	2	3	5	7	10	21
35–49	641	3.8	18	1	2	3	5	7	10	18
50–64	434	4.5	18	1	2	3	6	9	11	27
65+	349	6.3	34	1	2	4	8	14	17	27
GRAND TOTAL	**1,930**	**4.5**	**23**	**1**	**2**	**3**	**6**	**9**	**14**	**23**

54.59: PERITON ADHESIOLYSIS NEC

Type of Patients	Observed Patients	Avg. Stay	Vari-ance	Percentiles						
				10th	25th	50th	75th	90th	95th	99th
1. SINGLE DX										
0–19 Years	35	6.0	7	4	4	5	7	9	11	15
20–34	45	5.1	10	2	2	4	8	9	11	14
35–49	77	4.9	7	2	3	4	6	8	10	16
50–64	49	5.5	6	2	4	6	7	8	10	15
65+	20	6.0	9	2	4	6	8	9	13	13
2. MULTIPLE DX										
0–19 Years	225	8.5	45	3	5	6	10	16	22	29
20–34	466	6.5	38	2	3	5	8	11	17	29
35–49	1,333	6.9	32	2	3	5	9	13	18	27
50–64	1,622	9.0	41	3	5	7	11	17	21	33
65+	2,425	10.5	42	4	6	9	13	19	22	34
TOTAL SINGLE DX	**226**	**5.3**	**8**	**2**	**4**	**5**	**7**	**9**	**11**	**15**
TOTAL MULTIPLE DX	**6,071**	**9.0**	**42**	**3**	**5**	**8**	**11**	**17**	**21**	**32**
TOTAL										
0–19 Years	260	8.2	41	3	5	6	10	16	22	29
20–34	511	6.4	36	2	3	5	8	11	16	29
35–49	1,410	6.8	31	2	3	5	8	13	18	27
50–64	1,671	8.9	41	3	5	7	11	17	21	33
65+	2,445	10.5	42	4	6	9	13	18	22	33
GRAND TOTAL	**6,297**	**8.9**	**41**	**3**	**5**	**7**	**11**	**17**	**21**	**32**

54.6: ABD WALL/PERITON SUTURE

Type of Patients	Observed Patients	Avg. Stay	Vari-ance	Percentiles						
				10th	25th	50th	75th	90th	95th	99th
1. SINGLE DX										
0–19 Years	2	1.5	<1	1	1	2	2	2	2	2
20–34	25	2.3	2	1	1	2	3	4	5	7
35–49	6	1.8	1	1	1	1	2	4	4	4
50–64	6	2.3	2	1	2	2	2	6	6	6
65+	7	3.2	3	1	2	3	5	5	5	5
2. MULTIPLE DX										
0–19 Years	14	9.0	60	1	3	7	21	21	24	>99
20–34	59	4.1	23	1	1	3	5	7	13	35
35–49	63	5.0	21	1	2	4	6	9	11	19
50–64	72	6.7	31	2	3	5	8	12	19	29
65+	103	6.5	37	2	3	5	7	13	18	41
TOTAL SINGLE DX	**46**	**2.4**	**2**	**1**	**1**	**2**	**3**	**5**	**5**	**7**
TOTAL MULTIPLE DX	**311**	**6.0**	**33**	**1**	**3**	**5**	**7**	**12**	**19**	**30**
TOTAL										
0–19 Years	16	8.4	59	1	3	7	21	21	24	>99
20–34	84	3.6	18	1	1	3	4	7	9	19
35–49	69	4.7	20	1	2	4	6	9	10	19
50–64	78	6.3	30	1	3	5	8	12	19	25
65+	110	6.3	36	2	3	5	7	12	18	30
GRAND TOTAL	**357**	**5.6**	**31**	**1**	**2**	**4**	**7**	**11**	**19**	**30**

54.61: RECLOSE POSTOP DISRUPT

Type of Patients	Observed Patients	Avg. Stay	Vari-ance	Percentiles						
				10th	25th	50th	75th	90th	95th	99th
1. SINGLE DX										
0–19 Years	0									
20–34	14	2.9	2	1	2	3	4	5	7	7
35–49	4	1.9	2	1	1	1	2	4	4	4
50–64	5	1.9	<1	1	1	2	2	3	3	3
65+	6	3.4	2	1	2	3	5	5	5	5
2. MULTIPLE DX										
0–19 Years	2	17.7	33	9	9	21	21	21	21	21
20–34	19	5.4	43	1	3	3	7	7	19	35
35–49	35	5.8	28	2	3	5	7	10	16	36
50–64	53	5.9	24	2	3	5	8	10	12	29
65+	89	6.1	24	2	3	5	7	12	16	30
TOTAL SINGLE DX	**29**	**2.6**	**2**	**1**	**2**	**2**	**3**	**5**	**5**	**7**
TOTAL MULTIPLE DX	**198**	**6.2**	**30**	**2**	**3**	**5**	**7**	**12**	**19**	**30**
TOTAL										
0–19 Years	2	17.7	33	9	9	21	21	21	21	21
20–34	33	4.6	30	1	2	3	5	7	14	35
35–49	39	5.4	26	2	3	4	6	9	16	36
50–64	58	5.5	23	1	2	4	7	10	12	29
65+	95	5.9	23	2	3	5	7	12	16	30
GRAND TOTAL	**227**	**5.8**	**28**	**2**	**3**	**4**	**7**	**12**	**17**	**29**

54.7: OTH ABD WALL PERITON REP

Type of Patients	Observed Patients	Avg. Stay	Vari-ance	Percentiles 10th	25th	50th	75th	90th	95th	99th
1. SINGLE DX										
0–19 Years	4	2.5	2	1	1	3	4	4	4	4
20–34	2	1.2	<1	1	1	1	1	2	2	2
35–49	5	2.8	2	1	2	4	4	4	4	4
50–64	2	1.4	<1	1	1	1	2	2	2	2
65+	0									
2. MULTIPLE DX										
0–19 Years	110	28.2	554	5	14	23	33	68	97	>99
20–34	35	6.6	33	1	3	5	8	9	14	30
35–49	40	5.3	19	1	3	5	6	11	14	21
50–64	26	5.8	47	1	3	3	6	11	23	35
65+	26	6.1	20	1	3	6	9	13	16	17
TOTAL SINGLE DX	**13**	**2.1**	**2**	**1**	**1**	**2**	**3**	**4**	**4**	**4**
TOTAL MULTIPLE DX	**237**	**18.2**	**441**	**3**	**5**	**10**	**26**	**42**	**79**	**>99**
TOTAL										
0–19 Years	114	27.4	557	5	12	23	32	68	97	>99
20–34	37	5.9	32	1	3	5	8	9	14	30
35–49	45	5.0	17	1	3	4	5	10	14	21
50–64	28	5.6	46	1	3	3	6	11	21	35
65+	26	6.1	20	1	3	6	9	13	16	17
GRAND TOTAL	**250**	**17.4**	**431**	**2**	**4**	**9**	**25**	**41**	**70**	**>99**

54.71: REPAIR OF GASTROSCHISIS

Type of Patients	Observed Patients	Avg. Stay	Vari-ance	Percentiles 10th	25th	50th	75th	90th	95th	99th
1. SINGLE DX										
0–19 Years	0									
20–34	0									
35–49	0									
50–64	0									
65+	0									
2. MULTIPLE DX										
0–19 Years	100	33.6	547	15	19	26	40	93	97	>99
20–34	0									
35–49	0									
50–64	0									
65+	0									
TOTAL SINGLE DX	**0**									
TOTAL MULTIPLE DX	**100**	**33.6**	**547**	**15**	**19**	**26**	**40**	**93**	**97**	**>99**
TOTAL										
0–19 Years	100	33.6	547	15	19	26	40	93	97	>99
20–34	0									
35–49	0									
50–64	0									
65+	0									
GRAND TOTAL	**100**	**33.6**	**547**	**15**	**19**	**26**	**40**	**93**	**97**	**>99**

54.9: OTHER ABD REGION OPS

Type of Patients	Observed Patients	Avg. Stay	Vari-ance	Percentiles 10th	25th	50th	75th	90th	95th	99th
1. SINGLE DX										
0–19 Years	69	5.0	16	1	2	4	7	10	13	22
20–34	65	3.6	5	1	2	3	5	6	7	12
35–49	84	3.9	10	1	2	3	5	7	12	15
50–64	51	3.5	8	1	2	2	5	8	10	11
65+	20	4.2	6	1	2	4	5	7	9	10
2. MULTIPLE DX										
0–19 Years	591	7.5	83	1	3	5	9	15	23	64
20–34	977	5.7	38	2	2	4	7	11	15	24
35–49	3,504	5.7	28	1	2	4	7	12	15	27
50–64	5,015	5.8	29	2	3	4	7	12	16	26
65+	4,057	6.0	27	2	3	5	8	12	15	26
TOTAL SINGLE DX	**289**	**4.1**	**10**	**1**	**2**	**3**	**5**	**8**	**11**	**15**
TOTAL MULTIPLE DX	**14,144**	**5.9**	**32**	**2**	**3**	**4**	**7**	**12**	**16**	**27**
TOTAL										
0–19 Years	660	7.2	76	1	3	5	9	15	22	64
20–34	1,042	5.5	36	1	2	4	7	10	15	24
35–49	3,588	5.7	28	1	2	4	7	11	15	27
50–64	5,066	5.8	28	2	3	4	7	12	16	26
65+	4,077	6.0	27	2	3	5	8	12	15	26
GRAND TOTAL	**14,433**	**5.9**	**31**	**2**	**3**	**4**	**7**	**12**	**16**	**27**

54.91: PERC ABD DRAINAGE

Type of Patients	Observed Patients	Avg. Stay	Vari-ance	Percentiles 10th	25th	50th	75th	90th	95th	99th
1. SINGLE DX										
0–19 Years	52	5.4	20	2	2	4	7	11	14	22
20–34	53	4.0	5	1	2	4	5	7	8	12
35–49	75	3.8	9	1	2	3	4	7	11	15
50–64	42	3.7	8	1	2	3	5	9	11	11
65+	17	4.3	6	1	2	5	6	9	10	10
2. MULTIPLE DX										
0–19 Years	239	7.6	80	2	4	6	8	13	17	64
20–34	595	5.6	32	2	3	4	7	10	14	22
35–49	2,815	6.0	30	1	3	4	7	12	16	27
50–64	4,016	5.8	28	2	3	4	7	11	15	26
65+	3,089	6.1	25	2	3	5	8	12	15	24
TOTAL SINGLE DX	**239**	**4.3**	**11**	**1**	**2**	**3**	**5**	**9**	**11**	**16**
TOTAL MULTIPLE DX	**10,754**	**6.0**	**29**	**2**	**3**	**5**	**8**	**12**	**15**	**26**
TOTAL										
0–19 Years	291	7.2	69	2	4	6	8	13	16	64
20–34	648	5.5	30	2	3	4	7	10	13	22
35–49	2,890	5.9	29	1	3	4	7	12	16	27
50–64	4,058	5.8	28	2	3	4	7	11	15	26
65+	3,106	6.1	25	2	3	5	8	12	15	24
GRAND TOTAL	**10,993**	**5.9**	**29**	**2**	**3**	**5**	**7**	**12**	**15**	**26**

54.92: RMVL FB PERITON CAVITY

Type of Patients	Observed Patients	Avg. Stay	Vari-ance	10th	25th	50th	75th	90th	95th	99th
1. SINGLE DX										
0–19 Years	1	2.0	0	2	2	2	2	2	2	2
20–34	3	2.1	2	1	1	2	2	4	4	4
35–49	3	2.0	2	1	1	1	4	4	4	4
50–64	2	4.3	4	3	3	3	6	6	6	6
65+	1	5.0	0	5	5	5	5	5	5	5
2. MULTIPLE DX										
0–19 Years	4	9.5	36	2	9	9	9	21	21	21
20–34	18	6.1	37	1	2	4	6	19	23	23
35–49	37	5.9	24	2	3	4	7	9	21	23
50–64	49	6.5	68	1	3	4	7	11	21	60
65+	39	7.2	19	2	4	6	10	15	18	>99
TOTAL SINGLE DX	**10**	**2.8**	**3**	**1**	**1**	**2**	**4**	**5**	**6**	**6**
TOTAL MULTIPLE DX	**147**	**6.7**	**39**	**2**	**3**	**5**	**9**	**14**	**21**	**60**
TOTAL										
0–19 Years	5	8.4	38	2	2	9	9	21	21	21
20–34	21	5.5	33	1	2	3	6	11	23	23
35–49	40	5.6	24	1	3	4	7	9	19	23
50–64	51	6.4	66	1	3	4	7	9	21	60
65+	40	7.2	19	2	4	6	10	15	15	>99
GRAND TOTAL	**157**	**6.4**	**38**	**2**	**3**	**4**	**9**	**13**	**21**	**60**

54.93: CREATE CUTANEOPERIT FIST

Type of Patients	Observed Patients	Avg. Stay	Vari-ance	10th	25th	50th	75th	90th	95th	99th
1. SINGLE DX										
0–19 Years	2	2.4	3	1	1	1	4	4	4	4
20–34	3	1.0	0	1	1	1	1	1	1	1
35–49	0									
50–64	3	1.3	<1	1	1	1	2	2	2	2
65+	1	1.0	0	1	1	1	1	1	1	1
2. MULTIPLE DX										
0–19 Years	80	10.9	175	1	2	5	15	27	38	58
20–34	62	5.5	25	1	2	4	7	10	15	26
35–49	107	5.6	37	1	2	4	7	14	18	27
50–64	186	6.5	41	1	2	4	9	14	19	26
65+	200	6.4	27	1	2	5	9	13	17	23
TOTAL SINGLE DX	**9**	**1.5**	**1**	**1**	**1**	**1**	**1**	**4**	**4**	**4**
TOTAL MULTIPLE DX	**635**	**7.0**	**60**	**1**	**2**	**4**	**9**	**15**	**21**	**38**
TOTAL										
0–19 Years	82	10.8	173	1	2	5	15	24	38	58
20–34	65	5.3	24	1	2	4	7	10	15	26
35–49	107	5.6	37	1	2	4	7	14	18	27
50–64	189	6.5	40	1	2	4	8	14	19	26
65+	201	6.3	27	1	2	5	9	13	17	23
GRAND TOTAL	**644**	**6.9**	**60**	**1**	**2**	**4**	**9**	**15**	**21**	**38**

54.94: CREAT PERITONEOVAS SHUNT

Type of Patients	Observed Patients	Avg. Stay	Vari-ance	10th	25th	50th	75th	90th	95th	99th
1. SINGLE DX										
0–19 Years	0									
20–34	0									
35–49	0									
50–64	0									
65+	0									
2. MULTIPLE DX										
0–19 Years	5	12.8	122	2	5	8	23	28	28	28
20–34	2	21.8	618	2	2	2	42	42	42	42
35–49	21	6.0	45	1	1	4	7	19	23	24
50–64	30	7.7	49	2	3	7	10	17	28	31
65+	32	6.9	75	1	2	3	9	15	21	43
TOTAL SINGLE DX	**0**									
TOTAL MULTIPLE DX	**90**	**7.6**	**72**	**1**	**2**	**4**	**9**	**19**	**28**	**42**
TOTAL										
0–19 Years	5	12.8	122	2	5	8	23	28	28	28
20–34	2	21.8	618	2	2	2	42	42	42	42
35–49	21	6.0	45	1	1	4	7	19	23	24
50–64	30	7.7	49	2	3	7	10	17	28	31
65+	32	6.9	75	1	2	3	9	15	21	43
GRAND TOTAL	**90**	**7.6**	**72**	**1**	**2**	**4**	**9**	**19**	**28**	**42**

54.95: PERITONEAL INCISION

Type of Patients	Observed Patients	Avg. Stay	Vari-ance	10th	25th	50th	75th	90th	95th	99th
1. SINGLE DX										
0–19 Years	12	3.9	3	1	3	4	4	7	7	7
20–34	6	2.9	3	1	2	2	4	6	6	6
35–49	4	6.5	24	3	3	5	13	13	13	13
50–64	2	1.0	0	1	1	1	1	1	1	1
65+	1	4.0	0	4	4	4	4	4	4	4
2. MULTIPLE DX										
0–19 Years	159	6.5	56	1	2	5	8	14	19	>99
20–34	115	7.6	103	1	2	4	9	18	22	65
35–49	123	6.1	29	1	2	4	8	13	16	25
50–64	187	7.3	46	1	2	5	11	16	20	38
65+	159	8.5	72	1	3	5	11	18	24	47
TOTAL SINGLE DX	**25**	**3.8**	**6**	**1**	**2**	**4**	**4**	**7**	**7**	**13**
TOTAL MULTIPLE DX	**743**	**7.2**	**60**	**1**	**2**	**5**	**9**	**16**	**20**	**39**
TOTAL										
0–19 Years	171	6.3	52	1	2	5	8	14	19	>99
20–34	121	7.4	99	1	2	4	9	18	20	65
35–49	127	6.1	29	1	2	4	8	13	16	25
50–64	189	7.3	46	1	2	5	11	16	20	38
65+	160	8.4	72	1	3	5	11	18	24	47
GRAND TOTAL	**768**	**7.0**	**58**	**1**	**2**	**5**	**9**	**16**	**20**	**39**

54.98: PERITONEAL DIALYSIS

Type of Patients	Observed Patients	Avg. Stay	Vari-ance	10th	25th	50th	75th	90th	95th	99th
1. SINGLE DX										
0–19 Years	1	9.0	0	9	9	9	9	9	9	9
20–34	0									
35–49	0									
50–64	0									
65+	0									
2. MULTIPLE DX										
0–19 Years	99	5.2	31	1	2	4	6	10	22	26
20–34	179	4.4	13	1	2	3	5	9	12	18
35–49	383	4.1	10	1	2	3	5	8	10	14
50–64	531	4.9	15	2	3	4	6	10	13	20
65+	524	4.9	21	2	2	4	6	9	11	33
TOTAL SINGLE DX	**1**	**9.0**	**0**	**9**	**9**	**9**	**9**	**9**	**9**	**9**
TOTAL MULTIPLE DX	**1,716**	**4.7**	**17**	**1**	**2**	**4**	**6**	**9**	**12**	**22**
TOTAL										
0–19 Years	100	5.2	31	1	2	4	6	10	22	26
20–34	179	4.4	13	1	2	3	5	9	12	18
35–49	383	4.1	10	1	2	3	5	8	10	14
50–64	531	4.9	15	2	3	4	6	10	13	20
65+	524	4.9	21	2	2	4	6	9	11	33
GRAND TOTAL	**1,717**	**4.7**	**17**	**1**	**2**	**4**	**6**	**9**	**12**	**22**

55.0: NEPHROTOMY & NEPHROSTOMY

Type of Patients	Observed Patients	Avg. Stay	Vari-ance	10th	25th	50th	75th	90th	95th	99th
1. SINGLE DX										
0–19 Years	3	5.9	6	2	4	8	8	8	8	8
20–34	63	3.0	5	1	2	2	3	5	6	18
35–49	89	2.3	2	1	1	2	3	4	5	9
50–64	63	2.3	2	1	1	2	3	4	6	7
65+	18	2.0	<1	1	1	2	3	3	3	3
2. MULTIPLE DX										
0–19 Years	91	7.4	147	1	3	4	7	14	22	85
20–34	342	4.2	14	1	2	3	5	9	12	21
35–49	617	5.1	22	1	2	4	6	11	15	22
50–64	932	6.0	36	1	2	4	8	13	19	29
65+	1,201	7.8	53	2	3	6	10	15	20	41
TOTAL SINGLE DX	**236**	**2.5**	**3**	**1**	**1**	**2**	**3**	**4**	**6**	**9**
TOTAL MULTIPLE DX	**3,183**	**6.4**	**44**	**1**	**2**	**4**	**8**	**14**	**18**	**30**
TOTAL										
0–19 Years	94	7.3	143	1	3	4	7	14	22	85
20–34	405	4.0	13	1	2	3	5	8	11	20
35–49	706	4.8	21	1	2	3	6	11	14	21
50–64	995	5.8	34	1	2	4	7	13	18	29
65+	1,219	7.7	53	2	3	6	10	15	20	41
GRAND TOTAL	**3,419**	**6.1**	**43**	**1**	**2**	**4**	**8**	**13**	**18**	**29**

55.01: NEPHROTOMY

Type of Patients	Observed Patients	Avg. Stay	Vari-ance	10th	25th	50th	75th	90th	95th	99th
1. SINGLE DX										
0–19 Years	1	4.0	0	4	4	4	4	4	4	4
20–34	9	2.7	2	1	2	2	3	6	6	6
35–49	14	2.6	6	1	1	1	3	5	9	9
50–64	5	2.6	3	1	2	2	2	6	6	6
65+	2	2.3	1	1	1	3	3	3	3	3
2. MULTIPLE DX										
0–19 Years	9	4.9	7	1	3	5	6	7	11	11
20–34	30	4.5	17	2	3	3	5	8	15	23
35–49	45	5.4	24	2	3	3	6	13	17	26
50–64	80	4.3	15	1	2	3	5	10	12	18
65+	50	5.5	19	1	2	4	7	11	15	20
TOTAL SINGLE DX	**31**	**2.7**	**4**	**1**	**1**	**2**	**3**	**5**	**6**	**9**
TOTAL MULTIPLE DX	**214**	**4.9**	**18**	**1**	**2**	**3**	**6**	**10**	**15**	**20**
TOTAL										
0–19 Years	10	4.8	6	1	3	5	6	7	11	11
20–34	39	4.1	15	2	2	3	4	8	9	23
35–49	59	4.7	21	1	2	3	5	11	17	26
50–64	85	4.2	15	1	2	3	5	9	12	18
65+	52	5.3	19	1	2	4	7	11	15	20
GRAND TOTAL	**245**	**4.6**	**17**	**1**	**2**	**3**	**6**	**10**	**13**	**20**

55.02: NEPHROSTOMY

Type of Patients	Observed Patients	Avg. Stay	Vari-ance	10th	25th	50th	75th	90th	95th	99th
1. SINGLE DX										
0–19 Years	0									
20–34	2	3.5	12	1	1	4	6	6	6	6
35–49	1	1.0	0	1	1	1	1	1	1	1
50–64	2	1.6	<1	1	1	2	2	2	2	2
65+	0									
2. MULTIPLE DX										
0–19 Years	12	19.1	778	2	3	4	22	85	85	85
20–34	26	5.9	21	2	3	6	7	12	12	25
35–49	45	8.6	41	1	3	8	12	18	20	31
50–64	85	7.8	69	1	3	6	10	17	22	37
65+	146	8.9	73	3	4	7	11	17	20	42
TOTAL SINGLE DX	**5**	**2.1**	**4**	**1**	**1**	**1**	**2**	**6**	**6**	**6**
TOTAL MULTIPLE DX	**314**	**9.1**	**121**	**2**	**3**	**6**	**11**	**18**	**22**	**85**
TOTAL										
0–19 Years	12	19.1	778	2	3	4	22	85	85	85
20–34	28	5.8	21	1	3	6	7	12	12	25
35–49	46	8.4	42	1	3	7	12	18	20	31
50–64	87	7.7	68	1	3	6	9	17	22	37
65+	146	8.9	73	3	4	7	11	17	20	42
GRAND TOTAL	**319**	**9.0**	**120**	**2**	**3**	**6**	**11**	**18**	**22**	**85**

55.03: PERC NEPHROSTOMY S FRAG

Type of Patients	Observed Patients	Avg. Stay	Vari-ance	Percentiles						
				10th	25th	50th	75th	90th	95th	99th
1. SINGLE DX										
0–19 Years	1	2.0	0	2	2	2	2	2	2	2
20–34	26	3.0	9	1	2	2	3	4	7	18
35–49	34	2.4	3	1	1	2	3	5	5	9
50–64	21	2.2	2	1	1	2	3	4	4	7
65+	7	1.8	<1	1	1	2	2	3	3	3
2. MULTIPLE DX										
0–19 Years	62	5.7	21	1	2	5	7	12	14	22
20–34	210	4.4	17	1	2	3	5	10	13	21
35–49	375	5.7	25	1	2	4	7	12	15	26
50–64	534	7.0	37	2	3	5	9	15	20	29
65+	872	8.3	55	2	4	6	10	16	21	42
TOTAL SINGLE DX	**89**	**2.5**	**4**	**1**	**1**	**2**	**3**	**4**	**5**	**9**
TOTAL MULTIPLE DX	**2,053**	**7.0**	**42**	**2**	**3**	**5**	**9**	**14**	**19**	**30**
TOTAL										
0–19 Years	63	5.7	21	1	2	5	7	12	14	22
20–34	236	4.2	17	1	2	3	5	10	13	21
35–49	409	5.5	24	1	2	4	7	12	15	26
50–64	555	6.8	37	2	3	5	9	14	20	29
65+	879	8.2	55	2	4	6	10	16	21	42
GRAND TOTAL	**2,142**	**6.8**	**41**	**2**	**3**	**5**	**9**	**14**	**19**	**30**

55.04: PERC NEPHROSTOMY W FRAG

Type of Patients	Observed Patients	Avg. Stay	Vari-ance	Percentiles						
				10th	25th	50th	75th	90th	95th	99th
1. SINGLE DX										
0–19 Years	1	8.0	0	8	8	8	8	8	8	8
20–34	26	3.0	2	2	2	3	4	5	5	7
35–49	40	2.1	<1	1	2	2	2	3	3	7
50–64	35	2.3	2	1	1	2	3	4	4	9
65+	9	2.1	<1	1	1	2	3	3	3	3
2. MULTIPLE DX										
0–19 Years	8	3.8	3	2	2	4	5	6	6	6
20–34	76	3.3	4	2	2	3	4	6	9	10
35–49	152	3.0	4	1	2	3	4	5	7	11
50–64	233	3.7	17	1	2	2	4	7	12	26
65+	133	4.2	18	1	2	3	5	9	13	25
TOTAL SINGLE DX	**111**	**2.5**	**2**	**1**	**2**	**2**	**3**	**4**	**5**	**8**
TOTAL MULTIPLE DX	**602**	**3.6**	**12**	**1**	**2**	**3**	**4**	**7**	**9**	**25**
TOTAL										
0–19 Years	9	4.4	4	2	3	4	6	8	8	8
20–34	102	3.2	4	2	2	3	4	5	7	10
35–49	192	2.8	3	1	2	2	3	4	7	10
50–64	268	3.5	16	1	2	2	4	6	11	26
65+	142	4.1	17	1	2	3	5	8	10	25
GRAND TOTAL	**713**	**3.4**	**11**	**1**	**2**	**3**	**4**	**6**	**9**	**20**

55.1: PYELOTOMY & PYELOSTOMY

Type of Patients	Observed Patients	Avg. Stay	Vari-ance	Percentiles						
				10th	25th	50th	75th	90th	95th	99th
1. SINGLE DX										
0–19 Years	3	3.4	<1	3	3	3	4	4	4	4
20–34	2	2.1	2	1	1	3	3	3	3	3
35–49	8	2.5	<1	1	2	3	3	4	4	4
50–64	4	4.2	12	2	2	2	5	10	10	10
65+	2	3.0	0	3	3	3	3	3	3	3
2. MULTIPLE DX										
0–19 Years	9	4.7	7	2	3	3	6	6	13	13
20–34	27	3.5	5	1	1	3	5	5	7	12
35–49	28	4.0	13	1	2	3	5	6	8	22
50–64	37	4.4	8	1	3	5	5	7	8	19
65+	38	6.1	41	2	2	4	8	14	14	46
TOTAL SINGLE DX	**19**	**3.2**	**2**	**2**	**3**	**3**	**3**	**4**	**5**	**10**
TOTAL MULTIPLE DX	**139**	**4.6**	**18**	**1**	**2**	**4**	**5**	**8**	**12**	**19**
TOTAL										
0–19 Years	12	4.2	5	3	3	3	6	6	6	13
20–34	29	3.4	5	1	1	3	5	5	7	12
35–49	36	3.8	11	1	2	3	5	5	6	22
50–64	41	4.3	8	1	2	5	5	7	10	19
65+	40	5.9	40	2	2	4	8	14	14	46
GRAND TOTAL	**158**	**4.4**	**16**	**1**	**2**	**4**	**5**	**8**	**11**	**19**

55.11: PYELOTOMY

Type of Patients	Observed Patients	Avg. Stay	Vari-ance	Percentiles						
				10th	25th	50th	75th	90th	95th	99th
1. SINGLE DX										
0–19 Years	3	3.4	<1	3	3	3	4	4	4	4
20–34	2	2.1	2	1	1	3	3	3	3	3
35–49	8	2.5	<1	1	2	3	3	4	4	4
50–64	4	4.2	12	2	2	2	5	10	10	10
65+	2	3.0	0	3	3	3	3	3	3	3
2. MULTIPLE DX										
0–19 Years	7	4.3	3	2	3	3	6	6	6	6
20–34	23	2.7	3	1	1	3	4	5	6	7
35–49	22	3.2	3	1	2	3	5	5	6	8
50–64	30	4.0	3	1	3	4	5	5	7	8
65+	28	4.8	15	1	2	3	7	10	14	14
TOTAL SINGLE DX	**19**	**3.2**	**2**	**2**	**3**	**3**	**3**	**4**	**5**	**10**
TOTAL MULTIPLE DX	**110**	**3.8**	**7**	**1**	**2**	**3**	**5**	**7**	**8**	**14**
TOTAL										
0–19 Years	10	3.9	2	3	3	3	6	6	6	6
20–34	25	2.7	3	1	1	3	4	5	5	7
35–49	30	3.1	3	1	2	3	5	5	6	8
50–64	34	4.0	4	2	2	4	5	6	8	10
65+	30	4.7	14	2	2	3	7	10	14	14
GRAND TOTAL	**129**	**3.7**	**6**	**1**	**2**	**3**	**5**	**6**	**8**	**14**

55.2: RENAL DIAGNOSTIC PX

Type of Patients	Observed Patients	Avg. Stay	Vari-ance	Percentiles						
				10th	25th	50th	75th	90th	95th	99th
1. SINGLE DX										
0–19 Years	78	1.6	2	1	1	1	1	3	5	8
20–34	25	1.4	<1	1	1	1	2	2	3	4
35–49	23	1.5	2	1	1	1	1	2	2	9
50–64	14	2.8	4	1	1	3	4	4	4	10
65+	4	1.5	<1	1	1	1	2	3	3	3
2. MULTIPLE DX										
0–19 Years	328	5.1	29	1	1	4	7	11	17	22
20–34	419	5.6	24	1	2	5	7	10	16	26
35–49	501	5.5	25	1	2	5	8	11	15	23
50–64	579	6.1	37	1	2	5	8	13	16	30
65+	427	7.0	23	1	3	7	10	13	15	22
TOTAL SINGLE DX	**144**	**1.7**	**2**	**1**	**1**	**1**	**1**	**3**	**4**	**9**
TOTAL MULTIPLE DX	**2,254**	**5.9**	**28**	**1**	**2**	**5**	**8**	**12**	**16**	**27**
TOTAL										
0–19 Years	406	4.4	25	1	1	3	6	10	15	21
20–34	444	5.4	23	1	2	4	7	10	16	25
35–49	524	5.4	24	1	2	4	7	11	15	23
50–64	593	6.0	37	1	2	4	8	13	16	30
65+	431	7.0	23	1	3	7	9	13	15	22
GRAND TOTAL	**2,398**	**5.6**	**28**	**1**	**2**	**4**	**8**	**12**	**15**	**26**

55.23: CLOSED RENAL BIOPSY

Type of Patients	Observed Patients	Avg. Stay	Vari-ance	Percentiles						
				10th	25th	50th	75th	90th	95th	99th
1. SINGLE DX										
0–19 Years	73	1.5	2	1	1	1	1	3	3	8
20–34	24	1.4	<1	1	1	1	2	2	3	4
35–49	23	1.5	2	1	1	1	1	2	2	9
50–64	12	2.2	5	1	1	1	3	3	10	10
65+	3	1.2	<1	1	1	1	1	2	2	2
2. MULTIPLE DX										
0–19 Years	301	4.7	20	1	1	3	7	10	15	21
20–34	409	5.6	24	1	2	5	7	10	16	26
35–49	487	5.7	25	1	2	5	8	11	15	23
50–64	552	6.2	38	1	2	5	8	13	17	30
65+	407	7.1	22	2	4	7	10	13	15	22
TOTAL SINGLE DX	**135**	**1.5**	**2**	**1**	**1**	**1**	**1**	**3**	**3**	**9**
TOTAL MULTIPLE DX	**2,156**	**5.9**	**27**	**1**	**2**	**5**	**8**	**12**	**15**	**26**
TOTAL										
0–19 Years	374	4.1	18	1	1	2	5	9	13	21
20–34	433	5.4	24	1	2	4	7	10	16	26
35–49	510	5.5	25	1	2	4	8	11	15	23
50–64	564	6.1	38	1	2	4	8	13	17	30
65+	410	7.1	22	2	4	7	10	13	15	22
GRAND TOTAL	**2,291**	**5.6**	**27**	**1**	**2**	**4**	**8**	**12**	**15**	**25**

55.24: OPEN BIOPSY OF KIDNEY

Type of Patients	Observed Patients	Avg. Stay	Vari-ance	Percentiles						
				10th	25th	50th	75th	90th	95th	99th
1. SINGLE DX										
0–19 Years	4	3.4	10	1	1	1	4	8	8	8
20–34	0									
35–49	0									
50–64	1	4.0	0	4	4	4	4	4	4	4
65+	1	3.0	0	3	3	3	3	3	3	3
2. MULTIPLE DX										
0–19 Years	25	8.6	104	1	1	6	11	17	30	59
20–34	5	6.4	40	1	4	4	4	19	19	19
35–49	10	3.9	20	1	1	2	5	7	19	19
50–64	19	6.3	14	2	4	6	8	12	12	16
65+	13	4.1	37	1	1	3	4	6	29	29
TOTAL SINGLE DX	**6**	**3.7**	**4**	**1**	**3**	**4**	**4**	**4**	**8**	**8**
TOTAL MULTIPLE DX	**72**	**6.7**	**64**	**1**	**2**	**4**	**8**	**16**	**19**	**30**
TOTAL										
0–19 Years	29	8.1	97	1	1	6	10	17	19	59
20–34	5	6.4	40	1	4	4	4	19	19	19
35–49	10	3.9	20	1	1	2	5	7	19	19
50–64	20	5.7	11	2	4	4	7	11	12	16
65+	14	4.1	35	1	1	3	4	6	6	29
GRAND TOTAL	**78**	**6.4**	**59**	**1**	**2**	**4**	**8**	**16**	**19**	**30**

55.3: LOC EXC/DESTR RENAL LES

Type of Patients	Observed Patients	Avg. Stay	Vari-ance	Percentiles						
				10th	25th	50th	75th	90th	95th	99th
1. SINGLE DX										
0–19 Years	2	2.5	<1	2	2	2	3	3	3	3
20–34	2	2.5	<1	2	2	3	3	3	3	3
35–49	6	4.2	2	3	3	4	5	7	7	7
50–64	11	2.4	<1	1	2	3	3	3	3	3
65+	5	2.4	<1	1	2	2	3	3	3	3
2. MULTIPLE DX										
0–19 Years	1	1.0	0	1	1	1	1	1	1	1
20–34	11	3.2	2	1	2	4	4	4	5	5
35–49	39	3.6	9	1	2	3	5	6	8	20
50–64	59	2.4	2	1	1	2	3	4	5	7
65+	82	3.6	9	1	2	2	5	8	10	11
TOTAL SINGLE DX	**26**	**2.7**	**1**	**2**	**2**	**3**	**3**	**3**	**5**	**7**
TOTAL MULTIPLE DX	**192**	**3.2**	**6**	**1**	**2**	**3**	**4**	**6**	**8**	**11**
TOTAL										
0–19 Years	3	2.2	<1	1	2	2	3	3	3	3
20–34	13	3.1	2	1	2	4	4	4	5	5
35–49	45	3.7	8	1	2	3	5	6	8	20
50–64	70	2.4	1	1	1	2	3	4	5	7
65+	87	3.5	9	1	2	2	4	8	10	11
GRAND TOTAL	**218**	**3.1**	**6**	**1**	**2**	**3**	**4**	**6**	**8**	**11**

55.39: LOC DESTR RENAL LES NEC

Type of Patients	Observed Patients	Avg. Stay	Vari-ance	Percentiles 10th	25th	50th	75th	90th	95th	99th
1. SINGLE DX										
0–19 Years	2	2.5	<1	2	2	2	3	3	3	3
20–34	2	2.5	<1	2	2	3	3	3	3	3
35–49	4	3.6	1	3	3	3	5	5	5	5
50–64	10	2.5	<1	1	2	3	3	3	3	3
65+	4	2.5	<1	1	2	3	3	3	3	3
2. MULTIPLE DX										
0–19 Years	1	1.0	0	1	1	1	1	1	1	1
20–34	11	3.2	2	1	2	4	4	4	5	5
35–49	31	3.9	9	1	3	3	5	6	6	20
50–64	52	2.4	2	1	2	2	3	4	4	7
65+	79	3.7	9	1	2	3	5	8	10	11
TOTAL SINGLE DX	**22**	**2.6**	**<1**	**1**	**2**	**3**	**3**	**3**	**3**	**5**
TOTAL MULTIPLE DX	**174**	**3.3**	**7**	**1**	**2**	**3**	**4**	**6**	**8**	**11**
TOTAL										
0–19 Years	3	2.2	<1	1	2	2	3	3	3	3
20–34	13	3.1	2	1	2	4	4	4	5	5
35–49	35	3.9	8	1	3	3	5	6	6	20
50–64	62	2.4	1	1	2	2	3	4	4	7
65+	83	3.6	9	1	2	3	5	8	10	11
GRAND TOTAL	**196**	**3.2**	**6**	**1**	**2**	**3**	**4**	**6**	**8**	**11**

55.4: PARTIAL NEPHRECTOMY

Type of Patients	Observed Patients	Avg. Stay	Vari-ance	Percentiles 10th	25th	50th	75th	90th	95th	99th
1. SINGLE DX										
0–19 Years	11	2.7	<1	2	2	3	3	4	5	5
20–34	7	3.7	2	3	3	3	3	5	8	8
35–49	21	3.4	2	1	2	4	4	5	5	6
50–64	27	3.9	3	2	2	3	6	6	7	7
65+	15	3.9	3	2	2	4	5	6	6	6
2. MULTIPLE DX										
0–19 Years	57	2.9	3	1	2	2	4	5	6	10
20–34	29	4.1	3	2	3	4	5	6	7	10
35–49	132	4.7	5	3	3	4	6	7	9	12
50–64	288	4.5	4	3	3	4	5	7	8	12
65+	275	5.2	25	2	3	4	6	8	9	27
TOTAL SINGLE DX	**81**	**3.5**	**2**	**2**	**2**	**3**	**5**	**6**	**6**	**7**
TOTAL MULTIPLE DX	**781**	**4.6**	**12**	**2**	**3**	**4**	**5**	**7**	**8**	**14**
TOTAL										
0–19 Years	68	2.9	3	1	2	2	4	5	6	10
20–34	36	4.0	3	3	3	4	5	6	7	10
35–49	153	4.5	4	2	3	4	5	7	9	12
50–64	315	4.5	4	2	3	4	6	7	8	12
65+	290	5.2	24	2	3	4	6	8	9	21
GRAND TOTAL	**862**	**4.5**	**11**	**2**	**3**	**4**	**5**	**7**	**8**	**13**

55.5: COMPLETE NEPHRECTOMY

Type of Patients	Observed Patients	Avg. Stay	Vari-ance	Percentiles 10th	25th	50th	75th	90th	95th	99th
1. SINGLE DX										
0–19 Years	52	4.0	11	1	1	3	6	10	10	12
20–34	170	3.2	2	2	2	3	4	4	6	7
35–49	269	3.2	2	2	2	3	4	5	6	8
50–64	229	3.3	2	2	2	3	4	5	5	6
65+	50	3.8	2	2	3	4	4	6	6	11
2. MULTIPLE DX										
0–19 Years	205	4.9	31	1	2	3	6	11	14	29
20–34	281	4.9	29	2	3	4	5	8	11	29
35–49	812	5.3	19	2	3	4	6	9	14	23
50–64	1,584	5.5	20	2	3	4	6	9	12	24
65+	1,922	6.1	18	3	4	5	7	10	13	26
TOTAL SINGLE DX	**770**	**3.4**	**3**	**2**	**2**	**3**	**4**	**5**	**6**	**10**
TOTAL MULTIPLE DX	**4,804**	**5.6**	**21**	**2**	**3**	**4**	**6**	**10**	**13**	**25**
TOTAL										
0–19 Years	257	4.8	27	1	2	3	6	10	13	29
20–34	451	4.4	20	2	3	4	4	6	9	23
35–49	1,081	4.8	15	2	3	4	5	8	13	21
50–64	1,813	5.2	18	2	3	4	6	9	11	23
65+	1,972	6.1	18	3	4	5	7	10	13	26
GRAND TOTAL	**5,574**	**5.4**	**19**	**2**	**3**	**4**	**6**	**9**	**13**	**25**

55.51: NEPHROURETERECTOMY

Type of Patients	Observed Patients	Avg. Stay	Vari-ance	Percentiles 10th	25th	50th	75th	90th	95th	99th
1. SINGLE DX										
0–19 Years	51	4.0	11	1	1	3	6	10	10	12
20–34	168	3.2	2	2	2	3	4	4	6	7
35–49	268	3.2	2	2	2	3	4	5	6	8
50–64	226	3.3	2	2	2	3	4	5	5	6
65+	50	3.8	2	2	3	4	4	6	6	11
2. MULTIPLE DX										
0–19 Years	188	4.5	27	1	2	3	5	10	14	29
20–34	245	4.9	31	2	3	4	4	7	11	29
35–49	714	5.1	16	2	3	4	6	9	13	21
50–64	1,490	5.3	14	2	3	4	6	9	11	22
65+	1,895	6.1	18	3	4	5	7	10	13	26
TOTAL SINGLE DX	**763**	**3.4**	**3**	**2**	**2**	**3**	**4**	**5**	**6**	**10**
TOTAL MULTIPLE DX	**4,532**	**5.5**	**18**	**2**	**3**	**4**	**6**	**9**	**13**	**24**
TOTAL										
0–19 Years	239	4.4	24	1	2	3	5	10	12	25
20–34	413	4.3	21	2	3	4	4	6	9	24
35–49	982	4.6	13	2	3	4	5	8	11	21
50–64	1,716	5.1	13	2	3	4	6	8	11	21
65+	1,945	6.1	18	3	4	5	7	10	13	25
GRAND TOTAL	**5,295**	**5.3**	**17**	**2**	**3**	**4**	**6**	**9**	**12**	**23**

55.53: REJECTED KID NEPHRECTOMY

Type of Patients	Observed Patients	Avg. Stay	Vari-ance	Percentiles						
				10th	25th	50th	75th	90th	95th	99th
1. SINGLE DX										
0–19 Years	0									
20–34	0									
35–49	0									
50–64	0									
65+	0									
2. MULTIPLE DX										
0–19 Years	10	7.7	24	2	3	10	11	13	13	23
20–34	31	4.9	14	2	3	4	6	10	10	19
35–49	70	6.8	48	2	3	5	8	13	25	25
50–64	47	6.6	32	2	3	4	8	12	19	28
65+	10	4.5	15	1	2	4	6	7	7	18
TOTAL SINGLE DX	**0**									
TOTAL MULTIPLE DX	**168**	**6.3**	**33**	**2**	**3**	**4**	**8**	**12**	**18**	**26**
TOTAL										
0–19 Years	10	7.7	24	2	3	10	11	13	13	23
20–34	31	4.9	14	2	3	4	6	10	10	19
35–49	70	6.8	48	2	3	5	8	13	25	25
50–64	47	6.6	32	2	3	4	8	12	19	28
65+	10	4.5	15	1	2	4	6	7	7	18
GRAND TOTAL	**168**	**6.3**	**33**	**2**	**3**	**4**	**8**	**12**	**18**	**26**

55.54: BILATERAL NEPHRECTOMY

Type of Patients	Observed Patients	Avg. Stay	Vari-ance	Percentiles						
				10th	25th	50th	75th	90th	95th	99th
1. SINGLE DX										
0–19 Years	1	4.0	0	4	4	4	4	4	4	4
20–34	1	5.0	0	5	5	5	5	5	5	5
35–49	0									
50–64	2	1.0	0	1	1	1	1	1	1	1
65+	0									
2. MULTIPLE DX										
0–19 Years	3	22.1	238	4	11	35	35	35	35	35
20–34	5	6.6	11	3	4	6	9	11	11	11
35–49	25	6.3	8	3	4	6	7	13	13	13
50–64	37	11.8	169	4	6	8	9	46	46	46
65+	11	10.6	43	3	7	10	11	15	28	28
TOTAL SINGLE DX	**4**	**3.0**	**3**	**1**	**1**	**4**	**4**	**4**	**5**	**5**
TOTAL MULTIPLE DX	**81**	**10.1**	**107**	**3**	**5**	**7**	**10**	**15**	**46**	**46**
TOTAL										
0–19 Years	4	12.2	185	4	4	4	11	35	35	35
20–34	6	6.3	9	3	4	6	9	11	11	11
35–49	25	6.3	8	3	4	6	7	13	13	13
50–64	39	11.2	166	2	5	8	9	46	46	46
65+	11	10.6	43	3	7	10	11	15	28	28
GRAND TOTAL	**85**	**9.6**	**103**	**3**	**4**	**7**	**9**	**15**	**46**	**46**

55.6: KIDNEY TRANSPLANT

Type of Patients	Observed Patients	Avg. Stay	Vari-ance	Percentiles						
				10th	25th	50th	75th	90th	95th	99th
1. SINGLE DX										
0–19 Years	3	5.7	3	3	3	6	7	7	7	7
20–34	12	4.9	<1	4	4	5	5	6	6	6
35–49	12	4.6	1	3	3	5	5	6	6	7
50–64	10	4.9	<1	3	5	5	5	6	6	6
65+	3	5.4	<1	5	5	5	6	6	6	6
2. MULTIPLE DX										
0–19 Years	115	9.2	28	5	6	8	11	15	20	30
20–34	322	6.2	14	3	4	5	7	10	13	22
35–49	562	6.9	15	4	5	6	8	11	14	22
50–64	800	7.4	21	4	5	6	8	13	15	29
65+	215	7.3	17	4	5	6	8	12	16	25
TOTAL SINGLE DX	**40**	**4.9**	**1**	**3**	**5**	**5**	**5**	**6**	**7**	**7**
TOTAL MULTIPLE DX	**2,014**	**7.2**	**19**	**4**	**5**	**6**	**8**	**12**	**15**	**27**
TOTAL										
0–19 Years	118	9.2	28	5	6	8	11	15	20	30
20–34	334	6.2	13	3	4	5	7	9	13	21
35–49	574	6.8	14	4	5	6	8	11	14	22
50–64	810	7.3	21	4	5	6	8	13	15	29
65+	218	7.3	17	4	5	6	8	12	16	25
GRAND TOTAL	**2,054**	**7.2**	**19**	**4**	**5**	**6**	**8**	**12**	**15**	**26**

55.69: KIDNEY TRANSPLANT NEC

Type of Patients	Observed Patients	Avg. Stay	Vari-ance	Percentiles						
				10th	25th	50th	75th	90th	95th	99th
1. SINGLE DX										
0–19 Years	2	6.6	<1	6	6	7	7	7	7	7
20–34	12	4.9	<1	4	4	5	5	6	6	6
35–49	12	4.6	1	3	3	5	5	6	6	7
50–64	10	4.9	<1	3	5	5	5	6	6	6
65+	3	5.4	<1	5	5	5	6	6	6	6
2. MULTIPLE DX										
0–19 Years	115	9.2	28	5	6	8	11	15	20	30
20–34	322	6.2	14	3	4	5	7	10	13	22
35–49	557	6.9	15	4	5	6	8	11	15	22
50–64	799	7.4	21	4	5	6	8	13	15	29
65+	214	7.4	17	4	5	6	8	12	16	25
TOTAL SINGLE DX	**39**	**4.9**	**1**	**3**	**5**	**5**	**5**	**6**	**7**	**7**
TOTAL MULTIPLE DX	**2,007**	**7.2**	**19**	**4**	**5**	**6**	**8**	**12**	**15**	**27**
TOTAL										
0–19 Years	117	9.2	28	5	6	8	11	15	20	30
20–34	334	6.2	13	3	4	5	7	9	13	21
35–49	569	6.8	15	4	5	6	8	11	14	22
50–64	809	7.3	21	4	5	6	8	13	15	29
65+	217	7.3	17	4	5	6	8	12	16	25
GRAND TOTAL	**2,046**	**7.2**	**19**	**4**	**5**	**6**	**8**	**12**	**15**	**27**

55.7: NEPHROPEXY

Type of Patients	Observed Patients	Avg. Stay	Vari-ance	Percentiles						
				10th	25th	50th	75th	90th	95th	99th
1. SINGLE DX										
0–19 Years	0									
20–34	1	1.0	0	1	1	1	1	1	1	1
35–49	1	2.0	0	2	2	2	2	2	2	2
50–64	0									
65+	0									
2. MULTIPLE DX										
0–19 Years	0									
20–34	2	2.0	0	2	2	2	2	2	2	2
35–49	2	6.7	8	2	8	8	8	8	8	8
50–64	0									
65+	0									
TOTAL SINGLE DX	**2**	**1.5**	**<1**	**1**	**1**	**2**	**2**	**2**	**2**	**2**
TOTAL MULTIPLE DX	**4**	**4.8**	**10**	**2**	**2**	**2**	**8**	**8**	**8**	**8**
TOTAL										
0–19 Years	0									
20–34	3	1.8	<1	1	2	2	2	2	2	2
35–49	3	5.9	10	2	2	8	8	8	8	8
50–64	0									
65+	0									
GRAND TOTAL	**6**	**4.1**	**10**	**1**	**2**	**2**	**8**	**8**	**8**	**8**

55.8: OTHER KIDNEY REPAIR

Type of Patients	Observed Patients	Avg. Stay	Vari-ance	Percentiles						
				10th	25th	50th	75th	90th	95th	99th
1. SINGLE DX										
0–19 Years	97	2.3	<1	1	1	2	3	4	4	4
20–34	32	2.6	1	2	2	2	3	3	5	7
35–49	16	2.9	4	1	2	2	4	4	10	10
50–64	13	3.5	2	1	2	4	5	5	5	5
65+	1	3.0	0	3	3	3	3	3	3	3
2. MULTIPLE DX										
0–19 Years	279	2.9	5	1	2	2	3	5	7	13
20–34	113	3.4	6	2	2	3	4	5	6	12
35–49	80	4.1	6	2	3	4	4	7	8	14
50–64	87	4.0	11	2	2	3	5	7	7	10
65+	41	4.8	10	2	4	4	5	7	11	19
TOTAL SINGLE DX	**159**	**2.5**	**1**	**1**	**2**	**2**	**3**	**4**	**4**	**5**
TOTAL MULTIPLE DX	**600**	**3.3**	**7**	**1**	**2**	**3**	**4**	**5**	**7**	**14**
TOTAL										
0–19 Years	376	2.7	4	1	2	2	3	4	5	13
20–34	145	3.2	5	2	2	3	4	5	6	12
35–49	96	3.9	6	2	3	3	4	6	8	14
50–64	100	3.9	10	2	2	3	5	7	7	10
65+	42	4.8	9	2	4	4	5	7	11	19
GRAND TOTAL	**759**	**3.1**	**5**	**1**	**2**	**3**	**4**	**5**	**7**	**13**

55.87: CORRECTION OF UPJ

Type of Patients	Observed Patients	Avg. Stay	Vari-ance	Percentiles						
				10th	25th	50th	75th	90th	95th	99th
1. SINGLE DX										
0–19 Years	97	2.3	<1	1	1	2	3	4	4	4
20–34	32	2.6	1	2	2	2	3	3	5	7
35–49	16	2.9	4	1	2	2	4	4	10	10
50–64	13	3.5	2	1	2	4	5	5	5	5
65+	1	3.0	0	3	3	3	3	3	3	3
2. MULTIPLE DX										
0–19 Years	271	2.8	4	1	2	2	3	4	6	10
20–34	98	3.1	2	2	2	3	4	5	6	8
35–49	76	3.9	5	2	3	3	4	6	8	18
50–64	81	3.7	3	2	2	3	5	7	7	8
65+	40	4.8	10	2	4	4	5	7	11	19
TOTAL SINGLE DX	**159**	**2.5**	**1**	**1**	**2**	**2**	**3**	**4**	**4**	**5**
TOTAL MULTIPLE DX	**566**	**3.2**	**5**	**1**	**2**	**3**	**4**	**5**	**7**	**12**
TOTAL										
0–19 Years	368	2.6	3	1	2	2	3	4	5	9
20–34	130	3.0	2	2	2	3	4	5	6	8
35–49	92	3.8	5	2	3	3	4	6	8	10
50–64	94	3.6	3	2	2	3	5	6	7	8
65+	41	4.8	10	2	4	4	5	7	11	19
GRAND TOTAL	**725**	**3.0**	**4**	**1**	**2**	**3**	**4**	**5**	**6**	**10**

55.9: OTHER RENAL OPERATIONS

Type of Patients	Observed Patients	Avg. Stay	Vari-ance	Percentiles						
				10th	25th	50th	75th	90th	95th	99th
1. SINGLE DX										
0–19 Years	1	2.0	0	2	2	2	2	2	2	2
20–34	0									
35–49	2	2.2	1	1	1	3	3	3	3	3
50–64	3	1.0	0	1	1	1	1	1	1	1
65+	1	1.0	0	1	1	1	1	1	1	1
2. MULTIPLE DX										
0–19 Years	17	7.2	53	2	3	4	6	19	30	30
20–34	51	4.0	9	2	2	3	5	6	10	22
35–49	103	6.0	20	1	3	4	8	12	16	18
50–64	96	6.3	34	2	2	5	7	14	20	26
65+	170	6.4	40	1	3	5	8	13	15	37
TOTAL SINGLE DX	**7**	**1.4**	**<1**	**1**	**1**	**1**	**2**	**2**	**3**	**3**
TOTAL MULTIPLE DX	**437**	**6.1**	**33**	**1**	**3**	**4**	**8**	**13**	**15**	**30**
TOTAL										
0–19 Years	18	6.8	51	2	3	4	6	19	30	30
20–34	51	4.0	9	2	2	3	5	6	10	22
35–49	105	5.9	20	1	3	4	8	12	16	18
50–64	99	6.0	34	1	2	4	7	14	20	26
65+	171	6.4	40	1	2	5	8	13	15	37
GRAND TOTAL	**444**	**6.0**	**33**	**1**	**2**	**4**	**8**	**13**	**15**	**30**

55.92: PERC RENAL ASPIRATION

Type of Patients	Observed Patients	Avg. Stay	Variance	10th	25th	50th	75th	90th	95th	99th
1. SINGLE DX										
0–19 Years	0									
20–34	0									
35–49	0									
50–64	1	1.0	0	1	1	1	1	1	1	1
65+	0									
2. MULTIPLE DX										
0–19 Years	5	13.3	134	2	8	8	30	30	30	30
20–34	22	4.8	14	2	3	4	5	7	14	22
35–49	28	6.9	19	3	3	5	10	15	16	16
50–64	25	8.5	58	2	3	5	13	26	26	26
65+	29	8.0	85	1	2	6	12	14	14	52
TOTAL SINGLE DX	**1**	**1.0**	**0**	**1**	**1**	**1**	**1**	**1**	**1**	**1**
TOTAL MULTIPLE DX	**109**	**7.4**	**53**	**2**	**3**	**5**	**10**	**14**	**25**	**30**
TOTAL										
0–19 Years	5	13.3	134	2	8	8	30	30	30	30
20–34	22	4.8	14	2	3	4	5	7	14	22
35–49	28	6.9	19	3	3	5	10	15	16	16
50–64	26	8.3	58	2	2	5	13	26	26	26
65+	29	8.0	85	1	2	6	12	14	14	52
GRAND TOTAL	**110**	**7.4**	**53**	**2**	**3**	**5**	**10**	**14**	**22**	**30**

55.93: REPL NEPHROSTOMY TUBE

Type of Patients	Observed Patients	Avg. Stay	Variance	10th	25th	50th	75th	90th	95th	99th
1. SINGLE DX										
0–19 Years	1	2.0	0	2	2	2	2	2	2	2
20–34	0									
35–49	1	1.0	0	1	1	1	1	1	1	1
50–64	1	1.0	0	1	1	1	1	1	1	1
65+	0									
2. MULTIPLE DX										
0–19 Years	11	5.6	24	3	3	4	6	19	19	19
20–34	28	3.8	5	1	2	3	5	6	8	10
35–49	72	5.5	20	1	2	4	8	12	14	22
50–64	68	5.6	23	2	3	4	7	12	15	30
65+	138	6.0	24	1	3	5	8	11	15	28
TOTAL SINGLE DX	**3**	**1.3**	**<1**	**1**	**1**	**1**	**2**	**2**	**2**	**2**
TOTAL MULTIPLE DX	**317**	**5.6**	**22**	**1**	**3**	**4**	**7**	**11**	**15**	**22**
TOTAL										
0–19 Years	12	5.3	23	2	3	4	6	9	19	19
20–34	28	3.8	5	1	2	3	5	6	8	10
35–49	73	5.4	20	1	2	4	8	12	14	22
50–64	69	5.3	23	1	2	4	7	11	15	30
65+	138	6.0	24	1	3	5	8	11	15	28
GRAND TOTAL	**320**	**5.5**	**22**	**1**	**2**	**4**	**7**	**11**	**15**	**22**

56.0: TU RMVL URETERAL OBSTR

Type of Patients	Observed Patients	Avg. Stay	Variance	10th	25th	50th	75th	90th	95th	99th
1. SINGLE DX										
0–19 Years	36	1.5	<1	1	1	1	2	2	2	4
20–34	160	1.4	<1	1	1	1	2	2	3	5
35–49	201	1.7	1	1	1	1	2	3	4	6
50–64	112	1.3	<1	1	1	1	1	2	2	4
65+	28	1.5	<1	1	1	1	2	4	4	4
2. MULTIPLE DX										
0–19 Years	85	2.4	4	1	1	2	3	4	5	14
20–34	596	2.2	3	1	1	2	3	4	5	9
35–49	939	2.5	7	1	1	2	3	4	6	11
50–64	946	2.7	7	1	1	2	3	5	8	15
65+	701	3.5	12	1	1	2	4	8	11	16
TOTAL SINGLE DX	**537**	**1.5**	**<1**	**1**	**1**	**1**	**2**	**2**	**3**	**5**
TOTAL MULTIPLE DX	**3,267**	**2.7**	**8**	**1**	**1**	**2**	**3**	**5**	**8**	**14**
TOTAL										
0–19 Years	121	2.1	3	1	1	2	2	4	5	8
20–34	756	2.0	3	1	1	2	2	3	5	8
35–49	1,140	2.3	6	1	1	2	3	4	6	11
50–64	1,058	2.5	7	1	1	2	3	5	8	15
65+	729	3.5	12	1	1	2	4	8	11	15
GRAND TOTAL	**3,804**	**2.5**	**7**	**1**	**1**	**2**	**3**	**5**	**7**	**14**

56.1: URETERAL MEATOTOMY

Type of Patients	Observed Patients	Avg. Stay	Variance	10th	25th	50th	75th	90th	95th	99th
1. SINGLE DX										
0–19 Years	0									
20–34	0									
35–49	2	1.4	<1	1	1	1	2	2	2	2
50–64	0									
65+	1	2.0	0	2	2	2	2	2	2	2
2. MULTIPLE DX										
0–19 Years	1	19.0	0	19	19	19	19	19	19	19
20–34	5	2.4	7	1	1	1	2	7	7	7
35–49	3	6.4	53	1	1	2	14	14	14	14
50–64	13	2.8	11	1	1	2	3	6	7	17
65+	8	5.2	31	1	2	5	5	5	21	21
TOTAL SINGLE DX	**3**	**1.6**	**<1**	**1**	**1**	**2**	**2**	**2**	**2**	**2**
TOTAL MULTIPLE DX	**30**	**3.9**	**23**	**1**	**1**	**2**	**5**	**7**	**17**	**21**
TOTAL										
0–19 Years	1	19.0	0	19	19	19	19	19	19	19
20–34	5	2.4	7	1	1	1	2	7	7	7
35–49	5	3.9	29	1	1	2	2	14	14	14
50–64	13	2.8	11	1	1	2	3	6	7	17
65+	9	4.9	29	1	2	5	5	5	21	21
GRAND TOTAL	**33**	**3.7**	**22**	**1**	**1**	**2**	**5**	**7**	**17**	**21**

56.2: URETEROTOMY

Type of Patients	Observed Patients	Avg. Stay	Vari-ance	Percentiles						
				10th	25th	50th	75th	90th	95th	99th
1. SINGLE DX										
0–19 Years	0									
20–34	7	1.8	<1	1	1	2	2	3	3	3
35–49	6	1.9	<1	1	1	2	3	3	3	3
50–64	1	2.0	0	2	2	2	2	2	2	2
65+	1	2.0	0	2	2	2	2	2	2	2
2. MULTIPLE DX										
0–19 Years	7	2.9	7	1	1	2	5	5	9	9
20–34	26	2.6	2	1	1	2	3	5	6	6
35–49	34	3.3	7	1	2	2	4	6	8	15
50–64	39	4.3	11	1	2	4	5	9	10	15
65+	41	4.7	9	1	2	4	8	9	9	12
TOTAL SINGLE DX	**15**	**1.9**	**<1**	**1**	**1**	**2**	**2**	**3**	**3**	**3**
TOTAL MULTIPLE DX	**147**	**3.9**	**9**	**1**	**2**	**3**	**5**	**9**	**9**	**15**
TOTAL										
0–19 Years	7	2.9	7	1	1	2	5	5	9	9
20–34	33	2.4	2	1	1	2	3	5	6	6
35–49	40	3.1	6	1	2	2	4	6	8	15
50–64	40	4.3	11	1	2	4	5	9	10	15
65+	42	4.7	9	1	2	4	8	9	9	12
GRAND TOTAL	**162**	**3.7**	**8**	**1**	**2**	**3**	**5**	**8**	**9**	**15**

56.3: URETERAL DIAGNOSTIC PX

Type of Patients	Observed Patients	Avg. Stay	Vari-ance	Percentiles						
				10th	25th	50th	75th	90th	95th	99th
1. SINGLE DX										
0–19 Years	1	1.0	0	1	1	1	1	1	1	1
20–34	11	2.0	<1	1	1	2	2	4	4	4
35–49	14	1.9	2	1	1	1	2	4	7	7
50–64	2	3.3	1	2	2	4	4	4	4	4
65+	0									
2. MULTIPLE DX										
0–19 Years	4	6.2	7	1	7	7	7	10	10	10
20–34	58	2.5	4	1	1	2	3	5	8	9
35–49	77	3.1	10	1	2	2	3	6	8	21
50–64	64	5.4	35	1	1	3	7	20	21	21
65+	110	4.2	12	1	2	3	5	8	11	19
TOTAL SINGLE DX	**28**	**2.0**	**2**	**1**	**1**	**2**	**2**	**4**	**4**	**7**
TOTAL MULTIPLE DX	**313**	**3.9**	**16**	**1**	**1**	**3**	**5**	**8**	**11**	**21**
TOTAL										
0–19 Years	5	5.1	11	1	1	7	7	10	10	10
20–34	69	2.5	4	1	1	2	3	5	8	9
35–49	91	3.0	9	1	1	2	3	6	7	21
50–64	66	5.4	34	1	2	3	7	20	21	21
65+	110	4.2	12	1	2	3	5	8	11	19
GRAND TOTAL	**341**	**3.8**	**15**	**1**	**1**	**3**	**5**	**8**	**10**	**21**

56.31: URETEROSCOPY

Type of Patients	Observed Patients	Avg. Stay	Vari-ance	Percentiles						
				10th	25th	50th	75th	90th	95th	99th
1. SINGLE DX										
0–19 Years	1	1.0	0	1	1	1	1	1	1	1
20–34	10	1.8	<1	1	1	2	2	2	4	4
35–49	14	1.9	2	1	1	1	2	4	7	7
50–64	2	3.3	1	2	2	4	4	4	4	4
65+	0									
2. MULTIPLE DX										
0–19 Years	4	6.2	7	1	7	7	7	10	10	10
20–34	56	2.5	4	1	1	2	3	5	8	9
35–49	70	3.0	9	1	2	2	3	6	7	21
50–64	59	4.0	13	1	1	3	6	8	9	20
65+	66	4.1	9	1	2	3	5	8	9	12
TOTAL SINGLE DX	**27**	**1.9**	**2**	**1**	**1**	**2**	**2**	**4**	**4**	**7**
TOTAL MULTIPLE DX	**255**	**3.5**	**9**	**1**	**1**	**3**	**5**	**7**	**8**	**20**
TOTAL										
0–19 Years	5	5.1	11	1	1	7	7	10	10	10
20–34	66	2.5	4	1	1	2	3	5	8	9
35–49	84	2.9	8	1	1	2	3	6	7	21
50–64	61	4.0	13	1	1	3	6	8	9	20
65+	66	4.1	9	1	2	3	5	8	9	12
GRAND TOTAL	**282**	**3.4**	**9**	**1**	**1**	**2**	**4**	**7**	**8**	**20**

56.4: URETERECTOMY

Type of Patients	Observed Patients	Avg. Stay	Vari-ance	Percentiles						
				10th	25th	50th	75th	90th	95th	99th
1. SINGLE DX										
0–19 Years	6	1.9	<1	1	1	2	2	3	3	3
20–34	4	2.8	3	1	2	2	4	5	5	5
35–49	1	4.0	0	4	4	4	4	4	4	4
50–64	4	4.1	1	2	4	4	5	5	5	5
65+	3	4.9	1	4	4	5	5	7	7	7
2. MULTIPLE DX										
0–19 Years	47	4.4	21	1	2	3	5	11	11	22
20–34	16	3.6	3	2	2	4	5	6	7	7
35–49	16	4.5	3	2	3	6	6	6	6	6
50–64	54	4.2	20	1	2	3	4	8	11	20
65+	136	5.0	14	1	3	4	6	8	14	20
TOTAL SINGLE DX	**18**	**3.1**	**3**	**1**	**2**	**3**	**4**	**5**	**7**	**7**
TOTAL MULTIPLE DX	**269**	**4.6**	**16**	**1**	**2**	**4**	**6**	**8**	**11**	**22**
TOTAL										
0–19 Years	53	4.1	19	1	2	3	5	11	11	22
20–34	20	3.5	3	1	2	3	4	6	7	7
35–49	17	4.5	3	2	3	5	6	6	6	6
50–64	58	4.2	19	1	2	3	4	8	11	20
65+	139	5.0	14	1	3	4	6	8	14	20
GRAND TOTAL	**287**	**4.5**	**15**	**1**	**2**	**4**	**6**	**8**	**11**	**22**

56.41: PARTIAL URETERECTOMY

Type of Patients	Observed Patients	Avg. Stay	Vari-ance	10th	25th	50th	75th	90th	95th	99th
1. SINGLE DX										
0–19 Years	6	1.9	<1	1	1	2	2	3	3	3
20–34	1	5.0	0	5	5	5	5	5	5	5
35–49	1	4.0	0	4	4	4	4	4	4	4
50–64	3	4.2	2	2	4	5	5	5	5	5
65+	3	4.9	1	4	4	5	5	7	7	7
2. MULTIPLE DX										
0–19 Years	46	4.4	21	1	2	3	5	11	11	22
20–34	12	4.1	3	2	3	4	5	7	7	7
35–49	16	4.5	3	2	3	6	6	6	6	6
50–64	44	4.2	22	1	2	3	4	8	12	34
65+	120	5.0	16	1	3	4	6	8	14	20
TOTAL SINGLE DX	**14**	**3.2**	**3**	**1**	**2**	**3**	**5**	**5**	**7**	**7**
TOTAL MULTIPLE DX	**238**	**4.6**	**17**	**1**	**2**	**4**	**6**	**8**	**12**	**22**
TOTAL										
0–19 Years	52	4.1	19	1	2	2	5	11	11	22
20–34	13	4.2	3	2	3	4	5	7	7	7
35–49	17	4.5	3	2	3	5	6	6	6	6
50–64	47	4.2	21	1	2	3	4	8	10	34
65+	123	5.0	15	1	3	4	6	8	14	20
GRAND TOTAL	**252**	**4.5**	**16**	**1**	**2**	**4**	**6**	**8**	**11**	**22**

56.5: CUTAN URETERO-ILEOSTOMY

Type of Patients	Observed Patients	Avg. Stay	Vari-ance	10th	25th	50th	75th	90th	95th	99th
1. SINGLE DX										
0–19 Years	0									
20–34	1	5.0	0	5	5	5	5	5	5	5
35–49	1	9.0	0	9	9	9	9	9	9	9
50–64	0									
65+	1	8.0	0	8	8	8	8	8	8	8
2. MULTIPLE DX										
0–19 Years	5	11.4	103	1	7	9	9	29	29	29
20–34	11	7.4	13	5	5	7	9	14	15	15
35–49	35	9.2	75	3	3	7	11	20	20	57
50–64	68	10.2	32	5	7	9	12	16	22	30
65+	104	10.7	50	5	7	9	12	19	27	30
TOTAL SINGLE DX	**3**	**6.6**	**4**	**5**	**5**	**5**	**8**	**9**	**9**	**9**
TOTAL MULTIPLE DX	**223**	**10.2**	**48**	**4**	**6**	**9**	**12**	**17**	**24**	**30**
TOTAL										
0–19 Years	5	11.4	103	1	7	9	9	29	29	29
20–34	12	7.1	12	5	5	6	8	14	15	15
35–49	36	9.2	74	3	3	7	11	20	20	57
50–64	68	10.2	32	5	7	9	12	16	22	30
65+	105	10.7	50	5	7	9	12	19	27	30
GRAND TOTAL	**226**	**10.2**	**47**	**4**	**6**	**9**	**12**	**17**	**24**	**30**

56.51: FORM CUTAN ILEOURETEROST

Type of Patients	Observed Patients	Avg. Stay	Vari-ance	10th	25th	50th	75th	90th	95th	99th
1. SINGLE DX										
0–19 Years	0									
20–34	0									
35–49	1	9.0	0	9	9	9	9	9	9	9
50–64	0									
65+	1	8.0	0	8	8	8	8	8	8	8
2. MULTIPLE DX										
0–19 Years	2	20.8	147	8	8	29	29	29	29	29
20–34	4	10.7	18	6	6	9	14	15	15	15
35–49	21	9.9	101	3	3	7	11	20	25	57
50–64	53	11.2	23	7	8	10	12	16	22	30
65+	86	11.6	50	6	8	9	13	21	27	30
TOTAL SINGLE DX	**2**	**8.5**	**<1**	**8**	**8**	**8**	**9**	**9**	**9**	**9**
TOTAL MULTIPLE DX	**166**	**11.3**	**49**	**6**	**7**	**9**	**13**	**20**	**26**	**30**
TOTAL										
0–19 Years	2	20.8	147	8	8	29	29	29	29	29
20–34	4	10.7	18	6	6	9	14	15	15	15
35–49	22	9.9	98	3	3	7	11	20	25	57
50–64	53	11.2	23	7	8	10	12	16	22	30
65+	87	11.5	50	6	8	9	13	21	27	30
GRAND TOTAL	**168**	**11.3**	**49**	**6**	**7**	**9**	**13**	**20**	**26**	**30**

56.6: EXT URIN DIVERSION NEC

Type of Patients	Observed Patients	Avg. Stay	Vari-ance	10th	25th	50th	75th	90th	95th	99th
1. SINGLE DX										
0–19 Years	1	1.0	0	1	1	1	1	1	1	1
20–34	0									
35–49	3	2.3	2	1	1	2	4	4	4	4
50–64	1	3.0	0	3	3	3	3	3	3	3
65+	0									
2. MULTIPLE DX										
0–19 Years	18	3.8	7	1	1	4	6	6	9	10
20–34	0									
35–49	4	9.5	163	1	1	2	26	26	26	26
50–64	7	3.1	3	1	1	3	3	7	7	7
65+	4	3.1	15	1	1	2	2	10	10	10
TOTAL SINGLE DX	**5**	**2.0**	**2**	**1**	**1**	**1**	**3**	**4**	**4**	**4**
TOTAL MULTIPLE DX	**33**	**4.1**	**19**	**1**	**1**	**3**	**6**	**7**	**10**	**26**
TOTAL										
0–19 Years	19	3.7	7	1	1	4	6	6	9	10
20–34	0									
35–49	7	7.1	115	1	1	2	4	26	26	26
50–64	8	3.1	3	1	3	3	3	7	7	7
65+	4	3.1	15	1	1	2	2	10	10	10
GRAND TOTAL	**38**	**3.9**	**18**	**1**	**1**	**3**	**5**	**7**	**10**	**26**

56.7: OTHER URETERAL ANAST

Type of Patients	Observed Patients	Avg. Stay	Variance	Percentiles 10th	25th	50th	75th	90th	95th	99th
1. SINGLE DX										
0–19 Years	306	2.3	1	1	2	2	3	4	4	5
20–34	6	4.3	2	2	3	4	6	6	6	6
35–49	16	2.8	2	1	2	3	4	5	5	5
50–64	1	5.0	0	5	5	5	5	5	5	5
65+	2	2.0	2	1	1	3	3	3	3	3
2. MULTIPLE DX										
0–19 Years	690	2.9	8	1	2	3	3	5	6	10
20–34	47	4.6	4	3	3	5	5	6	9	13
35–49	87	5.5	10	3	4	4	6	10	13	14
50–64	82	6.1	12	3	4	6	8	10	10	17
65+	56	5.6	14	2	3	5	7	10	16	18
TOTAL SINGLE DX	**331**	**2.3**	**1**	**1**	**2**	**2**	**3**	**4**	**4**	**5**
TOTAL MULTIPLE DX	**962**	**3.4**	**10**	**1**	**2**	**3**	**4**	**6**	**8**	**13**
TOTAL										
0–19 Years	996	2.7	6	1	2	2	3	4	5	10
20–34	53	4.6	4	3	3	5	5	6	8	11
35–49	103	5.1	10	2	3	4	6	10	13	14
50–64	83	6.0	12	3	4	5	8	10	10	17
65+	58	5.5	14	2	3	5	6	9	16	18
GRAND TOTAL	**1,293**	**3.0**	**7**	**1**	**2**	**3**	**4**	**5**	**7**	**12**

56.74: URETERONEOCYSTOSTOMY

Type of Patients	Observed Patients	Avg. Stay	Variance	Percentiles 10th	25th	50th	75th	90th	95th	99th
1. SINGLE DX										
0–19 Years	305	2.3	1	1	2	2	3	4	4	5
20–34	6	4.3	2	2	3	4	6	6	6	6
35–49	15	2.7	1	1	2	2	4	4	5	5
50–64	1	5.0	0	5	5	5	5	5	5	5
65+	0									
2. MULTIPLE DX										
0–19 Years	670	2.8	6	1	2	3	3	5	6	10
20–34	37	4.3	3	2	3	4	5	5	6	11
35–49	77	5.4	10	3	3	4	6	10	13	15
50–64	62	5.6	7	3	3	5	7	10	10	12
65+	45	5.3	14	2	3	4	6	8	17	20
TOTAL SINGLE DX	**327**	**2.3**	**1**	**1**	**2**	**2**	**3**	**4**	**4**	**5**
TOTAL MULTIPLE DX	**891**	**3.2**	**7**	**1**	**2**	**3**	**4**	**5**	**7**	**12**
TOTAL										
0–19 Years	975	2.6	4	1	2	2	3	4	5	9
20–34	43	4.3	3	2	3	4	5	5	6	11
35–49	92	5.0	9	2	3	4	5	10	13	14
50–64	63	5.6	7	3	4	5	7	10	10	12
65+	45	5.3	14	2	3	4	6	8	17	20
GRAND TOTAL	**1,218**	**2.9**	**5**	**1**	**2**	**3**	**3**	**5**	**6**	**11**

56.8: REPAIR OF URETER

Type of Patients	Observed Patients	Avg. Stay	Variance	Percentiles 10th	25th	50th	75th	90th	95th	99th
1. SINGLE DX										
0–19 Years	2	1.0	0	1	1	1	1	1	1	1
20–34	0									
35–49	0									
50–64	1	1.0	0	1	1	1	1	1	1	1
65+	0									
2. MULTIPLE DX										
0–19 Years	16	3.4	7	1	1	2	5	7	9	9
20–34	6	7.0	31	2	2	6	10	17	17	17
35–49	10	5.8	13	2	4	5	5	10	15	15
50–64	14	5.5	11	1	4	5	6	9	11	16
65+	6	7.7	201	1	1	1	5	34	46	46
TOTAL SINGLE DX	**3**	**1.0**	**0**	**1**	**1**	**1**	**1**	**1**	**1**	**1**
TOTAL MULTIPLE DX	**52**	**5.3**	**41**	**1**	**2**	**4**	**6**	**9**	**15**	**46**
TOTAL										
0–19 Years	18	3.1	7	1	1	2	5	7	8	9
20–34	6	7.0	31	2	2	6	10	17	17	17
35–49	10	5.8	13	2	4	5	5	10	15	15
50–64	15	5.2	12	1	4	4	6	9	11	16
65+	6	7.7	201	1	1	1	5	34	46	46
GRAND TOTAL	**55**	**5.0**	**40**	**1**	**1**	**4**	**6**	**9**	**15**	**34**

56.9: OTHER URETERAL OPERATION

Type of Patients	Observed Patients	Avg. Stay	Variance	Percentiles 10th	25th	50th	75th	90th	95th	99th
1. SINGLE DX										
0–19 Years	0									
20–34	0									
35–49	0									
50–64	1	2.0	0	2	2	2	2	2	2	2
65+	0									
2. MULTIPLE DX										
0–19 Years	1	1.0	0	1	1	1	1	1	1	1
20–34	2	1.5	<1	1	1	1	2	2	2	2
35–49	2	5.7	16	1	1	8	8	8	8	8
50–64	4	4.0	1	3	3	4	4	6	6	6
65+	6	5.3	23	2	2	5	5	11	20	20
TOTAL SINGLE DX	**1**	**2.0**	**0**	**2**	**2**	**2**	**2**	**2**	**2**	**2**
TOTAL MULTIPLE DX	**15**	**4.4**	**16**	**1**	**2**	**4**	**5**	**8**	**11**	**20**
TOTAL										
0–19 Years	1	1.0	0	1	1	1	1	1	1	1
20–34	2	1.5	<1	1	1	1	2	2	2	2
35–49	2	5.7	16	1	1	8	8	8	8	8
50–64	5	3.7	2	2	3	4	4	6	6	6
65+	6	5.3	23	2	2	5	5	11	20	20
GRAND TOTAL	**16**	**4.3**	**15**	**1**	**2**	**3**	**5**	**8**	**11**	**20**

57.0: TU BLADDER CLEARANCE

Type of Patients	Observed Patients	Avg. Stay	Vari-ance	Percentiles						
				10th	25th	50th	75th	90th	95th	99th
1. SINGLE DX										
0–19 Years	2	1.7	<1	1	1	2	2	2	2	2
20–34	3	1.0	0	1	1	1	1	1	1	1
35–49	3	1.3	<1	1	1	1	2	2	2	2
50–64	8	1.4	<1	1	1	1	2	2	3	3
65+	5	1.4	<1	1	1	1	1	3	3	3
2. MULTIPLE DX										
0–19 Years	12	3.2	5	1	1	3	4	7	9	9
20–34	32	3.5	9	1	1	2	5	7	11	11
35–49	54	4.0	14	1	2	3	5	8	12	21
50–64	141	3.7	25	1	1	2	3	8	17	28
65+	491	4.1	19	1	1	3	5	9	12	21
TOTAL SINGLE DX	**21**	**1.4**	**<1**	**1**	**1**	**1**	**2**	**2**	**3**	**3**
TOTAL MULTIPLE DX	**730**	**4.0**	**19**	**1**	**1**	**2**	**5**	**8**	**12**	**23**
TOTAL										
0–19 Years	14	3.0	5	1	1	2	4	7	9	9
20–34	35	3.2	9	1	1	2	4	7	11	11
35–49	57	3.9	14	1	1	3	5	8	12	21
50–64	149	3.6	24	1	1	2	3	8	12	28
65+	496	4.0	19	1	1	2	5	9	12	21
GRAND TOTAL	**751**	**3.9**	**19**	**1**	**1**	**2**	**5**	**8**	**12**	**23**

57.1: CYSTOTOMY & CYSTOSTOMY

Type of Patients	Observed Patients	Avg. Stay	Vari-ance	Percentiles						
				10th	25th	50th	75th	90th	95th	99th
1. SINGLE DX										
0–19 Years	3	1.5	<1	1	1	1	2	3	3	3
20–34	8	2.2	3	1	1	2	2	7	7	7
35–49	23	2.4	<1	1	2	2	3	3	4	5
50–64	26	1.8	<1	1	1	2	2	3	3	5
65+	11	1.8	<1	1	1	1	3	3	3	3
2. MULTIPLE DX										
0–19 Years	50	4.9	81	1	1	2	5	8	10	50
20–34	43	5.3	38	1	1	3	8	18	23	23
35–49	131	4.9	48	1	1	3	5	9	18	41
50–64	219	4.3	24	1	2	3	5	9	13	22
65+	578	5.4	35	1	2	3	7	12	16	28
TOTAL SINGLE DX	**71**	**2.0**	**1**	**1**	**1**	**2**	**3**	**3**	**4**	**5**
TOTAL MULTIPLE DX	**1,021**	**5.1**	**37**	**1**	**2**	**3**	**6**	**11**	**16**	**32**
TOTAL										
0–19 Years	53	4.7	76	1	1	2	5	8	10	50
20–34	51	5.0	36	1	1	2	7	18	23	23
35–49	154	4.5	40	1	1	3	5	9	16	41
50–64	245	4.0	22	1	2	3	4	9	11	22
65+	589	5.3	34	1	2	3	7	12	16	28
GRAND TOTAL	**1,092**	**4.9**	**35**	**1**	**2**	**3**	**6**	**10**	**16**	**31**

57.17: PERCUTANEOUS CYSTOSTOMY

Type of Patients	Observed Patients	Avg. Stay	Vari-ance	Percentiles						
				10th	25th	50th	75th	90th	95th	99th
1. SINGLE DX										
0–19 Years	1	3.0	0	3	3	3	3	3	3	3
20–34	2	1.0	0	1	1	1	1	1	1	1
35–49	1	1.0	0	1	1	1	1	1	1	1
50–64	2	1.0	0	1	1	1	1	1	1	1
65+	1	1.0	0	1	1	1	1	1	1	1
2. MULTIPLE DX										
0–19 Years	11	7.3	186	1	1	2	5	46	46	46
20–34	13	11.6	62	2	5	9	18	23	23	23
35–49	22	5.2	29	1	1	4	7	11	21	21
50–64	26	8.4	81	2	3	7	9	19	31	49
65+	148	5.7	28	1	2	4	7	13	18	25
TOTAL SINGLE DX	**7**	**1.2**	**<1**	**1**	**1**	**1**	**1**	**1**	**3**	**3**
TOTAL MULTIPLE DX	**220**	**6.5**	**47**	**1**	**2**	**4**	**8**	**15**	**21**	**31**
TOTAL										
0–19 Years	12	7.1	177	1	1	2	5	8	46	46
20–34	15	10.4	66	1	3	9	18	23	23	23
35–49	23	4.8	28	1	1	3	7	11	21	21
50–64	28	7.8	79	1	3	6	9	19	22	49
65+	149	5.7	28	1	2	4	7	13	18	24
GRAND TOTAL	**227**	**6.3**	**47**	**1**	**2**	**4**	**7**	**15**	**21**	**31**

57.18: S/P CYSTOSTOMY NEC

Type of Patients	Observed Patients	Avg. Stay	Vari-ance	Percentiles						
				10th	25th	50th	75th	90th	95th	99th
1. SINGLE DX										
0–19 Years	0									
20–34	2	2.4	<1	2	2	2	3	3	3	3
35–49	19	2.4	<1	1	2	2	3	4	4	5
50–64	21	1.9	1	1	1	2	3	3	3	5
65+	8	2.2	<1	1	2	2	3	3	3	3
2. MULTIPLE DX										
0–19 Years	19	6.3	101	1	2	3	6	9	17	50
20–34	14	2.6	6	1	1	1	3	8	8	8
35–49	81	4.7	35	1	1	3	6	9	16	22
50–64	154	3.7	16	1	1	2	4	8	11	21
65+	312	5.4	43	1	2	3	7	12	16	43
TOTAL SINGLE DX	**50**	**2.2**	**<1**	**1**	**1**	**2**	**3**	**3**	**4**	**5**
TOTAL MULTIPLE DX	**580**	**4.8**	**36**	**1**	**1**	**3**	**6**	**10**	**15**	**32**
TOTAL										
0–19 Years	19	6.3	101	1	2	3	6	9	17	50
20–34	16	2.6	6	1	1	1	3	8	8	8
35–49	100	4.2	28	1	1	2	5	9	15	22
50–64	175	3.5	15	1	1	2	4	7	10	21
65+	320	5.3	42	1	2	3	7	12	16	43
GRAND TOTAL	**630**	**4.6**	**34**	**1**	**1**	**3**	**5**	**9**	**15**	**32**

57.19: CYSTOTOMY NEC

Type of Patients	Observed Patients	Avg. Stay	Vari-ance	Percentiles						
				10th	25th	50th	75th	90th	95th	99th
1. SINGLE DX										
0–19 Years	1	1.0	0	1	1	1	1	1	1	1
20–34	4	2.9	7	1	2	2	2	7	7	7
35–49	3	2.5	<1	2	2	2	3	3	3	3
50–64	3	2.0	0	2	2	2	2	2	2	2
65+	2	1.0	0	1	1	1	1	1	1	1
2. MULTIPLE DX										
0–19 Years	15	1.7	2	1	1	1	2	3	4	8
20–34	15	2.7	3	1	1	2	3	5	8	8
35–49	27	5.5	88	1	2	3	3	7	37	41
50–64	38	4.0	13	2	2	3	4	9	13	22
65+	114	5.1	21	1	2	3	7	11	12	23
TOTAL SINGLE DX	**13**	**1.9**	**1**	**1**	**1**	**2**	**2**	**3**	**3**	**7**
TOTAL MULTIPLE DX	**209**	**4.6**	**28**	**1**	**2**	**3**	**5**	**9**	**12**	**28**
TOTAL										
0–19 Years	16	1.6	2	1	1	1	2	3	4	8
20–34	19	2.7	3	1	1	2	3	5	7	8
35–49	30	5.1	78	1	2	3	3	7	37	41
50–64	41	3.8	12	2	2	3	4	8	13	22
65+	116	5.0	21	1	2	3	7	11	12	23
GRAND TOTAL	**222**	**4.4**	**27**	**1**	**2**	**3**	**5**	**9**	**12**	**28**

57.2: VESICOSTOMY

Type of Patients	Observed Patients	Avg. Stay	Vari-ance	Percentiles						
				10th	25th	50th	75th	90th	95th	99th
1. SINGLE DX										
0–19 Years	1	6.0	0	6	6	6	6	6	6	6
20–34	0									
35–49	0									
50–64	0									
65+	0									
2. MULTIPLE DX										
0–19 Years	52	5.1	24	1	2	4	7	8	11	26
20–34	4	5.5	2	3	4	6	6	7	7	7
35–49	2	4.0	8	2	2	2	6	6	6	6
50–64	2	2.5	<1	2	2	3	3	3	3	3
65+	5	3.9	6	1	3	4	5	8	8	8
TOTAL SINGLE DX	**1**	**6.0**	**0**	**6**	**6**	**6**	**6**	**6**	**6**	**6**
TOTAL MULTIPLE DX	**65**	**5.0**	**22**	**1**	**2**	**4**	**7**	**8**	**11**	**26**
TOTAL										
0–19 Years	53	5.1	24	1	2	4	7	8	11	26
20–34	4	5.5	2	3	4	6	6	7	7	7
35–49	2	4.0	8	2	2	2	6	6	6	6
50–64	2	2.5	<1	2	2	3	3	3	3	3
65+	5	3.9	6	1	3	4	5	8	8	8
GRAND TOTAL	**66**	**5.0**	**22**	**1**	**2**	**4**	**7**	**8**	**11**	**26**

57.3: BLADDER DIAGNOSTIC PX

Type of Patients	Observed Patients	Avg. Stay	Vari-ance	Percentiles						
				10th	25th	50th	75th	90th	95th	99th
1. SINGLE DX										
0–19 Years	11	2.2	3	1	1	1	4	4	4	7
20–34	22	1.8	2	1	1	1	2	5	5	5
35–49	19	2.9	7	1	1	2	3	8	8	11
50–64	20	1.4	<1	1	1	1	1	2	3	4
65+	8	1.1	<1	1	1	1	1	2	2	2
2. MULTIPLE DX										
0–19 Years	52	4.7	57	1	2	3	4	7	9	60
20–34	123	3.9	9	1	2	3	6	8	9	14
35–49	248	5.0	25	1	2	4	7	10	15	27
50–64	389	5.8	36	1	2	4	8	13	17	29
65+	1,052	6.0	27	1	2	5	8	12	16	26
TOTAL SINGLE DX	**80**	**1.9**	**3**	**1**	**1**	**1**	**2**	**4**	**5**	**8**
TOTAL MULTIPLE DX	**1,864**	**5.7**	**29**	**1**	**2**	**4**	**7**	**12**	**16**	**26**
TOTAL										
0–19 Years	63	4.3	49	1	1	3	4	7	8	60
20–34	145	3.5	8	1	1	3	5	7	9	14
35–49	267	4.9	24	1	2	3	6	10	14	25
50–64	409	5.6	35	1	2	4	7	12	16	29
65+	1,060	6.0	27	1	2	5	8	12	16	25
GRAND TOTAL	**1,944**	**5.5**	**29**	**1**	**2**	**4**	**7**	**11**	**16**	**25**

57.32: CYSTOSCOPY NEC

Type of Patients	Observed Patients	Avg. Stay	Vari-ance	Percentiles						
				10th	25th	50th	75th	90th	95th	99th
1. SINGLE DX										
0–19 Years	11	2.2	3	1	1	1	4	4	4	7
20–34	21	1.9	2	1	1	1	2	5	5	5
35–49	17	3.0	8	1	1	2	4	8	8	11
50–64	16	1.3	<1	1	1	1	1	3	3	4
65+	2	1.0	0	1	1	1	1	1	1	1
2. MULTIPLE DX										
0–19 Years	45	4.8	64	1	1	3	4	8	9	60
20–34	98	3.5	7	1	1	3	5	7	9	14
35–49	178	4.8	23	1	2	3	6	10	14	27
50–64	251	5.5	27	1	2	4	8	12	16	24
65+	665	6.1	24	1	3	5	8	13	16	24
TOTAL SINGLE DX	**67**	**2.0**	**3**	**1**	**1**	**1**	**2**	**4**	**5**	**8**
TOTAL MULTIPLE DX	**1,237**	**5.6**	**26**	**1**	**2**	**4**	**7**	**12**	**16**	**24**
TOTAL										
0–19 Years	56	4.3	54	1	1	3	4	7	9	60
20–34	119	3.1	6	1	1	2	4	7	8	14
35–49	195	4.6	22	1	2	3	6	10	13	27
50–64	267	5.2	27	1	2	3	7	12	16	24
65+	667	6.1	24	1	3	5	8	13	16	24
GRAND TOTAL	**1,304**	**5.3**	**26**	**1**	**2**	**4**	**7**	**11**	**15**	**24**

57.33: CLOSED BLADDER BIOPSY

Type of Patients	Observed Patients	Avg. Stay	Vari-ance	10th	25th	50th	75th	90th	95th	99th
1. SINGLE DX										
0–19 Years	0									
20–34	1	1.0	0	1	1	1	1	1	1	1
35–49	2	2.2	1	1	1	3	3	3	3	3
50–64	4	1.6	<1	1	1	2	2	2	2	2
65+	5	1.2	<1	1	1	1	1	2	2	2
2. MULTIPLE DX										
0–19 Years	4	4.2	1	3	4	4	4	7	7	7
20–34	22	5.8	15	1	3	6	8	9	10	18
35–49	66	5.7	29	1	1	5	8	11	19	25
50–64	132	6.6	54	1	3	4	8	13	21	34
65+	378	5.8	32	1	2	4	8	12	17	27
TOTAL SINGLE DX	**12**	**1.5**	**<1**	**1**	**1**	**1**	**2**	**3**	**3**	**3**
TOTAL MULTIPLE DX	**602**	**6.0**	**36**	**1**	**2**	**4**	**8**	**12**	**18**	**27**
TOTAL										
0–19 Years	4	4.2	1	3	4	4	4	7	7	7
20–34	23	5.6	15	1	3	6	8	9	10	18
35–49	68	5.6	28	1	1	4	8	11	19	25
50–64	136	6.4	53	1	3	4	8	13	21	34
65+	383	5.8	32	1	2	4	8	12	17	27
GRAND TOTAL	**614**	**5.9**	**36**	**1**	**2**	**4**	**8**	**12**	**18**	**27**

57.4: TU EXC/DESTR BLADDER LES

Type of Patients	Observed Patients	Avg. Stay	Vari-ance	10th	25th	50th	75th	90th	95th	99th
1. SINGLE DX										
0–19 Years	1	1.0	0	1	1	1	1	1	1	1
20–34	3	1.3	<1	1	1	1	2	2	2	2
35–49	15	2.1	3	1	1	2	2	3	8	8
50–64	51	1.4	<1	1	1	1	2	2	3	4
65+	102	1.4	<1	1	1	1	2	2	3	4
2. MULTIPLE DX										
0–19 Years	6	10.8	109	1	1	3	23	23	23	23
20–34	18	2.0	4	1	1	2	2	3	3	10
35–49	97	4.5	33	1	1	3	5	8	12	19
50–64	567	2.8	10	1	1	2	3	7	9	15
65+	2,856	3.5	18	1	1	2	4	8	12	21
TOTAL SINGLE DX	**172**	**1.4**	**<1**	**1**	**1**	**1**	**2**	**2**	**3**	**4**
TOTAL MULTIPLE DX	**3,544**	**3.4**	**17**	**1**	**1**	**2**	**4**	**8**	**12**	**22**
TOTAL										
0–19 Years	7	10.3	108	1	1	3	23	23	23	23
20–34	21	1.9	3	1	1	1	2	3	3	10
35–49	112	4.2	30	1	1	3	5	8	12	19
50–64	618	2.7	10	1	1	1	3	6	9	14
65+	2,958	3.5	17	1	1	2	4	8	12	21
GRAND TOTAL	**3,716**	**3.4**	**17**	**1**	**1**	**2**	**4**	**8**	**11**	**21**

57.49: TU DESTR BLADDER LES NEC

Type of Patients	Observed Patients	Avg. Stay	Vari-ance	10th	25th	50th	75th	90th	95th	99th
1. SINGLE DX										
0–19 Years	1	1.0	0	1	1	1	1	1	1	1
20–34	3	1.3	<1	1	1	1	2	2	2	2
35–49	15	2.1	3	1	1	2	2	3	8	8
50–64	51	1.4	<1	1	1	1	2	2	3	4
65+	102	1.4	<1	1	1	1	2	2	3	4
2. MULTIPLE DX										
0–19 Years	6	10.8	109	1	1	3	23	23	23	23
20–34	18	2.0	4	1	1	2	2	3	3	10
35–49	97	4.5	33	1	1	3	5	8	12	19
50–64	567	2.8	10	1	1	2	3	7	9	15
65+	2,855	3.5	18	1	1	2	4	8	12	21
TOTAL SINGLE DX	**172**	**1.4**	**<1**	**1**	**1**	**1**	**2**	**2**	**3**	**4**
TOTAL MULTIPLE DX	**3,543**	**3.4**	**17**	**1**	**1**	**2**	**4**	**8**	**12**	**22**
TOTAL										
0–19 Years	7	10.3	108	1	1	3	23	23	23	23
20–34	21	1.9	3	1	1	1	2	3	3	10
35–49	112	4.2	30	1	1	3	5	8	12	19
50–64	618	2.7	10	1	1	1	3	6	9	14
65+	2,957	3.5	17	1	1	2	4	8	12	21
GRAND TOTAL	**3,715**	**3.4**	**17**	**1**	**1**	**2**	**4**	**8**	**11**	**21**

57.5: BLADDER LES DESTR NEC

Type of Patients	Observed Patients	Avg. Stay	Vari-ance	10th	25th	50th	75th	90th	95th	99th
1. SINGLE DX										
0–19 Years	14	1.9	<1	1	2	2	2	2	3	3
20–34	1	3.0	0	3	3	3	3	3	3	3
35–49	4	2.9	<1	2	2	3	3	4	4	4
50–64	3	2.3	<1	2	2	2	3	3	3	3
65+	2	2.1	1	1	1	3	3	3	3	3
2. MULTIPLE DX										
0–19 Years	18	3.7	8	2	2	3	4	6	13	13
20–34	11	5.0	4	3	3	4	5	9	9	9
35–49	17	6.0	29	2	3	4	8	13	23	23
50–64	40	5.8	38	2	2	4	5	16	21	29
65+	60	5.3	11	2	3	4	7	9	12	17
TOTAL SINGLE DX	**24**	**2.2**	**<1**	**1**	**2**	**2**	**3**	**3**	**3**	**4**
TOTAL MULTIPLE DX	**146**	**5.2**	**18**	**2**	**3**	**4**	**6**	**9**	**14**	**23**
TOTAL										
0–19 Years	32	2.8	5	1	2	2	3	4	6	13
20–34	12	4.0	3	3	3	3	4	7	9	9
35–49	21	5.3	24	2	3	4	6	8	23	23
50–64	43	5.6	36	2	2	4	5	16	21	29
65+	62	5.2	11	2	3	4	6	9	12	17
GRAND TOTAL	**170**	**4.5**	**16**	**2**	**2**	**3**	**5**	**8**	**13**	**21**

57.59: OTH BLADDER LESION DESTR

Type of Patients	Observed Patients	Avg. Stay	Vari-ance	Percentiles						
				10th	25th	50th	75th	90th	95th	99th
1. SINGLE DX										
0–19 Years	1	3.0	0	3	3	3	3	3	3	3
20–34	0									
35–49	2	2.8	1	2	2	2	4	4	4	4
50–64	2	2.0	0	2	2	2	2	2	2	2
65+	2	2.1	1	1	1	3	3	3	3	3
2. MULTIPLE DX										
0–19 Years	7	2.5	<1	1	2	2	3	3	5	5
20–34	9	4.7	4	3	3	4	5	7	9	9
35–49	14	6.2	35	2	3	4	6	13	23	23
50–64	37	5.6	37	2	2	4	5	14	21	29
65+	57	5.4	12	2	3	4	7	10	12	18
TOTAL SINGLE DX	**7**	**2.4**	**<1**	**1**	**2**	**2**	**3**	**4**	**4**	**4**
TOTAL MULTIPLE DX	**124**	**5.2**	**19**	**2**	**3**	**4**	**6**	**9**	**14**	**23**
TOTAL										
0–19 Years	8	2.6	<1	1	2	3	3	3	5	5
20–34	9	4.7	4	3	3	4	5	7	9	9
35–49	16	5.7	31	2	2	4	6	13	23	23
50–64	39	5.4	36	2	2	4	5	14	21	29
65+	59	5.3	12	2	3	4	7	9	12	17
GRAND TOTAL	**131**	**5.1**	**19**	**2**	**3**	**4**	**6**	**9**	**14**	**23**

57.6: PARTIAL CYSTECTOMY

Type of Patients	Observed Patients	Avg. Stay	Vari-ance	Percentiles						
				10th	25th	50th	75th	90th	95th	99th
1. SINGLE DX										
0–19 Years	0									
20–34	0									
35–49	0									
50–64	5	2.3	1	1	1	2	3	4	4	4
65+	4	2.4	2	1	1	2	3	4	4	4
2. MULTIPLE DX										
0–19 Years	4	3.4	2	1	2	3	5	5	5	5
20–34	7	3.8	8	1	1	3	7	7	8	8
35–49	11	4.6	5	1	3	5	6	7	8	8
50–64	30	6.3	24	2	3	4	7	17	17	17
65+	89	5.4	13	2	3	4	7	10	13	19
TOTAL SINGLE DX	**9**	**2.3**	**1**	**1**	**1**	**2**	**3**	**4**	**4**	**4**
TOTAL MULTIPLE DX	**141**	**5.4**	**14**	**2**	**3**	**4**	**7**	**10**	**14**	**17**
TOTAL										
0–19 Years	4	3.4	2	1	2	3	5	5	5	5
20–34	7	3.8	8	1	1	3	7	7	8	8
35–49	11	4.6	5	1	3	5	6	7	8	8
50–64	35	5.6	22	2	3	4	7	13	17	17
65+	93	5.3	13	2	3	4	7	10	13	19
GRAND TOTAL	**150**	**5.2**	**14**	**2**	**3**	**4**	**6**	**10**	**13**	**17**

57.7: TOTAL CYSTECTOMY

Type of Patients	Observed Patients	Avg. Stay	Vari-ance	Percentiles						
				10th	25th	50th	75th	90th	95th	99th
1. SINGLE DX										
0–19 Years	0									
20–34	0									
35–49	1	8.0	0	8	8	8	8	8	8	8
50–64	11	6.6	8	2	5	7	8	8	13	13
65+	7	9.1	5	7	8	8	9	14	14	14
2. MULTIPLE DX										
0–19 Years	3	10.9	1	9	11	11	12	12	12	12
20–34	3	23.3	564	9	9	10	51	51	51	51
35–49	52	10.4	24	7	8	9	12	13	18	37
50–64	277	10.1	28	6	7	9	11	16	20	31
65+	630	10.8	33	6	7	9	12	18	21	32
TOTAL SINGLE DX	**19**	**7.8**	**8**	**5**	**7**	**8**	**8**	**11**	**14**	**14**
TOTAL MULTIPLE DX	**965**	**10.6**	**32**	**6**	**7**	**9**	**12**	**17**	**21**	**32**
TOTAL										
0–19 Years	3	10.9	1	9	11	11	12	12	12	12
20–34	3	23.3	564	9	9	10	51	51	51	51
35–49	53	10.3	24	7	8	9	12	13	18	37
50–64	288	10.0	28	5	7	9	11	16	20	31
65+	637	10.8	32	6	7	9	12	18	21	32
GRAND TOTAL	**984**	**10.5**	**31**	**6**	**7**	**9**	**12**	**17**	**21**	**32**

57.71: RADICAL CYSTECTOMY

Type of Patients	Observed Patients	Avg. Stay	Vari-ance	Percentiles						
				10th	25th	50th	75th	90th	95th	99th
1. SINGLE DX										
0–19 Years	0									
20–34	0									
35–49	1	8.0	0	8	8	8	8	8	8	8
50–64	11	6.6	8	2	5	7	8	8	13	13
65+	7	9.1	5	7	8	8	9	14	14	14
2. MULTIPLE DX										
0–19 Years	3	10.9	1	9	11	11	12	12	12	12
20–34	0									
35–49	47	9.6	17	6	8	8	10	13	18	28
50–64	257	10.1	28	5	7	9	11	16	20	31
65+	583	10.9	34	6	7	9	12	18	21	33
TOTAL SINGLE DX	**19**	**7.8**	**8**	**5**	**7**	**8**	**8**	**11**	**14**	**14**
TOTAL MULTIPLE DX	**890**	**10.6**	**31**	**6**	**7**	**9**	**12**	**17**	**21**	**32**
TOTAL										
0–19 Years	3	10.9	1	9	11	11	12	12	12	12
20–34	0									
35–49	48	9.6	17	6	8	8	10	13	18	28
50–64	268	10.0	28	5	7	9	11	16	20	31
65+	590	10.9	33	6	7	9	12	18	21	33
GRAND TOTAL	**909**	**10.6**	**31**	**6**	**7**	**9**	**12**	**17**	**21**	**32**

57.8: OTH URIN BLADDER REPAIR

Type of Patients	Observed Patients	Avg. Stay	Vari-ance	Percentiles						
				10th	25th	50th	75th	90th	95th	99th
1. SINGLE DX										
0–19 Years	6	3.2	7	1	1	1	7	7	7	7
20–34	5	3.1	1	1	3	3	4	5	5	5
35–49	11	1.7	2	1	1	1	2	2	7	7
50–64	3	1.9	2	1	1	2	2	4	4	4
65+	2	1.0	0	1	1	1	1	1	1	1
2. MULTIPLE DX										
0–19 Years	99	9.0	35	4	5	8	11	15	20	30
20–34	74	6.6	23	2	3	6	8	12	17	26
35–49	150	6.0	26	1	3	5	7	11	15	28
50–64	137	7.3	39	2	3	6	9	16	21	23
65+	154	8.6	35	2	5	8	11	17	20	28
TOTAL SINGLE DX	**27**	**2.4**	**4**	**1**	**1**	**1**	**3**	**7**	**7**	**7**
TOTAL MULTIPLE DX	**614**	**7.7**	**34**	**2**	**4**	**7**	**10**	**15**	**19**	**28**
TOTAL										
0–19 Years	105	8.7	35	3	5	8	11	15	20	30
20–34	79	6.4	22	2	3	6	8	11	17	26
35–49	161	5.7	26	1	3	5	7	10	15	28
50–64	140	7.2	38	1	3	5	9	16	21	23
65+	156	8.5	35	2	4	8	11	17	20	28
GRAND TOTAL	**641**	**7.5**	**34**	**2**	**4**	**6**	**9**	**14**	**19**	**28**

57.81: SUTURE BLADDER LAC

Type of Patients	Observed Patients	Avg. Stay	Vari-ance	Percentiles						
				10th	25th	50th	75th	90th	95th	99th
1. SINGLE DX										
0–19 Years	1	7.0	0	7	7	7	7	7	7	7
20–34	2	3.2	<1	3	3	3	3	4	4	4
35–49	1	1.0	0	1	1	1	1	1	1	1
50–64	0									
65+	0									
2. MULTIPLE DX										
0–19 Years	12	10.5	71	5	5	9	11	21	21	49
20–34	25	7.0	16	2	3	6	9	12	15	19
35–49	39	8.5	36	2	5	7	9	16	22	28
50–64	14	7.5	64	2	3	6	8	8	9	43
65+	31	7.9	31	3	4	7	10	14	21	28
TOTAL SINGLE DX	**4**	**4.2**	**4**	**3**	**3**	**3**	**7**	**7**	**7**	**7**
TOTAL MULTIPLE DX	**121**	**8.4**	**42**	**3**	**5**	**7**	**10**	**15**	**21**	**43**
TOTAL										
0–19 Years	13	10.2	66	5	5	9	11	21	21	49
20–34	27	6.4	15	3	3	6	8	12	15	19
35–49	40	8.4	36	2	5	7	9	16	22	28
50–64	14	7.5	64	2	3	6	8	8	9	43
65+	31	7.9	31	3	4	7	10	14	21	28
GRAND TOTAL	**125**	**8.2**	**41**	**3**	**5**	**7**	**10**	**14**	**21**	**43**

57.83: ENTEROVESICAL FIST REP

Type of Patients	Observed Patients	Avg. Stay	Vari-ance	Percentiles						
				10th	25th	50th	75th	90th	95th	99th
1. SINGLE DX										
0–19 Years	1	1.0	0	1	1	1	1	1	1	1
20–34	1	5.0	0	5	5	5	5	5	5	5
35–49	0									
50–64	0									
65+	0									
2. MULTIPLE DX										
0–19 Years	2	6.7	17	4	4	4	12	12	12	12
20–34	7	8.5	54	3	6	7	8	26	26	26
35–49	26	7.7	47	4	5	6	8	9	20	41
50–64	49	8.1	20	4	5	6	11	16	17	21
65+	68	10.7	36	5	7	8	14	19	25	32
TOTAL SINGLE DX	**2**	**1.7**	**3**	**1**	**1**	**1**	**1**	**5**	**5**	**5**
TOTAL MULTIPLE DX	**152**	**9.3**	**34**	**4**	**5**	**7**	**12**	**18**	**20**	**32**
TOTAL										
0–19 Years	3	4.5	18	1	1	4	4	12	12	12
20–34	8	8.1	49	3	5	6	7	26	26	26
35–49	26	7.7	47	4	5	6	8	9	20	41
50–64	49	8.1	20	4	5	6	11	16	17	21
65+	68	10.7	36	5	7	8	14	19	25	32
GRAND TOTAL	**154**	**9.1**	**34**	**4**	**5**	**7**	**12**	**18**	**20**	**32**

57.84: REP OTH FISTULA BLADDER

Type of Patients	Observed Patients	Avg. Stay	Vari-ance	Percentiles						
				10th	25th	50th	75th	90th	95th	99th
1. SINGLE DX										
0–19 Years	0									
20–34	1	2.0	0	2	2	2	2	2	2	2
35–49	9	1.7	3	1	1	1	2	2	7	7
50–64	1	2.0	0	2	2	2	2	2	2	2
65+	1	1.0	0	1	1	1	1	1	1	1
2. MULTIPLE DX										
0–19 Years	4	3.3	1	2	2	4	4	5	5	5
20–34	11	3.5	3	1	3	3	3	7	7	7
35–49	58	3.5	6	1	1	3	5	6	7	15
50–64	28	3.2	10	1	1	2	4	5	6	19
65+	21	5.7	29	1	2	3	8	16	18	20
TOTAL SINGLE DX	**12**	**1.7**	**2**	**1**	**1**	**1**	**2**	**2**	**7**	**7**
TOTAL MULTIPLE DX	**122**	**3.8**	**10**	**1**	**2**	**3**	**5**	**7**	**10**	**18**
TOTAL										
0–19 Years	4	3.3	1	2	2	4	4	5	5	5
20–34	12	3.4	3	2	3	3	3	7	7	7
35–49	67	3.2	6	1	1	3	4	6	7	10
50–64	29	3.1	9	1	1	2	4	5	6	19
65+	22	5.5	28	1	2	3	7	16	18	20
GRAND TOTAL	**134**	**3.6**	**10**	**1**	**2**	**3**	**4**	**7**	**9**	**18**

57.87: URINARY BLADDER RECONST

Type of Patients	Observed Patients	Avg. Stay	Vari-ance	10th	25th	50th	75th	90th	95th	99th
1. SINGLE DX										
0–19 Years	2	3.0	0	3	3	3	3	3	3	3
20–34	0									
35–49	0									
50–64	0									
65+	0									
2. MULTIPLE DX										
0–19 Years	54	9.4	14	6	7	8	11	14	17	27
20–34	15	8.6	10	6	6	8	10	11	12	20
35–49	11	7.0	4	5	6	6	9	9	12	12
50–64	20	12.1	60	4	7	10	15	23	23	37
65+	11	7.7	5	3	7	8	8	11	11	12
TOTAL SINGLE DX	**2**	**3.0**	**0**	**3**	**3**	**3**	**3**	**3**	**3**	**3**
TOTAL MULTIPLE DX	**111**	**9.5**	**21**	**6**	**7**	**8**	**11**	**14**	**20**	**27**
TOTAL										
0–19 Years	56	9.3	15	6	7	8	11	14	17	27
20–34	15	8.6	10	6	6	8	10	11	12	20
35–49	11	7.0	4	5	6	6	9	9	12	12
50–64	20	12.1	60	4	7	10	15	23	23	37
65+	11	7.7	5	3	7	8	8	11	11	12
GRAND TOTAL	**113**	**9.4**	**21**	**5**	**7**	**8**	**11**	**14**	**18**	**27**

57.9: OTHER BLADDER OPERATIONS

Type of Patients	Observed Patients	Avg. Stay	Vari-ance	10th	25th	50th	75th	90th	95th	99th
1. SINGLE DX										
0–19 Years	8	2.8	2	1	2	3	3	6	6	6
20–34	14	1.5	<1	1	1	1	2	2	2	4
35–49	0									
50–64	7	4.0	23	1	2	2	2	15	15	15
65+	8	2.1	3	1	1	1	2	6	6	6
2. MULTIPLE DX										
0–19 Years	96	2.8	5	1	1	2	4	5	8	11
20–34	172	3.9	21	1	2	3	4	7	9	23
35–49	322	5.0	40	1	2	3	6	9	13	40
50–64	538	4.5	24	1	2	3	5	8	12	28
65+	3,185	4.6	12	1	2	4	6	8	11	18
TOTAL SINGLE DX	**37**	**2.2**	**5**	**1**	**1**	**2**	**2**	**4**	**6**	**15**
TOTAL MULTIPLE DX	**4,313**	**4.5**	**16**	**1**	**2**	**4**	**6**	**8**	**11**	**20**
TOTAL										
0–19 Years	104	2.8	5	1	1	2	3	5	8	11
20–34	186	3.6	19	1	2	3	4	6	8	23
35–49	322	5.0	40	1	2	3	6	9	13	40
50–64	545	4.5	24	1	2	3	5	8	13	28
65+	3,193	4.6	12	1	2	4	6	8	11	18
GRAND TOTAL	**4,350**	**4.5**	**16**	**1**	**2**	**4**	**6**	**8**	**11**	**19**

57.91: BLADDER SPHINCTEROTOMY

Type of Patients	Observed Patients	Avg. Stay	Vari-ance	10th	25th	50th	75th	90th	95th	99th
1. SINGLE DX										
0–19 Years	0									
20–34	0									
35–49	0									
50–64	2	9.6	73	1	1	15	15	15	15	15
65+	1	1.0	0	1	1	1	1	1	1	1
2. MULTIPLE DX										
0–19 Years	1	1.0	0	1	1	1	1	1	1	1
20–34	5	4.1	2	2	3	5	5	5	5	5
35–49	13	1.6	1	1	1	1	1	4	4	4
50–64	27	2.1	6	1	1	1	2	4	10	10
65+	189	2.8	11	1	1	2	3	6	10	15
TOTAL SINGLE DX	**3**	**7.3**	**66**	**1**	**1**	**1**	**15**	**15**	**15**	**15**
TOTAL MULTIPLE DX	**235**	**2.7**	**10**	**1**	**1**	**1**	**3**	**6**	**10**	**15**
TOTAL										
0–19 Years	1	1.0	0	1	1	1	1	1	1	1
20–34	5	4.1	2	2	3	5	5	5	5	5
35–49	13	1.6	1	1	1	1	1	4	4	4
50–64	29	2.5	11	1	1	1	2	6	10	15
65+	190	2.8	11	1	1	2	3	6	10	15
GRAND TOTAL	**238**	**2.7**	**10**	**1**	**1**	**1**	**3**	**6**	**10**	**15**

57.93: CONTROL BLADDER HEMOR

Type of Patients	Observed Patients	Avg. Stay	Vari-ance	10th	25th	50th	75th	90th	95th	99th
1. SINGLE DX										
0–19 Years	0									
20–34	0									
35–49	0									
50–64	0									
65+	1	2.0	0	2	2	2	2	2	2	2
2. MULTIPLE DX										
0–19 Years	1	1.0	0	1	1	1	1	1	1	1
20–34	2	7.4	12	5	5	5	10	10	10	10
35–49	8	4.6	23	1	2	3	4	9	19	19
50–64	26	2.6	10	1	1	1	3	4	13	14
65+	173	4.7	20	1	2	3	6	9	13	24
TOTAL SINGLE DX	**1**	**2.0**	**0**	**2**	**2**	**2**	**2**	**2**	**2**	**2**
TOTAL MULTIPLE DX	**210**	**4.5**	**19**	**1**	**1**	**3**	**6**	**9**	**13**	**22**
TOTAL										
0–19 Years	1	1.0	0	1	1	1	1	1	1	1
20–34	2	7.4	12	5	5	5	10	10	10	10
35–49	8	4.6	23	1	2	3	4	9	19	19
50–64	26	2.6	10	1	1	1	3	4	13	14
65+	174	4.7	20	1	2	3	6	9	13	24
GRAND TOTAL	**211**	**4.5**	**19**	**1**	**1**	**3**	**6**	**9**	**13**	**22**

57.94: INSERT INDWELL URIN CATH

Type of Patients	Observed Patients	Avg. Stay	Vari-ance	10th	25th	50th	75th	90th	95th	99th
1. SINGLE DX										
0–19 Years	8	2.8	2	1	2	3	3	6	6	6
20–34	13	1.7	<1	1	1	2	2	2	2	4
35–49	0									
50–64	5	2.3	1	1	2	2	2	5	5	5
65+	4	1.5	2	1	1	1	1	5	5	5
2. MULTIPLE DX										
0–19 Years	93	2.7	4	1	1	2	4	4	6	9
20–34	158	3.9	22	1	2	3	4	7	9	23
35–49	283	4.7	29	1	2	3	5	8	11	33
50–64	451	4.8	26	1	2	4	5	8	13	31
65+	2,673	4.7	11	2	3	4	6	8	11	17
TOTAL SINGLE DX	**30**	**2.1**	**1**	**1**	**1**	**2**	**2**	**3**	**5**	**6**
TOTAL MULTIPLE DX	**3,658**	**4.6**	**15**	**1**	**2**	**4**	**6**	**8**	**11**	**19**
TOTAL										
0–19 Years	101	2.7	4	1	1	2	3	4	6	9
20–34	171	3.7	20	1	2	3	4	6	8	23
35–49	283	4.7	29	1	2	3	5	8	11	33
50–64	456	4.7	25	1	2	4	5	8	13	31
65+	2,677	4.7	11	2	3	4	6	8	11	17
GRAND TOTAL	**3,688**	**4.6**	**15**	**1**	**2**	**4**	**6**	**8**	**11**	**19**

57.95: REPL INDWELL URIN CATH

Type of Patients	Observed Patients	Avg. Stay	Vari-ance	10th	25th	50th	75th	90th	95th	99th
1. SINGLE DX										
0–19 Years	0									
20–34	0									
35–49	0									
50–64	0									
65+	2	4.3	6	2	2	6	6	6	6	6
2. MULTIPLE DX										
0–19 Years	0									
20–34	7	3.7	5	1	2	3	6	7	7	7
35–49	11	13.7	275	1	2	4	40	40	40	40
50–64	22	5.1	15	1	2	5	6	7	14	19
65+	113	4.3	14	1	2	4	5	8	9	19
TOTAL SINGLE DX	**2**	**4.3**	**6**	**2**	**2**	**6**	**6**	**6**	**6**	**6**
TOTAL MULTIPLE DX	**153**	**5.2**	**42**	**1**	**2**	**4**	**6**	**8**	**14**	**40**
TOTAL										
0–19 Years	0									
20–34	7	3.7	5	1	2	3	6	7	7	7
35–49	11	13.7	275	1	2	4	40	40	40	40
50–64	22	5.1	15	1	2	5	6	7	14	19
65+	115	4.3	13	1	2	4	6	8	9	19
GRAND TOTAL	**155**	**5.2**	**41**	**1**	**2**	**4**	**6**	**8**	**14**	**40**

58.0: URETHROTOMY

Type of Patients	Observed Patients	Avg. Stay	Vari-ance	10th	25th	50th	75th	90th	95th	99th
1. SINGLE DX										
0–19 Years	0									
20–34	2	1.0	0	1	1	1	1	1	1	1
35–49	0									
50–64	1	3.0	0	3	3	3	3	3	3	3
65+	0									
2. MULTIPLE DX										
0–19 Years	3	5.2	20	1	1	6	10	10	10	10
20–34	5	2.4	<1	1	2	3	3	3	3	3
35–49	4	1.3	<1	1	1	1	2	2	2	2
50–64	7	4.0	38	1	1	1	3	17	17	17
65+	11	6.5	17	1	3	6	10	12	12	12
TOTAL SINGLE DX	**3**	**1.7**	**1**	**1**	**1**	**1**	**3**	**3**	**3**	**3**
TOTAL MULTIPLE DX	**30**	**4.6**	**19**	**1**	**1**	**3**	**6**	**12**	**12**	**17**
TOTAL										
0–19 Years	3	5.2	20	1	1	6	10	10	10	10
20–34	7	2.2	<1	1	1	2	3	3	3	3
35–49	4	1.3	<1	1	1	1	2	2	2	2
50–64	8	3.9	34	1	1	1	3	17	17	17
65+	11	6.5	17	1	3	6	10	12	12	12
GRAND TOTAL	**33**	**4.5**	**18**	**1**	**1**	**3**	**6**	**12**	**12**	**17**

58.1: URETHRAL MEATOTOMY

Type of Patients	Observed Patients	Avg. Stay	Vari-ance	10th	25th	50th	75th	90th	95th	99th
1. SINGLE DX										
0–19 Years	1	3.0	0	3	3	3	3	3	3	3
20–34	0									
35–49	1	1.0	0	1	1	1	1	1	1	1
50–64	0									
65+	0									
2. MULTIPLE DX										
0–19 Years	4	5.1	68	1	1	1	1	19	19	19
20–34	0									
35–49	2	3.9	17	1	1	1	7	7	7	7
50–64	7	2.6	1	1	1	3	3	3	5	5
65+	4	4.9	21	1	1	5	6	15	15	15
TOTAL SINGLE DX	**2**	**2.1**	**2**	**1**	**1**	**3**	**3**	**3**	**3**	**3**
TOTAL MULTIPLE DX	**17**	**3.9**	**20**	**1**	**1**	**3**	**5**	**7**	**15**	**19**
TOTAL										
0–19 Years	5	4.7	55	1	1	1	3	19	19	19
20–34	0									
35–49	3	2.9	12	1	1	1	7	7	7	7
50–64	7	2.6	1	1	1	3	3	3	5	5
65+	4	4.9	21	1	1	5	6	15	15	15
GRAND TOTAL	**19**	**3.7**	**19**	**1**	**1**	**3**	**5**	**7**	**15**	**19**

58.2: URETHRAL DIAGNOSTIC PX

Type of Patients	Observed Patients	Avg. Stay	Vari-ance	Percentiles 10th	25th	50th	75th	90th	95th	99th
1. SINGLE DX										
0–19 Years	2	1.0	0	1	1	1	1	1	1	1
20–34	1	3.0	0	3	3	3	3	3	3	3
35–49	2	1.0	0	1	1	1	1	1	1	1
50–64	0									
65+	0									
2. MULTIPLE DX										
0–19 Years	4	3.3	10	2	2	2	2	10	10	10
20–34	3	7.3	48	1	1	6	15	15	15	15
35–49	12	3.7	26	1	1	2	3	8	21	21
50–64	13	3.7	5	1	2	3	6	6	6	6
65+	21	7.2	28	1	4	6	10	13	15	23
TOTAL SINGLE DX	**5**	**1.5**	**<1**	**1**	**1**	**1**	**1**	**3**	**3**	**3**
TOTAL MULTIPLE DX	**53**	**5.2**	**23**	**1**	**2**	**5**	**6**	**12**	**15**	**23**
TOTAL										
0–19 Years	6	2.8	9	1	2	2	2	10	10	10
20–34	4	5.9	33	1	3	3	6	15	15	15
35–49	14	3.4	24	1	1	2	3	8	21	21
50–64	13	3.7	5	1	2	3	6	6	6	6
65+	21	7.2	28	1	4	6	10	13	15	23
GRAND TOTAL	**58**	**5.0**	**22**	**1**	**1**	**3**	**6**	**12**	**15**	**23**

58.3: EXC/DESTR URETHRAL LES

Type of Patients	Observed Patients	Avg. Stay	Vari-ance	Percentiles 10th	25th	50th	75th	90th	95th	99th
1. SINGLE DX										
0–19 Years	4	1.7	<1	1	1	2	2	2	2	2
20–34	6	1.5	<1	1	1	1	2	3	3	3
35–49	4	1.1	<1	1	1	1	1	2	2	2
50–64	4	1.0	0	1	1	1	1	1	1	1
65+	1	1.0	0	1	1	1	1	1	1	1
2. MULTIPLE DX										
0–19 Years	14	5.6	34	1	1	2	8	16	16	17
20–34	13	3.8	10	1	1	2	8	8	8	8
35–49	21	3.1	23	1	1	1	2	9	20	20
50–64	32	1.8	2	1	1	1	2	4	4	5
65+	53	3.5	16	1	1	3	4	7	8	33
TOTAL SINGLE DX	**19**	**1.3**	**<1**	**1**	**1**	**1**	**2**	**2**	**2**	**3**
TOTAL MULTIPLE DX	**133**	**3.4**	**16**	**1**	**1**	**2**	**4**	**8**	**11**	**20**
TOTAL										
0–19 Years	18	4.6	28	1	1	2	8	16	16	17
20–34	19	3.2	8	1	1	2	4	8	8	8
35–49	25	2.5	17	1	1	1	2	4	9	20
50–64	36	1.7	1	1	1	1	2	4	4	5
65+	54	3.5	15	1	1	2	4	7	8	33
GRAND TOTAL	**152**	**3.1**	**14**	**1**	**1**	**2**	**4**	**8**	**9**	**20**

58.39: URETHRA LES DESTR NEC

Type of Patients	Observed Patients	Avg. Stay	Vari-ance	Percentiles 10th	25th	50th	75th	90th	95th	99th
1. SINGLE DX										
0–19 Years	3	1.3	<1	1	1	1	2	2	2	2
20–34	5	1.6	<1	1	1	1	2	3	3	3
35–49	4	1.1	<1	1	1	1	1	2	2	2
50–64	3	1.0	0	1	1	1	1	1	1	1
65+	0									
2. MULTIPLE DX										
0–19 Years	8	2.9	7	1	1	1	4	8	8	8
20–34	9	1.7	1	1	1	1	2	4	4	4
35–49	12	2.4	6	1	1	1	3	6	9	9
50–64	24	1.5	<1	1	1	1	2	3	4	5
65+	18	2.6	2	1	2	2	4	4	5	5
TOTAL SINGLE DX	**15**	**1.2**	**<1**	**1**	**1**	**1**	**1**	**2**	**2**	**3**
TOTAL MULTIPLE DX	**71**	**2.1**	**3**	**1**	**1**	**1**	**3**	**4**	**5**	**8**
TOTAL										
0–19 Years	11	2.6	6	1	1	1	4	8	8	8
20–34	14	1.7	<1	1	1	1	2	3	4	4
35–49	16	1.9	4	1	1	1	2	4	6	9
50–64	27	1.4	<1	1	1	1	2	3	4	5
65+	18	2.6	2	1	2	2	4	4	5	5
GRAND TOTAL	**86**	**2.0**	**3**	**1**	**1**	**1**	**2**	**4**	**5**	**8**

58.4: REPAIR OF URETHRA

Type of Patients	Observed Patients	Avg. Stay	Vari-ance	Percentiles 10th	25th	50th	75th	90th	95th	99th
1. SINGLE DX										
0–19 Years	100	2.3	3	1	1	2	3	6	7	7
20–34	14	1.8	<1	1	1	2	2	2	3	4
35–49	14	1.9	1	1	1	2	2	4	5	5
50–64	17	2.1	1	1	1	2	3	3	3	5
65+	0									
2. MULTIPLE DX										
0–19 Years	118	2.8	5	1	1	2	4	6	7	10
20–34	29	2.6	2	1	2	2	3	5	5	6
35–49	38	3.6	16	1	2	2	4	8	10	25
50–64	66	2.9	7	1	1	2	3	7	7	21
65+	42	3.4	13	1	1	2	4	6	8	21
TOTAL SINGLE DX	**145**	**2.2**	**3**	**1**	**1**	**2**	**3**	**5**	**7**	**7**
TOTAL MULTIPLE DX	**293**	**3.0**	**7**	**1**	**1**	**2**	**4**	**6**	**7**	**11**
TOTAL										
0–19 Years	218	2.6	4	1	1	2	4	6	7	7
20–34	43	2.3	2	1	1	2	3	4	5	6
35–49	52	3.0	12	1	1	2	3	6	8	25
50–64	83	2.8	6	1	1	2	3	6	7	8
65+	42	3.4	13	1	1	2	4	6	8	21
GRAND TOTAL	**438**	**2.7**	**6**	**1**	**1**	**2**	**3**	**6**	**7**	**10**

58.45: HYPOSPAD/EPISPADIAS REP

Type of Patients	Observed Patients	Avg. Stay	Vari-ance	Percentiles						
				10th	25th	50th	75th	90th	95th	99th
1. SINGLE DX										
0–19 Years	86	2.5	4	1	1	2	3	6	7	7
20–34	1	3.0	0	3	3	3	3	3	3	3
35–49	1	1.0	0	1	1	1	1	1	1	1
50–64	7	2.5	1	1	2	2	3	3	5	5
65+	0									
2. MULTIPLE DX										
0–19 Years	92	2.7	4	1	1	1	4	6	6	10
20–34	1	5.0	0	5	5	5	5	5	5	5
35–49	2	2.0	2	1	1	1	3	3	3	3
50–64	6	3.1	8	1	1	1	6	7	7	7
65+	1	1.0	0	1	1	1	1	1	1	1
TOTAL SINGLE DX	**95**	**2.5**	**3**	**1**	**1**	**2**	**3**	**6**	**7**	**7**
TOTAL MULTIPLE DX	**102**	**2.7**	**4**	**1**	**1**	**1**	**4**	**6**	**6**	**10**
TOTAL										
0–19 Years	178	2.6	4	1	1	2	4	6	7	7
20–34	2	4.0	2	3	3	5	5	5	5	5
35–49	3	1.7	1	1	1	1	3	3	3	3
50–64	13	2.7	4	1	1	2	3	6	7	7
65+	1	1.0	0	1	1	1	1	1	1	1
GRAND TOTAL	**197**	**2.6**	**4**	**1**	**1**	**2**	**4**	**6**	**7**	**7**

58.49: URETHRAL REPAIR NEC

Type of Patients	Observed Patients	Avg. Stay	Vari-ance	Percentiles						
				10th	25th	50th	75th	90th	95th	99th
1. SINGLE DX										
0–19 Years	4	1.4	<1	1	1	1	2	2	2	2
20–34	6	2.0	<1	1	1	2	2	4	4	4
35–49	9	2.1	<1	1	2	2	2	3	4	4
50–64	4	1.4	<1	1	1	1	2	2	2	2
65+	0									
2. MULTIPLE DX										
0–19 Years	3	3.2	4	1	1	5	5	5	5	5
20–34	10	1.9	1	1	1	2	2	3	4	5
35–49	14	2.8	4	1	2	2	3	5	5	10
50–64	23	3.1	13	1	1	2	3	6	8	21
65+	13	2.4	3	1	1	2	3	6	6	6
TOTAL SINGLE DX	**23**	**1.8**	**<1**	**1**	**1**	**2**	**2**	**2**	**4**	**4**
TOTAL MULTIPLE DX	**63**	**2.7**	**6**	**1**	**1**	**2**	**3**	**5**	**6**	**10**
TOTAL										
0–19 Years	7	2.2	3	1	1	2	2	5	5	5
20–34	16	1.9	1	1	1	2	2	4	4	5
35–49	23	2.5	3	1	2	2	3	4	5	10
50–64	27	2.9	12	1	1	2	3	6	8	21
65+	13	2.4	3	1	1	2	3	6	6	6
GRAND TOTAL	**86**	**2.5**	**5**	**1**	**1**	**2**	**3**	**5**	**6**	**10**

58.5: URETHRAL STRICTURE REL

Type of Patients	Observed Patients	Avg. Stay	Vari-ance	Percentiles						
				10th	25th	50th	75th	90th	95th	99th
1. SINGLE DX										
0–19 Years	3	1.4	<1	1	1	1	2	2	2	2
20–34	5	1.1	<1	1	1	1	1	1	2	2
35–49	4	1.2	<1	1	1	1	1	2	2	2
50–64	6	1.2	<1	1	1	1	1	2	2	2
65+	2	1.0	0	1	1	1	1	1	1	1
2. MULTIPLE DX										
0–19 Years	10	2.4	4	1	1	2	3	4	8	8
20–34	16	2.3	3	1	1	1	3	6	6	7
35–49	41	3.8	19	1	1	3	4	7	11	25
50–64	116	3.6	20	1	1	2	4	9	12	26
65+	267	3.7	23	1	1	2	4	9	12	23
TOTAL SINGLE DX	**20**	**1.2**	**<1**	**1**	**1**	**1**	**1**	**2**	**2**	**2**
TOTAL MULTIPLE DX	**450**	**3.6**	**21**	**1**	**1**	**2**	**4**	**9**	**12**	**23**
TOTAL										
0–19 Years	13	2.1	3	1	1	1	2	4	8	8
20–34	21	1.8	2	1	1	1	2	3	6	7
35–49	45	3.6	18	1	1	2	4	7	10	25
50–64	122	3.6	19	1	1	2	4	9	10	26
65+	269	3.7	23	1	1	2	4	9	12	23
GRAND TOTAL	**470**	**3.5**	**20**	**1**	**1**	**2**	**4**	**9**	**12**	**23**

58.6: URETHRAL DILATION

Type of Patients	Observed Patients	Avg. Stay	Vari-ance	Percentiles						
				10th	25th	50th	75th	90th	95th	99th
1. SINGLE DX										
0–19 Years	1	1.0	0	1	1	1	1	1	1	1
20–34	0									
35–49	1	1.0	0	1	1	1	1	1	1	1
50–64	5	1.2	<1	1	1	1	1	2	2	2
65+	1	1.0	0	1	1	1	1	1	1	1
2. MULTIPLE DX										
0–19 Years	12	5.1	42	1	1	2	8	13	25	25
20–34	25	3.7	14	1	1	3	5	10	12	17
35–49	43	5.7	19	1	3	5	7	10	11	28
50–64	74	5.4	40	1	1	3	7	13	15	33
65+	312	5.4	21	1	2	4	7	10	13	24
TOTAL SINGLE DX	**8**	**1.1**	**<1**	**1**	**1**	**1**	**1**	**2**	**2**	**2**
TOTAL MULTIPLE DX	**466**	**5.3**	**24**	**1**	**2**	**4**	**7**	**10**	**13**	**25**
TOTAL										
0–19 Years	13	4.7	39	1	1	2	8	13	25	25
20–34	25	3.7	14	1	1	3	5	10	12	17
35–49	44	5.6	19	1	3	5	7	10	11	28
50–64	79	5.2	38	1	1	3	7	13	15	33
65+	313	5.4	21	1	2	4	7	10	13	24
GRAND TOTAL	**474**	**5.3**	**24**	**1**	**2**	**4**	**7**	**10**	**13**	**25**

58.9: OTHER URETHRAL OPS

Type of Patients	Observed Patients	Avg. Stay	Variance	10th	25th	50th	75th	90th	95th	99th
1. SINGLE DX										
0–19 Years	0									
20–34	2	1.5	<1	1	1	1	2	2	2	2
35–49	0									
50–64	5	1.6	2	1	1	1	1	4	4	4
65+	9	2.6	6	1	1	1	3	7	7	7
2. MULTIPLE DX										
0–19 Years	4	3.1	9	1	2	2	2	9	9	9
20–34	5	3.9	2	2	3	5	5	5	5	5
35–49	16	1.5	2	1	1	1	1	3	4	7
50–64	58	2.2	8	1	1	1	2	3	8	17
65+	270	2.1	7	1	1	1	2	5	7	14
TOTAL SINGLE DX	**16**	**2.2**	**5**	**1**	**1**	**1**	**2**	**7**	**7**	**7**
TOTAL MULTIPLE DX	**353**	**2.1**	**7**	**1**	**1**	**1**	**2**	**5**	**7**	**14**
TOTAL										
0–19 Years	4	3.1	9	1	2	2	2	9	9	9
20–34	7	3.5	2	2	2	4	5	5	5	5
35–49	16	1.5	2	1	1	1	1	3	4	7
50–64	63	2.2	8	1	1	1	2	4	8	17
65+	279	2.1	7	1	1	1	2	5	7	13
GRAND TOTAL	**369**	**2.1**	**7**	**1**	**1**	**1**	**2**	**5**	**7**	**14**

58.93: IMPLANTATION OF AUS

Type of Patients	Observed Patients	Avg. Stay	Variance	10th	25th	50th	75th	90th	95th	99th
1. SINGLE DX										
0–19 Years	0									
20–34	0									
35–49	0									
50–64	3	1.0	0	1	1	1	1	1	1	1
65+	5	1.5	<1	1	1	1	2	3	3	3
2. MULTIPLE DX										
0–19 Years	2	1.7	<1	1	1	2	2	2	2	2
20–34	3	4.1	2	2	2	5	5	5	5	5
35–49	5	1.5	<1	1	1	1	2	3	3	3
50–64	47	1.5	<1	1	1	1	2	3	3	7
65+	190	1.4	2	1	1	1	1	2	3	8
TOTAL SINGLE DX	**8**	**1.4**	**<1**	**1**	**1**	**1**	**1**	**3**	**3**	**3**
TOTAL MULTIPLE DX	**247**	**1.5**	**2**	**1**	**1**	**1**	**1**	**2**	**4**	**8**
TOTAL										
0–19 Years	2	1.7	<1	1	1	2	2	2	2	2
20–34	3	4.1	2	2	2	5	5	5	5	5
35–49	5	1.5	<1	1	1	1	2	3	3	3
50–64	50	1.5	<1	1	1	1	2	3	3	7
65+	195	1.4	2	1	1	1	1	2	3	8
GRAND TOTAL	**255**	**1.5**	**1**	**1**	**1**	**1**	**1**	**2**	**4**	**8**

58.99: PERIURETHRAL OPS NEC

Type of Patients	Observed Patients	Avg. Stay	Variance	10th	25th	50th	75th	90th	95th	99th
1. SINGLE DX										
0–19 Years	0									
20–34	1	2.0	0	2	2	2	2	2	2	2
35–49	0									
50–64	2	2.5	4	1	1	4	4	4	4	4
65+	4	3.5	10	1	1	1	7	7	7	7
2. MULTIPLE DX										
0–19 Years	1	9.0	0	9	9	9	9	9	9	9
20–34	2	3.5	<1	3	3	4	4	4	4	4
35–49	7	2.2	5	1	1	1	4	7	7	7
50–64	10	5.5	30	1	1	3	8	17	17	17
65+	79	4.1	18	1	1	3	6	8	11	25
TOTAL SINGLE DX	**7**	**3.2**	**8**	**1**	**1**	**1**	**7**	**7**	**7**	**7**
TOTAL MULTIPLE DX	**99**	**4.2**	**18**	**1**	**1**	**3**	**6**	**9**	**13**	**25**
TOTAL										
0–19 Years	1	9.0	0	9	9	9	9	9	9	9
20–34	3	3.0	<1	2	2	3	4	4	4	4
35–49	7	2.2	5	1	1	1	4	7	7	7
50–64	12	5.3	28	1	1	3	8	17	17	17
65+	83	4.0	17	1	1	3	6	8	11	25
GRAND TOTAL	**106**	**4.1**	**18**	**1**	**1**	**3**	**6**	**9**	**13**	**25**

59.0: RETROPERITON DISSECTION

Type of Patients	Observed Patients	Avg. Stay	Variance	10th	25th	50th	75th	90th	95th	99th
1. SINGLE DX										
0–19 Years	1	4.0	0	4	4	4	4	4	4	4
20–34	1	4.0	0	4	4	4	4	4	4	4
35–49	3	6.4	20	3	3	5	12	12	12	12
50–64	3	2.2	<1	2	2	2	2	3	3	3
65+	0									
2. MULTIPLE DX										
0–19 Years	4	3.2	<1	2	3	3	4	4	4	4
20–34	11	4.8	3	3	4	5	5	6	6	11
35–49	32	5.0	20	2	3	4	4	11	17	21
50–64	22	4.8	14	2	3	3	5	9	15	18
65+	33	6.6	20	3	4	5	9	10	21	23
TOTAL SINGLE DX	**8**	**3.8**	**6**	**2**	**2**	**3**	**4**	**5**	**12**	**12**
TOTAL MULTIPLE DX	**102**	**5.3**	**16**	**2**	**3**	**4**	**6**	**10**	**15**	**21**
TOTAL										
0–19 Years	5	3.5	<1	3	3	4	4	4	4	4
20–34	12	4.8	3	3	4	5	5	6	6	11
35–49	35	5.1	20	2	3	4	5	11	17	21
50–64	25	4.5	13	2	2	3	4	7	15	18
65+	33	6.6	20	3	4	5	9	10	21	23
GRAND TOTAL	**110**	**5.2**	**16**	**2**	**3**	**4**	**6**	**9**	**15**	**21**

59.1: PERIVESICAL INCISION

Type of Patients	Observed Patients	Avg. Stay	Vari-ance	Percentiles						
				10th	25th	50th	75th	90th	95th	99th
1. SINGLE DX										
0–19 Years	0									
20–34	0									
35–49	0									
50–64	0									
65+	0									
2. MULTIPLE DX										
0–19 Years	0									
20–34	3	3.0	2	1	3	4	4	4	4	4
35–49	3	4.3	20	2	2	2	11	11	11	11
50–64	0									
65+	2	1.8	<1	1	2	2	2	2	2	2
TOTAL SINGLE DX	**0**									
TOTAL MULTIPLE DX	**8**	**3.0**	**7**	**1**	**2**	**2**	**3**	**4**	**11**	**11**
TOTAL										
0–19 Years	0									
20–34	3	3.0	2	1	3	4	4	4	4	4
35–49	3	4.3	20	2	2	2	11	11	11	11
50–64	0									
65+	2	1.8	<1	1	2	2	2	2	2	2
GRAND TOTAL	**8**	**3.0**	**7**	**1**	**2**	**2**	**3**	**4**	**11**	**11**

59.2: PERIRENAL DXTIC PX

Type of Patients	Observed Patients	Avg. Stay	Vari-ance	Percentiles						
				10th	25th	50th	75th	90th	95th	99th
1. SINGLE DX										
0–19 Years	0									
20–34	0									
35–49	0									
50–64	0									
65+	0									
2. MULTIPLE DX										
0–19 Years	0									
20–34	0									
35–49	1	12.0	0	12	12	12	12	12	12	12
50–64	2	5.1	2	4	4	6	6	6	6	6
65+	3	5.0	0	5	5	5	5	5	5	5
TOTAL SINGLE DX	**0**									
TOTAL MULTIPLE DX	**6**	**6.0**	**7**	**4**	**5**	**5**	**6**	**12**	**12**	**12**
TOTAL										
0–19 Years	0									
20–34	0									
35–49	1	12.0	0	12	12	12	12	12	12	12
50–64	2	5.1	2	4	4	6	6	6	6	6
65+	3	5.0	0	5	5	5	5	5	5	5
GRAND TOTAL	**6**	**6.0**	**7**	**4**	**5**	**5**	**6**	**12**	**12**	**12**

59.3: URETHROVES JUNCT PLICAT

Type of Patients	Observed Patients	Avg. Stay	Vari-ance	Percentiles						
				10th	25th	50th	75th	90th	95th	99th
1. SINGLE DX										
0–19 Years	0									
20–34	0									
35–49	0									
50–64	0									
65+	0									
2. MULTIPLE DX										
0–19 Years	0									
20–34	0									
35–49	3	2.2	<1	1	1	2	3	3	3	3
50–64	2	2.0	0	2	2	2	2	2	2	2
65+	0									
TOTAL SINGLE DX	**0**									
TOTAL MULTIPLE DX	**5**	**2.1**	**<1**	**1**	**2**	**2**	**3**	**3**	**3**	**3**
TOTAL										
0–19 Years	0									
20–34	0									
35–49	3	2.2	<1	1	1	2	3	3	3	3
50–64	2	2.0	0	2	2	2	2	2	2	2
65+	0									
GRAND TOTAL	**5**	**2.1**	**<1**	**1**	**2**	**2**	**3**	**3**	**3**	**3**

59.4: SUPRAPUBIC SLING OP

Type of Patients	Observed Patients	Avg. Stay	Vari-ance	Percentiles						
				10th	25th	50th	75th	90th	95th	99th
1. SINGLE DX										
0–19 Years	1	1.0	0	1	1	1	1	1	1	1
20–34	3	1.6	1	1	1	1	3	3	3	3
35–49	16	1.1	<1	1	1	1	1	1	2	2
50–64	19	1.3	<1	1	1	1	2	2	2	2
65+	9	1.4	<1	1	1	1	2	2	2	2
2. MULTIPLE DX										
0–19 Years	0									
20–34	14	1.4	<1	1	1	1	2	2	3	3
35–49	85	1.7	2	1	1	1	2	3	4	6
50–64	152	1.8	1	1	1	1	2	3	4	6
65+	157	1.6	<1	1	1	1	2	3	3	5
TOTAL SINGLE DX	**48**	**1.2**	**<1**	**1**	**1**	**1**	**1**	**2**	**2**	**3**
TOTAL MULTIPLE DX	**408**	**1.7**	**1**	**1**	**1**	**1**	**2**	**3**	**4**	**6**
TOTAL										
0–19 Years	1	1.0	0	1	1	1	1	1	1	1
20–34	17	1.5	<1	1	1	1	2	3	3	3
35–49	101	1.6	2	1	1	1	2	2	3	6
50–64	171	1.7	1	1	1	1	2	3	4	6
65+	166	1.6	<1	1	1	1	2	3	3	5
GRAND TOTAL	**456**	**1.6**	**1**	**1**	**1**	**1**	**2**	**3**	**3**	**6**

59.5: RETROPUBIC URETHRAL SUSP

Type of Patients	Observed Patients	Avg. Stay	Vari-ance	Percentiles						
				10th	25th	50th	75th	90th	95th	99th
1. SINGLE DX										
0–19 Years	0									
20–34	16	1.9	2	1	1	2	2	3	3	8
35–49	89	2.0	<1	1	2	2	2	3	3	4
50–64	69	2.0	<1	1	1	2	3	3	3	4
65+	17	2.4	1	1	2	2	3	4	4	4
2. MULTIPLE DX										
0–19 Years	3	4.8	3	4	4	4	4	8	8	8
20–34	50	2.0	<1	1	1	2	3	3	3	4
35–49	356	2.3	1	1	2	2	3	3	4	5
50–64	467	2.3	2	1	1	2	3	4	4	7
65+	282	2.7	3	1	2	3	3	5	6	8
TOTAL SINGLE DX	**191**	**2.0**	**<1**	**1**	**1**	**2**	**2**	**3**	**3**	**4**
TOTAL MULTIPLE DX	**1,158**	**2.4**	**2**	**1**	**2**	**2**	**3**	**4**	**4**	**8**
TOTAL										
0–19 Years	3	4.8	3	4	4	4	4	8	8	8
20–34	66	2.0	1	1	1	2	2	3	3	8
35–49	445	2.3	1	1	2	2	3	3	4	5
50–64	536	2.3	2	1	1	2	3	4	4	7
65+	299	2.7	3	1	2	3	3	4	6	8
GRAND TOTAL	**1,349**	**2.4**	**2**	**1**	**2**	**2**	**3**	**4**	**4**	**7**

59.6: PARAURETHRAL SUSPENSION

Type of Patients	Observed Patients	Avg. Stay	Vari-ance	Percentiles						
				10th	25th	50th	75th	90th	95th	99th
1. SINGLE DX										
0–19 Years	0									
20–34	0									
35–49	1	1.0	0	1	1	1	1	1	1	1
50–64	3	1.2	<1	1	1	1	1	2	2	2
65+	2	1.6	<1	1	1	2	2	2	2	2
2. MULTIPLE DX										
0–19 Years	0									
20–34	2	1.5	<1	1	1	2	2	2	2	2
35–49	16	2.0	<1	1	2	2	2	3	3	3
50–64	32	1.8	<1	1	1	2	2	3	3	6
65+	21	2.0	2	1	1	2	3	3	4	6
TOTAL SINGLE DX	**6**	**1.4**	**<1**	**1**	**1**	**1**	**2**	**2**	**2**	**2**
TOTAL MULTIPLE DX	**71**	**1.9**	**<1**	**1**	**1**	**2**	**2**	**3**	**3**	**6**
TOTAL										
0–19 Years	0									
20–34	2	1.5	<1	1	1	2	2	2	2	2
35–49	17	1.9	<1	1	2	2	2	3	3	3
50–64	35	1.8	<1	1	1	2	2	3	3	6
65+	23	1.9	1	1	1	2	3	3	4	6
GRAND TOTAL	**77**	**1.8**	**<1**	**1**	**1**	**2**	**2**	**3**	**3**	**6**

59.7: OTH URINARY INCONT REP

Type of Patients	Observed Patients	Avg. Stay	Vari-ance	Percentiles						
				10th	25th	50th	75th	90th	95th	99th
1. SINGLE DX										
0–19 Years	0									
20–34	28	1.3	<1	1	1	1	2	2	2	2
35–49	158	1.3	<1	1	1	1	2	2	2	3
50–64	182	1.2	<1	1	1	1	1	2	2	3
65+	99	1.4	2	1	1	1	1	2	2	11
2. MULTIPLE DX										
0–19 Years	6	2.7	5	1	1	2	6	6	6	6
20–34	88	1.6	<1	1	1	1	2	3	3	4
35–49	793	1.6	<1	1	1	1	2	3	3	4
50–64	1,447	1.6	<1	1	1	1	2	3	3	5
65+	1,399	1.7	1	1	1	1	2	3	4	6
TOTAL SINGLE DX	**467**	**1.3**	**<1**	**1**	**1**	**1**	**1**	**2**	**2**	**3**
TOTAL MULTIPLE DX	**3,733**	**1.6**	**<1**	**1**	**1**	**1**	**2**	**3**	**3**	**6**
TOTAL										
0–19 Years	6	2.7	5	1	1	2	6	6	6	6
20–34	116	1.5	<1	1	1	1	2	2	3	4
35–49	951	1.5	<1	1	1	1	2	3	3	4
50–64	1,629	1.5	<1	1	1	1	2	2	3	5
65+	1,498	1.7	1	1	1	1	2	3	3	6
GRAND TOTAL	**4,200**	**1.6**	**<1**	**1**	**1**	**1**	**2**	**3**	**3**	**5**

59.71: LEVATOR MUSC SUSPENSION

Type of Patients	Observed Patients	Avg. Stay	Vari-ance	Percentiles						
				10th	25th	50th	75th	90th	95th	99th
1. SINGLE DX										
0–19 Years	0									
20–34	0									
35–49	5	1.2	<1	1	1	1	1	2	2	2
50–64	3	1.4	<1	1	1	1	2	2	2	2
65+	1	1.0	0	1	1	1	1	1	1	1
2. MULTIPLE DX										
0–19 Years	1	6.0	0	6	6	6	6	6	6	6
20–34	2	3.6	<1	3	3	4	4	4	4	4
35–49	8	1.1	<1	1	1	1	1	2	2	2
50–64	24	1.7	2	1	1	1	2	3	3	7
65+	25	2.2	1	1	1	2	3	3	4	7
TOTAL SINGLE DX	**9**	**1.3**	**<1**	**1**	**1**	**1**	**2**	**2**	**2**	**2**
TOTAL MULTIPLE DX	**60**	**1.9**	**2**	**1**	**1**	**2**	**2**	**3**	**4**	**7**
TOTAL										
0–19 Years	1	6.0	0	6	6	6	6	6	6	6
20–34	2	3.6	<1	3	3	4	4	4	4	4
35–49	13	1.1	<1	1	1	1	1	2	2	2
50–64	27	1.7	2	1	1	1	2	3	3	7
65+	26	2.2	1	1	1	2	3	3	4	7
GRAND TOTAL	**69**	**1.9**	**2**	**1**	**1**	**1**	**2**	**3**	**4**	**7**

59.79: URIN INCONT REPAIR NEC

Type of Patients	Observed Patients	Avg. Stay	Variance	10th	25th	50th	75th	90th	95th	99th
1. SINGLE DX										
0–19 Years	0									
20–34	28	1.3	<1	1	1	1	2	2	2	2
35–49	153	1.3	<1	1	1	1	2	2	2	3
50–64	179	1.2	<1	1	1	1	1	2	2	3
65+	98	1.4	2	1	1	1	1	2	2	11
2. MULTIPLE DX										
0–19 Years	3	1.5	<1	1	1	2	2	2	2	2
20–34	86	1.5	<1	1	1	1	2	3	3	4
35–49	784	1.6	<1	1	1	1	2	3	3	4
50–64	1,423	1.6	<1	1	1	1	2	3	3	5
65+	1,366	1.7	1	1	1	1	2	3	3	6
TOTAL SINGLE DX	**458**	**1.3**	**<1**	**1**	**1**	**1**	**1**	**2**	**2**	**3**
TOTAL MULTIPLE DX	**3,662**	**1.6**	**<1**	**1**	**1**	**1**	**2**	**3**	**3**	**5**
TOTAL										
0–19 Years	3	1.5	<1	1	1	2	2	2	2	2
20–34	114	1.5	<1	1	1	1	2	2	3	4
35–49	937	1.6	<1	1	1	1	2	3	3	4
50–64	1,602	1.5	<1	1	1	1	2	2	3	5
65+	1,464	1.7	1	1	1	1	2	3	3	6
GRAND TOTAL	**4,120**	**1.6**	**<1**	**1**	**1**	**1**	**2**	**3**	**3**	**5**

59.8: URETERAL CATHETERIZATION

Type of Patients	Observed Patients	Avg. Stay	Variance	10th	25th	50th	75th	90th	95th	99th
1. SINGLE DX										
0–19 Years	20	1.7	<1	1	1	1	2	3	3	6
20–34	90	1.9	1	1	1	1	2	4	4	5
35–49	104	1.6	1	1	1	1	2	3	4	8
50–64	70	1.4	<1	1	1	1	1	2	4	5
65+	10	2.2	4	1	1	1	2	5	7	7
2. MULTIPLE DX										
0–19 Years	113	3.4	8	1	2	2	5	7	8	14
20–34	743	3.0	8	1	1	2	3	6	9	12
35–49	1,064	3.3	18	1	1	2	4	6	9	18
50–64	1,132	3.9	23	1	1	2	5	8	11	23
65+	1,329	5.1	22	1	2	4	7	10	14	22
TOTAL SINGLE DX	**294**	**1.7**	**1**	**1**	**1**	**1**	**2**	**3**	**4**	**6**
TOTAL MULTIPLE DX	**4,381**	**4.0**	**19**	**1**	**1**	**3**	**5**	**8**	**11**	**21**
TOTAL										
0–19 Years	133	3.1	7	1	1	2	4	6	8	14
20–34	833	2.9	7	1	1	2	3	6	9	11
35–49	1,168	3.2	17	1	1	2	4	6	9	17
50–64	1,202	3.7	22	1	1	2	4	8	11	23
65+	1,339	5.1	22	1	2	4	7	10	14	22
GRAND TOTAL	**4,675**	**3.9**	**19**	**1**	**1**	**2**	**5**	**8**	**11**	**20**

59.9: OTHER URINARY SYSTEM OPS

Type of Patients	Observed Patients	Avg. Stay	Variance	10th	25th	50th	75th	90th	95th	99th
1. SINGLE DX										
0–19 Years	0									
20–34	0									
35–49	0									
50–64	0									
65+	0									
2. MULTIPLE DX										
0–19 Years	5	8.0	61	1	1	4	18	18	18	18
20–34	20	5.5	25	1	2	4	6	14	17	19
35–49	47	3.9	9	1	2	3	6	8	9	15
50–64	45	4.0	13	1	2	3	6	8	8	22
65+	88	4.7	17	2	2	3	6	8	12	29
TOTAL SINGLE DX	**0**									
TOTAL MULTIPLE DX	**205**	**4.6**	**17**	**1**	**2**	**3**	**6**	**8**	**13**	**20**
TOTAL										
0–19 Years	5	8.0	61	1	1	4	18	18	18	18
20–34	20	5.5	25	1	2	4	6	14	17	19
35–49	47	3.9	9	1	2	3	6	8	9	15
50–64	45	4.0	13	1	2	3	6	8	8	22
65+	88	4.7	17	2	2	3	6	8	12	29
GRAND TOTAL	**205**	**4.6**	**17**	**1**	**2**	**3**	**6**	**8**	**13**	**20**

59.94: REPL CYSTOSTOMY TUBE

Type of Patients	Observed Patients	Avg. Stay	Variance	10th	25th	50th	75th	90th	95th	99th
1. SINGLE DX										
0–19 Years	0									
20–34	0									
35–49	0									
50–64	0									
65+	0									
2. MULTIPLE DX										
0–19 Years	3	3.0	1	1	3	3	4	4	4	4
20–34	4	9.8	50	1	7	14	14	17	17	17
35–49	24	4.8	9	2	2	4	6	7	9	15
50–64	24	4.8	16	1	2	4	7	8	8	22
65+	64	4.8	12	2	3	4	7	8	13	17
TOTAL SINGLE DX	**0**									
TOTAL MULTIPLE DX	**119**	**4.9**	**13**	**2**	**3**	**4**	**7**	**8**	**13**	**20**
TOTAL										
0–19 Years	3	3.0	1	1	3	3	4	4	4	4
20–34	4	9.8	50	1	7	14	14	17	17	17
35–49	24	4.8	9	2	2	4	6	7	9	15
50–64	24	4.8	16	1	2	4	7	8	8	22
65+	64	4.8	12	2	3	4	7	8	13	17
GRAND TOTAL	**119**	**4.9**	**13**	**2**	**3**	**4**	**7**	**8**	**13**	**20**

60.0: INCISION OF PROSTATE

Type of Patients	Observed Patients	Avg. Stay	Vari-ance	Percentiles 10th	25th	50th	75th	90th	95th	99th
1. SINGLE DX										
0–19 Years	0									
20–34	0									
35–49	1	1.0	0	1	1	1	1	1	1	1
50–64	3	1.0	0	1	1	1	1	1	1	1
65+	2	1.0	0	1	1	1	1	1	1	1
2. MULTIPLE DX										
0–19 Years	0									
20–34	1	1.0	0	1	1	1	1	1	1	1
35–49	11	2.0	4	1	1	1	2	3	9	9
50–64	38	2.6	26	1	1	1	2	4	7	34
65+	54	2.6	14	1	1	1	2	5	6	24
TOTAL SINGLE DX	**6**	**1.0**	**0**	**1**	**1**	**1**	**1**	**1**	**1**	**1**
TOTAL MULTIPLE DX	**104**	**2.5**	**17**	**1**	**1**	**1**	**2**	**4**	**7**	**24**
TOTAL										
0–19 Years	0									
20–34	1	1.0	0	1	1	1	1	1	1	1
35–49	12	2.0	4	1	1	1	2	3	9	9
50–64	41	2.3	23	1	1	1	2	4	5	34
65+	56	2.6	14	1	1	1	2	5	6	24
GRAND TOTAL	**110**	**2.4**	**16**	**1**	**1**	**1**	**2**	**4**	**6**	**24**

60.1: PROS/SEM VESICL DXTIC PX

Type of Patients	Observed Patients	Avg. Stay	Vari-ance	Percentiles 10th	25th	50th	75th	90th	95th	99th
1. SINGLE DX										
0–19 Years	0									
20–34	0									
35–49	0									
50–64	1	2.0	0	2	2	2	2	2	2	2
65+	0									
2. MULTIPLE DX										
0–19 Years	1	1.0	0	1	1	1	1	1	1	1
20–34	0									
35–49	4	5.6	26	1	1	5	9	13	13	13
50–64	35	6.7	27	1	3	6	9	13	17	26
65+	101	6.5	27	1	3	4	9	15	17	24
TOTAL SINGLE DX	**1**	**2.0**	**0**	**2**	**2**	**2**	**2**	**2**	**2**	**2**
TOTAL MULTIPLE DX	**141**	**6.5**	**27**	**1**	**3**	**4**	**9**	**14**	**17**	**24**
TOTAL										
0–19 Years	1	1.0	0	1	1	1	1	1	1	1
20–34	0									
35–49	4	5.6	26	1	1	5	9	13	13	13
50–64	36	6.5	27	1	2	6	9	13	17	26
65+	101	6.5	27	1	3	4	9	15	17	24
GRAND TOTAL	**142**	**6.4**	**27**	**1**	**3**	**4**	**9**	**14**	**17**	**24**

60.11: CLSD PROSTATIC BX

Type of Patients	Observed Patients	Avg. Stay	Vari-ance	Percentiles 10th	25th	50th	75th	90th	95th	99th
1. SINGLE DX										
0–19 Years	0									
20–34	0									
35–49	0									
50–64	1	2.0	0	2	2	2	2	2	2	2
65+	0									
2. MULTIPLE DX										
0–19 Years	1	1.0	0	1	1	1	1	1	1	1
20–34	0									
35–49	4	5.6	26	1	1	5	9	13	13	13
50–64	34	6.8	27	1	4	6	9	13	17	26
65+	99	6.5	27	1	3	4	9	15	17	24
TOTAL SINGLE DX	**1**	**2.0**	**0**	**2**	**2**	**2**	**2**	**2**	**2**	**2**
TOTAL MULTIPLE DX	**138**	**6.6**	**27**	**1**	**3**	**5**	**9**	**15**	**17**	**24**
TOTAL										
0–19 Years	1	1.0	0	1	1	1	1	1	1	1
20–34	0									
35–49	4	5.6	26	1	1	5	9	13	13	13
50–64	35	6.6	27	1	3	6	9	13	17	26
65+	99	6.5	27	1	3	4	9	15	17	24
GRAND TOTAL	**139**	**6.5**	**27**	**1**	**3**	**4**	**9**	**14**	**17**	**24**

60.2: TU PROSTATECTOMY

Type of Patients	Observed Patients	Avg. Stay	Vari-ance	Percentiles 10th	25th	50th	75th	90th	95th	99th
1. SINGLE DX										
0–19 Years	0									
20–34	1	3.0	0	3	3	3	3	3	3	3
35–49	11	1.2	<1	1	1	1	1	2	2	2
50–64	126	1.5	<1	1	1	1	2	2	3	3
65+	277	1.6	<1	1	1	1	2	2	3	4
2. MULTIPLE DX										
0–19 Years	1	5.0	0	5	5	5	5	5	5	5
20–34	4	1.0	0	1	1	1	1	1	1	1
35–49	132	2.3	7	1	1	2	2	4	7	15
50–64	2,226	2.0	4	1	1	2	2	3	5	11
65+	10,048	2.5	8	1	1	2	3	4	7	14
TOTAL SINGLE DX	**415**	**1.6**	**<1**	**1**	**1**	**1**	**2**	**2**	**3**	**4**
TOTAL MULTIPLE DX	**12,411**	**2.4**	**7**	**1**	**1**	**2**	**2**	**4**	**7**	**14**
TOTAL										
0–19 Years	1	5.0	0	5	5	5	5	5	5	5
20–34	5	1.6	<1	1	1	1	3	3	3	3
35–49	143	2.2	6	1	1	1	2	3	7	15
50–64	2,352	2.0	3	1	1	2	2	3	5	11
65+	10,325	2.5	8	1	1	2	3	4	7	14
GRAND TOTAL	**12,826**	**2.4**	**7**	**1**	**1**	**2**	**2**	**4**	**7**	**14**

60.21: TULIP PROCEDURE

Type of Patients	Observed Patients	Avg. Stay	Vari-ance	10th	25th	50th	75th	90th	95th	99th
1. SINGLE DX										
0–19 Years	0									
20–34	0									
35–49	2	1.0	0	1	1	1	1	1	1	1
50–64	4	1.0	0	1	1	1	1	1	1	1
65+	18	1.2	<1	1	1	1	1	2	2	3
2. MULTIPLE DX										
0–19 Years	0									
20–34	0									
35–49	4	1.0	0	1	1	1	1	1	1	1
50–64	43	2.6	11	1	1	1	3	4	7	26
65+	286	2.9	13	1	1	2	3	6	10	18
TOTAL SINGLE DX	**24**	**1.1**	**<1**	**1**	**1**	**1**	**1**	**2**	**2**	**3**
TOTAL MULTIPLE DX	**333**	**2.9**	**13**	**1**	**1**	**2**	**3**	**6**	**10**	**18**
TOTAL										
0–19 Years	0									
20–34	0									
35–49	6	1.0	0	1	1	1	1	1	1	1
50–64	47	2.5	11	1	1	1	3	4	7	26
65+	304	2.8	12	1	1	1	3	6	10	18
GRAND TOTAL	**357**	**2.7**	**12**	**1**	**1**	**1**	**3**	**6**	**9**	**18**

60.29: TU PROSTATECTOMY NEC

Type of Patients	Observed Patients	Avg. Stay	Vari-ance	10th	25th	50th	75th	90th	95th	99th
1. SINGLE DX										
0–19 Years	0									
20–34	1	3.0	0	3	3	3	3	3	3	3
35–49	9	1.2	<1	1	1	1	1	2	2	2
50–64	122	1.5	<1	1	1	1	2	2	3	3
65+	259	1.6	<1	1	1	1	2	2	3	4
2. MULTIPLE DX										
0–19 Years	1	5.0	0	5	5	5	5	5	5	5
20–34	4	1.0	0	1	1	1	1	1	1	1
35–49	128	2.4	7	1	1	2	2	4	7	15
50–64	2,183	2.0	3	1	1	2	2	3	5	11
65+	9,762	2.5	8	1	1	2	3	4	7	14
TOTAL SINGLE DX	**391**	**1.6**	**<1**	**1**	**1**	**1**	**2**	**2**	**3**	**4**
TOTAL MULTIPLE DX	**12,078**	**2.4**	**7**	**1**	**1**	**2**	**2**	**4**	**7**	**14**
TOTAL										
0–19 Years	1	5.0	0	5	5	5	5	5	5	5
20–34	5	1.6	<1	1	1	1	3	3	3	3
35–49	137	2.3	7	1	1	2	2	4	7	15
50–64	2,305	2.0	3	1	1	2	2	3	4	11
65+	10,021	2.5	8	1	1	2	3	4	7	14
GRAND TOTAL	**12,469**	**2.4**	**7**	**1**	**1**	**2**	**2**	**4**	**7**	**14**

60.3: SUPRAPUBIC PROSTATECTOMY

Type of Patients	Observed Patients	Avg. Stay	Vari-ance	10th	25th	50th	75th	90th	95th	99th
1. SINGLE DX										
0–19 Years	0									
20–34	0									
35–49	0									
50–64	4	3.6	5	2	2	2	5	7	7	7
65+	1	4.0	0	4	4	4	4	4	4	4
2. MULTIPLE DX										
0–19 Years	0									
20–34	0									
35–49	0									
50–64	75	4.8	6	2	3	4	6	8	9	14
65+	340	5.5	10	3	3	5	7	9	11	18
TOTAL SINGLE DX	**5**	**3.7**	**4**	**2**	**2**	**2**	**5**	**7**	**7**	**7**
TOTAL MULTIPLE DX	**415**	**5.4**	**10**	**3**	**3**	**5**	**7**	**9**	**11**	**17**
TOTAL										
0–19 Years	0									
20–34	0									
35–49	0									
50–64	79	4.7	6	2	3	4	6	8	9	14
65+	341	5.5	10	3	3	5	7	9	11	18
GRAND TOTAL	**420**	**5.3**	**10**	**3**	**3**	**4**	**7**	**9**	**11**	**17**

60.4: RETROPUBIC PROSTATECTOMY

Type of Patients	Observed Patients	Avg. Stay	Vari-ance	10th	25th	50th	75th	90th	95th	99th
1. SINGLE DX										
0–19 Years	0									
20–34	0									
35–49	0									
50–64	27	2.6	1	2	2	2	3	4	5	7
65+	12	3.1	1	2	2	3	4	5	5	5
2. MULTIPLE DX										
0–19 Years	1	4.0	0	4	4	4	4	4	4	4
20–34	0									
35–49	3	3.0	<1	2	2	3	4	4	4	4
50–64	112	3.5	2	2	2	3	4	6	7	8
65+	338	4.3	7	2	3	4	5	6	9	14
TOTAL SINGLE DX	**39**	**2.7**	**1**	**2**	**2**	**2**	**3**	**5**	**5**	**7**
TOTAL MULTIPLE DX	**454**	**4.0**	**6**	**2**	**3**	**3**	**5**	**6**	**8**	**13**
TOTAL										
0–19 Years	1	4.0	0	4	4	4	4	4	4	4
20–34	0									
35–49	3	3.0	<1	2	2	3	4	4	4	4
50–64	139	3.3	2	2	2	3	4	6	7	7
65+	350	4.2	7	2	3	4	5	6	9	13
GRAND TOTAL	**493**	**3.9**	**6**	**2**	**3**	**3**	**4**	**6**	**8**	**13**

60.5: RADICAL PROSTATECTOMY

Type of Patients	Observed Patients	Avg. Stay	Vari-ance	Percentiles						
				10th	25th	50th	75th	90th	95th	99th
1. SINGLE DX										
0–19 Years	1	2.0	0	2	2	2	2	2	2	2
20–34	0									
35–49	120	2.6	<1	2	2	3	3	4	4	5
50–64	1,083	2.6	<1	2	2	2	3	4	4	5
65+	411	2.7	<1	2	2	3	3	4	4	5
2. MULTIPLE DX										
0–19 Years	0									
20–34	0									
35–49	262	2.9	2	2	2	3	3	4	5	9
50–64	3,805	3.0	2	2	2	3	3	4	5	8
65+	2,626	3.2	3	2	2	3	4	5	6	9
TOTAL SINGLE DX	**1,615**	**2.6**	**<1**	**2**	**2**	**2**	**3**	**4**	**4**	**5**
TOTAL MULTIPLE DX	**6,693**	**3.1**	**2**	**2**	**2**	**3**	**4**	**5**	**6**	**9**
TOTAL										
0–19 Years	1	2.0	0	2	2	2	2	2	2	2
20–34	0									
35–49	382	2.9	2	2	2	3	3	4	5	7
50–64	4,888	2.9	2	2	2	3	3	4	5	8
65+	3,037	3.2	3	2	2	3	4	5	6	9
GRAND TOTAL	**8,308**	**3.0**	**2**	**2**	**2**	**3**	**3**	**4**	**5**	**8**

60.6: OTHER PROSTATECTOMY

Type of Patients	Observed Patients	Avg. Stay	Vari-ance	Percentiles						
				10th	25th	50th	75th	90th	95th	99th
1. SINGLE DX										
0–19 Years	0									
20–34	0									
35–49	0									
50–64	7	1.4	<1	1	1	1	1	3	3	3
65+	25	1.3	<1	1	1	1	1	2	3	3
2. MULTIPLE DX										
0–19 Years	0									
20–34	0									
35–49	1	4.0	0	4	4	4	4	4	4	4
50–64	37	1.6	4	1	1	1	1	2	3	14
65+	170	2.0	9	1	1	1	2	4	5	20
TOTAL SINGLE DX	**32**	**1.3**	**<1**	**1**	**1**	**1**	**1**	**3**	**3**	**3**
TOTAL MULTIPLE DX	**208**	**2.0**	**8**	**1**	**1**	**1**	**2**	**4**	**5**	**20**
TOTAL										
0–19 Years	0									
20–34	0									
35–49	1	4.0	0	4	4	4	4	4	4	4
50–64	44	1.6	4	1	1	1	1	2	3	14
65+	195	2.0	8	1	1	1	2	4	5	20
GRAND TOTAL	**240**	**1.9**	**7**	**1**	**1**	**1**	**2**	**3**	**5**	**20**

60.62: PERINEAL PROSTATECTOMY

Type of Patients	Observed Patients	Avg. Stay	Vari-ance	Percentiles						
				10th	25th	50th	75th	90th	95th	99th
1. SINGLE DX										
0–19 Years	0									
20–34	0									
35–49	0									
50–64	7	1.4	<1	1	1	1	1	3	3	3
65+	22	1.0	<1	1	1	1	1	1	1	2
2. MULTIPLE DX										
0–19 Years	0									
20–34	0									
35–49	0									
50–64	27	1.3	<1	1	1	1	1	2	2	3
65+	122	1.5	5	1	1	1	1	2	3	20
TOTAL SINGLE DX	**29**	**1.1**	**<1**	**1**	**1**	**1**	**1**	**1**	**3**	**3**
TOTAL MULTIPLE DX	**149**	**1.5**	**4**	**1**	**1**	**1**	**1**	**2**	**3**	**10**
TOTAL										
0–19 Years	0									
20–34	0									
35–49	0									
50–64	34	1.3	<1	1	1	1	1	2	2	3
65+	144	1.4	4	1	1	1	1	2	3	10
GRAND TOTAL	**178**	**1.4**	**3**	**1**	**1**	**1**	**1**	**2**	**3**	**10**

60.7: SEMINAL VESICLE OPS

Type of Patients	Observed Patients	Avg. Stay	Vari-ance	Percentiles						
				10th	25th	50th	75th	90th	95th	99th
1. SINGLE DX										
0–19 Years	0									
20–34	0									
35–49	0									
50–64	0									
65+	0									
2. MULTIPLE DX										
0–19 Years	0									
20–34	0									
35–49	0									
50–64	1	4.0	0	4	4	4	4	4	4	4
65+	1	7.0	0	7	7	7	7	7	7	7
TOTAL SINGLE DX	**0**									
TOTAL MULTIPLE DX	**2**	**5.6**	**4**	**4**	**4**	**7**	**7**	**7**	**7**	**7**
TOTAL										
0–19 Years	0									
20–34	0									
35–49	0									
50–64	1	4.0	0	4	4	4	4	4	4	4
65+	1	7.0	0	7	7	7	7	7	7	7
GRAND TOTAL	**2**	**5.6**	**4**	**4**	**4**	**7**	**7**	**7**	**7**	**7**

60.8: PERIPROSTATIC INC OR EXC

Type of Patients	Observed Patients	Avg. Stay	Vari-ance	10th	25th	50th	75th	90th	95th	99th
				Percentiles						
1. SINGLE DX										
0–19 Years	0									
20–34	0									
35–49	0									
50–64	0									
65+	0									
2. MULTIPLE DX										
0–19 Years	0									
20–34	0									
35–49	0									
50–64	0									
65+	0									
TOTAL SINGLE DX	**0**									
TOTAL MULTIPLE DX	**0**									
TOTAL										
0–19 Years	0									
20–34	0									
35–49	0									
50–64	0									
65+	0									
GRAND TOTAL	**0**									

60.9: OTHER PROSTATIC OPS

Type of Patients	Observed Patients	Avg. Stay	Vari-ance	10th	25th	50th	75th	90th	95th	99th
				Percentiles						
1. SINGLE DX										
0–19 Years	0									
20–34	1	1.0	0	1	1	1	1	1	1	1
35–49	0									
50–64	1	2.0	0	2	2	2	2	2	2	2
65+	3	1.5	<1	1	1	1	1	3	3	3
2. MULTIPLE DX										
0–19 Years	1	9.0	0	9	9	9	9	9	9	9
20–34	0									
35–49	3	5.8	69	1	1	1	16	16	16	16
50–64	31	3.9	14	1	1	3	5	8	8	19
65+	157	3.8	10	1	2	3	5	8	10	19
TOTAL SINGLE DX	**5**	**1.5**	**<1**	**1**	**1**	**1**	**2**	**3**	**3**	**3**
TOTAL MULTIPLE DX	**192**	**3.8**	**11**	**1**	**2**	**3**	**5**	**8**	**10**	**19**
TOTAL										
0–19 Years	1	9.0	0	9	9	9	9	9	9	9
20–34	1	1.0	0	1	1	1	1	1	1	1
35–49	3	5.8	69	1	1	1	16	16	16	16
50–64	32	3.9	14	1	1	3	5	8	8	19
65+	160	3.7	10	1	2	3	5	8	10	19
GRAND TOTAL	**197**	**3.8**	**11**	**1**	**1**	**3**	**5**	**8**	**10**	**19**

60.94: CNTRL POSTOP PROS HEMOR

Type of Patients	Observed Patients	Avg. Stay	Vari-ance	10th	25th	50th	75th	90th	95th	99th
				Percentiles						
1. SINGLE DX										
0–19 Years	0									
20–34	0									
35–49	0									
50–64	1	2.0	0	2	2	2	2	2	2	2
65+	1	3.0	0	3	3	3	3	3	3	3
2. MULTIPLE DX										
0–19 Years	0									
20–34	0									
35–49	2	1.0	0	1	1	1	1	1	1	1
50–64	22	4.2	11	1	2	3	5	8	8	19
65+	123	3.9	11	1	2	3	5	8	10	19
TOTAL SINGLE DX	**2**	**2.6**	**<1**	**2**	**2**	**3**	**3**	**3**	**3**	**3**
TOTAL MULTIPLE DX	**147**	**3.9**	**11**	**1**	**2**	**3**	**5**	**8**	**10**	**19**
TOTAL										
0–19 Years	0									
20–34	0									
35–49	2	1.0	0	1	1	1	1	1	1	1
50–64	23	4.2	11	1	2	3	5	8	8	19
65+	124	3.9	11	1	2	3	5	8	10	19
GRAND TOTAL	**149**	**3.9**	**11**	**1**	**2**	**3**	**5**	**8**	**10**	**19**

61.0: SCROTUM & TUNICA VAG I&D

Type of Patients	Observed Patients	Avg. Stay	Vari-ance	10th	25th	50th	75th	90th	95th	99th
				Percentiles						
1. SINGLE DX										
0–19 Years	10	2.4	3	1	1	2	4	5	5	5
20–34	9	2.1	1	1	1	2	3	4	4	4
35–49	14	3.6	2	2	2	4	4	6	7	7
50–64	4	2.6	3	1	1	2	4	5	5	5
65+	1	1.0	0	1	1	1	1	1	1	1
2. MULTIPLE DX										
0–19 Years	14	4.6	9	1	2	5	6	10	10	10
20–34	58	3.8	8	1	2	2	5	8	10	11
35–49	152	4.9	15	1	2	3	6	11	14	16
50–64	108	5.0	17	1	3	4	7	10	11	26
65+	54	4.5	7	2	3	4	6	8	10	11
TOTAL SINGLE DX	**38**	**2.7**	**3**	**1**	**1**	**2**	**4**	**5**	**5**	**7**
TOTAL MULTIPLE DX	**386**	**4.6**	**13**	**1**	**2**	**4**	**6**	**9**	**11**	**16**
TOTAL										
0–19 Years	24	3.5	7	1	1	3	5	8	10	10
20–34	67	3.6	7	1	2	2	5	8	10	11
35–49	166	4.7	14	1	2	3	6	10	14	16
50–64	112	4.9	17	1	2	4	6	10	11	26
65+	55	4.4	7	1	3	4	6	8	10	11
GRAND TOTAL	**424**	**4.5**	**12**	**1**	**2**	**3**	**6**	**9**	**11**	**15**

61.1: SCROTUM/TUNICA DXTIC PX

Type of Patients	Observed Patients	Avg. Stay	Vari-ance	Percentiles						
				10th	25th	50th	75th	90th	95th	99th
1. SINGLE DX										
0–19 Years	0									
20–34	0									
35–49	0									
50–64	0									
65+	0									
2. MULTIPLE DX										
0–19 Years	0									
20–34	1	6.0	0	6	6	6	6	6	6	6
35–49	3	4.1	12	2	2	2	8	8	8	8
50–64	0									
65+	1	11.0	0	11	11	11	11	11	11	11
TOTAL SINGLE DX	**0**									
TOTAL MULTIPLE DX	**5**	**5.9**	**15**	**2**	**2**	**6**	**8**	**11**	**11**	**11**
TOTAL										
0–19 Years	0									
20–34	1	6.0	0	6	6	6	6	6	6	6
35–49	3	4.1	12	2	2	2	8	8	8	8
50–64	0									
65+	1	11.0	0	11	11	11	11	11	11	11
GRAND TOTAL	**5**	**5.9**	**15**	**2**	**2**	**6**	**8**	**11**	**11**	**11**

61.2: EXCISION OF HYDROCELE

Type of Patients	Observed Patients	Avg. Stay	Vari-ance	Percentiles						
				10th	25th	50th	75th	90th	95th	99th
1. SINGLE DX										
0–19 Years	3	1.0	0	1	1	1	1	1	1	1
20–34	1	1.0	0	1	1	1	1	1	1	1
35–49	3	1.0	0	1	1	1	1	1	1	1
50–64	2	1.0	0	1	1	1	1	1	1	1
65+	0									
2. MULTIPLE DX										
0–19 Years	7	1.4	<1	1	1	1	1	2	4	4
20–34	5	4.0	5	1	2	4	6	6	6	6
35–49	6	1.9	<1	1	1	2	2	3	3	3
50–64	13	5.7	28	1	2	6	8	10	20	20
65+	34	2.8	14	1	1	2	2	7	12	18
TOTAL SINGLE DX	**9**	**1.0**	**0**	**1**	**1**	**1**	**1**	**1**	**1**	**1**
TOTAL MULTIPLE DX	**65**	**3.1**	**14**	**1**	**1**	**2**	**3**	**7**	**12**	**20**
TOTAL										
0–19 Years	10	1.2	<1	1	1	1	1	2	4	4
20–34	6	3.7	5	1	1	4	6	6	6	6
35–49	9	1.6	<1	1	1	2	2	3	3	3
50–64	15	5.1	27	1	1	2	8	10	20	20
65+	34	2.8	14	1	1	2	2	7	12	18
GRAND TOTAL	**74**	**2.9**	**12**	**1**	**1**	**1**	**2**	**7**	**12**	**18**

61.3: SCROTAL LES EXC/DESTR

Type of Patients	Observed Patients	Avg. Stay	Vari-ance	Percentiles						
				10th	25th	50th	75th	90th	95th	99th
1. SINGLE DX										
0–19 Years	1	1.0	0	1	1	1	1	1	1	1
20–34	1	6.0	0	6	6	6	6	6	6	6
35–49	4	2.3	5	1	1	1	2	6	6	6
50–64	2	5.4	8	2	2	7	7	7	7	7
65+	0									
2. MULTIPLE DX										
0–19 Years	3	3.3	14	1	1	1	8	8	8	8
20–34	2	7.9	30	4	4	4	12	12	12	12
35–49	35	7.6	40	2	3	6	10	18	19	31
50–64	25	8.9	34	4	4	6	12	18	20	27
65+	12	10.1	66	1	4	8	13	30	30	30
TOTAL SINGLE DX	**8**	**2.9**	**7**	**1**	**1**	**1**	**6**	**7**	**7**	**7**
TOTAL MULTIPLE DX	**77**	**8.3**	**41**	**2**	**4**	**6**	**12**	**18**	**19**	**31**
TOTAL										
0–19 Years	4	2.0	7	1	1	1	1	8	8	8
20–34	3	7.3	16	4	4	6	12	12	12	12
35–49	39	7.2	39	2	2	6	9	17	19	31
50–64	27	8.6	33	4	4	6	12	18	20	27
65+	12	10.1	66	1	4	8	13	30	30	30
GRAND TOTAL	**85**	**7.7**	**40**	**1**	**3**	**6**	**11**	**17**	**19**	**30**

61.4: SCROTUM & TUNICA VAG REP

Type of Patients	Observed Patients	Avg. Stay	Vari-ance	Percentiles						
				10th	25th	50th	75th	90th	95th	99th
1. SINGLE DX										
0–19 Years	11	1.2	<1	1	1	1	1	2	2	2
20–34	0									
35–49	0									
50–64	0									
65+	0									
2. MULTIPLE DX										
0–19 Years	11	2.5	9	1	1	1	4	4	13	13
20–34	6	5.7	28	2	2	4	4	15	15	15
35–49	10	7.1	68	2	2	2	5	22	23	23
50–64	17	11.2	87	2	5	7	16	21	31	41
65+	6	7.9	30	4	5	6	7	16	21	21
TOTAL SINGLE DX	**11**	**1.2**	**<1**	**1**	**1**	**1**	**1**	**2**	**2**	**2**
TOTAL MULTIPLE DX	**50**	**7.6**	**62**	**1**	**2**	**5**	**13**	**16**	**22**	**41**
TOTAL										
0–19 Years	22	1.9	5	1	1	1	2	4	4	13
20–34	6	5.7	28	2	2	4	4	15	15	15
35–49	10	7.1	68	2	2	2	5	22	23	23
50–64	17	11.2	87	2	5	7	16	21	31	41
65+	6	7.9	30	4	5	6	7	16	21	21
GRAND TOTAL	**61**	**6.5**	**57**	**1**	**1**	**4**	**7**	**16**	**21**	**41**

61.9: OTH SCROT/TUNICA VAG OPS

Type of Patients	Observed Patients	Avg. Stay	Vari-ance	Percentiles 10th	25th	50th	75th	90th	95th	99th
1. SINGLE DX										
0–19 Years	1	1.0	0	1	1	1	1	1	1	1
20–34	0									
35–49	2	3.5	<1	3	3	3	4	4	4	4
50–64	0									
65+	0									
2. MULTIPLE DX										
0–19 Years	0									
20–34	1	1.0	0	1	1	1	1	1	1	1
35–49	3	2.6	8	1	1	1	6	6	6	6
50–64	2	5.4	24	2	2	2	9	9	9	9
65+	4	9.7	87	1	7	7	8	27	27	27
TOTAL SINGLE DX	**3**	**2.5**	**2**	**1**	**1**	**3**	**4**	**4**	**4**	**4**
TOTAL MULTIPLE DX	**10**	**6.0**	**53**	**1**	**1**	**6**	**7**	**9**	**27**	**27**
TOTAL										
0–19 Years	1	1.0	0	1	1	1	1	1	1	1
20–34	1	1.0	0	1	1	1	1	1	1	1
35–49	5	3.0	4	1	1	3	4	6	6	6
50–64	2	5.4	24	2	2	2	9	9	9	9
65+	4	9.7	87	1	7	7	8	27	27	27
GRAND TOTAL	**13**	**5.3**	**43**	**1**	**1**	**3**	**7**	**9**	**27**	**27**

62.0: INCISION OF TESTIS

Type of Patients	Observed Patients	Avg. Stay	Vari-ance	Percentiles 10th	25th	50th	75th	90th	95th	99th
1. SINGLE DX										
0–19 Years	6	1.7	<1	1	1	2	2	2	4	4
20–34	3	1.0	0	1	1	1	1	1	1	1
35–49	0									
50–64	0									
65+	0									
2. MULTIPLE DX										
0–19 Years	1	1.0	0	1	1	1	1	1	1	1
20–34	1	2.0	0	2	2	2	2	2	2	2
35–49	1	1.0	0	1	1	1	1	1	1	1
50–64	3	2.9	5	1	2	2	6	6	6	6
65+	0									
TOTAL SINGLE DX	**9**	**1.6**	**<1**	**1**	**1**	**1**	**2**	**2**	**4**	**4**
TOTAL MULTIPLE DX	**6**	**2.4**	**4**	**1**	**1**	**2**	**2**	**6**	**6**	**6**
TOTAL										
0–19 Years	7	1.7	<1	1	1	2	2	2	4	4
20–34	4	1.2	<1	1	1	1	1	2	2	2
35–49	1	1.0	0	1	1	1	1	1	1	1
50–64	3	2.9	5	1	2	2	6	6	6	6
65+	0									
GRAND TOTAL	**15**	**1.8**	**2**	**1**	**1**	**2**	**2**	**2**	**6**	**6**

62.1: TESTES DXTIC PX

Type of Patients	Observed Patients	Avg. Stay	Vari-ance	Percentiles 10th	25th	50th	75th	90th	95th	99th
1. SINGLE DX										
0–19 Years	1	2.0	0	2	2	2	2	2	2	2
20–34	2	2.5	4	1	1	3	4	4	4	4
35–49	1	1.0	0	1	1	1	1	1	1	1
50–64	0									
65+	0									
2. MULTIPLE DX										
0–19 Years	2	2.7	<1	1	3	3	3	3	3	3
20–34	1	4.0	0	4	4	4	4	4	4	4
35–49	0									
50–64	0									
65+	1	6.0	0	6	6	6	6	6	6	6
TOTAL SINGLE DX	**4**	**2.0**	**2**	**1**	**1**	**1**	**2**	**4**	**4**	**4**
TOTAL MULTIPLE DX	**4**	**3.2**	**1**	**1**	**3**	**3**	**3**	**4**	**6**	**6**
TOTAL										
0–19 Years	3	2.7	<1	1	3	3	3	3	3	3
20–34	3	3.0	3	1	1	4	4	4	4	4
35–49	1	1.0	0	1	1	1	1	1	1	1
50–64	0									
65+	1	6.0	0	6	6	6	6	6	6	6
GRAND TOTAL	**8**	**2.9**	**2**	**1**	**2**	**3**	**3**	**4**	**6**	**6**

62.2: TESTICULAR LES EXC/DESTR

Type of Patients	Observed Patients	Avg. Stay	Vari-ance	Percentiles 10th	25th	50th	75th	90th	95th	99th
1. SINGLE DX										
0–19 Years	5	1.0	0	1	1	1	1	1	1	1
20–34	1	2.0	0	2	2	2	2	2	2	2
35–49	0									
50–64	0									
65+	0									
2. MULTIPLE DX										
0–19 Years	7	1.0	0	1	1	1	1	1	1	1
20–34	1	2.0	0	2	2	2	2	2	2	2
35–49	2	9.5	68	3	3	10	16	16	16	16
50–64	1	11.0	0	11	11	11	11	11	11	11
65+	1	1.0	0	1	1	1	1	1	1	1
TOTAL SINGLE DX	**6**	**1.1**	**<1**	**1**	**1**	**1**	**1**	**2**	**2**	**2**
TOTAL MULTIPLE DX	**12**	**3.0**	**21**	**1**	**1**	**1**	**2**	**11**	**16**	**16**
TOTAL										
0–19 Years	12	1.0	0	1	1	1	1	1	1	1
20–34	2	2.0	0	2	2	2	2	2	2	2
35–49	2	9.5	68	3	3	10	16	16	16	16
50–64	1	11.0	0	11	11	11	11	11	11	11
65+	1	1.0	0	1	1	1	1	1	1	1
GRAND TOTAL	**18**	**2.3**	**14**	**1**	**1**	**1**	**1**	**3**	**11**	**16**

62.3: UNILATERAL ORCHIECTOMY

Type of Patients	Observed Patients	Avg. Stay	Vari-ance	Percentiles						
				10th	25th	50th	75th	90th	95th	99th
1. SINGLE DX										
0–19 Years	39	1.1	<1	1	1	1	1	1	2	2
20–34	54	1.4	1	1	1	1	1	2	3	7
35–49	27	1.7	1	1	1	1	2	2	4	6
50–64	7	2.1	3	1	1	1	3	6	6	6
65+	3	1.5	<1	1	1	1	1	3	3	3
2. MULTIPLE DX										
0–19 Years	69	2.8	11	1	1	1	3	9	12	14
20–34	75	5.0	27	1	1	3	7	10	14	28
35–49	96	4.7	20	1	2	3	6	15	19	>99
50–64	53	5.1	22	1	2	3	8	12	15	20
65+	71	6.1	39	1	2	5	8	12	20	41
TOTAL SINGLE DX	**130**	**1.4**	**<1**	**1**	**1**	**1**	**1**	**2**	**3**	**6**
TOTAL MULTIPLE DX	**364**	**4.7**	**25**	**1**	**1**	**3**	**7**	**12**	**15**	**41**
TOTAL										
0–19 Years	108	2.1	7	1	1	1	2	3	11	12
20–34	129	3.4	19	1	1	2	4	7	12	28
35–49	123	4.0	18	1	1	2	5	11	15	>99
50–64	60	4.9	21	1	1	3	7	12	12	20
65+	74	5.9	39	1	2	4	7	12	20	41
GRAND TOTAL	**494**	**3.8**	**20**	**1**	**1**	**2**	**5**	**10**	**14**	**28**

62.4: BILATERAL ORCHIECTOMY

Type of Patients	Observed Patients	Avg. Stay	Vari-ance	Percentiles						
				10th	25th	50th	75th	90th	95th	99th
1. SINGLE DX										
0–19 Years	4	1.9	1	1	1	1	3	3	3	3
20–34	4	1.7	1	1	1	1	3	3	3	3
35–49	1	2.0	0	2	2	2	2	2	2	2
50–64	0									
65+	1	1.0	0	1	1	1	1	1	1	1
2. MULTIPLE DX										
0–19 Years	2	1.9	1	1	1	1	3	3	3	3
20–34	5	2.5	10	1	1	1	2	9	9	9
35–49	2	5.6	4	4	4	7	7	7	7	7
50–64	21	9.4	35	5	6	8	10	22	22	25
65+	81	4.5	26	1	1	2	6	11	13	23
TOTAL SINGLE DX	**10**	**1.8**	**<1**	**1**	**1**	**1**	**3**	**3**	**3**	**3**
TOTAL MULTIPLE DX	**111**	**5.3**	**30**	**1**	**1**	**3**	**8**	**12**	**13**	**25**
TOTAL										
0–19 Years	6	1.9	1	1	1	1	3	3	3	3
20–34	9	2.1	5	1	1	1	3	3	9	9
35–49	3	4.5	6	2	2	4	7	7	7	7
50–64	21	9.4	35	5	6	8	10	22	22	25
65+	82	4.5	26	1	1	2	6	11	13	23
GRAND TOTAL	**121**	**5.0**	**29**	**1**	**1**	**3**	**8**	**12**	**13**	**25**

62.41: RMVL BOTH TESTES

Type of Patients	Observed Patients	Avg. Stay	Vari-ance	Percentiles						
				10th	25th	50th	75th	90th	95th	99th
1. SINGLE DX										
0–19 Years	1	1.0	0	1	1	1	1	1	1	1
20–34	4	1.7	1	1	1	1	3	3	3	3
35–49	1	2.0	0	2	2	2	2	2	2	2
50–64	0									
65+	1	1.0	0	1	1	1	1	1	1	1
2. MULTIPLE DX										
0–19 Years	1	1.0	0	1	1	1	1	1	1	1
20–34	0									
35–49	1	7.0	0	7	7	7	7	7	7	7
50–64	21	9.4	35	5	6	8	10	22	22	25
65+	80	4.6	26	1	1	2	6	11	13	23
TOTAL SINGLE DX	**7**	**1.5**	**<1**	**1**	**1**	**1**	**2**	**3**	**3**	**3**
TOTAL MULTIPLE DX	**103**	**5.5**	**31**	**1**	**1**	**3**	**8**	**13**	**17**	**25**
TOTAL										
0–19 Years	2	1.0	0	1	1	1	1	1	1	1
20–34	4	1.7	1	1	1	1	3	3	3	3
35–49	2	4.7	11	2	2	7	7	7	7	7
50–64	21	9.4	35	5	6	8	10	22	22	25
65+	81	4.5	26	1	1	2	6	11	13	23
GRAND TOTAL	**110**	**5.3**	**30**	**1**	**1**	**3**	**8**	**13**	**13**	**25**

62.5: ORCHIOPEXY

Type of Patients	Observed Patients	Avg. Stay	Vari-ance	Percentiles						
				10th	25th	50th	75th	90th	95th	99th
1. SINGLE DX										
0–19 Years	95	1.0	<1	1	1	1	1	1	1	3
20–34	25	2.2	12	1	1	1	1	7	14	14
35–49	5	1.0	0	1	1	1	1	1	1	1
50–64	0									
65+	0									
2. MULTIPLE DX										
0–19 Years	85	1.4	8	1	1	1	1	2	3	4
20–34	20	1.1	<1	1	1	1	1	1	2	2
35–49	4	4.5	39	1	1	1	2	14	14	14
50–64	5	1.4	<1	1	1	1	1	3	3	3
65+	0									
TOTAL SINGLE DX	**125**	**1.2**	**2**	**1**	**1**	**1**	**1**	**1**	**1**	**7**
TOTAL MULTIPLE DX	**114**	**1.4**	**7**	**1**	**1**	**1**	**1**	**2**	**3**	**4**
TOTAL										
0–19 Years	180	1.2	4	1	1	1	1	1	2	4
20–34	45	1.6	6	1	1	1	1	2	7	14
35–49	9	2.4	16	1	1	1	1	2	14	14
50–64	5	1.4	<1	1	1	1	1	3	3	3
65+	0									
GRAND TOTAL	**239**	**1.3**	**4**	**1**	**1**	**1**	**1**	**1**	**2**	**7**

62.6: TESTES REPAIR

Type of Patients	Observed Patients	Avg. Stay	Vari-ance	Percentiles 10th	25th	50th	75th	90th	95th	99th
1. SINGLE DX										
0–19 Years	3	1.0	0	1	1	1	1	1	1	1
20–34	7	1.4	<1	1	1	1	2	2	2	2
35–49	1	1.0	0	1	1	1	1	1	1	1
50–64	0									
65+	0									
2. MULTIPLE DX										
0–19 Years	2	3.4	3	2	2	2	5	5	5	5
20–34	5	2.0	1	1	1	2	2	4	4	4
35–49	2	2.0	1	1	1	2	3	3	3	3
50–64	0									
65+	0									
TOTAL SINGLE DX	**11**	**1.2**	**<1**	**1**	**1**	**1**	**1**	**2**	**2**	**2**
TOTAL MULTIPLE DX	**9**	**2.4**	**2**	**1**	**1**	**2**	**3**	**5**	**5**	**5**
TOTAL										
0–19 Years	5	1.8	2	1	1	1	2	5	5	5
20–34	12	1.6	<1	1	1	1	2	2	4	4
35–49	3	1.8	1	1	1	1	3	3	3	3
50–64	0									
65+	0									
GRAND TOTAL	**20**	**1.7**	**1**	**1**	**1**	**1**	**2**	**3**	**5**	**5**

62.7: INSERT TESTICULAR PROSTH

Type of Patients	Observed Patients	Avg. Stay	Vari-ance	Percentiles 10th	25th	50th	75th	90th	95th	99th
1. SINGLE DX										
0–19 Years	0									
20–34	0									
35–49	0									
50–64	0									
65+	0									
2. MULTIPLE DX										
0–19 Years	1	2.0	0	2	2	2	2	2	2	2
20–34	0									
35–49	0									
50–64	0									
65+	0									
TOTAL SINGLE DX	**0**									
TOTAL MULTIPLE DX	**1**	**2.0**	**0**	**2**	**2**	**2**	**2**	**2**	**2**	**2**
TOTAL										
0–19 Years	1	2.0	0	2	2	2	2	2	2	2
20–34	0									
35–49	0									
50–64	0									
65+	0									
GRAND TOTAL	**1**	**2.0**	**0**	**2**	**2**	**2**	**2**	**2**	**2**	**2**

62.9: OTHER TESTICULAR OPS

Type of Patients	Observed Patients	Avg. Stay	Vari-ance	Percentiles 10th	25th	50th	75th	90th	95th	99th
1. SINGLE DX										
0–19 Years	0									
20–34	0									
35–49	0									
50–64	0									
65+	0									
2. MULTIPLE DX										
0–19 Years	2	1.0	0	1	1	1	1	1	1	1
20–34	0									
35–49	2	17.1	236	6	6	28	28	28	28	28
50–64	1	14.0	0	14	14	14	14	14	14	14
65+	2	4.7	7	3	3	3	7	7	7	7
TOTAL SINGLE DX	**0**									
TOTAL MULTIPLE DX	**7**	**7.2**	**80**	**1**	**1**	**3**	**7**	**28**	**28**	**28**
TOTAL										
0–19 Years	2	1.0	0	1	1	1	1	1	1	1
20–34	0									
35–49	2	17.1	236	6	6	28	28	28	28	28
50–64	1	14.0	0	14	14	14	14	14	14	14
65+	2	4.7	7	3	3	3	7	7	7	7
GRAND TOTAL	**7**	**7.2**	**80**	**1**	**1**	**3**	**7**	**28**	**28**	**28**

63.0: SPERMATIC CORD DXTIC PX

Type of Patients	Observed Patients	Avg. Stay	Vari-ance	Percentiles 10th	25th	50th	75th	90th	95th	99th
1. SINGLE DX										
0–19 Years	0									
20–34	0									
35–49	0									
50–64	0									
65+	0									
2. MULTIPLE DX										
0–19 Years	0									
20–34	0									
35–49	0									
50–64	0									
65+	0									
TOTAL SINGLE DX	**0**									
TOTAL MULTIPLE DX	**0**									
TOTAL										
0–19 Years	0									
20–34	0									
35–49	0									
50–64	0									
65+	0									
GRAND TOTAL	**0**									

63.1: EXC SPERMATIC VARICOCELE

Type of Patients	Observed Patients	Avg. Stay	Vari-ance	Percentiles						
				10th	25th	50th	75th	90th	95th	99th
1. SINGLE DX										
0–19 Years	6	1.1	<1	1	1	1	1	2	2	2
20–34	2	1.0	0	1	1	1	1	1	1	1
35–49	1	1.0	0	1	1	1	1	1	1	1
50–64	3	1.0	0	1	1	1	1	1	1	1
65+	1	1.0	0	1	1	1	1	1	1	1
2. MULTIPLE DX										
0–19 Years	5	1.3	<1	1	1	1	1	3	3	3
20–34	5	3.5	5	1	1	4	5	6	6	6
35–49	5	3.9	9	1	2	2	6	8	8	8
50–64	15	2.1	5	1	1	1	2	5	8	8
65+	20	2.0	2	1	1	1	3	4	4	7
TOTAL SINGLE DX	**13**	**1.1**	**<1**	**1**	**1**	**1**	**1**	**1**	**2**	**2**
TOTAL MULTIPLE DX	**50**	**2.2**	**3**	**1**	**1**	**1**	**3**	**5**	**7**	**8**
TOTAL										
0–19 Years	11	1.2	<1	1	1	1	1	2	3	3
20–34	7	2.8	5	1	1	1	5	6	6	6
35–49	6	3.4	9	1	1	2	6	8	8	8
50–64	18	2.0	4	1	1	1	2	5	8	8
65+	21	2.0	2	1	1	1	3	4	4	7
GRAND TOTAL	**63**	**2.0**	**3**	**1**	**1**	**1**	**3**	**4**	**6**	**8**

63.2: EXC EPIDIDYMIS CYST

Type of Patients	Observed Patients	Avg. Stay	Vari-ance	Percentiles						
				10th	25th	50th	75th	90th	95th	99th
1. SINGLE DX										
0–19 Years	0									
20–34	1	1.0	0	1	1	1	1	1	1	1
35–49	1	1.0	0	1	1	1	1	1	1	1
50–64	0									
65+	0									
2. MULTIPLE DX										
0–19 Years	0									
20–34	1	2.0	0	2	2	2	2	2	2	2
35–49	3	2.0	4	1	1	1	1	5	5	5
50–64	7	1.7	2	1	1	1	2	4	4	4
65+	11	2.1	1	1	2	2	2	3	6	6
TOTAL SINGLE DX	**2**	**1.0**	**0**	**1**	**1**	**1**	**1**	**1**	**1**	**1**
TOTAL MULTIPLE DX	**22**	**2.0**	**1**	**1**	**1**	**2**	**2**	**4**	**5**	**6**
TOTAL										
0–19 Years	0									
20–34	2	1.5	<1	1	1	2	2	2	2	2
35–49	4	1.8	3	1	1	1	1	5	5	5
50–64	7	1.7	2	1	1	1	2	4	4	4
65+	11	2.1	1	1	2	2	2	3	6	6
GRAND TOTAL	**24**	**1.9**	**1**	**1**	**1**	**2**	**2**	**4**	**5**	**6**

63.3: EXC SPERM CORD LES NEC

Type of Patients	Observed Patients	Avg. Stay	Vari-ance	Percentiles						
				10th	25th	50th	75th	90th	95th	99th
1. SINGLE DX										
0–19 Years	3	2.2	<1	1	1	2	3	3	3	3
20–34	1	1.0	0	1	1	1	1	1	1	1
35–49	0									
50–64	0									
65+	0									
2. MULTIPLE DX										
0–19 Years	2	1.0	0	1	1	1	1	1	1	1
20–34	1	2.0	0	2	2	2	2	2	2	2
35–49	2	4.6	2	4	4	4	4	7	7	7
50–64	5	2.0	1	1	1	2	2	5	5	5
65+	0									
TOTAL SINGLE DX	**4**	**1.9**	**<1**	**1**	**1**	**2**	**3**	**3**	**3**	**3**
TOTAL MULTIPLE DX	**10**	**2.4**	**3**	**1**	**1**	**2**	**4**	**4**	**5**	**7**
TOTAL										
0–19 Years	5	1.6	<1	1	1	1	2	3	3	3
20–34	2	1.3	<1	1	1	1	2	2	2	2
35–49	2	4.6	2	4	4	4	4	7	7	7
50–64	5	2.0	1	1	1	2	2	5	5	5
65+	0									
GRAND TOTAL	**14**	**2.3**	**2**	**1**	**1**	**2**	**3**	**4**	**5**	**7**

63.4: EPIDIDYMECTOMY

Type of Patients	Observed Patients	Avg. Stay	Vari-ance	Percentiles						
				10th	25th	50th	75th	90th	95th	99th
1. SINGLE DX										
0–19 Years	0									
20–34	0									
35–49	0									
50–64	0									
65+	0									
2. MULTIPLE DX										
0–19 Years	1	3.0	0	3	3	3	3	3	3	3
20–34	0									
35–49	1	1.0	0	1	1	1	1	1	1	1
50–64	3	4.8	13	1	4	4	4	14	14	14
65+	4	3.5	<1	3	3	4	4	4	4	4
TOTAL SINGLE DX	**0**									
TOTAL MULTIPLE DX	**9**	**3.9**	**6**	**3**	**3**	**4**	**4**	**4**	**14**	**14**
TOTAL										
0–19 Years	1	3.0	0	3	3	3	3	3	3	3
20–34	0									
35–49	1	1.0	0	1	1	1	1	1	1	1
50–64	3	4.8	13	1	4	4	4	14	14	14
65+	4	3.5	<1	3	3	4	4	4	4	4
GRAND TOTAL	**9**	**3.9**	**6**	**3**	**3**	**4**	**4**	**4**	**14**	**14**

63.5: SPERM CORD/EPID REPAIR

Type of Patients	Observed Patients	Avg. Stay	Vari-ance	10th	25th	50th	75th	90th	95th	99th
1. SINGLE DX										
0–19 Years	2	1.0	0	1	1	1	1	1	1	1
20–34	2	1.0	0	1	1	1	1	1	1	1
35–49	1	1.0	0	1	1	1	1	1	1	1
50–64	1	1.0	0	1	1	1	1	1	1	1
65+	0									
2. MULTIPLE DX										
0–19 Years	1	1.0	0	1	1	1	1	1	1	1
20–34	1	1.0	0	1	1	1	1	1	1	1
35–49	0									
50–64	1	13.0	0	13	13	13	13	13	13	13
65+	0									
TOTAL SINGLE DX	**6**	**1.0**	**0**	**1**	**1**	**1**	**1**	**1**	**1**	**1**
TOTAL MULTIPLE DX	**3**	**2.9**	**22**	**1**	**1**	**1**	**1**	**13**	**13**	**13**
TOTAL										
0–19 Years	3	1.0	0	1	1	1	1	1	1	1
20–34	3	1.0	0	1	1	1	1	1	1	1
35–49	1	1.0	0	1	1	1	1	1	1	1
50–64	2	7.2	70	1	1	13	13	13	13	13
65+	0									
GRAND TOTAL	**9**	**1.8**	**10**	**1**	**1**	**1**	**1**	**1**	**13**	**13**

63.6: VASOTOMY

Type of Patients	Observed Patients	Avg. Stay	Vari-ance	10th	25th	50th	75th	90th	95th	99th
1. SINGLE DX										
0–19 Years	0									
20–34	0									
35–49	0									
50–64	0									
65+	0									
2. MULTIPLE DX										
0–19 Years	0									
20–34	0									
35–49	0									
50–64	0									
65+	1	1.0	0	1	1	1	1	1	1	1
TOTAL SINGLE DX	**0**									
TOTAL MULTIPLE DX	**1**	**1.0**	**0**	**1**	**1**	**1**	**1**	**1**	**1**	**1**
TOTAL										
0–19 Years	0									
20–34	0									
35–49	0									
50–64	0									
65+	1	1.0	0	1	1	1	1	1	1	1
GRAND TOTAL	**1**	**1.0**	**0**	**1**	**1**	**1**	**1**	**1**	**1**	**1**

63.7: VASECTOMY & VAS DEF LIG

Type of Patients	Observed Patients	Avg. Stay	Vari-ance	10th	25th	50th	75th	90th	95th	99th
1. SINGLE DX										
0–19 Years	0									
20–34	0									
35–49	0									
50–64	0									
65+	0									
2. MULTIPLE DX										
0–19 Years	0									
20–34	0									
35–49	0									
50–64	1	1.0	0	1	1	1	1	1	1	1
65+	0									
TOTAL SINGLE DX	**0**									
TOTAL MULTIPLE DX	**1**	**1.0**	**0**	**1**	**1**	**1**	**1**	**1**	**1**	**1**
TOTAL										
0–19 Years	0									
20–34	0									
35–49	0									
50–64	1	1.0	0	1	1	1	1	1	1	1
65+	0									
GRAND TOTAL	**1**	**1.0**	**0**	**1**	**1**	**1**	**1**	**1**	**1**	**1**

63.8: VAS DEF & EPID REPAIR

Type of Patients	Observed Patients	Avg. Stay	Vari-ance	10th	25th	50th	75th	90th	95th	99th
1. SINGLE DX										
0–19 Years	0									
20–34	1	1.0	0	1	1	1	1	1	1	1
35–49	0									
50–64	0									
65+	0									
2. MULTIPLE DX										
0–19 Years	0									
20–34	0									
35–49	0									
50–64	0									
65+	0									
TOTAL SINGLE DX	**1**	**1.0**	**0**	**1**	**1**	**1**	**1**	**1**	**1**	**1**
TOTAL MULTIPLE DX	**0**									
TOTAL										
0–19 Years	0									
20–34	1	1.0	0	1	1	1	1	1	1	1
35–49	0									
50–64	0									
65+	0									
GRAND TOTAL	**1**	**1.0**	**0**	**1**	**1**	**1**	**1**	**1**	**1**	**1**

63.9: OTH SPERM CORD/EPID OPS

Type of Patients	Observed Patients	Avg. Stay	Variance	10th	25th	50th	75th	90th	95th	99th
1. SINGLE DX										
0–19 Years	1	1.0	0	1	1	1	1	1	1	1
20–34	0									
35–49	0									
50–64	0									
65+	0									
2. MULTIPLE DX										
0–19 Years	0									
20–34	1	4.0	0	4	4	4	4	4	4	4
35–49	0									
50–64	1	2.0	0	2	2	2	2	2	2	2
65+	0									
TOTAL SINGLE DX	**1**	**1.0**	**0**	**1**	**1**	**1**	**1**	**1**	**1**	**1**
TOTAL MULTIPLE DX	**2**	**3.4**	**1**	**2**	**2**	**4**	**4**	**4**	**4**	**4**
TOTAL										
0–19 Years	1	1.0	0	1	1	1	1	1	1	1
20–34	1	4.0	0	4	4	4	4	4	4	4
35–49	0									
50–64	1	2.0	0	2	2	2	2	2	2	2
65+	0									
GRAND TOTAL	**3**	**2.8**	**2**	**1**	**2**	**4**	**4**	**4**	**4**	**4**

64.0: CIRCUMCISION

Type of Patients	Observed Patients	Avg. Stay	Variance	10th	25th	50th	75th	90th	95th	99th
1. SINGLE DX										
0–19 Years	43,424	1.9	<1	1	1	2	2	3	4	4
20–34	2	1.0	0	1	1	1	1	1	1	1
35–49	0									
50–64	0									
65+	1	1.0	0	1	1	1	1	1	1	1
2. MULTIPLE DX										
0–19 Years	45,709	2.7	9	1	2	2	3	4	5	16
20–34	1	1.0	0	1	1	1	1	1	1	1
35–49	6	11.9	377	1	2	3	10	50	50	50
50–64	16	2.7	23	1	1	1	2	4	8	26
65+	82	4.1	16	1	1	3	6	9	11	24
TOTAL SINGLE DX	**43,427**	**1.9**	**<1**	**1**	**1**	**2**	**2**	**3**	**4**	**4**
TOTAL MULTIPLE DX	**45,814**	**2.7**	**9**	**1**	**2**	**2**	**3**	**4**	**5**	**16**
TOTAL										
0–19 Years	89,133	2.3	5	1	1	2	3	4	4	10
20–34	3	1.0	0	1	1	1	1	1	1	1
35–49	6	11.9	377	1	2	3	10	50	50	50
50–64	16	2.7	23	1	1	1	2	4	8	26
65+	83	4.1	16	1	1	3	6	9	11	24
GRAND TOTAL	**89,241**	**2.3**	**5**	**1**	**1**	**2**	**3**	**4**	**4**	**10**

64.1: PENILE DIAGNOSTIC PX

Type of Patients	Observed Patients	Avg. Stay	Variance	10th	25th	50th	75th	90th	95th	99th
1. SINGLE DX										
0–19 Years	0									
20–34	2	1.3	<1	1	1	1	2	2	2	2
35–49	0									
50–64	0									
65+	0									
2. MULTIPLE DX										
0–19 Years	0									
20–34	0									
35–49	4	3.7	<1	3	3	4	4	4	6	6
50–64	7	4.8	22	2	2	2	9	15	15	15
65+	10	3.0	13	1	1	1	2	8	12	12
TOTAL SINGLE DX	**2**	**1.3**	**<1**	**1**	**1**	**1**	**2**	**2**	**2**	**2**
TOTAL MULTIPLE DX	**21**	**3.7**	**11**	**1**	**1**	**3**	**4**	**9**	**12**	**15**
TOTAL										
0–19 Years	0									
20–34	2	1.3	<1	1	1	1	2	2	2	2
35–49	4	3.7	<1	3	3	4	4	4	6	6
50–64	7	4.8	22	2	2	2	9	15	15	15
65+	10	3.0	13	1	1	1	2	8	12	12
GRAND TOTAL	**23**	**3.5**	**11**	**1**	**1**	**2**	**4**	**8**	**12**	**15**

64.2: LOC EXC/DESTR PENILE LES

Type of Patients	Observed Patients	Avg. Stay	Variance	10th	25th	50th	75th	90th	95th	99th
1. SINGLE DX										
0–19 Years	0									
20–34	1	1.0	0	1	1	1	1	1	1	1
35–49	0									
50–64	0									
65+	1	1.0	0	1	1	1	1	1	1	1
2. MULTIPLE DX										
0–19 Years	3	1.7	<1	1	1	2	2	3	3	3
20–34	7	4.4	21	1	1	3	8	14	14	14
35–49	9	6.7	21	1	4	6	8	15	15	15
50–64	24	5.1	21	1	1	4	8	14	14	19
65+	15	3.8	13	1	1	2	5	10	10	14
TOTAL SINGLE DX	**2**	**1.0**	**0**	**1**	**1**	**1**	**1**	**1**	**1**	**1**
TOTAL MULTIPLE DX	**58**	**4.5**	**18**	**1**	**1**	**3**	**6**	**10**	**14**	**16**
TOTAL										
0–19 Years	3	1.7	<1	1	1	2	2	3	3	3
20–34	8	4.1	20	1	1	3	4	14	14	14
35–49	9	6.7	21	1	4	6	8	15	15	15
50–64	24	5.1	21	1	1	4	8	14	14	19
65+	16	3.7	13	1	1	2	5	10	10	14
GRAND TOTAL	**60**	**4.5**	**18**	**1**	**1**	**3**	**6**	**10**	**14**	**16**

64.3: AMPUTATION OF PENIS

Type of Patients	Observed Patients	Avg. Stay	Vari-ance	Percentiles						
				10th	25th	50th	75th	90th	95th	99th
1. SINGLE DX										
0–19 Years	0									
20–34	1	3.0	0	3	3	3	3	3	3	3
35–49	1	4.0	0	4	4	4	4	4	4	4
50–64	2	1.3	<1	1	1	1	2	2	2	2
65+	1	1.0	0	1	1	1	1	1	1	1
2. MULTIPLE DX										
0–19 Years	0									
20–34	1	7.0	0	7	7	7	7	7	7	7
35–49	6	4.6	8	1	2	6	7	8	8	8
50–64	15	5.3	61	1	2	2	5	13	35	35
65+	38	4.2	15	1	1	3	7	10	10	16
TOTAL SINGLE DX	**5**	**1.8**	**1**	**1**	**1**	**1**	**3**	**4**	**4**	**4**
TOTAL MULTIPLE DX	**60**	**4.5**	**26**	**1**	**1**	**3**	**6**	**10**	**13**	**35**
TOTAL										
0–19 Years	0									
20–34	2	5.1	7	3	3	7	7	7	7	7
35–49	7	4.5	7	1	2	4	7	8	8	8
50–64	17	4.8	54	1	2	2	5	13	13	35
65+	39	4.1	15	1	1	3	6	10	10	16
GRAND TOTAL	**65**	**4.3**	**25**	**1**	**1**	**2**	**6**	**10**	**13**	**35**

64.4: PENILE REP/PLASTIC OPS

Type of Patients	Observed Patients	Avg. Stay	Vari-ance	Percentiles						
				10th	25th	50th	75th	90th	95th	99th
1. SINGLE DX										
0–19 Years	4	1.0	0	1	1	1	1	1	1	1
20–34	14	1.5	1	1	1	1	2	2	5	5
35–49	14	1.2	<1	1	1	1	1	2	3	3
50–64	9	1.1	<1	1	1	1	1	1	2	2
65+	1	1.0	0	1	1	1	1	1	1	1
2. MULTIPLE DX										
0–19 Years	24	3.0	6	1	1	2	5	6	10	10
20–34	25	1.7	1	1	1	1	2	3	4	5
35–49	20	2.7	5	1	1	2	3	7	7	10
50–64	22	2.6	7	1	1	1	3	6	9	11
65+	9	2.2	2	1	1	1	3	4	6	6
TOTAL SINGLE DX	**42**	**1.2**	**<1**	**1**	**1**	**1**	**1**	**2**	**2**	**5**
TOTAL MULTIPLE DX	**100**	**2.5**	**5**	**1**	**1**	**2**	**3**	**6**	**7**	**10**
TOTAL										
0–19 Years	28	2.7	6	1	1	2	4	6	10	10
20–34	39	1.6	1	1	1	1	2	3	4	5
35–49	34	2.2	4	1	1	1	2	5	7	10
50–64	31	2.0	5	1	1	1	2	5	6	11
65+	10	2.0	2	1	1	1	3	4	6	6
GRAND TOTAL	**142**	**2.1**	**4**	**1**	**1**	**1**	**2**	**5**	**6**	**10**

64.5: SEX TRANSFORMATION NEC

Type of Patients	Observed Patients	Avg. Stay	Vari-ance	Percentiles						
				10th	25th	50th	75th	90th	95th	99th
1. SINGLE DX										
0–19 Years	0									
20–34	0									
35–49	0									
50–64	0									
65+	0									
2. MULTIPLE DX										
0–19 Years	1	1.0	0	1	1	1	1	1	1	1
20–34	0									
35–49	0									
50–64	0									
65+	0									
TOTAL SINGLE DX	**0**									
TOTAL MULTIPLE DX	**1**	**1.0**	**0**	**1**	**1**	**1**	**1**	**1**	**1**	**1**
TOTAL										
0–19 Years	1	1.0	0	1	1	1	1	1	1	1
20–34	0									
35–49	0									
50–64	0									
65+	0									
GRAND TOTAL	**1**	**1.0**	**0**	**1**	**1**	**1**	**1**	**1**	**1**	**1**

64.9: OTHER MALE GENITAL OPS

Type of Patients	Observed Patients	Avg. Stay	Vari-ance	Percentiles						
				10th	25th	50th	75th	90th	95th	99th
1. SINGLE DX										
0–19 Years	6	1.4	<1	1	1	1	2	2	2	2
20–34	13	2.2	1	1	1	2	3	3	4	4
35–49	24	2.1	1	1	1	2	3	3	5	5
50–64	28	1.4	<1	1	1	1	2	2	3	5
65+	34	1.4	1	1	1	1	1	2	4	6
2. MULTIPLE DX										
0–19 Years	43	2.5	3	1	1	2	3	5	6	9
20–34	41	4.0	32	1	1	3	4	7	10	32
35–49	131	3.1	8	1	1	2	5	7	10	12
50–64	354	1.9	6	1	1	1	2	3	6	14
65+	485	2.1	7	1	1	1	2	4	9	15
TOTAL SINGLE DX	**105**	**1.6**	**1**	**1**	**1**	**1**	**2**	**3**	**4**	**5**
TOTAL MULTIPLE DX	**1,054**	**2.2**	**8**	**1**	**1**	**1**	**2**	**5**	**8**	**14**
TOTAL										
0–19 Years	49	2.3	3	1	1	2	2	5	6	9
20–34	54	3.6	25	1	1	3	4	6	10	32
35–49	155	2.9	7	1	1	2	4	7	8	11
50–64	382	1.9	5	1	1	1	2	3	5	14
65+	519	2.1	7	1	1	1	2	4	7	15
GRAND TOTAL	**1,159**	**2.2**	**7**	**1**	**1**	**1**	**2**	**4**	**7**	**14**

64.95: INSERT/REPL NON-IPP NOS

Type of Patients	Observed Patients	Avg. Stay	Variance	Percentiles 10th	25th	50th	75th	90th	95th	99th
1. SINGLE DX										
0–19 Years	0									
20–34	0									
35–49	1	3.0	0	3	3	3	3	3	3	3
50–64	0									
65+	6	1.0	0	1	1	1	1	1	1	1
2. MULTIPLE DX										
0–19 Years	0									
20–34	1	3.0	0	3	3	3	3	3	3	3
35–49	8	1.8	2	1	1	1	2	4	4	4
50–64	42	1.3	3	1	1	1	1	1	2	14
65+	55	1.4	<1	1	1	1	1	3	3	6
TOTAL SINGLE DX	**7**	**1.1**	**<1**	**1**	**1**	**1**	**1**	**1**	**3**	**3**
TOTAL MULTIPLE DX	**106**	**1.5**	**2**	**1**	**1**	**1**	**1**	**3**	**3**	**6**
TOTAL										
0–19 Years	0									
20–34	1	3.0	0	3	3	3	3	3	3	3
35–49	9	1.9	2	1	1	1	3	4	4	4
50–64	42	1.3	3	1	1	1	1	1	2	14
65+	61	1.4	<1	1	1	1	1	2	3	6
GRAND TOTAL	**113**	**1.4**	**2**	**1**	**1**	**1**	**1**	**3**	**3**	**6**

64.96: RMVL INT PENILE PROSTH

Type of Patients	Observed Patients	Avg. Stay	Variance	Percentiles 10th	25th	50th	75th	90th	95th	99th
1. SINGLE DX										
0–19 Years	0									
20–34	0									
35–49	1	2.0	0	2	2	2	2	2	2	2
50–64	1	3.0	0	3	3	3	3	3	3	3
65+	2	2.5	7	1	1	1	6	6	6	6
2. MULTIPLE DX										
0–19 Years	0									
20–34	1	3.0	0	3	3	3	3	3	3	3
35–49	9	5.7	9	2	5	5	8	8	12	12
50–64	27	4.1	16	1	1	3	5	9	14	19
65+	67	4.4	19	1	1	3	5	10	15	19
TOTAL SINGLE DX	**4**	**2.5**	**3**	**1**	**1**	**2**	**3**	**6**	**6**	**6**
TOTAL MULTIPLE DX	**104**	**4.4**	**17**	**1**	**1**	**3**	**5**	**9**	**15**	**19**
TOTAL										
0–19 Years	0									
20–34	1	3.0	0	3	3	3	3	3	3	3
35–49	10	5.0	9	2	2	5	8	8	12	12
50–64	28	4.1	16	1	2	3	5	9	14	19
65+	69	4.3	18	1	1	3	5	9	15	19
GRAND TOTAL	**108**	**4.3**	**17**	**1**	**1**	**3**	**5**	**9**	**15**	**19**

64.97: INSERT OR REPL IPP

Type of Patients	Observed Patients	Avg. Stay	Variance	Percentiles 10th	25th	50th	75th	90th	95th	99th
1. SINGLE DX										
0–19 Years	0									
20–34	0									
35–49	3	2.0	<1	1	1	2	3	3	3	3
50–64	18	1.2	<1	1	1	1	1	2	2	2
65+	24	1.3	<1	1	1	1	1	2	2	4
2. MULTIPLE DX										
0–19 Years	0									
20–34	1	1.0	0	1	1	1	1	1	1	1
35–49	53	1.7	3	1	1	1	2	3	4	11
50–64	231	1.4	1	1	1	1	1	2	3	5
65+	329	1.3	<1	1	1	1	1	2	3	5
TOTAL SINGLE DX	**45**	**1.3**	**<1**	**1**	**1**	**1**	**1**	**2**	**2**	**4**
TOTAL MULTIPLE DX	**614**	**1.4**	**1**	**1**	**1**	**1**	**1**	**2**	**3**	**5**
TOTAL										
0–19 Years	0									
20–34	1	1.0	0	1	1	1	1	1	1	1
35–49	56	1.7	3	1	1	1	2	3	4	11
50–64	249	1.4	1	1	1	1	1	2	3	5
65+	353	1.3	<1	1	1	1	1	2	3	5
GRAND TOTAL	**659**	**1.4**	**1**	**1**	**1**	**1**	**1**	**2**	**3**	**5**

64.98: PENILE OPERATION NEC

Type of Patients	Observed Patients	Avg. Stay	Variance	Percentiles 10th	25th	50th	75th	90th	95th	99th
1. SINGLE DX										
0–19 Years	1	1.0	0	1	1	1	1	1	1	1
20–34	6	2.4	2	1	1	2	3	4	4	4
35–49	13	2.3	2	1	1	2	3	5	5	5
50–64	2	1.5	<1	1	1	1	2	2	2	2
65+	0									
2. MULTIPLE DX										
0–19 Years	2	4.9	2	4	4	4	6	6	6	6
20–34	22	4.7	52	1	1	3	4	10	32	32
35–49	36	3.1	6	1	1	2	4	6	7	11
50–64	26	3.4	14	1	1	2	5	8	14	14
65+	7	2.3	4	1	1	1	2	7	7	7
TOTAL SINGLE DX	**22**	**2.1**	**2**	**1**	**1**	**2**	**3**	**4**	**5**	**5**
TOTAL MULTIPLE DX	**93**	**3.6**	**21**	**1**	**1**	**2**	**4**	**7**	**10**	**32**
TOTAL										
0–19 Years	3	3.2	6	1	1	4	4	6	6	6
20–34	28	4.3	43	1	1	3	4	7	10	32
35–49	49	2.9	5	1	1	2	4	6	7	11
50–64	28	3.2	13	1	1	2	4	8	14	14
65+	7	2.3	4	1	1	1	2	7	7	7
GRAND TOTAL	**115**	**3.3**	**17**	**1**	**1**	**2**	**4**	**7**	**10**	**32**

65.0: OOPHOROTOMY

Type of Patients	Observed Patients	Avg. Stay	Vari-ance	Percentiles						
				10th	25th	50th	75th	90th	95th	99th
1. SINGLE DX										
0–19 Years	8	1.6	<1	1	1	1	2	3	3	3
20–34	17	2.4	2	1	2	2	3	4	4	7
35–49	5	1.5	<1	1	1	2	2	2	2	2
50–64	0									
65+	0									
2. MULTIPLE DX										
0–19 Years	25	2.1	3	1	1	1	2	5	6	8
20–34	87	2.6	4	1	1	2	3	5	7	9
35–49	57	3.8	10	1	2	3	4	8	11	15
50–64	6	2.6	2	1	1	2	4	4	4	4
65+	1	4.0	0	4	4	4	4	4	4	4
TOTAL SINGLE DX	**30**	**2.0**	**1**	**1**	**1**	**2**	**2**	**4**	**4**	**7**
TOTAL MULTIPLE DX	**176**	**2.9**	**6**	**1**	**1**	**2**	**4**	**6**	**8**	**12**
TOTAL										
0–19 Years	33	2.0	3	1	1	1	2	4	6	8
20–34	104	2.6	4	1	1	2	3	5	7	9
35–49	62	3.7	10	1	2	3	4	8	11	15
50–64	6	2.6	2	1	1	2	4	4	4	4
65+	1	4.0	0	4	4	4	4	4	4	4
GRAND TOTAL	**206**	**2.8**	**5**	**1**	**1**	**2**	**3**	**6**	**8**	**12**

65.01: LAPSCP OOPHOROTOMY

Type of Patients	Observed Patients	Avg. Stay	Vari-ance	Percentiles						
				10th	25th	50th	75th	90th	95th	99th
1. SINGLE DX										
0–19 Years	8	1.6	<1	1	1	1	2	3	3	3
20–34	12	1.9	<1	1	1	2	2	3	4	4
35–49	3	1.5	<1	1	1	2	2	2	2	2
50–64	0									
65+	0									
2. MULTIPLE DX										
0–19 Years	18	1.4	<1	1	1	1	2	2	3	3
20–34	51	2.1	4	1	1	1	2	4	7	12
35–49	30	3.7	9	1	2	3	4	10	11	11
50–64	4	1.9	2	1	1	1	2	4	4	4
65+	0									
TOTAL SINGLE DX	**23**	**1.8**	**<1**	**1**	**1**	**2**	**2**	**3**	**3**	**4**
TOTAL MULTIPLE DX	**103**	**2.4**	**5**	**1**	**1**	**2**	**3**	**4**	**7**	**11**
TOTAL										
0–19 Years	26	1.4	<1	1	1	1	2	2	3	3
20–34	63	2.1	3	1	1	2	2	4	7	9
35–49	33	3.5	8	1	2	3	4	8	11	11
50–64	4	1.9	2	1	1	1	2	4	4	4
65+	0									
GRAND TOTAL	**126**	**2.3**	**4**	**1**	**1**	**2**	**3**	**4**	**7**	**11**

65.1: DXTIC PX ON OVARIES

Type of Patients	Observed Patients	Avg. Stay	Vari-ance	Percentiles						
				10th	25th	50th	75th	90th	95th	99th
1. SINGLE DX										
0–19 Years	5	1.1	<1	1	1	1	1	2	2	2
20–34	3	2.0	<1	1	1	2	3	3	3	3
35–49	3	1.4	<1	1	1	1	2	2	2	2
50–64	2	1.5	<1	1	1	2	2	2	2	2
65+	0									
2. MULTIPLE DX										
0–19 Years	4	2.5	1	1	2	2	4	4	4	4
20–34	33	2.1	4	1	1	1	2	4	5	13
35–49	19	1.8	<1	1	1	2	2	2	3	3
50–64	10	5.1	19	1	2	4	7	9	16	16
65+	10	7.1	19	2	3	6	12	13	13	13
TOTAL SINGLE DX	**13**	**1.4**	**<1**	**1**	**1**	**1**	**2**	**2**	**2**	**3**
TOTAL MULTIPLE DX	**76**	**3.2**	**11**	**1**	**1**	**2**	**3**	**7**	**13**	**13**
TOTAL										
0–19 Years	9	1.7	1	1	1	1	2	4	4	4
20–34	36	2.1	4	1	1	1	3	4	5	13
35–49	22	1.7	<1	1	1	2	2	2	3	3
50–64	12	4.5	18	1	2	3	7	9	16	16
65+	10	7.1	19	2	3	6	12	13	13	13
GRAND TOTAL	**89**	**2.9**	**10**	**1**	**1**	**2**	**3**	**6**	**12**	**13**

65.2: LOC EXC/DESTR OVARY LES

Type of Patients	Observed Patients	Avg. Stay	Vari-ance	Percentiles						
				10th	25th	50th	75th	90th	95th	99th
1. SINGLE DX										
0–19 Years	133	1.9	1	1	1	2	2	3	3	6
20–34	416	1.9	<1	1	1	2	2	3	3	5
35–49	155	2.1	<1	1	1	2	3	3	4	6
50–64	15	1.5	<1	1	1	1	2	3	3	3
65+	3	2.3	3	1	1	2	2	5	5	5
2. MULTIPLE DX										
0–19 Years	248	2.7	3	1	2	3	3	5	5	9
20–34	1,535	2.4	2	1	2	2	3	4	5	8
35–49	769	2.8	9	1	2	2	3	4	5	25
50–64	144	3.3	7	1	2	3	4	6	8	16
65+	59	5.9	35	1	3	3	8	11	24	27
TOTAL SINGLE DX	**722**	**1.9**	**<1**	**1**	**1**	**2**	**2**	**3**	**3**	**5**
TOTAL MULTIPLE DX	**2,755**	**2.7**	**5**	**1**	**2**	**2**	**3**	**4**	**5**	**11**
TOTAL										
0–19 Years	381	2.4	2	1	1	2	3	4	5	9
20–34	1,951	2.3	2	1	1	2	3	4	4	8
35–49	924	2.6	7	1	2	2	3	4	5	21
50–64	159	3.1	7	1	1	2	4	6	8	11
65+	62	5.7	34	1	3	3	6	11	24	27
GRAND TOTAL	**3,477**	**2.5**	**4**	**1**	**2**	**2**	**3**	**4**	**5**	**10**

65.25: LAPSCP OV LES EXC NEC

Type of Patients	Observed Patients	Avg. Stay	Vari-ance	Percentiles						
				10th	25th	50th	75th	90th	95th	99th
1. SINGLE DX										
0–19 Years	40	1.3	<1	1	1	1	1	3	3	3
20–34	112	1.5	<1	1	1	1	2	2	3	5
35–49	36	1.5	<1	1	1	1	2	3	3	3
50–64	6	1.0	0	1	1	1	1	1	1	1
65+	0									
2. MULTIPLE DX										
0–19 Years	71	2.3	4	1	1	2	3	4	5	15
20–34	464	2.0	2	1	1	2	3	3	4	8
35–49	210	2.0	3	1	1	1	2	4	5	7
50–64	27	1.8	2	1	1	1	2	3	4	6
65+	7	1.2	<1	1	1	1	1	2	2	2
TOTAL SINGLE DX	**194**	**1.4**	**<1**	**1**	**1**	**1**	**2**	**3**	**3**	**4**
TOTAL MULTIPLE DX	**779**	**2.0**	**2**	**1**	**1**	**2**	**3**	**4**	**5**	**8**
TOTAL										
0–19 Years	111	2.0	3	1	1	1	2	4	4	9
20–34	576	1.9	2	1	1	1	2	3	4	8
35–49	246	2.0	2	1	1	1	2	4	5	7
50–64	33	1.6	1	1	1	1	2	3	4	6
65+	7	1.2	<1	1	1	1	1	2	2	2
GRAND TOTAL	**973**	**1.9**	**2**	**1**	**1**	**1**	**2**	**3**	**4**	**7**

65.29: LOC EXC/DESTR OV LES NEC

Type of Patients	Observed Patients	Avg. Stay	Vari-ance	Percentiles						
				10th	25th	50th	75th	90th	95th	99th
1. SINGLE DX										
0–19 Years	88	2.1	1	1	1	2	2	3	4	6
20–34	295	2.1	<1	1	2	2	2	3	3	4
35–49	118	2.2	<1	1	2	2	3	3	4	6
50–64	9	1.8	<1	1	1	2	2	3	3	3
65+	3	2.3	3	1	1	2	2	5	5	5
2. MULTIPLE DX										
0–19 Years	165	2.9	2	1	2	3	3	5	5	9
20–34	1,032	2.6	2	1	2	2	3	4	5	8
35–49	540	3.0	11	1	2	2	3	4	5	25
50–64	116	3.6	7	1	2	3	5	7	9	16
65+	51	6.5	37	3	3	4	8	11	24	27
TOTAL SINGLE DX	**513**	**2.1**	**<1**	**1**	**2**	**2**	**3**	**3**	**3**	**5**
TOTAL MULTIPLE DX	**1,904**	**2.9**	**6**	**1**	**2**	**2**	**3**	**4**	**6**	**13**
TOTAL										
0–19 Years	253	2.6	2	1	2	2	3	4	5	9
20–34	1,327	2.5	2	1	2	2	3	4	5	8
35–49	658	2.9	9	1	2	2	3	4	5	25
50–64	125	3.5	7	1	2	3	4	6	9	16
65+	54	6.3	36	2	3	4	8	11	24	27
GRAND TOTAL	**2,417**	**2.8**	**5**	**1**	**2**	**2**	**3**	**4**	**5**	**11**

65.3: UNILATERAL OOPHORECTOMY

Type of Patients	Observed Patients	Avg. Stay	Vari-ance	Percentiles						
				10th	25th	50th	75th	90th	95th	99th
1. SINGLE DX										
0–19 Years	26	2.2	2	1	1	2	3	3	6	6
20–34	89	2.4	<1	1	2	2	3	4	4	5
35–49	63	2.2	2	1	1	2	3	4	4	10
50–64	19	2.1	<1	1	1	2	3	3	3	3
65+	2	3.0	0	3	3	3	3	3	3	3
2. MULTIPLE DX										
0–19 Years	58	3.2	8	2	2	3	3	5	6	19
20–34	296	2.7	3	1	2	2	3	4	5	11
35–49	295	2.7	2	1	2	2	3	4	6	8
50–64	94	4.0	46	1	2	3	4	7	11	20
65+	72	3.8	12	1	2	3	4	8	10	15
TOTAL SINGLE DX	**199**	**2.3**	**1**	**1**	**2**	**2**	**3**	**4**	**4**	**6**
TOTAL MULTIPLE DX	**815**	**3.0**	**9**	**1**	**2**	**2**	**3**	**5**	**7**	**12**
TOTAL										
0–19 Years	84	2.9	6	1	2	2	3	4	6	19
20–34	385	2.6	2	1	2	2	3	4	5	9
35–49	358	2.6	2	1	2	2	3	4	6	8
50–64	113	3.6	38	1	2	3	3	7	11	20
65+	74	3.8	11	1	2	3	4	8	10	15
GRAND TOTAL	**1,014**	**2.8**	**7**	**1**	**2**	**2**	**3**	**4**	**6**	**11**

65.31: LAPSCP UNILAT OOPHORECT

Type of Patients	Observed Patients	Avg. Stay	Vari-ance	Percentiles						
				10th	25th	50th	75th	90th	95th	99th
1. SINGLE DX										
0–19 Years	6	1.7	<1	1	1	1	3	3	3	3
20–34	13	2.0	2	1	1	1	3	4	4	4
35–49	12	1.8	4	1	1	1	2	3	3	10
50–64	8	2.0	<1	1	1	2	3	3	3	3
65+	0									
2. MULTIPLE DX										
0–19 Years	7	2.0	<1	1	2	2	2	3	3	3
20–34	47	2.0	3	1	1	2	2	3	3	13
35–49	70	1.9	2	1	1	1	3	3	4	7
50–64	18	1.7	1	1	1	1	3	3	4	5
65+	15	1.5	2	1	1	1	2	3	3	8
TOTAL SINGLE DX	**39**	**1.9**	**2**	**1**	**1**	**1**	**3**	**3**	**4**	**10**
TOTAL MULTIPLE DX	**157**	**1.9**	**2**	**1**	**1**	**1**	**2**	**3**	**4**	**8**
TOTAL										
0–19 Years	13	1.9	<1	1	1	2	3	3	3	3
20–34	60	2.0	2	1	1	2	2	3	4	13
35–49	82	1.9	2	1	1	1	2	3	4	7
50–64	26	1.8	1	1	1	1	3	3	3	5
65+	15	1.5	2	1	1	1	2	3	3	8
GRAND TOTAL	**196**	**1.9**	**2**	**1**	**1**	**1**	**2**	**3**	**4**	**8**

65.39: UNILAT OOPHORECTOMY NEC

Type of Patients	Observed Patients	Avg. Stay	Vari-ance	Percentiles						
				10th	25th	50th	75th	90th	95th	99th
1. SINGLE DX										
0–19 Years	20	2.3	2	1	1	2	3	3	6	6
20–34	76	2.5	<1	2	2	2	3	4	4	5
35–49	51	2.4	<1	1	2	2	3	4	4	4
50–64	11	2.1	<1	1	2	2	3	3	3	3
65+	2	3.0	0	3	3	3	3	3	3	3
2. MULTIPLE DX										
0–19 Years	51	3.3	8	2	2	3	3	5	6	19
20–34	249	2.8	3	1	2	2	3	4	5	11
35–49	225	2.9	2	2	2	3	3	4	6	8
50–64	76	4.5	56	2	2	3	4	7	12	70
65+	57	4.4	13	2	2	3	5	8	10	15
TOTAL SINGLE DX	**160**	**2.4**	**<1**	**1**	**2**	**2**	**3**	**4**	**4**	**6**
TOTAL MULTIPLE DX	**658**	**3.2**	**10**	**2**	**2**	**3**	**3**	**5**	**7**	**12**
TOTAL										
0–19 Years	71	3.0	7	1	2	3	3	5	6	19
20–34	325	2.7	2	1	2	2	3	4	5	9
35–49	276	2.8	2	2	2	3	3	4	6	8
50–64	87	4.3	50	1	2	3	4	7	11	20
65+	59	4.3	12	2	2	3	5	8	10	15
GRAND TOTAL	**818**	**3.1**	**8**	**1**	**2**	**3**	**3**	**5**	**7**	**11**

65.4: UNILATERAL S-O

Type of Patients	Observed Patients	Avg. Stay	Vari-ance	Percentiles						
				10th	25th	50th	75th	90th	95th	99th
1. SINGLE DX										
0–19 Years	60	3.3	3	2	2	3	4	5	6	8
20–34	213	2.4	1	1	2	2	3	4	4	6
35–49	207	2.1	<1	1	1	2	3	3	3	5
50–64	50	2.4	2	1	1	2	3	4	5	7
65+	11	2.1	<1	1	1	2	3	3	4	4
2. MULTIPLE DX										
0–19 Years	192	3.4	6	2	2	3	4	6	8	11
20–34	1,111	2.9	3	1	2	3	3	5	7	9
35–49	1,607	3.0	4	1	2	2	3	5	7	13
50–64	498	3.2	9	1	2	3	4	5	7	12
65+	247	4.2	13	1	2	3	5	8	11	18
TOTAL SINGLE DX	**541**	**2.4**	**1**	**1**	**2**	**2**	**3**	**4**	**4**	**6**
TOTAL MULTIPLE DX	**3,655**	**3.1**	**6**	**1**	**2**	**3**	**3**	**5**	**7**	**12**
TOTAL										
0–19 Years	252	3.4	5	2	2	3	4	6	7	11
20–34	1,324	2.8	3	1	2	2	3	5	6	9
35–49	1,814	2.9	4	1	2	2	3	5	6	12
50–64	548	3.2	8	1	2	3	4	5	6	12
65+	258	4.1	13	1	2	3	5	8	11	18
GRAND TOTAL	**4,196**	**3.0**	**5**	**1**	**2**	**3**	**3**	**5**	**7**	**12**

65.41: LAPSCP UNILATERAL S-O

Type of Patients	Observed Patients	Avg. Stay	Vari-ance	Percentiles						
				10th	25th	50th	75th	90th	95th	99th
1. SINGLE DX										
0–19 Years	7	2.0	<1	1	1	2	3	3	3	3
20–34	41	1.8	<1	1	1	2	2	3	4	5
35–49	51	1.7	<1	1	1	1	2	3	4	4
50–64	14	1.3	<1	1	1	1	1	2	4	4
65+	4	1.3	<1	1	1	1	1	3	3	3
2. MULTIPLE DX										
0–19 Years	30	2.6	2	1	1	2	3	5	5	6
20–34	188	2.1	3	1	1	2	3	4	6	9
35–49	308	2.2	4	1	1	2	3	4	6	13
50–64	103	2.0	2	1	1	1	2	4	4	10
65+	47	2.6	10	1	1	1	3	5	8	18
TOTAL SINGLE DX	**117**	**1.7**	**<1**	**1**	**1**	**1**	**2**	**3**	**4**	**4**
TOTAL MULTIPLE DX	**676**	**2.2**	**4**	**1**	**1**	**2**	**3**	**4**	**6**	**10**
TOTAL										
0–19 Years	37	2.5	2	1	1	2	3	5	5	6
20–34	229	2.1	3	1	1	2	2	4	6	8
35–49	359	2.1	4	1	1	1	2	4	5	13
50–64	117	1.9	2	1	1	1	2	4	4	10
65+	51	2.5	9	1	1	1	3	5	8	18
GRAND TOTAL	**793**	**2.1**	**3**	**1**	**1**	**1**	**3**	**4**	**5**	**10**

65.49: UNILATERAL S-O NEC

Type of Patients	Observed Patients	Avg. Stay	Vari-ance	Percentiles						
				10th	25th	50th	75th	90th	95th	99th
1. SINGLE DX										
0–19 Years	53	3.4	3	2	2	3	4	6	7	8
20–34	172	2.6	1	1	2	2	3	4	5	6
35–49	156	2.3	<1	1	2	2	3	3	3	5
50–64	36	2.7	2	2	2	2	3	5	6	7
65+	7	2.5	<1	2	2	2	3	4	4	4
2. MULTIPLE DX										
0–19 Years	162	3.6	6	2	2	3	4	6	8	19
20–34	923	3.1	3	2	2	3	3	5	7	10
35–49	1,299	3.1	4	2	2	3	3	5	7	12
50–64	395	3.5	10	2	2	3	4	6	7	13
65+	200	4.5	14	2	2	3	5	9	11	18
TOTAL SINGLE DX	**424**	**2.6**	**1**	**1**	**2**	**2**	**3**	**4**	**5**	**7**
TOTAL MULTIPLE DX	**2,979**	**3.3**	**6**	**2**	**2**	**3**	**4**	**6**	**7**	**13**
TOTAL										
0–19 Years	215	3.6	5	2	2	3	4	6	8	11
20–34	1,095	3.0	3	2	2	3	3	5	6	9
35–49	1,455	3.0	4	2	2	3	3	5	6	12
50–64	431	3.5	9	2	2	3	4	5	7	13
65+	207	4.5	13	2	2	3	5	8	11	18
GRAND TOTAL	**3,403**	**3.2**	**5**	**2**	**2**	**3**	**4**	**5**	**7**	**12**

65.5: BILATERAL OOPHORECTOMY

Type of Patients	Observed Patients	Avg. Stay	Vari-ance	Percentiles 10th	25th	50th	75th	90th	95th	99th
1. SINGLE DX										
0–19 Years	1	1.0	0	1	1	1	1	1	1	1
20–34	2	2.0	0	2	2	2	2	2	2	2
35–49	3	2.3	1	1	1	3	3	3	3	3
50–64	0									
65+	2	3.3	2	1	4	4	4	4	4	4
2. MULTIPLE DX										
0–19 Years	4	2.4	2	1	2	2	4	4	4	4
20–34	21	2.4	2	1	2	2	3	4	5	8
35–49	94	2.7	4	1	1	2	3	6	7	10
50–64	76	2.9	7	1	2	2	3	4	7	9
65+	53	4.5	29	1	2	3	4	11	20	29
TOTAL SINGLE DX	**8**	**2.4**	**1**	**1**	**1**	**2**	**3**	**4**	**4**	**4**
TOTAL MULTIPLE DX	**248**	**3.1**	**11**	**1**	**2**	**2**	**3**	**6**	**7**	**20**
TOTAL										
0–19 Years	5	2.2	2	1	1	2	4	4	4	4
20–34	23	2.4	2	1	2	2	2	4	5	8
35–49	97	2.7	3	1	1	2	3	6	7	10
50–64	76	2.9	7	1	2	2	3	4	7	9
65+	55	4.4	28	1	2	3	4	10	15	29
GRAND TOTAL	**256**	**3.1**	**11**	**1**	**2**	**2**	**3**	**6**	**7**	**20**

65.51: RMVL BOTH OVARIES NEC

Type of Patients	Observed Patients	Avg. Stay	Vari-ance	Percentiles 10th	25th	50th	75th	90th	95th	99th
1. SINGLE DX										
0–19 Years	0									
20–34	2	2.0	0	2	2	2	2	2	2	2
35–49	0									
50–64	0									
65+	2	3.3	2	1	4	4	4	4	4	4
2. MULTIPLE DX										
0–19 Years	3	2.5	2	1	2	2	4	4	4	4
20–34	6	3.5	5	2	2	2	4	8	8	8
35–49	47	3.4	4	1	2	3	4	6	7	10
50–64	50	3.2	9	2	2	2	3	7	8	25
65+	31	6.3	47	2	3	3	6	15	20	29
TOTAL SINGLE DX	**4**	**2.7**	**2**	**1**	**2**	**2**	**4**	**4**	**4**	**4**
TOTAL MULTIPLE DX	**137**	**4.0**	**17**	**2**	**2**	**3**	**4**	**7**	**10**	**25**
TOTAL										
0–19 Years	3	2.5	2	1	2	2	4	4	4	4
20–34	8	3.0	4	2	2	2	3	8	8	8
35–49	47	3.4	4	1	2	3	4	6	7	10
50–64	50	3.2	9	2	2	2	3	7	8	25
65+	33	6.0	43	2	3	3	6	15	20	29
GRAND TOTAL	**141**	**3.9**	**17**	**2**	**2**	**3**	**4**	**7**	**10**	**25**

65.6: BILAT SALPINGO-OOPHORECT

Type of Patients	Observed Patients	Avg. Stay	Vari-ance	Percentiles 10th	25th	50th	75th	90th	95th	99th
1. SINGLE DX										
0–19 Years	1	1.0	0	1	1	1	1	1	1	1
20–34	12	2.5	2	1	2	2	2	5	5	6
35–49	36	1.9	<1	1	1	2	3	3	3	5
50–64	66	2.2	1	1	1	2	3	3	4	5
65+	18	2.5	<1	1	2	3	3	4	4	5
2. MULTIPLE DX										
0–19 Years	4	2.9	<1	2	3	3	3	3	3	3
20–34	195	3.0	8	2	2	2	3	4	6	17
35–49	1,159	3.2	5	1	2	3	4	5	7	13
50–64	1,349	3.7	21	1	2	3	4	6	8	22
65+	946	4.7	18	2	2	3	5	9	13	24
TOTAL SINGLE DX	**133**	**2.2**	**1**	**1**	**1**	**2**	**3**	**3**	**4**	**5**
TOTAL MULTIPLE DX	**3,653**	**3.8**	**15**	**1**	**2**	**3**	**4**	**7**	**10**	**18**
TOTAL										
0–19 Years	5	2.6	<1	1	2	3	3	3	3	3
20–34	207	2.9	8	2	2	2	3	4	6	17
35–49	1,195	3.1	5	1	2	3	4	5	7	13
50–64	1,415	3.6	20	1	2	3	4	6	8	20
65+	964	4.6	18	1	2	3	5	9	13	24
GRAND TOTAL	**3,786**	**3.7**	**15**	**1**	**2**	**3**	**4**	**7**	**9**	**18**

65.61: RMVL BOTH OV & FALL NEC

Type of Patients	Observed Patients	Avg. Stay	Vari-ance	Percentiles 10th	25th	50th	75th	90th	95th	99th
1. SINGLE DX										
0–19 Years	0									
20–34	6	2.5	2	2	2	2	2	3	6	6
35–49	22	2.3	<1	1	1	2	3	3	3	5
50–64	41	2.7	<1	2	2	3	3	4	5	5
65+	15	2.9	<1	2	2	3	3	4	4	5
2. MULTIPLE DX										
0–19 Years	2	2.5	<1	2	2	3	3	3	3	3
20–34	130	3.3	11	2	2	3	3	4	6	26
35–49	818	3.4	6	2	2	3	4	5	8	14
50–64	1,062	4.0	25	2	2	3	4	6	8	24
65+	745	5.2	20	2	3	4	6	10	14	25
TOTAL SINGLE DX	**84**	**2.6**	**<1**	**2**	**2**	**3**	**3**	**4**	**5**	**5**
TOTAL MULTIPLE DX	**2,757**	**4.2**	**18**	**2**	**2**	**3**	**4**	**7**	**10**	**22**
TOTAL										
0–19 Years	2	2.5	<1	2	2	3	3	3	3	3
20–34	136	3.2	11	2	2	3	3	4	6	26
35–49	840	3.4	6	2	2	3	4	5	8	14
50–64	1,103	4.0	24	2	2	3	4	6	8	24
65+	760	5.2	20	2	3	4	6	10	14	25
GRAND TOTAL	**2,841**	**4.1**	**18**	**2**	**2**	**3**	**4**	**7**	**10**	**21**

65.62: RMVL REM OV & FALL NEC

Type of Patients	Observed Patients	Avg. Stay	Vari-ance	10th	25th	50th	75th	90th	95th	99th
1. SINGLE DX										
0–19 Years	0									
20–34	5	2.5	3	1	1	2	5	5	5	5
35–49	4	1.2	<1	1	1	1	1	2	2	2
50–64	6	2.0	<1	2	2	2	2	3	3	3
65+	0									
2. MULTIPLE DX										
0–19 Years	1	3.0	0	3	3	3	3	3	3	3
20–34	39	2.6	2	2	2	2	3	4	5	8
35–49	150	3.4	4	2	2	3	4	6	7	10
50–64	97	3.2	3	1	2	3	4	6	7	8
65+	48	4.1	6	2	3	3	5	6	8	15
TOTAL SINGLE DX	**15**	**2.1**	**1**	**1**	**1**	**2**	**2**	**5**	**5**	**5**
TOTAL MULTIPLE DX	**335**	**3.4**	**4**	**2**	**2**	**3**	**4**	**6**	**7**	**11**
TOTAL										
0–19 Years	1	3.0	0	3	3	3	3	3	3	3
20–34	44	2.6	2	1	2	2	3	4	5	8
35–49	154	3.4	4	2	2	3	4	6	7	10
50–64	103	3.1	3	1	2	3	3	6	7	8
65+	48	4.1	6	2	3	3	5	6	8	15
GRAND TOTAL	**350**	**3.3**	**4**	**2**	**2**	**3**	**4**	**6**	**7**	**11**

65.63: LAPSCP RMVL BOTH OV/FALL

Type of Patients	Observed Patients	Avg. Stay	Vari-ance	10th	25th	50th	75th	90th	95th	99th
1. SINGLE DX										
0–19 Years	1	1.0	0	1	1	1	1	1	1	1
20–34	1	2.0	0	2	2	2	2	2	2	2
35–49	9	1.5	<1	1	1	1	2	3	3	3
50–64	18	1.6	<1	1	1	1	2	3	3	4
65+	2	1.3	<1	1	1	1	2	2	2	2
2. MULTIPLE DX										
0–19 Years	0									
20–34	20	2.0	<1	1	1	2	2	3	4	4
35–49	161	1.8	2	1	1	1	2	3	4	7
50–64	177	2.0	2	1	1	2	2	4	4	7
65+	147	2.2	5	1	1	1	2	5	8	9
TOTAL SINGLE DX	**31**	**1.5**	**<1**	**1**	**1**	**1**	**2**	**3**	**3**	**4**
TOTAL MULTIPLE DX	**505**	**2.0**	**3**	**1**	**1**	**1**	**2**	**4**	**5**	**8**
TOTAL										
0–19 Years	1	1.0	0	1	1	1	1	1	1	1
20–34	21	2.0	<1	1	1	2	2	3	4	4
35–49	170	1.8	2	1	1	1	2	3	4	7
50–64	195	2.0	2	1	1	1	2	4	4	7
65+	149	2.2	5	1	1	1	2	4	7	9
GRAND TOTAL	**536**	**2.0**	**3**	**1**	**1**	**1**	**2**	**4**	**5**	**8**

65.7: REPAIR OF OVARY

Type of Patients	Observed Patients	Avg. Stay	Vari-ance	10th	25th	50th	75th	90th	95th	99th
1. SINGLE DX										
0–19 Years	2	1.7	<1	1	1	2	2	2	2	2
20–34	3	2.4	1	1	1	3	3	3	3	3
35–49	1	3.0	0	3	3	3	3	3	3	3
50–64	0									
65+	0									
2. MULTIPLE DX										
0–19 Years	15	3.3	8	1	2	2	3	5	14	14
20–34	36	2.7	3	1	2	2	3	4	9	9
35–49	13	2.3	2	1	1	2	3	3	4	6
50–64	3	2.5	<1	2	2	2	3	3	3	3
65+	1	2.0	0	2	2	2	2	2	2	2
TOTAL SINGLE DX	**6**	**2.1**	**<1**	**1**	**1**	**2**	**3**	**3**	**3**	**3**
TOTAL MULTIPLE DX	**68**	**2.7**	**4**	**1**	**2**	**2**	**3**	**4**	**6**	**14**
TOTAL										
0–19 Years	17	3.1	8	1	2	2	3	5	7	14
20–34	39	2.7	3	1	2	2	3	4	6	9
35–49	14	2.3	1	1	1	2	3	3	4	6
50–64	3	2.5	<1	2	2	2	3	3	3	3
65+	1	2.0	0	2	2	2	2	2	2	2
GRAND TOTAL	**74**	**2.7**	**4**	**1**	**2**	**2**	**3**	**4**	**6**	**14**

65.8: TUBO-OVARIAN ADHESIO

Type of Patients	Observed Patients	Avg. Stay	Vari-ance	10th	25th	50th	75th	90th	95th	99th
1. SINGLE DX										
0–19 Years	1	1.0	0	1	1	1	1	1	1	1
20–34	4	1.9	<1	1	1	2	3	3	3	3
35–49	6	1.9	<1	1	1	2	2	3	3	3
50–64	0									
65+	1	1.0	0	1	1	1	1	1	1	1
2. MULTIPLE DX										
0–19 Years	12	3.3	4	1	1	4	4	6	7	7
20–34	149	2.5	2	1	1	2	3	4	6	10
35–49	159	2.7	3	1	2	2	3	4	6	9
50–64	39	3.5	7	1	2	3	4	7	9	15
65+	11	7.6	124	1	2	3	5	33	33	33
TOTAL SINGLE DX	**12**	**1.7**	**<1**	**1**	**1**	**2**	**2**	**3**	**3**	**3**
TOTAL MULTIPLE DX	**370**	**2.9**	**8**	**1**	**2**	**2**	**3**	**5**	**6**	**11**
TOTAL										
0–19 Years	13	2.9	4	1	1	2	4	6	6	7
20–34	153	2.5	2	1	1	2	3	4	5	10
35–49	165	2.6	2	1	2	2	3	4	6	9
50–64	39	3.5	7	1	2	3	4	7	9	15
65+	12	7.0	117	1	1	2	4	33	33	33
GRAND TOTAL	**382**	**2.8**	**8**	**1**	**2**	**2**	**3**	**5**	**6**	**11**

65.81: LAPSCP ADHESIO OV/FALL

Type of Patients	Observed Patients	Avg. Stay	Vari-ance	Percentiles 10th	25th	50th	75th	90th	95th	99th
1. SINGLE DX										
0–19 Years	1	1.0	0	1	1	1	1	1	1	1
20–34	0									
35–49	3	1.3	<1	1	1	1	2	2	2	2
50–64	0									
65+	1	1.0	0	1	1	1	1	1	1	1
2. MULTIPLE DX										
0–19 Years	10	3.3	3	1	2	4	4	6	6	6
20–34	58	2.3	3	1	1	2	3	4	5	10
35–49	56	2.6	4	1	1	2	3	5	7	10
50–64	16	2.2	3	1	1	1	3	5	5	5
65+	3	2.0	4	1	1	1	1	5	5	5
TOTAL SINGLE DX	**5**	**1.1**	**<1**	**1**	**1**	**1**	**1**	**2**	**2**	**2**
TOTAL MULTIPLE DX	**143**	**2.5**	**3**	**1**	**1**	**2**	**3**	**5**	**6**	**10**
TOTAL										
0–19 Years	11	2.9	4	1	1	2	4	6	6	6
20–34	58	2.3	3	1	1	2	3	4	5	10
35–49	59	2.5	4	1	1	2	3	5	7	10
50–64	16	2.2	3	1	1	1	3	5	5	5
65+	4	1.7	3	1	1	1	1	5	5	5
GRAND TOTAL	**148**	**2.4**	**3**	**1**	**1**	**2**	**3**	**5**	**6**	**10**

65.89: ADHESIO OV/FALL TUBE NEC

Type of Patients	Observed Patients	Avg. Stay	Vari-ance	Percentiles 10th	25th	50th	75th	90th	95th	99th
1. SINGLE DX										
0–19 Years	0									
20–34	4	1.9	<1	1	1	2	3	3	3	3
35–49	3	2.3	<1	2	2	2	3	3	3	3
50–64	0									
65+	0									
2. MULTIPLE DX										
0–19 Years	2	3.0	12	1	1	1	7	7	7	7
20–34	91	2.6	2	1	2	2	3	4	6	8
35–49	103	2.7	2	1	2	2	3	4	5	8
50–64	23	4.1	8	2	2	3	5	7	10	15
65+	8	9.8	156	2	2	4	18	33	33	33
TOTAL SINGLE DX	**7**	**2.1**	**<1**	**1**	**1**	**2**	**3**	**3**	**3**	**3**
TOTAL MULTIPLE DX	**227**	**3.1**	**11**	**1**	**2**	**2**	**3**	**5**	**6**	**18**
TOTAL										
0–19 Years	2	3.0	12	1	1	1	7	7	7	7
20–34	95	2.6	2	1	2	2	3	4	6	8
35–49	106	2.7	2	1	2	2	3	4	5	8
50–64	23	4.1	8	2	2	3	5	7	10	15
65+	8	9.8	156	2	2	4	18	33	33	33
GRAND TOTAL	**234**	**3.1**	**10**	**1**	**2**	**2**	**3**	**4**	**6**	**18**

65.9: OTHER OVARIAN OPERATIONS

Type of Patients	Observed Patients	Avg. Stay	Vari-ance	Percentiles 10th	25th	50th	75th	90th	95th	99th
1. SINGLE DX										
0–19 Years	8	1.7	<1	1	1	2	2	2	2	2
20–34	29	1.6	<1	1	1	1	2	3	4	4
35–49	9	4.9	27	1	1	3	8	14	14	14
50–64	1	1.0	0	1	1	1	1	1	1	1
65+	0									
2. MULTIPLE DX										
0–19 Years	47	2.1	1	1	1	2	2	4	4	5
20–34	133	2.8	6	1	1	2	3	5	7	15
35–49	75	3.1	8	1	2	2	3	5	8	15
50–64	12	5.6	31	1	1	3	9	15	15	15
65+	9	6.3	18	3	3	7	7	8	18	18
TOTAL SINGLE DX	**47**	**2.0**	**4**	**1**	**1**	**1**	**2**	**3**	**4**	**14**
TOTAL MULTIPLE DX	**276**	**3.0**	**8**	**1**	**1**	**2**	**3**	**5**	**7**	**15**
TOTAL										
0–19 Years	55	2.0	<1	1	1	2	2	4	4	5
20–34	162	2.5	5	1	1	2	3	5	6	15
35–49	84	3.3	10	1	2	2	3	5	10	15
50–64	13	5.2	30	1	1	3	9	15	15	15
65+	9	6.3	18	3	3	7	7	8	18	18
GRAND TOTAL	**323**	**2.8**	**7**	**1**	**1**	**2**	**3**	**5**	**7**	**15**

65.91: ASPIRATION OF OVARY

Type of Patients	Observed Patients	Avg. Stay	Vari-ance	Percentiles 10th	25th	50th	75th	90th	95th	99th
1. SINGLE DX										
0–19 Years	6	1.6	<1	1	1	2	2	2	2	2
20–34	29	1.6	<1	1	1	1	2	3	4	4
35–49	8	5.5	28	1	1	3	8	14	14	14
50–64	1	1.0	0	1	1	1	1	1	1	1
65+	0									
2. MULTIPLE DX										
0–19 Years	37	2.0	1	1	1	2	2	4	4	5
20–34	118	2.8	6	1	1	2	3	5	7	15
35–49	71	3.1	8	1	2	2	3	5	8	21
50–64	11	5.9	31	1	3	3	9	15	15	15
65+	9	6.3	18	3	3	7	7	8	18	18
TOTAL SINGLE DX	**44**	**2.0**	**5**	**1**	**1**	**1**	**2**	**4**	**4**	**14**
TOTAL MULTIPLE DX	**246**	**3.0**	**8**	**1**	**1**	**2**	**3**	**6**	**8**	**15**
TOTAL										
0–19 Years	43	2.0	1	1	1	2	2	3	4	5
20–34	147	2.5	5	1	1	2	3	5	6	15
35–49	79	3.3	10	1	2	3	3	6	10	15
50–64	12	5.5	30	1	1	3	9	15	15	15
65+	9	6.3	18	3	3	7	7	8	18	18
GRAND TOTAL	**290**	**2.9**	**8**	**1**	**1**	**2**	**3**	**5**	**8**	**15**

66.0: SALPINGOSTOMY/SALPINGOT

Type of Patients	Observed Patients	Avg. Stay	Vari-ance	10th	25th	50th	75th	90th	95th	99th
1. SINGLE DX										
0–19 Years	25	1.8	<1	1	1	2	2	3	3	3
20–34	229	1.5	<1	1	1	1	2	3	3	3
35–49	36	1.2	<1	1	1	1	1	2	2	3
50–64	6	2.2	<1	1	1	3	3	3	3	3
65+	0									
2. MULTIPLE DX										
0–19 Years	36	2.3	4	1	1	2	3	3	6	14
20–34	375	1.9	1	1	1	2	2	3	4	5
35–49	64	2.1	2	1	1	2	3	3	5	7
50–64	7	5.7	15	1	1	7	10	10	10	10
65+	0									
TOTAL SINGLE DX	**296**	**1.5**	**<1**	**1**	**1**	**1**	**2**	**3**	**3**	**3**
TOTAL MULTIPLE DX	**482**	**2.0**	**2**	**1**	**1**	**2**	**2**	**3**	**4**	**7**
TOTAL										
0–19 Years	61	2.2	3	1	1	2	3	3	6	9
20–34	604	1.7	<1	1	1	1	2	3	3	5
35–49	100	1.7	1	1	1	1	2	3	4	6
50–64	13	4.4	12	1	1	3	7	10	10	10
65+	0									
GRAND TOTAL	**778**	**1.8**	**1**	**1**	**1**	**1**	**2**	**3**	**4**	**7**

66.01: SALPINGOTOMY

Type of Patients	Observed Patients	Avg. Stay	Vari-ance	10th	25th	50th	75th	90th	95th	99th
1. SINGLE DX										
0–19 Years	2	2.2	<1	2	2	2	2	3	3	3
20–34	30	1.4	<1	1	1	1	2	2	3	3
35–49	4	1.1	<1	1	1	1	1	2	2	2
50–64	2	1.0	0	1	1	1	1	1	1	1
65+	0									
2. MULTIPLE DX										
0–19 Years	12	3.2	8	2	2	2	3	6	9	14
20–34	68	1.8	1	1	1	1	2	3	5	5
35–49	15	2.8	2	1	2	2	3	5	6	6
50–64	3	7.9	10	3	5	10	10	10	10	10
65+	0									
TOTAL SINGLE DX	**38**	**1.4**	**<1**	**1**	**1**	**1**	**2**	**2**	**3**	**3**
TOTAL MULTIPLE DX	**98**	**2.4**	**5**	**1**	**1**	**2**	**3**	**5**	**7**	**10**
TOTAL										
0–19 Years	14	3.0	7	2	2	2	3	6	9	14
20–34	98	1.7	1	1	1	1	2	3	4	5
35–49	19	2.1	2	1	1	2	3	4	5	6
50–64	5	6.0	17	1	1	5	10	10	10	10
65+	0									
GRAND TOTAL	**136**	**2.1**	**4**	**1**	**1**	**2**	**2**	**3**	**5**	**10**

66.02: SALPINGOSTOMY

Type of Patients	Observed Patients	Avg. Stay	Vari-ance	10th	25th	50th	75th	90th	95th	99th
1. SINGLE DX										
0–19 Years	23	1.7	<1	1	1	1	2	3	3	3
20–34	199	1.5	<1	1	1	1	2	3	3	3
35–49	32	1.3	<1	1	1	1	1	2	3	3
50–64	4	2.8	<1	2	3	3	3	3	3	3
65+	0									
2. MULTIPLE DX										
0–19 Years	24	2.0	2	1	1	2	2	3	6	6
20–34	307	1.9	<1	1	1	2	2	3	4	5
35–49	49	1.9	1	1	1	2	2	3	4	7
50–64	4	3.2	10	1	1	1	7	7	7	7
65+	0									
TOTAL SINGLE DX	**258**	**1.5**	**<1**	**1**	**1**	**1**	**2**	**3**	**3**	**3**
TOTAL MULTIPLE DX	**384**	**1.9**	**1**	**1**	**1**	**2**	**2**	**3**	**4**	**6**
TOTAL										
0–19 Years	47	1.9	1	1	1	2	2	3	3	6
20–34	506	1.7	<1	1	1	2	2	3	3	5
35–49	81	1.6	<1	1	1	1	2	3	3	5
50–64	8	3.0	5	1	1	3	3	7	7	7
65+	0									
GRAND TOTAL	**642**	**1.8**	**<1**	**1**	**1**	**1**	**2**	**3**	**3**	**5**

66.1: FALLOPIAN TUBE DXTIC PX

Type of Patients	Observed Patients	Avg. Stay	Vari-ance	10th	25th	50th	75th	90th	95th	99th
1. SINGLE DX										
0–19 Years	0									
20–34	1	3.0	0	3	3	3	3	3	3	3
35–49	0									
50–64	0									
65+	0									
2. MULTIPLE DX										
0–19 Years	2	4.3	1	3	3	5	5	5	5	5
20–34	0									
35–49	5	1.5	<1	1	1	1	2	2	2	2
50–64	0									
65+	0									
TOTAL SINGLE DX	**1**	**3.0**	**0**	**3**	**3**	**3**	**3**	**3**	**3**	**3**
TOTAL MULTIPLE DX	**7**	**2.5**	**3**	**1**	**1**	**2**	**3**	**5**	**5**	**5**
TOTAL										
0–19 Years	2	4.3	1	3	3	5	5	5	5	5
20–34	1	3.0	0	3	3	3	3	3	3	3
35–49	5	1.5	<1	1	1	1	2	2	2	2
50–64	0									
65+	0									
GRAND TOTAL	**8**	**2.6**	**2**	**1**	**1**	**2**	**3**	**5**	**5**	**5**

66.2: BILAT ENDO OCCL FALL

Type of Patients	Observed Patients	Avg. Stay	Vari-ance	Percentiles						
				10th	25th	50th	75th	90th	95th	99th
1. SINGLE DX										
0–19 Years	0									
20–34	6	1.3	<1	1	1	1	2	2	2	2
35–49	4	1.2	<1	1	1	1	1	2	2	2
50–64	3	2.0	<1	1	1	2	3	3	3	3
65+	0									
2. MULTIPLE DX										
0–19 Years	0									
20–34	288	2.1	1	1	2	2	2	3	3	8
35–49	103	2.1	2	1	1	2	2	3	4	10
50–64	7	2.1	<1	2	2	2	2	3	3	3
65+	0									
TOTAL SINGLE DX	**13**	**1.4**	**<1**	**1**	**1**	**1**	**2**	**2**	**3**	**3**
TOTAL MULTIPLE DX	**398**	**2.1**	**1**	**1**	**2**	**2**	**2**	**3**	**3**	**9**
TOTAL										
0–19 Years	0									
20–34	294	2.1	1	1	2	2	2	3	3	8
35–49	107	2.1	2	1	1	2	2	3	4	10
50–64	10	2.1	<1	1	2	2	2	3	3	3
65+	0									
GRAND TOTAL	**411**	**2.1**	**1**	**1**	**2**	**2**	**2**	**3**	**3**	**8**

66.22: BILAT ENDO LIG/DIV FALL

Type of Patients	Observed Patients	Avg. Stay	Vari-ance	Percentiles						
				10th	25th	50th	75th	90th	95th	99th
1. SINGLE DX										
0–19 Years	0									
20–34	2	1.6	<1	1	1	2	2	2	2	2
35–49	1	1.0	0	1	1	1	1	1	1	1
50–64	2	2.5	<1	2	2	2	3	3	3	3
65+	0									
2. MULTIPLE DX										
0–19 Years	0									
20–34	193	2.1	<1	1	2	2	2	3	3	3
35–49	60	2.3	3	1	2	2	2	3	4	10
50–64	5	2.2	<1	2	2	2	2	3	3	3
65+	0									
TOTAL SINGLE DX	**5**	**1.7**	**<1**	**1**	**1**	**2**	**2**	**3**	**3**	**3**
TOTAL MULTIPLE DX	**258**	**2.1**	**1**	**1**	**2**	**2**	**2**	**3**	**3**	**10**
TOTAL										
0–19 Years	0									
20–34	195	2.1	<1	1	2	2	2	3	3	3
35–49	61	2.3	3	1	2	2	2	3	4	10
50–64	7	2.3	<1	2	2	2	3	3	3	3
65+	0									
GRAND TOTAL	**263**	**2.1**	**1**	**1**	**2**	**2**	**2**	**3**	**3**	**10**

66.29: BILAT ENDO OCCL FALL NEC

Type of Patients	Observed Patients	Avg. Stay	Vari-ance	Percentiles						
				10th	25th	50th	75th	90th	95th	99th
1. SINGLE DX										
0–19 Years	0									
20–34	4	1.2	<1	1	1	1	1	2	2	2
35–49	3	1.3	<1	1	1	1	2	2	2	2
50–64	1	1.0	0	1	1	1	1	1	1	1
65+	0									
2. MULTIPLE DX										
0–19 Years	0									
20–34	94	2.2	2	1	2	2	2	3	5	8
35–49	43	1.8	<1	1	1	2	2	3	3	3
50–64	2	2.0	0	2	2	2	2	2	2	2
65+	0									
TOTAL SINGLE DX	**8**	**1.2**	**<1**	**1**	**1**	**1**	**1**	**2**	**2**	**2**
TOTAL MULTIPLE DX	**139**	**2.1**	**2**	**1**	**2**	**2**	**2**	**3**	**3**	**8**
TOTAL										
0–19 Years	0									
20–34	98	2.1	2	1	2	2	2	3	3	8
35–49	46	1.8	<1	1	1	2	2	3	3	3
50–64	3	1.7	<1	1	1	2	2	2	2	2
65+	0									
GRAND TOTAL	**147**	**2.0**	**2**	**1**	**1**	**2**	**2**	**3**	**3**	**8**

66.3: OTH BILAT FALL DESTR/EXC

Type of Patients	Observed Patients	Avg. Stay	Vari-ance	Percentiles						
				10th	25th	50th	75th	90th	95th	99th
1. SINGLE DX										
0–19 Years	0									
20–34	87	1.9	<1	1	2	2	2	3	3	3
35–49	22	1.7	<1	1	1	2	2	2	3	3
50–64	1	4.0	0	4	4	4	4	4	4	4
65+	0									
2. MULTIPLE DX										
0–19 Years	9	2.3	<1	2	2	2	2	4	4	4
20–34	8,199	2.1	2	1	2	2	2	3	3	5
35–49	2,476	2.2	2	1	2	2	2	3	3	5
50–64	132	2.4	5	1	2	2	3	3	3	15
65+	0									
TOTAL SINGLE DX	**110**	**1.9**	**<1**	**1**	**2**	**2**	**2**	**3**	**3**	**4**
TOTAL MULTIPLE DX	**10,816**	**2.2**	**2**	**1**	**2**	**2**	**2**	**3**	**3**	**5**
TOTAL										
0–19 Years	9	2.3	<1	2	2	2	2	4	4	4
20–34	8,286	2.1	2	1	2	2	2	3	3	5
35–49	2,498	2.2	2	1	2	2	2	3	3	5
50–64	133	2.4	5	1	2	2	3	3	3	15
65+	0									
GRAND TOTAL	**10,926**	**2.2**	**2**	**1**	**2**	**2**	**2**	**3**	**3**	**5**

66.32: BILAT FALL LIG & DIV NEC

Type of Patients	Observed Patients	Avg. Stay	Vari-ance	Percentiles						
				10th	25th	50th	75th	90th	95th	99th
1. SINGLE DX										
0–19 Years	0									
20–34	79	1.9	<1	1	2	2	2	3	3	3
35–49	17	1.8	<1	1	1	2	2	3	3	3
50–64	1	4.0	0	4	4	4	4	4	4	4
65+	0									
2. MULTIPLE DX										
0–19 Years	8	2.4	<1	2	2	2	3	4	4	4
20–34	6,898	2.2	3	1	2	2	2	3	3	5
35–49	2,084	2.2	2	1	2	2	2	3	3	5
50–64	109	2.6	6	2	2	2	3	3	4	15
65+	0									
TOTAL SINGLE DX	**97**	**1.9**	**<1**	**1**	**2**	**2**	**2**	**3**	**3**	**4**
TOTAL MULTIPLE DX	**9,099**	**2.2**	**2**	**1**	**2**	**2**	**2**	**3**	**3**	**5**
TOTAL										
0–19 Years	8	2.4	<1	2	2	2	3	4	4	4
20–34	6,977	2.2	3	1	2	2	2	3	3	5
35–49	2,101	2.2	2	1	2	2	2	3	3	5
50–64	110	2.6	6	2	2	2	3	3	4	15
65+	0									
GRAND TOTAL	**9,196**	**2.2**	**2**	**1**	**2**	**2**	**2**	**3**	**3**	**5**

66.39: BILAT FALL DESTR NEC

Type of Patients	Observed Patients	Avg. Stay	Vari-ance	Percentiles						
				10th	25th	50th	75th	90th	95th	99th
1. SINGLE DX										
0–19 Years	0									
20–34	8	1.7	<1	1	1	2	2	2	3	3
35–49	5	1.4	<1	1	1	1	2	2	2	2
50–64	0									
65+	0									
2. MULTIPLE DX										
0–19 Years	1	2.0	0	2	2	2	2	2	2	2
20–34	1,279	2.1	1	1	2	2	2	3	3	5
35–49	376	2.2	1	1	2	2	2	3	3	5
50–64	23	1.7	<1	1	1	2	2	3	3	3
65+	0									
TOTAL SINGLE DX	**13**	**1.6**	**<1**	**1**	**1**	**2**	**2**	**2**	**3**	**3**
TOTAL MULTIPLE DX	**1,679**	**2.1**	**1**	**1**	**2**	**2**	**2**	**3**	**3**	**5**
TOTAL										
0–19 Years	1	2.0	0	2	2	2	2	2	2	2
20–34	1,287	2.1	1	1	2	2	2	3	3	5
35–49	381	2.2	1	1	2	2	2	3	3	5
50–64	23	1.7	<1	1	1	2	2	3	3	3
65+	0									
GRAND TOTAL	**1,692**	**2.1**	**1**	**1**	**2**	**2**	**2**	**3**	**3**	**5**

66.4: TOT UNILAT SALPINGECTOMY

Type of Patients	Observed Patients	Avg. Stay	Vari-ance	Percentiles						
				10th	25th	50th	75th	90th	95th	99th
1. SINGLE DX										
0–19 Years	7	2.5	1	1	2	2	3	5	5	5
20–34	32	2.1	<1	1	2	2	2	3	4	6
35–49	26	2.3	<1	1	2	2	3	4	4	4
50–64	2	2.6	4	1	1	4	4	4	4	4
65+	0									
2. MULTIPLE DX										
0–19 Years	23	3.5	13	1	1	3	4	7	7	19
20–34	156	2.4	2	1	2	2	3	4	5	7
35–49	124	2.7	3	1	1	2	4	5	6	10
50–64	24	3.6	12	1	2	2	4	8	14	14
65+	14	2.9	15	1	2	2	2	4	6	19
TOTAL SINGLE DX	**67**	**2.3**	**<1**	**1**	**2**	**2**	**3**	**4**	**4**	**6**
TOTAL MULTIPLE DX	**341**	**2.7**	**4**	**1**	**1**	**2**	**3**	**5**	**6**	**10**
TOTAL										
0–19 Years	30	3.2	10	1	2	3	4	6	7	19
20–34	188	2.4	2	1	2	2	3	3	5	7
35–49	150	2.6	3	1	1	2	4	5	5	8
50–64	26	3.6	11	1	2	2	4	8	14	14
65+	14	2.9	15	1	2	2	2	4	6	19
GRAND TOTAL	**408**	**2.6**	**4**	**1**	**1**	**2**	**3**	**5**	**6**	**10**

66.5: TOT BILAT SALPINGECTOMY

Type of Patients	Observed Patients	Avg. Stay	Vari-ance	Percentiles						
				10th	25th	50th	75th	90th	95th	99th
1. SINGLE DX										
0–19 Years	0									
20–34	8	2.6	2	1	1	2	3	5	5	5
35–49	6	2.4	3	1	1	2	2	6	6	6
50–64	0									
65+	0									
2. MULTIPLE DX										
0–19 Years	3	2.7	2	1	1	3	4	4	4	4
20–34	31	2.5	3	1	2	2	3	4	5	11
35–49	61	3.3	5	1	2	3	4	7	8	11
50–64	16	3.4	4	1	2	3	5	7	7	7
65+	8	4.6	3	3	4	4	5	6	9	9
TOTAL SINGLE DX	**14**	**2.5**	**2**	**1**	**1**	**2**	**3**	**5**	**6**	**6**
TOTAL MULTIPLE DX	**119**	**3.2**	**4**	**1**	**2**	**3**	**4**	**7**	**7**	**11**
TOTAL										
0–19 Years	3	2.7	2	1	1	3	4	4	4	4
20–34	39	2.5	3	1	2	2	3	4	5	11
35–49	67	3.2	5	1	2	3	4	7	8	11
50–64	16	3.4	4	1	2	3	5	7	7	7
65+	8	4.6	3	3	4	4	5	6	9	9
GRAND TOTAL	**133**	**3.1**	**4**	**1**	**2**	**3**	**4**	**6**	**7**	**11**

66.51: RMVL BOTH FALL TUBES

Type of Patients	Observed Patients	Avg. Stay	Vari-ance	Percentiles						
				10th	25th	50th	75th	90th	95th	99th
1. SINGLE DX										
0–19 Years	0									
20–34	7	2.5	2	1	1	2	4	5	5	5
35–49	2	1.5	<1	1	1	1	2	2	2	2
50–64	0									
65+	0									
2. MULTIPLE DX										
0–19 Years	3	2.7	2	1	1	3	4	4	4	4
20–34	26	2.7	4	1	2	2	3	5	7	11
35–49	55	3.4	5	1	2	3	4	7	8	11
50–64	16	3.4	4	1	2	3	5	7	7	7
65+	7	4.2	<1	3	4	4	5	5	6	6
TOTAL SINGLE DX	**9**	**2.3**	**2**	**1**	**1**	**2**	**3**	**5**	**5**	**5**
TOTAL MULTIPLE DX	**107**	**3.3**	**4**	**1**	**2**	**3**	**4**	**7**	**7**	**11**
TOTAL										
0–19 Years	3	2.7	2	1	1	3	4	4	4	4
20–34	33	2.7	4	1	2	2	3	5	5	11
35–49	57	3.3	5	1	2	3	4	7	8	11
50–64	16	3.4	4	1	2	3	5	7	7	7
65+	7	4.2	<1	3	4	4	5	5	6	6
GRAND TOTAL	**116**	**3.2**	**4**	**1**	**2**	**3**	**4**	**6**	**7**	**11**

66.6: OTHER SALPINGECTOMY

Type of Patients	Observed Patients	Avg. Stay	Vari-ance	Percentiles						
				10th	25th	50th	75th	90th	95th	99th
1. SINGLE DX										
0–19 Years	47	1.7	<1	1	1	1	2	3	3	4
20–34	644	1.8	<1	1	1	2	2	3	3	4
35–49	224	1.9	<1	1	1	2	3	3	4	4
50–64	12	2.3	3	1	1	2	3	4	7	7
65+	0									
2. MULTIPLE DX										
0–19 Years	134	2.2	1	1	1	2	3	4	4	5
20–34	1,530	2.2	2	1	1	2	3	4	4	7
35–49	584	2.2	1	1	1	2	3	4	4	7
50–64	44	2.7	2	1	2	3	3	5	6	6
65+	9	4.4	23	1	2	3	3	10	18	18
TOTAL SINGLE DX	**927**	**1.8**	**<1**	**1**	**1**	**2**	**2**	**3**	**3**	**4**
TOTAL MULTIPLE DX	**2,301**	**2.3**	**2**	**1**	**1**	**2**	**3**	**4**	**4**	**7**
TOTAL										
0–19 Years	181	2.1	1	1	1	2	3	3	4	5
20–34	2,174	2.1	1	1	1	2	3	3	4	6
35–49	808	2.1	1	1	1	2	3	3	4	6
50–64	56	2.6	2	1	2	2	3	4	6	7
65+	9	4.4	23	1	2	3	3	10	18	18
GRAND TOTAL	**3,228**	**2.1**	**1**	**1**	**1**	**2**	**3**	**3**	**4**	**6**

66.61: EXC/DESTR FALL LES

Type of Patients	Observed Patients	Avg. Stay	Vari-ance	Percentiles						
				10th	25th	50th	75th	90th	95th	99th
1. SINGLE DX										
0–19 Years	11	1.6	<1	1	1	1	2	3	4	4
20–34	13	2.1	<1	1	2	2	3	3	3	3
35–49	11	2.1	<1	1	2	2	3	3	3	3
50–64	2	3.0	0	3	3	3	3	3	3	3
65+	0									
2. MULTIPLE DX										
0–19 Years	28	2.2	<1	1	1	2	3	3	4	4
20–34	72	2.5	5	1	1	2	3	4	10	10
35–49	46	2.2	1	1	1	2	3	3	4	5
50–64	8	3.6	3	2	2	3	6	6	6	6
65+	6	6.2	42	1	3	3	10	18	18	18
TOTAL SINGLE DX	**37**	**1.9**	**<1**	**1**	**1**	**2**	**3**	**3**	**3**	**4**
TOTAL MULTIPLE DX	**160**	**2.6**	**4**	**1**	**1**	**2**	**3**	**4**	**6**	**10**
TOTAL										
0–19 Years	39	2.0	<1	1	1	2	3	3	4	4
20–34	85	2.4	4	1	1	2	3	4	6	10
35–49	57	2.2	<1	1	1	2	3	3	4	5
50–64	10	3.5	2	2	2	3	6	6	6	6
65+	6	6.2	42	1	3	3	10	18	18	18
GRAND TOTAL	**197**	**2.4**	**4**	**1**	**1**	**2**	**3**	**4**	**6**	**10**

66.62: RMVL FALL & TUBAL PREG

Type of Patients	Observed Patients	Avg. Stay	Vari-ance	Percentiles						
				10th	25th	50th	75th	90th	95th	99th
1. SINGLE DX										
0–19 Years	27	1.8	<1	1	1	2	2	3	3	4
20–34	583	1.8	<1	1	1	1	2	3	3	4
35–49	197	1.8	<1	1	1	2	2	3	3	5
50–64	10	2.1	4	1	1	1	2	4	7	7
65+	0									
2. MULTIPLE DX										
0–19 Years	92	2.2	1	1	1	2	3	4	4	5
20–34	1,287	2.2	1	1	1	2	3	4	4	6
35–49	461	2.2	1	1	1	2	3	4	4	7
50–64	22	2.6	1	1	2	2	3	4	4	6
65+	0									
TOTAL SINGLE DX	**817**	**1.8**	**<1**	**1**	**1**	**1**	**2**	**3**	**3**	**5**
TOTAL MULTIPLE DX	**1,862**	**2.2**	**1**	**1**	**1**	**2**	**3**	**4**	**4**	**6**
TOTAL										
0–19 Years	119	2.1	1	1	1	2	3	4	4	5
20–34	1,870	2.1	1	1	1	2	3	3	4	5
35–49	658	2.1	1	1	1	2	3	3	4	6
50–64	32	2.4	2	1	1	2	3	4	4	7
65+	0									
GRAND TOTAL	**2,679**	**2.1**	**1**	**1**	**1**	**2**	**3**	**3**	**4**	**5**

66.69: PARTIAL FALL RMVL NEC

Type of Patients	Observed Patients	Avg. Stay	Vari-ance	Percentiles						
				10th	25th	50th	75th	90th	95th	99th
1. SINGLE DX										
0–19 Years	9	1.6	<1	1	1	1	2	3	3	3
20–34	47	2.2	<1	1	2	2	3	3	4	4
35–49	16	2.8	<1	2	2	3	3	4	4	4
50–64	0									
65+	0									
2. MULTIPLE DX										
0–19 Years	14	2.4	<1	2	2	2	3	3	3	4
20–34	147	2.4	2	1	2	2	3	4	5	7
35–49	63	2.3	2	1	1	2	3	4	5	8
50–64	14	2.1	1	1	1	2	3	3	5	5
65+	3	2.6	<1	2	2	3	3	3	3	3
TOTAL SINGLE DX	**72**	**2.2**	**<1**	**1**	**2**	**2**	**3**	**3**	**4**	**4**
TOTAL MULTIPLE DX	**241**	**2.4**	**1**	**1**	**2**	**2**	**3**	**4**	**5**	**7**
TOTAL										
0–19 Years	23	2.1	<1	1	1	2	3	3	3	4
20–34	194	2.4	1	1	2	2	3	4	4	7
35–49	79	2.4	2	1	2	2	3	4	5	8
50–64	14	2.1	1	1	1	2	3	3	5	5
65+	3	2.6	<1	2	2	3	3	3	3	3
GRAND TOTAL	**313**	**2.4**	**1**	**1**	**2**	**2**	**3**	**4**	**4**	**7**

66.7: REPAIR OF FALLOPIAN TUBE

Type of Patients	Observed Patients	Avg. Stay	Vari-ance	Percentiles						
				10th	25th	50th	75th	90th	95th	99th
1. SINGLE DX										
0–19 Years	0									
20–34	26	1.4	<1	1	1	1	2	2	2	3
35–49	29	1.5	<1	1	1	1	2	2	3	3
50–64	6	1.9	<1	1	1	2	2	3	3	3
65+	0									
2. MULTIPLE DX										
0–19 Years	1	1.0	0	1	1	1	1	1	1	1
20–34	38	1.9	<1	1	1	2	2	3	4	5
35–49	29	2.3	2	1	1	2	3	5	6	6
50–64	5	1.8	<1	1	1	2	2	3	3	3
65+	0									
TOTAL SINGLE DX	**61**	**1.5**	**<1**	**1**	**1**	**1**	**2**	**2**	**3**	**3**
TOTAL MULTIPLE DX	**73**	**2.1**	**1**	**1**	**1**	**2**	**2**	**3**	**5**	**6**
TOTAL										
0–19 Years	1	1.0	0	1	1	1	1	1	1	1
20–34	64	1.7	<1	1	1	2	2	3	3	5
35–49	58	1.8	1	1	1	1	2	3	3	6
50–64	11	1.8	<1	1	1	2	2	3	3	3
65+	0									
GRAND TOTAL	**134**	**1.8**	**<1**	**1**	**1**	**2**	**2**	**3**	**3**	**6**

66.79: FALL TUBE REPAIR NEC

Type of Patients	Observed Patients	Avg. Stay	Vari-ance	Percentiles						
				10th	25th	50th	75th	90th	95th	99th
1. SINGLE DX										
0–19 Years	0									
20–34	24	1.3	<1	1	1	1	2	2	2	3
35–49	28	1.4	<1	1	1	1	2	2	3	3
50–64	6	1.9	<1	1	1	2	2	3	3	3
65+	0									
2. MULTIPLE DX										
0–19 Years	1	1.0	0	1	1	1	1	1	1	1
20–34	29	1.9	<1	1	1	2	2	3	3	5
35–49	26	2.0	1	1	1	2	3	3	3	5
50–64	5	1.8	<1	1	1	2	2	3	3	3
65+	0									
TOTAL SINGLE DX	**58**	**1.4**	**<1**	**1**	**1**	**1**	**2**	**2**	**3**	**3**
TOTAL MULTIPLE DX	**61**	**1.9**	**<1**	**1**	**1**	**2**	**2**	**3**	**3**	**5**
TOTAL										
0–19 Years	1	1.0	0	1	1	1	1	1	1	1
20–34	53	1.6	<1	1	1	1	2	2	3	5
35–49	54	1.7	<1	1	1	1	2	3	3	5
50–64	11	1.8	<1	1	1	2	2	3	3	3
65+	0									
GRAND TOTAL	**119**	**1.6**	**<1**	**1**	**1**	**1**	**2**	**3**	**3**	**5**

66.8: FALL TUBE INSUFFLATION

Type of Patients	Observed Patients	Avg. Stay	Vari-ance	Percentiles						
				10th	25th	50th	75th	90th	95th	99th
1. SINGLE DX										
0–19 Years	0									
20–34	1	1.0	0	1	1	1	1	1	1	1
35–49	0									
50–64	0									
65+	0									
2. MULTIPLE DX										
0–19 Years	0									
20–34	1	1.0	0	1	1	1	1	1	1	1
35–49	0									
50–64	1	1.0	0	1	1	1	1	1	1	1
65+	0									
TOTAL SINGLE DX	**1**	**1.0**	**0**	**1**	**1**	**1**	**1**	**1**	**1**	**1**
TOTAL MULTIPLE DX	**2**	**1.0**	**0**	**1**	**1**	**1**	**1**	**1**	**1**	**1**
TOTAL										
0–19 Years	0									
20–34	2	1.0	0	1	1	1	1	1	1	1
35–49	0									
50–64	1	1.0	0	1	1	1	1	1	1	1
65+	0									
GRAND TOTAL	**3**	**1.0**	**0**	**1**	**1**	**1**	**1**	**1**	**1**	**1**

66.9: OTHER FALLOPIAN TUBE OPS

Type of Patients	Observed Patients	Avg. Stay	Vari-ance	Percentiles						
				10th	25th	50th	75th	90th	95th	99th
1. SINGLE DX										
0–19 Years	1	1.0	0	1	1	1	1	1	1	1
20–34	8	1.4	<1	1	1	1	2	2	2	2
35–49	0									
50–64	0									
65+	0									
2. MULTIPLE DX										
0–19 Years	3	1.7	<1	1	1	2	2	2	2	2
20–34	44	2.1	1	1	1	2	2	3	4	6
35–49	23	1.9	<1	1	1	2	2	3	4	5
50–64	1	2.0	0	2	2	2	2	2	2	2
65+	1	2.0	0	2	2	2	2	2	2	2
TOTAL SINGLE DX	**9**	**1.3**	**<1**	**1**	**1**	**1**	**2**	**2**	**2**	**2**
TOTAL MULTIPLE DX	**72**	**2.0**	**1**	**1**	**1**	**2**	**2**	**3**	**4**	**6**
TOTAL										
0–19 Years	4	1.5	<1	1	1	1	2	2	2	2
20–34	52	2.0	1	1	1	2	2	3	4	6
35–49	23	1.9	<1	1	1	2	2	3	4	5
50–64	1	2.0	0	2	2	2	2	2	2	2
65+	1	2.0	0	2	2	2	2	2	2	2
GRAND TOTAL	**81**	**1.9**	**1**	**1**	**1**	**2**	**2**	**3**	**4**	**6**

67.0: CERVICAL CANAL DILATION

Type of Patients	Observed Patients	Avg. Stay	Vari-ance	Percentiles						
				10th	25th	50th	75th	90th	95th	99th
1. SINGLE DX										
0–19 Years	0									
20–34	0									
35–49	0									
50–64	0									
65+	0									
2. MULTIPLE DX										
0–19 Years	0									
20–34	4	1.8	<1	1	1	2	2	3	3	3
35–49	5	1.8	<1	1	2	2	2	2	2	2
50–64	1	1.0	0	1	1	1	1	1	1	1
65+	3	1.0	0	1	1	1	1	1	1	1
TOTAL SINGLE DX	**0**									
TOTAL MULTIPLE DX	**13**	**1.5**	**<1**	**1**	**1**	**1**	**2**	**2**	**3**	**3**
TOTAL										
0–19 Years	0									
20–34	4	1.8	<1	1	1	2	2	3	3	3
35–49	5	1.8	<1	1	2	2	2	2	2	2
50–64	1	1.0	0	1	1	1	1	1	1	1
65+	3	1.0	0	1	1	1	1	1	1	1
GRAND TOTAL	**13**	**1.5**	**<1**	**1**	**1**	**1**	**2**	**2**	**3**	**3**

67.1: CERVICAL DIAGNOSTIC PX

Type of Patients	Observed Patients	Avg. Stay	Vari-ance	Percentiles						
				10th	25th	50th	75th	90th	95th	99th
1. SINGLE DX										
0–19 Years	0									
20–34	3	1.0	0	1	1	1	1	1	1	1
35–49	2	1.0	0	1	1	1	1	1	1	1
50–64	3	1.0	0	1	1	1	1	1	1	1
65+	0									
2. MULTIPLE DX										
0–19 Years	3	2.3	<1	2	2	2	3	3	3	3
20–34	18	8.3	288	1	2	3	7	15	15	82
35–49	58	4.7	28	1	2	3	5	12	16	31
50–64	47	4.4	72	1	1	2	4	8	11	65
65+	32	6.2	19	2	3	5	9	13	15	15
TOTAL SINGLE DX	**8**	**1.0**	**0**	**1**	**1**	**1**	**1**	**1**	**1**	**1**
TOTAL MULTIPLE DX	**158**	**5.3**	**64**	**1**	**2**	**3**	**6**	**12**	**15**	**31**
TOTAL										
0–19 Years	3	2.3	<1	2	2	2	3	3	3	3
20–34	21	7.4	254	1	1	2	7	13	15	82
35–49	60	4.6	28	1	1	3	5	12	16	31
50–64	50	4.2	69	1	1	2	4	8	11	65
65+	32	6.2	19	2	3	5	9	13	15	15
GRAND TOTAL	**166**	**5.1**	**62**	**1**	**2**	**3**	**6**	**12**	**15**	**31**

67.12: CERVICAL BIOPSY NEC

Type of Patients	Observed Patients	Avg. Stay	Vari-ance	Percentiles						
				10th	25th	50th	75th	90th	95th	99th
1. SINGLE DX										
0–19 Years	0									
20–34	2	1.0	0	1	1	1	1	1	1	1
35–49	1	1.0	0	1	1	1	1	1	1	1
50–64	3	1.0	0	1	1	1	1	1	1	1
65+	0									
2. MULTIPLE DX										
0–19 Years	2	2.5	<1	2	2	2	3	3	3	3
20–34	12	9.7	402	1	2	6	7	13	82	82
35–49	38	4.8	34	1	2	3	5	14	16	31
50–64	37	4.6	91	1	1	2	4	8	14	65
65+	27	7.0	20	2	3	5	11	14	15	15
TOTAL SINGLE DX	**6**	**1.0**	**0**	**1**	**1**	**1**	**1**	**1**	**1**	**1**
TOTAL MULTIPLE DX	**116**	**5.7**	**82**	**1**	**2**	**3**	**7**	**13**	**15**	**65**
TOTAL										
0–19 Years	2	2.5	<1	2	2	2	3	3	3	3
20–34	14	8.5	354	1	1	3	7	13	82	82
35–49	39	4.7	33	1	2	3	5	13	16	31
50–64	40	4.4	86	1	1	2	4	7	14	65
65+	27	7.0	20	2	3	5	11	14	15	15
GRAND TOTAL	**122**	**5.5**	**79**	**1**	**2**	**3**	**6**	**13**	**15**	**65**

67.2: CONIZATION OF CERVIX

Type of Patients	Observed Patients	Avg. Stay	Vari-ance	10th	25th	50th	75th	90th	95th	99th
1. SINGLE DX										
0–19 Years	0									
20–34	2	1.0	0	1	1	1	1	1	1	1
35–49	4	1.0	0	1	1	1	1	1	1	1
50–64	2	1.0	0	1	1	1	1	1	1	1
65+	0									
2. MULTIPLE DX										
0–19 Years	0									
20–34	14	1.5	<1	1	1	1	1	3	4	4
35–49	9	3.7	3	1	2	4	5	5	5	5
50–64	11	1.5	2	1	1	1	1	3	6	6
65+	5	2.4	11	1	1	1	1	9	9	9
TOTAL SINGLE DX	8	1.0	0	1	1	1	1	1	1	1
TOTAL MULTIPLE DX	39	2.4	4	1	1	1	4	5	5	9
TOTAL										
0–19 Years	0									
20–34	16	1.5	<1	1	1	1	1	3	3	4
35–49	13	3.3	3	1	1	4	5	5	5	5
50–64	13	1.5	2	1	1	1	1	3	6	6
65+	5	2.4	11	1	1	1	1	9	9	9
GRAND TOTAL	47	2.2	3	1	1	1	4	5	5	9

67.3: EXC/DESTR CERV LES NEC

Type of Patients	Observed Patients	Avg. Stay	Vari-ance	10th	25th	50th	75th	90th	95th	99th
1. SINGLE DX										
0–19 Years	1	3.0	0	3	3	3	3	3	3	3
20–34	12	1.2	<1	1	1	1	1	2	3	3
35–49	5	1.4	<1	1	1	1	1	3	3	3
50–64	2	1.6	<1	1	1	2	2	2	2	2
65+	1	1.0	0	1	1	1	1	1	1	1
2. MULTIPLE DX										
0–19 Years	2	2.2	1	1	1	3	3	3	3	3
20–34	39	2.3	3	1	1	2	3	3	8	8
35–49	53	1.8	1	1	1	2	2	3	3	6
50–64	26	3.1	18	1	1	1	4	6	19	19
65+	14	3.7	12	1	1	2	6	8	13	13
TOTAL SINGLE DX	21	1.3	<1	1	1	1	1	3	3	3
TOTAL MULTIPLE DX	134	2.4	6	1	1	2	3	5	7	19
TOTAL										
0–19 Years	3	2.4	1	1	1	3	3	3	3	3
20–34	51	2.0	3	1	1	1	3	3	6	8
35–49	58	1.8	1	1	1	1	2	3	3	6
50–64	28	3.0	17	1	1	1	4	6	19	19
65+	15	3.5	12	1	1	2	6	8	13	13
GRAND TOTAL	155	2.3	6	1	1	1	3	4	6	13

67.39: CERV LES EXC/DESTR NEC

Type of Patients	Observed Patients	Avg. Stay	Vari-ance	10th	25th	50th	75th	90th	95th	99th
1. SINGLE DX										
0–19 Years	0									
20–34	4	1.2	<1	1	1	1	1	3	3	3
35–49	4	1.5	<1	1	1	1	1	3	3	3
50–64	2	1.6	<1	1	1	2	2	2	2	2
65+	1	1.0	0	1	1	1	1	1	1	1
2. MULTIPLE DX										
0–19 Years	0									
20–34	24	2.3	1	1	1	2	3	3	4	6
35–49	40	1.7	<1	1	1	2	2	3	3	3
50–64	22	3.4	21	1	1	1	4	6	19	19
65+	10	3.9	7	1	2	3	7	8	8	8
TOTAL SINGLE DX	11	1.3	<1	1	1	1	1	3	3	3
TOTAL MULTIPLE DX	96	2.4	6	1	1	2	3	4	6	19
TOTAL										
0–19 Years	0									
20–34	28	2.1	1	1	1	2	3	3	4	6
35–49	44	1.7	<1	1	1	2	2	3	3	3
50–64	24	3.3	19	1	1	1	4	6	19	19
65+	11	3.6	7	1	1	3	5	8	8	8
GRAND TOTAL	107	2.3	6	1	1	2	3	4	6	19

67.4: AMPUTATION OF CERVIX

Type of Patients	Observed Patients	Avg. Stay	Vari-ance	10th	25th	50th	75th	90th	95th	99th
1. SINGLE DX										
0–19 Years	0									
20–34	3	2.3	<1	1	2	3	3	3	3	3
35–49	6	1.7	<1	1	1	2	2	2	2	2
50–64	2	2.0	0	2	2	2	2	2	2	2
65+	2	2.5	<1	2	2	3	3	3	3	3
2. MULTIPLE DX										
0–19 Years	0									
20–34	7	2.2	2	1	1	2	4	4	4	4
35–49	28	2.0	3	1	1	1	3	3	3	11
50–64	27	2.4	2	1	1	3	3	3	4	9
65+	28	3.7	30	1	2	2	3	7	13	37
TOTAL SINGLE DX	13	2.0	<1	1	2	2	2	3	3	3
TOTAL MULTIPLE DX	90	2.7	13	1	1	2	3	4	7	13
TOTAL										
0–19 Years	0									
20–34	10	2.2	1	1	1	2	3	4	4	4
35–49	34	2.0	2	1	1	1	3	3	3	11
50–64	29	2.4	2	1	1	2	3	3	4	9
65+	30	3.7	29	1	2	2	3	7	13	37
GRAND TOTAL	103	2.7	12	1	1	2	3	4	6	13

67.5: INT CERVICAL OS REPAIR

Type of Patients	Observed Patients	Avg. Stay	Vari-ance	Percentiles						
				10th	25th	50th	75th	90th	95th	99th
1. SINGLE DX										
0–19 Years	22	3.1	6	1	1	2	6	6	6	9
20–34	260	2.1	4	1	1	1	3	5	6	10
35–49	42	1.5	1	1	1	1	2	3	4	6
50–64	5	1.0	0	1	1	1	1	1	1	1
65+	0									
2. MULTIPLE DX										
0–19 Years	16	4.9	9	2	2	4	9	9	9	10
20–34	337	5.6	104	1	1	3	6	9	18	59
35–49	169	5.8	180	1	1	2	4	8	21	75
50–64	12	3.3	12	1	1	2	3	6	14	14
65+	1	3.0	0	3	3	3	3	3	3	3
TOTAL SINGLE DX	**329**	**2.1**	**4**	**1**	**1**	**1**	**2**	**5**	**6**	**9**
TOTAL MULTIPLE DX	**535**	**5.6**	**125**	**1**	**1**	**3**	**5**	**9**	**16**	**75**
TOTAL										
0–19 Years	38	3.8	8	1	1	3	6	9	9	10
20–34	597	4.1	64	1	1	2	4	7	11	57
35–49	211	5.0	152	1	1	2	4	7	15	75
50–64	17	2.6	10	1	1	1	3	6	14	14
65+	1	3.0	0	3	3	3	3	3	3	3
GRAND TOTAL	**864**	**4.3**	**83**	**1**	**1**	**2**	**4**	**7**	**12**	**59**

67.59: INT CERVICAL OS REP NEC

Type of Patients	Observed Patients	Avg. Stay	Vari-ance	Percentiles						
				10th	25th	50th	75th	90th	95th	99th
1. SINGLE DX										
0–19 Years	22	3.1	6	1	1	2	6	6	6	9
20–34	250	2.1	4	1	1	1	2	5	6	10
35–49	41	1.5	1	1	1	1	2	2	3	6
50–64	5	1.0	0	1	1	1	1	1	1	1
65+	0									
2. MULTIPLE DX										
0–19 Years	16	4.9	9	2	2	4	9	9	9	10
20–34	328	5.7	106	1	1	3	7	9	18	59
35–49	165	5.8	184	1	1	2	4	8	21	75
50–64	11	3.5	14	1	1	3	3	6	14	14
65+	1	3.0	0	3	3	3	3	3	3	3
TOTAL SINGLE DX	**318**	**2.1**	**4**	**1**	**1**	**1**	**2**	**5**	**6**	**9**
TOTAL MULTIPLE DX	**521**	**5.7**	**128**	**1**	**1**	**3**	**5**	**9**	**16**	**75**
TOTAL										
0–19 Years	38	3.8	8	1	1	3	6	9	9	10
20–34	578	4.2	65	1	1	2	4	7	12	57
35–49	206	5.1	156	1	1	2	4	7	15	75
50–64	16	2.6	10	1	1	1	3	6	14	14
65+	1	3.0	0	3	3	3	3	3	3	3
GRAND TOTAL	**839**	**4.3**	**85**	**1**	**1**	**2**	**4**	**7**	**12**	**59**

67.6: OTHER REPAIR OF CERVIX

Type of Patients	Observed Patients	Avg. Stay	Vari-ance	Percentiles						
				10th	25th	50th	75th	90th	95th	99th
1. SINGLE DX										
0–19 Years	1	1.0	0	1	1	1	1	1	1	1
20–34	2	1.0	0	1	1	1	1	1	1	1
35–49	2	1.0	0	1	1	1	1	1	1	1
50–64	1	1.0	0	1	1	1	1	1	1	1
65+	0									
2. MULTIPLE DX										
0–19 Years	2	2.6	<1	2	2	3	3	3	3	3
20–34	5	2.7	3	1	1	2	5	5	5	5
35–49	6	1.9	<1	1	1	2	3	3	3	3
50–64	2	2.1	2	1	1	3	3	3	3	3
65+	0									
TOTAL SINGLE DX	**6**	**1.0**	**0**	**1**	**1**	**1**	**1**	**1**	**1**	**1**
TOTAL MULTIPLE DX	**15**	**2.2**	**2**	**1**	**1**	**2**	**3**	**5**	**5**	**5**
TOTAL										
0–19 Years	3	1.8	<1	1	1	2	3	3	3	3
20–34	7	2.0	3	1	1	1	2	5	5	5
35–49	8	1.7	<1	1	1	1	3	3	3	3
50–64	3	1.7	1	1	1	1	3	3	3	3
65+	0									
GRAND TOTAL	**21**	**1.9**	**1**	**1**	**1**	**1**	**3**	**3**	**5**	**5**

68.0: HYSTEROTOMY

Type of Patients	Observed Patients	Avg. Stay	Vari-ance	Percentiles						
				10th	25th	50th	75th	90th	95th	99th
1. SINGLE DX										
0–19 Years	0									
20–34	0									
35–49	1	3.0	0	3	3	3	3	3	3	3
50–64	0									
65+	0									
2. MULTIPLE DX										
0–19 Years	0									
20–34	10	3.3	2	1	2	3	5	5	6	6
35–49	5	3.0	2	1	2	3	4	5	5	5
50–64	0									
65+	1	1.0	0	1	1	1	1	1	1	1
TOTAL SINGLE DX	**1**	**3.0**	**0**	**3**	**3**	**3**	**3**	**3**	**3**	**3**
TOTAL MULTIPLE DX	**16**	**3.2**	**2**	**1**	**2**	**3**	**5**	**5**	**5**	**6**
TOTAL										
0–19 Years	0									
20–34	10	3.3	2	1	2	3	5	5	6	6
35–49	6	3.0	2	1	2	3	4	5	5	5
50–64	0									
65+	1	1.0	0	1	1	1	1	1	1	1
GRAND TOTAL	**17**	**3.2**	**2**	**1**	**2**	**3**	**5**	**5**	**5**	**6**

68.1: UTER/ADNEXA DXTIC PX

Type of Patients	Observed Patients	Avg. Stay	Vari-ance	10th	25th	50th	75th	90th	95th	99th
1. SINGLE DX										
0–19 Years	0									
20–34	1	5.0	0	5	5	5	5	5	5	5
35–49	2	5.9	10	3	3	8	8	8	8	8
50–64	1	1.0	0	1	1	1	1	1	1	1
65+	0									
2. MULTIPLE DX										
0–19 Years	1	4.0	0	4	4	4	4	4	4	4
20–34	33	2.8	5	1	1	2	4	5	7	10
35–49	111	3.0	10	1	1	2	4	6	11	17
50–64	67	4.5	37	1	2	2	5	9	21	27
65+	54	5.5	42	1	2	3	6	9	14	35
TOTAL SINGLE DX	**4**	**4.5**	**9**	**1**	**3**	**5**	**8**	**8**	**8**	**8**
TOTAL MULTIPLE DX	**266**	**3.9**	**24**	**1**	**1**	**2**	**4**	**8**	**11**	**34**
TOTAL										
0–19 Years	1	4.0	0	4	4	4	4	4	4	4
20–34	34	2.8	5	1	1	2	4	5	7	10
35–49	113	3.1	10	1	1	2	4	6	11	17
50–64	68	4.5	37	1	2	2	5	9	21	27
65+	54	5.5	42	1	2	3	6	9	14	35
GRAND TOTAL	**270**	**3.9**	**24**	**1**	**1**	**2**	**4**	**8**	**11**	**34**

68.16: CLOSED UTERINE BIOPSY

Type of Patients	Observed Patients	Avg. Stay	Vari-ance	10th	25th	50th	75th	90th	95th	99th
1. SINGLE DX										
0–19 Years	0									
20–34	1	5.0	0	5	5	5	5	5	5	5
35–49	1	8.0	0	8	8	8	8	8	8	8
50–64	1	1.0	0	1	1	1	1	1	1	1
65+	0									
2. MULTIPLE DX										
0–19 Years	1	4.0	0	4	4	4	4	4	4	4
20–34	24	2.9	5	1	1	2	4	5	9	10
35–49	91	3.3	12	1	1	2	4	7	11	17
50–64	51	4.8	39	1	2	2	5	10	12	41
65+	47	6.1	50	2	3	4	7	13	14	35
TOTAL SINGLE DX	**3**	**4.9**	**10**	**1**	**1**	**5**	**8**	**8**	**8**	**8**
TOTAL MULTIPLE DX	**214**	**4.2**	**27**	**1**	**2**	**3**	**5**	**9**	**12**	**34**
TOTAL										
0–19 Years	1	4.0	0	4	4	4	4	4	4	4
20–34	25	2.9	5	1	1	2	4	5	7	10
35–49	92	3.3	12	1	1	2	4	7	11	17
50–64	52	4.8	39	1	2	2	5	9	12	41
65+	47	6.1	50	2	3	4	7	13	14	35
GRAND TOTAL	**217**	**4.2**	**27**	**1**	**2**	**3**	**5**	**9**	**12**	**34**

68.2: UTERINE LES EXC/DESTR

Type of Patients	Observed Patients	Avg. Stay	Vari-ance	10th	25th	50th	75th	90th	95th	99th
1. SINGLE DX										
0–19 Years	2	3.7	<1	3	3	4	4	4	4	4
20–34	250	2.4	<1	1	2	2	3	3	3	4
35–49	378	2.3	<1	1	2	2	3	3	4	6
50–64	72	2.4	2	1	2	2	3	3	4	9
65+	1	4.0	0	4	4	4	4	4	4	4
2. MULTIPLE DX										
0–19 Years	5	2.5	2	1	1	3	3	5	5	5
20–34	997	2.5	1	1	2	2	3	4	4	7
35–49	2,025	2.6	2	1	2	2	3	4	5	8
50–64	372	2.7	12	1	2	2	3	4	5	12
65+	42	5.8	59	1	1	2	6	24	24	24
TOTAL SINGLE DX	**703**	**2.4**	**<1**	**1**	**2**	**2**	**3**	**3**	**4**	**5**
TOTAL MULTIPLE DX	**3,441**	**2.7**	**4**	**1**	**2**	**2**	**3**	**4**	**5**	**9**
TOTAL										
0–19 Years	7	2.8	2	1	2	3	4	4	5	5
20–34	1,247	2.5	1	1	2	2	3	4	4	7
35–49	2,403	2.6	2	1	2	2	3	4	5	8
50–64	444	2.6	10	1	2	2	3	4	5	9
65+	43	5.7	58	1	1	2	6	24	24	24
GRAND TOTAL	**4,144**	**2.6**	**3**	**1**	**2**	**2**	**3**	**4**	**5**	**8**

68.23: ENDOMETRIAL ABLATION

Type of Patients	Observed Patients	Avg. Stay	Vari-ance	10th	25th	50th	75th	90th	95th	99th
1. SINGLE DX										
0–19 Years	0									
20–34	3	1.0	0	1	1	1	1	1	1	1
35–49	2	1.0	0	1	1	1	1	1	1	1
50–64	2	1.0	0	1	1	1	1	1	1	1
65+	0									
2. MULTIPLE DX										
0–19 Years	1	3.0	0	3	3	3	3	3	3	3
20–34	28	2.5	10	1	1	1	2	5	12	12
35–49	121	2.1	6	1	1	1	2	4	6	19
50–64	27	4.6	132	1	1	1	2	8	12	57
65+	4	1.9	3	1	1	1	2	5	5	5
TOTAL SINGLE DX	**7**	**1.0**	**0**	**1**	**1**	**1**	**1**	**1**	**1**	**1**
TOTAL MULTIPLE DX	**181**	**2.5**	**24**	**1**	**1**	**1**	**2**	**5**	**7**	**19**
TOTAL										
0–19 Years	1	3.0	0	3	3	3	3	3	3	3
20–34	31	2.4	9	1	1	1	2	5	12	12
35–49	123	2.1	6	1	1	1	2	4	6	19
50–64	29	4.3	125	1	1	1	2	8	12	57
65+	4	1.9	3	1	1	1	2	5	5	5
GRAND TOTAL	**188**	**2.4**	**23**	**1**	**1**	**1**	**2**	**4**	**7**	**19**

68.29: UTER LES EXC/DESTR NEC

Type of Patients	Observed Patients	Avg. Stay	Vari-ance	10th	25th	50th	75th	90th	95th	99th
1. SINGLE DX										
0–19 Years	2	3.7	<1	3	3	4	4	4	4	4
20–34	246	2.4	<1	2	2	2	3	3	3	4
35–49	376	2.4	<1	1	2	2	3	3	4	6
50–64	70	2.5	2	1	2	2	3	3	4	9
65+	1	4.0	0	4	4	4	4	4	4	4
2. MULTIPLE DX										
0–19 Years	4	2.1	3	1	1	1	2	5	5	5
20–34	968	2.5	1	1	2	2	3	4	4	7
35–49	1,903	2.7	2	1	2	2	3	4	5	8
50–64	345	2.5	3	1	2	2	3	4	5	8
65+	38	6.1	62	1	1	2	8	24	24	24
TOTAL SINGLE DX	**695**	**2.4**	**<1**	**1**	**2**	**2**	**3**	**3**	**4**	**5**
TOTAL MULTIPLE DX	**3,258**	**2.7**	**3**	**1**	**2**	**2**	**3**	**4**	**5**	**8**
TOTAL										
0–19 Years	6	2.8	2	1	1	3	4	5	5	5
20–34	1,214	2.5	1	1	2	2	3	4	4	6
35–49	2,279	2.6	2	1	2	2	3	4	5	8
50–64	415	2.5	2	1	2	2	3	4	5	9
65+	39	6.0	61	1	1	2	8	24	24	24
GRAND TOTAL	**3,953**	**2.6**	**2**	**1**	**2**	**2**	**3**	**4**	**5**	**8**

68.3: SUBTOT ABD HYSTERECTOMY

Type of Patients	Observed Patients	Avg. Stay	Vari-ance	10th	25th	50th	75th	90th	95th	99th
1. SINGLE DX										
0–19 Years	0									
20–34	23	1.7	<1	1	1	2	2	3	3	3
35–49	171	2.2	<1	1	2	2	3	3	3	5
50–64	45	2.0	<1	1	1	2	3	3	3	4
65+	2	2.1	2	1	1	3	3	3	3	3
2. MULTIPLE DX										
0–19 Years	6	4.7	25	1	2	3	3	16	16	16
20–34	356	2.6	3	1	2	2	3	4	5	10
35–49	3,668	2.7	3	1	2	3	3	4	4	9
50–64	1,363	2.9	3	1	2	3	3	4	5	11
65+	153	4.4	13	2	3	3	5	8	12	22
TOTAL SINGLE DX	**241**	**2.1**	**<1**	**1**	**1**	**2**	**3**	**3**	**3**	**4**
TOTAL MULTIPLE DX	**5,546**	**2.8**	**4**	**1**	**2**	**3**	**3**	**4**	**5**	**11**
TOTAL										
0–19 Years	6	4.7	25	1	2	3	3	16	16	16
20–34	379	2.5	3	1	1	2	3	4	5	10
35–49	3,839	2.6	3	1	2	2	3	4	4	9
50–64	1,408	2.8	3	1	2	3	3	4	5	11
65+	155	4.4	13	2	3	3	5	8	12	22
GRAND TOTAL	**5,787**	**2.7**	**4**	**1**	**2**	**3**	**3**	**4**	**5**	**11**

68.4: TOTAL ABD HYSTERECTOMY

Type of Patients	Observed Patients	Avg. Stay	Vari-ance	10th	25th	50th	75th	90th	95th	99th
1. SINGLE DX										
0–19 Years	1	4.0	0	4	4	4	4	4	4	4
20–34	193	2.7	<1	2	2	3	3	3	4	6
35–49	772	2.6	<1	2	2	3	3	3	4	5
50–64	361	2.7	<1	2	2	3	3	4	4	5
65+	88	3.1	<1	2	3	3	3	4	4	5
2. MULTIPLE DX										
0–19 Years	15	2.9	1	2	2	3	3	4	5	6
20–34	3,423	2.9	2	2	2	3	3	4	5	8
35–49	23,906	2.9	2	2	2	3	3	4	5	8
50–64	10,496	3.3	4	2	2	3	3	5	6	11
65+	3,089	4.4	12	2	3	3	5	7	10	18
TOTAL SINGLE DX	**1,415**	**2.7**	**<1**	**2**	**2**	**3**	**3**	**4**	**4**	**5**
TOTAL MULTIPLE DX	**40,929**	**3.2**	**4**	**2**	**2**	**3**	**3**	**4**	**6**	**11**
TOTAL										
0–19 Years	16	2.9	1	2	2	3	3	4	5	6
20–34	3,616	2.9	2	2	2	3	3	4	5	8
35–49	24,678	2.9	2	2	2	3	3	4	5	8
50–64	10,857	3.3	4	2	2	3	3	5	6	11
65+	3,177	4.4	11	2	3	3	5	7	10	18
GRAND TOTAL	**42,344**	**3.1**	**4**	**2**	**2**	**3**	**3**	**4**	**6**	**11**

68.5: VAGINAL HYSTERECTOMY

Type of Patients	Observed Patients	Avg. Stay	Vari-ance	10th	25th	50th	75th	90th	95th	99th
1. SINGLE DX										
0–19 Years	0									
20–34	239	1.7	<1	1	1	2	2	2	3	5
35–49	644	1.7	<1	1	1	2	2	3	3	3
50–64	343	2.0	<1	1	2	2	2	3	3	4
65+	128	2.1	<1	1	1	2	3	3	3	5
2. MULTIPLE DX										
0–19 Years	2	1.5	<1	1	1	1	2	2	2	2
20–34	3,388	1.8	<1	1	1	2	2	3	3	4
35–49	14,418	1.9	<1	1	1	2	2	3	3	4
50–64	6,064	2.0	<1	1	1	2	2	3	3	5
65+	2,646	2.5	2	1	2	2	3	4	4	8
TOTAL SINGLE DX	**1,354**	**1.8**	**<1**	**1**	**1**	**2**	**2**	**3**	**3**	**4**
TOTAL MULTIPLE DX	**26,518**	**2.0**	**1**	**1**	**1**	**2**	**2**	**3**	**3**	**5**
TOTAL										
0–19 Years	2	1.5	<1	1	1	1	2	2	2	2
20–34	3,627	1.8	<1	1	1	2	2	3	3	4
35–49	15,062	1.8	<1	1	1	2	2	3	3	4
50–64	6,407	2.0	<1	1	1	2	2	3	3	5
65+	2,774	2.5	2	1	2	2	3	4	4	8
GRAND TOTAL	**27,872**	**2.0**	**1**	**1**	**1**	**2**	**2**	**3**	**3**	**5**

68.51: LAVH

Type of Patients	Observed Patients	Avg. Stay	Vari-ance	Percentiles 10th	25th	50th	75th	90th	95th	99th
1. SINGLE DX										
0–19 Years	0									
20–34	56	1.6	<1	1	1	2	2	2	3	3
35–49	165	1.6	<1	1	1	2	2	2	3	3
50–64	86	2.0	<1	1	1	2	2	3	4	4
65+	11	1.8	<1	1	1	2	2	2	2	3
2. MULTIPLE DX										
0–19 Years	0									
20–34	1,136	1.7	<1	1	1	2	2	3	3	4
35–49	4,558	1.8	1	1	1	2	2	3	3	5
50–64	1,697	1.9	<1	1	1	2	2	3	3	5
65+	358	2.2	2	1	1	2	3	3	4	7
TOTAL SINGLE DX	**318**	**1.7**	**<1**	**1**	**1**	**2**	**2**	**3**	**3**	**4**
TOTAL MULTIPLE DX	**7,749**	**1.8**	**1**	**1**	**1**	**2**	**2**	**3**	**3**	**5**
TOTAL										
0–19 Years	0									
20–34	1,192	1.7	<1	1	1	2	2	3	3	4
35–49	4,723	1.8	1	1	1	2	2	3	3	5
50–64	1,783	1.9	<1	1	1	2	2	3	3	5
65+	369	2.2	2	1	1	2	3	3	4	7
GRAND TOTAL	**8,067**	**1.8**	**<1**	**1**	**1**	**2**	**2**	**3**	**3**	**5**

68.59: VAGINAL HYSTERECTOMY NEC

Type of Patients	Observed Patients	Avg. Stay	Vari-ance	Percentiles 10th	25th	50th	75th	90th	95th	99th
1. SINGLE DX										
0–19 Years	0									
20–34	183	1.7	<1	1	1	2	2	2	3	5
35–49	479	1.7	<1	1	1	2	2	3	3	3
50–64	257	2.0	<1	1	2	2	2	3	3	4
65+	117	2.1	<1	1	1	2	3	3	3	5
2. MULTIPLE DX										
0–19 Years	2	1.5	<1	1	1	1	2	2	2	2
20–34	2,252	1.8	1	1	1	2	2	3	3	5
35–49	9,860	1.9	<1	1	1	2	2	3	3	4
50–64	4,367	2.1	<1	1	2	2	3	3	3	5
65+	2,288	2.5	2	1	2	2	3	4	4	8
TOTAL SINGLE DX	**1,036**	**1.8**	**<1**	**1**	**1**	**2**	**2**	**3**	**3**	**4**
TOTAL MULTIPLE DX	**18,769**	**2.0**	**1**	**1**	**1**	**2**	**2**	**3**	**3**	**5**
TOTAL										
0–19 Years	2	1.5	<1	1	1	1	2	2	2	2
20–34	2,435	1.8	1	1	1	2	2	3	3	5
35–49	10,339	1.9	<1	1	1	2	2	3	3	4
50–64	4,624	2.1	<1	1	2	2	3	3	3	5
65+	2,405	2.5	2	1	2	2	3	4	4	8
GRAND TOTAL	**19,805**	**2.0**	**1**	**1**	**1**	**2**	**2**	**3**	**3**	**5**

68.6: RADICAL ABD HYSTERECTOMY

Type of Patients	Observed Patients	Avg. Stay	Vari-ance	Percentiles 10th	25th	50th	75th	90th	95th	99th
1. SINGLE DX										
0–19 Years	0									
20–34	27	3.6	<1	3	3	4	4	4	5	5
35–49	36	3.5	<1	2	3	4	4	5	5	6
50–64	17	4.0	2	2	3	4	5	6	6	6
65+	8	5.0	3	3	4	5	5	8	8	8
2. MULTIPLE DX										
0–19 Years	1	5.0	0	5	5	5	5	5	5	5
20–34	87	4.4	3	3	3	4	5	7	8	13
35–49	246	4.5	5	2	3	4	5	7	9	13
50–64	272	5.4	13	3	3	5	6	9	13	18
65+	156	6.0	12	3	4	5	7	9	12	20
TOTAL SINGLE DX	**88**	**3.8**	**1**	**2**	**3**	**4**	**4**	**5**	**6**	**8**
TOTAL MULTIPLE DX	**762**	**5.2**	**10**	**3**	**3**	**4**	**6**	**8**	**10**	**16**
TOTAL										
0–19 Years	1	5.0	0	5	5	5	5	5	5	5
20–34	114	4.2	3	3	3	4	5	6	8	13
35–49	282	4.4	5	2	3	4	5	7	9	13
50–64	289	5.4	13	3	3	4	6	9	12	18
65+	164	6.0	11	3	4	5	7	9	12	20
GRAND TOTAL	**850**	**5.0**	**9**	**3**	**3**	**4**	**6**	**8**	**10**	**15**

68.7: RADICAL VAG HYSTERECTOMY

Type of Patients	Observed Patients	Avg. Stay	Vari-ance	Percentiles 10th	25th	50th	75th	90th	95th	99th
1. SINGLE DX										
0–19 Years	0									
20–34	1	3.0	0	3	3	3	3	3	3	3
35–49	4	2.2	<1	2	2	2	2	3	3	3
50–64	3	3.2	<1	2	2	3	4	4	4	4
65+	1	4.0	0	4	4	4	4	4	4	4
2. MULTIPLE DX										
0–19 Years	0									
20–34	18	2.9	2	1	2	3	4	4	4	7
35–49	35	2.2	3	1	1	2	2	3	4	14
50–64	23	3.5	14	2	2	2	3	4	17	17
65+	12	4.4	9	1	2	5	7	8	10	10
TOTAL SINGLE DX	**9**	**2.8**	**<1**	**2**	**2**	**3**	**4**	**4**	**4**	**4**
TOTAL MULTIPLE DX	**88**	**3.0**	**7**	**1**	**2**	**2**	**3**	**5**	**8**	**17**
TOTAL										
0–19 Years	0									
20–34	19	2.9	2	1	2	3	4	4	4	7
35–49	39	2.2	3	1	1	2	2	3	4	14
50–64	26	3.4	13	2	2	3	3	4	17	17
65+	13	4.4	9	1	2	4	7	8	10	10
GRAND TOTAL	**97**	**3.0**	**7**	**1**	**2**	**2**	**3**	**5**	**8**	**17**

68.8: PELVIC EVISCERATION

Type of Patients	Observed Patients	Avg. Stay	Vari-ance	Percentiles 10th	25th	50th	75th	90th	95th	99th
1. SINGLE DX										
0–19 Years	0									
20–34	0									
35–49	1	18.0	0	18	18	18	18	18	18	18
50–64	0									
65+	0									
2. MULTIPLE DX										
0–19 Years	1	25.0	0	25	25	25	25	25	25	25
20–34	5	22.2	69	7	18	25	29	29	29	29
35–49	18	12.6	36	8	8	10	15	19	26	27
50–64	58	13.5	65	6	9	11	15	27	31	47
65+	47	18.0	104	8	11	15	23	34	47	47
TOTAL SINGLE DX	**1**	**18.0**	**0**	**18**	**18**	**18**	**18**	**18**	**18**	**18**
TOTAL MULTIPLE DX	**129**	**15.7**	**84**	**7**	**9**	**13**	**19**	**27**	**34**	**47**
TOTAL										
0–19 Years	1	25.0	0	25	25	25	25	25	25	25
20–34	5	22.2	69	7	18	25	29	29	29	29
35–49	19	12.8	35	8	8	11	17	19	26	27
50–64	58	13.5	65	6	9	11	15	27	31	47
65+	47	18.0	104	8	11	15	23	34	47	47
GRAND TOTAL	**130**	**15.7**	**83**	**7**	**9**	**13**	**19**	**27**	**34**	**47**

68.9: HYSTERECTOMY NEC & NOS

Type of Patients	Observed Patients	Avg. Stay	Vari-ance	Percentiles 10th	25th	50th	75th	90th	95th	99th
1. SINGLE DX										
0–19 Years	0									
20–34	0									
35–49	3	2.6	<1	2	2	3	3	3	3	3
50–64	2	2.6	<1	2	2	3	3	3	3	3
65+	0									
2. MULTIPLE DX										
0–19 Years	2	29.1	385	3	3	40	40	40	40	40
20–34	19	3.1	2	1	2	3	4	5	7	7
35–49	60	3.7	54	1	2	3	4	4	4	60
50–64	34	4.0	29	1	2	3	3	5	11	27
65+	5	3.9	21	1	1	3	3	14	14	14
TOTAL SINGLE DX	**5**	**2.6**	**<1**	**2**	**2**	**3**	**3**	**3**	**3**	**3**
TOTAL MULTIPLE DX	**120**	**4.2**	**54**	**1**	**2**	**3**	**4**	**4**	**7**	**40**
TOTAL										
0–19 Years	2	29.1	385	3	3	40	40	40	40	40
20–34	19	3.1	2	1	2	3	4	5	7	7
35–49	63	3.6	52	1	2	3	4	4	4	60
50–64	36	3.9	28	1	2	3	3	5	11	27
65+	5	3.9	21	1	1	3	3	14	14	14
GRAND TOTAL	**125**	**4.1**	**52**	**1**	**2**	**3**	**3**	**4**	**7**	**40**

69.0: UTERINE D&C

Type of Patients	Observed Patients	Avg. Stay	Vari-ance	Percentiles 10th	25th	50th	75th	90th	95th	99th
1. SINGLE DX										
0–19 Years	106	1.3	<1	1	1	1	1	2	2	3
20–34	902	1.3	<1	1	1	1	1	2	3	4
35–49	264	1.2	<1	1	1	1	1	2	2	5
50–64	36	1.2	<1	1	1	1	1	2	2	4
65+	4	3.0	3	1	2	2	4	5	5	5
2. MULTIPLE DX										
0–19 Years	254	2.5	3	1	1	2	3	5	5	7
20–34	2,143	2.4	6	1	1	2	3	4	6	12
35–49	1,158	2.3	6	1	1	2	3	4	6	15
50–64	230	2.9	14	1	1	2	3	5	9	20
65+	172	5.5	31	1	2	4	7	12	15	28
TOTAL SINGLE DX	**1,312**	**1.3**	**<1**	**1**	**1**	**1**	**1**	**2**	**3**	**4**
TOTAL MULTIPLE DX	**3,957**	**2.6**	**8**	**1**	**1**	**2**	**3**	**4**	**7**	**15**
TOTAL										
0–19 Years	360	2.2	3	1	1	2	3	4	5	7
20–34	3,045	2.1	5	1	1	2	2	3	5	11
35–49	1,422	2.1	6	1	1	1	2	4	5	14
50–64	266	2.7	12	1	1	2	3	5	9	20
65+	176	5.5	31	1	2	4	7	12	15	28
GRAND TOTAL	**5,269**	**2.3**	**6**	**1**	**1**	**2**	**3**	**4**	**6**	**13**

69.01: D&C FOR TERM OF PREG

Type of Patients	Observed Patients	Avg. Stay	Vari-ance	Percentiles 10th	25th	50th	75th	90th	95th	99th
1. SINGLE DX										
0–19 Years	4	1.0	0	1	1	1	1	1	1	1
20–34	21	1.2	<1	1	1	1	1	2	2	2
35–49	5	1.2	<1	1	1	1	1	2	2	2
50–64	0									
65+	0									
2. MULTIPLE DX										
0–19 Years	6	4.2	3	2	2	5	5	8	8	8
20–34	66	2.4	7	1	1	1	3	5	7	20
35–49	21	3.5	14	1	1	2	3	9	14	14
50–64	5	2.4	<1	1	2	2	3	4	4	4
65+	0									
TOTAL SINGLE DX	**30**	**1.1**	**<1**	**1**	**1**	**1**	**1**	**2**	**2**	**2**
TOTAL MULTIPLE DX	**98**	**2.7**	**8**	**1**	**1**	**2**	**3**	**5**	**8**	**14**
TOTAL										
0–19 Years	10	3.1	5	1	1	2	5	5	8	8
20–34	87	2.1	6	1	1	1	2	4	6	20
35–49	26	3.1	12	1	1	2	3	8	14	14
50–64	5	2.4	<1	1	2	2	3	4	4	4
65+	0									
GRAND TOTAL	**128**	**2.4**	**7**	**1**	**1**	**1**	**3**	**5**	**8**	**14**

69.02: D&C POST DEL OR AB

Type of Patients	Observed Patients	Avg. Stay	Vari-ance	10th	25th	50th	75th	90th	95th	99th
1. SINGLE DX										
0–19 Years	94	1.3	<1	1	1	1	2	2	2	3
20–34	803	1.3	<1	1	1	1	1	2	3	4
35–49	220	1.2	<1	1	1	1	1	2	2	4
50–64	19	1.1	<1	1	1	1	1	1	2	2
65+	0									
2. MULTIPLE DX										
0–19 Years	213	2.5	3	1	1	2	3	4	5	7
20–34	1,805	2.5	6	1	1	2	3	4	5	12
35–49	609	2.3	4	1	1	2	3	4	5	13
50–64	20	3.0	29	1	1	2	3	3	4	29
65+	0									
TOTAL SINGLE DX	**1,136**	**1.3**	**<1**	**1**	**1**	**1**	**1**	**2**	**3**	**4**
TOTAL MULTIPLE DX	**2,647**	**2.4**	**5**	**1**	**1**	**2**	**3**	**4**	**5**	**12**
TOTAL										
0–19 Years	307	2.2	3	1	1	2	3	4	5	7
20–34	2,608	2.1	5	1	1	2	3	3	4	11
35–49	829	2.0	3	1	1	1	2	4	5	11
50–64	39	2.0	15	1	1	1	2	3	3	29
65+	0									
GRAND TOTAL	**3,783**	**2.1**	**4**	**1**	**1**	**2**	**3**	**4**	**5**	**11**

69.09: D&C NEC

Type of Patients	Observed Patients	Avg. Stay	Vari-ance	10th	25th	50th	75th	90th	95th	99th
1. SINGLE DX										
0–19 Years	8	1.1	<1	1	1	1	1	1	2	2
20–34	78	1.5	<1	1	1	1	2	3	3	4
35–49	39	1.3	<1	1	1	1	1	2	3	5
50–64	17	1.4	<1	1	1	1	1	3	4	4
65+	4	3.0	3	1	2	2	4	5	5	5
2. MULTIPLE DX										
0–19 Years	35	2.5	2	1	1	2	4	5	5	6
20–34	272	2.3	6	1	1	1	3	4	7	12
35–49	528	2.3	9	1	1	1	3	4	6	17
50–64	205	3.0	13	1	1	2	3	6	9	18
65+	172	5.5	31	1	2	4	7	12	15	28
TOTAL SINGLE DX	**146**	**1.4**	**<1**	**1**	**1**	**1**	**2**	**3**	**3**	**5**
TOTAL MULTIPLE DX	**1,212**	**2.9**	**13**	**1**	**1**	**2**	**3**	**6**	**9**	**18**
TOTAL										
0–19 Years	43	2.2	2	1	1	2	3	4	5	6
20–34	350	2.1	5	1	1	1	2	4	6	12
35–49	567	2.3	8	1	1	1	2	4	6	17
50–64	222	2.9	12	1	1	2	3	5	9	18
65+	176	5.5	31	1	2	4	7	12	15	28
GRAND TOTAL	**1,358**	**2.8**	**12**	**1**	**1**	**2**	**3**	**6**	**8**	**18**

69.1: EXC/DESTR UTER/SUPP LES

Type of Patients	Observed Patients	Avg. Stay	Vari-ance	10th	25th	50th	75th	90th	95th	99th
1. SINGLE DX										
0–19 Years	7	2.1	1	1	1	2	3	4	4	4
20–34	25	2.2	<1	1	1	2	3	4	4	4
35–49	11	2.0	2	1	1	1	4	4	4	4
50–64	1	3.0	0	3	3	3	3	3	3	3
65+	1	5.0	0	5	5	5	5	5	5	5
2. MULTIPLE DX										
0–19 Years	22	2.4	2	1	1	3	3	5	5	6
20–34	92	2.3	1	1	1	2	3	4	4	5
35–49	59	2.6	5	1	2	2	3	4	5	19
50–64	11	4.5	9	1	2	4	5	9	9	9
65+	10	2.6	3	1	2	2	3	4	4	9
TOTAL SINGLE DX	**45**	**2.3**	**2**	**1**	**1**	**2**	**3**	**4**	**5**	**5**
TOTAL MULTIPLE DX	**194**	**2.5**	**3**	**1**	**2**	**2**	**3**	**4**	**5**	**9**
TOTAL										
0–19 Years	29	2.4	2	1	1	3	3	4	5	6
20–34	117	2.2	1	1	1	2	3	4	4	5
35–49	70	2.5	5	1	2	2	3	4	4	19
50–64	12	4.4	8	1	2	3	5	9	9	9
65+	11	3.0	4	1	2	2	4	5	5	9
GRAND TOTAL	**239**	**2.5**	**3**	**1**	**1**	**2**	**3**	**4**	**5**	**9**

69.19: EXC UTER/SUPP STRUCT NEC

Type of Patients	Observed Patients	Avg. Stay	Vari-ance	10th	25th	50th	75th	90th	95th	99th
1. SINGLE DX										
0–19 Years	7	2.1	1	1	1	2	3	4	4	4
20–34	25	2.2	<1	1	1	2	3	4	4	4
35–49	11	2.0	2	1	1	1	4	4	4	4
50–64	1	3.0	0	3	3	3	3	3	3	3
65+	1	5.0	0	5	5	5	5	5	5	5
2. MULTIPLE DX										
0–19 Years	22	2.4	2	1	1	3	3	5	5	6
20–34	92	2.3	1	1	1	2	3	4	4	5
35–49	59	2.6	5	1	2	2	3	4	5	19
50–64	11	4.5	9	1	2	4	5	9	9	9
65+	10	2.6	3	1	2	2	3	4	4	9
TOTAL SINGLE DX	**45**	**2.3**	**2**	**1**	**1**	**2**	**3**	**4**	**5**	**5**
TOTAL MULTIPLE DX	**194**	**2.5**	**3**	**1**	**2**	**2**	**3**	**4**	**5**	**9**
TOTAL										
0–19 Years	29	2.4	2	1	1	3	3	4	5	6
20–34	117	2.2	1	1	1	2	3	4	4	5
35–49	70	2.5	5	1	2	2	3	4	4	19
50–64	12	4.4	8	1	2	3	5	9	9	9
65+	11	3.0	4	1	2	2	4	5	5	9
GRAND TOTAL	**239**	**2.5**	**3**	**1**	**1**	**2**	**3**	**4**	**5**	**9**

69.2: UTERINE SUPP STRUCT REP

Type of Patients	Observed Patients	Avg. Stay	Vari-ance	Percentiles 10th	25th	50th	75th	90th	95th	99th
1. SINGLE DX										
0–19 Years	0									
20–34	1	1.0	0	1	1	1	1	1	1	1
35–49	3	1.3	<1	1	1	1	2	2	2	2
50–64	1	3.0	0	3	3	3	3	3	3	3
65+	1	2.0	0	2	2	2	2	2	2	2
2. MULTIPLE DX										
0–19 Years	0									
20–34	18	2.3	1	1	1	2	3	3	4	6
35–49	7	2.0	<1	2	2	2	2	2	3	3
50–64	11	2.4	5	1	1	2	2	6	9	9
65+	11	2.5	7	1	1	1	2	5	11	11
TOTAL SINGLE DX	**6**	**1.7**	**<1**	**1**	**1**	**2**	**2**	**3**	**3**	**3**
TOTAL MULTIPLE DX	**47**	**2.3**	**3**	**1**	**1**	**2**	**2**	**4**	**6**	**11**
TOTAL										
0–19 Years	0									
20–34	19	2.2	1	1	1	2	3	3	4	6
35–49	10	1.9	<1	1	2	2	2	2	3	3
50–64	12	2.5	4	1	1	2	2	6	6	9
65+	12	2.4	6	1	1	1	2	5	11	11
GRAND TOTAL	**53**	**2.3**	**3**	**1**	**1**	**2**	**2**	**4**	**6**	**11**

69.3: PARACERV UTERINE DENERV

Type of Patients	Observed Patients	Avg. Stay	Vari-ance	Percentiles 10th	25th	50th	75th	90th	95th	99th
1. SINGLE DX										
0–19 Years	0									
20–34	0									
35–49	0									
50–64	0									
65+	0									
2. MULTIPLE DX										
0–19 Years	0									
20–34	0									
35–49	1	1.0	0	1	1	1	1	1	1	1
50–64	1	2.0	0	2	2	2	2	2	2	2
65+	0									
TOTAL SINGLE DX	**0**									
TOTAL MULTIPLE DX	**2**	**1.5**	**<1**	**1**	**1**	**2**	**2**	**2**	**2**	**2**
TOTAL										
0–19 Years	0									
20–34	0									
35–49	1	1.0	0	1	1	1	1	1	1	1
50–64	1	2.0	0	2	2	2	2	2	2	2
65+	0									
GRAND TOTAL	**2**	**1.5**	**<1**	**1**	**1**	**2**	**2**	**2**	**2**	**2**

69.4: UTERINE REPAIR

Type of Patients	Observed Patients	Avg. Stay	Vari-ance	Percentiles 10th	25th	50th	75th	90th	95th	99th
1. SINGLE DX										
0–19 Years	0									
20–34	1	3.0	0	3	3	3	3	3	3	3
35–49	0									
50–64	0									
65+	0									
2. MULTIPLE DX										
0–19 Years	4	2.8	<1	2	3	3	3	3	3	3
20–34	18	3.2	6	1	2	2	4	8	9	9
35–49	4	3.0	1	2	2	4	4	4	4	4
50–64	2	8.2	34	3	3	12	12	12	12	12
65+	0									
TOTAL SINGLE DX	**1**	**3.0**	**0**	**3**	**3**	**3**	**3**	**3**	**3**	**3**
TOTAL MULTIPLE DX	**28**	**3.4**	**7**	**1**	**2**	**3**	**4**	**8**	**9**	**12**
TOTAL										
0–19 Years	4	2.8	<1	2	3	3	3	3	3	3
20–34	19	3.2	5	1	2	2	4	8	9	9
35–49	4	3.0	1	2	2	4	4	4	4	4
50–64	2	8.2	34	3	3	12	12	12	12	12
65+	0									
GRAND TOTAL	**29**	**3.4**	**6**	**1**	**2**	**3**	**4**	**8**	**9**	**12**

69.5: ASP CURETTAGE UTERUS

Type of Patients	Observed Patients	Avg. Stay	Vari-ance	Percentiles 10th	25th	50th	75th	90th	95th	99th
1. SINGLE DX										
0–19 Years	111	1.3	<1	1	1	1	1	2	3	5
20–34	922	1.2	<1	1	1	1	1	2	2	3
35–49	328	1.2	<1	1	1	1	1	2	2	3
50–64	28	1.0	<1	1	1	1	1	1	1	2
65+	0									
2. MULTIPLE DX										
0–19 Years	111	2.4	5	1	1	2	2	4	7	13
20–34	970	2.3	5	1	1	2	3	4	6	13
35–49	371	2.4	9	1	1	1	3	5	7	19
50–64	41	3.6	23	1	1	2	3	7	11	29
65+	8	6.3	13	2	3	5	11	11	12	12
TOTAL SINGLE DX	**1,389**	**1.2**	**<1**	**1**	**1**	**1**	**1**	**2**	**2**	**3**
TOTAL MULTIPLE DX	**1,501**	**2.4**	**6**	**1**	**1**	**2**	**3**	**4**	**7**	**13**
TOTAL										
0–19 Years	222	1.9	4	1	1	1	2	4	5	11
20–34	1,892	1.8	3	1	1	1	2	3	4	10
35–49	699	1.8	5	1	1	1	2	3	5	10
50–64	69	2.4	14	1	1	1	3	4	7	29
65+	8	6.3	13	2	3	5	11	11	12	12
GRAND TOTAL	**2,890**	**1.8**	**4**	**1**	**1**	**1**	**2**	**3**	**5**	**11**

69.51: ASP CURETTAGE-PREG TERM

Type of Patients	Observed Patients	Avg. Stay	Vari-ance	Percentiles						
				10th	25th	50th	75th	90th	95th	99th
1. SINGLE DX										
0–19 Years	3	1.3	<1	1	1	1	2	2	2	2
20–34	19	2.0	3	1	1	1	2	4	4	8
35–49	5	1.0	0	1	1	1	1	1	1	1
50–64	1	1.0	0	1	1	1	1	1	1	1
65+	0									
2. MULTIPLE DX										
0–19 Years	8	3.5	5	1	2	3	5	7	9	9
20–34	88	4.1	20	1	1	2	5	10	15	20
35–49	30	3.8	13	1	1	2	6	8	11	18
50–64	1	2.0	0	2	2	2	2	2	2	2
65+	0									
TOTAL SINGLE DX	**28**	**1.7**	**2**	**1**	**1**	**1**	**2**	**4**	**4**	**8**
TOTAL MULTIPLE DX	**127**	**4.0**	**16**	**1**	**1**	**2**	**5**	**9**	**12**	**19**
TOTAL										
0–19 Years	11	3.0	5	1	1	2	4	7	9	9
20–34	107	3.8	18	1	1	2	4	9	14	19
35–49	35	3.4	12	1	1	2	5	8	8	18
50–64	2	1.5	<1	1	1	2	2	2	2	2
65+	0									
GRAND TOTAL	**155**	**3.6**	**15**	**1**	**1**	**2**	**4**	**8**	**12**	**19**

69.52: ASP CURETTE POST DEL/AB

Type of Patients	Observed Patients	Avg. Stay	Vari-ance	Percentiles						
				10th	25th	50th	75th	90th	95th	99th
1. SINGLE DX										
0–19 Years	98	1.3	<1	1	1	1	1	2	3	5
20–34	820	1.2	<1	1	1	1	1	2	2	3
35–49	290	1.1	<1	1	1	1	1	1	2	3
50–64	24	1.0	<1	1	1	1	1	1	1	2
65+	0									
2. MULTIPLE DX										
0–19 Years	84	2.1	3	1	1	2	2	4	4	11
20–34	797	2.1	3	1	1	2	3	4	5	10
35–49	267	2.3	8	1	1	1	3	4	7	19
50–64	19	2.6	2	1	2	3	3	3	6	7
65+	0									
TOTAL SINGLE DX	**1,232**	**1.2**	**<1**	**1**	**1**	**1**	**1**	**2**	**2**	**3**
TOTAL MULTIPLE DX	**1,167**	**2.2**	**4**	**1**	**1**	**2**	**3**	**4**	**5**	**11**
TOTAL										
0–19 Years	182	1.7	2	1	1	1	2	3	4	7
20–34	1,617	1.7	2	1	1	1	2	3	4	8
35–49	557	1.7	4	1	1	1	2	3	4	9
50–64	43	1.7	1	1	1	1	2	3	3	7
65+	0									
GRAND TOTAL	**2,399**	**1.7**	**3**	**1**	**1**	**1**	**2**	**3**	**4**	**8**

69.59: ASP CURETTAGE UTERUS NEC

Type of Patients	Observed Patients	Avg. Stay	Vari-ance	Percentiles						
				10th	25th	50th	75th	90th	95th	99th
1. SINGLE DX										
0–19 Years	10	1.3	<1	1	1	1	1	2	3	3
20–34	83	1.3	<1	1	1	1	1	2	2	3
35–49	33	1.6	<1	1	1	1	2	3	3	3
50–64	3	1.0	0	1	1	1	1	1	1	1
65+	0									
2. MULTIPLE DX										
0–19 Years	19	3.3	13	1	1	2	3	9	13	13
20–34	85	1.9	2	1	1	1	2	4	4	7
35–49	74	2.2	9	1	1	1	2	4	5	10
50–64	21	4.6	42	1	1	2	4	11	18	29
65+	8	6.3	13	2	3	5	11	11	12	12
TOTAL SINGLE DX	**129**	**1.4**	**<1**	**1**	**1**	**1**	**2**	**2**	**3**	**3**
TOTAL MULTIPLE DX	**207**	**2.6**	**11**	**1**	**1**	**2**	**3**	**5**	**9**	**18**
TOTAL										
0–19 Years	29	2.7	10	1	1	1	2	9	13	13
20–34	168	1.6	1	1	1	1	2	3	4	7
35–49	107	2.0	6	1	1	1	2	3	5	10
50–64	24	4.1	37	1	1	2	4	11	18	29
65+	8	6.3	13	2	3	5	11	11	12	12
GRAND TOTAL	**336**	**2.1**	**7**	**1**	**1**	**1**	**2**	**4**	**6**	**13**

69.6: MENSTRUAL EXTRACTION

Type of Patients	Observed Patients	Avg. Stay	Vari-ance	Percentiles						
				10th	25th	50th	75th	90th	95th	99th
1. SINGLE DX										
0–19 Years	0									
20–34	0									
35–49	0									
50–64	0									
65+	0									
2. MULTIPLE DX										
0–19 Years	0									
20–34	0									
35–49	0									
50–64	0									
65+	0									
TOTAL SINGLE DX	**0**									
TOTAL MULTIPLE DX	**0**									
TOTAL										
0–19 Years	0									
20–34	0									
35–49	0									
50–64	0									
65+	0									
GRAND TOTAL	**0**									

69.7: INSERTION OF IUD

Type of Patients	Observed Patients	Avg. Stay	Vari-ance	10th	25th	50th	75th	90th	95th	99th
1. SINGLE DX										
0–19 Years	0									
20–34	0									
35–49	0									
50–64	0									
65+	0									
2. MULTIPLE DX										
0–19 Years	0									
20–34	0									
35–49	0									
50–64	0									
65+	0									
TOTAL SINGLE DX	**0**									
TOTAL MULTIPLE DX	**0**									
TOTAL										
0–19 Years	0									
20–34	0									
35–49	0									
50–64	0									
65+	0									
GRAND TOTAL	**0**									

69.9: OTHER OPS UTERUS/ADNEXA

Type of Patients	Observed Patients	Avg. Stay	Vari-ance	10th	25th	50th	75th	90th	95th	99th
1. SINGLE DX										
0–19 Years	3	2.0	<1	1	1	2	3	3	3	3
20–34	35	1.8	4	1	1	1	2	3	5	12
35–49	17	1.5	<1	1	1	1	2	3	3	3
50–64	1	3.0	0	3	3	3	3	3	3	3
65+	1	2.0	0	2	2	2	2	2	2	2
2. MULTIPLE DX										
0–19 Years	10	2.3	2	1	1	2	3	5	5	5
20–34	110	6.3	239	1	1	2	3	13	40	90
35–49	46	4.4	69	1	1	2	4	7	19	57
50–64	7	1.9	<1	1	1	1	3	3	3	3
65+	6	2.7	<1	2	2	3	3	3	3	3
TOTAL SINGLE DX	**57**	**1.7**	**2**	**1**	**1**	**1**	**2**	**3**	**4**	**12**
TOTAL MULTIPLE DX	**179**	**5.3**	**169**	**1**	**1**	**2**	**3**	**9**	**19**	**75**
TOTAL										
0–19 Years	13	2.3	2	1	1	2	3	5	5	5
20–34	145	5.5	198	1	1	2	3	10	24	75
35–49	63	3.5	51	1	1	2	3	6	10	57
50–64	8	2.0	<1	1	1	2	3	3	3	3
65+	7	2.6	<1	2	2	3	3	3	3	3
GRAND TOTAL	**236**	**4.6**	**136**	**1**	**1**	**2**	**3**	**6**	**14**	**75**

69.93: INSERTION OF LAMINARIA

Type of Patients	Observed Patients	Avg. Stay	Vari-ance	10th	25th	50th	75th	90th	95th	99th
1. SINGLE DX										
0–19 Years	2	1.9	2	1	1	1	3	3	3	3
20–34	15	1.9	1	1	1	2	2	4	5	5
35–49	6	1.3	<1	1	1	1	2	2	2	2
50–64	0									
65+	0									
2. MULTIPLE DX										
0–19 Years	7	1.7	<1	1	1	2	2	2	3	3
20–34	42	1.8	1	1	1	1	2	3	4	5
35–49	20	2.2	1	1	1	2	2	4	5	6
50–64	1	3.0	0	3	3	3	3	3	3	3
65+	0									
TOTAL SINGLE DX	**23**	**1.6**	**<1**	**1**	**1**	**1**	**2**	**3**	**4**	**5**
TOTAL MULTIPLE DX	**70**	**1.9**	**1**	**1**	**1**	**2**	**2**	**3**	**4**	**5**
TOTAL										
0–19 Years	9	1.7	<1	1	1	2	2	3	3	3
20–34	57	1.8	1	1	1	1	2	3	4	5
35–49	26	1.9	1	1	1	2	2	3	5	6
50–64	1	3.0	0	3	3	3	3	3	3	3
65+	0									
GRAND TOTAL	**93**	**1.8**	**1**	**1**	**1**	**2**	**2**	**3**	**4**	**5**

69.96: RMVL CERVICAL CERCLAGE

Type of Patients	Observed Patients	Avg. Stay	Vari-ance	10th	25th	50th	75th	90th	95th	99th
1. SINGLE DX										
0–19 Years	1	2.0	0	2	2	2	2	2	2	2
20–34	19	1.7	6	1	1	1	1	2	7	12
35–49	5	1.4	<1	1	1	1	1	3	3	3
50–64	0									
65+	0									
2. MULTIPLE DX										
0–19 Years	1	2.0	0	2	2	2	2	2	2	2
20–34	64	11.6	473	1	2	2	12	40	75	>99
35–49	17	9.0	191	1	2	4	10	19	57	57
50–64	2	2.6	<1	2	2	3	3	3	3	3
65+	0									
TOTAL SINGLE DX	**25**	**1.7**	**5**	**1**	**1**	**1**	**1**	**2**	**7**	**12**
TOTAL MULTIPLE DX	**84**	**10.7**	**398**	**1**	**2**	**2**	**10**	**35**	**75**	**90**
TOTAL										
0–19 Years	2	2.0	0	2	2	2	2	2	2	2
20–34	83	9.4	382	1	1	2	6	34	75	90
35–49	22	7.5	163	1	1	3	7	19	19	57
50–64	2	2.6	<1	2	2	3	3	3	3	3
65+	0									
GRAND TOTAL	**109**	**8.7**	**325**	**1**	**1**	**2**	**6**	**19**	**75**	**90**

70.0: CULDOCENTESIS

Type of Patients	Observed Patients	Avg. Stay	Vari-ance	10th	25th	50th	75th	90th	95th	99th
1. SINGLE DX										
0–19 Years	0									
20–34	5	2.6	2	2	2	2	2	5	5	5
35–49	0									
50–64	1	1.0	0	1	1	1	1	1	1	1
65+	0									
2. MULTIPLE DX										
0–19 Years	2	7.1	19	3	3	10	10	10	10	10
20–34	17	4.4	6	1	2	4	7	7	7	7
35–49	11	5.4	15	2	3	3	6	12	13	13
50–64	6	7.9	15	3	5	7	10	15	15	15
65+	1	4.0	0	4	4	4	4	4	4	4
TOTAL SINGLE DX	**6**	**2.4**	**2**	**1**	**2**	**2**	**2**	**5**	**5**	**5**
TOTAL MULTIPLE DX	**37**	**5.3**	**11**	**2**	**3**	**4**	**7**	**10**	**12**	**15**
TOTAL										
0–19 Years	2	7.1	19	3	3	10	10	10	10	10
20–34	22	4.1	5	2	2	4	7	7	7	7
35–49	11	5.4	15	2	3	3	6	12	13	13
50–64	7	7.1	19	1	5	6	10	15	15	15
65+	1	4.0	0	4	4	4	4	4	4	4
GRAND TOTAL	**43**	**5.0**	**11**	**2**	**2**	**4**	**7**	**10**	**12**	**15**

70.1: INC VAGINA & CUL-DE-SAC

Type of Patients	Observed Patients	Avg. Stay	Vari-ance	10th	25th	50th	75th	90th	95th	99th
1. SINGLE DX										
0–19 Years	2	1.0	0	1	1	1	1	1	1	1
20–34	9	3.4	8	1	1	2	6	8	9	9
35–49	21	3.3	2	1	3	4	4	5	5	6
50–64	4	2.9	1	2	2	2	3	5	5	5
65+	1	1.0	0	1	1	1	1	1	1	1
2. MULTIPLE DX										
0–19 Years	18	3.4	11	1	1	2	4	9	13	13
20–34	67	4.2	11	1	2	3	5	10	12	15
35–49	101	5.4	17	2	3	5	6	12	13	23
50–64	46	4.7	25	1	1	3	7	10	18	24
65+	30	4.4	15	1	1	3	7	11	11	15
TOTAL SINGLE DX	**37**	**3.1**	**3**	**1**	**1**	**3**	**4**	**5**	**6**	**9**
TOTAL MULTIPLE DX	**262**	**4.8**	**17**	**1**	**2**	**3**	**6**	**11**	**12**	**23**
TOTAL										
0–19 Years	20	3.2	10	1	1	2	4	9	13	13
20–34	76	4.1	11	1	2	3	5	10	12	12
35–49	122	5.1	15	2	3	4	6	11	12	23
50–64	50	4.6	24	1	1	3	6	9	18	24
65+	31	4.3	15	1	1	2	7	11	11	15
GRAND TOTAL	**299**	**4.6**	**16**	**1**	**2**	**3**	**6**	**10**	**12**	**23**

70.12: CULDOTOMY

Type of Patients	Observed Patients	Avg. Stay	Vari-ance	10th	25th	50th	75th	90th	95th	99th
1. SINGLE DX										
0–19 Years	0									
20–34	5	5.7	8	2	4	6	8	9	9	9
35–49	6	3.3	2	1	2	4	4	5	5	5
50–64	1	5.0	0	5	5	5	5	5	5	5
65+	1	1.0	0	1	1	1	1	1	1	1
2. MULTIPLE DX										
0–19 Years	3	4.1	13	1	1	5	9	9	9	9
20–34	23	6.0	20	1	2	4	10	12	12	15
35–49	39	6.6	17	3	4	5	8	12	13	23
50–64	17	7.0	28	3	3	5	8	18	18	18
65+	13	6.3	13	2	3	7	7	11	15	15
TOTAL SINGLE DX	**13**	**4.0**	**5**	**1**	**2**	**4**	**5**	**8**	**9**	**9**
TOTAL MULTIPLE DX	**95**	**6.4**	**19**	**2**	**3**	**5**	**9**	**12**	**15**	**18**
TOTAL										
0–19 Years	3	4.1	13	1	1	5	9	9	9	9
20–34	28	5.9	18	1	2	5	10	12	12	15
35–49	45	6.2	16	3	4	5	7	12	13	23
50–64	18	6.9	27	3	3	5	8	18	18	18
65+	14	6.1	14	2	3	6	7	11	15	15
GRAND TOTAL	**108**	**6.2**	**18**	**2**	**3**	**5**	**8**	**12**	**13**	**18**

70.14: VAGINOTOMY NEC

Type of Patients	Observed Patients	Avg. Stay	Vari-ance	10th	25th	50th	75th	90th	95th	99th
1. SINGLE DX										
0–19 Years	0									
20–34	3	1.8	<1	1	1	2	2	3	3	3
35–49	15	3.3	2	1	3	3	4	5	5	6
50–64	3	2.4	<1	2	2	2	3	3	3	3
65+	0									
2. MULTIPLE DX										
0–19 Years	9	4.5	16	1	2	4	5	13	13	13
20–34	41	3.2	3	1	2	3	5	6	6	10
35–49	61	4.6	16	2	2	3	6	8	10	23
50–64	27	3.7	21	1	1	2	4	9	10	24
65+	14	1.9	2	1	1	1	2	5	5	5
TOTAL SINGLE DX	**21**	**3.0**	**2**	**1**	**2**	**3**	**4**	**5**	**5**	**6**
TOTAL MULTIPLE DX	**152**	**3.8**	**13**	**1**	**2**	**3**	**5**	**7**	**9**	**23**
TOTAL										
0–19 Years	9	4.5	16	1	2	4	5	13	13	13
20–34	44	3.1	3	1	2	2	5	6	6	10
35–49	76	4.3	13	1	2	3	5	7	9	23
50–64	30	3.6	19	1	1	2	3	9	9	24
65+	14	1.9	2	1	1	1	2	5	5	5
GRAND TOTAL	**173**	**3.7**	**12**	**1**	**2**	**3**	**5**	**7**	**9**	**23**

70.2: VAG/CUL-DE-SAC DXTIC PX

Type of Patients	Observed Patients	Avg. Stay	Vari-ance	10th	25th	50th	75th	90th	95th	99th
1. SINGLE DX										
0–19 Years	3	1.7	<1	1	1	2	2	2	2	2
20–34	0									
35–49	0									
50–64	0									
65+	0									
2. MULTIPLE DX										
0–19 Years	3	2.0	3	1	1	1	1	5	5	5
20–34	14	2.8	12	1	1	1	4	4	6	16
35–49	23	3.5	8	1	2	3	4	6	6	14
50–64	32	7.1	60	1	4	5	9	12	16	45
65+	34	7.2	41	1	3	6	9	15	24	27
TOTAL SINGLE DX	**3**	**1.7**	**<1**	**1**	**1**	**2**	**2**	**2**	**2**	**2**
TOTAL MULTIPLE DX	**106**	**5.7**	**38**	**1**	**2**	**4**	**7**	**11**	**16**	**27**
TOTAL										
0–19 Years	6	1.8	2	1	1	1	2	5	5	5
20–34	14	2.8	12	1	1	1	4	4	6	16
35–49	23	3.5	8	1	2	3	4	6	6	14
50–64	32	7.1	60	1	4	5	9	12	16	45
65+	34	7.2	41	1	3	6	9	15	24	27
GRAND TOTAL	**109**	**5.6**	**38**	**1**	**2**	**4**	**7**	**11**	**16**	**27**

70.24: VAGINAL BIOPSY

Type of Patients	Observed Patients	Avg. Stay	Vari-ance	10th	25th	50th	75th	90th	95th	99th
1. SINGLE DX										
0–19 Years	1	2.0	0	2	2	2	2	2	2	2
20–34	0									
35–49	0									
50–64	0									
65+	0									
2. MULTIPLE DX										
0–19 Years	1	5.0	0	5	5	5	5	5	5	5
20–34	6	3.0	4	1	1	4	4	6	6	6
35–49	16	3.3	10	1	1	2	4	6	14	14
50–64	29	7.4	66	1	3	5	9	12	16	45
65+	33	7.4	41	1	3	6	10	15	24	27
TOTAL SINGLE DX	**1**	**2.0**	**0**	**2**	**2**	**2**	**2**	**2**	**2**	**2**
TOTAL MULTIPLE DX	**85**	**6.5**	**44**	**1**	**2**	**5**	**8**	**14**	**16**	**45**
TOTAL										
0–19 Years	2	3.5	3	2	2	2	5	5	5	5
20–34	6	3.0	4	1	1	4	4	6	6	6
35–49	16	3.3	10	1	1	2	4	6	14	14
50–64	29	7.4	66	1	3	5	9	12	16	45
65+	33	7.4	41	1	3	6	10	15	24	27
GRAND TOTAL	**86**	**6.4**	**43**	**1**	**2**	**5**	**8**	**14**	**16**	**45**

70.3: LOC EXC/DESTR VAG/CUL

Type of Patients	Observed Patients	Avg. Stay	Vari-ance	10th	25th	50th	75th	90th	95th	99th
1. SINGLE DX										
0–19 Years	2	1.6	<1	1	1	2	2	2	2	2
20–34	7	1.6	<1	1	1	2	2	3	3	3
35–49	8	1.2	<1	1	1	1	1	2	2	2
50–64	1	1.0	0	1	1	1	1	1	1	1
65+	0									
2. MULTIPLE DX										
0–19 Years	25	2.1	2	1	1	2	3	3	5	7
20–34	187	1.9	<1	1	1	2	2	3	3	4
35–49	78	1.8	2	1	1	1	2	3	4	6
50–64	55	2.6	14	1	1	1	2	5	10	26
65+	48	3.4	7	1	1	3	5	7	7	13
TOTAL SINGLE DX	**18**	**1.4**	**<1**	**1**	**1**	**1**	**2**	**2**	**2**	**3**
TOTAL MULTIPLE DX	**393**	**2.2**	**4**	**1**	**1**	**2**	**2**	**4**	**5**	**11**
TOTAL										
0–19 Years	27	2.0	2	1	1	2	3	3	5	7
20–34	194	1.9	<1	1	1	2	2	3	3	4
35–49	86	1.8	2	1	1	1	2	3	4	6
50–64	56	2.6	14	1	1	1	2	5	10	26
65+	48	3.4	7	1	1	3	5	7	7	13
GRAND TOTAL	**411**	**2.1**	**4**	**1**	**1**	**2**	**2**	**4**	**5**	**11**

70.33: EXC/DESTR VAGINAL LESION

Type of Patients	Observed Patients	Avg. Stay	Vari-ance	10th	25th	50th	75th	90th	95th	99th
1. SINGLE DX										
0–19 Years	0									
20–34	6	1.6	<1	1	1	1	2	3	3	3
35–49	7	1.1	<1	1	1	1	1	2	2	2
50–64	1	1.0	0	1	1	1	1	1	1	1
65+	0									
2. MULTIPLE DX										
0–19 Years	18	2.3	2	1	1	2	3	3	4	7
20–34	134	1.7	<1	1	1	2	2	3	3	4
35–49	63	1.8	2	1	1	1	2	3	4	6
50–64	52	2.6	15	1	1	1	2	5	10	26
65+	42	3.5	8	1	1	2	5	7	10	13
TOTAL SINGLE DX	**14**	**1.3**	**<1**	**1**	**1**	**1**	**2**	**2**	**3**	**3**
TOTAL MULTIPLE DX	**309**	**2.2**	**5**	**1**	**1**	**2**	**2**	**4**	**6**	**11**
TOTAL										
0–19 Years	18	2.3	2	1	1	2	3	3	4	7
20–34	140	1.7	<1	1	1	2	2	3	3	4
35–49	70	1.7	2	1	1	1	2	3	4	6
50–64	53	2.6	15	1	1	1	2	5	10	26
65+	42	3.5	8	1	1	2	5	7	10	13
GRAND TOTAL	**323**	**2.2**	**5**	**1**	**1**	**2**	**2**	**4**	**6**	**11**

70.4: VAGINAL OBLITERATION

Type of Patients	Observed Patients	Avg. Stay	Vari-ance	Percentiles						
				10th	25th	50th	75th	90th	95th	99th
1. SINGLE DX										
0–19 Years	0									
20–34	0									
35–49	2	9.8	47	5	5	5	15	15	15	15
50–64	3	1.7	<1	1	1	2	2	2	2	2
65+	3	1.8	1	1	1	1	3	3	3	3
2. MULTIPLE DX										
0–19 Years	0									
20–34	2	3.7	<1	3	3	4	4	4	4	4
35–49	11	3.0	2	1	2	3	4	5	6	6
50–64	17	4.9	7	1	2	5	6	8	8	12
65+	45	2.8	5	1	1	2	3	4	8	13
TOTAL SINGLE DX	**8**	**3.4**	**18**	**1**	**1**	**2**	**3**	**5**	**15**	**15**
TOTAL MULTIPLE DX	**75**	**3.2**	**6**	**1**	**1**	**3**	**4**	**6**	**8**	**13**
TOTAL										
0–19 Years	0									
20–34	2	3.7	<1	3	3	4	4	4	4	4
35–49	13	3.7	9	1	2	4	4	6	15	15
50–64	20	4.5	8	1	2	5	6	8	8	12
65+	48	2.7	5	1	1	2	3	4	8	13
GRAND TOTAL	**83**	**3.2**	**6**	**1**	**1**	**3**	**4**	**6**	**8**	**13**

70.5: CYSTOCELE/RECTOCELE REP

Type of Patients	Observed Patients	Avg. Stay	Vari-ance	Percentiles						
				10th	25th	50th	75th	90th	95th	99th
1. SINGLE DX										
0–19 Years	0									
20–34	27	1.6	<1	1	1	1	2	3	3	3
35–49	130	1.5	<1	1	1	1	2	2	3	4
50–64	234	1.6	<1	1	1	1	2	2	3	4
65+	190	1.6	<1	1	1	1	2	3	3	3
2. MULTIPLE DX										
0–19 Years	2	1.5	<1	1	1	1	2	2	2	2
20–34	101	1.9	1	1	1	2	2	4	4	6
35–49	704	1.8	<1	1	1	2	2	3	3	5
50–64	1,789	1.8	2	1	1	2	2	3	3	6
65+	2,330	2.0	2	1	1	2	2	3	4	6
TOTAL SINGLE DX	**581**	**1.6**	**<1**	**1**	**1**	**1**	**2**	**2**	**3**	**3**
TOTAL MULTIPLE DX	**4,926**	**1.9**	**2**	**1**	**1**	**2**	**2**	**3**	**4**	**6**
TOTAL										
0–19 Years	2	1.5	<1	1	1	1	2	2	2	2
20–34	128	1.9	1	1	1	2	2	3	4	6
35–49	834	1.8	<1	1	1	2	2	3	3	5
50–64	2,023	1.8	2	1	1	2	2	3	3	5
65+	2,520	2.0	2	1	1	2	2	3	4	6
GRAND TOTAL	**5,507**	**1.9**	**2**	**1**	**1**	**2**	**2**	**3**	**3**	**6**

70.50: REP CYSTOCELE/RECTOCELE

Type of Patients	Observed Patients	Avg. Stay	Vari-ance	Percentiles						
				10th	25th	50th	75th	90th	95th	99th
1. SINGLE DX										
0–19 Years	0									
20–34	14	1.9	<1	1	2	2	2	3	3	3
35–49	64	1.7	<1	1	1	2	2	3	3	3
50–64	116	1.8	<1	1	1	2	2	3	3	3
65+	93	1.7	<1	1	1	2	2	3	3	3
2. MULTIPLE DX										
0–19 Years	2	1.5	<1	1	1	1	2	2	2	2
20–34	38	1.9	1	1	1	2	2	3	3	8
35–49	309	1.9	<1	1	1	2	2	3	3	4
50–64	855	1.9	<1	1	1	2	2	3	3	5
65+	1,136	2.2	1	1	1	2	3	3	4	5
TOTAL SINGLE DX	**287**	**1.7**	**<1**	**1**	**1**	**2**	**2**	**3**	**3**	**3**
TOTAL MULTIPLE DX	**2,340**	**2.1**	**1**	**1**	**1**	**2**	**3**	**3**	**4**	**5**
TOTAL										
0–19 Years	2	1.5	<1	1	1	1	2	2	2	2
20–34	52	1.9	1	1	1	2	2	3	3	8
35–49	373	1.9	<1	1	1	2	2	3	3	4
50–64	971	1.9	<1	1	1	2	2	3	3	5
65+	1,229	2.1	1	1	1	2	3	3	4	5
GRAND TOTAL	**2,627**	**2.0**	**<1**	**1**	**1**	**2**	**2**	**3**	**4**	**5**

70.51: CYSTOCELE REPAIR

Type of Patients	Observed Patients	Avg. Stay	Vari-ance	Percentiles						
				10th	25th	50th	75th	90th	95th	99th
1. SINGLE DX										
0–19 Years	0									
20–34	1	1.0	0	1	1	1	1	1	1	1
35–49	13	1.3	<1	1	1	1	2	2	3	3
50–64	49	1.3	<1	1	1	1	2	2	2	2
65+	48	1.4	<1	1	1	1	2	2	3	3
2. MULTIPLE DX										
0–19 Years	0									
20–34	27	1.5	<1	1	1	1	2	3	4	5
35–49	200	1.7	<1	1	1	1	2	3	3	3
50–64	513	1.6	5	1	1	1	2	2	3	4
65+	707	1.7	2	1	1	1	2	3	3	6
TOTAL SINGLE DX	**111**	**1.4**	**<1**	**1**	**1**	**1**	**2**	**2**	**2**	**3**
TOTAL MULTIPLE DX	**1,447**	**1.7**	**3**	**1**	**1**	**1**	**2**	**3**	**3**	**5**
TOTAL										
0–19 Years	0									
20–34	28	1.5	<1	1	1	1	2	3	4	5
35–49	213	1.6	<1	1	1	1	2	3	3	3
50–64	562	1.6	5	1	1	1	2	2	3	4
65+	755	1.7	1	1	1	1	2	3	3	6
GRAND TOTAL	**1,558**	**1.6**	**3**	**1**	**1**	**1**	**2**	**3**	**3**	**5**

70.52: RECTOCELE REPAIR

Type of Patients	Observed Patients	Avg. Stay	Variance	10th	25th	50th	75th	90th	95th	99th
1. SINGLE DX										
0–19 Years	0									
20–34	12	1.3	<1	1	1	1	1	2	3	3
35–49	53	1.3	<1	1	1	1	1	2	3	4
50–64	69	1.4	<1	1	1	1	2	2	3	4
65+	49	1.6	<1	1	1	1	2	3	3	3
2. MULTIPLE DX										
0–19 Years	0									
20–34	36	2.2	2	1	1	2	2	4	5	6
35–49	195	1.9	1	1	1	2	2	3	4	6
50–64	421	1.8	1	1	1	1	2	3	3	7
65+	487	1.9	2	1	1	2	2	3	4	7
TOTAL SINGLE DX	**183**	**1.4**	**<1**	**1**	**1**	**1**	**2**	**2**	**3**	**4**
TOTAL MULTIPLE DX	**1,139**	**1.9**	**2**	**1**	**1**	**2**	**2**	**3**	**4**	**7**
TOTAL										
0–19 Years	0									
20–34	48	2.0	2	1	1	2	2	4	5	6
35–49	248	1.8	1	1	1	1	2	3	4	6
50–64	490	1.7	1	1	1	1	2	3	3	6
65+	536	1.9	2	1	1	2	2	3	4	7
GRAND TOTAL	**1,322**	**1.8**	**2**	**1**	**1**	**2**	**2**	**3**	**4**	**7**

70.6: VAGINAL CONSTR/RECONST

Type of Patients	Observed Patients	Avg. Stay	Variance	10th	25th	50th	75th	90th	95th	99th
1. SINGLE DX										
0–19 Years	0									
20–34	1	8.0	0	8	8	8	8	8	8	8
35–49	0									
50–64	0									
65+	0									
2. MULTIPLE DX										
0–19 Years	2	4.8	28	1	1	1	10	10	10	10
20–34	0									
35–49	4	4.7	6	1	5	5	6	7	7	7
50–64	3	2.5	<1	2	2	2	3	3	3	3
65+	1	2.0	0	2	2	2	2	2	2	2
TOTAL SINGLE DX	**1**	**8.0**	**0**	**8**	**8**	**8**	**8**	**8**	**8**	**8**
TOTAL MULTIPLE DX	**10**	**3.8**	**9**	**1**	**2**	**3**	**6**	**10**	**10**	**10**
TOTAL										
0–19 Years	2	4.8	28	1	1	1	10	10	10	10
20–34	1	8.0	0	8	8	8	8	8	8	8
35–49	4	4.7	6	1	5	5	6	7	7	7
50–64	3	2.5	<1	2	2	2	3	3	3	3
65+	1	2.0	0	2	2	2	2	2	2	2
GRAND TOTAL	**11**	**4.1**	**9**	**1**	**2**	**3**	**6**	**8**	**10**	**10**

70.7: OTHER VAGINAL REPAIR

Type of Patients	Observed Patients	Avg. Stay	Variance	10th	25th	50th	75th	90th	95th	99th
1. SINGLE DX										
0–19 Years	12	1.9	4	1	1	1	2	7	7	7
20–34	29	1.5	<1	1	1	1	2	2	3	3
35–49	37	1.9	<1	1	1	2	3	3	4	4
50–64	49	3.0	8	1	2	2	3	6	14	14
65+	27	2.0	<1	1	1	2	3	3	3	4
2. MULTIPLE DX										
0–19 Years	54	3.9	15	1	2	3	4	7	16	17
20–34	125	2.5	5	1	1	2	3	4	6	14
35–49	213	3.3	10	1	2	3	4	6	9	18
50–64	408	3.2	7	1	2	3	3	5	8	13
65+	525	3.5	9	1	2	3	4	6	8	17
TOTAL SINGLE DX	**154**	**2.2**	**4**	**1**	**1**	**2**	**3**	**3**	**4**	**14**
TOTAL MULTIPLE DX	**1,325**	**3.3**	**8**	**1**	**2**	**3**	**3**	**6**	**8**	**16**
TOTAL										
0–19 Years	66	3.5	13	1	1	2	4	7	15	17
20–34	154	2.3	4	1	1	2	3	4	6	14
35–49	250	3.1	9	1	1	2	3	5	7	18
50–64	457	3.1	7	1	2	3	3	5	8	14
65+	552	3.4	8	1	2	3	4	6	8	17
GRAND TOTAL	**1,479**	**3.2**	**8**	**1**	**2**	**3**	**3**	**6**	**8**	**15**

70.71: SUTURE VAGINA LACERATION

Type of Patients	Observed Patients	Avg. Stay	Variance	10th	25th	50th	75th	90th	95th	99th
1. SINGLE DX										
0–19 Years	8	1.2	<1	1	1	1	1	2	2	2
20–34	5	1.2	<1	1	1	1	1	2	2	2
35–49	10	1.5	<1	1	1	1	2	3	3	3
50–64	4	1.3	<1	1	1	1	2	2	2	2
65+	2	1.0	0	1	1	1	1	1	1	1
2. MULTIPLE DX										
0–19 Years	13	2.7	3	1	1	2	4	6	6	6
20–34	43	1.9	4	1	1	1	2	3	5	15
35–49	33	2.9	10	1	1	2	3	7	7	18
50–64	20	2.2	7	1	1	1	2	3	12	12
65+	16	2.2	3	1	1	2	2	3	8	8
TOTAL SINGLE DX	**29**	**1.2**	**<1**	**1**	**1**	**1**	**1**	**2**	**2**	**3**
TOTAL MULTIPLE DX	**125**	**2.3**	**6**	**1**	**1**	**2**	**3**	**4**	**7**	**15**
TOTAL										
0–19 Years	21	2.0	2	1	1	1	3	5	6	6
20–34	48	1.9	4	1	1	1	2	3	4	15
35–49	43	2.6	8	1	1	2	3	4	7	18
50–64	24	2.1	6	1	1	1	2	3	12	12
65+	18	2.0	3	1	1	2	2	3	8	8
GRAND TOTAL	**154**	**2.1**	**5**	**1**	**1**	**1**	**2**	**3**	**6**	**12**

70.73: REP RECTOVAGINAL FISTULA

Type of Patients	Observed Patients	Avg. Stay	Vari-ance	Percentiles 10th	25th	50th	75th	90th	95th	99th
1. SINGLE DX										
0–19 Years	1	7.0	0	7	7	7	7	7	7	7
20–34	21	1.5	<1	1	1	1	2	2	3	3
35–49	9	2.3	<1	1	2	2	3	4	4	4
50–64	6	2.9	4	1	2	2	4	7	7	7
65+	0									
2. MULTIPLE DX										
0–19 Years	11	5.9	30	2	2	4	6	17	17	17
20–34	49	2.7	5	1	2	2	3	4	6	14
35–49	67	3.1	7	1	1	2	4	6	9	18
50–64	52	4.1	16	1	1	3	5	13	13	16
65+	37	7.5	28	1	3	7	12	15	17	22
TOTAL SINGLE DX	**37**	**2.2**	**2**	**1**	**1**	**2**	**3**	**4**	**7**	**7**
TOTAL MULTIPLE DX	**216**	**4.2**	**17**	**1**	**2**	**3**	**5**	**12**	**13**	**17**
TOTAL										
0–19 Years	12	6.0	27	2	2	4	7	17	17	17
20–34	70	2.4	4	1	1	2	3	4	4	14
35–49	76	3.0	7	1	1	2	4	5	8	13
50–64	58	4.0	15	1	1	2	5	12	13	16
65+	37	7.5	28	1	3	7	12	15	17	22
GRAND TOTAL	**253**	**3.9**	**15**	**1**	**1**	**3**	**4**	**10**	**13**	**17**

70.77: VAGINAL SUSP & FIXATION

Type of Patients	Observed Patients	Avg. Stay	Vari-ance	Percentiles 10th	25th	50th	75th	90th	95th	99th
1. SINGLE DX										
0–19 Years	0									
20–34	0									
35–49	10	2.1	<1	1	1	2	3	3	4	4
50–64	32	2.4	1	1	2	2	3	3	4	6
65+	24	2.0	<1	1	1	2	3	3	3	3
2. MULTIPLE DX										
0–19 Years	0									
20–34	5	2.0	1	1	1	2	2	4	4	4
35–49	60	3.3	14	1	2	3	3	4	6	28
50–64	262	2.8	3	1	2	3	3	4	5	13
65+	394	2.9	3	1	2	3	3	4	5	10
TOTAL SINGLE DX	**66**	**2.2**	**<1**	**1**	**2**	**2**	**3**	**3**	**3**	**6**
TOTAL MULTIPLE DX	**721**	**2.9**	**4**	**1**	**2**	**3**	**3**	**4**	**5**	**12**
TOTAL										
0–19 Years	0									
20–34	5	2.0	1	1	1	2	2	4	4	4
35–49	70	3.2	13	1	2	3	3	4	6	28
50–64	294	2.7	3	1	2	3	3	4	5	13
65+	418	2.9	3	1	2	3	3	4	5	10
GRAND TOTAL	**787**	**2.9**	**4**	**1**	**2**	**3**	**3**	**4**	**5**	**12**

70.79: VAGINAL REPAIR NEC

Type of Patients	Observed Patients	Avg. Stay	Vari-ance	Percentiles 10th	25th	50th	75th	90th	95th	99th
1. SINGLE DX										
0–19 Years	3	1.6	1	1	1	1	3	3	3	3
20–34	2	2.0	0	2	2	2	2	2	2	2
35–49	8	1.2	<1	1	1	1	1	2	2	2
50–64	3	3.6	6	2	2	3	7	7	7	7
65+	1	4.0	0	4	4	4	4	4	4	4
2. MULTIPLE DX										
0–19 Years	26	3.7	13	1	1	3	4	7	15	16
20–34	23	3.1	5	1	2	2	3	6	9	9
35–49	33	3.2	5	1	2	3	4	6	9	9
50–64	50	2.7	7	1	1	2	3	4	5	21
65+	42	2.8	3	1	2	2	4	6	6	7
TOTAL SINGLE DX	**17**	**2.0**	**2**	**1**	**1**	**2**	**2**	**4**	**4**	**7**
TOTAL MULTIPLE DX	**174**	**3.0**	**6**	**1**	**1**	**2**	**4**	**6**	**7**	**15**
TOTAL										
0–19 Years	29	3.5	13	1	1	2	4	7	15	16
20–34	25	2.9	5	1	2	2	3	6	9	9
35–49	41	2.8	5	1	1	2	3	6	9	9
50–64	53	2.7	7	1	1	2	3	4	7	21
65+	43	2.9	3	1	2	2	4	6	6	7
GRAND TOTAL	**191**	**2.9**	**6**	**1**	**1**	**2**	**4**	**6**	**7**	**15**

70.8: VAGINAL VAULT OBLIT

Type of Patients	Observed Patients	Avg. Stay	Vari-ance	Percentiles 10th	25th	50th	75th	90th	95th	99th
1. SINGLE DX										
0–19 Years	0									
20–34	0									
35–49	1	1.0	0	1	1	1	1	1	1	1
50–64	2	2.5	4	1	1	4	4	4	4	4
65+	9	1.7	<1	1	1	2	2	3	3	3
2. MULTIPLE DX										
0–19 Years	0									
20–34	1	4.0	0	4	4	4	4	4	4	4
35–49	3	1.2	<1	1	1	1	1	2	2	2
50–64	1	4.0	0	4	4	4	4	4	4	4
65+	155	1.9	2	1	1	2	2	4	4	5
TOTAL SINGLE DX	**12**	**1.7**	**<1**	**1**	**1**	**1**	**2**	**3**	**3**	**4**
TOTAL MULTIPLE DX	**160**	**2.0**	**2**	**1**	**1**	**2**	**2**	**4**	**4**	**5**
TOTAL										
0–19 Years	0									
20–34	1	4.0	0	4	4	4	4	4	4	4
35–49	4	1.2	<1	1	1	1	1	2	2	2
50–64	3	3.0	3	1	1	4	4	4	4	4
65+	164	1.9	2	1	1	2	2	3	4	5
GRAND TOTAL	**172**	**1.9**	**2**	**1**	**1**	**2**	**2**	**4**	**4**	**5**

70.9: OTH VAG & CUL-DE-SAC OPS

Type of Patients	Observed Patients	Avg. Stay	Vari- ance	Percentiles						
				10th	25th	50th	75th	90th	95th	99th
1. SINGLE DX										
0–19 Years	0									
20–34	0									
35–49	8	1.5	<1	1	1	1	2	2	3	3
50–64	16	1.9	<1	1	1	2	2	3	4	4
65+	18	1.8	<1	1	1	2	2	2	3	3
2. MULTIPLE DX										
0–19 Years	2	27.8	>999	3	3	3	75	75	75	75
20–34	13	2.4	1	1	2	2	3	4	5	5
35–49	146	2.3	1	1	2	2	3	4	4	7
50–64	665	2.2	2	1	1	2	3	3	4	6
65+	1,200	2.4	2	1	1	2	3	4	5	8
TOTAL SINGLE DX	**42**	**1.7**	**<1**	**1**	**1**	**2**	**2**	**3**	**3**	**4**
TOTAL MULTIPLE DX	**2,026**	**2.4**	**4**	**1**	**1**	**2**	**3**	**4**	**5**	**8**
TOTAL										
0–19 Years	2	27.8	>999	3	3	3	75	75	75	75
20–34	13	2.4	1	1	2	2	3	4	5	5
35–49	154	2.3	1	1	2	2	3	4	4	7
50–64	681	2.2	2	1	1	2	3	3	4	6
65+	1,218	2.4	2	1	1	2	3	4	5	8
GRAND TOTAL	**2,068**	**2.3**	**4**	**1**	**1**	**2**	**3**	**4**	**5**	**8**

70.92: CUL-DE-SAC OPERATION NEC

Type of Patients	Observed Patients	Avg. Stay	Vari- ance	Percentiles						
				10th	25th	50th	75th	90th	95th	99th
1. SINGLE DX										
0–19 Years	0									
20–34	0									
35–49	7	1.6	<1	1	1	2	2	2	3	3
50–64	16	1.9	<1	1	1	2	2	3	4	4
65+	17	1.8	<1	1	1	2	2	3	3	3
2. MULTIPLE DX										
0–19 Years	1	3.0	0	3	3	3	3	3	3	3
20–34	11	2.5	2	1	1	2	4	4	5	5
35–49	143	2.3	1	1	2	2	3	4	4	7
50–64	658	2.2	2	1	1	2	3	3	4	6
65+	1,190	2.4	2	1	1	2	3	4	5	8
TOTAL SINGLE DX	**40**	**1.8**	**<1**	**1**	**1**	**2**	**2**	**3**	**3**	**4**
TOTAL MULTIPLE DX	**2,003**	**2.3**	**2**	**1**	**1**	**2**	**3**	**4**	**5**	**8**
TOTAL										
0–19 Years	1	3.0	0	3	3	3	3	3	3	3
20–34	11	2.5	2	1	1	2	4	4	5	5
35–49	150	2.3	1	1	2	2	3	4	4	7
50–64	674	2.2	2	1	1	2	3	3	4	6
65+	1,207	2.4	2	1	1	2	3	4	5	8
GRAND TOTAL	**2,043**	**2.3**	**2**	**1**	**1**	**2**	**3**	**4**	**5**	**8**

71.0: INC VULVA & PERINEUM

Type of Patients	Observed Patients	Avg. Stay	Vari- ance	Percentiles						
				10th	25th	50th	75th	90th	95th	99th
1. SINGLE DX										
0–19 Years	16	1.9	2	1	1	1	3	4	5	5
20–34	25	1.9	<1	1	1	2	2	4	4	4
35–49	14	1.9	1	1	1	1	3	3	4	5
50–64	4	2.0	1	1	1	1	3	3	3	3
65+	1	1.0	0	1	1	1	1	1	1	1
2. MULTIPLE DX										
0–19 Years	37	2.7	3	1	1	2	4	5	7	7
20–34	91	3.1	5	1	2	3	3	7	9	9
35–49	110	4.6	9	1	2	4	6	8	10	15
50–64	75	5.2	21	1	3	4	6	11	13	30
65+	46	4.3	7	1	2	4	6	7	8	15
TOTAL SINGLE DX	**60**	**1.9**	**1**	**1**	**1**	**2**	**2**	**4**	**4**	**5**
TOTAL MULTIPLE DX	**359**	**4.2**	**11**	**1**	**2**	**3**	**5**	**8**	**10**	**15**
TOTAL										
0–19 Years	53	2.5	3	1	1	2	3	5	7	7
20–34	116	2.9	4	1	2	2	3	5	8	9
35–49	124	4.2	9	1	2	4	5	8	10	15
50–64	79	5.1	21	1	3	4	6	11	13	30
65+	47	4.3	7	1	2	4	6	7	8	15
GRAND TOTAL	**419**	**3.9**	**10**	**1**	**2**	**3**	**5**	**7**	**9**	**15**

71.09: INC VULVA/PERINEUM NEC

Type of Patients	Observed Patients	Avg. Stay	Vari- ance	Percentiles						
				10th	25th	50th	75th	90th	95th	99th
1. SINGLE DX										
0–19 Years	15	2.0	2	1	1	1	3	4	5	5
20–34	25	1.9	<1	1	1	2	2	4	4	4
35–49	14	1.9	1	1	1	1	3	3	4	5
50–64	4	2.0	1	1	1	1	3	3	3	3
65+	0									
2. MULTIPLE DX										
0–19 Years	36	2.7	3	1	1	2	4	5	7	7
20–34	91	3.1	5	1	2	3	3	7	9	9
35–49	110	4.6	9	1	2	4	6	8	10	15
50–64	75	5.2	21	1	3	4	6	11	13	30
65+	43	4.4	7	1	3	4	6	7	8	15
TOTAL SINGLE DX	**58**	**1.9**	**1**	**1**	**1**	**2**	**2**	**4**	**4**	**5**
TOTAL MULTIPLE DX	**355**	**4.2**	**11**	**1**	**2**	**3**	**5**	**8**	**10**	**15**
TOTAL										
0–19 Years	51	2.5	3	1	1	2	3	5	7	7
20–34	116	2.9	4	1	2	2	3	5	8	9
35–49	124	4.2	9	1	2	4	5	8	10	15
50–64	79	5.1	21	1	3	4	6	11	13	30
65+	43	4.4	7	1	3	4	6	7	8	15
GRAND TOTAL	**413**	**3.9**	**10**	**1**	**2**	**3**	**5**	**7**	**9**	**15**

71.1: VULVAR DIAGNOSTIC PX

Type of Patients	Observed Patients	Avg. Stay	Vari-ance	Percentiles						
				10th	25th	50th	75th	90th	95th	99th
1. SINGLE DX										
0–19 Years	1	2.0	0	2	2	2	2	2	2	2
20–34	0									
35–49	1	1.0	0	1	1	1	1	1	1	1
50–64	0									
65+	1	2.0	0	2	2	2	2	2	2	2
2. MULTIPLE DX										
0–19 Years	3	3.8	2	2	2	5	5	5	5	5
20–34	17	1.9	<1	1	1	2	2	3	3	4
35–49	11	7.8	56	2	2	4	17	19	19	19
50–64	13	4.1	21	1	1	3	5	13	13	18
65+	24	4.1	13	1	1	3	5	11	12	12
TOTAL SINGLE DX	**3**	**1.7**	**<1**	**1**	**1**	**2**	**2**	**2**	**2**	**2**
TOTAL MULTIPLE DX	**68**	**4.4**	**24**	**1**	**1**	**2**	**5**	**12**	**19**	**19**
TOTAL										
0–19 Years	4	3.4	2	2	2	3	5	5	5	5
20–34	17	1.9	<1	1	1	2	2	3	3	4
35–49	12	7.5	56	2	2	4	17	19	19	19
50–64	13	4.1	21	1	1	3	5	13	13	18
65+	25	4.0	13	1	1	3	5	11	12	12
GRAND TOTAL	**71**	**4.3**	**23**	**1**	**1**	**2**	**5**	**12**	**18**	**19**

71.11: VULVAR BIOPSY

Type of Patients	Observed Patients	Avg. Stay	Vari-ance	Percentiles						
				10th	25th	50th	75th	90th	95th	99th
1. SINGLE DX										
0–19 Years	1	2.0	0	2	2	2	2	2	2	2
20–34	0									
35–49	1	1.0	0	1	1	1	1	1	1	1
50–64	0									
65+	1	2.0	0	2	2	2	2	2	2	2
2. MULTIPLE DX										
0–19 Years	3	3.8	2	2	2	5	5	5	5	5
20–34	17	1.9	<1	1	1	2	2	3	3	4
35–49	11	7.8	56	2	2	4	17	19	19	19
50–64	13	4.1	21	1	1	3	5	13	13	18
65+	24	4.1	13	1	1	3	5	11	12	12
TOTAL SINGLE DX	**3**	**1.7**	**<1**	**1**	**1**	**2**	**2**	**2**	**2**	**2**
TOTAL MULTIPLE DX	**68**	**4.4**	**24**	**1**	**1**	**2**	**5**	**12**	**19**	**19**
TOTAL										
0–19 Years	4	3.4	2	2	2	3	5	5	5	5
20–34	17	1.9	<1	1	1	2	2	3	3	4
35–49	12	7.5	56	2	2	4	17	19	19	19
50–64	13	4.1	21	1	1	3	5	13	13	18
65+	25	4.0	13	1	1	3	5	11	12	12
GRAND TOTAL	**71**	**4.3**	**23**	**1**	**1**	**2**	**5**	**12**	**18**	**19**

71.2: BARTHOLIN'S GLAND OPS

Type of Patients	Observed Patients	Avg. Stay	Vari-ance	Percentiles						
				10th	25th	50th	75th	90th	95th	99th
1. SINGLE DX										
0–19 Years	6	1.1	<1	1	1	1	1	2	2	2
20–34	15	1.5	<1	1	1	1	2	3	3	3
35–49	9	1.5	<1	1	1	1	2	3	3	3
50–64	3	1.7	<1	1	1	2	2	2	2	2
65+	2	1.0	0	1	1	1	1	1	1	1
2. MULTIPLE DX										
0–19 Years	12	2.5	3	1	1	2	3	3	8	8
20–34	43	2.3	2	1	1	2	3	5	5	6
35–49	18	2.3	2	1	1	2	3	4	6	6
50–64	20	7.4	84	1	1	3	11	24	24	24
65+	7	1.5	<1	1	1	1	2	3	3	3
TOTAL SINGLE DX	**35**	**1.4**	**<1**	**1**	**1**	**1**	**2**	**2**	**3**	**3**
TOTAL MULTIPLE DX	**100**	**3.5**	**26**	**1**	**1**	**2**	**3**	**6**	**24**	**24**
TOTAL										
0–19 Years	18	2.0	2	1	1	2	2	3	5	8
20–34	58	2.1	2	1	1	2	3	5	5	6
35–49	27	2.0	2	1	1	2	2	3	6	6
50–64	23	6.5	75	1	1	2	6	24	24	24
65+	9	1.2	<1	1	1	1	1	2	3	3
GRAND TOTAL	**135**	**2.9**	**19**	**1**	**1**	**2**	**3**	**5**	**6**	**24**

71.22: INC BARTHOLIN'S GLAND

Type of Patients	Observed Patients	Avg. Stay	Vari-ance	Percentiles						
				10th	25th	50th	75th	90th	95th	99th
1. SINGLE DX										
0–19 Years	5	1.0	0	1	1	1	1	1	1	1
20–34	8	1.6	<1	1	1	2	2	2	2	2
35–49	2	1.8	1	1	1	1	3	3	3	3
50–64	0									
65+	0									
2. MULTIPLE DX										
0–19 Years	6	2.4	3	1	1	2	3	3	8	8
20–34	24	2.6	2	1	1	2	3	5	5	5
35–49	7	2.8	4	1	1	2	4	6	6	6
50–64	7	13.0	107	2	3	11	24	24	24	24
65+	0									
TOTAL SINGLE DX	**15**	**1.4**	**<1**	**1**	**1**	**1**	**2**	**2**	**3**	**3**
TOTAL MULTIPLE DX	**44**	**5.0**	**45**	**1**	**2**	**2**	**5**	**24**	**24**	**24**
TOTAL										
0–19 Years	11	1.8	2	1	1	1	2	3	3	8
20–34	32	2.4	2	1	1	2	3	5	5	5
35–49	9	2.6	3	1	1	2	3	6	6	6
50–64	7	13.0	107	2	3	11	24	24	24	24
65+	0									
GRAND TOTAL	**59**	**4.1**	**37**	**1**	**1**	**2**	**4**	**6**	**24**	**24**

71.3: LOC VULVAR/PERI EXC NEC

Type of Patients	Observed Patients	Avg. Stay	Vari-ance	Percentiles						
				10th	25th	50th	75th	90th	95th	99th
1. SINGLE DX										
0–19 Years	2	1.0	0	1	1	1	1	1	1	1
20–34	8	2.1	2	1	1	2	2	3	6	6
35–49	5	1.1	<1	1	1	1	1	1	1	2
50–64	5	1.8	2	1	1	1	3	4	4	4
65+	2	1.0	0	1	1	1	1	1	1	1
2. MULTIPLE DX										
0–19 Years	30	2.6	5	1	2	2	3	3	4	13
20–34	263	1.9	<1	1	1	2	2	3	3	4
35–49	80	3.4	17	1	1	2	3	8	14	21
50–64	60	2.8	11	1	1	2	2	6	11	21
65+	56	4.4	95	1	1	2	3	8	14	66
TOTAL SINGLE DX	**22**	**1.4**	**<1**	**1**	**1**	**1**	**1**	**2**	**3**	**6**
TOTAL MULTIPLE DX	**489**	**2.6**	**18**	**1**	**1**	**2**	**2**	**4**	**8**	**17**
TOTAL										
0–19 Years	32	2.6	5	1	1	2	3	3	4	13
20–34	271	1.9	<1	1	1	2	2	3	3	6
35–49	85	3.0	15	1	1	2	3	6	14	21
50–64	65	2.8	11	1	1	2	2	6	9	21
65+	58	4.3	93	1	1	2	3	8	14	66
GRAND TOTAL	**511**	**2.6**	**17**	**1**	**1**	**2**	**2**	**3**	**7**	**15**

71.4: OPERATIONS ON CLITORIS

Type of Patients	Observed Patients	Avg. Stay	Vari-ance	Percentiles						
				10th	25th	50th	75th	90th	95th	99th
1. SINGLE DX										
0–19 Years	1	1.0	0	1	1	1	1	1	1	1
20–34	0									
35–49	0									
50–64	0									
65+	0									
2. MULTIPLE DX										
0–19 Years	7	1.9	1	1	1	2	2	4	4	4
20–34	2	2.0	2	1	1	1	3	3	3	3
35–49	0									
50–64	1	2.0	0	2	2	2	2	2	2	2
65+	1	1.0	0	1	1	1	1	1	1	1
TOTAL SINGLE DX	**1**	**1.0**	**0**	**1**	**1**	**1**	**1**	**1**	**1**	**1**
TOTAL MULTIPLE DX	**11**	**1.8**	**<1**	**1**	**1**	**2**	**2**	**3**	**4**	**4**
TOTAL										
0–19 Years	8	1.8	1	1	1	1	2	4	4	4
20–34	2	2.0	2	1	1	1	3	3	3	3
35–49	0									
50–64	1	2.0	0	2	2	2	2	2	2	2
65+	1	1.0	0	1	1	1	1	1	1	1
GRAND TOTAL	**12**	**1.7**	**<1**	**1**	**1**	**1**	**2**	**3**	**4**	**4**

71.5: RADICAL VULVECTOMY

Type of Patients	Observed Patients	Avg. Stay	Vari-ance	Percentiles						
				10th	25th	50th	75th	90th	95th	99th
1. SINGLE DX										
0–19 Years	0									
20–34	0									
35–49	4	2.5	2	1	1	2	4	4	4	4
50–64	3	3.2	2	2	2	2	4	5	5	5
65+	6	2.2	<1	1	2	2	3	3	4	4
2. MULTIPLE DX										
0–19 Years	0									
20–34	2	2.7	<1	2	2	3	3	3	3	3
35–49	27	4.7	14	2	2	3	7	11	12	15
50–64	53	3.9	19	1	2	3	5	6	9	36
65+	118	5.5	17	2	3	4	6	11	15	20
TOTAL SINGLE DX	**13**	**2.4**	**1**	**1**	**2**	**2**	**3**	**4**	**4**	**5**
TOTAL MULTIPLE DX	**200**	**5.0**	**18**	**2**	**2**	**4**	**6**	**9**	**12**	**20**
TOTAL										
0–19 Years	0									
20–34	2	2.7	<1	2	2	3	3	3	3	3
35–49	31	4.3	12	2	2	3	5	10	12	15
50–64	56	3.9	18	1	2	3	5	6	9	36
65+	124	5.2	17	2	3	4	6	10	14	20
GRAND TOTAL	**213**	**4.7**	**17**	**2**	**2**	**4**	**6**	**9**	**12**	**20**

71.6: OTHER VULVECTOMY

Type of Patients	Observed Patients	Avg. Stay	Vari-ance	Percentiles						
				10th	25th	50th	75th	90th	95th	99th
1. SINGLE DX										
0–19 Years	1	1.0	0	1	1	1	1	1	1	1
20–34	2	1.8	2	1	1	1	3	3	3	3
35–49	3	1.0	0	1	1	1	1	1	1	1
50–64	8	1.8	1	1	1	2	2	2	5	5
65+	6	1.3	<1	1	1	1	2	2	2	2
2. MULTIPLE DX										
0–19 Years	1	6.0	0	6	6	6	6	6	6	6
20–34	10	4.0	26	1	2	2	3	16	16	16
35–49	45	3.2	19	1	1	1	3	6	11	31
50–64	56	4.7	71	1	1	2	3	9	30	30
65+	90	3.2	15	1	1	3	3	5	6	27
TOTAL SINGLE DX	**20**	**1.5**	**<1**	**1**	**1**	**1**	**2**	**2**	**3**	**5**
TOTAL MULTIPLE DX	**202**	**3.8**	**36**	**1**	**1**	**2**	**3**	**6**	**16**	**30**
TOTAL										
0–19 Years	2	2.9	8	1	1	1	6	6	6	6
20–34	12	3.7	24	1	2	2	3	16	16	16
35–49	48	3.1	18	1	1	1	3	6	11	31
50–64	64	4.5	66	1	1	2	3	7	30	30
65+	96	3.1	14	1	1	2	3	5	6	27
GRAND TOTAL	**222**	**3.6**	**34**	**1**	**1**	**2**	**3**	**6**	**15**	**30**

71.61: UNILATERAL VULVECTOMY

Type of Patients	Observed Patients	Avg. Stay	Vari-ance	10th	25th	50th	75th	90th	95th	99th
1. SINGLE DX										
0–19 Years	0									
20–34	2	1.8	2	1	1	1	3	3	3	3
35–49	3	1.0	0	1	1	1	1	1	1	1
50–64	5	1.5	<1	1	1	1	2	2	2	2
65+	5	1.3	<1	1	1	1	2	2	2	2
2. MULTIPLE DX										
0–19 Years	1	6.0	0	6	6	6	6	6	6	6
20–34	5	5.9	42	2	2	2	16	16	16	16
35–49	28	3.2	22	1	1	2	3	5	7	31
50–64	45	5.2	81	1	1	2	3	30	30	30
65+	65	3.3	19	1	1	2	4	4	6	27
TOTAL SINGLE DX	**15**	**1.4**	**<1**	**1**	**1**	**1**	**2**	**2**	**2**	**3**
TOTAL MULTIPLE DX	**144**	**4.1**	**45**	**1**	**1**	**2**	**3**	**6**	**27**	**30**
TOTAL										
0–19 Years	1	6.0	0	6	6	6	6	6	6	6
20–34	7	5.1	36	1	2	2	3	16	16	16
35–49	31	3.0	21	1	1	2	3	5	7	31
50–64	50	4.9	76	1	1	2	3	30	30	30
65+	70	3.2	18	1	1	2	3	4	6	27
GRAND TOTAL	**159**	**3.9**	**42**	**1**	**1**	**2**	**3**	**5**	**27**	**30**

71.7: VULVAR & PERINEAL REPAIR

Type of Patients	Observed Patients	Avg. Stay	Vari-ance	10th	25th	50th	75th	90th	95th	99th
1. SINGLE DX										
0–19 Years	23	1.2	<1	1	1	1	1	2	2	3
20–34	13	1.3	<1	1	1	1	1	2	3	3
35–49	12	1.1	<1	1	1	1	1	1	2	2
50–64	10	1.7	<1	1	1	1	2	3	3	3
65+	7	1.3	<1	1	1	1	1	2	3	3
2. MULTIPLE DX										
0–19 Years	20	2.2	4	1	1	1	2	6	8	8
20–34	62	2.0	2	1	1	2	2	4	5	9
35–49	79	2.1	6	1	1	1	2	5	5	19
50–64	117	1.9	<1	1	1	2	2	3	3	4
65+	159	2.3	3	1	1	2	2	4	5	10
TOTAL SINGLE DX	**65**	**1.3**	**<1**	**1**	**1**	**1**	**1**	**2**	**3**	**3**
TOTAL MULTIPLE DX	**437**	**2.1**	**3**	**1**	**1**	**2**	**2**	**3**	**5**	**10**
TOTAL										
0–19 Years	43	1.7	2	1	1	1	2	3	6	8
20–34	75	1.9	2	1	1	2	2	3	5	9
35–49	91	2.0	6	1	1	1	2	4	5	19
50–64	127	1.9	<1	1	1	2	2	3	3	4
65+	166	2.3	3	1	1	2	2	4	5	10
GRAND TOTAL	**502**	**2.0**	**3**	**1**	**1**	**2**	**2**	**3**	**4**	**9**

71.71: SUTURE VULVAR/PERI LAC

Type of Patients	Observed Patients	Avg. Stay	Vari-ance	10th	25th	50th	75th	90th	95th	99th
1. SINGLE DX										
0–19 Years	18	1.2	<1	1	1	1	1	2	2	3
20–34	6	1.2	<1	1	1	1	1	2	2	2
35–49	3	1.3	<1	1	1	1	2	2	2	2
50–64	2	2.6	<1	1	3	3	3	3	3	3
65+	3	1.5	<1	1	1	1	1	3	3	3
2. MULTIPLE DX										
0–19 Years	15	2.3	5	1	1	1	2	7	8	8
20–34	12	1.9	<1	1	1	2	2	3	4	4
35–49	15	1.2	<1	1	1	1	1	2	2	3
50–64	29	2.1	1	1	1	2	3	4	4	4
65+	49	2.5	5	1	1	2	3	4	10	10
TOTAL SINGLE DX	**32**	**1.3**	**<1**	**1**	**1**	**1**	**1**	**3**	**3**	**3**
TOTAL MULTIPLE DX	**120**	**2.2**	**3**	**1**	**1**	**2**	**2**	**4**	**6**	**10**
TOTAL										
0–19 Years	33	1.7	3	1	1	1	2	3	7	8
20–34	18	1.7	<1	1	1	1	2	3	3	4
35–49	18	1.2	<1	1	1	1	1	2	2	3
50–64	31	2.1	<1	1	1	2	3	4	4	4
65+	52	2.5	5	1	1	2	3	4	10	10
GRAND TOTAL	**152**	**2.0**	**3**	**1**	**1**	**1**	**2**	**4**	**4**	**10**

71.79: VULVAR/PERINEUM REP NEC

Type of Patients	Observed Patients	Avg. Stay	Vari-ance	10th	25th	50th	75th	90th	95th	99th
1. SINGLE DX										
0–19 Years	4	1.0	0	1	1	1	1	1	1	1
20–34	7	1.4	<1	1	1	1	2	3	3	3
35–49	9	1.0	0	1	1	1	1	1	1	1
50–64	8	1.4	<1	1	1	1	2	2	2	2
65+	4	1.2	<1	1	1	1	1	2	2	2
2. MULTIPLE DX										
0–19 Years	3	1.6	<1	1	1	2	2	2	2	2
20–34	45	2.1	3	1	1	2	2	5	6	9
35–49	61	2.3	7	1	1	2	2	5	5	19
50–64	88	1.9	<1	1	1	2	2	3	3	4
65+	108	2.2	2	1	1	2	2	3	4	9
TOTAL SINGLE DX	**32**	**1.2**	**<1**	**1**	**1**	**1**	**1**	**2**	**2**	**3**
TOTAL MULTIPLE DX	**305**	**2.1**	**3**	**1**	**1**	**2**	**2**	**3**	**5**	**9**
TOTAL										
0–19 Years	7	1.3	<1	1	1	1	2	2	2	2
20–34	52	2.1	2	1	1	2	2	4	5	9
35–49	70	2.2	7	1	1	1	2	5	5	19
50–64	96	1.8	<1	1	1	2	2	3	3	4
65+	112	2.2	2	1	1	2	2	3	4	9
GRAND TOTAL	**337**	**2.0**	**3**	**1**	**1**	**2**	**2**	**3**	**4**	**9**

71.8: VULVAR OPERATIONS NEC

Type of Patients	Observed Patients	Avg. Stay	Vari-ance	Percentiles 10th	25th	50th	75th	90th	95th	99th
1. SINGLE DX										
0–19 Years	0									
20–34	0									
35–49	0									
50–64	0									
65+	0									
2. MULTIPLE DX										
0–19 Years	1	1.0	0	1	1	1	1	1	1	1
20–34	0									
35–49	0									
50–64	0									
65+	0									
TOTAL SINGLE DX	**0**									
TOTAL MULTIPLE DX	**1**	**1.0**	**0**	**1**	**1**	**1**	**1**	**1**	**1**	**1**
TOTAL										
0–19 Years	1	1.0	0	1	1	1	1	1	1	1
20–34	0									
35–49	0									
50–64	0									
65+	0									
GRAND TOTAL	**1**	**1.0**	**0**	**1**	**1**	**1**	**1**	**1**	**1**	**1**

71.9: FEMALE GENITAL OPS NEC

Type of Patients	Observed Patients	Avg. Stay	Vari-ance	Percentiles 10th	25th	50th	75th	90th	95th	99th
1. SINGLE DX										
0–19 Years	0									
20–34	0									
35–49	0									
50–64	0									
65+	0									
2. MULTIPLE DX										
0–19 Years	0									
20–34	1	2.0	0	2	2	2	2	2	2	2
35–49	0									
50–64	0									
65+	0									
TOTAL SINGLE DX	**0**									
TOTAL MULTIPLE DX	**1**	**2.0**	**0**	**2**	**2**	**2**	**2**	**2**	**2**	**2**
TOTAL										
0–19 Years	0									
20–34	1	2.0	0	2	2	2	2	2	2	2
35–49	0									
50–64	0									
65+	0									
GRAND TOTAL	**1**	**2.0**	**0**	**2**	**2**	**2**	**2**	**2**	**2**	**2**

72.0: LOW FORCEPS OPERATION

Type of Patients	Observed Patients	Avg. Stay	Vari-ance	Percentiles 10th	25th	50th	75th	90th	95th	99th
1. SINGLE DX										
0–19 Years	4	2.0	<1	1	2	2	3	3	3	3
20–34	62	1.9	<1	1	1	2	2	3	3	4
35–49	6	1.8	<1	1	1	2	2	3	3	3
50–64	0									
65+	0									
2. MULTIPLE DX										
0–19 Years	214	2.5	2	1	2	2	3	4	5	9
20–34	1,441	2.4	2	1	2	2	3	3	4	6
35–49	284	2.4	2	1	2	2	3	3	4	7
50–64	8	2.1	<1	1	2	2	3	3	3	3
65+	0									
TOTAL SINGLE DX	**72**	**1.9**	**<1**	**1**	**1**	**2**	**2**	**3**	**3**	**4**
TOTAL MULTIPLE DX	**1,947**	**2.4**	**2**	**1**	**2**	**2**	**3**	**3**	**4**	**7**
TOTAL										
0–19 Years	218	2.5	2	1	2	2	3	4	5	9
20–34	1,503	2.4	2	1	2	2	3	3	4	5
35–49	290	2.4	2	1	2	2	3	3	4	7
50–64	8	2.1	<1	1	2	2	3	3	3	3
65+	0									
GRAND TOTAL	**2,019**	**2.4**	**2**	**1**	**2**	**2**	**3**	**3**	**4**	**6**

72.1: LOW FORCEPS W EPISIOTOMY

Type of Patients	Observed Patients	Avg. Stay	Vari-ance	Percentiles 10th	25th	50th	75th	90th	95th	99th
1. SINGLE DX										
0–19 Years	58	2.0	<1	1	2	2	2	3	3	6
20–34	305	2.0	<1	1	2	2	2	3	3	3
35–49	18	2.0	<1	1	1	2	2	3	3	4
50–64	0									
65+	0									
2. MULTIPLE DX										
0–19 Years	259	2.4	3	1	2	2	3	4	4	5
20–34	1,693	2.3	<1	1	2	2	3	3	4	5
35–49	290	2.4	<1	1	2	2	3	3	4	5
50–64	17	2.8	<1	2	2	3	3	4	4	4
65+	0									
TOTAL SINGLE DX	**381**	**2.0**	**<1**	**1**	**2**	**2**	**2**	**3**	**3**	**4**
TOTAL MULTIPLE DX	**2,259**	**2.3**	**1**	**1**	**2**	**2**	**3**	**3**	**4**	**5**
TOTAL										
0–19 Years	317	2.4	3	1	2	2	3	3	4	5
20–34	1,998	2.3	<1	1	2	2	3	3	3	5
35–49	308	2.4	<1	1	2	2	3	3	4	5
50–64	17	2.8	<1	2	2	3	3	4	4	4
65+	0									
GRAND TOTAL	**2,640**	**2.3**	**1**	**1**	**2**	**2**	**3**	**3**	**4**	**5**

72.2: MID FORCEPS OPERATION

Type of Patients	Observed Patients	Avg. Stay	Vari-ance	10th	25th	50th	75th	90th	95th	99th
1. SINGLE DX										
0–19 Years	8	1.4	<1	1	1	1	2	2	2	2
20–34	28	1.8	<1	1	1	2	2	3	3	3
35–49	2	1.5	<1	1	1	2	2	2	2	2
50–64	1	2.0	0	2	2	2	2	2	2	2
65+	0									
2. MULTIPLE DX										
0–19 Years	36	2.4	<1	2	2	2	3	3	4	6
20–34	230	2.4	<1	2	2	2	3	3	4	6
35–49	34	2.6	2	2	2	2	3	6	6	6
50–64	4	2.3	<1	1	1	3	3	3	3	3
65+	0									
TOTAL SINGLE DX	**39**	**1.7**	**<1**	**1**	**1**	**2**	**2**	**3**	**3**	**3**
TOTAL MULTIPLE DX	**304**	**2.4**	**<1**	**2**	**2**	**2**	**3**	**3**	**4**	**6**
TOTAL										
0–19 Years	44	2.2	<1	1	2	2	3	3	4	6
20–34	258	2.4	<1	1	2	2	3	3	4	6
35–49	36	2.6	2	2	2	2	3	6	6	6
50–64	5	2.2	<1	1	2	2	3	3	3	3
65+	0									
GRAND TOTAL	**343**	**2.4**	**<1**	**1**	**2**	**2**	**3**	**3**	**4**	**6**

72.21: MID FORCEPS W EPISIOTOMY

Type of Patients	Observed Patients	Avg. Stay	Vari-ance	10th	25th	50th	75th	90th	95th	99th
1. SINGLE DX										
0–19 Years	6	1.7	<1	1	1	2	2	2	2	2
20–34	20	1.9	<1	1	1	2	2	3	3	3
35–49	2	1.5	<1	1	1	2	2	2	2	2
50–64	0									
65+	0									
2. MULTIPLE DX										
0–19 Years	22	2.5	1	2	2	2	3	3	6	6
20–34	140	2.4	<1	2	2	2	3	3	4	5
35–49	22	2.8	3	2	2	2	3	6	6	6
50–64	4	2.3	<1	1	1	3	3	3	3	3
65+	0									
TOTAL SINGLE DX	**28**	**1.8**	**<1**	**1**	**1**	**2**	**2**	**2**	**3**	**3**
TOTAL MULTIPLE DX	**188**	**2.5**	**1**	**2**	**2**	**2**	**3**	**4**	**5**	**6**
TOTAL										
0–19 Years	28	2.4	1	2	2	2	3	3	4	6
20–34	160	2.4	<1	2	2	2	3	3	4	5
35–49	24	2.8	3	2	2	2	3	6	6	6
50–64	4	2.3	<1	1	1	3	3	3	3	3
65+	0									
GRAND TOTAL	**216**	**2.4**	**1**	**2**	**2**	**2**	**3**	**3**	**4**	**6**

72.29: MID FORCEPS OP NEC

Type of Patients	Observed Patients	Avg. Stay	Vari-ance	10th	25th	50th	75th	90th	95th	99th
1. SINGLE DX										
0–19 Years	2	1.1	<1	1	1	1	1	2	2	2
20–34	8	1.8	<1	1	1	2	2	3	3	3
35–49	0									
50–64	1	2.0	0	2	2	2	2	2	2	2
65+	0									
2. MULTIPLE DX										
0–19 Years	14	2.3	<1	1	2	2	3	4	4	4
20–34	90	2.4	<1	2	2	2	3	3	4	6
35–49	12	2.3	<1	2	2	2	3	3	3	3
50–64	0									
65+	0									
TOTAL SINGLE DX	**11**	**1.5**	**<1**	**1**	**1**	**1**	**2**	**3**	**3**	**3**
TOTAL MULTIPLE DX	**116**	**2.4**	**<1**	**2**	**2**	**2**	**3**	**3**	**4**	**6**
TOTAL										
0–19 Years	16	2.0	<1	1	1	2	3	3	4	4
20–34	98	2.4	<1	1	2	2	3	3	4	6
35–49	12	2.3	<1	2	2	2	3	3	3	3
50–64	1	2.0	0	2	2	2	2	2	2	2
65+	0									
GRAND TOTAL	**127**	**2.3**	**<1**	**1**	**2**	**2**	**3**	**3**	**3**	**6**

72.3: HIGH FORCEPS OPERATION

Type of Patients	Observed Patients	Avg. Stay	Vari-ance	10th	25th	50th	75th	90th	95th	99th
1. SINGLE DX										
0–19 Years	0									
20–34	0									
35–49	0									
50–64	0									
65+	0									
2. MULTIPLE DX										
0–19 Years	1	3.0	0	3	3	3	3	3	3	3
20–34	7	1.7	<1	1	1	2	2	2	2	2
35–49	0									
50–64	0									
65+	0									
TOTAL SINGLE DX	**0**									
TOTAL MULTIPLE DX	**8**	**1.8**	**<1**	**1**	**1**	**2**	**2**	**3**	**3**	**3**
TOTAL										
0–19 Years	1	3.0	0	3	3	3	3	3	3	3
20–34	7	1.7	<1	1	1	2	2	2	2	2
35–49	0									
50–64	0									
65+	0									
GRAND TOTAL	**8**	**1.8**	**<1**	**1**	**1**	**2**	**2**	**3**	**3**	**3**

72.4: FORCEPS ROT FETAL HEAD

Type of Patients	Observed Patients	Avg. Stay	Vari-ance	Percentiles						
				10th	25th	50th	75th	90th	95th	99th
1. SINGLE DX										
0–19 Years	0									
20–34	1	2.0	0	2	2	2	2	2	2	2
35–49	0									
50–64	0									
65+	0									
2. MULTIPLE DX										
0–19 Years	7	1.7	<1	1	1	2	2	3	3	3
20–34	37	2.2	<1	1	2	2	3	3	3	3
35–49	7	2.2	<1	1	2	2	3	3	3	3
50–64	0									
65+	0									
TOTAL SINGLE DX	**1**	**2.0**	**0**	**2**	**2**	**2**	**2**	**2**	**2**	**2**
TOTAL MULTIPLE DX	**51**	**2.1**	**<1**	**1**	**2**	**2**	**3**	**3**	**3**	**3**
TOTAL										
0–19 Years	7	1.7	<1	1	1	2	2	3	3	3
20–34	38	2.2	<1	1	2	2	3	3	3	3
35–49	7	2.2	<1	1	2	2	3	3	3	3
50–64	0									
65+	0									
GRAND TOTAL	**52**	**2.1**	**<1**	**1**	**2**	**2**	**3**	**3**	**3**	**3**

72.5: BREECH EXTRACTION

Type of Patients	Observed Patients	Avg. Stay	Vari-ance	Percentiles						
				10th	25th	50th	75th	90th	95th	99th
1. SINGLE DX										
0–19 Years	0									
20–34	19	1.7	<1	1	1	2	2	2	2	2
35–49	4	2.8	<1	2	2	3	3	3	3	3
50–64	0									
65+	0									
2. MULTIPLE DX										
0–19 Years	32	2.0	4	1	1	1	2	3	5	11
20–34	254	2.9	14	1	1	2	3	4	11	18
35–49	72	2.9	20	1	2	2	2	4	5	36
50–64	4	3.4	3	2	3	3	3	6	6	6
65+	0									
TOTAL SINGLE DX	**23**	**1.9**	**<1**	**1**	**2**	**2**	**2**	**2**	**3**	**3**
TOTAL MULTIPLE DX	**362**	**2.8**	**14**	**1**	**1**	**2**	**3**	**4**	**9**	**18**
TOTAL										
0–19 Years	32	2.0	4	1	1	1	2	3	5	11
20–34	273	2.9	13	1	1	2	3	4	10	18
35–49	76	2.9	20	1	2	2	3	4	5	36
50–64	4	3.4	3	2	3	3	3	6	6	6
65+	0									
GRAND TOTAL	**385**	**2.8**	**13**	**1**	**1**	**2**	**3**	**4**	**9**	**18**

72.52: PART BREECH EXTRACT NEC

Type of Patients	Observed Patients	Avg. Stay	Vari-ance	Percentiles						
				10th	25th	50th	75th	90th	95th	99th
1. SINGLE DX										
0–19 Years	0									
20–34	6	1.8	<1	1	2	2	2	2	2	2
35–49	4	2.8	<1	2	2	3	3	3	3	3
50–64	0									
65+	0									
2. MULTIPLE DX										
0–19 Years	7	2.3	2	1	1	2	4	5	5	5
20–34	84	2.9	12	1	1	2	3	5	15	18
35–49	23	2.6	<1	2	2	2	3	4	5	5
50–64	1	3.0	0	3	3	3	3	3	3	3
65+	0									
TOTAL SINGLE DX	**10**	**2.2**	**<1**	**2**	**2**	**2**	**3**	**3**	**3**	**3**
TOTAL MULTIPLE DX	**115**	**2.8**	**9**	**1**	**2**	**2**	**3**	**4**	**10**	**15**
TOTAL										
0–19 Years	7	2.3	2	1	1	2	4	5	5	5
20–34	90	2.9	12	1	1	2	3	5	15	18
35–49	27	2.6	<1	2	2	2	3	4	4	5
50–64	1	3.0	0	3	3	3	3	3	3	3
65+	0									
GRAND TOTAL	**125**	**2.8**	**9**	**1**	**2**	**2**	**3**	**4**	**5**	**15**

72.54: TOT BREECH EXTRACT NEC

Type of Patients	Observed Patients	Avg. Stay	Vari-ance	Percentiles						
				10th	25th	50th	75th	90th	95th	99th
1. SINGLE DX										
0–19 Years	0									
20–34	11	1.7	<1	1	1	2	2	2	2	2
35–49	0									
50–64	0									
65+	0									
2. MULTIPLE DX										
0–19 Years	24	1.9	5	1	1	1	2	2	11	11
20–34	151	3.1	16	1	1	2	3	5	11	23
35–49	44	3.3	37	1	2	2	2	3	5	36
50–64	3	3.7	4	2	2	3	6	6	6	6
65+	0									
TOTAL SINGLE DX	**11**	**1.7**	**<1**	**1**	**1**	**2**	**2**	**2**	**2**	**2**
TOTAL MULTIPLE DX	**222**	**2.9**	**18**	**1**	**1**	**2**	**3**	**4**	**11**	**25**
TOTAL										
0–19 Years	24	1.9	5	1	1	1	2	2	11	11
20–34	162	3.0	15	1	1	2	3	4	9	23
35–49	44	3.3	37	1	2	2	2	3	5	36
50–64	3	3.7	4	2	2	3	6	6	6	6
65+	0									
GRAND TOTAL	**233**	**2.9**	**17**	**1**	**1**	**2**	**3**	**4**	**9**	**23**

72.6: FORCEPS-AFTERCOMING HEAD

Type of Patients	Observed Patients	Avg. Stay	Vari-ance	Percentiles						
				10th	25th	50th	75th	90th	95th	99th
1. SINGLE DX										
0–19 Years	0									
20–34	3	1.7	1	1	1	1	3	3	3	3
35–49	0									
50–64	0									
65+	0									
2. MULTIPLE DX										
0–19 Years	1	3.0	0	3	3	3	3	3	3	3
20–34	3	2.4	<1	2	2	2	3	3	3	3
35–49	1	2.0	0	2	2	2	2	2	2	2
50–64	0									
65+	0									
TOTAL SINGLE DX	**3**	**1.7**	**1**	**1**	**1**	**1**	**3**	**3**	**3**	**3**
TOTAL MULTIPLE DX	**5**	**2.3**	**<1**	**2**	**2**	**2**	**3**	**3**	**3**	**3**
TOTAL										
0–19 Years	1	3.0	0	3	3	3	3	3	3	3
20–34	6	2.0	<1	1	1	2	3	3	3	3
35–49	1	2.0	0	2	2	2	2	2	2	2
50–64	0									
65+	0									
GRAND TOTAL	**8**	**2.1**	**<1**	**1**	**2**	**2**	**3**	**3**	**3**	**3**

72.7: VACUUM EXTRACTION DEL

Type of Patients	Observed Patients	Avg. Stay	Vari-ance	Percentiles						
				10th	25th	50th	75th	90th	95th	99th
1. SINGLE DX										
0–19 Years	854	1.9	<1	1	2	2	2	3	3	4
20–34	5,151	1.9	2	1	1	2	2	3	3	3
35–49	326	1.9	<1	1	1	2	2	3	3	4
50–64	25	2.0	<1	1	2	2	2	3	3	3
65+	0									
2. MULTIPLE DX										
0–19 Years	3,045	2.2	<1	1	2	2	3	3	4	5
20–34	22,859	2.1	<1	1	2	2	3	3	3	5
35–49	4,651	2.2	3	1	2	2	3	3	3	5
50–64	232	2.3	2	1	2	2	3	3	4	5
65+	0									
TOTAL SINGLE DX	**6,356**	**1.9**	**2**	**1**	**1**	**2**	**2**	**3**	**3**	**3**
TOTAL MULTIPLE DX	**30,787**	**2.2**	**1**	**1**	**2**	**2**	**3**	**3**	**3**	**5**
TOTAL										
0–19 Years	3,899	2.1	<1	1	2	2	3	3	3	5
20–34	28,010	2.1	1	1	2	2	3	3	3	4
35–49	4,977	2.2	2	1	2	2	3	3	3	5
50–64	257	2.3	2	1	2	2	3	3	4	5
65+	0									
GRAND TOTAL	**37,143**	**2.1**	**1**	**1**	**2**	**2**	**3**	**3**	**3**	**4**

72.71: VED W EPISIOTOMY

Type of Patients	Observed Patients	Avg. Stay	Vari-ance	Percentiles						
				10th	25th	50th	75th	90th	95th	99th
1. SINGLE DX										
0–19 Years	638	2.0	<1	1	2	2	2	3	3	4
20–34	3,659	2.0	3	1	1	2	2	3	3	3
35–49	203	2.0	<1	1	2	2	2	3	3	4
50–64	14	2.0	<1	1	2	2	2	3	3	3
65+	0									
2. MULTIPLE DX										
0–19 Years	1,696	2.2	<1	1	2	2	3	3	4	5
20–34	11,187	2.2	<1	1	2	2	3	3	3	5
35–49	2,186	2.3	3	1	2	2	3	3	3	5
50–64	121	2.4	4	1	2	2	3	3	4	5
65+	0									
TOTAL SINGLE DX	**4,514**	**2.0**	**2**	**1**	**1**	**2**	**2**	**3**	**3**	**4**
TOTAL MULTIPLE DX	**15,190**	**2.2**	**1**	**1**	**2**	**2**	**3**	**3**	**3**	**5**
TOTAL										
0–19 Years	2,334	2.2	<1	1	2	2	3	3	3	5
20–34	14,846	2.1	1	1	2	2	3	3	3	4
35–49	2,389	2.3	3	1	2	2	3	3	3	5
50–64	135	2.4	3	1	2	2	3	3	4	5
65+	0									
GRAND TOTAL	**19,704**	**2.2**	**1**	**1**	**2**	**2**	**3**	**3**	**3**	**4**

72.79: VACUUM EXTRACT DEL NEC

Type of Patients	Observed Patients	Avg. Stay	Vari-ance	Percentiles						
				10th	25th	50th	75th	90th	95th	99th
1. SINGLE DX										
0–19 Years	216	1.8	<1	1	1	2	2	3	3	3
20–34	1,492	1.7	<1	1	1	2	2	3	3	3
35–49	123	1.8	<1	1	1	2	2	3	3	4
50–64	11	2.0	<1	1	1	2	2	3	3	3
65+	0									
2. MULTIPLE DX										
0–19 Years	1,349	2.1	1	1	2	2	3	3	3	5
20–34	11,672	2.1	<1	1	2	2	2	3	3	5
35–49	2,465	2.1	2	1	2	2	3	3	3	4
50–64	111	2.2	<1	1	2	2	3	3	4	5
65+	0									
TOTAL SINGLE DX	**1,842**	**1.8**	**<1**	**1**	**1**	**2**	**2**	**3**	**3**	**3**
TOTAL MULTIPLE DX	**15,597**	**2.1**	**1**	**1**	**2**	**2**	**3**	**3**	**3**	**5**
TOTAL										
0–19 Years	1,565	2.1	1	1	2	2	2	3	3	5
20–34	13,164	2.1	<1	1	2	2	2	3	3	4
35–49	2,588	2.1	2	1	2	2	2	3	3	4
50–64	122	2.2	<1	1	2	2	3	3	4	5
65+	0									
GRAND TOTAL	**17,439**	**2.1**	**1**	**1**	**2**	**2**	**2**	**3**	**3**	**5**

72.8: INSTRUMENTAL DEL NEC

Type of Patients	Observed Patients	Avg. Stay	Vari-ance	Percentiles						
				10th	25th	50th	75th	90th	95th	99th
1. SINGLE DX										
0–19 Years	1	3.0	0	3	3	3	3	3	3	3
20–34	3	1.3	<1	1	1	1	2	2	2	2
35–49	1	2.0	0	2	2	2	2	2	2	2
50–64	0									
65+	0									
2. MULTIPLE DX										
0–19 Years	2	2.5	4	1	1	4	4	4	4	4
20–34	9	2.2	<1	1	2	2	3	3	3	3
35–49	3	2.3	<1	2	2	2	3	3	3	3
50–64	0									
65+	0									
TOTAL SINGLE DX	**5**	**2.0**	**<1**	**1**	**1**	**2**	**3**	**3**	**3**	**3**
TOTAL MULTIPLE DX	**14**	**2.3**	**<1**	**1**	**2**	**2**	**3**	**3**	**4**	**4**
TOTAL										
0–19 Years	3	2.8	1	1	3	3	3	4	4	4
20–34	12	2.1	<1	1	2	2	3	3	3	3
35–49	4	2.2	<1	2	2	2	2	3	3	3
50–64	0									
65+	0									
GRAND TOTAL	**19**	**2.2**	**<1**	**1**	**2**	**2**	**3**	**3**	**3**	**4**

72.9: INSTRUMENTAL DEL NOS

Type of Patients	Observed Patients	Avg. Stay	Vari-ance	Percentiles						
				10th	25th	50th	75th	90th	95th	99th
1. SINGLE DX										
0–19 Years	1	2.0	0	2	2	2	2	2	2	2
20–34	12	1.8	<1	1	2	2	2	2	3	3
35–49	0									
50–64	0									
65+	0									
2. MULTIPLE DX										
0–19 Years	15	2.5	<1	2	2	2	3	3	4	4
20–34	74	2.5	1	2	2	2	3	3	5	7
35–49	16	2.7	1	2	2	2	4	4	4	4
50–64	1	2.0	0	2	2	2	2	2	2	2
65+	0									
TOTAL SINGLE DX	**13**	**1.8**	**<1**	**1**	**2**	**2**	**2**	**2**	**3**	**3**
TOTAL MULTIPLE DX	**106**	**2.6**	**<1**	**2**	**2**	**2**	**3**	**4**	**4**	**7**
TOTAL										
0–19 Years	16	2.4	<1	2	2	2	3	3	3	4
20–34	86	2.5	1	1	2	2	3	3	4	7
35–49	16	2.7	1	2	2	2	4	4	4	4
50–64	1	2.0	0	2	2	2	2	2	2	2
65+	0									
GRAND TOTAL	**119**	**2.5**	**<1**	**2**	**2**	**2**	**3**	**4**	**4**	**7**

73.0: ARTIFICIAL RUPT MEMBRANE

Type of Patients	Observed Patients	Avg. Stay	Vari-ance	Percentiles						
				10th	25th	50th	75th	90th	95th	99th
1. SINGLE DX										
0–19 Years	595	1.6	<1	1	1	2	2	2	3	3
20–34	4,775	1.6	<1	1	1	2	2	2	3	3
35–49	288	1.6	<1	1	1	2	2	2	3	3
50–64	9	1.8	<1	1	1	2	2	3	3	3
65+	0									
2. MULTIPLE DX										
0–19 Years	873	2.0	3	1	1	2	2	3	3	6
20–34	6,083	1.9	1	1	1	2	2	3	3	4
35–49	993	2.0	10	1	1	2	2	3	3	4
50–64	29	1.9	<1	1	1	2	2	2	4	4
65+	0									
TOTAL SINGLE DX	**5,667**	**1.6**	**<1**	**1**	**1**	**2**	**2**	**2**	**3**	**3**
TOTAL MULTIPLE DX	**7,978**	**1.9**	**2**	**1**	**1**	**2**	**2**	**3**	**3**	**4**
TOTAL										
0–19 Years	1,468	1.9	2	1	1	2	2	3	3	5
20–34	10,858	1.8	<1	1	1	2	2	3	3	4
35–49	1,281	1.9	8	1	1	2	2	3	3	4
50–64	38	1.9	<1	1	1	2	2	3	4	4
65+	0									
GRAND TOTAL	**13,645**	**1.8**	**2**	**1**	**1**	**2**	**2**	**3**	**3**	**4**

73.01: INDUCTION LABOR BY AROM

Type of Patients	Observed Patients	Avg. Stay	Vari-ance	Percentiles						
				10th	25th	50th	75th	90th	95th	99th
1. SINGLE DX										
0–19 Years	38	1.8	1	1	1	2	2	3	3	10
20–34	485	1.6	<1	1	1	2	2	2	3	3
35–49	32	1.7	<1	1	1	2	2	2	3	3
50–64	1	1.0	0	1	1	1	1	1	1	1
65+	0									
2. MULTIPLE DX										
0–19 Years	86	2.1	<1	1	2	2	2	3	3	4
20–34	965	1.9	<1	1	1	2	2	3	3	4
35–49	205	2.0	<1	1	2	2	2	3	3	4
50–64	5	1.6	<1	1	1	2	2	2	2	2
65+	0									
TOTAL SINGLE DX	**556**	**1.7**	**<1**	**1**	**1**	**2**	**2**	**2**	**3**	**3**
TOTAL MULTIPLE DX	**1,261**	**2.0**	**<1**	**1**	**1**	**2**	**2**	**3**	**3**	**4**
TOTAL										
0–19 Years	124	2.0	<1	1	1	2	2	3	3	4
20–34	1,450	1.8	<1	1	1	2	2	3	3	4
35–49	237	1.9	<1	1	2	2	2	3	3	4
50–64	6	1.5	<1	1	1	1	2	2	2	2
65+	0									
GRAND TOTAL	**1,817**	**1.9**	**<1**	**1**	**1**	**2**	**2**	**3**	**3**	**4**

73.09: ARTIF RUPT MEMBRANES NEC

Type of Patients	Observed Patients	Avg. Stay	Vari-ance	Percentiles						
				10th	25th	50th	75th	90th	95th	99th
1. SINGLE DX										
0–19 Years	557	1.6	<1	1	1	2	2	2	3	3
20–34	4,290	1.6	<1	1	1	2	2	2	3	3
35–49	256	1.6	<1	1	1	2	2	2	3	3
50–64	8	1.9	<1	1	2	2	2	3	3	3
65+	0									
2. MULTIPLE DX										
0–19 Years	787	2.0	3	1	1	2	2	3	3	6
20–34	5,118	1.9	1	1	1	2	2	3	3	4
35–49	788	2.0	13	1	1	2	2	3	3	4
50–64	24	1.9	<1	1	1	2	2	3	4	4
65+	0									
TOTAL SINGLE DX	**5,111**	**1.6**	**<1**	**1**	**1**	**2**	**2**	**2**	**3**	**3**
TOTAL MULTIPLE DX	**6,717**	**1.9**	**3**	**1**	**1**	**2**	**2**	**3**	**3**	**4**
TOTAL										
0–19 Years	1,344	1.9	2	1	1	2	2	3	3	5
20–34	9,408	1.7	<1	1	1	2	2	3	3	4
35–49	1,044	1.9	10	1	1	2	2	3	3	4
50–64	32	1.9	<1	1	1	2	2	3	4	4
65+	0									
GRAND TOTAL	**11,828**	**1.8**	**2**	**1**	**1**	**2**	**2**	**3**	**3**	**4**

73.1: SURG INDUCTION LABOR NEC

Type of Patients	Observed Patients	Avg. Stay	Vari-ance	Percentiles						
				10th	25th	50th	75th	90th	95th	99th
1. SINGLE DX										
0–19 Years	3	2.4	1	1	1	3	3	3	3	3
20–34	36	1.7	<1	1	1	2	2	3	3	4
35–49	5	2.3	2	1	1	2	3	4	4	4
50–64	0									
65+	0									
2. MULTIPLE DX										
0–19 Years	10	2.2	1	1	1	2	3	4	4	4
20–34	79	2.4	2	1	2	2	3	4	4	10
35–49	18	2.0	<1	1	1	2	3	3	3	3
50–64	0									
65+	0									
TOTAL SINGLE DX	**44**	**1.8**	**<1**	**1**	**1**	**2**	**2**	**3**	**3**	**4**
TOTAL MULTIPLE DX	**107**	**2.4**	**2**	**1**	**2**	**2**	**3**	**3**	**4**	**10**
TOTAL										
0–19 Years	13	2.3	1	1	1	3	3	4	4	4
20–34	115	2.2	2	1	1	2	3	3	4	10
35–49	23	2.1	<1	1	1	2	3	3	4	4
50–64	0									
65+	0									
GRAND TOTAL	**151**	**2.2**	**2**	**1**	**1**	**2**	**3**	**3**	**4**	**10**

73.2: INT/COMB VERSION/EXTRACT

Type of Patients	Observed Patients	Avg. Stay	Vari-ance	Percentiles						
				10th	25th	50th	75th	90th	95th	99th
1. SINGLE DX										
0–19 Years	0									
20–34	12	1.5	<1	1	1	1	2	3	4	4
35–49	1	2.0	0	2	2	2	2	2	2	2
50–64	0									
65+	0									
2. MULTIPLE DX										
0–19 Years	2	1.3	<1	1	1	1	1	3	3	3
20–34	33	2.0	<1	1	1	2	2	3	4	4
35–49	6	2.1	<1	1	1	2	3	3	3	3
50–64	0									
65+	0									
TOTAL SINGLE DX	**13**	**1.6**	**<1**	**1**	**1**	**1**	**2**	**3**	**4**	**4**
TOTAL MULTIPLE DX	**41**	**2.0**	**<1**	**1**	**1**	**2**	**2**	**3**	**4**	**4**
TOTAL										
0–19 Years	2	1.3	<1	1	1	1	1	3	3	3
20–34	45	1.9	<1	1	1	2	2	3	4	4
35–49	7	2.1	<1	1	2	2	3	3	3	3
50–64	0									
65+	0									
GRAND TOTAL	**54**	**1.9**	**<1**	**1**	**1**	**2**	**2**	**3**	**4**	**4**

73.3: FAILED FORCEPS

Type of Patients	Observed Patients	Avg. Stay	Vari-ance	Percentiles						
				10th	25th	50th	75th	90th	95th	99th
1. SINGLE DX										
0–19 Years	1	2.0	0	2	2	2	2	2	2	2
20–34	0									
35–49	0									
50–64	0									
65+	0									
2. MULTIPLE DX										
0–19 Years	1	2.0	0	2	2	2	2	2	2	2
20–34	3	4.0	1	3	3	3	5	5	5	5
35–49	1	3.0	0	3	3	3	3	3	3	3
50–64	0									
65+	0									
TOTAL SINGLE DX	**1**	**2.0**	**0**	**2**	**2**	**2**	**2**	**2**	**2**	**2**
TOTAL MULTIPLE DX	**5**	**3.4**	**1**	**2**	**3**	**3**	**5**	**5**	**5**	**5**
TOTAL										
0–19 Years	2	2.0	0	2	2	2	2	2	2	2
20–34	3	4.0	1	3	3	3	5	5	5	5
35–49	1	3.0	0	3	3	3	3	3	3	3
50–64	0									
65+	0									
GRAND TOTAL	**6**	**3.1**	**1**	**2**	**2**	**3**	**3**	**5**	**5**	**5**

73.4: MEDICAL INDUCTION LABOR

Type of Patients	Observed Patients	Avg. Stay	Vari-ance	Percentiles						
				10th	25th	50th	75th	90th	95th	99th
1. SINGLE DX										
0–19 Years	235	1.7	<1	1	1	2	2	3	3	5
20–34	2,560	1.7	1	1	1	2	2	3	3	3
35–49	211	1.6	<1	1	1	2	2	3	3	3
50–64	4	2.0	<1	1	1	2	3	3	3	3
65+	0									
2. MULTIPLE DX										
0–19 Years	756	2.4	3	1	2	2	3	3	4	7
20–34	7,192	2.2	4	1	1	2	2	3	4	6
35–49	1,370	2.2	5	1	1	2	2	3	4	9
50–64	50	2.3	<1	1	2	2	3	3	4	6
65+	0									
TOTAL SINGLE DX	**3,010**	**1.7**	**<1**	**1**	**1**	**2**	**2**	**3**	**3**	**3**
TOTAL MULTIPLE DX	**9,368**	**2.2**	**4**	**1**	**1**	**2**	**3**	**3**	**4**	**6**
TOTAL										
0–19 Years	991	2.2	2	1	1	2	3	3	4	6
20–34	9,752	2.0	3	1	1	2	2	3	4	5
35–49	1,581	2.1	4	1	1	2	2	3	4	7
50–64	54	2.3	<1	1	2	2	3	3	4	6
65+	0									
GRAND TOTAL	**12,378**	**2.1**	**3**	**1**	**1**	**2**	**2**	**3**	**4**	**6**

73.5: MANUALLY ASSISTED DEL

Type of Patients	Observed Patients	Avg. Stay	Vari-ance	Percentiles						
				10th	25th	50th	75th	90th	95th	99th
1. SINGLE DX										
0–19 Years	7,505	1.8	<1	1	1	2	2	3	3	3
20–34	67,872	1.7	<1	1	1	2	2	2	3	3
35–49	5,091	1.7	<1	1	1	2	2	2	3	3
50–64	272	1.8	<1	1	1	2	2	3	3	4
65+	0									
2. MULTIPLE DX										
0–19 Years	10,187	2.2	4	1	1	2	2	3	3	7
20–34	92,049	2.0	3	1	1	2	2	3	3	6
35–49	19,724	2.0	3	1	1	2	2	3	3	6
50–64	1,028	2.1	2	1	2	2	2	3	3	9
65+	0									
TOTAL SINGLE DX	**80,740**	**1.7**	**<1**	**1**	**1**	**2**	**2**	**2**	**3**	**3**
TOTAL MULTIPLE DX	**122,988**	**2.0**	**3**	**1**	**1**	**2**	**2**	**3**	**3**	**6**
TOTAL										
0–19 Years	17,692	2.0	3	1	1	2	2	3	3	5
20–34	159,921	1.9	2	1	1	2	2	3	3	5
35–49	24,815	2.0	2	1	1	2	2	3	3	6
50–64	1,300	2.1	2	1	1	2	2	3	3	7
65+	0									
GRAND TOTAL	**203,728**	**1.9**	**2**	**1**	**1**	**2**	**2**	**3**	**3**	**5**

73.51: MANUAL ROT FETAL HEAD

Type of Patients	Observed Patients	Avg. Stay	Vari-ance	Percentiles						
				10th	25th	50th	75th	90th	95th	99th
1. SINGLE DX										
0–19 Years	5	1.7	<1	1	1	2	2	2	2	2
20–34	49	1.6	<1	1	1	2	2	2	2	3
35–49	1	1.0	0	1	1	1	1	1	1	1
50–64	0									
65+	0									
2. MULTIPLE DX										
0–19 Years	23	1.9	<1	1	1	2	2	3	3	3
20–34	176	1.9	<1	1	1	2	2	3	3	4
35–49	53	2.0	<1	1	2	2	2	3	3	3
50–64	2	2.5	<1	2	2	3	3	3	3	3
65+	0									
TOTAL SINGLE DX	**55**	**1.6**	**<1**	**1**	**1**	**2**	**2**	**2**	**2**	**3**
TOTAL MULTIPLE DX	**254**	**2.0**	**<1**	**1**	**1**	**2**	**2**	**3**	**3**	**4**
TOTAL										
0–19 Years	28	1.9	<1	1	1	2	2	3	3	3
20–34	225	1.9	<1	1	1	2	2	3	3	4
35–49	54	2.0	<1	1	1	2	2	3	3	3
50–64	2	2.5	<1	2	2	3	3	3	3	3
65+	0									
GRAND TOTAL	**309**	**1.9**	**<1**	**1**	**1**	**2**	**2**	**3**	**3**	**3**

73.59: MANUAL ASSISTED DEL NEC

Type of Patients	Observed Patients	Avg. Stay	Vari-ance	Percentiles						
				10th	25th	50th	75th	90th	95th	99th
1. SINGLE DX										
0–19 Years	7,500	1.8	<1	1	1	2	2	3	3	3
20–34	67,823	1.7	<1	1	1	2	2	2	3	3
35–49	5,090	1.7	<1	1	1	2	2	2	3	3
50–64	272	1.8	<1	1	1	2	2	3	3	4
65+	0									
2. MULTIPLE DX										
0–19 Years	10,164	2.2	4	1	1	2	2	3	3	7
20–34	91,873	2.0	3	1	1	2	2	3	3	6
35–49	19,671	2.0	3	1	1	2	2	3	3	6
50–64	1,026	2.1	2	1	2	2	2	3	3	9
65+	0									
TOTAL SINGLE DX	**80,685**	**1.7**	**<1**	**1**	**1**	**2**	**2**	**2**	**3**	**3**
TOTAL MULTIPLE DX	**122,734**	**2.0**	**3**	**1**	**1**	**2**	**2**	**3**	**3**	**6**
TOTAL										
0–19 Years	17,664	2.0	3	1	1	2	2	3	3	5
20–34	159,696	1.9	2	1	1	2	2	3	3	5
35–49	24,761	2.0	2	1	1	2	2	3	3	6
50–64	1,298	2.1	2	1	1	2	2	3	3	7
65+	0									
GRAND TOTAL	**203,419**	**1.9**	**2**	**1**	**1**	**2**	**2**	**3**	**3**	**5**

73.6: EPISIOTOMY

Type of Patients	Observed Patients	Avg. Stay	Vari-ance	10th	25th	50th	75th	90th	95th	99th
1. SINGLE DX										
0–19 Years	3,768	1.9	<1	1	1	2	2	3	3	4
20–34	21,976	1.8	<1	1	1	2	2	3	3	3
35–49	1,752	1.8	<1	1	1	2	2	3	3	3
50–64	93	1.9	<1	1	2	2	2	3	3	5
65+	0									
2. MULTIPLE DX										
0–19 Years	2,927	2.2	3	1	2	2	3	3	3	7
20–34	18,431	2.1	2	1	2	2	2	3	3	5
35–49	3,899	2.2	8	1	2	2	2	3	3	6
50–64	189	2.1	2	1	2	2	2	3	3	8
65+	0									
TOTAL SINGLE DX	**27,589**	**1.8**	**<1**	**1**	**1**	**2**	**2**	**3**	**3**	**3**
TOTAL MULTIPLE DX	**25,446**	**2.1**	**3**	**1**	**2**	**2**	**2**	**3**	**3**	**5**
TOTAL										
0–19 Years	6,695	2.1	2	1	2	2	2	3	3	5
20–34	40,407	2.0	1	1	1	2	2	3	3	4
35–49	5,651	2.1	5	1	1	2	2	3	3	5
50–64	282	2.0	1	1	2	2	2	3	3	6
65+	0									
GRAND TOTAL	**53,035**	**2.0**	**2**	**1**	**1**	**2**	**2**	**3**	**3**	**4**

73.8: FETAL OPS-FACILITATE DEL

Type of Patients	Observed Patients	Avg. Stay	Vari-ance	10th	25th	50th	75th	90th	95th	99th
1. SINGLE DX										
0–19 Years	0									
20–34	0									
35–49	0									
50–64	0									
65+	0									
2. MULTIPLE DX										
0–19 Years	0									
20–34	0									
35–49	0									
50–64	0									
65+	0									
TOTAL SINGLE DX	**0**									
TOTAL MULTIPLE DX	**0**									
TOTAL										
0–19 Years	0									
20–34	0									
35–49	0									
50–64	0									
65+	0									
GRAND TOTAL	**0**									

73.9: OTH OPS ASSISTING DEL

Type of Patients	Observed Patients	Avg. Stay	Vari-ance	10th	25th	50th	75th	90th	95th	99th
1. SINGLE DX										
0–19 Years	2	1.0	0	1	1	1	1	1	1	1
20–34	28	1.4	<1	1	1	1	2	2	3	3
35–49	8	1.3	<1	1	1	1	1	3	3	3
50–64	0									
65+	0									
2. MULTIPLE DX										
0–19 Years	3	1.6	1	1	1	1	3	3	3	3
20–34	73	2.4	4	1	1	2	3	3	6	14
35–49	33	1.8	1	1	1	2	2	2	3	6
50–64	1	5.0	0	5	5	5	5	5	5	5
65+	0									
TOTAL SINGLE DX	**38**	**1.4**	**<1**	**1**	**1**	**1**	**2**	**2**	**3**	**3**
TOTAL MULTIPLE DX	**110**	**2.2**	**3**	**1**	**1**	**2**	**2**	**3**	**6**	**14**
TOTAL										
0–19 Years	5	1.4	<1	1	1	1	1	3	3	3
20–34	101	2.2	3	1	1	2	2	3	5	14
35–49	41	1.7	1	1	1	1	2	2	3	6
50–64	1	5.0	0	5	5	5	5	5	5	5
65+	0									
GRAND TOTAL	**148**	**2.0**	**3**	**1**	**1**	**2**	**2**	**3**	**5**	**6**

73.91: EXT VERSION-ASSIST DEL

Type of Patients	Observed Patients	Avg. Stay	Vari-ance	10th	25th	50th	75th	90th	95th	99th
1. SINGLE DX										
0–19 Years	2	1.0	0	1	1	1	1	1	1	1
20–34	26	1.5	<1	1	1	1	2	2	3	3
35–49	8	1.3	<1	1	1	1	1	3	3	3
50–64	0									
65+	0									
2. MULTIPLE DX										
0–19 Years	2	1.0	0	1	1	1	1	1	1	1
20–34	64	2.5	5	1	1	2	3	5	6	14
35–49	29	1.7	1	1	1	1	2	2	6	6
50–64	1	5.0	0	5	5	5	5	5	5	5
65+	0									
TOTAL SINGLE DX	**36**	**1.4**	**<1**	**1**	**1**	**1**	**2**	**2**	**3**	**3**
TOTAL MULTIPLE DX	**96**	**2.2**	**4**	**1**	**1**	**2**	**2**	**3**	**6**	**14**
TOTAL										
0–19 Years	4	1.0	0	1	1	1	1	1	1	1
20–34	90	2.2	4	1	1	2	3	3	6	14
35–49	37	1.6	1	1	1	1	2	2	3	6
50–64	1	5.0	0	5	5	5	5	5	5	5
65+	0									
GRAND TOTAL	**132**	**2.0**	**3**	**1**	**1**	**2**	**2**	**3**	**5**	**14**

74.0: CLASSICAL CD

Type of Patients	Observed Patients	Avg. Stay	Vari-ance	Percentiles						
				10th	25th	50th	75th	90th	95th	99th
1. SINGLE DX										
0–19 Years	2	3.5	<1	3	3	4	4	4	4	4
20–34	68	3.0	2	2	2	3	3	4	4	12
35–49	9	2.7	<1	2	2	2	3	4	5	5
50–64	1	3.0	0	3	3	3	3	3	3	3
65+	0									
2. MULTIPLE DX										
0–19 Years	45	6.1	33	2	3	4	7	14	14	29
20–34	894	6.7	71	2	3	4	6	15	22	50
35–49	346	7.5	73	3	3	4	7	18	26	38
50–64	18	6.1	14	3	4	4	7	9	11	19
65+	0									
TOTAL SINGLE DX	**80**	**3.0**	**1**	**2**	**2**	**3**	**3**	**4**	**4**	**5**
TOTAL MULTIPLE DX	**1,303**	**6.8**	**69**	**2**	**3**	**4**	**7**	**15**	**23**	**46**
TOTAL										
0–19 Years	47	6.1	32	2	3	4	7	14	14	29
20–34	962	6.4	67	2	3	4	6	13	22	46
35–49	355	7.4	72	3	3	4	7	18	26	38
50–64	19	5.9	14	3	4	4	7	9	11	19
65+	0									
GRAND TOTAL	**1,383**	**6.6**	**67**	**2**	**3**	**4**	**6**	**15**	**23**	**44**

74.1: LOW CERVICAL CD

Type of Patients	Observed Patients	Avg. Stay	Vari-ance	Percentiles						
				10th	25th	50th	75th	90th	95th	99th
1. SINGLE DX										
0–19 Years	1,290	3.0	<1	2	2	3	3	4	4	5
20–34	21,141	2.9	<1	2	2	3	3	4	4	5
35–49	1,646	3.1	<1	2	2	3	4	4	4	5
50–64	116	3.1	<1	2	3	3	4	4	4	5
65+	0									
2. MULTIPLE DX										
0–19 Years	7,434	3.7	5	2	3	3	4	5	6	12
20–34	97,878	3.6	8	2	3	3	4	5	6	12
35–49	30,587	3.8	11	2	3	3	4	5	6	15
50–64	1,749	4.0	18	2	3	4	4	5	6	16
65+	0									
TOTAL SINGLE DX	**24,193**	**2.9**	**<1**	**2**	**2**	**3**	**3**	**4**	**4**	**5**
TOTAL MULTIPLE DX	**137,648**	**3.7**	**8**	**2**	**3**	**3**	**4**	**5**	**6**	**13**
TOTAL										
0–19 Years	8,724	3.6	5	2	3	3	4	5	6	11
20–34	119,019	3.5	7	2	3	3	4	5	5	11
35–49	32,233	3.7	10	2	3	3	4	5	6	15
50–64	1,865	3.9	17	2	3	3	4	5	5	16
65+	0									
GRAND TOTAL	**161,841**	**3.6**	**7**	**2**	**3**	**3**	**4**	**5**	**5**	**12**

74.2: EXTRAPERITONEAL CD

Type of Patients	Observed Patients	Avg. Stay	Vari-ance	Percentiles						
				10th	25th	50th	75th	90th	95th	99th
1. SINGLE DX										
0–19 Years	0									
20–34	3	2.7	<1	2	2	3	3	3	3	3
35–49	0									
50–64	0									
65+	0									
2. MULTIPLE DX										
0–19 Years	2	3.5	<1	3	3	4	4	4	4	4
20–34	29	4.0	1	3	3	4	5	6	6	6
35–49	2	4.0	2	3	3	4	5	5	5	5
50–64	0									
65+	0									
TOTAL SINGLE DX	**3**	**2.7**	**<1**	**2**	**2**	**3**	**3**	**3**	**3**	**3**
TOTAL MULTIPLE DX	**33**	**4.0**	**1**	**3**	**3**	**4**	**5**	**5**	**6**	**6**
TOTAL										
0–19 Years	2	3.5	<1	3	3	4	4	4	4	4
20–34	32	3.8	1	3	3	4	5	5	6	6
35–49	2	4.0	2	3	3	4	5	5	5	5
50–64	0									
65+	0									
GRAND TOTAL	**36**	**3.8**	**1**	**3**	**3**	**4**	**5**	**5**	**6**	**6**

74.3: RMVL EXTRATUBAL PREG

Type of Patients	Observed Patients	Avg. Stay	Vari-ance	Percentiles						
				10th	25th	50th	75th	90th	95th	99th
1. SINGLE DX										
0–19 Years	1	2.0	0	2	2	2	2	2	2	2
20–34	30	2.1	1	1	1	2	3	3	4	5
35–49	14	2.3	2	1	1	2	4	4	4	4
50–64	1	2.0	0	2	2	2	2	2	2	2
65+	0									
2. MULTIPLE DX										
0–19 Years	4	1.7	<1	1	1	1	2	3	3	3
20–34	74	2.4	1	1	2	2	3	4	4	5
35–49	24	2.8	4	1	1	3	3	6	8	10
50–64	3	1.6	<1	1	1	2	2	2	2	2
65+	0									
TOTAL SINGLE DX	**46**	**2.1**	**1**	**1**	**1**	**2**	**3**	**4**	**4**	**5**
TOTAL MULTIPLE DX	**105**	**2.5**	**2**	**1**	**1**	**2**	**3**	**4**	**5**	**8**
TOTAL										
0–19 Years	5	1.8	<1	1	1	2	2	3	3	3
20–34	104	2.3	1	1	1	2	3	4	4	5
35–49	38	2.6	3	1	1	2	3	4	6	10
50–64	4	1.7	<1	1	1	2	2	2	2	2
65+	0									
GRAND TOTAL	**151**	**2.4**	**2**	**1**	**1**	**2**	**3**	**4**	**5**	**8**

74.4: CESAREAN SECTION NEC

Type of Patients	Observed Patients	Avg. Stay	Vari-ance	Percentiles						
				10th	25th	50th	75th	90th	95th	99th
1. SINGLE DX										
0–19 Years	2	3.3	<1	3	3	3	4	4	4	4
20–34	22	2.6	<1	2	2	3	3	3	3	3
35–49	2	3.0	0	3	3	3	3	3	3	3
50–64	0									
65+	0									
2. MULTIPLE DX										
0–19 Years	14	4.1	7	2	3	4	4	5	5	15
20–34	173	4.1	14	2	3	3	4	5	7	21
35–49	53	3.5	1	3	3	3	4	5	5	10
50–64	4	4.2	<1	3	3	4	5	5	5	5
65+	0									
TOTAL SINGLE DX	**26**	**2.7**	**<1**	**2**	**2**	**3**	**3**	**3**	**4**	**4**
TOTAL MULTIPLE DX	**244**	**3.9**	**10**	**2**	**3**	**3**	**4**	**5**	**7**	**15**
TOTAL										
0–19 Years	16	3.9	5	2	3	4	4	4	5	15
20–34	195	3.9	12	2	3	3	4	5	7	21
35–49	55	3.5	1	3	3	3	4	5	5	5
50–64	4	4.2	<1	3	3	4	5	5	5	5
65+	0									
GRAND TOTAL	**270**	**3.8**	**9**	**2**	**3**	**3**	**4**	**5**	**7**	**15**

74.9: CESAREAN SECTION NOS

Type of Patients	Observed Patients	Avg. Stay	Vari-ance	Percentiles						
				10th	25th	50th	75th	90th	95th	99th
1. SINGLE DX										
0–19 Years	1	3.0	0	3	3	3	3	3	3	3
20–34	37	3.1	<1	2	2	3	4	4	4	5
35–49	4	2.7	2	2	2	2	3	6	6	6
50–64	1	5.0	0	5	5	5	5	5	5	5
65+	0									
2. MULTIPLE DX										
0–19 Years	7	3.4	<1	2	3	4	4	4	4	4
20–34	128	3.6	2	2	3	3	4	5	6	10
35–49	46	4.1	12	2	3	3	4	6	17	17
50–64	2	3.0	0	3	3	3	3	3	3	3
65+	0									
TOTAL SINGLE DX	**43**	**3.0**	**<1**	**2**	**2**	**3**	**4**	**4**	**5**	**6**
TOTAL MULTIPLE DX	**183**	**3.7**	**5**	**2**	**3**	**3**	**4**	**5**	**6**	**17**
TOTAL										
0–19 Years	8	3.2	<1	3	3	3	4	4	4	4
20–34	165	3.4	2	2	3	3	4	5	6	10
35–49	50	3.9	11	2	2	3	4	6	17	17
50–64	3	3.8	1	3	3	3	5	5	5	5
65+	0									
GRAND TOTAL	**226**	**3.5**	**4**	**2**	**3**	**3**	**4**	**5**	**6**	**17**

74.99: OTHER CD TYPE NOS

Type of Patients	Observed Patients	Avg. Stay	Vari-ance	Percentiles						
				10th	25th	50th	75th	90th	95th	99th
1. SINGLE DX										
0–19 Years	1	3.0	0	3	3	3	3	3	3	3
20–34	37	3.1	<1	2	2	3	4	4	4	5
35–49	3	2.3	<1	2	2	2	3	3	3	3
50–64	1	5.0	0	5	5	5	5	5	5	5
65+	0									
2. MULTIPLE DX										
0–19 Years	6	3.3	<1	2	3	3	4	4	4	4
20–34	120	3.5	2	2	3	3	4	5	6	9
35–49	43	4.1	13	2	3	3	4	6	17	17
50–64	2	3.0	0	3	3	3	3	3	3	3
65+	0									
TOTAL SINGLE DX	**42**	**3.0**	**<1**	**2**	**2**	**3**	**4**	**4**	**5**	**5**
TOTAL MULTIPLE DX	**171**	**3.6**	**5**	**2**	**3**	**3**	**4**	**5**	**6**	**17**
TOTAL										
0–19 Years	7	3.2	<1	3	3	3	4	4	4	4
20–34	157	3.4	2	2	3	3	4	5	6	9
35–49	46	3.9	12	2	2	3	4	5	17	17
50–64	3	3.8	1	3	3	3	5	5	5	5
65+	0									
GRAND TOTAL	**213**	**3.5**	**4**	**2**	**3**	**3**	**4**	**5**	**6**	**17**

75.0: INTRA-AMNIO INJECT-AB

Type of Patients	Observed Patients	Avg. Stay	Vari-ance	Percentiles						
				10th	25th	50th	75th	90th	95th	99th
1. SINGLE DX										
0–19 Years	0									
20–34	4	1.2	<1	1	1	1	1	2	2	2
35–49	2	6.7	19	1	1	9	9	9	9	9
50–64	0									
65+	0									
2. MULTIPLE DX										
0–19 Years	1	2.0	0	2	2	2	2	2	2	2
20–34	18	1.3	<1	1	1	1	1	2	3	4
35–49	4	1.0	0	1	1	1	1	1	1	1
50–64	2	2.0	2	1	1	3	3	3	3	3
65+	0									
TOTAL SINGLE DX	**6**	**3.2**	**13**	**1**	**1**	**1**	**9**	**9**	**9**	**9**
TOTAL MULTIPLE DX	**25**	**1.3**	**<1**	**1**	**1**	**1**	**1**	**3**	**3**	**4**
TOTAL										
0–19 Years	1	2.0	0	2	2	2	2	2	2	2
20–34	22	1.3	<1	1	1	1	1	2	3	4
35–49	6	3.5	16	1	1	1	9	9	9	9
50–64	2	2.0	2	1	1	3	3	3	3	3
65+	0									
GRAND TOTAL	**31**	**1.6**	**3**	**1**	**1**	**1**	**1**	**3**	**4**	**9**

75.1: DIAGNOSTIC AMNIOCENTESIS

Type of Patients	Observed Patients	Avg. Stay	Vari-ance	Percentiles						
				10th	25th	50th	75th	90th	95th	99th
1. SINGLE DX										
0–19 Years	11	5.9	42	1	3	4	5	11	26	26
20–34	93	3.8	12	1	2	3	4	8	10	14
35–49	10	2.4	<1	1	2	3	3	3	4	4
50–64	0									
65+	0									
2. MULTIPLE DX										
0–19 Years	66	7.7	74	2	3	4	10	18	28	50
20–34	375	5.7	42	1	2	4	7	15	18	33
35–49	85	4.6	18	1	2	3	6	11	13	24
50–64	1	1.0	0	1	1	1	1	1	1	1
65+	0									
TOTAL SINGLE DX	**114**	**3.8**	**13**	**1**	**2**	**3**	**4**	**8**	**10**	**26**
TOTAL MULTIPLE DX	**527**	**5.8**	**43**	**1**	**2**	**4**	**7**	**13**	**18**	**34**
TOTAL										
0–19 Years	77	7.5	70	2	3	4	10	18	26	50
20–34	468	5.3	36	1	2	3	7	11	18	32
35–49	95	4.4	17	1	2	3	5	11	13	24
50–64	1	1.0	0	1	1	1	1	1	1	1
65+	0									
GRAND TOTAL	**641**	**5.4**	**38**	**1**	**2**	**3**	**7**	**11**	**18**	**32**

75.2: INTRAUTERINE TRANSFUSION

Type of Patients	Observed Patients	Avg. Stay	Vari-ance	Percentiles						
				10th	25th	50th	75th	90th	95th	99th
1. SINGLE DX										
0–19 Years	0									
20–34	8	1.6	<1	1	1	1	2	3	3	3
35–49	0									
50–64	0									
65+	0									
2. MULTIPLE DX										
0–19 Years	1	1.0	0	1	1	1	1	1	1	1
20–34	5	2.2	2	1	1	2	3	4	4	4
35–49	3	1.0	0	1	1	1	1	1	1	1
50–64	0									
65+	0									
TOTAL SINGLE DX	**8**	**1.6**	**<1**	**1**	**1**	**1**	**2**	**3**	**3**	**3**
TOTAL MULTIPLE DX	**9**	**1.5**	**1**	**1**	**1**	**1**	**2**	**3**	**4**	**4**
TOTAL										
0–19 Years	1	1.0	0	1	1	1	1	1	1	1
20–34	13	1.8	1	1	1	1	3	3	4	4
35–49	3	1.0	0	1	1	1	1	1	1	1
50–64	0									
65+	0									
GRAND TOTAL	**17**	**1.6**	**<1**	**1**	**1**	**1**	**2**	**3**	**3**	**4**

75.3: IU OPS FETUS & AMNIO NEC

Type of Patients	Observed Patients	Avg. Stay	Vari-ance	Percentiles						
				10th	25th	50th	75th	90th	95th	99th
1. SINGLE DX										
0–19 Years	313	1.8	1	1	1	1	2	3	4	6
20–34	2,306	1.7	4	1	1	1	2	3	3	7
35–49	219	1.9	7	1	1	1	2	4	5	7
50–64	9	2.0	<1	1	1	2	3	3	3	3
65+	0									
2. MULTIPLE DX										
0–19 Years	506	2.4	9	1	1	2	3	4	5	12
20–34	3,395	2.5	11	1	1	2	3	4	6	17
35–49	774	2.7	14	1	1	2	3	5	7	18
50–64	30	2.1	2	1	1	2	3	4	5	6
65+	0									
TOTAL SINGLE DX	**2,847**	**1.8**	**4**	**1**	**1**	**1**	**2**	**3**	**4**	**7**
TOTAL MULTIPLE DX	**4,705**	**2.5**	**11**	**1**	**1**	**2**	**3**	**4**	**6**	**16**
TOTAL										
0–19 Years	819	2.2	6	1	1	2	2	3	5	11
20–34	5,701	2.2	8	1	1	2	2	4	5	13
35–49	993	2.5	13	1	1	2	3	5	6	16
50–64	39	2.1	1	1	1	2	3	4	5	6
65+	0									
GRAND TOTAL	**7,552**	**2.2**	**9**	**1**	**1**	**2**	**2**	**4**	**5**	**13**

75.32: FETAL EKG

Type of Patients	Observed Patients	Avg. Stay	Vari-ance	Percentiles						
				10th	25th	50th	75th	90th	95th	99th
1. SINGLE DX										
0–19 Years	37	1.9	<1	1	2	2	2	3	3	3
20–34	278	1.7	<1	1	1	2	2	2	3	3
35–49	17	1.7	<1	1	1	2	2	3	3	3
50–64	2	1.0	0	1	1	1	1	1	1	1
65+	0									
2. MULTIPLE DX										
0–19 Years	44	2.1	<1	1	2	2	2	3	3	4
20–34	389	2.2	6	1	1	2	2	3	4	10
35–49	78	2.0	<1	1	1	2	2	3	3	6
50–64	1	2.0	0	2	2	2	2	2	2	2
65+	0									
TOTAL SINGLE DX	**334**	**1.7**	**<1**	**1**	**1**	**2**	**2**	**3**	**3**	**3**
TOTAL MULTIPLE DX	**512**	**2.1**	**5**	**1**	**1**	**2**	**2**	**3**	**3**	**8**
TOTAL										
0–19 Years	81	2.0	<1	1	2	2	2	3	3	4
20–34	667	2.0	4	1	1	2	2	3	3	8
35–49	95	1.9	<1	1	1	2	2	3	3	6
50–64	3	1.3	<1	1	1	1	2	2	2	2
65+	0									
GRAND TOTAL	**846**	**2.0**	**3**	**1**	**1**	**2**	**2**	**3**	**3**	**6**

75.34: FETAL MONITORING NEC

Type of Patients	Observed Patients	Avg. Stay	Vari-ance	Percentiles						
				10th	25th	50th	75th	90th	95th	99th
1. SINGLE DX										
0–19 Years	209	1.8	1	1	1	1	2	3	4	6
20–34	1,627	1.6	1	1	1	1	2	3	3	7
35–49	157	2.1	9	1	1	1	2	4	6	9
50–64	7	2.2	<1	1	1	3	3	3	3	3
65+	0									
2. MULTIPLE DX										
0–19 Years	316	2.3	3	1	1	2	3	4	5	11
20–34	2,039	2.5	12	1	1	2	3	4	7	16
35–49	470	2.7	18	1	1	2	3	5	8	21
50–64	23	2.4	2	1	1	2	3	5	5	6
65+	0									
TOTAL SINGLE DX	**2,000**	**1.7**	**2**	**1**	**1**	**1**	**2**	**3**	**4**	**7**
TOTAL MULTIPLE DX	**2,848**	**2.5**	**12**	**1**	**1**	**2**	**3**	**4**	**6**	**16**
TOTAL										
0–19 Years	525	2.1	3	1	1	2	3	4	5	10
20–34	3,666	2.1	8	1	1	1	2	4	5	13
35–49	627	2.5	16	1	1	1	2	5	6	21
50–64	30	2.4	2	1	1	2	3	4	5	6
65+	0									
GRAND TOTAL	**4,848**	**2.2**	**8**	**1**	**1**	**1**	**2**	**4**	**5**	**13**

75.35: DXTIC PX FETUS/AMNIO NEC

Type of Patients	Observed Patients	Avg. Stay	Vari-ance	Percentiles						
				10th	25th	50th	75th	90th	95th	99th
1. SINGLE DX										
0–19 Years	60	1.5	<1	1	1	1	2	2	3	5
20–34	353	2.1	17	1	1	1	2	3	4	18
35–49	44	1.6	1	1	1	1	2	3	3	6
50–64	0									
65+	0									
2. MULTIPLE DX										
0–19 Years	111	2.9	29	1	1	2	3	5	6	22
20–34	714	2.8	15	1	1	2	3	5	9	20
35–49	182	3.0	14	1	1	2	4	6	9	16
50–64	5	1.2	<1	1	1	1	1	2	2	2
65+	0									
TOTAL SINGLE DX	**457**	**2.0**	**13**	**1**	**1**	**1**	**2**	**3**	**4**	**12**
TOTAL MULTIPLE DX	**1,012**	**2.9**	**16**	**1**	**1**	**2**	**3**	**5**	**8**	**20**
TOTAL										
0–19 Years	171	2.4	18	1	1	2	2	4	6	21
20–34	1,067	2.6	16	1	1	2	3	5	7	20
35–49	226	2.8	12	1	1	2	3	5	7	16
50–64	5	1.2	<1	1	1	1	1	2	2	2
65+	0									
GRAND TOTAL	**1,469**	**2.6**	**15**	**1**	**1**	**2**	**3**	**5**	**7**	**19**

75.37: AMNIOINFUSION

Type of Patients	Observed Patients	Avg. Stay	Vari-ance	Percentiles						
				10th	25th	50th	75th	90th	95th	99th
1. SINGLE DX										
0–19 Years	7	1.4	<1	1	1	1	2	2	2	2
20–34	39	1.7	<1	1	1	2	2	3	3	3
35–49	0									
50–64	0									
65+	0									
2. MULTIPLE DX										
0–19 Years	35	2.2	<1	1	2	2	3	3	3	3
20–34	241	2.2	2	1	2	2	2	3	4	8
35–49	42	2.3	1	1	2	2	3	4	4	6
50–64	1	2.0	0	2	2	2	2	2	2	2
65+	0									
TOTAL SINGLE DX	**46**	**1.7**	**<1**	**1**	**1**	**2**	**2**	**3**	**3**	**3**
TOTAL MULTIPLE DX	**319**	**2.2**	**2**	**1**	**2**	**2**	**3**	**3**	**4**	**8**
TOTAL										
0–19 Years	42	2.1	<1	1	2	2	3	3	3	3
20–34	280	2.1	2	1	2	2	2	3	4	8
35–49	42	2.3	1	1	2	2	3	4	4	6
50–64	1	2.0	0	2	2	2	2	2	2	2
65+	0									
GRAND TOTAL	**365**	**2.2**	**2**	**1**	**2**	**2**	**2**	**3**	**4**	**8**

75.4: MAN RMVL OF RET PLACENTA

Type of Patients	Observed Patients	Avg. Stay	Vari-ance	Percentiles						
				10th	25th	50th	75th	90th	95th	99th
1. SINGLE DX										
0–19 Years	7	1.3	<1	1	1	1	2	2	2	2
20–34	153	1.6	<1	1	1	1	2	2	3	3
35–49	16	1.6	<1	1	1	2	2	2	2	3
50–64	0									
65+	0									
2. MULTIPLE DX										
0–19 Years	51	1.9	<1	1	2	2	2	3	4	4
20–34	471	2.0	2	1	1	2	2	3	3	6
35–49	107	2.5	4	1	2	2	3	4	6	12
50–64	4	2.3	2	1	1	2	4	4	4	4
65+	0									
TOTAL SINGLE DX	**176**	**1.5**	**<1**	**1**	**1**	**1**	**2**	**2**	**3**	**3**
TOTAL MULTIPLE DX	**633**	**2.1**	**2**	**1**	**1**	**2**	**2**	**3**	**4**	**6**
TOTAL										
0–19 Years	58	1.9	<1	1	1	2	2	2	4	4
20–34	624	1.9	1	1	1	2	2	3	3	6
35–49	123	2.4	4	1	1	2	3	4	6	12
50–64	4	2.3	2	1	1	2	4	4	4	4
65+	0									
GRAND TOTAL	**809**	**2.0**	**2**	**1**	**1**	**2**	**2**	**3**	**3**	**6**

75.5: REP CURRENT OB LAC UTER

Type of Patients	Observed Patients	Avg. Stay	Vari-ance	10th	25th	50th	75th	90th	95th	99th
1. SINGLE DX										
0–19 Years	5	2.3	<1	2	2	2	2	4	4	4
20–34	33	2.1	1	1	1	2	2	4	4	4
35–49	2	2.0	0	2	2	2	2	2	2	2
50–64	1	3.0	0	3	3	3	3	3	3	3
65+	0									
2. MULTIPLE DX										
0–19 Years	46	2.6	4	1	2	2	3	3	4	19
20–34	301	2.2	<1	1	2	2	3	3	4	5
35–49	53	2.4	2	1	2	2	3	3	4	11
50–64	8	3.0	1	2	2	3	4	5	5	5
65+	0									
TOTAL SINGLE DX	**41**	**2.1**	**<1**	**1**	**2**	**2**	**2**	**4**	**4**	**4**
TOTAL MULTIPLE DX	**408**	**2.3**	**1**	**1**	**2**	**2**	**3**	**3**	**4**	**5**
TOTAL										
0–19 Years	51	2.6	3	2	2	2	3	3	4	5
20–34	334	2.2	<1	1	2	2	3	3	4	5
35–49	55	2.4	2	1	2	2	3	3	4	11
50–64	9	3.0	1	2	2	3	4	5	5	5
65+	0									
GRAND TOTAL	**449**	**2.3**	**1**	**1**	**2**	**2**	**3**	**3**	**4**	**5**

75.51: REP CURRENT OB LAC CERV

Type of Patients	Observed Patients	Avg. Stay	Vari-ance	10th	25th	50th	75th	90th	95th	99th
1. SINGLE DX										
0–19 Years	4	2.1	<1	2	2	2	2	3	3	3
20–34	32	2.1	<1	1	1	2	2	4	4	4
35–49	2	2.0	0	2	2	2	2	2	2	2
50–64	1	3.0	0	3	3	3	3	3	3	3
65+	0									
2. MULTIPLE DX										
0–19 Years	45	2.6	4	1	2	2	3	3	4	19
20–34	294	2.2	<1	1	2	2	3	3	4	5
35–49	50	2.4	2	1	2	2	3	3	4	11
50–64	8	3.0	1	2	2	3	4	5	5	5
65+	0									
TOTAL SINGLE DX	**39**	**2.1**	**<1**	**1**	**2**	**2**	**2**	**4**	**4**	**4**
TOTAL MULTIPLE DX	**397**	**2.3**	**1**	**1**	**2**	**2**	**3**	**3**	**4**	**5**
TOTAL										
0–19 Years	49	2.6	3	2	2	2	3	3	4	5
20–34	326	2.2	<1	1	2	2	3	3	4	5
35–49	52	2.3	2	1	2	2	3	3	4	11
50–64	9	3.0	1	2	2	3	4	5	5	5
65+	0									
GRAND TOTAL	**436**	**2.3**	**1**	**1**	**2**	**2**	**3**	**3**	**4**	**5**

75.6: REP OTH CURRENT OB LAC

Type of Patients	Observed Patients	Avg. Stay	Vari-ance	10th	25th	50th	75th	90th	95th	99th
1. SINGLE DX										
0–19 Years	3,236	1.8	<1	1	1	2	2	3	3	3
20–34	24,801	1.7	<1	1	1	2	2	2	3	3
35–49	1,445	1.7	<1	1	1	2	2	2	3	3
50–64	72	1.8	<1	1	1	2	2	2	3	3
65+	0									
2. MULTIPLE DX										
0–19 Years	8,549	2.1	2	1	2	2	2	3	3	5
20–34	65,371	2.0	2	1	1	2	2	3	3	5
35–49	12,382	2.0	1	1	1	2	2	3	3	5
50–64	546	2.0	<1	1	2	2	2	3	3	5
65+	0									
TOTAL SINGLE DX	**29,554**	**1.7**	**<1**	**1**	**1**	**2**	**2**	**2**	**3**	**3**
TOTAL MULTIPLE DX	**86,848**	**2.0**	**2**	**1**	**1**	**2**	**2**	**3**	**3**	**5**
TOTAL										
0–19 Years	11,785	2.0	2	1	1	2	2	3	3	5
20–34	90,172	1.9	1	1	1	2	2	3	3	4
35–49	13,827	2.0	1	1	1	2	2	3	3	5
50–64	618	2.0	<1	1	2	2	2	3	3	5
65+	0									
GRAND TOTAL	**116,402**	**1.9**	**1**	**1**	**1**	**2**	**2**	**3**	**3**	**4**

75.61: REP OB LAC BLAD/URETHRA

Type of Patients	Observed Patients	Avg. Stay	Vari-ance	10th	25th	50th	75th	90th	95th	99th
1. SINGLE DX										
0–19 Years	66	1.6	<1	1	1	2	2	2	3	3
20–34	465	1.7	<1	1	1	2	2	2	3	3
35–49	10	2.1	<1	1	2	2	2	3	3	3
50–64	0									
65+	0									
2. MULTIPLE DX										
0–19 Years	382	2.1	1	1	1	2	2	3	3	6
20–34	2,354	2.0	<1	1	1	2	2	3	3	4
35–49	278	2.1	<1	1	2	2	2	3	4	5
50–64	16	2.2	<1	2	2	2	2	3	3	3
65+	0									
TOTAL SINGLE DX	**541**	**1.7**	**<1**	**1**	**1**	**2**	**2**	**2**	**3**	**3**
TOTAL MULTIPLE DX	**3,030**	**2.0**	**<1**	**1**	**1**	**2**	**2**	**3**	**3**	**4**
TOTAL										
0–19 Years	448	2.0	1	1	1	2	2	3	3	6
20–34	2,819	1.9	<1	1	1	2	2	3	3	4
35–49	288	2.1	<1	1	2	2	2	3	3	5
50–64	16	2.2	<1	2	2	2	2	3	3	3
65+	0									
GRAND TOTAL	**3,571**	**1.9**	**<1**	**1**	**1**	**2**	**2**	**3**	**3**	**4**

75.62: REP OB LAC RECTUM/ANUS

Type of Patients	Observed Patients	Avg. Stay	Vari-ance	Percentiles						
				10th	25th	50th	75th	90th	95th	99th
1. SINGLE DX										
0–19 Years	193	1.9	<1	1	1	2	2	3	3	3
20–34	1,258	1.9	<1	1	2	2	2	3	3	4
35–49	54	2.0	1	1	1	2	2	3	3	6
50–64	1	1.0	0	1	1	1	1	1	1	1
65+	0									
2. MULTIPLE DX										
0–19 Years	646	2.2	1	1	2	2	3	3	3	5
20–34	4,315	2.2	1	1	2	2	3	3	3	5
35–49	605	2.2	<1	1	2	2	3	3	3	5
50–64	27	2.1	<1	1	2	2	2	3	3	3
65+	0									
TOTAL SINGLE DX	**1,506**	**1.9**	**<1**	**1**	**2**	**2**	**2**	**3**	**3**	**4**
TOTAL MULTIPLE DX	**5,593**	**2.2**	**1**	**1**	**2**	**2**	**3**	**3**	**3**	**5**
TOTAL										
0–19 Years	839	2.1	1	1	2	2	2	3	3	5
20–34	5,573	2.2	1	1	2	2	3	3	3	4
35–49	659	2.1	<1	1	2	2	3	3	3	5
50–64	28	2.1	<1	1	2	2	2	3	3	3
65+	0									
GRAND TOTAL	**7,099**	**2.2**	**1**	**1**	**2**	**2**	**3**	**3**	**3**	**4**

75.69: REP CURRENT OB LAC NEC

Type of Patients	Observed Patients	Avg. Stay	Vari-ance	Percentiles						
				10th	25th	50th	75th	90th	95th	99th
1. SINGLE DX										
0–19 Years	2,977	1.8	<1	1	1	2	2	3	3	3
20–34	23,078	1.7	<1	1	1	2	2	2	3	3
35–49	1,381	1.7	<1	1	1	2	2	2	3	3
50–64	71	1.8	<1	1	1	2	2	2	3	3
65+	0									
2. MULTIPLE DX										
0–19 Years	7,521	2.1	3	1	2	2	2	3	3	5
20–34	58,702	2.0	2	1	1	2	2	3	3	5
35–49	11,499	2.0	1	1	1	2	2	3	3	5
50–64	503	2.0	<1	1	1	2	2	3	3	5
65+	0									
TOTAL SINGLE DX	**27,507**	**1.7**	**<1**	**1**	**1**	**2**	**2**	**2**	**3**	**3**
TOTAL MULTIPLE DX	**78,225**	**2.0**	**2**	**1**	**1**	**2**	**2**	**3**	**3**	**5**
TOTAL										
0–19 Years	10,498	2.0	2	1	1	2	2	3	3	5
20–34	81,780	1.9	1	1	1	2	2	3	3	4
35–49	12,880	1.9	1	1	1	2	2	3	3	4
50–64	574	2.0	<1	1	1	2	2	3	3	5
65+	0									
GRAND TOTAL	**105,732**	**1.9**	**1**	**1**	**1**	**2**	**2**	**3**	**3**	**4**

75.7: PP MANUAL EXPL UTERUS

Type of Patients	Observed Patients	Avg. Stay	Vari-ance	Percentiles						
				10th	25th	50th	75th	90th	95th	99th
1. SINGLE DX										
0–19 Years	0									
20–34	11	1.9	<1	1	2	2	2	2	3	3
35–49	2	1.2	<1	1	1	1	1	2	2	2
50–64	0									
65+	0									
2. MULTIPLE DX										
0–19 Years	12	2.0	<1	1	1	2	2	3	3	5
20–34	54	2.1	<1	1	1	2	3	3	4	4
35–49	7	2.4	<1	2	2	2	3	3	3	3
50–64	0									
65+	0									
TOTAL SINGLE DX	**13**	**1.7**	**<1**	**1**	**1**	**2**	**2**	**2**	**3**	**3**
TOTAL MULTIPLE DX	**73**	**2.1**	**<1**	**1**	**1**	**2**	**3**	**3**	**4**	**4**
TOTAL										
0–19 Years	12	2.0	<1	1	1	2	2	3	3	5
20–34	65	2.0	<1	1	1	2	2	3	4	4
35–49	9	1.9	<1	1	1	2	3	3	3	3
50–64	0									
65+	0									
GRAND TOTAL	**86**	**2.0**	**<1**	**1**	**1**	**2**	**2**	**3**	**4**	**4**

75.8: OB TAMPONADE UTERUS/VAG

Type of Patients	Observed Patients	Avg. Stay	Vari-ance	Percentiles						
				10th	25th	50th	75th	90th	95th	99th
1. SINGLE DX										
0–19 Years	0									
20–34	0									
35–49	0									
50–64	0									
65+	0									
2. MULTIPLE DX										
0–19 Years	0									
20–34	3	2.4	<1	2	2	2	3	3	3	3
35–49	1	2.0	0	2	2	2	2	2	2	2
50–64	1	5.0	0	5	5	5	5	5	5	5
65+	0									
TOTAL SINGLE DX	**0**									
TOTAL MULTIPLE DX	**5**	**2.8**	**2**	**2**	**2**	**2**	**3**	**5**	**5**	**5**
TOTAL										
0–19 Years	0									
20–34	3	2.4	<1	2	2	2	3	3	3	3
35–49	1	2.0	0	2	2	2	2	2	2	2
50–64	1	5.0	0	5	5	5	5	5	5	5
65+	0									
GRAND TOTAL	**5**	**2.8**	**2**	**2**	**2**	**2**	**3**	**5**	**5**	**5**

75.9: OTHER OBSTETRICAL OPS

Type of Patients	Observed Patients	Avg. Stay	Variance	10th	25th	50th	75th	90th	95th	99th
1. SINGLE DX										
0–19 Years	0									
20–34	23	2.3	<1	1	2	2	3	3	3	4
35–49	2	1.0	0	1	1	1	1	1	1	1
50–64	0									
65+	0									
2. MULTIPLE DX										
0–19 Years	18	2.0	1	1	1	2	2	3	5	5
20–34	98	2.6	1	1	2	2	3	4	4	6
35–49	16	3.2	3	2	2	3	3	6	6	9
50–64	1	1.0	0	1	1	1	1	1	1	1
65+	0									
TOTAL SINGLE DX	**25**	**2.2**	**<1**	**1**	**2**	**2**	**3**	**3**	**3**	**4**
TOTAL MULTIPLE DX	**133**	**2.6**	**1**	**1**	**2**	**2**	**3**	**4**	**5**	**6**
TOTAL										
0–19 Years	18	2.0	1	1	1	2	2	3	5	5
20–34	121	2.5	1	1	2	2	3	4	4	6
35–49	18	3.0	3	1	2	3	3	6	6	9
50–64	1	1.0	0	1	1	1	1	1	1	1
65+	0									
GRAND TOTAL	**158**	**2.5**	**1**	**1**	**2**	**2**	**3**	**4**	**4**	**6**

76.0: FACIAL BONE INCISION

Type of Patients	Observed Patients	Avg. Stay	Variance	10th	25th	50th	75th	90th	95th	99th
1. SINGLE DX										
0–19 Years	0									
20–34	0									
35–49	0									
50–64	0									
65+	0									
2. MULTIPLE DX										
0–19 Years	3	5.2	<1	4	5	5	6	6	6	6
20–34	4	5.4	14	1	2	3	9	9	9	9
35–49	3	2.1	4	1	1	1	5	5	5	5
50–64	7	2.2	3	1	1	1	3	6	6	6
65+	4	1.5	1	1	1	1	1	4	4	4
TOTAL SINGLE DX	**0**									
TOTAL MULTIPLE DX	**21**	**3.1**	**7**	**1**	**1**	**2**	**5**	**6**	**9**	**9**
TOTAL										
0–19 Years	3	5.2	<1	4	5	5	6	6	6	6
20–34	4	5.4	14	1	2	3	9	9	9	9
35–49	3	2.1	4	1	1	1	5	5	5	5
50–64	7	2.2	3	1	1	1	3	6	6	6
65+	4	1.5	1	1	1	1	1	4	4	4
GRAND TOTAL	**21**	**3.1**	**7**	**1**	**1**	**2**	**5**	**6**	**9**	**9**

76.1: DXTIC PX FACIAL BONE/JT

Type of Patients	Observed Patients	Avg. Stay	Variance	10th	25th	50th	75th	90th	95th	99th
1. SINGLE DX										
0–19 Years	3	5.7	24	1	1	10	10	10	10	10
20–34	0									
35–49	1	1.0	0	1	1	1	1	1	1	1
50–64	0									
65+	0									
2. MULTIPLE DX										
0–19 Years	5	4.4	14	1	1	5	6	12	12	12
20–34	1	1.0	0	1	1	1	1	1	1	1
35–49	5	6.3	3	3	7	7	7	8	8	8
50–64	1	3.0	0	3	3	3	3	3	3	3
65+	3	8.8	49	2	2	8	17	17	17	17
TOTAL SINGLE DX	**4**	**4.0**	**20**	**1**	**1**	**1**	**10**	**10**	**10**	**10**
TOTAL MULTIPLE DX	**15**	**5.6**	**16**	**1**	**2**	**5**	**7**	**12**	**17**	**17**
TOTAL										
0–19 Years	8	4.9	17	1	1	5	10	10	12	12
20–34	1	1.0	0	1	1	1	1	1	1	1
35–49	6	4.8	8	1	1	7	7	7	8	8
50–64	1	3.0	0	3	3	3	3	3	3	3
65+	3	8.8	49	2	2	8	17	17	17	17
GRAND TOTAL	**19**	**5.2**	**17**	**1**	**1**	**5**	**7**	**10**	**12**	**17**

76.2: EXC/DESTR FAC BONE LES

Type of Patients	Observed Patients	Avg. Stay	Variance	10th	25th	50th	75th	90th	95th	99th
1. SINGLE DX										
0–19 Years	9	2.0	<1	1	1	2	3	3	3	3
20–34	8	2.5	1	1	2	2	4	4	4	4
35–49	6	1.2	<1	1	1	1	1	2	2	2
50–64	1	1.0	0	1	1	1	1	1	1	1
65+	2	1.0	0	1	1	1	1	1	1	1
2. MULTIPLE DX										
0–19 Years	15	3.5	14	1	1	2	4	8	14	14
20–34	14	2.4	8	1	1	1	2	9	9	12
35–49	30	3.1	8	1	2	2	4	6	7	20
50–64	36	3.1	10	1	1	2	3	9	9	12
65+	30	3.7	17	1	1	2	5	10	10	20
TOTAL SINGLE DX	**26**	**1.8**	**<1**	**1**	**1**	**1**	**2**	**3**	**4**	**4**
TOTAL MULTIPLE DX	**125**	**3.2**	**11**	**1**	**1**	**2**	**4**	**8**	**10**	**20**
TOTAL										
0–19 Years	24	2.8	9	1	1	2	3	4	14	14
20–34	22	2.4	6	1	1	1	3	6	9	12
35–49	36	2.9	8	1	1	2	4	5	7	20
50–64	37	3.0	10	1	1	2	3	9	9	12
65+	32	3.5	16	1	1	2	5	10	10	20
GRAND TOTAL	**151**	**3.0**	**10**	**1**	**1**	**2**	**3**	**7**	**10**	**17**

76.3: PARTIAL FACIAL OSTECTOMY

Type of Patients	Observed Patients	Avg. Stay	Variance	10th	25th	50th	75th	90th	95th	99th
1. SINGLE DX										
0–19 Years	5	3.4	13	1	1	1	9	9	9	9
20–34	5	5.5	6	2	2	7	7	7	7	7
35–49	3	5.1	11	1	1	7	7	7	7	7
50–64	8	2.5	4	1	1	2	3	7	7	7
65+	4	3.8	4	2	2	3	7	7	7	7
2. MULTIPLE DX										
0–19 Years	13	2.6	4	1	1	2	3	7	7	7
20–34	22	2.5	4	1	1	2	4	5	7	8
35–49	26	8.5	216	1	2	3	6	29	53	53
50–64	57	4.4	13	1	1	3	7	10	11	15
65+	59	5.3	16	1	3	4	7	10	14	21
TOTAL SINGLE DX	**25**	**3.9**	**8**	**1**	**1**	**3**	**7**	**7**	**9**	**9**
TOTAL MULTIPLE DX	**177**	**4.9**	**43**	**1**	**2**	**3**	**6**	**9**	**12**	**53**
TOTAL										
0–19 Years	18	2.8	6	1	1	2	4	7	9	9
20–34	27	3.1	6	1	1	2	5	7	7	8
35–49	29	8.3	205	1	2	3	7	26	53	53
50–64	65	4.1	12	1	1	3	7	10	11	15
65+	63	5.2	15	1	3	4	7	10	14	18
GRAND TOTAL	**202**	**4.7**	**39**	**1**	**2**	**3**	**7**	**9**	**11**	**53**

76.31: PARTIAL MANDIBULECTOMY

Type of Patients	Observed Patients	Avg. Stay	Variance	10th	25th	50th	75th	90th	95th	99th
1. SINGLE DX										
0–19 Years	3	5.2	17	1	1	2	9	9	9	9
20–34	5	5.5	6	2	2	7	7	7	7	7
35–49	2	7.0	0	7	7	7	7	7	7	7
50–64	5	3.7	4	2	2	3	4	7	7	7
65+	3	4.4	4	3	3	3	7	7	7	7
2. MULTIPLE DX										
0–19 Years	12	2.5	4	1	1	2	4	7	7	7
20–34	16	2.9	5	1	1	2	5	5	8	8
35–49	19	10.3	270	1	2	3	7	53	53	53
50–64	44	4.8	13	1	2	4	8	10	11	14
65+	39	5.9	15	2	4	4	7	12	17	18
TOTAL SINGLE DX	**18**	**5.0**	**7**	**2**	**2**	**7**	**7**	**7**	**9**	**9**
TOTAL MULTIPLE DX	**130**	**5.4**	**54**	**1**	**2**	**4**	**7**	**10**	**14**	**53**
TOTAL										
0–19 Years	15	3.0	7	1	1	2	5	7	9	9
20–34	21	3.5	6	1	1	2	5	7	7	8
35–49	21	10.1	257	1	2	3	7	53	53	53
50–64	49	4.7	12	1	2	4	8	10	11	14
65+	42	5.7	15	2	3	4	7	10	17	18
GRAND TOTAL	**148**	**5.4**	**48**	**1**	**2**	**4**	**7**	**10**	**12**	**53**

76.4: FACIAL BONE EXC/RECONST

Type of Patients	Observed Patients	Avg. Stay	Variance	10th	25th	50th	75th	90th	95th	99th
1. SINGLE DX										
0–19 Years	17	2.9	1	1	2	3	4	4	4	5
20–34	10	1.4	<1	1	1	1	2	2	2	2
35–49	7	2.0	2	1	1	1	3	4	4	4
50–64	5	1.0	0	1	1	1	1	1	1	1
65+	2	1.0	0	1	1	1	1	1	1	1
2. MULTIPLE DX										
0–19 Years	39	3.6	11	1	2	3	4	7	7	17
20–34	27	2.4	4	1	1	2	2	7	7	7
35–49	16	2.7	4	1	1	2	4	5	7	7
50–64	28	3.7	80	1	1	2	2	4	13	53
65+	13	5.5	13	2	3	4	8	13	13	13
TOTAL SINGLE DX	**41**	**2.2**	**2**	**1**	**1**	**2**	**3**	**4**	**4**	**5**
TOTAL MULTIPLE DX	**123**	**3.4**	**23**	**1**	**1**	**2**	**4**	**7**	**8**	**17**
TOTAL										
0–19 Years	56	3.4	8	1	2	3	4	5	7	17
20–34	37	2.2	4	1	1	1	2	7	7	7
35–49	23	2.5	3	1	1	2	4	5	7	7
50–64	33	3.3	71	1	1	2	2	4	4	53
65+	15	4.8	14	1	2	4	7	13	13	13
GRAND TOTAL	**164**	**3.1**	**18**	**1**	**1**	**2**	**4**	**7**	**7**	**17**

76.5: TMJ ARTHROPLASTY

Type of Patients	Observed Patients	Avg. Stay	Variance	10th	25th	50th	75th	90th	95th	99th
1. SINGLE DX										
0–19 Years	5	1.6	<1	1	1	2	2	2	2	2
20–34	18	1.3	<1	1	1	1	2	2	2	2
35–49	20	1.6	<1	1	1	2	2	2	2	2
50–64	11	1.4	<1	1	1	1	2	3	3	3
65+	0									
2. MULTIPLE DX										
0–19 Years	11	1.9	3	1	1	1	2	3	7	7
20–34	27	1.5	<1	1	1	1	2	2	2	3
35–49	35	2.1	2	1	1	2	2	3	4	8
50–64	26	1.7	<1	1	1	2	2	3	3	3
65+	6	1.6	<1	1	1	2	2	2	2	2
TOTAL SINGLE DX	**54**	**1.5**	**<1**	**1**	**1**	**1**	**2**	**2**	**2**	**3**
TOTAL MULTIPLE DX	**105**	**1.8**	**1**	**1**	**1**	**2**	**2**	**3**	**3**	**7**
TOTAL										
0–19 Years	16	1.8	2	1	1	1	2	3	3	7
20–34	45	1.4	<1	1	1	1	2	2	2	3
35–49	55	1.9	1	1	1	2	2	3	3	8
50–64	37	1.7	<1	1	1	2	2	3	3	3
65+	6	1.6	<1	1	1	2	2	2	2	2
GRAND TOTAL	**159**	**1.7**	**<1**	**1**	**1**	**2**	**2**	**2**	**3**	**7**

76.6: OTHER FACIAL BONE REPAIR

Type of Patients	Observed Patients	Avg. Stay	Vari-ance	Percentiles						
				10th	25th	50th	75th	90th	95th	99th
1. SINGLE DX										
0–19 Years	96	1.3	<1	1	1	1	1	2	2	4
20–34	161	1.3	<1	1	1	1	1	2	2	3
35–49	50	1.4	<1	1	1	1	2	2	3	4
50–64	24	1.3	<1	1	1	1	2	2	2	2
65+	2	1.0	0	1	1	1	1	1	1	1
2. MULTIPLE DX										
0–19 Years	375	1.9	2	1	1	2	2	3	4	7
20–34	460	1.7	2	1	1	1	2	3	3	9
35–49	181	1.8	2	1	1	1	2	3	4	8
50–64	112	1.4	<1	1	1	1	2	2	2	4
65+	12	3.6	12	1	1	2	3	11	11	11
TOTAL SINGLE DX	**333**	**1.3**	**<1**	**1**	**1**	**1**	**1**	**2**	**2**	**4**
TOTAL MULTIPLE DX	**1,140**	**1.8**	**2**	**1**	**1**	**1**	**2**	**3**	**4**	**9**
TOTAL										
0–19 Years	471	1.8	2	1	1	1	2	3	4	7
20–34	621	1.6	2	1	1	1	2	2	3	9
35–49	231	1.8	2	1	1	1	2	3	4	8
50–64	136	1.3	<1	1	1	1	2	2	2	4
65+	14	3.3	11	1	1	2	3	11	11	11
GRAND TOTAL	**1,473**	**1.7**	**2**	**1**	**1**	**1**	**2**	**3**	**3**	**8**

76.62: OPEN OSTY MAND RAMUS

Type of Patients	Observed Patients	Avg. Stay	Vari-ance	Percentiles						
				10th	25th	50th	75th	90th	95th	99th
1. SINGLE DX										
0–19 Years	42	1.1	<1	1	1	1	1	1	2	3
20–34	53	1.2	<1	1	1	1	1	2	2	6
35–49	13	1.4	<1	1	1	1	2	2	3	3
50–64	8	1.3	<1	1	1	1	2	2	2	2
65+	1	1.0	0	1	1	1	1	1	1	1
2. MULTIPLE DX										
0–19 Years	71	1.7	2	1	1	1	2	3	3	11
20–34	94	1.3	<1	1	1	1	2	2	2	3
35–49	44	1.4	<1	1	1	1	2	2	2	6
50–64	37	1.2	<1	1	1	1	1	2	2	4
65+	1	2.0	0	2	2	2	2	2	2	2
TOTAL SINGLE DX	**117**	**1.2**	**<1**	**1**	**1**	**1**	**1**	**2**	**2**	**3**
TOTAL MULTIPLE DX	**247**	**1.5**	**<1**	**1**	**1**	**1**	**2**	**2**	**3**	**4**
TOTAL										
0–19 Years	113	1.5	1	1	1	1	2	2	3	4
20–34	147	1.3	<1	1	1	1	2	2	2	3
35–49	57	1.4	<1	1	1	1	2	2	2	3
50–64	45	1.2	<1	1	1	1	1	2	2	4
65+	2	1.5	<1	1	1	2	2	2	2	2
GRAND TOTAL	**364**	**1.4**	**<1**	**1**	**1**	**1**	**2**	**2**	**2**	**4**

76.64: MAND ORTHOGNATHIC OP NEC

Type of Patients	Observed Patients	Avg. Stay	Vari-ance	Percentiles						
				10th	25th	50th	75th	90th	95th	99th
1. SINGLE DX										
0–19 Years	11	1.2	<1	1	1	1	1	2	2	2
20–34	25	1.2	<1	1	1	1	1	2	2	2
35–49	13	1.2	<1	1	1	1	1	2	2	2
50–64	3	1.0	0	1	1	1	1	1	1	1
65+	0									
2. MULTIPLE DX										
0–19 Years	26	2.0	5	1	1	1	2	4	4	14
20–34	42	1.8	7	1	1	1	2	3	3	22
35–49	28	2.1	2	1	1	1	3	4	5	5
50–64	17	1.6	<1	1	1	1	2	3	3	4
65+	2	1.3	<1	1	1	1	2	2	2	2
TOTAL SINGLE DX	**52**	**1.2**	**<1**	**1**	**1**	**1**	**1**	**2**	**2**	**2**
TOTAL MULTIPLE DX	**115**	**1.9**	**4**	**1**	**1**	**1**	**2**	**4**	**4**	**14**
TOTAL										
0–19 Years	37	1.7	4	1	1	1	2	3	4	14
20–34	67	1.6	4	1	1	1	2	2	3	4
35–49	41	1.9	2	1	1	1	2	4	5	5
50–64	20	1.6	<1	1	1	1	2	3	3	4
65+	2	1.3	<1	1	1	1	2	2	2	2
GRAND TOTAL	**167**	**1.7**	**3**	**1**	**1**	**1**	**2**	**3**	**4**	**5**

76.65: SEG OSTEOPLASTY MAXILLA

Type of Patients	Observed Patients	Avg. Stay	Vari-ance	Percentiles						
				10th	25th	50th	75th	90th	95th	99th
1. SINGLE DX										
0–19 Years	20	1.2	<1	1	1	1	1	2	2	3
20–34	51	1.4	<1	1	1	1	2	2	2	7
35–49	12	1.5	<1	1	1	2	2	2	2	2
50–64	9	1.4	<1	1	1	1	2	2	2	2
65+	0									
2. MULTIPLE DX										
0–19 Years	171	1.7	<1	1	1	1	2	3	3	5
20–34	221	1.6	<1	1	1	1	2	2	3	3
35–49	69	1.8	<1	1	1	2	2	3	4	5
50–64	42	1.3	<1	1	1	1	2	2	2	3
65+	4	2.5	2	1	2	2	3	5	5	5
TOTAL SINGLE DX	**92**	**1.3**	**<1**	**1**	**1**	**1**	**2**	**2**	**2**	**3**
TOTAL MULTIPLE DX	**507**	**1.6**	**<1**	**1**	**1**	**1**	**2**	**3**	**3**	**5**
TOTAL										
0–19 Years	191	1.7	<1	1	1	1	2	3	3	5
20–34	272	1.5	<1	1	1	1	2	2	3	3
35–49	81	1.7	<1	1	1	2	2	3	4	5
50–64	51	1.3	<1	1	1	1	2	2	2	3
65+	4	2.5	2	1	2	2	3	5	5	5
GRAND TOTAL	**599**	**1.6**	**<1**	**1**	**1**	**1**	**2**	**2**	**3**	**5**

76.66: TOT OSTEOPLASTY MAXILLA

Type of Patients	Observed Patients	Avg. Stay	Vari-ance	Percentiles						
				10th	25th	50th	75th	90th	95th	99th
1. SINGLE DX										
0–19 Years	9	1.7	<1	1	1	2	2	3	3	3
20–34	11	1.6	<1	1	1	2	2	2	2	2
35–49	3	3.0	3	1	1	4	4	4	4	4
50–64	0									
65+	0									
2. MULTIPLE DX										
0–19 Years	64	1.9	<1	1	1	2	2	3	3	5
20–34	57	1.7	<1	1	1	1	2	3	3	6
35–49	16	1.7	<1	1	1	2	2	2	2	2
50–64	6	2.0	<1	1	1	2	3	3	3	3
65+	0									
TOTAL SINGLE DX	**23**	**1.8**	**<1**	**1**	**1**	**2**	**2**	**3**	**3**	**4**
TOTAL MULTIPLE DX	**143**	**1.8**	**<1**	**1**	**1**	**2**	**2**	**3**	**3**	**5**
TOTAL										
0–19 Years	73	1.9	<1	1	1	2	2	3	3	5
20–34	68	1.7	<1	1	1	1	2	3	3	4
35–49	19	1.8	<1	1	1	2	2	2	4	4
50–64	6	2.0	<1	1	1	2	3	3	3	3
65+	0									
GRAND TOTAL	**166**	**1.8**	**<1**	**1**	**1**	**2**	**2**	**3**	**3**	**5**

76.7: REDUCTION OF FACIAL FX

Type of Patients	Observed Patients	Avg. Stay	Vari-ance	Percentiles						
				10th	25th	50th	75th	90th	95th	99th
1. SINGLE DX										
0–19 Years	119	1.6	1	1	1	1	2	3	3	9
20–34	250	2.0	2	1	1	1	3	4	5	6
35–49	90	2.4	4	1	1	2	3	5	6	10
50–64	38	2.4	3	1	1	2	3	5	6	9
65+	6	1.2	<1	1	1	1	1	2	2	2
2. MULTIPLE DX										
0–19 Years	378	2.9	8	1	1	2	3	6	8	15
20–34	1,004	3.2	10	1	1	2	4	7	9	16
35–49	630	3.9	13	1	1	3	5	9	11	19
50–64	271	4.4	15	1	1	3	6	9	14	17
65+	124	4.4	13	1	2	3	6	9	12	16
TOTAL SINGLE DX	**503**	**2.0**	**2**	**1**	**1**	**1**	**2**	**4**	**5**	**8**
TOTAL MULTIPLE DX	**2,407**	**3.5**	**11**	**1**	**1**	**2**	**4**	**8**	**10**	**17**
TOTAL										
0–19 Years	497	2.6	6	1	1	2	3	5	8	15
20–34	1,254	3.0	9	1	1	2	4	6	8	16
35–49	720	3.7	12	1	1	3	5	8	10	17
50–64	309	4.2	14	1	1	3	6	9	12	17
65+	130	4.3	12	1	1	3	6	9	10	16
GRAND TOTAL	**2,910**	**3.2**	**10**	**1**	**1**	**2**	**4**	**7**	**9**	**17**

76.72: OPEN RED MALAR/ZMC FX

Type of Patients	Observed Patients	Avg. Stay	Vari-ance	Percentiles						
				10th	25th	50th	75th	90th	95th	99th
1. SINGLE DX										
0–19 Years	6	1.5	<1	1	1	1	2	2	2	2
20–34	27	1.7	2	1	1	1	2	3	5	6
35–49	12	1.7	<1	1	1	2	2	3	3	3
50–64	3	1.5	<1	1	1	1	2	2	2	2
65+	2	1.2	<1	1	1	1	1	2	2	2
2. MULTIPLE DX										
0–19 Years	32	3.2	8	1	1	3	4	9	10	13
20–34	106	3.2	6	1	1	3	5	7	9	9
35–49	88	4.6	22	1	1	3	6	10	14	19
50–64	52	5.9	20	1	2	5	9	11	17	19
65+	20	4.5	7	1	1	5	7	8	9	9
TOTAL SINGLE DX	**50**	**1.6**	**<1**	**1**	**1**	**1**	**2**	**2**	**3**	**6**
TOTAL MULTIPLE DX	**298**	**4.1**	**13**	**1**	**1**	**3**	**6**	**9**	**10**	**19**
TOTAL										
0–19 Years	38	2.9	7	1	1	2	4	5	10	13
20–34	133	3.0	5	1	1	2	4	6	8	9
35–49	100	4.3	21	1	1	3	6	9	14	19
50–64	55	5.7	20	1	2	5	9	11	17	19
65+	22	4.2	8	1	1	5	7	8	9	9
GRAND TOTAL	**348**	**3.8**	**13**	**1**	**1**	**3**	**5**	**9**	**10**	**19**

76.74: OPEN RED MAXILLARY FX

Type of Patients	Observed Patients	Avg. Stay	Vari-ance	Percentiles						
				10th	25th	50th	75th	90th	95th	99th
1. SINGLE DX										
0–19 Years	3	4.3	2	3	3	4	6	6	6	6
20–34	8	2.6	3	1	1	2	5	5	5	5
35–49	0									
50–64	1	1.0	0	1	1	1	1	1	1	1
65+	0									
2. MULTIPLE DX										
0–19 Years	18	3.6	7	1	2	2	6	8	8	11
20–34	49	4.8	20	1	1	3	10	10	11	21
35–49	25	5.0	27	2	2	2	5	17	17	17
50–64	24	5.4	13	1	3	5	7	9	17	17
65+	11	6.5	8	2	4	7	8	10	10	10
TOTAL SINGLE DX	**12**	**2.5**	**3**	**1**	**1**	**2**	**4**	**5**	**6**	**6**
TOTAL MULTIPLE DX	**127**	**4.9**	**17**	**1**	**2**	**4**	**7**	**10**	**12**	**17**
TOTAL										
0–19 Years	21	3.7	7	1	2	2	6	8	8	11
20–34	57	4.6	19	1	1	3	7	10	11	21
35–49	25	5.0	27	2	2	2	5	17	17	17
50–64	25	4.9	14	1	2	4	6	9	9	17
65+	11	6.5	8	2	4	7	8	10	10	10
GRAND TOTAL	**139**	**4.7**	**17**	**1**	**2**	**3**	**7**	**10**	**11**	**17**

76.75: CLSD RED MANDIBULAR FX

Type of Patients	Observed Patients	Avg. Stay	Variance	10th	25th	50th	75th	90th	95th	99th
1. SINGLE DX										
0–19 Years	43	1.5	<1	1	1	1	2	3	3	6
20–34	50	1.8	2	1	1	1	2	4	6	6
35–49	16	3.3	6	1	1	2	5	7	8	8
50–64	4	2.0	0	2	2	2	2	2	2	2
65+	0									
2. MULTIPLE DX										
0–19 Years	75	2.1	4	1	1	1	2	4	8	9
20–34	135	2.4	3	1	1	2	3	4	5	8
35–49	66	3.7	13	1	1	2	5	9	9	12
50–64	20	4.0	12	1	1	2	5	11	12	12
65+	15	3.8	12	1	2	2	6	8	12	12
TOTAL SINGLE DX	**113**	**1.9**	**2**	**1**	**1**	**1**	**2**	**3**	**6**	**7**
TOTAL MULTIPLE DX	**311**	**2.7**	**6**	**1**	**1**	**2**	**3**	**6**	**9**	**12**
TOTAL										
0–19 Years	118	1.9	3	1	1	1	2	3	5	9
20–34	185	2.2	2	1	1	2	3	4	5	8
35–49	82	3.6	12	1	1	2	5	9	9	12
50–64	24	3.7	11	1	2	2	5	9	11	12
65+	15	3.8	12	1	2	2	6	8	12	12
GRAND TOTAL	**424**	**2.5**	**5**	**1**	**1**	**2**	**3**	**5**	**8**	**12**

76.76: OPEN RED MANDIBULAR FX

Type of Patients	Observed Patients	Avg. Stay	Variance	10th	25th	50th	75th	90th	95th	99th
1. SINGLE DX										
0–19 Years	56	1.7	2	1	1	1	2	3	4	9
20–34	147	2.1	2	1	1	2	3	4	5	6
35–49	52	2.5	4	1	1	2	3	5	5	10
50–64	21	3.2	5	1	1	3	5	6	7	9
65+	2	1.6	<1	1	1	2	2	2	2	2
2. MULTIPLE DX										
0–19 Years	194	2.9	8	1	1	2	3	6	8	15
20–34	551	3.2	10	1	1	2	4	6	8	20
35–49	330	4.0	11	1	2	3	5	9	11	15
50–64	118	3.1	7	1	1	2	4	7	8	17
65+	42	4.5	16	1	1	3	6	10	10	23
TOTAL SINGLE DX	**278**	**2.1**	**2**	**1**	**1**	**2**	**3**	**4**	**5**	**9**
TOTAL MULTIPLE DX	**1,235**	**3.4**	**10**	**1**	**1**	**2**	**4**	**7**	**9**	**17**
TOTAL										
0–19 Years	250	2.6	7	1	1	2	3	5	8	15
20–34	698	2.9	9	1	1	2	3	6	8	16
35–49	382	3.8	10	1	2	3	5	8	10	15
50–64	139	3.1	7	1	1	3	4	7	8	17
65+	44	4.4	16	1	1	3	6	10	10	23
GRAND TOTAL	**1,513**	**3.1**	**9**	**1**	**1**	**2**	**4**	**6**	**9**	**16**

76.79: OPEN RED FACIAL FX NEC

Type of Patients	Observed Patients	Avg. Stay	Variance	10th	25th	50th	75th	90th	95th	99th
1. SINGLE DX										
0–19 Years	10	1.1	<1	1	1	1	1	1	2	2
20–34	16	1.3	<1	1	1	1	1	2	4	4
35–49	7	1.0	0	1	1	1	1	1	1	1
50–64	7	1.8	1	1	1	1	3	3	4	4
65+	2	1.0	0	1	1	1	1	1	1	1
2. MULTIPLE DX										
0–19 Years	51	3.5	13	1	1	2	4	7	13	19
20–34	144	3.4	12	1	1	2	4	6	12	16
35–49	111	3.1	9	1	1	2	4	7	8	16
50–64	47	5.8	23	1	3	5	7	14	14	29
65+	34	4.4	13	1	1	3	6	9	13	13
TOTAL SINGLE DX	**42**	**1.2**	**<1**	**1**	**1**	**1**	**1**	**2**	**3**	**4**
TOTAL MULTIPLE DX	**387**	**3.7**	**13**	**1**	**1**	**2**	**5**	**7**	**12**	**16**
TOTAL										
0–19 Years	61	3.1	12	1	1	2	3	6	10	19
20–34	160	3.3	12	1	1	2	4	6	11	16
35–49	118	3.0	9	1	1	2	4	7	8	16
50–64	54	5.3	22	1	2	4	6	14	14	29
65+	36	4.1	13	1	1	3	6	9	13	13
GRAND TOTAL	**429**	**3.5**	**12**	**1**	**1**	**2**	**4**	**7**	**11**	**16**

76.9: OTH OPS FACIAL BONE/JT

Type of Patients	Observed Patients	Avg. Stay	Variance	10th	25th	50th	75th	90th	95th	99th
1. SINGLE DX										
0–19 Years	14	1.5	<1	1	1	1	2	3	3	4
20–34	19	1.5	<1	1	1	1	2	3	3	3
35–49	10	1.4	<1	1	1	1	1	2	5	5
50–64	10	1.6	1	1	1	1	1	4	4	4
65+	1	2.0	0	2	2	2	2	2	2	2
2. MULTIPLE DX										
0–19 Years	40	1.6	1	1	1	1	2	3	4	7
20–34	48	3.2	13	1	1	2	3	10	10	16
35–49	57	4.6	43	1	1	3	5	9	29	32
50–64	45	3.3	16	1	1	2	3	6	9	25
65+	31	4.8	34	1	1	2	6	13	13	26
TOTAL SINGLE DX	**54**	**1.5**	**<1**	**1**	**1**	**1**	**2**	**3**	**3**	**5**
TOTAL MULTIPLE DX	**221**	**3.4**	**23**	**1**	**1**	**2**	**3**	**8**	**10**	**29**
TOTAL										
0–19 Years	54	1.6	1	1	1	1	2	3	4	7
20–34	67	2.7	10	1	1	1	3	10	10	13
35–49	67	4.0	37	1	1	2	5	7	12	29
50–64	55	3.0	14	1	1	2	3	6	8	25
65+	32	4.8	34	1	1	2	6	13	13	26
GRAND TOTAL	**275**	**3.0**	**19**	**1**	**1**	**1**	**3**	**6**	**10**	**29**

76.97: RMVL INT FIX FACE BONE

Type of Patients	Observed Patients	Avg. Stay	Vari-ance	Percentiles						
				10th	25th	50th	75th	90th	95th	99th
1. SINGLE DX										
0–19 Years	2	1.0	0	1	1	1	1	1	1	1
20–34	8	2.1	1	1	1	2	3	3	3	3
35–49	3	2.5	4	1	1	2	5	5	5	5
50–64	4	1.2	<1	1	1	1	1	2	2	2
65+	0									
2. MULTIPLE DX										
0–19 Years	16	1.5	1	1	1	1	1	3	5	5
20–34	20	2.4	7	1	1	1	2	7	10	13
35–49	30	5.9	61	1	2	4	5	9	29	29
50–64	23	4.2	28	1	1	3	3	8	25	25
65+	14	2.3	3	1	1	2	2	5	6	8
TOTAL SINGLE DX	**17**	**1.8**	**1**	**1**	**1**	**1**	**3**	**3**	**3**	**5**
TOTAL MULTIPLE DX	**103**	**3.3**	**24**	**1**	**1**	**2**	**3**	**6**	**9**	**29**
TOTAL										
0–19 Years	18	1.4	1	1	1	1	1	3	5	5
20–34	28	2.3	5	1	1	2	2	4	8	13
35–49	33	5.7	57	1	2	4	5	9	29	29
50–64	27	3.8	26	1	1	3	3	8	9	25
65+	14	2.3	3	1	1	2	2	5	6	8
GRAND TOTAL	**120**	**3.2**	**22**	**1**	**1**	**2**	**3**	**5**	**9**	**29**

77.0: SEQUESTRECTOMY

Type of Patients	Observed Patients	Avg. Stay	Vari-ance	Percentiles						
				10th	25th	50th	75th	90th	95th	99th
1. SINGLE DX										
0–19 Years	1	4.0	0	4	4	4	4	4	4	4
20–34	0									
35–49	1	3.0	0	3	3	3	3	3	3	3
50–64	0									
65+	0									
2. MULTIPLE DX										
0–19 Years	1	1.0	0	1	1	1	1	1	1	1
20–34	15	6.9	100	1	1	2	8	28	37	37
35–49	26	5.8	18	1	3	4	6	13	15	19
50–64	21	4.5	18	1	2	3	5	12	13	20
65+	16	6.3	7	4	4	5	8	9	10	13
TOTAL SINGLE DX	**2**	**3.6**	**<1**	**3**	**3**	**4**	**4**	**4**	**4**	**4**
TOTAL MULTIPLE DX	**79**	**5.7**	**32**	**1**	**2**	**4**	**7**	**13**	**15**	**37**
TOTAL										
0–19 Years	2	2.8	3	1	1	4	4	4	4	4
20–34	15	6.9	100	1	1	2	8	28	37	37
35–49	27	5.7	18	1	3	4	6	13	15	19
50–64	21	4.5	18	1	2	3	5	12	13	20
65+	16	6.3	7	4	4	5	8	9	10	13
GRAND TOTAL	**81**	**5.7**	**31**	**1**	**2**	**4**	**6**	**12**	**15**	**37**

77.1: BONE INC NEC W/O DIV

Type of Patients	Observed Patients	Avg. Stay	Vari-ance	Percentiles						
				10th	25th	50th	75th	90th	95th	99th
1. SINGLE DX										
0–19 Years	23	2.3	5	1	1	1	3	7	8	8
20–34	12	2.3	6	1	1	1	3	4	6	11
35–49	9	2.1	1	1	1	2	2	4	4	4
50–64	2	2.4	4	1	1	1	4	4	4	4
65+	2	3.0	0	3	3	3	3	3	3	3
2. MULTIPLE DX										
0–19 Years	52	9.0	273	1	2	3	8	28	33	97
20–34	24	3.1	6	1	1	2	4	7	8	10
35–49	34	5.7	87	1	2	3	5	8	24	61
50–64	52	5.1	21	1	2	4	7	12	12	21
65+	34	5.3	23	1	2	4	7	9	14	24
TOTAL SINGLE DX	**48**	**2.3**	**4**	**1**	**1**	**1**	**3**	**6**	**8**	**11**
TOTAL MULTIPLE DX	**196**	**6.3**	**121**	**1**	**2**	**3**	**7**	**12**	**24**	**61**
TOTAL										
0–19 Years	75	6.9	196	1	1	3	6	14	28	97
20–34	36	2.8	6	1	1	2	4	6	8	11
35–49	43	5.1	75	1	2	3	4	8	24	61
50–64	54	5.0	20	1	2	4	7	12	12	21
65+	36	5.2	22	1	2	4	7	9	14	24
GRAND TOTAL	**244**	**5.5**	**98**	**1**	**1**	**3**	**6**	**10**	**19**	**36**

77.2: WEDGE OSTEOTOMY

Type of Patients	Observed Patients	Avg. Stay	Vari-ance	Percentiles						
				10th	25th	50th	75th	90th	95th	99th
1. SINGLE DX										
0–19 Years	59	1.9	<1	1	1	2	2	3	4	4
20–34	7	2.9	3	1	1	3	4	6	6	6
35–49	23	2.3	1	1	1	3	3	3	4	4
50–64	14	2.4	1	1	2	2	3	4	4	5
65+	1	2.0	0	2	2	2	2	2	2	2
2. MULTIPLE DX										
0–19 Years	178	2.9	5	1	2	3	4	5	6	12
20–34	34	2.6	3	1	2	2	3	6	8	8
35–49	100	2.9	3	1	2	2	3	6	7	9
50–64	91	2.9	2	1	2	3	4	4	5	8
65+	13	3.0	<1	2	3	3	3	4	4	6
TOTAL SINGLE DX	**104**	**2.1**	**1**	**1**	**1**	**2**	**2**	**4**	**4**	**6**
TOTAL MULTIPLE DX	**416**	**2.9**	**4**	**1**	**2**	**3**	**4**	**5**	**6**	**12**
TOTAL										
0–19 Years	237	2.7	4	1	1	2	3	4	5	12
20–34	41	2.7	3	1	2	2	3	6	6	8
35–49	123	2.8	3	1	2	3	3	4	6	9
50–64	105	2.8	2	1	2	3	4	4	5	8
65+	14	3.0	<1	2	2	3	3	4	4	6
GRAND TOTAL	**520**	**2.7**	**3**	**1**	**2**	**2**	**3**	**4**	**6**	**11**

77.25: FEMORAL WEDGE OSTEOTOMY

Type of Patients	Observed Patients	Avg. Stay	Vari-ance	Percentiles						
				10th	25th	50th	75th	90th	95th	99th
1. SINGLE DX										
0–19 Years	17	2.6	1	1	2	2	4	4	4	6
20–34	0									
35–49	5	3.0	1	1	3	3	4	4	4	4
50–64	2	2.4	<1	2	2	2	2	4	4	4
65+	0									
2. MULTIPLE DX										
0–19 Years	105	3.5	4	2	2	3	4	5	7	12
20–34	13	3.5	6	1	2	3	6	8	8	8
35–49	16	3.6	4	2	2	3	4	7	8	9
50–64	13	3.5	1	2	3	3	4	6	6	6
65+	4	3.5	1	3	3	3	3	6	6	6
TOTAL SINGLE DX	**24**	**2.7**	**1**	**1**	**2**	**2**	**4**	**4**	**4**	**6**
TOTAL MULTIPLE DX	**151**	**3.5**	**4**	**2**	**2**	**3**	**4**	**6**	**7**	**12**
TOTAL										
0–19 Years	122	3.4	4	2	2	3	4	5	6	12
20–34	13	3.5	6	1	2	3	6	8	8	8
35–49	21	3.5	3	2	2	3	4	7	8	9
50–64	15	3.4	1	2	3	3	4	4	6	6
65+	4	3.5	1	3	3	3	3	6	6	6
GRAND TOTAL	**175**	**3.4**	**4**	**2**	**2**	**3**	**4**	**5**	**7**	**12**

77.27: TIB & FIB WEDGE OSTY

Type of Patients	Observed Patients	Avg. Stay	Vari-ance	Percentiles						
				10th	25th	50th	75th	90th	95th	99th
1. SINGLE DX										
0–19 Years	16	1.9	<1	1	1	2	2	2	4	4
20–34	3	3.5	<1	3	3	3	4	4	4	4
35–49	14	2.3	<1	1	1	3	3	3	3	4
50–64	10	2.6	1	2	2	2	3	4	5	5
65+	0									
2. MULTIPLE DX										
0–19 Years	25	2.3	2	1	1	2	3	4	5	8
20–34	17	2.2	<1	1	2	2	3	3	4	4
35–49	72	2.6	2	1	2	2	3	4	6	6
50–64	63	2.8	2	1	2	3	4	4	5	5
65+	3	2.9	<1	1	3	3	3	4	4	4
TOTAL SINGLE DX	**43**	**2.2**	**<1**	**1**	**2**	**2**	**3**	**4**	**4**	**5**
TOTAL MULTIPLE DX	**180**	**2.6**	**2**	**1**	**2**	**2**	**3**	**4**	**5**	**8**
TOTAL										
0–19 Years	41	2.1	2	1	1	2	2	4	5	8
20–34	20	2.3	<1	1	2	2	3	4	4	4
35–49	86	2.5	2	1	2	2	3	4	6	6
50–64	73	2.7	2	1	2	3	4	4	5	5
65+	3	2.9	<1	1	3	3	3	4	4	4
GRAND TOTAL	**223**	**2.5**	**2**	**1**	**2**	**2**	**3**	**4**	**5**	**6**

77.3: OTHER DIVISION OF BONE

Type of Patients	Observed Patients	Avg. Stay	Vari-ance	Percentiles						
				10th	25th	50th	75th	90th	95th	99th
1. SINGLE DX										
0–19 Years	120	2.2	2	1	1	2	3	4	5	7
20–34	20	2.8	2	1	2	3	3	5	5	6
35–49	31	2.8	2	1	2	3	4	5	6	7
50–64	15	2.6	2	1	1	3	3	5	5	5
65+	2	1.6	<1	1	1	2	2	2	2	2
2. MULTIPLE DX										
0–19 Years	313	2.6	4	1	1	2	3	5	6	13
20–34	77	3.2	5	1	2	3	4	5	7	15
35–49	141	3.3	19	1	2	2	4	6	7	18
50–64	114	3.2	8	1	2	3	4	6	6	19
65+	46	3.5	9	1	2	3	4	6	6	25
TOTAL SINGLE DX	**188**	**2.3**	**2**	**1**	**1**	**2**	**3**	**4**	**5**	**7**
TOTAL MULTIPLE DX	**691**	**2.9**	**7**	**1**	**2**	**2**	**4**	**5**	**6**	**13**
TOTAL										
0–19 Years	433	2.5	3	1	1	2	3	5	5	10
20–34	97	3.1	4	1	2	3	4	5	6	15
35–49	172	3.2	16	1	2	2	4	6	7	11
50–64	129	3.1	8	1	2	3	4	5	6	19
65+	48	3.4	9	1	2	3	4	6	6	25
GRAND TOTAL	**879**	**2.7**	**6**	**1**	**1**	**2**	**3**	**5**	**6**	**11**

77.35: FEMORAL DIVISION NEC

Type of Patients	Observed Patients	Avg. Stay	Vari-ance	Percentiles						
				10th	25th	50th	75th	90th	95th	99th
1. SINGLE DX										
0–19 Years	37	2.6	1	1	2	2	3	4	5	6
20–34	7	3.4	2	1	3	3	4	5	6	6
35–49	8	4.3	2	2	3	4	5	7	7	7
50–64	0									
65+	1	2.0	0	2	2	2	2	2	2	2
2. MULTIPLE DX										
0–19 Years	156	3.2	3	2	2	3	4	5	6	9
20–34	23	3.2	2	2	2	3	4	5	5	6
35–49	21	2.9	2	2	2	3	3	5	6	7
50–64	18	4.7	14	2	2	3	6	7	14	16
65+	9	6.7	31	4	4	5	6	9	25	25
TOTAL SINGLE DX	**53**	**2.8**	**2**	**1**	**2**	**3**	**3**	**5**	**5**	**6**
TOTAL MULTIPLE DX	**227**	**3.4**	**4**	**2**	**2**	**3**	**4**	**5**	**6**	**10**
TOTAL										
0–19 Years	193	3.1	2	1	2	3	4	5	6	9
20–34	30	3.3	2	2	2	3	4	5	5	6
35–49	29	3.2	2	2	2	3	4	5	6	7
50–64	18	4.7	14	2	2	3	6	7	14	16
65+	10	6.2	29	2	4	5	6	9	25	25
GRAND TOTAL	**280**	**3.3**	**4**	**2**	**2**	**3**	**4**	**5**	**6**	**10**

77.37: TIBIA/FIBULA DIV NEC

Type of Patients	Observed Patients	Avg. Stay	Vari-ance	Percentiles						
				10th	25th	50th	75th	90th	95th	99th
1. SINGLE DX										
0–19 Years	40	1.9	1	1	1	1	2	3	5	6
20–34	7	2.3	<1	1	2	2	3	3	3	3
35–49	16	2.3	<1	1	2	2	3	3	3	4
50–64	10	2.7	2	1	1	3	4	5	5	5
65+	0									
2. MULTIPLE DX										
0–19 Years	106	2.2	5	1	1	2	2	3	4	13
20–34	32	2.8	3	1	1	2	4	4	7	9
35–49	74	3.3	34	1	2	2	3	5	7	54
50–64	55	2.6	1	1	2	2	3	4	5	6
65+	15	2.7	<1	2	2	3	3	4	4	4
TOTAL SINGLE DX	**73**	**2.0**	**1**	**1**	**1**	**2**	**3**	**3**	**5**	**6**
TOTAL MULTIPLE DX	**282**	**2.6**	**10**	**1**	**1**	**2**	**3**	**4**	**5**	**13**
TOTAL										
0–19 Years	146	2.1	4	1	1	2	2	3	5	13
20–34	39	2.7	3	1	2	2	4	4	5	9
35–49	90	3.1	27	1	2	2	3	4	7	11
50–64	65	2.6	2	1	2	3	3	4	5	6
65+	15	2.7	<1	2	2	3	3	4	4	4
GRAND TOTAL	**355**	**2.4**	**8**	**1**	**1**	**2**	**3**	**4**	**5**	**13**

77.4: BIOPSY OF BONE

Type of Patients	Observed Patients	Avg. Stay	Vari-ance	Percentiles						
				10th	25th	50th	75th	90th	95th	99th
1. SINGLE DX										
0–19 Years	89	3.0	7	1	1	2	4	7	9	14
20–34	22	3.4	15	1	1	2	4	13	13	14
35–49	16	2.0	3	1	1	1	2	5	7	7
50–64	26	1.8	2	1	1	1	2	4	6	6
65+	23	1.5	1	1	1	1	1	2	5	6
2. MULTIPLE DX										
0–19 Years	137	6.4	31	1	3	5	8	13	17	30
20–34	89	6.4	31	2	2	4	9	17	20	23
35–49	236	9.4	153	2	3	7	10	16	27	79
50–64	466	8.6	60	1	3	6	11	18	24	40
65+	1,263	6.8	40	1	3	5	9	14	19	29
TOTAL SINGLE DX	**176**	**2.6**	**6**	**1**	**1**	**1**	**4**	**6**	**8**	**14**
TOTAL MULTIPLE DX	**2,191**	**7.4**	**54**	**1**	**3**	**6**	**9**	**15**	**20**	**37**
TOTAL										
0–19 Years	226	5.0	24	1	2	4	7	10	14	30
20–34	111	5.8	29	1	2	4	8	13	19	23
35–49	252	8.9	146	1	3	6	9	16	24	79
50–64	492	8.2	60	1	2	6	11	18	23	40
65+	1,286	6.7	39	1	2	5	9	14	18	29
GRAND TOTAL	**2,367**	**7.0**	**52**	**1**	**2**	**5**	**9**	**14**	**20**	**37**

77.41: CHEST CAGE BONE BIOPSY

Type of Patients	Observed Patients	Avg. Stay	Vari-ance	Percentiles						
				10th	25th	50th	75th	90th	95th	99th
1. SINGLE DX										
0–19 Years	6	3.1	9	1	1	1	5	9	9	9
20–34	1	1.0	0	1	1	1	1	1	1	1
35–49	1	2.0	0	2	2	2	2	2	2	2
50–64	3	2.9	7	1	1	2	6	6	6	6
65+	0									
2. MULTIPLE DX										
0–19 Years	4	12.6	155	1	1	14	14	30	30	30
20–34	2	1.5	<1	1	1	2	2	2	2	2
35–49	15	12.1	457	1	2	6	12	27	93	93
50–64	37	6.7	30	1	2	5	9	17	17	19
65+	77	8.1	41	2	3	6	12	15	20	34
TOTAL SINGLE DX	**11**	**2.9**	**7**	**1**	**1**	**1**	**5**	**7**	**9**	**9**
TOTAL MULTIPLE DX	**135**	**8.1**	**74**	**2**	**3**	**6**	**12**	**16**	**20**	**34**
TOTAL										
0–19 Years	10	5.9	66	1	1	1	7	14	30	30
20–34	3	1.4	<1	1	1	1	2	2	2	2
35–49	16	11.5	434	1	2	5	12	27	93	93
50–64	40	6.5	30	1	2	5	9	17	17	19
65+	77	8.1	41	2	3	6	12	15	20	34
GRAND TOTAL	**146**	**7.6**	**70**	**1**	**2**	**6**	**10**	**15**	**19**	**34**

77.42: HUMERUS BIOPSY

Type of Patients	Observed Patients	Avg. Stay	Vari-ance	Percentiles						
				10th	25th	50th	75th	90th	95th	99th
1. SINGLE DX										
0–19 Years	11	2.3	2	1	1	2	3	4	6	6
20–34	2	3.9	17	1	1	1	7	7	7	7
35–49	0									
50–64	2	1.4	<1	1	1	1	2	2	2	2
65+	2	1.0	0	1	1	1	1	1	1	1
2. MULTIPLE DX										
0–19 Years	9	5.2	6	2	4	5	8	8	8	8
20–34	5	9.3	70	2	3	4	13	21	21	21
35–49	7	6.2	28	2	2	3	13	14	14	14
50–64	17	3.3	8	1	1	2	4	4	11	11
65+	47	6.4	26	1	2	5	10	12	15	24
TOTAL SINGLE DX	**17**	**2.0**	**2**	**1**	**1**	**2**	**2**	**4**	**6**	**7**
TOTAL MULTIPLE DX	**85**	**5.6**	**22**	**1**	**2**	**4**	**8**	**12**	**13**	**24**
TOTAL										
0–19 Years	20	4.0	6	1	2	4	5	8	8	8
20–34	7	7.9	59	1	2	4	13	21	21	21
35–49	7	6.2	28	2	2	3	13	14	14	14
50–64	19	2.9	7	1	1	2	4	4	11	11
65+	49	6.2	27	1	2	5	10	12	13	24
GRAND TOTAL	**102**	**5.0**	**21**	**1**	**2**	**4**	**8**	**11**	**13**	**21**

77.45: FEMORAL BIOPSY

Type of Patients	Observed Patients	Avg. Stay	Vari-ance	Percentiles						
				10th	25th	50th	75th	90th	95th	99th
1. SINGLE DX										
0–19 Years	27	3.3	9	1	1	2	4	7	10	14
20–34	8	2.1	5	1	1	1	2	2	9	9
35–49	8	1.6	<1	1	1	1	2	2	4	4
50–64	5	1.4	<1	1	1	1	2	2	2	2
65+	4	2.9	3	1	2	2	4	5	5	5
2. MULTIPLE DX										
0–19 Years	46	7.2	46	2	3	4	8	18	23	30
20–34	15	4.9	17	2	2	3	5	11	17	17
35–49	37	7.2	92	2	3	5	8	13	18	60
50–64	62	6.9	43	2	3	5	9	11	22	40
65+	135	7.4	33	2	3	6	9	15	20	28
TOTAL SINGLE DX	**52**	**2.8**	**7**	**1**	**1**	**2**	**4**	**6**	**7**	**14**
TOTAL MULTIPLE DX	**295**	**7.1**	**42**	**2**	**3**	**5**	**9**	**15**	**20**	**30**
TOTAL										
0–19 Years	73	5.5	34	1	2	4	7	12	18	30
20–34	23	3.9	15	1	1	3	4	9	11	17
35–49	45	5.9	77	1	2	4	7	11	16	60
50–64	67	6.6	42	1	3	5	9	11	22	40
65+	139	7.3	33	2	3	6	9	14	20	28
GRAND TOTAL	**347**	**6.4**	**39**	**1**	**3**	**4**	**8**	**13**	**18**	**28**

77.47: TIBIA & FIBULA BIOPSY

Type of Patients	Observed Patients	Avg. Stay	Vari-ance	Percentiles						
				10th	25th	50th	75th	90th	95th	99th
1. SINGLE DX										
0–19 Years	31	2.3	4	1	1	1	3	5	6	7
20–34	5	4.7	34	1	1	2	13	14	14	14
35–49	4	2.6	9	1	1	1	7	7	7	7
50–64	2	2.9	2	2	2	2	4	4	4	4
65+	2	4.2	7	2	2	6	6	6	6	6
2. MULTIPLE DX										
0–19 Years	41	4.2	8	1	2	4	7	9	10	11
20–34	18	4.3	21	2	2	2	4	9	18	19
35–49	25	7.3	82	1	2	5	8	16	20	50
50–64	22	6.2	31	2	2	4	11	12	16	25
65+	34	6.3	61	1	2	4	7	13	16	50
TOTAL SINGLE DX	**44**	**2.7**	**7**	**1**	**1**	**1**	**4**	**6**	**7**	**14**
TOTAL MULTIPLE DX	**140**	**5.5**	**37**	**1**	**2**	**4**	**7**	**11**	**16**	**31**
TOTAL										
0–19 Years	72	3.5	7	1	1	3	5	7	9	10
20–34	23	4.4	23	1	2	2	4	13	18	19
35–49	29	6.8	75	1	2	5	8	16	20	50
50–64	24	6.0	29	2	2	4	11	12	16	25
65+	36	6.2	59	1	2	4	7	13	16	50
GRAND TOTAL	**184**	**4.8**	**32**	**1**	**2**	**3**	**6**	**11**	**14**	**31**

77.48: METATARSAL/TARSAL BIOPSY

Type of Patients	Observed Patients	Avg. Stay	Vari-ance	Percentiles						
				10th	25th	50th	75th	90th	95th	99th
1. SINGLE DX										
0–19 Years	1	3.0	0	3	3	3	3	3	3	3
20–34	0									
35–49	1	2.0	0	2	2	2	2	2	2	2
50–64	1	1.0	0	1	1	1	1	1	1	1
65+	1	1.0	0	1	1	1	1	1	1	1
2. MULTIPLE DX										
0–19 Years	7	7.8	26	2	5	6	8	17	17	17
20–34	6	3.3	9	1	1	3	5	9	9	9
35–49	10	7.4	14	1	5	8	11	13	13	13
50–64	22	6.7	28	1	2	6	10	16	16	16
65+	20	5.7	10	3	4	5	6	10	13	19
TOTAL SINGLE DX	**4**	**1.9**	**<1**	**1**	**1**	**2**	**3**	**3**	**3**	**3**
TOTAL MULTIPLE DX	**65**	**6.3**	**19**	**1**	**3**	**5**	**8**	**13**	**16**	**19**
TOTAL										
0–19 Years	8	7.2	25	2	3	6	8	17	17	17
20–34	6	3.3	9	1	1	3	5	9	9	9
35–49	11	7.0	15	1	3	8	9	13	13	13
50–64	23	6.5	28	1	1	6	10	16	16	16
65+	21	5.6	10	3	4	5	6	10	13	19
GRAND TOTAL	**69**	**6.1**	**19**	**1**	**3**	**5**	**8**	**13**	**16**	**17**

77.49: BONE BIOPSY NEC

Type of Patients	Observed Patients	Avg. Stay	Vari-ance	Percentiles						
				10th	25th	50th	75th	90th	95th	99th
1. SINGLE DX										
0–19 Years	12	4.4	12	1	1	3	8	9	9	9
20–34	5	4.6	15	1	3	4	4	13	13	13
35–49	2	3.5	4	2	2	4	5	5	5	5
50–64	13	1.8	3	1	1	1	2	6	6	6
65+	14	1.0	<1	1	1	1	1	1	1	2
2. MULTIPLE DX										
0–19 Years	30	8.2	27	3	6	7	10	13	15	32
20–34	42	8.3	32	3	4	7	10	20	23	25
35–49	137	9.8	153	2	4	7	10	16	24	79
50–64	302	9.7	71	1	4	7	14	20	27	41
65+	946	6.7	41	1	2	5	9	14	18	29
TOTAL SINGLE DX	**46**	**2.6**	**7**	**1**	**1**	**1**	**3**	**8**	**9**	**13**
TOTAL MULTIPLE DX	**1,457**	**7.7**	**58**	**1**	**3**	**6**	**10**	**16**	**21**	**38**
TOTAL										
0–19 Years	42	7.1	25	1	3	7	9	13	13	32
20–34	47	7.9	31	3	4	7	10	17	20	25
35–49	139	9.7	152	2	4	7	10	16	24	79
50–64	315	9.3	71	1	3	7	13	20	27	41
65+	960	6.6	41	1	2	5	9	14	18	27
GRAND TOTAL	**1,503**	**7.5**	**57**	**1**	**2**	**6**	**9**	**16**	**20**	**37**

77.5: TOE DEFORMITY EXC/REP

Type of Patients	Observed Patients	Avg. Stay	Vari-ance	Percentiles						
				10th	25th	50th	75th	90th	95th	99th
1. SINGLE DX										
0–19 Years	11	1.2	<1	1	1	1	1	2	2	2
20–34	5	1.0	0	1	1	1	1	1	1	1
35–49	5	1.4	<1	1	1	1	2	2	2	2
50–64	6	1.6	<1	1	1	2	2	2	2	2
65+	1	1.0	0	1	1	1	1	1	1	1
2. MULTIPLE DX										
0–19 Years	33	1.6	2	1	1	1	2	3	5	5
20–34	19	1.8	<1	1	1	2	2	3	3	4
35–49	67	1.8	4	1	1	1	2	3	4	16
50–64	119	2.4	7	1	1	2	3	4	5	17
65+	113	2.4	5	1	1	2	3	4	6	12
TOTAL SINGLE DX	**28**	**1.3**	**<1**	**1**	**1**	**1**	**2**	**2**	**2**	**2**
TOTAL MULTIPLE DX	**351**	**2.2**	**5**	**1**	**1**	**2**	**2**	**4**	**5**	**16**
TOTAL										
0–19 Years	44	1.5	1	1	1	1	2	3	5	5
20–34	24	1.6	<1	1	1	1	2	3	3	4
35–49	72	1.8	3	1	1	1	2	3	4	16
50–64	125	2.4	7	1	1	2	3	4	5	17
65+	114	2.4	5	1	1	2	3	4	6	12
GRAND TOTAL	**379**	**2.1**	**5**	**1**	**1**	**2**	**2**	**4**	**5**	**16**

77.51: BUNIONECT/STC/OSTY

Type of Patients	Observed Patients	Avg. Stay	Vari-ance	Percentiles						
				10th	25th	50th	75th	90th	95th	99th
1. SINGLE DX										
0–19 Years	6	1.2	<1	1	1	1	1	2	2	2
20–34	3	1.0	0	1	1	1	1	1	1	1
35–49	1	2.0	0	2	2	2	2	2	2	2
50–64	0									
65+	0									
2. MULTIPLE DX										
0–19 Years	19	1.2	<1	1	1	1	1	2	3	3
20–34	10	1.9	<1	1	1	2	2	2	4	4
35–49	29	1.7	<1	1	1	1	2	3	3	5
50–64	56	2.7	10	1	1	2	3	4	7	17
65+	32	2.7	8	1	1	2	3	5	6	18
TOTAL SINGLE DX	**10**	**1.2**	**<1**	**1**	**1**	**1**	**1**	**2**	**2**	**2**
TOTAL MULTIPLE DX	**146**	**2.2**	**6**	**1**	**1**	**2**	**2**	**4**	**5**	**17**
TOTAL										
0–19 Years	25	1.2	<1	1	1	1	1	2	2	3
20–34	13	1.7	<1	1	1	2	2	2	4	4
35–49	30	1.7	<1	1	1	1	2	3	3	5
50–64	56	2.7	10	1	1	2	3	4	7	17
65+	32	2.7	8	1	1	2	3	5	6	18
GRAND TOTAL	**156**	**2.1**	**5**	**1**	**1**	**1**	**2**	**4**	**5**	**17**

77.6: LOC EXC BONE LESION

Type of Patients	Observed Patients	Avg. Stay	Vari-ance	Percentiles						
				10th	25th	50th	75th	90th	95th	99th
1. SINGLE DX										
0–19 Years	169	2.1	3	1	1	1	3	4	5	6
20–34	45	2.4	3	1	1	2	3	5	6	10
35–49	60	2.5	4	1	1	2	3	6	6	12
50–64	30	2.6	8	1	1	2	3	6	7	16
65+	9	2.4	3	1	1	2	3	4	6	6
2. MULTIPLE DX										
0–19 Years	127	6.0	122	1	1	3	6	14	21	90
20–34	209	5.7	39	1	2	4	6	12	20	28
35–49	408	5.9	44	1	2	4	7	13	17	35
50–64	600	6.3	31	1	2	5	8	13	18	29
65+	541	8.2	79	2	3	6	10	16	21	38
TOTAL SINGLE DX	**313**	**2.2**	**3**	**1**	**1**	**1**	**3**	**4**	**6**	**10**
TOTAL MULTIPLE DX	**1,885**	**6.7**	**58**	**1**	**2**	**5**	**8**	**14**	**20**	**33**
TOTAL										
0–19 Years	296	3.6	51	1	1	2	4	6	11	29
20–34	254	5.1	34	1	1	3	6	12	20	26
35–49	468	5.5	40	1	2	4	6	12	16	35
50–64	630	6.1	30	1	2	4	8	13	18	28
65+	550	8.1	78	2	3	6	10	16	21	38
GRAND TOTAL	**2,198**	**5.9**	**51**	**1**	**2**	**4**	**7**	**13**	**18**	**33**

77.61: EXC CHEST CAGE BONE LES

Type of Patients	Observed Patients	Avg. Stay	Vari-ance	Percentiles						
				10th	25th	50th	75th	90th	95th	99th
1. SINGLE DX										
0–19 Years	4	3.0	6	1	1	2	6	6	6	6
20–34	4	1.5	<1	1	1	2	2	2	2	2
35–49	2	1.5	<1	1	1	1	2	2	2	2
50–64	1	1.0	0	1	1	1	1	1	1	1
65+	1	1.0	0	1	1	1	1	1	1	1
2. MULTIPLE DX										
0–19 Years	10	7.4	49	1	2	3	18	18	18	18
20–34	9	8.2	81	1	1	3	18	18	26	26
35–49	21	6.4	63	1	3	4	6	17	21	43
50–64	73	7.1	50	1	2	4	10	18	22	30
65+	84	11.0	216	2	4	7	14	19	22	95
TOTAL SINGLE DX	**12**	**2.1**	**3**	**1**	**1**	**1**	**2**	**6**	**6**	**6**
TOTAL MULTIPLE DX	**197**	**8.8**	**130**	**1**	**2**	**6**	**12**	**18**	**22**	**64**
TOTAL										
0–19 Years	14	6.3	42	1	2	2	10	18	18	18
20–34	13	6.3	67	1	1	2	10	18	26	26
35–49	23	6.1	61	1	2	4	6	7	21	43
50–64	74	7.1	50	1	2	4	10	18	22	30
65+	85	10.9	215	2	4	7	14	19	22	95
GRAND TOTAL	**209**	**8.5**	**125**	**1**	**2**	**5**	**12**	**18**	**22**	**64**

77.62: LOC EXC HUMERUS LESION

Type of Patients	Observed Patients	Avg. Stay	Vari-ance	Percentiles 10th	25th	50th	75th	90th	95th	99th
1. SINGLE DX										
0–19 Years	27	1.2	<1	1	1	1	1	2	2	2
20–34	3	1.7	1	1	1	1	3	3	3	3
35–49	4	3.7	9	1	2	2	4	8	8	8
50–64	3	1.3	<1	1	1	1	2	2	2	2
65+	0									
2. MULTIPLE DX										
0–19 Years	9	2.6	3	1	1	2	5	5	5	5
20–34	8	7.0	52	2	2	5	10	25	25	25
35–49	18	4.4	13	1	2	4	5	10	12	16
50–64	18	5.0	16	1	2	3	7	10	14	14
65+	13	5.4	22	3	3	5	5	7	23	23
TOTAL SINGLE DX	**37**	**1.4**	**1**	**1**	**1**	**1**	**2**	**2**	**3**	**8**
TOTAL MULTIPLE DX	**66**	**4.7**	**18**	**1**	**2**	**4**	**5**	**10**	**14**	**25**
TOTAL										
0–19 Years	36	1.6	1	1	1	1	2	2	5	5
20–34	11	5.4	41	1	2	3	6	10	25	25
35–49	22	4.3	12	1	2	4	5	10	12	16
50–64	21	4.5	15	1	2	2	7	10	14	14
65+	13	5.4	22	3	3	5	5	7	23	23
GRAND TOTAL	**103**	**3.4**	**14**	**1**	**1**	**2**	**5**	**7**	**10**	**23**

77.63: LOC EXC RADIUS/ULNA LES

Type of Patients	Observed Patients	Avg. Stay	Vari-ance	Percentiles 10th	25th	50th	75th	90th	95th	99th
1. SINGLE DX										
0–19 Years	12	1.1	<1	1	1	1	1	1	3	3
20–34	4	2.2	1	1	1	3	3	3	3	3
35–49	4	3.2	12	1	2	2	3	12	12	12
50–64	5	2.5	5	1	1	2	2	7	7	7
65+	1	6.0	0	6	6	6	6	6	6	6
2. MULTIPLE DX										
0–19 Years	6	4.6	9	1	2	4	7	10	10	10
20–34	14	4.0	23	1	2	2	4	9	21	21
35–49	19	3.0	4	1	1	3	4	6	6	7
50–64	14	4.8	17	1	2	3	5	12	13	13
65+	16	4.1	7	1	2	4	6	8	8	8
TOTAL SINGLE DX	**26**	**1.8**	**3**	**1**	**1**	**1**	**2**	**3**	**3**	**12**
TOTAL MULTIPLE DX	**69**	**4.0**	**12**	**1**	**2**	**3**	**5**	**8**	**10**	**21**
TOTAL										
0–19 Years	18	1.9	4	1	1	1	1	4	7	10
20–34	18	3.5	17	1	2	2	3	7	9	21
35–49	23	3.0	5	1	1	2	4	6	7	12
50–64	19	4.2	15	1	1	3	5	12	13	13
65+	17	4.2	7	1	2	4	6	8	8	8
GRAND TOTAL	**95**	**3.2**	**10**	**1**	**1**	**2**	**4**	**7**	**9**	**13**

77.65: LOCAL EXC FEMUR LESION

Type of Patients	Observed Patients	Avg. Stay	Vari-ance	Percentiles 10th	25th	50th	75th	90th	95th	99th
1. SINGLE DX										
0–19 Years	40	2.7	3	1	1	2	5	5	6	6
20–34	7	3.5	3	2	2	3	6	6	6	6
35–49	21	2.2	3	1	1	2	3	3	3	9
50–64	12	1.9	1	1	1	1	3	3	3	5
65+	1	3.0	0	3	3	3	3	3	3	3
2. MULTIPLE DX										
0–19 Years	24	2.7	4	1	1	2	4	6	6	11
20–34	51	5.0	34	1	1	3	5	12	20	24
35–49	58	3.6	29	1	1	2	4	7	8	44
50–64	52	4.6	27	1	2	3	6	13	16	28
65+	40	7.0	29	1	3	6	10	14	18	21
TOTAL SINGLE DX	**81**	**2.5**	**3**	**1**	**1**	**2**	**3**	**5**	**6**	**6**
TOTAL MULTIPLE DX	**225**	**4.6**	**28**	**1**	**1**	**3**	**6**	**11**	**16**	**24**
TOTAL										
0–19 Years	64	2.7	4	1	1	2	4	5	6	8
20–34	58	4.8	30	1	1	3	5	12	20	24
35–49	79	3.2	22	1	1	2	3	6	8	20
50–64	64	4.1	23	1	1	3	5	8	15	22
65+	41	6.9	29	1	3	6	10	14	18	21
GRAND TOTAL	**306**	**3.9**	**21**	**1**	**1**	**2**	**5**	**8**	**13**	**22**

77.67: LOC EXC TIBIA/FIBULA LES

Type of Patients	Observed Patients	Avg. Stay	Vari-ance	Percentiles 10th	25th	50th	75th	90th	95th	99th
1. SINGLE DX										
0–19 Years	45	1.5	3	1	1	1	1	2	5	12
20–34	10	2.4	5	1	1	2	2	4	10	10
35–49	13	2.5	2	1	1	3	3	4	5	5
50–64	0									
65+	4	2.0	2	1	1	2	4	4	4	4
2. MULTIPLE DX										
0–19 Years	29	5.5	215	1	1	2	4	8	8	93
20–34	45	6.5	61	1	2	4	7	15	21	42
35–49	72	5.7	28	1	2	4	7	15	17	27
50–64	86	6.3	25	1	2	5	9	13	14	25
65+	48	6.1	20	2	3	5	9	11	17	19
TOTAL SINGLE DX	**72**	**1.7**	**3**	**1**	**1**	**1**	**2**	**3**	**5**	**12**
TOTAL MULTIPLE DX	**280**	**6.0**	**58**	**1**	**2**	**4**	**8**	**13**	**17**	**27**
TOTAL										
0–19 Years	74	3.0	85	1	1	1	2	5	8	46
20–34	55	5.8	53	1	2	3	6	14	21	42
35–49	85	5.2	25	1	2	3	6	13	17	21
50–64	86	6.3	25	1	2	5	9	13	14	25
65+	52	5.8	19	2	3	4	8	11	17	19
GRAND TOTAL	**352**	**4.9**	**48**	**1**	**1**	**3**	**6**	**11**	**15**	**25**

77.68: LOCAL EXC MT/TARSAL LES

Type of Patients	Observed Patients	Avg. Stay	Vari-ance	Percentiles						
				10th	25th	50th	75th	90th	95th	99th
1. SINGLE DX										
0–19 Years	10	1.8	<1	1	1	1	3	3	3	3
20–34	3	1.7	1	1	1	1	3	3	3	3
35–49	2	1.0	0	1	1	1	1	1	1	1
50–64	0									
65+	1	3.0	0	3	3	3	3	3	3	3
2. MULTIPLE DX										
0–19 Years	8	2.1	1	1	1	2	3	4	4	4
20–34	17	5.4	17	1	2	3	9	11	12	12
35–49	65	7.3	41	1	4	6	8	14	21	42
50–64	120	7.1	32	1	3	6	9	12	20	29
65+	125	8.4	46	3	4	7	11	16	20	28
TOTAL SINGLE DX	**16**	**1.7**	**<1**	**1**	**1**	**1**	**3**	**3**	**3**	**3**
TOTAL MULTIPLE DX	**335**	**7.3**	**39**	**1**	**3**	**6**	**9**	**14**	**20**	**29**
TOTAL										
0–19 Years	18	1.9	<1	1	1	2	3	3	3	4
20–34	20	5.0	16	1	1	3	9	11	12	12
35–49	67	7.0	41	1	3	6	8	14	21	42
50–64	120	7.1	32	1	3	6	9	12	20	29
65+	126	8.3	46	3	4	7	11	16	20	28
GRAND TOTAL	**351**	**6.9**	**38**	**1**	**3**	**6**	**9**	**13**	**18**	**29**

77.69: LOC EXC BONE LESION NEC

Type of Patients	Observed Patients	Avg. Stay	Vari-ance	Percentiles						
				10th	25th	50th	75th	90th	95th	99th
1. SINGLE DX										
0–19 Years	26	3.1	1	1	2	3	4	4	4	6
20–34	10	2.1	2	1	1	2	2	4	5	5
35–49	14	3.1	4	1	2	2	6	6	6	7
50–64	8	5.4	23	1	3	4	6	16	16	16
65+	1	1.0	0	1	1	1	1	1	1	1
2. MULTIPLE DX										
0–19 Years	32	11.4	212	2	3	7	17	26	33	90
20–34	49	5.4	31	1	2	4	6	11	20	28
35–49	133	7.2	68	1	2	5	9	16	26	47
50–64	216	6.4	28	1	3	5	9	13	18	23
65+	203	8.0	61	1	3	6	10	16	23	38
TOTAL SINGLE DX	**59**	**3.1**	**4**	**1**	**2**	**3**	**4**	**5**	**6**	**8**
TOTAL MULTIPLE DX	**633**	**7.3**	**61**	**1**	**2**	**5**	**9**	**16**	**21**	**35**
TOTAL										
0–19 Years	58	6.6	107	2	2	4	6	17	21	33
20–34	59	4.9	29	1	2	3	5	10	20	28
35–49	147	6.7	63	1	2	4	8	15	24	47
50–64	224	6.4	28	1	3	5	9	13	18	23
65+	204	8.0	61	1	3	6	10	16	23	38
GRAND TOTAL	**692**	**6.8**	**56**	**1**	**2**	**4**	**9**	**15**	**20**	**35**

77.7: EXC BONE FOR GRAFT

Type of Patients	Observed Patients	Avg. Stay	Vari-ance	Percentiles						
				10th	25th	50th	75th	90th	95th	99th
1. SINGLE DX										
0–19 Years	19	2.0	4	1	1	1	2	3	4	10
20–34	33	1.8	4	1	1	1	2	3	4	14
35–49	33	2.3	11	1	1	2	2	3	3	17
50–64	38	1.6	<1	1	1	2	2	2	3	3
65+	6	2.5	2	1	1	2	4	4	4	4
2. MULTIPLE DX										
0–19 Years	40	4.0	61	1	1	1	3	9	35	35
20–34	80	2.5	7	1	1	2	2	6	8	13
35–49	168	2.5	12	1	1	2	3	4	5	12
50–64	162	2.8	14	1	1	2	3	4	7	21
65+	78	2.6	2	1	2	2	3	4	5	7
TOTAL SINGLE DX	**129**	**1.9**	**4**	**1**	**1**	**1**	**2**	**3**	**4**	**14**
TOTAL MULTIPLE DX	**528**	**2.8**	**16**	**1**	**1**	**2**	**3**	**4**	**7**	**21**
TOTAL										
0–19 Years	59	3.4	45	1	1	1	2	5	15	35
20–34	113	2.3	6	1	1	2	2	4	7	14
35–49	201	2.4	12	1	1	2	3	4	5	17
50–64	200	2.6	12	1	1	2	3	4	6	21
65+	84	2.6	2	1	2	2	4	4	5	7
GRAND TOTAL	**657**	**2.6**	**14**	**1**	**1**	**2**	**3**	**4**	**6**	**21**

77.79: EXC BONE FOR GRAFT NEC

Type of Patients	Observed Patients	Avg. Stay	Vari-ance	Percentiles						
				10th	25th	50th	75th	90th	95th	99th
1. SINGLE DX										
0–19 Years	18	2.0	4	1	1	1	2	3	4	10
20–34	27	1.9	5	1	1	1	2	3	4	14
35–49	29	2.5	13	1	1	2	2	3	17	17
50–64	33	1.6	<1	1	1	2	2	2	3	3
65+	4	1.2	<1	1	1	1	1	2	2	2
2. MULTIPLE DX										
0–19 Years	31	2.6	11	1	1	1	2	5	9	15
20–34	70	2.3	5	1	1	2	2	6	7	13
35–49	139	2.5	14	1	1	2	3	4	4	16
50–64	129	3.1	18	1	1	2	3	5	8	21
65+	62	2.3	1	1	1	2	3	4	5	6
TOTAL SINGLE DX	**111**	**2.0**	**5**	**1**	**1**	**1**	**2**	**3**	**4**	**17**
TOTAL MULTIPLE DX	**431**	**2.6**	**11**	**1**	**1**	**2**	**3**	**4**	**6**	**21**
TOTAL										
0–19 Years	49	2.4	8	1	1	1	2	5	9	15
20–34	97	2.2	5	1	1	2	2	4	7	13
35–49	168	2.5	13	1	1	2	3	3	5	17
50–64	162	2.9	15	1	1	2	3	4	7	21
65+	66	2.2	1	1	1	2	3	4	5	6
GRAND TOTAL	**542**	**2.5**	**10**	**1**	**1**	**2**	**3**	**4**	**6**	**17**

77.8: OTHER PARTIAL OSTECTOMY

Type of Patients	Observed Patients	Avg. Stay	Vari-ance	Percentiles						
				10th	25th	50th	75th	90th	95th	99th
1. SINGLE DX										
0–19 Years	61	2.9	6	1	1	2	5	6	7	12
20–34	40	2.8	4	1	1	2	3	5	8	13
35–49	50	1.9	2	1	1	1	2	3	4	10
50–64	33	2.1	3	1	1	2	3	3	6	10
65+	10	3.8	5	2	2	3	7	7	8	8
2. MULTIPLE DX										
0–19 Years	67	6.0	64	1	1	3	7	16	18	45
20–34	114	5.0	39	1	2	3	6	10	14	47
35–49	289	5.9	72	1	2	3	7	13	17	45
50–64	418	6.2	47	1	2	4	7	15	21	37
65+	418	6.0	30	1	2	4	7	13	17	26
TOTAL SINGLE DX	**194**	**2.6**	**5**	**1**	**1**	**2**	**3**	**5**	**7**	**10**
TOTAL MULTIPLE DX	**1,306**	**5.9**	**47**	**1**	**2**	**4**	**7**	**13**	**18**	**37**
TOTAL										
0–19 Years	128	4.6	38	1	1	3	5	9	16	45
20–34	154	4.5	31	1	2	3	5	9	13	26
35–49	339	5.3	65	1	1	3	6	12	16	43
50–64	451	5.9	45	1	2	3	7	14	21	37
65+	428	5.9	29	1	2	4	7	13	17	26
GRAND TOTAL	**1,500**	**5.5**	**42**	**1**	**2**	**3**	**7**	**13**	**18**	**35**

77.81: CHEST CAGE OSTECTOMY NEC

Type of Patients	Observed Patients	Avg. Stay	Vari-ance	Percentiles						
				10th	25th	50th	75th	90th	95th	99th
1. SINGLE DX										
0–19 Years	8	1.3	<1	1	1	1	2	2	2	2
20–34	7	2.9	3	1	2	2	5	5	5	5
35–49	20	1.5	<1	1	1	1	2	3	3	3
50–64	7	1.5	<1	1	1	1	2	2	3	3
65+	0									
2. MULTIPLE DX										
0–19 Years	0									
20–34	21	2.6	2	1	1	2	4	4	5	5
35–49	59	3.9	54	1	1	2	3	5	14	45
50–64	90	3.9	35	1	1	2	3	11	18	21
65+	61	3.7	21	1	1	2	4	8	15	24
TOTAL SINGLE DX	**42**	**1.7**	**1**	**1**	**1**	**1**	**2**	**3**	**5**	**5**
TOTAL MULTIPLE DX	**231**	**3.7**	**32**	**1**	**1**	**2**	**4**	**7**	**16**	**39**
TOTAL										
0–19 Years	8	1.3	<1	1	1	1	2	2	2	2
20–34	28	2.7	2	1	1	2	4	5	5	5
35–49	79	3.3	41	1	1	2	3	5	9	45
50–64	97	3.7	32	1	1	2	3	10	18	21
65+	61	3.7	21	1	1	2	4	8	15	24
GRAND TOTAL	**273**	**3.3**	**27**	**1**	**1**	**2**	**3**	**7**	**14**	**24**

77.85: PART OSTECTOMY FEMUR

Type of Patients	Observed Patients	Avg. Stay	Vari-ance	Percentiles						
				10th	25th	50th	75th	90th	95th	99th
1. SINGLE DX										
0–19 Years	11	4.7	7	1	3	5	6	9	9	9
20–34	6	2.4	2	1	1	2	4	4	4	4
35–49	2	2.0	0	2	2	2	2	2	2	2
50–64	3	2.9	6	1	1	2	6	6	6	6
65+	5	5.7	6	2	4	7	7	8	8	8
2. MULTIPLE DX										
0–19 Years	24	9.9	162	1	2	4	13	27	45	45
20–34	26	5.9	15	2	3	4	7	13	15	16
35–49	43	12.1	275	3	3	7	10	29	43	91
50–64	40	11.0	106	4	5	7	14	32	37	>99
65+	61	9.4	33	4	5	8	13	18	21	27
TOTAL SINGLE DX	**27**	**4.2**	**7**	**1**	**2**	**4**	**6**	**8**	**9**	**9**
TOTAL MULTIPLE DX	**194**	**9.9**	**118**	**2**	**4**	**6**	**12**	**22**	**29**	**59**
TOTAL										
0–19 Years	35	8.0	112	1	2	4	9	23	45	45
20–34	32	5.3	14	2	3	4	7	13	15	16
35–49	45	11.8	268	2	3	6	10	29	43	91
50–64	43	10.5	103	3	5	6	14	26	37	>99
65+	66	9.2	32	4	5	8	13	18	21	27
GRAND TOTAL	**221**	**9.2**	**107**	**2**	**4**	**6**	**11**	**21**	**27**	**59**

77.86: PARTIAL PATELLECTOMY

Type of Patients	Observed Patients	Avg. Stay	Vari-ance	Percentiles						
				10th	25th	50th	75th	90th	95th	99th
1. SINGLE DX										
0–19 Years	1	1.0	0	1	1	1	1	1	1	1
20–34	10	4.1	12	1	2	3	3	8	13	13
35–49	11	2.0	3	1	1	2	2	2	7	7
50–64	11	3.2	6	2	2	3	3	9	10	10
65+	2	3.0	0	3	3	3	3	3	3	3
2. MULTIPLE DX										
0–19 Years	3	2.3	<1	2	2	2	3	3	3	3
20–34	20	3.4	7	1	2	3	4	6	7	13
35–49	29	4.3	10	2	2	3	5	6	10	17
50–64	47	3.9	6	1	2	4	5	7	8	15
65+	70	4.4	24	2	2	3	5	7	9	44
TOTAL SINGLE DX	**35**	**3.1**	**7**	**1**	**2**	**2**	**3**	**8**	**9**	**13**
TOTAL MULTIPLE DX	**169**	**4.1**	**15**	**2**	**2**	**3**	**5**	**7**	**8**	**17**
TOTAL										
0–19 Years	4	2.0	<1	1	2	2	3	3	3	3
20–34	30	3.6	8	1	2	3	4	8	13	13
35–49	40	3.8	10	2	2	3	5	6	10	17
50–64	58	3.8	6	1	2	3	5	7	8	15
65+	72	4.4	24	2	2	3	5	7	9	21
GRAND TOTAL	**204**	**4.0**	**14**	**2**	**2**	**3**	**5**	**7**	**9**	**17**

77.87: PART OSTECTOMY TIB/FIB

Type of Patients	Observed Patients	Avg. Stay	Vari-ance	Percentiles 10th	25th	50th	75th	90th	95th	99th
1. SINGLE DX										
0–19 Years	14	3.2	3	1	2	4	5	5	5	6
20–34	2	2.0	0	2	2	2	2	2	2	2
35–49	5	3.8	10	1	2	3	4	10	10	10
50–64	3	2.6	<1	2	2	3	3	3	3	3
65+	0									
2. MULTIPLE DX										
0–19 Years	11	5.4	14	2	3	6	7	8	18	18
20–34	7	5.3	18	1	2	3	12	12	12	12
35–49	16	7.0	33	1	3	5	12	15	20	20
50–64	14	3.7	11	1	1	3	4	9	13	13
65+	12	3.6	15	2	2	2	4	5	17	17
TOTAL SINGLE DX	**24**	**3.2**	**3**	**1**	**2**	**3**	**4**	**5**	**5**	**10**
TOTAL MULTIPLE DX	**60**	**5.0**	**19**	**1**	**2**	**3**	**7**	**12**	**13**	**20**
TOTAL										
0–19 Years	25	4.0	8	1	2	4	5	7	7	18
20–34	9	4.9	17	1	2	3	5	12	12	12
35–49	21	6.2	28	1	2	4	10	13	15	20
50–64	17	3.5	9	1	2	3	4	9	13	13
65+	12	3.6	15	2	2	2	4	5	17	17
GRAND TOTAL	**84**	**4.4**	**14**	**1**	**2**	**3**	**5**	**10**	**13**	**18**

77.88: PART OSTECTOMY MT/TARSAL

Type of Patients	Observed Patients	Avg. Stay	Vari-ance	Percentiles 10th	25th	50th	75th	90th	95th	99th
1. SINGLE DX										
0–19 Years	13	1.1	<1	1	1	1	1	1	1	2
20–34	1	1.0	0	1	1	1	1	1	1	1
35–49	2	1.5	<1	1	1	2	2	2	2	2
50–64	0									
65+	0									
2. MULTIPLE DX										
0–19 Years	11	2.3	6	1	1	1	2	7	8	8
20–34	12	4.6	8	2	2	4	7	7	12	12
35–49	63	6.0	18	2	3	5	8	13	15	20
50–64	125	7.4	48	2	3	5	10	19	21	35
65+	114	6.9	31	1	3	6	8	13	18	27
TOTAL SINGLE DX	**16**	**1.1**	**<1**	**1**	**1**	**1**	**1**	**1**	**2**	**2**
TOTAL MULTIPLE DX	**325**	**6.7**	**34**	**1**	**2**	**5**	**8**	**14**	**20**	**29**
TOTAL										
0–19 Years	24	1.6	3	1	1	1	1	2	7	8
20–34	13	4.3	8	1	2	4	7	7	12	12
35–49	65	5.9	18	2	2	5	8	13	15	20
50–64	125	7.4	48	2	3	5	10	19	21	35
65+	114	6.9	31	1	3	6	8	13	18	27
GRAND TOTAL	**341**	**6.3**	**34**	**1**	**2**	**5**	**8**	**13**	**19**	**29**

77.89: PARTIAL OSTECTOMY NEC

Type of Patients	Observed Patients	Avg. Stay	Vari-ance	Percentiles 10th	25th	50th	75th	90th	95th	99th
1. SINGLE DX										
0–19 Years	8	4.7	11	1	1	5	6	7	12	12
20–34	6	2.2	2	1	1	1	3	4	4	4
35–49	5	1.7	2	1	1	1	1	4	4	4
50–64	3	1.0	0	1	1	1	1	1	1	1
65+	1	3.0	0	3	3	3	3	3	3	3
2. MULTIPLE DX										
0–19 Years	10	6.4	38	1	1	3	16	16	16	16
20–34	17	8.3	103	1	1	5	10	17	26	47
35–49	54	5.4	27	1	1	3	9	14	16	21
50–64	75	7.4	46	1	3	5	10	18	22	33
65+	70	6.6	27	2	2	5	10	13	15	26
TOTAL SINGLE DX	**23**	**3.4**	**9**	**1**	**1**	**3**	**5**	**6**	**12**	**12**
TOTAL MULTIPLE DX	**226**	**6.7**	**40**	**1**	**2**	**5**	**10**	**16**	**18**	**26**
TOTAL										
0–19 Years	18	5.8	28	1	1	3	7	16	16	16
20–34	23	7.1	89	1	1	3	10	17	26	47
35–49	59	5.1	26	1	1	3	8	13	16	21
50–64	78	7.2	45	1	3	5	10	18	22	33
65+	71	6.6	27	2	2	5	10	13	15	26
GRAND TOTAL	**249**	**6.3**	**37**	**1**	**2**	**5**	**9**	**15**	**18**	**26**

77.9: TOTAL OSTECTOMY

Type of Patients	Observed Patients	Avg. Stay	Vari-ance	Percentiles 10th	25th	50th	75th	90th	95th	99th
1. SINGLE DX										
0–19 Years	17	2.0	<1	1	1	2	2	4	4	5
20–34	34	3.0	7	1	2	2	3	5	8	13
35–49	58	2.0	1	1	1	2	3	3	4	8
50–64	24	1.7	<1	1	1	2	2	3	3	4
65+	3	2.4	<1	1	1	3	3	3	3	3
2. MULTIPLE DX										
0–19 Years	22	8.3	96	1	2	8	11	16	18	46
20–34	76	3.1	6	1	1	3	3	6	7	12
35–49	153	4.4	62	1	2	2	4	7	15	43
50–64	97	5.1	128	1	2	3	4	7	13	84
65+	76	8.0	64	2	3	5	9	20	27	29
TOTAL SINGLE DX	**136**	**2.2**	**2**	**1**	**1**	**2**	**3**	**4**	**4**	**8**
TOTAL MULTIPLE DX	**424**	**5.3**	**72**	**1**	**2**	**3**	**5**	**11**	**18**	**46**
TOTAL										
0–19 Years	39	5.7	67	1	1	2	8	11	16	46
20–34	110	3.0	6	1	1	2	3	6	8	13
35–49	211	3.7	46	1	1	2	3	6	9	37
50–64	121	4.5	109	1	2	2	4	6	13	84
65+	79	7.4	60	1	3	4	9	20	27	29
GRAND TOTAL	**560**	**4.6**	**57**	**1**	**2**	**3**	**4**	**9**	**14**	**42**

77.91: TOT CHEST CAGE OSTECTOMY

Type of Patients	Observed Patients	Avg. Stay	Vari-ance	Percentiles						
				10th	25th	50th	75th	90th	95th	99th
1. SINGLE DX										
0–19 Years	11	1.9	<1	1	2	2	2	2	2	5
20–34	28	2.6	2	1	2	2	3	5	5	8
35–49	53	2.1	1	1	1	2	3	3	4	8
50–64	18	1.8	<1	1	1	2	2	3	4	4
65+	0									
2. MULTIPLE DX										
0–19 Years	13	5.6	23	1	2	3	10	12	16	16
20–34	65	2.9	5	1	1	2	3	6	7	12
35–49	118	3.5	53	1	2	2	3	4	7	62
50–64	68	3.7	12	1	2	3	4	7	12	16
65+	15	8.1	68	2	3	4	11	27	27	27
TOTAL SINGLE DX	**110**	**2.2**	**1**	**1**	**1**	**2**	**3**	**4**	**4**	**8**
TOTAL MULTIPLE DX	**279**	**3.8**	**32**	**1**	**2**	**2**	**4**	**7**	**11**	**27**
TOTAL										
0–19 Years	24	3.7	15	1	2	2	4	10	12	16
20–34	93	2.8	4	1	1	2	3	5	7	11
35–49	171	3.0	37	1	1	2	3	4	6	14
50–64	86	3.4	11	1	2	2	4	6	12	16
65+	15	8.1	68	2	3	4	11	27	27	27
GRAND TOTAL	**389**	**3.3**	**24**	**1**	**2**	**2**	**3**	**5**	**10**	**22**

78.0: BONE GRAFT

Type of Patients	Observed Patients	Avg. Stay	Vari-ance	Percentiles						
				10th	25th	50th	75th	90th	95th	99th
1. SINGLE DX										
0–19 Years	53	2.4	3	1	1	2	3	5	7	7
20–34	37	2.1	1	1	1	2	3	4	4	5
35–49	38	2.0	2	1	1	2	3	4	5	6
50–64	35	2.0	2	1	1	2	3	4	6	6
65+	5	1.8	<1	1	1	2	2	3	3	3
2. MULTIPLE DX										
0–19 Years	56	2.3	2	1	1	2	3	5	5	8
20–34	93	2.5	3	1	1	2	3	5	6	10
35–49	147	2.9	5	1	1	2	4	5	8	12
50–64	131	3.4	14	1	2	2	4	6	7	27
65+	86	3.8	22	1	1	3	5	6	10	36
TOTAL SINGLE DX	**168**	**2.2**	**2**	**1**	**1**	**2**	**3**	**4**	**5**	**7**
TOTAL MULTIPLE DX	**513**	**3.0**	**9**	**1**	**1**	**2**	**4**	**6**	**7**	**14**
TOTAL										
0–19 Years	109	2.3	3	1	1	2	3	5	5	8
20–34	130	2.4	3	1	1	2	3	5	5	10
35–49	185	2.7	4	1	1	2	3	5	7	12
50–64	166	3.2	12	1	1	2	4	6	7	27
65+	91	3.7	22	1	1	3	5	6	10	36
GRAND TOTAL	**681**	**2.8**	**8**	**1**	**1**	**2**	**3**	**5**	**7**	**12**

78.05: BONE GRAFT TO FEMUR

Type of Patients	Observed Patients	Avg. Stay	Vari-ance	Percentiles						
				10th	25th	50th	75th	90th	95th	99th
1. SINGLE DX										
0–19 Years	26	2.6	3	1	1	2	4	7	7	7
20–34	15	1.9	1	1	1	2	3	3	4	4
35–49	14	2.0	2	1	1	2	3	4	5	5
50–64	11	1.7	<1	1	1	2	2	3	3	3
65+	3	2.0	<1	1	1	2	3	3	3	3
2. MULTIPLE DX										
0–19 Years	32	2.2	2	1	1	2	3	4	4	9
20–34	27	3.0	5	1	2	2	4	6	10	10
35–49	49	3.5	8	1	2	3	4	8	8	15
50–64	49	3.7	6	1	2	3	4	7	10	12
65+	45	4.5	35	1	2	3	6	8	13	36
TOTAL SINGLE DX	**69**	**2.2**	**2**	**1**	**1**	**2**	**3**	**4**	**5**	**7**
TOTAL MULTIPLE DX	**202**	**3.4**	**12**	**1**	**1**	**2**	**4**	**6**	**9**	**14**
TOTAL										
0–19 Years	58	2.3	2	1	1	2	3	4	5	7
20–34	42	2.6	4	1	1	2	3	5	6	10
35–49	63	3.2	7	1	1	3	4	7	8	15
50–64	60	3.3	6	1	2	3	4	7	8	12
65+	48	4.4	34	1	2	3	5	8	13	36
GRAND TOTAL	**271**	**3.1**	**10**	**1**	**1**	**2**	**4**	**6**	**8**	**14**

78.07: BONE GRAFT TIBIA/FIBULA

Type of Patients	Observed Patients	Avg. Stay	Vari-ance	Percentiles						
				10th	25th	50th	75th	90th	95th	99th
1. SINGLE DX										
0–19 Years	19	1.9	3	1	1	1	2	3	7	7
20–34	13	2.3	2	1	1	2	3	4	5	5
35–49	19	1.9	1	1	1	2	2	3	4	6
50–64	13	2.8	3	1	1	3	4	6	6	6
65+	2	1.5	<1	1	1	2	2	2	2	2
2. MULTIPLE DX										
0–19 Years	15	3.4	4	1	2	4	5	5	5	8
20–34	46	2.2	2	1	1	2	3	4	5	7
35–49	71	2.7	3	1	2	2	3	4	7	12
50–64	49	3.3	15	1	2	2	4	5	7	27
65+	24	2.6	4	1	1	2	4	6	6	8
TOTAL SINGLE DX	**66**	**2.1**	**2**	**1**	**1**	**2**	**3**	**4**	**6**	**7**
TOTAL MULTIPLE DX	**205**	**2.8**	**6**	**1**	**1**	**2**	**4**	**5**	**6**	**8**
TOTAL										
0–19 Years	34	2.6	4	1	1	2	4	5	7	8
20–34	59	2.2	2	1	1	2	3	4	5	7
35–49	90	2.6	3	1	1	2	3	4	6	12
50–64	62	3.2	13	1	1	2	4	6	7	27
65+	26	2.5	4	1	1	2	4	6	6	8
GRAND TOTAL	**271**	**2.6**	**5**	**1**	**1**	**2**	**3**	**5**	**6**	**8**

78.1: APPL EXT FIXATION DEVICE

Type of Patients	Observed Patients	Avg. Stay	Vari-ance	Percentiles						
				10th	25th	50th	75th	90th	95th	99th
1. SINGLE DX										
0–19 Years	75	2.6	8	1	1	2	3	5	6	7
20–34	43	3.6	16	1	1	2	3	8	10	23
35–49	38	3.1	6	1	2	3	4	4	6	14
50–64	43	2.3	5	1	1	2	3	5	7	14
65+	18	2.1	2	1	1	2	3	4	6	6
2. MULTIPLE DX										
0–19 Years	76	5.7	52	1	1	4	6	15	20	30
20–34	86	7.2	65	1	2	5	10	15	24	51
35–49	149	7.4	92	1	3	4	9	15	20	61
50–64	149	4.9	29	1	2	3	6	10	14	34
65+	187	5.1	90	1	2	3	5	10	12	76
TOTAL SINGLE DX	**217**	**2.8**	**8**	**1**	**1**	**2**	**3**	**5**	**7**	**15**
TOTAL MULTIPLE DX	**647**	**5.9**	**69**	**1**	**2**	**4**	**7**	**12**	**18**	**51**
TOTAL										
0–19 Years	151	4.1	32	1	1	3	5	7	15	30
20–34	129	6.0	52	1	2	3	8	14	20	32
35–49	187	6.6	78	1	2	4	8	12	19	61
50–64	192	4.4	25	1	1	3	5	9	13	28
65+	205	4.8	84	1	1	3	5	9	12	76
GRAND TOTAL	**864**	**5.1**	**55**	**1**	**2**	**3**	**6**	**10**	**15**	**35**

78.13: APPL EXT FIX RAD/ULNA

Type of Patients	Observed Patients	Avg. Stay	Vari-ance	Percentiles						
				10th	25th	50th	75th	90th	95th	99th
1. SINGLE DX										
0–19 Years	5	1.2	<1	1	1	1	1	2	2	2
20–34	11	1.5	<1	1	1	1	2	2	3	3
35–49	15	1.8	1	1	1	1	2	4	4	4
50–64	27	2.1	6	1	1	1	2	3	8	14
65+	14	1.7	<1	1	1	1	2	3	3	3
2. MULTIPLE DX										
0–19 Years	8	1.9	2	1	1	1	4	4	5	5
20–34	24	4.1	16	1	1	2	5	12	12	14
35–49	32	3.0	10	1	1	2	3	7	8	17
50–64	57	2.3	4	1	1	2	3	5	7	11
65+	133	3.4	10	1	1	3	4	7	10	12
TOTAL SINGLE DX	**72**	**1.8**	**3**	**1**	**1**	**1**	**2**	**3**	**4**	**14**
TOTAL MULTIPLE DX	**254**	**3.1**	**9**	**1**	**1**	**2**	**4**	**7**	**10**	**13**
TOTAL										
0–19 Years	13	1.6	2	1	1	1	1	4	5	5
20–34	35	3.4	13	1	1	2	4	12	12	14
35–49	47	2.6	8	1	1	2	3	5	8	17
50–64	84	2.3	4	1	1	2	2	5	7	11
65+	147	3.2	9	1	1	2	4	7	10	12
GRAND TOTAL	**326**	**2.9**	**8**	**1**	**1**	**2**	**3**	**6**	**10**	**13**

78.15: APPL EXT FIX DEV FEMUR

Type of Patients	Observed Patients	Avg. Stay	Vari-ance	Percentiles						
				10th	25th	50th	75th	90th	95th	99th
1. SINGLE DX										
0–19 Years	35	3.0	12	1	2	3	3	5	5	27
20–34	2	4.8	11	3	3	3	10	10	10	10
35–49	1	1.0	0	1	1	1	1	1	1	1
50–64	1	5.0	0	5	5	5	5	5	5	5
65+	0									
2. MULTIPLE DX										
0–19 Years	36	6.1	70	1	2	3	6	15	23	57
20–34	5	16.0	336	2	8	8	12	51	51	51
35–49	10	8.6	26	4	5	8	10	12	23	23
50–64	9	6.9	17	2	2	8	10	14	14	14
65+	14	5.4	15	2	3	4	7	12	15	15
TOTAL SINGLE DX	**39**	**3.1**	**11**	**1**	**2**	**3**	**3**	**5**	**7**	**27**
TOTAL MULTIPLE DX	**74**	**7.0**	**76**	**1**	**3**	**5**	**8**	**15**	**23**	**51**
TOTAL										
0–19 Years	71	4.6	43	1	2	3	5	7	16	30
20–34	7	11.9	239	2	3	8	12	51	51	51
35–49	11	8.0	28	3	5	8	10	12	23	23
50–64	10	6.7	15	2	4	6	10	10	14	14
65+	14	5.4	15	2	3	4	7	12	15	15
GRAND TOTAL	**113**	**5.5**	**53**	**1**	**2**	**3**	**6**	**11**	**16**	**51**

78.17: APPL EXT FIX DEV TIB/FIB

Type of Patients	Observed Patients	Avg. Stay	Vari-ance	Percentiles						
				10th	25th	50th	75th	90th	95th	99th
1. SINGLE DX										
0–19 Years	22	2.5	3	1	1	2	3	6	6	7
20–34	24	4.6	24	2	2	3	6	9	15	23
35–49	20	3.9	8	2	2	3	4	6	13	14
50–64	14	2.5	3	1	1	2	3	6	7	7
65+	4	3.4	4	2	2	2	6	6	6	6
2. MULTIPLE DX										
0–19 Years	22	6.8	44	1	2	5	7	20	22	22
20–34	38	7.1	49	1	2	6	8	14	24	32
35–49	82	7.1	43	2	3	5	9	16	20	35
50–64	66	6.4	42	2	3	5	6	13	19	34
65+	30	11.8	406	3	4	5	7	16	76	76
TOTAL SINGLE DX	**84**	**3.4**	**10**	**1**	**2**	**2**	**4**	**6**	**9**	**15**
TOTAL MULTIPLE DX	**238**	**7.5**	**93**	**2**	**3**	**5**	**8**	**15**	**22**	**76**
TOTAL										
0–19 Years	44	4.3	25	1	1	2	5	10	20	22
20–34	62	6.2	41	1	2	4	7	14	24	32
35–49	102	6.4	37	2	3	4	8	13	19	35
50–64	80	5.7	37	1	2	4	6	11	17	34
65+	34	10.7	361	2	4	5	7	15	76	76
GRAND TOTAL	**322**	**6.4**	**74**	**1**	**2**	**4**	**7**	**12**	**19**	**35**

78.2: LIMB SHORTENING PX

Type of Patients	Observed Patients	Avg. Stay	Vari-ance	10th	25th	50th	75th	90th	95th	99th
				Percentiles						
1. SINGLE DX										
0–19 Years	42	1.4	<1	1	1	1	2	2	2	3
20–34	2	1.0	0	1	1	1	1	1	1	1
35–49	3	1.4	<1	1	1	1	2	2	2	2
50–64	1	1.0	0	1	1	1	1	1	1	1
65+	0									
2. MULTIPLE DX										
0–19 Years	126	2.0	4	1	1	1	2	4	4	11
20–34	13	2.2	3	1	1	1	3	6	6	6
35–49	13	2.3	5	1	1	1	2	5	10	10
50–64	11	3.1	3	1	1	3	4	6	6	6
65+	3	4.1	3	2	2	5	5	5	5	5
TOTAL SINGLE DX	**48**	**1.3**	**<1**	**1**	**1**	**1**	**2**	**2**	**2**	**3**
TOTAL MULTIPLE DX	**166**	**2.1**	**4**	**1**	**1**	**1**	**3**	**4**	**4**	**11**
TOTAL										
0–19 Years	168	1.8	3	1	1	1	2	3	4	11
20–34	15	2.1	3	1	1	1	3	5	6	6
35–49	16	2.1	4	1	1	1	2	3	5	10
50–64	12	3.0	3	1	1	3	4	6	6	6
65+	3	4.1	3	2	2	5	5	5	5	5
GRAND TOTAL	**214**	**1.9**	**3**	**1**	**1**	**1**	**2**	**4**	**4**	**11**

78.25: LIMB SHORT PX FEMUR

Type of Patients	Observed Patients	Avg. Stay	Vari-ance	10th	25th	50th	75th	90th	95th	99th
				Percentiles						
1. SINGLE DX										
0–19 Years	29	1.4	<1	1	1	1	2	2	3	3
20–34	0									
35–49	1	1.0	0	1	1	1	1	1	1	1
50–64	0									
65+	0									
2. MULTIPLE DX										
0–19 Years	83	2.4	6	1	1	2	3	4	4	11
20–34	7	3.7	3	2	2	3	5	6	6	6
35–49	5	4.0	11	2	2	3	3	10	10	10
50–64	5	3.2	<1	2	2	3	4	4	4	4
65+	1	5.0	0	5	5	5	5	5	5	5
TOTAL SINGLE DX	**30**	**1.4**	**<1**	**1**	**1**	**1**	**2**	**2**	**3**	**3**
TOTAL MULTIPLE DX	**101**	**2.5**	**5**	**1**	**1**	**2**	**3**	**4**	**5**	**11**
TOTAL										
0–19 Years	112	2.1	4	1	1	2	3	4	4	11
20–34	7	3.7	3	2	2	3	5	6	6	6
35–49	6	3.0	9	1	1	2	3	10	10	10
50–64	5	3.2	<1	2	2	3	4	4	4	4
65+	1	5.0	0	5	5	5	5	5	5	5
GRAND TOTAL	**131**	**2.2**	**4**	**1**	**1**	**2**	**3**	**4**	**4**	**11**

78.3: LIMB LENGTHENING PX

Type of Patients	Observed Patients	Avg. Stay	Vari-ance	10th	25th	50th	75th	90th	95th	99th
				Percentiles						
1. SINGLE DX										
0–19 Years	21	2.8	8	1	1	2	3	5	5	15
20–34	1	1.0	0	1	1	1	1	1	1	1
35–49	1	1.0	0	1	1	1	1	1	1	1
50–64	1	2.0	0	2	2	2	2	2	2	2
65+	0									
2. MULTIPLE DX										
0–19 Years	39	2.3	3	1	1	1	3	4	6	9
20–34	10	2.6	<1	2	2	3	3	3	4	4
35–49	9	3.5	9	1	1	2	5	10	10	10
50–64	5	2.6	1	1	2	3	3	4	4	4
65+	8	2.9	3	1	2	2	4	6	6	6
TOTAL SINGLE DX	**24**	**2.7**	**8**	**1**	**1**	**2**	**3**	**5**	**5**	**15**
TOTAL MULTIPLE DX	**71**	**2.5**	**3**	**1**	**1**	**2**	**3**	**5**	**6**	**9**
TOTAL										
0–19 Years	60	2.4	5	1	1	2	3	5	6	15
20–34	11	2.5	<1	2	2	2	3	3	4	4
35–49	10	3.3	9	1	1	2	5	7	10	10
50–64	6	2.5	1	1	2	3	3	4	4	4
65+	8	2.9	3	1	2	2	4	6	6	6
GRAND TOTAL	**95**	**2.5**	**4**	**1**	**1**	**2**	**3**	**5**	**6**	**10**

78.4: OTHER BONE REPAIR

Type of Patients	Observed Patients	Avg. Stay	Vari-ance	10th	25th	50th	75th	90th	95th	99th
				Percentiles						
1. SINGLE DX										
0–19 Years	15	2.0	2	1	1	1	3	4	4	7
20–34	12	3.7	14	1	1	2	4	7	14	14
35–49	15	2.4	5	1	1	1	3	5	9	9
50–64	9	1.9	2	1	1	1	3	4	4	4
65+	28	1.4	1	1	1	1	1	3	5	5
2. MULTIPLE DX										
0–19 Years	37	4.0	7	1	2	3	6	8	8	13
20–34	46	4.8	14	1	2	5	6	7	13	22
35–49	78	3.9	53	1	1	2	4	7	10	26
50–64	170	5.4	27	1	1	4	8	13	14	25
65+	1,081	4.9	18	1	1	4	7	10	12	20
TOTAL SINGLE DX	**79**	**2.0**	**4**	**1**	**1**	**1**	**3**	**4**	**5**	**9**
TOTAL MULTIPLE DX	**1,412**	**4.8**	**20**	**1**	**1**	**4**	**7**	**10**	**13**	**21**
TOTAL										
0–19 Years	52	3.3	6	1	1	3	5	7	8	9
20–34	58	4.6	14	1	2	4	6	7	13	22
35–49	93	3.7	46	1	1	2	4	7	9	26
50–64	179	5.3	27	1	1	4	8	13	14	25
65+	1,109	4.8	18	1	1	4	7	10	12	20
GRAND TOTAL	**1,491**	**4.7**	**19**	**1**	**1**	**4**	**7**	**10**	**13**	**20**

78.49: OTHER BONE REPAIR NEC

Type of Patients	Observed Patients	Avg. Stay	Vari-ance	Percentiles						
				10th	25th	50th	75th	90th	95th	99th
1. SINGLE DX										
0–19 Years	2	1.6	2	1	1	1	1	4	4	4
20–34	1	5.0	0	5	5	5	5	5	5	5
35–49	6	2.4	8	1	1	1	1	9	9	9
50–64	8	1.7	1	1	1	1	2	4	4	4
65+	22	1.1	<1	1	1	1	1	1	1	5
2. MULTIPLE DX										
0–19 Years	1	3.0	0	3	3	3	3	3	3	3
20–34	7	6.7	22	1	2	5	8	14	14	14
35–49	27	5.5	136	1	1	1	5	10	24	68
50–64	113	5.8	28	1	1	4	9	13	15	19
65+	1,052	4.9	18	1	1	4	7	10	13	20
TOTAL SINGLE DX	**39**	**1.5**	**2**	**1**	**1**	**1**	**1**	**4**	**5**	**9**
TOTAL MULTIPLE DX	**1,200**	**5.0**	**21**	**1**	**1**	**4**	**7**	**10**	**13**	**20**
TOTAL										
0–19 Years	3	1.8	2	1	1	1	3	4	4	4
20–34	8	6.6	20	1	5	5	8	14	14	14
35–49	33	4.8	109	1	1	1	5	9	13	68
50–64	121	5.6	27	1	1	4	9	13	14	19
65+	1,074	4.8	18	1	1	4	7	10	12	20
GRAND TOTAL	**1,239**	**4.9**	**21**	**1**	**1**	**4**	**7**	**10**	**13**	**20**

78.5: INT FIX W/O FX REDUCTION

Type of Patients	Observed Patients	Avg. Stay	Vari-ance	Percentiles						
				10th	25th	50th	75th	90th	95th	99th
1. SINGLE DX										
0–19 Years	340	2.2	5	1	1	2	3	4	5	14
20–34	169	2.6	4	1	1	2	3	4	6	11
35–49	109	2.5	3	1	1	2	3	4	5	11
50–64	99	2.4	2	1	1	2	3	4	5	7
65+	71	3.6	6	1	2	3	5	5	6	10
2. MULTIPLE DX										
0–19 Years	270	3.6	12	1	1	2	4	7	10	17
20–34	336	5.0	30	1	2	3	6	9	14	28
35–49	363	4.2	12	1	2	3	5	9	11	18
50–64	667	5.1	30	1	2	4	6	9	14	34
65+	2,402	5.0	12	2	3	4	6	8	11	20
TOTAL SINGLE DX	**788**	**2.5**	**5**	**1**	**1**	**2**	**3**	**4**	**5**	**11**
TOTAL MULTIPLE DX	**4,038**	**4.8**	**17**	**2**	**3**	**4**	**6**	**8**	**12**	**22**
TOTAL										
0–19 Years	610	2.8	9	1	1	2	3	5	7	17
20–34	505	4.1	22	1	2	3	5	8	12	27
35–49	472	3.8	10	1	2	3	5	8	11	15
50–64	766	4.7	28	1	2	3	5	9	13	33
65+	2,473	5.0	12	2	3	4	6	8	10	20
GRAND TOTAL	**4,826**	**4.4**	**15**	**1**	**2**	**4**	**5**	**8**	**10**	**21**

78.52: INT FIX W/O RED HUMERUS

Type of Patients	Observed Patients	Avg. Stay	Vari-ance	Percentiles						
				10th	25th	50th	75th	90th	95th	99th
1. SINGLE DX										
0–19 Years	14	1.3	<1	1	1	1	1	2	2	3
20–34	8	1.9	<1	1	1	2	2	3	3	3
35–49	6	1.6	<1	1	1	1	2	2	3	3
50–64	9	1.7	2	1	1	1	2	2	6	6
65+	2	1.0	0	1	1	1	1	1	1	1
2. MULTIPLE DX										
0–19 Years	14	2.9	5	1	1	2	5	7	7	7
20–34	15	6.3	45	2	2	6	6	16	28	28
35–49	14	4.0	12	1	1	2	6	9	13	13
50–64	85	3.2	12	1	1	2	3	7	11	21
65+	115	4.4	22	1	2	3	4	9	20	20
TOTAL SINGLE DX	**39**	**1.5**	**<1**	**1**	**1**	**1**	**2**	**2**	**3**	**6**
TOTAL MULTIPLE DX	**243**	**4.0**	**19**	**1**	**2**	**3**	**4**	**8**	**13**	**21**
TOTAL										
0–19 Years	28	1.9	3	1	1	1	2	5	7	7
20–34	23	4.9	35	1	2	3	6	7	16	28
35–49	20	3.0	9	1	1	2	6	6	9	13
50–64	94	3.1	11	1	1	2	3	6	9	21
65+	117	4.4	21	1	2	3	4	9	20	20
GRAND TOTAL	**282**	**3.6**	**17**	**1**	**1**	**2**	**4**	**7**	**12**	**20**

78.55: INT FIX W/O RED FEMUR

Type of Patients	Observed Patients	Avg. Stay	Vari-ance	Percentiles						
				10th	25th	50th	75th	90th	95th	99th
1. SINGLE DX										
0–19 Years	283	2.3	6	1	1	2	3	4	5	17
20–34	44	2.9	6	1	1	2	3	7	8	12
35–49	30	3.1	5	1	2	3	4	5	7	13
50–64	43	2.8	3	1	2	2	4	5	5	11
65+	63	3.6	3	2	2	3	5	5	6	10
2. MULTIPLE DX										
0–19 Years	179	3.8	15	1	1	3	4	7	13	25
20–34	156	6.1	46	2	3	4	7	13	18	35
35–49	146	5.0	13	2	3	4	6	10	14	18
50–64	381	5.4	26	2	3	4	6	10	14	37
65+	2,157	5.0	11	3	3	4	6	8	10	19
TOTAL SINGLE DX	**463**	**2.6**	**6**	**1**	**1**	**2**	**3**	**5**	**6**	**13**
TOTAL MULTIPLE DX	**3,019**	**5.0**	**15**	**2**	**3**	**4**	**6**	**8**	**11**	**21**
TOTAL										
0–19 Years	462	2.9	10	1	1	2	3	5	7	17
20–34	200	5.4	39	1	2	4	6	11	16	34
35–49	176	4.7	12	2	3	4	6	10	13	18
50–64	424	5.2	24	2	3	4	6	9	13	31
65+	2,220	5.0	11	3	3	4	6	8	10	19
GRAND TOTAL	**3,482**	**4.7**	**15**	**2**	**3**	**4**	**5**	**8**	**11**	**21**

78.57: INT FIX W/O RED TIB/FIB

Type of Patients	Observed Patients	Avg. Stay	Vari-ance	Percentiles						
				10th	25th	50th	75th	90th	95th	99th
1. SINGLE DX										
0–19 Years	30	2.0	1	1	1	2	3	4	5	5
20–34	102	2.5	3	1	2	2	3	4	5	11
35–49	57	2.5	2	1	2	2	3	4	5	11
50–64	37	2.2	2	1	1	2	3	4	4	7
65+	3	8.3	124	1	1	2	21	21	21	21
2. MULTIPLE DX										
0–19 Years	45	2.8	5	1	2	2	3	5	7	13
20–34	123	3.7	8	1	2	3	4	7	8	17
35–49	139	3.8	10	1	2	3	5	7	9	22
50–64	145	4.4	24	1	2	3	5	8	10	28
65+	73	5.3	14	2	3	4	7	10	15	16
TOTAL SINGLE DX	**229**	**2.5**	**3**	**1**	**1**	**2**	**3**	**4**	**5**	**11**
TOTAL MULTIPLE DX	**525**	**4.0**	**13**	**1**	**2**	**3**	**5**	**8**	**10**	**20**
TOTAL										
0–19 Years	75	2.6	4	1	2	2	3	5	5	13
20–34	225	3.2	6	1	2	2	4	6	8	16
35–49	196	3.4	8	1	2	3	4	6	8	15
50–64	182	4.0	20	1	2	3	4	7	9	28
65+	76	5.4	17	2	3	4	7	10	16	17
GRAND TOTAL	**754**	**3.5**	**11**	**1**	**2**	**3**	**4**	**7**	**9**	**18**

78.59: INT FIX W/O FX RED NEC

Type of Patients	Observed Patients	Avg. Stay	Vari-ance	Percentiles						
				10th	25th	50th	75th	90th	95th	99th
1. SINGLE DX										
0–19 Years	6	2.6	2	1	2	2	3	5	5	5
20–34	4	2.2	<1	1	2	2	3	3	3	3
35–49	9	2.9	7	1	1	2	3	9	9	9
50–64	4	1.2	<1	1	1	1	1	2	2	2
65+	1	1.0	0	1	1	1	1	1	1	1
2. MULTIPLE DX										
0–19 Years	17	3.4	13	1	1	2	5	8	8	17
20–34	21	4.6	14	1	2	4	6	11	12	12
35–49	29	4.4	10	1	3	3	5	10	11	12
50–64	28	8.3	138	1	1	4	6	33	37	45
65+	29	5.4	31	1	3	5	5	9	14	30
TOTAL SINGLE DX	**24**	**2.4**	**4**	**1**	**1**	**2**	**3**	**5**	**5**	**9**
TOTAL MULTIPLE DX	**124**	**5.3**	**44**	**1**	**1**	**3**	**5**	**11**	**14**	**37**
TOTAL										
0–19 Years	23	3.2	10	1	1	2	5	6	8	17
20–34	25	4.3	12	1	2	3	6	11	12	12
35–49	38	4.0	10	1	2	3	5	9	11	12
50–64	32	7.5	127	1	1	4	5	33	37	45
65+	30	5.3	30	1	3	5	5	9	14	30
GRAND TOTAL	**148**	**4.8**	**38**	**1**	**1**	**3**	**5**	**10**	**12**	**37**

78.6: RMVL IMPL DEV FROM BONE

Type of Patients	Observed Patients	Avg. Stay	Vari-ance	Percentiles						
				10th	25th	50th	75th	90th	95th	99th
1. SINGLE DX										
0–19 Years	92	1.7	5	1	1	1	2	2	4	6
20–34	90	1.6	2	1	1	1	2	3	4	10
35–49	157	1.8	1	1	1	2	2	3	4	5
50–64	110	1.7	1	1	1	1	2	3	5	6
65+	25	2.2	1	1	1	2	3	4	4	4
2. MULTIPLE DX										
0–19 Years	235	2.8	8	1	1	2	4	6	8	20
20–34	323	3.3	15	1	1	2	4	6	9	16
35–49	727	3.6	17	1	1	2	4	7	11	22
50–64	748	3.9	27	1	1	2	4	7	13	29
65+	661	4.7	31	1	1	3	5	10	14	30
TOTAL SINGLE DX	**474**	**1.8**	**2**	**1**	**1**	**1**	**2**	**3**	**4**	**6**
TOTAL MULTIPLE DX	**2,694**	**3.8**	**22**	**1**	**1**	**2**	**4**	**8**	**12**	**26**
TOTAL										
0–19 Years	327	2.4	7	1	1	1	3	6	7	20
20–34	413	3.0	13	1	1	2	3	6	9	16
35–49	884	3.2	15	1	1	2	4	6	9	21
50–64	858	3.6	24	1	1	2	4	7	11	29
65+	686	4.6	30	1	1	3	5	10	14	29
GRAND TOTAL	**3,168**	**3.5**	**20**	**1**	**1**	**2**	**4**	**7**	**11**	**24**

78.62: RMVL IMPL DEV HUMERUS

Type of Patients	Observed Patients	Avg. Stay	Vari-ance	Percentiles						
				10th	25th	50th	75th	90th	95th	99th
1. SINGLE DX										
0–19 Years	1	1.0	0	1	1	1	1	1	1	1
20–34	4	1.0	0	1	1	1	1	1	1	1
35–49	7	2.2	2	1	1	1	3	5	5	5
50–64	1	1.0	0	1	1	1	1	1	1	1
65+	0									
2. MULTIPLE DX										
0–19 Years	8	2.1	<1	1	1	2	3	3	3	3
20–34	18	2.5	2	1	1	3	4	4	5	5
35–49	16	3.0	16	1	1	2	3	8	16	16
50–64	28	2.9	22	1	1	1	3	4	11	29
65+	42	5.0	64	1	1	2	4	7	30	36
TOTAL SINGLE DX	**13**	**1.6**	**1**	**1**	**1**	**1**	**1**	**3**	**5**	**5**
TOTAL MULTIPLE DX	**112**	**3.6**	**32**	**1**	**1**	**2**	**4**	**6**	**11**	**36**
TOTAL										
0–19 Years	9	1.9	<1	1	1	2	3	3	3	3
20–34	22	2.3	2	1	1	2	3	4	5	5
35–49	23	2.8	12	1	1	2	3	5	16	16
50–64	29	2.8	22	1	1	1	3	4	11	29
65+	42	5.0	64	1	1	2	4	7	30	36
GRAND TOTAL	**125**	**3.4**	**30**	**1**	**1**	**2**	**3**	**6**	**11**	**36**

78.63: RMVL IMPL DEV RAD/ULNA

Type of Patients	Observed Patients	Avg. Stay	Vari- ance	Percentiles						
				10th	25th	50th	75th	90th	95th	99th
1. SINGLE DX										
0–19 Years	11	1.7	1	1	1	1	2	4	4	4
20–34	5	1.3	<1	1	1	1	2	2	2	2
35–49	12	1.5	<1	1	1	1	2	3	3	3
50–64	6	1.4	<1	1	1	1	2	2	2	2
65+	0									
2. MULTIPLE DX										
0–19 Years	12	1.4	<1	1	1	1	1	3	3	4
20–34	36	3.0	7	1	1	2	3	8	8	14
35–49	64	2.9	12	1	1	2	3	5	7	22
50–64	31	3.5	14	1	1	2	5	10	13	16
65+	51	3.8	14	1	2	3	4	6	8	26
TOTAL SINGLE DX	**34**	**1.5**	**<1**	**1**	**1**	**1**	**2**	**3**	**3**	**4**
TOTAL MULTIPLE DX	**194**	**3.1**	**11**	**1**	**1**	**2**	**3**	**6**	**8**	**22**
TOTAL										
0–19 Years	23	1.5	<1	1	1	1	2	3	4	4
20–34	41	2.8	7	1	1	2	3	7	8	14
35–49	76	2.6	10	1	1	2	3	4	6	22
50–64	37	3.2	13	1	1	2	3	8	11	16
65+	51	3.8	14	1	2	3	4	6	8	26
GRAND TOTAL	**228**	**2.9**	**10**	**1**	**1**	**2**	**3**	**6**	**8**	**16**

78.65: RMVL IMPL DEV FEMUR

Type of Patients	Observed Patients	Avg. Stay	Vari- ance	Percentiles						
				10th	25th	50th	75th	90th	95th	99th
1. SINGLE DX										
0–19 Years	48	1.7	7	1	1	1	2	2	4	24
20–34	21	1.4	<1	1	1	1	2	2	3	4
35–49	18	1.4	<1	1	1	1	2	2	3	3
50–64	24	1.5	1	1	1	1	2	3	5	5
65+	13	2.0	1	1	1	2	2	4	4	4
2. MULTIPLE DX										
0–19 Years	83	2.1	7	1	1	1	2	4	7	20
20–34	44	3.0	42	1	1	2	3	4	6	54
35–49	65	4.4	24	1	2	3	5	12	21	21
50–64	93	5.4	77	1	1	3	5	9	28	38
65+	197	4.9	29	1	2	3	5	11	14	23
TOTAL SINGLE DX	**124**	**1.6**	**4**	**1**	**1**	**1**	**2**	**2**	**4**	**6**
TOTAL MULTIPLE DX	**482**	**4.1**	**34**	**1**	**1**	**2**	**4**	**8**	**13**	**28**
TOTAL										
0–19 Years	131	1.9	7	1	1	1	2	3	7	20
20–34	65	2.5	29	1	1	1	2	4	4	13
35–49	83	3.8	20	1	1	2	4	6	16	21
50–64	117	4.7	66	1	1	2	4	7	26	38
65+	210	4.6	27	1	2	3	5	10	14	23
GRAND TOTAL	**606**	**3.5**	**28**	**1**	**1**	**2**	**4**	**7**	**12**	**28**

78.67: RMVL IMPL DEV TIB & FIB

Type of Patients	Observed Patients	Avg. Stay	Vari- ance	Percentiles						
				10th	25th	50th	75th	90th	95th	99th
1. SINGLE DX										
0–19 Years	7	1.3	<1	1	1	1	2	2	2	2
20–34	25	1.4	<1	1	1	1	2	2	2	4
35–49	33	1.8	2	1	1	1	2	5	5	5
50–64	20	1.6	<1	1	1	1	2	3	3	5
65+	2	2.0	2	1	1	3	3	3	3	3
2. MULTIPLE DX										
0–19 Years	26	4.3	18	1	2	3	5	8	13	22
20–34	73	4.8	18	1	2	3	7	11	13	22
35–49	148	5.5	32	1	2	4	7	11	16	29
50–64	140	5.2	38	1	2	3	6	13	16	36
65+	122	5.4	36	1	2	4	7	13	14	29
TOTAL SINGLE DX	**87**	**1.6**	**<1**	**1**	**1**	**1**	**2**	**2**	**4**	**5**
TOTAL MULTIPLE DX	**509**	**5.2**	**32**	**1**	**2**	**3**	**6**	**12**	**15**	**29**
TOTAL										
0–19 Years	33	3.7	16	1	1	2	5	6	13	22
20–34	98	3.9	16	1	1	2	6	9	11	19
35–49	181	4.9	29	1	1	3	6	10	16	29
50–64	160	4.8	35	1	1	3	5	12	16	30
65+	124	5.4	35	1	2	4	7	13	14	29
GRAND TOTAL	**596**	**4.8**	**30**	**1**	**1**	**3**	**6**	**11**	**14**	**29**

78.68: RMVL IMPL DEV MT/TARSAL

Type of Patients	Observed Patients	Avg. Stay	Vari- ance	Percentiles						
				10th	25th	50th	75th	90th	95th	99th
1. SINGLE DX										
0–19 Years	2	1.0	0	1	1	1	1	1	1	1
20–34	1	2.0	0	2	2	2	2	2	2	2
35–49	7	1.6	<1	1	1	1	3	3	3	3
50–64	3	1.8	<1	1	2	2	2	2	2	2
65+	0									
2. MULTIPLE DX										
0–19 Years	3	1.8	<1	1	1	2	3	3	3	3
20–34	16	2.9	4	1	1	2	4	6	7	7
35–49	35	4.1	13	1	2	3	4	8	15	16
50–64	46	3.8	8	1	2	3	5	7	10	15
65+	27	3.2	4	1	2	3	4	6	8	10
TOTAL SINGLE DX	**13**	**1.5**	**<1**	**1**	**1**	**1**	**2**	**3**	**3**	**3**
TOTAL MULTIPLE DX	**127**	**3.6**	**8**	**1**	**2**	**3**	**4**	**7**	**9**	**15**
TOTAL										
0–19 Years	5	1.4	<1	1	1	1	2	3	3	3
20–34	17	2.9	4	1	1	2	4	6	7	7
35–49	42	3.7	12	1	1	3	4	8	11	16
50–64	49	3.7	8	1	2	3	5	6	10	15
65+	27	3.2	4	1	2	3	4	6	8	10
GRAND TOTAL	**140**	**3.4**	**8**	**1**	**1**	**3**	**4**	**6**	**8**	**15**

78.69: RMVL IMPL DEV SITE NEC

Type of Patients	Observed Patients	Avg. Stay	Vari-ance	Percentiles						
				10th	25th	50th	75th	90th	95th	99th
1. SINGLE DX										
0–19 Years	21	1.9	1	1	1	2	2	3	6	6
20–34	28	1.9	2	1	1	1	2	3	4	7
35–49	69	2.0	1	1	1	2	2	3	3	7
50–64	51	1.9	2	1	1	1	2	4	5	6
65+	10	2.4	1	1	1	2	4	4	4	4
2. MULTIPLE DX										
0–19 Years	91	3.3	5	1	2	3	5	7	8	>99
20–34	117	2.7	7	1	1	2	3	5	6	14
35–49	354	2.7	9	1	1	2	3	5	7	12
50–64	371	3.2	12	1	1	2	4	6	10	15
65+	183	3.9	19	1	1	2	4	9	14	20
TOTAL SINGLE DX	**179**	**2.0**	**1**	**1**	**1**	**2**	**2**	**3**	**4**	**6**
TOTAL MULTIPLE DX	**1,116**	**3.1**	**11**	**1**	**1**	**2**	**4**	**6**	**9**	**16**
TOTAL										
0–19 Years	112	3.0	5	1	1	2	4	7	8	>99
20–34	145	2.6	6	1	1	2	3	4	6	14
35–49	423	2.5	7	1	1	2	3	4	7	12
50–64	422	3.0	11	1	1	2	3	6	10	15
65+	193	3.8	18	1	1	2	4	9	14	20
GRAND TOTAL	**1,295**	**3.0**	**10**	**1**	**1**	**2**	**3**	**6**	**8**	**15**

78.7: OSTEOCLASIS

Type of Patients	Observed Patients	Avg. Stay	Vari-ance	Percentiles						
				10th	25th	50th	75th	90th	95th	99th
1. SINGLE DX										
0–19 Years	2	1.0	0	1	1	1	1	1	1	1
20–34	0									
35–49	0									
50–64	0									
65+	0									
2. MULTIPLE DX										
0–19 Years	2	1.3	<1	1	1	1	1	3	3	3
20–34	4	1.6	<1	1	1	2	2	2	2	2
35–49	1	1.0	0	1	1	1	1	1	1	1
50–64	4	3.3	4	1	2	5	5	5	5	5
65+	2	3.0	2	2	2	2	4	4	4	4
TOTAL SINGLE DX	**2**	**1.0**	**0**	**1**	**1**	**1**	**1**	**1**	**1**	**1**
TOTAL MULTIPLE DX	**13**	**1.9**	**2**	**1**	**1**	**1**	**2**	**4**	**5**	**5**
TOTAL										
0–19 Years	4	1.2	<1	1	1	1	1	1	3	3
20–34	4	1.6	<1	1	1	2	2	2	2	2
35–49	1	1.0	0	1	1	1	1	1	1	1
50–64	4	3.3	4	1	2	5	5	5	5	5
65+	2	3.0	2	2	2	2	4	4	4	4
GRAND TOTAL	**15**	**1.7**	**1**	**1**	**1**	**1**	**2**	**4**	**5**	**5**

78.8: OTHER BONE DIAGNOSTIC PX

Type of Patients	Observed Patients	Avg. Stay	Vari-ance	Percentiles						
				10th	25th	50th	75th	90th	95th	99th
1. SINGLE DX										
0–19 Years	1	2.0	0	2	2	2	2	2	2	2
20–34	0									
35–49	1	3.0	0	3	3	3	3	3	3	3
50–64	0									
65+	0									
2. MULTIPLE DX										
0–19 Years	1	8.0	0	8	8	8	8	8	8	8
20–34	0									
35–49	0									
50–64	0									
65+	1	4.0	0	4	4	4	4	4	4	4
TOTAL SINGLE DX	**2**	**2.4**	**<1**	**2**	**2**	**2**	**3**	**3**	**3**	**3**
TOTAL MULTIPLE DX	**2**	**6.0**	**8**	**4**	**4**	**8**	**8**	**8**	**8**	**8**
TOTAL										
0–19 Years	2	4.1	12	2	2	2	8	8	8	8
20–34	0									
35–49	1	3.0	0	3	3	3	3	3	3	3
50–64	0									
65+	1	4.0	0	4	4	4	4	4	4	4
GRAND TOTAL	**4**	**3.9**	**6**	**2**	**2**	**3**	**4**	**8**	**8**	**8**

78.9: INSERT BONE GROWTH STIM

Type of Patients	Observed Patients	Avg. Stay	Vari-ance	Percentiles						
				10th	25th	50th	75th	90th	95th	99th
1. SINGLE DX										
0–19 Years	1	1.0	0	1	1	1	1	1	1	1
20–34	0									
35–49	1	1.0	0	1	1	1	1	1	1	1
50–64	0									
65+	0									
2. MULTIPLE DX										
0–19 Years	0									
20–34	0									
35–49	7	2.9	7	1	1	2	3	10	10	10
50–64	7	2.2	<1	1	2	2	2	4	4	4
65+	4	1.9	7	1	1	1	1	2	10	10
TOTAL SINGLE DX	**2**	**1.0**	**0**	**1**	**1**	**1**	**1**	**1**	**1**	**1**
TOTAL MULTIPLE DX	**18**	**2.3**	**5**	**1**	**1**	**2**	**2**	**4**	**10**	**10**
TOTAL										
0–19 Years	1	1.0	0	1	1	1	1	1	1	1
20–34	0									
35–49	8	2.7	7	1	1	2	3	3	10	10
50–64	7	2.2	<1	1	2	2	2	4	4	4
65+	4	1.9	7	1	1	1	1	2	10	10
GRAND TOTAL	**20**	**2.2**	**5**	**1**	**1**	**1**	**2**	**3**	**10**	**10**

79.0: CLSD FX RED W/O INT FIX

Type of Patients	Observed Patients	Avg. Stay	Vari-ance	Percentiles 10th	25th	50th	75th	90th	95th	99th
1. SINGLE DX										
0–19 Years	1,215	1.5	3	1	1	1	2	2	3	8
20–34	121	1.9	4	1	1	1	2	3	5	12
35–49	96	1.8	3	1	1	1	2	3	4	10
50–64	64	2.3	11	1	1	1	2	4	11	20
65+	32	1.3	<1	1	1	1	1	3	3	4
2. MULTIPLE DX										
0–19 Years	507	2.2	11	1	1	1	2	3	6	13
20–34	219	3.1	20	1	1	2	4	6	7	29
35–49	300	3.7	25	1	1	2	4	7	11	29
50–64	341	3.5	10	1	2	2	4	7	10	17
65+	954	3.7	8	1	2	3	4	7	8	16
TOTAL SINGLE DX	**1,528**	**1.6**	**3**	**1**	**1**	**1**	**2**	**2**	**3**	**10**
TOTAL MULTIPLE DX	**2,321**	**3.2**	**12**	**1**	**1**	**2**	**4**	**6**	**8**	**16**
TOTAL										
0–19 Years	1,722	1.7	5	1	1	1	2	3	4	11
20–34	340	2.7	15	1	1	2	3	5	7	19
35–49	396	3.2	20	1	1	2	3	7	10	29
50–64	405	3.4	10	1	1	2	4	7	10	17
65+	986	3.6	8	1	2	3	4	7	8	16
GRAND TOTAL	**3,849**	**2.4**	**9**	**1**	**1**	**1**	**3**	**5**	**7**	**15**

79.01: CLSD FX RED HUMERUS

Type of Patients	Observed Patients	Avg. Stay	Vari-ance	Percentiles 10th	25th	50th	75th	90th	95th	99th
1. SINGLE DX										
0–19 Years	123	1.2	<1	1	1	1	1	2	2	2
20–34	6	2.9	3	1	1	4	4	5	5	5
35–49	7	1.3	<1	1	1	1	2	2	2	2
50–64	8	1.3	<1	1	1	1	1	1	4	4
65+	5	1.3	<1	1	1	1	1	3	3	3
2. MULTIPLE DX										
0–19 Years	39	1.6	2	1	1	1	2	2	5	7
20–34	30	2.5	4	1	1	2	3	5	7	9
35–49	29	1.9	1	1	1	1	3	3	5	5
50–64	61	3.3	6	1	1	2	5	7	7	11
65+	198	2.9	4	1	1	3	4	5	7	11
TOTAL SINGLE DX	**149**	**1.2**	**<1**	**1**	**1**	**1**	**1**	**2**	**2**	**4**
TOTAL MULTIPLE DX	**357**	**2.7**	**4**	**1**	**1**	**2**	**3**	**5**	**7**	**10**
TOTAL										
0–19 Years	162	1.3	<1	1	1	1	1	2	2	6
20–34	36	2.6	4	1	1	2	3	5	7	9
35–49	36	1.8	1	1	1	1	2	3	4	5
50–64	69	3.0	6	1	1	2	5	7	7	11
65+	203	2.9	4	1	1	3	4	5	7	11
GRAND TOTAL	**506**	**2.1**	**3**	**1**	**1**	**1**	**3**	**4**	**6**	**9**

79.02: CLSD FX RED RADIUS/ULNA

Type of Patients	Observed Patients	Avg. Stay	Vari-ance	Percentiles 10th	25th	50th	75th	90th	95th	99th
1. SINGLE DX										
0–19 Years	496	1.1	<1	1	1	1	1	1	2	2
20–34	25	2.4	16	1	1	1	2	4	12	19
35–49	31	1.9	6	1	1	1	1	3	10	12
50–64	26	1.7	4	1	1	1	1	3	4	11
65+	11	1.2	<1	1	1	1	1	1	4	4
2. MULTIPLE DX										
0–19 Years	194	1.5	<1	1	1	1	2	3	3	5
20–34	58	3.2	34	1	1	2	3	6	6	48
35–49	92	3.4	20	1	1	2	4	7	9	29
50–64	84	3.1	8	1	1	2	4	8	9	14
65+	343	3.5	7	1	2	3	4	7	8	14
TOTAL SINGLE DX	**589**	**1.2**	**1**	**1**	**1**	**1**	**1**	**1**	**2**	**4**
TOTAL MULTIPLE DX	**771**	**2.8**	**9**	**1**	**1**	**2**	**3**	**6**	**8**	**13**
TOTAL										
0–19 Years	690	1.2	<1	1	1	1	1	2	2	3
20–34	83	2.9	29	1	1	1	3	6	8	48
35–49	123	3.0	17	1	1	1	3	7	9	29
50–64	110	2.8	7	1	1	2	3	6	9	13
65+	354	3.4	7	1	2	3	4	7	8	14
GRAND TOTAL	**1,360**	**2.1**	**6**	**1**	**1**	**1**	**2**	**4**	**6**	**11**

79.05: CLSD FX RED FEMUR

Type of Patients	Observed Patients	Avg. Stay	Vari-ance	Percentiles 10th	25th	50th	75th	90th	95th	99th
1. SINGLE DX										
0–19 Years	272	2.1	8	1	1	1	2	3	5	20
20–34	2	2.9	2	2	2	2	4	4	4	4
35–49	3	3.6	9	2	2	2	8	8	8	8
50–64	1	4.0	0	4	4	4	4	4	4	4
65+	4	1.0	0	1	1	1	1	1	1	1
2. MULTIPLE DX										
0–19 Years	114	3.0	28	1	1	2	3	5	9	17
20–34	10	9.4	149	3	3	4	8	29	38	38
35–49	9	5.6	23	3	3	4	5	18	18	18
50–64	15	3.9	7	1	2	4	5	6	11	11
65+	103	4.6	15	2	3	4	5	7	15	21
TOTAL SINGLE DX	**282**	**2.1**	**8**	**1**	**1**	**1**	**2**	**3**	**5**	**20**
TOTAL MULTIPLE DX	**251**	**3.7**	**27**	**1**	**2**	**2**	**4**	**6**	**12**	**29**
TOTAL										
0–19 Years	386	2.3	13	1	1	1	2	3	6	20
20–34	12	8.4	131	2	3	4	7	29	38	38
35–49	12	5.0	19	2	3	3	5	8	18	18
50–64	16	4.0	7	1	2	4	5	6	11	11
65+	107	4.5	15	1	3	4	5	7	13	21
GRAND TOTAL	**533**	**2.7**	**15**	**1**	**1**	**2**	**3**	**5**	**8**	**22**

79.06: CLSD FX RED TIBIA/FIBULA

Type of Patients	Observed Patients	Avg. Stay	Vari- ance	Percentiles						
				10th	25th	50th	75th	90th	95th	99th
1. SINGLE DX										
0–19 Years	302	1.4	<1	1	1	1	2	2	3	4
20–34	73	1.7	1	1	1	1	2	3	3	7
35–49	47	1.6	<1	1	1	1	2	3	3	5
50–64	28	3.2	21	1	1	2	2	4	16	20
65+	10	1.7	1	1	1	1	2	3	4	4
2. MULTIPLE DX										
0–19 Years	140	2.2	3	1	1	2	3	4	7	9
20–34	75	2.3	2	1	1	2	3	4	5	6
35–49	120	3.9	33	1	1	2	4	9	13	30
50–64	141	3.8	11	1	2	3	4	7	10	19
65+	256	4.0	9	1	3	3	5	7	9	18
TOTAL SINGLE DX	**460**	**1.6**	**2**	**1**	**1**	**1**	**2**	**3**	**3**	**6**
TOTAL MULTIPLE DX	**732**	**3.4**	**12**	**1**	**1**	**3**	**4**	**6**	**9**	**19**
TOTAL										
0–19 Years	442	1.7	2	1	1	1	2	3	4	8
20–34	148	2.0	2	1	1	1	3	4	5	7
35–49	167	3.3	25	1	1	2	3	6	11	27
50–64	169	3.7	13	1	2	2	4	7	13	20
65+	266	3.9	9	1	3	3	5	7	9	18
GRAND TOTAL	**1,192**	**2.6**	**8**	**1**	**1**	**2**	**3**	**5**	**7**	**15**

79.09: CLOSED FX REDUCTION NEC

Type of Patients	Observed Patients	Avg. Stay	Vari- ance	Percentiles						
				10th	25th	50th	75th	90th	95th	99th
1. SINGLE DX										
0–19 Years	4	1.2	<1	1	1	1	1	1	3	3
20–34	2	2.3	1	1	1	3	3	3	3	3
35–49	3	2.0	0	2	2	2	2	2	2	2
50–64	0									
65+	0									
2. MULTIPLE DX										
0–19 Years	5	3.7	23	1	1	2	2	12	12	12
20–34	20	5.0	8	2	3	4	7	9	11	11
35–49	13	5.5	20	1	2	5	10	11	16	16
50–64	13	5.5	29	1	2	2	9	17	17	17
65+	22	4.6	7	2	2	4	6	9	9	10
TOTAL SINGLE DX	**9**	**1.6**	**<1**	**1**	**1**	**1**	**2**	**3**	**3**	**3**
TOTAL MULTIPLE DX	**73**	**5.0**	**14**	**1**	**2**	**4**	**7**	**10**	**11**	**17**
TOTAL										
0–19 Years	9	2.1	9	1	1	1	2	3	12	12
20–34	22	4.7	8	2	3	4	6	9	11	11
35–49	16	4.8	18	1	2	3	7	11	16	16
50–64	13	5.5	29	1	2	2	9	17	17	17
65+	22	4.6	7	2	2	4	6	9	9	10
GRAND TOTAL	**82**	**4.5**	**13**	**1**	**2**	**3**	**6**	**10**	**11**	**17**

79.1: CLSD FX RED W INT FIX

Type of Patients	Observed Patients	Avg. Stay	Vari- ance	Percentiles						
				10th	25th	50th	75th	90th	95th	99th
1. SINGLE DX										
0–19 Years	1,905	1.4	1	1	1	1	1	2	3	5
20–34	334	2.2	2	1	1	2	3	4	5	6
35–49	263	2.4	3	1	1	2	3	4	5	8
50–64	204	2.5	3	1	1	2	3	5	5	10
65+	105	2.6	4	1	1	2	3	4	5	9
2. MULTIPLE DX										
0–19 Years	725	2.9	12	1	1	2	3	6	9	19
20–34	609	4.3	18	1	2	3	5	9	11	24
35–49	697	4.2	20	1	2	3	5	8	11	23
50–64	958	4.8	20	1	2	4	6	9	12	21
65+	4,492	5.2	9	3	3	4	6	8	11	16
TOTAL SINGLE DX	**2,811**	**1.6**	**2**	**1**	**1**	**1**	**2**	**3**	**4**	**6**
TOTAL MULTIPLE DX	**7,481**	**4.7**	**13**	**1**	**3**	**4**	**6**	**8**	**11**	**18**
TOTAL										
0–19 Years	2,630	1.8	4	1	1	1	2	3	4	11
20–34	943	3.6	13	1	1	3	4	7	9	17
35–49	960	3.7	16	1	2	3	4	7	10	18
50–64	1,162	4.4	18	1	2	3	5	9	11	21
65+	4,597	5.1	9	2	3	4	6	8	11	16
GRAND TOTAL	**10,292**	**3.7**	**11**	**1**	**1**	**3**	**5**	**7**	**9**	**16**

79.11: CRIF HUMERUS

Type of Patients	Observed Patients	Avg. Stay	Vari- ance	Percentiles						
				10th	25th	50th	75th	90th	95th	99th
1. SINGLE DX										
0–19 Years	1,356	1.2	<1	1	1	1	1	2	2	3
20–34	7	1.8	<1	1	1	2	2	3	3	3
35–49	6	1.5	<1	1	1	1	2	2	2	2
50–64	13	1.3	<1	1	1	1	1	2	3	3
65+	14	1.8	<1	1	1	1	2	3	4	4
2. MULTIPLE DX										
0–19 Years	300	1.7	5	1	1	1	2	3	4	13
20–34	24	2.8	2	1	2	2	4	4	5	7
35–49	47	3.7	40	1	1	3	3	6	9	48
50–64	58	3.6	10	1	1	3	4	8	10	16
65+	194	4.5	14	1	2	3	6	9	11	15
TOTAL SINGLE DX	**1,396**	**1.2**	**<1**	**1**	**1**	**1**	**1**	**2**	**2**	**3**
TOTAL MULTIPLE DX	**623**	**2.7**	**11**	**1**	**1**	**2**	**3**	**6**	**8**	**14**
TOTAL										
0–19 Years	1,656	1.3	1	1	1	1	1	2	2	4
20–34	31	2.5	2	1	2	2	4	4	4	7
35–49	53	3.5	35	1	1	2	3	6	9	48
50–64	71	3.3	9	1	1	3	4	8	10	16
65+	208	4.4	13	1	2	3	6	8	11	15
GRAND TOTAL	**2,019**	**1.6**	**3**	**1**	**1**	**1**	**2**	**3**	**4**	**10**

79.12: CRIF RADIUS/ULNA

Type of Patients	Observed Patients	Avg. Stay	Vari-ance	Percentiles						
				10th	25th	50th	75th	90th	95th	99th
1. SINGLE DX										
0–19 Years	168	1.3	<1	1	1	1	1	2	2	6
20–34	54	1.6	1	1	1	1	2	3	4	8
35–49	69	1.6	2	1	1	1	2	2	3	9
50–64	52	1.5	1	1	1	1	2	3	3	8
65+	26	1.4	<1	1	1	1	2	2	2	3
2. MULTIPLE DX										
0–19 Years	68	2.1	5	1	1	1	2	4	4	16
20–34	80	3.2	13	1	1	2	3	8	10	21
35–49	135	2.6	8	1	1	2	3	4	10	14
50–64	158	2.7	7	1	1	2	3	6	10	15
65+	326	2.9	7	1	1	2	4	6	8	12
TOTAL SINGLE DX	**369**	**1.4**	**<1**	**1**	**1**	**1**	**2**	**2**	**3**	**7**
TOTAL MULTIPLE DX	**767**	**2.8**	**8**	**1**	**1**	**2**	**3**	**6**	**9**	**14**
TOTAL										
0–19 Years	236	1.5	2	1	1	1	1	2	3	7
20–34	134	2.6	9	1	1	1	3	6	9	15
35–49	204	2.3	6	1	1	1	2	4	8	14
50–64	210	2.4	6	1	1	2	3	5	8	11
65+	352	2.8	6	1	1	2	4	5	8	12
GRAND TOTAL	**1,136**	**2.3**	**6**	**1**	**1**	**1**	**3**	**5**	**7**	**13**

79.13: CRIF MC/CARPALS

Type of Patients	Observed Patients	Avg. Stay	Vari-ance	Percentiles						
				10th	25th	50th	75th	90th	95th	99th
1. SINGLE DX										
0–19 Years	8	1.2	<1	1	1	1	1	2	2	2
20–34	31	1.5	<1	1	1	1	2	2	3	6
35–49	13	1.3	<1	1	1	1	2	2	3	3
50–64	3	1.3	<1	1	1	1	2	2	2	2
65+	1	1.0	0	1	1	1	1	1	1	1
2. MULTIPLE DX										
0–19 Years	19	2.1	3	1	1	1	3	3	7	7
20–34	31	2.9	5	1	1	3	4	7	8	9
35–49	17	2.2	7	1	1	1	2	3	7	13
50–64	11	4.6	40	1	1	2	7	9	24	24
65+	13	3.2	6	1	1	2	4	7	9	9
TOTAL SINGLE DX	**56**	**1.4**	**<1**	**1**	**1**	**1**	**2**	**2**	**2**	**6**
TOTAL MULTIPLE DX	**91**	**2.8**	**9**	**1**	**1**	**2**	**3**	**7**	**8**	**13**
TOTAL										
0–19 Years	27	1.9	2	1	1	1	2	3	7	7
20–34	62	2.3	4	1	1	1	3	5	7	9
35–49	30	1.8	4	1	1	1	2	3	3	13
50–64	14	4.0	34	1	1	2	3	9	24	24
65+	14	3.0	6	1	1	2	4	7	9	9
GRAND TOTAL	**147**	**2.3**	**6**	**1**	**1**	**1**	**3**	**5**	**7**	**13**

79.14: CRIF FINGER

Type of Patients	Observed Patients	Avg. Stay	Vari-ance	Percentiles						
				10th	25th	50th	75th	90th	95th	99th
1. SINGLE DX										
0–19 Years	15	2.1	7	1	1	1	1	5	11	11
20–34	17	1.6	<1	1	1	1	2	2	2	5
35–49	9	2.3	5	1	1	2	2	8	8	8
50–64	6	2.5	12	1	1	1	2	10	10	10
65+	2	1.5	<1	1	1	1	2	2	2	2
2. MULTIPLE DX										
0–19 Years	6	2.6	1	1	2	2	3	4	4	4
20–34	17	1.5	<1	1	1	1	2	2	3	4
35–49	21	3.8	24	1	1	3	5	6	8	28
50–64	10	2.1	2	1	1	2	3	4	5	5
65+	9	4.9	20	1	2	3	5	13	13	13
TOTAL SINGLE DX	**49**	**2.0**	**5**	**1**	**1**	**1**	**2**	**3**	**8**	**11**
TOTAL MULTIPLE DX	**63**	**3.0**	**13**	**1**	**1**	**2**	**4**	**5**	**8**	**28**
TOTAL										
0–19 Years	21	2.3	5	1	1	1	3	4	5	11
20–34	34	1.6	<1	1	1	1	2	2	3	5
35–49	30	3.5	20	1	1	2	5	6	8	28
50–64	16	2.2	5	1	1	1	2	5	10	10
65+	11	4.3	18	1	2	3	4	13	13	13
GRAND TOTAL	**112**	**2.6**	**10**	**1**	**1**	**2**	**3**	**5**	**8**	**13**

79.15: CRIF FEMUR

Type of Patients	Observed Patients	Avg. Stay	Vari-ance	Percentiles						
				10th	25th	50th	75th	90th	95th	99th
1. SINGLE DX										
0–19 Years	236	2.5	6	1	1	2	3	4	5	12
20–34	71	3.1	2	1	2	3	4	5	6	9
35–49	58	3.0	2	2	2	3	4	5	6	10
50–64	71	3.2	3	1	2	3	4	5	6	8
65+	53	3.5	2	2	3	3	4	5	6	9
2. MULTIPLE DX										
0–19 Years	230	5.0	22	2	2	3	5	12	15	22
20–34	256	6.0	30	2	3	5	7	11	15	30
35–49	231	5.5	25	2	3	4	6	11	13	24
50–64	509	5.5	17	2	3	4	6	10	12	21
65+	3,786	5.4	9	3	4	5	6	8	11	16
TOTAL SINGLE DX	**489**	**2.8**	**4**	**1**	**2**	**3**	**3**	**4**	**6**	**9**
TOTAL MULTIPLE DX	**5,012**	**5.4**	**12**	**3**	**3**	**5**	**6**	**9**	**11**	**19**
TOTAL										
0–19 Years	466	3.7	15	1	2	3	4	7	12	22
20–34	327	5.2	25	2	3	4	6	10	13	27
35–49	289	5.0	21	2	3	4	5	9	13	24
50–64	580	5.2	16	2	3	4	6	9	12	21
65+	3,839	5.4	9	3	4	5	6	8	11	16
GRAND TOTAL	**5,501**	**5.2**	**12**	**2**	**3**	**4**	**6**	**9**	**11**	**18**

79.16: CRIF TIBIA & FIBULA

Type of Patients	Observed Patients	Avg. Stay	Variance	10th	25th	50th	75th	90th	95th	99th
				Percentiles						
1. SINGLE DX										
0–19 Years	111	1.9	2	1	1	1	2	3	4	8
20–34	145	2.2	1	1	1	2	3	4	5	6
35–49	101	2.7	3	1	2	2	3	4	5	6
50–64	54	2.5	3	1	1	2	3	4	5	12
65+	9	2.8	16	1	1	2	3	3	19	19
2. MULTIPLE DX										
0–19 Years	90	3.4	6	1	1	3	4	8	9	11
20–34	170	3.4	4	1	2	3	4	6	7	10
35–49	211	4.0	16	1	2	3	5	7	9	16
50–64	191	4.8	35	2	3	3	5	9	14	21
65+	142	5.0	13	2	2	4	6	10	11	18
TOTAL SINGLE DX	**420**	**2.3**	**2**	**1**	**1**	**2**	**3**	**4**	**5**	**8**
TOTAL MULTIPLE DX	**804**	**4.1**	**16**	**1**	**2**	**3**	**5**	**8**	**10**	**17**
TOTAL										
0–19 Years	201	2.6	4	1	1	2	3	5	8	11
20–34	315	2.9	3	1	2	2	4	5	6	10
35–49	312	3.5	12	1	2	3	4	6	8	16
50–64	245	4.3	29	1	2	3	5	7	10	21
65+	151	4.8	14	1	2	4	6	10	11	19
GRAND TOTAL	**1,224**	**3.5**	**12**	**1**	**2**	**3**	**4**	**6**	**9**	**16**

79.17: CRIF METATARSAL/TARSAL

Type of Patients	Observed Patients	Avg. Stay	Variance	10th	25th	50th	75th	90th	95th	99th
				Percentiles						
1. SINGLE DX										
0–19 Years	7	1.3	<1	1	1	1	1	2	2	2
20–34	9	1.5	3	1	1	1	1	1	7	7
35–49	5	1.3	<1	1	1	1	2	2	2	2
50–64	4	2.1	2	1	1	2	4	4	4	4
65+	0									
2. MULTIPLE DX										
0–19 Years	9	1.9	<1	1	2	2	2	2	3	3
20–34	19	2.7	3	1	2	2	4	6	6	6
35–49	23	4.4	11	1	2	4	7	9	11	14
50–64	13	4.6	16	1	2	2	8	10	13	13
65+	11	3.7	5	1	2	3	5	7	7	7
TOTAL SINGLE DX	**25**	**1.5**	**2**	**1**	**1**	**1**	**1**	**2**	**4**	**7**
TOTAL MULTIPLE DX	**75**	**3.5**	**8**	**1**	**2**	**2**	**5**	**7**	**9**	**14**
TOTAL										
0–19 Years	16	1.6	<1	1	1	2	2	2	3	3
20–34	28	2.4	3	1	1	2	3	6	6	7
35–49	28	3.9	10	1	2	2	6	8	11	14
50–64	17	4.0	13	1	1	2	5	10	13	13
65+	11	3.7	5	1	2	3	5	7	7	7
GRAND TOTAL	**100**	**3.0**	**7**	**1**	**1**	**2**	**4**	**7**	**8**	**13**

79.2: OPEN FRACTURE REDUCTION

Type of Patients	Observed Patients	Avg. Stay	Variance	10th	25th	50th	75th	90th	95th	99th
				Percentiles						
1. SINGLE DX										
0–19 Years	78	2.0	5	1	1	1	3	4	5	5
20–34	36	2.4	4	1	1	2	3	5	6	10
35–49	21	1.6	1	1	1	1	2	3	4	6
50–64	17	2.5	2	1	2	2	3	5	6	6
65+	5	2.0	<1	1	1	2	3	3	3	3
2. MULTIPLE DX										
0–19 Years	58	3.7	10	1	2	3	4	8	11	14
20–34	65	5.2	43	1	2	3	5	13	14	34
35–49	77	5.1	26	1	2	3	6	11	19	22
50–64	69	6.6	92	1	2	4	6	20	41	41
65+	100	5.7	33	1	3	4	7	12	13	37
TOTAL SINGLE DX	**157**	**2.1**	**4**	**1**	**1**	**1**	**3**	**4**	**5**	**10**
TOTAL MULTIPLE DX	**369**	**5.3**	**40**	**1**	**2**	**3**	**6**	**10**	**15**	**41**
TOTAL										
0–19 Years	136	2.8	8	1	1	2	3	5	8	14
20–34	101	4.2	30	1	1	3	5	8	13	34
35–49	98	4.2	22	1	1	3	5	10	18	22
50–64	86	6.0	80	1	2	3	5	7	30	41
65+	105	5.5	32	1	3	4	7	12	12	37
GRAND TOTAL	**526**	**4.3**	**31**	**1**	**1**	**3**	**5**	**8**	**13**	**37**

79.22: OPEN RED RADIUS/ULNA FX

Type of Patients	Observed Patients	Avg. Stay	Variance	10th	25th	50th	75th	90th	95th	99th
				Percentiles						
1. SINGLE DX										
0–19 Years	31	1.7	2	1	1	1	2	5	5	5
20–34	10	2.0	1	1	1	2	2	3	5	5
35–49	7	1.1	<1	1	1	1	1	2	2	2
50–64	7	2.4	2	1	1	3	3	5	5	5
65+	3	2.2	1	1	1	3	3	3	3	3
2. MULTIPLE DX										
0–19 Years	13	3.3	15	1	1	2	3	13	13	13
20–34	14	5.1	18	2	3	3	5	13	15	15
35–49	13	2.2	3	1	1	1	3	6	7	7
50–64	13	2.1	1	1	1	2	3	4	5	5
65+	29	3.0	5	1	1	2	4	7	8	9
TOTAL SINGLE DX	**58**	**1.8**	**1**	**1**	**1**	**1**	**2**	**3**	**5**	**5**
TOTAL MULTIPLE DX	**82**	**3.2**	**9**	**1**	**1**	**2**	**4**	**7**	**9**	**15**
TOTAL										
0–19 Years	44	2.1	6	1	1	1	2	5	5	13
20–34	24	3.9	13	1	2	3	5	8	15	15
35–49	20	1.8	2	1	1	1	2	3	6	7
50–64	20	2.2	2	1	1	2	3	4	5	5
65+	32	2.9	4	1	1	2	4	6	7	9
GRAND TOTAL	**140**	**2.6**	**6**	**1**	**1**	**2**	**3**	**5**	**7**	**13**

79.26: OPEN RED TIBIA/FIB FX

Type of Patients	Observed Patients	Avg. Stay	Vari-ance	10th	25th	50th	75th	90th	95th	99th
				Percentiles						
1. SINGLE DX										
0–19 Years	26	2.6	10	1	1	2	3	4	4	22
20–34	12	3.0	7	1	1	2	3	7	10	10
35–49	8	1.5	1	1	1	1	1	3	4	4
50–64	7	2.8	2	1	2	3	3	6	6	6
65+	1	2.0	0	2	2	2	2	2	2	2
2. MULTIPLE DX										
0–19 Years	19	3.1	6	1	2	3	3	6	8	14
20–34	24	7.6	108	1	2	4	7	13	34	50
35–49	31	6.8	32	2	3	4	10	19	22	22
50–64	30	9.8	168	2	3	4	7	41	41	41
65+	25	6.7	40	3	3	5	8	12	15	37
TOTAL SINGLE DX	**54**	**2.5**	**7**	**1**	**1**	**2**	**3**	**4**	**6**	**22**
TOTAL MULTIPLE DX	**129**	**6.9**	**75**	**2**	**3**	**4**	**7**	**15**	**26**	**41**
TOTAL										
0–19 Years	45	2.8	8	1	1	2	3	4	6	22
20–34	36	5.7	70	1	2	3	6	10	13	50
35–49	39	5.5	30	1	2	4	6	11	19	22
50–64	37	8.9	150	2	2	4	7	30	41	41
65+	26	6.6	40	2	3	5	8	12	15	37
GRAND TOTAL	**183**	**5.5**	**58**	**1**	**2**	**3**	**5**	**10**	**22**	**41**

79.3: OP FX REDUCTION INT FIX

Type of Patients	Observed Patients	Avg. Stay	Vari-ance	10th	25th	50th	75th	90th	95th	99th
				Percentiles						
1. SINGLE DX										
0–19 Years	2,236	1.8	2	1	1	1	2	3	4	7
20–34	2,514	2.4	5	1	1	2	3	4	6	13
35–49	2,169	2.4	5	1	1	2	3	4	6	12
50–64	1,608	2.5	5	1	1	2	3	4	6	11
65+	564	2.7	3	1	1	2	4	5	5	8
2. MULTIPLE DX										
0–19 Years	1,751	3.6	15	1	1	2	4	8	11	19
20–34	3,977	4.2	21	1	2	3	5	9	12	23
35–49	5,334	4.2	20	1	2	3	5	8	12	22
50–64	6,758	4.5	20	1	2	3	5	9	12	22
65+	18,802	5.3	13	2	3	5	6	9	11	20
TOTAL SINGLE DX	**9,091**	**2.3**	**4**	**1**	**1**	**2**	**3**	**4**	**5**	**11**
TOTAL MULTIPLE DX	**36,622**	**4.8**	**16**	**1**	**2**	**4**	**6**	**9**	**12**	**21**
TOTAL										
0–19 Years	3,987	2.5	8	1	1	2	3	5	7	15
20–34	6,491	3.5	15	1	1	2	4	7	10	20
35–49	7,503	3.7	16	1	2	2	4	7	11	20
50–64	8,366	4.1	18	1	2	3	5	8	11	21
65+	19,366	5.3	13	2	3	4	6	9	11	20
GRAND TOTAL	**45,713**	**4.3**	**15**	**1**	**2**	**3**	**5**	**8**	**11**	**20**

79.31: ORIF HUMERUS

Type of Patients	Observed Patients	Avg. Stay	Vari-ance	10th	25th	50th	75th	90th	95th	99th
				Percentiles						
1. SINGLE DX										
0–19 Years	549	1.4	1	1	1	1	2	2	3	5
20–34	155	2.2	4	1	1	2	3	4	5	8
35–49	112	2.6	12	1	1	2	3	4	5	27
50–64	122	2.2	5	1	1	2	2	3	4	9
65+	50	1.8	<1	1	1	2	2	3	3	4
2. MULTIPLE DX										
0–19 Years	253	2.4	5	1	1	2	3	5	6	13
20–34	277	4.2	23	1	2	3	5	9	12	27
35–49	366	3.8	23	1	2	2	4	8	12	19
50–64	598	3.6	14	1	2	2	4	7	10	23
65+	1,117	4.0	11	1	2	3	5	7	10	17
TOTAL SINGLE DX	**988**	**1.7**	**3**	**1**	**1**	**1**	**2**	**3**	**4**	**7**
TOTAL MULTIPLE DX	**2,611**	**3.7**	**14**	**1**	**2**	**3**	**4**	**7**	**10**	**18**
TOTAL										
0–19 Years	802	1.7	2	1	1	1	2	3	4	8
20–34	432	3.5	17	1	1	2	4	8	10	20
35–49	478	3.5	21	1	2	2	4	7	11	19
50–64	720	3.3	13	1	2	2	4	6	9	23
65+	1,167	3.9	10	1	2	3	5	7	10	17
GRAND TOTAL	**3,599**	**3.1**	**11**	**1**	**1**	**2**	**3**	**6**	**9**	**17**

79.32: ORIF RADIUS/ULNA

Type of Patients	Observed Patients	Avg. Stay	Vari-ance	10th	25th	50th	75th	90th	95th	99th
				Percentiles						
1. SINGLE DX										
0–19 Years	593	1.6	1	1	1	1	2	3	3	6
20–34	367	2.1	5	1	1	1	2	4	6	13
35–49	313	2.0	4	1	1	2	2	3	5	12
50–64	200	1.9	3	1	1	1	2	3	5	12
65+	75	1.5	<1	1	1	1	2	2	3	4
2. MULTIPLE DX										
0–19 Years	331	2.4	9	1	1	2	2	4	6	21
20–34	537	3.3	11	1	1	2	4	7	9	17
35–49	609	3.1	15	1	1	2	3	6	10	18
50–64	583	3.1	12	1	1	2	3	6	10	19
65+	892	3.3	10	1	1	2	4	6	8	14
TOTAL SINGLE DX	**1,548**	**1.8**	**3**	**1**	**1**	**1**	**2**	**3**	**4**	**11**
TOTAL MULTIPLE DX	**2,952**	**3.1**	**11**	**1**	**1**	**2**	**4**	**6**	**9**	**18**
TOTAL										
0–19 Years	924	1.9	4	1	1	1	2	3	4	10
20–34	904	2.8	9	1	1	2	3	6	9	15
35–49	922	2.8	12	1	1	2	3	5	9	17
50–64	783	2.8	10	1	1	2	3	6	9	18
65+	967	3.1	9	1	1	2	4	6	8	14
GRAND TOTAL	**4,500**	**2.6**	**9**	**1**	**1**	**2**	**3**	**5**	**8**	**15**

79.33: ORIF CARPALS/METACARPALS

Type of Patients	Observed Patients	Avg. Stay	Vari-ance	Percentiles 10th	25th	50th	75th	90th	95th	99th
1. SINGLE DX										
0–19 Years	16	1.6	<1	1	1	1	2	3	4	4
20–34	50	1.5	<1	1	1	1	2	2	3	4
35–49	23	2.1	3	1	1	2	2	4	6	8
50–64	11	2.0	2	1	1	1	3	3	6	6
65+	2	1.0	0	1	1	1	1	1	1	1
2. MULTIPLE DX										
0–19 Years	35	2.4	6	1	1	1	3	5	6	12
20–34	116	3.0	11	1	1	2	4	7	8	13
35–49	79	3.0	8	1	1	2	4	7	11	14
50–64	49	4.4	20	1	1	2	6	11	16	23
65+	17	3.8	11	1	1	3	6	7	14	14
TOTAL SINGLE DX	**102**	**1.7**	**1**	**1**	**1**	**1**	**2**	**3**	**4**	**6**
TOTAL MULTIPLE DX	**296**	**3.2**	**11**	**1**	**1**	**2**	**4**	**7**	**10**	**16**
TOTAL										
0–19 Years	51	2.1	4	1	1	1	2	4	6	12
20–34	166	2.5	8	1	1	2	3	5	7	11
35–49	102	2.8	7	1	1	2	3	6	8	14
50–64	60	4.0	18	1	1	2	6	8	13	23
65+	19	3.5	11	1	1	2	5	7	14	14
GRAND TOTAL	**398**	**2.8**	**9**	**1**	**1**	**2**	**3**	**6**	**8**	**14**

79.34: ORIF FINGER

Type of Patients	Observed Patients	Avg. Stay	Vari-ance	Percentiles 10th	25th	50th	75th	90th	95th	99th
1. SINGLE DX										
0–19 Years	33	1.4	<1	1	1	1	2	2	2	4
20–34	42	2.0	2	1	1	1	2	5	5	6
35–49	34	1.4	<1	1	1	1	1	2	3	5
50–64	22	2.4	8	1	1	1	3	5	11	11
65+	3	1.0	0	1	1	1	1	1	1	1
2. MULTIPLE DX										
0–19 Years	57	2.5	5	1	1	2	3	6	9	9
20–34	173	2.6	10	1	1	2	3	6	6	12
35–49	140	2.2	3	1	1	2	3	5	6	7
50–64	97	2.1	3	1	1	2	2	4	5	8
65+	57	2.4	4	1	1	2	3	4	8	11
TOTAL SINGLE DX	**134**	**1.7**	**2**	**1**	**1**	**1**	**2**	**4**	**5**	**9**
TOTAL MULTIPLE DX	**524**	**2.4**	**6**	**1**	**1**	**2**	**3**	**5**	**6**	**11**
TOTAL										
0–19 Years	90	2.0	3	1	1	1	2	4	6	9
20–34	215	2.5	9	1	1	1	3	5	6	12
35–49	174	2.0	3	1	1	1	2	4	6	7
50–64	119	2.2	4	1	1	1	2	4	7	11
65+	60	2.3	4	1	1	2	3	4	5	11
GRAND TOTAL	**658**	**2.2**	**5**	**1**	**1**	**1**	**3**	**5**	**6**	**11**

79.35: ORIF FEMUR

Type of Patients	Observed Patients	Avg. Stay	Vari-ance	Percentiles 10th	25th	50th	75th	90th	95th	99th
1. SINGLE DX										
0–19 Years	207	2.8	3	1	2	3	4	5	6	8
20–34	149	3.5	7	2	2	3	4	6	7	13
35–49	127	3.5	3	2	2	3	5	6	6	10
50–64	130	3.9	4	2	3	4	5	6	8	10
65+	153	4.1	2	3	3	4	5	6	6	9
2. MULTIPLE DX										
0–19 Years	404	5.9	26	2	3	4	7	11	15	27
20–34	638	6.9	35	2	3	5	8	13	17	29
35–49	806	6.5	33	2	3	5	7	12	16	28
50–64	1,643	6.6	32	3	4	5	7	12	15	25
65+	13,497	5.9	13	3	4	5	7	9	12	22
TOTAL SINGLE DX	**766**	**3.5**	**4**	**2**	**2**	**3**	**4**	**6**	**7**	**10**
TOTAL MULTIPLE DX	**16,988**	**6.0**	**17**	**3**	**4**	**5**	**7**	**10**	**13**	**23**
TOTAL										
0–19 Years	611	4.8	20	2	2	3	6	9	13	23
20–34	787	6.2	32	2	3	5	7	12	16	28
35–49	933	6.0	30	2	3	5	7	11	16	24
50–64	1,773	6.4	31	3	4	5	7	11	15	25
65+	13,650	5.8	13	3	4	5	7	9	12	21
GRAND TOTAL	**17,754**	**5.9**	**16**	**3**	**4**	**5**	**7**	**10**	**12**	**23**

79.36: ORIF TIBIA & FIBULA

Type of Patients	Observed Patients	Avg. Stay	Vari-ance	Percentiles 10th	25th	50th	75th	90th	95th	99th
1. SINGLE DX										
0–19 Years	759	1.9	2	1	1	2	2	3	4	7
20–34	1,514	2.5	5	1	1	2	3	4	6	13
35–49	1,340	2.4	5	1	1	2	3	4	5	12
50–64	995	2.5	4	1	1	2	3	4	5	12
65+	264	2.3	2	1	1	2	3	4	4	6
2. MULTIPLE DX										
0–19 Years	554	3.0	7	1	1	2	4	6	7	15
20–34	1,790	3.5	12	1	2	3	4	7	10	19
35–49	2,835	3.7	14	1	2	3	4	7	10	21
50–64	3,301	3.7	12	1	2	3	4	7	10	19
65+	3,030	4.1	11	2	2	3	5	7	9	19
TOTAL SINGLE DX	**4,872**	**2.4**	**4**	**1**	**1**	**2**	**3**	**4**	**5**	**12**
TOTAL MULTIPLE DX	**11,510**	**3.8**	**12**	**1**	**2**	**3**	**4**	**7**	**9**	**19**
TOTAL										
0–19 Years	1,313	2.4	4	1	1	2	3	4	6	11
20–34	3,304	3.0	9	1	1	2	3	6	8	17
35–49	4,175	3.3	12	1	2	2	4	6	9	19
50–64	4,296	3.4	10	1	2	3	4	6	9	18
65+	3,294	4.0	10	1	2	3	5	7	9	19
GRAND TOTAL	**16,382**	**3.3**	**10**	**1**	**2**	**3**	**4**	**6**	**9**	**18**

79.37: ORIF METATARSAL/TARSAL

Type of Patients	Observed Patients	Avg. Stay	Variance	Percentiles 10th	25th	50th	75th	90th	95th	99th
1. SINGLE DX										
0–19 Years	50	1.8	<1	1	1	2	2	3	3	6
20–34	161	2.1	3	1	1	2	2	3	4	10
35–49	152	2.3	4	1	1	2	3	3	6	9
50–64	79	2.4	10	1	1	2	2	3	4	22
65+	8	2.4	<1	1	2	3	3	3	3	3
2. MULTIPLE DX										
0–19 Years	57	3.1	12	1	1	2	3	7	8	22
20–34	207	3.7	22	1	2	2	4	7	13	18
35–49	272	3.4	12	1	1	2	4	7	11	18
50–64	251	3.4	11	1	1	2	4	7	10	16
65+	74	3.5	8	1	2	3	4	8	9	14
TOTAL SINGLE DX	**450**	**2.2**	**4**	**1**	**1**	**2**	**2**	**3**	**4**	**10**
TOTAL MULTIPLE DX	**861**	**3.5**	**14**	**1**	**1**	**2**	**4**	**7**	**11**	**18**
TOTAL										
0–19 Years	107	2.5	7	1	1	2	2	5	7	22
20–34	368	3.0	15	1	1	2	3	5	9	16
35–49	424	3.0	9	1	1	2	3	6	9	16
50–64	330	3.1	11	1	1	2	3	6	10	22
65+	82	3.4	7	1	2	3	4	7	9	14
GRAND TOTAL	**1,311**	**3.0**	**11**	**1**	**1**	**2**	**3**	**6**	**9**	**16**

79.39: ORIF BONE NEC X FACIAL

Type of Patients	Observed Patients	Avg. Stay	Variance	Percentiles 10th	25th	50th	75th	90th	95th	99th
1. SINGLE DX										
0–19 Years	23	1.8	3	1	1	1	1	7	7	7
20–34	72	2.7	12	1	1	1	3	6	7	19
35–49	65	2.8	5	1	1	2	3	5	8	15
50–64	48	2.8	6	1	1	2	3	6	7	15
65+	9	2.2	3	1	1	2	2	4	8	8
2. MULTIPLE DX										
0–19 Years	52	7.8	22	1	3	8	11	12	15	21
20–34	223	7.3	49	1	2	6	10	16	21	27
35–49	217	7.4	33	1	2	6	11	14	19	25
50–64	228	7.4	47	1	2	6	10	16	22	33
65+	111	6.9	32	2	3	6	9	14	16	37
TOTAL SINGLE DX	**217**	**2.6**	**7**	**1**	**1**	**2**	**3**	**5**	**7**	**15**
TOTAL MULTIPLE DX	**831**	**7.3**	**40**	**1**	**2**	**6**	**10**	**15**	**19**	**29**
TOTAL										
0–19 Years	75	6.1	24	1	1	6	10	12	13	21
20–34	295	6.2	44	1	1	4	8	15	18	27
35–49	282	6.3	30	1	2	5	9	13	17	24
50–64	276	6.5	43	1	2	5	8	15	18	33
65+	120	6.5	31	1	3	6	9	13	15	27
GRAND TOTAL	**1,048**	**6.3**	**37**	**1**	**2**	**5**	**9**	**14**	**17**	**27**

79.4: CR SEP EPIPHYSIS

Type of Patients	Observed Patients	Avg. Stay	Variance	Percentiles 10th	25th	50th	75th	90th	95th	99th
1. SINGLE DX										
0–19 Years	103	1.7	1	1	1	1	2	3	4	7
20–34	3	4.3	31	1	1	1	12	12	12	12
35–49	4	2.0	<1	1	1	2	3	3	3	3
50–64	0									
65+	2	3.0	2	2	2	4	4	4	4	4
2. MULTIPLE DX										
0–19 Years	45	2.0	2	1	1	2	2	3	4	9
20–34	5	6.4	54	1	3	4	5	20	20	20
35–49	12	4.0	9	1	2	3	7	7	10	10
50–64	10	4.5	12	1	2	3	6	8	13	13
65+	16	5.3	45	2	2	3	5	6	32	32
TOTAL SINGLE DX	**112**	**1.8**	**2**	**1**	**1**	**1**	**2**	**3**	**4**	**7**
TOTAL MULTIPLE DX	**88**	**3.2**	**15**	**1**	**1**	**2**	**3**	**6**	**9**	**20**
TOTAL										
0–19 Years	148	1.8	2	1	1	1	2	3	4	7
20–34	8	5.4	40	1	1	3	5	12	20	20
35–49	16	3.6	8	1	2	2	5	7	10	10
50–64	10	4.5	12	1	2	3	6	8	13	13
65+	18	5.1	42	2	2	3	5	6	10	32
GRAND TOTAL	**200**	**2.4**	**8**	**1**	**1**	**2**	**3**	**4**	**7**	**12**

79.5: OPEN RED SEP EPIPHYSIS

Type of Patients	Observed Patients	Avg. Stay	Variance	Percentiles 10th	25th	50th	75th	90th	95th	99th
1. SINGLE DX										
0–19 Years	66	1.9	2	1	1	1	3	4	4	9
20–34	19	2.8	3	1	2	3	3	4	6	9
35–49	13	2.8	1	1	2	3	3	4	5	5
50–64	7	2.4	<1	2	2	2	3	4	4	4
65+	2	1.5	1	1	1	1	3	3	3	3
2. MULTIPLE DX										
0–19 Years	34	2.5	1	1	2	2	4	4	4	5
20–34	29	5.3	25	1	2	3	7	13	17	21
35–49	22	4.3	32	1	1	2	5	8	23	>99
50–64	24	4.7	27	1	2	3	6	7	16	27
65+	43	6.0	23	2	3	5	7	11	18	22
TOTAL SINGLE DX	**107**	**2.1**	**2**	**1**	**1**	**2**	**3**	**4**	**4**	**9**
TOTAL MULTIPLE DX	**152**	**4.6**	**21**	**1**	**2**	**3**	**6**	**9**	**18**	**23**
TOTAL										
0–19 Years	100	2.1	2	1	1	2	3	4	4	5
20–34	48	4.4	18	1	2	3	6	9	13	21
35–49	35	3.9	23	1	1	3	4	8	23	>99
50–64	31	4.2	22	2	2	2	5	7	16	27
65+	45	5.8	23	1	3	5	7	11	18	22
GRAND TOTAL	**259**	**3.6**	**15**	**1**	**1**	**3**	**4**	**7**	**11**	**23**

79.56: OP RED SEP EPIPH TIB/FIB

Type of Patients	Observed Patients	Avg. Stay	Variance	Percentiles						
				10th	25th	50th	75th	90th	95th	99th
1. SINGLE DX										
0–19 Years	34	1.6	<1	1	1	1	2	3	3	4
20–34	13	2.8	2	2	2	3	3	4	6	6
35–49	12	2.8	1	1	2	3	3	4	5	5
50–64	5	2.6	<1	2	2	2	3	4	4	4
65+	1	3.0	0	3	3	3	3	3	3	3
2. MULTIPLE DX										
0–19 Years	17	2.7	2	1	1	3	4	4	5	5
20–34	20	5.0	25	1	2	3	6	13	17	19
35–49	14	5.0	45	1	1	2	8	23	23	>99
50–64	15	3.4	4	1	2	3	6	6	7	7
65+	11	5.3	33	2	3	3	6	7	22	22
TOTAL SINGLE DX	**65**	**2.0**	**1**	**1**	**1**	**2**	**3**	**4**	**4**	**6**
TOTAL MULTIPLE DX	**77**	**4.2**	**21**	**1**	**2**	**3**	**5**	**8**	**19**	**23**
TOTAL										
0–19 Years	51	1.9	1	1	1	1	3	4	4	5
20–34	33	4.1	16	1	2	3	4	11	13	19
35–49	26	4.2	30	1	1	2	4	8	23	>99
50–64	20	3.2	3	1	2	2	4	6	6	7
65+	12	5.1	30	2	3	3	6	7	22	22
GRAND TOTAL	**142**	**3.1**	**12**	**1**	**1**	**2**	**3**	**6**	**8**	**23**

79.6: OPEN FX SITE DEBRIDEMENT

Type of Patients	Observed Patients	Avg. Stay	Variance	Percentiles						
				10th	25th	50th	75th	90th	95th	99th
1. SINGLE DX										
0–19 Years	132	2.5	5	1	1	2	3	5	6	11
20–34	79	2.8	4	1	1	2	4	6	6	10
35–49	70	3.3	8	1	2	3	4	7	9	15
50–64	33	3.2	7	1	1	2	4	6	9	13
65+	7	2.0	<1	1	1	2	3	3	3	3
2. MULTIPLE DX										
0–19 Years	126	4.8	34	1	2	3	6	9	12	66
20–34	280	5.4	41	1	2	3	6	11	18	35
35–49	252	6.0	41	1	2	4	8	14	19	28
50–64	187	6.4	75	1	2	4	8	15	20	29
65+	140	5.2	23	1	2	4	7	11	13	25
TOTAL SINGLE DX	**321**	**2.7**	**6**	**1**	**1**	**2**	**3**	**5**	**7**	**13**
TOTAL MULTIPLE DX	**985**	**5.6**	**43**	**1**	**2**	**4**	**7**	**12**	**18**	**29**
TOTAL										
0–19 Years	258	3.6	21	1	1	2	4	7	11	25
20–34	359	4.8	34	1	2	3	6	10	15	29
35–49	322	5.4	35	1	2	3	7	12	17	28
50–64	220	5.9	67	1	2	4	7	14	19	29
65+	147	5.0	22	1	2	3	6	10	13	25
GRAND TOTAL	**1,306**	**4.8**	**35**	**1**	**2**	**3**	**6**	**10**	**15**	**28**

79.62: DEBRIDE OPEN FX RAD/ULNA

Type of Patients	Observed Patients	Avg. Stay	Variance	Percentiles						
				10th	25th	50th	75th	90th	95th	99th
1. SINGLE DX										
0–19 Years	68	1.9	2	1	1	2	2	3	4	11
20–34	11	2.2	4	1	1	1	3	7	7	7
35–49	12	2.3	3	1	1	2	3	4	8	8
50–64	6	1.4	<1	1	1	1	2	2	2	2
65+	4	2.0	<1	1	1	2	3	3	3	3
2. MULTIPLE DX										
0–19 Years	12	2.0	2	1	1	2	2	3	7	7
20–34	31	3.6	10	1	2	3	5	6	10	20
35–49	32	4.7	23	2	2	3	4	13	15	23
50–64	23	5.1	33	1	1	3	6	10	17	26
65+	39	4.7	29	1	2	3	5	13	18	25
TOTAL SINGLE DX	**101**	**2.0**	**2**	**1**	**1**	**2**	**2**	**3**	**4**	**8**
TOTAL MULTIPLE DX	**137**	**4.2**	**21**	**1**	**2**	**3**	**4**	**10**	**14**	**25**
TOTAL										
0–19 Years	80	2.0	2	1	1	2	2	3	4	7
20–34	42	3.2	9	1	1	2	4	6	8	20
35–49	44	4.1	19	1	2	3	3	11	14	23
50–64	29	4.3	28	1	1	2	6	10	17	26
65+	43	4.5	27	1	2	3	4	13	18	25
GRAND TOTAL	**238**	**3.2**	**14**	**1**	**1**	**2**	**3**	**6**	**10**	**23**

79.64: DEBRIDE OPEN FX FINGER

Type of Patients	Observed Patients	Avg. Stay	Variance	Percentiles						
				10th	25th	50th	75th	90th	95th	99th
1. SINGLE DX										
0–19 Years	6	1.2	<1	1	1	1	1	1	3	3
20–34	10	3.2	4	1	2	2	5	6	6	6
35–49	7	2.7	2	1	2	2	3	5	5	5
50–64	5	1.0	0	1	1	1	1	1	1	1
65+	0									
2. MULTIPLE DX										
0–19 Years	19	2.3	2	1	1	2	3	4	6	8
20–34	47	2.3	7	1	1	1	3	4	6	18
35–49	34	3.1	14	1	1	1	3	10	12	18
50–64	22	2.5	17	1	1	1	2	4	4	22
65+	21	3.0	8	1	1	2	3	8	8	12
TOTAL SINGLE DX	**28**	**2.0**	**2**	**1**	**1**	**1**	**3**	**5**	**6**	**6**
TOTAL MULTIPLE DX	**143**	**2.6**	**9**	**1**	**1**	**2**	**3**	**5**	**8**	**18**
TOTAL										
0–19 Years	25	2.0	2	1	1	2	2	3	4	8
20–34	57	2.4	6	1	1	2	3	5	6	18
35–49	41	3.0	12	1	1	2	3	9	11	18
50–64	27	2.2	15	1	1	1	2	4	4	22
65+	21	3.0	8	1	1	2	3	8	8	12
GRAND TOTAL	**171**	**2.5**	**8**	**1**	**1**	**2**	**3**	**5**	**8**	**18**

79.65: DEBRIDE OPEN FEMUR FX

Type of Patients	Observed Patients	Avg. Stay	Variance	10th	25th	50th	75th	90th	95th	99th
1. SINGLE DX										
0–19 Years	3	1.7	<1	1	1	2	2	2	2	2
20–34	4	2.4	<1	2	2	2	3	3	3	3
35–49	3	2.3	1	1	1	3	3	3	3	3
50–64	0									
65+	0									
2. MULTIPLE DX										
0–19 Years	11	9.4	172	2	3	7	9	12	12	66
20–34	27	12.8	179	2	2	9	18	35	55	55
35–49	20	12.0	79	2	3	10	16	27	29	29
50–64	16	10.9	89	1	1	11	15	21	22	42
65+	9	12.3	38	8	8	11	11	17	30	30
TOTAL SINGLE DX	**10**	**2.1**	**<1**	**1**	**2**	**2**	**3**	**3**	**3**	**3**
TOTAL MULTIPLE DX	**83**	**11.6**	**119**	**2**	**4**	**9**	**14**	**25**	**30**	**55**
TOTAL										
0–19 Years	14	7.5	140	2	2	5	9	12	12	66
20–34	31	11.1	165	2	2	6	15	28	37	55
35–49	23	11.0	80	2	3	8	16	25	27	29
50–64	16	10.9	89	1	1	11	15	21	22	42
65+	9	12.3	38	8	8	11	11	17	30	30
GRAND TOTAL	**93**	**10.5**	**115**	**2**	**3**	**8**	**14**	**24**	**30**	**55**

79.66: DEBRIDE OPN FX TIBIA/FIB

Type of Patients	Observed Patients	Avg. Stay	Variance	10th	25th	50th	75th	90th	95th	99th
1. SINGLE DX										
0–19 Years	40	3.7	11	1	2	3	5	6	7	24
20–34	29	3.2	6	1	1	3	4	6	9	10
35–49	33	4.1	11	1	2	3	5	9	13	15
50–64	13	4.9	11	2	3	4	6	9	13	13
65+	2	2.4	<1	2	2	2	3	3	3	3
2. MULTIPLE DX										
0–19 Years	45	4.7	15	1	3	4	6	7	11	>99
20–34	96	5.8	27	1	3	4	7	12	17	25
35–49	104	7.4	51	2	3	5	10	15	20	36
50–64	78	8.1	125	2	3	5	9	16	24	91
65+	44	5.1	9	2	3	5	6	9	10	20
TOTAL SINGLE DX	**117**	**3.8**	**10**	**1**	**2**	**3**	**5**	**6**	**9**	**15**
TOTAL MULTIPLE DX	**367**	**6.4**	**49**	**2**	**3**	**5**	**7**	**12**	**18**	**36**
TOTAL										
0–19 Years	85	4.2	13	1	2	4	6	7	8	27
20–34	125	5.2	23	1	2	4	6	11	13	25
35–49	137	6.5	43	2	3	4	8	14	18	36
50–64	91	7.7	111	2	3	5	9	16	22	91
65+	46	5.0	9	2	3	5	6	9	10	20
GRAND TOTAL	**484**	**5.7**	**40**	**1**	**3**	**4**	**7**	**11**	**16**	**29**

79.7: CLOSED RED DISLOCATION

Type of Patients	Observed Patients	Avg. Stay	Variance	10th	25th	50th	75th	90th	95th	99th
1. SINGLE DX										
0–19 Years	69	1.3	<1	1	1	1	1	2	3	5
20–34	55	1.9	13	1	1	1	2	2	5	34
35–49	55	1.4	<1	1	1	1	2	2	3	6
50–64	83	1.3	<1	1	1	1	1	2	3	5
65+	109	1.4	<1	1	1	1	2	2	3	6
2. MULTIPLE DX										
0–19 Years	77	3.7	21	1	1	2	4	10	15	24
20–34	161	2.5	5	1	1	2	3	5	8	9
35–49	239	2.6	6	1	1	2	3	5	7	13
50–64	445	2.7	14	1	1	2	3	5	9	18
65+	1,366	2.7	7	1	1	2	3	5	7	13
TOTAL SINGLE DX	**371**	**1.4**	**3**	**1**	**1**	**1**	**1**	**2**	**3**	**6**
TOTAL MULTIPLE DX	**2,288**	**2.7**	**9**	**1**	**1**	**2**	**3**	**5**	**8**	**15**
TOTAL										
0–19 Years	146	2.5	12	1	1	1	2	5	10	17
20–34	216	2.3	7	1	1	1	3	5	7	9
35–49	294	2.4	5	1	1	2	3	5	7	13
50–64	528	2.5	13	1	1	1	3	5	7	16
65+	1,475	2.6	7	1	1	2	3	5	7	13
GRAND TOTAL	**2,659**	**2.5**	**8**	**1**	**1**	**2**	**3**	**5**	**7**	**14**

79.71: CLSD RED SHOULDER DISLOC

Type of Patients	Observed Patients	Avg. Stay	Variance	10th	25th	50th	75th	90th	95th	99th
1. SINGLE DX										
0–19 Years	1	1.0	0	1	1	1	1	1	1	1
20–34	8	1.0	0	1	1	1	1	1	1	1
35–49	9	1.2	<1	1	1	1	1	2	2	2
50–64	4	1.0	0	1	1	1	1	1	1	1
65+	8	1.1	<1	1	1	1	1	2	2	2
2. MULTIPLE DX										
0–19 Years	13	5.7	51	1	1	5	5	24	24	24
20–34	46	2.2	4	1	1	1	3	4	8	9
35–49	45	2.8	5	1	1	2	3	7	7	10
50–64	46	2.8	5	1	1	2	3	5	5	12
65+	226	3.3	10	1	1	3	4	6	8	21
TOTAL SINGLE DX	**30**	**1.1**	**<1**	**1**	**1**	**1**	**1**	**1**	**2**	**2**
TOTAL MULTIPLE DX	**376**	**3.1**	**10**	**1**	**1**	**2**	**4**	**6**	**9**	**22**
TOTAL										
0–19 Years	14	5.4	49	1	1	2	5	24	24	24
20–34	54	2.0	4	1	1	1	3	3	8	9
35–49	54	2.6	5	1	1	2	3	6	7	10
50–64	50	2.7	5	1	1	2	3	5	5	12
65+	234	3.2	10	1	1	2	4	6	8	21
GRAND TOTAL	**406**	**3.0**	**10**	**1**	**1**	**2**	**4**	**6**	**8**	**22**

79.72: CLSD RED ELBOW DISLOC

Type of Patients	Observed Patients	Avg. Stay	Vari-ance	10th	25th	50th	75th	90th	95th	99th
1. SINGLE DX										
0–19 Years	10	1.0	0	1	1	1	1	1	1	1
20–34	13	2.6	45	1	1	1	1	1	5	34
35–49	6	1.6	<1	1	1	1	2	3	3	3
50–64	4	1.4	<1	1	1	1	1	3	3	3
65+	0									
2. MULTIPLE DX										
0–19 Years	4	1.3	<1	1	1	1	2	2	2	2
20–34	12	2.3	3	1	1	2	4	5	5	5
35–49	16	1.3	<1	1	1	1	1	2	4	4
50–64	20	2.1	4	1	1	1	2	5	5	9
65+	15	3.4	5	1	2	2	5	8	8	9
TOTAL SINGLE DX	**33**	**1.9**	**21**	**1**	**1**	**1**	**1**	**2**	**3**	**34**
TOTAL MULTIPLE DX	**67**	**2.3**	**4**	**1**	**1**	**2**	**2**	**5**	**6**	**9**
TOTAL										
0–19 Years	14	1.1	<1	1	1	1	1	1	2	2
20–34	25	2.5	26	1	1	1	2	5	5	34
35–49	22	1.4	<1	1	1	1	2	2	3	4
50–64	24	2.0	3	1	1	1	2	4	5	9
65+	15	3.4	5	1	2	2	5	8	8	9
GRAND TOTAL	**100**	**2.1**	**10**	**1**	**1**	**1**	**2**	**5**	**5**	**9**

79.75: CLSD RED HIP DISLOC

Type of Patients	Observed Patients	Avg. Stay	Vari-ance	10th	25th	50th	75th	90th	95th	99th
1. SINGLE DX										
0–19 Years	43	1.3	<1	1	1	1	1	2	3	5
20–34	15	1.7	1	1	1	1	2	2	3	6
35–49	28	1.3	<1	1	1	1	1	2	3	6
50–64	71	1.3	<1	1	1	1	1	2	3	5
65+	99	1.5	<1	1	1	1	2	2	3	6
2. MULTIPLE DX										
0–19 Years	43	4.0	18	1	1	2	4	12	15	17
20–34	62	3.0	6	1	1	2	4	5	7	18
35–49	136	2.6	7	1	1	2	3	5	8	14
50–64	330	2.7	17	1	1	1	3	5	9	18
65+	1,048	2.5	6	1	1	2	3	5	7	13
TOTAL SINGLE DX	**256**	**1.4**	**<1**	**1**	**1**	**1**	**1**	**2**	**3**	**6**
TOTAL MULTIPLE DX	**1,619**	**2.6**	**9**	**1**	**1**	**2**	**3**	**5**	**7**	**15**
TOTAL										
0–19 Years	86	2.4	9	1	1	1	2	5	12	15
20–34	77	2.8	6	1	1	2	4	5	7	11
35–49	164	2.4	6	1	1	1	3	5	8	13
50–64	401	2.5	15	1	1	1	2	5	7	18
65+	1,147	2.4	5	1	1	2	3	5	6	13
GRAND TOTAL	**1,875**	**2.4**	**8**	**1**	**1**	**2**	**3**	**5**	**7**	**14**

79.76: CLSD RED KNEE DISLOC

Type of Patients	Observed Patients	Avg. Stay	Vari-ance	10th	25th	50th	75th	90th	95th	99th
1. SINGLE DX										
0–19 Years	4	1.0	0	1	1	1	1	1	1	1
20–34	5	1.3	<1	1	1	1	2	2	2	2
35–49	2	2.4	4	1	1	1	4	4	4	4
50–64	3	1.8	<1	1	2	2	2	2	2	2
65+	1	3.0	0	3	3	3	3	3	3	3
2. MULTIPLE DX										
0–19 Years	4	1.2	<1	1	1	1	1	2	2	2
20–34	14	1.6	<1	1	1	1	2	3	3	3
35–49	9	2.8	4	1	1	2	4	7	7	7
50–64	15	2.7	7	1	1	2	3	4	12	12
65+	32	2.8	2	1	1	3	4	5	5	7
TOTAL SINGLE DX	**15**	**1.6**	**<1**	**1**	**1**	**1**	**2**	**3**	**4**	**4**
TOTAL MULTIPLE DX	**74**	**2.4**	**3**	**1**	**1**	**2**	**3**	**5**	**5**	**12**
TOTAL										
0–19 Years	8	1.1	<1	1	1	1	1	1	2	2
20–34	19	1.5	<1	1	1	1	2	3	3	3
35–49	11	2.8	4	1	1	2	4	5	7	7
50–64	18	2.5	5	1	1	2	2	4	4	12
65+	33	2.8	2	1	1	3	4	5	5	7
GRAND TOTAL	**89**	**2.3**	**3**	**1**	**1**	**2**	**3**	**4**	**5**	**7**

79.8: OPEN RED DISLOCATION

Type of Patients	Observed Patients	Avg. Stay	Vari-ance	10th	25th	50th	75th	90th	95th	99th
1. SINGLE DX										
0–19 Years	90	2.0	8	1	1	1	2	3	5	20
20–34	32	1.9	1	1	1	1	2	4	4	5
35–49	25	2.3	10	1	1	1	2	3	14	15
50–64	14	2.5	3	1	1	2	3	6	6	6
65+	2	2.7	1	2	2	2	4	4	4	4
2. MULTIPLE DX										
0–19 Years	116	2.5	4	1	1	2	3	4	6	11
20–34	62	4.5	32	1	1	3	7	10	12	29
35–49	67	4.5	35	1	1	2	5	12	14	42
50–64	73	4.0	14	1	2	3	6	9	10	25
65+	105	4.3	7	1	3	4	5	9	10	13
TOTAL SINGLE DX	**163**	**2.1**	**7**	**1**	**1**	**1**	**2**	**3**	**5**	**15**
TOTAL MULTIPLE DX	**423**	**3.5**	**13**	**1**	**1**	**2**	**4**	**7**	**10**	**20**
TOTAL										
0–19 Years	206	2.3	6	1	1	2	2	4	6	15
20–34	94	3.7	23	1	1	2	4	7	12	29
35–49	92	3.7	27	1	1	2	4	8	14	21
50–64	87	3.8	13	1	1	3	5	8	10	25
65+	107	4.3	7	1	3	4	5	9	10	13
GRAND TOTAL	**586**	**2.9**	**11**	**1**	**1**	**2**	**3**	**6**	**9**	**18**

79.85: OPEN RED HIP DISLOC

Type of Patients	Observed Patients	Avg. Stay	Vari-ance	Percentiles						
				10th	25th	50th	75th	90th	95th	99th
1. SINGLE DX										
0–19 Years	65	2.1	9	1	1	1	2	3	6	20
20–34	1	3.0	0	3	3	3	3	3	3	3
35–49	0									
50–64	1	6.0	0	6	6	6	6	6	6	6
65+	1	4.0	0	4	4	4	4	4	4	4
2. MULTIPLE DX										
0–19 Years	98	2.5	5	1	1	2	3	4	6	11
20–34	6	6.6	21	1	2	6	10	14	14	14
35–49	11	7.7	102	3	4	4	6	12	42	42
50–64	11	7.5	35	3	3	6	10	10	25	25
65+	61	4.9	8	3	3	4	6	9	10	16
TOTAL SINGLE DX	**68**	**2.1**	**9**	**1**	**1**	**1**	**2**	**3**	**6**	**20**
TOTAL MULTIPLE DX	**187**	**3.4**	**11**	**1**	**2**	**2**	**4**	**6**	**9**	**15**
TOTAL										
0–19 Years	163	2.3	7	1	1	2	2	4	6	15
20–34	7	6.1	20	1	3	6	10	14	14	14
35–49	11	7.7	102	3	4	4	6	12	42	42
50–64	12	7.2	30	3	3	6	10	10	25	25
65+	62	4.9	8	3	3	4	6	9	10	16
GRAND TOTAL	**255**	**2.9**	**11**	**1**	**1**	**2**	**3**	**6**	**9**	**16**

79.9: BONE INJURY OP NOS

Type of Patients	Observed Patients	Avg. Stay	Vari-ance	Percentiles						
				10th	25th	50th	75th	90th	95th	99th
1. SINGLE DX										
0–19 Years	0									
20–34	0									
35–49	0									
50–64	0									
65+	0									
2. MULTIPLE DX										
0–19 Years	0									
20–34	0									
35–49	0									
50–64	1	3.0	0	3	3	3	3	3	3	3
65+	2	4.2	14	1	1	7	7	7	7	7
TOTAL SINGLE DX	**0**									
TOTAL MULTIPLE DX	**3**	**3.8**	**8**	**1**	**1**	**3**	**7**	**7**	**7**	**7**
TOTAL										
0–19 Years	0									
20–34	0									
35–49	0									
50–64	1	3.0	0	3	3	3	3	3	3	3
65+	2	4.2	14	1	1	7	7	7	7	7
GRAND TOTAL	**3**	**3.8**	**8**	**1**	**1**	**3**	**7**	**7**	**7**	**7**

80.0: ARTHROTOMY RMVL PROSTH

Type of Patients	Observed Patients	Avg. Stay	Vari-ance	Percentiles						
				10th	25th	50th	75th	90th	95th	99th
1. SINGLE DX										
0–19 Years	0									
20–34	0									
35–49	5	5.0	15	1	3	4	5	11	11	11
50–64	7	3.7	2	3	3	3	5	5	5	5
65+	9	5.9	5	3	4	6	7	10	10	10
2. MULTIPLE DX										
0–19 Years	3	5.1	<1	4	5	5	5	6	6	6
20–34	17	6.1	31	1	2	5	8	17	17	20
35–49	81	7.3	23	3	4	6	9	13	18	23
50–64	230	8.3	76	3	4	6	10	14	18	49
65+	430	8.3	44	3	4	7	10	15	21	36
TOTAL SINGLE DX	**21**	**5.0**	**6**	**1**	**3**	**5**	**6**	**7**	**10**	**11**
TOTAL MULTIPLE DX	**761**	**8.2**	**51**	**3**	**4**	**6**	**10**	**14**	**20**	**39**
TOTAL										
0–19 Years	3	5.1	<1	4	5	5	5	6	6	6
20–34	17	6.1	31	1	2	5	8	17	17	20
35–49	86	7.2	23	3	4	5	9	13	18	23
50–64	237	8.2	74	3	4	6	10	14	18	49
65+	439	8.3	43	3	4	6	10	15	20	36
GRAND TOTAL	**782**	**8.1**	**50**	**3**	**4**	**6**	**10**	**14**	**19**	**39**

80.05: RMVL PROSTH HIP INC

Type of Patients	Observed Patients	Avg. Stay	Vari-ance	Percentiles						
				10th	25th	50th	75th	90th	95th	99th
1. SINGLE DX										
0–19 Years	0									
20–34	0									
35–49	0									
50–64	1	3.0	0	3	3	3	3	3	3	3
65+	2	6.4	<1	6	6	6	7	7	7	7
2. MULTIPLE DX										
0–19 Years	1	5.0	0	5	5	5	5	5	5	5
20–34	4	13.3	45	5	5	17	17	20	20	20
35–49	33	8.9	29	4	5	7	12	17	23	23
50–64	66	12.0	156	3	6	8	11	23	44	84
65+	164	9.3	50	3	5	8	11	18	24	47
TOTAL SINGLE DX	**3**	**6.1**	**1**	**3**	**6**	**6**	**7**	**7**	**7**	**7**
TOTAL MULTIPLE DX	**268**	**9.9**	**73**	**3**	**5**	**8**	**12**	**18**	**24**	**48**
TOTAL										
0–19 Years	1	5.0	0	5	5	5	5	5	5	5
20–34	4	13.3	45	5	5	17	17	20	20	20
35–49	33	8.9	29	4	5	7	12	17	23	23
50–64	67	11.9	155	3	6	8	11	23	44	84
65+	166	9.2	48	3	5	7	11	17	24	47
GRAND TOTAL	**271**	**9.8**	**71**	**3**	**5**	**7**	**11**	**18**	**24**	**48**

80.06: RMVL PROSTH KNEE INC

Type of Patients	Observed Patients	Avg. Stay	Variance	10th	25th	50th	75th	90th	95th	99th
1. SINGLE DX										
0–19 Years	0									
20–34	0									
35–49	4	5.2	18	1	3	5	11	11	11	11
50–64	4	4.3	1	3	3	5	5	5	5	5
65+	6	5.6	12	1	3	6	10	10	10	10
2. MULTIPLE DX										
0–19 Years	1	4.0	0	4	4	4	4	4	4	4
20–34	6	5.6	10	2	2	6	8	10	10	10
35–49	41	6.9	17	3	4	5	9	12	15	21
50–64	134	7.4	38	3	4	6	9	14	15	45
65+	240	8.0	41	3	4	6	9	14	20	36
TOTAL SINGLE DX	14	5.0	8	1	3	5	6	10	11	11
TOTAL MULTIPLE DX	422	7.7	38	3	4	6	9	14	18	36
TOTAL										
0–19 Years	1	4.0	0	4	4	4	4	4	4	4
20–34	6	5.6	10	2	2	6	8	10	10	10
35–49	45	6.7	17	3	4	5	9	12	15	21
50–64	138	7.3	37	3	4	6	9	13	15	45
65+	246	7.9	41	3	4	6	9	14	20	36
GRAND TOTAL	436	7.6	37	3	4	6	9	14	18	36

80.1: OTHER ARTHROTOMY

Type of Patients	Observed Patients	Avg. Stay	Variance	10th	25th	50th	75th	90th	95th	99th
1. SINGLE DX										
0–19 Years	74	4.5	15	1	2	4	6	7	11	24
20–34	88	2.4	3	1	1	2	3	4	5	8
35–49	47	2.8	6	1	2	2	3	5	7	16
50–64	32	3.2	2	2	2	3	4	4	6	9
65+	12	3.8	5	1	2	3	5	8	8	8
2. MULTIPLE DX										
0–19 Years	214	7.0	37	2	3	5	8	14	21	28
20–34	301	4.8	20	1	2	3	6	9	14	21
35–49	489	6.4	68	1	2	4	7	13	18	51
50–64	519	6.4	37	2	3	5	8	13	18	37
65+	603	7.0	32	2	3	5	8	14	18	27
TOTAL SINGLE DX	253	3.5	9	1	2	3	4	6	7	15
TOTAL MULTIPLE DX	2,126	6.4	40	2	3	5	8	13	18	29
TOTAL										
0–19 Years	288	6.4	33	2	3	5	7	13	20	28
20–34	389	4.3	17	1	2	3	5	9	12	20
35–49	536	6.1	64	1	2	4	7	12	17	42
50–64	551	6.2	35	2	3	4	8	12	17	37
65+	615	6.9	31	2	3	5	8	14	18	27
GRAND TOTAL	2,379	6.1	37	2	3	4	7	12	17	29

80.11: ARTHROTOMY NEC SHOULDER

Type of Patients	Observed Patients	Avg. Stay	Variance	10th	25th	50th	75th	90th	95th	99th
1. SINGLE DX										
0–19 Years	1	4.0	0	4	4	4	4	4	4	4
20–34	4	1.8	<1	1	1	2	2	3	3	3
35–49	0									
50–64	2	3.4	2	1	4	4	4	4	4	4
65+	2	1.6	<1	1	1	2	2	2	2	2
2. MULTIPLE DX										
0–19 Years	3	8.8	21	1	8	8	13	13	13	13
20–34	9	2.5	4	1	1	2	3	4	8	8
35–49	35	5.3	21	1	2	4	8	9	15	24
50–64	40	6.3	55	1	2	4	8	12	13	37
65+	59	5.8	19	2	3	5	7	11	15	27
TOTAL SINGLE DX	9	2.6	2	1	1	2	4	4	4	4
TOTAL MULTIPLE DX	146	5.8	29	1	2	4	8	12	14	37
TOTAL										
0–19 Years	4	8.1	20	1	4	8	13	13	13	13
20–34	13	2.3	3	1	1	2	3	4	8	8
35–49	35	5.3	21	1	2	4	8	9	15	24
50–64	42	6.1	51	1	2	4	8	10	13	37
65+	61	5.7	19	2	3	4	7	9	15	27
GRAND TOTAL	155	5.6	28	1	2	4	8	11	14	37

80.12: ARTHROTOMY NEC ELBOW

Type of Patients	Observed Patients	Avg. Stay	Variance	10th	25th	50th	75th	90th	95th	99th
1. SINGLE DX										
0–19 Years	4	4.0	6	1	1	6	6	6	6	6
20–34	1	1.0	0	1	1	1	1	1	1	1
35–49	6	4.2	22	1	2	3	3	16	16	16
50–64	2	2.8	<1	2	3	3	3	3	3	3
65+	0									
2. MULTIPLE DX										
0–19 Years	10	3.7	9	1	2	2	5	11	11	11
20–34	16	4.7	17	1	2	3	8	10	15	15
35–49	39	4.2	12	1	2	3	6	9	11	16
50–64	41	5.4	21	1	2	4	6	12	13	22
65+	36	4.5	6	2	3	4	6	7	8	13
TOTAL SINGLE DX	13	3.6	10	1	2	3	6	6	6	16
TOTAL MULTIPLE DX	142	4.7	13	1	2	4	6	9	12	22
TOTAL										
0–19 Years	14	3.8	7	1	2	4	6	6	11	11
20–34	17	4.5	17	1	2	3	5	10	15	15
35–49	45	4.2	13	1	2	3	6	10	11	16
50–64	43	5.2	20	1	2	4	6	9	13	22
65+	36	4.5	6	2	3	4	6	7	8	13
GRAND TOTAL	155	4.5	13	1	2	3	6	9	12	16

80.14: ARTHROTOMY NEC HAND/FING

Type of Patients	Observed Patients	Avg. Stay	Vari-ance	Percentiles						
				10th	25th	50th	75th	90th	95th	99th
1. SINGLE DX										
0–19 Years	3	1.5	<1	1	1	1	2	2	2	2
20–34	18	2.7	1	1	2	3	4	4	4	4
35–49	6	2.8	<1	2	2	3	3	4	4	4
50–64	7	3.5	2	2	3	3	4	6	6	6
65+	1	5.0	0	5	5	5	5	5	5	5
2. MULTIPLE DX										
0–19 Years	20	3.5	4	1	2	3	5	7	7	7
20–34	79	3.6	8	1	2	3	4	7	8	22
35–49	86	4.1	8	2	2	3	5	7	9	14
50–64	49	4.7	13	2	2	4	5	11	11	18
65+	26	3.6	9	1	2	2	5	7	8	17
TOTAL SINGLE DX	**35**	**2.8**	**2**	**1**	**2**	**3**	**3**	**4**	**5**	**6**
TOTAL MULTIPLE DX	**260**	**4.0**	**9**	**1**	**2**	**3**	**5**	**7**	**10**	**18**
TOTAL										
0–19 Years	23	3.2	4	1	2	2	5	5	7	7
20–34	97	3.5	7	1	2	3	4	6	7	11
35–49	92	4.1	8	2	2	3	5	7	9	14
50–64	56	4.5	12	2	2	4	5	11	11	18
65+	27	3.7	9	1	2	3	5	7	8	17
GRAND TOTAL	**295**	**3.8**	**8**	**1**	**2**	**3**	**5**	**7**	**9**	**17**

80.15: ARTHROTOMY NEC HIP

Type of Patients	Observed Patients	Avg. Stay	Vari-ance	Percentiles						
				10th	25th	50th	75th	90th	95th	99th
1. SINGLE DX										
0–19 Years	19	5.0	12	2	4	4	5	6	11	24
20–34	9	3.0	5	1	1	3	4	6	8	8
35–49	5	2.4	1	1	2	2	2	5	5	5
50–64	1	4.0	0	4	4	4	4	4	4	4
65+	3	2.2	2	1	1	2	4	4	4	4
2. MULTIPLE DX										
0–19 Years	68	8.9	53	3	4	6	11	22	28	28
20–34	28	8.2	41	4	4	8	9	11	12	43
35–49	65	8.7	56	2	4	6	10	19	25	42
50–64	66	8.2	52	2	4	7	10	17	28	>99
65+	134	8.0	37	3	4	6	10	16	21	29
TOTAL SINGLE DX	**37**	**4.3**	**10**	**2**	**2**	**4**	**5**	**6**	**8**	**24**
TOTAL MULTIPLE DX	**361**	**8.5**	**47**	**3**	**4**	**6**	**10**	**18**	**26**	**38**
TOTAL										
0–19 Years	87	8.2	47	3	4	5	10	21	26	28
20–34	37	7.0	37	2	4	6	9	11	12	43
35–49	70	8.2	54	2	3	5	10	17	20	42
50–64	67	8.2	51	2	4	7	10	17	28	>99
65+	137	7.9	37	3	4	6	9	16	21	29
GRAND TOTAL	**398**	**8.0**	**45**	**2**	**4**	**6**	**10**	**17**	**25**	**35**

80.16: ARTHROTOMY NEC KNEE

Type of Patients	Observed Patients	Avg. Stay	Vari-ance	Percentiles						
				10th	25th	50th	75th	90th	95th	99th
1. SINGLE DX										
0–19 Years	32	4.9	19	2	3	4	6	7	8	32
20–34	46	2.4	4	1	1	2	3	4	5	15
35–49	25	2.5	3	1	2	2	3	5	7	7
50–64	17	3.1	4	2	2	3	4	4	7	9
65+	4	5.1	5	3	3	5	8	8	8	8
2. MULTIPLE DX										
0–19 Years	82	5.3	22	1	2	4	7	13	15	26
20–34	128	4.6	18	1	2	3	6	9	12	20
35–49	195	7.4	131	2	2	4	7	14	28	82
50–64	237	6.3	29	2	3	5	8	12	15	29
65+	284	6.8	23	3	3	5	9	14	16	25
TOTAL SINGLE DX	**124**	**3.5**	**11**	**1**	**2**	**3**	**4**	**7**	**7**	**15**
TOTAL MULTIPLE DX	**926**	**6.3**	**44**	**2**	**3**	**4**	**7**	**12**	**16**	**30**
TOTAL										
0–19 Years	114	5.1	21	1	2	4	7	9	15	29
20–34	174	4.0	15	1	2	3	4	8	12	20
35–49	220	6.9	119	1	2	4	7	13	24	51
50–64	254	6.1	28	2	3	5	7	12	15	26
65+	288	6.8	23	3	3	5	9	14	16	25
GRAND TOTAL	**1,050**	**5.9**	**41**	**2**	**3**	**4**	**7**	**12**	**15**	**30**

80.17: ARTHROTOMY NEC ANKLE

Type of Patients	Observed Patients	Avg. Stay	Vari-ance	Percentiles						
				10th	25th	50th	75th	90th	95th	99th
1. SINGLE DX										
0–19 Years	11	4.0	14	1	1	3	7	11	11	11
20–34	5	1.8	<1	1	1	2	2	3	3	3
35–49	0									
50–64	2	2.8	2	2	2	2	4	4	4	4
65+	0									
2. MULTIPLE DX										
0–19 Years	20	8.1	19	4	5	7	9	14	14	23
20–34	20	5.3	33	1	1	2	7	16	17	17
35–49	37	6.1	50	1	2	4	7	15	28	28
50–64	49	6.4	54	1	2	4	5	19	28	28
65+	21	12.3	122	2	5	11	13	27	27	57
TOTAL SINGLE DX	**18**	**3.3**	**11**	**1**	**1**	**2**	**4**	**11**	**11**	**11**
TOTAL MULTIPLE DX	**147**	**7.6**	**60**	**1**	**2**	**5**	**10**	**17**	**27**	**28**
TOTAL										
0–19 Years	31	7.1	20	2	4	7	9	14	14	23
20–34	25	4.7	29	1	1	2	5	16	17	17
35–49	37	6.1	50	1	2	4	7	15	28	28
50–64	51	6.3	52	2	2	4	5	19	28	28
65+	21	12.3	122	2	5	11	13	27	27	57
GRAND TOTAL	**165**	**7.2**	**57**	**1**	**2**	**4**	**9**	**16**	**27**	**28**

80.2: ARTHROSCOPY

Type of Patients	Observed Patients	Avg. Stay	Vari-ance	Percentiles 10th	25th	50th	75th	90th	95th	99th
1. SINGLE DX										
0–19 Years	9	3.0	7	1	1	2	5	8	8	8
20–34	12	1.4	<1	1	1	1	2	2	3	3
35–49	14	1.7	<1	1	1	1	2	3	5	5
50–64	13	1.5	<1	1	1	1	2	3	3	3
65+	8	1.6	<1	1	1	2	2	2	2	2
2. MULTIPLE DX										
0–19 Years	17	3.5	7	1	1	3	4	7	10	10
20–34	29	2.2	2	1	1	2	3	4	5	6
35–49	52	3.0	14	1	1	2	3	5	8	24
50–64	96	3.2	15	1	1	2	3	12	12	19
65+	103	2.3	7	1	1	1	2	6	6	12
TOTAL SINGLE DX	**56**	**1.8**	**2**	**1**	**1**	**1**	**2**	**3**	**5**	**8**
TOTAL MULTIPLE DX	**297**	**2.8**	**10**	**1**	**1**	**2**	**3**	**6**	**10**	**19**
TOTAL										
0–19 Years	26	3.4	7	1	1	3	4	8	9	10
20–34	41	2.0	2	1	1	1	3	4	5	6
35–49	66	2.7	11	1	1	2	2	5	6	24
50–64	109	3.0	14	1	1	2	3	9	12	19
65+	111	2.3	7	1	1	1	2	5	6	12
GRAND TOTAL	**353**	**2.6**	**9**	**1**	**1**	**2**	**3**	**5**	**8**	**14**

80.21: SHOULDER ARTHROSCOPY

Type of Patients	Observed Patients	Avg. Stay	Vari-ance	Percentiles 10th	25th	50th	75th	90th	95th	99th
1. SINGLE DX										
0–19 Years	4	1.2	<1	1	1	1	1	2	2	2
20–34	8	1.5	<1	1	1	1	2	3	3	3
35–49	6	1.4	<1	1	1	1	2	2	2	2
50–64	11	1.6	<1	1	1	1	2	3	3	3
65+	6	1.5	<1	1	1	2	2	2	2	2
2. MULTIPLE DX										
0–19 Years	4	2.0	2	1	1	1	4	4	4	4
20–34	12	1.4	<1	1	1	1	1	3	4	4
35–49	28	1.8	<1	1	1	2	2	3	4	5
50–64	71	1.8	3	1	1	1	2	3	4	13
65+	83	1.6	5	1	1	1	2	2	2	23
TOTAL SINGLE DX	**35**	**1.5**	**<1**	**1**	**1**	**1**	**2**	**2**	**3**	**3**
TOTAL MULTIPLE DX	**198**	**1.7**	**4**	**1**	**1**	**1**	**2**	**3**	**4**	**8**
TOTAL										
0–19 Years	8	1.7	1	1	1	1	2	4	4	4
20–34	20	1.4	<1	1	1	1	2	3	3	4
35–49	34	1.7	<1	1	1	1	2	2	4	5
50–64	82	1.8	3	1	1	1	2	3	4	13
65+	89	1.6	5	1	1	1	2	2	2	6
GRAND TOTAL	**233**	**1.6**	**3**	**1**	**1**	**1**	**2**	**3**	**3**	**8**

80.26: KNEE ARTHROSCOPY

Type of Patients	Observed Patients	Avg. Stay	Vari-ance	Percentiles 10th	25th	50th	75th	90th	95th	99th
1. SINGLE DX										
0–19 Years	4	4.7	7	1	3	3	8	8	8	8
20–34	3	1.3	<1	1	1	1	2	2	2	2
35–49	6	1.7	<1	1	1	2	2	2	3	3
50–64	1	1.0	0	1	1	1	1	1	1	1
65+	2	1.7	<1	1	1	2	2	2	2	2
2. MULTIPLE DX										
0–19 Years	9	4.2	5	1	3	3	7	7	9	9
20–34	14	2.8	2	1	2	3	4	5	6	6
35–49	23	4.2	26	1	2	2	5	8	19	24
50–64	21	7.4	31	1	3	6	12	14	19	19
65+	19	4.9	6	3	3	4	6	8	12	12
TOTAL SINGLE DX	**16**	**2.4**	**4**	**1**	**1**	**2**	**3**	**5**	**8**	**8**
TOTAL MULTIPLE DX	**86**	**4.9**	**17**	**1**	**2**	**3**	**6**	**12**	**12**	**19**
TOTAL										
0–19 Years	13	4.3	6	1	3	3	7	8	8	9
20–34	17	2.6	2	1	1	2	4	5	5	6
35–49	29	3.5	20	1	1	2	4	6	8	24
50–64	22	6.8	32	1	2	4	12	14	19	19
65+	21	4.5	6	2	3	4	6	7	12	12
GRAND TOTAL	**102**	**4.4**	**16**	**1**	**2**	**3**	**6**	**11**	**12**	**19**

80.3: BIOPSY JOINT STRUCTURE

Type of Patients	Observed Patients	Avg. Stay	Vari-ance	Percentiles 10th	25th	50th	75th	90th	95th	99th
1. SINGLE DX										
0–19 Years	9	3.6	2	1	3	4	4	6	6	6
20–34	4	3.5	9	1	1	2	5	8	8	8
35–49	7	2.9	10	1	1	1	4	9	9	9
50–64	1	2.0	0	2	2	2	2	2	2	2
65+	2	3.0	2	2	2	4	4	4	4	4
2. MULTIPLE DX										
0–19 Years	12	6.6	18	1	4	6	9	14	14	14
20–34	13	9.0	73	1	3	5	12	23	28	28
35–49	35	7.4	46	2	3	5	10	18	21	35
50–64	50	6.0	22	2	2	5	8	12	19	21
65+	107	6.4	18	3	3	6	8	11	13	26
TOTAL SINGLE DX	**23**	**3.4**	**4**	**1**	**1**	**4**	**4**	**6**	**8**	**9**
TOTAL MULTIPLE DX	**217**	**6.6**	**26**	**2**	**3**	**5**	**8**	**13**	**18**	**26**
TOTAL										
0–19 Years	21	4.9	12	1	3	4	6	9	14	14
20–34	17	7.7	63	1	2	5	10	23	23	28
35–49	42	6.9	43	2	2	4	10	14	21	35
50–64	51	6.0	22	2	2	5	8	12	19	21
65+	109	6.4	18	2	3	6	8	11	13	26
GRAND TOTAL	**240**	**6.3**	**25**	**2**	**3**	**5**	**8**	**12**	**15**	**26**

80.4: JT CAPSULE/LIG/CART DIV

Type of Patients	Observed Patients	Avg. Stay	Vari-ance	Percentiles						
				10th	25th	50th	75th	90th	95th	99th
1. SINGLE DX										
0–19 Years	91	1.2	<1	1	1	1	1	2	3	4
20–34	23	1.6	<1	1	1	1	2	2	3	5
35–49	21	2.1	<1	1	1	2	3	3	4	4
50–64	12	2.3	<1	1	2	3	3	3	3	3
65+	6	1.4	<1	1	1	1	2	2	2	2
2. MULTIPLE DX										
0–19 Years	111	1.8	1	1	1	1	2	4	4	5
20–34	73	2.6	7	1	1	2	3	5	7	17
35–49	115	2.6	5	1	1	2	3	4	5	14
50–64	128	2.6	4	1	1	2	3	5	8	9
65+	67	3.0	5	1	2	2	4	5	6	16
TOTAL SINGLE DX	**153**	**1.4**	**<1**	**1**	**1**	**1**	**1**	**2**	**3**	**4**
TOTAL MULTIPLE DX	**494**	**2.3**	**4**	**1**	**1**	**2**	**3**	**4**	**5**	**10**
TOTAL										
0–19 Years	202	1.5	<1	1	1	1	2	3	4	4
20–34	96	2.3	5	1	1	2	3	4	7	13
35–49	136	2.5	4	1	1	2	3	4	5	14
50–64	140	2.5	3	1	1	2	3	5	7	9
65+	73	2.9	5	1	2	2	4	5	5	16
GRAND TOTAL	**647**	**2.0**	**3**	**1**	**1**	**1**	**3**	**4**	**5**	**9**

80.46: KNEE STRUCTURE DIVISION

Type of Patients	Observed Patients	Avg. Stay	Vari-ance	Percentiles						
				10th	25th	50th	75th	90th	95th	99th
1. SINGLE DX										
0–19 Years	12	1.6	1	1	1	1	2	3	4	4
20–34	20	1.6	<1	1	1	1	2	2	3	5
35–49	16	2.2	<1	1	1	2	3	3	4	4
50–64	7	2.4	<1	1	2	3	3	3	3	3
65+	4	1.6	<1	1	1	2	2	2	2	2
2. MULTIPLE DX										
0–19 Years	47	2.0	1	1	1	2	3	3	4	5
20–34	49	2.6	6	1	1	2	3	5	7	13
35–49	78	2.4	2	1	1	2	3	4	5	9
50–64	75	2.7	4	1	2	2	3	5	8	9
65+	46	2.8	2	1	2	2	4	5	5	9
TOTAL SINGLE DX	**59**	**1.8**	**<1**	**1**	**1**	**2**	**2**	**3**	**4**	**5**
TOTAL MULTIPLE DX	**295**	**2.5**	**3**	**1**	**1**	**2**	**3**	**4**	**5**	**9**
TOTAL										
0–19 Years	59	1.9	1	1	1	2	3	3	4	5
20–34	69	2.3	4	1	1	2	3	4	7	11
35–49	94	2.4	2	1	1	2	3	4	5	6
50–64	82	2.7	4	1	2	2	3	5	8	9
65+	50	2.7	2	1	2	2	4	5	5	9
GRAND TOTAL	**354**	**2.4**	**3**	**1**	**1**	**2**	**3**	**4**	**5**	**9**

80.5: IV DISC EXC/DESTRUCTION

Type of Patients	Observed Patients	Avg. Stay	Vari-ance	Percentiles						
				10th	25th	50th	75th	90th	95th	99th
1. SINGLE DX										
0–19 Years	70	1.6	2	1	1	1	2	4	4	8
20–34	1,565	1.5	<1	1	1	1	2	2	3	6
35–49	2,936	1.4	<1	1	1	1	2	2	3	5
50–64	1,554	1.5	<1	1	1	1	2	3	3	5
65+	335	1.7	1	1	1	1	2	3	4	5
2. MULTIPLE DX										
0–19 Years	63	3.2	23	1	1	1	4	7	13	32
20–34	1,745	2.0	5	1	1	1	2	4	6	10
35–49	5,036	2.1	5	1	1	1	2	4	5	10
50–64	4,982	2.3	6	1	1	2	3	4	6	11
65+	3,419	3.0	9	1	1	2	3	6	8	16
TOTAL SINGLE DX	**6,460**	**1.5**	**<1**	**1**	**1**	**1**	**2**	**2**	**3**	**5**
TOTAL MULTIPLE DX	**15,245**	**2.4**	**7**	**1**	**1**	**2**	**3**	**5**	**6**	**13**
TOTAL										
0–19 Years	133	2.4	13	1	1	1	2	5	8	20
20–34	3,310	1.8	3	1	1	1	2	3	4	8
35–49	7,972	1.8	4	1	1	1	2	3	5	9
50–64	6,536	2.1	5	1	1	1	2	4	5	11
65+	3,754	2.9	8	1	1	2	3	6	8	15
GRAND TOTAL	**21,705**	**2.1**	**5**	**1**	**1**	**1**	**2**	**4**	**6**	**11**

80.51: IV DISC EXCISION

Type of Patients	Observed Patients	Avg. Stay	Vari-ance	Percentiles						
				10th	25th	50th	75th	90th	95th	99th
1. SINGLE DX										
0–19 Years	70	1.6	2	1	1	1	2	4	4	8
20–34	1,558	1.5	<1	1	1	1	2	2	3	6
35–49	2,920	1.4	<1	1	1	1	2	2	3	5
50–64	1,543	1.5	<1	1	1	1	2	3	3	5
65+	330	1.7	1	1	1	1	2	3	4	5
2. MULTIPLE DX										
0–19 Years	63	3.2	23	1	1	1	4	7	13	32
20–34	1,734	2.0	5	1	1	1	2	4	6	10
35–49	5,013	2.1	5	1	1	1	2	4	5	10
50–64	4,952	2.3	6	1	1	2	3	4	6	11
65+	3,405	3.0	9	1	1	2	3	6	8	16
TOTAL SINGLE DX	**6,421**	**1.5**	**<1**	**1**	**1**	**1**	**2**	**2**	**3**	**5**
TOTAL MULTIPLE DX	**15,167**	**2.4**	**7**	**1**	**1**	**2**	**3**	**5**	**6**	**13**
TOTAL										
0–19 Years	133	2.4	13	1	1	1	2	5	8	20
20–34	3,292	1.8	3	1	1	1	2	3	4	8
35–49	7,933	1.8	3	1	1	1	2	3	5	9
50–64	6,495	2.1	5	1	1	1	2	4	5	10
65+	3,735	2.9	8	1	1	2	3	5	8	15
GRAND TOTAL	**21,588**	**2.1**	**5**	**1**	**1**	**1**	**2**	**4**	**5**	**11**

80.59: IV DISC DESTRUCTION NEC

Type of Patients	Observed Patients	Avg. Stay	Vari-ance	Percentiles						
				10th	25th	50th	75th	90th	95th	99th
1. SINGLE DX										
0–19 Years	0									
20–34	3	1.0	0	1	1	1	1	1	1	1
35–49	12	1.3	<1	1	1	1	1	2	3	3
50–64	3	1.3	<1	1	1	1	2	2	2	2
65+	3	1.8	<1	1	2	2	2	2	2	2
2. MULTIPLE DX										
0–19 Years	0									
20–34	7	2.3	4	1	1	1	3	6	6	6
35–49	12	4.8	141	1	1	1	3	7	50	50
50–64	16	4.5	34	1	1	2	6	18	19	19
65+	7	5.9	20	1	1	5	10	13	13	13
TOTAL SINGLE DX	**21**	**1.3**	**<1**	**1**	**1**	**1**	**2**	**2**	**2**	**3**
TOTAL MULTIPLE DX	**42**	**4.4**	**61**	**1**	**1**	**2**	**5**	**10**	**18**	**50**
TOTAL										
0–19 Years	0									
20–34	10	2.0	3	1	1	1	2	6	6	6
35–49	24	3.3	81	1	1	1	2	3	7	50
50–64	19	4.0	30	1	1	1	4	12	18	19
65+	10	4.4	16	1	1	2	6	13	13	13
GRAND TOTAL	**63**	**3.4**	**43**	**1**	**1**	**1**	**3**	**7**	**13**	**50**

80.6: EXC KNEE SEMILUNAR CART

Type of Patients	Observed Patients	Avg. Stay	Vari-ance	Percentiles						
				10th	25th	50th	75th	90th	95th	99th
1. SINGLE DX										
0–19 Years	2	1.0	0	1	1	1	1	1	1	1
20–34	4	1.0	0	1	1	1	1	1	1	1
35–49	20	1.4	<1	1	1	1	2	2	3	3
50–64	20	2.9	26	1	1	2	2	4	5	28
65+	3	1.5	<1	1	1	2	2	2	2	2
2. MULTIPLE DX										
0–19 Years	22	1.7	2	1	1	1	3	3	4	7
20–34	104	2.2	4	1	1	1	2	5	7	9
35–49	235	2.5	9	1	1	2	3	5	7	21
50–64	263	2.7	12	1	1	1	3	5	8	21
65+	219	4.4	20	1	1	3	6	11	13	22
TOTAL SINGLE DX	**49**	**2.0**	**12**	**1**	**1**	**1**	**2**	**2**	**4**	**28**
TOTAL MULTIPLE DX	**843**	**3.0**	**13**	**1**	**1**	**2**	**3**	**7**	**10**	**21**
TOTAL										
0–19 Years	24	1.7	2	1	1	1	2	3	4	7
20–34	108	2.1	3	1	1	1	2	5	7	9
35–49	255	2.4	8	1	1	2	2	4	7	21
50–64	283	2.7	13	1	1	1	3	5	8	21
65+	222	4.4	19	1	1	3	6	10	13	22
GRAND TOTAL	**892**	**3.0**	**13**	**1**	**1**	**2**	**3**	**7**	**10**	**21**

80.7: SYNOVECTOMY

Type of Patients	Observed Patients	Avg. Stay	Vari-ance	Percentiles						
				10th	25th	50th	75th	90th	95th	99th
1. SINGLE DX										
0–19 Years	12	4.4	129	1	1	1	3	4	49	49
20–34	12	2.3	4	1	1	1	4	6	6	6
35–49	14	2.5	1	1	2	2	3	4	4	4
50–64	9	5.4	30	1	1	4	7	7	20	20
65+	4	3.1	1	2	2	3	3	5	5	5
2. MULTIPLE DX										
0–19 Years	30	3.9	16	1	2	3	4	7	10	27
20–34	74	4.0	9	1	2	3	5	8	10	16
35–49	140	6.3	37	1	2	4	7	15	21	28
50–64	171	6.3	43	1	2	4	8	15	20	31
65+	225	6.5	31	1	3	5	8	14	16	35
TOTAL SINGLE DX	**51**	**3.4**	**40**	**1**	**1**	**2**	**4**	**6**	**7**	**49**
TOTAL MULTIPLE DX	**640**	**5.9**	**32**	**1**	**2**	**4**	**7**	**13**	**18**	**28**
TOTAL										
0–19 Years	42	4.0	42	1	1	3	3	7	10	49
20–34	86	3.8	9	1	1	3	5	8	9	13
35–49	154	5.9	35	1	2	4	7	14	21	28
50–64	180	6.3	42	1	2	4	8	15	20	31
65+	229	6.5	31	1	3	5	8	14	16	35
GRAND TOTAL	**691**	**5.7**	**33**	**1**	**2**	**4**	**7**	**12**	**18**	**28**

80.76: KNEE SYNOVECTOMY

Type of Patients	Observed Patients	Avg. Stay	Vari-ance	Percentiles						
				10th	25th	50th	75th	90th	95th	99th
1. SINGLE DX										
0–19 Years	11	4.7	140	1	1	1	3	4	49	49
20–34	10	2.1	4	1	1	1	2	6	6	6
35–49	12	2.4	1	1	2	2	3	4	4	4
50–64	7	6.5	32	1	2	6	7	20	20	20
65+	3	3.5	1	3	3	3	5	5	5	5
2. MULTIPLE DX										
0–19 Years	24	4.4	19	1	2	3	6	9	11	27
20–34	62	3.7	5	1	2	3	5	7	8	10
35–49	106	7.0	40	2	3	6	8	18	23	28
50–64	144	6.5	39	1	3	5	8	14	19	32
65+	173	6.8	30	2	4	5	8	14	16	28
TOTAL SINGLE DX	**43**	**3.6**	**47**	**1**	**1**	**2**	**3**	**6**	**7**	**49**
TOTAL MULTIPLE DX	**509**	**6.2**	**31**	**1**	**3**	**5**	**7**	**14**	**18**	**28**
TOTAL										
0–19 Years	35	4.5	52	1	1	3	4	7	11	49
20–34	72	3.4	5	1	1	3	5	7	8	10
35–49	118	6.5	38	1	2	5	7	17	22	28
50–64	151	6.5	39	1	3	5	8	14	20	32
65+	176	6.8	29	2	4	5	8	14	16	28
GRAND TOTAL	**552**	**6.0**	**33**	**1**	**3**	**4**	**7**	**13**	**18**	**28**

80.8: OTH EXC/DESTR JOINT LES

Type of Patients	Observed Patients	Avg. Stay	Vari-ance	Percentiles						
				10th	25th	50th	75th	90th	95th	99th
1. SINGLE DX										
0–19 Years	17	2.4	2	1	1	2	4	5	6	6
20–34	65	2.2	3	1	1	2	2	4	5	11
35–49	64	2.3	2	1	1	2	3	4	5	7
50–64	54	2.1	3	1	1	1	3	5	6	7
65+	5	4.6	10	1	1	4	8	8	8	8
2. MULTIPLE DX										
0–19 Years	71	4.8	15	1	2	3	6	10	11	24
20–34	199	4.2	11	1	2	3	6	8	10	21
35–49	482	4.7	39	1	1	3	5	10	18	33
50–64	730	4.7	47	1	1	3	5	10	16	33
65+	759	5.4	28	1	2	4	7	12	16	25
TOTAL SINGLE DX	**205**	**2.3**	**3**	**1**	**1**	**2**	**3**	**5**	**6**	**8**
TOTAL MULTIPLE DX	**2,241**	**4.9**	**34**	**1**	**1**	**3**	**6**	**11**	**15**	**28**
TOTAL										
0–19 Years	88	4.3	13	1	2	3	5	10	11	15
20–34	264	3.7	10	1	2	3	5	8	9	14
35–49	546	4.5	35	1	1	2	5	10	15	33
50–64	784	4.6	44	1	1	2	5	10	15	32
65+	764	5.4	28	1	2	4	7	12	16	25
GRAND TOTAL	**2,446**	**4.7**	**32**	**1**	**1**	**3**	**6**	**11**	**15**	**26**

80.81: EXC/DESTR SHOULD LES NEC

Type of Patients	Observed Patients	Avg. Stay	Vari-ance	Percentiles						
				10th	25th	50th	75th	90th	95th	99th
1. SINGLE DX										
0–19 Years	1	1.0	0	1	1	1	1	1	1	1
20–34	9	1.6	<1	1	1	1	2	2	4	4
35–49	13	1.7	<1	1	1	2	2	3	3	4
50–64	21	1.9	3	1	1	1	2	4	7	7
65+	2	2.9	3	1	1	4	4	4	4	4
2. MULTIPLE DX										
0–19 Years	8	5.1	20	1	1	5	11	11	11	11
20–34	33	2.4	4	1	1	2	3	4	7	10
35–49	168	2.8	17	1	1	1	3	6	10	15
50–64	353	2.4	10	1	1	1	2	5	7	14
65+	374	4.1	24	1	1	2	5	11	14	21
TOTAL SINGLE DX	**46**	**1.7**	**2**	**1**	**1**	**1**	**2**	**4**	**4**	**7**
TOTAL MULTIPLE DX	**936**	**3.2**	**18**	**1**	**1**	**2**	**4**	**8**	**12**	**20**
TOTAL										
0–19 Years	9	3.8	17	1	1	1	8	11	11	11
20–34	42	2.2	3	1	1	2	2	4	7	10
35–49	181	2.7	15	1	1	1	3	6	9	15
50–64	374	2.4	10	1	1	1	2	5	7	14
65+	376	4.1	24	1	1	2	5	11	14	21
GRAND TOTAL	**982**	**3.2**	**17**	**1**	**1**	**2**	**3**	**7**	**12**	**20**

80.82: EXC/DESTR ELBOW LES NEC

Type of Patients	Observed Patients	Avg. Stay	Vari-ance	Percentiles						
				10th	25th	50th	75th	90th	95th	99th
1. SINGLE DX										
0–19 Years	0									
20–34	2	1.5	<1	1	1	1	2	2	2	2
35–49	6	2.3	2	1	1	2	3	5	5	5
50–64	4	1.5	<1	1	1	1	1	3	3	3
65+	1	1.0	0	1	1	1	1	1	1	1
2. MULTIPLE DX										
0–19 Years	6	5.0	4	2	4	5	5	5	10	10
20–34	16	3.6	6	1	2	3	7	7	7	7
35–49	35	3.0	5	1	2	3	3	6	9	12
50–64	33	4.4	25	1	1	3	6	12	15	23
65+	23	3.2	8	1	1	2	4	7	8	13
TOTAL SINGLE DX	**13**	**1.9**	**1**	**1**	**1**	**1**	**3**	**3**	**5**	**5**
TOTAL MULTIPLE DX	**113**	**3.7**	**11**	**1**	**1**	**3**	**5**	**7**	**10**	**15**
TOTAL										
0–19 Years	6	5.0	4	2	4	5	5	5	10	10
20–34	18	3.4	5	1	2	3	6	7	7	7
35–49	41	2.9	4	1	2	3	3	5	9	12
50–64	37	4.1	24	1	1	3	5	7	15	23
65+	24	3.1	7	1	1	2	4	7	8	13
GRAND TOTAL	**126**	**3.5**	**10**	**1**	**1**	**3**	**5**	**7**	**9**	**15**

80.84: EXC/DESTR HAND LES NEC

Type of Patients	Observed Patients	Avg. Stay	Vari-ance	Percentiles						
				10th	25th	50th	75th	90th	95th	99th
1. SINGLE DX										
0–19 Years	0									
20–34	11	2.7	3	1	2	2	3	7	7	7
35–49	5	1.7	2	1	1	1	1	5	5	5
50–64	4	2.4	3	1	1	2	2	5	5	5
65+	0									
2. MULTIPLE DX										
0–19 Years	9	5.1	29	1	2	3	4	15	15	15
20–34	21	3.8	8	2	2	3	5	7	9	14
35–49	22	3.6	8	2	2	3	4	7	9	13
50–64	25	6.0	31	2	3	3	5	17	17	23
65+	23	4.2	9	1	2	3	6	10	10	10
TOTAL SINGLE DX	**20**	**2.4**	**3**	**1**	**1**	**2**	**3**	**5**	**7**	**7**
TOTAL MULTIPLE DX	**100**	**4.5**	**16**	**1**	**2**	**3**	**5**	**10**	**15**	**17**
TOTAL										
0–19 Years	9	5.1	29	1	2	3	4	15	15	15
20–34	32	3.4	6	2	2	2	4	7	7	14
35–49	27	3.2	7	1	2	2	3	7	9	13
50–64	29	5.6	29	2	3	3	5	17	17	23
65+	23	4.2	9	1	2	3	6	10	10	10
GRAND TOTAL	**120**	**4.2**	**14**	**1**	**2**	**3**	**5**	**9**	**14**	**17**

80.85: EXC/DESTR HIP LESION NEC

Type of Patients	Observed Patients	Avg. Stay	Variance	Percentiles 10th	25th	50th	75th	90th	95th	99th
1. SINGLE DX										
0–19 Years	2	3.3	1	2	2	4	4	4	4	4
20–34	6	1.0	0	1	1	1	1	1	1	1
35–49	8	2.2	3	1	1	2	4	5	5	5
50–64	6	1.2	<1	1	1	1	1	2	2	2
65+	0									
2. MULTIPLE DX										
0–19 Years	8	4.3	4	2	3	4	5	6	9	9
20–34	12	7.1	36	1	3	6	9	21	22	22
35–49	40	7.0	79	1	1	4	9	14	30	43
50–64	53	9.3	222	1	2	4	8	18	64	64
65+	68	7.9	50	2	3	5	11	18	25	34
TOTAL SINGLE DX	**22**	**1.7**	**2**	**1**	**1**	**1**	**2**	**4**	**4**	**5**
TOTAL MULTIPLE DX	**181**	**7.9**	**99**	**1**	**2**	**5**	**9**	**17**	**25**	**64**
TOTAL										
0–19 Years	10	4.1	4	2	3	4	5	6	9	9
20–34	18	5.6	34	1	1	3	9	11	21	22
35–49	48	6.3	71	1	1	4	8	13	30	43
50–64	59	8.6	207	1	2	4	7	16	46	64
65+	68	7.9	50	2	3	5	11	18	25	34
GRAND TOTAL	**203**	**7.3**	**94**	**1**	**2**	**4**	**9**	**16**	**25**	**64**

80.86: EXC/DESTR KNEE LES NEC

Type of Patients	Observed Patients	Avg. Stay	Variance	Percentiles 10th	25th	50th	75th	90th	95th	99th
1. SINGLE DX										
0–19 Years	12	2.7	3	1	1	2	4	5	6	6
20–34	25	2.5	5	1	1	2	3	5	6	11
35–49	21	2.7	4	1	1	2	3	7	7	7
50–64	15	3.1	3	1	1	3	4	6	6	6
65+	2	6.4	10	1	8	8	8	8	8	8
2. MULTIPLE DX										
0–19 Years	26	3.9	6	1	3	3	4	8	11	11
20–34	84	4.6	9	1	3	4	6	9	9	15
35–49	151	6.7	59	1	2	4	7	18	21	33
50–64	197	6.8	47	2	3	5	8	15	20	32
65+	194	6.5	20	2	3	6	8	12	16	22
TOTAL SINGLE DX	**75**	**2.9**	**5**	**1**	**1**	**2**	**4**	**6**	**8**	**11**
TOTAL MULTIPLE DX	**652**	**6.2**	**34**	**2**	**3**	**4**	**8**	**12**	**18**	**32**
TOTAL										
0–19 Years	38	3.5	6	1	2	3	4	6	8	11
20–34	109	4.2	9	1	2	4	5	8	9	15
35–49	172	6.2	54	1	2	4	7	17	21	33
50–64	212	6.6	45	1	3	4	8	14	20	32
65+	196	6.5	20	2	3	6	8	12	16	22
GRAND TOTAL	**727**	**5.9**	**32**	**1**	**3**	**4**	**7**	**12**	**17**	**31**

80.87: EXC/DESTR ANKLE LES NEC

Type of Patients	Observed Patients	Avg. Stay	Variance	Percentiles 10th	25th	50th	75th	90th	95th	99th
1. SINGLE DX										
0–19 Years	1	2.0	0	2	2	2	2	2	2	2
20–34	7	2.4	2	1	1	2	4	4	4	4
35–49	6	3.2	3	1	1	4	4	5	5	5
50–64	3	2.0	0	2	2	2	2	2	2	2
65+	0									
2. MULTIPLE DX										
0–19 Years	9	6.5	15	1	1	9	9	10	10	10
20–34	22	4.2	10	1	1	3	8	8	10	11
35–49	47	4.8	39	1	1	3	5	13	23	27
50–64	37	6.8	69	1	2	3	9	12	26	46
65+	35	7.4	58	1	3	4	9	21	21	35
TOTAL SINGLE DX	**17**	**2.5**	**2**	**1**	**2**	**2**	**4**	**4**	**4**	**5**
TOTAL MULTIPLE DX	**150**	**5.9**	**45**	**1**	**2**	**3**	**8**	**12**	**21**	**29**
TOTAL										
0–19 Years	10	6.2	15	1	2	9	9	10	10	10
20–34	29	3.7	8	1	1	2	6	8	9	11
35–49	53	4.7	36	1	1	3	4	13	23	27
50–64	40	6.3	64	1	2	3	9	12	26	46
65+	35	7.4	58	1	3	4	9	21	21	35
GRAND TOTAL	**167**	**5.5**	**41**	**1**	**2**	**3**	**8**	**12**	**21**	**29**

80.9: OTHER JOINT EXCISION

Type of Patients	Observed Patients	Avg. Stay	Variance	Percentiles 10th	25th	50th	75th	90th	95th	99th
1. SINGLE DX										
0–19 Years	4	1.5	<1	1	1	1	2	2	2	2
20–34	3	1.0	0	1	1	1	1	1	1	1
35–49	2	1.5	<1	1	1	1	2	2	2	2
50–64	1	3.0	0	3	3	3	3	3	3	3
65+	0									
2. MULTIPLE DX										
0–19 Years	12	3.1	22	1	1	1	3	15	15	18
20–34	10	4.6	39	1	1	3	5	9	28	28
35–49	23	5.2	28	2	2	3	5	11	12	28
50–64	30	4.8	21	1	2	3	6	9	17	23
65+	20	6.7	12	2	4	6	10	10	14	14
TOTAL SINGLE DX	**10**	**1.6**	**<1**	**1**	**1**	**1**	**2**	**3**	**3**	**3**
TOTAL MULTIPLE DX	**95**	**4.9**	**24**	**1**	**1**	**3**	**6**	**10**	**14**	**28**
TOTAL										
0–19 Years	16	2.5	14	1	1	1	2	4	15	18
20–34	13	4.0	35	1	1	3	4	9	9	28
35–49	25	4.9	27	2	2	3	5	11	12	28
50–64	31	4.7	20	1	2	3	6	9	12	23
65+	20	6.7	12	2	4	6	10	10	14	14
GRAND TOTAL	**105**	**4.4**	**22**	**1**	**1**	**3**	**6**	**10**	**13**	**28**

81.0: SPINAL FUSION

Type of Patients	Observed Patients	Avg. Stay	Vari-ance	Percentiles 10th	25th	50th	75th	90th	95th	99th
1. SINGLE DX										
0–19 Years	271	5.1	4	3	4	5	6	7	9	12
20–34	537	2.8	4	1	1	2	4	5	6	10
35–49	2,150	2.2	3	1	1	2	3	4	5	7
50–64	1,538	2.3	3	1	1	2	3	4	5	8
65+	238	2.5	2	1	1	2	3	4	5	7
2. MULTIPLE DX										
0–19 Years	806	7.4	31	4	5	6	8	13	16	27
20–34	1,839	4.5	16	1	2	4	5	8	12	20
35–49	8,747	3.4	11	1	1	3	4	6	8	17
50–64	10,791	3.9	12	1	2	3	5	7	9	17
65+	6,627	4.8	17	1	3	4	6	8	12	23
TOTAL SINGLE DX	**4,734**	**2.6**	**3**	**1**	**1**	**2**	**4**	**5**	**6**	**9**
TOTAL MULTIPLE DX	**28,810**	**4.2**	**15**	**1**	**2**	**3**	**5**	**7**	**10**	**20**
TOTAL										
0–19 Years	1,077	6.8	25	4	4	6	7	11	15	23
20–34	2,376	4.1	14	1	2	3	5	8	11	19
35–49	10,897	3.1	9	1	1	2	4	6	7	16
50–64	12,329	3.7	12	1	2	3	5	7	9	16
65+	6,865	4.8	17	1	3	4	6	8	12	22
GRAND TOTAL	**33,544**	**3.9**	**14**	**1**	**2**	**3**	**5**	**7**	**9**	**19**

81.01: ATLAS-AXIS SPINAL FUSION

Type of Patients	Observed Patients	Avg. Stay	Vari-ance	Percentiles 10th	25th	50th	75th	90th	95th	99th
1. SINGLE DX										
0–19 Years	4	6.0	16	2	3	4	11	11	11	11
20–34	2	1.6	<1	1	1	2	2	2	2	2
35–49	2	4.0	1	3	3	5	5	5	5	5
50–64	7	2.3	<1	1	2	2	3	4	4	4
65+	1	4.0	0	4	4	4	4	4	4	4
2. MULTIPLE DX										
0–19 Years	9	7.3	9	3	6	7	10	11	11	11
20–34	11	8.9	37	2	3	8	14	15	20	20
35–49	33	5.1	28	1	1	3	7	14	19	21
50–64	49	5.7	52	2	2	3	6	12	20	42
65+	95	7.5	30	2	3	6	11	14	16	28
TOTAL SINGLE DX	**16**	**3.8**	**9**	**1**	**2**	**3**	**4**	**11**	**11**	**11**
TOTAL MULTIPLE DX	**197**	**6.8**	**33**	**2**	**3**	**5**	**10**	**13**	**16**	**28**
TOTAL										
0–19 Years	13	7.1	10	3	4	7	11	11	11	11
20–34	13	7.6	39	2	2	6	13	15	20	20
35–49	35	5.0	26	1	1	3	7	14	19	21
50–64	56	5.3	47	2	2	3	5	10	20	42
65+	96	7.5	29	2	3	6	11	13	16	28
GRAND TOTAL	**213**	**6.6**	**32**	**2**	**2**	**5**	**10**	**13**	**16**	**28**

81.02: ANT CERVICAL FUSION NEC

Type of Patients	Observed Patients	Avg. Stay	Vari-ance	Percentiles 10th	25th	50th	75th	90th	95th	99th
1. SINGLE DX										
0–19 Years	10	2.7	10	1	1	2	2	5	13	13
20–34	228	1.5	<1	1	1	1	2	2	4	5
35–49	1,438	1.5	<1	1	1	1	2	2	3	4
50–64	973	1.6	1	1	1	1	2	3	3	5
65+	125	1.7	1	1	1	1	2	3	4	6
2. MULTIPLE DX										
0–19 Years	28	9.7	320	2	3	5	8	13	31	91
20–34	516	2.4	11	1	1	1	2	5	7	19
35–49	4,263	2.0	4	1	1	1	2	3	5	11
50–64	4,466	2.3	6	1	1	2	2	4	6	14
65+	1,562	3.4	21	1	1	2	3	7	12	26
TOTAL SINGLE DX	**2,774**	**1.5**	**<1**	**1**	**1**	**1**	**2**	**2**	**3**	**5**
TOTAL MULTIPLE DX	**10,835**	**2.4**	**9**	**1**	**1**	**2**	**2**	**4**	**7**	**15**
TOTAL										
0–19 Years	38	8.0	253	1	2	4	8	13	17	91
20–34	744	2.1	8	1	1	1	2	4	6	14
35–49	5,701	1.9	4	1	1	1	2	3	4	10
50–64	5,439	2.1	5	1	1	1	2	4	6	13
65+	1,687	3.3	20	1	1	2	3	7	12	26
GRAND TOTAL	**13,609**	**2.2**	**8**	**1**	**1**	**1**	**2**	**4**	**6**	**14**

81.03: POST CERVICAL FUSION NEC

Type of Patients	Observed Patients	Avg. Stay	Vari-ance	Percentiles 10th	25th	50th	75th	90th	95th	99th
1. SINGLE DX										
0–19 Years	7	4.2	11	2	2	2	5	10	10	10
20–34	7	3.3	5	1	2	3	3	9	9	9
35–49	32	2.9	5	1	1	2	4	5	6	14
50–64	40	2.5	1	1	2	2	3	4	4	6
65+	12	2.8	3	1	2	2	3	5	8	8
2. MULTIPLE DX										
0–19 Years	25	7.3	25	3	4	5	12	15	18	19
20–34	50	6.3	27	2	3	5	8	12	20	25
35–49	169	4.8	21	1	2	3	5	11	17	27
50–64	320	4.5	19	1	2	3	5	9	11	19
65+	272	5.3	21	2	2	4	7	11	13	23
TOTAL SINGLE DX	**98**	**2.9**	**4**	**1**	**2**	**2**	**3**	**5**	**6**	**10**
TOTAL MULTIPLE DX	**836**	**5.0**	**21**	**2**	**2**	**4**	**6**	**10**	**13**	**22**
TOTAL										
0–19 Years	32	6.7	24	2	3	4	10	14	16	19
20–34	57	5.8	25	2	3	4	8	11	20	25
35–49	201	4.5	19	1	2	3	5	9	14	25
50–64	360	4.3	18	1	2	3	5	8	11	17
65+	284	5.2	20	2	2	4	7	10	13	23
GRAND TOTAL	**934**	**4.8**	**20**	**1**	**2**	**4**	**6**	**10**	**13**	**22**

81.04: ANTERIOR DORSAL FUSION

Type of Patients	Observed Patients	Avg. Stay	Vari-ance	Percentiles						
				10th	25th	50th	75th	90th	95th	99th
1. SINGLE DX										
0–19 Years	35	6.0	5	4	5	5	6	8	10	15
20–34	9	7.7	10	5	6	6	10	14	14	14
35–49	6	5.7	1	4	5	6	6	7	8	8
50–64	6	6.9	6	2	6	7	9	9	9	9
65+	0									
2. MULTIPLE DX										
0–19 Years	137	8.9	42	5	5	7	9	15	19	40
20–34	50	9.7	33	3	6	8	12	18	20	33
35–49	79	9.5	39	4	5	7	12	20	22	28
50–64	95	10.7	54	2	6	8	15	21	24	28
65+	52	10.9	98	1	5	8	14	22	29	56
TOTAL SINGLE DX	**56**	**6.2**	**6**	**4**	**5**	**5**	**6**	**9**	**10**	**15**
TOTAL MULTIPLE DX	**413**	**9.7**	**50**	**4**	**6**	**7**	**12**	**19**	**22**	**40**
TOTAL										
0–19 Years	172	8.4	36	5	5	6	9	15	18	40
20–34	59	9.5	30	3	6	8	12	16	20	33
35–49	85	9.1	36	4	5	7	12	20	21	28
50–64	101	10.6	52	2	6	8	15	21	24	28
65+	52	10.9	98	1	5	8	14	22	29	56
GRAND TOTAL	**469**	**9.2**	**46**	**4**	**5**	**7**	**11**	**18**	**21**	**40**

81.05: POSTERIOR DORSAL FUSION

Type of Patients	Observed Patients	Avg. Stay	Vari-ance	Percentiles						
				10th	25th	50th	75th	90th	95th	99th
1. SINGLE DX										
0–19 Years	175	5.1	2	4	4	5	6	7	8	11
20–34	26	5.7	10	2	3	5	8	9	11	14
35–49	18	6.2	28	2	3	5	7	10	19	23
50–64	15	5.0	4	2	4	5	6	8	9	9
65+	0									
2. MULTIPLE DX										
0–19 Years	489	7.1	16	4	5	6	8	12	15	20
20–34	174	8.7	42	4	5	7	10	16	18	45
35–49	176	9.0	50	3	5	7	11	16	20	43
50–64	289	9.1	54	4	5	7	11	17	22	50
65+	237	9.6	54	4	5	8	11	18	22	44
TOTAL SINGLE DX	**234**	**5.2**	**4**	**3**	**4**	**5**	**6**	**8**	**9**	**12**
TOTAL MULTIPLE DX	**1,365**	**8.1**	**35**	**4**	**5**	**7**	**9**	**15**	**18**	**32**
TOTAL										
0–19 Years	664	6.6	13	4	5	6	7	10	14	20
20–34	200	8.3	38	3	5	7	10	15	18	45
35–49	194	8.7	49	3	4	7	11	16	20	43
50–64	304	8.9	52	4	5	7	10	16	22	50
65+	237	9.6	54	4	5	8	11	18	22	44
GRAND TOTAL	**1,599**	**7.6**	**31**	**4**	**5**	**6**	**8**	**14**	**17**	**29**

81.06: ANTERIOR LUMBAR FUSION

Type of Patients	Observed Patients	Avg. Stay	Vari-ance	Percentiles						
				10th	25th	50th	75th	90th	95th	99th
1. SINGLE DX										
0–19 Years	8	4.8	1	4	5	5	5	7	7	7
20–34	60	3.6	2	2	3	3	4	6	6	7
35–49	162	3.5	2	2	2	3	4	5	6	8
50–64	98	3.6	3	2	2	3	4	6	6	11
65+	5	2.2	<1	2	2	2	2	3	3	3
2. MULTIPLE DX										
0–19 Years	20	6.8	15	4	4	6	8	10	10	27
20–34	203	4.4	7	2	3	4	5	7	10	16
35–49	732	4.8	18	2	3	4	5	7	9	22
50–64	718	5.6	25	2	3	4	6	9	12	22
65+	182	6.8	45	2	3	4	7	15	20	35
TOTAL SINGLE DX	**333**	**3.6**	**2**	**2**	**2**	**3**	**4**	**6**	**6**	**8**
TOTAL MULTIPLE DX	**1,855**	**5.3**	**23**	**2**	**3**	**4**	**6**	**9**	**12**	**24**
TOTAL										
0–19 Years	28	6.1	11	4	4	5	7	10	10	27
20–34	263	4.2	6	2	3	4	5	7	9	16
35–49	894	4.6	15	2	3	4	5	7	9	20
50–64	816	5.3	23	2	3	4	6	9	12	21
65+	187	6.7	44	2	3	4	7	15	20	35
GRAND TOTAL	**2,188**	**5.0**	**20**	**2**	**3**	**4**	**6**	**8**	**11**	**23**

81.07: LAT TRANS LUMBAR FUSION

Type of Patients	Observed Patients	Avg. Stay	Vari-ance	Percentiles						
				10th	25th	50th	75th	90th	95th	99th
1. SINGLE DX										
0–19 Years	1	4.0	0	4	4	4	4	4	4	4
20–34	16	3.4	3	2	2	3	4	7	7	7
35–49	37	3.1	2	1	2	3	4	5	5	7
50–64	35	3.0	2	1	2	3	4	5	5	6
65+	8	4.0	4	2	3	3	7	7	7	7
2. MULTIPLE DX										
0–19 Years	3	8.2	41	3	3	4	16	16	16	16
20–34	51	5.2	9	3	3	4	6	9	12	15
35–49	230	4.2	6	2	3	4	5	6	7	15
50–64	368	4.5	8	2	3	4	5	7	8	13
65+	468	4.8	6	3	3	4	6	7	9	16
TOTAL SINGLE DX	**97**	**3.2**	**2**	**1**	**2**	**3**	**4**	**5**	**6**	**7**
TOTAL MULTIPLE DX	**1,120**	**4.6**	**7**	**2**	**3**	**4**	**5**	**7**	**8**	**16**
TOTAL										
0–19 Years	4	7.7	38	3	4	4	16	16	16	16
20–34	67	4.8	8	2	3	4	6	7	12	15
35–49	267	4.0	5	2	3	4	5	6	7	15
50–64	403	4.4	7	2	3	4	5	6	7	12
65+	476	4.8	6	3	3	4	6	7	9	16
GRAND TOTAL	**1,217**	**4.5**	**7**	**2**	**3**	**4**	**5**	**7**	**8**	**16**

81.08: POSTERIOR LUMBAR FUSION

Type of Patients	Observed Patients	Avg. Stay	Vari-ance	Percentiles						
				10th	25th	50th	75th	90th	95th	99th
1. SINGLE DX										
0–19 Years	31	4.3	5	2	3	4	5	6	7	16
20–34	189	3.7	2	2	3	4	4	6	7	9
35–49	452	3.6	2	2	3	4	4	5	6	8
50–64	361	3.6	2	2	3	4	4	5	6	8
65+	86	3.3	2	2	2	3	4	5	6	7
2. MULTIPLE DX										
0–19 Years	93	6.7	33	3	4	5	8	14	17	23
20–34	779	4.5	7	2	3	4	5	7	9	13
35–49	3,058	4.3	7	2	3	4	5	7	8	15
50–64	4,474	4.6	7	2	3	4	5	7	8	15
65+	3,748	4.9	9	3	3	4	6	8	9	16
TOTAL SINGLE DX	**1,119**	**3.6**	**2**	**2**	**3**	**4**	**4**	**6**	**6**	**8**
TOTAL MULTIPLE DX	**12,152**	**4.7**	**8**	**2**	**3**	**4**	**5**	**7**	**9**	**16**
TOTAL										
0–19 Years	124	6.1	27	3	3	4	7	11	17	23
20–34	968	4.3	6	2	3	4	5	6	9	13
35–49	3,510	4.2	6	2	3	4	5	6	8	13
50–64	4,835	4.5	7	2	3	4	5	7	8	14
65+	3,834	4.9	9	2	3	4	6	8	9	16
GRAND TOTAL	**13,271**	**4.6**	**8**	**2**	**3**	**4**	**5**	**7**	**9**	**15**

81.1: FOOT & ANKLE ARTHRODESIS

Type of Patients	Observed Patients	Avg. Stay	Vari-ance	Percentiles						
				10th	25th	50th	75th	90th	95th	99th
1. SINGLE DX										
0–19 Years	11	1.7	1	1	1	1	2	3	5	5
20–34	27	2.0	1	1	1	2	2	3	5	6
35–49	61	1.9	<1	1	1	2	2	3	3	5
50–64	72	1.9	<1	1	1	2	2	3	3	6
65+	22	2.0	1	1	1	2	2	3	6	6
2. MULTIPLE DX										
0–19 Years	60	1.9	<1	1	1	2	2	3	4	5
20–34	126	2.3	5	1	1	2	3	4	4	9
35–49	347	2.7	6	1	2	2	3	5	6	13
50–64	602	2.5	3	1	2	2	3	4	4	11
65+	493	2.6	2	1	2	2	3	4	5	7
TOTAL SINGLE DX	**193**	**1.9**	**1**	**1**	**1**	**2**	**2**	**3**	**3**	**6**
TOTAL MULTIPLE DX	**1,628**	**2.5**	**3**	**1**	**2**	**2**	**3**	**4**	**5**	**9**
TOTAL										
0–19 Years	71	1.9	<1	1	1	2	2	3	4	5
20–34	153	2.2	4	1	1	2	3	3	4	9
35–49	408	2.6	6	1	1	2	3	4	6	11
50–64	674	2.4	3	1	2	2	3	4	4	7
65+	515	2.5	2	1	2	2	3	4	5	7
GRAND TOTAL	**1,821**	**2.4**	**3**	**1**	**2**	**2**	**3**	**4**	**5**	**9**

81.11: ANKLE FUSION

Type of Patients	Observed Patients	Avg. Stay	Vari-ance	Percentiles						
				10th	25th	50th	75th	90th	95th	99th
1. SINGLE DX										
0–19 Years	1	5.0	0	5	5	5	5	5	5	5
20–34	9	1.6	<1	1	1	1	2	3	3	3
35–49	35	2.0	<1	1	1	2	3	3	3	5
50–64	35	2.1	1	1	1	2	3	3	5	6
65+	13	2.1	2	1	1	2	2	2	6	6
2. MULTIPLE DX										
0–19 Years	6	1.8	2	1	1	1	2	5	5	5
20–34	44	2.6	11	1	1	2	3	4	4	29
35–49	163	3.1	11	1	2	2	3	6	9	21
50–64	286	2.6	4	1	2	2	3	4	5	12
65+	237	2.6	2	1	2	2	3	4	5	8
TOTAL SINGLE DX	**93**	**2.0**	**1**	**1**	**1**	**2**	**2**	**3**	**5**	**6**
TOTAL MULTIPLE DX	**736**	**2.7**	**5**	**1**	**2**	**2**	**3**	**4**	**6**	**12**
TOTAL										
0–19 Years	7	2.0	2	1	1	1	3	5	5	5
20–34	53	2.4	9	1	1	2	3	4	4	29
35–49	198	2.9	10	1	1	2	3	5	7	21
50–64	321	2.5	4	1	1	2	3	4	5	12
65+	250	2.6	2	1	2	2	3	4	5	8
GRAND TOTAL	**829**	**2.6**	**5**	**1**	**2**	**2**	**3**	**4**	**5**	**12**

81.12: TRIPLE ARTHRODESIS

Type of Patients	Observed Patients	Avg. Stay	Vari-ance	Percentiles						
				10th	25th	50th	75th	90th	95th	99th
1. SINGLE DX										
0–19 Years	4	1.9	<1	1	1	2	2	3	3	3
20–34	9	2.4	2	1	2	2	3	3	6	6
35–49	7	1.6	<1	1	1	1	2	3	3	3
50–64	17	2.0	<1	1	2	2	2	3	3	3
65+	4	1.7	<1	1	1	2	2	2	2	2
2. MULTIPLE DX										
0–19 Years	33	2.1	<1	1	1	2	3	3	4	5
20–34	31	2.0	<1	1	1	2	2	3	3	5
35–49	65	2.6	2	1	2	2	3	5	5	6
50–64	138	2.4	1	1	2	2	3	4	4	6
65+	120	2.8	2	1	2	3	3	5	5	7
TOTAL SINGLE DX	**41**	**2.0**	**<1**	**1**	**1**	**2**	**2**	**3**	**3**	**6**
TOTAL MULTIPLE DX	**387**	**2.5**	**1**	**1**	**2**	**2**	**3**	**4**	**5**	**6**
TOTAL										
0–19 Years	37	2.1	<1	1	1	2	3	3	4	5
20–34	40	2.1	1	1	1	2	2	3	4	6
35–49	72	2.5	2	1	2	2	3	4	5	6
50–64	155	2.4	1	1	2	2	3	4	4	6
65+	124	2.8	2	1	2	2	3	5	5	7
GRAND TOTAL	**428**	**2.5**	**1**	**1**	**2**	**2**	**3**	**4**	**5**	**6**

81.13: SUBTALAR FUSION

Type of Patients	Observed Patients	Avg. Stay	Vari-ance	Percentiles						
				10th	25th	50th	75th	90th	95th	99th
1. SINGLE DX										
0–19 Years	4	1.0	0	1	1	1	1	1	1	1
20–34	6	1.9	2	1	1	1	2	5	5	5
35–49	8	1.8	<1	1	1	2	2	3	3	3
50–64	11	1.6	<1	1	1	2	2	2	3	3
65+	2	2.5	<1	1	3	3	3	3	3	3
2. MULTIPLE DX										
0–19 Years	12	1.5	<1	1	1	2	2	2	2	2
20–34	30	2.0	1	1	1	2	2	4	5	6
35–49	60	2.0	1	1	1	2	2	3	4	6
50–64	74	2.4	1	1	2	2	3	3	4	6
65+	56	2.2	1	1	1	2	3	4	4	5
TOTAL SINGLE DX	**31**	**1.7**	**<1**	**1**	**1**	**1**	**2**	**3**	**3**	**5**
TOTAL MULTIPLE DX	**232**	**2.2**	**1**	**1**	**1**	**2**	**3**	**4**	**4**	**6**
TOTAL										
0–19 Years	16	1.4	<1	1	1	1	2	2	2	2
20–34	36	2.0	1	1	1	2	2	4	5	6
35–49	68	2.0	1	1	1	2	2	3	4	6
50–64	85	2.3	1	1	2	2	3	3	4	6
65+	58	2.2	1	1	1	2	3	4	4	5
GRAND TOTAL	**263**	**2.1**	**1**	**1**	**1**	**2**	**3**	**3**	**4**	**6**

81.2: ARTHRODESIS OF OTH JOINT

Type of Patients	Observed Patients	Avg. Stay	Vari-ance	Percentiles						
				10th	25th	50th	75th	90th	95th	99th
1. SINGLE DX										
0–19 Years	5	4.0	47	1	1	1	2	20	20	20
20–34	6	1.6	<1	1	1	1	2	3	3	3
35–49	16	1.6	<1	1	1	1	2	3	3	3
50–64	10	1.4	<1	1	1	1	1	3	4	4
65+	2	2.7	6	1	1	1	5	5	5	5
2. MULTIPLE DX										
0–19 Years	10	2.3	3	1	1	1	4	4	6	6
20–34	28	3.2	6	1	1	2	4	8	8	9
35–49	62	3.2	16	1	1	2	4	5	11	29
50–64	72	4.0	15	1	1	2	5	9	15	16
65+	71	5.7	27	1	2	4	7	12	17	31
TOTAL SINGLE DX	**39**	**2.0**	**9**	**1**	**1**	**1**	**2**	**3**	**4**	**20**
TOTAL MULTIPLE DX	**243**	**4.1**	**19**	**1**	**1**	**3**	**5**	**8**	**14**	**17**
TOTAL										
0–19 Years	15	2.9	18	1	1	1	4	4	20	20
20–34	34	2.9	6	1	1	2	4	7	8	9
35–49	78	2.8	13	1	1	2	3	5	7	29
50–64	82	3.6	14	1	1	2	5	8	15	16
65+	73	5.6	27	1	2	4	7	12	17	31
GRAND TOTAL	**282**	**3.8**	**18**	**1**	**1**	**2**	**5**	**8**	**13**	**20**

81.26: METACARPOCARPAL FUSION

Type of Patients	Observed Patients	Avg. Stay	Vari-ance	Percentiles						
				10th	25th	50th	75th	90th	95th	99th
1. SINGLE DX										
0–19 Years	0									
20–34	2	1.9	1	1	1	1	3	3	3	3
35–49	5	1.9	<1	1	1	2	2	3	3	3
50–64	4	1.0	0	1	1	1	1	1	1	1
65+	0									
2. MULTIPLE DX										
0–19 Years	1	1.0	0	1	1	1	1	1	1	1
20–34	10	2.4	5	1	1	1	3	5	8	8
35–49	21	1.5	<1	1	1	1	2	3	3	4
50–64	14	1.6	<1	1	1	1	2	3	3	3
65+	24	2.8	6	1	1	2	3	7	8	9
TOTAL SINGLE DX	**11**	**1.5**	**<1**	**1**	**1**	**1**	**2**	**3**	**3**	**3**
TOTAL MULTIPLE DX	**70**	**2.1**	**3**	**1**	**1**	**1**	**2**	**5**	**6**	**8**
TOTAL										
0–19 Years	1	1.0	0	1	1	1	1	1	1	1
20–34	12	2.3	4	1	1	1	3	5	8	8
35–49	26	1.6	<1	1	1	1	2	3	3	4
50–64	18	1.4	<1	1	1	1	2	2	3	3
65+	24	2.8	6	1	1	2	3	7	8	9
GRAND TOTAL	**81**	**2.0**	**3**	**1**	**1**	**1**	**2**	**4**	**6**	**8**

81.3: SPINAL REFUSION

Type of Patients	Observed Patients	Avg. Stay	Vari-ance	Percentiles						
				10th	25th	50th	75th	90th	95th	99th
1. SINGLE DX										
0–19 Years	4	4.4	2	3	3	4	6	6	6	6
20–34	26	3.1	1	2	2	3	4	4	4	7
35–49	91	2.5	2	1	1	2	3	4	5	7
50–64	57	3.1	4	1	2	3	4	6	7	8
65+	11	3.7	9	1	2	2	4	9	9	9
2. MULTIPLE DX										
0–19 Years	36	4.7	15	2	3	4	5	7	7	31
20–34	120	4.4	14	2	3	3	5	7	9	27
35–49	652	3.8	7	1	2	3	5	7	9	15
50–64	734	4.3	11	1	2	4	5	7	10	17
65+	374	5.7	20	2	3	4	7	10	13	23
TOTAL SINGLE DX	**189**	**2.9**	**3**	**1**	**2**	**3**	**4**	**5**	**7**	**9**
TOTAL MULTIPLE DX	**1,916**	**4.5**	**13**	**2**	**2**	**4**	**5**	**8**	**10**	**19**
TOTAL										
0–19 Years	40	4.6	14	2	3	4	5	7	7	31
20–34	146	4.2	12	2	3	3	5	6	8	27
35–49	743	3.7	7	1	2	3	4	7	9	14
50–64	791	4.3	10	1	2	4	5	7	9	16
65+	385	5.6	20	2	3	4	7	10	13	23
GRAND TOTAL	**2,105**	**4.3**	**12**	**1**	**2**	**4**	**5**	**7**	**10**	**19**

81.32: ANT CERV REFUSION NEC

Type of Patients	Observed Patients	Avg. Stay	Vari-ance	Percentiles						
				10th	25th	50th	75th	90th	95th	99th
1. SINGLE DX										
0–19 Years	0									
20–34	1	1.0	0	1	1	1	1	1	1	1
35–49	24	1.6	<1	1	1	1	2	3	4	4
50–64	17	1.6	<1	1	1	1	2	3	3	3
65+	3	1.6	2	1	1	1	1	4	4	4
2. MULTIPLE DX										
0–19 Years	0									
20–34	6	2.3	<1	2	2	2	3	3	3	3
35–49	151	2.2	3	1	1	2	3	4	5	7
50–64	133	2.6	17	1	1	2	3	4	7	16
65+	28	4.1	23	1	1	2	7	9	15	24
TOTAL SINGLE DX	**45**	**1.6**	**<1**	**1**	**1**	**1**	**2**	**3**	**4**	**4**
TOTAL MULTIPLE DX	**318**	**2.6**	**11**	**1**	**1**	**2**	**3**	**5**	**7**	**15**
TOTAL										
0–19 Years	0									
20–34	7	2.2	<1	1	2	2	3	3	3	3
35–49	175	2.1	2	1	1	2	2	4	5	7
50–64	150	2.5	15	1	1	2	3	4	6	16
65+	31	3.9	21	1	1	2	7	8	15	24
GRAND TOTAL	**363**	**2.5**	**10**	**1**	**1**	**2**	**3**	**4**	**7**	**15**

81.33: POST CERV REFUSION NEC

Type of Patients	Observed Patients	Avg. Stay	Vari-ance	Percentiles						
				10th	25th	50th	75th	90th	95th	99th
1. SINGLE DX										
0–19 Years	0									
20–34	1	3.0	0	3	3	3	3	3	3	3
35–49	17	2.5	3	1	1	2	3	5	7	7
50–64	5	2.4	1	1	2	2	3	4	4	4
65+	1	9.0	0	9	9	9	9	9	9	9
2. MULTIPLE DX										
0–19 Years	2	4.6	10	2	2	7	7	7	7	7
20–34	9	3.7	1	3	3	4	4	5	5	5
35–49	103	3.4	5	1	2	3	4	7	9	11
50–64	80	3.5	5	1	2	3	4	7	7	14
65+	21	5.5	14	2	3	4	6	12	12	14
TOTAL SINGLE DX	**24**	**3.3**	**7**	**1**	**1**	**2**	**4**	**9**	**9**	**9**
TOTAL MULTIPLE DX	**215**	**3.7**	**6**	**1**	**2**	**3**	**4**	**7**	**10**	**12**
TOTAL										
0–19 Years	2	4.6	10	2	2	7	7	7	7	7
20–34	10	3.6	1	3	3	4	4	5	5	5
35–49	120	3.3	5	1	2	3	4	6	9	11
50–64	85	3.4	5	1	2	3	4	7	7	14
65+	22	6.0	13	2	3	5	9	12	12	14
GRAND TOTAL	**239**	**3.7**	**7**	**1**	**2**	**3**	**4**	**7**	**9**	**12**

81.35: POST DORSAL REFUSION

Type of Patients	Observed Patients	Avg. Stay	Vari-ance	Percentiles						
				10th	25th	50th	75th	90th	95th	99th
1. SINGLE DX										
0–19 Years	2	5.5	<1	4	4	6	6	6	6	6
20–34	3	4.5	4	3	3	4	7	7	7	7
35–49	2	2.9	2	2	2	2	4	4	4	4
50–64	4	2.9	7	1	1	1	6	7	7	7
65+	1	3.0	0	3	3	3	3	3	3	3
2. MULTIPLE DX										
0–19 Years	18	5.7	30	2	4	5	6	7	8	31
20–34	23	5.7	23	2	3	4	7	10	18	21
35–49	28	5.5	10	2	3	5	7	9	13	14
50–64	37	6.9	22	3	4	5	9	14	16	22
65+	34	8.3	58	4	5	6	9	15	25	41
TOTAL SINGLE DX	**12**	**3.8**	**5**	**1**	**2**	**4**	**6**	**7**	**7**	**7**
TOTAL MULTIPLE DX	**140**	**6.8**	**33**	**3**	**4**	**5**	**8**	**12**	**17**	**41**
TOTAL										
0–19 Years	20	5.6	26	2	4	5	6	7	8	31
20–34	26	5.6	21	3	3	4	7	10	18	21
35–49	30	5.4	10	2	3	5	7	9	13	14
50–64	41	6.3	21	1	3	5	9	14	16	22
65+	35	8.2	58	3	5	6	9	15	21	41
GRAND TOTAL	**152**	**6.5**	**31**	**2**	**4**	**5**	**7**	**11**	**16**	**41**

81.36: ANT LUMBAR REFUSION

Type of Patients	Observed Patients	Avg. Stay	Vari-ance	Percentiles						
				10th	25th	50th	75th	90th	95th	99th
1. SINGLE DX										
0–19 Years	0									
20–34	2	4.0	0	4	4	4	4	4	4	4
35–49	3	4.1	3	3	3	3	6	6	6	6
50–64	5	4.6	3	2	4	4	7	7	7	7
65+	0									
2. MULTIPLE DX										
0–19 Years	3	5.8	6	2	7	7	7	7	7	7
20–34	9	3.6	2	3	3	3	4	6	7	7
35–49	41	5.2	9	2	3	4	8	8	10	15
50–64	45	5.6	16	2	3	5	7	9	12	23
65+	25	7.6	25	2	5	7	7	19	19	19
TOTAL SINGLE DX	**10**	**4.3**	**2**	**3**	**4**	**4**	**4**	**7**	**7**	**7**
TOTAL MULTIPLE DX	**123**	**5.8**	**15**	**2**	**3**	**5**	**7**	**9**	**15**	**21**
TOTAL										
0–19 Years	3	5.8	6	2	7	7	7	7	7	7
20–34	11	3.7	2	3	3	3	4	6	7	7
35–49	44	5.2	9	2	3	4	7	8	10	15
50–64	50	5.5	14	2	3	5	7	9	12	23
65+	25	7.6	25	2	5	7	7	19	19	19
GRAND TOTAL	**133**	**5.7**	**15**	**2**	**3**	**5**	**7**	**9**	**15**	**21**

81.37: LAT TRANS LUMB REFUSION

Type of Patients	Observed Patients	Avg. Stay	Vari-ance	Percentiles						
				10th	25th	50th	75th	90th	95th	99th
1. SINGLE DX										
0–19 Years	0									
20–34	1	2.0	0	2	2	2	2	2	2	2
35–49	7	2.8	<1	2	3	3	3	3	3	3
50–64	2	2.0	0	2	2	2	2	2	2	2
65+	1	2.0	0	2	2	2	2	2	2	2
2. MULTIPLE DX										
0–19 Years	0									
20–34	5	3.7	1	3	3	3	5	5	5	5
35–49	19	3.4	4	2	2	3	4	6	6	10
50–64	31	4.3	5	2	3	4	5	7	11	11
65+	20	4.5	2	3	3	5	5	6	7	7
TOTAL SINGLE DX	**11**	**2.6**	**<1**	**2**	**2**	**3**	**3**	**3**	**3**	**3**
TOTAL MULTIPLE DX	**75**	**4.1**	**4**	**2**	**3**	**4**	**5**	**6**	**7**	**11**
TOTAL										
0–19 Years	0									
20–34	6	3.6	1	2	3	3	5	5	5	5
35–49	26	3.2	3	2	2	3	4	5	6	10
50–64	33	4.1	5	2	3	4	5	6	11	11
65+	21	4.4	2	3	3	5	5	6	7	7
GRAND TOTAL	**86**	**3.9**	**4**	**2**	**3**	**3**	**5**	**6**	**7**	**11**

81.38: POST LUMBAR REFUSION

Type of Patients	Observed Patients	Avg. Stay	Vari-ance	Percentiles						
				10th	25th	50th	75th	90th	95th	99th
1. SINGLE DX										
0–19 Years	1	3.0	0	3	3	3	3	3	3	3
20–34	18	3.0	<1	2	2	3	4	4	4	4
35–49	37	2.9	2	1	2	3	4	4	5	7
50–64	24	4.1	2	2	3	4	5	7	7	8
65+	5	2.6	<1	2	2	2	3	4	4	4
2. MULTIPLE DX										
0–19 Years	9	3.5	2	1	3	4	4	5	7	7
20–34	62	4.5	17	2	3	4	5	6	9	27
35–49	290	4.4	7	2	3	4	5	7	9	16
50–64	391	4.7	7	2	3	4	6	7	9	16
65+	240	5.4	12	2	3	4	7	10	12	23
TOTAL SINGLE DX	**85**	**3.2**	**2**	**2**	**2**	**3**	**4**	**4**	**5**	**7**
TOTAL MULTIPLE DX	**992**	**4.7**	**9**	**2**	**3**	**4**	**6**	**7**	**10**	**18**
TOTAL										
0–19 Years	10	3.4	2	1	3	3	4	5	7	7
20–34	80	4.1	13	2	3	3	4	6	7	27
35–49	327	4.2	7	2	3	4	5	7	9	16
50–64	415	4.7	7	2	3	4	6	7	8	16
65+	245	5.3	12	2	3	4	7	10	12	23
GRAND TOTAL	**1,077**	**4.6**	**9**	**2**	**3**	**4**	**5**	**7**	**10**	**17**

81.4: OTHER LOW LIMB JOINT REP

Type of Patients	Observed Patients	Avg. Stay	Vari-ance	Percentiles						
				10th	25th	50th	75th	90th	95th	99th
1. SINGLE DX										
0–19 Years	131	1.5	1	1	1	1	2	3	4	5
20–34	178	1.4	<1	1	1	1	2	2	3	4
35–49	151	1.5	<1	1	1	1	2	2	3	5
50–64	69	2.1	2	1	1	2	3	4	5	8
65+	25	3.3	4	1	2	3	4	6	7	10
2. MULTIPLE DX										
0–19 Years	308	1.7	2	1	1	1	2	3	4	7
20–34	708	2.1	4	1	1	1	2	4	6	10
35–49	762	2.3	4	1	1	2	3	4	6	11
50–64	482	2.7	4	1	1	2	3	5	6	14
65+	225	4.0	9	1	2	3	5	8	10	12
TOTAL SINGLE DX	**554**	**1.6**	**1**	**1**	**1**	**1**	**2**	**3**	**4**	**6**
TOTAL MULTIPLE DX	**2,485**	**2.4**	**5**	**1**	**1**	**2**	**3**	**4**	**6**	**11**
TOTAL										
0–19 Years	439	1.7	2	1	1	1	2	3	4	5
20–34	886	1.9	3	1	1	1	2	4	5	10
35–49	913	2.2	4	1	1	2	2	4	6	10
50–64	551	2.6	4	1	1	2	3	5	6	13
65+	250	3.9	8	1	2	3	5	8	10	12
GRAND TOTAL	**3,039**	**2.2**	**4**	**1**	**1**	**2**	**3**	**4**	**6**	**10**

81.44: PATELLAR STABILIZATION

Type of Patients	Observed Patients	Avg. Stay	Vari-ance	Percentiles						
				10th	25th	50th	75th	90th	95th	99th
1. SINGLE DX										
0–19 Years	27	2.0	2	1	1	1	2	5	5	5
20–34	15	1.9	1	1	1	2	2	2	4	6
35–49	4	1.2	<1	1	1	1	1	2	2	2
50–64	1	1.0	0	1	1	1	1	1	1	1
65+	0									
2. MULTIPLE DX										
0–19 Years	53	1.8	1	1	1	1	3	3	3	6
20–34	41	2.2	2	1	1	2	3	5	6	6
35–49	27	2.3	5	1	1	2	2	4	4	15
50–64	20	2.8	4	1	2	2	3	7	7	8
65+	27	3.5	3	2	3	3	4	5	6	11
TOTAL SINGLE DX	**47**	**1.9**	**2**	**1**	**1**	**1**	**2**	**5**	**5**	**6**
TOTAL MULTIPLE DX	**168**	**2.3**	**3**	**1**	**1**	**2**	**3**	**4**	**6**	**8**
TOTAL										
0–19 Years	80	1.9	2	1	1	1	3	4	5	5
20–34	56	2.1	2	1	1	2	2	4	6	6
35–49	31	2.1	5	1	1	2	2	4	4	15
50–64	21	2.7	4	1	1	2	3	7	7	8
65+	27	3.5	3	2	3	3	4	5	6	11
GRAND TOTAL	**215**	**2.2**	**3**	**1**	**1**	**2**	**3**	**4**	**5**	**7**

81.45: CRUCIATE LIG REPAIR NEC

Type of Patients	Observed Patients	Avg. Stay	Vari-ance	10th	25th	50th	75th	90th	95th	99th
1. SINGLE DX										
0–19 Years	68	1.1	<1	1	1	1	1	2	2	3
20–34	111	1.2	<1	1	1	1	1	2	2	3
35–49	95	1.2	<1	1	1	1	1	2	2	3
50–64	11	1.5	<1	1	1	2	2	2	2	2
65+	1	3.0	0	3	3	3	3	3	3	3
2. MULTIPLE DX										
0–19 Years	180	1.4	2	1	1	1	2	2	3	5
20–34	456	1.6	2	1	1	1	2	3	4	8
35–49	396	1.7	3	1	1	1	2	3	3	9
50–64	110	1.5	<1	1	1	1	2	2	4	5
65+	5	3.2	4	1	2	3	3	7	7	7
TOTAL SINGLE DX	**286**	**1.2**	**<1**	**1**	**1**	**1**	**1**	**2**	**2**	**3**
TOTAL MULTIPLE DX	**1,147**	**1.6**	**2**	**1**	**1**	**1**	**2**	**3**	**4**	**8**
TOTAL										
0–19 Years	248	1.3	1	1	1	1	1	2	3	4
20–34	567	1.5	2	1	1	1	2	3	4	8
35–49	491	1.6	2	1	1	1	2	3	3	8
50–64	121	1.5	<1	1	1	1	2	2	4	5
65+	6	3.2	4	2	2	3	3	7	7	7
GRAND TOTAL	**1,433**	**1.5**	**2**	**1**	**1**	**1**	**2**	**2**	**3**	**7**

81.47: REPAIR OF KNEE NEC

Type of Patients	Observed Patients	Avg. Stay	Vari-ance	10th	25th	50th	75th	90th	95th	99th
1. SINGLE DX										
0–19 Years	19	1.8	1	1	1	1	3	3	4	5
20–34	36	1.7	<1	1	1	1	2	3	3	4
35–49	41	2.3	2	1	1	2	3	4	5	6
50–64	50	2.3	2	1	1	2	3	4	6	8
65+	23	3.1	3	1	2	3	4	5	6	10
2. MULTIPLE DX										
0–19 Years	38	2.0	5	1	1	1	2	3	5	17
20–34	124	2.6	5	1	1	2	3	5	6	12
35–49	253	2.9	5	1	1	2	3	5	9	11
50–64	280	3.1	5	1	2	3	4	5	7	14
65+	150	3.9	7	1	2	3	4	8	10	12
TOTAL SINGLE DX	**169**	**2.2**	**2**	**1**	**1**	**2**	**3**	**4**	**5**	**7**
TOTAL MULTIPLE DX	**845**	**3.0**	**6**	**1**	**1**	**2**	**4**	**5**	**8**	**12**
TOTAL										
0–19 Years	57	1.9	4	1	1	1	2	3	5	10
20–34	160	2.4	4	1	1	2	3	4	6	12
35–49	294	2.8	5	1	1	2	3	5	8	11
50–64	330	3.0	5	1	2	2	4	5	7	14
65+	173	3.8	7	1	2	3	4	8	10	12
GRAND TOTAL	**1,014**	**2.9**	**5**	**1**	**1**	**2**	**4**	**5**	**7**	**12**

81.49: REPAIR OF ANKLE NEC

Type of Patients	Observed Patients	Avg. Stay	Vari-ance	10th	25th	50th	75th	90th	95th	99th
1. SINGLE DX										
0–19 Years	4	1.3	<1	1	1	1	1	3	3	3
20–34	13	1.6	<1	1	1	1	2	3	3	3
35–49	8	1.4	<1	1	1	1	2	2	2	2
50–64	4	1.7	<1	1	1	2	2	3	3	3
65+	0									
2. MULTIPLE DX										
0–19 Years	10	2.1	<1	1	2	2	2	3	4	4
20–34	34	1.7	2	1	1	1	2	4	5	6
35–49	47	2.0	2	1	1	1	3	4	4	7
50–64	50	2.5	2	1	1	2	3	4	4	7
65+	18	2.9	4	1	2	2	4	7	8	8
TOTAL SINGLE DX	**29**	**1.5**	**<1**	**1**	**1**	**1**	**2**	**3**	**3**	**3**
TOTAL MULTIPLE DX	**159**	**2.2**	**2**	**1**	**1**	**2**	**3**	**4**	**5**	**7**
TOTAL										
0–19 Years	14	1.9	<1	1	1	2	2	3	3	4
20–34	47	1.6	1	1	1	1	2	3	5	6
35–49	55	1.9	2	1	1	1	2	4	4	7
50–64	54	2.4	2	1	1	2	3	4	4	7
65+	18	2.9	4	1	2	2	4	7	8	8
GRAND TOTAL	**188**	**2.1**	**2**	**1**	**1**	**2**	**3**	**4**	**4**	**7**

81.5: JOINT REPL LOWER EXT

Type of Patients	Observed Patients	Avg. Stay	Vari-ance	10th	25th	50th	75th	90th	95th	99th
1. SINGLE DX										
0–19 Years	12	5.3	3	3	4	5	7	8	8	8
20–34	89	3.4	3	2	3	3	4	5	6	9
35–49	968	3.3	1	2	3	3	4	5	5	7
50–64	3,034	3.5	1	2	3	3	4	5	5	7
65+	3,412	3.6	1	3	3	3	4	5	6	7
2. MULTIPLE DX										
0–19 Years	57	5.5	12	2	3	5	7	10	11	13
20–34	490	4.6	13	3	3	4	5	7	9	17
35–49	4,631	4.1	7	2	3	4	4	6	7	13
50–64	22,231	4.1	5	3	3	4	4	6	7	12
65+	57,334	4.6	6	3	3	4	5	7	8	15
TOTAL SINGLE DX	**7,515**	**3.5**	**1**	**2**	**3**	**3**	**4**	**5**	**5**	**7**
TOTAL MULTIPLE DX	**84,743**	**4.4**	**6**	**3**	**3**	**4**	**5**	**7**	**8**	**14**
TOTAL										
0–19 Years	69	5.5	11	2	3	5	7	9	11	13
20–34	579	4.5	11	2	3	4	5	7	9	16
35–49	5,599	3.9	6	2	3	4	4	5	7	13
50–64	25,265	4.0	4	3	3	4	4	6	7	12
65+	60,746	4.5	6	3	3	4	5	7	8	14
GRAND TOTAL	**92,258**	**4.3**	**6**	**3**	**3**	**4**	**5**	**6**	**8**	**14**

81.51: TOTAL HIP REPLACEMENT

Type of Patients	Observed Patients	Avg. Stay	Vari-ance	Percentiles 10th	25th	50th	75th	90th	95th	99th
1. SINGLE DX										
0–19 Years	6	4.3	2	3	3	4	6	6	6	6
20–34	53	3.4	2	2	3	3	4	4	5	9
35–49	446	3.4	1	2	3	3	4	5	5	7
50–64	1,120	3.5	1	2	3	3	4	5	5	7
65+	1,010	3.7	1	3	3	4	4	5	5	6
2. MULTIPLE DX										
0–19 Years	16	4.6	4	2	3	5	5	8	8	9
20–34	299	4.1	3	3	3	4	5	6	7	10
35–49	2,092	4.0	3	3	3	4	4	6	7	12
50–64	7,020	4.0	3	3	3	4	4	6	7	11
65+	14,969	4.3	5	3	3	4	5	6	7	12
TOTAL SINGLE DX	**2,635**	**3.6**	**1**	**2**	**3**	**3**	**4**	**5**	**5**	**7**
TOTAL MULTIPLE DX	**24,396**	**4.2**	**4**	**3**	**3**	**4**	**5**	**6**	**7**	**12**
TOTAL										
0–19 Years	22	4.5	3	2	3	4	5	7	8	9
20–34	352	4.0	3	3	3	4	4	5	7	10
35–49	2,538	3.9	3	2	3	4	4	5	7	11
50–64	8,140	3.9	3	3	3	4	4	5	6	10
65+	15,979	4.2	4	3	3	4	5	6	7	12
GRAND TOTAL	**27,031**	**4.1**	**4**	**3**	**3**	**4**	**5**	**6**	**7**	**12**

81.52: PARTIAL HIP REPLACEMENT

Type of Patients	Observed Patients	Avg. Stay	Vari-ance	Percentiles 10th	25th	50th	75th	90th	95th	99th
1. SINGLE DX										
0–19 Years	1	5.0	0	5	5	5	5	5	5	5
20–34	4	3.0	0	3	3	3	3	3	3	3
35–49	18	3.6	3	2	3	3	4	6	8	8
50–64	28	4.7	4	2	4	4	5	8	10	10
65+	159	4.2	2	3	3	4	5	6	7	9
2. MULTIPLE DX										
0–19 Years	12	4.6	6	2	3	3	6	8	11	11
20–34	38	5.8	18	2	3	4	7	12	14	21
35–49	177	6.3	44	3	3	5	7	10	17	43
50–64	754	6.6	20	3	4	5	7	11	16	25
65+	10,869	6.0	11	3	4	5	7	9	12	19
TOTAL SINGLE DX	**210**	**4.2**	**2**	**3**	**3**	**4**	**5**	**6**	**7**	**10**
TOTAL MULTIPLE DX	**11,850**	**6.0**	**12**	**3**	**4**	**5**	**7**	**10**	**12**	**20**
TOTAL										
0–19 Years	13	4.6	6	2	3	3	6	8	8	11
20–34	42	5.6	17	2	3	4	7	12	14	21
35–49	195	6.0	40	2	3	4	7	10	14	30
50–64	782	6.5	20	3	4	5	7	11	16	25
65+	11,028	6.0	11	3	4	5	7	9	12	19
GRAND TOTAL	**12,060**	**6.0**	**12**	**3**	**4**	**5**	**7**	**9**	**12**	**20**

81.53: HIP REPLACEMENT REVISION

Type of Patients	Observed Patients	Avg. Stay	Vari-ance	Percentiles 10th	25th	50th	75th	90th	95th	99th
1. SINGLE DX										
0–19 Years	0									
20–34	12	3.5	<1	3	3	3	4	5	5	5
35–49	51	3.6	2	3	3	3	4	5	5	11
50–64	114	3.6	5	2	3	3	4	5	5	13
65+	127	4.0	3	3	3	4	4	6	6	13
2. MULTIPLE DX										
0–19 Years	5	6.6	47	4	4	5	5	5	27	27
20–34	39	5.6	58	2	3	4	5	7	16	47
35–49	419	5.0	28	3	3	4	5	7	9	24
50–64	1,112	4.9	13	3	3	4	5	7	10	20
65+	2,931	5.3	15	3	3	4	6	8	12	19
TOTAL SINGLE DX	**304**	**3.8**	**3**	**2**	**3**	**3**	**4**	**5**	**6**	**13**
TOTAL MULTIPLE DX	**4,506**	**5.2**	**16**	**3**	**3**	**4**	**6**	**8**	**11**	**20**
TOTAL										
0–19 Years	5	6.6	47	4	4	5	5	5	27	27
20–34	51	5.1	46	2	3	4	5	7	12	47
35–49	470	4.8	25	3	3	4	5	7	9	24
50–64	1,226	4.8	12	3	3	4	5	7	10	20
65+	3,058	5.3	14	3	3	4	6	8	12	19
GRAND TOTAL	**4,810**	**5.1**	**15**	**3**	**3**	**4**	**6**	**8**	**11**	**20**

81.54: TOTAL KNEE REPLACEMENT

Type of Patients	Observed Patients	Avg. Stay	Vari-ance	Percentiles 10th	25th	50th	75th	90th	95th	99th
1. SINGLE DX										
0–19 Years	5	6.6	4	3	6	7	8	8	8	8
20–34	17	3.9	7	2	3	3	4	6	8	14
35–49	414	3.2	1	2	3	3	4	4	5	6
50–64	1,687	3.4	1	2	3	3	4	5	5	6
65+	2,017	3.6	1	2	3	3	4	5	5	7
2. MULTIPLE DX										
0–19 Years	14	7.2	11	4	4	6	10	13	13	13
20–34	80	5.2	22	2	3	4	6	8	10	37
35–49	1,700	3.7	2	2	3	4	4	5	6	9
50–64	12,262	3.9	3	3	3	4	4	5	6	10
65+	26,384	4.1	3	3	3	4	5	6	7	11
TOTAL SINGLE DX	**4,140**	**3.5**	**1**	**2**	**3**	**3**	**4**	**5**	**5**	**7**
TOTAL MULTIPLE DX	**40,440**	**4.0**	**3**	**3**	**3**	**4**	**4**	**6**	**7**	**10**
TOTAL										
0–19 Years	19	7.1	9	4	4	7	10	13	13	13
20–34	97	5.0	20	2	3	4	6	8	10	37
35–49	2,114	3.6	2	2	3	3	4	5	6	9
50–64	13,949	3.8	3	3	3	4	4	5	6	9
65+	28,401	4.0	3	3	3	4	4	6	7	11
GRAND TOTAL	**44,580**	**4.0**	**3**	**3**	**3**	**4**	**4**	**6**	**7**	**10**

81.55: KNEE REPLACEMENT REV

Type of Patients	Observed Patients	Avg. Stay	Vari-ance	Percentiles						
				10th	25th	50th	75th	90th	95th	99th
1. SINGLE DX										
0–19 Years	0									
20–34	3	1.8	<1	1	1	1	3	3	3	3
35–49	35	3.8	4	1	3	3	4	6	6	11
50–64	80	3.5	1	2	3	3	4	5	6	8
65+	97	3.5	2	2	2	4	4	5	6	7
2. MULTIPLE DX										
0–19 Years	9	5.4	7	2	3	4	8	9	9	9
20–34	31	6.8	23	2	4	5	9	10	15	25
35–49	221	4.0	7	2	3	3	4	6	7	14
50–64	1,037	4.3	9	2	3	4	5	6	8	19
65+	2,123	4.5	7	3	3	4	5	7	9	17
TOTAL SINGLE DX	**215**	**3.5**	**2**	**2**	**3**	**3**	**4**	**5**	**6**	**8**
TOTAL MULTIPLE DX	**3,421**	**4.5**	**8**	**3**	**3**	**4**	**5**	**7**	**9**	**17**
TOTAL										
0–19 Years	9	5.4	7	2	3	4	8	9	9	9
20–34	34	6.2	23	2	3	5	9	10	15	25
35–49	256	3.9	7	2	3	3	4	6	7	14
50–64	1,117	4.3	8	2	3	4	5	6	8	18
65+	2,220	4.5	7	3	3	4	5	7	9	17
GRAND TOTAL	**3,636**	**4.4**	**8**	**2**	**3**	**4**	**5**	**7**	**9**	**17**

81.56: TOTAL ANKLE REPLACEMENT

Type of Patients	Observed Patients	Avg. Stay	Vari-ance	Percentiles						
				10th	25th	50th	75th	90th	95th	99th
1. SINGLE DX										
0–19 Years	0									
20–34	0									
35–49	3	2.0	0	2	2	2	2	2	2	2
50–64	4	3.1	<1	2	3	3	4	4	4	4
65+	2	2.8	<1	2	3	3	3	3	3	3
2. MULTIPLE DX										
0–19 Years	1	1.0	0	1	1	1	1	1	1	1
20–34	2	4.8	1	4	4	4	6	6	6	6
35–49	21	2.3	<1	1	2	2	3	3	4	4
50–64	40	2.1	1	1	1	2	2	3	4	6
65+	52	2.7	<1	2	2	3	3	4	4	7
TOTAL SINGLE DX	**9**	**2.8**	**<1**	**2**	**2**	**3**	**3**	**4**	**4**	**4**
TOTAL MULTIPLE DX	**116**	**2.5**	**1**	**1**	**2**	**2**	**3**	**4**	**4**	**6**
TOTAL										
0–19 Years	1	1.0	0	1	1	1	1	1	1	1
20–34	2	4.8	1	4	4	4	6	6	6	6
35–49	24	2.3	<1	1	2	2	3	3	4	4
50–64	44	2.2	1	1	2	2	2	4	4	6
65+	54	2.8	<1	2	2	3	3	4	4	7
GRAND TOTAL	**125**	**2.5**	**1**	**1**	**2**	**2**	**3**	**4**	**4**	**6**

81.6: OTH SPINAL PROCEDURES

Type of Patients	Observed Patients	Avg. Stay	Vari-ance	Percentiles						
				10th	25th	50th	75th	90th	95th	99th
1. SINGLE DX										
0–19 Years	0									
20–34	2	2.0	0	2	2	2	2	2	2	2
35–49	7	3.4	4	1	1	4	5	6	6	6
50–64	4	3.5	2	2	2	3	5	5	5	5
65+	0									
2. MULTIPLE DX										
0–19 Years	1	8.0	0	8	8	8	8	8	8	8
20–34	14	5.9	20	3	3	4	7	8	22	22
35–49	50	4.2	7	1	3	4	5	7	8	18
50–64	57	5.2	13	2	3	5	6	8	10	21
65+	45	4.9	5	3	3	5	6	7	8	16
TOTAL SINGLE DX	**13**	**3.0**	**2**	**1**	**2**	**2**	**4**	**5**	**6**	**6**
TOTAL MULTIPLE DX	**167**	**5.0**	**10**	**2**	**3**	**4**	**6**	**8**	**9**	**21**
TOTAL										
0–19 Years	1	8.0	0	8	8	8	8	8	8	8
20–34	16	5.0	18	2	3	4	7	8	8	22
35–49	57	4.1	7	1	3	4	5	7	8	18
50–64	61	5.1	12	2	3	5	6	8	10	21
65+	45	4.9	5	3	3	5	6	7	8	16
GRAND TOTAL	**180**	**4.8**	**9**	**2**	**3**	**4**	**6**	**8**	**9**	**21**

81.61: 360 DEG SPINAL FUS-1 INC

Type of Patients	Observed Patients	Avg. Stay	Vari-ance	Percentiles						
				10th	25th	50th	75th	90th	95th	99th
1. SINGLE DX										
0–19 Years	0									
20–34	2	2.0	0	2	2	2	2	2	2	2
35–49	7	3.4	4	1	1	4	5	6	6	6
50–64	4	3.5	2	2	2	3	5	5	5	5
65+	0									
2. MULTIPLE DX										
0–19 Years	1	8.0	0	8	8	8	8	8	8	8
20–34	14	5.9	20	3	3	4	7	8	22	22
35–49	50	4.2	7	1	3	4	5	7	8	18
50–64	57	5.2	13	2	3	5	6	8	10	21
65+	45	4.9	5	3	3	5	6	7	8	16
TOTAL SINGLE DX	**13**	**3.0**	**2**	**1**	**2**	**2**	**4**	**5**	**6**	**6**
TOTAL MULTIPLE DX	**167**	**5.0**	**10**	**2**	**3**	**4**	**6**	**8**	**9**	**21**
TOTAL										
0–19 Years	1	8.0	0	8	8	8	8	8	8	8
20–34	16	5.0	18	2	3	4	7	8	8	22
35–49	57	4.1	7	1	3	4	5	7	8	18
50–64	61	5.1	12	2	3	5	6	8	10	21
65+	45	4.9	5	3	3	5	6	7	8	16
GRAND TOTAL	**180**	**4.8**	**9**	**2**	**3**	**4**	**6**	**8**	**9**	**21**

81.7: HAND/FINGER ARTHROPLASTY

Type of Patients	Observed Patients	Avg. Stay	Vari-ance	Percentiles 10th	25th	50th	75th	90th	95th	99th
1. SINGLE DX										
0–19 Years	5	1.4	<1	1	1	1	1	3	3	3
20–34	14	2.7	9	1	1	1	2	9	9	9
35–49	16	2.3	3	1	1	2	3	5	6	6
50–64	17	2.7	23	1	1	2	2	4	22	22
65+	9	1.2	<1	1	1	1	1	2	2	3
2. MULTIPLE DX										
0–19 Years	7	1.2	<1	1	1	1	1	2	2	2
20–34	25	2.8	6	1	1	2	3	7	10	10
35–49	51	2.2	4	1	1	1	3	4	6	13
50–64	80	2.1	2	1	1	2	2	4	5	8
65+	70	1.7	1	1	1	1	2	3	4	7
TOTAL SINGLE DX	**61**	**2.1**	**8**	**1**	**1**	**1**	**2**	**4**	**8**	**22**
TOTAL MULTIPLE DX	**233**	**2.0**	**3**	**1**	**1**	**1**	**2**	**4**	**6**	**10**
TOTAL										
0–19 Years	12	1.2	<1	1	1	1	1	2	3	3
20–34	39	2.8	7	1	1	2	3	7	9	10
35–49	67	2.2	4	1	1	1	3	5	6	13
50–64	97	2.2	5	1	1	2	2	4	5	9
65+	79	1.6	1	1	1	1	2	3	4	6
GRAND TOTAL	**294**	**2.0**	**4**	**1**	**1**	**1**	**2**	**4**	**6**	**10**

81.75: CARPAL/CMC ARTHROPLASTY

Type of Patients	Observed Patients	Avg. Stay	Vari-ance	Percentiles 10th	25th	50th	75th	90th	95th	99th
1. SINGLE DX										
0–19 Years	1	1.0	0	1	1	1	1	1	1	1
20–34	4	1.2	<1	1	1	1	1	2	2	2
35–49	3	2.9	7	1	1	2	6	6	6	6
50–64	10	1.5	<1	1	1	2	2	2	2	2
65+	4	1.4	<1	1	1	1	2	3	3	3
2. MULTIPLE DX										
0–19 Years	2	2.0	0	2	2	2	2	2	2	2
20–34	7	1.4	<1	1	1	1	2	2	2	2
35–49	17	1.8	<1	1	1	2	2	3	4	4
50–64	31	2.0	2	1	1	2	2	4	4	6
65+	17	1.7	2	1	1	1	2	4	5	5
TOTAL SINGLE DX	**22**	**1.6**	**1**	**1**	**1**	**1**	**2**	**2**	**3**	**6**
TOTAL MULTIPLE DX	**74**	**1.8**	**1**	**1**	**1**	**1**	**2**	**4**	**4**	**5**
TOTAL										
0–19 Years	3	1.8	<1	1	1	2	2	2	2	2
20–34	11	1.4	<1	1	1	1	2	2	2	2
35–49	20	1.9	2	1	1	2	2	4	4	6
50–64	41	1.9	1	1	1	2	2	4	4	6
65+	21	1.7	1	1	1	1	2	4	4	5
GRAND TOTAL	**96**	**1.8**	**1**	**1**	**1**	**1**	**2**	**4**	**4**	**6**

81.8: SHOULD/ELB ARTHROPLASTY

Type of Patients	Observed Patients	Avg. Stay	Vari-ance	Percentiles 10th	25th	50th	75th	90th	95th	99th
1. SINGLE DX										
0–19 Years	46	1.4	<1	1	1	1	1	2	3	5
20–34	111	1.8	7	1	1	1	1	3	7	19
35–49	135	1.8	3	1	1	1	2	3	3	8
50–64	231	1.9	3	1	1	1	2	3	4	6
65+	211	1.9	1	1	1	2	2	3	3	5
2. MULTIPLE DX										
0–19 Years	41	1.3	<1	1	1	1	1	2	3	3
20–34	208	2.0	5	1	1	1	2	3	4	19
35–49	553	2.0	4	1	1	2	2	3	5	11
50–64	1,489	2.3	4	1	1	2	3	4	5	12
65+	2,769	2.8	5	1	2	2	3	5	6	14
TOTAL SINGLE DX	**734**	**1.8**	**3**	**1**	**1**	**1**	**2**	**3**	**3**	**9**
TOTAL MULTIPLE DX	**5,060**	**2.6**	**5**	**1**	**1**	**2**	**3**	**4**	**6**	**13**
TOTAL										
0–19 Years	87	1.3	<1	1	1	1	1	2	3	5
20–34	319	1.9	6	1	1	1	2	3	4	19
35–49	688	2.0	3	1	1	1	2	3	4	11
50–64	1,720	2.2	4	1	1	2	3	4	5	11
65+	2,980	2.8	5	1	2	2	3	5	6	13
GRAND TOTAL	**5,794**	**2.5**	**5**	**1**	**1**	**2**	**3**	**4**	**6**	**13**

81.80: TOTAL SHOULDER REPL

Type of Patients	Observed Patients	Avg. Stay	Vari-ance	Percentiles 10th	25th	50th	75th	90th	95th	99th
1. SINGLE DX										
0–19 Years	1	5.0	0	5	5	5	5	5	5	5
20–34	0									
35–49	11	2.1	<1	1	2	2	2	3	3	3
50–64	56	2.1	<1	1	1	2	3	3	3	4
65+	77	1.9	<1	1	2	2	2	3	3	3
2. MULTIPLE DX										
0–19 Years	0									
20–34	3	1.5	<1	1	1	2	2	2	2	2
35–49	49	2.7	2	1	2	2	3	5	5	8
50–64	350	2.5	2	1	2	2	3	4	4	9
65+	864	2.6	2	1	2	2	3	4	5	8
TOTAL SINGLE DX	**145**	**2.0**	**<1**	**1**	**2**	**2**	**2**	**3**	**3**	**5**
TOTAL MULTIPLE DX	**1,266**	**2.6**	**2**	**1**	**2**	**2**	**3**	**4**	**5**	**8**
TOTAL										
0–19 Years	1	5.0	0	5	5	5	5	5	5	5
20–34	3	1.5	<1	1	1	2	2	2	2	2
35–49	60	2.6	2	1	2	2	3	4	5	8
50–64	406	2.5	2	1	2	2	3	4	4	8
65+	941	2.5	2	1	2	2	3	4	5	8
GRAND TOTAL	**1,411**	**2.5**	**2**	**1**	**2**	**2**	**3**	**4**	**5**	**8**

81.81: PARTIAL SHOULDER REPL

Type of Patients	Observed Patients	Avg. Stay	Vari-ance	10th	25th	50th	75th	90th	95th	99th
				Percentiles						
1. SINGLE DX										
0–19 Years	1	3.0	0	3	3	3	3	3	3	3
20–34	5	3.3	4	1	2	3	3	7	7	7
35–49	25	1.9	<1	1	1	2	2	3	4	4
50–64	66	1.9	1	1	1	2	3	3	3	5
65+	84	2.2	2	1	1	2	3	3	3	4
2. MULTIPLE DX										
0–19 Years	0									
20–34	18	2.5	<1	1	2	2	3	4	4	4
35–49	124	2.9	9	1	2	2	3	4	9	16
50–64	470	2.9	6	1	2	2	3	5	7	14
65+	1,219	3.4	7	1	2	3	4	6	8	14
TOTAL SINGLE DX	**181**	**2.1**	**1**	**1**	**1**	**2**	**3**	**3**	**3**	**6**
TOTAL MULTIPLE DX	**1,831**	**3.2**	**7**	**1**	**2**	**3**	**4**	**6**	**8**	**14**
TOTAL										
0–19 Years	1	3.0	0	3	3	3	3	3	3	3
20–34	23	2.7	2	1	2	3	3	4	4	7
35–49	149	2.7	7	1	1	2	3	4	7	16
50–64	536	2.7	5	1	2	2	3	4	7	14
65+	1,303	3.3	7	1	2	3	4	6	8	14
GRAND TOTAL	**2,012**	**3.1**	**6**	**1**	**2**	**2**	**3**	**5**	**8**	**14**

81.82: RECUR SHOULD DISLOC REP

Type of Patients	Observed Patients	Avg. Stay	Vari-ance	10th	25th	50th	75th	90th	95th	99th
				Percentiles						
1. SINGLE DX										
0–19 Years	39	1.1	<1	1	1	1	1	1	2	2
20–34	72	1.3	<1	1	1	1	1	2	2	3
35–49	30	1.3	<1	1	1	1	1	2	2	3
50–64	8	1.1	<1	1	1	1	1	2	2	2
65+	1	1.0	0	1	1	1	1	1	1	1
2. MULTIPLE DX										
0–19 Years	26	1.2	<1	1	1	1	1	2	2	3
20–34	96	1.5	<1	1	1	1	2	3	3	6
35–49	54	1.5	<1	1	1	1	2	2	3	5
50–64	29	1.6	1	1	1	1	2	3	3	6
65+	28	2.6	3	1	2	2	3	4	6	10
TOTAL SINGLE DX	**150**	**1.2**	**<1**	**1**	**1**	**1**	**1**	**2**	**2**	**3**
TOTAL MULTIPLE DX	**233**	**1.6**	**1**	**1**	**1**	**1**	**2**	**3**	**4**	**6**
TOTAL										
0–19 Years	65	1.1	<1	1	1	1	1	2	2	2
20–34	168	1.4	<1	1	1	1	2	2	3	6
35–49	84	1.4	<1	1	1	1	2	2	3	4
50–64	37	1.5	<1	1	1	1	2	3	3	6
65+	29	2.5	3	1	1	2	3	4	6	10
GRAND TOTAL	**383**	**1.5**	**<1**	**1**	**1**	**1**	**2**	**2**	**3**	**6**

81.83: SHOULD ARTHROPLASTY NEC

Type of Patients	Observed Patients	Avg. Stay	Vari-ance	10th	25th	50th	75th	90th	95th	99th
				Percentiles						
1. SINGLE DX										
0–19 Years	2	1.0	0	1	1	1	1	1	1	1
20–34	26	1.1	<1	1	1	1	1	1	2	2
35–49	49	1.3	<1	1	1	1	1	2	3	5
50–64	78	1.3	<1	1	1	1	1	2	2	5
65+	42	1.4	<1	1	1	1	2	2	3	3
2. MULTIPLE DX										
0–19 Years	15	1.4	<1	1	1	1	2	3	3	3
20–34	60	1.4	<1	1	1	1	2	2	3	3
35–49	264	1.4	<1	1	1	1	2	2	3	4
50–64	543	1.4	<1	1	1	1	2	2	3	5
65+	550	1.8	2	1	1	1	2	3	4	7
TOTAL SINGLE DX	**197**	**1.3**	**<1**	**1**	**1**	**1**	**1**	**2**	**3**	**4**
TOTAL MULTIPLE DX	**1,432**	**1.6**	**1**	**1**	**1**	**1**	**2**	**3**	**3**	**6**
TOTAL										
0–19 Years	17	1.4	<1	1	1	1	2	3	3	3
20–34	86	1.3	<1	1	1	1	1	2	2	3
35–49	313	1.4	<1	1	1	1	2	2	3	5
50–64	621	1.4	<1	1	1	1	2	2	3	5
65+	592	1.8	2	1	1	1	2	3	4	7
GRAND TOTAL	**1,629**	**1.5**	**1**	**1**	**1**	**1**	**2**	**3**	**3**	**6**

81.84: TOTAL ELBOW REPLACEMENT

Type of Patients	Observed Patients	Avg. Stay	Vari-ance	10th	25th	50th	75th	90th	95th	99th
				Percentiles						
1. SINGLE DX										
0–19 Years	0									
20–34	6	6.9	43	1	1	7	12	19	19	19
35–49	16	3.4	18	1	1	2	3	8	12	19
50–64	19	3.9	20	1	2	2	4	6	17	19
65+	4	3.6	7	2	2	3	3	9	9	9
2. MULTIPLE DX										
0–19 Years	0									
20–34	15	7.1	43	2	2	4	8	19	19	19
35–49	40	2.9	7	1	2	2	3	4	10	15
50–64	76	3.8	19	1	2	2	4	7	10	22
65+	95	3.9	22	1	2	2	4	7	17	21
TOTAL SINGLE DX	**45**	**4.1**	**22**	**1**	**1**	**2**	**4**	**12**	**19**	**19**
TOTAL MULTIPLE DX	**226**	**3.9**	**20**	**1**	**2**	**2**	**4**	**7**	**17**	**22**
TOTAL										
0–19 Years	0									
20–34	21	7.1	42	1	2	4	12	19	19	19
35–49	56	3.1	10	1	2	2	3	4	11	19
50–64	95	3.8	19	1	2	2	4	6	17	22
65+	99	3.9	21	1	2	2	4	7	17	21
GRAND TOTAL	**271**	**3.9**	**21**	**1**	**2**	**2**	**4**	**8**	**17**	**22**

81.85: ELBOW ARTHROPLASTY NEC

Type of Patients	Observed Patients	Avg. Stay	Vari-ance	Percentiles						
				10th	25th	50th	75th	90th	95th	99th
1. SINGLE DX										
0–19 Years	3	1.9	<1	1	1	2	3	3	3	3
20–34	2	11.4	120	3	3	3	20	20	20	20
35–49	4	2.4	<1	1	1	3	3	3	3	3
50–64	4	3.5	5	1	1	4	4	7	7	7
65+	3	4.2	19	1	1	2	9	9	9	9
2. MULTIPLE DX										
0–19 Years	0									
20–34	16	2.3	2	1	1	2	3	4	5	7
35–49	22	3.1	3	1	2	2	5	6	6	6
50–64	21	2.4	2	1	1	2	3	5	5	6
65+	13	2.3	1	1	2	2	2	5	5	5
TOTAL SINGLE DX	**16**	**3.6**	**17**	**1**	**1**	**3**	**3**	**7**	**9**	**20**
TOTAL MULTIPLE DX	**72**	**2.5**	**2**	**1**	**1**	**2**	**3**	**5**	**6**	**7**
TOTAL										
0–19 Years	3	1.9	<1	1	1	2	3	3	3	3
20–34	18	3.1	15	1	1	2	3	5	7	20
35–49	26	3.0	3	1	2	3	3	6	6	6
50–64	25	2.6	3	1	1	2	4	5	6	7
65+	16	2.5	4	1	1	2	3	5	5	9
GRAND TOTAL	**88**	**2.7**	**5**	**1**	**1**	**2**	**3**	**5**	**6**	**9**

81.9: OTHER JOINT STRUCTURE OP

Type of Patients	Observed Patients	Avg. Stay	Vari-ance	Percentiles						
				10th	25th	50th	75th	90th	95th	99th
1. SINGLE DX										
0–19 Years	100	3.2	6	1	1	3	4	6	7	14
20–34	50	2.4	3	1	1	2	3	4	6	9
35–49	42	2.9	6	1	1	2	4	7	8	10
50–64	28	2.7	5	1	1	2	3	7	9	10
65+	21	2.1	<1	1	1	2	3	3	4	4
2. MULTIPLE DX										
0–19 Years	170	4.6	16	1	2	4	6	8	13	15
20–34	254	4.1	12	1	2	3	5	7	11	18
35–49	622	5.1	46	1	2	4	6	10	13	42
50–64	866	5.0	33	1	2	4	6	9	12	25
65+	2,355	5.2	16	2	3	4	6	9	12	20
TOTAL SINGLE DX	**241**	**2.8**	**5**	**1**	**1**	**2**	**3**	**6**	**7**	**14**
TOTAL MULTIPLE DX	**4,267**	**5.0**	**23**	**2**	**2**	**4**	**6**	**9**	**12**	**22**
TOTAL										
0–19 Years	270	4.1	13	1	2	3	5	8	11	14
20–34	304	3.8	11	1	2	3	5	7	10	18
35–49	664	5.0	44	1	2	3	6	9	13	29
50–64	894	4.9	32	1	2	4	6	9	12	25
65+	2,376	5.1	16	2	3	4	6	9	12	20
GRAND TOTAL	**4,508**	**4.9**	**22**	**1**	**2**	**4**	**6**	**9**	**12**	**22**

81.91: ARTHROCENTESIS

Type of Patients	Observed Patients	Avg. Stay	Vari-ance	Percentiles						
				10th	25th	50th	75th	90th	95th	99th
1. SINGLE DX										
0–19 Years	91	3.4	6	1	2	3	4	6	7	14
20–34	35	2.4	2	1	1	2	4	4	5	7
35–49	32	3.3	6	1	1	3	4	7	9	10
50–64	14	2.7	4	1	1	3	3	3	9	9
65+	13	2.3	<1	1	2	2	3	3	4	4
2. MULTIPLE DX										
0–19 Years	150	4.6	11	1	2	4	6	8	12	13
20–34	197	4.4	12	1	2	3	6	8	11	18
35–49	514	5.2	38	1	2	4	6	10	13	42
50–64	700	4.9	19	1	2	4	6	9	12	22
65+	1,737	5.2	15	2	3	4	7	9	12	20
TOTAL SINGLE DX	**185**	**3.1**	**5**	**1**	**1**	**3**	**4**	**6**	**7**	**14**
TOTAL MULTIPLE DX	**3,298**	**5.1**	**18**	**2**	**3**	**4**	**6**	**9**	**12**	**21**
TOTAL										
0–19 Years	241	4.2	9	1	2	3	5	8	11	14
20–34	232	4.1	11	1	2	3	5	7	11	18
35–49	546	5.1	36	1	2	4	6	9	13	29
50–64	714	4.8	18	1	2	4	6	9	12	22
65+	1,750	5.2	15	2	3	4	6	9	12	20
GRAND TOTAL	**3,483**	**4.9**	**18**	**2**	**2**	**4**	**6**	**9**	**12**	**20**

81.92: INJECTION INTO JOINT

Type of Patients	Observed Patients	Avg. Stay	Vari-ance	Percentiles						
				10th	25th	50th	75th	90th	95th	99th
1. SINGLE DX										
0–19 Years	1	1.0	0	1	1	1	1	1	1	1
20–34	0									
35–49	3	2.3	<1	2	2	2	3	3	3	3
50–64	4	2.7	9	1	1	1	7	7	7	7
65+	1	4.0	0	4	4	4	4	4	4	4
2. MULTIPLE DX										
0–19 Years	7	10.7	195	2	3	4	15	45	45	45
20–34	27	3.9	12	1	2	3	4	7	9	19
35–49	56	7.4	167	1	3	4	7	12	23	98
50–64	93	7.4	138	2	2	5	8	11	17	75
65+	475	5.6	22	2	3	4	7	10	14	24
TOTAL SINGLE DX	**9**	**2.6**	**4**	**1**	**1**	**2**	**4**	**7**	**7**	**7**
TOTAL MULTIPLE DX	**658**	**5.9**	**50**	**2**	**3**	**4**	**7**	**11**	**15**	**31**
TOTAL										
0–19 Years	8	9.7	182	1	2	3	11	45	45	45
20–34	27	3.9	12	1	2	3	4	7	9	19
35–49	59	7.2	161	1	2	4	7	12	19	98
50–64	97	7.2	134	2	2	5	8	11	17	75
65+	476	5.6	22	2	3	4	7	10	14	24
GRAND TOTAL	**667**	**5.9**	**50**	**2**	**3**	**4**	**7**	**11**	**15**	**31**

81.97: REV JOINT REPL UE

Type of Patients	Observed Patients	Avg. Stay	Vari-ance	10th	25th	50th	75th	90th	95th	99th
				Percentiles						
1. SINGLE DX										
0–19 Years	0									
20–34	3	5.6	16	2	2	9	9	9	9	9
35–49	1	1.0	0	1	1	1	1	1	1	1
50–64	7	2.3	2	1	1	3	3	4	4	4
65+	6	1.6	<1	1	1	1	2	3	3	3
2. MULTIPLE DX										
0–19 Years	2	4.0	0	4	4	4	4	4	4	4
20–34	3	6.5	49	3	3	3	17	17	17	17
35–49	25	3.2	2	2	3	3	3	4	7	9
50–64	46	2.9	4	2	2	2	3	5	6	15
65+	130	3.1	3	1	2	3	4	5	6	9
TOTAL SINGLE DX	**17**	**2.4**	**5**	**1**	**1**	**2**	**3**	**4**	**9**	**9**
TOTAL MULTIPLE DX	**206**	**3.1**	**3**	**2**	**2**	**3**	**4**	**5**	**6**	**9**
TOTAL										
0–19 Years	2	4.0	0	4	4	4	4	4	4	4
20–34	6	6.0	28	2	3	3	9	17	17	17
35–49	26	3.1	2	2	3	3	3	4	4	9
50–64	53	2.8	4	1	2	2	3	4	6	15
65+	136	3.1	3	1	2	3	4	5	6	9
GRAND TOTAL	**223**	**3.1**	**3**	**1**	**2**	**3**	**4**	**5**	**6**	**9**

82.0: INC HAND SOFT TISSUE

Type of Patients	Observed Patients	Avg. Stay	Vari-ance	10th	25th	50th	75th	90th	95th	99th
				Percentiles						
1. SINGLE DX										
0–19 Years	10	1.5	<1	1	1	1	2	3	4	4
20–34	25	2.3	2	1	1	2	4	4	4	4
35–49	29	3.0	5	1	2	2	4	6	9	10
50–64	15	1.7	<1	1	1	1	2	3	4	4
65+	1	3.0	0	3	3	3	3	3	3	3
2. MULTIPLE DX										
0–19 Years	43	3.4	7	1	2	3	4	8	9	10
20–34	133	3.8	8	1	2	3	5	6	9	18
35–49	221	4.5	12	2	2	4	6	8	10	22
50–64	159	5.0	20	2	2	4	6	10	14	21
65+	84	3.8	8	1	2	3	5	6	7	14
TOTAL SINGLE DX	**80**	**2.3**	**3**	**1**	**1**	**2**	**3**	**4**	**4**	**9**
TOTAL MULTIPLE DX	**640**	**4.3**	**12**	**1**	**2**	**3**	**5**	**8**	**10**	**19**
TOTAL										
0–19 Years	53	3.1	6	1	1	2	4	8	9	10
20–34	158	3.5	8	1	2	3	4	6	9	14
35–49	250	4.3	11	1	2	4	5	8	10	17
50–64	174	4.8	19	2	2	3	6	10	13	21
65+	85	3.8	8	1	2	3	5	6	7	14
GRAND TOTAL	**720**	**4.1**	**12**	**1**	**2**	**3**	**5**	**8**	**10**	**18**

82.01: EXPL TENDON SHEATH HAND

Type of Patients	Observed Patients	Avg. Stay	Vari-ance	10th	25th	50th	75th	90th	95th	99th
				Percentiles						
1. SINGLE DX										
0–19 Years	6	1.5	1	1	1	1	1	3	4	4
20–34	12	2.6	2	1	1	2	4	4	4	4
35–49	16	3.1	6	1	2	2	4	6	9	9
50–64	15	1.7	<1	1	1	1	2	3	4	4
65+	1	3.0	0	3	3	3	3	3	3	3
2. MULTIPLE DX										
0–19 Years	23	3.7	8	1	2	3	4	9	10	10
20–34	75	4.0	9	2	2	3	5	6	9	20
35–49	137	4.2	6	2	2	4	5	7	8	15
50–64	92	4.2	9	2	2	3	6	7	10	14
65+	41	3.4	9	1	2	3	4	5	6	22
TOTAL SINGLE DX	**50**	**2.3**	**3**	**1**	**1**	**2**	**3**	**4**	**4**	**9**
TOTAL MULTIPLE DX	**368**	**4.1**	**8**	**2**	**2**	**3**	**5**	**7**	**9**	**17**
TOTAL										
0–19 Years	29	3.2	7	1	1	3	4	9	10	10
20–34	87	3.8	9	1	2	3	4	6	9	18
35–49	153	4.1	6	2	2	4	5	7	8	15
50–64	107	4.0	9	1	2	3	6	7	10	14
65+	42	3.4	9	1	2	3	4	5	6	22
GRAND TOTAL	**418**	**3.8**	**8**	**1**	**2**	**3**	**5**	**7**	**9**	**15**

82.09: INC SOFT TISSUE HAND NEC

Type of Patients	Observed Patients	Avg. Stay	Vari-ance	10th	25th	50th	75th	90th	95th	99th
				Percentiles						
1. SINGLE DX										
0–19 Years	2	2.0	0	2	2	2	2	2	2	2
20–34	10	2.3	1	1	1	2	3	4	4	4
35–49	10	2.8	6	1	1	2	3	5	10	10
50–64	0									
65+	0									
2. MULTIPLE DX										
0–19 Years	16	3.8	5	1	2	3	6	8	8	8
20–34	50	3.5	7	1	2	3	4	6	10	14
35–49	69	4.6	20	1	2	3	6	10	13	24
50–64	58	6.6	38	2	3	5	7	17	19	40
65+	37	4.1	8	1	2	3	6	7	9	14
TOTAL SINGLE DX	**22**	**2.5**	**3**	**1**	**1**	**2**	**3**	**4**	**5**	**10**
TOTAL MULTIPLE DX	**230**	**4.7**	**19**	**1**	**2**	**3**	**6**	**9**	**14**	**21**
TOTAL										
0–19 Years	18	3.7	5	1	2	3	6	8	8	8
20–34	60	3.3	6	1	2	3	4	6	9	14
35–49	79	4.3	18	1	2	3	5	10	13	24
50–64	58	6.6	38	2	3	5	7	17	19	40
65+	37	4.1	8	1	2	3	6	7	9	14
GRAND TOTAL	**252**	**4.5**	**18**	**1**	**2**	**3**	**6**	**9**	**13**	**21**

82.1: DIV HAND MUSC/TEND/FASC

Type of Patients	Observed Patients	Avg. Stay	Variance	10th	25th	50th	75th	90th	95th	99th
				Percentiles						
1. SINGLE DX										
0–19 Years	2	1.0	0	1	1	1	1	1	1	1
20–34	2	2.0	2	1	1	1	3	3	3	3
35–49	6	2.5	2	1	2	2	3	4	5	5
50–64	1	12.0	0	12	12	12	12	12	12	12
65+	1	4.0	0	4	4	4	4	4	4	4
2. MULTIPLE DX										
0–19 Years	9	3.4	8	1	1	3	7	7	8	8
20–34	18	3.9	11	1	2	2	7	9	11	11
35–49	22	5.5	45	2	3	3	6	10	12	41
50–64	18	3.9	17	1	2	3	5	5	5	23
65+	11	8.8	90	2	3	7	8	14	37	37
TOTAL SINGLE DX	**12**	**2.8**	**7**	**1**	**1**	**2**	**4**	**5**	**12**	**12**
TOTAL MULTIPLE DX	**78**	**4.9**	**33**	**1**	**2**	**3**	**6**	**8**	**12**	**37**
TOTAL										
0–19 Years	11	3.0	7	1	1	1	4	7	8	8
20–34	20	3.8	10	1	1	2	7	9	11	11
35–49	28	4.9	38	2	3	3	5	8	12	41
50–64	19	4.2	19	1	2	3	5	5	12	23
65+	12	8.5	84	2	3	7	8	14	37	37
GRAND TOTAL	**90**	**4.6**	**30**	**1**	**2**	**3**	**5**	**8**	**12**	**37**

82.2: EXC LES HAND SOFT TISSUE

Type of Patients	Observed Patients	Avg. Stay	Variance	10th	25th	50th	75th	90th	95th	99th
				Percentiles						
1. SINGLE DX										
0–19 Years	0									
20–34	1	1.0	0	1	1	1	1	1	1	1
35–49	2	1.0	0	1	1	1	1	1	1	1
50–64	1	2.0	0	2	2	2	2	2	2	2
65+	0									
2. MULTIPLE DX										
0–19 Years	3	2.3	1	1	1	3	3	3	3	3
20–34	6	3.0	12	1	1	1	3	11	11	11
35–49	10	6.2	16	2	3	6	9	14	14	14
50–64	7	3.7	14	1	2	3	4	4	15	15
65+	13	4.7	19	1	1	3	8	12	13	13
TOTAL SINGLE DX	**4**	**1.2**	**<1**	**1**	**1**	**1**	**1**	**2**	**2**	**2**
TOTAL MULTIPLE DX	**39**	**4.3**	**15**	**1**	**1**	**3**	**6**	**11**	**13**	**15**
TOTAL										
0–19 Years	3	2.3	1	1	1	3	3	3	3	3
20–34	7	2.8	11	1	1	1	3	11	11	11
35–49	12	5.1	18	1	1	3	7	10	14	14
50–64	8	3.5	13	1	2	3	4	4	15	15
65+	13	4.7	19	1	1	3	8	12	13	13
GRAND TOTAL	**43**	**4.0**	**14**	**1**	**1**	**3**	**5**	**11**	**13**	**15**

82.3: OTH EXC HAND SOFT TISSUE

Type of Patients	Observed Patients	Avg. Stay	Variance	10th	25th	50th	75th	90th	95th	99th
				Percentiles						
1. SINGLE DX										
0–19 Years	1	1.0	0	1	1	1	1	1	1	1
20–34	1	1.0	0	1	1	1	1	1	1	1
35–49	3	2.5	5	1	1	1	5	5	5	5
50–64	2	3.2	6	1	1	5	5	5	5	5
65+	0									
2. MULTIPLE DX										
0–19 Years	4	2.0	6	1	1	1	2	9	9	9
20–34	13	3.0	1	2	2	3	4	4	4	6
35–49	23	4.9	10	1	2	5	7	11	11	12
50–64	23	4.0	20	1	1	2	4	9	13	21
65+	29	3.9	22	1	1	2	5	8	15	24
TOTAL SINGLE DX	**7**	**2.3**	**4**	**1**	**1**	**1**	**5**	**5**	**5**	**5**
TOTAL MULTIPLE DX	**92**	**3.9**	**15**	**1**	**1**	**2**	**5**	**8**	**12**	**21**
TOTAL										
0–19 Years	5	1.9	6	1	1	1	2	2	9	9
20–34	14	2.9	1	2	2	3	4	4	4	6
35–49	26	4.7	10	1	2	5	7	11	11	12
50–64	25	3.9	19	1	1	2	5	9	13	21
65+	29	3.9	22	1	1	2	5	8	15	24
GRAND TOTAL	**99**	**3.8**	**15**	**1**	**1**	**2**	**5**	**8**	**11**	**21**

82.4: SUTURE HAND SOFT TISSUE

Type of Patients	Observed Patients	Avg. Stay	Variance	10th	25th	50th	75th	90th	95th	99th
				Percentiles						
1. SINGLE DX										
0–19 Years	18	1.7	1	1	1	1	2	3	3	6
20–34	47	1.9	5	1	1	1	2	3	7	12
35–49	27	1.6	2	1	1	1	2	3	5	8
50–64	17	1.9	3	1	1	1	1	5	7	7
65+	1	2.0	0	2	2	2	2	2	2	2
2. MULTIPLE DX										
0–19 Years	42	1.8	2	1	1	1	2	4	5	7
20–34	144	2.7	7	1	1	2	3	6	7	13
35–49	93	2.2	4	1	1	1	3	4	7	9
50–64	48	2.0	3	1	1	1	2	5	7	10
65+	28	4.1	21	1	1	3	5	8	12	25
TOTAL SINGLE DX	**110**	**1.8**	**3**	**1**	**1**	**1**	**2**	**3**	**6**	**11**
TOTAL MULTIPLE DX	**355**	**2.4**	**6**	**1**	**1**	**2**	**3**	**5**	**7**	**13**
TOTAL										
0–19 Years	60	1.8	2	1	1	1	2	3	4	7
20–34	191	2.5	6	1	1	1	3	5	7	13
35–49	120	2.0	3	1	1	1	2	4	5	9
50–64	65	2.0	3	1	1	1	2	5	7	10
65+	29	4.0	20	1	1	3	5	8	12	25
GRAND TOTAL	**465**	**2.3**	**6**	**1**	**1**	**1**	**3**	**5**	**7**	**12**

82.44: SUT FLEXOR TEND HAND NEC

Type of Patients	Observed Patients	Avg. Stay	Vari-ance	10th	25th	50th	75th	90th	95th	99th
1. SINGLE DX										
0–19 Years	13	1.6	<1	1	1	1	2	3	3	3
20–34	16	2.9	9	1	1	2	3	7	12	12
35–49	9	1.7	2	1	1	1	2	5	5	5
50–64	6	2.3	6	1	1	1	4	7	7	7
65+	0									
2. MULTIPLE DX										
0–19 Years	27	1.6	1	1	1	1	2	3	4	5
20–34	65	2.9	6	1	1	2	4	7	8	13
35–49	41	2.4	5	1	1	2	3	5	8	13
50–64	21	2.4	6	1	1	1	2	7	7	10
65+	10	2.1	1	1	1	2	3	4	4	4
TOTAL SINGLE DX	**44**	**2.2**	**5**	**1**	**1**	**1**	**2**	**5**	**7**	**12**
TOTAL MULTIPLE DX	**164**	**2.4**	**5**	**1**	**1**	**2**	**3**	**5**	**7**	**10**
TOTAL										
0–19 Years	40	1.6	<1	1	1	1	2	3	4	5
20–34	81	2.9	7	1	1	2	4	7	9	13
35–49	50	2.3	5	1	1	2	2	5	8	13
50–64	27	2.4	5	1	1	1	2	7	7	10
65+	10	2.1	1	1	1	2	3	4	4	4
GRAND TOTAL	**208**	**2.4**	**5**	**1**	**1**	**1**	**3**	**5**	**7**	**12**

82.45: SUTURE HAND TENDON NEC

Type of Patients	Observed Patients	Avg. Stay	Vari-ance	10th	25th	50th	75th	90th	95th	99th
1. SINGLE DX										
0–19 Years	3	1.0	0	1	1	1	1	1	1	1
20–34	28	1.3	<1	1	1	1	1	2	2	3
35–49	13	1.2	<1	1	1	1	1	2	3	3
50–64	9	1.4	1	1	1	1	1	1	5	5
65+	1	2.0	0	2	2	2	2	2	2	2
2. MULTIPLE DX										
0–19 Years	9	2.6	4	1	1	2	4	6	7	7
20–34	59	2.5	8	1	1	2	3	5	6	21
35–49	43	1.9	2	1	1	1	3	3	5	7
50–64	19	1.6	1	1	1	1	2	2	3	6
65+	12	4.1	8	1	1	4	8	8	8	8
TOTAL SINGLE DX	**54**	**1.3**	**<1**	**1**	**1**	**1**	**1**	**2**	**2**	**5**
TOTAL MULTIPLE DX	**142**	**2.4**	**6**	**1**	**1**	**1**	**3**	**5**	**7**	**13**
TOTAL										
0–19 Years	12	2.3	4	1	1	1	3	6	7	7
20–34	87	2.1	6	1	1	1	2	5	5	13
35–49	56	1.8	2	1	1	1	2	3	5	7
50–64	28	1.5	1	1	1	1	2	2	5	6
65+	13	4.0	8	1	1	4	8	8	8	8
GRAND TOTAL	**196**	**2.1**	**4**	**1**	**1**	**1**	**2**	**5**	**6**	**8**

82.5: HAND MUSC/TEND TRANSPL

Type of Patients	Observed Patients	Avg. Stay	Vari-ance	10th	25th	50th	75th	90th	95th	99th
1. SINGLE DX										
0–19 Years	0									
20–34	1	1.0	0	1	1	1	1	1	1	1
35–49	0									
50–64	0									
65+	0									
2. MULTIPLE DX										
0–19 Years	3	1.0	0	1	1	1	1	1	1	1
20–34	2	1.0	0	1	1	1	1	1	1	1
35–49	2	2.0	2	1	1	1	3	3	3	3
50–64	5	1.4	<1	1	1	1	1	3	3	3
65+	6	4.0	11	1	1	1	7	8	8	8
TOTAL SINGLE DX	**1**	**1.0**	**0**	**1**	**1**	**1**	**1**	**1**	**1**	**1**
TOTAL MULTIPLE DX	**18**	**2.1**	**5**	**1**	**1**	**1**	**3**	**7**	**7**	**8**
TOTAL										
0–19 Years	3	1.0	0	1	1	1	1	1	1	1
20–34	3	1.0	0	1	1	1	1	1	1	1
35–49	2	2.0	2	1	1	1	3	3	3	3
50–64	5	1.4	<1	1	1	1	1	3	3	3
65+	6	4.0	11	1	1	1	7	8	8	8
GRAND TOTAL	**19**	**2.1**	**5**	**1**	**1**	**1**	**1**	**7**	**7**	**8**

82.6: RECONSTRUCTION OF THUMB

Type of Patients	Observed Patients	Avg. Stay	Vari-ance	10th	25th	50th	75th	90th	95th	99th
1. SINGLE DX										
0–19 Years	1	1.0	0	1	1	1	1	1	1	1
20–34	0									
35–49	0									
50–64	1	7.0	0	7	7	7	7	7	7	7
65+	0									
2. MULTIPLE DX										
0–19 Years	5	1.1	<1	1	1	1	1	1	1	2
20–34	3	6.2	1	5	5	7	7	7	7	7
35–49	3	10.4	26	7	7	8	17	17	17	17
50–64	2	4.7	20	1	1	8	8	8	8	8
65+	4	3.2	3	1	1	3	5	5	5	5
TOTAL SINGLE DX	**2**	**2.3**	**7**	**1**	**1**	**1**	**1**	**7**	**7**	**7**
TOTAL MULTIPLE DX	**17**	**3.1**	**12**	**1**	**1**	**1**	**5**	**8**	**8**	**17**
TOTAL										
0–19 Years	6	1.0	<1	1	1	1	1	1	1	2
20–34	3	6.2	1	5	5	7	7	7	7	7
35–49	3	10.4	26	7	7	8	17	17	17	17
50–64	3	5.4	13	1	1	7	8	8	8	8
65+	4	3.2	3	1	1	3	5	5	5	5
GRAND TOTAL	**19**	**3.0**	**12**	**1**	**1**	**1**	**5**	**7**	**8**	**17**

82.7: PLASTIC OP HND GRFT/IMPL

Type of Patients	Observed Patients	Avg. Stay	Vari-ance	Percentiles						
				10th	25th	50th	75th	90th	95th	99th
1. SINGLE DX										
0–19 Years	1	2.0	0	2	2	2	2	2	2	2
20–34	4	1.9	2	1	1	1	2	4	4	4
35–49	5	1.3	<1	1	1	1	2	2	2	2
50–64	2	1.0	0	1	1	1	1	1	1	1
65+	0									
2. MULTIPLE DX										
0–19 Years	3	1.0	0	1	1	1	1	1	1	1
20–34	9	1.8	2	1	1	1	2	5	5	5
35–49	7	2.8	2	1	2	2	4	5	6	6
50–64	1	1.0	0	1	1	1	1	1	1	1
65+	1	1.0	0	1	1	1	1	1	1	1
TOTAL SINGLE DX	**12**	**1.5**	**<1**	**1**	**1**	**1**	**2**	**2**	**4**	**4**
TOTAL MULTIPLE DX	**21**	**2.0**	**2**	**1**	**1**	**2**	**2**	**5**	**5**	**6**
TOTAL										
0–19 Years	4	1.2	<1	1	1	1	1	2	2	2
20–34	13	1.8	2	1	1	1	2	4	5	5
35–49	12	2.1	2	1	1	2	2	4	6	6
50–64	3	1.0	0	1	1	1	1	1	1	1
65+	1	1.0	0	1	1	1	1	1	1	1
GRAND TOTAL	**33**	**1.8**	**2**	**1**	**1**	**1**	**2**	**4**	**5**	**6**

82.8: OTHER PLASTIC OPS HAND

Type of Patients	Observed Patients	Avg. Stay	Vari-ance	Percentiles						
				10th	25th	50th	75th	90th	95th	99th
1. SINGLE DX										
0–19 Years	1	3.0	0	3	3	3	3	3	3	3
20–34	5	1.7	1	1	1	1	2	4	4	4
35–49	2	1.0	0	1	1	1	1	1	1	1
50–64	0									
65+	0									
2. MULTIPLE DX										
0–19 Years	4	1.6	<1	1	1	1	2	3	3	3
20–34	7	3.0	5	1	2	2	4	7	7	7
35–49	10	2.7	6	1	1	2	4	4	10	10
50–64	8	3.0	5	1	1	3	3	8	8	8
65+	3	1.6	1	1	1	1	3	3	3	3
TOTAL SINGLE DX	**8**	**1.7**	**1**	**1**	**1**	**1**	**2**	**4**	**4**	**4**
TOTAL MULTIPLE DX	**32**	**2.5**	**4**	**1**	**1**	**2**	**3**	**4**	**8**	**10**
TOTAL										
0–19 Years	5	1.7	<1	1	1	1	2	3	3	3
20–34	12	2.4	4	1	1	2	4	6	7	7
35–49	12	2.5	6	1	1	1	3	4	10	10
50–64	8	3.0	5	1	1	3	3	8	8	8
65+	3	1.6	1	1	1	1	3	3	3	3
GRAND TOTAL	**40**	**2.4**	**4**	**1**	**1**	**2**	**3**	**4**	**7**	**10**

82.9: OTH HAND SOFT TISSUE OPS

Type of Patients	Observed Patients	Avg. Stay	Vari-ance	Percentiles						
				10th	25th	50th	75th	90th	95th	99th
1. SINGLE DX										
0–19 Years	0									
20–34	1	2.0	0	2	2	2	2	2	2	2
35–49	0									
50–64	0									
65+	0									
2. MULTIPLE DX										
0–19 Years	1	1.0	0	1	1	1	1	1	1	1
20–34	3	1.4	<1	1	1	1	1	3	3	3
35–49	6	5.7	10	2	3	6	10	10	10	10
50–64	10	2.4	7	1	1	1	2	4	11	11
65+	7	3.4	3	1	2	4	4	5	8	8
TOTAL SINGLE DX	**1**	**2.0**	**0**	**2**	**2**	**2**	**2**	**2**	**2**	**2**
TOTAL MULTIPLE DX	**27**	**3.1**	**7**	**1**	**1**	**2**	**4**	**6**	**10**	**11**
TOTAL										
0–19 Years	1	1.0	0	1	1	1	1	1	1	1
20–34	4	1.6	<1	1	1	1	2	3	3	3
35–49	6	5.7	10	2	3	6	10	10	10	10
50–64	10	2.4	7	1	1	1	2	4	11	11
65+	7	3.4	3	1	2	4	4	5	8	8
GRAND TOTAL	**28**	**3.1**	**6**	**1**	**1**	**2**	**4**	**6**	**10**	**11**

83.0: INC MUSC/TEND/FASC/BURSA

Type of Patients	Observed Patients	Avg. Stay	Vari-ance	Percentiles						
				10th	25th	50th	75th	90th	95th	99th
1. SINGLE DX										
0–19 Years	44	2.3	2	1	1	2	3	4	5	8
20–34	49	2.7	4	1	1	2	3	5	7	11
35–49	46	2.6	7	1	1	2	3	6	6	20
50–64	19	2.7	5	1	1	2	3	6	8	9
65+	7	2.5	4	1	1	2	4	6	6	6
2. MULTIPLE DX										
0–19 Years	144	7.1	68	1	2	5	8	14	25	42
20–34	298	5.5	33	1	2	4	7	12	16	22
35–49	542	6.1	36	2	3	4	8	13	17	27
50–64	472	6.4	45	2	3	5	8	12	15	34
65+	430	6.1	24	2	3	5	8	12	17	24
TOTAL SINGLE DX	**165**	**2.5**	**4**	**1**	**1**	**2**	**3**	**5**	**6**	**11**
TOTAL MULTIPLE DX	**1,886**	**6.2**	**39**	**2**	**3**	**5**	**8**	**12**	**17**	**32**
TOTAL										
0–19 Years	188	6.0	57	1	2	4	7	12	17	42
20–34	347	5.1	30	1	2	4	6	11	14	22
35–49	588	5.8	35	1	2	4	7	12	17	27
50–64	491	6.3	44	2	3	5	8	12	15	34
65+	437	6.1	24	2	3	5	8	12	17	24
GRAND TOTAL	**2,051**	**5.9**	**37**	**1**	**2**	**4**	**7**	**12**	**16**	**31**

83.02: MYOTOMY

Type of Patients	Observed Patients	Avg. Stay	Vari-ance	Percentiles						
				10th	25th	50th	75th	90th	95th	99th
1. SINGLE DX										
0–19 Years	4	2.6	3	1	1	2	5	5	5	5
20–34	9	1.7	<1	1	1	2	2	3	3	3
35–49	12	1.7	<1	1	1	1	2	3	4	4
50–64	1	1.0	0	1	1	1	1	1	1	1
65+	0									
2. MULTIPLE DX										
0–19 Years	14	4.4	34	1	2	2	4	10	25	25
20–34	41	5.5	68	1	1	3	5	14	18	50
35–49	70	5.6	24	1	2	4	8	11	18	23
50–64	64	7.6	55	2	3	6	9	13	14	42
65+	38	8.5	51	2	4	7	10	17	24	32
TOTAL SINGLE DX	**26**	**1.9**	**1**	**1**	**1**	**1**	**2**	**3**	**5**	**5**
TOTAL MULTIPLE DX	**227**	**6.5**	**48**	**1**	**2**	**4**	**8**	**14**	**18**	**38**
TOTAL										
0–19 Years	18	3.9	26	1	1	2	4	6	10	25
20–34	50	4.7	56	1	1	3	4	9	17	50
35–49	82	5.0	23	1	2	3	7	11	18	23
50–64	65	7.5	55	2	3	6	8	13	14	42
65+	38	8.5	51	2	4	7	10	17	24	32
GRAND TOTAL	**253**	**6.0**	**45**	**1**	**2**	**4**	**8**	**13**	**18**	**34**

83.03: BURSOTOMY

Type of Patients	Observed Patients	Avg. Stay	Vari-ance	Percentiles						
				10th	25th	50th	75th	90th	95th	99th
1. SINGLE DX										
0–19 Years	3	2.6	1	2	2	2	4	4	4	4
20–34	6	3.5	5	1	2	3	4	8	8	8
35–49	11	2.3	3	1	1	2	3	5	7	7
50–64	9	3.1	5	1	1	2	4	8	8	8
65+	1	2.0	0	2	2	2	2	2	2	2
2. MULTIPLE DX										
0–19 Years	20	5.3	23	2	2	3	6	17	17	17
20–34	55	5.6	20	2	3	5	7	9	13	27
35–49	110	5.4	54	2	3	4	6	9	11	21
50–64	93	4.8	11	2	3	4	6	8	9	23
65+	90	5.2	15	2	2	5	6	8	11	23
TOTAL SINGLE DX	**30**	**2.8**	**4**	**1**	**1**	**2**	**3**	**6**	**8**	**8**
TOTAL MULTIPLE DX	**368**	**5.2**	**26**	**2**	**3**	**4**	**6**	**9**	**11**	**23**
TOTAL										
0–19 Years	23	5.1	22	2	2	3	6	17	17	17
20–34	61	5.4	19	2	2	5	7	9	10	27
35–49	121	5.1	50	2	3	4	5	9	10	21
50–64	102	4.6	10	2	2	4	6	8	9	23
65+	91	5.2	15	2	2	4	6	8	11	23
GRAND TOTAL	**398**	**5.0**	**25**	**2**	**2**	**4**	**6**	**9**	**10**	**23**

83.09: SOFT TISSUE INCISION NEC

Type of Patients	Observed Patients	Avg. Stay	Vari-ance	Percentiles						
				10th	25th	50th	75th	90th	95th	99th
1. SINGLE DX										
0–19 Years	37	2.3	2	1	1	2	3	4	4	8
20–34	31	3.0	5	1	1	3	3	6	7	11
35–49	23	3.1	12	1	1	2	4	6	7	20
50–64	8	2.4	6	1	1	2	2	9	9	9
65+	5	2.9	4	1	1	2	4	6	6	6
2. MULTIPLE DX										
0–19 Years	105	7.9	79	1	3	6	9	14	38	42
20–34	191	5.7	30	1	2	4	7	12	14	19
35–49	343	6.5	32	2	3	5	9	14	18	27
50–64	299	6.9	53	2	3	5	8	13	16	32
65+	295	6.2	23	2	3	5	8	13	17	22
TOTAL SINGLE DX	**104**	**2.7**	**5**	**1**	**1**	**2**	**3**	**5**	**6**	**11**
TOTAL MULTIPLE DX	**1,233**	**6.6**	**41**	**2**	**3**	**5**	**8**	**13**	**17**	**32**
TOTAL										
0–19 Years	142	6.4	65	1	2	4	7	12	16	42
20–34	222	5.3	28	1	2	4	6	12	14	19
35–49	366	6.3	32	1	3	4	8	14	17	27
50–64	307	6.7	53	2	3	5	8	13	16	32
65+	300	6.1	23	2	3	5	8	12	17	22
GRAND TOTAL	**1,337**	**6.2**	**39**	**1**	**3**	**4**	**8**	**13**	**16**	**31**

83.1: MUSC/TEND/FASC DIVISION

Type of Patients	Observed Patients	Avg. Stay	Vari-ance	Percentiles						
				10th	25th	50th	75th	90th	95th	99th
1. SINGLE DX										
0–19 Years	70	2.0	7	1	1	1	2	3	9	15
20–34	28	2.3	2	1	1	2	3	5	6	6
35–49	8	2.1	1	1	1	2	2	5	5	5
50–64	5	1.5	1	1	1	1	1	4	4	4
65+	4	1.6	2	1	1	1	1	4	4	4
2. MULTIPLE DX										
0–19 Years	219	2.8	9	1	1	2	3	5	8	17
20–34	113	6.5	40	1	2	5	8	13	18	41
35–49	136	6.8	44	1	2	5	8	16	24	31
50–64	148	6.2	47	1	2	4	8	15	21	32
65+	117	6.9	57	1	2	4	10	21	21	31
TOTAL SINGLE DX	**115**	**2.1**	**6**	**1**	**1**	**1**	**2**	**3**	**6**	**15**
TOTAL MULTIPLE DX	**733**	**5.1**	**36**	**1**	**1**	**3**	**6**	**12**	**18**	**31**
TOTAL										
0–19 Years	289	2.6	9	1	1	2	3	5	8	17
20–34	141	5.7	35	1	2	4	7	13	16	35
35–49	144	6.6	43	1	2	4	8	16	21	31
50–64	153	6.1	46	1	1	3	8	15	21	32
65+	121	6.6	56	1	2	3	10	20	21	31
GRAND TOTAL	**848**	**4.5**	**31**	**1**	**1**	**2**	**5**	**11**	**16**	**28**

83.12: ADDUCTOR TENOTOMY OF HIP

Type of Patients	Observed Patients	Avg. Stay	Vari-ance	Percentiles						
				10th	25th	50th	75th	90th	95th	99th
1. SINGLE DX										
0–19 Years	19	2.9	18	1	1	1	2	10	15	15
20–34	0									
35–49	0									
50–64	0									
65+	0									
2. MULTIPLE DX										
0–19 Years	85	2.3	3	1	1	2	3	4	6	8
20–34	2	3.4	6	2	2	2	7	7	7	7
35–49	3	10.5	71	1	2	17	17	17	17	17
50–64	6	1.8	2	1	1	1	2	6	6	6
65+	10	5.7	51	1	2	3	6	12	27	27
TOTAL SINGLE DX	**19**	**2.9**	**18**	**1**	**1**	**1**	**2**	**10**	**15**	**15**
TOTAL MULTIPLE DX	**106**	**2.6**	**8**	**1**	**1**	**2**	**3**	**5**	**8**	**17**
TOTAL										
0–19 Years	104	2.4	7	1	1	1	3	5	8	15
20–34	2	3.4	6	2	2	2	7	7	7	7
35–49	3	10.5	71	1	2	17	17	17	17	17
50–64	6	1.8	2	1	1	1	2	6	6	6
65+	10	5.7	51	1	2	3	6	12	27	27
GRAND TOTAL	**125**	**2.7**	**10**	**1**	**1**	**2**	**3**	**6**	**8**	**17**

83.13: TENOTOMY NEC

Type of Patients	Observed Patients	Avg. Stay	Vari-ance	Percentiles						
				10th	25th	50th	75th	90th	95th	99th
1. SINGLE DX										
0–19 Years	18	1.4	<1	1	1	1	2	3	3	3
20–34	2	1.7	1	1	1	1	3	3	3	3
35–49	2	1.0	0	1	1	1	1	1	1	1
50–64	0									
65+	2	1.8	2	1	1	1	4	4	4	4
2. MULTIPLE DX										
0–19 Years	65	2.3	4	1	1	2	3	5	5	17
20–34	12	4.2	19	1	1	2	6	8	18	18
35–49	17	3.2	15	1	1	2	3	7	7	19
50–64	39	2.4	3	1	1	2	3	5	5	7
65+	41	3.0	8	1	1	2	3	7	9	15
TOTAL SINGLE DX	**24**	**1.4**	**<1**	**1**	**1**	**1**	**2**	**3**	**3**	**4**
TOTAL MULTIPLE DX	**174**	**2.7**	**7**	**1**	**1**	**2**	**3**	**5**	**7**	**17**
TOTAL										
0–19 Years	83	2.0	3	1	1	1	2	4	5	6
20–34	14	3.9	17	1	1	2	6	8	18	18
35–49	19	3.0	14	1	1	2	3	4	7	19
50–64	39	2.4	3	1	1	2	3	5	5	7
65+	43	2.9	7	1	1	2	3	7	9	15
GRAND TOTAL	**198**	**2.4**	**6**	**1**	**1**	**2**	**3**	**5**	**6**	**17**

83.14: FASCIOTOMY

Type of Patients	Observed Patients	Avg. Stay	Vari-ance	Percentiles						
				10th	25th	50th	75th	90th	95th	99th
1. SINGLE DX										
0–19 Years	20	2.3	2	1	2	2	3	3	5	7
20–34	24	2.5	2	1	1	2	3	5	6	6
35–49	4	2.1	<1	2	2	2	2	3	3	3
50–64	4	2.0	2	1	1	1	2	4	4	4
65+	1	1.0	0	1	1	1	1	1	1	1
2. MULTIPLE DX										
0–19 Years	53	5.2	30	1	2	3	6	13	18	24
20–34	90	7.2	44	2	3	5	9	13	21	41
35–49	99	7.8	48	2	3	6	9	18	24	31
50–64	85	8.4	58	1	3	6	11	20	25	33
65+	54	10.0	77	2	3	7	13	21	25	44
TOTAL SINGLE DX	**53**	**2.3**	**2**	**1**	**1**	**2**	**3**	**4**	**5**	**7**
TOTAL MULTIPLE DX	**381**	**7.7**	**53**	**1**	**3**	**5**	**10**	**18**	**24**	**35**
TOTAL										
0–19 Years	73	4.4	23	1	2	3	5	11	17	24
20–34	114	6.2	39	1	2	5	8	13	18	41
35–49	103	7.5	47	2	3	6	9	16	24	31
50–64	89	8.2	58	1	3	6	11	20	25	33
65+	55	9.9	77	2	3	7	13	21	25	44
GRAND TOTAL	**434**	**7.0**	**50**	**1**	**2**	**4**	**10**	**16**	**24**	**34**

83.2: SOFT TISSUE DXTIC PX

Type of Patients	Observed Patients	Avg. Stay	Vari-ance	Percentiles						
				10th	25th	50th	75th	90th	95th	99th
1. SINGLE DX										
0–19 Years	32	4.9	17	1	1	3	8	12	13	14
20–34	19	4.3	20	1	1	3	6	14	14	14
35–49	28	2.0	2	1	1	1	3	3	5	6
50–64	22	2.9	13	1	1	1	3	6	8	17
65+	5	1.7	1	1	1	1	2	4	4	4
2. MULTIPLE DX										
0–19 Years	59	13.5	266	1	2	7	17	45	55	76
20–34	84	10.4	92	2	4	8	13	22	33	49
35–49	211	8.2	51	2	4	6	11	15	24	42
50–64	308	8.3	59	2	3	6	10	19	27	35
65+	414	8.2	40	2	4	7	11	17	21	33
TOTAL SINGLE DX	**106**	**3.7**	**14**	**1**	**1**	**2**	**5**	**10**	**12**	**14**
TOTAL MULTIPLE DX	**1,076**	**8.8**	**70**	**2**	**3**	**7**	**11**	**18**	**26**	**45**
TOTAL										
0–19 Years	91	10.6	196	1	2	5	14	28	45	76
20–34	103	9.4	85	1	3	7	12	20	29	49
35–49	239	7.5	49	1	3	5	10	15	21	42
50–64	330	8.0	58	1	3	6	10	18	26	35
65+	419	8.1	40	2	4	7	11	16	21	33
GRAND TOTAL	**1,182**	**8.3**	**67**	**1**	**3**	**6**	**11**	**17**	**24**	**44**

83.21: SOFT TISSUE BIOPSY

Type of Patients	Observed Patients	Avg. Stay	Vari-ance	Percentiles						
				10th	25th	50th	75th	90th	95th	99th
1. SINGLE DX										
0–19 Years	32	4.9	17	1	1	3	8	12	13	14
20–34	19	4.3	20	1	1	3	6	14	14	14
35–49	28	2.0	2	1	1	1	3	3	5	6
50–64	22	2.9	13	1	1	1	3	6	8	17
65+	5	1.7	1	1	1	1	2	4	4	4
2. MULTIPLE DX										
0–19 Years	59	13.5	266	1	2	7	17	45	55	76
20–34	84	10.4	92	2	4	8	13	22	33	49
35–49	211	8.2	51	2	4	6	11	15	24	42
50–64	308	8.3	59	2	3	6	10	19	27	35
65+	414	8.2	40	2	4	7	11	17	21	33
TOTAL SINGLE DX	**106**	**3.7**	**14**	**1**	**1**	**2**	**5**	**10**	**12**	**14**
TOTAL MULTIPLE DX	**1,076**	**8.8**	**70**	**2**	**3**	**7**	**11**	**18**	**26**	**45**
TOTAL										
0–19 Years	91	10.6	196	1	2	5	14	28	45	76
20–34	103	9.4	85	1	3	7	12	20	29	49
35–49	239	7.5	49	1	3	5	10	15	21	42
50–64	330	8.0	58	1	3	6	10	18	26	35
65+	419	8.1	40	2	4	7	11	16	21	33
GRAND TOTAL	**1,182**	**8.3**	**67**	**1**	**3**	**6**	**11**	**17**	**24**	**44**

83.3: EXC LESION SOFT TISSUE

Type of Patients	Observed Patients	Avg. Stay	Vari-ance	Percentiles						
				10th	25th	50th	75th	90th	95th	99th
1. SINGLE DX										
0–19 Years	71	2.3	7	1	1	1	2	4	9	13
20–34	49	2.2	2	1	1	2	3	4	6	8
35–49	82	2.1	2	1	1	2	3	4	6	6
50–64	66	2.5	5	1	1	2	3	5	6	14
65+	21	1.8	<1	1	1	2	2	3	4	4
2. MULTIPLE DX										
0–19 Years	41	3.4	18	1	2	2	3	9	9	31
20–34	60	4.0	29	1	1	3	5	9	10	38
35–49	219	4.4	42	1	1	3	4	9	13	38
50–64	334	4.4	38	1	1	3	5	9	12	24
65+	331	4.5	28	1	1	3	5	9	17	26
TOTAL SINGLE DX	**289**	**2.2**	**5**	**1**	**1**	**2**	**2**	**4**	**6**	**13**
TOTAL MULTIPLE DX	**985**	**4.4**	**34**	**1**	**1**	**3**	**5**	**9**	**13**	**28**
TOTAL										
0–19 Years	112	2.6	11	1	1	2	2	6	9	13
20–34	109	3.2	18	1	1	2	4	6	9	17
35–49	301	3.8	32	1	1	2	4	7	12	38
50–64	400	4.1	34	1	1	2	5	9	12	21
65+	352	4.4	27	1	1	3	5	8	17	26
GRAND TOTAL	**1,274**	**3.8**	**27**	**1**	**1**	**2**	**4**	**8**	**12**	**26**

83.32: EXC MUSCLE LESION

Type of Patients	Observed Patients	Avg. Stay	Vari-ance	Percentiles						
				10th	25th	50th	75th	90th	95th	99th
1. SINGLE DX										
0–19 Years	21	1.4	2	1	1	1	1	2	3	8
20–34	21	2.0	2	1	1	2	3	4	4	8
35–49	29	2.5	3	1	1	2	3	6	6	6
50–64	21	2.2	3	1	1	2	3	4	5	8
65+	8	1.9	<1	1	1	2	2	3	4	4
2. MULTIPLE DX										
0–19 Years	8	2.4	2	1	2	2	3	3	6	6
20–34	11	2.8	15	1	1	2	3	4	17	17
35–49	49	2.8	5	1	1	3	3	4	7	12
50–64	86	3.9	16	1	1	3	5	8	11	28
65+	86	4.6	34	1	2	3	5	8	26	26
TOTAL SINGLE DX	**100**	**2.0**	**2**	**1**	**1**	**1**	**2**	**4**	**6**	**8**
TOTAL MULTIPLE DX	**240**	**3.9**	**21**	**1**	**1**	**3**	**4**	**8**	**12**	**26**
TOTAL										
0–19 Years	29	1.7	2	1	1	1	2	3	3	8
20–34	32	2.3	7	1	1	2	3	4	4	17
35–49	78	2.7	4	1	1	2	3	5	6	12
50–64	107	3.6	14	1	1	2	4	8	9	28
65+	94	4.4	32	1	2	3	4	8	26	26
GRAND TOTAL	**340**	**3.3**	**16**	**1**	**1**	**2**	**3**	**6**	**9**	**26**

83.39: EXC LES SOFT TISSUE NEC

Type of Patients	Observed Patients	Avg. Stay	Vari-ance	Percentiles						
				10th	25th	50th	75th	90th	95th	99th
1. SINGLE DX										
0–19 Years	47	2.6	9	1	1	1	2	8	13	13
20–34	28	2.3	2	1	1	2	3	4	6	7
35–49	52	1.9	1	1	1	2	3	3	4	6
50–64	45	2.6	6	1	1	2	3	5	9	14
65+	13	1.8	<1	1	1	2	2	3	3	4
2. MULTIPLE DX										
0–19 Years	32	3.6	21	1	2	2	3	9	10	31
20–34	48	4.4	33	1	1	4	5	9	10	38
35–49	159	5.0	54	1	1	3	6	9	15	38
50–64	241	4.6	47	1	1	3	6	10	14	24
65+	240	4.6	26	1	1	3	5	9	17	25
TOTAL SINGLE DX	**185**	**2.3**	**6**	**1**	**1**	**2**	**2**	**4**	**8**	**13**
TOTAL MULTIPLE DX	**720**	**4.6**	**38**	**1**	**1**	**3**	**5**	**9**	**15**	**31**
TOTAL										
0–19 Years	79	3.0	14	1	1	2	3	9	10	13
20–34	76	3.6	23	1	1	2	4	7	9	38
35–49	211	4.3	44	1	1	2	4	8	13	38
50–64	286	4.4	41	1	1	2	5	9	14	21
65+	253	4.4	25	1	1	3	5	9	17	25
GRAND TOTAL	**905**	**4.1**	**32**	**1**	**1**	**2**	**5**	**9**	**13**	**28**

83.4: OTHER EXC MUSC/TEND/FASC

Type of Patients	Observed Patients	Avg. Stay	Vari-ance	Percentiles 10th	25th	50th	75th	90th	95th	99th
1. SINGLE DX										
0–19 Years	17	1.8	<1	1	1	2	2	3	3	3
20–34	32	2.4	3	1	1	2	3	4	7	7
35–49	22	2.3	13	1	1	1	2	3	6	22
50–64	9	2.7	2	1	1	2	4	5	5	5
65+	6	1.5	<1	1	1	2	2	2	2	2
2. MULTIPLE DX										
0–19 Years	52	6.2	113	1	1	3	7	13	15	84
20–34	142	6.1	49	1	2	4	8	13	18	41
35–49	285	7.2	64	1	3	5	9	14	20	46
50–64	262	8.1	59	1	3	6	11	19	23	37
65+	311	9.2	76	1	3	7	12	21	25	46
TOTAL SINGLE DX	**86**	**2.2**	**5**	**1**	**1**	**2**	**3**	**4**	**5**	**7**
TOTAL MULTIPLE DX	**1,052**	**7.8**	**69**	**1**	**3**	**5**	**10**	**17**	**23**	**42**
TOTAL										
0–19 Years	69	5.2	91	1	1	2	6	12	15	84
20–34	174	5.4	42	1	2	3	7	12	16	41
35–49	307	6.9	62	1	3	5	9	14	20	30
50–64	271	7.9	59	1	3	5	10	19	23	37
65+	317	9.1	76	1	3	7	12	21	24	46
GRAND TOTAL	**1,138**	**7.4**	**66**	**1**	**2**	**5**	**10**	**16**	**22**	**41**

83.42: TENONECTOMY NEC

Type of Patients	Observed Patients	Avg. Stay	Vari-ance	Percentiles 10th	25th	50th	75th	90th	95th	99th
1. SINGLE DX										
0–19 Years	0									
20–34	0									
35–49	1	1.0	0	1	1	1	1	1	1	1
50–64	2	2.1	2	1	1	3	3	3	3	3
65+	0									
2. MULTIPLE DX										
0–19 Years	1	1.0	0	1	1	1	1	1	1	1
20–34	2	8.1	7	6	6	10	10	10	10	10
35–49	15	4.0	5	2	3	3	4	7	9	9
50–64	22	5.6	50	1	2	3	6	14	21	31
65+	32	5.0	16	1	2	4	7	10	13	20
TOTAL SINGLE DX	**3**	**1.8**	**1**	**1**	**1**	**1**	**3**	**3**	**3**	**3**
TOTAL MULTIPLE DX	**72**	**4.9**	**23**	**1**	**2**	**3**	**6**	**10**	**13**	**31**
TOTAL										
0–19 Years	1	1.0	0	1	1	1	1	1	1	1
20–34	2	8.1	7	6	6	10	10	10	10	10
35–49	16	3.9	5	2	2	3	4	7	9	9
50–64	24	5.3	47	1	2	3	6	14	21	31
65+	32	5.0	16	1	2	4	7	10	13	20
GRAND TOTAL	**75**	**4.8**	**23**	**1**	**2**	**3**	**6**	**10**	**13**	**31**

83.44: FASCIECTOMY NEC

Type of Patients	Observed Patients	Avg. Stay	Vari-ance	Percentiles 10th	25th	50th	75th	90th	95th	99th
1. SINGLE DX										
0–19 Years	0									
20–34	1	5.0	0	5	5	5	5	5	5	5
35–49	1	22.0	0	22	22	22	22	22	22	22
50–64	0									
65+	1	1.0	0	1	1	1	1	1	1	1
2. MULTIPLE DX										
0–19 Years	5	4.1	13	1	1	1	9	9	9	9
20–34	9	6.6	24	3	4	4	8	15	18	18
35–49	34	8.2	42	1	4	6	10	18	23	30
50–64	24	10.4	77	3	5	7	13	30	30	37
65+	24	7.8	37	3	3	5	11	16	22	27
TOTAL SINGLE DX	**3**	**8.3**	**102**	**1**	**1**	**5**	**22**	**22**	**22**	**22**
TOTAL MULTIPLE DX	**96**	**8.0**	**46**	**1**	**3**	**5**	**10**	**16**	**23**	**30**
TOTAL										
0–19 Years	5	4.1	13	1	1	1	9	9	9	9
20–34	10	6.5	23	3	4	4	8	15	18	18
35–49	35	8.5	45	1	4	7	11	22	23	30
50–64	24	10.4	77	3	5	7	13	30	30	37
65+	25	7.7	37	3	3	5	11	16	22	27
GRAND TOTAL	**99**	**8.0**	**46**	**1**	**3**	**5**	**10**	**17**	**22**	**30**

83.45: MYECTOMY NEC

Type of Patients	Observed Patients	Avg. Stay	Vari-ance	Percentiles 10th	25th	50th	75th	90th	95th	99th
1. SINGLE DX										
0–19 Years	9	2.0	<1	1	1	2	3	3	3	3
20–34	28	2.1	2	1	1	2	3	4	4	7
35–49	14	1.9	1	1	1	2	2	3	3	6
50–64	7	2.8	3	1	2	2	5	5	5	5
65+	2	1.0	0	1	1	1	1	1	1	1
2. MULTIPLE DX										
0–19 Years	34	7.6	175	1	2	4	8	13	19	84
20–34	115	6.1	58	1	2	4	7	13	19	41
35–49	210	7.7	76	2	3	6	10	15	21	81
50–64	188	8.7	61	2	4	6	12	20	23	39
65+	218	10.1	76	2	4	8	14	21	24	36
TOTAL SINGLE DX	**60**	**2.1**	**2**	**1**	**1**	**2**	**3**	**4**	**5**	**7**
TOTAL MULTIPLE DX	**765**	**8.4**	**76**	**1**	**3**	**6**	**11**	**19**	**23**	**42**
TOTAL										
0–19 Years	43	6.5	144	1	2	3	6	13	19	84
20–34	143	5.3	49	1	1	3	7	12	18	41
35–49	224	7.3	73	1	3	5	9	15	20	46
50–64	195	8.6	60	2	3	6	11	20	23	39
65+	220	10.1	76	2	4	8	14	21	24	36
GRAND TOTAL	**825**	**8.0**	**74**	**1**	**3**	**5**	**11**	**17**	**23**	**41**

83.49: SOFT TISSUE EXC NEC

Type of Patients	Observed Patients	Avg. Stay	Vari-ance	Percentiles						
				10th	25th	50th	75th	90th	95th	99th
1. SINGLE DX										
0–19 Years	8	1.5	<1	1	1	1	2	3	3	3
20–34	3	4.2	6	1	1	4	7	7	7	7
35–49	5	1.6	<1	1	1	1	2	3	3	3
50–64	0									
65+	3	1.8	<1	1	2	2	2	2	2	2
2. MULTIPLE DX										
0–19 Years	11	5.2	33	1	1	2	6	15	15	15
20–34	12	6.3	15	1	3	6	11	11	11	11
35–49	25	4.2	14	1	1	3	5	8	10	19
50–64	23	4.9	20	1	2	3	7	9	14	21
65+	35	9.0	150	1	2	5	8	26	46	46
TOTAL SINGLE DX	**19**	**2.0**	**2**	**1**	**1**	**2**	**2**	**4**	**4**	**7**
TOTAL MULTIPLE DX	**106**	**6.3**	**65**	**1**	**2**	**4**	**8**	**11**	**21**	**46**
TOTAL										
0–19 Years	19	3.6	22	1	1	2	3	15	15	15
20–34	15	5.8	13	1	3	6	9	11	11	11
35–49	30	3.8	13	1	1	3	5	8	10	19
50–64	23	4.9	20	1	2	3	7	9	14	21
65+	38	8.2	138	1	2	4	8	25	46	46
GRAND TOTAL	**125**	**5.6**	**57**	**1**	**1**	**3**	**7**	**11**	**15**	**46**

83.5: BURSECTOMY

Type of Patients	Observed Patients	Avg. Stay	Vari-ance	Percentiles						
				10th	25th	50th	75th	90th	95th	99th
1. SINGLE DX										
0–19 Years	3	4.5	5	2	4	4	4	8	8	8
20–34	11	4.8	18	1	2	3	7	14	14	14
35–49	13	2.6	1	1	2	2	3	5	5	5
50–64	14	2.4	1	1	1	2	3	4	4	4
65+	5	1.3	<1	1	1	1	1	3	3	3
2. MULTIPLE DX										
0–19 Years	8	2.8	8	1	1	2	3	9	9	9
20–34	37	3.7	8	1	2	3	4	8	10	15
35–49	117	3.6	7	1	1	3	5	7	9	11
50–64	152	3.7	12	1	1	3	5	6	7	26
65+	161	3.6	11	1	1	3	4	7	11	16
TOTAL SINGLE DX	**46**	**3.1**	**7**	**1**	**2**	**2**	**4**	**5**	**8**	**14**
TOTAL MULTIPLE DX	**475**	**3.6**	**10**	**1**	**1**	**3**	**5**	**7**	**9**	**15**
TOTAL										
0–19 Years	11	3.2	7	1	1	2	4	9	9	9
20–34	48	3.9	10	1	2	3	4	8	12	15
35–49	130	3.5	7	1	1	3	5	7	9	11
50–64	166	3.6	12	1	1	3	5	6	7	19
65+	166	3.6	11	1	1	3	4	7	10	16
GRAND TOTAL	**521**	**3.6**	**10**	**1**	**1**	**3**	**5**	**7**	**9**	**15**

83.6: SUTURE MUSC/TENDON/FASC

Type of Patients	Observed Patients	Avg. Stay	Vari-ance	Percentiles						
				10th	25th	50th	75th	90th	95th	99th
1. SINGLE DX										
0–19 Years	49	1.3	<1	1	1	1	1	2	2	3
20–34	154	1.7	2	1	1	1	2	3	4	9
35–49	263	1.5	1	1	1	1	2	2	3	7
50–64	268	1.4	<1	1	1	1	2	2	3	4
65+	141	1.4	<1	1	1	1	2	2	3	4
2. MULTIPLE DX										
0–19 Years	116	2.2	4	1	1	1	3	4	5	9
20–34	321	2.4	7	1	1	2	3	5	6	14
35–49	558	2.1	5	1	1	1	2	4	6	11
50–64	1,211	1.8	3	1	1	1	2	3	4	9
65+	1,625	1.9	3	1	1	1	2	3	4	9
TOTAL SINGLE DX	**875**	**1.5**	**<1**	**1**	**1**	**1**	**2**	**2**	**3**	**6**
TOTAL MULTIPLE DX	**3,831**	**2.0**	**4**	**1**	**1**	**1**	**2**	**3**	**5**	**10**
TOTAL										
0–19 Years	165	2.0	3	1	1	1	2	4	5	9
20–34	475	2.2	5	1	1	1	2	4	6	12
35–49	821	1.9	4	1	1	1	2	3	5	9
50–64	1,479	1.7	3	1	1	1	2	3	4	9
65+	1,766	1.9	3	1	1	1	2	3	4	8
GRAND TOTAL	**4,706**	**1.9**	**3**	**1**	**1**	**1**	**2**	**3**	**4**	**9**

83.61: TENDON SHEATH SUTURE

Type of Patients	Observed Patients	Avg. Stay	Vari-ance	Percentiles						
				10th	25th	50th	75th	90th	95th	99th
1. SINGLE DX										
0–19 Years	6	1.3	<1	1	1	1	2	2	2	2
20–34	10	1.6	1	1	1	1	2	3	4	4
35–49	19	1.4	<1	1	1	1	1	2	4	4
50–64	7	1.2	<1	1	1	1	1	2	2	2
65+	0									
2. MULTIPLE DX										
0–19 Years	8	4.2	33	1	2	2	3	5	22	22
20–34	23	1.9	3	1	1	1	2	3	6	8
35–49	27	3.9	31	1	1	2	4	7	7	28
50–64	21	2.7	9	1	1	2	2	6	12	12
65+	25	2.9	4	1	1	3	4	5	7	10
TOTAL SINGLE DX	**42**	**1.4**	**<1**	**1**	**1**	**1**	**2**	**2**	**4**	**4**
TOTAL MULTIPLE DX	**104**	**3.0**	**13**	**1**	**1**	**2**	**3**	**6**	**7**	**22**
TOTAL										
0–19 Years	14	3.0	21	1	1	2	3	5	22	22
20–34	33	1.8	2	1	1	1	2	3	5	8
35–49	46	2.8	19	1	1	1	3	4	7	28
50–64	28	2.3	7	1	1	1	2	4	12	12
65+	25	2.9	4	1	1	3	4	5	7	10
GRAND TOTAL	**146**	**2.5**	**10**	**1**	**1**	**2**	**3**	**5**	**7**	**22**

83.63: ROTATOR CUFF REPAIR

Type of Patients	Observed Patients	Avg. Stay	Vari-ance	Percentiles 10th	25th	50th	75th	90th	95th	99th
1. SINGLE DX										
0–19 Years	1	1.0	0	1	1	1	1	1	1	1
20–34	4	1.5	<1	1	1	1	2	2	2	2
35–49	74	1.4	<1	1	1	1	2	2	3	4
50–64	194	1.4	<1	1	1	1	2	2	3	3
65+	129	1.4	<1	1	1	1	2	2	3	4
2. MULTIPLE DX										
0–19 Years	2	2.6	4	1	1	4	4	4	4	4
20–34	18	1.1	<1	1	1	1	1	1	3	3
35–49	268	1.5	<1	1	1	1	2	2	3	4
50–64	976	1.6	1	1	1	1	2	3	3	6
65+	1,439	1.7	1	1	1	1	2	3	4	6
TOTAL SINGLE DX	**402**	**1.4**	**<1**	**1**	**1**	**1**	**2**	**2**	**3**	**4**
TOTAL MULTIPLE DX	**2,703**	**1.7**	**1**	**1**	**1**	**1**	**2**	**3**	**3**	**6**
TOTAL										
0–19 Years	3	2.0	3	1	1	1	4	4	4	4
20–34	22	1.2	<1	1	1	1	1	2	2	3
35–49	342	1.5	<1	1	1	1	2	2	3	4
50–64	1,170	1.6	1	1	1	1	2	2	3	5
65+	1,568	1.7	1	1	1	1	2	3	3	6
GRAND TOTAL	**3,105**	**1.6**	**1**	**1**	**1**	**1**	**2**	**3**	**3**	**6**

83.64: SUTURE OF TENDON NEC

Type of Patients	Observed Patients	Avg. Stay	Vari-ance	Percentiles 10th	25th	50th	75th	90th	95th	99th
1. SINGLE DX										
0–19 Years	22	1.2	<1	1	1	1	1	2	2	3
20–34	113	1.6	2	1	1	1	2	3	4	10
35–49	139	1.6	2	1	1	1	2	3	3	8
50–64	56	1.5	<1	1	1	1	2	3	4	6
65+	12	2.1	<1	1	2	2	3	3	3	3
2. MULTIPLE DX										
0–19 Years	46	1.9	3	1	1	1	2	4	5	9
20–34	156	2.4	4	1	1	2	3	5	6	11
35–49	162	2.4	5	1	1	2	3	6	7	11
50–64	140	2.4	6	1	1	2	3	4	7	15
65+	109	3.2	11	1	1	2	4	5	11	17
TOTAL SINGLE DX	**342**	**1.6**	**1**	**1**	**1**	**1**	**2**	**3**	**4**	**8**
TOTAL MULTIPLE DX	**613**	**2.5**	**6**	**1**	**1**	**2**	**3**	**5**	**7**	**13**
TOTAL										
0–19 Years	68	1.7	2	1	1	1	2	3	5	9
20–34	269	2.0	3	1	1	1	2	4	5	11
35–49	301	2.0	3	1	1	1	2	4	6	9
50–64	196	2.2	5	1	1	2	3	4	6	15
65+	121	3.1	10	1	1	2	3	5	10	17
GRAND TOTAL	**955**	**2.2**	**4**	**1**	**1**	**1**	**3**	**4**	**6**	**12**

83.65: MUSCLE/FASC SUTURE NEC

Type of Patients	Observed Patients	Avg. Stay	Vari-ance	Percentiles 10th	25th	50th	75th	90th	95th	99th
1. SINGLE DX										
0–19 Years	20	1.3	<1	1	1	1	1	2	2	3
20–34	25	2.1	3	1	1	2	2	4	6	9
35–49	26	1.4	<1	1	1	1	2	3	3	3
50–64	9	1.7	<1	1	1	2	2	3	3	3
65+	0									
2. MULTIPLE DX										
0–19 Years	60	2.2	3	1	1	2	3	5	5	9
20–34	120	2.7	11	1	1	2	3	5	8	18
35–49	96	2.8	8	1	1	2	3	5	7	20
50–64	66	3.5	15	1	1	2	3	7	10	20
65+	48	4.1	27	1	1	2	5	10	11	36
TOTAL SINGLE DX	**80**	**1.6**	**1**	**1**	**1**	**1**	**2**	**3**	**3**	**6**
TOTAL MULTIPLE DX	**390**	**2.9**	**12**	**1**	**1**	**2**	**3**	**5**	**8**	**20**
TOTAL										
0–19 Years	80	2.1	2	1	1	1	3	4	5	7
20–34	145	2.6	10	1	1	2	3	5	7	18
35–49	122	2.5	7	1	1	2	3	4	7	13
50–64	75	3.3	14	1	1	2	3	6	10	20
65+	48	4.1	27	1	1	2	5	10	11	36
GRAND TOTAL	**470**	**2.7**	**10**	**1**	**1**	**2**	**3**	**5**	**8**	**19**

83.7: MUSCLE/TENDON RECONST

Type of Patients	Observed Patients	Avg. Stay	Vari-ance	Percentiles 10th	25th	50th	75th	90th	95th	99th
1. SINGLE DX										
0–19 Years	39	1.5	<1	1	1	1	2	3	3	4
20–34	4	1.0	0	1	1	1	1	1	1	1
35–49	12	1.4	<1	1	1	1	2	2	3	3
50–64	17	1.6	<1	1	1	1	2	3	3	4
65+	5	1.7	1	1	1	1	3	3	3	3
2. MULTIPLE DX										
0–19 Years	118	1.9	2	1	1	1	2	3	5	8
20–34	39	2.6	14	1	1	2	3	6	6	24
35–49	69	2.3	3	1	1	2	3	4	5	8
50–64	124	2.2	2	1	1	2	3	4	4	9
65+	85	3.3	30	1	2	2	3	5	6	51
TOTAL SINGLE DX	**77**	**1.5**	**<1**	**1**	**1**	**1**	**2**	**3**	**3**	**4**
TOTAL MULTIPLE DX	**435**	**2.4**	**9**	**1**	**1**	**2**	**3**	**4**	**6**	**9**
TOTAL										
0–19 Years	157	1.8	2	1	1	1	2	3	4	8
20–34	43	2.5	13	1	1	1	2	6	6	24
35–49	81	2.2	2	1	1	2	3	4	5	8
50–64	141	2.1	2	1	1	2	3	4	4	9
65+	90	3.2	29	1	1	2	3	5	6	51
GRAND TOTAL	**512**	**2.2**	**8**	**1**	**1**	**2**	**3**	**4**	**5**	**9**

83.75: TENDON TRANSF/TRANSPL

Type of Patients	Observed Patients	Avg. Stay	Vari-ance	Percentiles						
				10th	25th	50th	75th	90th	95th	99th
1. SINGLE DX										
0–19 Years	26	1.6	<1	1	1	1	2	3	3	4
20–34	1	1.0	0	1	1	1	1	1	1	1
35–49	7	1.4	<1	1	1	1	2	2	3	3
50–64	11	1.4	<1	1	1	1	1	3	3	3
65+	4	1.4	<1	1	1	1	1	3	3	3
2. MULTIPLE DX										
0–19 Years	81	1.7	1	1	1	1	2	3	4	5
20–34	25	2.1	3	1	1	1	2	6	6	6
35–49	38	2.1	3	1	1	2	3	4	5	11
50–64	63	2.2	2	1	1	2	3	4	5	9
65+	46	2.5	1	1	2	2	3	4	5	6
TOTAL SINGLE DX	**49**	**1.5**	**<1**	**1**	**1**	**1**	**2**	**3**	**3**	**4**
TOTAL MULTIPLE DX	**253**	**2.0**	**2**	**1**	**1**	**2**	**3**	**3**	**5**	**6**
TOTAL										
0–19 Years	107	1.7	1	1	1	1	2	3	3	5
20–34	26	2.1	2	1	1	1	2	6	6	6
35–49	45	2.0	2	1	1	1	3	3	4	11
50–64	74	2.0	2	1	1	2	2	4	5	9
65+	50	2.4	1	1	2	2	3	3	5	6
GRAND TOTAL	**302**	**1.9**	**2**	**1**	**1**	**2**	**3**	**3**	**4**	**6**

83.8: MUSC/TEND/FASC OP NEC

Type of Patients	Observed Patients	Avg. Stay	Vari-ance	Percentiles						
				10th	25th	50th	75th	90th	95th	99th
1. SINGLE DX										
0–19 Years	112	1.5	<1	1	1	1	2	3	4	4
20–34	40	1.7	<1	1	1	1	2	3	3	5
35–49	90	1.6	<1	1	1	1	2	3	3	3
50–64	56	1.8	<1	1	1	2	2	3	3	4
65+	11	1.8	<1	1	1	2	2	3	3	3
2. MULTIPLE DX										
0–19 Years	298	2.1	16	1	1	1	2	3	4	11
20–34	86	3.3	9	1	1	2	4	6	12	14
35–49	219	3.8	32	1	1	2	4	9	15	36
50–64	308	3.2	18	1	1	2	3	7	10	19
65+	293	4.1	18	1	2	3	5	10	12	18
TOTAL SINGLE DX	**309**	**1.6**	**<1**	**1**	**1**	**1**	**2**	**3**	**4**	**4**
TOTAL MULTIPLE DX	**1,204**	**3.2**	**19**	**1**	**1**	**2**	**3**	**7**	**11**	**20**
TOTAL										
0–19 Years	410	1.9	11	1	1	1	2	3	4	11
20–34	126	2.7	7	1	1	2	3	5	7	14
35–49	309	3.2	24	1	1	2	3	6	11	35
50–64	364	3.0	16	1	1	2	3	7	9	19
65+	304	4.1	17	1	2	3	5	9	12	18
GRAND TOTAL	**1,513**	**2.8**	**15**	**1**	**1**	**2**	**3**	**5**	**9**	**17**

83.82: MUSCLE OR FASCIA GRAFT

Type of Patients	Observed Patients	Avg. Stay	Vari-ance	Percentiles						
				10th	25th	50th	75th	90th	95th	99th
1. SINGLE DX										
0–19 Years	2	2.5	<1	1	3	3	3	3	3	3
20–34	3	2.4	<1	1	2	3	3	3	3	3
35–49	2	1.8	<1	1	2	2	2	2	2	2
50–64	2	3.5	<1	3	3	4	4	4	4	4
65+	0									
2. MULTIPLE DX										
0–19 Years	1	8.0	0	8	8	8	8	8	8	8
20–34	14	5.8	24	1	3	4	7	14	17	17
35–49	31	11.4	119	1	4	9	13	35	36	36
50–64	27	8.3	88	2	3	7	10	14	42	42
65+	40	9.1	44	3	4	7	12	17	26	30
TOTAL SINGLE DX	**9**	**2.4**	**<1**	**1**	**2**	**3**	**3**	**3**	**4**	**4**
TOTAL MULTIPLE DX	**113**	**9.1**	**69**	**2**	**4**	**7**	**12**	**17**	**30**	**42**
TOTAL										
0–19 Years	3	3.4	6	1	3	3	3	8	8	8
20–34	17	5.1	21	1	2	4	5	14	14	17
35–49	33	10.2	114	1	2	7	12	33	36	36
50–64	29	8.1	85	3	3	5	9	14	42	42
65+	40	9.1	44	3	4	7	12	17	26	30
GRAND TOTAL	**122**	**8.4**	**67**	**2**	**3**	**5**	**11**	**17**	**29**	**42**

83.84: CLUBFOOT RELEASE NEC

Type of Patients	Observed Patients	Avg. Stay	Vari-ance	Percentiles						
				10th	25th	50th	75th	90th	95th	99th
1. SINGLE DX										
0–19 Years	47	1.2	<1	1	1	1	1	2	2	5
20–34	0									
35–49	5	1.8	<1	1	1	2	2	3	3	3
50–64	0									
65+	0									
2. MULTIPLE DX										
0–19 Years	29	1.4	<1	1	1	1	2	2	3	3
20–34	0									
35–49	4	2.2	4	1	1	1	5	5	5	5
50–64	0									
65+	2	1.4	<1	1	1	1	2	2	2	2
TOTAL SINGLE DX	**52**	**1.3**	**<1**	**1**	**1**	**1**	**1**	**2**	**2**	**5**
TOTAL MULTIPLE DX	**35**	**1.5**	**<1**	**1**	**1**	**1**	**2**	**2**	**3**	**5**
TOTAL										
0–19 Years	76	1.3	<1	1	1	1	1	2	3	5
20–34	0									
35–49	9	2.0	2	1	1	1	2	5	5	5
50–64	0									
65+	2	1.4	<1	1	1	1	2	2	2	2
GRAND TOTAL	**87**	**1.3**	**<1**	**1**	**1**	**1**	**1**	**2**	**3**	**5**

83.85: CHANGE IN M/T LENGTH NEC

Type of Patients	Observed Patients	Avg. Stay	Variance	10th	25th	50th	75th	90th	95th	99th
1. SINGLE DX										
0–19 Years	58	1.8	1	1	1	1	2	4	4	4
20–34	1	1.0	0	1	1	1	1	1	1	1
35–49	5	1.2	<1	1	1	1	1	2	2	2
50–64	3	2.8	1	2	2	2	4	4	4	4
65+	0									
2. MULTIPLE DX										
0–19 Years	247	2.2	20	1	1	1	2	3	4	14
20–34	25	3.1	8	1	1	2	5	7	8	12
35–49	47	3.0	10	1	1	2	3	7	11	15
50–64	77	3.1	9	1	2	2	3	6	10	20
65+	48	3.7	10	1	2	3	4	12	12	12
TOTAL SINGLE DX	**67**	**1.7**	**1**	**1**	**1**	**1**	**2**	**4**	**4**	**4**
TOTAL MULTIPLE DX	**444**	**2.6**	**16**	**1**	**1**	**2**	**3**	**4**	**7**	**14**
TOTAL										
0–19 Years	305	2.1	16	1	1	1	2	3	4	11
20–34	26	3.1	8	1	1	2	4	7	8	12
35–49	52	2.8	9	1	1	2	3	7	11	15
50–64	80	3.1	9	1	2	2	3	6	10	20
65+	48	3.7	10	1	2	3	4	12	12	12
GRAND TOTAL	**511**	**2.4**	**14**	**1**	**1**	**2**	**3**	**4**	**6**	**13**

83.86: QUADRICEPSPLASTY

Type of Patients	Observed Patients	Avg. Stay	Variance	10th	25th	50th	75th	90th	95th	99th
1. SINGLE DX										
0–19 Years	1	2.0	0	2	2	2	2	2	2	2
20–34	1	2.0	0	2	2	2	2	2	2	2
35–49	11	1.8	<1	1	1	2	2	3	3	3
50–64	10	2.2	<1	1	2	2	3	3	4	4
65+	1	2.0	0	2	2	2	2	2	2	2
2. MULTIPLE DX										
0–19 Years	7	3.5	2	2	2	4	4	6	6	6
20–34	7	4.3	4	2	3	4	6	7	7	7
35–49	12	3.7	7	2	2	3	4	5	11	11
50–64	26	2.9	4	1	1	2	4	7	7	7
65+	42	2.6	3	1	1	2	3	5	6	8
TOTAL SINGLE DX	**24**	**2.0**	**<1**	**1**	**2**	**2**	**2**	**3**	**3**	**4**
TOTAL MULTIPLE DX	**94**	**3.0**	**4**	**1**	**2**	**2**	**4**	**6**	**7**	**8**
TOTAL										
0–19 Years	8	3.4	2	2	2	4	4	6	6	6
20–34	8	3.9	4	2	2	4	6	7	7	7
35–49	23	2.9	5	1	2	2	4	4	11	11
50–64	36	2.7	4	1	1	2	3	7	7	7
65+	43	2.6	3	1	1	2	3	5	6	8
GRAND TOTAL	**118**	**2.8**	**3**	**1**	**2**	**2**	**4**	**6**	**7**	**8**

83.88: PLASTIC OPS TENDON NEC

Type of Patients	Observed Patients	Avg. Stay	Variance	10th	25th	50th	75th	90th	95th	99th
1. SINGLE DX										
0–19 Years	3	1.0	0	1	1	1	1	1	1	1
20–34	28	1.6	<1	1	1	1	2	3	3	5
35–49	50	1.6	<1	1	1	1	2	3	3	4
50–64	39	1.6	<1	1	1	1	2	3	3	3
65+	6	1.9	<1	1	1	2	3	3	3	3
2. MULTIPLE DX										
0–19 Years	12	2.3	2	1	1	2	3	5	5	5
20–34	28	2.6	6	1	1	2	3	5	5	12
35–49	98	1.9	2	1	1	1	2	3	4	11
50–64	152	2.3	7	1	1	2	2	4	7	19
65+	134	3.2	7	1	1	2	4	7	9	13
TOTAL SINGLE DX	**126**	**1.6**	**<1**	**1**	**1**	**1**	**2**	**3**	**3**	**5**
TOTAL MULTIPLE DX	**424**	**2.5**	**6**	**1**	**1**	**2**	**3**	**5**	**7**	**13**
TOTAL										
0–19 Years	15	2.0	2	1	1	1	3	4	5	5
20–34	56	2.1	3	1	1	1	2	5	5	12
35–49	148	1.8	2	1	1	1	2	3	4	6
50–64	191	2.1	6	1	1	2	2	3	5	11
65+	140	3.2	7	1	1	2	4	7	9	13
GRAND TOTAL	**550**	**2.3**	**5**	**1**	**1**	**2**	**3**	**4**	**6**	**13**

83.9: OTHER CONN TISSUE OPS

Type of Patients	Observed Patients	Avg. Stay	Variance	10th	25th	50th	75th	90th	95th	99th
1. SINGLE DX										
0–19 Years	6	2.2	2	1	1	2	3	4	5	5
20–34	2	3.6	<1	3	3	4	4	4	4	4
35–49	10	1.8	2	1	1	1	2	3	6	6
50–64	1	1.0	0	1	1	1	1	1	1	1
65+	0									
2. MULTIPLE DX										
0–19 Years	24	5.4	28	1	1	3	9	12	17	24
20–34	48	5.4	27	1	2	4	6	18	18	21
35–49	133	5.6	31	1	2	4	8	11	14	20
50–64	156	5.4	27	2	2	4	6	11	12	35
65+	228	5.3	18	2	3	4	7	10	14	24
TOTAL SINGLE DX	**19**	**2.1**	**2**	**1**	**1**	**1**	**3**	**4**	**5**	**6**
TOTAL MULTIPLE DX	**589**	**5.4**	**24**	**1**	**2**	**4**	**7**	**11**	**14**	**26**
TOTAL										
0–19 Years	30	4.7	24	1	1	3	5	12	15	24
20–34	50	5.4	26	1	2	4	6	18	18	21
35–49	143	5.3	30	1	2	4	7	10	14	20
50–64	157	5.4	27	1	2	4	6	11	12	35
65+	228	5.3	18	2	3	4	7	10	14	24
GRAND TOTAL	**608**	**5.3**	**24**	**1**	**2**	**4**	**7**	**10**	**14**	**26**

83.94: ASPIRATION OF BURSA

Type of Patients	Observed Patients	Avg. Stay	Vari-ance	10th	25th	50th	75th	90th	95th	99th
1. SINGLE DX										
0–19 Years	0									
20–34	0									
35–49	6	2.5	3	1	1	2	3	6	6	6
50–64	1	1.0	0	1	1	1	1	1	1	1
65+	0									
2. MULTIPLE DX										
0–19 Years	3	2.8	<1	2	2	3	3	4	4	4
20–34	14	3.4	7	1	2	2	5	5	7	12
35–49	36	4.1	9	1	2	3	7	8	12	13
50–64	41	3.9	5	2	2	3	5	6	7	13
65+	67	4.3	9	1	2	4	5	7	8	17
TOTAL SINGLE DX	**7**	**2.3**	**3**	**1**	**1**	**2**	**3**	**6**	**6**	**6**
TOTAL MULTIPLE DX	**161**	**4.0**	**7**	**1**	**2**	**4**	**5**	**7**	**8**	**14**
TOTAL										
0–19 Years	3	2.8	<1	2	2	3	3	4	4	4
20–34	14	3.4	7	1	2	2	5	5	7	12
35–49	42	3.9	9	1	2	3	6	7	8	13
50–64	42	3.8	5	2	2	3	5	6	7	13
65+	67	4.3	9	1	2	4	5	7	8	17
GRAND TOTAL	**168**	**4.0**	**7**	**1**	**2**	**4**	**5**	**7**	**8**	**14**

83.95: SOFT TISSUE ASP NEC

Type of Patients	Observed Patients	Avg. Stay	Vari-ance	10th	25th	50th	75th	90th	95th	99th
1. SINGLE DX										
0–19 Years	5	2.9	2	1	2	3	4	5	5	5
20–34	1	4.0	0	4	4	4	4	4	4	4
35–49	1	3.0	0	3	3	3	3	3	3	3
50–64	0									
65+	0									
2. MULTIPLE DX										
0–19 Years	18	5.9	33	1	1	3	10	14	17	24
20–34	23	4.8	19	1	2	4	6	8	14	21
35–49	75	6.3	29	2	3	5	8	13	15	20
50–64	62	7.5	48	2	3	5	9	12	26	35
65+	80	7.6	28	3	4	6	10	14	20	27
TOTAL SINGLE DX	**7**	**3.0**	**2**	**1**	**2**	**3**	**4**	**5**	**5**	**5**
TOTAL MULTIPLE DX	**258**	**6.8**	**34**	**2**	**3**	**5**	**9**	**14**	**16**	**35**
TOTAL										
0–19 Years	23	5.3	28	1	1	3	9	12	17	24
20–34	24	4.8	18	1	2	4	6	8	14	21
35–49	76	6.3	29	2	3	5	8	13	15	20
50–64	62	7.5	48	2	3	5	9	12	26	35
65+	80	7.6	28	3	4	6	10	14	20	27
GRAND TOTAL	**265**	**6.7**	**33**	**2**	**3**	**5**	**9**	**13**	**16**	**29**

83.96: INJECTION INTO BURSA

Type of Patients	Observed Patients	Avg. Stay	Vari-ance	10th	25th	50th	75th	90th	95th	99th
1. SINGLE DX										
0–19 Years	0									
20–34	0									
35–49	0									
50–64	0									
65+	0									
2. MULTIPLE DX										
0–19 Years	1	3.0	0	3	3	3	3	3	3	3
20–34	1	4.0	0	4	4	4	4	4	4	4
35–49	5	5.1	15	1	3	3	8	10	10	10
50–64	16	3.9	4	2	2	4	4	8	8	8
65+	51	4.2	5	2	3	4	5	6	8	16
TOTAL SINGLE DX	**0**									
TOTAL MULTIPLE DX	**74**	**4.1**	**5**	**2**	**3**	**4**	**5**	**7**	**8**	**16**
TOTAL										
0–19 Years	1	3.0	0	3	3	3	3	3	3	3
20–34	1	4.0	0	4	4	4	4	4	4	4
35–49	5	5.1	15	1	3	3	8	10	10	10
50–64	16	3.9	4	2	2	4	4	8	8	8
65+	51	4.2	5	2	3	4	5	6	8	16
GRAND TOTAL	**74**	**4.1**	**5**	**2**	**3**	**4**	**5**	**7**	**8**	**16**

84.0: AMPUTATION OF UPPER LIMB

Type of Patients	Observed Patients	Avg. Stay	Vari-ance	10th	25th	50th	75th	90th	95th	99th
1. SINGLE DX										
0–19 Years	20	1.3	<1	1	1	1	1	2	2	5
20–34	42	2.4	10	1	1	1	2	5	7	20
35–49	25	1.7	1	1	1	1	2	3	5	5
50–64	20	2.2	4	1	1	1	3	4	8	8
65+	7	1.3	<1	1	1	1	1	3	3	3
2. MULTIPLE DX										
0–19 Years	17	2.8	6	1	1	2	3	6	9	9
20–34	88	4.1	43	1	1	2	3	7	17	32
35–49	162	4.9	28	1	1	3	7	13	17	22
50–64	205	5.4	35	1	1	3	7	13	19	32
65+	147	5.5	25	1	1	3	8	13	16	20
TOTAL SINGLE DX	**114**	**1.9**	**5**	**1**	**1**	**1**	**2**	**4**	**5**	**14**
TOTAL MULTIPLE DX	**619**	**5.0**	**31**	**1**	**1**	**3**	**7**	**13**	**17**	**29**
TOTAL										
0–19 Years	37	2.0	4	1	1	1	2	5	6	9
20–34	130	3.5	33	1	1	2	3	7	14	32
35–49	187	4.5	26	1	1	2	5	12	17	22
50–64	225	5.1	33	1	1	3	6	13	16	29
65+	154	5.2	24	1	1	3	8	13	16	20
GRAND TOTAL	**733**	**4.5**	**28**	**1**	**1**	**2**	**6**	**11**	**16**	**27**

84.01: FINGER AMPUTATION

Type of Patients	Observed Patients	Avg. Stay	Variance	10th	25th	50th	75th	90th	95th	99th
1. SINGLE DX										
0–19 Years	15	1.4	<1	1	1	1	1	2	5	5
20–34	32	1.9	5	1	1	1	2	3	6	14
35–49	21	1.7	1	1	1	1	2	3	5	5
50–64	13	2.2	4	1	1	1	4	4	8	8
65+	4	1.3	<1	1	1	1	1	3	3	3
2. MULTIPLE DX										
0–19 Years	12	2.7	5	1	1	2	3	6	6	8
20–34	65	3.2	23	1	1	2	3	6	14	29
35–49	130	4.6	28	1	1	3	6	12	20	27
50–64	170	5.4	38	1	1	3	6	14	21	32
65+	98	4.8	17	1	1	3	8	12	13	17
TOTAL SINGLE DX	**85**	**1.8**	**3**	**1**	**1**	**1**	**2**	**4**	**5**	**8**
TOTAL MULTIPLE DX	**475**	**4.7**	**29**	**1**	**1**	**3**	**6**	**12**	**16**	**29**
TOTAL										
0–19 Years	27	2.0	3	1	1	1	3	6	6	8
20–34	97	2.8	17	1	1	2	2	6	7	27
35–49	151	4.3	26	1	1	2	5	10	16	20
50–64	183	5.2	37	1	1	3	6	13	19	32
65+	102	4.6	17	1	1	3	8	11	13	17
GRAND TOTAL	**560**	**4.3**	**26**	**1**	**1**	**2**	**5**	**10**	**15**	**27**

84.1: AMPUTATION OF LOWER LIMB

Type of Patients	Observed Patients	Avg. Stay	Variance	10th	25th	50th	75th	90th	95th	99th
1. SINGLE DX										
0–19 Years	23	2.6	4	1	1	2	4	5	7	9
20–34	16	5.7	29	1	3	4	6	16	16	16
35–49	10	4.9	14	2	2	5	5	5	15	15
50–64	18	4.6	13	1	2	4	7	8	15	15
65+	15	3.9	4	1	2	3	5	6	8	8
2. MULTIPLE DX										
0–19 Years	48	5.7	40	1	1	4	7	12	20	37
20–34	183	10.6	120	2	4	7	12	25	37	64
35–49	1,273	9.7	84	2	4	7	12	19	25	51
50–64	3,220	9.8	67	3	4	8	13	19	25	43
65+	5,137	9.2	53	3	4	7	12	18	23	36
TOTAL SINGLE DX	**82**	**3.8**	**11**	**1**	**2**	**3**	**5**	**7**	**13**	**16**
TOTAL MULTIPLE DX	**9,861**	**9.4**	**63**	**3**	**4**	**7**	**12**	**19**	**24**	**40**
TOTAL										
0–19 Years	71	4.5	28	1	1	3	5	9	16	27
20–34	199	10.2	114	2	4	7	12	22	34	56
35–49	1,283	9.7	84	2	4	7	12	19	25	51
50–64	3,238	9.7	67	3	4	8	13	19	25	43
65+	5,152	9.2	53	3	4	7	12	18	23	36
GRAND TOTAL	**9,943**	**9.4**	**62**	**3**	**4**	**7**	**12**	**18**	**24**	**40**

84.11: TOE AMPUTATION

Type of Patients	Observed Patients	Avg. Stay	Variance	10th	25th	50th	75th	90th	95th	99th
1. SINGLE DX										
0–19 Years	12	1.4	<1	1	1	1	2	2	3	3
20–34	5	1.7	<1	1	1	2	2	3	3	3
35–49	4	3.0	3	1	2	4	4	5	5	5
50–64	6	4.2	4	1	4	4	7	7	7	7
65+	5	2.0	1	1	1	2	2	2	5	5
2. MULTIPLE DX										
0–19 Years	12	3.5	38	1	1	1	3	7	27	27
20–34	84	8.9	83	2	3	7	11	15	21	64
35–49	650	7.8	36	2	4	7	10	15	19	27
50–64	1,332	7.5	35	2	3	6	10	15	19	27
65+	1,484	7.2	29	2	4	6	9	14	17	26
TOTAL SINGLE DX	**32**	**2.1**	**2**	**1**	**1**	**2**	**2**	**4**	**5**	**7**
TOTAL MULTIPLE DX	**3,562**	**7.5**	**33**	**2**	**4**	**6**	**10**	**14**	**18**	**27**
TOTAL										
0–19 Years	24	2.3	18	1	1	1	2	3	7	27
20–34	89	8.5	81	1	3	6	11	15	21	37
35–49	654	7.8	35	2	4	7	10	15	19	27
50–64	1,338	7.5	35	2	3	6	10	14	19	27
65+	1,489	7.2	29	2	3	6	9	14	17	26
GRAND TOTAL	**3,594**	**7.4**	**33**	**2**	**3**	**6**	**10**	**14**	**18**	**27**

84.12: AMPUTATION THROUGH FOOT

Type of Patients	Observed Patients	Avg. Stay	Variance	10th	25th	50th	75th	90th	95th	99th
1. SINGLE DX										
0–19 Years	1	4.0	0	4	4	4	4	4	4	4
20–34	2	4.0	0	4	4	4	4	4	4	4
35–49	1	15.0	0	15	15	15	15	15	15	15
50–64	1	1.0	0	1	1	1	1	1	1	1
65+	1	8.0	0	8	8	8	8	8	8	8
2. MULTIPLE DX										
0–19 Years	1	2.0	0	2	2	2	2	2	2	2
20–34	14	10.7	48	3	7	9	12	25	25	25
35–49	174	9.9	80	2	4	7	13	19	23	44
50–64	461	10.6	65	3	5	9	14	20	26	41
65+	544	9.7	65	2	4	7	13	19	24	46
TOTAL SINGLE DX	**6**	**5.1**	**13**	**4**	**4**	**4**	**4**	**8**	**15**	**15**
TOTAL MULTIPLE DX	**1,194**	**10.1**	**67**	**2**	**5**	**8**	**14**	**19**	**25**	**46**
TOTAL										
0–19 Years	2	3.1	1	2	2	4	4	4	4	4
20–34	16	9.6	46	3	4	8	10	25	25	25
35–49	175	9.9	80	2	4	7	13	19	23	44
50–64	462	10.6	65	3	5	9	14	20	26	41
65+	545	9.7	65	2	4	7	13	19	24	46
GRAND TOTAL	**1,200**	**10.0**	**67**	**2**	**4**	**8**	**14**	**19**	**25**	**46**

84.15: BK AMPUTATION NEC

Type of Patients	Observed Patients	Avg. Stay	Vari-ance	Percentiles						
				10th	25th	50th	75th	90th	95th	99th
1. SINGLE DX										
0–19 Years	2	5.0	0	5	5	5	5	5	5	5
20–34	2	3.5	<1	3	3	3	4	4	4	4
35–49	5	4.3	1	2	4	5	5	5	5	5
50–64	10	5.0	21	2	2	3	7	13	15	15
65+	8	4.1	3	3	3	4	5	5	8	8
2. MULTIPLE DX										
0–19 Years	11	6.4	22	2	2	6	8	16	16	16
20–34	57	10.8	83	2	4	9	14	25	32	39
35–49	329	12.0	124	3	5	8	15	24	32	59
50–64	996	11.1	75	3	5	9	14	22	28	46
65+	1,798	10.3	67	3	5	8	13	20	25	43
TOTAL SINGLE DX	**27**	**4.5**	**8**	**2**	**3**	**4**	**5**	**7**	**13**	**15**
TOTAL MULTIPLE DX	**3,191**	**10.7**	**75**	**3**	**5**	**8**	**14**	**21**	**27**	**44**
TOTAL										
0–19 Years	13	6.2	20	2	3	5	6	16	16	16
20–34	59	10.6	82	2	4	8	14	25	32	39
35–49	334	11.9	123	3	5	8	15	24	32	59
50–64	1,006	11.1	75	3	5	9	14	22	27	46
65+	1,806	10.3	67	3	5	8	13	20	25	43
GRAND TOTAL	**3,218**	**10.6**	**75**	**3**	**5**	**8**	**14**	**21**	**27**	**44**

84.17: ABOVE KNEE AMPUTATION

Type of Patients	Observed Patients	Avg. Stay	Vari-ance	Percentiles						
				10th	25th	50th	75th	90th	95th	99th
1. SINGLE DX										
0–19 Years	1	4.0	0	4	4	4	4	4	4	4
20–34	4	9.8	46	3	3	16	16	16	16	16
35–49	0									
50–64	0									
65+	1	6.0	0	6	6	6	6	6	6	6
2. MULTIPLE DX										
0–19 Years	8	9.2	34	4	4	8	12	12	24	24
20–34	15	12.2	185	3	4	5	12	42	42	42
35–49	80	13.4	190	3	5	10	17	34	45	56
50–64	339	12.7	136	4	5	9	16	28	36	74
65+	1,202	9.6	49	3	5	8	12	19	24	33
TOTAL SINGLE DX	**6**	**6.7**	**23**	**3**	**4**	**4**	**6**	**16**	**16**	**16**
TOTAL MULTIPLE DX	**1,644**	**10.5**	**77**	**3**	**5**	**8**	**13**	**21**	**27**	**44**
TOTAL										
0–19 Years	9	7.2	27	4	4	4	10	12	24	24
20–34	19	11.6	148	3	4	5	16	42	42	42
35–49	80	13.4	190	3	5	10	17	34	45	56
50–64	339	12.7	136	4	5	9	16	28	36	74
65+	1,203	9.6	49	3	5	8	12	19	24	33
GRAND TOTAL	**1,650**	**10.4**	**76**	**3**	**5**	**8**	**13**	**21**	**27**	**44**

84.2: EXTREMITY REATTACHMENT

Type of Patients	Observed Patients	Avg. Stay	Vari-ance	Percentiles						
				10th	25th	50th	75th	90th	95th	99th
1. SINGLE DX										
0–19 Years	9	2.3	1	1	1	3	3	4	4	4
20–34	11	4.6	7	2	2	5	6	8	11	11
35–49	12	6.4	7	4	4	5	7	9	13	13
50–64	7	6.1	9	1	4	6	8	11	11	11
65+	1	2.0	0	2	2	2	2	2	2	2
2. MULTIPLE DX										
0–19 Years	10	4.8	9	1	3	5	5	8	13	13
20–34	18	9.7	162	4	4	6	8	15	45	52
35–49	25	7.3	22	1	4	5	12	13	16	17
50–64	14	7.0	26	1	5	6	7	11	26	26
65+	6	3.1	3	1	2	3	4	6	6	6
TOTAL SINGLE DX	**40**	**4.4**	**8**	**1**	**2**	**4**	**6**	**8**	**11**	**13**
TOTAL MULTIPLE DX	**73**	**7.1**	**55**	**1**	**4**	**5**	**8**	**13**	**16**	**52**
TOTAL										
0–19 Years	19	3.5	7	1	1	3	5	5	8	13
20–34	29	7.9	112	2	4	5	7	11	45	52
35–49	37	7.1	18	3	4	5	10	13	16	17
50–64	21	6.7	21	1	5	6	8	11	11	26
65+	7	2.9	2	1	2	3	4	6	6	6
GRAND TOTAL	**113**	**6.1**	**40**	**1**	**3**	**5**	**7**	**12**	**13**	**45**

84.3: AMPUTATION STUMP REV

Type of Patients	Observed Patients	Avg. Stay	Vari-ance	Percentiles						
				10th	25th	50th	75th	90th	95th	99th
1. SINGLE DX										
0–19 Years	2	2.1	1	1	1	3	3	3	3	3
20–34	8	2.6	3	1	1	2	3	6	6	6
35–49	13	3.3	3	1	2	4	4	5	6	6
50–64	12	2.2	11	1	1	1	1	3	12	12
65+	1	1.0	0	1	1	1	1	1	1	1
2. MULTIPLE DX										
0–19 Years	12	7.1	29	1	2	7	14	14	14	14
20–34	30	5.7	43	1	2	4	5	12	18	37
35–49	211	7.7	44	2	3	6	10	17	21	33
50–64	428	8.1	63	2	3	6	11	16	21	42
65+	454	7.9	60	2	4	6	9	17	20	45
TOTAL SINGLE DX	**36**	**2.6**	**5**	**1**	**1**	**2**	**4**	**5**	**6**	**12**
TOTAL MULTIPLE DX	**1,135**	**7.9**	**58**	**2**	**3**	**6**	**10**	**16**	**21**	**42**
TOTAL										
0–19 Years	14	6.3	27	1	1	3	10	14	14	14
20–34	38	5.1	36	1	2	4	5	11	17	37
35–49	224	7.4	43	2	3	5	10	17	21	27
50–64	440	8.0	63	1	3	6	11	16	21	42
65+	455	7.9	60	2	4	6	9	17	20	45
GRAND TOTAL	**1,171**	**7.8**	**57**	**2**	**3**	**6**	**10**	**16**	**21**	**42**

84.4: IMPL OR FIT PROSTH LIMB

Type of Patients	Observed Patients	Avg. Stay	Vari-ance	Percentiles 10th	25th	50th	75th	90th	95th	99th
1. SINGLE DX										
0–19 Years	0									
20–34	0									
35–49	0									
50–64	1	5.0	0	5	5	5	5	5	5	5
65+	0									
2. MULTIPLE DX										
0–19 Years	0									
20–34	0									
35–49	1	16.0	0	16	16	16	16	16	16	16
50–64	1	2.0	0	2	2	2	2	2	2	2
65+	1	3.0	0	3	3	3	3	3	3	3
TOTAL SINGLE DX	**1**	**5.0**	**0**	**5**	**5**	**5**	**5**	**5**	**5**	**5**
TOTAL MULTIPLE DX	**3**	**5.0**	**28**	**2**	**3**	**3**	**3**	**16**	**16**	**16**
TOTAL										
0–19 Years	0									
20–34	0									
35–49	1	16.0	0	16	16	16	16	16	16	16
50–64	2	3.6	4	2	2	5	5	5	5	5
65+	1	3.0	0	3	3	3	3	3	3	3
GRAND TOTAL	**4**	**5.0**	**23**	**2**	**3**	**3**	**5**	**16**	**16**	**16**

84.5: IMPL OTH MS DEV & SUBST

Type of Patients	Observed Patients	Avg. Stay	Vari-ance	Percentiles 10th	25th	50th	75th	90th	95th	99th
1. SINGLE DX										
0–19 Years	0									
20–34	0									
35–49	0									
50–64	0									
65+	0									
2. MULTIPLE DX										
0–19 Years	0									
20–34	0									
35–49	1	4.0	0	4	4	4	4	4	4	4
50–64	1	1.0	0	1	1	1	1	1	1	1
65+	1	11.0	0	11	11	11	11	11	11	11
TOTAL SINGLE DX	**0**									
TOTAL MULTIPLE DX	**3**	**4.7**	**24**	**1**	**1**	**4**	**11**	**11**	**11**	**11**
TOTAL										
0–19 Years	0									
20–34	0									
35–49	1	4.0	0	4	4	4	4	4	4	4
50–64	1	1.0	0	1	1	1	1	1	1	1
65+	1	11.0	0	11	11	11	11	11	11	11
GRAND TOTAL	**3**	**4.7**	**24**	**1**	**1**	**4**	**11**	**11**	**11**	**11**

84.9: OTHER MUSCULOSKELETAL OP

Type of Patients	Observed Patients	Avg. Stay	Vari-ance	Percentiles 10th	25th	50th	75th	90th	95th	99th
1. SINGLE DX										
0–19 Years	0									
20–34	1	1.0	0	1	1	1	1	1	1	1
35–49	0									
50–64	0									
65+	0									
2. MULTIPLE DX										
0–19 Years	0									
20–34	0									
35–49	1	1.0	0	1	1	1	1	1	1	1
50–64	0									
65+	0									
TOTAL SINGLE DX	**1**	**1.0**	**0**	**1**	**1**	**1**	**1**	**1**	**1**	**1**
TOTAL MULTIPLE DX	**1**	**1.0**	**0**	**1**	**1**	**1**	**1**	**1**	**1**	**1**
TOTAL										
0–19 Years	0									
20–34	1	1.0	0	1	1	1	1	1	1	1
35–49	1	1.0	0	1	1	1	1	1	1	1
50–64	0									
65+	0									
GRAND TOTAL	**2**	**1.0**	**0**	**1**	**1**	**1**	**1**	**1**	**1**	**1**

85.0: MASTOTOMY

Type of Patients	Observed Patients	Avg. Stay	Vari-ance	Percentiles 10th	25th	50th	75th	90th	95th	99th
1. SINGLE DX										
0–19 Years	22	2.9	2	1	2	3	4	4	5	5
20–34	69	2.3	2	1	1	2	3	4	5	7
35–49	37	2.3	2	1	1	2	3	4	5	7
50–64	23	1.7	3	1	1	1	2	3	3	11
65+	3	4.8	27	1	1	2	11	11	11	11
2. MULTIPLE DX										
0–19 Years	19	4.8	10	1	3	5	7	10	11	11
20–34	74	3.2	5	1	1	2	4	6	8	11
35–49	125	2.9	6	1	1	2	4	5	7	11
50–64	103	3.9	10	1	1	3	6	8	11	14
65+	66	4.3	20	1	2	3	5	8	16	19
TOTAL SINGLE DX	**154**	**2.4**	**3**	**1**	**1**	**2**	**3**	**4**	**5**	**11**
TOTAL MULTIPLE DX	**387**	**3.7**	**10**	**1**	**1**	**3**	**4**	**8**	**10**	**19**
TOTAL										
0–19 Years	41	3.8	6	1	2	4	5	8	10	11
20–34	143	2.8	4	1	1	2	4	5	7	10
35–49	162	2.8	5	1	1	2	3	5	7	11
50–64	126	3.5	10	1	1	2	4	8	9	14
65+	69	4.4	20	1	2	3	5	8	16	19
GRAND TOTAL	**541**	**3.3**	**8**	**1**	**1**	**2**	**4**	**7**	**8**	**14**

85.1: BREAST DIAGNOSTIC PX

Type of Patients	Observed Patients	Avg. Stay	Vari-ance	10th	25th	50th	75th	90th	95th	99th
1. SINGLE DX										
0–19 Years	1	1.0	0	1	1	1	1	1	1	1
20–34	7	2.3	1	1	1	2	3	4	4	4
35–49	8	3.5	6	1	2	3	4	9	9	9
50–64	4	1.2	<1	1	1	1	1	2	2	2
65+	3	2.2	1	1	1	3	3	3	3	3
2. MULTIPLE DX										
0–19 Years	1	3.0	0	3	3	3	3	3	3	3
20–34	22	10.0	141	1	3	4	10	33	33	33
35–49	64	4.9	24	1	1	3	7	13	14	23
50–64	99	6.9	55	1	2	4	10	14	35	>99
65+	164	6.1	21	1	2	5	8	13	15	20
TOTAL SINGLE DX	**23**	**2.5**	**3**	**1**	**1**	**2**	**3**	**4**	**4**	**9**
TOTAL MULTIPLE DX	**350**	**6.3**	**39**	**1**	**2**	**4**	**8**	**13**	**19**	**35**
TOTAL										
0–19 Years	2	2.4	1	1	1	3	3	3	3	3
20–34	29	8.4	121	1	2	3	8	33	33	33
35–49	72	4.7	22	1	1	3	7	13	14	20
50–64	103	6.7	54	1	2	4	9	14	35	>99
65+	167	6.0	21	1	2	5	8	13	15	20
GRAND TOTAL	**373**	**6.1**	**38**	**1**	**2**	**4**	**8**	**13**	**16**	**35**

85.11: PERC BREAST BIOPSY

Type of Patients	Observed Patients	Avg. Stay	Vari-ance	10th	25th	50th	75th	90th	95th	99th
1. SINGLE DX										
0–19 Years	1	1.0	0	1	1	1	1	1	1	1
20–34	1	1.0	0	1	1	1	1	1	1	1
35–49	2	5.4	27	1	1	9	9	9	9	9
50–64	1	1.0	0	1	1	1	1	1	1	1
65+	1	3.0	0	3	3	3	3	3	3	3
2. MULTIPLE DX										
0–19 Years	0									
20–34	11	6.6	10	1	5	7	10	11	11	11
35–49	30	6.0	23	1	2	4	8	14	16	20
50–64	64	8.4	74	2	3	6	10	25	35	>99
65+	114	6.6	23	2	3	5	9	14	16	20
TOTAL SINGLE DX	**6**	**2.8**	**10**	**1**	**1**	**1**	**3**	**9**	**9**	**9**
TOTAL MULTIPLE DX	**219**	**7.0**	**38**	**2**	**3**	**6**	**10**	**14**	**20**	**35**
TOTAL										
0–19 Years	1	1.0	0	1	1	1	1	1	1	1
20–34	12	6.1	12	1	3	6	8	10	11	11
35–49	32	5.9	23	1	2	5	8	13	14	20
50–64	65	8.4	74	2	3	6	10	25	35	>99
65+	115	6.5	23	2	3	5	9	14	16	20
GRAND TOTAL	**225**	**6.9**	**38**	**2**	**3**	**5**	**10**	**14**	**20**	**35**

85.12: OPEN BIOPSY OF BREAST

Type of Patients	Observed Patients	Avg. Stay	Vari-ance	10th	25th	50th	75th	90th	95th	99th
1. SINGLE DX										
0–19 Years	0									
20–34	6	2.6	1	1	2	3	3	4	4	4
35–49	6	3.0	1	1	2	3	4	4	4	4
50–64	3	1.3	<1	1	1	1	2	2	2	2
65+	2	1.9	2	1	1	1	3	3	3	3
2. MULTIPLE DX										
0–19 Years	1	3.0	0	3	3	3	3	3	3	3
20–34	11	12.1	213	1	2	3	33	33	33	33
35–49	33	4.1	23	1	1	2	4	11	14	23
50–64	34	4.5	15	1	2	3	6	12	14	14
65+	48	5.0	15	1	2	4	7	9	14	21
TOTAL SINGLE DX	**17**	**2.4**	**1**	**1**	**1**	**3**	**3**	**4**	**4**	**4**
TOTAL MULTIPLE DX	**127**	**5.3**	**39**	**1**	**2**	**3**	**6**	**12**	**15**	**33**
TOTAL										
0–19 Years	1	3.0	0	3	3	3	3	3	3	3
20–34	17	9.6	173	1	2	3	4	33	33	33
35–49	39	4.0	20	1	1	3	4	10	13	23
50–64	37	4.3	15	1	2	3	6	12	14	14
65+	50	4.9	15	1	2	4	7	9	14	21
GRAND TOTAL	**144**	**5.0**	**36**	**1**	**2**	**3**	**6**	**11**	**14**	**33**

85.2: EXC/DESTR BREAST TISSUE

Type of Patients	Observed Patients	Avg. Stay	Vari-ance	10th	25th	50th	75th	90th	95th	99th
1. SINGLE DX										
0–19 Years	4	2.1	2	1	1	2	4	4	4	4
20–34	30	2.0	6	1	1	1	2	4	5	15
35–49	131	1.3	<1	1	1	1	1	2	3	5
50–64	179	1.2	<1	1	1	1	1	2	2	3
65+	109	1.1	<1	1	1	1	1	2	2	2
2. MULTIPLE DX										
0–19 Years	3	2.8	1	1	3	3	4	4	4	4
20–34	48	2.5	5	1	1	2	3	5	7	11
35–49	421	2.1	7	1	1	1	2	4	8	15
50–64	810	1.7	3	1	1	1	2	3	5	11
65+	993	1.9	8	1	1	1	2	3	5	16
TOTAL SINGLE DX	**453**	**1.3**	**<1**	**1**	**1**	**1**	**1**	**2**	**2**	**5**
TOTAL MULTIPLE DX	**2,275**	**1.9**	**6**	**1**	**1**	**1**	**2**	**3**	**6**	**14**
TOTAL										
0–19 Years	7	2.5	2	1	1	3	4	4	4	4
20–34	78	2.3	5	1	1	1	3	5	6	15
35–49	552	1.9	6	1	1	1	2	4	7	13
50–64	989	1.6	3	1	1	1	1	2	4	11
65+	1,102	1.8	8	1	1	1	2	3	5	15
GRAND TOTAL	**2,728**	**1.8**	**6**	**1**	**1**	**1**	**2**	**3**	**5**	**13**

85.21: LOCAL EXC BREAST LESION

Type of Patients	Observed Patients	Avg. Stay	Vari-ance	Percentiles						
				10th	25th	50th	75th	90th	95th	99th
1. SINGLE DX										
0–19 Years	4	2.1	2	1	1	2	4	4	4	4
20–34	26	2.2	7	1	1	1	3	4	5	15
35–49	68	1.4	<1	1	1	1	2	2	3	5
50–64	88	1.2	<1	1	1	1	1	2	2	3
65+	54	1.1	<1	1	1	1	1	2	2	2
2. MULTIPLE DX										
0–19 Years	3	2.8	1	1	3	3	4	4	4	4
20–34	38	2.6	5	1	1	2	3	6	7	11
35–49	254	2.5	9	1	1	1	2	6	8	19
50–64	469	1.9	5	1	1	1	2	4	6	13
65+	538	2.0	8	1	1	1	2	3	6	15
TOTAL SINGLE DX	**240**	**1.4**	**1**	**1**	**1**	**1**	**1**	**2**	**3**	**5**
TOTAL MULTIPLE DX	**1,302**	**2.0**	**7**	**1**	**1**	**1**	**2**	**4**	**7**	**15**
TOTAL										
0–19 Years	7	2.5	2	1	1	3	4	4	4	4
20–34	64	2.4	6	1	1	1	3	5	7	15
35–49	322	2.3	8	1	1	1	2	4	8	15
50–64	557	1.8	4	1	1	1	2	3	5	13
65+	592	1.9	7	1	1	1	2	3	6	15
GRAND TOTAL	**1,542**	**1.9**	**6**	**1**	**1**	**1**	**2**	**4**	**6**	**14**

85.22: QUADRANT RESECT BREAST

Type of Patients	Observed Patients	Avg. Stay	Vari-ance	Percentiles						
				10th	25th	50th	75th	90th	95th	99th
1. SINGLE DX										
0–19 Years	0									
20–34	1	1.0	0	1	1	1	1	1	1	1
35–49	8	1.4	2	1	1	1	1	5	5	5
50–64	11	1.1	<1	1	1	1	1	1	2	2
65+	12	1.2	<1	1	1	1	1	2	2	2
2. MULTIPLE DX										
0–19 Years	0									
20–34	1	2.0	0	2	2	2	2	2	2	2
35–49	33	1.6	2	1	1	1	2	2	3	8
50–64	66	1.5	<1	1	1	1	2	2	3	5
65+	71	1.4	<1	1	1	1	2	2	3	3
TOTAL SINGLE DX	**32**	**1.2**	**<1**	**1**	**1**	**1**	**1**	**2**	**2**	**5**
TOTAL MULTIPLE DX	**171**	**1.4**	**<1**	**1**	**1**	**1**	**2**	**2**	**3**	**6**
TOTAL										
0–19 Years	0									
20–34	2	1.6	<1	1	1	2	2	2	2	2
35–49	41	1.6	2	1	1	1	2	2	3	8
50–64	77	1.4	<1	1	1	1	2	2	2	5
65+	83	1.4	<1	1	1	1	2	2	3	3
GRAND TOTAL	**203**	**1.4**	**<1**	**1**	**1**	**1**	**2**	**2**	**3**	**5**

85.23: SUBTOTAL MASTECTOMY

Type of Patients	Observed Patients	Avg. Stay	Vari-ance	Percentiles						
				10th	25th	50th	75th	90th	95th	99th
1. SINGLE DX										
0–19 Years	0									
20–34	3	1.0	0	1	1	1	1	1	1	1
35–49	53	1.2	<1	1	1	1	1	1	2	5
50–64	79	1.2	<1	1	1	1	1	2	2	3
65+	43	1.1	<1	1	1	1	1	1	2	2
2. MULTIPLE DX										
0–19 Years	0									
20–34	7	1.7	2	1	1	1	2	5	5	5
35–49	129	1.2	<1	1	1	1	1	2	2	5
50–64	273	1.5	1	1	1	1	1	2	3	7
65+	379	1.9	11	1	1	1	2	2	4	23
TOTAL SINGLE DX	**178**	**1.1**	**<1**	**1**	**1**	**1**	**1**	**2**	**2**	**3**
TOTAL MULTIPLE DX	**788**	**1.6**	**6**	**1**	**1**	**1**	**1**	**2**	**3**	**12**
TOTAL										
0–19 Years	0									
20–34	10	1.5	1	1	1	1	1	2	5	5
35–49	182	1.2	<1	1	1	1	1	2	2	5
50–64	352	1.4	1	1	1	1	1	2	3	6
65+	422	1.8	10	1	1	1	1	2	4	23
GRAND TOTAL	**966**	**1.6**	**5**	**1**	**1**	**1**	**1**	**2**	**3**	**12**

85.3: RED MAMMOPLASTY/ECTOMY

Type of Patients	Observed Patients	Avg. Stay	Vari-ance	Percentiles						
				10th	25th	50th	75th	90th	95th	99th
1. SINGLE DX										
0–19 Years	30	1.1	<1	1	1	1	1	1	2	2
20–34	232	1.1	<1	1	1	1	1	1	2	2
35–49	217	1.2	<1	1	1	1	1	2	2	4
50–64	147	1.4	<1	1	1	1	1	2	4	6
65+	17	1.2	<1	1	1	1	1	2	2	4
2. MULTIPLE DX										
0–19 Years	39	1.3	<1	1	1	1	1	2	2	3
20–34	290	1.2	<1	1	1	1	1	2	2	3
35–49	486	1.5	<1	1	1	1	2	2	3	6
50–64	483	1.6	1	1	1	1	2	3	4	6
65+	129	1.5	<1	1	1	1	2	3	3	4
TOTAL SINGLE DX	**643**	**1.2**	**<1**	**1**	**1**	**1**	**1**	**2**	**2**	**4**
TOTAL MULTIPLE DX	**1,427**	**1.5**	**1**	**1**	**1**	**1**	**2**	**2**	**3**	**5**
TOTAL										
0–19 Years	69	1.2	<1	1	1	1	1	2	2	3
20–34	522	1.2	<1	1	1	1	1	2	2	3
35–49	703	1.4	<1	1	1	1	2	2	3	5
50–64	630	1.5	1	1	1	1	2	3	4	6
65+	146	1.5	<1	1	1	1	2	3	3	4
GRAND TOTAL	**2,070**	**1.4**	**<1**	**1**	**1**	**1**	**1**	**2**	**3**	**5**

85.32: BILAT RED MAMMOPLASTY

Type of Patients	Observed Patients	Avg. Stay	Vari-ance	Percentiles						
				10th	25th	50th	75th	90th	95th	99th
1. SINGLE DX										
0–19 Years	26	1.1	<1	1	1	1	1	1	2	2
20–34	225	1.1	<1	1	1	1	1	1	2	2
35–49	191	1.2	<1	1	1	1	1	2	2	3
50–64	113	1.1	<1	1	1	1	1	2	2	2
65+	14	1.0	0	1	1	1	1	1	1	1
2. MULTIPLE DX										
0–19 Years	34	1.3	<1	1	1	1	1	2	2	3
20–34	276	1.2	<1	1	1	1	1	2	2	3
35–49	387	1.2	<1	1	1	1	1	2	2	3
50–64	364	1.4	<1	1	1	1	2	2	3	4
65+	90	1.4	<1	1	1	1	2	2	2	3
TOTAL SINGLE DX	**569**	**1.1**	**<1**	**1**	**1**	**1**	**1**	**2**	**2**	**2**
TOTAL MULTIPLE DX	**1,151**	**1.3**	**<1**	**1**	**1**	**1**	**1**	**2**	**2**	**4**
TOTAL										
0–19 Years	60	1.2	<1	1	1	1	1	2	2	3
20–34	501	1.2	<1	1	1	1	1	2	2	3
35–49	578	1.2	<1	1	1	1	1	2	2	3
50–64	477	1.3	<1	1	1	1	1	2	3	4
65+	104	1.3	<1	1	1	1	2	2	2	3
GRAND TOTAL	**1,720**	**1.2**	**<1**	**1**	**1**	**1**	**1**	**2**	**2**	**3**

85.4: MASTECTOMY

Type of Patients	Observed Patients	Avg. Stay	Vari-ance	Percentiles						
				10th	25th	50th	75th	90th	95th	99th
1. SINGLE DX										
0–19 Years	1	1.0	0	1	1	1	1	1	1	1
20–34	59	1.5	<1	1	1	1	2	2	3	3
35–49	403	1.7	1	1	1	1	2	3	4	5
50–64	562	1.7	1	1	1	1	2	3	4	6
65+	330	1.5	<1	1	1	1	2	3	3	5
2. MULTIPLE DX										
0–19 Years	0									
20–34	147	2.2	2	1	1	2	3	4	5	7
35–49	1,577	2.2	6	1	1	2	3	4	5	7
50–64	2,833	2.1	3	1	1	2	2	4	5	9
65+	3,577	2.0	3	1	1	2	2	3	4	9
TOTAL SINGLE DX	**1,355**	**1.7**	**<1**	**1**	**1**	**1**	**2**	**3**	**4**	**5**
TOTAL MULTIPLE DX	**8,134**	**2.1**	**4**	**1**	**1**	**2**	**2**	**4**	**5**	**9**
TOTAL										
0–19 Years	1	1.0	0	1	1	1	1	1	1	1
20–34	206	2.0	2	1	1	2	2	4	5	7
35–49	1,980	2.1	5	1	1	2	2	4	5	7
50–64	3,395	2.1	3	1	1	2	2	4	5	9
65+	3,907	1.9	3	1	1	1	2	3	4	9
GRAND TOTAL	**9,489**	**2.0**	**3**	**1**	**1**	**2**	**2**	**4**	**5**	**8**

85.41: UNILAT SIMPLE MASTECTOMY

Type of Patients	Observed Patients	Avg. Stay	Vari-ance	Percentiles						
				10th	25th	50th	75th	90th	95th	99th
1. SINGLE DX										
0–19 Years	1	1.0	0	1	1	1	1	1	1	1
20–34	15	1.4	<1	1	1	1	2	2	3	3
35–49	118	1.8	1	1	1	1	2	4	4	5
50–64	174	1.7	1	1	1	1	2	3	4	5
65+	102	1.4	<1	1	1	1	2	2	3	4
2. MULTIPLE DX										
0–19 Years	0									
20–34	17	2.2	2	1	1	2	3	4	4	7
35–49	343	2.2	5	1	1	2	3	4	6	10
50–64	650	2.0	3	1	1	1	3	4	5	8
65+	920	1.8	4	1	1	1	2	3	4	10
TOTAL SINGLE DX	**410**	**1.6**	**<1**	**1**	**1**	**1**	**2**	**3**	**4**	**5**
TOTAL MULTIPLE DX	**1,930**	**2.0**	**4**	**1**	**1**	**1**	**2**	**4**	**5**	**10**
TOTAL										
0–19 Years	1	1.0	0	1	1	1	1	1	1	1
20–34	32	1.8	1	1	1	1	2	3	4	7
35–49	461	2.1	4	1	1	1	3	4	5	10
50–64	824	2.0	3	1	1	1	2	4	5	8
65+	1,022	1.8	4	1	1	1	2	3	4	10
GRAND TOTAL	**2,340**	**1.9**	**3**	**1**	**1**	**1**	**2**	**3**	**5**	**10**

85.42: BILAT SIMPLE MASTECTOMY

Type of Patients	Observed Patients	Avg. Stay	Vari-ance	Percentiles						
				10th	25th	50th	75th	90th	95th	99th
1. SINGLE DX										
0–19 Years	0									
20–34	4	1.6	<1	1	1	2	2	2	2	2
35–49	36	1.9	1	1	1	2	2	4	4	6
50–64	26	1.7	<1	1	1	2	2	3	3	4
65+	7	1.8	<1	1	1	2	2	3	3	3
2. MULTIPLE DX										
0–19 Years	0									
20–34	26	2.5	2	1	2	2	3	5	6	7
35–49	241	2.4	2	1	1	2	3	4	5	6
50–64	266	2.5	6	1	1	2	3	4	6	17
65+	144	2.0	2	1	1	2	2	4	4	9
TOTAL SINGLE DX	**73**	**1.8**	**1**	**1**	**1**	**2**	**2**	**3**	**4**	**6**
TOTAL MULTIPLE DX	**677**	**2.4**	**3**	**1**	**1**	**2**	**3**	**4**	**5**	**10**
TOTAL										
0–19 Years	0									
20–34	30	2.4	2	1	1	2	2	5	5	7
35–49	277	2.3	2	1	1	2	3	4	5	6
50–64	292	2.5	5	1	1	2	3	4	6	17
65+	151	2.0	2	1	1	2	2	4	4	6
GRAND TOTAL	**750**	**2.3**	**3**	**1**	**1**	**2**	**3**	**4**	**5**	**10**

85.43: UNILAT EXTEN SIMPLE MAST

Type of Patients	Observed Patients	Avg. Stay	Vari-ance	Percentiles 10th	25th	50th	75th	90th	95th	99th
1. SINGLE DX										
0–19 Years	0									
20–34	39	1.5	<1	1	1	1	2	2	3	3
35–49	232	1.6	<1	1	1	1	2	3	3	5
50–64	337	1.7	1	1	1	1	2	3	4	6
65+	210	1.6	<1	1	1	1	2	3	3	5
2. MULTIPLE DX										
0–19 Years	0									
20–34	96	2.2	2	1	1	2	2	4	6	8
35–49	903	2.2	7	1	1	2	2	4	5	7
50–64	1,758	2.0	3	1	1	2	2	4	5	9
65+	2,376	2.0	3	1	1	2	2	3	4	8
TOTAL SINGLE DX	**818**	**1.6**	**<1**	**1**	**1**	**1**	**2**	**3**	**3**	**5**
TOTAL MULTIPLE DX	**5,133**	**2.0**	**4**	**1**	**1**	**2**	**2**	**4**	**5**	**8**
TOTAL										
0–19 Years	0									
20–34	135	2.0	2	1	1	2	2	3	5	7
35–49	1,135	2.0	6	1	1	2	2	4	5	7
50–64	2,095	2.0	2	1	1	2	2	4	5	8
65+	2,586	2.0	3	1	1	2	2	3	4	8
GRAND TOTAL	**5,951**	**2.0**	**3**	**1**	**1**	**2**	**2**	**3**	**5**	**8**

85.44: BILAT EXTEN SIMPLE MAST

Type of Patients	Observed Patients	Avg. Stay	Vari-ance	Percentiles 10th	25th	50th	75th	90th	95th	99th
1. SINGLE DX										
0–19 Years	0									
20–34	1	2.0	0	2	2	2	2	2	2	2
35–49	12	2.0	1	1	1	2	2	4	5	5
50–64	17	2.6	3	1	2	2	2	6	6	6
65+	4	1.5	<1	1	1	2	2	2	2	2
2. MULTIPLE DX										
0–19 Years	0									
20–34	5	2.2	2	1	1	2	3	4	4	4
35–49	64	2.4	2	1	2	2	3	4	5	6
50–64	112	2.4	2	1	1	2	3	4	6	8
65+	88	2.2	8	1	1	2	3	3	4	13
TOTAL SINGLE DX	**34**	**2.2**	**2**	**1**	**1**	**2**	**2**	**5**	**6**	**6**
TOTAL MULTIPLE DX	**269**	**2.3**	**4**	**1**	**1**	**2**	**3**	**4**	**5**	**8**
TOTAL										
0–19 Years	0									
20–34	6	2.1	1	1	1	2	3	4	4	4
35–49	76	2.3	1	1	2	2	3	4	5	6
50–64	129	2.4	3	1	1	2	3	5	6	8
65+	92	2.2	8	1	1	2	2	3	4	13
GRAND TOTAL	**303**	**2.3**	**4**	**1**	**1**	**2**	**3**	**4**	**5**	**8**

85.45: UNILAT RAD MASTECTOMY

Type of Patients	Observed Patients	Avg. Stay	Vari-ance	Percentiles 10th	25th	50th	75th	90th	95th	99th
1. SINGLE DX										
0–19 Years	0									
20–34	0									
35–49	5	1.4	<1	1	1	1	2	2	2	2
50–64	5	2.1	2	1	1	1	4	4	4	4
65+	5	1.4	<1	1	1	1	2	2	2	2
2. MULTIPLE DX										
0–19 Years	0									
20–34	3	1.7	<1	1	1	2	2	2	2	2
35–49	18	2.5	5	1	1	2	2	4	10	10
50–64	39	2.9	5	1	2	2	3	4	7	16
65+	37	2.3	6	1	1	1	3	4	6	14
TOTAL SINGLE DX	**15**	**1.6**	**<1**	**1**	**1**	**1**	**2**	**4**	**4**	**4**
TOTAL MULTIPLE DX	**97**	**2.5**	**5**	**1**	**1**	**2**	**3**	**4**	**7**	**14**
TOTAL										
0–19 Years	0									
20–34	3	1.7	<1	1	1	2	2	2	2	2
35–49	23	2.3	4	1	1	2	2	4	8	10
50–64	44	2.8	5	1	1	2	3	4	7	16
65+	42	2.1	5	1	1	1	2	4	6	14
GRAND TOTAL	**112**	**2.4**	**5**	**1**	**1**	**2**	**3**	**4**	**7**	**14**

85.5: AUGMENTATION MAMMOPLASTY

Type of Patients	Observed Patients	Avg. Stay	Vari-ance	Percentiles 10th	25th	50th	75th	90th	95th	99th
1. SINGLE DX										
0–19 Years	1	1.0	0	1	1	1	1	1	1	1
20–34	8	1.3	<1	1	1	1	2	2	2	2
35–49	6	1.0	0	1	1	1	1	1	1	1
50–64	5	1.2	<1	1	1	1	1	2	2	2
65+	1	1.0	0	1	1	1	1	1	1	1
2. MULTIPLE DX										
0–19 Years	2	1.5	<1	1	1	1	2	2	2	2
20–34	18	1.1	<1	1	1	1	1	1	2	2
35–49	46	1.4	<1	1	1	1	1	3	4	4
50–64	38	1.5	1	1	1	1	2	3	3	7
65+	3	1.0	0	1	1	1	1	1	1	1
TOTAL SINGLE DX	**21**	**1.1**	**<1**	**1**	**1**	**1**	**1**	**2**	**2**	**2**
TOTAL MULTIPLE DX	**107**	**1.4**	**<1**	**1**	**1**	**1**	**1**	**2**	**3**	**5**
TOTAL										
0–19 Years	3	1.2	<1	1	1	1	1	2	2	2
20–34	26	1.1	<1	1	1	1	1	2	2	2
35–49	52	1.3	<1	1	1	1	1	3	4	4
50–64	43	1.5	1	1	1	1	1	3	3	7
65+	4	1.0	0	1	1	1	1	1	1	1
GRAND TOTAL	**128**	**1.3**	**<1**	**1**	**1**	**1**	**1**	**2**	**3**	**5**

85.54: BILATERAL BREAST IMPLANT

Type of Patients	Observed Patients	Avg. Stay	Vari-ance	10th	25th	50th	75th	90th	95th	99th
1. SINGLE DX										
0–19 Years	1	1.0	0	1	1	1	1	1	1	1
20–34	8	1.3	<1	1	1	1	2	2	2	2
35–49	5	1.0	0	1	1	1	1	1	1	1
50–64	4	1.2	<1	1	1	1	1	2	2	2
65+	0									
2. MULTIPLE DX										
0–19 Years	2	1.5	<1	1	1	1	2	2	2	2
20–34	17	1.1	<1	1	1	1	1	1	2	2
35–49	31	1.3	<1	1	1	1	1	3	3	4
50–64	20	1.4	<1	1	1	1	1	2	3	5
65+	1	1.0	0	1	1	1	1	1	1	1
TOTAL SINGLE DX	**18**	**1.2**	**<1**	**1**	**1**	**1**	**1**	**2**	**2**	**2**
TOTAL MULTIPLE DX	**71**	**1.3**	**<1**	**1**	**1**	**1**	**1**	**2**	**3**	**4**
TOTAL										
0–19 Years	3	1.2	<1	1	1	1	1	2	2	2
20–34	25	1.2	<1	1	1	1	1	2	2	2
35–49	36	1.3	<1	1	1	1	1	2	3	4
50–64	24	1.4	<1	1	1	1	1	2	3	5
65+	1	1.0	0	1	1	1	1	1	1	1
GRAND TOTAL	**89**	**1.3**	**<1**	**1**	**1**	**1**	**1**	**2**	**3**	**4**

85.6: MASTOPEXY

Type of Patients	Observed Patients	Avg. Stay	Vari-ance	10th	25th	50th	75th	90th	95th	99th
1. SINGLE DX										
0–19 Years	1	1.0	0	1	1	1	1	1	1	1
20–34	1	1.0	0	1	1	1	1	1	1	1
35–49	1	1.0	0	1	1	1	1	1	1	1
50–64	5	1.4	<1	1	1	1	2	2	2	2
65+	0									
2. MULTIPLE DX										
0–19 Years	0									
20–34	5	1.2	<1	1	1	1	1	2	2	2
35–49	13	1.4	<1	1	1	1	2	2	3	3
50–64	21	1.6	<1	1	1	1	2	3	4	4
65+	7	1.1	<1	1	1	1	1	2	2	2
TOTAL SINGLE DX	**8**	**1.2**	**<1**	**1**	**1**	**1**	**1**	**2**	**2**	**2**
TOTAL MULTIPLE DX	**46**	**1.5**	**<1**	**1**	**1**	**1**	**2**	**2**	**3**	**4**
TOTAL										
0–19 Years	1	1.0	0	1	1	1	1	1	1	1
20–34	6	1.1	<1	1	1	1	1	2	2	2
35–49	14	1.4	<1	1	1	1	2	2	3	3
50–64	26	1.6	<1	1	1	1	2	3	4	4
65+	7	1.1	<1	1	1	1	1	2	2	2
GRAND TOTAL	**54**	**1.4**	**<1**	**1**	**1**	**1**	**2**	**2**	**3**	**4**

85.7: TOTAL BREAST RECONST

Type of Patients	Observed Patients	Avg. Stay	Vari-ance	10th	25th	50th	75th	90th	95th	99th
1. SINGLE DX										
0–19 Years	0									
20–34	1	2.0	0	2	2	2	2	2	2	2
35–49	5	4.0	1	3	3	4	4	6	6	6
50–64	14	3.3	1	1	3	4	4	4	5	5
65+	0									
2. MULTIPLE DX										
0–19 Years	0									
20–34	13	4.5	3	3	3	4	6	6	9	9
35–49	104	3.5	3	1	2	3	4	6	7	8
50–64	169	3.7	3	2	3	4	5	6	6	8
65+	22	4.5	7	2	3	4	6	6	9	14
TOTAL SINGLE DX	**20**	**3.4**	**1**	**1**	**3**	**4**	**4**	**4**	**5**	**6**
TOTAL MULTIPLE DX	**308**	**3.7**	**3**	**1**	**3**	**4**	**5**	**6**	**7**	**8**
TOTAL										
0–19 Years	0									
20–34	14	4.4	3	3	3	4	6	6	9	9
35–49	109	3.5	3	1	2	3	4	6	7	8
50–64	183	3.7	2	1	3	4	5	5	6	8
65+	22	4.5	7	2	3	4	6	6	9	14
GRAND TOTAL	**328**	**3.7**	**3**	**1**	**3**	**4**	**5**	**6**	**7**	**8**

85.8: OTHER BREAST REPAIR

Type of Patients	Observed Patients	Avg. Stay	Vari-ance	10th	25th	50th	75th	90th	95th	99th
1. SINGLE DX										
0–19 Years	0									
20–34	3	3.2	2	1	1	4	4	4	4	4
35–49	17	2.1	<1	1	1	2	2	3	4	5
50–64	13	2.6	2	1	1	3	3	4	5	5
65+	3	3.4	10	1	1	2	7	7	7	7
2. MULTIPLE DX										
0–19 Years	5	2.2	<1	2	2	2	2	2	4	4
20–34	27	3.7	14	1	1	2	4	10	12	17
35–49	130	3.5	17	1	2	3	4	5	8	25
50–64	205	3.1	9	1	1	2	3	5	9	16
65+	73	2.6	5	1	1	2	3	5	6	14
TOTAL SINGLE DX	**36**	**2.5**	**2**	**1**	**1**	**2**	**3**	**4**	**5**	**7**
TOTAL MULTIPLE DX	**440**	**3.1**	**11**	**1**	**2**	**2**	**3**	**5**	**8**	**17**
TOTAL										
0–19 Years	5	2.2	<1	2	2	2	2	2	4	4
20–34	30	3.6	12	1	1	2	4	8	12	17
35–49	147	3.3	15	1	2	2	4	5	7	25
50–64	218	3.0	9	1	1	2	3	5	9	16
65+	76	2.7	5	1	1	2	3	6	7	14
GRAND TOTAL	**476**	**3.1**	**10**	**1**	**1**	**2**	**3**	**5**	**8**	**17**

85.85: BREAST MUSCLE FLAP GRAFT

Type of Patients	Observed Patients	Avg. Stay	Vari-ance	10th	25th	50th	75th	90th	95th	99th
1. SINGLE DX										
0–19 Years	0									
20–34	1	4.0	0	4	4	4	4	4	4	4
35–49	10	2.3	<1	1	2	2	3	3	4	4
50–64	10	2.8	1	1	2	3	3	4	5	5
65+	2	1.4	<1	1	1	1	2	2	2	2
2. MULTIPLE DX										
0–19 Years	2	2.0	0	2	2	2	2	2	2	2
20–34	9	3.2	1	2	2	3	4	5	5	5
35–49	72	3.3	3	2	2	3	4	5	6	14
50–64	113	2.8	2	2	2	3	3	4	5	9
65+	32	3.2	5	2	2	2	4	6	6	14
TOTAL SINGLE DX	**23**	**2.5**	**1**	**1**	**2**	**2**	**3**	**4**	**4**	**5**
TOTAL MULTIPLE DX	**228**	**3.0**	**3**	**2**	**2**	**3**	**3**	**5**	**6**	**9**
TOTAL										
0–19 Years	2	2.0	0	2	2	2	2	2	2	2
20–34	10	3.3	1	2	2	3	4	5	5	5
35–49	82	3.2	3	2	2	3	3	5	6	14
50–64	123	2.8	2	2	2	3	3	4	5	7
65+	34	3.1	5	1	2	2	3	6	6	14
GRAND TOTAL	**251**	**3.0**	**3**	**2**	**2**	**3**	**3**	**5**	**6**	**9**

85.9: OTHER BREAST OPERATIONS

Type of Patients	Observed Patients	Avg. Stay	Vari-ance	10th	25th	50th	75th	90th	95th	99th
1. SINGLE DX										
0–19 Years	4	2.0	4	1	1	1	1	5	5	5
20–34	11	2.7	3	1	1	3	3	4	7	7
35–49	18	2.4	6	1	1	2	2	5	11	11
50–64	26	2.1	4	1	1	1	3	6	7	8
65+	7	1.1	<1	1	1	1	1	1	2	2
2. MULTIPLE DX										
0–19 Years	5	4.2	5	1	3	3	7	7	7	7
20–34	38	3.3	9	1	1	2	5	7	10	14
35–49	162	2.3	4	1	1	2	3	4	6	13
50–64	244	2.7	6	1	1	2	3	6	7	10
65+	118	2.5	4	1	1	2	3	5	8	10
TOTAL SINGLE DX	**66**	**2.1**	**4**	**1**	**1**	**1**	**3**	**5**	**7**	**11**
TOTAL MULTIPLE DX	**567**	**2.6**	**5**	**1**	**1**	**2**	**3**	**6**	**7**	**10**
TOTAL										
0–19 Years	9	3.5	6	1	1	3	7	7	7	7
20–34	49	3.2	8	1	1	2	4	7	10	14
35–49	180	2.3	4	1	1	2	3	4	6	11
50–64	270	2.7	6	1	1	2	3	6	7	10
65+	125	2.4	4	1	1	1	3	4	8	10
GRAND TOTAL	**633**	**2.6**	**5**	**1**	**1**	**2**	**3**	**5**	**7**	**10**

85.91: ASPIRATION OF BREAST

Type of Patients	Observed Patients	Avg. Stay	Vari-ance	10th	25th	50th	75th	90th	95th	99th
1. SINGLE DX										
0–19 Years	1	5.0	0	5	5	5	5	5	5	5
20–34	6	2.5	<1	1	2	3	3	3	3	3
35–49	3	5.7	19	2	2	4	11	11	11	11
50–64	0									
65+	0									
2. MULTIPLE DX										
0–19 Years	4	4.7	4	3	3	3	7	7	7	7
20–34	15	3.6	4	1	2	3	5	7	7	7
35–49	18	4.2	6	2	3	4	5	5	8	13
50–64	28	4.9	6	3	3	4	7	9	9	9
65+	27	4.3	5	2	3	4	5	8	10	10
TOTAL SINGLE DX	**10**	**3.7**	**8**	**2**	**2**	**3**	**4**	**11**	**11**	**11**
TOTAL MULTIPLE DX	**92**	**4.4**	**5**	**2**	**3**	**4**	**6**	**8**	**9**	**10**
TOTAL										
0–19 Years	5	4.8	4	3	3	3	7	7	7	7
20–34	21	3.3	3	1	2	3	5	6	7	7
35–49	21	4.4	8	2	3	4	5	8	11	13
50–64	28	4.9	6	3	3	4	7	9	9	9
65+	27	4.3	5	2	3	4	5	8	10	10
GRAND TOTAL	**102**	**4.4**	**5**	**2**	**3**	**4**	**6**	**8**	**9**	**11**

85.94: BREAST IMPLANT REMOVAL

Type of Patients	Observed Patients	Avg. Stay	Vari-ance	10th	25th	50th	75th	90th	95th	99th
1. SINGLE DX										
0–19 Years	0									
20–34	4	2.7	9	1	1	1	7	7	7	7
35–49	10	1.8	1	1	1	2	2	2	5	5
50–64	16	2.4	6	1	1	1	3	7	8	8
65+	5	1.1	<1	1	1	1	1	2	2	2
2. MULTIPLE DX										
0–19 Years	0									
20–34	15	3.5	13	1	1	2	3	10	14	14
35–49	76	2.4	4	1	1	1	3	4	6	13
50–64	118	2.6	6	1	1	2	3	5	7	11
65+	60	1.9	3	1	1	1	2	4	5	10
TOTAL SINGLE DX	**35**	**2.0**	**4**	**1**	**1**	**1**	**2**	**6**	**7**	**8**
TOTAL MULTIPLE DX	**269**	**2.4**	**5**	**1**	**1**	**2**	**3**	**5**	**7**	**11**
TOTAL										
0–19 Years	0									
20–34	19	3.4	12	1	1	2	7	7	10	14
35–49	86	2.3	4	1	1	1	3	4	6	13
50–64	134	2.6	6	1	1	2	3	5	7	11
65+	65	1.9	3	1	1	1	2	4	5	10
GRAND TOTAL	**304**	**2.4**	**5**	**1**	**1**	**1**	**3**	**5**	**7**	**11**

85.96: RMVL BRST TISS EXPANDER

Type of Patients	Observed Patients	Avg. Stay	Vari-ance	Percentiles						
				10th	25th	50th	75th	90th	95th	99th
1. SINGLE DX										
0–19 Years	0									
20–34	0									
35–49	3	1.8	1	1	1	1	3	3	3	3
50–64	2	2.0	2	1	1	3	3	3	3	3
65+	0									
2. MULTIPLE DX										
0–19 Years	0									
20–34	4	3.0	17	1	1	1	1	10	10	10
35–49	37	1.9	3	1	1	1	2	4	6	8
50–64	55	2.7	5	1	1	2	4	6	7	10
65+	17	2.0	3	1	1	1	2	4	8	8
TOTAL SINGLE DX	**5**	**1.8**	**1**	**1**	**1**	**1**	**3**	**3**	**3**	**3**
TOTAL MULTIPLE DX	**113**	**2.4**	**4**	**1**	**1**	**1**	**3**	**6**	**7**	**10**
TOTAL										
0–19 Years	0									
20–34	4	3.0	17	1	1	1	1	10	10	10
35–49	40	1.9	2	1	1	1	2	4	5	8
50–64	57	2.7	5	1	1	2	4	6	7	10
65+	17	2.0	3	1	1	1	2	4	8	8
GRAND TOTAL	**118**	**2.3**	**4**	**1**	**1**	**1**	**3**	**6**	**7**	**10**

86.0: INCISION SKIN & SUBCU

Type of Patients	Observed Patients	Avg. Stay	Vari-ance	Percentiles						
				10th	25th	50th	75th	90th	95th	99th
1. SINGLE DX										
0–19 Years	546	2.9	6	1	1	2	4	6	8	13
20–34	421	2.7	3	1	1	2	4	5	6	10
35–49	413	2.9	5	1	1	2	4	5	7	12
50–64	211	2.7	13	1	1	2	3	4	6	31
65+	54	2.5	3	1	1	2	4	5	7	8
2. MULTIPLE DX										
0–19 Years	1,872	6.0	45	1	2	4	7	13	17	33
20–34	2,552	4.8	22	1	2	4	6	9	13	24
35–49	5,113	5.2	22	1	2	4	6	10	14	24
50–64	4,847	6.1	31	1	3	4	8	12	16	29
65+	4,188	6.6	35	2	3	5	8	13	18	29
TOTAL SINGLE DX	**1,645**	**2.8**	**6**	**1**	**1**	**2**	**4**	**5**	**7**	**12**
TOTAL MULTIPLE DX	**18,572**	**5.8**	**31**	**1**	**2**	**4**	**7**	**12**	**16**	**28**
TOTAL										
0–19 Years	2,418	5.3	38	1	2	4	6	11	16	30
20–34	2,973	4.6	20	1	2	3	5	9	12	22
35–49	5,526	5.0	21	1	2	4	6	10	14	24
50–64	5,058	5.9	31	1	2	4	7	12	16	29
65+	4,242	6.5	34	2	3	5	8	13	17	29
GRAND TOTAL	**20,217**	**5.6**	**29**	**1**	**2**	**4**	**7**	**11**	**15**	**28**

86.01: ASPIRATION SKIN & SUBCU

Type of Patients	Observed Patients	Avg. Stay	Vari-ance	Percentiles						
				10th	25th	50th	75th	90th	95th	99th
1. SINGLE DX										
0–19 Years	16	2.9	3	1	2	3	3	4	9	9
20–34	8	2.1	3	1	1	1	2	4	6	6
35–49	18	3.7	4	1	3	3	4	5	7	12
50–64	9	1.6	<1	1	1	1	2	3	3	3
65+	0									
2. MULTIPLE DX										
0–19 Years	73	4.2	16	1	2	3	5	8	10	16
20–34	106	4.4	23	2	2	3	5	9	10	27
35–49	186	5.4	28	1	3	4	7	11	13	37
50–64	226	5.4	19	1	3	4	7	11	14	20
65+	280	5.9	31	2	2	4	7	12	15	31
TOTAL SINGLE DX	**51**	**2.9**	**4**	**1**	**1**	**3**	**4**	**5**	**6**	**12**
TOTAL MULTIPLE DX	**871**	**5.4**	**25**	**2**	**2**	**4**	**7**	**11**	**14**	**31**
TOTAL										
0–19 Years	89	4.0	14	1	2	3	5	8	10	16
20–34	114	4.3	22	1	2	3	5	8	10	27
35–49	204	5.2	26	1	3	4	6	10	13	37
50–64	235	5.3	19	1	2	4	7	11	14	20
65+	280	5.9	31	2	2	4	7	12	15	31
GRAND TOTAL	**922**	**5.2**	**24**	**1**	**2**	**4**	**6**	**10**	**14**	**31**

86.03: INCISION PILONIDAL SINUS

Type of Patients	Observed Patients	Avg. Stay	Vari-ance	Percentiles						
				10th	25th	50th	75th	90th	95th	99th
1. SINGLE DX										
0–19 Years	30	2.5	3	1	1	2	3	5	7	7
20–34	26	1.8	2	1	1	1	2	3	4	8
35–49	7	1.6	2	1	1	1	1	5	5	5
50–64	0									
65+	0									
2. MULTIPLE DX										
0–19 Years	29	2.9	4	1	2	2	4	5	9	9
20–34	27	2.3	3	1	1	2	4	5	5	8
35–49	19	3.7	20	1	1	3	4	6	20	20
50–64	5	4.4	1	3	4	4	5	6	6	6
65+	2	1.0	0	1	1	1	1	1	1	1
TOTAL SINGLE DX	**63**	**2.2**	**3**	**1**	**1**	**2**	**3**	**5**	**5**	**8**
TOTAL MULTIPLE DX	**82**	**2.9**	**7**	**1**	**1**	**2**	**4**	**5**	**6**	**20**
TOTAL										
0–19 Years	59	2.7	4	1	1	2	3	5	7	9
20–34	53	2.1	3	1	1	1	2	4	5	8
35–49	26	3.1	16	1	1	2	4	5	6	20
50–64	5	4.4	1	3	4	4	5	6	6	6
65+	2	1.0	0	1	1	1	1	1	1	1
GRAND TOTAL	**145**	**2.6**	**5**	**1**	**1**	**2**	**3**	**5**	**6**	**9**

86.04: SKIN & SUBCU I&D NEC

Type of Patients	Observed Patients	Avg. Stay	Vari-ance	Percentiles						
				10th	25th	50th	75th	90th	95th	99th
1. SINGLE DX										
0–19 Years	350	2.9	4	1	2	2	4	5	6	10
20–34	311	2.8	3	1	2	2	4	5	6	9
35–49	316	3.0	6	1	1	2	4	5	7	14
50–64	150	2.6	4	1	1	2	3	5	6	9
65+	34	2.8	4	1	1	2	4	6	7	8
2. MULTIPLE DX										
0–19 Years	918	4.4	17	2	2	3	5	7	10	17
20–34	1,796	4.4	15	1	2	4	5	8	11	18
35–49	3,543	4.7	15	1	2	4	6	9	12	20
50–64	2,617	5.3	17	2	2	4	7	10	13	20
65+	1,857	5.9	20	2	3	5	7	11	14	23
TOTAL SINGLE DX	**1,161**	**2.9**	**4**	**1**	**1**	**2**	**4**	**5**	**6**	**11**
TOTAL MULTIPLE DX	**10,731**	**5.0**	**17**	**2**	**2**	**4**	**6**	**9**	**13**	**21**
TOTAL										
0–19 Years	1,268	4.0	14	1	2	3	5	7	9	15
20–34	2,107	4.1	13	1	2	3	5	7	10	17
35–49	3,859	4.6	14	1	2	4	6	9	12	20
50–64	2,767	5.1	17	1	2	4	7	10	13	20
65+	1,891	5.8	20	2	3	5	7	11	14	23
GRAND TOTAL	**11,892**	**4.8**	**16**	**1**	**2**	**4**	**6**	**9**	**12**	**20**

86.05: INC W RMVL FB SKIN/SUBCU

Type of Patients	Observed Patients	Avg. Stay	Vari-ance	Percentiles						
				10th	25th	50th	75th	90th	95th	99th
1. SINGLE DX										
0–19 Years	42	1.5	1	1	1	1	2	2	4	6
20–34	37	1.8	<1	1	1	2	2	3	4	4
35–49	21	1.5	<1	1	1	1	2	2	3	3
50–64	8	1.6	<1	1	1	1	2	3	3	3
65+	3	1.0	0	1	1	1	1	1	1	1
2. MULTIPLE DX										
0–19 Years	275	7.9	68	1	3	5	10	17	27	44
20–34	189	5.7	45	1	2	3	8	12	17	29
35–49	390	6.8	39	2	3	5	8	13	21	32
50–64	496	7.0	35	1	3	6	9	14	17	28
65+	436	6.9	32	2	3	6	9	14	18	28
TOTAL SINGLE DX	**111**	**1.6**	**<1**	**1**	**1**	**1**	**2**	**3**	**3**	**5**
TOTAL MULTIPLE DX	**1,786**	**7.0**	**42**	**1**	**3**	**5**	**9**	**14**	**19**	**32**
TOTAL										
0–19 Years	317	6.9	63	1	2	4	9	15	24	44
20–34	226	5.3	41	1	2	3	7	11	15	29
35–49	411	6.6	38	1	3	5	8	13	20	31
50–64	504	6.9	35	1	3	5	9	14	17	28
65+	439	6.9	32	2	3	5	9	14	18	28
GRAND TOTAL	**1,897**	**6.7**	**42**	**1**	**2**	**5**	**9**	**14**	**19**	**31**

86.06: INSERTION INFUSION PUMP

Type of Patients	Observed Patients	Avg. Stay	Vari-ance	Percentiles						
				10th	25th	50th	75th	90th	95th	99th
1. SINGLE DX										
0–19 Years	12	3.3	7	1	2	2	4	8	8	8
20–34	10	2.8	4	1	1	2	4	6	7	7
35–49	19	1.9	<1	1	1	2	3	3	3	4
50–64	20	2.0	1	1	1	2	3	4	4	4
65+	7	1.8	<1	1	1	2	3	3	3	3
2. MULTIPLE DX										
0–19 Years	87	3.8	20	1	1	2	4	8	15	25
20–34	53	4.6	36	1	1	2	5	12	18	30
35–49	206	3.9	21	1	1	2	4	8	15	24
50–64	285	4.5	32	1	1	2	5	10	16	27
65+	234	5.3	36	1	1	3	6	13	17	27
TOTAL SINGLE DX	**68**	**2.4**	**3**	**1**	**1**	**2**	**3**	**4**	**8**	**8**
TOTAL MULTIPLE DX	**865**	**4.5**	**29**	**1**	**1**	**2**	**5**	**11**	**16**	**26**
TOTAL										
0–19 Years	99	3.7	18	1	1	2	4	8	13	25
20–34	63	4.3	31	1	1	2	5	7	18	30
35–49	225	3.7	19	1	1	2	4	8	15	24
50–64	305	4.3	30	1	1	2	5	10	16	26
65+	241	5.3	35	1	1	3	6	13	17	27
GRAND TOTAL	**933**	**4.4**	**28**	**1**	**1**	**2**	**5**	**10**	**16**	**25**

86.07: VAD INSERTION

Type of Patients	Observed Patients	Avg. Stay	Vari-ance	Percentiles						
				10th	25th	50th	75th	90th	95th	99th
1. SINGLE DX										
0–19 Years	71	4.1	17	1	1	2	6	10	13	17
20–34	10	6.2	12	3	4	5	9	10	14	14
35–49	12	1.9	1	1	1	2	2	4	5	5
50–64	17	6.2	92	1	1	2	4	31	31	31
65+	7	2.4	3	1	1	2	4	5	5	5
2. MULTIPLE DX										
0–19 Years	327	9.1	67	2	4	7	12	20	26	38
20–34	219	8.4	46	2	4	7	10	17	23	38
35–49	475	7.8	44	2	3	6	10	15	24	29
50–64	857	8.5	64	2	4	6	10	17	23	43
65+	982	8.4	59	2	3	6	11	18	24	36
TOTAL SINGLE DX	**117**	**4.3**	**25**	**1**	**1**	**2**	**5**	**10**	**14**	**31**
TOTAL MULTIPLE DX	**2,860**	**8.4**	**58**	**2**	**4**	**6**	**11**	**17**	**24**	**38**
TOTAL										
0–19 Years	398	8.1	61	1	3	6	11	18	23	38
20–34	229	8.3	45	2	4	7	10	17	23	38
35–49	487	7.6	44	2	3	6	10	15	24	29
50–64	874	8.4	64	2	4	6	10	17	24	43
65+	989	8.4	59	2	3	6	11	18	24	36
GRAND TOTAL	**2,977**	**8.2**	**57**	**2**	**3**	**6**	**10**	**17**	**23**	**38**

86.09: SKIN/SUBCU INCISION NEC

Type of Patients	Observed Patients	Avg. Stay	Vari-ance	Percentiles						
				10th	25th	50th	75th	90th	95th	99th
1. SINGLE DX										
0–19 Years	25	2.5	2	1	1	3	3	5	5	6
20–34	19	2.3	3	1	1	2	3	5	5	8
35–49	20	2.6	2	1	1	3	4	4	5	6
50–64	7	1.7	2	1	1	1	2	5	5	5
65+	3	1.4	<1	1	1	1	2	2	2	2
2. MULTIPLE DX										
0–19 Years	162	8.0	90	1	3	5	10	16	20	33
20–34	162	4.2	11	1	2	4	6	8	11	15
35–49	292	5.3	22	1	2	4	7	11	15	24
50–64	361	5.9	35	1	2	4	7	12	18	30
65+	397	6.1	32	1	3	4	8	13	18	25
TOTAL SINGLE DX	**74**	**2.4**	**2**	**1**	**1**	**2**	**3**	**5**	**5**	**6**
TOTAL MULTIPLE DX	**1,374**	**6.0**	**38**	**1**	**2**	**4**	**8**	**13**	**17**	**26**
TOTAL										
0–19 Years	187	7.4	83	1	3	5	10	15	17	33
20–34	181	4.1	10	1	2	3	5	8	10	15
35–49	312	5.2	21	1	2	4	7	10	15	24
50–64	368	5.9	35	1	2	4	7	12	18	30
65+	400	6.0	32	1	3	4	8	13	18	25
GRAND TOTAL	**1,448**	**5.8**	**37**	**1**	**2**	**4**	**7**	**12**	**16**	**26**

86.1: SKIN & SUBCU DXTIC PX

Type of Patients	Observed Patients	Avg. Stay	Vari-ance	Percentiles						
				10th	25th	50th	75th	90th	95th	99th
1. SINGLE DX										
0–19 Years	10	3.9	9	1	2	3	4	10	10	10
20–34	11	2.2	1	1	1	2	3	4	4	4
35–49	18	2.3	4	1	1	1	4	6	7	7
50–64	13	1.6	2	1	1	1	1	3	5	6
65+	3	1.5	<1	1	1	1	2	2	2	2
2. MULTIPLE DX										
0–19 Years	73	6.7	72	1	2	5	8	11	15	59
20–34	132	6.0	74	1	2	4	7	12	14	68
35–49	269	6.4	37	2	3	5	8	13	16	29
50–64	305	6.4	32	2	3	5	8	12	16	29
65+	394	6.6	22	2	4	5	8	13	15	21
TOTAL SINGLE DX	**55**	**2.4**	**4**	**1**	**1**	**1**	**3**	**5**	**7**	**10**
TOTAL MULTIPLE DX	**1,173**	**6.5**	**37**	**2**	**3**	**5**	**8**	**13**	**15**	**29**
TOTAL										
0–19 Years	83	6.3	65	1	2	5	7	11	15	59
20–34	143	5.8	70	1	2	4	6	12	14	68
35–49	287	6.1	36	1	2	4	8	13	15	29
50–64	318	6.2	31	1	3	5	8	11	16	29
65+	397	6.6	22	2	3	5	8	13	15	21
GRAND TOTAL	**1,228**	**6.3**	**36**	**2**	**3**	**5**	**8**	**12**	**15**	**29**

86.11: SKIN & SUBCU BIOPSY

Type of Patients	Observed Patients	Avg. Stay	Vari-ance	Percentiles						
				10th	25th	50th	75th	90th	95th	99th
1. SINGLE DX										
0–19 Years	10	3.9	9	1	2	3	4	10	10	10
20–34	11	2.2	1	1	1	2	3	4	4	4
35–49	18	2.3	4	1	1	1	4	6	7	7
50–64	13	1.6	2	1	1	1	1	3	5	6
65+	3	1.5	<1	1	1	1	2	2	2	2
2. MULTIPLE DX										
0–19 Years	73	6.7	72	1	2	5	8	11	15	59
20–34	132	6.0	74	1	2	4	7	12	14	68
35–49	269	6.4	37	2	3	5	8	13	16	29
50–64	305	6.4	32	2	3	5	8	12	16	29
65+	394	6.6	22	2	4	5	8	13	15	21
TOTAL SINGLE DX	**55**	**2.4**	**4**	**1**	**1**	**1**	**3**	**5**	**7**	**10**
TOTAL MULTIPLE DX	**1,173**	**6.5**	**37**	**2**	**3**	**5**	**8**	**13**	**15**	**29**
TOTAL										
0–19 Years	83	6.3	65	1	2	5	7	11	15	59
20–34	143	5.8	70	1	2	4	6	12	14	68
35–49	287	6.1	36	1	2	4	8	13	15	29
50–64	318	6.2	31	1	3	5	8	11	16	29
65+	397	6.6	22	2	3	5	8	13	15	21
GRAND TOTAL	**1,228**	**6.3**	**36**	**2**	**3**	**5**	**8**	**12**	**15**	**29**

86.2: EXC/DESTR SKIN LESION

Type of Patients	Observed Patients	Avg. Stay	Vari-ance	Percentiles						
				10th	25th	50th	75th	90th	95th	99th
1. SINGLE DX										
0–19 Years	195	2.5	9	1	1	1	2	5	8	17
20–34	335	2.9	12	1	1	2	3	6	8	20
35–49	255	3.3	8	1	2	2	4	7	9	15
50–64	141	3.3	6	1	1	3	4	6	7	12
65+	49	3.7	6	1	2	3	6	7	9	12
2. MULTIPLE DX										
0–19 Years	1,379	5.4	50	1	2	3	6	13	18	33
20–34	2,506	6.7	54	1	2	4	8	15	21	36
35–49	4,731	7.9	69	2	3	5	10	16	23	46
50–64	5,534	8.7	72	2	4	6	11	18	25	48
65+	7,829	8.8	63	3	4	7	11	18	23	41
TOTAL SINGLE DX	**975**	**3.0**	**9**	**1**	**1**	**2**	**4**	**6**	**8**	**15**
TOTAL MULTIPLE DX	**21,979**	**8.1**	**66**	**2**	**3**	**6**	**10**	**17**	**23**	**42**
TOTAL										
0–19 Years	1,574	5.0	45	1	2	3	6	12	17	33
20–34	2,841	6.3	51	1	2	4	7	14	19	36
35–49	4,986	7.6	67	2	3	5	9	15	23	44
50–64	5,675	8.5	71	2	3	6	11	18	24	47
65+	7,878	8.8	63	3	4	7	11	18	23	41
GRAND TOTAL	**22,954**	**7.9**	**64**	**2**	**3**	**6**	**10**	**17**	**23**	**41**

86.21: EXCISION PILONIDAL CYST

Type of Patients	Observed Patients	Avg. Stay	Vari-ance	Percentiles						
				10th	25th	50th	75th	90th	95th	99th
1. SINGLE DX										
0–19 Years	30	1.2	<1	1	1	1	1	2	2	7
20–34	27	1.8	3	1	1	1	2	3	4	10
35–49	4	2.2	<1	1	1	2	3	3	3	3
50–64	2	1.0	0	1	1	1	1	1	1	1
65+	1	2.0	0	2	2	2	2	2	2	2
2. MULTIPLE DX										
0–19 Years	15	4.2	46	1	1	2	5	6	31	31
20–34	29	2.3	2	1	1	2	3	4	5	6
35–49	21	3.5	23	1	1	1	5	8	12	24
50–64	9	2.9	4	1	2	2	3	6	8	8
65+	3	5.3	65	2	2	2	2	27	27	27
TOTAL SINGLE DX	**64**	**1.5**	**1**	**1**	**1**	**1**	**2**	**2**	**3**	**7**
TOTAL MULTIPLE DX	**77**	**3.3**	**20**	**1**	**1**	**2**	**4**	**6**	**8**	**31**
TOTAL										
0–19 Years	45	2.0	14	1	1	1	2	4	5	31
20–34	56	2.1	2	1	1	2	3	4	5	10
35–49	25	3.3	20	1	1	2	3	8	12	24
50–64	11	2.7	4	1	2	2	3	6	8	8
65+	4	4.9	57	2	2	2	2	8	27	27
GRAND TOTAL	**141**	**2.4**	**12**	**1**	**1**	**1**	**2**	**5**	**6**	**24**

86.22: EXC DEBRIDE WND/INFECT

Type of Patients	Observed Patients	Avg. Stay	Vari-ance	Percentiles						
				10th	25th	50th	75th	90th	95th	99th
1. SINGLE DX										
0–19 Years	138	2.8	11	1	1	2	3	6	8	20
20–34	262	3.1	14	1	1	2	3	6	8	20
35–49	219	3.3	8	1	2	2	4	7	9	15
50–64	117	3.3	6	1	1	3	4	6	7	12
65+	47	3.7	6	1	2	3	6	7	9	12
2. MULTIPLE DX										
0–19 Years	827	6.5	56	1	2	4	8	14	20	33
20–34	2,122	7.1	55	1	3	5	9	16	22	36
35–49	4,143	8.0	67	2	3	6	10	16	23	44
50–64	4,764	9.0	77	2	4	6	11	19	25	51
65+	6,200	9.0	61	3	4	7	11	18	24	41
TOTAL SINGLE DX	**783**	**3.1**	**10**	**1**	**1**	**2**	**4**	**6**	**9**	**16**
TOTAL MULTIPLE DX	**18,056**	**8.4**	**66**	**2**	**3**	**6**	**10**	**18**	**24**	**42**
TOTAL										
0–19 Years	965	5.9	51	1	2	3	7	13	19	33
20–34	2,384	6.6	52	1	2	4	8	15	21	36
35–49	4,362	7.8	65	2	3	5	10	16	23	44
50–64	4,881	8.8	76	2	4	6	11	19	25	50
65+	6,247	8.9	60	3	4	7	11	18	24	41
GRAND TOTAL	**18,839**	**8.2**	**65**	**2**	**3**	**6**	**10**	**17**	**23**	**42**

86.23: NAIL REMOVAL

Type of Patients	Observed Patients	Avg. Stay	Vari-ance	Percentiles						
				10th	25th	50th	75th	90th	95th	99th
1. SINGLE DX										
0–19 Years	0									
20–34	1	1.0	0	1	1	1	1	1	1	1
35–49	1	1.0	0	1	1	1	1	1	1	1
50–64	1	2.0	0	2	2	2	2	2	2	2
65+	0									
2. MULTIPLE DX										
0–19 Years	17	10.6	453	1	1	4	9	26	93	93
20–34	22	3.5	3	2	2	3	5	6	7	8
35–49	35	6.3	114	2	2	3	5	13	20	52
50–64	48	6.0	29	2	3	4	7	13	15	37
65+	103	7.0	40	2	3	5	8	14	19	29
TOTAL SINGLE DX	**3**	**1.4**	**<1**	**1**	**1**	**1**	**2**	**2**	**2**	**2**
TOTAL MULTIPLE DX	**225**	**6.7**	**76**	**2**	**3**	**4**	**7**	**14**	**18**	**52**
TOTAL										
0–19 Years	17	10.6	453	1	1	4	9	26	93	93
20–34	23	3.4	3	1	2	3	5	6	7	8
35–49	36	6.2	113	1	2	3	5	13	20	52
50–64	49	5.9	29	2	3	4	7	13	15	37
65+	103	7.0	40	2	3	5	8	14	19	29
GRAND TOTAL	**228**	**6.6**	**76**	**2**	**3**	**4**	**7**	**14**	**18**	**52**

86.26: LIG DERMAL APPENDAGE

Type of Patients	Observed Patients	Avg. Stay	Vari-ance	Percentiles						
				10th	25th	50th	75th	90th	95th	99th
1. SINGLE DX										
0–19 Years	2	1.0	0	1	1	1	1	1	1	1
20–34	0									
35–49	0									
50–64	0									
65+	0									
2. MULTIPLE DX										
0–19 Years	335	2.3	4	1	1	2	3	4	4	14
20–34	0									
35–49	0									
50–64	0									
65+	0									
TOTAL SINGLE DX	**2**	**1.0**	**0**	**1**	**1**	**1**	**1**	**1**	**1**	**1**
TOTAL MULTIPLE DX	**335**	**2.3**	**4**	**1**	**1**	**2**	**3**	**4**	**4**	**14**
TOTAL										
0–19 Years	337	2.3	4	1	1	2	3	4	4	14
20–34	0									
35–49	0									
50–64	0									
65+	0									
GRAND TOTAL	**337**	**2.3**	**4**	**1**	**1**	**2**	**3**	**4**	**4**	**14**

86.27: DEBRIDEMENT OF NAIL

Type of Patients	Observed Patients	Avg. Stay	Vari-ance	10th	25th	50th	75th	90th	95th	99th
1. SINGLE DX										
0–19 Years	1	1.0	0	1	1	1	1	1	1	1
20–34	0									
35–49	0									
50–64	1	1.0	0	1	1	1	1	1	1	1
65+	0									
2. MULTIPLE DX										
0–19 Years	4	14.3	277	4	5	5	36	42	42	42
20–34	12	8.6	216	2	2	3	7	26	61	61
35–49	56	13.3	142	2	4	11	18	27	37	55
50–64	122	11.7	94	4	5	8	16	27	31	55
65+	505	10.2	89	3	4	7	13	20	26	49
TOTAL SINGLE DX	**2**	**1.0**	**0**	**1**	**1**	**1**	**1**	**1**	**1**	**1**
TOTAL MULTIPLE DX	**699**	**10.7**	**98**	**3**	**4**	**7**	**14**	**22**	**28**	**54**
TOTAL										
0–19 Years	5	11.5	244	1	4	5	5	42	42	42
20–34	12	8.6	216	2	2	3	7	26	61	61
35–49	56	13.3	142	2	4	11	18	27	37	55
50–64	123	11.6	94	3	5	8	16	27	31	55
65+	505	10.2	89	3	4	7	13	20	26	49
GRAND TOTAL	**701**	**10.6**	**98**	**3**	**4**	**7**	**14**	**22**	**28**	**54**

86.28: NONEXC DEBRIDEMENT WOUND

Type of Patients	Observed Patients	Avg. Stay	Vari-ance	10th	25th	50th	75th	90th	95th	99th
1. SINGLE DX										
0–19 Years	24	2.6	6	1	1	2	3	7	7	15
20–34	45	2.6	5	1	1	2	3	6	8	11
35–49	31	3.5	13	1	2	3	4	6	7	23
50–64	20	3.7	5	1	3	3	5	6	6	12
65+	1	3.0	0	3	3	3	3	3	3	3
2. MULTIPLE DX										
0–19 Years	179	4.3	20	1	1	3	6	9	12	21
20–34	319	4.8	38	1	2	3	6	10	13	32
35–49	474	6.3	68	1	2	4	7	13	18	29
50–64	586	5.9	26	2	3	4	8	11	15	28
65+	1,018	7.3	63	2	3	5	8	14	18	38
TOTAL SINGLE DX	**121**	**3.0**	**7**	**1**	**1**	**2**	**4**	**6**	**7**	**15**
TOTAL MULTIPLE DX	**2,576**	**6.3**	**51**	**1**	**3**	**4**	**8**	**12**	**17**	**30**
TOTAL										
0–19 Years	203	4.1	18	1	1	3	5	9	12	21
20–34	364	4.6	35	1	1	3	5	9	12	32
35–49	505	6.1	65	1	2	4	7	12	18	29
50–64	606	5.8	26	2	3	4	7	11	15	28
65+	1,019	7.3	63	2	3	5	8	13	18	38
GRAND TOTAL	**2,697**	**6.2**	**49**	**1**	**3**	**4**	**7**	**12**	**16**	**29**

86.3: LOC EXC/DESTR SKIN NEC

Type of Patients	Observed Patients	Avg. Stay	Vari-ance	10th	25th	50th	75th	90th	95th	99th
1. SINGLE DX										
0–19 Years	63	1.5	1	1	1	1	2	3	4	8
20–34	39	1.5	2	1	1	1	1	3	5	6
35–49	43	1.7	4	1	1	1	2	3	5	12
50–64	27	2.6	11	1	1	1	2	9	10	16
65+	12	1.9	3	1	1	1	1	5	5	5
2. MULTIPLE DX										
0–19 Years	104	2.8	10	1	1	2	3	5	8	26
20–34	93	4.5	19	1	1	3	6	11	15	18
35–49	208	4.3	26	1	1	3	5	8	11	28
50–64	234	4.9	22	1	2	3	7	10	12	24
65+	310	5.3	26	1	1	4	7	12	14	21
TOTAL SINGLE DX	**184**	**1.7**	**3**	**1**	**1**	**1**	**2**	**3**	**5**	**10**
TOTAL MULTIPLE DX	**949**	**4.6**	**23**	**1**	**1**	**3**	**6**	**11**	**14**	**23**
TOTAL										
0–19 Years	167	2.3	7	1	1	1	3	5	6	14
20–34	132	3.6	16	1	1	2	5	11	14	18
35–49	251	3.9	24	1	1	3	5	8	10	28
50–64	261	4.7	21	1	1	3	7	10	12	24
65+	322	5.2	25	1	1	3	7	12	14	21
GRAND TOTAL	**1,133**	**4.2**	**21**	**1**	**1**	**2**	**5**	**10**	**13**	**21**

86.4: RAD EXCISION SKIN LESION

Type of Patients	Observed Patients	Avg. Stay	Vari-ance	10th	25th	50th	75th	90th	95th	99th
1. SINGLE DX										
0–19 Years	24	1.4	1	1	1	1	1	2	4	7
20–34	14	2.6	3	1	1	2	3	5	7	7
35–49	29	1.8	2	1	1	1	2	4	6	6
50–64	29	2.0	2	1	1	2	2	3	5	7
65+	28	2.0	3	1	1	1	2	5	6	7
2. MULTIPLE DX										
0–19 Years	26	2.7	5	1	1	2	3	5	8	11
20–34	52	10.3	183	1	1	4	14	26	45	68
35–49	113	6.3	54	1	2	3	8	15	29	31
50–64	189	6.0	59	1	1	3	7	14	22	44
65+	418	4.8	31	1	1	3	6	11	14	27
TOTAL SINGLE DX	**124**	**1.9**	**2**	**1**	**1**	**1**	**2**	**4**	**5**	**7**
TOTAL MULTIPLE DX	**798**	**5.5**	**50**	**1**	**1**	**3**	**7**	**13**	**20**	**44**
TOTAL										
0–19 Years	50	2.1	4	1	1	1	2	4	6	11
20–34	66	8.4	150	1	1	3	10	22	45	68
35–49	142	5.5	47	1	1	3	7	15	25	31
50–64	218	5.5	54	1	1	3	7	13	20	44
65+	446	4.7	30	1	1	3	6	11	13	27
GRAND TOTAL	**922**	**5.0**	**45**	**1**	**1**	**3**	**6**	**12**	**16**	**40**

86.5: SKIN/SUBCU SUTURE/CLOSE

Type of Patients	Observed Patients	Avg. Stay	Vari-ance	Percentiles						
				10th	25th	50th	75th	90th	95th	99th
1. SINGLE DX										
0–19 Years	105	1.5	<1	1	1	1	2	3	3	6
20–34	92	1.3	<1	1	1	1	1	2	3	8
35–49	57	1.4	<1	1	1	1	1	2	3	4
50–64	27	1.7	2	1	1	1	2	4	6	6
65+	15	1.4	<1	1	1	1	2	2	4	4
2. MULTIPLE DX										
0–19 Years	989	2.2	5	1	1	1	3	5	7	16
20–34	2,000	2.4	7	1	1	2	3	5	7	13
35–49	1,650	3.1	13	1	1	2	3	7	9	19
50–64	1,284	3.5	20	1	1	2	4	7	10	21
65+	3,292	3.6	10	1	2	3	4	7	9	15
TOTAL SINGLE DX	**296**	**1.4**	**<1**	**1**	**1**	**1**	**1**	**2**	**3**	**6**
TOTAL MULTIPLE DX	**9,215**	**3.1**	**11**	**1**	**1**	**2**	**4**	**6**	**9**	**16**
TOTAL										
0–19 Years	1,094	2.1	5	1	1	1	3	4	6	15
20–34	2,092	2.4	7	1	1	1	3	5	7	13
35–49	1,707	3.0	12	1	1	2	3	7	8	19
50–64	1,311	3.5	20	1	1	2	4	7	10	21
65+	3,307	3.6	10	1	2	3	4	7	9	15
GRAND TOTAL	**9,511**	**3.1**	**10**	**1**	**1**	**2**	**4**	**6**	**9**	**16**

86.59: SKIN CLOSURE NEC

Type of Patients	Observed Patients	Avg. Stay	Vari-ance	Percentiles						
				10th	25th	50th	75th	90th	95th	99th
1. SINGLE DX										
0–19 Years	104	1.5	<1	1	1	1	2	3	3	6
20–34	92	1.3	<1	1	1	1	1	2	3	8
35–49	57	1.4	<1	1	1	1	1	2	3	4
50–64	27	1.7	2	1	1	1	2	4	6	6
65+	15	1.4	<1	1	1	1	2	2	4	4
2. MULTIPLE DX										
0–19 Years	987	2.2	5	1	1	1	3	4	7	15
20–34	1,999	2.4	7	1	1	2	3	5	7	13
35–49	1,646	3.1	13	1	1	2	3	7	9	19
50–64	1,283	3.5	20	1	1	2	4	7	10	21
65+	3,287	3.6	10	1	2	3	4	7	9	15
TOTAL SINGLE DX	**295**	**1.4**	**<1**	**1**	**1**	**1**	**1**	**2**	**3**	**6**
TOTAL MULTIPLE DX	**9,202**	**3.1**	**11**	**1**	**1**	**2**	**4**	**6**	**9**	**16**
TOTAL										
0–19 Years	1,091	2.1	4	1	1	1	3	4	6	13
20–34	2,091	2.4	7	1	1	1	3	5	7	13
35–49	1,703	3.0	12	1	1	2	3	7	8	19
50–64	1,310	3.5	20	1	1	2	4	7	10	21
65+	3,302	3.6	10	1	2	3	4	7	9	15
GRAND TOTAL	**9,497**	**3.1**	**10**	**1**	**1**	**2**	**4**	**6**	**9**	**16**

86.6: FREE SKIN GRAFT

Type of Patients	Observed Patients	Avg. Stay	Vari-ance	Percentiles						
				10th	25th	50th	75th	90th	95th	99th
1. SINGLE DX										
0–19 Years	36	5.0	30	1	1	2	8	17	17	17
20–34	48	4.7	15	1	1	4	6	9	14	20
35–49	56	4.4	15	1	1	4	6	9	12	20
50–64	42	4.1	10	1	2	3	6	8	12	12
65+	27	2.8	14	1	1	2	3	6	7	22
2. MULTIPLE DX										
0–19 Years	260	9.6	86	1	3	7	14	20	28	48
20–34	453	10.5	91	1	4	8	13	21	29	46
35–49	591	11.2	109	1	4	8	15	24	34	50
50–64	542	9.5	88	1	3	7	12	22	29	49
65+	598	8.4	66	1	3	6	11	19	24	41
TOTAL SINGLE DX	**209**	**4.4**	**19**	**1**	**1**	**3**	**6**	**12**	**16**	**18**
TOTAL MULTIPLE DX	**2,444**	**9.7**	**88**	**1**	**3**	**7**	**13**	**21**	**28**	**46**
TOTAL										
0–19 Years	296	8.8	79	1	2	6	13	18	23	45
20–34	501	9.9	87	1	4	8	12	21	27	41
35–49	647	10.6	105	1	4	7	14	23	32	48
50–64	584	9.1	84	1	3	6	12	21	28	47
65+	625	8.2	66	1	3	6	11	18	23	41
GRAND TOTAL	**2,653**	**9.3**	**84**	**1**	**3**	**7**	**13**	**21**	**27**	**45**

86.62: HAND SKIN GRAFT NEC

Type of Patients	Observed Patients	Avg. Stay	Vari-ance	Percentiles						
				10th	25th	50th	75th	90th	95th	99th
1. SINGLE DX										
0–19 Years	1	1.0	0	1	1	1	1	1	1	1
20–34	1	3.0	0	3	3	3	3	3	3	3
35–49	3	2.6	3	1	2	2	5	5	5	5
50–64	2	6.8	42	2	2	2	12	12	12	12
65+	2	9.8	173	1	1	1	22	22	22	22
2. MULTIPLE DX										
0–19 Years	17	9.4	29	4	5	7	13	17	23	23
20–34	39	6.2	30	1	2	5	8	14	18	26
35–49	31	14.1	153	1	4	12	16	35	43	43
50–64	18	8.9	112	1	3	4	10	32	40	40
65+	7	12.0	33	3	9	14	16	18	18	18
TOTAL SINGLE DX	**9**	**4.6**	**40**	**1**	**1**	**2**	**5**	**12**	**22**	**22**
TOTAL MULTIPLE DX	**112**	**9.7**	**82**	**1**	**3**	**7**	**14**	**18**	**32**	**43**
TOTAL										
0–19 Years	18	8.9	32	4	4	7	13	17	17	23
20–34	40	6.1	29	1	2	5	8	14	18	26
35–49	34	13.1	150	1	3	12	16	35	43	43
50–64	20	8.7	104	1	2	4	12	17	32	40
65+	9	11.6	47	1	3	14	16	18	22	22
GRAND TOTAL	**121**	**9.4**	**81**	**1**	**3**	**7**	**14**	**18**	**31**	**43**

86.63: FTHICK SKIN GRAFT NEC

Type of Patients	Observed Patients	Avg. Stay	Vari-ance	10th	25th	50th	75th	90th	95th	99th
1. SINGLE DX										
0–19 Years	10	2.6	5	1	1	2	3	8	8	8
20–34	2	2.4	4	1	1	1	4	4	4	4
35–49	8	2.9	4	1	1	2	4	6	6	6
50–64	1	2.0	0	2	2	2	2	2	2	2
65+	4	3.0	5	1	1	2	4	6	6	6
2. MULTIPLE DX										
0–19 Years	16	4.6	18	1	1	4	5	13	15	16
20–34	14	5.4	20	1	1	3	8	11	11	17
35–49	33	5.3	29	1	1	4	7	13	15	24
50–64	22	6.9	46	1	1	3	11	18	18	21
65+	54	5.0	24	1	2	3	7	11	17	23
TOTAL SINGLE DX	**25**	**2.7**	**4**	**1**	**1**	**2**	**3**	**6**	**8**	**8**
TOTAL MULTIPLE DX	**139**	**5.3**	**27**	**1**	**1**	**4**	**7**	**13**	**17**	**23**
TOTAL										
0–19 Years	26	3.7	13	1	1	2	5	8	13	16
20–34	16	5.1	19	1	1	3	8	11	11	17
35–49	41	4.9	25	1	1	4	6	13	15	24
50–64	23	6.2	42	1	1	2	10	18	18	21
65+	58	4.9	23	1	2	3	7	11	17	23
GRAND TOTAL	**164**	**4.8**	**24**	**1**	**1**	**3**	**6**	**11**	**16**	**23**

86.66: HOMOGRAFT TO SKIN

Type of Patients	Observed Patients	Avg. Stay	Vari-ance	10th	25th	50th	75th	90th	95th	99th
1. SINGLE DX										
0–19 Years	0									
20–34	1	14.0	0	14	14	14	14	14	14	14
35–49	3	7.9	43	1	1	12	13	13	13	13
50–64	1	4.0	0	4	4	4	4	4	4	4
65+	0									
2. MULTIPLE DX										
0–19 Years	35	10.3	87	2	2	9	13	18	35	45
20–34	50	11.7	106	1	8	10	13	19	29	68
35–49	57	14.7	210	2	5	11	20	29	45	91
50–64	33	11.1	49	3	4	10	16	21	22	35
65+	23	18.9	192	2	5	15	33	41	41	45
TOTAL SINGLE DX	**5**	**8.3**	**35**	**1**	**4**	**12**	**13**	**14**	**14**	**14**
TOTAL MULTIPLE DX	**198**	**12.8**	**133**	**2**	**5**	**10**	**17**	**27**	**35**	**48**
TOTAL										
0–19 Years	35	10.3	87	2	2	9	13	18	35	45
20–34	51	11.8	105	1	8	10	13	19	29	68
35–49	60	14.4	203	1	5	11	19	29	45	91
50–64	34	10.9	49	4	4	10	14	21	22	35
65+	23	18.9	192	2	5	15	33	41	41	45
GRAND TOTAL	**203**	**12.7**	**131**	**2**	**5**	**10**	**17**	**27**	**35**	**48**

86.67: DERMAL REGENERATIVE GRFT

Type of Patients	Observed Patients	Avg. Stay	Vari-ance	10th	25th	50th	75th	90th	95th	99th
1. SINGLE DX										
0–19 Years	0									
20–34	2	1.0	0	1	1	1	1	1	1	1
35–49	1	1.0	0	1	1	1	1	1	1	1
50–64	1	2.0	0	2	2	2	2	2	2	2
65+	0									
2. MULTIPLE DX										
0–19 Years	23	10.1	216	1	4	7	8	22	61	61
20–34	14	12.2	137	2	3	9	14	32	40	40
35–49	8	8.7	49	1	4	8	15	21	21	21
50–64	11	10.6	282	2	2	4	8	54	54	54
65+	13	6.4	27	1	1	6	9	14	17	17
TOTAL SINGLE DX	**4**	**1.3**	**<1**	**1**	**1**	**1**	**2**	**2**	**2**	**2**
TOTAL MULTIPLE DX	**69**	**9.7**	**168**	**1**	**3**	**6**	**10**	**22**	**40**	**61**
TOTAL										
0–19 Years	23	10.1	216	1	4	7	8	22	61	61
20–34	16	10.5	132	1	2	8	12	32	40	40
35–49	9	7.9	50	1	2	7	8	21	21	21
50–64	12	10.1	268	2	2	4	8	54	54	54
65+	13	6.4	27	1	1	6	9	14	17	17
GRAND TOTAL	**73**	**9.4**	**164**	**1**	**2**	**6**	**9**	**22**	**40**	**61**

86.69: FREE SKIN GRAFT NEC

Type of Patients	Observed Patients	Avg. Stay	Vari-ance	10th	25th	50th	75th	90th	95th	99th
1. SINGLE DX										
0–19 Years	20	8.1	38	1	2	6	12	17	17	17
20–34	37	5.3	14	1	3	5	7	9	9	20
35–49	38	4.9	16	1	1	5	6	9	12	20
50–64	37	4.2	10	1	1	3	7	8	12	12
65+	21	2.2	3	1	1	2	3	6	6	7
2. MULTIPLE DX										
0–19 Years	155	10.3	76	1	4	8	15	21	28	35
20–34	326	11.2	97	2	5	9	14	23	30	48
35–49	450	11.2	98	2	4	8	15	24	33	56
50–64	445	9.6	83	1	3	7	12	23	29	44
65+	491	8.3	58	1	3	6	11	19	23	38
TOTAL SINGLE DX	**153**	**5.3**	**21**	**1**	**1**	**4**	**7**	**12**	**17**	**18**
TOTAL MULTIPLE DX	**1,867**	**9.8**	**82**	**1**	**4**	**7**	**13**	**22**	**28**	**43**
TOTAL										
0–19 Years	175	9.9	70	1	3	8	15	20	24	35
20–34	363	10.6	92	2	4	8	14	23	29	41
35–49	488	10.7	95	2	4	7	15	23	30	50
50–64	482	9.2	80	1	3	6	12	22	28	44
65+	512	8.1	58	1	3	6	11	18	23	37
GRAND TOTAL	**2,020**	**9.5**	**78**	**1**	**3**	**7**	**13**	**21**	**27**	**43**

86.7: PEDICLE GRAFTS OR FLAPS

Type of Patients	Observed Patients	Avg. Stay	Vari-ance	10th	25th	50th	75th	90th	95th	99th
				Percentiles						
1. SINGLE DX										
0–19 Years	26	2.9	24	1	1	2	2	6	9	35
20–34	28	5.0	14	1	1	6	7	10	12	15
35–49	18	2.1	5	1	1	1	2	5	9	9
50–64	18	2.2	2	1	1	2	3	5	5	5
65+	10	2.3	2	1	1	2	3	4	6	6
2. MULTIPLE DX										
0–19 Years	88	4.6	24	1	1	3	6	12	14	30
20–34	175	9.8	98	1	2	6	15	21	29	50
35–49	307	10.2	139	1	3	6	13	22	36	60
50–64	392	8.1	76	1	2	5	11	20	27	>99
65+	402	7.8	81	1	2	6	9	17	24	40
TOTAL SINGLE DX	**100**	**3.1**	**14**	**1**	**1**	**2**	**4**	**7**	**9**	**15**
TOTAL MULTIPLE DX	**1,364**	**8.3**	**90**	**1**	**2**	**5**	**11**	**20**	**28**	**59**
TOTAL										
0–19 Years	114	4.2	25	1	1	2	6	9	13	35
20–34	203	9.2	90	1	2	6	14	21	28	50
35–49	325	9.7	135	1	2	6	13	22	36	60
50–64	410	7.9	74	1	2	5	11	20	26	>99
65+	412	7.7	80	1	2	5	9	17	24	40
GRAND TOTAL	**1,464**	**8.0**	**87**	**1**	**2**	**5**	**10**	**19**	**26**	**56**

86.70: PEDICLE/FLAP GRAFT NOS

Type of Patients	Observed Patients	Avg. Stay	Vari-ance	10th	25th	50th	75th	90th	95th	99th
				Percentiles						
1. SINGLE DX										
0–19 Years	0									
20–34	1	4.0	0	4	4	4	4	4	4	4
35–49	4	2.8	10	1	1	2	2	9	9	9
50–64	1	1.0	0	1	1	1	1	1	1	1
65+	1	3.0	0	3	3	3	3	3	3	3
2. MULTIPLE DX										
0–19 Years	3	6.9	16	1	7	7	10	10	10	10
20–34	12	4.5	41	1	1	2	3	18	23	23
35–49	14	6.8	12	2	5	6	10	10	15	15
50–64	21	4.1	13	1	1	3	6	7	11	18
65+	16	3.6	13	1	1	2	6	12	12	13
TOTAL SINGLE DX	**7**	**3.0**	**6**	**1**	**1**	**2**	**4**	**4**	**9**	**9**
TOTAL MULTIPLE DX	**66**	**4.5**	**18**	**1**	**1**	**3**	**6**	**10**	**13**	**18**
TOTAL										
0–19 Years	3	6.9	16	1	7	7	10	10	10	10
20–34	13	4.5	35	1	1	2	4	12	18	23
35–49	18	5.8	14	1	2	6	9	10	10	15
50–64	22	4.0	13	1	1	3	6	7	11	18
65+	17	3.5	12	1	1	2	6	12	12	13
GRAND TOTAL	**73**	**4.4**	**17**	**1**	**1**	**3**	**6**	**10**	**12**	**18**

86.72: PEDICLE GRAFT ADV

Type of Patients	Observed Patients	Avg. Stay	Vari-ance	10th	25th	50th	75th	90th	95th	99th
				Percentiles						
1. SINGLE DX										
0–19 Years	2	1.7	<1	1	1	2	2	2	2	2
20–34	2	8.7	87	1	1	15	15	15	15	15
35–49	4	3.1	11	1	1	1	3	9	9	9
50–64	2	2.0	0	2	2	2	2	2	2	2
65+	0									
2. MULTIPLE DX										
0–19 Years	5	2.9	4	1	2	2	6	6	6	6
20–34	13	8.2	54	2	2	3	15	18	18	21
35–49	17	2.9	4	1	1	3	4	6	7	7
50–64	24	9.9	121	1	2	7	14	21	24	56
65+	29	8.5	77	1	3	6	11	24	25	40
TOTAL SINGLE DX	**10**	**3.0**	**14**	**1**	**1**	**2**	**2**	**9**	**15**	**15**
TOTAL MULTIPLE DX	**88**	**7.7**	**76**	**1**	**2**	**4**	**11**	**18**	**21**	**40**
TOTAL										
0–19 Years	7	2.4	3	1	2	2	2	6	6	6
20–34	15	8.2	54	1	2	3	15	18	18	21
35–49	21	2.9	5	1	1	3	4	6	7	9
50–64	26	9.3	116	1	2	7	14	21	24	56
65+	29	8.5	77	1	3	6	11	24	25	40
GRAND TOTAL	**98**	**7.2**	**71**	**1**	**2**	**3**	**11**	**18**	**21**	**40**

86.74: ATTACH PEDICLE GRAFT NEC

Type of Patients	Observed Patients	Avg. Stay	Vari-ance	10th	25th	50th	75th	90th	95th	99th
				Percentiles						
1. SINGLE DX										
0–19 Years	20	3.3	31	1	1	2	3	7	9	35
20–34	17	5.4	12	1	2	6	8	11	12	12
35–49	2	2.0	0	2	2	2	2	2	2	2
50–64	10	2.5	3	1	1	2	3	5	5	5
65+	6	1.9	1	1	1	2	3	4	4	4
2. MULTIPLE DX										
0–19 Years	65	4.9	29	1	1	3	7	13	17	>99
20–34	118	11.9	116	1	4	8	16	28	36	50
35–49	210	11.4	150	2	3	7	15	28	37	60
50–64	277	8.8	73	1	3	6	12	21	28	>99
65+	300	8.2	96	1	2	5	10	18	26	59
TOTAL SINGLE DX	**55**	**3.5**	**19**	**1**	**1**	**2**	**5**	**8**	**9**	**35**
TOTAL MULTIPLE DX	**970**	**9.1**	**99**	**1**	**3**	**6**	**12**	**21**	**29**	**64**
TOTAL										
0–19 Years	85	4.5	30	1	1	2	6	13	16	35
20–34	135	11.2	109	1	4	8	16	24	35	50
35–49	212	11.3	149	2	3	7	15	28	37	60
50–64	287	8.6	72	1	3	6	12	21	28	>99
65+	306	8.1	94	1	2	5	9	18	26	59
GRAND TOTAL	**1,025**	**8.8**	**96**	**1**	**3**	**6**	**11**	**20**	**29**	**60**

86.75: REV PEDICLE/FLAP GRAFT

Type of Patients	Observed Patients	Avg. Stay	Vari-ance	10th	25th	50th	75th	90th	95th	99th
1. SINGLE DX										
0–19 Years	0									
20–34	3	5.2	20	1	1	6	10	10	10	10
35–49	2	2.9	7	1	1	1	5	5	5	5
50–64	1	4.0	0	4	4	4	4	4	4	4
65+	2	4.1	6	2	2	6	6	6	6	6
2. MULTIPLE DX										
0–19 Years	10	3.6	5	1	1	4	6	6	6	6
20–34	15	5.6	21	1	2	4	9	15	16	16
35–49	44	11.2	196	1	2	6	19	22	41	72
50–64	55	5.2	48	1	1	3	6	12	18	>99
65+	43	6.2	30	1	3	6	6	11	18	32
TOTAL SINGLE DX	**8**	**4.2**	**9**	**1**	**1**	**4**	**6**	**10**	**10**	**10**
TOTAL MULTIPLE DX	**167**	**6.9**	**79**	**1**	**2**	**4**	**7**	**18**	**22**	**72**
TOTAL										
0–19 Years	10	3.6	5	1	1	4	6	6	6	6
20–34	18	5.6	20	1	2	5	9	10	15	16
35–49	46	10.9	191	1	2	5	19	22	41	72
50–64	56	5.2	48	1	1	3	6	12	18	>99
65+	45	6.2	29	1	3	6	6	11	18	32
GRAND TOTAL	**175**	**6.8**	**76**	**1**	**2**	**4**	**7**	**16**	**22**	**44**

86.8: OTHER SKIN & SUBCU REP

Type of Patients	Observed Patients	Avg. Stay	Vari-ance	10th	25th	50th	75th	90th	95th	99th
1. SINGLE DX										
0–19 Years	24	1.5	1	1	1	1	1	3	5	5
20–34	48	1.6	<1	1	1	1	2	3	3	5
35–49	102	1.6	3	1	1	1	2	2	3	8
50–64	111	1.4	<1	1	1	1	2	2	2	4
65+	19	1.9	3	1	1	2	2	2	2	9
2. MULTIPLE DX										
0–19 Years	83	2.5	7	1	1	1	3	6	6	16
20–34	300	2.0	4	1	1	2	2	4	5	9
35–49	667	2.3	8	1	1	2	3	4	5	10
50–64	758	2.5	8	1	1	2	3	4	7	13
65+	189	2.7	9	1	1	2	3	6	8	14
TOTAL SINGLE DX	**304**	**1.5**	**2**	**1**	**1**	**1**	**2**	**2**	**3**	**8**
TOTAL MULTIPLE DX	**1,997**	**2.4**	**8**	**1**	**1**	**2**	**3**	**4**	**6**	**13**
TOTAL										
0–19 Years	107	2.3	6	1	1	1	3	5	6	14
20–34	348	2.0	3	1	1	1	2	3	5	8
35–49	769	2.3	8	1	1	2	3	4	5	10
50–64	869	2.4	7	1	1	2	3	4	7	13
65+	208	2.6	8	1	1	2	3	6	8	14
GRAND TOTAL	**2,301**	**2.3**	**7**	**1**	**1**	**2**	**3**	**4**	**6**	**13**

86.82: FACIAL RHYTIDECTOMY

Type of Patients	Observed Patients	Avg. Stay	Vari-ance	10th	25th	50th	75th	90th	95th	99th
1. SINGLE DX										
0–19 Years	0									
20–34	1	2.0	0	2	2	2	2	2	2	2
35–49	24	1.2	<1	1	1	1	1	2	2	2
50–64	49	1.2	<1	1	1	1	1	2	2	3
65+	6	1.6	<1	1	1	2	2	2	2	2
2. MULTIPLE DX										
0–19 Years	2	2.6	<1	2	2	3	3	3	3	3
20–34	0									
35–49	42	1.3	1	1	1	1	1	2	3	8
50–64	182	1.4	<1	1	1	1	2	2	3	3
65+	53	1.4	<1	1	1	1	2	2	2	3
TOTAL SINGLE DX	**80**	**1.3**	**<1**	**1**	**1**	**1**	**2**	**2**	**2**	**2**
TOTAL MULTIPLE DX	**279**	**1.4**	**<1**	**1**	**1**	**1**	**2**	**2**	**3**	**3**
TOTAL										
0–19 Years	2	2.6	<1	2	2	3	3	3	3	3
20–34	1	2.0	0	2	2	2	2	2	2	2
35–49	66	1.3	<1	1	1	1	1	2	2	8
50–64	231	1.3	<1	1	1	1	2	2	3	3
65+	59	1.4	<1	1	1	1	2	2	2	3
GRAND TOTAL	**359**	**1.4**	**<1**	**1**	**1**	**1**	**2**	**2**	**3**	**3**

86.83: SIZE RED PLASTIC OP

Type of Patients	Observed Patients	Avg. Stay	Vari-ance	10th	25th	50th	75th	90th	95th	99th
1. SINGLE DX										
0–19 Years	2	1.4	<1	1	1	1	2	2	2	2
20–34	39	1.6	<1	1	1	1	2	2	3	5
35–49	70	1.7	4	1	1	1	2	2	5	16
50–64	56	1.5	<1	1	1	1	2	2	3	4
65+	11	1.3	<1	1	1	1	2	2	2	2
2. MULTIPLE DX										
0–19 Years	6	2.0	2	1	1	1	2	5	5	5
20–34	213	1.9	1	1	1	2	2	3	4	6
35–49	536	2.2	2	1	1	2	3	4	5	9
50–64	522	2.8	8	1	1	2	3	6	8	13
65+	79	3.1	11	1	1	2	3	7	9	21
TOTAL SINGLE DX	**178**	**1.6**	**2**	**1**	**1**	**1**	**2**	**2**	**3**	**8**
TOTAL MULTIPLE DX	**1,356**	**2.4**	**5**	**1**	**1**	**2**	**3**	**4**	**6**	**13**
TOTAL										
0–19 Years	8	1.8	2	1	1	1	2	5	5	5
20–34	252	1.8	1	1	1	2	2	3	4	6
35–49	606	2.1	3	1	1	2	3	4	5	9
50–64	578	2.7	7	1	1	2	3	5	8	13
65+	90	2.9	10	1	1	2	3	6	9	21
GRAND TOTAL	**1,534**	**2.3**	**5**	**1**	**1**	**2**	**3**	**4**	**6**	**13**

86.89: SKIN REP & RECONST NEC

Type of Patients	Observed Patients	Avg. Stay	Vari-ance	Percentiles 10th	25th	50th	75th	90th	95th	99th
1. SINGLE DX										
0–19 Years	15	1.7	2	1	1	1	2	4	5	5
20–34	6	2.0	1	1	1	2	3	4	4	4
35–49	7	1.4	<1	1	1	1	2	2	2	2
50–64	5	2.0	2	1	1	2	2	4	4	4
65+	2	5.8	21	1	1	9	9	9	9	9
2. MULTIPLE DX										
0–19 Years	51	2.8	8	1	1	2	3	5	7	16
20–34	80	2.6	11	1	1	2	3	5	8	26
35–49	68	4.7	61	1	1	4	5	9	11	72
50–64	40	3.7	44	1	1	2	3	6	7	45
65+	51	4.0	13	1	1	3	6	8	9	20
TOTAL SINGLE DX	**35**	**2.0**	**3**	**1**	**1**	**1**	**2**	**4**	**5**	**9**
TOTAL MULTIPLE DX	**290**	**3.5**	**26**	**1**	**1**	**2**	**4**	**7**	**9**	**20**
TOTAL										
0–19 Years	66	2.6	7	1	1	1	3	5	6	16
20–34	86	2.6	10	1	1	2	3	4	8	15
35–49	75	4.4	57	1	1	3	5	9	10	16
50–64	45	3.6	40	1	1	2	3	6	7	45
65+	53	4.0	13	1	1	3	6	9	9	20
GRAND TOTAL	**325**	**3.3**	**23**	**1**	**1**	**2**	**4**	**6**	**9**	**20**

86.9: OTHER SKIN & SUBCU OPS

Type of Patients	Observed Patients	Avg. Stay	Vari-ance	Percentiles 10th	25th	50th	75th	90th	95th	99th
1. SINGLE DX										
0–19 Years	7	1.0	0	1	1	1	1	1	1	1
20–34	1	1.0	0	1	1	1	1	1	1	1
35–49	2	1.5	<1	1	1	1	2	2	2	2
50–64	1	1.0	0	1	1	1	1	1	1	1
65+	0									
2. MULTIPLE DX										
0–19 Years	12	2.1	3	1	1	1	3	4	4	7
20–34	10	1.3	<1	1	1	1	1	2	3	3
35–49	12	4.5	10	1	2	3	8	8	8	10
50–64	9	1.2	<1	1	1	1	1	2	2	2
65+	3	3.5	13	1	1	2	8	8	8	8
TOTAL SINGLE DX	**11**	**1.0**	**<1**	**1**	**1**	**1**	**1**	**1**	**1**	**2**
TOTAL MULTIPLE DX	**46**	**2.5**	**6**	**1**	**1**	**1**	**3**	**8**	**8**	**10**
TOTAL										
0–19 Years	19	1.6	2	1	1	1	1	4	4	7
20–34	11	1.3	<1	1	1	1	1	2	3	3
35–49	14	4.2	10	1	1	3	8	8	8	10
50–64	10	1.2	<1	1	1	1	1	2	2	2
65+	3	3.5	13	1	1	2	8	8	8	8
GRAND TOTAL	**57**	**2.2**	**5**	**1**	**1**	**1**	**2**	**4**	**8**	**10**

87.0: HEAD/NECK SFT TISS X-RAY

Type of Patients	Observed Patients	Avg. Stay	Vari-ance	Percentiles 10th	25th	50th	75th	90th	95th	99th
1. SINGLE DX										
0–19 Years	509	1.7	2	1	1	1	2	3	4	7
20–34	176	2.3	7	1	1	1	3	4	6	18
35–49	130	2.4	5	1	1	2	3	6	8	12
50–64	86	2.9	25	1	1	2	3	5	9	42
65+	62	2.1	3	1	1	1	3	4	4	14
2. MULTIPLE DX										
0–19 Years	1,363	2.8	11	1	1	2	3	6	8	17
20–34	1,271	2.9	12	1	1	2	3	6	9	21
35–49	2,293	3.4	13	1	1	2	4	7	9	20
50–64	3,592	3.7	14	1	1	3	5	7	10	19
65+	11,072	4.0	12	1	2	3	5	7	10	17
TOTAL SINGLE DX	**963**	**2.0**	**5**	**1**	**1**	**1**	**2**	**4**	**5**	**10**
TOTAL MULTIPLE DX	**19,591**	**3.7**	**12**	**1**	**2**	**3**	**5**	**7**	**10**	**18**
TOTAL										
0–19 Years	1,872	2.5	9	1	1	2	3	5	7	16
20–34	1,447	2.8	12	1	1	2	3	5	8	18
35–49	2,423	3.4	13	1	1	2	4	7	9	19
50–64	3,678	3.7	14	1	1	3	4	7	10	19
65+	11,134	4.0	12	1	2	3	5	7	10	17
GRAND TOTAL	**20,554**	**3.6**	**12**	**1**	**1**	**3**	**4**	**7**	**9**	**17**

87.02: BRAIN/SKULL CONTR X-RAY

Type of Patients	Observed Patients	Avg. Stay	Vari-ance	Percentiles 10th	25th	50th	75th	90th	95th	99th
1. SINGLE DX										
0–19 Years	0									
20–34	0									
35–49	0									
50–64	1	13.0	0	13	13	13	13	13	13	13
65+	0									
2. MULTIPLE DX										
0–19 Years	1	1.0	0	1	1	1	1	1	1	1
20–34	5	2.9	4	1	1	3	3	6	6	6
35–49	2	5.5	<1	5	5	5	6	6	6	6
50–64	1	5.0	0	5	5	5	5	5	5	5
65+	21	8.7	27	3	5	7	13	15	21	21
TOTAL SINGLE DX	**1**	**13.0**	**0**	**13**	**13**	**13**	**13**	**13**	**13**	**13**
TOTAL MULTIPLE DX	**30**	**7.3**	**27**	**1**	**3**	**6**	**9**	**13**	**21**	**21**
TOTAL										
0–19 Years	1	1.0	0	1	1	1	1	1	1	1
20–34	5	2.9	4	1	1	3	3	6	6	6
35–49	2	5.5	<1	5	5	5	6	6	6	6
50–64	2	8.3	26	5	5	5	13	13	13	13
65+	21	8.7	27	3	5	7	13	15	21	21
GRAND TOTAL	**31**	**7.4**	**27**	**1**	**3**	**6**	**11**	**13**	**21**	**21**

87.03: CAT SCAN HEAD

Type of Patients	Observed Patients	Avg. Stay	Vari-ance	Percentiles						
				10th	25th	50th	75th	90th	95th	99th
1. SINGLE DX										
0–19 Years	506	1.7	2	1	1	1	2	3	4	7
20–34	174	2.3	7	1	1	1	3	4	6	18
35–49	128	2.4	5	1	1	2	3	6	8	12
50–64	85	2.8	24	1	1	2	3	5	8	42
65+	61	2.1	3	1	1	1	3	4	4	14
2. MULTIPLE DX										
0–19 Years	1,351	2.8	11	1	1	2	3	6	8	17
20–34	1,263	2.9	13	1	1	2	3	6	9	21
35–49	2,283	3.4	13	1	1	2	4	7	9	20
50–64	3,581	3.7	14	1	1	3	4	7	10	19
65+	11,036	4.0	12	1	2	3	5	7	10	17
TOTAL SINGLE DX	**954**	**2.0**	**5**	**1**	**1**	**1**	**2**	**4**	**5**	**10**
TOTAL MULTIPLE DX	**19,514**	**3.7**	**12**	**1**	**2**	**3**	**5**	**7**	**10**	**17**
TOTAL										
0–19 Years	1,857	2.5	9	1	1	2	3	5	7	16
20–34	1,437	2.8	12	1	1	2	3	5	8	18
35–49	2,411	3.4	13	1	1	2	4	7	9	19
50–64	3,666	3.7	14	1	1	3	4	7	10	19
65+	11,097	4.0	12	1	2	3	5	7	10	17
GRAND TOTAL	**20,468**	**3.6**	**12**	**1**	**1**	**3**	**4**	**7**	**9**	**17**

87.1: OTHER HEAD/NECK X-RAY

Type of Patients	Observed Patients	Avg. Stay	Vari-ance	Percentiles						
				10th	25th	50th	75th	90th	95th	99th
1. SINGLE DX										
0–19 Years	3	2.6	3	1	1	2	5	5	5	5
20–34	0									
35–49	2	5.2	16	2	2	8	8	8	8	8
50–64	0									
65+	0									
2. MULTIPLE DX										
0–19 Years	8	6.3	62	3	4	4	4	28	28	28
20–34	6	2.3	2	1	2	2	2	5	5	5
35–49	12	3.9	9	1	2	2	4	8	10	10
50–64	6	3.1	4	1	2	2	4	7	7	7
65+	4	1.7	2	1	1	1	2	4	4	4
TOTAL SINGLE DX	**5**	**3.3**	**7**	**1**	**2**	**2**	**5**	**8**	**8**	**8**
TOTAL MULTIPLE DX	**36**	**3.6**	**17**	**1**	**2**	**2**	**4**	**7**	**8**	**28**
TOTAL										
0–19 Years	11	5.0	43	1	2	4	4	5	28	28
20–34	6	2.3	2	1	2	2	2	5	5	5
35–49	14	4.1	9	1	2	4	8	8	10	10
50–64	6	3.1	4	1	2	2	4	7	7	7
65+	4	1.7	2	1	1	1	2	4	4	4
GRAND TOTAL	**41**	**3.5**	**16**	**1**	**2**	**2**	**4**	**7**	**8**	**28**

87.2: X-RAY OF SPINE

Type of Patients	Observed Patients	Avg. Stay	Vari-ance	Percentiles						
				10th	25th	50th	75th	90th	95th	99th
1. SINGLE DX										
0–19 Years	2	2.9	7	1	1	1	5	5	5	5
20–34	13	4.1	20	1	1	2	5	15	15	15
35–49	13	2.2	2	1	1	1	3	5	5	5
50–64	12	2.4	7	1	1	1	3	6	11	11
65+	6	1.4	<1	1	1	1	2	2	2	2
2. MULTIPLE DX										
0–19 Years	9	2.8	2	1	2	2	3	5	6	6
20–34	45	2.7	11	1	1	1	3	6	8	22
35–49	119	4.6	11	1	2	4	6	9	11	15
50–64	132	3.9	11	1	1	3	5	9	10	16
65+	148	5.7	36	2	3	5	7	11	13	41
TOTAL SINGLE DX	**46**	**2.6**	**9**	**1**	**1**	**1**	**3**	**5**	**8**	**15**
TOTAL MULTIPLE DX	**453**	**4.6**	**21**	**1**	**2**	**4**	**6**	**9**	**12**	**17**
TOTAL										
0–19 Years	11	2.9	3	1	2	2	3	5	6	6
20–34	58	3.0	13	1	1	2	4	7	12	22
35–49	132	4.4	10	1	2	4	6	8	11	15
50–64	144	3.8	11	1	1	3	5	9	10	16
65+	154	5.6	35	1	2	5	7	9	13	41
GRAND TOTAL	**499**	**4.5**	**20**	**1**	**2**	**3**	**6**	**9**	**12**	**17**

87.21: CONTRAST MYELOGRAM

Type of Patients	Observed Patients	Avg. Stay	Vari-ance	Percentiles						
				10th	25th	50th	75th	90th	95th	99th
1. SINGLE DX										
0–19 Years	0									
20–34	4	7.3	31	3	3	5	15	15	15	15
35–49	7	2.6	3	1	1	3	4	5	5	5
50–64	9	2.7	8	1	1	1	4	6	11	11
65+	3	1.0	0	1	1	1	1	1	1	1
2. MULTIPLE DX										
0–19 Years	0									
20–34	16	4.7	22	1	1	4	6	8	12	22
35–49	90	4.9	10	1	2	4	7	9	12	15
50–64	92	4.5	12	1	2	4	5	10	10	15
65+	106	6.5	46	2	3	5	8	12	14	55
TOTAL SINGLE DX	**23**	**3.2**	**12**	**1**	**1**	**1**	**4**	**6**	**15**	**15**
TOTAL MULTIPLE DX	**304**	**5.3**	**25**	**1**	**2**	**4**	**7**	**10**	**13**	**21**
TOTAL										
0–19 Years	0									
20–34	20	5.3	24	1	3	4	6	12	15	22
35–49	97	4.7	10	1	2	4	6	9	11	15
50–64	101	4.3	12	1	1	4	5	9	10	15
65+	109	6.3	45	1	3	5	8	12	13	55
GRAND TOTAL	**327**	**5.2**	**25**	**1**	**2**	**4**	**7**	**10**	**13**	**18**

87.3: THORAX SOFT TISSUE X-RAY

Type of Patients	Observed Patients	Avg. Stay	Vari-ance	10th	25th	50th	75th	90th	95th	99th
1. SINGLE DX										
0–19 Years	9	2.8	4	1	1	2	4	7	7	7
20–34	11	2.6	7	1	1	2	3	3	11	11
35–49	1	1.0	0	1	1	1	1	1	1	1
50–64	3	3.0	3	1	1	4	4	4	4	4
65+	2	2.4	3	1	1	1	4	4	4	4
2. MULTIPLE DX										
0–19 Years	46	3.3	5	1	2	2	5	7	7	9
20–34	25	4.0	11	1	2	3	5	9	9	15
35–49	64	3.4	18	1	1	2	3	7	11	30
50–64	71	3.5	6	1	1	3	5	7	8	10
65+	95	3.2	5	1	2	3	4	5	8	16
TOTAL SINGLE DX	**26**	**2.6**	**5**	**1**	**1**	**2**	**4**	**5**	**7**	**11**
TOTAL MULTIPLE DX	**301**	**3.4**	**8**	**1**	**2**	**3**	**4**	**7**	**8**	**15**
TOTAL										
0–19 Years	55	3.2	5	1	2	2	5	7	7	9
20–34	36	3.5	10	1	1	3	4	9	11	15
35–49	65	3.3	18	1	1	2	3	7	11	30
50–64	74	3.5	6	1	1	3	5	7	8	10
65+	97	3.2	5	1	2	3	4	5	8	16
GRAND TOTAL	**327**	**3.3**	**8**	**1**	**2**	**3**	**4**	**7**	**8**	**15**

87.39: THOR SOFT TISS X-RAY NEC

Type of Patients	Observed Patients	Avg. Stay	Vari-ance	10th	25th	50th	75th	90th	95th	99th
1. SINGLE DX										
0–19 Years	9	2.8	4	1	1	2	4	7	7	7
20–34	11	2.6	7	1	1	2	3	3	11	11
35–49	1	1.0	0	1	1	1	1	1	1	1
50–64	3	3.0	3	1	1	4	4	4	4	4
65+	2	2.4	3	1	1	1	4	4	4	4
2. MULTIPLE DX										
0–19 Years	41	3.3	5	1	2	2	5	7	7	9
20–34	24	3.8	11	1	1	3	5	9	9	15
35–49	60	2.9	9	1	1	2	3	6	7	16
50–64	68	3.3	6	1	1	3	5	6	8	14
65+	88	3.1	4	1	2	3	4	5	8	8
TOTAL SINGLE DX	**26**	**2.6**	**5**	**1**	**1**	**2**	**4**	**5**	**7**	**11**
TOTAL MULTIPLE DX	**281**	**3.2**	**6**	**1**	**2**	**3**	**4**	**6**	**8**	**14**
TOTAL										
0–19 Years	50	3.2	5	1	1	2	5	7	7	9
20–34	35	3.4	10	1	1	3	4	9	11	15
35–49	61	2.8	9	1	1	2	3	6	7	16
50–64	71	3.3	5	1	1	3	5	6	8	10
65+	90	3.1	4	1	2	3	4	5	8	8
GRAND TOTAL	**307**	**3.1**	**5**	**1**	**1**	**3**	**4**	**6**	**8**	**11**

87.4: OTHER X-RAY OF THORAX

Type of Patients	Observed Patients	Avg. Stay	Vari-ance	10th	25th	50th	75th	90th	95th	99th
1. SINGLE DX										
0–19 Years	209	2.6	6	1	1	2	3	5	6	10
20–34	111	2.2	4	1	1	1	3	5	7	12
35–49	114	2.2	19	1	1	1	2	4	5	7
50–64	104	1.9	5	1	1	1	2	3	5	7
65+	38	2.2	8	1	1	1	2	4	8	15
2. MULTIPLE DX										
0–19 Years	605	4.2	28	1	2	3	5	8	11	22
20–34	573	3.9	19	1	1	3	5	8	10	20
35–49	1,506	3.6	13	1	1	3	5	7	10	18
50–64	2,160	3.6	11	1	1	3	5	7	10	15
65+	3,331	4.3	11	1	2	4	6	8	10	16
TOTAL SINGLE DX	**576**	**2.3**	**8**	**1**	**1**	**1**	**3**	**4**	**6**	**12**
TOTAL MULTIPLE DX	**8,175**	**4.0**	**13**	**1**	**2**	**3**	**5**	**8**	**10**	**17**
TOTAL										
0–19 Years	814	3.8	23	1	2	3	4	7	11	19
20–34	684	3.7	17	1	1	3	5	8	9	19
35–49	1,620	3.5	13	1	1	2	4	7	10	18
50–64	2,264	3.5	10	1	1	3	5	7	9	15
65+	3,369	4.3	11	1	2	4	6	8	10	16
GRAND TOTAL	**8,751**	**3.9**	**13**	**1**	**2**	**3**	**5**	**8**	**10**	**17**

87.41: CAT SCAN THORAX

Type of Patients	Observed Patients	Avg. Stay	Vari-ance	10th	25th	50th	75th	90th	95th	99th
1. SINGLE DX										
0–19 Years	27	2.9	3	1	1	3	4	5	6	10
20–34	41	2.6	6	1	1	1	3	6	8	12
35–49	35	2.6	2	1	1	2	3	5	6	7
50–64	29	2.5	13	1	1	1	2	4	6	21
65+	10	4.7	24	1	1	2	8	12	15	15
2. MULTIPLE DX										
0–19 Years	117	5.3	27	1	2	4	7	12	16	22
20–34	300	4.4	25	1	2	3	6	9	12	20
35–49	766	4.0	15	1	2	3	5	8	10	19
50–64	1,219	4.1	13	1	2	3	5	8	11	16
65+	2,413	4.7	12	1	2	4	6	9	11	17
TOTAL SINGLE DX	**142**	**2.8**	**7**	**1**	**1**	**2**	**3**	**5**	**8**	**15**
TOTAL MULTIPLE DX	**4,815**	**4.5**	**14**	**1**	**2**	**4**	**6**	**9**	**11**	**18**
TOTAL										
0–19 Years	144	4.9	24	1	2	3	6	11	14	22
20–34	341	4.2	23	1	1	3	5	9	11	20
35–49	801	4.0	14	1	2	3	5	8	10	19
50–64	1,248	4.1	13	1	2	3	5	8	11	16
65+	2,423	4.7	12	1	2	4	6	9	11	17
GRAND TOTAL	**4,957**	**4.4**	**14**	**1**	**2**	**4**	**6**	**9**	**11**	**18**

87.44: ROUTINE CHEST X-RAY

Type of Patients	Observed Patients	Avg. Stay	Vari- ance	Percentiles						
				10th	25th	50th	75th	90th	95th	99th
1. SINGLE DX										
0–19 Years	177	2.6	6	1	1	2	3	5	7	19
20–34	57	2.3	4	1	1	1	3	5	6	10
35–49	60	2.3	36	1	1	1	2	3	5	49
50–64	64	1.6	1	1	1	1	2	3	4	7
65+	21	1.4	<1	1	1	1	2	2	2	4
2. MULTIPLE DX										
0–19 Years	423	4.0	32	1	2	3	5	8	10	25
20–34	237	3.4	11	1	1	2	4	7	9	23
35–49	616	3.2	10	1	1	2	4	6	9	18
50–64	738	3.0	8	1	1	2	4	6	8	13
65+	453	3.8	9	1	2	3	5	7	9	18
TOTAL SINGLE DX	**379**	**2.3**	**9**	**1**	**1**	**1**	**3**	**4**	**6**	**10**
TOTAL MULTIPLE DX	**2,467**	**3.5**	**14**	**1**	**1**	**2**	**4**	**7**	**9**	**18**
TOTAL										
0–19 Years	600	3.6	25	1	1	2	4	7	10	19
20–34	294	3.2	10	1	1	2	4	6	9	23
35–49	676	3.1	12	1	1	2	4	6	8	18
50–64	802	2.9	8	1	1	2	4	6	8	13
65+	474	3.7	9	1	2	3	5	7	9	18
GRAND TOTAL	**2,846**	**3.3**	**13**	**1**	**1**	**2**	**4**	**7**	**9**	**17**

87.49: CHEST X-RAY NEC

Type of Patients	Observed Patients	Avg. Stay	Vari- ance	Percentiles						
				10th	25th	50th	75th	90th	95th	99th
1. SINGLE DX										
0–19 Years	5	2.4	4	1	1	2	2	6	6	6
20–34	13	1.0	0	1	1	1	1	1	1	1
35–49	18	1.5	<1	1	1	1	2	3	4	4
50–64	11	2.4	<1	1	2	3	3	3	4	4
65+	7	1.4	<1	1	1	1	1	3	3	3
2. MULTIPLE DX										
0–19 Years	48	2.3	2	1	1	2	3	4	6	7
20–34	34	2.3	5	1	1	2	2	4	5	15
35–49	121	3.3	8	1	1	3	4	6	7	13
50–64	189	2.7	4	1	1	2	4	5	7	10
65+	440	3.1	7	1	1	3	4	5	7	10
TOTAL SINGLE DX	**54**	**1.6**	**1**	**1**	**1**	**1**	**2**	**3**	**4**	**6**
TOTAL MULTIPLE DX	**832**	**3.0**	**6**	**1**	**1**	**3**	**4**	**5**	**7**	**10**
TOTAL										
0–19 Years	53	2.3	2	1	1	2	3	4	6	7
20–34	47	2.0	4	1	1	1	2	3	4	15
35–49	139	3.0	8	1	1	2	4	6	7	13
50–64	200	2.7	4	1	1	2	4	5	7	10
65+	447	3.1	7	1	1	3	4	5	7	10
GRAND TOTAL	**886**	**2.9**	**6**	**1**	**1**	**2**	**4**	**5**	**7**	**10**

87.5: BILIARY TRACT X-RAY

Type of Patients	Observed Patients	Avg. Stay	Vari- ance	Percentiles						
				10th	25th	50th	75th	90th	95th	99th
1. SINGLE DX										
0–19 Years	2	2.2	2	1	1	3	3	3	3	3
20–34	6	3.1	3	1	2	3	4	6	6	6
35–49	1	4.0	0	4	4	4	4	4	4	4
50–64	1	1.0	0	1	1	1	1	1	1	1
65+	3	1.8	3	1	1	1	1	5	5	5
2. MULTIPLE DX										
0–19 Years	8	5.9	72	1	2	4	5	28	28	28
20–34	34	5.9	51	1	2	3	9	12	13	40
35–49	55	6.5	28	2	3	5	9	12	18	25
50–64	107	6.1	30	2	3	5	7	11	15	36
65+	177	5.6	22	2	2	4	7	11	15	25
TOTAL SINGLE DX	**13**	**2.4**	**3**	**1**	**1**	**2**	**4**	**5**	**5**	**6**
TOTAL MULTIPLE DX	**381**	**5.9**	**28**	**2**	**2**	**4**	**7**	**11**	**16**	**25**
TOTAL										
0–19 Years	10	5.2	60	1	1	3	5	5	28	28
20–34	40	5.5	45	1	2	3	6	11	13	40
35–49	56	6.4	28	2	3	5	8	12	18	25
50–64	108	6.1	30	1	3	5	7	11	15	36
65+	180	5.5	22	1	2	4	7	11	15	25
GRAND TOTAL	**394**	**5.8**	**27**	**1**	**2**	**4**	**7**	**11**	**16**	**25**

87.51: PERC HEPAT CHOLANGIOGRAM

Type of Patients	Observed Patients	Avg. Stay	Vari- ance	Percentiles						
				10th	25th	50th	75th	90th	95th	99th
1. SINGLE DX										
0–19 Years	1	1.0	0	1	1	1	1	1	1	1
20–34	1	1.0	0	1	1	1	1	1	1	1
35–49	1	4.0	0	4	4	4	4	4	4	4
50–64	1	1.0	0	1	1	1	1	1	1	1
65+	2	1.0	0	1	1	1	1	1	1	1
2. MULTIPLE DX										
0–19 Years	1	2.0	0	2	2	2	2	2	2	2
20–34	8	7.0	23	1	4	7	12	13	13	13
35–49	21	8.0	46	3	3	5	10	22	23	23
50–64	62	6.0	27	1	2	5	7	11	16	36
65+	91	6.4	25	2	3	6	8	14	16	25
TOTAL SINGLE DX	**6**	**1.5**	**1**	**1**	**1**	**1**	**1**	**4**	**4**	**4**
TOTAL MULTIPLE DX	**183**	**6.4**	**28**	**2**	**3**	**5**	**8**	**14**	**17**	**24**
TOTAL										
0–19 Years	2	1.5	<1	1	1	2	2	2	2	2
20–34	9	6.3	24	1	1	5	11	13	13	13
35–49	22	7.8	44	3	3	4	10	18	23	23
50–64	63	5.9	27	1	2	5	7	11	16	36
65+	93	6.2	25	1	2	5	8	12	16	25
GRAND TOTAL	**189**	**6.2**	**28**	**1**	**2**	**5**	**8**	**13**	**17**	**24**

87.54: CHOLANGIOGRAM NEC

Type of Patients	Observed Patients	Avg. Stay	Vari-ance	Percentiles						
				10th	25th	50th	75th	90th	95th	99th
1. SINGLE DX										
0–19 Years	0									
20–34	3	3.0	<1	2	2	3	4	4	4	4
35–49	0									
50–64	0									
65+	1	5.0	0	5	5	5	5	5	5	5
2. MULTIPLE DX										
0–19 Years	3	1.5	1	1	1	1	3	3	3	3
20–34	19	5.9	80	1	2	3	5	9	23	40
35–49	22	5.9	19	2	3	5	7	9	11	25
50–64	24	6.4	48	1	4	5	7	10	13	39
65+	57	3.9	10	1	2	3	5	9	10	15
TOTAL SINGLE DX	**4**	**3.6**	**2**	**2**	**3**	**4**	**5**	**5**	**5**	**5**
TOTAL MULTIPLE DX	**125**	**4.9**	**28**	**1**	**2**	**4**	**6**	**9**	**11**	**39**
TOTAL										
0–19 Years	3	1.5	1	1	1	1	3	3	3	3
20–34	22	5.5	69	1	2	3	5	9	23	40
35–49	22	5.9	19	2	3	5	7	9	11	25
50–64	24	6.4	48	1	4	5	7	10	13	39
65+	58	3.9	9	1	2	3	5	9	10	15
GRAND TOTAL	**129**	**4.9**	**27**	**1**	**2**	**4**	**5**	**9**	**11**	**39**

87.6: OTH DIGESTIVE SYST X-RAY

Type of Patients	Observed Patients	Avg. Stay	Vari-ance	Percentiles						
				10th	25th	50th	75th	90th	95th	99th
1. SINGLE DX										
0–19 Years	108	2.2	3	1	1	2	3	4	6	9
20–34	11	3.1	6	1	1	2	4	5	11	11
35–49	10	3.5	<1	3	3	3	4	5	6	6
50–64	13	3.2	4	1	1	3	4	5	8	8
65+	7	2.0	2	1	1	2	3	3	5	5
2. MULTIPLE DX										
0–19 Years	297	3.5	21	1	1	2	4	6	8	19
20–34	55	3.9	12	1	2	3	5	6	9	26
35–49	140	4.2	10	1	2	3	6	8	10	17
50–64	165	4.4	8	1	2	4	6	9	10	15
65+	559	5.2	14	2	3	4	7	9	11	17
TOTAL SINGLE DX	**149**	**2.4**	**3**	**1**	**1**	**2**	**3**	**5**	**6**	**9**
TOTAL MULTIPLE DX	**1,216**	**4.4**	**16**	**1**	**2**	**3**	**6**	**8**	**10**	**17**
TOTAL										
0–19 Years	405	3.1	16	1	1	2	4	6	8	17
20–34	66	3.7	11	1	2	3	4	6	9	26
35–49	150	4.1	9	1	2	3	5	8	10	17
50–64	178	4.3	8	1	2	4	5	8	10	15
65+	566	5.1	14	2	3	4	7	9	11	17
GRAND TOTAL	**1,365**	**4.1**	**14**	**1**	**2**	**3**	**5**	**8**	**10**	**16**

87.61: BARIUM SWALLOW

Type of Patients	Observed Patients	Avg. Stay	Vari-ance	Percentiles						
				10th	25th	50th	75th	90th	95th	99th
1. SINGLE DX										
0–19 Years	10	2.0	1	1	1	2	3	4	4	4
20–34	3	6.0	19	3	3	4	11	11	11	11
35–49	0									
50–64	1	4.0	0	4	4	4	4	4	4	4
65+	0									
2. MULTIPLE DX										
0–19 Years	30	2.9	2	1	1	3	4	5	5	6
20–34	7	5.3	65	1	2	2	3	26	26	26
35–49	29	4.2	14	1	2	3	5	8	13	17
50–64	38	5.0	10	2	2	4	7	10	12	12
65+	218	5.6	23	2	3	4	7	9	12	24
TOTAL SINGLE DX	**14**	**2.7**	**5**	**1**	**1**	**2**	**4**	**4**	**4**	**11**
TOTAL MULTIPLE DX	**322**	**5.1**	**19**	**2**	**3**	**4**	**6**	**9**	**12**	**24**
TOTAL										
0–19 Years	40	2.7	2	1	1	3	4	5	5	6
20–34	10	5.5	51	1	2	3	6	11	26	26
35–49	29	4.2	14	1	2	3	5	8	13	17
50–64	39	4.9	10	2	2	4	7	10	12	12
65+	218	5.6	23	2	3	4	7	9	12	24
GRAND TOTAL	**336**	**4.9**	**19**	**1**	**2**	**4**	**6**	**9**	**12**	**24**

87.62: UPPER GI SERIES

Type of Patients	Observed Patients	Avg. Stay	Vari-ance	Percentiles						
				10th	25th	50th	75th	90th	95th	99th
1. SINGLE DX										
0–19 Years	61	2.8	4	1	1	2	4	6	7	9
20–34	5	2.0	1	1	1	2	3	4	4	4
35–49	3	3.5	<1	3	3	3	4	4	4	4
50–64	4	4.1	7	1	4	4	4	8	8	8
65+	1	1.0	0	1	1	1	1	1	1	1
2. MULTIPLE DX										
0–19 Years	209	3.8	28	1	1	2	4	7	9	26
20–34	24	3.1	4	1	2	3	4	6	8	9
35–49	62	4.0	6	2	2	3	5	7	9	14
50–64	65	4.2	8	1	2	4	5	9	10	15
65+	147	4.9	8	2	3	4	7	9	11	13
TOTAL SINGLE DX	**74**	**2.7**	**4**	**1**	**1**	**2**	**4**	**5**	**7**	**9**
TOTAL MULTIPLE DX	**507**	**4.1**	**18**	**1**	**2**	**3**	**5**	**8**	**10**	**17**
TOTAL										
0–19 Years	270	3.5	23	1	1	2	4	6	9	19
20–34	29	2.9	3	1	2	2	4	5	6	9
35–49	65	3.9	6	2	2	3	5	7	9	14
50–64	69	4.2	8	1	2	4	5	8	10	15
65+	148	4.8	8	2	3	4	7	9	11	13
GRAND TOTAL	**581**	**3.9**	**16**	**1**	**2**	**3**	**5**	**7**	**9**	**15**

87.64: LOWER GI SERIES

Type of Patients	Observed Patients	Avg. Stay	Vari-ance	10th	25th	50th	75th	90th	95th	99th
1. SINGLE DX										
0–19 Years	35	1.4	<1	1	1	1	1	2	4	4
20–34	3	4.0	3	2	2	5	5	5	5	5
35–49	4	4.3	2	3	3	5	5	6	6	6
50–64	7	2.6	2	1	1	2	4	5	5	5
65+	4	2.8	1	1	2	3	3	5	5	5
2. MULTIPLE DX										
0–19 Years	35	2.3	3	1	1	2	3	6	6	7
20–34	13	3.9	4	1	3	4	5	6	9	9
35–49	17	5.5	18	1	3	6	6	10	12	20
50–64	25	3.5	2	2	3	3	4	5	6	6
65+	76	4.2	9	1	2	3	5	8	11	13
TOTAL SINGLE DX	**53**	**1.8**	**2**	**1**	**1**	**1**	**2**	**4**	**5**	**5**
TOTAL MULTIPLE DX	**166**	**3.7**	**8**	**1**	**2**	**3**	**5**	**7**	**9**	**13**
TOTAL										
0–19 Years	70	1.8	2	1	1	1	2	4	6	7
20–34	16	4.0	4	1	3	4	5	6	9	9
35–49	21	5.3	16	1	3	6	6	10	12	20
50–64	32	3.3	2	1	2	3	4	5	6	6
65+	80	4.2	8	1	2	3	5	8	10	13
GRAND TOTAL	**219**	**3.2**	**7**	**1**	**1**	**2**	**4**	**6**	**8**	**12**

87.7: X-RAY OF URINARY SYSTEM

Type of Patients	Observed Patients	Avg. Stay	Vari-ance	10th	25th	50th	75th	90th	95th	99th
1. SINGLE DX										
0–19 Years	93	2.7	3	1	2	2	3	5	5	7
20–34	63	1.7	1	1	1	1	2	3	4	5
35–49	56	1.9	2	1	1	1	2	3	6	9
50–64	36	1.8	2	1	1	1	2	3	4	8
65+	7	1.2	<1	1	1	1	1	1	4	4
2. MULTIPLE DX										
0–19 Years	665	4.4	12	2	2	3	6	8	10	17
20–34	415	3.3	14	1	1	3	4	6	8	15
35–49	494	3.6	17	1	2	2	4	7	10	17
50–64	499	4.0	20	1	2	3	5	7	9	28
65+	703	5.0	18	1	2	4	7	11	13	20
TOTAL SINGLE DX	**255**	**2.2**	**2**	**1**	**1**	**2**	**3**	**4**	**5**	**8**
TOTAL MULTIPLE DX	**2,776**	**4.2**	**16**	**1**	**2**	**3**	**5**	**8**	**11**	**18**
TOTAL										
0–19 Years	758	4.2	11	2	2	3	5	8	10	17
20–34	478	3.1	13	1	1	2	4	6	7	13
35–49	550	3.4	16	1	1	2	4	7	9	17
50–64	535	3.8	19	1	2	3	5	7	9	28
65+	710	5.0	18	1	2	4	7	11	13	20
GRAND TOTAL	**3,031**	**4.0**	**15**	**1**	**2**	**3**	**5**	**8**	**11**	**18**

87.71: CAT SCAN OF KIDNEY

Type of Patients	Observed Patients	Avg. Stay	Vari-ance	10th	25th	50th	75th	90th	95th	99th
1. SINGLE DX										
0–19 Years	1	2.0	0	2	2	2	2	2	2	2
20–34	4	2.2	4	1	1	1	5	5	5	5
35–49	7	1.6	2	1	1	1	1	3	6	6
50–64	6	1.2	<1	1	1	1	1	1	3	3
65+	0									
2. MULTIPLE DX										
0–19 Years	8	2.7	5	1	1	2	4	7	7	7
20–34	36	2.1	2	1	1	2	3	4	5	7
35–49	34	2.7	8	1	1	2	3	5	12	14
50–64	25	3.1	4	1	1	3	4	7	7	7
65+	36	3.6	9	1	1	3	4	7	11	13
TOTAL SINGLE DX	**18**	**1.6**	**2**	**1**	**1**	**1**	**1**	**3**	**5**	**6**
TOTAL MULTIPLE DX	**139**	**2.9**	**6**	**1**	**1**	**2**	**4**	**6**	**7**	**13**
TOTAL										
0–19 Years	9	2.6	4	1	1	2	4	7	7	7
20–34	40	2.1	2	1	1	1	3	4	5	7
35–49	41	2.5	7	1	1	2	3	5	6	14
50–64	31	2.6	4	1	1	2	3	7	7	7
65+	36	3.6	9	1	1	3	4	7	11	13
GRAND TOTAL	**157**	**2.8**	**6**	**1**	**1**	**2**	**3**	**5**	**7**	**13**

87.73: IV PYELOGRAM

Type of Patients	Observed Patients	Avg. Stay	Vari-ance	10th	25th	50th	75th	90th	95th	99th
1. SINGLE DX										
0–19 Years	4	2.2	<1	1	2	2	3	3	3	3
20–34	16	1.8	1	1	1	1	2	4	4	4
35–49	18	1.5	<1	1	1	1	2	2	4	4
50–64	14	1.6	<1	1	1	1	2	3	3	4
65+	1	1.0	0	1	1	1	1	1	1	1
2. MULTIPLE DX										
0–19 Years	33	3.1	4	1	2	3	4	5	7	12
20–34	153	3.3	5	1	2	3	5	6	7	10
35–49	165	3.3	6	1	2	2	4	6	8	14
50–64	142	3.1	5	1	2	2	4	6	7	14
65+	155	4.7	21	2	2	4	5	9	11	20
TOTAL SINGLE DX	**53**	**1.7**	**<1**	**1**	**1**	**1**	**2**	**3**	**4**	**4**
TOTAL MULTIPLE DX	**648**	**3.6**	**10**	**1**	**2**	**3**	**5**	**6**	**9**	**14**
TOTAL										
0–19 Years	37	3.0	4	1	2	2	3	5	7	12
20–34	169	3.1	5	1	1	2	4	6	6	10
35–49	183	3.1	6	1	2	2	4	6	7	14
50–64	156	2.9	5	1	1	2	4	6	7	14
65+	156	4.7	21	2	2	4	5	9	11	20
GRAND TOTAL	**701**	**3.5**	**10**	**1**	**2**	**3**	**4**	**6**	**8**	**14**

87.74: RETROGRADE PYELOGRAM

Type of Patients	Observed Patients	Avg. Stay	Variance	10th	25th	50th	75th	90th	95th	99th
1. SINGLE DX										
0–19 Years	5	2.4	2	1	1	2	3	5	5	5
20–34	25	1.4	<1	1	1	1	2	2	3	3
35–49	19	1.6	<1	1	1	2	2	2	3	4
50–64	6	1.1	<1	1	1	1	1	2	2	2
65+	3	1.0	0	1	1	1	1	1	1	1
2. MULTIPLE DX										
0–19 Years	26	3.6	12	1	1	2	6	8	9	16
20–34	140	2.9	5	1	1	2	3	5	6	11
35–49	177	3.8	29	1	2	2	4	8	10	15
50–64	205	4.0	11	1	2	3	5	8	11	15
65+	295	5.4	19	1	2	4	7	11	14	20
TOTAL SINGLE DX	**58**	**1.5**	**<1**	**1**	**1**	**1**	**2**	**2**	**3**	**5**
TOTAL MULTIPLE DX	**843**	**4.3**	**18**	**1**	**2**	**3**	**5**	**9**	**11**	**18**
TOTAL										
0–19 Years	31	3.5	11	1	1	2	5	8	9	16
20–34	165	2.7	5	1	1	2	3	5	6	10
35–49	196	3.6	26	1	1	2	4	8	10	15
50–64	211	3.9	11	1	2	3	5	8	11	15
65+	298	5.3	19	1	2	4	7	11	13	20
GRAND TOTAL	**901**	**4.1**	**17**	**1**	**2**	**3**	**5**	**9**	**11**	**18**

87.76: RETRO CYSTOURETHROGRAM

Type of Patients	Observed Patients	Avg. Stay	Variance	10th	25th	50th	75th	90th	95th	99th
1. SINGLE DX										
0–19 Years	46	3.3	3	2	2	3	4	5	7	13
20–34	0									
35–49	1	1.0	0	1	1	1	1	1	1	1
50–64	0									
65+	0									
2. MULTIPLE DX										
0–19 Years	477	4.6	12	2	3	4	6	8	10	17
20–34	13	3.3	3	2	2	3	4	4	4	10
35–49	13	4.8	19	1	2	3	8	11	15	15
50–64	20	3.9	4	1	2	3	6	7	8	8
65+	19	6.9	18	2	4	5	10	14	14	15
TOTAL SINGLE DX	**47**	**3.3**	**3**	**2**	**2**	**3**	**4**	**5**	**7**	**13**
TOTAL MULTIPLE DX	**542**	**4.6**	**12**	**2**	**3**	**4**	**6**	**8**	**10**	**17**
TOTAL										
0–19 Years	523	4.5	11	2	2	3	6	8	10	17
20–34	13	3.3	3	2	2	3	4	4	4	10
35–49	14	4.6	18	1	1	3	8	11	15	15
50–64	20	3.9	4	1	2	3	6	7	8	8
65+	19	6.9	18	2	4	5	10	14	14	15
GRAND TOTAL	**589**	**4.5**	**11**	**2**	**2**	**4**	**6**	**8**	**10**	**17**

87.77: CYSTOGRAM NEC

Type of Patients	Observed Patients	Avg. Stay	Variance	10th	25th	50th	75th	90th	95th	99th
1. SINGLE DX										
0–19 Years	8	1.7	<1	1	1	2	2	2	2	2
20–34	1	2.0	0	2	2	2	2	2	2	2
35–49	0									
50–64	3	6.5	4	4	4	7	8	8	8	8
65+	1	1.0	0	1	1	1	1	1	1	1
2. MULTIPLE DX										
0–19 Years	41	4.0	12	2	2	3	6	7	11	24
20–34	14	4.9	11	1	2	4	6	10	12	12
35–49	18	4.3	8	1	2	5	5	8	10	12
50–64	32	8.9	132	1	3	5	7	39	39	39
65+	105	4.9	17	1	3	4	6	8	11	18
TOTAL SINGLE DX	**13**	**2.3**	**4**	**1**	**1**	**2**	**2**	**7**	**8**	**8**
TOTAL MULTIPLE DX	**210**	**5.3**	**35**	**1**	**2**	**4**	**6**	**10**	**12**	**39**
TOTAL										
0–19 Years	49	3.7	11	1	2	2	5	6	11	14
20–34	15	4.7	11	1	2	4	6	10	12	12
35–49	18	4.3	8	1	2	5	5	8	10	12
50–64	35	8.7	125	1	3	5	7	39	39	39
65+	106	4.9	17	1	2	4	6	8	11	18
GRAND TOTAL	**223**	**5.1**	**33**	**1**	**2**	**4**	**6**	**9**	**12**	**39**

87.79: URINARY SYSTEM X-RAY NEC

Type of Patients	Observed Patients	Avg. Stay	Variance	10th	25th	50th	75th	90th	95th	99th
1. SINGLE DX										
0–19 Years	28	2.1	2	1	1	2	3	4	5	6
20–34	15	1.8	1	1	1	1	2	4	5	5
35–49	11	3.5	8	1	1	2	6	8	9	9
50–64	7	2.2	<1	1	1	2	3	3	3	3
65+	2	2.5	4	1	1	4	4	4	4	4
2. MULTIPLE DX										
0–19 Years	77	4.3	17	1	2	3	6	9	13	22
20–34	46	4.2	19	1	2	3	4	12	15	19
35–49	66	3.7	9	1	2	3	5	6	8	19
50–64	58	3.0	3	1	2	3	4	6	7	10
65+	57	3.9	7	1	2	3	5	7	7	18
TOTAL SINGLE DX	**63**	**2.3**	**3**	**1**	**1**	**2**	**3**	**4**	**6**	**9**
TOTAL MULTIPLE DX	**304**	**3.9**	**11**	**1**	**2**	**3**	**5**	**7**	**10**	**19**
TOTAL										
0–19 Years	105	3.7	14	1	1	2	4	7	11	22
20–34	61	3.6	16	1	1	2	4	7	12	19
35–49	77	3.7	9	1	2	3	5	6	8	19
50–64	65	2.9	3	1	2	3	3	6	7	10
65+	59	3.9	7	1	2	3	5	7	7	18
GRAND TOTAL	**367**	**3.6**	**10**	**1**	**2**	**3**	**4**	**7**	**9**	**19**

87.8: FEMALE GENITAL X-RAY

Type of Patients	Observed Patients	Avg. Stay	Vari-ance	Percentiles						
				10th	25th	50th	75th	90th	95th	99th
1. SINGLE DX										
0–19 Years	0									
20–34	0									
35–49	0									
50–64	0									
65+	0									
2. MULTIPLE DX										
0–19 Years	0									
20–34	0									
35–49	0									
50–64	0									
65+	0									
TOTAL SINGLE DX	**0**									
TOTAL MULTIPLE DX	**0**									
TOTAL										
0–19 Years	0									
20–34	0									
35–49	0									
50–64	0									
65+	0									
GRAND TOTAL	**0**									

87.9: MALE GENITAL X-RAY

Type of Patients	Observed Patients	Avg. Stay	Vari-ance	Percentiles						
				10th	25th	50th	75th	90th	95th	99th
1. SINGLE DX										
0–19 Years	0									
20–34	0									
35–49	0									
50–64	0									
65+	0									
2. MULTIPLE DX										
0–19 Years	0									
20–34	0									
35–49	0									
50–64	1	11.0	0	11	11	11	11	11	11	11
65+	0									
TOTAL SINGLE DX	**0**									
TOTAL MULTIPLE DX	**1**	**11.0**	**0**	**11**	**11**	**11**	**11**	**11**	**11**	**11**
TOTAL										
0–19 Years	0									
20–34	0									
35–49	0									
50–64	1	11.0	0	11	11	11	11	11	11	11
65+	0									
GRAND TOTAL	**1**	**11.0**	**0**	**11**	**11**	**11**	**11**	**11**	**11**	**11**

88.0: ABD SOFT TISSUE X-RAY

Type of Patients	Observed Patients	Avg. Stay	Vari-ance	Percentiles						
				10th	25th	50th	75th	90th	95th	99th
1. SINGLE DX										
0–19 Years	388	1.9	3	1	1	1	2	4	5	7
20–34	364	2.5	4	1	1	2	3	5	6	9
35–49	359	2.6	5	1	1	2	3	5	6	9
50–64	194	2.7	5	1	1	2	4	5	6	11
65+	48	2.6	4	1	1	2	3	5	6	12
2. MULTIPLE DX										
0–19 Years	930	3.0	12	1	1	2	4	6	8	15
20–34	1,457	3.3	10	1	1	2	4	6	8	15
35–49	2,409	3.7	9	1	2	3	5	7	9	15
50–64	2,531	3.9	11	1	2	3	5	7	10	17
65+	4,039	4.3	12	1	2	3	5	8	10	17
TOTAL SINGLE DX	**1,353**	**2.3**	**4**	**1**	**1**	**2**	**3**	**5**	**6**	**9**
TOTAL MULTIPLE DX	**11,366**	**3.8**	**11**	**1**	**2**	**3**	**5**	**7**	**10**	**16**
TOTAL										
0–19 Years	1,318	2.7	9	1	1	2	3	6	8	14
20–34	1,821	3.1	9	1	1	2	4	6	8	15
35–49	2,768	3.6	9	1	2	3	5	7	9	15
50–64	2,725	3.8	11	1	2	3	5	7	9	16
65+	4,087	4.2	12	1	2	3	5	8	10	17
GRAND TOTAL	**12,719**	**3.7**	**11**	**1**	**2**	**3**	**5**	**7**	**9**	**16**

88.01: ABDOMEN CAT SCAN

Type of Patients	Observed Patients	Avg. Stay	Vari-ance	Percentiles						
				10th	25th	50th	75th	90th	95th	99th
1. SINGLE DX										
0–19 Years	381	1.9	3	1	1	1	2	4	5	7
20–34	360	2.4	3	1	1	2	3	5	6	9
35–49	348	2.6	5	1	1	2	3	5	6	9
50–64	183	2.7	5	1	1	2	4	5	6	11
65+	46	2.6	4	1	1	2	3	5	7	12
2. MULTIPLE DX										
0–19 Years	911	3.0	12	1	1	2	4	6	8	15
20–34	1,429	3.3	10	1	1	2	4	6	9	15
35–49	2,346	3.7	9	1	2	3	5	7	9	15
50–64	2,467	3.9	11	1	2	3	5	7	10	17
65+	3,982	4.2	11	1	2	3	5	8	10	16
TOTAL SINGLE DX	**1,318**	**2.3**	**4**	**1**	**1**	**2**	**3**	**5**	**6**	**8**
TOTAL MULTIPLE DX	**11,135**	**3.8**	**11**	**1**	**2**	**3**	**5**	**7**	**10**	**16**
TOTAL										
0–19 Years	1,292	2.7	9	1	1	2	3	6	8	15
20–34	1,789	3.1	9	1	1	2	4	6	8	15
35–49	2,694	3.6	9	1	2	3	5	7	9	15
50–64	2,650	3.8	11	1	2	3	5	7	9	16
65+	4,028	4.2	11	1	2	3	5	8	10	16
GRAND TOTAL	**12,453**	**3.7**	**10**	**1**	**2**	**3**	**5**	**7**	**9**	**16**

88.1: OTHER ABDOMINAL X-RAY

Type of Patients	Observed Patients	Avg. Stay	Vari-ance	Percentiles						
				10th	25th	50th	75th	90th	95th	99th
1. SINGLE DX										
0–19 Years	4	1.6	<1	1	1	1	2	3	3	3
20–34	3	2.0	<1	1	1	2	3	3	3	3
35–49	1	1.0	0	1	1	1	1	1	1	1
50–64	3	3.0	2	1	3	3	3	5	5	5
65+	0									
2. MULTIPLE DX										
0–19 Years	13	4.8	20	1	1	4	7	8	17	17
20–34	9	2.3	1	1	2	2	3	4	4	4
35–49	22	2.7	5	1	1	2	3	6	9	9
50–64	46	4.0	8	1	2	3	5	8	9	13
65+	64	3.3	9	1	1	2	4	8	10	15
TOTAL SINGLE DX	**11**	**2.0**	**1**	**1**	**1**	**2**	**3**	**3**	**5**	**5**
TOTAL MULTIPLE DX	**154**	**3.5**	**9**	**1**	**1**	**2**	**4**	**8**	**9**	**15**
TOTAL										
0–19 Years	17	3.9	17	1	1	2	7	8	17	17
20–34	12	2.3	1	1	2	2	3	4	4	4
35–49	23	2.6	5	1	1	2	3	6	9	9
50–64	49	3.9	8	1	2	3	5	8	9	13
65+	64	3.3	9	1	1	2	4	8	10	15
GRAND TOTAL	**165**	**3.4**	**9**	**1**	**1**	**2**	**4**	**7**	**9**	**15**

88.11: PELV DYE CONTRAST X-RAY

Type of Patients	Observed Patients	Avg. Stay	Vari-ance	Percentiles						
				10th	25th	50th	75th	90th	95th	99th
1. SINGLE DX										
0–19 Years	0									
20–34	0									
35–49	0									
50–64	1	3.0	0	3	3	3	3	3	3	3
65+	0									
2. MULTIPLE DX										
0–19 Years	0									
20–34	0									
35–49	6	2.4	4	1	1	1	3	6	6	6
50–64	13	5.1	7	2	3	4	8	9	9	9
65+	14	2.8	3	1	1	2	5	6	6	6
TOTAL SINGLE DX	**1**	**3.0**	**0**	**3**	**3**	**3**	**3**	**3**	**3**	**3**
TOTAL MULTIPLE DX	**33**	**3.7**	**6**	**1**	**1**	**3**	**6**	**8**	**8**	**9**
TOTAL										
0–19 Years	0									
20–34	0									
35–49	6	2.4	4	1	1	1	3	6	6	6
50–64	14	4.9	7	2	3	4	7	9	9	9
65+	14	2.8	3	1	1	2	5	6	6	6
GRAND TOTAL	**34**	**3.6**	**6**	**1**	**1**	**3**	**6**	**8**	**8**	**9**

88.19: ABDOMINAL X-RAY NEC

Type of Patients	Observed Patients	Avg. Stay	Vari-ance	Percentiles						
				10th	25th	50th	75th	90th	95th	99th
1. SINGLE DX										
0–19 Years	4	1.6	<1	1	1	1	2	3	3	3
20–34	3	2.0	<1	1	1	2	3	3	3	3
35–49	1	1.0	0	1	1	1	1	1	1	1
50–64	1	1.0	0	1	1	1	1	1	1	1
65+	0									
2. MULTIPLE DX										
0–19 Years	13	4.8	20	1	1	4	7	8	17	17
20–34	8	2.4	1	1	2	2	3	4	4	4
35–49	14	2.1	2	1	1	2	3	4	6	6
50–64	28	3.2	7	1	2	2	3	5	7	13
65+	43	2.9	6	1	1	2	3	7	8	10
TOTAL SINGLE DX	**9**	**1.6**	**<1**	**1**	**1**	**1**	**2**	**3**	**3**	**3**
TOTAL MULTIPLE DX	**106**	**3.0**	**7**	**1**	**1**	**2**	**3**	**7**	**8**	**13**
TOTAL										
0–19 Years	17	3.9	17	1	1	2	7	8	17	17
20–34	11	2.3	1	1	1	2	3	4	4	4
35–49	15	2.0	2	1	1	2	2	4	6	6
50–64	29	3.1	6	1	2	2	3	5	7	13
65+	43	2.9	6	1	1	2	3	7	8	10
GRAND TOTAL	**115**	**2.9**	**7**	**1**	**1**	**2**	**3**	**7**	**8**	**13**

88.2: EXT & PELVIS SKEL X-RAY

Type of Patients	Observed Patients	Avg. Stay	Vari-ance	Percentiles						
				10th	25th	50th	75th	90th	95th	99th
1. SINGLE DX										
0–19 Years	34	2.6	4	1	1	2	3	6	6	8
20–34	34	2.8	5	1	1	2	4	5	8	9
35–49	32	2.6	7	1	1	2	3	4	5	16
50–64	12	1.9	3	1	1	1	2	4	7	7
65+	5	1.5	<1	1	1	1	2	3	3	3
2. MULTIPLE DX										
0–19 Years	55	5.4	33	1	1	3	7	14	20	>99
20–34	78	3.0	4	1	2	2	4	6	7	10
35–49	127	4.0	12	1	2	3	5	7	10	18
50–64	119	4.1	15	1	2	3	5	8	13	17
65+	88	4.0	8	1	2	3	6	7	9	16
TOTAL SINGLE DX	**117**	**2.6**	**5**	**1**	**1**	**2**	**3**	**5**	**7**	**9**
TOTAL MULTIPLE DX	**467**	**4.0**	**13**	**1**	**2**	**3**	**5**	**8**	**11**	**22**
TOTAL										
0–19 Years	89	4.4	24	1	1	3	5	12	20	>99
20–34	112	2.9	5	1	1	2	4	6	8	10
35–49	159	3.7	11	1	2	3	5	7	10	18
50–64	131	3.9	15	1	1	3	5	7	10	17
65+	93	3.9	8	1	2	3	6	7	9	16
GRAND TOTAL	**584**	**3.8**	**12**	**1**	**2**	**3**	**5**	**7**	**10**	**20**

88.3: OTHER X-RAY

Type of Patients	Observed Patients	Avg. Stay	Vari-ance	Percentiles 10th	25th	50th	75th	90th	95th	99th
1. SINGLE DX										
0–19 Years	111	2.3	3	1	1	2	3	5	6	7
20–34	67	2.4	3	1	1	2	4	5	6	7
35–49	43	2.3	3	1	1	2	3	5	5	8
50–64	35	1.9	1	1	1	1	3	4	4	4
65+	14	2.4	1	1	2	2	3	3	5	5
2. MULTIPLE DX										
0–19 Years	263	3.8	22	1	1	2	4	7	12	27
20–34	283	2.9	7	1	1	2	3	6	8	16
35–49	390	3.5	12	1	1	3	4	8	10	14
50–64	398	4.1	12	1	2	3	5	8	10	18
65+	668	4.3	9	1	2	4	5	8	10	17
TOTAL SINGLE DX	**270**	**2.3**	**3**	**1**	**1**	**2**	**3**	**5**	**5**	**7**
TOTAL MULTIPLE DX	**2,002**	**3.9**	**12**	**1**	**2**	**3**	**5**	**8**	**10**	**18**
TOTAL										
0–19 Years	374	3.3	17	1	1	2	4	6	9	25
20–34	350	2.8	6	1	1	2	3	6	7	16
35–49	433	3.4	11	1	1	2	4	8	10	14
50–64	433	3.9	11	1	2	3	5	8	10	17
65+	682	4.3	9	1	2	4	5	8	10	17
GRAND TOTAL	**2,272**	**3.7**	**11**	**1**	**1**	**3**	**5**	**7**	**9**	**17**

88.38: CAT SCAN NEC

Type of Patients	Observed Patients	Avg. Stay	Vari-ance	Percentiles 10th	25th	50th	75th	90th	95th	99th
1. SINGLE DX										
0–19 Years	97	2.3	3	1	1	2	3	5	6	7
20–34	62	2.4	3	1	1	2	4	5	6	7
35–49	41	2.3	3	1	1	2	3	5	5	8
50–64	32	1.9	1	1	1	1	2	4	4	4
65+	13	2.5	1	1	2	2	3	5	5	5
2. MULTIPLE DX										
0–19 Years	232	3.2	13	1	1	2	4	6	7	15
20–34	273	2.9	7	1	1	2	3	6	8	16
35–49	368	3.6	13	1	1	3	4	8	10	14
50–64	371	4.1	12	1	2	3	5	8	10	18
65+	646	4.3	9	1	2	4	5	8	9	17
TOTAL SINGLE DX	**245**	**2.3**	**3**	**1**	**1**	**2**	**3**	**5**	**6**	**7**
TOTAL MULTIPLE DX	**1,890**	**3.8**	**11**	**1**	**2**	**3**	**5**	**7**	**9**	**16**
TOTAL										
0–19 Years	329	3.0	10	1	1	2	4	6	7	14
20–34	335	2.8	6	1	1	2	3	5	7	16
35–49	409	3.4	12	1	1	2	4	8	10	14
50–64	403	3.9	11	1	2	3	5	8	10	18
65+	659	4.3	9	1	2	4	5	8	9	17
GRAND TOTAL	**2,135**	**3.6**	**10**	**1**	**1**	**3**	**5**	**7**	**9**	**16**

88.4: CONTRAST ARTERIOGRAPHY

Type of Patients	Observed Patients	Avg. Stay	Vari-ance	Percentiles 10th	25th	50th	75th	90th	95th	99th
1. SINGLE DX										
0–19 Years	34	2.3	4	1	1	1	3	5	7	8
20–34	87	2.8	6	1	1	2	3	6	8	11
35–49	86	3.0	10	1	1	2	3	6	8	19
50–64	81	3.0	5	1	1	2	4	6	7	10
65+	53	2.2	4	1	1	2	3	5	8	8
2. MULTIPLE DX										
0–19 Years	122	3.9	22	1	1	2	5	8	11	16
20–34	523	4.2	15	1	2	3	5	9	11	18
35–49	1,196	4.6	16	1	2	4	6	9	12	22
50–64	1,975	4.6	15	1	2	4	6	9	11	18
65+	4,036	4.6	13	1	2	4	6	9	11	17
TOTAL SINGLE DX	**341**	**2.7**	**6**	**1**	**1**	**2**	**3**	**6**	**8**	**11**
TOTAL MULTIPLE DX	**7,852**	**4.6**	**14**	**1**	**2**	**4**	**6**	**9**	**11**	**18**
TOTAL										
0–19 Years	156	3.6	19	1	1	2	4	7	10	16
20–34	610	4.0	14	1	1	3	5	8	11	18
35–49	1,282	4.5	16	1	2	3	6	9	12	22
50–64	2,056	4.5	14	1	2	4	6	9	11	18
65+	4,089	4.6	13	1	2	4	6	9	11	17
GRAND TOTAL	**8,193**	**4.5**	**14**	**1**	**2**	**4**	**6**	**9**	**11**	**18**

88.41: CEREBRAL ARTERIOGRAM

Type of Patients	Observed Patients	Avg. Stay	Vari-ance	Percentiles 10th	25th	50th	75th	90th	95th	99th
1. SINGLE DX										
0–19 Years	12	3.1	6	1	1	3	4	7	8	8
20–34	42	3.0	8	1	1	2	3	8	11	11
35–49	46	3.0	6	1	1	2	3	8	8	14
50–64	50	3.6	6	1	1	3	6	7	9	10
65+	15	1.8	3	1	1	1	1	5	8	8
2. MULTIPLE DX										
0–19 Years	45	4.8	40	1	2	2	7	9	16	46
20–34	202	4.4	15	1	2	3	6	9	11	17
35–49	429	5.6	23	1	2	4	8	12	14	23
50–64	720	4.8	16	1	2	4	7	10	13	17
65+	1,239	4.5	13	1	2	4	6	8	11	16
TOTAL SINGLE DX	**165**	**3.1**	**6**	**1**	**1**	**2**	**4**	**7**	**8**	**11**
TOTAL MULTIPLE DX	**2,635**	**4.7**	**16**	**1**	**2**	**4**	**6**	**9**	**12**	**19**
TOTAL										
0–19 Years	57	4.5	35	1	2	2	7	9	12	46
20–34	244	4.2	14	1	2	3	5	9	11	16
35–49	475	5.3	21	1	2	4	7	11	13	23
50–64	770	4.7	16	1	2	4	6	10	12	17
65+	1,254	4.4	13	1	2	4	6	8	11	16
GRAND TOTAL	**2,800**	**4.6**	**16**	**1**	**2**	**4**	**6**	**9**	**12**	**18**

88.42: CONTRAST AORTOGRAM

Type of Patients	Observed Patients	Avg. Stay	Vari-ance	Percentiles						
				10th	25th	50th	75th	90th	95th	99th
1. SINGLE DX										
0–19 Years	4	1.1	<1	1	1	1	1	2	2	2
20–34	10	3.3	4	1	1	3	6	6	6	6
35–49	5	5.7	55	1	1	2	6	20	20	20
50–64	11	1.8	3	1	1	1	1	5	7	7
65+	19	2.3	5	1	1	2	2	8	8	8
2. MULTIPLE DX										
0–19 Years	20	3.0	5	1	2	2	4	5	7	11
20–34	50	4.0	18	1	1	2	5	11	12	22
35–49	123	4.7	13	1	2	4	6	11	13	15
50–64	344	4.7	17	1	2	4	6	9	11	23
65+	940	4.7	16	1	2	4	6	10	12	20
TOTAL SINGLE DX	**49**	**2.5**	**8**	**1**	**1**	**1**	**2**	**6**	**8**	**20**
TOTAL MULTIPLE DX	**1,477**	**4.7**	**16**	**1**	**2**	**4**	**6**	**10**	**12**	**20**
TOTAL										
0–19 Years	24	2.6	4	1	1	2	3	5	7	11
20–34	60	3.9	16	1	1	2	5	9	11	22
35–49	128	4.8	14	1	2	4	6	11	13	16
50–64	355	4.6	17	1	2	3	6	9	11	23
65+	959	4.7	16	1	2	4	6	10	12	19
GRAND TOTAL	**1,526**	**4.6**	**16**	**1**	**2**	**4**	**6**	**10**	**12**	**20**

88.43: PULMONARY ARTERIOGRAM

Type of Patients	Observed Patients	Avg. Stay	Vari-ance	Percentiles						
				10th	25th	50th	75th	90th	95th	99th
1. SINGLE DX										
0–19 Years	1	2.0	0	2	2	2	2	2	2	2
20–34	12	2.6	2	1	1	2	3	5	6	6
35–49	15	2.4	3	1	1	2	3	5	6	8
50–64	6	2.7	2	1	1	2	4	4	4	4
65+	6	3.0	2	1	2	3	4	5	5	5
2. MULTIPLE DX										
0–19 Years	22	2.6	4	1	1	2	4	6	8	8
20–34	142	3.9	7	1	2	3	5	8	10	11
35–49	361	3.8	9	1	2	3	5	7	9	15
50–64	437	4.3	11	1	2	3	6	8	11	14
65+	886	4.5	10	1	2	4	6	8	11	16
TOTAL SINGLE DX	**40**	**2.6**	**2**	**1**	**1**	**2**	**4**	**4**	**5**	**8**
TOTAL MULTIPLE DX	**1,848**	**4.3**	**10**	**1**	**2**	**4**	**6**	**8**	**10**	**15**
TOTAL										
0–19 Years	23	2.5	4	1	1	2	3	6	6	8
20–34	154	3.8	7	1	2	3	5	8	10	11
35–49	376	3.7	9	1	2	3	5	7	9	15
50–64	443	4.3	10	1	2	3	6	8	11	14
65+	892	4.5	10	1	2	4	6	8	10	16
GRAND TOTAL	**1,888**	**4.2**	**10**	**1**	**2**	**3**	**6**	**8**	**10**	**15**

88.44: THOR ARTERIOGRAM NEC

Type of Patients	Observed Patients	Avg. Stay	Vari-ance	Percentiles						
				10th	25th	50th	75th	90th	95th	99th
1. SINGLE DX										
0–19 Years	0									
20–34	2	4.0	2	3	3	3	5	5	5	5
35–49	2	1.5	<1	1	1	1	2	2	2	2
50–64	3	2.7	<1	1	3	3	3	3	3	3
65+	0									
2. MULTIPLE DX										
0–19 Years	1	5.0	0	5	5	5	5	5	5	5
20–34	17	3.2	3	1	2	4	5	5	5	5
35–49	48	3.7	9	1	2	3	5	6	7	18
50–64	50	4.0	18	1	1	3	4	8	13	27
65+	86	3.8	9	1	2	3	5	8	10	13
TOTAL SINGLE DX	**7**	**2.7**	**1**	**1**	**2**	**3**	**3**	**3**	**5**	**5**
TOTAL MULTIPLE DX	**202**	**3.8**	**11**	**1**	**2**	**3**	**5**	**8**	**10**	**18**
TOTAL										
0–19 Years	1	5.0	0	5	5	5	5	5	5	5
20–34	19	3.3	3	1	2	4	5	5	5	5
35–49	50	3.7	9	1	1	3	5	6	7	18
50–64	53	3.9	17	1	1	3	4	8	9	27
65+	86	3.8	9	1	2	3	5	8	10	13
GRAND TOTAL	**209**	**3.8**	**11**	**1**	**2**	**3**	**5**	**8**	**10**	**18**

88.45: RENAL ARTERIOGRAM

Type of Patients	Observed Patients	Avg. Stay	Vari-ance	Percentiles						
				10th	25th	50th	75th	90th	95th	99th
1. SINGLE DX										
0–19 Years	3	2.0	4	1	1	1	5	5	5	5
20–34	1	1.0	0	1	1	1	1	1	1	1
35–49	4	3.2	3	1	3	3	4	5	5	5
50–64	1	4.0	0	4	4	4	4	4	4	4
65+	2	1.4	<1	1	1	1	2	2	2	2
2. MULTIPLE DX										
0–19 Years	6	5.9	6	2	4	6	7	9	9	9
20–34	21	5.6	19	3	4	5	6	8	9	27
35–49	47	5.9	37	2	3	5	7	10	11	46
50–64	64	5.8	21	1	2	4	10	11	13	23
65+	142	4.7	13	1	2	4	7	9	11	17
TOTAL SINGLE DX	**11**	**2.3**	**3**	**1**	**1**	**1**	**4**	**5**	**5**	**5**
TOTAL MULTIPLE DX	**280**	**5.2**	**19**	**1**	**2**	**4**	**7**	**10**	**11**	**23**
TOTAL										
0–19 Years	9	4.7	8	1	2	5	7	9	9	9
20–34	22	5.4	19	2	4	5	6	8	9	27
35–49	51	5.8	35	2	3	5	7	9	11	46
50–64	65	5.8	21	1	2	4	10	11	13	23
65+	144	4.7	13	1	2	4	7	9	11	17
GRAND TOTAL	**291**	**5.1**	**19**	**1**	**2**	**4**	**7**	**10**	**11**	**23**

88.47: ABD ARTERIOGRAM NEC

Type of Patients	Observed Patients	Avg. Stay	Vari-ance	Percentiles						
				10th	25th	50th	75th	90th	95th	99th
1. SINGLE DX										
0–19 Years	1	6.0	0	6	6	6	6	6	6	6
20–34	2	3.0	8	1	1	5	5	5	5	5
35–49	6	2.6	11	1	1	1	2	10	10	10
50–64	2	2.0	2	1	1	3	3	3	3	3
65+	2	1.0	0	1	1	1	1	1	1	1
2. MULTIPLE DX										
0–19 Years	7	5.6	20	1	1	4	8	12	12	12
20–34	23	5.3	15	1	2	5	7	11	11	17
35–49	46	4.3	11	1	2	4	6	8	11	14
50–64	104	4.4	17	1	2	3	5	8	12	21
65+	180	5.7	20	2	3	5	7	11	15	24
TOTAL SINGLE DX	**13**	**2.6**	**8**	**1**	**1**	**1**	**3**	**6**	**10**	**10**
TOTAL MULTIPLE DX	**360**	**5.1**	**18**	**1**	**2**	**4**	**7**	**10**	**13**	**22**
TOTAL										
0–19 Years	8	5.7	17	1	1	5	8	12	12	12
20–34	25	5.2	15	1	1	5	7	11	11	17
35–49	52	4.1	11	1	1	3	6	10	11	14
50–64	106	4.4	17	1	2	3	5	8	12	21
65+	182	5.6	20	2	3	5	7	11	14	24
GRAND TOTAL	**373**	**5.0**	**18**	**1**	**2**	**4**	**6**	**10**	**13**	**22**

88.48: CONTRAST ARTERIOGRAM-LEG

Type of Patients	Observed Patients	Avg. Stay	Vari-ance	Percentiles						
				10th	25th	50th	75th	90th	95th	99th
1. SINGLE DX										
0–19 Years	11	1.9	<1	1	1	2	3	3	3	3
20–34	14	1.8	<1	1	1	1	2	3	4	4
35–49	3	1.0	0	1	1	1	1	1	1	1
50–64	4	1.9	<1	1	2	2	2	2	2	2
65+	7	2.4	2	1	1	2	3	6	6	6
2. MULTIPLE DX										
0–19 Years	9	2.4	3	1	1	2	3	4	7	7
20–34	35	3.7	17	1	1	2	4	9	13	18
35–49	65	4.4	12	1	2	4	6	8	10	19
50–64	162	4.7	14	1	2	4	7	9	11	16
65+	451	4.9	16	1	2	4	7	9	12	20
TOTAL SINGLE DX	**39**	**1.9**	**1**	**1**	**1**	**2**	**2**	**3**	**3**	**6**
TOTAL MULTIPLE DX	**722**	**4.7**	**15**	**1**	**2**	**4**	**7**	**9**	**11**	**19**
TOTAL										
0–19 Years	20	2.2	2	1	1	2	3	3	4	7
20–34	49	3.2	13	1	1	2	3	7	13	18
35–49	68	4.3	12	1	1	4	6	8	10	19
50–64	166	4.6	14	1	2	3	6	9	11	16
65+	458	4.8	16	1	2	4	7	9	12	20
GRAND TOTAL	**761**	**4.6**	**15**	**1**	**2**	**3**	**7**	**9**	**11**	**18**

88.49: CONTRAST ARTERIOGRAM NEC

Type of Patients	Observed Patients	Avg. Stay	Vari-ance	Percentiles						
				10th	25th	50th	75th	90th	95th	99th
1. SINGLE DX										
0–19 Years	2	1.0	0	1	1	1	1	1	1	1
20–34	4	2.1	9	1	1	1	1	9	9	9
35–49	5	5.1	55	1	1	2	3	19	19	19
50–64	4	2.9	10	1	1	1	7	7	7	7
65+	2	2.5	4	1	1	1	4	4	4	4
2. MULTIPLE DX										
0–19 Years	12	3.6	18	1	1	2	4	14	14	14
20–34	32	4.1	36	1	1	2	4	9	23	23
35–49	77	4.0	11	1	2	3	5	8	10	15
50–64	93	4.1	9	1	2	3	5	9	10	14
65+	109	4.3	10	1	2	4	5	8	12	17
TOTAL SINGLE DX	**17**	**3.0**	**19**	**1**	**1**	**1**	**3**	**7**	**19**	**19**
TOTAL MULTIPLE DX	**323**	**4.1**	**13**	**1**	**2**	**3**	**5**	**8**	**11**	**21**
TOTAL										
0–19 Years	14	3.3	16	1	1	2	4	14	14	14
20–34	36	3.9	33	1	1	1	4	9	23	23
35–49	82	4.0	13	1	2	3	5	8	10	19
50–64	97	4.1	9	1	2	3	5	9	10	14
65+	111	4.3	10	1	2	4	5	8	12	17
GRAND TOTAL	**340**	**4.1**	**13**	**1**	**2**	**3**	**5**	**8**	**11**	**21**

88.5: CONTRAST ANGIOCARDIOGRAM

Type of Patients	Observed Patients	Avg. Stay	Vari-ance	Percentiles						
				10th	25th	50th	75th	90th	95th	99th
1. SINGLE DX										
0–19 Years	0									
20–34	2	1.0	0	1	1	1	1	1	1	1
35–49	3	1.3	<1	1	1	1	2	2	2	2
50–64	8	1.1	<1	1	1	1	1	2	2	2
65+	6	1.0	0	1	1	1	1	1	1	1
2. MULTIPLE DX										
0–19 Years	8	2.5	2	1	1	3	3	6	6	6
20–34	29	3.9	15	1	1	2	5	11	13	14
35–49	185	3.0	8	1	1	2	3	6	8	15
50–64	466	2.6	6	1	1	2	3	5	8	12
65+	657	3.5	10	1	1	2	5	7	10	15
TOTAL SINGLE DX	**19**	**1.1**	**<1**	**1**	**1**	**1**	**1**	**1**	**2**	**2**
TOTAL MULTIPLE DX	**1,345**	**3.1**	**9**	**1**	**1**	**2**	**4**	**7**	**9**	**14**
TOTAL										
0–19 Years	8	2.5	2	1	1	3	3	6	6	6
20–34	31	3.8	15	1	1	2	5	11	11	14
35–49	188	3.0	8	1	1	2	3	6	8	15
50–64	474	2.6	6	1	1	2	3	5	8	12
65+	663	3.5	10	1	1	2	5	7	10	15
GRAND TOTAL	**1,364**	**3.1**	**9**	**1**	**1**	**2**	**4**	**7**	**9**	**14**

88.51: VC ANGIOCARDIOGRAM

Type of Patients	Observed Patients	Avg. Stay	Variance	Percentiles 10th	25th	50th	75th	90th	95th	99th
1. SINGLE DX										
0–19 Years	0									
20–34	0									
35–49	0									
50–64	0									
65+	0									
2. MULTIPLE DX										
0–19 Years	4	2.7	<1	1	3	3	3	3	3	3
20–34	11	6.3	18	3	3	5	11	13	14	14
35–49	15	3.7	5	1	2	3	6	7	8	8
50–64	22	5.8	14	2	4	5	7	10	12	20
65+	44	6.5	17	3	3	6	8	11	17	21
TOTAL SINGLE DX	**0**									
TOTAL MULTIPLE DX	**96**	**5.8**	**15**	**2**	**3**	**5**	**7**	**11**	**13**	**21**
TOTAL										
0–19 Years	4	2.7	<1	1	3	3	3	3	3	3
20–34	11	6.3	18	3	3	5	11	13	14	14
35–49	15	3.7	5	1	2	3	6	7	8	8
50–64	22	5.8	14	2	4	5	7	10	12	20
65+	44	6.5	17	3	3	6	8	11	17	21
GRAND TOTAL	**96**	**5.8**	**15**	**2**	**3**	**5**	**7**	**11**	**13**	**21**

88.53: LT HEART ANGIOCARDIOGRAM

Type of Patients	Observed Patients	Avg. Stay	Variance	Percentiles 10th	25th	50th	75th	90th	95th	99th
1. SINGLE DX										
0–19 Years	0									
20–34	1	1.0	0	1	1	1	1	1	1	1
35–49	1	1.0	0	1	1	1	1	1	1	1
50–64	3	1.3	<1	1	1	1	2	2	2	2
65+	1	1.0	0	1	1	1	1	1	1	1
2. MULTIPLE DX										
0–19 Years	0									
20–34	1	11.0	0	11	11	11	11	11	11	11
35–49	24	2.3	1	1	1	2	3	4	4	4
50–64	41	2.3	2	1	1	2	3	5	5	8
65+	51	3.2	12	1	1	2	4	7	11	20
TOTAL SINGLE DX	**6**	**1.2**	**<1**	**1**	**1**	**1**	**1**	**2**	**2**	**2**
TOTAL MULTIPLE DX	**117**	**2.7**	**7**	**1**	**1**	**2**	**4**	**5**	**7**	**13**
TOTAL										
0–19 Years	0									
20–34	2	6.3	47	1	1	11	11	11	11	11
35–49	25	2.2	1	1	1	2	3	4	4	4
50–64	44	2.3	2	1	1	2	3	5	5	8
65+	52	3.2	12	1	1	2	4	7	11	20
GRAND TOTAL	**123**	**2.7**	**7**	**1**	**1**	**2**	**3**	**5**	**7**	**13**

88.56: COR ARTERIOGRAM-2 CATH

Type of Patients	Observed Patients	Avg. Stay	Variance	Percentiles 10th	25th	50th	75th	90th	95th	99th
1. SINGLE DX										
0–19 Years	0									
20–34	1	1.0	0	1	1	1	1	1	1	1
35–49	2	1.4	<1	1	1	1	2	2	2	2
50–64	5	1.0	0	1	1	1	1	1	1	1
65+	4	1.0	0	1	1	1	1	1	1	1
2. MULTIPLE DX										
0–19 Years	1	6.0	0	6	6	6	6	6	6	6
20–34	16	2.2	6	1	1	1	2	5	6	11
35–49	132	3.0	8	1	1	2	3	6	9	15
50–64	381	2.5	5	1	1	2	3	5	8	11
65+	495	3.3	9	1	1	2	5	7	10	14
TOTAL SINGLE DX	**12**	**1.1**	**<1**	**1**	**1**	**1**	**1**	**1**	**2**	**2**
TOTAL MULTIPLE DX	**1,025**	**2.9**	**8**	**1**	**1**	**2**	**4**	**6**	**8**	**14**
TOTAL										
0–19 Years	1	6.0	0	6	6	6	6	6	6	6
20–34	17	2.2	6	1	1	1	2	5	6	11
35–49	134	2.9	8	1	1	2	3	6	9	15
50–64	386	2.5	5	1	1	2	3	5	8	11
65+	499	3.3	9	1	1	2	5	7	10	14
GRAND TOTAL	**1,037**	**2.9**	**8**	**1**	**1**	**2**	**4**	**6**	**8**	**14**

88.57: CORONARY ARTERIOGRAM NEC

Type of Patients	Observed Patients	Avg. Stay	Variance	Percentiles 10th	25th	50th	75th	90th	95th	99th
1. SINGLE DX										
0–19 Years	0									
20–34	0									
35–49	0									
50–64	0									
65+	1	1.0	0	1	1	1	1	1	1	1
2. MULTIPLE DX										
0–19 Years	0									
20–34	1	11.0	0	11	11	11	11	11	11	11
35–49	7	5.4	21	1	3	4	11	13	13	13
50–64	11	2.5	5	1	1	1	3	5	8	8
65+	40	3.3	7	1	2	3	3	7	8	13
TOTAL SINGLE DX	**1**	**1.0**	**0**	**1**	**1**	**1**	**1**	**1**	**1**	**1**
TOTAL MULTIPLE DX	**59**	**3.4**	**8**	**1**	**1**	**3**	**4**	**7**	**11**	**13**
TOTAL										
0–19 Years	0									
20–34	1	11.0	0	11	11	11	11	11	11	11
35–49	7	5.4	21	1	3	4	11	13	13	13
50–64	11	2.5	5	1	1	1	3	5	8	8
65+	41	3.3	7	1	2	3	3	7	8	13
GRAND TOTAL	**60**	**3.4**	**8**	**1**	**1**	**3**	**4**	**7**	**11**	**13**

88.6: PHLEBOGRAPHY

Type of Patients	Observed Patients	Avg. Stay	Vari-ance	10th	25th	50th	75th	90th	95th	99th
1. SINGLE DX										
0–19 Years	1	3.0	0	3	3	3	3	3	3	3
20–34	1	3.0	0	3	3	3	3	3	3	3
35–49	4	3.2	<1	2	2	3	4	4	4	4
50–64	3	3.0	1	2	2	3	4	4	4	4
65+	0									
2. MULTIPLE DX										
0–19 Years	12	9.3	127	1	3	4	12	38	38	38
20–34	43	4.7	10	1	2	4	7	10	11	15
35–49	84	5.9	20	2	3	5	7	11	14	17
50–64	82	5.7	29	2	3	4	8	12	17	29
65+	98	5.2	10	1	3	5	7	9	11	15
TOTAL SINGLE DX	9	3.1	<1	2	3	3	4	4	4	4
TOTAL MULTIPLE DX	319	5.7	23	1	3	4	7	11	14	29
TOTAL										
0–19 Years	13	8.6	116	1	3	3	12	13	38	38
20–34	44	4.7	10	1	2	4	7	10	11	15
35–49	88	5.8	19	2	3	4	7	11	14	17
50–64	85	5.7	29	2	2	4	8	11	17	29
65+	98	5.2	10	1	3	5	7	9	11	15
GRAND TOTAL	328	5.6	23	1	3	4	7	11	13	29

88.66: CONTRAST PHLEBOGRAM-LEG

Type of Patients	Observed Patients	Avg. Stay	Vari-ance	10th	25th	50th	75th	90th	95th	99th
1. SINGLE DX										
0–19 Years	0									
20–34	1	3.0	0	3	3	3	3	3	3	3
35–49	3	3.3	1	2	2	4	4	4	4	4
50–64	3	3.0	1	2	2	3	4	4	4	4
65+	0									
2. MULTIPLE DX										
0–19 Years	3	6.9	23	3	3	3	13	13	13	13
20–34	10	4.4	6	1	2	5	6	9	9	9
35–49	31	6.7	13	3	4	7	8	12	12	17
50–64	22	7.7	60	2	3	4	10	17	17	38
65+	39	6.1	8	3	5	6	7	10	13	15
TOTAL SINGLE DX	7	3.1	<1	2	2	3	4	4	4	4
TOTAL MULTIPLE DX	105	6.5	20	2	4	6	7	12	15	17
TOTAL										
0–19 Years	3	6.9	23	3	3	3	13	13	13	13
20–34	11	4.3	6	1	3	4	6	9	9	9
35–49	34	6.5	13	3	4	6	8	12	12	17
50–64	25	7.2	56	2	3	4	10	17	17	38
65+	39	6.1	8	3	5	6	7	10	13	15
GRAND TOTAL	112	6.4	20	2	3	6	7	12	15	17

88.67: CONTRAST PHLEBOGRAM NEC

Type of Patients	Observed Patients	Avg. Stay	Vari-ance	10th	25th	50th	75th	90th	95th	99th
1. SINGLE DX										
0–19 Years	0									
20–34	0									
35–49	0									
50–64	0									
65+	0									
2. MULTIPLE DX										
0–19 Years	5	15.8	251	1	3	12	38	38	38	38
20–34	26	4.6	8	2	2	4	7	10	11	11
35–49	36	5.6	18	1	2	4	9	11	11	17
50–64	38	5.5	24	2	3	4	7	8	13	29
65+	47	4.7	10	1	2	4	6	9	10	15
TOTAL SINGLE DX	0									
TOTAL MULTIPLE DX	152	5.5	27	1	2	4	7	11	13	38
TOTAL										
0–19 Years	5	15.8	251	1	3	12	38	38	38	38
20–34	26	4.6	8	2	2	4	7	10	11	11
35–49	36	5.6	18	1	2	4	9	11	11	17
50–64	38	5.5	24	2	3	4	7	8	13	29
65+	47	4.7	10	1	2	4	6	9	10	15
GRAND TOTAL	152	5.5	27	1	2	4	7	11	13	38

88.7: DIAGNOSTIC ULTRASOUND

Type of Patients	Observed Patients	Avg. Stay	Vari-ance	10th	25th	50th	75th	90th	95th	99th
1. SINGLE DX										
0–19 Years	454	2.2	2	1	1	2	3	4	5	9
20–34	550	2.4	6	1	1	2	3	4	6	10
35–49	332	2.3	3	1	1	2	3	5	6	8
50–64	200	2.5	5	1	1	2	3	5	6	10
65+	83	2.6	4	1	1	2	4	5	7	9
2. MULTIPLE DX										
0–19 Years	2,850	4.3	26	1	2	3	5	8	13	27
20–34	2,933	3.7	15	1	2	3	4	7	10	21
35–49	5,028	4.0	16	1	2	3	5	8	10	20
50–64	8,014	4.1	13	1	2	3	5	8	10	18
65+	19,149	4.4	12	1	2	4	6	8	11	18
TOTAL SINGLE DX	1,619	2.3	4	1	1	2	3	4	6	9
TOTAL MULTIPLE DX	37,974	4.2	14	1	2	3	5	8	11	19
TOTAL										
0–19 Years	3,304	4.0	23	1	2	3	4	7	12	26
20–34	3,483	3.5	14	1	1	2	4	7	10	20
35–49	5,360	3.9	16	1	2	3	5	7	10	20
50–64	8,214	4.0	13	1	2	3	5	8	10	18
65+	19,232	4.4	12	1	2	4	6	8	11	18
GRAND TOTAL	39,593	4.2	14	1	2	3	5	8	10	19

88.71: HEAD & NECK ULTRASOUND

Type of Patients	Observed Patients	Avg. Stay	Vari-ance	Percentiles						
				10th	25th	50th	75th	90th	95th	99th
1. SINGLE DX										
0–19 Years	18	2.9	6	1	1	2	4	7	9	9
20–34	2	5.1	29	1	1	9	9	9	9	9
35–49	7	2.8	4	2	2	2	2	7	8	8
50–64	9	1.7	<1	1	1	2	2	3	3	3
65+	6	4.0	6	1	2	3	7	7	7	7
2. MULTIPLE DX										
0–19 Years	203	11.9	118	2	3	8	19	27	36	45
20–34	21	4.1	16	2	2	3	6	6	7	21
35–49	114	3.5	10	1	1	2	4	7	8	14
50–64	380	3.0	6	1	1	2	4	5	8	11
65+	1,345	3.5	6	1	2	3	4	7	8	14
TOTAL SINGLE DX	**42**	**2.9**	**5**	**1**	**1**	**2**	**3**	**7**	**8**	**9**
TOTAL MULTIPLE DX	**2,063**	**4.2**	**24**	**1**	**2**	**3**	**5**	**8**	**13**	**27**
TOTAL										
0–19 Years	221	10.9	113	2	3	7	17	27	36	45
20–34	23	4.2	16	1	2	3	6	7	9	21
35–49	121	3.4	9	1	2	2	4	7	8	14
50–64	389	3.0	6	1	1	2	4	5	8	11
65+	1,351	3.5	6	1	2	3	4	7	8	14
GRAND TOTAL	**2,105**	**4.2**	**24**	**1**	**2**	**3**	**5**	**8**	**12**	**27**

88.72: HEART ULTRASOUND

Type of Patients	Observed Patients	Avg. Stay	Vari-ance	Percentiles						
				10th	25th	50th	75th	90th	95th	99th
1. SINGLE DX										
0–19 Years	102	2.4	2	1	2	2	3	4	5	7
20–34	42	2.3	3	1	1	2	3	4	5	8
35–49	89	1.5	<1	1	1	1	2	2	3	5
50–64	80	1.8	2	1	1	1	2	4	4	10
65+	41	1.7	1	1	1	1	2	3	4	6
2. MULTIPLE DX										
0–19 Years	1,109	4.5	28	1	2	3	5	8	14	25
20–34	682	4.2	16	1	2	3	5	9	11	19
35–49	2,420	4.0	18	1	2	3	5	8	10	21
50–64	4,912	4.0	13	1	2	3	5	8	10	17
65+	13,023	4.4	12	1	2	4	6	8	11	18
TOTAL SINGLE DX	**354**	**2.0**	**2**	**1**	**1**	**2**	**2**	**4**	**4**	**8**
TOTAL MULTIPLE DX	**22,146**	**4.3**	**14**	**1**	**2**	**3**	**5**	**8**	**11**	**18**
TOTAL										
0–19 Years	1,211	4.3	26	1	2	3	5	8	13	25
20–34	724	4.1	15	1	2	3	5	8	11	19
35–49	2,509	3.9	18	1	1	3	5	8	10	21
50–64	4,992	3.9	13	1	2	3	5	8	10	17
65+	13,064	4.4	12	1	2	4	6	8	11	18
GRAND TOTAL	**22,500**	**4.2**	**14**	**1**	**2**	**3**	**5**	**8**	**11**	**18**

88.73: THORAX ULTRASOUND NEC

Type of Patients	Observed Patients	Avg. Stay	Vari-ance	Percentiles						
				10th	25th	50th	75th	90th	95th	99th
1. SINGLE DX										
0–19 Years	1	5.0	0	5	5	5	5	5	5	5
20–34	0									
35–49	3	1.4	<1	1	1	1	2	2	2	2
50–64	0									
65+	0									
2. MULTIPLE DX										
0–19 Years	7	6.4	5	3	6	7	8	9	9	9
20–34	9	5.6	13	1	3	4	7	12	12	12
35–49	15	4.4	13	2	2	4	6	10	16	16
50–64	24	4.2	6	1	2	4	7	8	8	9
65+	42	5.8	19	1	3	5	8	9	13	22
TOTAL SINGLE DX	**4**	**3.1**	**4**	**1**	**1**	**2**	**5**	**5**	**5**	**5**
TOTAL MULTIPLE DX	**97**	**5.2**	**14**	**1**	**2**	**4**	**7**	**9**	**10**	**19**
TOTAL										
0–19 Years	8	6.1	4	3	5	6	8	8	9	9
20–34	9	5.6	13	1	3	4	7	12	12	12
35–49	18	4.0	12	1	2	2	6	6	10	16
50–64	24	4.2	6	1	2	4	7	8	8	9
65+	42	5.8	19	1	3	5	8	9	13	22
GRAND TOTAL	**101**	**5.2**	**14**	**1**	**2**	**4**	**7**	**9**	**10**	**19**

88.74: DIGEST SYSTEM ULTRASOUND

Type of Patients	Observed Patients	Avg. Stay	Vari-ance	Percentiles						
				10th	25th	50th	75th	90th	95th	99th
1. SINGLE DX										
0–19 Years	11	1.3	<1	1	1	1	2	2	3	3
20–34	19	2.4	4	1	1	1	3	6	6	7
35–49	28	3.2	3	1	2	3	5	6	6	6
50–64	15	4.6	8	1	2	5	6	8	11	11
65+	3	2.8	4	1	1	3	5	5	5	5
2. MULTIPLE DX										
0–19 Years	27	4.6	29	1	1	3	6	8	16	26
20–34	102	3.8	12	1	2	2	5	8	10	21
35–49	145	4.2	14	1	2	3	5	8	11	20
50–64	155	4.3	13	1	2	3	5	9	12	19
65+	152	4.2	14	1	2	3	5	8	13	20
TOTAL SINGLE DX	**76**	**2.9**	**5**	**1**	**1**	**2**	**5**	**6**	**6**	**8**
TOTAL MULTIPLE DX	**581**	**4.2**	**14**	**1**	**2**	**3**	**5**	**8**	**12**	**20**
TOTAL										
0–19 Years	38	3.5	22	1	1	2	3	8	12	26
20–34	121	3.5	11	1	1	2	5	8	9	17
35–49	173	4.0	12	1	2	3	5	7	9	20
50–64	170	4.3	12	1	2	3	6	8	11	19
65+	155	4.2	14	1	2	3	5	8	13	20
GRAND TOTAL	**657**	**4.0**	**13**	**1**	**2**	**3**	**5**	**8**	**11**	**20**

88.75: URINARY SYST ULTRASOUND

Type of Patients	Observed Patients	Avg. Stay	Vari-ance	Percentiles						
				10th	25th	50th	75th	90th	95th	99th
1. SINGLE DX										
0–19 Years	79	2.7	3	1	2	2	3	4	7	10
20–34	17	2.5	<1	1	2	2	3	4	4	4
35–49	11	2.1	1	1	1	2	3	3	4	4
50–64	9	2.0	1	1	1	2	3	4	4	4
65+	1	1.0	0	1	1	1	1	1	1	1
2. MULTIPLE DX										
0–19 Years	666	3.4	5	1	2	3	4	6	7	12
20–34	290	3.2	5	1	2	3	4	6	8	12
35–49	269	3.7	6	1	2	3	5	6	7	15
50–64	329	4.7	13	2	3	4	6	9	10	22
65+	945	5.0	14	2	3	4	6	9	12	18
TOTAL SINGLE DX	117	2.6	3	1	1	2	3	4	7	9
TOTAL MULTIPLE DX	2,499	4.1	10	1	2	3	5	7	10	17
TOTAL										
0–19 Years	745	3.3	5	1	2	3	4	6	7	12
20–34	307	3.2	5	1	2	3	4	5	7	12
35–49	280	3.7	6	1	2	3	5	6	7	15
50–64	338	4.6	13	2	2	4	6	9	10	22
65+	946	5.0	14	2	3	4	6	9	12	18
GRAND TOTAL	2,616	4.0	10	1	2	3	5	7	9	16

88.76: ABD & RETROPERITON US

Type of Patients	Observed Patients	Avg. Stay	Vari-ance	Percentiles						
				10th	25th	50th	75th	90th	95th	99th
1. SINGLE DX										
0–19 Years	174	1.7	1	1	1	1	2	3	4	6
20–34	160	2.3	10	1	1	2	3	4	5	6
35–49	102	2.8	3	1	1	2	4	6	7	8
50–64	50	2.9	8	1	1	2	4	5	6	17
65+	16	4.0	5	1	2	4	5	7	7	9
2. MULTIPLE DX										
0–19 Years	548	3.5	12	1	2	3	4	7	9	15
20–34	791	3.3	10	1	2	2	4	6	8	18
35–49	1,153	3.7	9	1	2	3	5	7	9	14
50–64	1,156	4.2	16	1	2	3	5	8	10	20
65+	1,706	4.5	11	1	2	4	6	9	11	17
TOTAL SINGLE DX	502	2.2	5	1	1	2	3	4	5	9
TOTAL MULTIPLE DX	5,354	4.0	12	1	2	3	5	7	10	17
TOTAL										
0–19 Years	722	3.1	10	1	1	2	4	6	9	14
20–34	951	3.1	10	1	1	2	4	6	8	18
35–49	1,255	3.6	9	1	2	3	5	6	9	14
50–64	1,206	4.2	16	1	2	3	5	7	10	20
65+	1,722	4.5	10	1	2	4	6	8	11	17
GRAND TOTAL	5,856	3.8	11	1	2	3	5	7	10	17

88.77: PERIPH VASC ULTRASOUND

Type of Patients	Observed Patients	Avg. Stay	Vari-ance	Percentiles						
				10th	25th	50th	75th	90th	95th	99th
1. SINGLE DX										
0–19 Years	9	1.3	<1	1	1	1	1	3	3	3
20–34	41	3.8	12	1	2	3	5	7	8	22
35–49	42	3.2	7	1	2	2	4	8	10	12
50–64	29	2.7	4	1	1	2	4	5	6	8
65+	14	3.1	4	1	1	3	5	6	6	6
2. MULTIPLE DX										
0–19 Years	32	5.2	14	2	3	4	7	8	16	16
20–34	206	3.7	10	1	2	3	5	7	10	16
35–49	617	4.4	13	1	2	4	6	8	10	23
50–64	889	4.5	14	1	2	4	6	8	11	18
65+	1,796	4.8	15	2	3	4	6	9	11	19
TOTAL SINGLE DX	135	3.1	7	1	1	2	4	6	8	12
TOTAL MULTIPLE DX	3,540	4.6	14	1	2	4	6	8	11	19
TOTAL										
0–19 Years	41	4.6	14	1	2	3	6	8	16	16
20–34	247	3.7	10	1	2	3	5	7	10	18
35–49	659	4.4	13	1	2	4	6	8	10	21
50–64	918	4.4	13	1	2	4	5	8	11	18
65+	1,810	4.8	15	2	3	4	6	9	11	19
GRAND TOTAL	3,675	4.6	14	1	2	4	6	8	11	19

88.78: GRAVID UTERUS ULTRASOUND

Type of Patients	Observed Patients	Avg. Stay	Vari-ance	Percentiles						
				10th	25th	50th	75th	90th	95th	99th
1. SINGLE DX										
0–19 Years	29	2.3	2	1	1	2	3	5	5	6
20–34	221	2.3	4	1	1	2	3	4	6	10
35–49	20	1.8	2	1	1	1	2	3	3	7
50–64	1	1.0	0	1	1	1	1	1	1	1
65+	0									
2. MULTIPLE DX										
0–19 Years	122	3.2	8	1	2	3	4	5	7	15
20–34	697	3.7	28	1	1	2	4	7	12	28
35–49	150	5.4	74	1	1	3	5	13	17	43
50–64	9	8.6	88	1	2	3	22	22	22	22
65+	0									
TOTAL SINGLE DX	271	2.3	4	1	1	2	3	4	6	10
TOTAL MULTIPLE DX	978	4.0	34	1	1	2	4	7	13	32
TOTAL										
0–19 Years	151	3.1	7	1	1	2	4	5	6	15
20–34	918	3.4	23	1	1	2	3	6	10	25
35–49	170	5.0	68	1	1	3	5	12	17	43
50–64	10	8.0	85	1	1	3	22	22	22	22
65+	0									
GRAND TOTAL	1,249	3.6	28	1	1	2	4	6	11	29

88.79: ULTRASOUND NEC

Type of Patients	Observed Patients	Avg. Stay	Vari-ance	Percentiles 10th	25th	50th	75th	90th	95th	99th
1. SINGLE DX										
0–19 Years	31	2.4	2	1	1	2	3	5	5	6
20–34	48	1.9	2	1	1	1	2	4	5	8
35–49	30	1.9	1	1	1	2	2	3	4	5
50–64	7	3.4	2	1	3	4	4	5	5	5
65+	2	1.0	0	1	1	1	1	1	1	1
2. MULTIPLE DX										
0–19 Years	136	2.9	4	1	2	2	3	5	8	11
20–34	135	3.6	11	1	1	3	4	7	9	18
35–49	145	4.1	13	1	2	3	5	9	11	23
50–64	160	4.1	9	1	2	3	6	7	11	16
65+	140	5.6	26	2	3	4	6	9	15	28
TOTAL SINGLE DX	**118**	**2.1**	**2**	**1**	**1**	**2**	**2**	**4**	**5**	**6**
TOTAL MULTIPLE DX	**716**	**4.1**	**14**	**1**	**2**	**3**	**5**	**8**	**11**	**20**
TOTAL										
0–19 Years	167	2.8	4	1	2	2	3	5	8	11
20–34	183	3.2	10	1	1	2	4	6	8	18
35–49	175	3.7	12	1	1	3	5	8	11	14
50–64	167	4.1	9	1	2	3	5	7	9	16
65+	142	5.5	26	1	3	4	6	9	15	28
GRAND TOTAL	**834**	**3.8**	**12**	**1**	**2**	**3**	**5**	**7**	**10**	**20**

88.8: THERMOGRAPHY

Type of Patients	Observed Patients	Avg. Stay	Vari-ance	Percentiles 10th	25th	50th	75th	90th	95th	99th
1. SINGLE DX										
0–19 Years	0									
20–34	0									
35–49	0									
50–64	0									
65+	0									
2. MULTIPLE DX										
0–19 Years	0									
20–34	0									
35–49	0									
50–64	0									
65+	1	5.0	0	5	5	5	5	5	5	5
TOTAL SINGLE DX	**0**									
TOTAL MULTIPLE DX	**1**	**5.0**	**0**	**5**	**5**	**5**	**5**	**5**	**5**	**5**
TOTAL										
0–19 Years	0									
20–34	0									
35–49	0									
50–64	0									
65+	1	5.0	0	5	5	5	5	5	5	5
GRAND TOTAL	**1**	**5.0**	**0**	**5**	**5**	**5**	**5**	**5**	**5**	**5**

88.9: OTHER DIAGNOSTIC IMAGING

Type of Patients	Observed Patients	Avg. Stay	Vari-ance	Percentiles 10th	25th	50th	75th	90th	95th	99th
1. SINGLE DX										
0–19 Years	313	2.7	5	1	1	2	3	5	7	13
20–34	121	3.4	9	1	1	2	4	7	9	15
35–49	138	3.0	6	1	1	2	4	6	8	13
50–64	83	3.1	7	1	1	2	4	7	9	13
65+	27	2.6	5	1	1	2	3	5	9	11
2. MULTIPLE DX										
0–19 Years	1,114	4.9	37	1	2	3	6	10	15	26
20–34	728	4.6	21	1	2	3	6	9	12	22
35–49	1,550	5.0	24	1	2	4	6	10	13	29
50–64	2,377	4.7	17	1	2	4	6	9	12	21
65+	4,353	4.8	16	1	2	4	6	9	12	21
TOTAL SINGLE DX	**682**	**2.9**	**6**	**1**	**1**	**2**	**4**	**6**	**7**	**13**
TOTAL MULTIPLE DX	**10,122**	**4.8**	**21**	**1**	**2**	**4**	**6**	**9**	**13**	**23**
TOTAL										
0–19 Years	1,427	4.4	30	1	2	3	5	9	14	26
20–34	849	4.5	19	1	2	3	5	9	12	22
35–49	1,688	4.9	23	1	2	3	6	9	13	29
50–64	2,460	4.6	17	1	2	3	6	9	12	20
65+	4,380	4.8	16	1	2	4	6	9	12	21
GRAND TOTAL	**10,804**	**4.7**	**20**	**1**	**2**	**3**	**6**	**9**	**12**	**22**

88.91: BRAIN & BRAIN STEM MRI

Type of Patients	Observed Patients	Avg. Stay	Vari-ance	Percentiles 10th	25th	50th	75th	90th	95th	99th
1. SINGLE DX										
0–19 Years	187	2.5	3	1	1	2	3	4	6	8
20–34	67	2.9	6	1	1	2	3	7	8	13
35–49	55	3.2	9	1	1	2	4	7	10	16
50–64	45	3.1	8	1	1	2	4	7	7	13
65+	17	2.4	5	1	1	2	3	4	11	11
2. MULTIPLE DX										
0–19 Years	726	4.8	24	1	2	3	6	10	15	23
20–34	406	4.5	26	1	2	3	5	9	13	24
35–49	898	4.8	23	1	2	3	6	9	13	29
50–64	1,540	4.3	15	1	2	3	5	8	11	20
65+	3,083	4.6	15	1	2	4	6	8	12	19
TOTAL SINGLE DX	**371**	**2.7**	**5**	**1**	**1**	**2**	**3**	**5**	**7**	**13**
TOTAL MULTIPLE DX	**6,653**	**4.6**	**18**	**1**	**2**	**3**	**6**	**9**	**12**	**22**
TOTAL										
0–19 Years	913	4.3	21	1	2	3	5	9	14	23
20–34	473	4.3	24	1	2	3	5	9	12	24
35–49	953	4.7	22	1	2	3	5	9	13	29
50–64	1,585	4.3	15	1	2	3	5	8	11	20
65+	3,100	4.6	15	1	2	4	6	8	12	19
GRAND TOTAL	**7,024**	**4.5**	**18**	**1**	**2**	**3**	**5**	**8**	**12**	**22**

88.92: CHEST & MYOCARDIUM MRI

Type of Patients	Observed Patients	Avg. Stay	Variance	10th	25th	50th	75th	90th	95th	99th
1. SINGLE DX										
0–19 Years	1	1.0	0	1	1	1	1	1	1	1
20–34	0									
35–49	0									
50–64	0									
65+	1	3.0	0	3	3	3	3	3	3	3
2. MULTIPLE DX										
0–19 Years	5	8.5	60	3	3	5	10	25	25	25
20–34	4	4.5	8	1	4	5	5	8	8	8
35–49	12	5.3	28	2	3	4	5	8	22	22
50–64	18	5.0	9	2	2	4	7	10	11	11
65+	25	5.2	17	2	2	4	7	8	17	19
TOTAL SINGLE DX	**2**	**1.8**	**1**	**1**	**1**	**1**	**3**	**3**	**3**	**3**
TOTAL MULTIPLE DX	**64**	**5.5**	**22**	**2**	**3**	**4**	**7**	**10**	**17**	**25**
TOTAL										
0–19 Years	6	7.4	58	1	3	4	10	25	25	25
20–34	4	4.5	8	1	4	5	5	8	8	8
35–49	12	5.3	28	2	3	4	5	8	22	22
50–64	18	5.0	9	2	2	4	7	10	11	11
65+	26	5.1	17	2	2	4	7	8	17	19
GRAND TOTAL	**66**	**5.4**	**22**	**2**	**2**	**4**	**7**	**10**	**17**	**25**

88.93: SPINAL CANAL MRI

Type of Patients	Observed Patients	Avg. Stay	Variance	10th	25th	50th	75th	90th	95th	99th
1. SINGLE DX										
0–19 Years	28	3.4	10	1	1	2	4	7	13	13
20–34	34	3.7	10	1	2	3	5	5	7	20
35–49	56	2.6	3	1	1	2	3	6	6	7
50–64	27	3.7	8	1	2	3	4	9	10	12
65+	4	3.3	11	1	1	2	3	9	9	9
2. MULTIPLE DX										
0–19 Years	118	4.5	18	1	2	3	6	9	11	22
20–34	160	4.3	12	1	2	3	5	8	11	19
35–49	346	4.6	24	1	2	3	5	9	12	30
50–64	398	5.0	18	1	2	4	6	10	13	21
65+	657	5.3	17	2	3	4	6	10	13	21
TOTAL SINGLE DX	**149**	**3.3**	**8**	**1**	**1**	**2**	**4**	**6**	**7**	**13**
TOTAL MULTIPLE DX	**1,679**	**4.9**	**18**	**1**	**2**	**4**	**6**	**10**	**12**	**23**
TOTAL										
0–19 Years	146	4.3	17	1	2	3	5	9	11	22
20–34	194	4.2	11	1	2	3	5	8	9	19
35–49	402	4.4	22	1	2	3	5	8	11	30
50–64	425	4.9	17	1	2	4	6	10	12	19
65+	661	5.2	17	2	3	4	6	10	13	21
GRAND TOTAL	**1,828**	**4.8**	**18**	**1**	**2**	**4**	**6**	**9**	**12**	**22**

88.94: MUSCULOSKELETAL MRI

Type of Patients	Observed Patients	Avg. Stay	Variance	10th	25th	50th	75th	90th	95th	99th
1. SINGLE DX										
0–19 Years	43	3.7	11	1	2	2	5	7	9	20
20–34	9	5.6	25	1	3	4	6	15	15	15
35–49	11	3.6	9	1	1	3	5	7	12	12
50–64	2	2.5	<1	2	2	3	3	3	3	3
65+	1	2.0	0	2	2	2	2	2	2	2
2. MULTIPLE DX										
0–19 Years	77	4.9	15	1	2	4	6	10	12	15
20–34	66	6.5	21	2	4	5	8	12	15	30
35–49	139	6.4	18	2	3	5	8	11	13	26
50–64	180	6.4	22	2	3	5	8	12	14	24
65+	225	5.9	18	2	3	5	7	12	15	22
TOTAL SINGLE DX	**66**	**3.8**	**12**	**1**	**2**	**3**	**5**	**7**	**11**	**20**
TOTAL MULTIPLE DX	**687**	**6.0**	**19**	**2**	**3**	**5**	**8**	**12**	**14**	**24**
TOTAL										
0–19 Years	120	4.5	14	1	2	3	6	9	12	20
20–34	75	6.4	21	2	3	5	7	13	15	30
35–49	150	6.2	18	2	3	5	8	11	13	26
50–64	182	6.3	22	2	3	5	8	12	14	24
65+	226	5.9	18	2	3	5	7	12	15	22
GRAND TOTAL	**753**	**5.8**	**19**	**2**	**3**	**5**	**7**	**12**	**14**	**23**

88.95: PELVIS/PROS/BLADDER MRI

Type of Patients	Observed Patients	Avg. Stay	Variance	10th	25th	50th	75th	90th	95th	99th
1. SINGLE DX										
0–19 Years	8	2.3	3	1	1	2	3	4	7	7
20–34	0									
35–49	1	1.0	0	1	1	1	1	1	1	1
50–64	0									
65+	2	3.5	6	1	1	5	5	5	5	5
2. MULTIPLE DX										
0–19 Years	14	4.0	11	1	1	3	6	9	13	13
20–34	10	4.8	15	1	1	3	8	9	11	11
35–49	11	6.6	59	2	3	4	7	10	32	32
50–64	26	5.8	35	2	3	4	6	10	20	33
65+	37	4.5	18	1	2	3	6	9	14	22
TOTAL SINGLE DX	**11**	**2.5**	**3**	**1**	**1**	**2**	**3**	**5**	**7**	**7**
TOTAL MULTIPLE DX	**98**	**5.0**	**25**	**1**	**2**	**3**	**6**	**9**	**13**	**32**
TOTAL										
0–19 Years	22	3.4	9	1	1	3	4	7	9	13
20–34	10	4.8	15	1	1	3	8	9	11	11
35–49	12	6.2	57	2	3	4	7	10	32	32
50–64	26	5.8	35	2	3	4	6	10	20	33
65+	39	4.4	17	1	2	3	5	9	14	22
GRAND TOTAL	**109**	**4.7**	**23**	**1**	**2**	**3**	**6**	**9**	**13**	**32**

88.97: MRI SITE NEC & NOS

Type of Patients	Observed Patients	Avg. Stay	Vari-ance	Percentiles						
				10th	25th	50th	75th	90th	95th	99th
1. SINGLE DX										
0–19 Years	40	2.2	3	1	1	1	3	5	7	8
20–34	11	3.1	7	1	1	3	3	8	11	11
35–49	15	3.6	6	1	2	3	5	8	9	9
50–64	9	1.9	<1	1	1	2	2	3	4	4
65+	2	2.0	0	2	2	2	2	2	2	2
2. MULTIPLE DX										
0–19 Years	165	5.6	121	1	1	2	5	15	26	71
20–34	82	4.5	10	2	2	4	6	9	11	16
35–49	141	5.9	32	2	2	4	7	13	22	24
50–64	207	5.1	17	2	2	4	7	9	12	18
65+	319	5.1	18	2	2	4	7	10	13	27
TOTAL SINGLE DX	**77**	**2.5**	**4**	**1**	**1**	**2**	**3**	**5**	**8**	**9**
TOTAL MULTIPLE DX	**914**	**5.3**	**40**	**1**	**2**	**4**	**6**	**10**	**15**	**27**
TOTAL										
0–19 Years	205	5.0	100	1	1	2	4	11	20	71
20–34	93	4.3	9	1	2	3	6	9	11	13
35–49	156	5.7	30	2	2	4	7	13	22	22
50–64	216	4.9	16	1	2	4	6	9	12	18
65+	321	5.1	18	2	2	4	7	10	13	27
GRAND TOTAL	**991**	**5.0**	**38**	**1**	**2**	**3**	**6**	**10**	**14**	**27**

89.0: DX INTERVIEW/CONSUL/EXAM

Type of Patients	Observed Patients	Avg. Stay	Vari-ance	Percentiles						
				10th	25th	50th	75th	90th	95th	99th
1. SINGLE DX										
0–19 Years	240	2.3	1	1	2	2	3	3	4	6
20–34	20	2.5	3	1	1	1	5	5	6	6
35–49	25	2.9	5	1	1	2	4	6	6	8
50–64	18	2.1	2	1	1	2	2	3	6	6
65+	15	2.5	2	1	1	2	3	5	5	6
2. MULTIPLE DX										
0–19 Years	238	3.0	14	1	1	2	3	4	6	20
20–34	222	2.6	5	1	1	2	3	5	7	11
35–49	568	2.7	4	1	1	2	3	5	7	11
50–64	931	3.0	7	1	1	2	4	6	7	13
65+	2,266	3.6	7	1	2	3	4	7	8	12
TOTAL SINGLE DX	**318**	**2.4**	**2**	**1**	**1**	**2**	**3**	**4**	**5**	**6**
TOTAL MULTIPLE DX	**4,225**	**3.3**	**7**	**1**	**2**	**3**	**4**	**6**	**8**	**12**
TOTAL										
0–19 Years	478	2.7	7	1	2	2	3	4	5	11
20–34	242	2.6	5	1	1	2	3	5	7	11
35–49	593	2.7	4	1	1	2	3	5	7	10
50–64	949	3.0	7	1	1	2	4	6	7	13
65+	2,281	3.6	7	1	2	3	4	7	8	12
GRAND TOTAL	**4,543**	**3.2**	**7**	**1**	**2**	**3**	**4**	**6**	**7**	**12**

89.03: COMPR INTERVIEW/EVAL

Type of Patients	Observed Patients	Avg. Stay	Vari-ance	Percentiles						
				10th	25th	50th	75th	90th	95th	99th
1. SINGLE DX										
0–19 Years	23	2.0	<1	1	1	2	2	3	4	4
20–34	14	2.4	3	1	1	1	5	5	5	5
35–49	11	3.5	4	1	2	2	6	6	6	6
50–64	10	2.6	2	1	2	2	3	6	6	6
65+	7	2.8	2	1	1	3	3	5	5	5
2. MULTIPLE DX										
0–19 Years	58	2.5	3	1	1	2	3	4	7	8
20–34	62	2.4	3	1	1	2	3	5	5	8
35–49	139	2.2	2	1	1	2	3	4	4	7
50–64	222	3.1	9	1	1	2	4	6	7	25
65+	506	3.4	12	1	2	3	4	6	9	13
TOTAL SINGLE DX	**65**	**2.5**	**3**	**1**	**1**	**2**	**3**	**5**	**6**	**6**
TOTAL MULTIPLE DX	**987**	**3.0**	**9**	**1**	**1**	**2**	**4**	**5**	**7**	**13**
TOTAL										
0–19 Years	81	2.4	2	1	1	2	3	4	4	8
20–34	76	2.4	3	1	1	2	3	5	5	8
35–49	150	2.3	2	1	1	2	3	4	6	7
50–64	232	3.1	9	1	1	2	4	6	7	25
65+	513	3.4	12	1	2	3	4	6	9	13
GRAND TOTAL	**1,052**	**3.0**	**8**	**1**	**1**	**2**	**4**	**5**	**7**	**11**

89.04: INTERVIEW & EVAL NEC

Type of Patients	Observed Patients	Avg. Stay	Vari-ance	Percentiles						
				10th	25th	50th	75th	90th	95th	99th
1. SINGLE DX										
0–19 Years	14	1.3	<1	1	1	1	2	2	2	3
20–34	4	1.2	<1	1	1	1	1	2	2	2
35–49	8	1.1	<1	1	1	1	1	2	2	2
50–64	5	1.0	0	1	1	1	1	1	1	1
65+	2	1.0	0	1	1	1	1	1	1	1
2. MULTIPLE DX										
0–19 Years	42	1.5	<1	1	1	1	2	3	3	5
20–34	72	2.0	1	1	1	2	3	4	4	6
35–49	226	2.6	3	1	1	2	3	5	6	9
50–64	385	2.5	4	1	1	2	3	5	6	10
65+	1,080	3.3	6	1	2	3	4	6	8	12
TOTAL SINGLE DX	**33**	**1.2**	**<1**	**1**	**1**	**1**	**1**	**2**	**2**	**3**
TOTAL MULTIPLE DX	**1,805**	**2.9**	**5**	**1**	**1**	**2**	**4**	**6**	**7**	**12**
TOTAL										
0–19 Years	56	1.5	<1	1	1	1	2	3	3	5
20–34	76	1.9	1	1	1	2	3	4	4	6
35–49	234	2.5	3	1	1	2	3	5	6	9
50–64	390	2.4	4	1	1	2	3	5	6	10
65+	1,082	3.3	6	1	2	3	4	6	8	12
GRAND TOTAL	**1,838**	**2.9**	**5**	**1**	**1**	**2**	**4**	**5**	**7**	**12**

89.06: LIMITED CONSULTATION

Type of Patients	Observed Patients	Avg. Stay	Variance	10th	25th	50th	75th	90th	95th	99th
1. SINGLE DX										
0–19 Years	1	3.0	0	3	3	3	3	3	3	3
20–34	0									
35–49	3	3.1	2	1	3	4	4	4	4	4
50–64	3	1.2	<1	1	1	1	1	2	2	2
65+	0									
2. MULTIPLE DX										
0–19 Years	15	8.8	137	2	2	3	8	36	36	36
20–34	35	3.7	11	1	2	3	4	9	9	19
35–49	100	3.0	5	1	1	3	4	5	8	11
50–64	170	3.5	9	1	2	3	4	6	8	17
65+	346	4.1	6	2	3	3	5	7	9	12
TOTAL SINGLE DX	**7**	**2.3**	**2**	**1**	**1**	**3**	**3**	**4**	**4**	**4**
TOTAL MULTIPLE DX	**666**	**3.8**	**10**	**1**	**2**	**3**	**5**	**7**	**9**	**14**
TOTAL										
0–19 Years	16	8.5	131	2	2	3	8	36	36	36
20–34	35	3.7	11	1	2	3	4	9	9	19
35–49	103	3.0	5	1	1	3	4	5	8	11
50–64	173	3.5	9	1	2	3	4	6	8	17
65+	346	4.1	6	2	3	3	5	7	9	12
GRAND TOTAL	**673**	**3.8**	**10**	**1**	**2**	**3**	**5**	**7**	**9**	**14**

89.07: COMPREHENSIVE CONSULT

Type of Patients	Observed Patients	Avg. Stay	Variance	10th	25th	50th	75th	90th	95th	99th
1. SINGLE DX										
0–19 Years	0									
20–34	1	6.0	0	6	6	6	6	6	6	6
35–49	0									
50–64	0									
65+	0									
2. MULTIPLE DX										
0–19 Years	6	4.4	48	1	1	1	3	20	20	20
20–34	19	3.8	14	1	1	3	5	8	8	19
35–49	57	3.3	8	1	2	2	4	7	8	17
50–64	96	3.6	4	1	2	3	5	6	7	10
65+	194	4.4	7	2	3	4	6	8	9	14
TOTAL SINGLE DX	**1**	**6.0**	**0**	**6**	**6**	**6**	**6**	**6**	**6**	**6**
TOTAL MULTIPLE DX	**372**	**4.0**	**7**	**1**	**2**	**3**	**5**	**7**	**8**	**14**
TOTAL										
0–19 Years	6	4.4	48	1	1	1	3	20	20	20
20–34	20	4.0	13	1	1	3	6	8	8	19
35–49	57	3.3	8	1	2	2	4	7	8	17
50–64	96	3.6	4	1	2	3	5	6	7	10
65+	194	4.4	7	2	3	4	6	8	9	14
GRAND TOTAL	**373**	**4.0**	**7**	**1**	**2**	**3**	**5**	**7**	**8**	**14**

89.08: CONSULTATION NEC

Type of Patients	Observed Patients	Avg. Stay	Variance	10th	25th	50th	75th	90th	95th	99th
1. SINGLE DX										
0–19 Years	174	2.6	1	1	2	2	3	4	4	6
20–34	0									
35–49	0									
50–64	0									
65+	0									
2. MULTIPLE DX										
0–19 Years	97	3.3	5	2	2	3	4	4	5	20
20–34	1	2.0	0	2	2	2	2	2	2	2
35–49	0									
50–64	2	3.4	4	2	2	2	5	5	5	5
65+	3	3.3	<1	3	3	3	4	4	4	4
TOTAL SINGLE DX	**174**	**2.6**	**1**	**1**	**2**	**2**	**3**	**4**	**4**	**6**
TOTAL MULTIPLE DX	**103**	**3.2**	**5**	**2**	**2**	**3**	**4**	**4**	**5**	**20**
TOTAL										
0–19 Years	271	2.8	3	1	2	3	3	4	5	6
20–34	1	2.0	0	2	2	2	2	2	2	2
35–49	0									
50–64	2	3.4	4	2	2	2	5	5	5	5
65+	3	3.3	<1	3	3	3	4	4	4	4
GRAND TOTAL	**277**	**2.8**	**3**	**1**	**2**	**3**	**3**	**4**	**5**	**6**

89.1: NERVOUS SYSTEM EXAMS

Type of Patients	Observed Patients	Avg. Stay	Variance	10th	25th	50th	75th	90th	95th	99th
1. SINGLE DX										
0–19 Years	521	2.2	3	1	1	2	3	4	5	9
20–34	132	3.6	6	1	2	3	4	6	7	15
35–49	88	3.6	5	1	2	4	5	6	7	14
50–64	49	3.1	3	1	2	3	4	6	7	9
65+	6	1.4	<1	1	1	1	2	3	3	3
2. MULTIPLE DX										
0–19 Years	984	3.2	16	1	1	2	4	6	10	17
20–34	367	5.5	110	1	2	3	5	7	12	69
35–49	517	4.2	25	1	2	3	5	8	12	19
50–64	479	4.9	25	1	2	4	6	9	13	37
65+	863	5.1	15	2	3	4	6	9	13	21
TOTAL SINGLE DX	**796**	**2.6**	**4**	**1**	**1**	**2**	**3**	**5**	**6**	**10**
TOTAL MULTIPLE DX	**3,210**	**4.3**	**30**	**1**	**2**	**3**	**5**	**8**	**12**	**21**
TOTAL										
0–19 Years	1,505	2.9	11	1	1	2	3	5	8	16
20–34	499	5.0	86	1	2	3	5	7	11	69
35–49	605	4.1	22	1	2	3	5	7	11	16
50–64	528	4.8	23	1	2	4	6	9	12	37
65+	869	5.0	15	2	3	4	6	9	13	20
GRAND TOTAL	**4,006**	**3.9**	**24**	**1**	**2**	**3**	**4**	**7**	**10**	**19**

89.14: ELECTROENCEPHALOGRAM

Type of Patients	Observed Patients	Avg. Stay	Vari-ance	Percentiles						
				10th	25th	50th	75th	90th	95th	99th
1. SINGLE DX										
0–19 Years	194	2.1	4	1	1	2	2	4	5	10
20–34	24	2.9	10	1	1	2	3	6	8	15
35–49	12	3.0	6	1	1	2	5	7	7	7
50–64	5	1.6	1	1	1	1	2	4	4	4
65+	5	1.5	<1	1	1	1	2	3	3	3
2. MULTIPLE DX										
0–19 Years	497	3.5	17	1	1	2	4	7	10	18
20–34	142	4.1	12	1	2	3	5	9	11	16
35–49	265	5.0	49	1	2	3	6	12	14	21
50–64	303	5.4	34	1	2	4	6	11	14	39
65+	804	5.1	15	2	3	4	6	9	13	19
TOTAL SINGLE DX	**240**	**2.2**	**4**	**1**	**1**	**2**	**2**	**4**	**5**	**10**
TOTAL MULTIPLE DX	**2,011**	**4.5**	**22**	**1**	**2**	**3**	**5**	**9**	**13**	**20**
TOTAL										
0–19 Years	691	3.1	14	1	1	2	3	6	10	16
20–34	166	3.9	12	1	2	3	5	9	11	15
35–49	277	4.9	47	1	2	3	6	11	14	21
50–64	308	5.2	34	1	2	4	6	11	14	39
65+	809	5.0	15	2	3	4	6	9	13	19
GRAND TOTAL	**2,251**	**4.2**	**21**	**1**	**2**	**3**	**5**	**9**	**12**	**20**

89.17: POLYSOMNOGRAM

Type of Patients	Observed Patients	Avg. Stay	Vari-ance	Percentiles						
				10th	25th	50th	75th	90th	95th	99th
1. SINGLE DX										
0–19 Years	7	1.7	<1	1	1	1	2	3	3	3
20–34	0									
35–49	0									
50–64	0									
65+	0									
2. MULTIPLE DX										
0–19 Years	31	4.0	12	1	1	4	5	8	12	15
20–34	2	2.4	4	1	1	1	4	4	4	4
35–49	5	3.2	5	1	2	3	4	7	7	7
50–64	2	5.9	5	2	7	7	7	7	7	7
65+	4	3.9	9	2	2	3	3	9	9	9
TOTAL SINGLE DX	**7**	**1.7**	**<1**	**1**	**1**	**1**	**2**	**3**	**3**	**3**
TOTAL MULTIPLE DX	**44**	**4.0**	**10**	**1**	**1**	**3**	**6**	**8**	**11**	**15**
TOTAL										
0–19 Years	38	3.6	11	1	1	2	5	8	11	15
20–34	2	2.4	4	1	1	1	4	4	4	4
35–49	5	3.2	5	1	2	3	4	7	7	7
50–64	2	5.9	5	2	7	7	7	7	7	7
65+	4	3.9	9	2	2	3	3	9	9	9
GRAND TOTAL	**51**	**3.7**	**10**	**1**	**1**	**3**	**5**	**7**	**11**	**15**

89.19: VIDEO/TELEMETRIC EEG MON

Type of Patients	Observed Patients	Avg. Stay	Vari-ance	Percentiles						
				10th	25th	50th	75th	90th	95th	99th
1. SINGLE DX										
0–19 Years	296	2.3	2	1	1	2	3	4	5	8
20–34	105	3.6	5	1	2	3	5	6	6	12
35–49	73	3.8	5	1	2	4	5	6	7	15
50–64	42	3.5	3	1	2	3	4	6	7	9
65+	1	1.0	0	1	1	1	1	1	1	1
2. MULTIPLE DX										
0–19 Years	416	2.6	5	1	1	2	3	5	6	11
20–34	217	3.8	6	1	2	3	5	6	8	13
35–49	234	3.6	5	1	2	3	4	6	8	12
50–64	158	4.1	9	1	2	4	5	7	9	15
65+	36	3.9	4	2	2	3	5	8	8	9
TOTAL SINGLE DX	**517**	**2.8**	**3**	**1**	**2**	**2**	**4**	**5**	**6**	**9**
TOTAL MULTIPLE DX	**1,061**	**3.3**	**6**	**1**	**2**	**3**	**4**	**6**	**8**	**13**
TOTAL										
0–19 Years	712	2.5	4	1	1	2	3	4	5	10
20–34	322	3.7	6	1	2	3	5	6	7	13
35–49	307	3.7	5	1	2	3	4	6	8	13
50–64	200	4.0	8	1	2	3	5	7	9	15
65+	37	3.8	5	2	2	3	5	8	8	9
GRAND TOTAL	**1,578**	**3.1**	**5**	**1**	**2**	**3**	**4**	**5**	**7**	**12**

89.2: GU SYSTEM-EXAMINATION

Type of Patients	Observed Patients	Avg. Stay	Vari-ance	Percentiles						
				10th	25th	50th	75th	90th	95th	99th
1. SINGLE DX										
0–19 Years	3	1.3	<1	1	1	1	2	2	2	2
20–34	3	1.5	<1	1	1	1	2	2	2	2
35–49	3	1.0	0	1	1	1	1	1	1	1
50–64	4	1.0	0	1	1	1	1	1	1	1
65+	0									
2. MULTIPLE DX										
0–19 Years	20	8.0	113	1	2	3	8	28	28	41
20–34	17	2.4	3	1	1	2	3	5	7	7
35–49	18	3.1	8	1	1	2	4	5	10	11
50–64	13	2.8	4	1	1	2	4	6	8	8
65+	35	6.0	25	1	3	4	8	11	13	29
TOTAL SINGLE DX	**13**	**1.2**	**<1**	**1**	**1**	**1**	**1**	**2**	**2**	**2**
TOTAL MULTIPLE DX	**103**	**5.1**	**39**	**1**	**2**	**3**	**6**	**10**	**13**	**29**
TOTAL										
0–19 Years	23	7.4	106	1	2	3	7	28	28	41
20–34	20	2.3	3	1	1	2	3	3	7	7
35–49	21	2.8	7	1	1	2	4	5	10	11
50–64	17	2.5	3	1	1	2	4	4	6	8
65+	35	6.0	25	1	3	4	8	11	13	29
GRAND TOTAL	**116**	**4.8**	**37**	**1**	**1**	**3**	**6**	**10**	**13**	**29**

89.22: CYSTOMETROGRAM

Type of Patients	Observed Patients	Avg. Stay	Vari-ance	10th	25th	50th	75th	90th	95th	99th
				Percentiles						
1. SINGLE DX										
0–19 Years	0									
20–34	0									
35–49	0									
50–64	0									
65+	0									
2. MULTIPLE DX										
0–19 Years	1	7.0	0	7	7	7	7	7	7	7
20–34	0									
35–49	2	7.2	21	4	4	4	11	11	11	11
50–64	1	8.0	0	8	8	8	8	8	8	8
65+	7	8.4	62	3	3	5	11	12	29	29
TOTAL SINGLE DX	**0**									
TOTAL MULTIPLE DX	**11**	**8.1**	**49**	**3**	**3**	**7**	**11**	**12**	**29**	**29**
TOTAL										
0–19 Years	1	7.0	0	7	7	7	7	7	7	7
20–34	0									
35–49	2	7.2	21	4	4	4	11	11	11	11
50–64	1	8.0	0	8	8	8	8	8	8	8
65+	7	8.4	62	3	3	5	11	12	29	29
GRAND TOTAL	**11**	**8.1**	**49**	**3**	**3**	**7**	**11**	**12**	**29**	**29**

89.26: GYNECOLOGIC EXAMINATION

Type of Patients	Observed Patients	Avg. Stay	Vari-ance	10th	25th	50th	75th	90th	95th	99th
				Percentiles						
1. SINGLE DX										
0–19 Years	2	1.5	<1	1	1	2	2	2	2	2
20–34	3	1.5	<1	1	1	1	2	2	2	2
35–49	3	1.0	0	1	1	1	1	1	1	1
50–64	2	1.0	0	1	1	1	1	1	1	1
65+	0									
2. MULTIPLE DX										
0–19 Years	15	9.6	138	1	3	3	11	28	41	41
20–34	15	2.2	2	1	1	2	3	3	5	7
35–49	16	2.6	5	1	1	2	3	5	10	10
50–64	9	2.1	2	1	1	2	3	3	6	6
65+	17	4.2	8	1	1	4	6	9	9	10
TOTAL SINGLE DX	**10**	**1.3**	**<1**	**1**	**1**	**1**	**2**	**2**	**2**	**2**
TOTAL MULTIPLE DX	**72**	**4.5**	**43**	**1**	**1**	**3**	**4**	**9**	**11**	**41**
TOTAL										
0–19 Years	17	9.0	132	1	2	3	11	28	41	41
20–34	18	2.1	2	1	1	2	3	3	5	7
35–49	19	2.3	4	1	1	2	3	4	5	10
50–64	11	1.9	2	1	1	1	2	3	6	6
65+	17	4.2	8	1	1	4	6	9	9	10
GRAND TOTAL	**82**	**4.2**	**40**	**1**	**1**	**2**	**4**	**8**	**11**	**41**

89.3: OTHER EXAMINATIONS

Type of Patients	Observed Patients	Avg. Stay	Vari-ance	10th	25th	50th	75th	90th	95th	99th
				Percentiles						
1. SINGLE DX										
0–19 Years	106	2.4	5	1	1	2	3	5	6	11
20–34	9	2.0	1	1	1	2	3	4	4	4
35–49	4	2.2	3	1	1	1	2	5	5	5
50–64	4	2.7	7	1	1	2	2	7	7	7
65+	2	4.8	12	1	1	7	7	7	7	7
2. MULTIPLE DX										
0–19 Years	471	5.8	34	1	2	4	8	13	17	26
20–34	33	3.0	4	1	1	3	4	6	8	8
35–49	76	3.9	22	1	2	3	4	8	9	41
50–64	120	4.2	13	1	2	3	5	8	11	17
65+	163	4.0	11	1	2	3	5	9	10	13
TOTAL SINGLE DX	**125**	**2.4**	**5**	**1**	**1**	**2**	**3**	**5**	**7**	**11**
TOTAL MULTIPLE DX	**863**	**5.1**	**27**	**1**	**2**	**4**	**6**	**11**	**14**	**25**
TOTAL										
0–19 Years	577	5.1	30	1	1	3	7	11	16	25
20–34	42	2.7	3	1	1	2	3	5	6	8
35–49	80	3.8	21	1	2	3	4	6	9	41
50–64	124	4.2	13	1	2	3	5	8	11	17
65+	165	4.0	11	1	2	3	5	9	10	13
GRAND TOTAL	**988**	**4.7**	**24**	**1**	**2**	**3**	**6**	**10**	**13**	**24**

89.37: VITAL CAPACITY

Type of Patients	Observed Patients	Avg. Stay	Vari-ance	10th	25th	50th	75th	90th	95th	99th
				Percentiles						
1. SINGLE DX										
0–19 Years	2	3.4	3	2	2	2	5	5	5	5
20–34	1	1.0	0	1	1	1	1	1	1	1
35–49	2	3.5	4	2	2	2	5	5	5	5
50–64	2	1.4	<1	1	1	1	2	2	2	2
65+	1	7.0	0	7	7	7	7	7	7	7
2. MULTIPLE DX										
0–19 Years	14	5.2	14	2	2	3	8	13	13	13
20–34	14	2.9	3	1	2	3	4	5	6	6
35–49	32	3.3	3	1	2	3	4	6	8	8
50–64	50	4.9	10	2	3	4	6	8	10	17
65+	73	4.1	5	2	2	3	5	8	9	10
TOTAL SINGLE DX	**8**	**3.4**	**5**	**1**	**2**	**2**	**5**	**7**	**7**	**7**
TOTAL MULTIPLE DX	**183**	**4.2**	**7**	**2**	**2**	**3**	**6**	**8**	**9**	**13**
TOTAL										
0–19 Years	16	4.9	13	2	2	3	7	9	13	13
20–34	15	2.8	3	1	1	3	4	5	6	6
35–49	34	3.3	3	1	2	3	4	6	8	8
50–64	52	4.8	10	2	3	4	6	8	10	17
65+	74	4.1	6	2	3	3	5	8	9	10
GRAND TOTAL	**191**	**4.1**	**7**	**2**	**2**	**3**	**5**	**8**	**9**	**13**

89.38: RESPIRATORY MEASURE NEC

Type of Patients	Observed Patients	Avg. Stay	Vari-ance	Percentiles 10th	25th	50th	75th	90th	95th	99th
1. SINGLE DX										
0–19 Years	51	2.4	6	1	1	2	2	5	11	11
20–34	1	2.0	0	2	2	2	2	2	2	2
35–49	0									
50–64	0									
65+	0									
2. MULTIPLE DX										
0–19 Years	206	6.2	32	1	2	5	9	12	17	25
20–34	1	6.0	0	6	6	6	6	6	6	6
35–49	4	6.9	35	2	2	6	14	14	14	14
50–64	10	3.8	1	2	3	4	4	5	6	6
65+	9	3.2	4	1	2	3	5	6	7	7
TOTAL SINGLE DX	**52**	**2.4**	**6**	**1**	**1**	**2**	**2**	**5**	**11**	**11**
TOTAL MULTIPLE DX	**230**	**6.0**	**30**	**1**	**2**	**4**	**8**	**12**	**16**	**25**
TOTAL										
0–19 Years	257	5.2	28	1	2	3	7	11	15	25
20–34	2	3.7	7	2	2	2	6	6	6	6
35–49	4	6.9	35	2	2	6	14	14	14	14
50–64	10	3.8	1	2	3	4	4	5	6	6
65+	9	3.2	4	1	2	3	5	6	7	7
GRAND TOTAL	**282**	**5.1**	**27**	**1**	**2**	**3**	**7**	**11**	**15**	**25**

89.39: NONOPERATIVE EXAMS NEC

Type of Patients	Observed Patients	Avg. Stay	Vari-ance	Percentiles 10th	25th	50th	75th	90th	95th	99th
1. SINGLE DX										
0–19 Years	51	2.4	3	1	1	2	3	5	6	10
20–34	7	2.1	1	1	1	2	3	4	4	4
35–49	2	1.0	0	1	1	1	1	1	1	1
50–64	0									
65+	1	1.0	0	1	1	1	1	1	1	1
2. MULTIPLE DX										
0–19 Years	239	5.7	38	1	2	4	7	13	18	37
20–34	14	3.6	6	1	2	3	4	8	8	8
35–49	31	4.8	50	1	2	3	5	9	12	41
50–64	45	3.0	8	1	1	2	4	7	11	14
65+	65	4.1	19	1	1	2	6	10	11	28
TOTAL SINGLE DX	**61**	**2.3**	**3**	**1**	**1**	**2**	**3**	**4**	**6**	**10**
TOTAL MULTIPLE DX	**394**	**5.1**	**33**	**1**	**1**	**3**	**6**	**11**	**15**	**28**
TOTAL										
0–19 Years	290	5.1	33	1	1	4	6	11	16	28
20–34	21	2.8	4	1	1	2	3	6	8	8
35–49	33	4.6	47	1	2	3	5	9	12	41
50–64	45	3.0	8	1	1	2	4	7	11	14
65+	66	4.0	19	1	1	2	6	10	11	28
GRAND TOTAL	**455**	**4.7**	**30**	**1**	**1**	**3**	**6**	**10**	**13**	**28**

89.4: PACER/CARD STRESS TEST

Type of Patients	Observed Patients	Avg. Stay	Vari-ance	Percentiles 10th	25th	50th	75th	90th	95th	99th
1. SINGLE DX										
0–19 Years	8	1.2	<1	1	1	1	1	1	3	3
20–34	17	1.2	<1	1	1	1	1	1	3	3
35–49	139	1.4	<1	1	1	1	2	2	3	5
50–64	135	1.2	<1	1	1	1	1	2	3	3
65+	45	1.2	<1	1	1	1	1	2	2	3
2. MULTIPLE DX										
0–19 Years	15	2.4	8	1	1	1	3	6	11	11
20–34	190	1.8	2	1	1	1	2	4	5	6
35–49	2,343	1.8	2	1	1	1	2	3	4	7
50–64	4,982	2.0	3	1	1	1	2	4	5	8
65+	6,173	2.6	5	1	1	2	3	5	7	11
TOTAL SINGLE DX	**344**	**1.3**	**<1**	**1**	**1**	**1**	**1**	**2**	**3**	**4**
TOTAL MULTIPLE DX	**13,703**	**2.2**	**4**	**1**	**1**	**2**	**3**	**4**	**6**	**9**
TOTAL										
0–19 Years	23	1.9	5	1	1	1	1	5	6	11
20–34	207	1.8	2	1	1	1	2	4	4	6
35–49	2,482	1.8	2	1	1	1	2	3	4	7
50–64	5,117	2.0	3	1	1	1	2	4	5	8
65+	6,218	2.6	5	1	1	2	3	5	7	11
GRAND TOTAL	**14,047**	**2.2**	**4**	**1**	**1**	**2**	**3**	**4**	**6**	**9**

89.41: TREADMILL STRESS TEST

Type of Patients	Observed Patients	Avg. Stay	Vari-ance	Percentiles 10th	25th	50th	75th	90th	95th	99th
1. SINGLE DX										
0–19 Years	6	1.2	<1	1	1	1	1	3	3	3
20–34	11	1.0	0	1	1	1	1	1	1	1
35–49	97	1.3	<1	1	1	1	1	2	2	6
50–64	92	1.1	<1	1	1	1	1	1	2	3
65+	23	1.1	<1	1	1	1	1	1	2	3
2. MULTIPLE DX										
0–19 Years	12	2.7	10	1	1	1	3	6	11	11
20–34	115	1.6	2	1	1	1	2	3	4	6
35–49	1,261	1.5	1	1	1	1	2	3	4	6
50–64	2,318	1.6	2	1	1	1	2	3	4	7
65+	1,602	1.9	3	1	1	1	2	4	5	9
TOTAL SINGLE DX	**229**	**1.2**	**<1**	**1**	**1**	**1**	**1**	**2**	**2**	**4**
TOTAL MULTIPLE DX	**5,308**	**1.7**	**2**	**1**	**1**	**1**	**2**	**3**	**4**	**7**
TOTAL										
0–19 Years	18	2.1	6	1	1	1	2	6	6	11
20–34	126	1.6	1	1	1	1	2	3	4	6
35–49	1,358	1.5	1	1	1	1	2	3	4	6
50–64	2,410	1.6	2	1	1	1	2	3	4	7
65+	1,625	1.9	3	1	1	1	2	4	5	9
GRAND TOTAL	**5,537**	**1.7**	**2**	**1**	**1**	**1**	**2**	**3**	**4**	**7**

89.44: CV STRESS TEST NEC

Type of Patients	Observed Patients	Avg. Stay	Vari-ance	Percentiles						
				10th	25th	50th	75th	90th	95th	99th
1. SINGLE DX										
0–19 Years	1	1.0	0	1	1	1	1	1	1	1
20–34	6	1.4	<1	1	1	1	1	3	3	3
35–49	42	1.5	<1	1	1	1	2	3	3	5
50–64	42	1.3	<1	1	1	1	1	3	3	3
65+	22	1.4	<1	1	1	1	2	2	3	3
2. MULTIPLE DX										
0–19 Years	1	5.0	0	5	5	5	5	5	5	5
20–34	72	2.1	2	1	1	2	3	4	5	6
35–49	1,069	2.1	3	1	1	2	3	4	5	8
50–64	2,619	2.4	3	1	1	2	3	5	6	9
65+	4,353	2.8	5	1	1	2	3	5	7	12
TOTAL SINGLE DX	**113**	**1.4**	**<1**	**1**	**1**	**1**	**2**	**3**	**3**	**4**
TOTAL MULTIPLE DX	**8,114**	**2.6**	**4**	**1**	**1**	**2**	**3**	**5**	**6**	**10**
TOTAL										
0–19 Years	2	3.0	7	1	1	1	5	5	5	5
20–34	78	2.1	2	1	1	2	3	4	5	6
35–49	1,111	2.1	2	1	1	2	3	4	5	8
50–64	2,661	2.4	3	1	1	2	3	5	6	9
65+	4,375	2.8	5	1	1	2	3	5	7	12
GRAND TOTAL	**8,227**	**2.5**	**4**	**1**	**1**	**2**	**3**	**5**	**6**	**10**

89.45: PACEMAKER RATE CHECK

Type of Patients	Observed Patients	Avg. Stay	Vari-ance	Percentiles						
				10th	25th	50th	75th	90th	95th	99th
1. SINGLE DX										
0–19 Years	1	1.0	0	1	1	1	1	1	1	1
20–34	0									
35–49	0									
50–64	0									
65+	0									
2. MULTIPLE DX										
0–19 Years	1	1.0	0	1	1	1	1	1	1	1
20–34	3	2.9	6	1	1	2	6	6	6	6
35–49	2	1.0	0	1	1	1	1	1	1	1
50–64	15	2.7	8	1	1	2	3	5	7	14
65+	164	3.5	8	1	1	3	5	7	9	11
TOTAL SINGLE DX	**1**	**1.0**	**0**	**1**	**1**	**1**	**1**	**1**	**1**	**1**
TOTAL MULTIPLE DX	**185**	**3.4**	**8**	**1**	**1**	**3**	**5**	**7**	**8**	**13**
TOTAL										
0–19 Years	2	1.0	0	1	1	1	1	1	1	1
20–34	3	2.9	6	1	1	2	6	6	6	6
35–49	2	1.0	0	1	1	1	1	1	1	1
50–64	15	2.7	8	1	1	2	3	5	7	14
65+	164	3.5	8	1	1	3	5	7	9	11
GRAND TOTAL	**186**	**3.4**	**8**	**1**	**1**	**3**	**5**	**7**	**8**	**13**

89.5: OTHER CARDIAC FUNCT TEST

Type of Patients	Observed Patients	Avg. Stay	Vari-ance	Percentiles						
				10th	25th	50th	75th	90th	95th	99th
1. SINGLE DX										
0–19 Years	55	2.0	5	1	1	1	2	3	4	15
20–34	76	3.5	15	1	1	2	4	9	14	18
35–49	137	2.3	11	1	1	1	2	6	9	16
50–64	107	2.7	23	1	1	1	2	6	12	27
65+	40	1.5	<1	1	1	1	2	2	4	4
2. MULTIPLE DX										
0–19 Years	184	4.8	47	1	1	3	5	11	20	31
20–34	362	2.6	8	1	1	2	3	5	6	9
35–49	1,180	2.6	7	1	1	2	3	5	6	14
50–64	1,851	2.7	17	1	1	2	3	5	7	13
65+	2,976	3.2	6	1	1	3	4	6	8	13
TOTAL SINGLE DX	**415**	**2.5**	**13**	**1**	**1**	**1**	**2**	**5**	**11**	**19**
TOTAL MULTIPLE DX	**6,553**	**3.0**	**11**	**1**	**1**	**2**	**4**	**6**	**8**	**14**
TOTAL										
0–19 Years	239	4.1	38	1	1	2	4	9	15	28
20–34	438	2.7	9	1	1	2	3	5	7	15
35–49	1,317	2.5	7	1	1	2	3	5	6	14
50–64	1,958	2.7	17	1	1	2	3	5	7	13
65+	3,016	3.2	6	1	1	3	4	6	8	13
GRAND TOTAL	**6,968**	**3.0**	**11**	**1**	**1**	**2**	**4**	**6**	**8**	**15**

89.50: AMBULATORY CARD MONITOR

Type of Patients	Observed Patients	Avg. Stay	Vari-ance	Percentiles						
				10th	25th	50th	75th	90th	95th	99th
1. SINGLE DX										
0–19 Years	3	1.0	0	1	1	1	1	1	1	1
20–34	0									
35–49	0									
50–64	0									
65+	0									
2. MULTIPLE DX										
0–19 Years	4	9.6	96	1	2	2	22	22	22	22
20–34	5	2.7	8	1	1	2	2	8	8	8
35–49	5	3.5	2	2	3	3	3	6	6	6
50–64	13	3.1	4	1	1	3	4	6	8	8
65+	35	4.8	6	2	3	5	6	7	7	15
TOTAL SINGLE DX	**3**	**1.0**	**0**	**1**	**1**	**1**	**1**	**1**	**1**	**1**
TOTAL MULTIPLE DX	**62**	**4.6**	**14**	**1**	**2**	**4**	**6**	**7**	**11**	**22**
TOTAL										
0–19 Years	7	5.8	69	1	1	1	11	22	22	22
20–34	5	2.7	8	1	1	2	2	8	8	8
35–49	5	3.5	2	2	3	3	3	6	6	6
50–64	13	3.1	4	1	1	3	4	6	8	8
65+	35	4.8	6	2	3	5	6	7	7	15
GRAND TOTAL	**65**	**4.4**	**14**	**1**	**2**	**3**	**6**	**7**	**8**	**22**

89.51: RHYTHM ELECTROCARDIOGRAM

Type of Patients	Observed Patients	Avg. Stay	Vari-ance	Percentiles						
				10th	25th	50th	75th	90th	95th	99th
1. SINGLE DX										
0–19 Years	0									
20–34	0									
35–49	0									
50–64	0									
65+	0									
2. MULTIPLE DX										
0–19 Years	1	4.0	0	4	4	4	4	4	4	4
20–34	1	2.0	0	2	2	2	2	2	2	2
35–49	0									
50–64	2	2.2	<1	2	2	2	2	3	3	3
65+	6	2.4	2	1	1	3	3	5	5	5
TOTAL SINGLE DX	**0**									
TOTAL MULTIPLE DX	**10**	**2.4**	**1**	**1**	**1**	**2**	**3**	**4**	**5**	**5**
TOTAL										
0–19 Years	1	4.0	0	4	4	4	4	4	4	4
20–34	1	2.0	0	2	2	2	2	2	2	2
35–49	0									
50–64	2	2.2	<1	2	2	2	2	3	3	3
65+	6	2.4	2	1	1	3	3	5	5	5
GRAND TOTAL	**10**	**2.4**	**1**	**1**	**1**	**2**	**3**	**4**	**5**	**5**

89.52: ELECTROCARDIOGRAM

Type of Patients	Observed Patients	Avg. Stay	Vari-ance	Percentiles						
				10th	25th	50th	75th	90th	95th	99th
1. SINGLE DX										
0–19 Years	21	2.9	14	1	1	2	3	10	14	15
20–34	62	3.9	17	1	1	2	5	11	14	18
35–49	109	2.5	13	1	1	1	2	6	11	16
50–64	89	3.0	27	1	1	1	2	10	14	27
65+	27	1.3	<1	1	1	1	1	2	2	4
2. MULTIPLE DX										
0–19 Years	86	5.9	72	1	2	3	6	12	22	35
20–34	220	2.6	11	1	1	2	3	4	5	15
35–49	712	2.5	9	1	1	2	3	5	6	14
50–64	1,038	2.6	18	1	1	2	3	5	7	13
65+	1,032	3.0	6	1	1	2	4	6	8	15
TOTAL SINGLE DX	**308**	**2.8**	**17**	**1**	**1**	**1**	**2**	**7**	**12**	**22**
TOTAL MULTIPLE DX	**3,088**	**2.8**	**13**	**1**	**1**	**2**	**3**	**5**	**8**	**15**
TOTAL										
0–19 Years	107	5.3	62	1	1	3	5	11	20	35
20–34	282	2.9	13	1	1	2	3	5	8	16
35–49	821	2.5	9	1	1	2	3	5	6	16
50–64	1,127	2.7	19	1	1	2	3	5	7	19
65+	1,059	3.0	6	1	1	2	4	6	8	15
GRAND TOTAL	**3,396**	**2.8**	**14**	**1**	**1**	**2**	**3**	**5**	**8**	**15**

89.54: ECG MONITORING

Type of Patients	Observed Patients	Avg. Stay	Vari-ance	Percentiles						
				10th	25th	50th	75th	90th	95th	99th
1. SINGLE DX										
0–19 Years	13	1.7	1	1	1	1	3	3	4	4
20–34	11	1.6	<1	1	1	1	2	2	4	4
35–49	25	1.6	2	1	1	1	2	3	3	8
50–64	17	1.6	<1	1	1	1	2	3	4	4
65+	13	1.9	1	1	1	2	2	4	4	4
2. MULTIPLE DX										
0–19 Years	54	2.5	3	1	1	2	3	4	5	12
20–34	123	2.5	3	1	1	2	3	5	6	7
35–49	434	2.5	5	1	1	2	3	5	7	9
50–64	741	2.7	15	1	1	2	3	5	7	11
65+	1,700	3.3	6	1	1	3	4	6	8	11
TOTAL SINGLE DX	**79**	**1.7**	**1**	**1**	**1**	**1**	**2**	**3**	**4**	**4**
TOTAL MULTIPLE DX	**3,052**	**3.0**	**8**	**1**	**1**	**2**	**4**	**6**	**7**	**11**
TOTAL										
0–19 Years	67	2.3	3	1	1	2	3	4	5	6
20–34	134	2.4	3	1	1	2	3	5	6	7
35–49	459	2.5	5	1	1	2	3	5	7	9
50–64	758	2.7	15	1	1	2	3	5	7	11
65+	1,713	3.3	6	1	1	3	4	6	8	11
GRAND TOTAL	**3,131**	**3.0**	**8**	**1**	**1**	**2**	**4**	**6**	**7**	**11**

89.59: NONOP CARD/VASC EXAM NEC

Type of Patients	Observed Patients	Avg. Stay	Vari-ance	Percentiles						
				10th	25th	50th	75th	90th	95th	99th
1. SINGLE DX										
0–19 Years	18	1.5	<1	1	1	2	2	2	2	2
20–34	3	1.7	<1	1	1	2	2	2	2	2
35–49	3	2.4	1	1	1	3	3	3	3	3
50–64	1	1.0	0	1	1	1	1	1	1	1
65+	0									
2. MULTIPLE DX										
0–19 Years	39	5.3	45	1	2	2	5	15	22	31
20–34	12	3.0	3	1	2	2	4	6	7	7
35–49	29	3.3	6	1	2	2	4	7	7	14
50–64	53	3.8	10	1	2	3	4	8	11	18
65+	203	3.9	6	2	2	3	5	6	9	14
TOTAL SINGLE DX	**25**	**1.6**	**<1**	**1**	**1**	**2**	**2**	**2**	**2**	**3**
TOTAL MULTIPLE DX	**336**	**4.0**	**13**	**1**	**2**	**3**	**5**	**7**	**9**	**22**
TOTAL										
0–19 Years	57	4.0	32	1	1	2	4	9	16	28
20–34	15	2.8	3	1	2	2	4	6	7	7
35–49	32	3.2	6	1	2	3	4	7	7	14
50–64	54	3.8	10	1	2	3	4	8	11	18
65+	203	3.9	6	2	2	3	5	6	9	14
GRAND TOTAL	**361**	**3.8**	**12**	**1**	**2**	**3**	**5**	**7**	**9**	**18**

89.6: CIRCULATORY MONITORING

Type of Patients	Observed Patients	Avg. Stay	Vari-ance	Percentiles						
				10th	25th	50th	75th	90th	95th	99th
1. SINGLE DX										
0–19 Years	199	2.4	2	1	2	2	3	4	4	8
20–34	15	2.1	<1	1	2	2	3	3	4	4
35–49	18	2.2	3	1	1	2	3	6	6	6
50–64	13	2.9	1	2	2	3	4	4	5	5
65+	4	1.5	<1	1	1	1	1	3	3	3
2. MULTIPLE DX										
0–19 Years	522	6.0	56	1	2	3	6	15	23	35
20–34	194	4.5	18	1	2	3	5	10	13	22
35–49	412	5.8	47	1	2	4	7	12	17	27
50–64	710	6.0	34	2	3	5	8	12	15	23
65+	1,502	6.2	20	2	3	5	8	12	15	22
TOTAL SINGLE DX	**249**	**2.4**	**2**	**1**	**2**	**2**	**3**	**4**	**4**	**8**
TOTAL MULTIPLE DX	**3,340**	**6.0**	**32**	**2**	**3**	**4**	**7**	**12**	**16**	**26**
TOTAL										
0–19 Years	721	5.1	45	1	2	3	5	10	20	31
20–34	209	4.3	17	1	2	3	4	10	13	22
35–49	430	5.7	46	1	2	4	7	12	17	27
50–64	723	6.0	34	2	3	5	8	11	15	21
65+	1,506	6.2	20	2	3	5	8	12	15	22
GRAND TOTAL	**3,589**	**5.7**	**31**	**2**	**2**	**4**	**7**	**12**	**15**	**25**

89.62: CVP MONITORING

Type of Patients	Observed Patients	Avg. Stay	Vari-ance	Percentiles						
				10th	25th	50th	75th	90th	95th	99th
1. SINGLE DX										
0–19 Years	0									
20–34	1	2.0	0	2	2	2	2	2	2	2
35–49	0									
50–64	0									
65+	0									
2. MULTIPLE DX										
0–19 Years	11	12.7	91	7	7	7	20	27	27	42
20–34	11	5.3	27	2	2	3	6	10	21	21
35–49	31	7.9	25	4	4	6	11	16	20	20
50–64	34	9.5	190	3	3	6	11	16	17	94
65+	73	9.2	30	3	5	8	12	15	22	29
TOTAL SINGLE DX	**1**	**2.0**	**0**	**2**	**2**	**2**	**2**	**2**	**2**	**2**
TOTAL MULTIPLE DX	**160**	**9.2**	**71**	**3**	**4**	**7**	**11**	**17**	**21**	**30**
TOTAL										
0–19 Years	11	12.7	91	7	7	7	20	27	27	42
20–34	12	5.1	26	2	2	3	6	10	21	21
35–49	31	7.9	25	4	4	6	11	16	20	20
50–64	34	9.5	190	3	3	6	11	16	17	94
65+	73	9.2	30	3	5	8	12	15	22	29
GRAND TOTAL	**161**	**9.2**	**71**	**3**	**4**	**7**	**11**	**17**	**21**	**30**

89.64: PA WEDGE MONITORING

Type of Patients	Observed Patients	Avg. Stay	Vari-ance	Percentiles						
				10th	25th	50th	75th	90th	95th	99th
1. SINGLE DX										
0–19 Years	0									
20–34	1	3.0	0	3	3	3	3	3	3	3
35–49	2	1.3	<1	1	1	1	2	2	2	2
50–64	0									
65+	0									
2. MULTIPLE DX										
0–19 Years	3	2.8	9	1	1	1	7	7	7	7
20–34	21	8.4	27	1	4	9	12	14	15	19
35–49	60	9.5	144	1	3	6	11	19	27	65
50–64	145	8.0	42	2	4	7	11	15	16	23
65+	221	9.8	31	4	6	9	12	18	21	28
TOTAL SINGLE DX	**3**	**1.8**	**<1**	**1**	**1**	**2**	**3**	**3**	**3**	**3**
TOTAL MULTIPLE DX	**450**	**9.1**	**51**	**2**	**4**	**8**	**12**	**16**	**20**	**28**
TOTAL										
0–19 Years	3	2.8	9	1	1	1	7	7	7	7
20–34	22	8.1	27	1	3	9	12	14	15	19
35–49	62	9.3	142	1	3	6	11	19	27	65
50–64	145	8.0	42	2	4	7	11	15	16	23
65+	221	9.8	31	4	6	9	12	18	21	28
GRAND TOTAL	**453**	**9.0**	**51**	**2**	**4**	**8**	**12**	**16**	**20**	**28**

89.65: ARTERIAL BLD GAS MEASURE

Type of Patients	Observed Patients	Avg. Stay	Vari-ance	Percentiles						
				10th	25th	50th	75th	90th	95th	99th
1. SINGLE DX										
0–19 Years	196	2.4	2	1	2	2	3	4	4	8
20–34	12	2.0	<1	1	1	2	2	4	4	4
35–49	15	2.4	3	1	1	2	3	6	6	6
50–64	11	2.8	1	1	2	3	3	4	5	5
65+	3	1.6	1	1	1	1	3	3	3	3
2. MULTIPLE DX										
0–19 Years	462	5.4	49	1	2	3	6	12	19	33
20–34	140	3.7	14	1	2	3	4	7	8	25
35–49	254	4.1	14	1	2	3	5	8	12	22
50–64	416	4.6	13	1	2	4	6	8	11	18
65+	989	5.0	12	2	3	4	6	9	11	17
TOTAL SINGLE DX	**237**	**2.4**	**2**	**1**	**2**	**2**	**3**	**4**	**4**	**8**
TOTAL MULTIPLE DX	**2,261**	**4.9**	**20**	**1**	**2**	**4**	**6**	**9**	**12**	**23**
TOTAL										
0–19 Years	658	4.6	37	1	2	3	4	9	17	30
20–34	152	3.6	13	1	2	3	4	7	8	25
35–49	269	4.0	14	1	2	3	5	8	11	21
50–64	427	4.6	13	1	2	4	6	8	11	18
65+	992	5.0	12	2	3	4	6	9	11	17
GRAND TOTAL	**2,498**	**4.6**	**19**	**1**	**2**	**3**	**6**	**9**	**12**	**23**

89.68: CARDIAC OUTPUT MON NEC

Type of Patients	Observed Patients	Avg. Stay	Vari-ance	10th	25th	50th	75th	90th	95th	99th
1. SINGLE DX										
0–19 Years	0									
20–34	0									
35–49	0									
50–64	1	4.0	0	4	4	4	4	4	4	4
65+	1	1.0	0	1	1	1	1	1	1	1
2. MULTIPLE DX										
0–19 Years	7	3.1	3	1	2	3	4	7	7	7
20–34	14	5.5	22	2	2	4	7	14	15	15
35–49	45	5.6	14	2	3	5	7	10	15	17
50–64	88	6.3	29	2	3	6	8	10	16	21
65+	154	5.5	13	2	3	5	7	10	13	15
TOTAL SINGLE DX	**2**	**2.5**	**4**	**1**	**1**	**1**	**4**	**4**	**4**	**4**
TOTAL MULTIPLE DX	**308**	**5.7**	**18**	**2**	**3**	**5**	**7**	**10**	**14**	**20**
TOTAL										
0–19 Years	7	3.1	3	1	2	3	4	7	7	7
20–34	14	5.5	22	2	2	4	7	14	15	15
35–49	45	5.6	14	2	3	5	7	10	15	17
50–64	89	6.2	28	2	3	6	8	10	16	21
65+	155	5.5	13	2	3	5	7	10	13	15
GRAND TOTAL	**310**	**5.7**	**18**	**2**	**3**	**5**	**7**	**10**	**14**	**20**

89.7: GENERAL PHYSICAL EXAM

Type of Patients	Observed Patients	Avg. Stay	Vari-ance	10th	25th	50th	75th	90th	95th	99th
1. SINGLE DX										
0–19 Years	0									
20–34	1	1.0	0	1	1	1	1	1	1	1
35–49	0									
50–64	0									
65+	0									
2. MULTIPLE DX										
0–19 Years	2	3.0	3	1	1	4	4	4	4	4
20–34	0									
35–49	1	2.0	0	2	2	2	2	2	2	2
50–64	1	11.0	0	11	11	11	11	11	11	11
65+	0									
TOTAL SINGLE DX	**1**	**1.0**	**0**	**1**	**1**	**1**	**1**	**1**	**1**	**1**
TOTAL MULTIPLE DX	**4**	**4.5**	**16**	**1**	**2**	**4**	**4**	**11**	**11**	**11**
TOTAL										
0–19 Years	2	3.0	3	1	1	4	4	4	4	4
20–34	1	1.0	0	1	1	1	1	1	1	1
35–49	1	2.0	0	2	2	2	2	2	2	2
50–64	1	11.0	0	11	11	11	11	11	11	11
65+	0									
GRAND TOTAL	**5**	**3.7**	**14**	**1**	**1**	**2**	**4**	**11**	**11**	**11**

89.8: AUTOPSY

Type of Patients	Observed Patients	Avg. Stay	Vari-ance	10th	25th	50th	75th	90th	95th	99th
1. SINGLE DX										
0–19 Years	0									
20–34	0									
35–49	0									
50–64	0									
65+	0									
2. MULTIPLE DX										
0–19 Years	0									
20–34	0									
35–49	0									
50–64	0									
65+	0									
TOTAL SINGLE DX	**0**									
TOTAL MULTIPLE DX	**0**									
TOTAL										
0–19 Years	0									
20–34	0									
35–49	0									
50–64	0									
65+	0									
GRAND TOTAL	**0**									

90.0: MICRO EXAM-NERVOUS SYST

Type of Patients	Observed Patients	Avg. Stay	Vari-ance	10th	25th	50th	75th	90th	95th	99th
1. SINGLE DX										
0–19 Years	0									
20–34	0									
35–49	0									
50–64	0									
65+	0									
2. MULTIPLE DX										
0–19 Years	0									
20–34	0									
35–49	1	1.0	0	1	1	1	1	1	1	1
50–64	0									
65+	0									
TOTAL SINGLE DX	**0**									
TOTAL MULTIPLE DX	**1**	**1.0**	**0**	**1**	**1**	**1**	**1**	**1**	**1**	**1**
TOTAL										
0–19 Years	0									
20–34	0									
35–49	1	1.0	0	1	1	1	1	1	1	1
50–64	0									
65+	0									
GRAND TOTAL	**1**	**1.0**	**0**	**1**	**1**	**1**	**1**	**1**	**1**	**1**

90.1: MICRO EXAM-ENDOCRINE

Type of Patients	Observed Patients	Avg. Stay	Vari-ance	10th	25th	50th	75th	90th	95th	99th
1. SINGLE DX										
0–19 Years	0									
20–34	0									
35–49	0									
50–64	0									
65+	0									
2. MULTIPLE DX										
0–19 Years	0									
20–34	0									
35–49	0									
50–64	0									
65+	0									
TOTAL SINGLE DX	**0**									
TOTAL MULTIPLE DX	**0**									
TOTAL										
0–19 Years	0									
20–34	0									
35–49	0									
50–64	0									
65+	0									
GRAND TOTAL	**0**									

90.2: MICRO EXAM-EYE

Type of Patients	Observed Patients	Avg. Stay	Vari-ance	10th	25th	50th	75th	90th	95th	99th
1. SINGLE DX										
0–19 Years	1	2.0	0	2	2	2	2	2	2	2
20–34	0									
35–49	0									
50–64	0									
65+	0									
2. MULTIPLE DX										
0–19 Years	0									
20–34	1	3.0	0	3	3	3	3	3	3	3
35–49	0									
50–64	1	5.0	0	5	5	5	5	5	5	5
65+	0									
TOTAL SINGLE DX	**1**	**2.0**	**0**	**2**	**2**	**2**	**2**	**2**	**2**	**2**
TOTAL MULTIPLE DX	**2**	**4.0**	**2**	**3**	**3**	**3**	**5**	**5**	**5**	**5**
TOTAL										
0–19 Years	1	2.0	0	2	2	2	2	2	2	2
20–34	1	3.0	0	3	3	3	3	3	3	3
35–49	0									
50–64	1	5.0	0	5	5	5	5	5	5	5
65+	0									
GRAND TOTAL	**3**	**3.2**	**2**	**2**	**2**	**3**	**5**	**5**	**5**	**5**

90.3: MICRO EXAM-ENT/LARYNX

Type of Patients	Observed Patients	Avg. Stay	Vari-ance	10th	25th	50th	75th	90th	95th	99th
1. SINGLE DX										
0–19 Years	1	1.0	0	1	1	1	1	1	1	1
20–34	1	6.0	0	6	6	6	6	6	6	6
35–49	0									
50–64	1	27.0	0	27	27	27	27	27	27	27
65+	0									
2. MULTIPLE DX										
0–19 Years	1	2.0	0	2	2	2	2	2	2	2
20–34	3	2.3	2	1	1	2	4	4	4	4
35–49	0									
50–64	0									
65+	0									
TOTAL SINGLE DX	**3**	**10.6**	**156**	**1**	**1**	**6**	**27**	**27**	**27**	**27**
TOTAL MULTIPLE DX	**4**	**2.2**	**2**	**1**	**1**	**2**	**4**	**4**	**4**	**4**
TOTAL										
0–19 Years	2	1.6	<1	1	1	2	2	2	2	2
20–34	4	3.2	5	1	1	4	4	6	6	6
35–49	0									
50–64	1	27.0	0	27	27	27	27	27	27	27
65+	0									
GRAND TOTAL	**7**	**5.3**	**66**	**1**	**1**	**2**	**6**	**27**	**27**	**27**

90.4: MICRO EXAM-LOWER RESP

Type of Patients	Observed Patients	Avg. Stay	Vari-ance	10th	25th	50th	75th	90th	95th	99th
1. SINGLE DX										
0–19 Years	0									
20–34	0									
35–49	0									
50–64	0									
65+	0									
2. MULTIPLE DX										
0–19 Years	0									
20–34	1	1.0	0	1	1	1	1	1	1	1
35–49	3	13.3	176	5	5	6	29	29	29	29
50–64	2	5.9	2	5	5	5	7	7	7	7
65+	1	4.0	0	4	4	4	4	4	4	4
TOTAL SINGLE DX	**0**									
TOTAL MULTIPLE DX	**7**	**7.1**	**73**	**1**	**4**	**5**	**6**	**29**	**29**	**29**
TOTAL										
0–19 Years	0									
20–34	1	1.0	0	1	1	1	1	1	1	1
35–49	3	13.3	176	5	5	6	29	29	29	29
50–64	2	5.9	2	5	5	5	7	7	7	7
65+	1	4.0	0	4	4	4	4	4	4	4
GRAND TOTAL	**7**	**7.1**	**73**	**1**	**4**	**5**	**6**	**29**	**29**	**29**

90.5: MICRO EXAM-BLOOD

Type of Patients	Observed Patients	Avg. Stay	Vari-ance	Percentiles 10th	25th	50th	75th	90th	95th	99th
1. SINGLE DX										
0–19 Years	81	1.8	<1	1	1	2	2	2	3	6
20–34	1	2.0	0	2	2	2	2	2	2	2
35–49	0									
50–64	0									
65+	2	3.0	0	3	3	3	3	3	3	3
2. MULTIPLE DX										
0–19 Years	943	3.1	8	1	2	2	3	5	8	16
20–34	4	2.9	<1	2	2	3	4	4	4	4
35–49	8	3.2	9	1	1	3	3	11	11	11
50–64	13	4.0	22	2	2	3	4	4	20	20
65+	47	4.4	7	2	3	4	5	8	9	13
TOTAL SINGLE DX	**84**	**1.8**	**<1**	**1**	**1**	**2**	**2**	**3**	**3**	**6**
TOTAL MULTIPLE DX	**1,015**	**3.2**	**8**	**1**	**2**	**2**	**4**	**6**	**8**	**16**
TOTAL										
0–19 Years	1,024	3.0	7	1	2	2	3	5	8	15
20–34	5	2.7	<1	2	2	2	4	4	4	4
35–49	8	3.2	9	1	1	3	3	11	11	11
50–64	13	4.0	22	2	2	3	4	4	20	20
65+	49	4.3	7	2	3	4	5	8	9	13
GRAND TOTAL	**1,099**	**3.1**	**8**	**1**	**2**	**2**	**3**	**5**	**8**	**15**

90.52: CULTURE-BLOOD

Type of Patients	Observed Patients	Avg. Stay	Vari-ance	Percentiles 10th	25th	50th	75th	90th	95th	99th
1. SINGLE DX										
0–19 Years	78	1.8	<1	1	1	2	2	2	3	6
20–34	0									
35–49	0									
50–64	0									
65+	2	3.0	0	3	3	3	3	3	3	3
2. MULTIPLE DX										
0–19 Years	896	3.1	8	1	2	2	3	5	8	16
20–34	4	2.9	<1	2	2	3	4	4	4	4
35–49	7	3.3	10	1	1	3	3	11	11	11
50–64	13	4.0	22	2	2	3	4	4	20	20
65+	44	4.3	6	2	3	4	5	8	9	13
TOTAL SINGLE DX	**80**	**1.8**	**<1**	**1**	**1**	**2**	**2**	**3**	**3**	**6**
TOTAL MULTIPLE DX	**964**	**3.2**	**8**	**1**	**2**	**2**	**3**	**5**	**8**	**16**
TOTAL										
0–19 Years	974	3.0	7	1	2	2	3	5	7	16
20–34	4	2.9	<1	2	2	3	4	4	4	4
35–49	7	3.3	10	1	1	3	3	11	11	11
50–64	13	4.0	22	2	2	3	4	4	20	20
65+	46	4.3	6	2	3	4	5	8	9	13
GRAND TOTAL	**1,044**	**3.1**	**7**	**1**	**2**	**2**	**3**	**5**	**8**	**16**

90.59: MICRO EXAM NEC-BLOOD

Type of Patients	Observed Patients	Avg. Stay	Vari-ance	Percentiles 10th	25th	50th	75th	90th	95th	99th
1. SINGLE DX										
0–19 Years	1	2.0	0	2	2	2	2	2	2	2
20–34	1	2.0	0	2	2	2	2	2	2	2
35–49	0									
50–64	0									
65+	0									
2. MULTIPLE DX										
0–19 Years	1	5.0	0	5	5	5	5	5	5	5
20–34	0									
35–49	0									
50–64	0									
65+	2	2.3	5	1	1	1	5	5	5	5
TOTAL SINGLE DX	**2**	**2.0**	**0**	**2**	**2**	**2**	**2**	**2**	**2**	**2**
TOTAL MULTIPLE DX	**3**	**3.2**	**5**	**1**	**1**	**5**	**5**	**5**	**5**	**5**
TOTAL										
0–19 Years	2	3.7	3	2	2	5	5	5	5	5
20–34	1	2.0	0	2	2	2	2	2	2	2
35–49	0									
50–64	0									
65+	2	2.3	5	1	1	1	5	5	5	5
GRAND TOTAL	**5**	**2.8**	**3**	**1**	**1**	**2**	**5**	**5**	**5**	**5**

90.6: MICRO EXAM-SPLEEN/MARROW

Type of Patients	Observed Patients	Avg. Stay	Vari-ance	Percentiles 10th	25th	50th	75th	90th	95th	99th
1. SINGLE DX										
0–19 Years	0									
20–34	0									
35–49	0									
50–64	0									
65+	0									
2. MULTIPLE DX										
0–19 Years	1	2.0	0	2	2	2	2	2	2	2
20–34	0									
35–49	0									
50–64	0									
65+	0									
TOTAL SINGLE DX	**0**									
TOTAL MULTIPLE DX	**1**	**2.0**	**0**	**2**	**2**	**2**	**2**	**2**	**2**	**2**
TOTAL										
0–19 Years	1	2.0	0	2	2	2	2	2	2	2
20–34	0									
35–49	0									
50–64	0									
65+	0									
GRAND TOTAL	**1**	**2.0**	**0**	**2**	**2**	**2**	**2**	**2**	**2**	**2**

90.7: MICRO EXAM-LYMPH SYSTEM

Type of Patients	Observed Patients	Avg. Stay	Vari-ance	Percentiles						
				10th	25th	50th	75th	90th	95th	99th
1. SINGLE DX										
0–19 Years	0									
20–34	0									
35–49	0									
50–64	0									
65+	0									
2. MULTIPLE DX										
0–19 Years	0									
20–34	0									
35–49	1	7.0	0	7	7	7	7	7	7	7
50–64	0									
65+	0									
TOTAL SINGLE DX	**0**									
TOTAL MULTIPLE DX	**1**	**7.0**	**0**	**7**	**7**	**7**	**7**	**7**	**7**	**7**
TOTAL										
0–19 Years	0									
20–34	0									
35–49	1	7.0	0	7	7	7	7	7	7	7
50–64	0									
65+	0									
GRAND TOTAL	**1**	**7.0**	**0**	**7**	**7**	**7**	**7**	**7**	**7**	**7**

90.8: MICRO EXAM-UPPER GI

Type of Patients	Observed Patients	Avg. Stay	Vari-ance	Percentiles						
				10th	25th	50th	75th	90th	95th	99th
1. SINGLE DX										
0–19 Years	0									
20–34	0									
35–49	0									
50–64	0									
65+	0									
2. MULTIPLE DX										
0–19 Years	1	3.0	0	3	3	3	3	3	3	3
20–34	0									
35–49	0									
50–64	0									
65+	0									
TOTAL SINGLE DX	**0**									
TOTAL MULTIPLE DX	**1**	**3.0**	**0**	**3**	**3**	**3**	**3**	**3**	**3**	**3**
TOTAL										
0–19 Years	1	3.0	0	3	3	3	3	3	3	3
20–34	0									
35–49	0									
50–64	0									
65+	0									
GRAND TOTAL	**1**	**3.0**	**0**	**3**	**3**	**3**	**3**	**3**	**3**	**3**

90.9: MICRO EXAM-LOWER GI

Type of Patients	Observed Patients	Avg. Stay	Vari-ance	Percentiles						
				10th	25th	50th	75th	90th	95th	99th
1. SINGLE DX										
0–19 Years	0									
20–34	0									
35–49	0									
50–64	0									
65+	0									
2. MULTIPLE DX										
0–19 Years	6	2.4	<1	1	2	3	3	3	3	3
20–34	0									
35–49	0									
50–64	0									
65+	1	5.0	0	5	5	5	5	5	5	5
TOTAL SINGLE DX	**0**									
TOTAL MULTIPLE DX	**7**	**3.6**	**2**	**2**	**3**	**3**	**5**	**5**	**5**	**5**
TOTAL										
0–19 Years	6	2.4	<1	1	2	3	3	3	3	3
20–34	0									
35–49	0									
50–64	0									
65+	1	5.0	0	5	5	5	5	5	5	5
GRAND TOTAL	**7**	**3.6**	**2**	**2**	**3**	**3**	**5**	**5**	**5**	**5**

91.0: MICRO EXAM-BIL/PANCREAS

Type of Patients	Observed Patients	Avg. Stay	Vari-ance	Percentiles						
				10th	25th	50th	75th	90th	95th	99th
1. SINGLE DX										
0–19 Years	0									
20–34	0									
35–49	0									
50–64	0									
65+	0									
2. MULTIPLE DX										
0–19 Years	0									
20–34	0									
35–49	0									
50–64	0									
65+	0									
TOTAL SINGLE DX	**0**									
TOTAL MULTIPLE DX	**0**									
TOTAL										
0–19 Years	0									
20–34	0									
35–49	0									
50–64	0									
65+	0									
GRAND TOTAL	**0**									

91.1: MICRO EXAM-PERITONEUM

Type of Patients	Observed Patients	Avg. Stay	Vari- ance	Percentiles						
				10th	25th	50th	75th	90th	95th	99th
1. SINGLE DX										
0–19 Years	0									
20–34	0									
35–49	0									
50–64	0									
65+	0									
2. MULTIPLE DX										
0–19 Years	1	7.0	0	7	7	7	7	7	7	7
20–34	0									
35–49	0									
50–64	1	7.0	0	7	7	7	7	7	7	7
65+	0									
TOTAL SINGLE DX	**0**									
TOTAL MULTIPLE DX	**2**	**7.0**	**0**	**7**	**7**	**7**	**7**	**7**	**7**	**7**
TOTAL										
0–19 Years	1	7.0	0	7	7	7	7	7	7	7
20–34	0									
35–49	0									
50–64	1	7.0	0	7	7	7	7	7	7	7
65+	0									
GRAND TOTAL	**2**	**7.0**	**0**	**7**	**7**	**7**	**7**	**7**	**7**	**7**

91.2: MICRO EXAM-UPPER URINARY

Type of Patients	Observed Patients	Avg. Stay	Vari- ance	Percentiles						
				10th	25th	50th	75th	90th	95th	99th
1. SINGLE DX										
0–19 Years	0									
20–34	0									
35–49	0									
50–64	0									
65+	0									
2. MULTIPLE DX										
0–19 Years	0									
20–34	0									
35–49	1	7.0	0	7	7	7	7	7	7	7
50–64	0									
65+	0									
TOTAL SINGLE DX	**0**									
TOTAL MULTIPLE DX	**1**	**7.0**	**0**	**7**	**7**	**7**	**7**	**7**	**7**	**7**
TOTAL										
0–19 Years	0									
20–34	0									
35–49	1	7.0	0	7	7	7	7	7	7	7
50–64	0									
65+	0									
GRAND TOTAL	**1**	**7.0**	**0**	**7**	**7**	**7**	**7**	**7**	**7**	**7**

91.3: MICRO EXAM-LOWER URINARY

Type of Patients	Observed Patients	Avg. Stay	Vari- ance	Percentiles						
				10th	25th	50th	75th	90th	95th	99th
1. SINGLE DX										
0–19 Years	19	2.0	<1	1	1	2	3	3	3	3
20–34	15	2.2	6	1	1	1	2	6	10	10
35–49	0									
50–64	0									
65+	0									
2. MULTIPLE DX										
0–19 Years	98	2.4	4	1	1	2	3	4	6	13
20–34	31	4.0	25	1	1	2	4	11	13	24
35–49	10	2.1	1	1	1	2	3	3	4	4
50–64	9	8.9	76	2	3	3	11	27	27	27
65+	1	10.0	0	10	10	10	10	10	10	10
TOTAL SINGLE DX	**34**	**2.1**	**3**	**1**	**1**	**2**	**3**	**3**	**6**	**10**
TOTAL MULTIPLE DX	**149**	**3.1**	**14**	**1**	**1**	**2**	**3**	**6**	**11**	**24**
TOTAL										
0–19 Years	117	2.3	4	1	1	2	3	4	6	12
20–34	46	3.3	19	1	1	2	3	10	13	24
35–49	10	2.1	1	1	1	2	3	3	4	4
50–64	9	8.9	76	2	3	3	11	27	27	27
65+	1	10.0	0	10	10	10	10	10	10	10
GRAND TOTAL	**183**	**2.9**	**12**	**1**	**1**	**2**	**3**	**6**	**11**	**24**

91.4: MICRO EXAM-FEMALE GENIT

Type of Patients	Observed Patients	Avg. Stay	Vari- ance	Percentiles						
				10th	25th	50th	75th	90th	95th	99th
1. SINGLE DX										
0–19 Years	0									
20–34	0									
35–49	0									
50–64	0									
65+	0									
2. MULTIPLE DX										
0–19 Years	0									
20–34	3	1.7	<1	1	1	2	2	2	2	2
35–49	4	4.9	5	1	3	6	6	7	7	7
50–64	2	3.5	<1	3	3	3	4	4	4	4
65+	2	1.0	0	1	1	1	1	1	1	1
TOTAL SINGLE DX	**0**									
TOTAL MULTIPLE DX	**11**	**3.1**	**5**	**1**	**1**	**2**	**6**	**6**	**7**	**7**
TOTAL										
0–19 Years	0									
20–34	3	1.7	<1	1	1	2	2	2	2	2
35–49	4	4.9	5	1	3	6	6	7	7	7
50–64	2	3.5	<1	3	3	3	4	4	4	4
65+	2	1.0	0	1	1	1	1	1	1	1
GRAND TOTAL	**11**	**3.1**	**5**	**1**	**1**	**2**	**6**	**6**	**7**	**7**

91.5: MICRO EXAM-MS/JT FLUID

Type of Patients	Observed Patients	Avg. Stay	Vari-ance	10th	25th	50th	75th	90th	95th	99th
1. SINGLE DX										
0–19 Years	0									
20–34	0									
35–49	0									
50–64	0									
65+	0									
2. MULTIPLE DX										
0–19 Years	0									
20–34	0									
35–49	0									
50–64	0									
65+	2	4.6	4	3	3	6	6	6	6	6
TOTAL SINGLE DX	**0**									
TOTAL MULTIPLE DX	**2**	**4.6**	**4**	**3**	**3**	**6**	**6**	**6**	**6**	**6**
TOTAL										
0–19 Years	0									
20–34	0									
35–49	0									
50–64	0									
65+	2	4.6	4	3	3	6	6	6	6	6
GRAND TOTAL	**2**	**4.6**	**4**	**3**	**3**	**6**	**6**	**6**	**6**	**6**

91.6: MICRO EXAM-INTEGUMENT

Type of Patients	Observed Patients	Avg. Stay	Vari-ance	10th	25th	50th	75th	90th	95th	99th
1. SINGLE DX										
0–19 Years	0									
20–34	0									
35–49	0									
50–64	0									
65+	0									
2. MULTIPLE DX										
0–19 Years	2	2.5	<1	2	2	3	3	3	3	3
20–34	0									
35–49	2	3.0	1	2	2	4	4	4	4	4
50–64	2	5.0	2	4	4	4	6	6	6	6
65+	4	4.6	6	3	3	3	8	9	9	9
TOTAL SINGLE DX	**0**									
TOTAL MULTIPLE DX	**10**	**4.0**	**4**	**2**	**3**	**3**	**4**	**8**	**9**	**9**
TOTAL										
0–19 Years	2	2.5	<1	2	2	3	3	3	3	3
20–34	0									
35–49	2	3.0	1	2	2	4	4	4	4	4
50–64	2	5.0	2	4	4	4	6	6	6	6
65+	4	4.6	6	3	3	3	8	9	9	9
GRAND TOTAL	**10**	**4.0**	**4**	**2**	**3**	**3**	**4**	**8**	**9**	**9**

91.7: MICRO EXAM-OP WOUND

Type of Patients	Observed Patients	Avg. Stay	Vari-ance	10th	25th	50th	75th	90th	95th	99th
1. SINGLE DX										
0–19 Years	0									
20–34	1	3.0	0	3	3	3	3	3	3	3
35–49	0									
50–64	0									
65+	0									
2. MULTIPLE DX										
0–19 Years	0									
20–34	0									
35–49	1	18.0	0	18	18	18	18	18	18	18
50–64	0									
65+	0									
TOTAL SINGLE DX	**1**	**3.0**	**0**	**3**	**3**	**3**	**3**	**3**	**3**	**3**
TOTAL MULTIPLE DX	**1**	**18.0**	**0**	**18**	**18**	**18**	**18**	**18**	**18**	**18**
TOTAL										
0–19 Years	0									
20–34	1	3.0	0	3	3	3	3	3	3	3
35–49	1	18.0	0	18	18	18	18	18	18	18
50–64	0									
65+	0									
GRAND TOTAL	**2**	**10.8**	**105**	**3**	**3**	**18**	**18**	**18**	**18**	**18**

91.8: MICRO EXAM NEC

Type of Patients	Observed Patients	Avg. Stay	Vari-ance	10th	25th	50th	75th	90th	95th	99th
1. SINGLE DX										
0–19 Years	1	2.0	0	2	2	2	2	2	2	2
20–34	0									
35–49	0									
50–64	0									
65+	0									
2. MULTIPLE DX										
0–19 Years	2	2.6	<1	2	2	3	3	3	3	3
20–34	0									
35–49	0									
50–64	0									
65+	1	6.0	0	6	6	6	6	6	6	6
TOTAL SINGLE DX	**1**	**2.0**	**0**	**2**	**2**	**2**	**2**	**2**	**2**	**2**
TOTAL MULTIPLE DX	**3**	**4.1**	**4**	**2**	**3**	**3**	**6**	**6**	**6**	**6**
TOTAL										
0–19 Years	3	2.4	<1	2	2	2	3	3	3	3
20–34	0									
35–49	0									
50–64	0									
65+	1	6.0	0	6	6	6	6	6	6	6
GRAND TOTAL	**4**	**3.8**	**4**	**2**	**2**	**3**	**6**	**6**	**6**	**6**

91.9: MICRO EXAM NOS

Type of Patients	Observed Patients	Avg. Stay	Vari-ance	Percentiles 10th	25th	50th	75th	90th	95th	99th
1. SINGLE DX										
0–19 Years	0									
20–34	0									
35–49	0									
50–64	1	8.0	0	8	8	8	8	8	8	8
65+	0									
2. MULTIPLE DX										
0–19 Years	1	3.0	0	3	3	3	3	3	3	3
20–34	0									
35–49	0									
50–64	0									
65+	0									
TOTAL SINGLE DX	**1**	**8.0**	**0**	**8**	**8**	**8**	**8**	**8**	**8**	**8**
TOTAL MULTIPLE DX	**1**	**3.0**	**0**	**3**	**3**	**3**	**3**	**3**	**3**	**3**
TOTAL										
0–19 Years	1	3.0	0	3	3	3	3	3	3	3
20–34	0									
35–49	0									
50–64	1	8.0	0	8	8	8	8	8	8	8
65+	0									
GRAND TOTAL	**2**	**5.4**	**11**	**3**	**3**	**3**	**8**	**8**	**8**	**8**

92.0: ISOTOPE SCAN & FUNCTION

Type of Patients	Observed Patients	Avg. Stay	Vari-ance	Percentiles 10th	25th	50th	75th	90th	95th	99th
1. SINGLE DX										
0–19 Years	10	2.3	1	1	2	2	3	4	5	5
20–34	20	2.3	2	1	1	2	3	4	5	6
35–49	33	1.6	<1	1	1	1	2	3	4	4
50–64	26	1.6	1	1	1	1	2	2	2	7
65+	17	1.9	1	1	1	2	2	4	5	5
2. MULTIPLE DX										
0–19 Years	64	5.5	22	2	3	4	6	14	17	20
20–34	120	3.4	11	1	1	3	4	7	11	17
35–49	498	2.8	7	1	1	2	4	6	8	14
50–64	1,072	2.7	6	1	1	2	3	5	7	12
65+	1,816	3.4	10	1	1	2	4	7	9	14
TOTAL SINGLE DX	**106**	**1.9**	**1**	**1**	**1**	**2**	**2**	**4**	**4**	**6**
TOTAL MULTIPLE DX	**3,570**	**3.2**	**9**	**1**	**1**	**2**	**4**	**6**	**9**	**15**
TOTAL										
0–19 Years	74	5.1	21	2	2	4	6	14	17	20
20–34	140	3.2	10	1	1	2	4	6	10	17
35–49	531	2.7	6	1	1	2	3	6	7	13
50–64	1,098	2.7	6	1	1	2	3	5	7	12
65+	1,833	3.4	10	1	1	2	4	7	9	14
GRAND TOTAL	**3,676**	**3.1**	**9**	**1**	**1**	**2**	**4**	**6**	**9**	**15**

92.02: LIVER SCAN/ISOTOPE FUNCT

Type of Patients	Observed Patients	Avg. Stay	Vari-ance	Percentiles 10th	25th	50th	75th	90th	95th	99th
1. SINGLE DX										
0–19 Years	1	2.0	0	2	2	2	2	2	2	2
20–34	11	2.9	3	1	1	3	4	5	6	6
35–49	6	2.1	2	1	1	2	3	4	4	4
50–64	3	2.8	11	1	1	1	7	7	7	7
65+	4	2.5	<1	2	2	2	2	4	4	4
2. MULTIPLE DX										
0–19 Years	5	4.3	26	1	1	1	5	6	18	18
20–34	56	3.3	7	1	1	3	4	7	10	11
35–49	79	4.4	10	1	2	4	6	9	11	19
50–64	82	3.8	12	1	2	3	5	7	9	18
65+	157	5.2	10	2	3	4	7	10	11	14
TOTAL SINGLE DX	**25**	**2.6**	**3**	**1**	**1**	**2**	**4**	**5**	**6**	**7**
TOTAL MULTIPLE DX	**379**	**4.5**	**11**	**1**	**2**	**4**	**6**	**9**	**11**	**16**
TOTAL										
0–19 Years	6	4.0	23	1	1	2	5	6	18	18
20–34	67	3.3	6	1	1	3	4	6	10	11
35–49	85	4.2	10	1	2	4	5	8	11	19
50–64	85	3.8	12	1	2	3	5	7	8	18
65+	161	5.1	10	2	3	4	7	10	11	14
GRAND TOTAL	**404**	**4.4**	**10**	**1**	**2**	**4**	**6**	**9**	**10**	**16**

92.03: RENAL SCAN/ISOTOPE STUDY

Type of Patients	Observed Patients	Avg. Stay	Vari-ance	Percentiles 10th	25th	50th	75th	90th	95th	99th
1. SINGLE DX										
0–19 Years	2	3.6	<1	3	3	4	4	4	4	4
20–34	1	2.0	0	2	2	2	2	2	2	2
35–49	2	2.0	2	1	1	3	3	3	3	3
50–64	0									
65+	1	3.0	0	3	3	3	3	3	3	3
2. MULTIPLE DX										
0–19 Years	18	5.7	25	3	3	4	4	15	15	20
20–34	9	6.0	47	1	1	3	17	17	17	17
35–49	6	3.0	2	1	2	4	4	5	5	5
50–64	13	5.6	12	3	4	5	5	10	16	16
65+	54	6.4	13	3	4	6	8	11	14	21
TOTAL SINGLE DX	**6**	**2.7**	**1**	**1**	**2**	**3**	**3**	**4**	**4**	**4**
TOTAL MULTIPLE DX	**100**	**5.9**	**18**	**2**	**3**	**4**	**7**	**14**	**16**	**20**
TOTAL										
0–19 Years	20	5.6	23	3	3	4	4	15	15	20
20–34	10	5.8	44	1	1	2	4	17	17	17
35–49	8	2.8	2	1	2	3	4	5	5	5
50–64	13	5.6	12	3	4	5	5	10	16	16
65+	55	6.3	13	3	4	6	8	11	14	21
GRAND TOTAL	**106**	**5.8**	**18**	**2**	**3**	**4**	**7**	**12**	**16**	**20**

92.04: GI SCAN & ISOTOPE STUDY

Type of Patients	Observed Patients	Avg. Stay	Vari-ance	10th	25th	50th	75th	90th	95th	99th
1. SINGLE DX										
0–19 Years	4	1.6	<1	1	1	2	2	2	2	2
20–34	2	1.7	<1	1	1	2	2	2	2	2
35–49	1	4.0	0	4	4	4	4	4	4	4
50–64	1	2.0	0	2	2	2	2	2	2	2
65+	0									
2. MULTIPLE DX										
0–19 Years	30	5.6	21	2	2	4	7	14	14	20
20–34	15	3.2	4	1	1	3	4	6	8	8
35–49	27	5.0	15	1	3	4	6	11	12	19
50–64	27	4.8	16	1	2	4	5	7	18	18
65+	70	4.8	8	2	3	5	6	7	11	16
TOTAL SINGLE DX	**8**	**1.9**	**<1**	**1**	**1**	**2**	**2**	**4**	**4**	**4**
TOTAL MULTIPLE DX	**169**	**4.9**	**13**	**2**	**2**	**4**	**6**	**8**	**14**	**19**
TOTAL										
0–19 Years	34	5.2	20	2	2	4	6	14	14	20
20–34	17	3.0	4	1	1	2	4	6	8	8
35–49	28	5.0	14	1	3	4	6	9	12	19
50–64	28	4.6	16	1	2	4	5	7	18	18
65+	70	4.8	8	2	3	5	6	7	11	16
GRAND TOTAL	**177**	**4.7**	**13**	**2**	**2**	**4**	**6**	**8**	**13**	**19**

92.05: CV SCAN/ISOTOPE STUDY

Type of Patients	Observed Patients	Avg. Stay	Vari-ance	10th	25th	50th	75th	90th	95th	99th
1. SINGLE DX										
0–19 Years	1	5.0	0	5	5	5	5	5	5	5
20–34	5	1.2	<1	1	1	1	1	2	2	2
35–49	21	1.3	<1	1	1	1	1	2	3	3
50–64	20	1.4	<1	1	1	1	2	2	2	2
65+	12	1.6	1	1	1	1	2	2	5	5
2. MULTIPLE DX										
0–19 Years	6	6.0	34	1	3	4	5	17	17	17
20–34	31	2.9	8	1	1	2	3	6	11	13
35–49	371	2.4	5	1	1	2	3	5	6	12
50–64	939	2.5	4	1	1	2	3	5	6	10
65+	1,520	3.0	9	1	1	2	4	6	8	14
TOTAL SINGLE DX	**59**	**1.4**	**<1**	**1**	**1**	**1**	**2**	**2**	**3**	**5**
TOTAL MULTIPLE DX	**2,867**	**2.8**	**7**	**1**	**1**	**2**	**3**	**5**	**7**	**13**
TOTAL										
0–19 Years	7	5.9	30	1	3	4	5	17	17	17
20–34	36	2.6	7	1	1	1	3	6	11	13
35–49	392	2.3	5	1	1	2	3	5	6	12
50–64	959	2.4	4	1	1	2	3	5	6	10
65+	1,532	3.0	9	1	1	2	4	6	8	14
GRAND TOTAL	**2,926**	**2.8**	**7**	**1**	**1**	**2**	**3**	**5**	**7**	**13**

92.1: OTHER RADIOISOTOPE SCAN

Type of Patients	Observed Patients	Avg. Stay	Vari-ance	10th	25th	50th	75th	90th	95th	99th
1. SINGLE DX										
0–19 Years	31	4.0	15	1	1	3	5	7	7	21
20–34	12	4.7	24	1	2	4	5	16	16	16
35–49	17	3.4	7	1	1	3	4	6	8	12
50–64	13	3.3	4	1	2	3	4	7	8	8
65+	6	3.4	5	1	1	3	6	6	6	6
2. MULTIPLE DX										
0–19 Years	88	4.3	23	1	1	3	6	9	10	34
20–34	170	4.2	11	1	2	3	6	9	12	15
35–49	468	4.2	11	1	2	3	6	8	11	16
50–64	893	4.5	14	1	2	4	6	9	11	21
65+	1,907	4.9	13	2	3	4	6	9	11	19
TOTAL SINGLE DX	**79**	**3.8**	**12**	**1**	**2**	**3**	**5**	**7**	**8**	**21**
TOTAL MULTIPLE DX	**3,526**	**4.7**	**13**	**1**	**2**	**4**	**6**	**9**	**11**	**19**
TOTAL										
0–19 Years	119	4.2	21	1	1	3	6	7	10	29
20–34	182	4.3	12	1	2	3	6	9	12	15
35–49	485	4.2	11	1	2	3	6	8	11	16
50–64	906	4.5	14	1	2	3	6	9	11	21
65+	1,913	4.9	12	2	3	4	6	9	11	19
GRAND TOTAL	**3,605**	**4.7**	**13**	**1**	**2**	**4**	**6**	**9**	**11**	**19**

92.14: BONE SCAN

Type of Patients	Observed Patients	Avg. Stay	Vari-ance	10th	25th	50th	75th	90th	95th	99th
1. SINGLE DX										
0–19 Years	26	4.2	17	1	2	3	5	7	7	21
20–34	3	3.3	1	2	2	4	4	4	4	4
35–49	8	4.4	10	1	2	4	5	8	12	12
50–64	5	4.3	8	1	3	3	7	8	8	8
65+	1	3.0	0	3	3	3	3	3	3	3
2. MULTIPLE DX										
0–19 Years	59	4.3	14	1	2	4	6	9	10	15
20–34	28	6.4	14	3	4	5	8	13	15	15
35–49	102	5.6	13	2	3	4	8	11	14	15
50–64	212	6.0	19	2	3	5	8	11	16	22
65+	546	5.4	11	2	3	5	7	9	12	19
TOTAL SINGLE DX	**43**	**4.2**	**14**	**1**	**2**	**3**	**5**	**7**	**8**	**21**
TOTAL MULTIPLE DX	**947**	**5.5**	**14**	**2**	**3**	**5**	**7**	**10**	**13**	**21**
TOTAL										
0–19 Years	85	4.3	15	1	2	3	6	8	9	21
20–34	31	6.1	14	3	4	5	7	13	15	15
35–49	110	5.5	13	2	3	4	7	11	13	15
50–64	217	6.0	19	2	3	4	8	11	16	22
65+	547	5.4	11	2	3	5	7	9	12	19
GRAND TOTAL	**990**	**5.4**	**14**	**2**	**3**	**5**	**7**	**10**	**13**	**21**

92.15: PULMONARY SCAN

Type of Patients	Observed Patients	Avg. Stay	Vari- ance	Percentiles						
				10th	25th	50th	75th	90th	95th	99th
1. SINGLE DX										
0–19 Years	1	1.0	0	1	1	1	1	1	1	1
20–34	9	5.1	31	1	1	2	6	16	16	16
35–49	8	2.3	3	1	1	1	3	6	6	6
50–64	8	2.8	2	2	2	2	3	4	6	6
65+	5	3.5	6	1	1	3	6	6	6	6
2. MULTIPLE DX										
0–19 Years	16	3.4	9	1	1	2	6	6	7	13
20–34	133	3.6	9	1	1	2	5	8	11	14
35–49	347	3.7	9	1	2	3	5	7	9	16
50–64	653	4.0	11	1	2	3	5	7	9	18
65+	1,265	4.6	13	1	2	4	6	9	11	18
TOTAL SINGLE DX	**31**	**3.4**	**12**	**1**	**1**	**2**	**5**	**6**	**6**	**16**
TOTAL MULTIPLE DX	**2,414**	**4.3**	**12**	**1**	**2**	**3**	**6**	**8**	**11**	**18**
TOTAL										
0–19 Years	17	3.3	9	1	1	2	6	6	7	13
20–34	142	3.7	11	1	1	2	5	8	11	16
35–49	355	3.7	9	1	1	3	5	7	9	15
50–64	661	3.9	11	1	2	3	5	7	9	18
65+	1,270	4.6	13	1	2	4	6	9	11	18
GRAND TOTAL	**2,445**	**4.3**	**12**	**1**	**2**	**3**	**6**	**8**	**11**	**18**

92.18: TOTAL BODY SCAN

Type of Patients	Observed Patients	Avg. Stay	Vari- ance	Percentiles						
				10th	25th	50th	75th	90th	95th	99th
1. SINGLE DX										
0–19 Years	2	1.0	0	1	1	1	1	1	1	1
20–34	0									
35–49	1	3.0	0	3	3	3	3	3	3	3
50–64	0									
65+	0									
2. MULTIPLE DX										
0–19 Years	9	2.4	4	1	1	2	3	5	7	7
20–34	4	6.1	2	4	6	7	7	7	7	7
35–49	13	6.3	45	2	3	4	7	12	27	27
50–64	15	7.5	48	2	3	4	11	24	24	24
65+	66	5.7	12	2	4	5	7	10	14	15
TOTAL SINGLE DX	**3**	**1.6**	**1**	**1**	**1**	**1**	**3**	**3**	**3**	**3**
TOTAL MULTIPLE DX	**107**	**5.7**	**19**	**2**	**3**	**4**	**7**	**10**	**15**	**24**
TOTAL										
0–19 Years	11	2.2	4	1	1	1	3	5	7	7
20–34	4	6.1	2	4	6	7	7	7	7	7
35–49	14	6.1	42	2	3	4	7	12	27	27
50–64	15	7.5	48	2	3	4	11	24	24	24
65+	66	5.7	12	2	4	5	7	10	14	15
GRAND TOTAL	**110**	**5.6**	**19**	**1**	**3**	**4**	**7**	**10**	**14**	**24**

92.19: SCAN OF SITE NEC

Type of Patients	Observed Patients	Avg. Stay	Vari- ance	Percentiles						
				10th	25th	50th	75th	90th	95th	99th
1. SINGLE DX										
0–19 Years	1	2.0	0	2	2	2	2	2	2	2
20–34	0									
35–49	0									
50–64	0									
65+	0									
2. MULTIPLE DX										
0–19 Years	1	1.0	0	1	1	1	1	1	1	1
20–34	4	7.6	15	4	6	6	8	14	14	14
35–49	3	3.2	4	2	2	2	6	6	6	6
50–64	8	5.7	22	2	2	3	10	14	14	14
65+	18	5.7	11	2	3	5	8	9	15	15
TOTAL SINGLE DX	**1**	**2.0**	**0**	**2**	**2**	**2**	**2**	**2**	**2**	**2**
TOTAL MULTIPLE DX	**34**	**5.5**	**14**	**2**	**2**	**5**	**8**	**10**	**14**	**15**
TOTAL										
0–19 Years	2	1.5	<1	1	1	2	2	2	2	2
20–34	4	7.6	15	4	6	6	8	14	14	14
35–49	3	3.2	4	2	2	2	6	6	6	6
50–64	8	5.7	22	2	2	3	10	14	14	14
65+	18	5.7	11	2	3	5	8	9	15	15
GRAND TOTAL	**35**	**5.4**	**14**	**2**	**2**	**5**	**7**	**10**	**14**	**15**

92.2: THER RADIOLOGY & NU MED

Type of Patients	Observed Patients	Avg. Stay	Vari- ance	Percentiles						
				10th	25th	50th	75th	90th	95th	99th
1. SINGLE DX										
0–19 Years	12	1.8	<1	1	1	2	2	3	4	4
20–34	138	1.8	<1	1	1	2	2	3	3	5
35–49	287	1.8	<1	1	1	2	2	3	3	4
50–64	218	1.7	<1	1	1	1	2	3	3	4
65+	137	1.6	1	1	1	1	2	2	3	5
2. MULTIPLE DX										
0–19 Years	83	4.3	24	1	2	2	5	10	18	23
20–34	331	2.9	12	1	1	2	3	6	8	21
35–49	862	3.9	30	1	2	2	4	8	13	23
50–64	1,534	4.9	31	1	2	3	6	11	16	26
65+	1,958	5.4	31	1	2	4	7	12	15	28
TOTAL SINGLE DX	**792**	**1.7**	**<1**	**1**	**1**	**2**	**2**	**3**	**3**	**4**
TOTAL MULTIPLE DX	**4,768**	**4.8**	**30**	**1**	**2**	**3**	**6**	**10**	**15**	**26**
TOTAL										
0–19 Years	95	4.0	22	1	2	2	5	9	16	23
20–34	469	2.6	9	1	1	2	2	4	7	21
35–49	1,149	3.4	23	1	2	2	3	7	10	23
50–64	1,752	4.5	29	1	2	3	5	10	15	26
65+	2,095	5.1	30	1	2	3	7	11	15	27
GRAND TOTAL	**5,560**	**4.4**	**27**	**1**	**2**	**2**	**5**	**10**	**14**	**25**

92.23: ISOTOPE TELERADIOTHERAPY

Type of Patients	Observed Patients	Avg. Stay	Vari-ance	Percentiles						
				10th	25th	50th	75th	90th	95th	99th
1. SINGLE DX										
0–19 Years	0									
20–34	6	1.7	<1	1	1	2	2	2	2	2
35–49	12	1.5	<1	1	1	1	2	2	3	3
50–64	8	1.9	1	1	1	2	2	2	5	5
65+	2	5.8	36	2	2	2	12	12	12	12
2. MULTIPLE DX										
0–19 Years	6	3.1	8	1	1	1	5	7	7	7
20–34	22	1.8	<1	1	1	2	2	3	3	3
35–49	38	2.6	4	1	2	2	3	6	7	9
50–64	47	3.4	11	1	2	2	3	7	10	17
65+	34	5.9	27	2	3	4	7	16	18	24
TOTAL SINGLE DX	**28**	**2.0**	**4**	**1**	**1**	**2**	**2**	**2**	**5**	**12**
TOTAL MULTIPLE DX	**147**	**3.5**	**13**	**1**	**2**	**2**	**4**	**7**	**9**	**18**
TOTAL										
0–19 Years	6	3.1	8	1	1	1	5	7	7	7
20–34	28	1.8	<1	1	1	2	2	3	3	3
35–49	50	2.4	3	1	1	2	2	5	7	9
50–64	55	3.2	9	1	2	2	3	7	10	17
65+	36	5.9	27	2	3	4	7	12	17	24
GRAND TOTAL	**175**	**3.3**	**12**	**1**	**2**	**2**	**4**	**7**	**9**	**18**

92.24: PHOTON TELERADIOTHERAPY

Type of Patients	Observed Patients	Avg. Stay	Vari-ance	Percentiles						
				10th	25th	50th	75th	90th	95th	99th
1. SINGLE DX										
0–19 Years	0									
20–34	0									
35–49	2	1.5	<1	1	1	1	2	2	2	2
50–64	2	1.8	1	1	1	1	3	3	3	3
65+	0									
2. MULTIPLE DX										
0–19 Years	22	5.5	29	1	2	5	6	16	18	23
20–34	13	10.3	68	2	4	8	17	21	28	28
35–49	102	7.2	36	2	4	5	9	15	20	27
50–64	227	6.9	49	2	3	5	8	13	18	43
65+	327	7.8	51	2	3	6	9	16	23	39
TOTAL SINGLE DX	**4**	**1.7**	**<1**	**1**	**1**	**1**	**2**	**3**	**3**	**3**
TOTAL MULTIPLE DX	**691**	**7.4**	**48**	**2**	**3**	**5**	**9**	**15**	**21**	**39**
TOTAL										
0–19 Years	22	5.5	29	1	2	5	6	16	18	23
20–34	13	10.3	68	2	4	8	17	21	28	28
35–49	104	7.1	36	2	4	5	9	14	20	27
50–64	229	6.8	49	2	3	5	8	13	18	43
65+	327	7.8	51	2	3	6	9	16	23	39
GRAND TOTAL	**695**	**7.4**	**48**	**2**	**3**	**5**	**9**	**15**	**21**	**39**

92.26: PARTIC TELERADIOTX NEC

Type of Patients	Observed Patients	Avg. Stay	Vari-ance	Percentiles						
				10th	25th	50th	75th	90th	95th	99th
1. SINGLE DX										
0–19 Years	0									
20–34	0									
35–49	0									
50–64	0									
65+	1	3.0	0	3	3	3	3	3	3	3
2. MULTIPLE DX										
0–19 Years	1	12.0	0	12	12	12	12	12	12	12
20–34	2	5.6	<1	5	5	6	6	6	6	6
35–49	19	5.6	17	2	3	5	5	13	15	18
50–64	49	7.0	29	2	3	5	9	15	19	23
65+	57	7.9	18	3	5	7	12	13	14	22
TOTAL SINGLE DX	**1**	**3.0**	**0**	**3**	**3**	**3**	**3**	**3**	**3**	**3**
TOTAL MULTIPLE DX	**128**	**7.2**	**22**	**2**	**3**	**6**	**10**	**14**	**16**	**22**
TOTAL										
0–19 Years	1	12.0	0	12	12	12	12	12	12	12
20–34	2	5.6	<1	5	5	6	6	6	6	6
35–49	19	5.6	17	2	3	5	5	13	15	18
50–64	49	7.0	29	2	3	5	9	15	19	23
65+	58	7.8	18	3	4	7	12	13	14	22
GRAND TOTAL	**129**	**7.2**	**22**	**2**	**3**	**6**	**10**	**14**	**16**	**22**

92.27: RADIOACTIVE ELEMENT IMPL

Type of Patients	Observed Patients	Avg. Stay	Vari-ance	Percentiles						
				10th	25th	50th	75th	90th	95th	99th
1. SINGLE DX										
0–19 Years	2	1.5	<1	1	1	2	2	2	2	2
20–34	20	2.2	<1	1	2	2	3	3	3	5
35–49	71	1.9	<1	1	1	2	2	3	3	3
50–64	112	1.6	<1	1	1	1	2	3	3	3
65+	86	1.4	<1	1	1	1	2	2	3	3
2. MULTIPLE DX										
0–19 Years	1	2.0	0	2	2	2	2	2	2	2
20–34	35	2.5	1	1	2	2	3	4	4	7
35–49	137	2.3	3	1	1	2	3	4	6	9
50–64	351	2.1	4	1	1	2	3	3	4	10
65+	494	2.5	13	1	1	2	2	4	8	14
TOTAL SINGLE DX	**291**	**1.7**	**<1**	**1**	**1**	**2**	**2**	**3**	**3**	**3**
TOTAL MULTIPLE DX	**1,018**	**2.3**	**8**	**1**	**1**	**2**	**2**	**4**	**6**	**14**
TOTAL										
0–19 Years	3	1.7	<1	1	1	2	2	2	2	2
20–34	55	2.4	1	1	2	2	3	4	4	7
35–49	208	2.2	2	1	1	2	2	3	5	9
50–64	463	2.0	3	1	1	2	2	3	4	9
65+	580	2.3	11	1	1	1	2	4	7	14
GRAND TOTAL	**1,309**	**2.2**	**7**	**1**	**1**	**2**	**2**	**4**	**5**	**13**

92.28: ISOTOPE INJECT/INSTILL

Type of Patients	Observed Patients	Avg. Stay	Vari-ance	10th	25th	50th	75th	90th	95th	99th
				Percentiles						
1. SINGLE DX										
0–19 Years	3	1.6	<1	1	1	2	2	2	2	2
20–34	7	2.0	3	1	1	1	2	5	5	5
35–49	20	1.8	<1	1	1	2	2	3	3	4
50–64	9	1.2	<1	1	1	1	1	2	2	2
65+	5	2.0	<1	1	2	2	2	3	3	3
2. MULTIPLE DX										
0–19 Years	7	5.4	32	1	1	5	6	18	18	18
20–34	17	2.2	<1	2	2	2	2	3	3	4
35–49	32	2.8	3	1	2	2	4	5	6	11
50–64	48	2.1	2	1	1	2	2	5	5	8
65+	32	3.7	11	1	2	2	4	10	10	15
TOTAL SINGLE DX	**44**	**1.7**	**<1**	**1**	**1**	**2**	**2**	**3**	**3**	**5**
TOTAL MULTIPLE DX	**136**	**2.9**	**6**	**1**	**2**	**2**	**3**	**5**	**9**	**15**
TOTAL										
0–19 Years	10	3.9	22	1	1	2	6	6	18	18
20–34	24	2.1	<1	1	2	2	2	3	4	5
35–49	52	2.5	3	1	2	2	3	4	5	11
50–64	57	2.0	2	1	1	2	2	3	5	8
65+	37	3.4	10	1	2	2	3	9	10	15
GRAND TOTAL	**180**	**2.6**	**5**	**1**	**1**	**2**	**2**	**5**	**6**	**11**

92.29: RADIOTHERAPEUTIC PX NEC

Type of Patients	Observed Patients	Avg. Stay	Vari-ance	10th	25th	50th	75th	90th	95th	99th
				Percentiles						
1. SINGLE DX										
0–19 Years	7	2.0	<1	1	1	2	2	4	4	4
20–34	105	1.7	<1	1	1	2	2	2	3	4
35–49	182	1.8	<1	1	1	2	2	3	3	4
50–64	86	1.7	<1	1	1	2	2	3	3	3
65+	42	1.6	1	1	1	1	2	2	2	9
2. MULTIPLE DX										
0–19 Years	42	3.6	15	1	2	2	4	9	11	19
20–34	241	2.7	9	1	1	2	3	4	8	21
35–49	527	3.8	37	1	2	2	4	8	11	24
50–64	788	5.7	36	1	2	4	7	13	17	29
65+	990	6.0	28	2	3	4	8	12	15	28
TOTAL SINGLE DX	**422**	**1.7**	**<1**	**1**	**1**	**2**	**2**	**3**	**3**	**4**
TOTAL MULTIPLE DX	**2,588**	**5.2**	**32**	**1**	**2**	**3**	**7**	**11**	**15**	**27**
TOTAL										
0–19 Years	49	3.3	13	1	2	2	3	6	10	19
20–34	346	2.3	7	1	1	2	2	4	7	14
35–49	709	3.3	28	1	1	2	3	7	10	20
50–64	874	5.3	34	1	2	3	7	12	16	29
65+	1,032	5.8	28	2	2	4	8	12	15	28
GRAND TOTAL	**3,010**	**4.7**	**29**	**1**	**2**	**3**	**6**	**10**	**14**	**25**

92.3: STEREOTACTIC RADIOSURG

Type of Patients	Observed Patients	Avg. Stay	Vari-ance	10th	25th	50th	75th	90th	95th	99th
				Percentiles						
1. SINGLE DX										
0–19 Years	2	2.0	1	1	1	3	3	3	3	3
20–34	1	1.0	0	1	1	1	1	1	1	1
35–49	17	1.1	<1	1	1	1	1	1	1	3
50–64	30	1.0	<1	1	1	1	1	1	1	4
65+	18	1.0	0	1	1	1	1	1	1	1
2. MULTIPLE DX										
0–19 Years	9	3.9	11	1	2	4	4	4	15	15
20–34	16	2.4	4	1	1	1	4	4	6	9
35–49	47	1.5	3	1	1	1	1	2	3	13
50–64	95	2.3	14	1	1	1	1	6	7	21
65+	127	1.5	5	1	1	1	1	2	4	11
TOTAL SINGLE DX	**68**	**1.1**	**<1**	**1**	**1**	**1**	**1**	**1**	**1**	**3**
TOTAL MULTIPLE DX	**294**	**1.8**	**8**	**1**	**1**	**1**	**1**	**4**	**6**	**21**
TOTAL										
0–19 Years	11	3.7	11	1	2	4	4	4	15	15
20–34	17	2.3	4	1	1	1	4	4	6	9
35–49	64	1.4	2	1	1	1	1	2	3	12
50–64	125	1.9	10	1	1	1	1	3	7	21
65+	145	1.4	5	1	1	1	1	1	3	11
GRAND TOTAL	**362**	**1.7**	**6**	**1**	**1**	**1**	**1**	**3**	**5**	**15**

92.32: MULTI-SOURCE PHOTON SURG

Type of Patients	Observed Patients	Avg. Stay	Vari-ance	10th	25th	50th	75th	90th	95th	99th
				Percentiles						
1. SINGLE DX										
0–19 Years	1	1.0	0	1	1	1	1	1	1	1
20–34	1	1.0	0	1	1	1	1	1	1	1
35–49	15	1.0	0	1	1	1	1	1	1	1
50–64	26	1.0	0	1	1	1	1	1	1	1
65+	17	1.0	0	1	1	1	1	1	1	1
2. MULTIPLE DX										
0–19 Years	2	1.0	0	1	1	1	1	1	1	1
20–34	12	2.1	2	1	1	1	4	4	4	4
35–49	37	1.1	<1	1	1	1	1	1	1	2
50–64	79	1.9	13	1	1	1	1	2	7	21
65+	111	1.5	5	1	1	1	1	1	3	11
TOTAL SINGLE DX	**60**	**1.0**	**0**	**1**	**1**	**1**	**1**	**1**	**1**	**1**
TOTAL MULTIPLE DX	**241**	**1.6**	**7**	**1**	**1**	**1**	**1**	**1**	**4**	**21**
TOTAL										
0–19 Years	3	1.0	0	1	1	1	1	1	1	1
20–34	13	2.0	2	1	1	1	4	4	4	4
35–49	52	1.0	<1	1	1	1	1	1	1	2
50–64	105	1.6	8	1	1	1	1	1	2	21
65+	128	1.4	5	1	1	1	1	1	3	11
GRAND TOTAL	**301**	**1.4**	**5**	**1**	**1**	**1**	**1**	**1**	**3**	**11**

93.0: DXTIC PHYSICAL TX

Type of Patients	Observed Patients	Avg. Stay	Vari-ance	10th	25th	50th	75th	90th	95th	99th
1. SINGLE DX										
0–19 Years	5	1.9	<1	1	2	2	2	2	2	2
20–34	7	2.5	1	1	2	2	3	4	4	4
35–49	1	1.0	0	1	1	1	1	1	1	1
50–64	6	4.9	3	2	3	6	6	6	6	6
65+	5	3.0	6	1	1	2	3	7	7	7
2. MULTIPLE DX										
0–19 Years	51	8.0	55	2	2	4	11	20	22	23
20–34	36	4.0	9	2	2	3	5	7	8	17
35–49	65	5.6	28	2	2	5	8	10	12	42
50–64	116	5.6	40	1	2	4	6	14	22	29
65+	414	6.3	50	2	3	4	7	13	18	48
TOTAL SINGLE DX	**24**	**3.2**	**4**	**1**	**2**	**2**	**6**	**6**	**6**	**7**
TOTAL MULTIPLE DX	**682**	**6.2**	**46**	**2**	**2**	**4**	**7**	**13**	**20**	**47**
TOTAL										
0–19 Years	56	7.5	53	1	2	4	11	20	22	23
20–34	43	3.8	8	2	2	3	5	7	8	17
35–49	66	5.6	28	2	2	5	8	10	11	42
50–64	122	5.5	37	1	2	4	6	12	17	29
65+	419	6.3	50	2	3	4	7	13	18	48
GRAND TOTAL	**706**	**6.1**	**44**	**2**	**2**	**4**	**7**	**13**	**20**	**47**

93.01: FUNCTIONAL PT EVALUATION

Type of Patients	Observed Patients	Avg. Stay	Vari-ance	10th	25th	50th	75th	90th	95th	99th
1. SINGLE DX										
0–19 Years	4	2.0	0	2	2	2	2	2	2	2
20–34	3	2.7	<1	2	2	3	3	3	3	3
35–49	0									
50–64	2	4.5	6	2	2	6	6	6	6	6
65+	3	3.5	9	1	1	2	7	7	7	7
2. MULTIPLE DX										
0–19 Years	45	8.3	59	2	2	5	19	20	22	23
20–34	29	4.4	12	1	2	3	6	8	12	17
35–49	54	5.4	30	2	2	4	7	10	11	42
50–64	91	5.8	44	1	2	4	7	15	22	29
65+	381	6.2	53	2	3	4	6	12	20	48
TOTAL SINGLE DX	**12**	**2.9**	**3**	**2**	**2**	**2**	**3**	**6**	**7**	**7**
TOTAL MULTIPLE DX	**600**	**6.2**	**49**	**2**	**2**	**4**	**7**	**13**	**20**	**48**
TOTAL										
0–19 Years	49	7.8	57	2	2	4	11	20	22	23
20–34	32	4.2	11	1	2	3	6	7	12	17
35–49	54	5.4	30	2	2	4	7	10	11	42
50–64	93	5.8	43	1	2	4	6	15	22	29
65+	384	6.2	52	2	3	4	7	12	20	48
GRAND TOTAL	**612**	**6.2**	**48**	**2**	**2**	**4**	**7**	**13**	**20**	**48**

93.08: ELECTROMYOGRAPHY

Type of Patients	Observed Patients	Avg. Stay	Vari-ance	10th	25th	50th	75th	90th	95th	99th
1. SINGLE DX										
0–19 Years	0									
20–34	3	2.4	2	1	1	2	4	4	4	4
35–49	0									
50–64	1	6.0	0	6	6	6	6	6	6	6
65+	1	3.0	0	3	3	3	3	3	3	3
2. MULTIPLE DX										
0–19 Years	2	6.2	6	4	4	8	8	8	8	8
20–34	5	3.3	3	2	2	3	4	6	6	6
35–49	8	7.7	10	4	5	8	8	14	14	14
50–64	15	6.5	30	2	3	5	6	14	22	22
65+	29	8.0	21	3	4	8	10	17	18	18
TOTAL SINGLE DX	**5**	**4.3**	**4**	**1**	**3**	**6**	**6**	**6**	**6**	**6**
TOTAL MULTIPLE DX	**59**	**7.1**	**21**	**2**	**4**	**6**	**9**	**14**	**18**	**22**
TOTAL										
0–19 Years	2	6.2	6	4	4	8	8	8	8	8
20–34	8	2.9	2	1	2	2	4	6	6	6
35–49	8	7.7	10	4	5	8	8	14	14	14
50–64	16	6.4	23	2	3	6	6	14	14	22
65+	30	7.8	21	3	4	8	10	17	18	18
GRAND TOTAL	**64**	**6.8**	**19**	**2**	**4**	**6**	**9**	**14**	**17**	**22**

93.1: PT EXERCISES

Type of Patients	Observed Patients	Avg. Stay	Vari-ance	10th	25th	50th	75th	90th	95th	99th
1. SINGLE DX										
0–19 Years	3	1.6	<1	1	1	1	2	3	3	3
20–34	1	2.0	0	2	2	2	2	2	2	2
35–49	3	1.7	<1	1	1	2	2	2	2	2
50–64	4	2.4	3	1	1	3	3	5	5	5
65+	3	1.8	<1	1	1	2	2	3	3	3
2. MULTIPLE DX										
0–19 Years	2	2.4	5	1	1	1	5	5	5	5
20–34	1	1.0	0	1	1	1	1	1	1	1
35–49	27	2.6	6	1	2	2	3	4	5	16
50–64	55	2.1	5	1	1	2	2	3	5	19
65+	72	5.1	89	1	1	2	5	10	14	73
TOTAL SINGLE DX	**14**	**1.9**	**1**	**1**	**1**	**2**	**3**	**3**	**3**	**5**
TOTAL MULTIPLE DX	**157**	**3.5**	**44**	**1**	**1**	**2**	**3**	**6**	**10**	**48**
TOTAL										
0–19 Years	5	1.9	2	1	1	1	3	5	5	5
20–34	2	1.5	<1	1	1	1	2	2	2	2
35–49	30	2.5	6	1	2	2	2	4	4	16
50–64	59	2.1	5	1	1	2	2	3	5	19
65+	75	4.9	85	1	1	2	5	9	14	73
GRAND TOTAL	**171**	**3.4**	**41**	**1**	**1**	**2**	**3**	**6**	**9**	**22**

93.16: JOINT MOBILIZATION NEC

Type of Patients	Observed Patients	Avg. Stay	Variance	Percentiles						
				10th	25th	50th	75th	90th	95th	99th
1. SINGLE DX										
0–19 Years	3	1.6	<1	1	1	1	2	3	3	3
20–34	1	2.0	0	2	2	2	2	2	2	2
35–49	3	1.7	<1	1	1	2	2	2	2	2
50–64	4	2.4	3	1	1	3	3	5	5	5
65+	3	1.8	<1	1	1	2	2	3	3	3
2. MULTIPLE DX										
0–19 Years	1	1.0	0	1	1	1	1	1	1	1
20–34	1	1.0	0	1	1	1	1	1	1	1
35–49	26	2.2	<1	1	2	2	2	4	4	5
50–64	52	1.9	1	1	1	2	2	3	3	7
65+	52	2.4	3	1	1	2	3	6	6	6
TOTAL SINGLE DX	**14**	**1.9**	**1**	**1**	**1**	**2**	**3**	**3**	**3**	**5**
TOTAL MULTIPLE DX	**132**	**2.1**	**2**	**1**	**1**	**2**	**2**	**4**	**6**	**6**
TOTAL										
0–19 Years	4	1.5	<1	1	1	1	2	3	3	3
20–34	2	1.5	<1	1	1	1	2	2	2	2
35–49	29	2.2	<1	1	2	2	2	4	4	5
50–64	56	1.9	1	1	1	2	2	3	5	7
65+	55	2.3	2	1	1	2	3	6	6	6
GRAND TOTAL	**146**	**2.1**	**2**	**1**	**1**	**2**	**2**	**3**	**5**	**6**

93.2: OTH PT MS MANIPULATION

Type of Patients	Observed Patients	Avg. Stay	Variance	Percentiles						
				10th	25th	50th	75th	90th	95th	99th
1. SINGLE DX										
0–19 Years	2	1.4	<1	1	1	1	2	2	2	2
20–34	5	2.6	<1	2	2	2	3	4	4	4
35–49	8	2.4	7	1	1	1	3	8	8	8
50–64	20	2.0	<1	1	1	2	2	3	4	4
65+	4	2.0	0	2	2	2	2	2	2	2
2. MULTIPLE DX										
0–19 Years	18	3.4	19	1	2	2	3	3	18	18
20–34	15	4.5	92	1	1	1	4	7	11	47
35–49	67	3.7	20	1	1	2	4	8	12	25
50–64	131	3.1	8	1	1	2	3	6	8	16
65+	290	6.1	38	1	2	4	7	14	17	30
TOTAL SINGLE DX	**39**	**2.1**	**2**	**1**	**1**	**2**	**2**	**4**	**4**	**8**
TOTAL MULTIPLE DX	**521**	**4.9**	**31**	**1**	**2**	**3**	**6**	**11**	**16**	**30**
TOTAL										
0–19 Years	20	3.2	18	1	2	2	3	3	18	18
20–34	20	4.1	72	1	1	2	3	7	11	47
35–49	75	3.5	19	1	1	2	4	8	11	25
50–64	151	3.0	8	1	1	2	3	6	8	16
65+	294	6.0	38	1	2	4	7	14	17	30
GRAND TOTAL	**560**	**4.8**	**30**	**1**	**2**	**3**	**6**	**11**	**16**	**30**

93.22: AMB & GAIT TRAINING

Type of Patients	Observed Patients	Avg. Stay	Variance	Percentiles						
				10th	25th	50th	75th	90th	95th	99th
1. SINGLE DX										
0–19 Years	1	2.0	0	2	2	2	2	2	2	2
20–34	0									
35–49	0									
50–64	2	2.5	<1	2	2	2	3	3	3	3
65+	0									
2. MULTIPLE DX										
0–19 Years	6	5.2	50	1	1	2	3	18	18	18
20–34	3	19.4	575	1	1	11	47	47	47	47
35–49	13	5.1	21	1	1	3	8	12	15	15
50–64	29	5.8	16	2	3	6	7	10	15	21
65+	200	7.4	37	2	4	6	9	16	18	24
TOTAL SINGLE DX	**3**	**2.3**	**<1**	**2**	**2**	**2**	**3**	**3**	**3**	**3**
TOTAL MULTIPLE DX	**251**	**7.1**	**39**	**2**	**3**	**5**	**9**	**15**	**18**	**24**
TOTAL										
0–19 Years	7	4.9	46	1	1	2	3	18	18	18
20–34	3	19.4	575	1	1	11	47	47	47	47
35–49	13	5.1	21	1	1	3	8	12	15	15
50–64	31	5.7	15	2	3	6	7	10	13	21
65+	200	7.4	37	2	4	6	9	16	18	24
GRAND TOTAL	**254**	**7.1**	**38**	**2**	**3**	**5**	**9**	**15**	**18**	**24**

93.26: MANUAL RUPT JOINT ADHES

Type of Patients	Observed Patients	Avg. Stay	Variance	Percentiles						
				10th	25th	50th	75th	90th	95th	99th
1. SINGLE DX										
0–19 Years	1	1.0	0	1	1	1	1	1	1	1
20–34	4	2.7	<1	2	2	2	3	4	4	4
35–49	4	1.7	<1	1	1	1	2	3	3	3
50–64	16	1.8	<1	1	1	2	2	3	4	4
65+	3	2.0	0	2	2	2	2	2	2	2
2. MULTIPLE DX										
0–19 Years	0									
20–34	9	2.0	2	1	1	1	3	5	5	5
35–49	41	2.4	5	1	1	1	3	5	6	11
50–64	89	2.3	3	1	1	2	3	4	4	10
65+	69	2.3	2	1	1	2	3	4	5	6
TOTAL SINGLE DX	**28**	**1.9**	**<1**	**1**	**1**	**2**	**2**	**3**	**4**	**4**
TOTAL MULTIPLE DX	**208**	**2.3**	**3**	**1**	**1**	**2**	**3**	**4**	**5**	**11**
TOTAL										
0–19 Years	1	1.0	0	1	1	1	1	1	1	1
20–34	13	2.2	2	1	1	2	3	4	5	5
35–49	45	2.3	5	1	1	1	3	4	6	11
50–64	105	2.2	3	1	1	2	3	4	4	10
65+	72	2.3	2	1	1	2	3	4	5	6
GRAND TOTAL	**236**	**2.3**	**3**	**1**	**1**	**2**	**3**	**4**	**5**	**11**

93.3: OTHER PT THERAPEUTIC PX

Type of Patients	Observed Patients	Avg. Stay	Vari-ance	Percentiles 10th	25th	50th	75th	90th	95th	99th
1. SINGLE DX										
0–19 Years	23	3.4	6	1	2	3	4	8	9	10
20–34	11	4.0	4	1	2	4	6	6	6	6
35–49	13	3.0	6	2	2	2	3	4	13	13
50–64	8	6.6	9	3	4	6	10	10	10	10
65+	16	5.3	16	2	3	4	5	10	16	16
2. MULTIPLE DX										
0–19 Years	141	7.8	60	2	3	5	10	20	22	44
20–34	153	9.6	107	2	4	7	12	22	29	60
35–49	403	9.6	95	2	4	7	11	22	27	53
50–64	1,071	10.0	70	2	4	7	13	21	27	37
65+	5,046	9.5	59	3	4	7	13	19	23	36
TOTAL SINGLE DX	**71**	**4.1**	**9**	**1**	**2**	**3**	**5**	**9**	**10**	**16**
TOTAL MULTIPLE DX	**6,814**	**9.5**	**63**	**3**	**4**	**7**	**13**	**19**	**24**	**39**
TOTAL										
0–19 Years	164	7.1	55	2	3	5	9	18	22	44
20–34	164	9.2	102	2	4	6	10	22	29	60
35–49	416	9.4	93	2	3	6	11	21	27	53
50–64	1,079	10.0	70	2	4	7	13	21	27	37
65+	5,062	9.5	59	3	4	7	13	19	23	36
GRAND TOTAL	**6,885**	**9.5**	**63**	**3**	**4**	**7**	**13**	**19**	**24**	**38**

93.32: WHIRLPOOL TREATMENT

Type of Patients	Observed Patients	Avg. Stay	Vari-ance	Percentiles 10th	25th	50th	75th	90th	95th	99th
1. SINGLE DX										
0–19 Years	0									
20–34	0									
35–49	3	5.9	29	3	3	3	13	13	13	13
50–64	1	5.0	0	5	5	5	5	5	5	5
65+	1	10.0	0	10	10	10	10	10	10	10
2. MULTIPLE DX										
0–19 Years	3	6.7	11	2	6	6	10	10	10	10
20–34	10	4.4	4	3	3	4	5	7	9	9
35–49	33	5.0	11	2	3	4	7	11	11	17
50–64	33	6.4	20	2	4	6	8	11	11	31
65+	36	8.9	32	4	5	6	11	16	23	23
TOTAL SINGLE DX	**5**	**6.4**	**18**	**3**	**3**	**5**	**10**	**13**	**13**	**13**
TOTAL MULTIPLE DX	**115**	**6.9**	**23**	**3**	**4**	**6**	**9**	**12**	**16**	**23**
TOTAL										
0–19 Years	3	6.7	11	2	6	6	10	10	10	10
20–34	10	4.4	4	3	3	4	5	7	9	9
35–49	36	5.1	12	2	3	4	7	11	11	17
50–64	34	6.4	20	2	4	6	8	11	11	31
65+	37	8.9	31	4	5	6	11	16	23	23
GRAND TOTAL	**120**	**6.9**	**23**	**3**	**4**	**6**	**9**	**12**	**16**	**23**

93.38: COMBINED PT NOS

Type of Patients	Observed Patients	Avg. Stay	Vari-ance	Percentiles 10th	25th	50th	75th	90th	95th	99th
1. SINGLE DX										
0–19 Years	0									
20–34	0									
35–49	0									
50–64	2	6.5	12	4	4	4	9	9	9	9
65+	1	2.0	0	2	2	2	2	2	2	2
2. MULTIPLE DX										
0–19 Years	3	4.1	3	2	2	4	6	6	6	6
20–34	7	13.2	64	2	4	15	18	25	25	25
35–49	29	9.9	44	4	5	7	16	21	22	27
50–64	84	10.2	62	4	5	7	15	21	27	38
65+	318	9.1	57	2	5	8	11	18	22	28
TOTAL SINGLE DX	**3**	**4.8**	**12**	**2**	**2**	**4**	**9**	**9**	**9**	**9**
TOTAL MULTIPLE DX	**441**	**9.3**	**57**	**3**	**5**	**7**	**11**	**19**	**23**	**30**
TOTAL										
0–19 Years	3	4.1	3	2	2	4	6	6	6	6
20–34	7	13.2	64	2	4	15	18	25	25	25
35–49	29	9.9	44	4	5	7	16	21	22	27
50–64	86	10.1	61	4	5	7	15	21	27	38
65+	319	9.1	57	2	5	8	11	18	22	28
GRAND TOTAL	**444**	**9.3**	**57**	**3**	**5**	**7**	**11**	**19**	**23**	**30**

93.39: PHYSICAL THERAPY NEC

Type of Patients	Observed Patients	Avg. Stay	Vari-ance	Percentiles 10th	25th	50th	75th	90th	95th	99th
1. SINGLE DX										
0–19 Years	23	3.4	6	1	2	3	4	8	9	10
20–34	9	3.7	4	1	2	3	6	6	6	6
35–49	10	2.3	<1	2	2	2	3	3	4	4
50–64	5	6.9	11	2	3	6	10	10	10	10
65+	14	5.2	16	2	3	4	4	10	16	16
2. MULTIPLE DX										
0–19 Years	124	8.0	64	2	3	5	10	20	22	44
20–34	129	10.1	118	2	4	7	12	23	30	60
35–49	339	10.0	104	2	4	7	12	23	28	53
50–64	952	10.2	72	2	4	8	14	22	27	37
65+	4,688	9.5	59	3	4	7	13	19	24	37
TOTAL SINGLE DX	**61**	**3.9**	**9**	**1**	**2**	**3**	**4**	**8**	**10**	**16**
TOTAL MULTIPLE DX	**6,232**	**9.6**	**64**	**3**	**4**	**7**	**13**	**20**	**24**	**39**
TOTAL										
0–19 Years	147	7.3	58	2	3	5	8	18	22	44
20–34	138	9.7	113	2	4	7	10	22	30	60
35–49	349	9.8	103	2	3	7	12	23	27	53
50–64	957	10.1	72	2	4	8	14	22	27	37
65+	4,702	9.5	59	3	4	7	13	19	24	37
GRAND TOTAL	**6,293**	**9.5**	**64**	**3**	**4**	**7**	**13**	**20**	**24**	**39**

93.4: SKELETAL & OTH TRACTION

Type of Patients	Observed Patients	Avg. Stay	Vari-ance	Percentiles 10th	25th	50th	75th	90th	95th	99th
1. SINGLE DX										
0–19 Years	23	15.2	82	3	6	12	22	27	28	28
20–34	3	2.6	2	1	1	2	4	4	4	4
35–49	4	3.7	16	1	1	2	2	10	10	10
50–64	1	4.0	0	4	4	4	4	4	4	4
65+	0									
2. MULTIPLE DX										
0–19 Years	16	11.1	83	2	3	5	20	22	29	29
20–34	4	8.0	71	3	3	4	7	23	23	23
35–49	10	6.1	9	3	4	5	8	10	11	11
50–64	18	14.7	435	2	4	9	16	28	98	>99
65+	52	5.0	19	2	2	4	6	12	14	24
TOTAL SINGLE DX	**31**	**12.8**	**89**	**2**	**4**	**12**	**22**	**27**	**28**	**28**
TOTAL MULTIPLE DX	**100**	**7.7**	**107**	**2**	**2**	**4**	**8**	**18**	**23**	**98**
TOTAL										
0–19 Years	39	13.5	85	2	4	12	21	27	28	29
20–34	7	5.8	47	1	3	4	4	23	23	23
35–49	14	5.3	12	2	2	4	8	10	11	11
50–64	19	14.1	416	2	4	8	15	28	98	>99
65+	52	5.0	19	2	2	4	6	12	14	24
GRAND TOTAL	**131**	**8.9**	**107**	**2**	**3**	**5**	**13**	**22**	**27**	**98**

93.46: LIMB SKIN TRACTION NEC

Type of Patients	Observed Patients	Avg. Stay	Vari-ance	Percentiles 10th	25th	50th	75th	90th	95th	99th
1. SINGLE DX										
0–19 Years	5	10.6	39	1	4	12	12	22	22	22
20–34	0									
35–49	1	2.0	0	2	2	2	2	2	2	2
50–64	0									
65+	0									
2. MULTIPLE DX										
0–19 Years	6	4.6	23	2	2	3	4	15	15	15
20–34	2	12.8	157	4	4	4	23	23	23	23
35–49	3	8.7	1	8	8	8	10	10	10	10
50–64	8	9.8	64	2	3	6	15	26	26	26
65+	34	4.5	15	1	2	3	6	8	14	17
TOTAL SINGLE DX	**6**	**9.7**	**42**	**1**	**4**	**12**	**12**	**22**	**22**	**22**
TOTAL MULTIPLE DX	**53**	**5.5**	**27**	**2**	**2**	**4**	**6**	**14**	**17**	**26**
TOTAL										
0–19 Years	11	7.8	39	2	2	4	12	15	22	22
20–34	2	12.8	157	4	4	4	23	23	23	23
35–49	4	6.7	13	2	2	8	8	10	10	10
50–64	8	9.8	64	2	3	6	15	26	26	26
65+	34	4.5	15	1	2	3	6	8	14	17
GRAND TOTAL	**59**	**6.0**	**30**	**2**	**2**	**4**	**8**	**14**	**17**	**26**

93.5: OTH IMMOB/PRESS/WND ATTN

Type of Patients	Observed Patients	Avg. Stay	Vari-ance	Percentiles 10th	25th	50th	75th	90th	95th	99th
1. SINGLE DX										
0–19 Years	252	2.1	7	1	1	1	2	4	6	18
20–34	95	1.9	2	1	1	1	2	3	5	8
35–49	68	1.8	1	1	1	1	2	4	5	6
50–64	31	1.8	1	1	1	2	2	3	4	5
65+	22	2.5	4	1	1	2	3	5	6	11
2. MULTIPLE DX										
0–19 Years	411	3.0	11	1	1	2	3	6	10	19
20–34	367	2.9	8	1	1	2	4	6	9	17
35–49	446	4.1	23	1	2	3	5	9	11	26
50–64	491	4.9	45	1	2	3	5	10	16	40
65+	1,492	4.1	11	1	2	3	5	7	10	17
TOTAL SINGLE DX	**468**	**2.1**	**5**	**1**	**1**	**1**	**2**	**3**	**5**	**11**
TOTAL MULTIPLE DX	**3,207**	**3.9**	**17**	**1**	**2**	**3**	**5**	**8**	**11**	**19**
TOTAL										
0–19 Years	663	2.7	10	1	1	2	3	5	9	19
20–34	462	2.7	7	1	1	2	3	5	8	17
35–49	514	3.8	21	1	1	2	4	8	11	19
50–64	522	4.7	43	1	2	3	5	10	15	40
65+	1,514	4.1	11	1	2	3	5	7	10	17
GRAND TOTAL	**3,675**	**3.7**	**16**	**1**	**1**	**3**	**4**	**7**	**10**	**19**

93.51: PLASTER JACKET APPL

Type of Patients	Observed Patients	Avg. Stay	Vari-ance	Percentiles 10th	25th	50th	75th	90th	95th	99th
1. SINGLE DX										
0–19 Years	42	2.9	11	1	1	2	3	7	10	19
20–34	0									
35–49	0									
50–64	0									
65+	3	1.2	<1	1	1	1	1	2	2	2
2. MULTIPLE DX										
0–19 Years	34	4.7	36	1	1	1	5	17	18	22
20–34	0									
35–49	1	67.0	0	67	67	67	67	67	67	67
50–64	2	3.0	0	3	3	3	3	3	3	3
65+	1	5.0	0	5	5	5	5	5	5	5
TOTAL SINGLE DX	**45**	**2.8**	**11**	**1**	**1**	**2**	**3**	**7**	**10**	**19**
TOTAL MULTIPLE DX	**38**	**5.4**	**80**	**1**	**1**	**2**	**5**	**17**	**19**	**67**
TOTAL										
0–19 Years	76	3.7	24	1	1	2	3	10	18	19
20–34	0									
35–49	1	67.0	0	67	67	67	67	67	67	67
50–64	2	3.0	0	3	3	3	3	3	3	3
65+	4	3.0	4	1	1	2	5	5	5	5
GRAND TOTAL	**83**	**4.0**	**45**	**1**	**1**	**2**	**4**	**10**	**18**	**22**

93.53: CAST APPLICATION NEC

Type of Patients	Observed Patients	Avg. Stay	Vari-ance	Percentiles						
				10th	25th	50th	75th	90th	95th	99th
1. SINGLE DX										
0–19 Years	137	2.2	9	1	1	1	2	3	5	18
20–34	31	1.6	<1	1	1	1	3	3	3	3
35–49	21	1.8	2	1	1	1	2	4	5	5
50–64	6	2.0	2	1	1	2	2	5	5	5
65+	9	3.1	6	1	2	3	3	5	11	11
2. MULTIPLE DX										
0–19 Years	141	3.0	9	1	1	2	3	5	8	19
20–34	59	3.5	9	1	2	3	4	7	9	19
35–49	89	3.8	17	1	1	3	4	7	11	28
50–64	101	5.8	60	1	2	3	6	15	19	57
65+	273	4.1	10	1	2	3	5	7	10	19
TOTAL SINGLE DX	**204**	**2.1**	**7**	**1**	**1**	**1**	**2**	**3**	**5**	**17**
TOTAL MULTIPLE DX	**663**	**4.0**	**18**	**1**	**2**	**3**	**4**	**7**	**11**	**19**
TOTAL										
0–19 Years	278	2.6	9	1	1	2	3	5	7	19
20–34	90	2.8	6	1	1	2	3	5	7	13
35–49	110	3.4	14	1	1	2	4	6	10	28
50–64	107	5.6	57	1	2	3	6	13	19	57
65+	282	4.0	10	1	2	3	5	7	10	19
GRAND TOTAL	**867**	**3.5**	**16**	**1**	**1**	**3**	**4**	**7**	**10**	**19**

93.54: APPLICATION OF SPLINT

Type of Patients	Observed Patients	Avg. Stay	Vari-ance	Percentiles						
				10th	25th	50th	75th	90th	95th	99th
1. SINGLE DX										
0–19 Years	59	1.4	<1	1	1	1	1	3	4	5
20–34	48	1.9	2	1	1	2	2	3	4	10
35–49	36	1.8	<1	1	1	1	2	3	4	4
50–64	18	1.8	<1	1	1	2	2	3	3	3
65+	4	3.1	4	1	1	3	3	6	6	6
2. MULTIPLE DX										
0–19 Years	121	2.3	7	1	1	1	3	5	7	14
20–34	188	2.6	7	1	1	2	3	5	8	18
35–49	183	3.2	9	1	2	2	4	6	9	17
50–64	218	4.2	47	1	1	3	4	7	9	50
65+	698	3.7	9	1	2	3	4	7	8	16
TOTAL SINGLE DX	**165**	**1.7**	**1**	**1**	**1**	**1**	**2**	**3**	**4**	**6**
TOTAL MULTIPLE DX	**1,408**	**3.4**	**14**	**1**	**1**	**3**	**4**	**6**	**8**	**17**
TOTAL										
0–19 Years	180	2.0	5	1	1	1	2	4	6	14
20–34	236	2.5	7	1	1	2	3	5	7	11
35–49	219	3.0	8	1	1	2	4	6	8	12
50–64	236	4.0	44	1	1	3	4	7	9	50
65+	702	3.7	9	1	2	3	4	7	8	16
GRAND TOTAL	**1,573**	**3.2**	**13**	**1**	**1**	**2**	**4**	**6**	**8**	**17**

93.56: PRESSURE DRESSING APPL

Type of Patients	Observed Patients	Avg. Stay	Vari-ance	Percentiles						
				10th	25th	50th	75th	90th	95th	99th
1. SINGLE DX										
0–19 Years	2	2.8	3	1	1	4	4	4	4	4
20–34	3	1.0	0	1	1	1	1	1	1	1
35–49	1	1.0	0	1	1	1	1	1	1	1
50–64	1	1.0	0	1	1	1	1	1	1	1
65+	1	1.0	0	1	1	1	1	1	1	1
2. MULTIPLE DX										
0–19 Years	2	1.4	<1	1	1	1	2	2	2	2
20–34	6	2.0	<1	1	1	2	3	3	3	3
35–49	10	7.1	27	1	2	7	14	14	14	14
50–64	14	4.0	18	1	1	2	7	12	12	12
65+	46	5.3	23	2	2	4	7	10	10	36
TOTAL SINGLE DX	**8**	**1.6**	**2**	**1**	**1**	**1**	**1**	**4**	**4**	**4**
TOTAL MULTIPLE DX	**78**	**4.9**	**22**	**1**	**2**	**3**	**7**	**10**	**14**	**18**
TOTAL										
0–19 Years	4	2.1	2	1	1	1	4	4	4	4
20–34	9	1.7	<1	1	1	1	3	3	3	3
35–49	11	6.7	27	1	1	7	14	14	14	14
50–64	15	3.8	17	1	1	1	6	12	12	12
65+	47	5.2	23	2	2	4	7	10	10	36
GRAND TOTAL	**86**	**4.7**	**21**	**1**	**1**	**3**	**7**	**10**	**13**	**18**

93.57: APPL WOUND DRESSING NEC

Type of Patients	Observed Patients	Avg. Stay	Vari-ance	Percentiles						
				10th	25th	50th	75th	90th	95th	99th
1. SINGLE DX										
0–19 Years	2	3.3	11	1	1	1	6	6	6	6
20–34	4	3.0	7	1	1	3	3	8	8	8
35–49	1	1.0	0	1	1	1	1	1	1	1
50–64	0									
65+	1	3.0	0	3	3	3	3	3	3	3
2. MULTIPLE DX										
0–19 Years	82	3.2	9	1	1	2	4	7	10	15
20–34	50	3.2	10	1	1	2	4	8	9	18
35–49	83	5.0	29	1	2	3	8	11	14	31
50–64	68	5.6	42	1	2	3	6	13	20	40
65+	136	5.2	13	2	3	4	6	9	12	16
TOTAL SINGLE DX	**8**	**2.8**	**6**	**1**	**1**	**3**	**3**	**6**	**8**	**8**
TOTAL MULTIPLE DX	**419**	**4.5**	**20**	**1**	**2**	**3**	**5**	**10**	**13**	**23**
TOTAL										
0–19 Years	84	3.2	9	1	1	2	4	7	10	15
20–34	54	3.2	10	1	1	2	4	8	9	18
35–49	84	5.0	29	1	2	3	8	11	14	31
50–64	68	5.6	42	1	2	3	6	13	20	40
65+	137	5.2	13	2	3	4	6	9	12	16
GRAND TOTAL	**427**	**4.5**	**20**	**1**	**2**	**3**	**5**	**10**	**13**	**22**

93.59: IMMOB/PRESS/WND ATTN NEC

Type of Patients	Observed Patients	Avg. Stay	Vari-ance	Percentiles						
				10th	25th	50th	75th	90th	95th	99th
1. SINGLE DX										
0–19 Years	9	1.9	1	1	1	2	2	4	4	4
20–34	6	3.5	8	1	1	3	7	7	7	7
35–49	8	2.7	3	1	1	2	3	6	6	6
50–64	6	1.9	2	1	1	1	3	4	4	4
65+	4	2.0	<1	1	2	2	2	3	3	3
2. MULTIPLE DX										
0–19 Years	27	3.1	11	1	1	2	4	5	5	17
20–34	50	3.3	6	1	1	3	4	7	9	11
35–49	70	4.5	20	1	2	3	5	9	13	32
50–64	80	5.6	32	1	2	3	9	14	16	28
65+	314	4.4	11	1	2	4	5	9	10	18
TOTAL SINGLE DX	**33**	**2.4**	**3**	**1**	**1**	**2**	**3**	**5**	**7**	**7**
TOTAL MULTIPLE DX	**541**	**4.4**	**15**	**1**	**2**	**3**	**5**	**9**	**12**	**20**
TOTAL										
0–19 Years	36	2.7	8	1	1	2	4	4	5	17
20–34	56	3.3	6	1	1	3	4	7	9	11
35–49	78	4.3	19	1	2	3	5	9	13	19
50–64	86	5.4	31	1	2	3	8	14	16	28
65+	318	4.4	11	1	2	4	5	9	10	18
GRAND TOTAL	**574**	**4.3**	**15**	**1**	**2**	**3**	**5**	**9**	**12**	**20**

93.6: OSTEOPATHIC MANIPULATION

Type of Patients	Observed Patients	Avg. Stay	Vari-ance	Percentiles						
				10th	25th	50th	75th	90th	95th	99th
1. SINGLE DX										
0–19 Years	0									
20–34	0									
35–49	0									
50–64	1	1.0	0	1	1	1	1	1	1	1
65+	0									
2. MULTIPLE DX										
0–19 Years	3	3.6	4	2	2	3	6	6	6	6
20–34	1	2.0	0	2	2	2	2	2	2	2
35–49	6	3.5	5	1	2	3	6	7	7	7
50–64	11	3.5	9	1	2	2	5	5	12	12
65+	16	3.5	6	1	2	3	5	6	8	11
TOTAL SINGLE DX	**1**	**1.0**	**0**	**1**	**1**	**1**	**1**	**1**	**1**	**1**
TOTAL MULTIPLE DX	**37**	**3.5**	**6**	**1**	**2**	**3**	**5**	**6**	**8**	**12**
TOTAL										
0–19 Years	3	3.6	4	2	2	3	6	6	6	6
20–34	1	2.0	0	2	2	2	2	2	2	2
35–49	6	3.5	5	1	2	3	6	7	7	7
50–64	12	3.3	9	1	1	2	5	5	12	12
65+	16	3.5	6	1	2	3	5	6	8	11
GRAND TOTAL	**38**	**3.4**	**6**	**1**	**2**	**3**	**5**	**6**	**8**	**12**

93.67: OMT NEC

Type of Patients	Observed Patients	Avg. Stay	Vari-ance	Percentiles						
				10th	25th	50th	75th	90th	95th	99th
1. SINGLE DX										
0–19 Years	0									
20–34	0									
35–49	0									
50–64	1	1.0	0	1	1	1	1	1	1	1
65+	0									
2. MULTIPLE DX										
0–19 Years	3	3.6	4	2	2	3	6	6	6	6
20–34	1	2.0	0	2	2	2	2	2	2	2
35–49	4	3.0	6	1	1	2	3	7	7	7
50–64	10	3.6	9	1	2	3	5	5	12	12
65+	14	3.6	7	1	2	3	5	8	11	11
TOTAL SINGLE DX	**1**	**1.0**	**0**	**1**	**1**	**1**	**1**	**1**	**1**	**1**
TOTAL MULTIPLE DX	**32**	**3.5**	**7**	**1**	**2**	**3**	**5**	**7**	**11**	**12**
TOTAL										
0–19 Years	3	3.6	4	2	2	3	6	6	6	6
20–34	1	2.0	0	2	2	2	2	2	2	2
35–49	4	3.0	6	1	1	2	3	7	7	7
50–64	11	3.4	9	1	1	2	5	5	12	12
65+	14	3.6	7	1	2	3	5	8	11	11
GRAND TOTAL	**33**	**3.4**	**7**	**1**	**2**	**2**	**5**	**6**	**11**	**12**

93.7: SPEECH/READ/BLIND REHAB

Type of Patients	Observed Patients	Avg. Stay	Vari-ance	Percentiles						
				10th	25th	50th	75th	90th	95th	99th
1. SINGLE DX										
0–19 Years	2	2.1	1	1	1	3	3	3	3	3
20–34	0									
35–49	1	2.0	0	2	2	2	2	2	2	2
50–64	1	4.0	0	4	4	4	4	4	4	4
65+	0									
2. MULTIPLE DX										
0–19 Years	11	5.8	30	1	2	4	10	13	17	17
20–34	10	5.2	37	1	1	3	5	18	18	18
35–49	19	7.9	53	2	4	5	7	21	21	28
50–64	47	5.6	22	2	3	4	8	9	15	29
65+	227	6.0	30	2	3	5	7	12	17	28
TOTAL SINGLE DX	**4**	**2.5**	**2**	**1**	**1**	**3**	**3**	**4**	**4**	**4**
TOTAL MULTIPLE DX	**314**	**6.0**	**30**	**2**	**3**	**4**	**7**	**13**	**17**	**28**
TOTAL										
0–19 Years	13	5.2	27	1	1	3	7	13	17	17
20–34	10	5.2	37	1	1	3	5	18	18	18
35–49	20	7.7	52	2	3	4	7	21	21	28
50–64	48	5.6	22	2	3	4	8	9	15	29
65+	227	6.0	30	2	3	5	7	12	17	28
GRAND TOTAL	**318**	**6.0**	**30**	**2**	**3**	**4**	**7**	**13**	**17**	**28**

93.75: SPEECH THERAPY NEC

Type of Patients	Observed Patients	Avg. Stay	Vari-ance	Percentiles						
				10th	25th	50th	75th	90th	95th	99th
1. SINGLE DX										
0–19 Years	2	2.1	1	1	1	3	3	3	3	3
20–34	0									
35–49	1	2.0	0	2	2	2	2	2	2	2
50–64	1	4.0	0	4	4	4	4	4	4	4
65+	0									
2. MULTIPLE DX										
0–19 Years	10	6.0	33	1	1	2	10	17	17	17
20–34	8	6.0	44	1	2	3	5	18	18	18
35–49	19	7.9	53	2	4	5	7	21	21	28
50–64	46	5.8	23	2	2	4	8	11	15	29
65+	217	6.1	31	2	3	5	7	12	17	28
TOTAL SINGLE DX	**4**	**2.5**	**2**	**1**	**1**	**3**	**3**	**4**	**4**	**4**
TOTAL MULTIPLE DX	**300**	**6.2**	**31**	**2**	**3**	**5**	**8**	**13**	**18**	**28**
TOTAL										
0–19 Years	12	5.3	29	1	1	2	10	13	17	17
20–34	8	6.0	44	1	2	3	5	18	18	18
35–49	20	7.7	52	2	3	4	7	21	21	28
50–64	47	5.7	23	2	2	4	8	11	15	29
65+	217	6.1	31	2	3	5	7	12	17	28
GRAND TOTAL	**304**	**6.1**	**31**	**2**	**3**	**4**	**8**	**13**	**18**	**28**

93.8: OTHER REHAB THERAPY

Type of Patients	Observed Patients	Avg. Stay	Vari-ance	Percentiles						
				10th	25th	50th	75th	90th	95th	99th
1. SINGLE DX										
0–19 Years	33	4.2	11	1	2	3	7	8	12	15
20–34	282	8.9	85	2	3	6	11	21	29	47
35–49	203	8.1	44	2	4	6	12	17	22	28
50–64	79	9.1	68	2	3	6	12	19	30	35
65+	4	4.3	4	2	3	5	5	7	7	7
2. MULTIPLE DX										
0–19 Years	87	11.6	279	2	4	6	10	27	69	69
20–34	684	7.6	55	2	3	5	9	16	22	38
35–49	995	7.9	57	2	3	6	9	17	24	41
50–64	643	9.3	82	2	4	6	11	20	28	48
65+	546	10.9	52	3	5	9	15	21	25	31
TOTAL SINGLE DX	**601**	**8.4**	**64**	**2**	**3**	**5**	**11**	**18**	**25**	**40**
TOTAL MULTIPLE DX	**2,955**	**9.0**	**70**	**2**	**4**	**6**	**11**	**20**	**25**	**43**
TOTAL										
0–19 Years	120	9.9	227	2	3	5	9	16	45	69
20–34	966	8.0	64	2	3	5	9	17	25	43
35–49	1,198	7.9	54	2	3	6	10	17	23	40
50–64	722	9.3	80	2	4	6	11	20	28	48
65+	550	10.9	52	3	5	9	15	21	25	31
GRAND TOTAL	**3,556**	**8.9**	**69**	**2**	**4**	**6**	**11**	**19**	**25**	**42**

93.81: RECREATIONAL THERAPY

Type of Patients	Observed Patients	Avg. Stay	Vari-ance	Percentiles						
				10th	25th	50th	75th	90th	95th	99th
1. SINGLE DX										
0–19 Years	4	2.1	2	1	1	2	4	4	4	4
20–34	41	6.9	67	1	3	5	7	12	20	43
35–49	33	5.5	11	2	3	5	6	10	12	17
50–64	12	9.1	71	3	3	5	14	17	30	30
65+	1	7.0	0	7	7	7	7	7	7	7
2. MULTIPLE DX										
0–19 Years	8	10.9	131	1	3	10	13	35	35	35
20–34	80	7.6	57	2	3	4	9	18	24	34
35–49	107	7.9	65	2	3	5	9	17	29	36
50–64	47	9.8	86	2	4	7	13	22	31	51
65+	27	12.0	59	3	7	11	15	25	26	34
TOTAL SINGLE DX	**91**	**6.5**	**44**	**2**	**3**	**5**	**7**	**12**	**17**	**43**
TOTAL MULTIPLE DX	**269**	**8.7**	**69**	**2**	**3**	**5**	**11**	**19**	**28**	**36**
TOTAL										
0–19 Years	12	8.4	108	1	1	4	11	35	35	35
20–34	121	7.4	60	1	3	5	8	18	24	34
35–49	140	7.3	53	2	3	5	8	16	21	36
50–64	59	9.6	82	3	4	7	13	22	30	51
65+	28	11.8	58	3	7	11	15	25	26	34
GRAND TOTAL	**360**	**8.2**	**63**	**2**	**3**	**5**	**10**	**17**	**26**	**36**

93.83: OCCUPATIONAL THERAPY

Type of Patients	Observed Patients	Avg. Stay	Vari-ance	Percentiles						
				10th	25th	50th	75th	90th	95th	99th
1. SINGLE DX										
0–19 Years	29	4.5	12	1	2	3	7	8	12	15
20–34	241	9.3	87	2	4	6	12	22	29	47
35–49	170	8.6	49	2	4	6	12	17	23	28
50–64	67	9.1	68	2	4	6	12	19	32	35
65+	3	3.6	2	2	2	3	5	5	5	5
2. MULTIPLE DX										
0–19 Years	74	11.8	314	2	4	5	10	27	69	69
20–34	598	7.4	54	2	3	5	8	15	22	42
35–49	863	7.6	53	2	3	6	9	16	22	41
50–64	537	8.8	81	2	3	6	10	19	28	48
65+	381	10.2	54	3	5	8	14	21	25	31
TOTAL SINGLE DX	**510**	**8.7**	**67**	**2**	**3**	**6**	**12**	**20**	**26**	**40**
TOTAL MULTIPLE DX	**2,453**	**8.5**	**70**	**2**	**3**	**6**	**10**	**18**	**25**	**46**
TOTAL										
0–19 Years	103	10.1	252	2	3	5	9	16	69	69
20–34	839	7.9	64	2	3	5	9	16	26	43
35–49	1,033	7.7	52	2	3	6	9	16	22	40
50–64	604	8.8	80	2	3	6	10	19	28	48
65+	384	10.2	54	3	4	8	14	21	25	31
GRAND TOTAL	**2,963**	**8.5**	**70**	**2**	**3**	**6**	**10**	**18**	**25**	**45**

93.89: REHABILITATION NEC

Type of Patients	Observed Patients	Avg. Stay	Variance	10th	25th	50th	75th	90th	95th	99th
1. SINGLE DX										
0–19 Years	0									
20–34	0									
35–49	0									
50–64	0									
65+	0									
2. MULTIPLE DX										
0–19 Years	5	9.3	27	4	4	9	12	18	18	18
20–34	6	17.5	33	6	14	21	22	22	22	22
35–49	25	15.7	62	5	11	17	22	25	25	39
50–64	59	12.9	68	5	7	11	17	27	28	39
65+	138	12.5	45	5	8	11	17	21	24	31
TOTAL SINGLE DX	**0**									
TOTAL MULTIPLE DX	**233**	**12.9**	**52**	**5**	**8**	**12**	**18**	**23**	**27**	**33**
TOTAL										
0–19 Years	5	9.3	27	4	4	9	12	18	18	18
20–34	6	17.5	33	6	14	21	22	22	22	22
35–49	25	15.7	62	5	11	17	22	25	25	39
50–64	59	12.9	68	5	7	11	17	27	28	39
65+	138	12.5	45	5	8	11	17	21	24	31
GRAND TOTAL	**233**	**12.9**	**52**	**5**	**8**	**12**	**18**	**23**	**27**	**33**

93.9: RESPIRATORY THERAPY

Type of Patients	Observed Patients	Avg. Stay	Variance	10th	25th	50th	75th	90th	95th	99th
1. SINGLE DX										
0–19 Years	3,477	2.2	2	1	1	2	3	4	4	8
20–34	66	2.3	2	1	1	2	3	4	6	6
35–49	65	2.3	3	1	1	2	3	5	6	9
50–64	58	2.3	3	1	1	2	3	4	5	12
65+	20	3.1	4	1	1	2	5	6	6	9
2. MULTIPLE DX										
0–19 Years	8,895	6.3	85	1	2	3	6	15	25	49
20–34	498	3.9	20	1	2	3	5	8	10	21
35–49	1,589	4.1	16	1	2	3	5	8	11	19
50–64	3,069	4.6	16	1	2	3	6	9	12	19
65+	6,557	5.0	15	2	3	4	6	10	12	18
TOTAL SINGLE DX	**3,686**	**2.2**	**2**	**1**	**1**	**2**	**3**	**4**	**4**	**8**
TOTAL MULTIPLE DX	**20,608**	**5.4**	**46**	**1**	**2**	**3**	**6**	**11**	**16**	**37**
TOTAL										
0–19 Years	12,372	5.2	65	1	2	3	4	11	20	45
20–34	564	3.7	18	1	2	3	4	7	10	19
35–49	1,654	4.0	15	1	2	3	5	8	11	19
50–64	3,127	4.5	16	1	2	3	6	9	12	18
65+	6,577	5.0	15	2	3	4	6	10	12	18
GRAND TOTAL	**24,294**	**4.9**	**41**	**1**	**2**	**3**	**5**	**10**	**14**	**34**

93.90: CPAP

Type of Patients	Observed Patients	Avg. Stay	Variance	10th	25th	50th	75th	90th	95th	99th
1. SINGLE DX										
0–19 Years	199	2.1	2	1	1	2	3	3	4	7
20–34	0									
35–49	3	1.3	<1	1	1	1	2	2	2	2
50–64	4	3.0	<1	2	2	3	4	4	4	4
65+	1	5.0	0	5	5	5	5	5	5	5
2. MULTIPLE DX										
0–19 Years	2,660	12.7	197	2	3	7	17	33	43	65
20–34	151	5.4	42	2	2	4	6	10	14	45
35–49	665	5.2	20	1	3	4	7	11	13	22
50–64	1,409	5.7	21	2	3	5	7	11	13	22
65+	2,856	6.3	21	2	3	5	8	12	14	22
TOTAL SINGLE DX	**207**	**2.2**	**2**	**1**	**1**	**2**	**3**	**3**	**4**	**7**
TOTAL MULTIPLE DX	**7,741**	**8.3**	**91**	**2**	**3**	**5**	**9**	**17**	**27**	**54**
TOTAL										
0–19 Years	2,859	12.1	192	2	3	7	16	31	42	65
20–34	151	5.4	42	2	2	4	6	10	14	45
35–49	668	5.2	20	1	3	4	6	11	13	22
50–64	1,413	5.7	21	2	3	5	7	11	13	22
65+	2,857	6.3	21	2	3	5	8	12	14	22
GRAND TOTAL	**7,948**	**8.1**	**90**	**2**	**3**	**5**	**9**	**17**	**27**	**52**

93.91: IPPB

Type of Patients	Observed Patients	Avg. Stay	Variance	10th	25th	50th	75th	90th	95th	99th
1. SINGLE DX										
0–19 Years	3	1.9	<1	1	1	2	3	3	3	3
20–34	0									
35–49	0									
50–64	0									
65+	0									
2. MULTIPLE DX										
0–19 Years	54	4.4	21	1	2	3	4	10	15	25
20–34	7	6.3	22	1	2	7	9	14	14	14
35–49	4	4.9	12	1	1	6	9	9	9	9
50–64	41	6.4	33	2	3	4	7	15	19	28
65+	54	6.7	31	2	3	5	8	12	18	33
TOTAL SINGLE DX	**3**	**1.9**	**<1**	**1**	**1**	**2**	**3**	**3**	**3**	**3**
TOTAL MULTIPLE DX	**160**	**5.7**	**28**	**1**	**3**	**4**	**7**	**13**	**15**	**28**
TOTAL										
0–19 Years	57	4.3	20	1	2	3	4	10	15	25
20–34	7	6.3	22	1	2	7	9	14	14	14
35–49	4	4.9	12	1	1	6	9	9	9	9
50–64	41	6.4	33	2	3	4	7	15	19	28
65+	54	6.7	31	2	3	5	8	12	18	33
GRAND TOTAL	**163**	**5.7**	**27**	**1**	**2**	**4**	**7**	**12**	**15**	**28**

93.93: NONMECH RESUSCITATION

Type of Patients	Observed Patients	Avg. Stay	Vari-ance	Percentiles						
				10th	25th	50th	75th	90th	95th	99th
1. SINGLE DX										
0–19 Years	35	1.9	<1	1	1	2	3	3	3	3
20–34	0									
35–49	1	6.0	0	6	6	6	6	6	6	6
50–64	0									
65+	0									
2. MULTIPLE DX										
0–19 Years	231	3.8	18	1	2	3	4	7	11	19
20–34	1	1.0	0	1	1	1	1	1	1	1
35–49	0									
50–64	1	14.0	0	14	14	14	14	14	14	14
65+	7	3.9	6	2	2	3	5	9	9	9
TOTAL SINGLE DX	**36**	**1.9**	**<1**	**1**	**1**	**2**	**3**	**3**	**3**	**6**
TOTAL MULTIPLE DX	**240**	**3.8**	**18**	**1**	**2**	**3**	**4**	**7**	**11**	**19**
TOTAL										
0–19 Years	266	3.5	16	1	2	3	3	6	10	19
20–34	1	1.0	0	1	1	1	1	1	1	1
35–49	1	6.0	0	6	6	6	6	6	6	6
50–64	1	14.0	0	14	14	14	14	14	14	14
65+	7	3.9	6	2	2	3	5	9	9	9
GRAND TOTAL	**276**	**3.5**	**16**	**1**	**2**	**3**	**3**	**6**	**10**	**19**

93.94: NEBULIZER THERAPY

Type of Patients	Observed Patients	Avg. Stay	Vari-ance	Percentiles						
				10th	25th	50th	75th	90th	95th	99th
1. SINGLE DX										
0–19 Years	744	2.3	3	1	1	2	3	4	6	9
20–34	36	2.3	2	1	1	2	3	4	6	6
35–49	32	2.1	3	1	1	2	3	3	7	9
50–64	32	2.8	4	1	2	2	3	5	6	12
65+	11	2.4	3	1	1	2	4	6	6	6
2. MULTIPLE DX										
0–19 Years	1,533	2.9	6	1	1	2	4	6	7	12
20–34	211	3.2	7	1	2	2	4	6	8	18
35–49	511	3.3	6	1	2	3	4	6	7	12
50–64	956	3.8	8	1	2	3	5	7	9	14
65+	2,120	4.3	9	2	2	4	5	8	10	15
TOTAL SINGLE DX	**855**	**2.3**	**3**	**1**	**1**	**2**	**3**	**4**	**6**	**9**
TOTAL MULTIPLE DX	**5,331**	**3.6**	**8**	**1**	**2**	**3**	**5**	**7**	**9**	**14**
TOTAL										
0–19 Years	2,277	2.7	5	1	1	2	3	5	7	11
20–34	247	3.0	7	1	2	2	4	6	8	14
35–49	543	3.2	6	1	2	3	4	6	7	12
50–64	988	3.7	7	1	2	3	5	7	9	13
65+	2,131	4.3	9	2	2	4	5	8	10	15
GRAND TOTAL	**6,186**	**3.4**	**7**	**1**	**2**	**3**	**4**	**6**	**8**	**13**

93.95: HYPERBARIC OXYGENATION

Type of Patients	Observed Patients	Avg. Stay	Vari-ance	Percentiles						
				10th	25th	50th	75th	90th	95th	99th
1. SINGLE DX										
0–19 Years	0									
20–34	0									
35–49	0									
50–64	1	1.0	0	1	1	1	1	1	1	1
65+	0									
2. MULTIPLE DX										
0–19 Years	2	4.1	11	1	1	7	7	7	7	7
20–34	4	3.4	33	1	1	1	1	15	15	15
35–49	9	2.0	1	1	1	2	2	4	4	4
50–64	19	5.4	18	1	2	4	7	12	16	17
65+	16	8.7	59	1	2	6	16	21	21	22
TOTAL SINGLE DX	**1**	**1.0**	**0**	**1**	**1**	**1**	**1**	**1**	**1**	**1**
TOTAL MULTIPLE DX	**50**	**5.4**	**31**	**1**	**1**	**4**	**7**	**16**	**18**	**22**
TOTAL										
0–19 Years	2	4.1	11	1	1	7	7	7	7	7
20–34	4	3.4	33	1	1	1	1	15	15	15
35–49	9	2.0	1	1	1	2	2	4	4	4
50–64	20	5.3	18	1	1	4	7	12	16	17
65+	16	8.7	59	1	2	6	16	21	21	22
GRAND TOTAL	**51**	**5.4**	**31**	**1**	**1**	**4**	**7**	**16**	**18**	**22**

93.96: OXYGEN ENRICHMENT NEC

Type of Patients	Observed Patients	Avg. Stay	Vari-ance	Percentiles						
				10th	25th	50th	75th	90th	95th	99th
1. SINGLE DX										
0–19 Years	2,470	2.1	1	1	1	2	3	3	4	6
20–34	27	2.4	2	1	1	2	4	4	5	6
35–49	26	2.6	3	1	1	2	4	5	5	6
50–64	20	1.4	<1	1	1	1	2	3	3	3
65+	8	3.9	6	1	2	3	5	9	9	9
2. MULTIPLE DX										
0–19 Years	4,327	4.2	26	1	2	3	4	8	12	30
20–34	112	3.2	7	1	2	3	3	6	9	14
35–49	384	3.2	16	1	1	2	4	6	7	14
50–64	619	3.3	11	1	2	2	4	6	8	12
65+	1,477	4.0	8	1	2	3	5	8	9	14
TOTAL SINGLE DX	**2,551**	**2.1**	**1**	**1**	**1**	**2**	**3**	**3**	**4**	**6**
TOTAL MULTIPLE DX	**6,919**	**4.0**	**19**	**1**	**2**	**3**	**4**	**8**	**10**	**24**
TOTAL										
0–19 Years	6,797	3.5	18	1	2	2	4	7	10	25
20–34	139	3.0	6	1	2	2	3	6	7	14
35–49	410	3.1	16	1	1	2	4	6	7	13
50–64	639	3.2	11	1	1	2	4	6	8	12
65+	1,485	4.0	8	1	2	3	5	8	9	14
GRAND TOTAL	**9,470**	**3.5**	**15**	**1**	**2**	**3**	**4**	**7**	**9**	**21**

93.99: RESPIRATORY THERAPY NEC

Type of Patients	Observed Patients	Avg. Stay	Vari-ance	Percentiles						
				10th	25th	50th	75th	90th	95th	99th
1. SINGLE DX										
0–19 Years	26	2.3	2	1	1	2	3	4	4	7
20–34	3	2.0	<1	1	1	2	3	3	3	3
35–49	3	1.3	<1	1	1	1	2	2	2	2
50–64	1	3.0	0	3	3	3	3	3	3	3
65+	0									
2. MULTIPLE DX										
0–19 Years	86	6.8	68	1	2	4	7	20	28	39
20–34	11	4.9	56	1	1	2	5	6	26	26
35–49	15	2.1	<1	1	2	2	2	3	4	4
50–64	22	4.0	18	1	1	3	4	15	15	15
65+	27	3.3	6	1	1	3	4	7	10	10
TOTAL SINGLE DX	**33**	**2.2**	**2**	**1**	**1**	**2**	**3**	**3**	**4**	**7**
TOTAL MULTIPLE DX	**161**	**5.3**	**46**	**1**	**2**	**3**	**5**	**11**	**20**	**34**
TOTAL										
0–19 Years	112	5.7	55	1	2	3	6	13	21	39
20–34	14	4.3	45	1	1	2	4	6	26	26
35–49	18	2.0	<1	1	1	2	2	3	4	4
50–64	23	3.9	17	1	1	3	4	15	15	15
65+	27	3.3	6	1	1	3	4	7	10	10
GRAND TOTAL	**194**	**4.7**	**40**	**1**	**2**	**3**	**4**	**10**	**20**	**34**

94.0: PSYCH EVAL & TESTING

Type of Patients	Observed Patients	Avg. Stay	Vari-ance	Percentiles						
				10th	25th	50th	75th	90th	95th	99th
1. SINGLE DX										
0–19 Years	0									
20–34	0									
35–49	0									
50–64	1	9.0	0	9	9	9	9	9	9	9
65+	0									
2. MULTIPLE DX										
0–19 Years	6	14.2	55	7	9	12	22	27	27	27
20–34	1	2.0	0	2	2	2	2	2	2	2
35–49	0									
50–64	1	16.0	0	16	16	16	16	16	16	16
65+	6	12.9	38	6	8	11	15	24	24	24
TOTAL SINGLE DX	**1**	**9.0**	**0**	**9**	**9**	**9**	**9**	**9**	**9**	**9**
TOTAL MULTIPLE DX	**14**	**13.2**	**48**	**6**	**9**	**12**	**16**	**24**	**27**	**27**
TOTAL										
0–19 Years	6	14.2	55	7	9	12	22	27	27	27
20–34	1	2.0	0	2	2	2	2	2	2	2
35–49	0									
50–64	2	12.8	21	9	9	16	16	16	16	16
65+	6	12.9	38	6	8	11	15	24	24	24
GRAND TOTAL	**15**	**13.0**	**46**	**6**	**9**	**11**	**16**	**24**	**27**	**27**

94.1: PSYCH EVAL/CONSULT

Type of Patients	Observed Patients	Avg. Stay	Vari-ance	Percentiles						
				10th	25th	50th	75th	90th	95th	99th
1. SINGLE DX										
0–19 Years	20	7.0	41	1	1	4	12	15	20	21
20–34	41	7.1	44	1	2	5	9	15	23	30
35–49	42	6.9	48	2	3	5	8	20	26	28
50–64	7	5.6	5	2	5	5	7	8	8	8
65+	0									
2. MULTIPLE DX										
0–19 Years	160	8.9	158	1	3	5	9	18	30	61
20–34	171	5.9	35	1	2	4	7	13	19	35
35–49	284	5.3	40	1	2	4	6	12	15	31
50–64	97	6.1	41	1	2	4	8	17	18	29
65+	15	6.8	17	2	4	7	11	13	14	14
TOTAL SINGLE DX	**110**	**6.9**	**41**	**1**	**2**	**5**	**9**	**15**	**21**	**28**
TOTAL MULTIPLE DX	**727**	**6.8**	**82**	**1**	**2**	**4**	**8**	**14**	**20**	**52**
TOTAL										
0–19 Years	180	8.7	146	1	3	5	9	18	30	61
20–34	212	6.1	37	1	2	4	8	13	19	33
35–49	326	5.5	41	1	2	4	6	12	17	31
50–64	104	6.1	38	1	2	4	8	15	18	29
65+	15	6.8	17	2	4	7	11	13	14	14
GRAND TOTAL	**837**	**6.8**	**77**	**1**	**2**	**4**	**8**	**14**	**20**	**51**

94.11: PSYCH MENTAL STATUS

Type of Patients	Observed Patients	Avg. Stay	Vari-ance	Percentiles						
				10th	25th	50th	75th	90th	95th	99th
1. SINGLE DX										
0–19 Years	20	7.0	41	1	1	4	12	15	20	21
20–34	40	7.2	45	1	2	5	9	15	23	30
35–49	41	7.1	48	2	3	5	8	20	26	28
50–64	7	5.6	5	2	5	5	7	8	8	8
65+	0									
2. MULTIPLE DX										
0–19 Years	159	9.0	158	1	3	5	9	18	30	61
20–34	166	5.6	25	1	2	4	7	12	14	20
35–49	274	5.0	29	1	2	4	6	10	14	24
50–64	91	5.8	34	1	2	3	8	15	17	29
65+	13	7.0	18	2	2	8	11	14	14	14
TOTAL SINGLE DX	**108**	**7.0**	**41**	**1**	**2**	**5**	**9**	**15**	**23**	**28**
TOTAL MULTIPLE DX	**703**	**6.6**	**77**	**1**	**2**	**4**	**7**	**14**	**19**	**52**
TOTAL										
0–19 Years	179	8.8	146	1	3	5	9	18	30	61
20–34	206	5.9	29	1	2	4	8	13	18	27
35–49	315	5.3	32	1	2	4	6	11	15	28
50–64	98	5.8	32	1	2	4	7	14	17	29
65+	13	7.0	18	2	2	8	11	14	14	14
GRAND TOTAL	**811**	**6.7**	**73**	**1**	**2**	**4**	**8**	**14**	**20**	**51**

94.19: PSYCH INTERVIEW/EVAL NEC

Type of Patients	Observed Patients	Avg. Stay	Vari-ance	Percentiles						
				10th	25th	50th	75th	90th	95th	99th
1. SINGLE DX										
0–19 Years	0									
20–34	1	2.0	0	2	2	2	2	2	2	2
35–49	1	1.0	0	1	1	1	1	1	1	1
50–64	0									
65+	0									
2. MULTIPLE DX										
0–19 Years	1	1.0	0	1	1	1	1	1	1	1
20–34	5	16.2	252	3	3	5	33	35	35	35
35–49	10	10.5	227	1	1	1	31	31	49	49
50–64	5	7.7	117	1	1	4	7	33	33	33
65+	2	5.0	2	4	4	4	6	6	6	6
TOTAL SINGLE DX	**2**	**1.4**	**<1**	**1**	**1**	**1**	**2**	**2**	**2**	**2**
TOTAL MULTIPLE DX	**23**	**10.5**	**199**	**1**	**1**	**3**	**10**	**33**	**35**	**49**
TOTAL										
0–19 Years	1	1.0	0	1	1	1	1	1	1	1
20–34	6	14.8	244	3	3	3	33	35	35	35
35–49	11	10.0	219	1	1	1	10	31	31	49
50–64	5	7.7	117	1	1	4	7	33	33	33
65+	2	5.0	2	4	4	4	6	6	6	6
GRAND TOTAL	**25**	**10.1**	**193**	**1**	**1**	**3**	**10**	**33**	**35**	**49**

94.2: PSYCH SOMATOTHERAPY

Type of Patients	Observed Patients	Avg. Stay	Vari-ance	Percentiles						
				10th	25th	50th	75th	90th	95th	99th
1. SINGLE DX										
0–19 Years	106	9.0	59	2	4	7	10	20	25	43
20–34	229	7.3	51	1	3	5	10	15	21	37
35–49	190	8.1	121	1	3	5	8	19	28	95
50–64	75	10.3	183	2	3	6	12	20	27	90
65+	14	10.0	35	3	5	12	12	20	20	23
2. MULTIPLE DX										
0–19 Years	644	9.6	108	2	4	7	12	22	28	55
20–34	1,386	6.4	48	2	2	4	7	14	19	34
35–49	1,615	7.6	75	2	3	5	9	17	23	49
50–64	824	9.2	88	2	3	6	12	20	27	54
65+	697	14.7	118	4	7	12	20	32	37	54
TOTAL SINGLE DX	**614**	**8.3**	**89**	**2**	**3**	**5**	**10**	**18**	**25**	**51**
TOTAL MULTIPLE DX	**5,166**	**8.8**	**88**	**2**	**3**	**6**	**11**	**20**	**27**	**49**
TOTAL										
0–19 Years	750	9.6	102	2	4	7	11	20	28	50
20–34	1,615	6.5	49	2	2	4	8	14	19	34
35–49	1,805	7.7	80	2	3	5	9	17	24	49
50–64	899	9.3	95	2	3	6	12	20	27	55
65+	711	14.6	116	4	7	12	20	31	36	54
GRAND TOTAL	**5,780**	**8.7**	**88**	**2**	**3**	**6**	**11**	**20**	**27**	**49**

94.22: LITHIUM THERAPY

Type of Patients	Observed Patients	Avg. Stay	Vari-ance	Percentiles						
				10th	25th	50th	75th	90th	95th	99th
1. SINGLE DX										
0–19 Years	2	6.4	9	2	2	8	8	8	8	8
20–34	1	6.0	0	6	6	6	6	6	6	6
35–49	3	12.9	8	10	10	12	16	16	16	16
50–64	1	3.0	0	3	3	3	3	3	3	3
65+	0									
2. MULTIPLE DX										
0–19 Years	5	5.2	2	3	4	5	6	7	7	7
20–34	12	6.9	47	1	3	4	9	21	21	21
35–49	24	6.6	14	2	3	6	10	12	13	14
50–64	11	5.0	19	2	2	3	6	9	17	17
65+	1	7.0	0	7	7	7	7	7	7	7
TOTAL SINGLE DX	**7**	**8.5**	**21**	**2**	**6**	**8**	**12**	**16**	**16**	**16**
TOTAL MULTIPLE DX	**53**	**6.2**	**21**	**2**	**3**	**5**	**8**	**12**	**17**	**21**
TOTAL										
0–19 Years	7	5.7	5	2	4	6	8	8	8	8
20–34	13	6.9	44	1	3	4	9	21	21	21
35–49	27	7.3	17	2	4	7	10	13	14	16
50–64	12	4.9	17	2	2	3	6	9	17	17
65+	1	7.0	0	7	7	7	7	7	7	7
GRAND TOTAL	**60**	**6.5**	**21**	**2**	**3**	**5**	**8**	**12**	**16**	**21**

94.23: NEUROLEPTIC THERAPY

Type of Patients	Observed Patients	Avg. Stay	Vari-ance	Percentiles						
				10th	25th	50th	75th	90th	95th	99th
1. SINGLE DX										
0–19 Years	0									
20–34	0									
35–49	0									
50–64	1	8.0	0	8	8	8	8	8	8	8
65+	0									
2. MULTIPLE DX										
0–19 Years	2	1.0	0	1	1	1	1	1	1	1
20–34	3	3.1	7	1	1	2	6	6	6	6
35–49	12	11.5	61	4	5	10	17	22	27	27
50–64	6	4.0	6	1	4	4	4	9	9	9
65+	11	22.5	128	6	13	24	34	34	34	34
TOTAL SINGLE DX	**1**	**8.0**	**0**	**8**	**8**	**8**	**8**	**8**	**8**	**8**
TOTAL MULTIPLE DX	**34**	**13.3**	**136**	**1**	**4**	**9**	**22**	**34**	**34**	**34**
TOTAL										
0–19 Years	2	1.0	0	1	1	1	1	1	1	1
20–34	3	3.1	7	1	1	2	6	6	6	6
35–49	12	11.5	61	4	5	10	17	22	27	27
50–64	7	4.4	7	1	4	4	5	9	9	9
65+	11	22.5	128	6	13	24	34	34	34	34
GRAND TOTAL	**35**	**13.2**	**133**	**1**	**4**	**9**	**21**	**34**	**34**	**34**

94.25: PSYCH DRUG THERAPY NEC

Type of Patients	Observed Patients	Avg. Stay	Vari-ance	Percentiles 10th	25th	50th	75th	90th	95th	99th
1. SINGLE DX										
0–19 Years	103	8.9	59	2	4	7	10	20	25	43
20–34	222	7.3	51	1	3	5	10	15	21	37
35–49	174	8.1	128	1	3	5	8	19	28	95
50–64	62	8.8	154	2	3	6	10	14	20	90
65+	6	6.5	24	1	3	8	8	14	14	14
2. MULTIPLE DX										
0–19 Years	637	9.7	109	2	4	7	12	22	28	55
20–34	1,301	6.1	43	2	2	4	7	13	17	31
35–49	1,375	6.9	65	2	3	5	8	14	20	49
50–64	642	7.9	62	2	3	6	10	16	21	54
65+	423	11.3	52	4	7	10	14	20	23	36
TOTAL SINGLE DX	**567**	**8.0**	**87**	**2**	**3**	**5**	**10**	**18**	**25**	**43**
TOTAL MULTIPLE DX	**4,378**	**7.7**	**68**	**2**	**3**	**5**	**9**	**16**	**21**	**48**
TOTAL										
0–19 Years	740	9.6	103	2	4	7	11	21	28	50
20–34	1,523	6.3	44	2	2	4	7	14	17	31
35–49	1,549	7.0	71	2	3	5	8	14	20	49
50–64	704	8.0	69	2	3	6	10	16	21	54
65+	429	11.2	52	4	7	10	14	20	23	36
GRAND TOTAL	**4,945**	**7.8**	**70**	**2**	**3**	**5**	**9**	**16**	**22**	**48**

94.27: ELECTROSHOCK THERAPY NEC

Type of Patients	Observed Patients	Avg. Stay	Vari-ance	Percentiles 10th	25th	50th	75th	90th	95th	99th
1. SINGLE DX										
0–19 Years	1	18.0	0	18	18	18	18	18	18	18
20–34	6	7.0	66	1	2	2	18	20	20	20
35–49	13	8.0	45	2	3	4	11	20	22	22
50–64	11	20.6	286	5	9	18	25	57	57	57
65+	8	12.4	30	4	8	12	16	20	23	23
2. MULTIPLE DX										
0–19 Years	0									
20–34	70	12.6	126	2	5	9	17	27	36	59
35–49	204	13.2	131	1	4	10	19	30	36	58
50–64	164	15.2	160	2	5	12	22	33	40	55
65+	262	20.7	179	3	10	19	28	39	46	56
TOTAL SINGLE DX	**39**	**12.6**	**127**	**2**	**4**	**12**	**18**	**24**	**27**	**57**
TOTAL MULTIPLE DX	**700**	**16.5**	**167**	**2**	**6**	**14**	**24**	**36**	**42**	**56**
TOTAL										
0–19 Years	1	18.0	0	18	18	18	18	18	18	18
20–34	76	12.1	123	2	5	8	17	27	36	59
35–49	217	12.9	127	1	3	10	19	30	36	53
50–64	175	15.5	167	2	5	12	22	33	45	57
65+	270	20.4	176	3	10	19	28	39	45	56
GRAND TOTAL	**739**	**16.3**	**165**	**2**	**6**	**14**	**23**	**35**	**41**	**56**

94.29: PSYCH SOMATOTHERAPY NEC

Type of Patients	Observed Patients	Avg. Stay	Vari-ance	Percentiles 10th	25th	50th	75th	90th	95th	99th
1. SINGLE DX										
0–19 Years	0									
20–34	0									
35–49	0									
50–64	0									
65+	0									
2. MULTIPLE DX										
0–19 Years	0									
20–34	0									
35–49	0									
50–64	0									
65+	0									
TOTAL SINGLE DX	**0**									
TOTAL MULTIPLE DX	**0**									
TOTAL										
0–19 Years	0									
20–34	0									
35–49	0									
50–64	0									
65+	0									
GRAND TOTAL	**0**									

94.3: INDIVIDUAL PSYCHOTHERAPY

Type of Patients	Observed Patients	Avg. Stay	Vari-ance	Percentiles 10th	25th	50th	75th	90th	95th	99th
1. SINGLE DX										
0–19 Years	5	7.6	6	2	7	8	8	11	11	11
20–34	85	4.3	17	1	1	3	6	11	11	13
35–49	36	8.5	136	1	1	4	10	34	34	34
50–64	15	4.4	13	1	2	3	7	11	11	11
65+	3	4.1	12	1	1	7	7	7	7	7
2. MULTIPLE DX										
0–19 Years	50	8.3	45	2	3	6	13	17	26	26
20–34	358	5.0	12	2	3	4	6	9	13	20
35–49	533	6.6	47	2	3	5	8	13	16	26
50–64	294	7.1	29	2	4	6	9	14	17	27
65+	237	9.8	38	3	5	9	14	17	21	29
TOTAL SINGLE DX	**144**	**5.7**	**51**	**1**	**1**	**3**	**7**	**11**	**13**	**34**
TOTAL MULTIPLE DX	**1,472**	**6.9**	**36**	**2**	**3**	**5**	**9**	**14**	**17**	**27**
TOTAL										
0–19 Years	55	8.2	42	2	3	7	11	17	26	26
20–34	443	4.9	13	1	2	4	6	9	12	20
35–49	569	6.7	52	2	3	5	8	14	19	34
50–64	309	7.0	29	2	4	6	9	14	16	27
65+	240	9.8	38	3	5	9	14	17	21	29
GRAND TOTAL	**1,616**	**6.8**	**38**	**2**	**3**	**5**	**8**	**14**	**17**	**28**

94.35: CRISIS INTERVENTION

Type of Patients	Observed Patients	Avg. Stay	Vari-ance	Percentiles						
				10th	25th	50th	75th	90th	95th	99th
1. SINGLE DX										
0–19 Years	0									
20–34	0									
35–49	0									
50–64	0									
65+	0									
2. MULTIPLE DX										
0–19 Years	0									
20–34	0									
35–49	0									
50–64	0									
65+	0									
TOTAL SINGLE DX	**0**									
TOTAL MULTIPLE DX	**0**									
TOTAL										
0–19 Years	0									
20–34	0									
35–49	0									
50–64	0									
65+	0									
GRAND TOTAL	**0**									

94.38: SUPP VERBAL PSYCHTX

Type of Patients	Observed Patients	Avg. Stay	Vari-ance	Percentiles						
				10th	25th	50th	75th	90th	95th	99th
1. SINGLE DX										
0–19 Years	0									
20–34	0									
35–49	0									
50–64	0									
65+	0									
2. MULTIPLE DX										
0–19 Years	0									
20–34	0									
35–49	0									
50–64	0									
65+	0									
TOTAL SINGLE DX	**0**									
TOTAL MULTIPLE DX	**0**									
TOTAL										
0–19 Years	0									
20–34	0									
35–49	0									
50–64	0									
65+	0									
GRAND TOTAL	**0**									

94.39: INDIVIDUAL PSYCHTX NEC

Type of Patients	Observed Patients	Avg. Stay	Vari-ance	Percentiles						
				10th	25th	50th	75th	90th	95th	99th
1. SINGLE DX										
0–19 Years	4	8.3	2	7	8	8	8	11	11	11
20–34	85	4.3	17	1	1	3	6	11	11	13
35–49	34	8.8	141	1	1	4	10	34	34	34
50–64	14	4.4	14	1	2	2	7	11	11	11
65+	2	7.0	0	7	7	7	7	7	7	7
2. MULTIPLE DX										
0–19 Years	45	8.5	46	2	3	7	13	17	26	26
20–34	336	5.1	12	2	3	4	7	9	12	19
35–49	508	6.6	47	2	3	5	8	13	16	25
50–64	277	7.2	29	2	4	6	9	14	17	27
65+	165	11.1	36	4	6	11	14	18	21	30
TOTAL SINGLE DX	**139**	**5.8**	**53**	**1**	**1**	**3**	**7**	**11**	**26**	**34**
TOTAL MULTIPLE DX	**1,331**	**7.0**	**37**	**2**	**3**	**5**	**9**	**14**	**17**	**27**
TOTAL										
0–19 Years	49	8.5	42	2	4	7	11	17	26	26
20–34	421	4.9	13	1	2	4	6	9	12	19
35–49	542	6.8	53	2	3	5	8	14	19	34
50–64	291	7.1	29	2	4	6	9	14	17	27
65+	167	11.0	36	4	6	11	14	18	21	30
GRAND TOTAL	**1,470**	**6.9**	**38**	**2**	**3**	**5**	**9**	**14**	**17**	**28**

94.4: OTH PSYCHTX/COUNSELLING

Type of Patients	Observed Patients	Avg. Stay	Vari-ance	Percentiles						
				10th	25th	50th	75th	90th	95th	99th
1. SINGLE DX										
0–19 Years	6	12.2	29	3	9	16	16	16	16	16
20–34	17	6.0	32	1	4	4	7	17	24	24
35–49	21	6.6	22	2	3	6	8	13	18	20
50–64	14	6.2	8	3	5	5	8	8	12	16
65+	1	36.0	0	36	36	36	36	36	36	36
2. MULTIPLE DX										
0–19 Years	36	9.3	36	4	7	7	10	16	20	34
20–34	166	7.7	46	2	3	6	10	15	20	29
35–49	476	10.0	57	3	6	8	13	18	24	38
50–64	378	11.0	80	3	5	8	14	22	28	44
65+	546	13.4	63	5	7	12	17	24	28	42
TOTAL SINGLE DX	**59**	**7.5**	**35**	**2**	**4**	**5**	**9**	**16**	**17**	**36**
TOTAL MULTIPLE DX	**1,602**	**10.9**	**65**	**3**	**6**	**9**	**14**	**21**	**27**	**38**
TOTAL										
0–19 Years	42	9.7	36	4	7	8	12	16	20	34
20–34	183	7.6	45	2	3	6	10	15	20	28
35–49	497	9.8	56	3	5	8	12	18	24	36
50–64	392	10.8	77	3	5	8	14	22	27	44
65+	547	13.4	64	5	7	12	17	24	28	42
GRAND TOTAL	**1,661**	**10.8**	**65**	**3**	**5**	**8**	**14**	**21**	**26**	**38**

94.44: GROUP THERAPY NEC

Type of Patients	Observed Patients	Avg. Stay	Vari-ance	Percentiles 10th	25th	50th	75th	90th	95th	99th
1. SINGLE DX										
0–19 Years	5	12.6	31	1	11	16	16	16	16	16
20–34	17	6.0	32	1	4	4	7	17	24	24
35–49	20	6.2	17	2	3	6	8	13	13	18
50–64	14	6.2	8	3	5	5	8	8	12	16
65+	1	36.0	0	36	36	36	36	36	36	36
2. MULTIPLE DX										
0–19 Years	35	9.7	37	4	7	7	10	17	20	34
20–34	161	7.8	47	2	4	6	10	15	20	29
35–49	464	10.2	59	3	6	8	13	18	24	38
50–64	377	11.1	80	3	5	8	14	22	28	44
65+	544	13.4	63	5	7	12	17	24	28	42
TOTAL SINGLE DX	**57**	**7.3**	**34**	**2**	**4**	**5**	**8**	**16**	**17**	**36**
TOTAL MULTIPLE DX	**1,581**	**11.0**	**66**	**3**	**6**	**9**	**14**	**21**	**27**	**38**
TOTAL										
0–19 Years	40	10.0	37	4	7	9	12	16	20	34
20–34	178	7.6	46	2	4	6	10	15	20	28
35–49	484	10.0	58	3	5	8	13	18	24	38
50–64	391	10.8	77	3	5	8	14	22	27	44
65+	545	13.4	64	5	7	12	17	24	28	42
GRAND TOTAL	**1,638**	**10.9**	**65**	**3**	**5**	**9**	**14**	**21**	**27**	**38**

94.49: COUNSELLING NEC

Type of Patients	Observed Patients	Avg. Stay	Vari-ance	Percentiles 10th	25th	50th	75th	90th	95th	99th
1. SINGLE DX										
0–19 Years	0									
20–34	0									
35–49	0									
50–64	0									
65+	0									
2. MULTIPLE DX										
0–19 Years	0									
20–34	0									
35–49	0									
50–64	0									
65+	0									
TOTAL SINGLE DX	**0**									
TOTAL MULTIPLE DX	**0**									
TOTAL										
0–19 Years	0									
20–34	0									
35–49	0									
50–64	0									
65+	0									
GRAND TOTAL	**0**									

94.5: REFERRAL PSYCH REHAB

Type of Patients	Observed Patients	Avg. Stay	Vari-ance	Percentiles 10th	25th	50th	75th	90th	95th	99th
1. SINGLE DX										
0–19 Years	0									
20–34	0									
35–49	0									
50–64	0									
65+	0									
2. MULTIPLE DX										
0–19 Years	0									
20–34	0									
35–49	0									
50–64	0									
65+	1	7.0	0	7	7	7	7	7	7	7
TOTAL SINGLE DX	**0**									
TOTAL MULTIPLE DX	**1**	**7.0**	**0**	**7**	**7**	**7**	**7**	**7**	**7**	**7**
TOTAL										
0–19 Years	0									
20–34	0									
35–49	0									
50–64	0									
65+	1	7.0	0	7	7	7	7	7	7	7
GRAND TOTAL	**1**	**7.0**	**0**	**7**	**7**	**7**	**7**	**7**	**7**	**7**

94.6: ALCOHOL/DRUG REHAB/DETOX

Type of Patients	Observed Patients	Avg. Stay	Vari-ance	Percentiles 10th	25th	50th	75th	90th	95th	99th
1. SINGLE DX										
0–19 Years	17	5.0	41	1	2	2	5	17	17	28
20–34	177	8.7	152	1	2	4	9	31	49	>99
35–49	315	10.2	209	1	2	4	11	29	42	>99
50–64	107	11.5	285	2	2	5	14	29	47	92
65+	15	7.7	155	1	2	3	9	14	26	59
2. MULTIPLE DX										
0–19 Years	456	17.5	218	2	4	13	28	42	42	42
20–34	3,730	6.1	40	1	2	4	7	14	21	28
35–49	9,505	5.7	27	2	3	4	7	12	16	28
50–64	5,144	5.8	24	2	3	4	7	12	15	26
65+	1,055	6.2	28	2	3	5	7	12	16	29
TOTAL SINGLE DX	**631**	**9.8**	**203**	**1**	**2**	**4**	**11**	**29**	**46**	**>99**
TOTAL MULTIPLE DX	**19,890**	**6.3**	**41**	**2**	**3**	**4**	**7**	**13**	**20**	**35**
TOTAL										
0–19 Years	473	17.2	217	2	4	13	27	42	42	42
20–34	3,907	6.2	44	1	2	4	7	14	21	29
35–49	9,820	5.8	33	2	3	4	7	12	17	28
50–64	5,251	5.9	30	2	3	4	7	12	15	28
65+	1,070	6.2	30	2	3	5	7	12	16	31
GRAND TOTAL	**20,521**	**6.4**	**45**	**2**	**3**	**4**	**7**	**14**	**20**	**41**

94.61: ALCOHOL REHABILITATION

Type of Patients	Observed Patients	Avg. Stay	Vari-ance	Percentiles						
				10th	25th	50th	75th	90th	95th	99th
1. SINGLE DX										
0–19 Years	1	17.0	0	17	17	17	17	17	17	17
20–34	22	25.8	360	4	14	27	33	91	>99	>99
35–49	49	24.7	413	5	8	25	34	74	>99	>99
50–64	18	33.5	634	2	14	28	39	92	92	>99
65+	2	11.7	7	10	10	10	14	14	14	14
2. MULTIPLE DX										
0–19 Years	6	7.0	26	3	3	3	14	14	14	14
20–34	79	9.8	74	1	2	7	16	21	28	28
35–49	289	7.4	52	1	2	5	11	18	21	33
50–64	148	8.8	57	1	2	7	14	21	22	28
65+	24	10.5	53	2	5	11	14	20	28	28
TOTAL SINGLE DX	**92**	**26.4**	**448**	**4**	**13**	**27**	**34**	**81**	**>99**	**>99**
TOTAL MULTIPLE DX	**546**	**8.3**	**56**	**1**	**2**	**5**	**13**	**20**	**23**	**28**
TOTAL										
0–19 Years	7	8.2	34	3	3	3	14	17	17	17
20–34	101	12.5	159	2	3	9	20	28	33	>99
35–49	338	10.0	145	1	2	6	14	28	33	84
50–64	166	11.4	172	1	3	8	15	27	28	92
65+	26	10.6	50	2	5	11	14	20	28	28
GRAND TOTAL	**638**	**10.8**	**149**	**1**	**3**	**7**	**14**	**28**	**31**	**92**

94.62: ALCOHOL DETOXIFICATION

Type of Patients	Observed Patients	Avg. Stay	Vari-ance	Percentiles						
				10th	25th	50th	75th	90th	95th	99th
1. SINGLE DX										
0–19 Years	0									
20–34	37	2.2	<1	1	1	2	3	3	3	6
35–49	96	2.6	5	1	1	2	3	4	6	12
50–64	40	3.0	4	1	2	3	3	6	6	11
65+	5	7.4	101	2	3	3	4	26	26	26
2. MULTIPLE DX										
0–19 Years	44	2.4	2	1	1	2	3	5	6	6
20–34	1,301	3.6	11	1	2	3	4	7	10	17
35–49	4,793	4.1	12	1	2	3	5	8	10	17
50–64	2,936	4.3	13	1	2	3	5	8	11	18
65+	761	5.3	21	2	3	4	6	10	14	23
TOTAL SINGLE DX	**178**	**2.7**	**6**	**1**	**1**	**2**	**3**	**4**	**6**	**12**
TOTAL MULTIPLE DX	**9,835**	**4.2**	**13**	**1**	**2**	**3**	**5**	**8**	**10**	**18**
TOTAL										
0–19 Years	44	2.4	2	1	1	2	3	5	6	6
20–34	1,338	3.6	11	1	2	3	4	7	10	17
35–49	4,889	4.0	12	1	2	3	5	8	10	17
50–64	2,976	4.3	13	1	2	3	5	8	11	18
65+	766	5.3	22	2	3	4	6	10	14	26
GRAND TOTAL	**10,013**	**4.2**	**13**	**1**	**2**	**3**	**5**	**8**	**10**	**18**

94.63: ALCOHOL REHAB/DETOX

Type of Patients	Observed Patients	Avg. Stay	Vari-ance	Percentiles						
				10th	25th	50th	75th	90th	95th	99th
1. SINGLE DX										
0–19 Years	5	3.3	7	1	1	2	7	7	7	7
20–34	29	5.7	24	2	3	5	7	9	10	31
35–49	91	8.1	71	2	4	5	9	27	32	36
50–64	32	10.3	98	2	4	6	14	29	29	47
65+	5	3.6	10	1	2	2	8	9	9	9
2. MULTIPLE DX										
0–19 Years	9	7.7	66	1	3	3	16	17	25	25
20–34	181	8.4	40	2	3	7	11	17	21	28
35–49	750	8.3	36	3	4	6	11	17	21	28
50–64	459	9.5	42	3	5	8	13	20	22	29
65+	118	8.6	26	3	5	6	12	16	17	23
TOTAL SINGLE DX	**162**	**7.7**	**66**	**2**	**3**	**5**	**8**	**16**	**29**	**35**
TOTAL MULTIPLE DX	**1,517**	**8.7**	**38**	**3**	**4**	**7**	**12**	**17**	**21**	**28**
TOTAL										
0–19 Years	14	5.8	45	1	2	3	7	17	17	25
20–34	210	8.1	39	2	3	6	10	17	21	28
35–49	841	8.2	39	3	4	6	11	17	21	29
50–64	491	9.5	46	3	5	8	13	20	22	29
65+	123	8.3	26	3	5	6	11	15	17	23
GRAND TOTAL	**1,679**	**8.6**	**40**	**3**	**4**	**6**	**11**	**17**	**21**	**29**

94.64: DRUG REHABILITATION

Type of Patients	Observed Patients	Avg. Stay	Vari-ance	Percentiles						
				10th	25th	50th	75th	90th	95th	99th
1. SINGLE DX										
0–19 Years	2	6.8	124	2	2	2	2	28	28	28
20–34	25	20.4	227	6	8	25	43	>99	>99	>99
35–49	20	27.4	542	7	13	27	39	88	>99	>99
50–64	2	21.4	84	14	14	28	28	28	28	28
65+	0									
2. MULTIPLE DX										
0–19 Years	38	11.8	41	2	7	12	15	21	22	28
20–34	108	10.7	85	1	3	8	18	27	28	41
35–49	150	10.5	61	2	3	9	16	21	24	29
50–64	41	7.7	35	1	2	7	13	15	21	21
65+	3	14.8	3	13	14	14	17	17	17	17
TOTAL SINGLE DX	**49**	**22.2**	**371**	**2**	**7**	**24**	**39**	**>99**	**>99**	**>99**
TOTAL MULTIPLE DX	**340**	**10.5**	**63**	**2**	**4**	**8**	**15**	**21**	**27**	**29**
TOTAL										
0–19 Years	40	11.5	46	2	7	12	15	21	22	28
20–34	133	11.9	113	2	4	8	20	28	41	>99
35–49	170	12.1	128	2	4	10	18	24	28	88
50–64	43	8.1	41	1	2	7	14	16	21	28
65+	3	14.8	3	13	14	14	17	17	17	17
GRAND TOTAL	**389**	**11.5**	**101**	**2**	**4**	**9**	**16**	**25**	**28**	**>99**

94.65: DRUG DETOXIFICATION

Type of Patients	Observed Patients	Avg. Stay	Variance	10th	25th	50th	75th	90th	95th	99th
1. SINGLE DX										
0–19 Years	3	2.1	1	1	1	3	3	3	3	3
20–34	35	3.4	9	1	2	3	4	6	9	20
35–49	36	4.2	8	2	2	4	5	7	10	16
50–64	12	3.5	3	2	2	3	5	5	5	8
65+	1	5.0	0	5	5	5	5	5	5	5
2. MULTIPLE DX										
0–19 Years	83	4.7	15	1	2	3	6	10	12	17
20–34	1,043	4.9	20	2	3	4	6	9	11	23
35–49	1,658	5.6	13	2	3	5	8	10	12	19
50–64	814	6.4	15	2	4	6	8	11	13	20
65+	75	8.0	73	2	3	5	8	17	35	35
TOTAL SINGLE DX	**87**	**3.7**	**7**	**1**	**2**	**3**	**5**	**6**	**9**	**16**
TOTAL MULTIPLE DX	**3,673**	**5.6**	**17**	**2**	**3**	**5**	**8**	**10**	**12**	**21**
TOTAL										
0–19 Years	86	4.7	15	1	2	3	6	10	12	17
20–34	1,078	4.9	19	2	3	4	6	8	11	23
35–49	1,694	5.6	13	2	3	5	8	10	12	19
50–64	826	6.4	15	2	4	6	8	11	13	20
65+	76	8.0	72	2	3	5	8	17	35	35
GRAND TOTAL	**3,760**	**5.6**	**17**	**2**	**3**	**5**	**8**	**10**	**12**	**21**

94.66: DRUG REHAB/DETOX

Type of Patients	Observed Patients	Avg. Stay	Variance	10th	25th	50th	75th	90th	95th	99th
1. SINGLE DX										
0–19 Years	6	2.8	1	2	2	3	3	5	5	5
20–34	28	6.0	56	1	2	4	6	11	28	31
35–49	22	9.4	52	2	4	7	14	18	28	28
50–64	3	4.7	6	2	2	5	7	7	7	7
65+	2	32.3	>999	5	5	59	59	59	59	59
2. MULTIPLE DX										
0–19 Years	50	12.6	68	3	5	13	18	25	26	28
20–34	352	11.1	74	3	5	8	16	26	28	31
35–49	442	10.2	61	3	5	7	14	22	28	31
50–64	195	10.0	33	4	6	9	12	20	21	28
65+	27	7.5	17	4	5	6	10	13	17	23
TOTAL SINGLE DX	**61**	**7.7**	**85**	**2**	**3**	**4**	**8**	**16**	**28**	**59**
TOTAL MULTIPLE DX	**1,066**	**10.5**	**60**	**3**	**5**	**8**	**14**	**23**	**28**	**31**
TOTAL										
0–19 Years	56	12.0	69	3	3	10	18	25	26	28
20–34	380	10.8	75	3	4	7	15	26	28	31
35–49	464	10.2	60	3	5	7	14	21	28	31
50–64	198	9.9	33	4	6	9	12	20	21	28
65+	29	8.5	71	4	5	6	10	13	17	59
GRAND TOTAL	**1,127**	**10.4**	**61**	**3**	**5**	**8**	**14**	**23**	**28**	**31**

94.67: ALC/DRUG REHABILITATION

Type of Patients	Observed Patients	Avg. Stay	Variance	10th	25th	50th	75th	90th	95th	99th
1. SINGLE DX										
0–19 Years	0									
20–34	1	8.0	0	8	8	8	8	8	8	8
35–49	0									
50–64	0									
65+	0									
2. MULTIPLE DX										
0–19 Years	156	27.3	225	8	13	33	42	42	42	42
20–34	138	12.8	69	3	5	13	20	23	28	50
35–49	204	11.2	61	2	4	10	17	21	28	28
50–64	42	10.9	62	3	6	8	17	22	28	29
65+	0									
TOTAL SINGLE DX	**1**	**8.0**	**0**	**8**	**8**	**8**	**8**	**8**	**8**	**8**
TOTAL MULTIPLE DX	**540**	**18.6**	**196**	**3**	**8**	**14**	**28**	**42**	**42**	**42**
TOTAL										
0–19 Years	156	27.3	225	8	13	33	42	42	42	42
20–34	139	12.7	69	3	5	13	20	22	28	50
35–49	204	11.2	61	2	4	10	17	21	28	28
50–64	42	10.9	62	3	6	8	17	22	28	29
65+	0									
GRAND TOTAL	**541**	**18.6**	**196**	**3**	**8**	**14**	**28**	**42**	**42**	**42**

94.68: ALC/DRUG DETOXIFICATION

Type of Patients	Observed Patients	Avg. Stay	Variance	10th	25th	50th	75th	90th	95th	99th
1. SINGLE DX										
0–19 Years	0									
20–34	0									
35–49	1	4.0	0	4	4	4	4	4	4	4
50–64	0									
65+	0									
2. MULTIPLE DX										
0–19 Years	29	7.9	60	1	2	5	13	15	16	42
20–34	351	4.5	17	2	2	4	5	8	11	22
35–49	817	5.0	13	2	3	4	6	8	11	19
50–64	360	5.4	12	2	3	5	7	10	12	16
65+	28	4.8	8	1	2	5	7	9	9	10
TOTAL SINGLE DX	**1**	**4.0**	**0**	**4**	**4**	**4**	**4**	**4**	**4**	**4**
TOTAL MULTIPLE DX	**1,585**	**5.0**	**15**	**2**	**3**	**4**	**6**	**9**	**12**	**19**
TOTAL										
0–19 Years	29	7.9	60	1	2	5	13	15	16	42
20–34	351	4.5	17	2	2	4	5	8	11	22
35–49	818	5.0	13	2	3	4	6	8	11	19
50–64	360	5.4	12	2	3	5	7	10	12	16
65+	28	4.8	8	1	2	5	7	9	9	10
GRAND TOTAL	**1,586**	**5.0**	**15**	**2**	**3**	**4**	**6**	**9**	**12**	**19**

94.69: ALC/DRUG REHAB/DETOX

Type of Patients	Observed Patients	Avg. Stay	Vari-ance	Percentiles						
				10th	25th	50th	75th	90th	95th	99th
1. SINGLE DX										
0–19 Years	0									
20–34	0									
35–49	0									
50–64	0									
65+	0									
2. MULTIPLE DX										
0–19 Years	41	15.7	55	3	13	15	21	23	29	29
20–34	177	10.2	70	2	4	6	16	24	28	29
35–49	402	10.3	57	3	5	7	14	22	28	31
50–64	149	10.4	50	4	6	8	13	20	28	32
65+	19	8.3	32	5	5	6	9	15	23	28
TOTAL SINGLE DX	**0**									
TOTAL MULTIPLE DX	**788**	**10.7**	**60**	**3**	**5**	**8**	**15**	**22**	**28**	**30**
TOTAL										
0–19 Years	41	15.7	55	3	13	15	21	23	29	29
20–34	177	10.2	70	2	4	6	16	24	28	29
35–49	402	10.3	57	3	5	7	14	22	28	31
50–64	149	10.4	50	4	6	8	13	20	28	32
65+	19	8.3	32	5	5	6	9	15	23	28
GRAND TOTAL	**788**	**10.7**	**60**	**3**	**5**	**8**	**15**	**22**	**28**	**30**

95.0: GEN/SUBJECTIVE EYE EXAM

Type of Patients	Observed Patients	Avg. Stay	Vari-ance	Percentiles						
				10th	25th	50th	75th	90th	95th	99th
1. SINGLE DX										
0–19 Years	10	2.1	2	1	1	1	3	4	4	4
20–34	0									
35–49	0									
50–64	1	2.0	0	2	2	2	2	2	2	2
65+	0									
2. MULTIPLE DX										
0–19 Years	81	3.0	12	1	1	2	3	7	11	17
20–34	2	2.6	1	2	2	2	4	4	4	4
35–49	2	1.4	<1	1	1	1	2	2	2	2
50–64	3	1.5	2	1	1	1	1	4	4	4
65+	2	9.5	55	4	4	15	15	15	15	15
TOTAL SINGLE DX	**11**	**2.1**	**2**	**1**	**1**	**2**	**3**	**4**	**4**	**4**
TOTAL MULTIPLE DX	**90**	**3.0**	**12**	**1**	**1**	**2**	**3**	**7**	**11**	**17**
TOTAL										
0–19 Years	91	2.9	11	1	1	2	3	6	11	17
20–34	2	2.6	1	2	2	2	4	4	4	4
35–49	2	1.4	<1	1	1	1	2	2	2	2
50–64	4	1.6	1	1	1	1	2	4	4	4
65+	2	9.5	55	4	4	15	15	15	15	15
GRAND TOTAL	**101**	**2.9**	**11**	**1**	**1**	**2**	**3**	**6**	**11**	**17**

95.1: FORM & STRUCT EYE EXAM

Type of Patients	Observed Patients	Avg. Stay	Vari-ance	Percentiles						
				10th	25th	50th	75th	90th	95th	99th
1. SINGLE DX										
0–19 Years	1	2.0	0	2	2	2	2	2	2	2
20–34	0									
35–49	0									
50–64	0									
65+	0									
2. MULTIPLE DX										
0–19 Years	2	8.5	138	1	1	1	20	20	20	20
20–34	1	11.0	0	11	11	11	11	11	11	11
35–49	0									
50–64	0									
65+	2	5.4	26	2	2	2	10	10	10	10
TOTAL SINGLE DX	**1**	**2.0**	**0**	**2**	**2**	**2**	**2**	**2**	**2**	**2**
TOTAL MULTIPLE DX	**5**	**7.9**	**54**	**1**	**2**	**10**	**11**	**20**	**20**	**20**
TOTAL										
0–19 Years	3	6.7	97	1	1	2	20	20	20	20
20–34	1	11.0	0	11	11	11	11	11	11	11
35–49	0									
50–64	0									
65+	2	5.4	26	2	2	2	10	10	10	10
GRAND TOTAL	**6**	**7.1**	**50**	**1**	**2**	**2**	**11**	**20**	**20**	**20**

95.2: OBJECTIVE FUNCT EYE TEST

Type of Patients	Observed Patients	Avg. Stay	Vari-ance	Percentiles						
				10th	25th	50th	75th	90th	95th	99th
1. SINGLE DX										
0–19 Years	0									
20–34	1	2.0	0	2	2	2	2	2	2	2
35–49	0									
50–64	0									
65+	0									
2. MULTIPLE DX										
0–19 Years	0									
20–34	1	3.0	0	3	3	3	3	3	3	3
35–49	0									
50–64	3	8.2	2	6	8	8	10	10	10	10
65+	2	6.1	25	2	2	10	10	10	10	10
TOTAL SINGLE DX	**1**	**2.0**	**0**	**2**	**2**	**2**	**2**	**2**	**2**	**2**
TOTAL MULTIPLE DX	**6**	**6.8**	**10**	**2**	**3**	**8**	**10**	**10**	**>99**	**>99**
TOTAL										
0–19 Years	0									
20–34	2	2.6	<1	2	2	3	3	3	3	3
35–49	0									
50–64	3	8.2	2	6	8	8	10	10	10	10
65+	2	6.1	25	2	2	10	10	10	10	10
GRAND TOTAL	**7**	**6.4**	**11**	**2**	**3**	**8**	**10**	**10**	**>99**	**>99**

95.3: SPECIAL VISION SERVICES

Type of Patients	Observed Patients	Avg. Stay	Vari-ance	Percentiles						
				10th	25th	50th	75th	90th	95th	99th
1. SINGLE DX										
0–19 Years	0									
20–34	0									
35–49	0									
50–64	0									
65+	0									
2. MULTIPLE DX										
0–19 Years	0									
20–34	0									
35–49	0									
50–64	0									
65+	0									
TOTAL SINGLE DX	**0**									
TOTAL MULTIPLE DX	**0**									
TOTAL										
0–19 Years	0									
20–34	0									
35–49	0									
50–64	0									
65+	0									
GRAND TOTAL	**0**									

95.4: NONOP HEARING PROCEDURE

Type of Patients	Observed Patients	Avg. Stay	Vari-ance	Percentiles						
				10th	25th	50th	75th	90th	95th	99th
1. SINGLE DX										
0–19 Years	5,817	1.8	<1	1	1	2	2	3	4	4
20–34	0									
35–49	1	3.0	0	3	3	3	3	3	3	3
50–64	0									
65+	0									
2. MULTIPLE DX										
0–19 Years	7,953	2.4	5	1	2	2	3	4	4	9
20–34	0									
35–49	1	2.0	0	2	2	2	2	2	2	2
50–64	2	2.0	0	2	2	2	2	2	2	2
65+	7	5.7	6	4	4	6	6	12	12	12
TOTAL SINGLE DX	**5,818**	**1.8**	**<1**	**1**	**1**	**2**	**2**	**3**	**4**	**4**
TOTAL MULTIPLE DX	**7,963**	**2.4**	**5**	**1**	**2**	**2**	**3**	**4**	**4**	**9**
TOTAL										
0–19 Years	13,770	2.2	3	1	1	2	2	4	4	7
20–34	0									
35–49	2	2.5	<1	2	2	2	3	3	3	3
50–64	2	2.0	0	2	2	2	2	2	2	2
65+	7	5.7	6	4	4	6	6	12	12	12
GRAND TOTAL	**13,781**	**2.2**	**3**	**1**	**1**	**2**	**2**	**4**	**4**	**7**

95.41: AUDIOMETRY

Type of Patients	Observed Patients	Avg. Stay	Vari-ance	Percentiles						
				10th	25th	50th	75th	90th	95th	99th
1. SINGLE DX										
0–19 Years	1,299	1.8	<1	1	1	2	2	3	3	4
20–34	0									
35–49	1	3.0	0	3	3	3	3	3	3	3
50–64	0									
65+	0									
2. MULTIPLE DX										
0–19 Years	1,269	2.7	12	1	2	2	3	4	5	17
20–34	0									
35–49	1	2.0	0	2	2	2	2	2	2	2
50–64	2	2.0	0	2	2	2	2	2	2	2
65+	7	5.7	6	4	4	6	6	12	12	12
TOTAL SINGLE DX	**1,300**	**1.8**	**<1**	**1**	**1**	**2**	**2**	**3**	**3**	**4**
TOTAL MULTIPLE DX	**1,279**	**2.8**	**12**	**1**	**2**	**2**	**3**	**4**	**6**	**17**
TOTAL										
0–19 Years	2,568	2.2	6	1	1	2	2	3	4	10
20–34	0									
35–49	2	2.5	<1	2	2	2	3	3	3	3
50–64	2	2.0	0	2	2	2	2	2	2	2
65+	7	5.7	6	4	4	6	6	12	12	12
GRAND TOTAL	**2,579**	**2.3**	**6**	**1**	**1**	**2**	**3**	**3**	**4**	**11**

95.42: CLINICAL HEARING TEST

Type of Patients	Observed Patients	Avg. Stay	Vari-ance	Percentiles						
				10th	25th	50th	75th	90th	95th	99th
1. SINGLE DX										
0–19 Years	1	2.0	0	2	2	2	2	2	2	2
20–34	0									
35–49	0									
50–64	0									
65+	0									
2. MULTIPLE DX										
0–19 Years	11	1.9	<1	1	1	2	3	3	3	3
20–34	0									
35–49	0									
50–64	0									
65+	0									
TOTAL SINGLE DX	**1**	**2.0**	**0**	**2**	**2**	**2**	**2**	**2**	**2**	**2**
TOTAL MULTIPLE DX	**11**	**1.9**	**<1**	**1**	**1**	**2**	**3**	**3**	**3**	**3**
TOTAL										
0–19 Years	12	1.9	<1	1	1	2	3	3	3	3
20–34	0									
35–49	0									
50–64	0									
65+	0									
GRAND TOTAL	**12**	**1.9**	**<1**	**1**	**1**	**2**	**3**	**3**	**3**	**3**

95.43: AUDIOLOGICAL EVALUATION

Type of Patients	Observed Patients	Avg. Stay	Vari-ance	10th	25th	50th	75th	90th	95th	99th
1. SINGLE DX										
0–19 Years	645	1.6	<1	1	1	2	2	2	3	4
20–34	0									
35–49	0									
50–64	0									
65+	0									
2. MULTIPLE DX										
0–19 Years	2,165	2.1	4	1	1	2	2	3	4	9
20–34	0									
35–49	0									
50–64	0									
65+	0									
TOTAL SINGLE DX	**645**	**1.6**	**<1**	**1**	**1**	**2**	**2**	**2**	**3**	**4**
TOTAL MULTIPLE DX	**2,165**	**2.1**	**4**	**1**	**1**	**2**	**2**	**3**	**4**	**9**
TOTAL										
0–19 Years	2,810	2.0	3	1	1	2	2	3	4	8
20–34	0									
35–49	0									
50–64	0									
65+	0									
GRAND TOTAL	**2,810**	**2.0**	**3**	**1**	**1**	**2**	**2**	**3**	**4**	**8**

95.46: AUDITORY & VEST TEST NEC

Type of Patients	Observed Patients	Avg. Stay	Vari-ance	10th	25th	50th	75th	90th	95th	99th
1. SINGLE DX										
0–19 Years	1,002	2.2	<1	1	2	2	2	4	4	4
20–34	0									
35–49	0									
50–64	0									
65+	0									
2. MULTIPLE DX										
0–19 Years	2,101	2.5	2	2	2	2	3	4	4	6
20–34	0									
35–49	0									
50–64	0									
65+	0									
TOTAL SINGLE DX	**1,002**	**2.2**	**<1**	**1**	**2**	**2**	**2**	**4**	**4**	**4**
TOTAL MULTIPLE DX	**2,101**	**2.5**	**2**	**2**	**2**	**2**	**3**	**4**	**4**	**6**
TOTAL										
0–19 Years	3,103	2.4	2	1	2	2	3	4	4	5
20–34	0									
35–49	0									
50–64	0									
65+	0									
GRAND TOTAL	**3,103**	**2.4**	**2**	**1**	**2**	**2**	**3**	**4**	**4**	**5**

95.47: HEARING EXAMINATION NOS

Type of Patients	Observed Patients	Avg. Stay	Vari-ance	10th	25th	50th	75th	90th	95th	99th
1. SINGLE DX										
0–19 Years	2,870	1.7	<1	1	1	2	2	3	4	4
20–34	0									
35–49	0									
50–64	0									
65+	0									
2. MULTIPLE DX										
0–19 Years	2,403	2.2	6	1	1	2	2	3	4	8
20–34	0									
35–49	0									
50–64	0									
65+	0									
TOTAL SINGLE DX	**2,870**	**1.7**	**<1**	**1**	**1**	**2**	**2**	**3**	**4**	**4**
TOTAL MULTIPLE DX	**2,403**	**2.2**	**6**	**1**	**1**	**2**	**2**	**3**	**4**	**8**
TOTAL										
0–19 Years	5,273	1.9	3	1	1	2	2	3	4	6
20–34	0									
35–49	0									
50–64	0									
65+	0									
GRAND TOTAL	**5,273**	**1.9**	**3**	**1**	**1**	**2**	**2**	**3**	**4**	**6**

95.49: NONOP HEARING PX NEC

Type of Patients	Observed Patients	Avg. Stay	Vari-ance	10th	25th	50th	75th	90th	95th	99th
1. SINGLE DX										
0–19 Years	0									
20–34	0									
35–49	0									
50–64	0									
65+	0									
2. MULTIPLE DX										
0–19 Years	4	3.8	11	1	1	3	8	8	8	8
20–34	0									
35–49	0									
50–64	0									
65+	0									
TOTAL SINGLE DX	**0**									
TOTAL MULTIPLE DX	**4**	**3.8**	**11**	**1**	**1**	**3**	**8**	**8**	**8**	**8**
TOTAL										
0–19 Years	4	3.8	11	1	1	3	8	8	8	8
20–34	0									
35–49	0									
50–64	0									
65+	0									
GRAND TOTAL	**4**	**3.8**	**11**	**1**	**1**	**3**	**8**	**8**	**8**	**8**

96.0: NONOP GI & RESP INTUB

Type of Patients	Observed Patients	Avg. Stay	Vari-ance	Percentiles 10th	25th	50th	75th	90th	95th	99th
1. SINGLE DX										
0–19 Years	290	2.2	3	1	1	2	2	4	5	11
20–34	55	2.8	3	1	1	2	4	4	6	12
35–49	60	2.8	3	1	1	2	3	5	7	9
50–64	53	2.2	2	1	1	2	3	4	4	6
65+	28	3.6	3	1	2	4	5	7	7	7
2. MULTIPLE DX										
0–19 Years	4,572	16.0	477	1	2	5	23	55	75	>99
20–34	1,241	4.9	45	1	2	3	5	11	17	35
35–49	2,211	5.8	38	1	2	4	7	13	19	28
50–64	2,390	6.9	49	2	3	5	9	15	21	34
65+	4,304	7.4	45	2	3	5	9	16	20	30
TOTAL SINGLE DX	**486**	**2.4**	**3**	**1**	**1**	**2**	**3**	**4**	**6**	**11**
TOTAL MULTIPLE DX	**14,718**	**9.5**	**195**	**1**	**2**	**5**	**10**	**23**	**42**	**90**
TOTAL										
0–19 Years	4,862	15.1	459	1	2	4	21	53	74	>99
20–34	1,296	4.8	43	1	2	3	5	10	16	33
35–49	2,271	5.7	37	1	2	4	7	13	19	28
50–64	2,443	6.7	49	1	3	4	8	15	20	34
65+	4,332	7.3	45	2	3	5	9	16	20	30
GRAND TOTAL	**15,204**	**9.2**	**190**	**1**	**2**	**4**	**10**	**22**	**41**	**89**

96.04: INSERT ENDOTRACHEAL TUBE

Type of Patients	Observed Patients	Avg. Stay	Vari-ance	Percentiles 10th	25th	50th	75th	90th	95th	99th
1. SINGLE DX										
0–19 Years	213	2.1	3	1	1	2	2	3	6	11
20–34	20	3.2	4	1	2	3	4	4	7	12
35–49	9	1.5	<1	1	1	1	2	2	2	2
50–64	4	2.2	4	1	1	1	2	6	6	6
65+	1	4.0	0	4	4	4	4	4	4	4
2. MULTIPLE DX										
0–19 Years	4,103	17.5	513	1	2	7	27	60	79	>99
20–34	943	5.2	50	1	1	3	6	12	19	35
35–49	1,522	6.7	49	1	2	4	9	17	22	30
50–64	1,430	8.9	67	2	3	7	12	19	25	41
65+	2,202	10.0	65	3	5	8	13	20	24	40
TOTAL SINGLE DX	**247**	**2.2**	**3**	**1**	**1**	**2**	**2**	**4**	**6**	**11**
TOTAL MULTIPLE DX	**10,200**	**12.0**	**266**	**1**	**3**	**6**	**14**	**32**	**54**	**98**
TOTAL										
0–19 Years	4,316	16.8	499	1	2	6	26	57	78	>99
20–34	963	5.1	49	1	1	3	6	12	18	33
35–49	1,531	6.7	49	1	2	4	9	17	22	30
50–64	1,434	8.9	67	2	3	7	12	19	25	41
65+	2,203	10.0	65	3	5	8	13	20	24	40
GRAND TOTAL	**10,447**	**11.8**	**262**	**1**	**3**	**6**	**14**	**31**	**53**	**97**

96.05: RESP TRACT INTUB NEC

Type of Patients	Observed Patients	Avg. Stay	Vari-ance	Percentiles 10th	25th	50th	75th	90th	95th	99th
1. SINGLE DX										
0–19 Years	29	2.2	1	1	1	2	3	4	4	4
20–34	0									
35–49	1	7.0	0	7	7	7	7	7	7	7
50–64	0									
65+	1	6.0	0	6	6	6	6	6	6	6
2. MULTIPLE DX										
0–19 Years	123	6.4	180	1	2	2	4	14	26	71
20–34	14	6.5	21	2	3	5	11	14	14	14
35–49	24	8.0	24	2	5	8	9	14	19	19
50–64	43	7.5	47	2	2	6	9	15	22	38
65+	112	9.0	40	3	4	7	12	17	22	30
TOTAL SINGLE DX	**31**	**2.4**	**2**	**1**	**1**	**2**	**4**	**4**	**4**	**7**
TOTAL MULTIPLE DX	**316**	**7.7**	**90**	**2**	**2**	**5**	**9**	**16**	**22**	**65**
TOTAL										
0–19 Years	152	5.5	142	1	2	2	4	9	26	71
20–34	14	6.5	21	2	3	5	11	14	14	14
35–49	25	7.9	24	2	5	8	9	14	19	19
50–64	43	7.5	47	2	2	6	9	15	22	38
65+	113	9.0	39	3	4	7	12	17	22	30
GRAND TOTAL	**347**	**7.2**	**84**	**1**	**2**	**4**	**9**	**15**	**22**	**65**

96.07: INSERT GASTRIC TUBE NEC

Type of Patients	Observed Patients	Avg. Stay	Vari-ance	Percentiles 10th	25th	50th	75th	90th	95th	99th
1. SINGLE DX										
0–19 Years	45	2.3	3	1	1	2	3	5	5	11
20–34	34	2.3	2	1	1	2	3	4	5	6
35–49	49	3.0	3	1	2	3	4	5	7	9
50–64	49	2.2	1	1	1	2	3	4	4	6
65+	25	3.6	4	1	2	3	5	7	7	7
2. MULTIPLE DX										
0–19 Years	306	3.5	20	1	1	2	4	7	11	25
20–34	274	3.3	10	1	2	2	4	6	7	12
35–49	645	4.0	10	1	2	3	5	7	10	16
50–64	882	4.0	11	1	2	3	5	7	10	14
65+	1,881	4.5	11	2	2	4	6	9	11	17
TOTAL SINGLE DX	**202**	**2.6**	**3**	**1**	**1**	**2**	**3**	**5**	**5**	**7**
TOTAL MULTIPLE DX	**3,988**	**4.2**	**12**	**1**	**2**	**3**	**5**	**8**	**10**	**17**
TOTAL										
0–19 Years	351	3.4	18	1	1	2	4	7	11	25
20–34	308	3.1	9	1	2	2	4	6	7	12
35–49	694	3.9	10	1	2	3	5	7	9	16
50–64	931	3.9	11	1	2	3	5	7	10	14
65+	1,906	4.5	11	2	2	4	6	9	11	17
GRAND TOTAL	**4,190**	**4.1**	**11**	**1**	**2**	**3**	**5**	**8**	**10**	**17**

96.08: INSERT INTESTINAL TUBE

Type of Patients	Observed Patients	Avg. Stay	Vari-ance	Percentiles 10th	25th	50th	75th	90th	95th	99th
1. SINGLE DX										
0–19 Years	0									
20–34	1	7.0	0	7	7	7	7	7	7	7
35–49	1	2.0	0	2	2	2	2	2	2	2
50–64	0									
65+	1	3.0	0	3	3	3	3	3	3	3
2. MULTIPLE DX										
0–19 Years	20	15.1	294	1	2	7	22	36	47	64
20–34	10	18.7	299	3	4	15	26	50	50	50
35–49	15	6.8	43	1	4	5	7	18	18	30
50–64	25	6.8	77	2	3	4	5	13	31	44
65+	75	7.6	36	2	3	7	8	17	22	26
TOTAL SINGLE DX	**3**	**4.3**	**6**	**2**	**3**	**3**	**7**	**7**	**7**	**7**
TOTAL MULTIPLE DX	**145**	**9.4**	**116**	**2**	**3**	**6**	**10**	**22**	**31**	**50**
TOTAL										
0–19 Years	20	15.1	294	1	2	7	22	36	47	64
20–34	11	17.7	284	3	4	15	18	50	50	50
35–49	16	6.6	42	1	3	5	6	18	18	30
50–64	25	6.8	77	2	3	4	5	13	31	44
65+	76	7.5	36	2	3	7	8	17	22	26
GRAND TOTAL	**148**	**9.3**	**114**	**2**	**3**	**6**	**10**	**22**	**31**	**50**

96.09: INSERT RECTAL TUBE

Type of Patients	Observed Patients	Avg. Stay	Vari-ance	Percentiles 10th	25th	50th	75th	90th	95th	99th
1. SINGLE DX										
0–19 Years	1	1.0	0	1	1	1	1	1	1	1
20–34	0									
35–49	0									
50–64	0									
65+	0									
2. MULTIPLE DX										
0–19 Years	5	2.6	1	1	2	3	3	4	4	4
20–34	0									
35–49	1	6.0	0	6	6	6	6	6	6	6
50–64	4	4.0	7	1	3	3	7	9	9	9
65+	24	6.9	16	2	3	8	9	14	14	15
TOTAL SINGLE DX	**1**	**1.0**	**0**	**1**	**1**	**1**	**1**	**1**	**1**	**1**
TOTAL MULTIPLE DX	**34**	**5.9**	**15**	**2**	**3**	**5**	**8**	**13**	**14**	**15**
TOTAL										
0–19 Years	6	2.3	1	1	1	3	3	4	4	4
20–34	0									
35–49	1	6.0	0	6	6	6	6	6	6	6
50–64	4	4.0	7	1	3	3	7	9	9	9
65+	24	6.9	16	2	3	8	9	14	14	15
GRAND TOTAL	**35**	**5.8**	**15**	**2**	**3**	**5**	**8**	**13**	**14**	**15**

96.1: OTHER NONOP INSERTION

Type of Patients	Observed Patients	Avg. Stay	Vari-ance	Percentiles 10th	25th	50th	75th	90th	95th	99th
1. SINGLE DX										
0–19 Years	0									
20–34	1	1.0	0	1	1	1	1	1	1	1
35–49	2	3.1	2	2	2	4	4	4	4	4
50–64	3	1.6	1	1	1	1	3	3	3	3
65+	1	1.0	0	1	1	1	1	1	1	1
2. MULTIPLE DX										
0–19 Years	2	5.1	32	2	2	2	13	13	13	13
20–34	3	1.3	<1	1	1	1	2	2	2	2
35–49	12	2.4	5	1	1	2	2	3	10	10
50–64	2	4.9	12	3	3	3	9	9	9	9
65+	21	4.4	8	1	2	4	6	9	10	11
TOTAL SINGLE DX	**7**	**1.9**	**2**	**1**	**1**	**1**	**3**	**4**	**4**	**4**
TOTAL MULTIPLE DX	**40**	**3.6**	**9**	**1**	**2**	**2**	**4**	**9**	**10**	**13**
TOTAL										
0–19 Years	2	5.1	32	2	2	2	13	13	13	13
20–34	4	1.2	<1	1	1	1	1	2	2	2
35–49	14	2.5	4	1	2	2	2	4	10	10
50–64	5	3.3	8	1	1	3	3	9	9	9
65+	22	4.3	8	1	2	4	6	9	10	11
GRAND TOTAL	**47**	**3.4**	**8**	**1**	**1**	**2**	**4**	**8**	**10**	**13**

96.2: NONOP DILATION & MANIP

Type of Patients	Observed Patients	Avg. Stay	Vari-ance	Percentiles 10th	25th	50th	75th	90th	95th	99th
1. SINGLE DX										
0–19 Years	48	1.1	<1	1	1	1	1	2	2	3
20–34	5	3.0	2	1	2	3	4	5	5	5
35–49	8	2.3	5	1	1	1	3	7	7	7
50–64	9	1.5	<1	1	1	1	2	2	4	4
65+	6	1.0	0	1	1	1	1	1	1	1
2. MULTIPLE DX										
0–19 Years	48	2.9	12	1	1	2	3	7	7	23
20–34	15	3.1	4	1	1	3	5	6	6	6
35–49	45	2.8	9	1	1	2	3	5	6	22
50–64	51	3.3	13	1	1	2	3	8	11	20
65+	109	3.4	7	1	1	3	5	7	9	14
TOTAL SINGLE DX	**76**	**1.3**	**<1**	**1**	**1**	**1**	**1**	**2**	**3**	**5**
TOTAL MULTIPLE DX	**268**	**3.2**	**9**	**1**	**1**	**2**	**4**	**7**	**9**	**16**
TOTAL										
0–19 Years	96	2.0	7	1	1	1	2	3	7	19
20–34	20	3.1	4	1	1	3	5	6	6	6
35–49	53	2.8	8	1	1	2	3	5	6	22
50–64	60	3.1	12	1	1	2	3	8	11	20
65+	115	3.2	7	1	1	2	5	7	9	14
GRAND TOTAL	**344**	**2.7**	**8**	**1**	**1**	**2**	**3**	**6**	**8**	**14**

96.27: MANUAL REDUCTION HERNIA

Type of Patients	Observed Patients	Avg. Stay	Vari-ance	Percentiles 10th	25th	50th	75th	90th	95th	99th
1. SINGLE DX										
0–19 Years	6	1.2	<1	1	1	1	1	2	2	2
20–34	1	2.0	0	2	2	2	2	2	2	2
35–49	5	1.6	2	1	1	1	1	4	4	4
50–64	2	1.0	0	1	1	1	1	1	1	1
65+	4	1.0	0	1	1	1	1	1	1	1
2. MULTIPLE DX										
0–19 Years	6	1.3	<1	1	1	1	2	2	2	2
20–34	6	3.1	5	1	1	2	6	6	6	6
35–49	18	1.9	2	1	1	1	3	4	5	5
50–64	25	2.7	9	1	1	1	3	6	11	13
65+	62	3.2	4	1	2	3	4	6	7	9
TOTAL SINGLE DX	**18**	**1.2**	**<1**	**1**	**1**	**1**	**1**	**2**	**2**	**4**
TOTAL MULTIPLE DX	**117**	**2.8**	**5**	**1**	**1**	**2**	**4**	**6**	**7**	**11**
TOTAL										
0–19 Years	12	1.2	<1	1	1	1	1	2	2	2
20–34	7	3.0	5	1	1	2	6	6	6	6
35–49	23	1.8	2	1	1	1	3	4	5	5
50–64	27	2.6	9	1	1	1	3	6	11	13
65+	66	3.0	4	1	1	2	4	6	7	9
GRAND TOTAL	**135**	**2.6**	**5**	**1**	**1**	**2**	**3**	**6**	**6**	**11**

96.3: NONOP GI IRRIG/INSTILL

Type of Patients	Observed Patients	Avg. Stay	Vari-ance	Percentiles 10th	25th	50th	75th	90th	95th	99th
1. SINGLE DX										
0–19 Years	220	1.8	<1	1	1	2	2	3	3	4
20–34	4	1.7	1	1	1	1	2	4	4	4
35–49	1	1.0	0	1	1	1	1	1	1	1
50–64	4	1.0	0	1	1	1	1	1	1	1
65+	1	4.0	0	4	4	4	4	4	4	4
2. MULTIPLE DX										
0–19 Years	721	7.6	50	1	2	6	11	17	21	30
20–34	185	2.1	4	1	1	1	3	4	5	11
35–49	177	3.1	18	1	1	2	3	5	9	27
50–64	116	3.9	31	1	1	2	4	8	10	37
65+	258	4.4	22	1	2	3	5	9	12	20
TOTAL SINGLE DX	**230**	**1.8**	**<1**	**1**	**1**	**2**	**2**	**3**	**3**	**4**
TOTAL MULTIPLE DX	**1,457**	**5.6**	**39**	**1**	**2**	**3**	**7**	**14**	**19**	**30**
TOTAL										
0–19 Years	941	6.6	46	1	2	4	9	16	21	30
20–34	189	2.1	4	1	1	1	3	4	5	11
35–49	178	3.1	18	1	1	2	3	5	9	27
50–64	120	3.8	31	1	1	2	4	8	10	37
65+	259	4.4	22	1	2	3	5	9	12	20
GRAND TOTAL	**1,687**	**5.2**	**37**	**1**	**1**	**3**	**7**	**13**	**18**	**28**

96.33: GASTRIC LAVAGE

Type of Patients	Observed Patients	Avg. Stay	Vari-ance	Percentiles 10th	25th	50th	75th	90th	95th	99th
1. SINGLE DX										
0–19 Years	193	1.9	<1	1	1	2	2	3	3	4
20–34	2	1.0	0	1	1	1	1	1	1	1
35–49	1	1.0	0	1	1	1	1	1	1	1
50–64	1	1.0	0	1	1	1	1	1	1	1
65+	0									
2. MULTIPLE DX										
0–19 Years	233	2.4	3	1	1	2	3	4	6	8
20–34	159	2.1	4	1	1	1	2	4	5	11
35–49	140	3.1	22	1	1	1	3	7	9	27
50–64	70	3.9	49	1	1	2	4	7	36	>99
65+	45	3.6	10	1	1	2	5	8	12	12
TOTAL SINGLE DX	**197**	**1.9**	**<1**	**1**	**1**	**2**	**2**	**3**	**3**	**4**
TOTAL MULTIPLE DX	**647**	**2.7**	**13**	**1**	**1**	**2**	**3**	**5**	**8**	**23**
TOTAL										
0–19 Years	426	2.3	3	1	1	2	3	3	5	8
20–34	161	2.0	4	1	1	1	2	4	5	11
35–49	141	3.1	22	1	1	1	3	7	9	27
50–64	71	3.9	48	1	1	2	4	7	36	>99
65+	45	3.6	10	1	1	2	5	8	12	12
GRAND TOTAL	**844**	**2.6**	**11**	**1**	**1**	**2**	**3**	**4**	**7**	**19**

96.35: GASTRIC GAVAGE

Type of Patients	Observed Patients	Avg. Stay	Vari-ance	Percentiles 10th	25th	50th	75th	90th	95th	99th
1. SINGLE DX										
0–19 Years	7	1.8	<1	1	1	2	2	3	3	3
20–34	0									
35–49	0									
50–64	0									
65+	0									
2. MULTIPLE DX										
0–19 Years	424	10.8	54	3	6	9	15	21	23	40
20–34	6	1.8	2	1	1	1	2	5	5	5
35–49	4	1.0	0	1	1	1	1	1	1	1
50–64	3	3.5	5	1	3	3	3	7	7	7
65+	6	3.4	2	2	2	3	4	6	6	6
TOTAL SINGLE DX	**7**	**1.8**	**<1**	**1**	**1**	**2**	**2**	**3**	**3**	**3**
TOTAL MULTIPLE DX	**443**	**10.5**	**54**	**3**	**5**	**9**	**14**	**20**	**23**	**40**
TOTAL										
0–19 Years	431	10.7	54	3	6	9	15	21	23	40
20–34	6	1.8	2	1	1	1	2	5	5	5
35–49	4	1.0	0	1	1	1	1	1	1	1
50–64	3	3.5	5	1	3	3	3	7	7	7
65+	6	3.4	2	2	2	3	4	6	6	6
GRAND TOTAL	**450**	**10.4**	**55**	**3**	**5**	**8**	**14**	**20**	**23**	**40**

96.38: IMPACTED FECES REMOVAL

Type of Patients	Observed Patients	Avg. Stay	Variance	Percentiles 10th	25th	50th	75th	90th	95th	99th
1. SINGLE DX										
0–19 Years	14	1.7	<1	1	1	2	2	3	3	3
20–34	1	2.0	0	2	2	2	2	2	2	2
35–49	0									
50–64	3	1.0	0	1	1	1	1	1	1	1
65+	1	4.0	0	4	4	4	4	4	4	4
2. MULTIPLE DX										
0–19 Years	46	3.7	11	1	1	2	5	8	10	14
20–34	10	3.3	6	1	1	3	4	8	8	8
35–49	22	3.1	5	1	2	2	4	4	9	12
50–64	31	4.4	16	1	2	3	6	9	14	19
65+	172	5.1	29	1	2	4	6	11	13	31
TOTAL SINGLE DX	**19**	**1.7**	**<1**	**1**	**1**	**2**	**2**	**3**	**3**	**4**
TOTAL MULTIPLE DX	**281**	**4.5**	**22**	**1**	**2**	**3**	**6**	**9**	**12**	**20**
TOTAL										
0–19 Years	60	3.2	9	1	1	2	3	8	9	14
20–34	11	3.1	5	1	2	3	4	8	8	8
35–49	22	3.1	5	1	2	2	4	4	9	12
50–64	34	4.2	16	1	2	3	6	9	10	19
65+	173	5.1	29	1	2	4	6	11	13	31
GRAND TOTAL	**300**	**4.3**	**21**	**1**	**2**	**3**	**5**	**9**	**12**	**20**

96.39: TRANSANAL ENEMA NEC

Type of Patients	Observed Patients	Avg. Stay	Variance	Percentiles 10th	25th	50th	75th	90th	95th	99th
1. SINGLE DX										
0–19 Years	5	1.5	2	1	1	1	1	5	5	5
20–34	1	4.0	0	4	4	4	4	4	4	4
35–49	0									
50–64	0									
65+	0									
2. MULTIPLE DX										
0–19 Years	12	3.0	3	1	2	3	3	6	8	8
20–34	4	2.7	2	1	2	3	4	4	4	4
35–49	5	3.1	<1	3	3	3	3	4	4	4
50–64	7	2.6	3	1	2	2	3	3	9	9
65+	24	2.5	3	1	2	2	3	3	8	8
TOTAL SINGLE DX	**6**	**1.7**	**2**	**1**	**1**	**1**	**1**	**5**	**5**	**5**
TOTAL MULTIPLE DX	**52**	**2.8**	**3**	**1**	**2**	**3**	**3**	**4**	**7**	**8**
TOTAL										
0–19 Years	17	2.6	3	1	1	3	3	6	7	8
20–34	5	3.0	2	1	2	3	4	4	4	4
35–49	5	3.1	<1	3	3	3	3	4	4	4
50–64	7	2.6	3	1	2	2	3	3	9	9
65+	24	2.5	3	1	2	2	3	3	8	8
GRAND TOTAL	**58**	**2.7**	**3**	**1**	**2**	**3**	**3**	**4**	**7**	**8**

96.4: DIGEST/GU IRRIG/INSTILL

Type of Patients	Observed Patients	Avg. Stay	Variance	Percentiles 10th	25th	50th	75th	90th	95th	99th
1. SINGLE DX										
0–19 Years	80	1.9	4	1	1	2	2	3	3	4
20–34	699	1.6	<1	1	1	1	2	3	3	3
35–49	123	1.4	<1	1	1	1	2	3	3	4
50–64	8	1.3	<1	1	1	1	2	2	2	2
65+	3	1.4	<1	1	1	1	2	2	2	2
2. MULTIPLE DX										
0–19 Years	205	2.3	2	1	1	2	3	4	4	6
20–34	1,544	2.2	4	1	1	2	3	3	4	7
35–49	370	2.2	4	1	1	2	3	3	4	14
50–64	65	3.0	11	1	1	2	3	6	8	25
65+	201	3.0	9	1	1	2	3	5	10	16
TOTAL SINGLE DX	**913**	**1.6**	**<1**	**1**	**1**	**1**	**2**	**3**	**3**	**4**
TOTAL MULTIPLE DX	**2,385**	**2.3**	**4**	**1**	**1**	**2**	**3**	**3**	**4**	**9**
TOTAL										
0–19 Years	285	2.2	2	1	1	2	3	4	4	6
20–34	2,243	2.0	3	1	1	2	3	3	4	6
35–49	493	2.0	3	1	1	2	2	3	4	7
50–64	73	2.9	10	1	1	2	3	6	7	25
65+	204	3.0	9	1	1	2	3	5	10	16
GRAND TOTAL	**3,298**	**2.1**	**3**	**1**	**1**	**2**	**3**	**3**	**4**	**8**

96.48: INDWELL CATH IRRIG NEC

Type of Patients	Observed Patients	Avg. Stay	Variance	Percentiles 10th	25th	50th	75th	90th	95th	99th
1. SINGLE DX										
0–19 Years	0									
20–34	0									
35–49	0									
50–64	0									
65+	1	2.0	0	2	2	2	2	2	2	2
2. MULTIPLE DX										
0–19 Years	0									
20–34	0									
35–49	5	2.3	2	1	1	2	4	5	5	5
50–64	24	2.4	4	1	1	2	2	5	8	9
65+	101	2.6	3	1	1	2	3	4	5	10
TOTAL SINGLE DX	**1**	**2.0**	**0**	**2**	**2**	**2**	**2**	**2**	**2**	**2**
TOTAL MULTIPLE DX	**130**	**2.5**	**3**	**1**	**1**	**2**	**3**	**4**	**6**	**10**
TOTAL										
0–19 Years	0									
20–34	0									
35–49	5	2.3	2	1	1	2	4	5	5	5
50–64	24	2.4	4	1	1	2	2	5	8	9
65+	102	2.5	3	1	1	2	3	4	5	10
GRAND TOTAL	**131**	**2.5**	**3**	**1**	**1**	**2**	**3**	**4**	**6**	**10**

96.49: GU INSTILLATION NEC

Type of Patients	Observed Patients	Avg. Stay	Vari-ance	Percentiles						
				10th	25th	50th	75th	90th	95th	99th
1. SINGLE DX										
0–19 Years	79	1.9	4	1	1	2	2	3	3	4
20–34	699	1.6	<1	1	1	1	2	3	3	3
35–49	122	1.4	<1	1	1	1	2	2	3	3
50–64	8	1.3	<1	1	1	1	2	2	2	2
65+	2	1.0	0	1	1	1	1	1	1	1
2. MULTIPLE DX										
0–19 Years	199	2.3	2	1	1	2	3	4	4	6
20–34	1,533	2.2	4	1	1	2	3	3	4	7
35–49	354	2.2	4	1	1	2	3	3	4	14
50–64	29	2.7	14	1	1	2	3	5	6	25
65+	88	3.3	15	1	1	2	3	10	12	16
TOTAL SINGLE DX	**910**	**1.6**	**<1**	**1**	**1**	**1**	**2**	**3**	**3**	**3**
TOTAL MULTIPLE DX	**2,203**	**2.3**	**4**	**1**	**1**	**2**	**3**	**3**	**4**	**9**
TOTAL										
0–19 Years	278	2.2	2	1	1	2	3	3	4	6
20–34	2,232	2.0	3	1	1	2	3	3	4	6
35–49	476	2.0	3	1	1	2	2	3	3	6
50–64	37	2.4	12	1	1	2	2	3	6	25
65+	90	3.3	14	1	1	2	3	10	12	16
GRAND TOTAL	**3,113**	**2.1**	**3**	**1**	**1**	**2**	**3**	**3**	**4**	**7**

96.5: OTHER NONOP IRRIG/CLEAN

Type of Patients	Observed Patients	Avg. Stay	Vari-ance	Percentiles						
				10th	25th	50th	75th	90th	95th	99th
1. SINGLE DX										
0–19 Years	16	2.0	2	1	1	1	3	3	6	7
20–34	13	3.6	4	1	2	3	5	6	7	7
35–49	6	2.7	5	1	1	3	3	7	7	7
50–64	4	2.9	3	1	1	2	4	5	5	5
65+	1	6.0	0	6	6	6	6	6	6	6
2. MULTIPLE DX										
0–19 Years	65	4.2	25	1	1	3	5	7	12	33
20–34	63	4.7	18	1	1	3	8	11	12	22
35–49	78	5.6	23	1	3	4	7	13	16	27
50–64	113	7.8	43	1	3	6	11	15	21	34
65+	300	8.9	46	2	4	7	11	18	25	29
TOTAL SINGLE DX	**40**	**2.7**	**4**	**1**	**1**	**2**	**4**	**6**	**6**	**7**
TOTAL MULTIPLE DX	**619**	**7.2**	**41**	**1**	**3**	**5**	**10**	**16**	**21**	**29**
TOTAL										
0–19 Years	81	3.8	22	1	1	3	4	7	12	33
20–34	76	4.5	16	1	2	3	6	10	11	22
35–49	84	5.4	22	1	3	4	7	13	16	19
50–64	117	7.7	42	1	3	6	11	15	21	34
65+	301	8.8	46	2	4	7	11	18	25	29
GRAND TOTAL	**659**	**6.9**	**40**	**1**	**2**	**5**	**9**	**16**	**21**	**29**

96.52: IRRIGATION OF EAR

Type of Patients	Observed Patients	Avg. Stay	Vari-ance	Percentiles						
				10th	25th	50th	75th	90th	95th	99th
1. SINGLE DX										
0–19 Years	0									
20–34	0									
35–49	0									
50–64	0									
65+	0									
2. MULTIPLE DX										
0–19 Years	23	3.2	32	1	1	2	3	7	7	33
20–34	3	2.2	<1	1	1	2	3	3	3	3
35–49	11	5.6	25	1	2	3	12	13	13	13
50–64	9	6.9	29	2	3	5	13	15	15	15
65+	40	7.6	42	1	3	7	10	18	25	25
TOTAL SINGLE DX	**0**									
TOTAL MULTIPLE DX	**86**	**5.6**	**38**	**1**	**1**	**3**	**8**	**15**	**18**	**33**
TOTAL										
0–19 Years	23	3.2	32	1	1	2	3	7	7	33
20–34	3	2.2	<1	1	1	2	3	3	3	3
35–49	11	5.6	25	1	2	3	12	13	13	13
50–64	9	6.9	29	2	3	5	13	15	15	15
65+	40	7.6	42	1	3	7	10	18	25	25
GRAND TOTAL	**86**	**5.6**	**38**	**1**	**1**	**3**	**8**	**15**	**18**	**33**

96.56: BRONCH/TRACH LAVAGE NEC

Type of Patients	Observed Patients	Avg. Stay	Vari-ance	Percentiles						
				10th	25th	50th	75th	90th	95th	99th
1. SINGLE DX										
0–19 Years	7	2.2	<1	1	1	2	3	3	3	3
20–34	1	1.0	0	1	1	1	1	1	1	1
35–49	1	1.0	0	1	1	1	1	1	1	1
50–64	2	3.0	2	2	2	4	4	4	4	4
65+	0									
2. MULTIPLE DX										
0–19 Years	18	5.4	10	3	3	4	6	12	12	12
20–34	26	7.2	23	2	3	7	10	12	21	22
35–49	33	6.7	31	1	3	5	9	16	19	27
50–64	65	8.1	27	2	5	8	11	14	18	26
65+	214	10.1	47	4	5	9	12	20	25	32
TOTAL SINGLE DX	**11**	**2.2**	**1**	**1**	**1**	**2**	**3**	**3**	**4**	**4**
TOTAL MULTIPLE DX	**356**	**8.9**	**40**	**3**	**4**	**8**	**12**	**17**	**23**	**29**
TOTAL										
0–19 Years	25	4.6	10	2	3	3	6	11	12	12
20–34	27	7.1	23	2	3	6	10	12	21	22
35–49	34	6.5	31	1	3	5	9	16	19	27
50–64	67	8.0	27	2	5	8	11	14	18	26
65+	214	10.1	47	4	5	9	12	20	25	32
GRAND TOTAL	**367**	**8.7**	**40**	**3**	**4**	**7**	**11**	**17**	**22**	**29**

96.59: WOUND IRRIGATION NEC

Type of Patients	Observed Patients	Avg. Stay	Variance	10th	25th	50th	75th	90th	95th	99th
1. SINGLE DX										
0–19 Years	6	2.3	4	1	1	2	3	7	7	7
20–34	12	3.7	3	2	2	4	5	6	7	7
35–49	5	3.0	5	1	1	3	3	7	7	7
50–64	2	2.8	7	1	1	1	5	5	5	5
65+	1	6.0	0	6	6	6	6	6	6	6
2. MULTIPLE DX										
0–19 Years	16	4.7	38	1	2	3	4	14	27	27
20–34	25	3.0	7	1	1	2	4	8	9	10
35–49	24	5.0	17	1	3	4	6	13	14	18
50–64	29	9.1	102	1	2	4	14	25	34	34
65+	25	4.9	28	1	2	3	6	8	9	27
TOTAL SINGLE DX	**26**	**3.3**	**4**	**1**	**2**	**3**	**5**	**6**	**7**	**7**
TOTAL MULTIPLE DX	**119**	**5.4**	**43**	**1**	**2**	**3**	**6**	**14**	**21**	**34**
TOTAL										
0–19 Years	22	4.0	29	1	2	3	3	7	14	27
20–34	37	3.2	6	1	1	2	4	7	9	10
35–49	29	4.7	15	1	3	4	6	9	14	18
50–64	31	8.7	98	1	2	4	14	25	34	34
65+	26	5.0	26	1	2	3	6	8	9	27
GRAND TOTAL	**145**	**5.0**	**36**	**1**	**2**	**3**	**6**	**9**	**18**	**34**

96.6: ENTERAL NUTRITION

Type of Patients	Observed Patients	Avg. Stay	Variance	10th	25th	50th	75th	90th	95th	99th
1. SINGLE DX										
0–19 Years	5	4.5	35	1	1	1	4	14	16	16
20–34	4	4.3	4	2	4	4	4	7	7	7
35–49	0									
50–64	1	4.0	0	4	4	4	4	4	4	4
65+	1	3.0	0	3	3	3	3	3	3	3
2. MULTIPLE DX										
0–19 Years	552	9.3	102	2	3	6	12	21	29	51
20–34	92	10.1	109	2	5	7	12	17	31	71
35–49	141	9.1	43	3	5	7	12	17	18	37
50–64	231	8.1	57	2	4	6	10	16	21	48
65+	1,111	8.1	38	3	4	7	10	16	20	32
TOTAL SINGLE DX	**11**	**4.3**	**27**	**1**	**1**	**1**	**4**	**14**	**16**	**16**
TOTAL MULTIPLE DX	**2,127**	**8.6**	**63**	**2**	**4**	**6**	**11**	**17**	**23**	**41**
TOTAL										
0–19 Years	557	9.2	102	2	3	6	12	21	29	51
20–34	96	10.0	107	2	5	7	12	17	31	71
35–49	141	9.1	43	3	5	7	12	17	18	37
50–64	232	8.1	57	2	4	6	10	16	21	48
65+	1,112	8.1	38	3	4	7	10	16	20	32
GRAND TOTAL	**2,138**	**8.6**	**63**	**2**	**4**	**6**	**11**	**17**	**23**	**41**

96.7: CONT MECH VENT NEC

Type of Patients	Observed Patients	Avg. Stay	Variance	10th	25th	50th	75th	90th	95th	99th
1. SINGLE DX										
0–19 Years	64	3.6	9	1	1	2	4	9	12	12
20–34	23	2.4	3	1	1	2	3	5	6	7
35–49	25	5.3	85	1	1	2	3	7	34	34
50–64	6	1.8	1	1	1	1	3	3	4	4
65+	3	4.7	10	3	3	3	9	9	9	9
2. MULTIPLE DX										
0–19 Years	3,853	18.1	407	2	4	11	24	52	73	>99
20–34	1,686	6.7	57	1	2	4	8	16	22	40
35–49	3,055	8.3	65	2	3	6	11	18	24	38
50–64	4,742	10.0	62	3	5	8	13	19	24	37
65+	8,592	10.3	55	3	5	8	13	20	24	36
TOTAL SINGLE DX	**121**	**3.7**	**23**	**1**	**1**	**2**	**4**	**7**	**10**	**34**
TOTAL MULTIPLE DX	**21,928**	**11.2**	**137**	**2**	**4**	**8**	**14**	**23**	**32**	**76**
TOTAL										
0–19 Years	3,917	17.9	404	2	4	10	24	51	73	>99
20–34	1,709	6.6	57	1	2	4	8	16	22	40
35–49	3,080	8.3	65	2	3	6	11	18	24	38
50–64	4,748	10.0	62	3	5	8	13	19	24	37
65+	8,595	10.3	55	3	5	8	13	20	24	36
GRAND TOTAL	**22,049**	**11.2**	**137**	**2**	**4**	**8**	**14**	**23**	**32**	**75**

96.70: CONT MECH VENT-TIME NOS

Type of Patients	Observed Patients	Avg. Stay	Variance	10th	25th	50th	75th	90th	95th	99th
1. SINGLE DX										
0–19 Years	0									
20–34	0									
35–49	0									
50–64	0									
65+	0									
2. MULTIPLE DX										
0–19 Years	18	16.1	274	1	3	10	31	51	>99	>99
20–34	3	13.2	6	10	11	15	15	15	15	15
35–49	10	11.1	56	4	5	9	18	19	25	25
50–64	19	9.9	43	4	4	9	14	18	19	24
65+	26	12.3	61	2	6	11	18	24	24	29
TOTAL SINGLE DX	**0**									
TOTAL MULTIPLE DX	**76**	**12.8**	**116**	**3**	**5**	**11**	**18**	**28**	**40**	**>99**
TOTAL										
0–19 Years	18	16.1	274	1	3	10	31	51	>99	>99
20–34	3	13.2	6	10	11	15	15	15	15	15
35–49	10	11.1	56	4	5	9	18	19	25	25
50–64	19	9.9	43	4	4	9	14	18	19	24
65+	26	12.3	61	2	6	11	18	24	24	29
GRAND TOTAL	**76**	**12.8**	**116**	**3**	**5**	**11**	**18**	**28**	**40**	**>99**

96.71: CONT MECH VENT-<96 HOURS

Type of Patients	Observed Patients	Avg. Stay	Variance	10th	25th	50th	75th	90th	95th	99th
				Percentiles						
1. SINGLE DX										
0–19 Years	57	3.2	8	1	1	2	4	7	12	12
20–34	23	2.4	3	1	1	2	3	5	6	7
35–49	23	2.5	3	1	1	2	3	6	6	7
50–64	6	1.8	1	1	1	1	3	3	4	4
65+	3	4.7	10	3	3	3	9	9	9	9
2. MULTIPLE DX										
0–19 Years	2,670	13.6	264	2	3	7	18	37	53	88
20–34	1,310	4.2	16	1	2	3	5	8	11	23
35–49	2,188	5.4	24	1	2	4	7	11	15	23
50–64	3,091	7.2	32	2	4	6	9	14	17	27
65+	5,726	7.9	30	3	4	7	10	15	19	28
TOTAL SINGLE DX	**112**	**2.9**	**6**	**1**	**1**	**2**	**3**	**6**	**9**	**12**
TOTAL MULTIPLE DX	**14,985**	**8.2**	**81**	**2**	**3**	**6**	**10**	**16**	**23**	**52**
TOTAL										
0–19 Years	2,727	13.4	261	1	3	7	18	36	52	88
20–34	1,333	4.2	16	1	2	3	5	8	11	23
35–49	2,211	5.4	24	1	2	4	7	11	15	23
50–64	3,097	7.2	32	2	4	6	9	14	17	27
65+	5,729	7.9	30	3	4	7	10	15	19	28
GRAND TOTAL	**15,097**	**8.2**	**81**	**2**	**3**	**6**	**10**	**16**	**23**	**52**

96.72: CONT MECH VENT->95 HOURS

Type of Patients	Observed Patients	Avg. Stay	Variance	10th	25th	50th	75th	90th	95th	99th
				Percentiles						
1. SINGLE DX										
0–19 Years	7	6.7	4	4	6	6	9	10	10	10
20–34	0									
35–49	2	26.9	211	4	34	34	34	34	34	34
50–64	0									
65+	0									
2. MULTIPLE DX										
0–19 Years	1,165	28.2	581	8	11	19	43	79	96	>99
20–34	373	15.4	105	6	9	13	19	28	39	>99
35–49	857	15.7	94	7	10	13	20	27	31	56
50–64	1,632	15.4	76	7	10	14	19	25	31	47
65+	2,840	15.3	69	7	10	14	19	25	31	47
TOTAL SINGLE DX	**9**	**12.5**	**143**	**4**	**6**	**7**	**10**	**34**	**34**	**34**
TOTAL MULTIPLE DX	**6,867**	**17.8**	**197**	**7**	**10**	**14**	**21**	**31**	**50**	**99**
TOTAL										
0–19 Years	1,172	28.1	580	8	11	19	43	79	96	>99
20–34	373	15.4	105	6	9	13	19	28	39	>99
35–49	859	15.8	94	7	10	13	20	27	32	56
50–64	1,632	15.4	76	7	10	14	19	25	31	47
65+	2,840	15.3	69	7	10	14	19	25	31	47
GRAND TOTAL	**6,876**	**17.8**	**197**	**7**	**10**	**14**	**21**	**31**	**50**	**99**

97.0: GI APPLIANCE REPLACEMENT

Type of Patients	Observed Patients	Avg. Stay	Variance	10th	25th	50th	75th	90th	95th	99th
				Percentiles						
1. SINGLE DX										
0–19 Years	2	4.0	0	4	4	4	4	4	4	4
20–34	0									
35–49	2	2.6	4	1	1	4	4	4	4	4
50–64	2	2.3	<1	2	2	2	3	3	3	3
65+	2	1.8	<1	1	2	2	2	2	2	2
2. MULTIPLE DX										
0–19 Years	137	5.2	38	1	2	4	6	10	21	32
20–34	73	5.6	21	1	2	4	8	14	14	19
35–49	133	5.4	23	1	2	4	7	11	13	27
50–64	261	6.2	35	1	2	4	8	14	17	27
65+	880	6.4	30	1	3	5	8	13	18	28
TOTAL SINGLE DX	**8**	**2.4**	**1**	**1**	**2**	**2**	**3**	**4**	**4**	**4**
TOTAL MULTIPLE DX	**1,484**	**6.1**	**31**	**1**	**2**	**5**	**8**	**13**	**17**	**29**
TOTAL										
0–19 Years	139	5.2	38	1	2	4	6	10	21	32
20–34	73	5.6	21	1	2	4	8	14	14	19
35–49	135	5.4	23	1	2	4	7	11	13	27
50–64	263	6.2	35	1	2	4	8	14	17	27
65+	882	6.4	30	1	3	5	8	13	18	28
GRAND TOTAL	**1,492**	**6.1**	**31**	**1**	**2**	**4**	**8**	**13**	**17**	**29**

97.02: REPL GASTROSTOMY TUBE

Type of Patients	Observed Patients	Avg. Stay	Variance	10th	25th	50th	75th	90th	95th	99th
				Percentiles						
1. SINGLE DX										
0–19 Years	1	4.0	0	4	4	4	4	4	4	4
20–34	0									
35–49	0									
50–64	2	2.3	<1	2	2	2	3	3	3	3
65+	1	1.0	0	1	1	1	1	1	1	1
2. MULTIPLE DX										
0–19 Years	107	5.1	32	1	2	4	6	11	19	31
20–34	47	6.0	23	1	3	4	8	14	14	26
35–49	73	5.9	29	2	2	4	7	11	15	28
50–64	127	5.8	28	1	2	4	8	11	14	23
65+	700	6.7	30	1	3	5	9	13	18	28
TOTAL SINGLE DX	**4**	**2.3**	**1**	**1**	**1**	**2**	**3**	**4**	**4**	**4**
TOTAL MULTIPLE DX	**1,054**	**6.3**	**30**	**1**	**3**	**5**	**8**	**13**	**17**	**29**
TOTAL										
0–19 Years	108	5.1	32	1	2	4	6	11	19	31
20–34	47	6.0	23	1	3	4	8	14	14	26
35–49	73	5.9	29	2	2	4	7	11	15	28
50–64	129	5.8	28	1	2	4	8	11	14	23
65+	701	6.7	31	1	3	5	9	13	18	28
GRAND TOTAL	**1,058**	**6.3**	**30**	**1**	**3**	**5**	**8**	**13**	**17**	**29**

97.03: REPL SMALL INTEST TUBE

Type of Patients	Observed Patients	Avg. Stay	Vari-ance	10th	25th	50th	75th	90th	95th	99th
1. SINGLE DX										
0–19 Years	0									
20–34	0									
35–49	0									
50–64	0									
65+	0									
2. MULTIPLE DX										
0–19 Years	19	6.1	63	1	2	4	6	10	32	32
20–34	6	5.6	9	1	1	7	8	8	8	8
35–49	13	5.8	35	1	1	4	11	11	12	26
50–64	24	10.7	70	2	4	7	15	27	27	27
65+	48	6.7	48	1	2	4	8	16	21	34
TOTAL SINGLE DX	**0**									
TOTAL MULTIPLE DX	**110**	**7.2**	**54**	**1**	**2**	**5**	**8**	**15**	**27**	**32**
TOTAL										
0–19 Years	19	6.1	63	1	2	4	6	10	32	32
20–34	6	5.6	9	1	1	7	8	8	8	8
35–49	13	5.8	35	1	1	4	11	11	12	26
50–64	24	10.7	70	2	4	7	15	27	27	27
65+	48	6.7	48	1	2	4	8	16	21	34
GRAND TOTAL	**110**	**7.2**	**54**	**1**	**2**	**5**	**8**	**15**	**27**	**32**

97.05: REPL PANC/BILIARY STENT

Type of Patients	Observed Patients	Avg. Stay	Vari-ance	10th	25th	50th	75th	90th	95th	99th
1. SINGLE DX										
0–19 Years	0									
20–34	0									
35–49	2	2.6	4	1	1	4	4	4	4	4
50–64	0									
65+	1	2.0	0	2	2	2	2	2	2	2
2. MULTIPLE DX										
0–19 Years	5	3.2	5	1	1	4	4	6	6	6
20–34	18	5.0	26	1	2	3	5	14	19	19
35–49	43	4.5	8	2	3	4	6	9	10	14
50–64	108	5.5	28	1	2	4	6	12	15	29
65+	125	5.1	21	1	2	4	7	9	13	22
TOTAL SINGLE DX	**3**	**2.2**	**<1**	**1**	**2**	**2**	**2**	**4**	**4**	**4**
TOTAL MULTIPLE DX	**299**	**5.1**	**21**	**1**	**2**	**4**	**6**	**9**	**13**	**27**
TOTAL										
0–19 Years	5	3.2	5	1	1	4	4	6	6	6
20–34	18	5.0	26	1	2	3	5	14	19	19
35–49	45	4.4	8	1	2	4	6	8	10	14
50–64	108	5.5	28	1	2	4	6	12	15	29
65+	126	5.0	20	1	2	4	7	9	13	22
GRAND TOTAL	**302**	**5.1**	**21**	**1**	**2**	**4**	**6**	**9**	**13**	**27**

97.1: REPL MS APPLIANCE

Type of Patients	Observed Patients	Avg. Stay	Vari-ance	10th	25th	50th	75th	90th	95th	99th
1. SINGLE DX										
0–19 Years	9	1.1	<1	1	1	1	1	1	3	3
20–34	0									
35–49	2	2.5	<1	2	2	3	3	3	3	3
50–64	0									
65+	0									
2. MULTIPLE DX										
0–19 Years	8	2.8	3	1	2	3	3	4	8	8
20–34	4	2.1	1	1	1	3	3	3	3	3
35–49	11	10.1	344	1	2	3	6	60	60	60
50–64	4	6.6	3	5	6	6	9	9	9	9
65+	12	6.1	43	2	3	5	5	15	28	28
TOTAL SINGLE DX	**11**	**1.3**	**<1**	**1**	**1**	**1**	**1**	**3**	**3**	**3**
TOTAL MULTIPLE DX	**39**	**5.9**	**118**	**1**	**2**	**3**	**5**	**9**	**15**	**60**
TOTAL										
0–19 Years	17	2.1	2	1	1	2	3	3	4	8
20–34	4	2.1	1	1	1	3	3	3	3	3
35–49	13	9.4	315	1	2	3	6	60	60	60
50–64	4	6.6	3	5	6	6	9	9	9	9
65+	12	6.1	43	2	3	5	5	15	28	28
GRAND TOTAL	**50**	**4.9**	**95**	**1**	**1**	**3**	**5**	**7**	**9**	**60**

97.2: OTHER NONOP REPLACEMENT

Type of Patients	Observed Patients	Avg. Stay	Vari-ance	10th	25th	50th	75th	90th	95th	99th
1. SINGLE DX										
0–19 Years	2	9.7	93	3	3	3	18	18	18	18
20–34	0									
35–49	2	1.5	<1	1	1	2	2	2	2	2
50–64	2	1.0	0	1	1	1	1	1	1	1
65+	0									
2. MULTIPLE DX										
0–19 Years	42	4.1	12	1	2	3	7	9	10	18
20–34	21	8.2	36	2	3	6	13	18	19	20
35–49	37	6.9	109	1	2	4	6	11	42	42
50–64	71	6.4	76	1	2	4	8	11	16	29
65+	67	4.9	18	1	2	4	6	13	16	21
TOTAL SINGLE DX	**6**	**4.1**	**39**	**1**	**1**	**2**	**3**	**18**	**18**	**18**
TOTAL MULTIPLE DX	**238**	**5.7**	**49**	**1**	**2**	**4**	**7**	**11**	**16**	**42**
TOTAL										
0–19 Years	44	4.3	14	1	2	3	7	9	10	18
20–34	21	8.2	36	2	3	6	13	18	19	20
35–49	39	6.6	105	1	1	4	6	11	42	42
50–64	73	6.3	75	1	2	4	8	11	16	29
65+	67	4.9	18	1	2	4	6	13	16	21
GRAND TOTAL	**244**	**5.7**	**49**	**1**	**2**	**4**	**7**	**11**	**16**	**42**

97.23: REPL TRACH TUBE

Type of Patients	Observed Patients	Avg. Stay	Vari-ance	10th	25th	50th	75th	90th	95th	99th
1. SINGLE DX										
0–19 Years	0									
20–34	0									
35–49	2	1.5	<1	1	1	2	2	2	2	2
50–64	2	1.0	0	1	1	1	1	1	1	1
65+	0									
2. MULTIPLE DX										
0–19 Years	41	4.1	12	1	2	3	7	9	10	18
20–34	15	8.6	40	1	2	8	14	18	20	20
35–49	34	7.1	116	1	2	5	6	13	42	42
50–64	59	7.0	86	1	2	5	8	13	16	79
65+	51	4.9	19	1	2	4	5	13	16	21
TOTAL SINGLE DX	**4**	**1.3**	**<1**	**1**	**1**	**1**	**2**	**2**	**2**	**2**
TOTAL MULTIPLE DX	**200**	**5.9**	**54**	**1**	**2**	**4**	**7**	**12**	**16**	**42**
TOTAL										
0–19 Years	41	4.1	12	1	2	3	7	9	10	18
20–34	15	8.6	40	1	2	8	14	18	20	20
35–49	36	6.8	111	1	1	4	6	11	42	42
50–64	61	6.8	85	1	2	5	8	11	16	79
65+	51	4.9	19	1	2	4	5	13	16	21
GRAND TOTAL	**204**	**5.8**	**54**	**1**	**2**	**4**	**7**	**12**	**16**	**42**

97.3: RMVL THER DEV-HEAD/NECK

Type of Patients	Observed Patients	Avg. Stay	Vari-ance	10th	25th	50th	75th	90th	95th	99th
1. SINGLE DX										
0–19 Years	5	1.4	<1	1	1	1	2	2	2	2
20–34	5	1.7	3	1	1	1	1	5	5	5
35–49	1	1.0	0	1	1	1	1	1	1	1
50–64	3	2.4	1	1	1	3	3	3	3	3
65+	0									
2. MULTIPLE DX										
0–19 Years	30	2.3	4	1	1	2	2	6	7	11
20–34	11	9.1	113	1	4	5	6	28	33	33
35–49	16	7.4	76	1	3	4	7	17	24	36
50–64	32	4.4	24	1	2	3	5	7	14	30
65+	48	5.2	22	1	2	4	7	11	11	29
TOTAL SINGLE DX	**14**	**1.7**	**1**	**1**	**1**	**1**	**2**	**3**	**5**	**5**
TOTAL MULTIPLE DX	**137**	**4.8**	**31**	**1**	**2**	**3**	**5**	**10**	**16**	**30**
TOTAL										
0–19 Years	35	2.1	4	1	1	2	2	4	6	11
20–34	16	6.1	80	1	1	4	5	16	33	33
35–49	17	7.0	74	1	2	4	7	17	24	36
50–64	35	4.1	21	1	2	3	5	7	14	30
65+	48	5.2	22	1	2	4	7	11	11	29
GRAND TOTAL	**151**	**4.4**	**29**	**1**	**1**	**2**	**5**	**10**	**15**	**30**

97.4: RMVL THOR THER DEVICE

Type of Patients	Observed Patients	Avg. Stay	Vari-ance	10th	25th	50th	75th	90th	95th	99th
1. SINGLE DX										
0–19 Years	2	2.6	3	1	1	4	4	4	4	4
20–34	2	4.0	3	3	3	3	6	6	6	6
35–49	1	1.0	0	1	1	1	1	1	1	1
50–64	1	2.0	0	2	2	2	2	2	2	2
65+	0									
2. MULTIPLE DX										
0–19 Years	42	8.1	39	2	4	6	12	16	22	27
20–34	34	5.8	11	2	3	5	9	11	11	11
35–49	75	5.4	79	1	2	3	6	8	14	63
50–64	119	6.8	35	2	3	5	9	13	19	34
65+	94	5.5	23	2	2	4	7	11	17	22
TOTAL SINGLE DX	**6**	**2.7**	**3**	**1**	**1**	**3**	**4**	**6**	**6**	**6**
TOTAL MULTIPLE DX	**364**	**6.2**	**39**	**2**	**2**	**4**	**8**	**12**	**16**	**27**
TOTAL										
0–19 Years	44	7.9	38	2	4	6	11	16	22	27
20–34	36	5.7	11	2	3	5	9	11	11	11
35–49	76	5.3	78	1	2	3	6	8	14	63
50–64	120	6.7	35	2	3	5	9	13	19	34
65+	94	5.5	23	2	2	4	7	11	17	22
GRAND TOTAL	**370**	**6.2**	**39**	**2**	**2**	**4**	**8**	**12**	**16**	**27**

97.49: RMVL DEV FROM THORAX NEC

Type of Patients	Observed Patients	Avg. Stay	Vari-ance	10th	25th	50th	75th	90th	95th	99th
1. SINGLE DX										
0–19 Years	1	1.0	0	1	1	1	1	1	1	1
20–34	0									
35–49	1	1.0	0	1	1	1	1	1	1	1
50–64	0									
65+	0									
2. MULTIPLE DX										
0–19 Years	39	8.2	39	2	4	6	12	16	22	27
20–34	29	6.0	12	2	3	6	9	11	11	11
35–49	72	5.4	83	1	2	3	6	8	14	63
50–64	106	7.0	38	2	3	5	9	13	20	34
65+	85	5.6	23	2	3	4	7	11	17	27
TOTAL SINGLE DX	**2**	**1.0**	**0**	**1**	**1**	**1**	**1**	**1**	**1**	**1**
TOTAL MULTIPLE DX	**331**	**6.4**	**41**	**2**	**2**	**5**	**8**	**13**	**17**	**34**
TOTAL										
0–19 Years	40	8.1	39	2	4	6	12	16	22	27
20–34	29	6.0	12	2	3	6	9	11	11	11
35–49	73	5.3	82	1	2	3	5	8	14	63
50–64	106	7.0	38	2	3	5	9	13	20	34
65+	85	5.6	23	2	3	4	7	11	17	27
GRAND TOTAL	**333**	**6.4**	**41**	**2**	**2**	**5**	**8**	**13**	**17**	**34**

97.5: NONOP RMVL GI THER DEV

Type of Patients	Observed Patients	Avg. Stay	Vari-ance	Percentiles						
				10th	25th	50th	75th	90th	95th	99th
1. SINGLE DX										
0–19 Years	0									
20–34	0									
35–49	0									
50–64	4	3.4	6	1	1	3	3	7	7	7
65+	0									
2. MULTIPLE DX										
0–19 Years	15	5.3	23	1	2	4	6	16	16	16
20–34	16	4.7	17	2	2	3	5	8	8	20
35–49	43	7.2	69	1	2	3	9	21	22	41
50–64	68	8.2	130	2	3	4	7	20	33	59
65+	146	7.1	60	1	2	5	9	16	27	39
TOTAL SINGLE DX	**4**	**3.4**	**6**	**1**	**1**	**3**	**3**	**7**	**7**	**7**
TOTAL MULTIPLE DX	**288**	**7.2**	**76**	**1**	**2**	**4**	**8**	**17**	**27**	**41**
TOTAL										
0–19 Years	15	5.3	23	1	2	4	6	16	16	16
20–34	16	4.7	17	2	2	3	5	8	8	20
35–49	43	7.2	69	1	2	3	9	21	22	41
50–64	72	8.1	126	1	3	4	7	20	33	59
65+	146	7.1	60	1	2	5	9	16	27	39
GRAND TOTAL	**292**	**7.2**	**76**	**1**	**2**	**4**	**8**	**17**	**27**	**41**

97.51: RMVL GASTROSTOMY TUBE

Type of Patients	Observed Patients	Avg. Stay	Vari-ance	Percentiles						
				10th	25th	50th	75th	90th	95th	99th
1. SINGLE DX										
0–19 Years	0									
20–34	0									
35–49	0									
50–64	0									
65+	0									
2. MULTIPLE DX										
0–19 Years	10	5.8	23	1	3	4	6	16	16	16
20–34	7	6.3	34	2	3	3	8	20	20	20
35–49	19	10.5	112	2	2	5	19	22	22	41
50–64	37	9.9	183	1	3	4	11	32	33	59
65+	89	8.3	83	1	2	5	11	27	31	39
TOTAL SINGLE DX	**0**									
TOTAL MULTIPLE DX	**162**	**8.7**	**107**	**1**	**3**	**4**	**11**	**22**	**31**	**59**
TOTAL										
0–19 Years	10	5.8	23	1	3	4	6	16	16	16
20–34	7	6.3	34	2	3	3	8	20	20	20
35–49	19	10.5	112	2	2	5	19	22	22	41
50–64	37	9.9	183	1	3	4	11	32	33	59
65+	89	8.3	83	1	2	5	11	27	31	39
GRAND TOTAL	**162**	**8.7**	**107**	**1**	**3**	**4**	**11**	**22**	**31**	**59**

97.6: NONOP RMVL URIN THER DEV

Type of Patients	Observed Patients	Avg. Stay	Vari-ance	Percentiles						
				10th	25th	50th	75th	90th	95th	99th
1. SINGLE DX										
0–19 Years	4	1.0	0	1	1	1	1	1	1	1
20–34	7	1.9	1	1	1	2	3	4	4	4
35–49	6	1.3	<1	1	1	1	2	2	2	2
50–64	1	2.0	0	2	2	2	2	2	2	2
65+	0									
2. MULTIPLE DX										
0–19 Years	30	3.4	5	1	2	3	5	6	7	11
20–34	75	2.9	5	1	1	2	4	7	7	10
35–49	69	3.9	10	1	2	3	5	8	13	15
50–64	67	5.3	17	1	2	4	6	11	13	26
65+	110	5.8	23	1	2	5	8	13	16	24
TOTAL SINGLE DX	**18**	**1.4**	**<1**	**1**	**1**	**1**	**2**	**2**	**3**	**4**
TOTAL MULTIPLE DX	**351**	**4.5**	**15**	**1**	**2**	**3**	**6**	**10**	**13**	**20**
TOTAL										
0–19 Years	34	2.9	5	1	1	2	4	5	7	11
20–34	82	2.8	5	1	1	2	4	6	7	10
35–49	75	3.7	9	1	2	3	5	7	11	15
50–64	68	5.3	17	2	2	4	6	11	13	26
65+	110	5.8	23	1	2	5	8	13	16	24
GRAND TOTAL	**369**	**4.3**	**15**	**1**	**2**	**3**	**6**	**10**	**13**	**19**

97.62: RMVL URETERAL DRAIN

Type of Patients	Observed Patients	Avg. Stay	Vari-ance	Percentiles						
				10th	25th	50th	75th	90th	95th	99th
1. SINGLE DX										
0–19 Years	4	1.0	0	1	1	1	1	1	1	1
20–34	7	1.9	1	1	1	2	3	4	4	4
35–49	6	1.3	<1	1	1	1	2	2	2	2
50–64	1	2.0	0	2	2	2	2	2	2	2
65+	0									
2. MULTIPLE DX										
0–19 Years	20	3.7	5	1	2	4	5	6	7	11
20–34	64	3.0	6	1	1	2	4	7	8	10
35–49	63	3.9	10	1	2	3	5	8	13	15
50–64	55	5.4	19	1	2	4	7	11	13	26
65+	79	6.2	24	1	2	5	8	13	16	21
TOTAL SINGLE DX	**18**	**1.4**	**<1**	**1**	**1**	**1**	**2**	**2**	**3**	**4**
TOTAL MULTIPLE DX	**281**	**4.6**	**16**	**1**	**2**	**4**	**6**	**10**	**13**	**20**
TOTAL										
0–19 Years	24	3.0	5	1	1	2	4	5	7	11
20–34	71	2.9	5	1	1	2	4	6	7	10
35–49	69	3.7	10	1	2	3	5	8	13	15
50–64	56	5.3	19	1	2	4	7	11	13	26
65+	79	6.2	24	1	2	5	8	13	16	21
GRAND TOTAL	**299**	**4.4**	**16**	**1**	**2**	**3**	**6**	**10**	**13**	**19**

97.7: RMVL THER DEV GENIT SYST

Type of Patients	Observed Patients	Avg. Stay	Vari-ance	Percentiles						
				10th	25th	50th	75th	90th	95th	99th
1. SINGLE DX										
0–19 Years	1	2.0	0	2	2	2	2	2	2	2
20–34	9	1.9	2	1	1	2	2	5	5	5
35–49	3	2.3	1	1	1	3	3	3	3	3
50–64	0									
65+	0									
2. MULTIPLE DX										
0–19 Years	1	2.0	0	2	2	2	2	2	2	2
20–34	43	2.5	3	1	1	2	3	4	4	10
35–49	27	3.3	2	2	2	3	4	6	6	7
50–64	7	5.0	7	2	2	4	6	9	9	9
65+	10	3.8	11	1	1	2	7	8	10	10
TOTAL SINGLE DX	**13**	**2.0**	**1**	**1**	**1**	**2**	**3**	**3**	**5**	**5**
TOTAL MULTIPLE DX	**88**	**3.0**	**4**	**1**	**2**	**3**	**4**	**6**	**7**	**10**
TOTAL										
0–19 Years	2	2.0	0	2	2	2	2	2	2	2
20–34	52	2.4	2	1	1	2	3	4	5	10
35–49	30	3.2	2	1	2	3	4	6	6	7
50–64	7	5.0	7	2	2	4	6	9	9	9
65+	10	3.8	11	1	1	2	7	8	10	10
GRAND TOTAL	**101**	**2.9**	**4**	**1**	**2**	**2**	**3**	**6**	**7**	**10**

97.8: OTH NONOP RMVL THER DEV

Type of Patients	Observed Patients	Avg. Stay	Vari-ance	Percentiles						
				10th	25th	50th	75th	90th	95th	99th
1. SINGLE DX										
0–19 Years	3	3.3	9	1	1	1	5	8	8	8
20–34	5	1.8	<1	1	1	2	2	3	3	3
35–49	2	1.4	<1	1	1	1	2	2	2	2
50–64	2	3.0	0	3	3	3	3	3	3	3
65+	1	1.0	0	1	1	1	1	1	1	1
2. MULTIPLE DX										
0–19 Years	17	5.1	27	1	1	3	5	17	17	17
20–34	23	3.7	10	1	2	3	4	9	11	11
35–49	51	4.9	18	1	2	4	6	11	14	25
50–64	68	8.6	83	1	2	5	13	22	32	36
65+	76	5.4	20	2	3	4	7	11	14	28
TOTAL SINGLE DX	**13**	**2.4**	**4**	**1**	**1**	**2**	**3**	**5**	**8**	**8**
TOTAL MULTIPLE DX	**235**	**5.9**	**38**	**1**	**2**	**4**	**7**	**14**	**17**	**32**
TOTAL										
0–19 Years	20	4.8	24	1	1	3	5	12	17	17
20–34	28	3.5	9	1	1	3	4	9	11	11
35–49	53	4.8	17	1	2	4	6	11	12	25
50–64	70	8.4	82	1	3	5	11	22	32	36
65+	77	5.3	20	1	2	4	7	11	14	28
GRAND TOTAL	**248**	**5.7**	**37**	**1**	**2**	**4**	**7**	**14**	**17**	**32**

97.89: RMVL THERAPEUTIC DEV NEC

Type of Patients	Observed Patients	Avg. Stay	Vari-ance	Percentiles						
				10th	25th	50th	75th	90th	95th	99th
1. SINGLE DX										
0–19 Years	1	8.0	0	8	8	8	8	8	8	8
20–34	2	2.4	<1	2	2	2	3	3	3	3
35–49	0									
50–64	1	3.0	0	3	3	3	3	3	3	3
65+	0									
2. MULTIPLE DX										
0–19 Years	8	3.2	3	1	1	3	5	5	7	7
20–34	9	5.4	19	1	1	4	11	11	11	11
35–49	25	4.2	13	2	2	3	4	7	14	15
50–64	30	8.8	120	1	3	5	9	32	36	36
65+	38	5.6	25	2	3	4	6	12	15	28
TOTAL SINGLE DX	**4**	**4.0**	**7**	**2**	**2**	**3**	**8**	**8**	**8**	**8**
TOTAL MULTIPLE DX	**110**	**5.9**	**48**	**1**	**2**	**4**	**6**	**12**	**25**	**36**
TOTAL										
0–19 Years	9	3.6	5	1	2	4	5	7	8	8
20–34	11	5.0	17	1	1	3	11	11	11	11
35–49	25	4.2	13	2	2	3	4	7	14	15
50–64	31	8.6	117	1	3	5	6	32	36	36
65+	38	5.6	25	2	3	4	6	12	15	28
GRAND TOTAL	**114**	**5.9**	**46**	**1**	**2**	**4**	**6**	**12**	**17**	**36**

98.0: RMVL INTRALUM GI FB

Type of Patients	Observed Patients	Avg. Stay	Vari-ance	Percentiles						
				10th	25th	50th	75th	90th	95th	99th
1. SINGLE DX										
0–19 Years	69	1.1	<1	1	1	1	1	1	1	2
20–34	12	1.2	<1	1	1	1	1	2	3	3
35–49	14	1.1	<1	1	1	1	1	2	2	2
50–64	11	1.2	<1	1	1	1	1	2	2	2
65+	4	1.0	0	1	1	1	1	1	1	1
2. MULTIPLE DX										
0–19 Years	44	8.6	368	1	1	1	2	59	59	59
20–34	18	1.7	1	1	1	1	2	3	3	6
35–49	41	1.7	2	1	1	1	2	3	4	11
50–64	29	1.9	4	1	1	1	3	4	6	10
65+	63	2.6	6	1	1	2	3	5	7	14
TOTAL SINGLE DX	**110**	**1.1**	**<1**	**1**	**1**	**1**	**1**	**1**	**2**	**2**
TOTAL MULTIPLE DX	**195**	**3.7**	**98**	**1**	**1**	**1**	**3**	**5**	**8**	**59**
TOTAL										
0–19 Years	113	4.1	163	1	1	1	1	2	59	59
20–34	30	1.5	1	1	1	1	2	2	3	6
35–49	55	1.6	2	1	1	1	2	3	3	11
50–64	40	1.7	3	1	1	1	1	3	6	10
65+	67	2.6	6	1	1	2	3	5	7	14
GRAND TOTAL	**305**	**2.8**	**65**	**1**	**1**	**1**	**2**	**3**	**6**	**59**

98.02: RMVL INTRALUM ESOPH FB

Type of Patients	Observed Patients	Avg. Stay	Vari-ance	10th	25th	50th	75th	90th	95th	99th
1. SINGLE DX										
0–19 Years	62	1.1	<1	1	1	1	1	1	2	2
20–34	1	1.0	0	1	1	1	1	1	1	1
35–49	1	1.0	0	1	1	1	1	1	1	1
50–64	1	1.0	0	1	1	1	1	1	1	1
65+	1	1.0	0	1	1	1	1	1	1	1
2. MULTIPLE DX										
0–19 Years	36	1.4	1	1	1	1	1	2	2	8
20–34	7	1.1	<1	1	1	1	1	1	2	2
35–49	11	2.4	5	1	1	2	3	3	3	11
50–64	15	2.1	5	1	1	1	3	4	10	10
65+	43	3.1	8	1	1	2	5	7	8	14
TOTAL SINGLE DX	**66**	**1.1**	**<1**	**1**	**1**	**1**	**1**	**1**	**1**	**2**
TOTAL MULTIPLE DX	**112**	**2.2**	**5**	**1**	**1**	**1**	**3**	**5**	**7**	**11**
TOTAL										
0–19 Years	98	1.2	<1	1	1	1	1	2	2	5
20–34	8	1.1	<1	1	1	1	1	1	2	2
35–49	12	2.3	5	1	1	2	3	3	3	11
50–64	16	2.1	4	1	1	1	3	4	4	10
65+	44	3.1	8	1	1	2	5	7	8	14
GRAND TOTAL	**178**	**1.8**	**3**	**1**	**1**	**1**	**2**	**3**	**5**	**10**

98.1: RMVL INTRALUM FB NEC

Type of Patients	Observed Patients	Avg. Stay	Vari-ance	10th	25th	50th	75th	90th	95th	99th
1. SINGLE DX										
0–19 Years	70	1.2	<1	1	1	1	1	2	2	3
20–34	1	1.0	0	1	1	1	1	1	1	1
35–49	4	1.4	<1	1	1	1	2	2	2	2
50–64	9	1.0	0	1	1	1	1	1	1	1
65+	0									
2. MULTIPLE DX										
0–19 Years	41	2.2	6	1	1	1	2	4	9	13
20–34	15	1.8	<1	1	1	1	2	3	4	4
35–49	16	8.3	213	1	2	2	4	47	47	47
50–64	23	3.1	18	1	1	1	4	6	14	18
65+	46	6.1	38	1	2	4	8	16	22	25
TOTAL SINGLE DX	**84**	**1.2**	**<1**	**1**	**1**	**1**	**1**	**2**	**2**	**3**
TOTAL MULTIPLE DX	**141**	**4.5**	**57**	**1**	**1**	**2**	**4**	**10**	**18**	**47**
TOTAL										
0–19 Years	111	1.6	3	1	1	1	1	2	4	10
20–34	16	1.7	<1	1	1	1	2	3	4	4
35–49	20	7.0	180	1	1	2	2	19	47	47
50–64	32	2.5	13	1	1	1	2	6	14	18
65+	46	6.1	38	1	2	4	8	16	22	25
GRAND TOTAL	**225**	**3.2**	**37**	**1**	**1**	**1**	**2**	**6**	**13**	**47**

98.2: RMVL OTH FB W/O INC

Type of Patients	Observed Patients	Avg. Stay	Vari-ance	10th	25th	50th	75th	90th	95th	99th
1. SINGLE DX										
0–19 Years	15	1.6	1	1	1	1	2	3	4	5
20–34	23	1.5	<1	1	1	1	2	3	4	4
35–49	10	3.1	9	1	1	2	4	5	11	11
50–64	3	1.3	<1	1	1	1	2	2	2	2
65+	0									
2. MULTIPLE DX										
0–19 Years	27	2.2	5	1	1	2	2	5	5	13
20–34	36	2.0	2	1	1	2	2	4	4	6
35–49	20	4.4	50	1	1	2	3	16	26	26
50–64	18	3.2	17	1	1	2	3	6	18	18
65+	15	3.7	5	1	2	3	6	7	7	10
TOTAL SINGLE DX	**51**	**1.8**	**3**	**1**	**1**	**1**	**2**	**4**	**4**	**11**
TOTAL MULTIPLE DX	**116**	**2.9**	**13**	**1**	**1**	**2**	**3**	**6**	**7**	**26**
TOTAL										
0–19 Years	42	2.0	4	1	1	2	2	3	5	13
20–34	59	1.8	1	1	1	1	2	4	4	6
35–49	30	4.0	37	1	1	2	3	11	26	26
50–64	21	3.0	15	1	1	2	2	6	10	18
65+	15	3.7	5	1	2	3	6	7	7	10
GRAND TOTAL	**167**	**2.6**	**10**	**1**	**1**	**2**	**3**	**5**	**7**	**18**

98.5: ESWL

Type of Patients	Observed Patients	Avg. Stay	Vari-ance	10th	25th	50th	75th	90th	95th	99th
1. SINGLE DX										
0–19 Years	3	2.7	3	1	1	4	4	5	5	5
20–34	20	1.5	<1	1	1	1	2	2	3	3
35–49	38	1.7	<1	1	1	1	3	3	3	5
50–64	23	1.5	<1	1	1	1	2	2	3	4
65+	9	1.3	<1	1	1	1	1	3	4	4
2. MULTIPLE DX										
0–19 Years	13	3.0	4	1	1	4	4	5	5	10
20–34	101	2.9	6	1	2	2	3	6	9	11
35–49	204	2.4	4	1	1	2	3	4	5	8
50–64	190	2.4	5	1	1	2	3	4	6	13
65+	216	3.4	18	1	1	2	4	8	12	19
TOTAL SINGLE DX	**93**	**1.7**	**<1**	**1**	**1**	**1**	**2**	**3**	**4**	**5**
TOTAL MULTIPLE DX	**724**	**2.8**	**9**	**1**	**1**	**2**	**3**	**5**	**9**	**18**
TOTAL										
0–19 Years	16	2.9	4	1	1	4	4	5	5	10
20–34	121	2.7	5	1	1	2	3	5	9	11
35–49	242	2.3	3	1	1	2	3	4	5	8
50–64	213	2.3	4	1	1	2	3	4	6	9
65+	225	3.3	17	1	1	2	4	8	12	19
GRAND TOTAL	**817**	**2.7**	**8**	**1**	**1**	**2**	**3**	**5**	**8**	**18**

98.51: RENAL/URETER/BLAD ESWL

Type of Patients	Observed Patients	Avg. Stay	Vari-ance	Percentiles 10th	25th	50th	75th	90th	95th	99th
1. SINGLE DX										
0–19 Years	3	2.7	3	1	1	4	4	5	5	5
20–34	20	1.5	<1	1	1	1	2	2	3	3
35–49	38	1.7	<1	1	1	1	3	3	3	5
50–64	23	1.5	<1	1	1	1	2	2	3	4
65+	9	1.3	<1	1	1	1	1	3	4	4
2. MULTIPLE DX										
0–19 Years	12	3.1	4	1	1	4	4	5	5	10
20–34	100	2.9	6	1	2	2	3	6	9	11
35–49	203	2.4	4	1	1	2	3	4	5	8
50–64	186	2.4	5	1	1	2	3	4	6	13
65+	213	3.4	18	1	1	2	4	8	12	19
TOTAL SINGLE DX	**93**	**1.7**	**<1**	**1**	**1**	**1**	**2**	**3**	**4**	**5**
TOTAL MULTIPLE DX	**714**	**2.8**	**9**	**1**	**1**	**2**	**3**	**5**	**9**	**18**
TOTAL										
0–19 Years	15	2.9	4	1	1	4	4	5	5	10
20–34	120	2.7	5	1	1	2	3	5	9	11
35–49	241	2.3	4	1	1	2	3	4	5	8
50–64	209	2.3	4	1	1	2	3	4	6	13
65+	222	3.3	17	1	1	2	4	8	12	19
GRAND TOTAL	**807**	**2.7**	**8**	**1**	**1**	**2**	**3**	**5**	**8**	**18**

99.0: BLOOD TRANSFUSION

Type of Patients	Observed Patients	Avg. Stay	Vari-ance	Percentiles 10th	25th	50th	75th	90th	95th	99th
1. SINGLE DX										
0–19 Years	258	2.4	5	1	1	2	3	5	6	12
20–34	133	3.6	12	1	1	2	4	9	11	15
35–49	122	2.6	6	1	1	1	3	7	8	12
50–64	100	1.8	3	1	1	1	2	4	6	9
65+	176	1.3	<1	1	1	1	1	2	3	4
2. MULTIPLE DX										
0–19 Years	2,288	5.3	56	1	2	3	6	11	16	40
20–34	2,218	4.8	26	1	2	3	6	10	14	25
35–49	5,129	4.5	18	1	2	3	6	9	13	21
50–64	8,458	5.0	23	1	2	4	6	10	13	23
65+	30,842	4.9	16	1	2	4	6	10	12	20
TOTAL SINGLE DX	**789**	**2.3**	**5**	**1**	**1**	**1**	**3**	**5**	**8**	**12**
TOTAL MULTIPLE DX	**48,935**	**4.9**	**20**	**1**	**2**	**4**	**6**	**10**	**13**	**21**
TOTAL										
0–19 Years	2,546	5.1	53	1	2	3	6	11	15	38
20–34	2,351	4.7	25	1	2	3	6	10	14	25
35–49	5,251	4.5	18	1	2	3	6	9	13	21
50–64	8,558	5.0	23	1	2	4	6	10	13	23
65+	31,018	4.9	16	1	2	4	6	9	12	20
GRAND TOTAL	**49,724**	**4.9**	**20**	**1**	**2**	**4**	**6**	**10**	**13**	**21**

99.01: EXCHANGE TRANSFUSION

Type of Patients	Observed Patients	Avg. Stay	Vari-ance	Percentiles 10th	25th	50th	75th	90th	95th	99th
1. SINGLE DX										
0–19 Years	5	3.4	3	1	2	3	4	6	6	6
20–34	5	2.1	<1	1	2	2	2	3	3	3
35–49	0									
50–64	1	8.0	0	8	8	8	8	8	8	8
65+	0									
2. MULTIPLE DX										
0–19 Years	82	9.6	229	2	3	4	9	17	67	67
20–34	25	4.6	16	2	2	2	6	10	11	17
35–49	19	4.4	8	1	3	4	4	8	11	12
50–64	4	6.7	12	5	5	5	5	13	13	13
65+	4	6.2	3	4	6	6	7	8	8	8
TOTAL SINGLE DX	**11**	**3.3**	**4**	**1**	**2**	**3**	**4**	**6**	**8**	**8**
TOTAL MULTIPLE DX	**134**	**7.8**	**153**	**2**	**3**	**4**	**8**	**15**	**25**	**67**
TOTAL										
0–19 Years	87	9.1	215	2	3	4	9	15	67	67
20–34	30	4.3	14	2	2	2	6	10	11	17
35–49	19	4.4	8	1	3	4	4	8	11	12
50–64	5	6.8	11	5	5	5	8	13	13	13
65+	4	6.2	3	4	6	6	7	8	8	8
GRAND TOTAL	**145**	**7.5**	**144**	**2**	**3**	**4**	**7**	**15**	**23**	**67**

99.03: WHOLE BLOOD TRANSFUS NEC

Type of Patients	Observed Patients	Avg. Stay	Vari-ance	Percentiles 10th	25th	50th	75th	90th	95th	99th
1. SINGLE DX										
0–19 Years	1	2.0	0	2	2	2	2	2	2	2
20–34	1	1.0	0	1	1	1	1	1	1	1
35–49	0									
50–64	0									
65+	3	1.3	<1	1	1	1	2	2	2	2
2. MULTIPLE DX										
0–19 Years	8	6.6	46	1	1	6	8	12	24	24
20–34	7	10.2	159	1	2	4	14	36	36	36
35–49	21	3.4	4	1	2	3	5	7	7	8
50–64	22	8.4	49	2	3	7	9	21	21	21
65+	99	4.7	17	1	2	3	6	9	12	20
TOTAL SINGLE DX	**5**	**1.4**	**<1**	**1**	**1**	**1**	**2**	**2**	**2**	**2**
TOTAL MULTIPLE DX	**157**	**5.5**	**30**	**1**	**2**	**3**	**7**	**12**	**21**	**25**
TOTAL										
0–19 Years	9	6.4	45	1	1	6	8	12	24	24
20–34	8	9.2	150	1	2	4	14	36	36	36
35–49	21	3.4	4	1	2	3	5	7	7	8
50–64	22	8.4	49	2	3	7	9	21	21	21
65+	102	4.6	17	1	2	3	6	9	12	20
GRAND TOTAL	**162**	**5.4**	**30**	**1**	**2**	**3**	**7**	**12**	**20**	**25**

99.04: PACKED CELL TRANSFUSION

Type of Patients	Observed Patients	Avg. Stay	Variance	Percentiles 10th	25th	50th	75th	90th	95th	99th
1. SINGLE DX										
0–19 Years	233	2.3	5	1	1	2	2	5	7	12
20–34	123	3.8	13	1	1	2	5	10	11	15
35–49	112	2.6	6	1	1	1	3	8	8	12
50–64	84	1.8	3	1	1	1	2	4	6	11
65+	159	1.3	<1	1	1	1	1	2	3	4
2. MULTIPLE DX										
0–19 Years	1,767	5.1	55	1	2	3	5	10	16	40
20–34	1,954	4.7	26	1	2	3	6	10	14	25
35–49	4,598	4.4	17	1	2	3	6	9	12	21
50–64	7,562	5.0	23	1	2	4	6	10	13	23
65+	28,438	4.9	16	1	2	4	6	9	12	20
TOTAL SINGLE DX	**711**	**2.3**	**6**	**1**	**1**	**1**	**2**	**5**	**8**	**12**
TOTAL MULTIPLE DX	**44,319**	**4.9**	**20**	**1**	**2**	**4**	**6**	**10**	**13**	**21**
TOTAL										
0–19 Years	2,000	4.8	51	1	2	3	5	10	15	38
20–34	2,077	4.7	25	1	2	3	6	10	14	25
35–49	4,710	4.4	17	1	2	3	6	9	12	21
50–64	7,646	5.0	23	1	2	4	6	10	13	23
65+	28,597	4.9	16	1	2	4	6	9	12	20
GRAND TOTAL	**45,030**	**4.8**	**20**	**1**	**2**	**4**	**6**	**10**	**13**	**21**

99.05: PLATELET TRANSFUSION

Type of Patients	Observed Patients	Avg. Stay	Variance	Percentiles 10th	25th	50th	75th	90th	95th	99th
1. SINGLE DX										
0–19 Years	12	2.7	4	1	1	3	3	6	7	7
20–34	2	2.0	0	2	2	2	2	2	2	2
35–49	7	2.2	1	1	1	2	3	4	4	4
50–64	11	1.5	<1	1	1	1	3	3	3	3
65+	8	1.3	<1	1	1	1	1	2	3	3
2. MULTIPLE DX										
0–19 Years	311	5.6	29	2	2	4	7	12	16	24
20–34	132	5.4	24	1	3	4	6	9	15	28
35–49	211	5.7	24	1	2	4	7	12	16	25
50–64	361	5.3	24	1	2	4	7	11	13	20
65+	586	5.6	23	1	2	4	7	11	15	24
TOTAL SINGLE DX	**40**	**2.0**	**2**	**1**	**1**	**1**	**3**	**3**	**5**	**7**
TOTAL MULTIPLE DX	**1,601**	**5.5**	**25**	**1**	**2**	**4**	**7**	**11**	**15**	**24**
TOTAL										
0–19 Years	323	5.5	29	1	2	4	7	12	16	24
20–34	134	5.3	23	1	2	4	6	9	15	28
35–49	218	5.6	24	1	2	4	7	12	16	25
50–64	372	5.2	23	1	2	4	7	11	12	20
65+	594	5.6	23	1	2	4	7	11	15	24
GRAND TOTAL	**1,641**	**5.4**	**25**	**1**	**2**	**4**	**7**	**11**	**15**	**23**

99.06: COAG FACTOR TRANSFUSION

Type of Patients	Observed Patients	Avg. Stay	Variance	Percentiles 10th	25th	50th	75th	90th	95th	99th
1. SINGLE DX										
0–19 Years	5	1.9	<1	1	1	2	3	3	3	3
20–34	0									
35–49	0									
50–64	2	1.0	0	1	1	1	1	1	1	1
65+	2	1.0	0	1	1	1	1	1	1	1
2. MULTIPLE DX										
0–19 Years	39	3.4	14	1	2	2	4	6	12	20
20–34	17	4.5	9	2	2	4	6	10	11	11
35–49	15	5.2	24	2	2	4	5	16	16	16
50–64	16	5.9	20	2	3	3	9	12	13	16
65+	10	4.4	7	2	2	4	6	8	8	10
TOTAL SINGLE DX	**9**	**1.4**	**<1**	**1**	**1**	**1**	**2**	**3**	**3**	**3**
TOTAL MULTIPLE DX	**97**	**4.3**	**15**	**1**	**2**	**3**	**5**	**10**	**12**	**20**
TOTAL										
0–19 Years	44	3.3	13	1	2	2	4	5	7	20
20–34	17	4.5	9	2	2	4	6	10	11	11
35–49	15	5.2	24	2	2	4	5	16	16	16
50–64	18	5.0	20	1	2	3	6	12	13	16
65+	12	4.2	7	1	2	3	6	8	8	10
GRAND TOTAL	**106**	**4.1**	**14**	**1**	**2**	**3**	**5**	**9**	**12**	**20**

99.07: SERUM TRANSFUSION NEC

Type of Patients	Observed Patients	Avg. Stay	Variance	Percentiles 10th	25th	50th	75th	90th	95th	99th
1. SINGLE DX										
0–19 Years	2	3.6	4	2	2	5	5	5	5	5
20–34	1	5.0	0	5	5	5	5	5	5	5
35–49	3	3.0	11	1	1	1	7	7	7	7
50–64	1	4.0	0	4	4	4	4	4	4	4
65+	4	1.4	<1	1	1	1	2	2	2	2
2. MULTIPLE DX										
0–19 Years	42	6.1	26	2	2	5	8	11	17	28
20–34	74	5.2	22	1	2	4	7	10	15	21
35–49	232	5.3	20	1	2	4	7	10	15	23
50–64	446	5.1	21	1	2	4	7	10	14	22
65+	1,609	4.9	18	1	2	4	6	9	12	20
TOTAL SINGLE DX	**11**	**2.7**	**4**	**1**	**1**	**2**	**5**	**5**	**7**	**7**
TOTAL MULTIPLE DX	**2,403**	**5.0**	**19**	**1**	**2**	**4**	**7**	**10**	**12**	**21**
TOTAL										
0–19 Years	44	6.0	25	2	2	5	8	10	17	28
20–34	75	5.2	21	1	2	4	7	10	15	21
35–49	235	5.2	20	1	2	4	7	10	15	23
50–64	447	5.1	21	1	2	4	7	10	14	22
65+	1,613	4.9	18	1	2	4	6	9	12	20
GRAND TOTAL	**2,414**	**5.0**	**19**	**1**	**2**	**4**	**7**	**10**	**12**	**21**

99.09: TRANSFUSION NEC

Type of Patients	Observed Patients	Avg. Stay	Vari-ance	Percentiles 10th	25th	50th	75th	90th	95th	99th
1. SINGLE DX										
0–19 Years	0									
20–34	0									
35–49	0									
50–64	1	1.0	0	1	1	1	1	1	1	1
65+	0									
2. MULTIPLE DX										
0–19 Years	39	5.6	20	1	2	4	8	14	14	16
20–34	9	5.4	14	2	2	3	10	10	11	11
35–49	26	6.5	29	1	2	6	8	17	17	19
50–64	29	5.1	30	2	2	3	7	8	12	29
65+	58	5.4	15	1	3	4	8	10	13	19
TOTAL SINGLE DX	**1**	**1.0**	**0**	**1**	**1**	**1**	**1**	**1**	**1**	**1**
TOTAL MULTIPLE DX	**161**	**5.6**	**21**	**1**	**2**	**4**	**8**	**12**	**14**	**19**
TOTAL										
0–19 Years	39	5.6	20	1	2	4	8	14	14	16
20–34	9	5.4	14	2	2	3	10	10	11	11
35–49	26	6.5	29	1	2	6	8	17	17	19
50–64	30	5.0	30	1	2	3	7	8	12	29
65+	58	5.4	15	1	3	4	8	10	13	19
GRAND TOTAL	**162**	**5.6**	**21**	**1**	**2**	**4**	**8**	**12**	**14**	**19**

99.1: INJECT/INFUSE THER SUBST

Type of Patients	Observed Patients	Avg. Stay	Vari-ance	Percentiles 10th	25th	50th	75th	90th	95th	99th
1. SINGLE DX										
0–19 Years	260	1.9	2	1	1	2	2	3	4	8
20–34	111	2.8	10	1	1	2	3	6	7	21
35–49	60	3.6	11	1	1	3	4	7	9	22
50–64	34	3.2	6	1	1	2	4	6	9	13
65+	28	3.3	5	1	1	2	5	7	7	9
2. MULTIPLE DX										
0–19 Years	2,465	9.7	105	1	2	6	14	23	31	48
20–34	755	5.7	67	1	2	3	7	11	17	36
35–49	1,201	6.5	44	1	2	4	8	15	21	33
50–64	1,644	5.9	33	1	2	4	7	12	15	32
65+	3,054	6.0	25	1	3	5	7	12	16	27
TOTAL SINGLE DX	**493**	**2.4**	**5**	**1**	**1**	**2**	**3**	**5**	**7**	**9**
TOTAL MULTIPLE DX	**9,119**	**7.1**	**59**	**1**	**2**	**5**	**9**	**16**	**22**	**38**
TOTAL										
0–19 Years	2,725	8.9	100	1	2	5	13	22	29	45
20–34	866	5.4	61	1	2	3	6	10	16	34
35–49	1,261	6.4	43	1	2	4	8	15	21	33
50–64	1,678	5.8	33	1	2	4	7	11	15	32
65+	3,082	6.0	25	1	3	5	7	12	16	27
GRAND TOTAL	**9,612**	**6.9**	**57**	**1**	**2**	**4**	**8**	**15**	**22**	**37**

99.10: INJECT THROMBOLYTIC

Type of Patients	Observed Patients	Avg. Stay	Vari-ance	Percentiles 10th	25th	50th	75th	90th	95th	99th
1. SINGLE DX										
0–19 Years	5	2.1	1	1	2	2	2	4	4	4
20–34	4	6.4	8	3	5	5	9	9	9	9
35–49	10	3.3	3	1	2	3	4	5	8	8
50–64	8	2.2	1	1	2	2	2	5	5	5
65+	8	2.4	4	1	1	2	3	7	7	7
2. MULTIPLE DX										
0–19 Years	15	5.2	13	2	2	4	7	12	12	14
20–34	53	4.6	6	1	3	4	7	7	9	11
35–49	171	4.5	13	1	2	4	6	9	11	18
50–64	367	4.8	13	1	2	4	6	9	11	16
65+	729	5.1	14	2	3	4	6	9	12	19
TOTAL SINGLE DX	**35**	**2.9**	**4**	**1**	**2**	**2**	**4**	**5**	**8**	**9**
TOTAL MULTIPLE DX	**1,335**	**4.9**	**13**	**1**	**3**	**4**	**6**	**9**	**12**	**19**
TOTAL										
0–19 Years	20	4.7	13	1	2	4	7	10	12	14
20–34	57	4.7	6	1	3	5	7	8	9	11
35–49	181	4.4	12	1	2	4	6	8	11	18
50–64	375	4.7	13	1	2	4	6	9	11	16
65+	737	5.1	14	2	3	4	6	9	12	19
GRAND TOTAL	**1,370**	**4.9**	**13**	**1**	**3**	**4**	**6**	**9**	**12**	**19**

99.11: INJECT RH IMMUNE GLOB

Type of Patients	Observed Patients	Avg. Stay	Vari-ance	Percentiles 10th	25th	50th	75th	90th	95th	99th
1. SINGLE DX										
0–19 Years	22	1.7	<1	1	1	2	2	2	2	3
20–34	45	1.8	1	1	1	2	2	2	4	7
35–49	6	1.9	1	1	1	1	3	4	4	4
50–64	0									
65+	0									
2. MULTIPLE DX										
0–19 Years	31	3.8	37	1	1	2	4	8	26	26
20–34	144	2.4	7	1	1	2	2	4	8	12
35–49	33	3.0	24	1	1	2	3	6	8	33
50–64	3	2.5	<1	2	2	2	2	4	4	4
65+	3	5.3	8	4	4	4	4	11	11	11
TOTAL SINGLE DX	**73**	**1.8**	**1**	**1**	**1**	**2**	**2**	**2**	**3**	**7**
TOTAL MULTIPLE DX	**214**	**2.7**	**14**	**1**	**1**	**2**	**3**	**4**	**8**	**26**
TOTAL										
0–19 Years	53	2.9	21	1	1	2	2	4	8	26
20–34	189	2.2	6	1	1	2	2	3	7	12
35–49	39	2.9	21	1	1	2	3	4	8	33
50–64	3	2.5	<1	2	2	2	2	4	4	4
65+	3	5.3	8	4	4	4	4	11	11	11
GRAND TOTAL	**287**	**2.5**	**11**	**1**	**1**	**2**	**2**	**4**	**8**	**26**

99.14: INJECT GAMMA GLOBULIN

Type of Patients	Observed Patients	Avg. Stay	Vari-ance	Percentiles 10th	25th	50th	75th	90th	95th	99th
1. SINGLE DX										
0–19 Years	176	1.9	2	1	1	1	2	3	4	8
20–34	14	3.1	6	1	1	2	6	7	7	7
35–49	13	1.5	1	1	1	1	2	2	5	5
50–64	9	2.3	3	1	1	1	3	6	6	6
65+	7	1.7	<1	1	1	2	2	2	2	2
2. MULTIPLE DX										
0–19 Years	577	2.7	6	1	1	2	3	5	7	14
20–34	54	4.0	22	1	1	2	5	6	12	36
35–49	100	2.9	7	1	1	2	4	6	8	16
50–64	61	3.5	7	1	2	3	5	7	10	12
65+	100	3.9	10	1	2	3	5	8	9	14
TOTAL SINGLE DX	219	1.9	2	1	1	1	2	3	5	8
TOTAL MULTIPLE DX	892	3.0	8	1	1	2	3	6	8	14
TOTAL										
0–19 Years	753	2.4	5	1	1	2	3	4	7	14
20–34	68	3.9	19	1	1	2	5	6	8	36
35–49	113	2.8	7	1	1	2	4	6	7	16
50–64	70	3.4	7	1	1	3	5	7	10	12
65+	107	3.8	10	1	2	3	5	8	9	14
GRAND TOTAL	1,111	2.7	7	1	1	2	3	5	7	14

99.15: PARENTERAL NUTRITION

Type of Patients	Observed Patients	Avg. Stay	Vari-ance	Percentiles 10th	25th	50th	75th	90th	95th	99th
1. SINGLE DX										
0–19 Years	7	5.1	3	1	4	6	6	7	7	7
20–34	16	5.6	33	2	2	3	6	19	21	21
35–49	10	8.2	30	3	3	8	9	14	22	22
50–64	7	5.7	14	2	3	4	9	13	13	13
65+	2	6.3	2	4	7	7	7	7	7	7
2. MULTIPLE DX										
0–19 Years	1,584	13.4	117	3	6	11	18	28	34	56
20–34	256	9.9	137	3	4	7	11	20	28	72
35–49	469	10.0	62	3	5	7	13	23	26	43
50–64	571	8.8	54	3	4	7	11	16	22	44
65+	870	9.2	38	3	5	8	12	17	22	30
TOTAL SINGLE DX	42	6.1	21	2	3	6	7	13	19	22
TOTAL MULTIPLE DX	3,750	11.1	88	3	5	8	14	23	30	48
TOTAL										
0–19 Years	1,591	13.4	117	3	6	11	18	28	34	56
20–34	272	9.6	132	2	4	6	10	19	28	72
35–49	479	10.0	61	3	5	7	13	23	26	43
50–64	578	8.7	54	3	4	7	11	16	22	44
65+	872	9.2	38	3	5	8	12	17	22	30
GRAND TOTAL	3,792	11.1	88	3	5	8	14	23	30	48

99.17: INJECT INSULIN

Type of Patients	Observed Patients	Avg. Stay	Vari-ance	Percentiles 10th	25th	50th	75th	90th	95th	99th
1. SINGLE DX										
0–19 Years	29	1.6	<1	1	1	2	2	3	3	3
20–34	7	2.1	<1	1	2	2	3	3	3	3
35–49	5	2.9	3	2	2	2	3	6	6	6
50–64	2	2.6	4	1	1	4	4	4	4	4
65+	0									
2. MULTIPLE DX										
0–19 Years	73	2.7	3	1	2	2	3	5	6	11
20–34	96	3.0	4	1	2	2	4	6	6	12
35–49	143	3.3	22	1	2	2	4	6	7	23
50–64	221	3.6	16	1	2	3	4	6	8	16
65+	427	3.5	9	1	2	3	4	6	8	15
TOTAL SINGLE DX	43	1.9	<1	1	1	2	2	3	3	6
TOTAL MULTIPLE DX	960	3.4	11	1	2	3	4	6	8	15
TOTAL										
0–19 Years	102	2.5	3	1	1	2	3	4	5	8
20–34	103	2.9	4	1	2	2	4	6	6	12
35–49	148	3.3	21	1	2	2	4	6	7	23
50–64	223	3.6	16	1	2	3	4	6	8	16
65+	427	3.5	9	1	2	3	4	6	8	15
GRAND TOTAL	1,003	3.3	11	1	2	3	4	6	8	13

99.18: INJECT ELECTROLYTES

Type of Patients	Observed Patients	Avg. Stay	Vari-ance	Percentiles 10th	25th	50th	75th	90th	95th	99th
1. SINGLE DX										
0–19 Years	13	1.7	<1	1	1	1	2	3	3	3
20–34	5	1.8	<1	1	2	2	2	2	2	2
35–49	0									
50–64	1	1.0	0	1	1	1	1	1	1	1
65+	0									
2. MULTIPLE DX										
0–19 Years	159	2.1	4	1	1	1	2	4	6	12
20–34	66	2.3	3	1	1	2	3	5	6	9
35–49	60	2.6	7	1	1	2	3	5	8	17
50–64	80	3.2	9	1	1	2	4	7	11	16
65+	177	2.9	6	1	1	2	4	6	7	14
TOTAL SINGLE DX	19	1.7	<1	1	1	1	2	3	3	3
TOTAL MULTIPLE DX	542	2.5	5	1	1	2	3	5	7	13
TOTAL										
0–19 Years	172	2.1	4	1	1	1	2	4	6	9
20–34	71	2.3	3	1	1	2	3	4	6	9
35–49	60	2.6	7	1	1	2	3	5	8	17
50–64	81	3.2	9	1	1	2	4	7	11	16
65+	177	2.9	6	1	1	2	4	6	7	14
GRAND TOTAL	561	2.5	5	1	1	2	3	5	7	13

99.19: INJECT ANTICOAGULANT

Type of Patients	Observed Patients	Avg. Stay	Vari-ance	10th	25th	50th	75th	90th	95th	99th
1. SINGLE DX										
0–19 Years	2	2.5	<1	1	3	3	3	3	3	3
20–34	15	2.9	5	1	1	2	4	7	8	8
35–49	9	3.9	4	2	3	3	5	7	7	7
50–64	6	3.4	2	1	1	4	4	5	5	5
65+	11	3.7	6	1	1	4	5	6	9	9
2. MULTIPLE DX										
0–19 Years	17	5.3	23	1	2	3	9	11	18	18
20–34	71	5.4	22	1	2	5	6	10	16	33
35–49	205	4.6	12	1	2	4	6	8	12	16
50–64	323	3.9	7	1	2	3	5	7	9	13
65+	740	4.7	11	1	2	4	6	8	11	17
TOTAL SINGLE DX	**43**	**3.4**	**4**	**1**	**1**	**3**	**4**	**7**	**7**	**9**
TOTAL MULTIPLE DX	**1,356**	**4.5**	**11**	**1**	**2**	**4**	**6**	**8**	**11**	**16**
TOTAL										
0–19 Years	19	4.9	21	1	2	3	7	11	18	18
20–34	86	5.0	20	1	2	4	6	8	14	33
35–49	214	4.5	12	1	2	4	6	8	12	16
50–64	329	3.9	7	1	2	4	5	7	9	13
65+	751	4.6	11	1	2	4	6	8	11	17
GRAND TOTAL	**1,399**	**4.5**	**11**	**1**	**2**	**4**	**6**	**8**	**11**	**16**

99.2: OTH INJECT THER SUBST

Type of Patients	Observed Patients	Avg. Stay	Vari-ance	10th	25th	50th	75th	90th	95th	99th
1. SINGLE DX										
0–19 Years	583	2.3	3	1	1	2	3	4	5	10
20–34	817	2.4	3	1	1	2	3	4	6	11
35–49	295	2.4	4	1	1	2	3	5	6	9
50–64	167	2.2	3	1	1	2	3	4	6	9
65+	74	2.6	7	1	1	2	3	5	7	14
2. MULTIPLE DX										
0–19 Years	7,015	4.0	19	1	2	3	4	7	10	25
20–34	3,732	4.5	34	1	2	3	5	7	13	31
35–49	5,098	4.3	22	1	2	3	5	7	11	26
50–64	7,237	4.5	26	1	2	3	5	8	12	28
65+	7,172	4.7	26	1	2	4	5	9	13	29
TOTAL SINGLE DX	**1,936**	**2.3**	**3**	**1**	**1**	**2**	**3**	**4**	**6**	**10**
TOTAL MULTIPLE DX	**30,254**	**4.4**	**24**	**1**	**2**	**3**	**5**	**7**	**12**	**27**
TOTAL										
0–19 Years	7,598	3.9	18	1	2	3	4	7	10	24
20–34	4,549	4.2	30	1	2	3	5	7	11	29
35–49	5,393	4.2	21	1	2	3	5	7	11	26
50–64	7,404	4.4	25	1	2	3	5	7	12	28
65+	7,246	4.7	26	1	2	4	5	9	13	29
GRAND TOTAL	**32,190**	**4.3**	**23**	**1**	**2**	**3**	**5**	**7**	**11**	**27**

99.20: INJECT PLATELET INHIB

Type of Patients	Observed Patients	Avg. Stay	Vari-ance	10th	25th	50th	75th	90th	95th	99th
1. SINGLE DX										
0–19 Years	1	2.0	0	2	2	2	2	2	2	2
20–34	0									
35–49	0									
50–64	0									
65+	1	1.0	0	1	1	1	1	1	1	1
2. MULTIPLE DX										
0–19 Years	1	4.0	0	4	4	4	4	4	4	4
20–34	2	6.0	0	6	6	6	6	6	6	6
35–49	34	2.5	2	1	1	2	3	5	5	8
50–64	115	3.5	8	1	2	3	4	5	9	16
65+	276	4.4	11	2	2	4	5	8	10	16
TOTAL SINGLE DX	**2**	**1.6**	**<1**	**1**	**1**	**2**	**2**	**2**	**2**	**2**
TOTAL MULTIPLE DX	**428**	**4.0**	**10**	**1**	**2**	**3**	**5**	**7**	**9**	**16**
TOTAL										
0–19 Years	2	3.0	1	2	2	3	4	4	4	4
20–34	2	6.0	0	6	6	6	6	6	6	6
35–49	34	2.5	2	1	1	2	3	5	5	8
50–64	115	3.5	8	1	2	3	4	5	9	16
65+	277	4.4	11	2	2	4	5	8	10	16
GRAND TOTAL	**430**	**4.0**	**10**	**1**	**2**	**3**	**5**	**7**	**9**	**16**

99.21: INJECT ANTIBIOTIC

Type of Patients	Observed Patients	Avg. Stay	Vari-ance	10th	25th	50th	75th	90th	95th	99th
1. SINGLE DX										
0–19 Years	188	2.3	2	1	1	2	3	4	5	8
20–34	87	2.3	1	1	1	2	3	4	5	6
35–49	62	2.8	3	1	2	2	3	5	7	9
50–64	35	2.6	3	1	1	2	3	5	7	8
65+	16	4.0	15	1	2	2	5	8	8	19
2. MULTIPLE DX										
0–19 Years	1,386	4.4	21	1	2	3	5	9	13	24
20–34	541	3.8	12	1	2	3	4	7	11	17
35–49	712	3.8	14	1	2	3	4	7	10	20
50–64	766	4.4	26	1	2	3	5	8	11	35
65+	1,282	4.2	13	1	2	3	5	7	10	16
TOTAL SINGLE DX	**388**	**2.5**	**3**	**1**	**1**	**2**	**3**	**4**	**6**	**8**
TOTAL MULTIPLE DX	**4,687**	**4.2**	**18**	**1**	**2**	**3**	**5**	**8**	**11**	**23**
TOTAL										
0–19 Years	1,574	4.2	19	1	2	3	5	8	12	24
20–34	628	3.6	11	1	2	3	4	7	10	16
35–49	774	3.7	13	1	2	3	4	7	9	20
50–64	801	4.4	26	1	2	3	5	8	11	35
65+	1,298	4.2	13	1	2	3	5	7	10	16
GRAND TOTAL	**5,075**	**4.1**	**17**	**1**	**2**	**3**	**5**	**7**	**11**	**22**

99.22: INJECT ANTI-INFECT NEC

Type of Patients	Observed Patients	Avg. Stay	Vari-ance	10th	25th	50th	75th	90th	95th	99th
1. SINGLE DX										
0–19 Years	1	3.0	0	3	3	3	3	3	3	3
20–34	0									
35–49	0									
50–64	0									
65+	0									
2. MULTIPLE DX										
0–19 Years	14	4.5	9	2	2	4	6	7	12	13
20–34	8	2.2	1	1	2	2	3	4	4	4
35–49	5	2.2	<1	2	2	2	2	2	4	4
50–64	7	3.5	2	1	3	4	5	5	5	5
65+	14	4.6	8	2	2	3	7	9	11	11
TOTAL SINGLE DX	**1**	**3.0**	**0**	**3**	**3**	**3**	**3**	**3**	**3**	**3**
TOTAL MULTIPLE DX	**48**	**3.9**	**7**	**2**	**2**	**3**	**5**	**7**	**10**	**13**
TOTAL										
0–19 Years	15	4.3	8	2	2	4	6	7	12	13
20–34	8	2.2	1	1	2	2	3	4	4	4
35–49	5	2.2	<1	2	2	2	2	2	4	4
50–64	7	3.5	2	1	3	4	5	5	5	5
65+	14	4.6	8	2	2	3	7	9	11	11
GRAND TOTAL	**49**	**3.9**	**6**	**2**	**2**	**3**	**5**	**7**	**10**	**13**

99.23: INJECT STEROID

Type of Patients	Observed Patients	Avg. Stay	Vari-ance	10th	25th	50th	75th	90th	95th	99th
1. SINGLE DX										
0–19 Years	20	1.5	2	1	1	1	1	2	4	8
20–34	14	3.2	6	1	2	2	3	8	8	8
35–49	7	2.5	3	1	1	1	4	5	5	5
50–64	6	3.0	3	1	1	3	4	6	6	6
65+	5	1.8	3	1	1	1	1	5	5	5
2. MULTIPLE DX										
0–19 Years	47	3.4	14	1	2	3	4	7	28	>99
20–34	67	5.6	59	1	1	3	5	20	25	28
35–49	64	3.3	9	1	2	2	4	5	7	27
50–64	94	4.2	13	1	2	3	5	7	11	19
65+	175	5.3	16	2	2	4	7	11	14	17
TOTAL SINGLE DX	**52**	**2.2**	**4**	**1**	**1**	**1**	**2**	**5**	**8**	**8**
TOTAL MULTIPLE DX	**447**	**4.6**	**21**	**1**	**2**	**3**	**5**	**9**	**15**	**28**
TOTAL										
0–19 Years	67	2.7	11	1	1	2	3	5	9	>99
20–34	81	5.1	49	1	2	3	4	17	24	28
35–49	71	3.2	9	1	2	2	4	5	7	9
50–64	100	4.1	13	1	2	3	5	7	10	19
65+	180	5.2	16	2	2	4	6	11	14	17
GRAND TOTAL	**499**	**4.4**	**20**	**1**	**2**	**3**	**5**	**9**	**14**	**28**

99.25: INJECT CA CHEMO AGENT

Type of Patients	Observed Patients	Avg. Stay	Vari-ance	10th	25th	50th	75th	90th	95th	99th
1. SINGLE DX										
0–19 Years	47	3.2	5	1	1	3	4	5	8	13
20–34	33	2.6	3	1	1	2	4	5	6	7
35–49	28	3.6	5	1	2	4	4	8	8	8
50–64	19	3.2	7	1	1	2	4	6	9	10
65+	11	1.9	2	1	1	1	3	4	5	5
2. MULTIPLE DX										
0–19 Years	4,766	4.0	17	1	2	3	4	6	10	25
20–34	1,717	5.2	38	1	3	4	5	7	13	36
35–49	2,679	5.0	26	1	2	4	5	8	14	28
50–64	4,600	4.8	31	1	2	4	5	8	15	30
65+	3,590	5.3	39	1	2	4	6	10	17	33
TOTAL SINGLE DX	**138**	**3.0**	**5**	**1**	**1**	**3**	**4**	**6**	**8**	**10**
TOTAL MULTIPLE DX	**17,352**	**4.7**	**28**	**1**	**2**	**4**	**5**	**8**	**13**	**29**
TOTAL										
0–19 Years	4,813	4.0	17	1	2	3	4	6	9	25
20–34	1,750	5.1	38	1	3	4	5	7	12	36
35–49	2,707	4.9	26	1	2	4	5	8	14	28
50–64	4,619	4.8	31	1	2	4	5	8	14	30
65+	3,601	5.3	39	1	2	4	6	10	17	33
GRAND TOTAL	**17,490**	**4.7**	**28**	**1**	**2**	**4**	**5**	**8**	**13**	**29**

99.28: INJECT BRM/ANTINEO AGENT

Type of Patients	Observed Patients	Avg. Stay	Vari-ance	10th	25th	50th	75th	90th	95th	99th
1. SINGLE DX										
0–19 Years	14	3.9	3	2	2	5	5	6	6	6
20–34	0									
35–49	8	3.1	2	1	2	3	4	5	5	5
50–64	10	2.8	3	1	2	2	4	6	6	6
65+	5	2.4	1	1	2	2	3	4	4	4
2. MULTIPLE DX										
0–19 Years	26	4.4	39	1	2	3	5	7	7	40
20–34	103	3.8	6	1	2	4	5	6	7	14
35–49	324	4.7	15	2	2	4	5	7	13	23
50–64	483	4.2	5	2	2	4	5	6	8	14
65+	203	5.5	35	1	3	4	6	9	15	42
TOTAL SINGLE DX	**37**	**3.4**	**3**	**2**	**2**	**3**	**5**	**6**	**6**	**6**
TOTAL MULTIPLE DX	**1,139**	**4.5**	**15**	**2**	**2**	**4**	**5**	**7**	**10**	**20**
TOTAL										
0–19 Years	40	4.2	25	1	2	3	5	6	7	40
20–34	103	3.8	6	1	2	4	5	6	7	14
35–49	332	4.7	15	2	2	4	5	7	13	20
50–64	493	4.1	5	2	2	4	5	6	8	14
65+	208	5.4	35	1	3	4	6	9	15	42
GRAND TOTAL	**1,176**	**4.5**	**14**	**2**	**2**	**4**	**5**	**7**	**10**	**20**

99.29: INJECT/INFUSE NEC

Type of Patients	Observed Patients	Avg. Stay	Vari-ance	Percentiles						
				10th	25th	50th	75th	90th	95th	99th
1. SINGLE DX										
0–19 Years	311	2.0	4	1	1	1	2	4	5	10
20–34	681	2.4	4	1	1	2	3	4	6	11
35–49	190	2.0	3	1	1	1	2	4	5	9
50–64	97	1.9	2	1	1	1	2	4	4	7
65+	36	2.2	4	1	1	2	2	4	5	14
2. MULTIPLE DX										
0–19 Years	770	3.2	24	1	1	2	3	7	10	25
20–34	1,291	4.1	38	1	1	2	4	8	13	34
35–49	1,276	3.4	17	1	1	2	4	7	8	17
50–64	1,163	3.4	13	1	1	2	4	7	9	19
65+	1,618	3.9	11	1	2	3	5	8	10	15
TOTAL SINGLE DX	**1,315**	**2.2**	**3**	**1**	**1**	**2**	**3**	**4**	**5**	**10**
TOTAL MULTIPLE DX	**6,118**	**3.6**	**20**	**1**	**1**	**2**	**4**	**7**	**10**	**21**
TOTAL										
0–19 Years	1,081	2.8	18	1	1	2	3	5	8	21
20–34	1,972	3.5	28	1	1	2	4	7	10	26
35–49	1,466	3.2	16	1	1	2	4	6	8	17
50–64	1,260	3.2	12	1	1	2	4	7	9	18
65+	1,654	3.8	11	1	2	3	5	8	10	15
GRAND TOTAL	**7,433**	**3.4**	**17**	**1**	**1**	**2**	**4**	**7**	**9**	**19**

99.3: PROPHYL VACC-BACT DIS

Type of Patients	Observed Patients	Avg. Stay	Vari-ance	Percentiles						
				10th	25th	50th	75th	90th	95th	99th
1. SINGLE DX										
0–19 Years	1	3.0	0	3	3	3	3	3	3	3
20–34	1	1.0	0	1	1	1	1	1	1	1
35–49	2	2.8	7	1	1	1	5	5	5	5
50–64	2	1.6	<1	1	1	2	2	2	2	2
65+	0									
2. MULTIPLE DX										
0–19 Years	18	5.2	17	1	1	6	9	9	13	15
20–34	12	2.2	1	1	1	2	3	3	4	4
35–49	17	2.3	3	1	1	2	3	5	6	7
50–64	15	3.5	11	1	1	2	3	8	12	12
65+	33	3.7	25	1	1	2	4	8	10	35
TOTAL SINGLE DX	**6**	**2.1**	**2**	**1**	**1**	**2**	**3**	**5**	**5**	**5**
TOTAL MULTIPLE DX	**95**	**3.5**	**16**	**1**	**1**	**2**	**4**	**8**	**10**	**15**
TOTAL										
0–19 Years	19	5.0	17	1	1	3	9	9	13	15
20–34	13	2.1	1	1	1	2	3	3	4	4
35–49	19	2.3	3	1	1	2	3	5	6	7
50–64	17	3.3	11	1	1	2	3	8	12	12
65+	33	3.7	25	1	1	2	4	8	10	35
GRAND TOTAL	**101**	**3.4**	**15**	**1**	**1**	**2**	**4**	**8**	**9**	**15**

99.38: TETANUS TOXOID ADMIN

Type of Patients	Observed Patients	Avg. Stay	Vari-ance	Percentiles						
				10th	25th	50th	75th	90th	95th	99th
1. SINGLE DX										
0–19 Years	1	3.0	0	3	3	3	3	3	3	3
20–34	0									
35–49	1	1.0	0	1	1	1	1	1	1	1
50–64	1	2.0	0	2	2	2	2	2	2	2
65+	0									
2. MULTIPLE DX										
0–19 Years	4	4.7	41	1	1	2	2	15	15	15
20–34	4	1.7	<1	1	1	2	2	3	3	3
35–49	2	1.6	<1	1	1	2	2	2	2	2
50–64	9	2.5	4	1	1	2	3	5	8	8
65+	8	2.8	5	1	1	2	4	4	9	9
TOTAL SINGLE DX	**3**	**2.2**	**<1**	**1**	**1**	**2**	**3**	**3**	**3**	**3**
TOTAL MULTIPLE DX	**27**	**2.7**	**7**	**1**	**1**	**2**	**3**	**5**	**9**	**15**
TOTAL										
0–19 Years	5	4.2	27	1	2	2	3	15	15	15
20–34	4	1.7	<1	1	1	2	2	3	3	3
35–49	3	1.4	<1	1	1	1	2	2	2	2
50–64	10	2.4	4	1	1	2	3	5	8	8
65+	8	2.8	5	1	1	2	4	4	9	9
GRAND TOTAL	**30**	**2.6**	**7**	**1**	**1**	**2**	**3**	**4**	**8**	**15**

99.4: VIRAL IMMUNIZATION

Type of Patients	Observed Patients	Avg. Stay	Vari-ance	Percentiles						
				10th	25th	50th	75th	90th	95th	99th
1. SINGLE DX										
0–19 Years	2	2.1	2	1	1	3	3	3	3	3
20–34	5	1.8	<1	1	1	2	2	3	3	3
35–49	0									
50–64	0									
65+	0									
2. MULTIPLE DX										
0–19 Years	11	1.7	<1	1	1	2	2	2	2	2
20–34	9	1.9	<1	1	2	2	2	2	3	3
35–49	4	1.7	<1	1	1	2	2	3	3	3
50–64	1	16.0	0	16	16	16	16	16	16	16
65+	1	5.0	0	5	5	5	5	5	5	5
TOTAL SINGLE DX	**7**	**1.9**	**<1**	**1**	**1**	**2**	**3**	**3**	**3**	**3**
TOTAL MULTIPLE DX	**26**	**2.6**	**11**	**1**	**1**	**2**	**2**	**3**	**16**	**16**
TOTAL										
0–19 Years	13	1.7	<1	1	1	2	2	2	3	3
20–34	14	1.9	<1	1	1	2	2	3	3	3
35–49	4	1.7	<1	1	1	2	2	3	3	3
50–64	1	16.0	0	16	16	16	16	16	16	16
65+	1	5.0	0	5	5	5	5	5	5	5
GRAND TOTAL	**33**	**2.5**	**10**	**1**	**1**	**2**	**2**	**3**	**5**	**16**

99.5: OTHER IMMUNIZATION

Type of Patients	Observed Patients	Avg. Stay	Vari-ance	Percentiles						
				10th	25th	50th	75th	90th	95th	99th
1. SINGLE DX										
0–19 Years	3,483	1.7	<1	1	1	2	2	3	3	4
20–34	5	1.4	<1	1	1	1	2	2	2	2
35–49	0									
50–64	0									
65+	1	1.0	0	1	1	1	1	1	1	1
2. MULTIPLE DX										
0–19 Years	48,664	2.0	3	1	1	2	2	3	4	7
20–34	9	3.0	10	1	1	2	3	11	11	11
35–49	23	4.4	22	1	2	3	5	7	16	>99
50–64	38	3.4	7	1	2	2	4	7	9	12
65+	83	3.5	4	1	2	3	5	6	8	9
TOTAL SINGLE DX	3,489	1.7	<1	1	1	2	2	3	3	4
TOTAL MULTIPLE DX	48,817	2.0	3	1	1	2	2	3	4	8
TOTAL										
0–19 Years	52,147	2.0	3	1	1	2	2	3	4	7
20–34	14	2.5	7	1	1	2	2	6	11	11
35–49	23	4.4	22	1	2	3	5	7	16	>99
50–64	38	3.4	7	1	2	2	4	7	9	12
65+	84	3.5	4	1	2	3	5	6	8	9
GRAND TOTAL	52,306	2.0	3	1	1	2	2	3	4	7

99.52: INFLUENZA VACCINATION

Type of Patients	Observed Patients	Avg. Stay	Vari-ance	Percentiles						
				10th	25th	50th	75th	90th	95th	99th
1. SINGLE DX										
0–19 Years	23	1.6	<1	1	1	2	2	2	3	3
20–34	0									
35–49	0									
50–64	0									
65+	1	1.0	0	1	1	1	1	1	1	1
2. MULTIPLE DX										
0–19 Years	100	2.7	44	1	1	2	2	3	5	64
20–34	2	1.5	<1	1	1	1	2	2	2	2
35–49	7	3.1	3	1	1	3	5	5	5	5
50–64	8	2.7	<1	2	2	2	4	4	4	4
65+	37	3.2	4	1	2	2	4	6	7	12
TOTAL SINGLE DX	24	1.6	<1	1	1	2	2	2	3	3
TOTAL MULTIPLE DX	154	2.9	24	1	2	2	3	5	6	12
TOTAL										
0–19 Years	123	2.5	37	1	1	2	2	3	4	11
20–34	2	1.5	<1	1	1	1	2	2	2	2
35–49	7	3.1	3	1	1	3	5	5	5	5
50–64	8	2.7	<1	2	2	2	4	4	4	4
65+	38	3.2	4	1	2	2	4	6	7	12
GRAND TOTAL	178	2.8	22	1	1	2	3	5	6	12

99.55: VACCINATION NEC

Type of Patients	Observed Patients	Avg. Stay	Vari-ance	Percentiles						
				10th	25th	50th	75th	90th	95th	99th
1. SINGLE DX										
0–19 Years	3,263	1.7	<1	1	1	2	2	3	3	4
20–34	2	1.5	<1	1	1	2	2	2	2	2
35–49	0									
50–64	0									
65+	0									
2. MULTIPLE DX										
0–19 Years	47,576	2.0	3	1	1	2	2	3	4	8
20–34	7	3.5	12	1	1	2	3	11	11	11
35–49	9	4.1	13	1	2	2	7	7	14	14
50–64	18	2.9	3	1	2	3	3	4	7	7
65+	44	3.7	4	1	2	4	5	7	8	8
TOTAL SINGLE DX	3,265	1.7	<1	1	1	2	2	3	3	4
TOTAL MULTIPLE DX	47,654	2.0	3	1	1	2	2	3	4	8
TOTAL										
0–19 Years	50,839	2.0	3	1	1	2	2	3	4	7
20–34	9	3.1	10	1	1	2	3	11	11	11
35–49	9	4.1	13	1	2	2	7	7	14	14
50–64	18	2.9	3	1	2	3	3	4	7	7
65+	44	3.7	4	1	2	4	5	7	8	8
GRAND TOTAL	50,919	2.0	3	1	1	2	2	3	4	7

99.59: VACC/INOCULATION NEC

Type of Patients	Observed Patients	Avg. Stay	Vari-ance	Percentiles						
				10th	25th	50th	75th	90th	95th	99th
1. SINGLE DX										
0–19 Years	193	1.7	<1	1	1	2	2	3	3	5
20–34	2	1.0	0	1	1	1	1	1	1	1
35–49	0									
50–64	0									
65+	0									
2. MULTIPLE DX										
0–19 Years	946	1.7	1	1	1	2	2	3	3	4
20–34	0									
35–49	3	1.4	<1	1	1	1	2	2	2	2
50–64	8	1.8	<1	1	1	2	2	4	4	4
65+	1	4.0	0	4	4	4	4	4	4	4
TOTAL SINGLE DX	195	1.7	<1	1	1	2	2	3	3	4
TOTAL MULTIPLE DX	958	1.7	1	1	1	2	2	3	3	4
TOTAL										
0–19 Years	1,139	1.7	<1	1	1	2	2	3	3	4
20–34	2	1.0	0	1	1	1	1	1	1	1
35–49	3	1.4	<1	1	1	1	2	2	2	2
50–64	8	1.8	<1	1	1	2	2	4	4	4
65+	1	4.0	0	4	4	4	4	4	4	4
GRAND TOTAL	1,153	1.7	<1	1	1	2	2	3	3	4

99.6: CARD RHYTHM CONVERSION

Type of Patients	Observed Patients	Avg. Stay	Vari-ance	Percentiles 10th	25th	50th	75th	90th	95th	99th
1. SINGLE DX										
0–19 Years	6	1.2	<1	1	1	1	1	1	3	3
20–34	21	1.3	<1	1	1	1	1	2	4	4
35–49	53	1.5	<1	1	1	1	2	2	3	5
50–64	64	1.8	<1	1	1	2	2	3	3	5
65+	70	1.5	1	1	1	1	1	4	5	5
2. MULTIPLE DX										
0–19 Years	108	5.1	159	1	2	3	4	6	9	97
20–34	108	3.3	16	1	1	2	4	9	10	26
35–49	477	3.1	10	1	1	2	4	6	9	16
50–64	1,391	3.1	11	1	1	2	4	6	8	14
65+	3,586	4.1	13	1	2	3	5	9	11	17
TOTAL SINGLE DX	**214**	**1.6**	**<1**	**1**	**1**	**1**	**2**	**3**	**4**	**5**
TOTAL MULTIPLE DX	**5,670**	**3.7**	**15**	**1**	**1**	**3**	**5**	**8**	**10**	**17**
TOTAL										
0–19 Years	114	4.8	148	1	1	3	4	6	9	97
20–34	129	2.9	14	1	1	1	3	8	10	26
35–49	530	3.0	10	1	1	2	4	6	9	15
50–64	1,455	3.1	10	1	1	2	4	6	8	14
65+	3,656	4.0	13	1	2	3	5	9	11	17
GRAND TOTAL	**5,884**	**3.7**	**15**	**1**	**1**	**3**	**5**	**8**	**10**	**17**

99.60: CPR NOS

Type of Patients	Observed Patients	Avg. Stay	Vari-ance	Percentiles 10th	25th	50th	75th	90th	95th	99th
1. SINGLE DX										
0–19 Years	0									
20–34	0									
35–49	0									
50–64	0									
65+	0									
2. MULTIPLE DX										
0–19 Years	57	7.4	321	2	2	3	4	9	31	99
20–34	6	11.0	95	1	3	8	11	26	26	26
35–49	35	8.4	44	1	4	7	12	19	20	35
50–64	51	7.0	34	1	2	6	10	16	18	30
65+	136	7.0	23	1	4	6	10	14	16	22
TOTAL SINGLE DX	**0**									
TOTAL MULTIPLE DX	**285**	**7.3**	**84**	**1**	**3**	**5**	**9**	**14**	**19**	**31**
TOTAL										
0–19 Years	57	7.4	321	2	2	3	4	9	31	99
20–34	6	11.0	95	1	3	8	11	26	26	26
35–49	35	8.4	44	1	4	7	12	19	20	35
50–64	51	7.0	34	1	2	6	10	16	18	30
65+	136	7.0	23	1	4	6	10	14	16	22
GRAND TOTAL	**285**	**7.3**	**84**	**1**	**3**	**5**	**9**	**14**	**19**	**31**

99.61: ATRIAL CARDIOVERSION

Type of Patients	Observed Patients	Avg. Stay	Vari-ance	Percentiles 10th	25th	50th	75th	90th	95th	99th
1. SINGLE DX										
0–19 Years	1	1.0	0	1	1	1	1	1	1	1
20–34	7	1.6	1	1	1	1	2	4	4	4
35–49	31	1.6	<1	1	1	1	2	2	3	5
50–64	33	1.6	<1	1	1	1	2	3	3	5
65+	31	1.4	<1	1	1	1	1	3	4	4
2. MULTIPLE DX										
0–19 Years	13	3.7	2	2	3	4	5	5	7	7
20–34	44	2.7	5	1	1	2	4	6	10	10
35–49	170	2.8	5	1	1	2	4	5	7	11
50–64	577	2.9	12	1	1	2	3	6	7	13
65+	1,508	3.8	11	1	2	3	5	8	10	16
TOTAL SINGLE DX	**103**	**1.5**	**<1**	**1**	**1**	**1**	**2**	**3**	**3**	**5**
TOTAL MULTIPLE DX	**2,312**	**3.5**	**11**	**1**	**1**	**2**	**4**	**7**	**10**	**16**
TOTAL										
0–19 Years	14	3.5	2	1	3	3	4	5	5	7
20–34	51	2.6	5	1	1	1	4	6	6	10
35–49	201	2.7	5	1	1	2	4	5	7	11
50–64	610	2.8	12	1	1	2	3	6	7	13
65+	1,539	3.8	11	1	1	3	5	8	10	16
GRAND TOTAL	**2,415**	**3.4**	**11**	**1**	**1**	**2**	**4**	**7**	**10**	**16**

99.62: HEART COUNTERSHOCK NEC

Type of Patients	Observed Patients	Avg. Stay	Vari-ance	Percentiles 10th	25th	50th	75th	90th	95th	99th
1. SINGLE DX										
0–19 Years	2	1.0	0	1	1	1	1	1	1	1
20–34	13	1.3	<1	1	1	1	1	2	4	4
35–49	17	1.4	<1	1	1	1	2	3	4	4
50–64	26	2.0	<1	1	1	2	3	3	3	4
65+	35	1.8	2	1	1	1	2	5	5	5
2. MULTIPLE DX										
0–19 Years	17	3.0	4	1	1	3	5	5	5	9
20–34	47	2.9	8	1	1	2	3	9	10	10
35–49	224	2.9	7	1	1	2	4	5	8	14
50–64	637	3.2	8	1	1	2	4	7	8	13
65+	1,616	4.1	14	1	2	3	5	9	11	17
TOTAL SINGLE DX	**93**	**1.7**	**1**	**1**	**1**	**1**	**2**	**3**	**4**	**5**
TOTAL MULTIPLE DX	**2,541**	**3.7**	**12**	**1**	**1**	**3**	**5**	**8**	**10**	**17**
TOTAL										
0–19 Years	19	2.9	4	1	1	2	5	5	5	9
20–34	60	2.5	7	1	1	1	3	6	10	10
35–49	241	2.8	6	1	1	2	4	5	8	14
50–64	663	3.1	8	1	1	2	4	6	8	13
65+	1,651	4.1	13	1	2	3	5	9	11	17
GRAND TOTAL	**2,634**	**3.7**	**11**	**1**	**1**	**3**	**5**	**8**	**10**	**17**

99.69: CARDIAC RHYTHM CONV NEC

Type of Patients	Observed Patients	Avg. Stay	Vari-ance	Percentiles 10th	25th	50th	75th	90th	95th	99th
1. SINGLE DX										
0–19 Years	2	1.0	0	1	1	1	1	1	1	1
20–34	1	1.0	0	1	1	1	1	1	1	1
35–49	5	1.0	0	1	1	1	1	1	1	1
50–64	5	1.8	<1	1	1	2	2	3	3	3
65+	4	1.0	0	1	1	1	1	1	1	1
2. MULTIPLE DX										
0–19 Years	9	2.6	8	1	1	1	2	7	10	10
20–34	11	2.7	16	1	1	1	2	14	14	14
35–49	45	2.0	2	1	1	1	3	4	5	6
50–64	124	2.5	5	1	1	2	3	5	7	13
65+	318	3.6	13	1	1	2	5	7	10	21
TOTAL SINGLE DX	**17**	**1.1**	**<1**	**1**	**1**	**1**	**1**	**2**	**2**	**3**
TOTAL MULTIPLE DX	**507**	**3.2**	**10**	**1**	**1**	**2**	**4**	**6**	**9**	**17**
TOTAL										
0–19 Years	11	2.0	6	1	1	1	1	7	7	10
20–34	12	2.2	11	1	1	1	2	2	14	14
35–49	50	1.9	2	1	1	1	3	4	5	6
50–64	129	2.5	5	1	1	2	3	5	7	13
65+	322	3.6	13	1	1	2	5	7	10	21
GRAND TOTAL	**524**	**3.1**	**10**	**1**	**1**	**2**	**4**	**6**	**9**	**15**

99.7: THER APHERESIS/ADMIN NEC

Type of Patients	Observed Patients	Avg. Stay	Vari-ance	Percentiles 10th	25th	50th	75th	90th	95th	99th
1. SINGLE DX										
0–19 Years	12	5.0	43	1	1	3	4	15	22	22
20–34	6	4.3	5	1	3	4	6	7	7	7
35–49	12	5.7	11	1	1	7	8	10	10	10
50–64	22	2.3	10	1	1	1	1	11	11	11
65+	6	1.0	0	1	1	1	1	1	1	1
2. MULTIPLE DX										
0–19 Years	48	6.2	26	1	2	5	8	12	20	24
20–34	74	7.9	75	1	2	5	11	17	25	38
35–49	151	7.1	51	1	3	5	9	15	21	28
50–64	150	7.4	55	1	2	5	9	14	21	39
65+	185	7.1	35	1	3	6	9	15	17	30
TOTAL SINGLE DX	**58**	**4.0**	**19**	**1**	**1**	**1**	**7**	**10**	**11**	**22**
TOTAL MULTIPLE DX	**608**	**7.1**	**47**	**1**	**3**	**5**	**9**	**15**	**20**	**37**
TOTAL										
0–19 Years	60	6.0	28	1	2	5	8	13	20	24
20–34	80	7.7	71	1	2	5	11	17	25	38
35–49	163	7.0	47	1	3	5	9	14	21	28
50–64	172	6.8	52	1	2	5	9	14	21	39
65+	191	6.9	35	1	3	5	9	15	17	30
GRAND TOTAL	**666**	**6.9**	**45**	**1**	**2**	**5**	**9**	**15**	**20**	**37**

99.71: THER PLASMAPHERESIS

Type of Patients	Observed Patients	Avg. Stay	Vari-ance	Percentiles 10th	25th	50th	75th	90th	95th	99th
1. SINGLE DX										
0–19 Years	3	13.7	71	1	15	15	22	22	22	22
20–34	4	4.7	7	1	1	5	6	7	7	7
35–49	10	5.9	11	1	3	7	8	10	10	10
50–64	18	1.2	<1	1	1	1	1	1	5	5
65+	4	1.0	0	1	1	1	1	1	1	1
2. MULTIPLE DX										
0–19 Years	13	6.7	24	1	3	6	9	11	12	24
20–34	51	8.0	62	1	4	5	11	16	18	48
35–49	90	8.3	68	1	3	6	10	21	24	34
50–64	81	8.8	62	2	4	7	10	16	27	39
65+	104	7.6	30	2	4	7	10	17	17	22
TOTAL SINGLE DX	**39**	**4.4**	**22**	**1**	**1**	**1**	**7**	**10**	**15**	**22**
TOTAL MULTIPLE DX	**339**	**8.0**	**51**	**1**	**4**	**6**	**10**	**17**	**21**	**39**
TOTAL										
0–19 Years	16	7.4	32	1	3	6	10	15	22	24
20–34	55	7.8	59	1	4	5	11	16	18	48
35–49	100	8.0	60	1	3	7	10	18	24	34
50–64	99	7.7	60	1	2	6	10	15	21	39
65+	108	7.4	31	1	3	6	9	17	17	22
GRAND TOTAL	**378**	**7.7**	**49**	**1**	**3**	**6**	**10**	**16**	**21**	**39**

99.74: THER PLATELETPHERESIS

Type of Patients	Observed Patients	Avg. Stay	Vari-ance	Percentiles 10th	25th	50th	75th	90th	95th	99th
1. SINGLE DX										
0–19 Years	1	4.0	0	4	4	4	4	4	4	4
20–34	1	3.0	0	3	3	3	3	3	3	3
35–49	1	4.0	0	4	4	4	4	4	4	4
50–64	2	1.0	0	1	1	1	1	1	1	1
65+	2	1.0	0	1	1	1	1	1	1	1
2. MULTIPLE DX										
0–19 Years	17	5.0	17	1	3	4	5	10	14	18
20–34	15	3.4	7	1	2	2	5	7	7	11
35–49	28	4.9	13	1	2	4	7	11	11	12
50–64	42	5.2	22	1	2	4	7	9	14	24
65+	66	5.3	21	1	2	4	7	13	15	22
TOTAL SINGLE DX	**7**	**2.1**	**2**	**1**	**1**	**1**	**4**	**4**	**4**	**4**
TOTAL MULTIPLE DX	**168**	**5.0**	**18**	**1**	**2**	**4**	**7**	**11**	**14**	**22**
TOTAL										
0–19 Years	18	5.0	16	1	3	4	5	10	14	18
20–34	16	3.4	7	1	2	2	4	7	7	11
35–49	29	4.9	12	1	2	4	7	11	11	12
50–64	44	5.0	22	1	2	4	7	9	14	24
65+	68	5.2	21	1	2	4	7	13	15	22
GRAND TOTAL	**175**	**4.9**	**18**	**1**	**2**	**4**	**7**	**11**	**14**	**22**

99.8: MISC PHYSICAL PROCEDURES

Type of Patients	Observed Patients	Avg. Stay	Vari-ance	10th	25th	50th	75th	90th	95th	99th
				Percentiles						
1. SINGLE DX										
0–19 Years	3,871	1.8	<1	1	1	2	2	3	3	5
20–34	1	3.0	0	3	3	3	3	3	3	3
35–49	2	1.0	0	1	1	1	1	1	1	1
50–64	1	4.0	0	4	4	4	4	4	4	4
65+	0									
2. MULTIPLE DX										
0–19 Years	13,395	6.6	54	2	3	4	7	15	21	37
20–34	78	2.4	7	1	1	2	3	4	6	27
35–49	60	3.0	7	1	1	2	4	6	7	21
50–64	36	4.0	11	1	1	2	5	10	10	13
65+	97	5.6	12	2	4	5	7	10	11	20
TOTAL SINGLE DX	**3,875**	**1.8**	**<1**	**1**	**1**	**2**	**2**	**3**	**3**	**5**
TOTAL MULTIPLE DX	**13,666**	**6.5**	**53**	**2**	**3**	**4**	**7**	**15**	**21**	**36**
TOTAL										
0–19 Years	17,266	5.2	43	1	2	3	5	12	19	33
20–34	79	2.5	7	1	1	2	3	4	6	27
35–49	62	3.0	7	1	1	2	4	6	7	21
50–64	37	4.0	11	1	1	2	5	10	10	13
65+	97	5.6	12	2	4	5	7	10	11	20
GRAND TOTAL	**17,541**	**5.2**	**43**	**1**	**2**	**3**	**5**	**12**	**18**	**33**

99.82: UV LIGHT THERAPY

Type of Patients	Observed Patients	Avg. Stay	Vari-ance	10th	25th	50th	75th	90th	95th	99th
				Percentiles						
1. SINGLE DX										
0–19 Years	413	2.0	<1	1	1	2	2	3	3	5
20–34	0									
35–49	0									
50–64	0									
65+	0									
2. MULTIPLE DX										
0–19 Years	1,114	5.1	25	2	3	4	6	9	13	31
20–34	0									
35–49	0									
50–64	1	13.0	0	13	13	13	13	13	13	13
65+	0									
TOTAL SINGLE DX	**413**	**2.0**	**<1**	**1**	**1**	**2**	**2**	**3**	**3**	**5**
TOTAL MULTIPLE DX	**1,115**	**5.1**	**25**	**2**	**3**	**4**	**6**	**9**	**13**	**31**
TOTAL										
0–19 Years	1,527	4.0	19	1	2	3	5	7	11	25
20–34	0									
35–49	0									
50–64	1	13.0	0	13	13	13	13	13	13	13
65+	0									
GRAND TOTAL	**1,528**	**4.1**	**19**	**1**	**2**	**3**	**5**	**7**	**11**	**25**

99.83: PHOTOTHERAPY NEC

Type of Patients	Observed Patients	Avg. Stay	Vari-ance	10th	25th	50th	75th	90th	95th	99th
				Percentiles						
1. SINGLE DX										
0–19 Years	3,457	1.8	<1	1	1	2	2	3	3	4
20–34	0									
35–49	1	1.0	0	1	1	1	1	1	1	1
50–64	0									
65+	0									
2. MULTIPLE DX										
0–19 Years	12,245	6.7	56	2	3	4	7	16	22	38
20–34	0									
35–49	2	2.8	7	1	1	1	5	5	5	5
50–64	1	2.0	0	2	2	2	2	2	2	2
65+	0									
TOTAL SINGLE DX	**3,458**	**1.8**	**<1**	**1**	**1**	**2**	**2**	**3**	**3**	**4**
TOTAL MULTIPLE DX	**12,248**	**6.7**	**56**	**2**	**3**	**4**	**7**	**16**	**22**	**38**
TOTAL										
0–19 Years	15,702	5.3	46	1	2	3	5	12	19	33
20–34	0									
35–49	3	2.2	5	1	1	1	5	5	5	5
50–64	1	2.0	0	2	2	2	2	2	2	2
65+	0									
GRAND TOTAL	**15,706**	**5.3**	**46**	**1**	**2**	**3**	**5**	**12**	**19**	**33**

99.84: ISOLATION

Type of Patients	Observed Patients	Avg. Stay	Vari-ance	10th	25th	50th	75th	90th	95th	99th
				Percentiles						
1. SINGLE DX										
0–19 Years	1	2.0	0	2	2	2	2	2	2	2
20–34	1	3.0	0	3	3	3	3	3	3	3
35–49	1	1.0	0	1	1	1	1	1	1	1
50–64	0									
65+	0									
2. MULTIPLE DX										
0–19 Years	32	2.2	1	1	1	2	3	4	5	5
20–34	78	2.4	7	1	1	2	3	4	6	27
35–49	53	3.0	7	1	1	2	4	6	7	21
50–64	29	3.1	6	1	1	2	5	6	9	11
65+	95	5.6	12	2	4	5	7	10	11	20
TOTAL SINGLE DX	**3**	**1.9**	**<1**	**1**	**1**	**2**	**3**	**3**	**3**	**3**
TOTAL MULTIPLE DX	**287**	**3.2**	**9**	**1**	**1**	**2**	**4**	**6**	**8**	**20**
TOTAL										
0–19 Years	33	2.2	1	1	1	2	3	4	5	5
20–34	79	2.5	7	1	1	2	3	4	6	27
35–49	54	3.0	7	1	1	2	4	6	7	21
50–64	29	3.1	6	1	1	2	5	6	9	11
65+	95	5.6	12	2	4	5	7	10	11	20
GRAND TOTAL	**290**	**3.2**	**9**	**1**	**1**	**2**	**4**	**6**	**8**	**20**

99.88: THER PHOTOPHERESIS

Type of Patients	Observed Patients	Avg. Stay	Vari-ance	Percentiles 10th	25th	50th	75th	90th	95th	99th
1. SINGLE DX										
0–19 Years	0									
20–34	0									
35–49	0									
50–64	0									
65+	0									
2. MULTIPLE DX										
0–19 Years	2	3.6	<1	3	3	4	4	4	4	4
20–34	0									
35–49	5	2.9	5	1	1	1	5	5	5	5
50–64	5	6.4	18	1	1	10	10	10	10	10
65+	0									
TOTAL SINGLE DX	**0**									
TOTAL MULTIPLE DX	**12**	**5.2**	**15**	**1**	**1**	**4**	**10**	**10**	**10**	**10**
TOTAL										
0–19 Years	2	3.6	<1	3	3	4	4	4	4	4
20–34	0									
35–49	5	2.9	5	1	1	1	5	5	5	5
50–64	5	6.4	18	1	1	10	10	10	10	10
65+	0									
GRAND TOTAL	**12**	**5.2**	**15**	**1**	**1**	**4**	**10**	**10**	**10**	**10**

99.9: OTHER MISC PROCEDURES

Type of Patients	Observed Patients	Avg. Stay	Vari-ance	Percentiles 10th	25th	50th	75th	90th	95th	99th
1. SINGLE DX										
0–19 Years	75	2.2	5	1	2	2	2	3	3	3
20–34	2	1.5	<1	1	1	1	2	2	2	2
35–49	3	2.4	<1	2	2	2	3	3	3	3
50–64	1	13.0	0	13	13	13	13	13	13	13
65+	1	7.0	0	7	7	7	7	7	7	7
2. MULTIPLE DX										
0–19 Years	68	2.8	44	1	1	2	2	3	4	22
20–34	16	3.4	12	1	1	2	4	10	13	13
35–49	52	4.2	10	1	2	3	6	9	9	15
50–64	32	5.5	12	2	3	4	8	11	13	15
65+	231	5.3	18	2	3	4	6	9	13	22
TOTAL SINGLE DX	**82**	**2.5**	**8**	**1**	**2**	**2**	**2**	**3**	**3**	**13**
TOTAL MULTIPLE DX	**399**	**4.5**	**25**	**1**	**2**	**3**	**5**	**9**	**12**	**19**
TOTAL										
0–19 Years	143	2.5	24	1	2	2	2	3	3	22
20–34	18	3.2	11	1	1	2	4	7	10	13
35–49	55	4.1	10	1	2	3	6	9	9	15
50–64	33	6.1	16	2	3	5	9	13	13	15
65+	232	5.3	18	2	3	4	6	9	13	22
GRAND TOTAL	**481**	**4.0**	**21**	**1**	**2**	**3**	**5**	**8**	**11**	**19**

99.99: MISC PROCEDURES NEC

Type of Patients	Observed Patients	Avg. Stay	Vari-ance	Percentiles 10th	25th	50th	75th	90th	95th	99th
1. SINGLE DX										
0–19 Years	73	2.3	5	1	2	2	2	3	3	3
20–34	2	1.5	<1	1	1	1	2	2	2	2
35–49	2	2.6	<1	2	2	3	3	3	3	3
50–64	1	13.0	0	13	13	13	13	13	13	13
65+	1	7.0	0	7	7	7	7	7	7	7
2. MULTIPLE DX										
0–19 Years	62	2.8	48	1	1	2	2	3	4	22
20–34	16	3.4	12	1	1	2	4	10	13	13
35–49	47	4.1	10	1	2	3	6	9	11	15
50–64	31	5.5	13	2	3	4	8	11	13	15
65+	224	5.2	16	2	3	4	6	9	12	19
TOTAL SINGLE DX	**79**	**2.5**	**8**	**1**	**2**	**2**	**2**	**3**	**3**	**13**
TOTAL MULTIPLE DX	**380**	**4.4**	**24**	**1**	**2**	**3**	**5**	**9**	**11**	**19**
TOTAL										
0–19 Years	135	2.5	25	1	2	2	2	3	3	22
20–34	18	3.2	11	1	1	2	4	7	10	13
35–49	49	4.0	10	1	2	3	5	9	11	15
50–64	32	6.2	16	2	3	5	9	13	13	15
65+	225	5.2	16	2	3	4	6	9	12	19
GRAND TOTAL	**459**	**4.0**	**21**	**1**	**2**	**3**	**5**	**8**	**11**	**19**

APPENDIX A
Hospital Characteristics
Short-Term, General, Nonfederal Hospitals[1]

HOSPITAL CATEGORY	U.S. TOTAL
Bed Size	
6–24 Beds	692
25–49	1,438
50–99	1,449
100–199	1,435
200–299	709
300–399	385
400–499	200
500+	300
Unknown	54
Total	**6,662**
Region and Census Division	
Northeast	**981**
New England	299
Middle Atlantic	682
North Central	**1,816**
East North Central	992
West North Central	824
South	**2,611**
South Atlantic	998
East South Central	545
West South Central	1,068
West	**1,254**
Mountain	461
Pacific	793
Location	
Urban	4,151
Rural	2,511
Teaching Intensity	
High/Medium	480
Low	6,182

[1] For a definition of short-term, general, and nonfederal hospitals, see "Description of the Database."

APPENDIX B
States Included in Each Region

Northeast	North Central	South	West
Connecticut	Illinois	Alabama	Alaska
Maine	Indiana	Arkansas	Arizona
Massachusetts	Iowa	Delaware	California
New Hampshire	Kansas	District of Columbia	Colorado
New Jersey	Michigan	Florida	Hawaii
New York	Minnesota	Georgia	Idaho
Pennsylvania	Missouri	Kentucky	Montana
Rhode Island	Nebraska	Louisiana	Nevada
Vermont	North Dakota	Maryland	New Mexico
	Ohio	Mississippi	Oregon
	South Dakota	North Carolina	Utah
	Wisconsin	Oklahoma	Washington
		South Carolina	Wyoming
		Tennessee	
		Texas	
		Virginia	
		West Virginia	

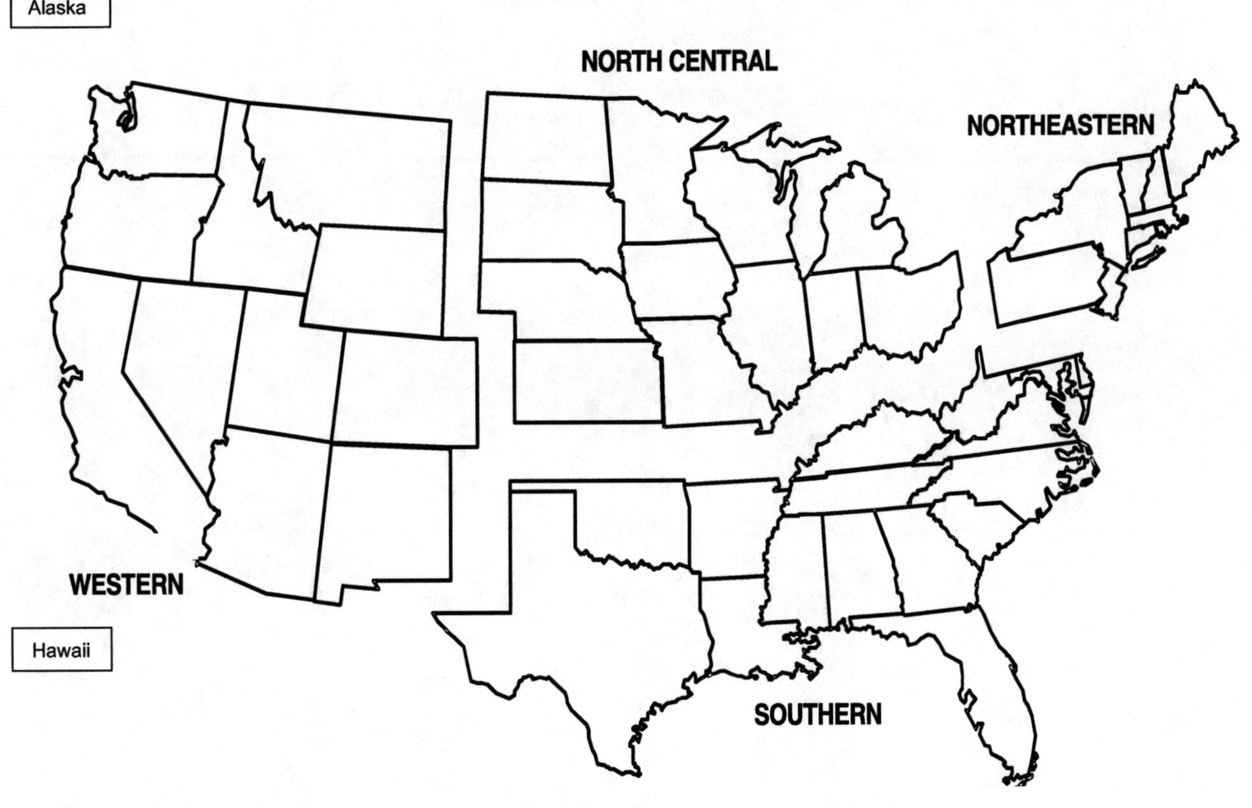

APPENDIX C
Operative Status of Procedure Codes

The following table lists every ICD-9-CM procedure code included in this book, its description, and its CMS-defined operative status (*i.e.*, operative or non-operative). Operative procedures are those classified by CMS as "operating room" procedures. CMS physician panels classify every ICD-9-CM procedure code according to whether the procedure would, in most hospitals, be performed in the operating room. For codes that contain both operative and non-operative detail codes, the notation "Mixed," followed by the number of each type, will appear in the "Operative Status" column. For example, a code containing three operative and two non-operative detail codes will be identified as "Mixed (3, 2)."

Code	Description	Operative Status
00.0	Therapeutic ultrasound	Non-Operative
00.1	Pharmaceuticals	Non-Operative
00.11	Infuse drotrecogin alfa	Non-Operative
00.13	Inject nesiritide	Non-Operative
00.5	Oth cardiovascular px	Mixed (5, 1)
00.50	Impl CRT-P total system	Operative
00.51	Impl CRT-D total system	Operative
00.52	Impl lead cor ven system	Operative
01.0	Cranial puncture	Non-Operative
01.02	Ventriculopunct via cath	Non-Operative
01.1	Dxtic px on skull/brain	Mixed (5, 2)
01.13	Closed brain biopsy	Non-Operative
01.14	Open biopsy of brain	Operative
01.18	Dxtic px brain/cereb NEC	Operative
01.2	Craniotomy & craniectomy	Operative
01.23	Reopen craniotomy site	Operative
01.24	Craniotomy NEC	Operative
01.25	Craniectomy NEC	Operative
01.3	Inc brain/cereb meninges	Operative
01.31	Inc cerebral meninges	Operative
01.39	Brain incision NEC	Operative
01.4	Thalamus/globus pall ops	Operative
01.5	Exc/destr brain/meninges	Operative
01.51	Exc cereb meningeal les	Operative
01.53	Brain lobectomy	Operative
01.59	Exc/destr brain les NEC	Operative
01.6	Excision of skull lesion	Operative
02.0	Cranioplasty	Operative
02.01	Opening cranial suture	Operative
02.02	Elevation skull fx frag	Operative
02.03	Cran bone flap formation	Operative
02.06	Cranial osteoplasty NEC	Operative
02.1	Cerebral meninges repair	Operative
02.12	REP cerebral mening NEC	Operative
02.2	Ventriculostomy	Operative
02.3	Extracranial vent shunt	Operative
02.34	Vent shunt to abd cavity	Operative
02.4	Vent shunt rev/rmvl	Mixed (2, 1)
02.42	Repl ventriclular shunt	Operative
02.43	Rmvl ventriclular shunt	Operative
02.9	Skull & brain ops NEC	Mixed (5, 2)
02.93	Impl IC neurostimulator	Operative
02.94	Insert/repl skull tongs	Operative
03.0	Spinal canal exploration	Operative
03.02	Reopen laminectomy site	Operative
03.09	Spinal canal expl NEC	Operative
03.1	Intraspin nerve root div	Operative
03.2	Chordotomy	Operative
03.3	Dxtic px on spinal canal	Mixed (2, 1)
03.31	Spinal tap	Non-Operative
03.32	Spinal cord/meninges Bx	Operative
03.4	Exc spinal cord lesion	Operative
03.5	Spinal cord plastic ops	Operative
03.51	Spinal meningocele REP	Operative
03.53	Vertebral fx repair	Operative
03.59	Spinal struct repair NEC	Operative
03.6	Spinal cord adhesiolysis	Operative
03.7	Spinal thecal shunt	Operative
03.71	Subarach-periton shunt	Operative
03.8	Destr inject-spine canal	Non-Operative
03.9	Spinal cord ops NEC	Mixed (5, 5)
03.90	Insert spinal canal cath	Non-Operative
03.91	Inject anes-spinal canal	Non-Operative
03.92	Inject spinal canal NEC	Non-Operative
03.93	Insert spinal neurostim	Operative
03.94	Rmvl spinal neurostim	Operative
03.95	Spinal blood patch	Non-Operative
03.97	Rev spinal thecal shunt	Operative
04.0	Periph nerve inc/div/exc	Operative
04.01	Exc acoustic neuroma	Operative
04.07	Periph/cran nerv exc NEC	Operative
04.1	Dxtic px periph nerv	Mixed (2, 1)
04.2	Destr periph/cran nerves	Non-Operative
04.3	Cran/periph nerve suture	Operative
04.4	Periph nerv adhesiolysis	Operative
04.41	Decomp trigeminal root	Operative
04.42	Cranial nerve decomp NEC	Operative
04.43	Carpal tunnel release	Operative
04.49	Periph nerv ADHESIO NEC	Operative
04.5	Cran or periph nerv grft	Operative
04.6	Periph nerves transpos	Operative
04.7	Other periph neuroplasty	Operative
04.8	Peripheral nerve inject	Non-Operative
04.81	Anes inject periph nerve	Non-Operative
04.9	Oth periph nerve ops	Operative
04.92	Impl periph neurostim	Operative
05.0	Sympath nerve division	Operative
05.1	Sympath nerve dxtic px	Operative
05.2	Sympathectomy	Operative
05.29	Other sympathectomy	Operative
05.3	Sympath nerve injection	Non-Operative
05.31	Anes inject sympath nerv	Non-Operative
05.8	Oth sympath nerve ops	Operative
05.9	Other nervous system ops	Operative

Code	Description	Operative Status
06.0	Thyroid field incision	Mixed (2, 1)
06.09	Inc thyroid field NEC	Operative
06.1	Thyroid/parathy dxtic px	Mixed (3, 1)
06.11	Closed thyroid biopsy	Non-Operative
06.2	Unilat thyroid lobectomy	Operative
06.3	Other part thyroidectomy	Operative
06.31	Excision thyroid lesion	Operative
06.39	Part thyroidectomy NEC	Operative
06.4	Complete thyroidectomy	Operative
06.5	Substernal thyroidectomy	Operative
06.51	Part substern thyroidect	Operative
06.52	Tot substern thyroidect	Operative
06.6	Lingual thyroid excision	Operative
06.7	Thyroglossal duct exc	Operative
06.8	Parathyroidectomy	Operative
06.81	Total parathyroidectomy	Operative
06.89	Other parathyroidectomy	Operative
06.9	Thyroid/parathy ops NEC	Operative
07.0	Adrenal field expl	Operative
07.1	Oth endocrine dxtic px	Mixed (7, 1)
07.11	Clsd adrenal gland Bx	Non-Operative
07.2	Partial adrenalectomy	Operative
07.22	Unilateral adrenalectomy	Operative
07.3	Bilateral adrenalectomy	Operative
07.4	Other adrenal operations	Operative
07.5	Pineal gland operations	Operative
07.6	Hypophysectomy	Operative
07.62	Exc pit les-transsphen	Operative
07.65	Tot exc pit-transsphen	Operative
07.7	Other hypophysis ops	Operative
07.8	Thymectomy	Operative
07.82	Total excision of thymus	Operative
07.9	Other thymus operations	Operative
08.0	Eyelid incision	Non-Operative
08.1	Dxtic px on eyelid	Mixed (1, 1)
08.2	Exc/destr eyelid lesion	Operative
08.3	Ptosis/lid retract REP	Operative
08.4	Entropion/ectropion REP	Operative
08.5	Oth adjust lid position	Operative
08.6	Eyelid reconst w graft	Operative
08.7	Other eyelid reconst	Operative
08.8	Other repair of eyelid	Non-Operative
08.81	Linear REP eyelid lac	Non-Operative
08.9	Other eyelid operations	Operative
09.0	Lacrimal gland incision	Operative
09.1	Lacrimal system dxtic px	Operative
09.2	Lacrimal gland les exc	Operative
09.3	Other lacrimal gland ops	Operative
09.4	Lacrimal passage manip	Operative
09.5	Inc lacrimal sac/passg	Operative
09.6	Lacrimal sac/passage exc	Operative
09.7	Canaliculus/punctum REP	Operative
09.8	NL fistulization	Operative
09.9	Oth lacrimal syst ops	Operative
10.0	Inc/rmvl FB-conjunctiva	Operative
10.1	Conjunctiva incision NEC	Operative
10.2	Conjunctiva dxtic px	Operative
10.3	Exc/destr conjunct les	Operative
10.4	Conjunctivoplasty	Operative
10.5	Conjunct/lid ADHESIO	Operative
10.6	Repair conjunct lac	Operative

Code	Description	Operative Status
10.9	Other conjunctival ops	Operative
11.0	Magnet removal cornea FB	Operative
11.1	Corneal incision	Operative
11.2	Dxtic px on cornea	Operative
11.3	Excision of pterygium	Operative
11.4	Exc/destr corneal lesion	Operative
11.5	Corneal repair	Operative
11.51	Suture of corneal lac	Operative
11.6	Corneal transplant	Operative
11.7	Other cornea reconst	Operative
11.9	Other corneal operations	Operative
12.0	Rmvl inOc FB ant segment	Operative
12.1	Iridotomy/smp iridectomy	Operative
12.2	Anterior SEG dxtic px	Operative
12.3	Iridoplasty/coreoplasty	Operative
12.4	Destr iris/cil body les	Operative
12.5	InOc circulat facilitat	Operative
12.6	Scleral fistulization	Operative
12.7	Elevat inOc press relief	Operative
12.8	Operations on sclera	Operative
12.9	Oth anterior segment ops	Operative
13.0	Removal FB from lens	Operative
13.1	Intracap lens extraction	Operative
13.2	Lin extracaps lens extr	Operative
13.3	Simp asp lens extraction	Operative
13.4	Frag-asp extracaps lens	Operative
13.41	Cataract PHACO & asp	Operative
13.5	Oth extracaps lens extr	Operative
13.6	Oth cataract extraction	Operative
13.7	Insert prosthetic lens	Operative
13.8	Implanted lens removal	Operative
13.9	Other operations on lens	Operative
14.0	Rmvl of post segment FB	Operative
14.1	Dxtic px posterior SEG	Operative
14.2	Retina-choroid les destr	Mixed (5, 3)
14.3	Repair of retinal tear	Mixed (3, 3)
14.4	REP retina detach/buckle	Operative
14.49	Scleral buckling NEC	Operative
14.5	Oth repair retina detach	Operative
14.6	Rmvl prosth mat post SEG	Operative
14.7	Operations on vitreous	Operative
14.74	Mech vitrectomy NEC	Operative
14.9	Other post segment ops	Operative
15.0	ExOc musc-tend dxtic px	Operative
15.1	1 ExOc musc ops w detach	Operative
15.2	Oth ops on 1 ExOc muscle	Operative
15.3	Temp detach >1 ExOc musc	Operative
15.4	Oth ops on >1 ExOc musc	Operative
15.5	ExOc musc transposition	Operative
15.6	Rev ExOc muscle surgery	Operative
15.7	ExOc muscle injury REP	Operative
15.9	Oth ExOc musc-tend ops	Operative
16.0	Orbitotomy	Operative
16.09	Orbitotomy NEC	Operative
16.1	Rmvl penetr FB eye NOS	Operative
16.2	Orbit & eyeball dxtic px	Mixed (3, 1)
16.3	Evisceration of eyeball	Operative
16.4	Enucleation of eyeball	Operative
16.5	Exenteration of orbit	Operative
16.6	2nd px post rmvl eyeball	Operative
16.7	Ocular/orbital impl rmvl	Operative

Code	Description	Operative Status
16.8	Eyeball/orbit inj repair	Operative
16.82	Repair eyeball rupture	Operative
16.9	Other eye & orbit ops	Mixed (4, 1)
18.0	External ear incision	Non-Operative
18.09	External ear inc NEC	Non-Operative
18.1	External ear dxtic px	Non-Operative
18.2	Exc/destr ext ear lesion	Mixed (1, 1)
18.29	Destr ext ear les NEC	Non-Operative
18.3	Other external ear exc	Operative
18.4	Suture ext ear lac	Non-Operative
18.5	Correction prominent ear	Operative
18.6	Ext audit canal reconst	Operative
18.7	Oth plastic REP ext ear	Operative
18.79	Plastic REP ext ear NEC	Operative
18.9	Other ext ear operations	Operative
19.0	Stapes mobilization	Operative
19.1	Stapedectomy	Operative
19.2	Stapedectomy revision	Operative
19.3	Ossicular chain ops NEC	Operative
19.4	Myringoplasty	Operative
19.5	Other tympanoplasty	Operative
19.6	Tympanoplasty revision	Operative
19.9	Middle ear repair NEC	Operative
20.0	Myringotomy	Mixed (1, 1)
20.01	Myringotomy w intubation	Operative
20.1	Tympanostomy tube rmvl	Non-Operative
20.2	Mastoid & mid ear inc	Operative
20.3	Mid & inner ear dxtic px	Mixed (2, 1)
20.4	Mastoidectomy	Operative
20.42	Radical mastoidectomy	Operative
20.49	Mastoidectomy NEC	Operative
20.5	Oth middle ear excision	Operative
20.6	Fenestration inner ear	Operative
20.7	Inc/exc/destr inner ear	Operative
20.8	Eustachian tube ops	Non-Operative
20.9	Other ME & IE ops	Mixed (8, 1)
21.0	Control of epistaxis	Mixed (5, 4)
21.01	Ant NAS pack for epistx	Non-Operative
21.02	Post NAS pack for epistx	Non-Operative
21.03	Caut to cntrl epistaxis	Non-Operative
21.09	Epistaxis control NEC	Operative
21.1	Nose incision	Non-Operative
21.2	Nasal diagnostic px	Non-Operative
21.21	Rhinoscopy	Non-Operative
21.3	Nasal lesion destr/exc	Non-Operative
21.4	Resection of nose	Operative
21.5	Submuc NAS septum resect	Operative
21.6	Turbinectomy	Operative
21.7	Nasal fracture reduction	Mixed (1, 1)
21.71	Clsd reduction nasal fx	Non-Operative
21.72	Open reduction nasal fx	Operative
21.8	Nasal REP & plastic ops	Mixed (8, 1)
21.81	Nasal laceration suture	Non-Operative
21.88	Septoplasty NEC	Operative
21.89	Nasal repair NEC	Operative
21.9	Other nasal operations	Mixed (1, 1)
22.0	Nasal sinus asp & lavage	Non-Operative
22.1	Nasal sinus dxtic px	Mixed (1, 2)
22.2	Intranasal antrotomy	Non-Operative
22.3	Ext maxillary antrotomy	Operative
22.4	Front sinusot & sinusect	Operative
22.5	Other nasal sinusotomy	Operative
22.6	Other nasal sinusectomy	Operative
22.62	Exc max sinus lesion NEC	Operative
22.63	Ethmoidectomy	Operative
22.7	Nasal sinus repair	Operative
22.9	Other nasal sinus ops	Operative
23.0	Forceps tooth extraction	Non-Operative
23.09	Tooth extraction NEC	Non-Operative
23.1	Surg removal of tooth	Non-Operative
23.19	Surg tooth extract NEC	Non-Operative
23.2	Tooth restor by filling	Non-Operative
23.3	Tooth restor by inlay	Non-Operative
23.4	Other dental restoration	Non-Operative
23.5	Tooth implantation	Non-Operative
23.6	Prosthetic dental impl	Non-Operative
23.7	Root canal Tx & apicoect	Non-Operative
24.0	Gum or alveolar incision	Non-Operative
24.1	Tooth & gum dxtic px	Non-Operative
24.2	Gingivoplasty	Operative
24.3	Other operations on gums	Non-Operative
24.4	Exc of dental les of jaw	Operative
24.5	Alveoloplasty	Operative
24.6	Exposure of tooth	Non-Operative
24.7	Appl orthodont appliance	Non-Operative
24.8	Other orthodontic op	Non-Operative
24.9	Other dental operation	Non-Operative
25.0	Dxtic px on tongue	Mixed (1, 2)
25.1	Exc/destr tongue les	Operative
25.2	Partial glossectomy	Operative
25.3	Complete glossectomy	Operative
25.4	Radical glossectomy	Operative
25.5	Repair of tongue	Mixed (1, 1)
25.9	Other tongue operations	Mixed (2, 3)
25.91	Lingual frenotomy	Non-Operative
26.0	Inc salivary gland/duct	Non-Operative
26.1	Salivary gland dxtic px	Mixed (1, 2)
26.2	Exc of SG lesion	Operative
26.29	Salivary les exc NEC	Operative
26.3	Sialoadenectomy	Operative
26.30	Sialoadenectomy NOS	Operative
26.31	Partial sialoadenectomy	Operative
26.32	Complete sialoadenectomy	Operative
26.4	SG & duct repair	Operative
26.9	Oth salivary operations	Mixed (1, 1)
27.0	Drain face & mouth floor	Operative
27.1	Incision of palate	Operative
27.2	Oral cavity dxtic px	Mixed (2, 3)
27.3	Exc bony palate les/tiss	Operative
27.4	Other excision of mouth	Mixed (3, 1)
27.49	Excision of mouth NEC	Operative
27.5	Mouth plastic repair	Mixed (6, 2)
27.51	Suture of lip laceration	Non-Operative
27.54	Repair of cleft lip	Operative
27.59	Mouth repair NEC	Operative
27.6	Palatoplasty	Operative
27.62	Cleft palate correction	Operative
27.63	Rev cleft palate repair	Operative
27.69	Other plastic REP palate	Operative
27.7	Operations on uvula	Operative
27.9	Oth ops on mouth & face	Mixed (2, 1)
28.0	Tonsil/peritonsillar I&D	Operative

Code	Description	Operative Status
28.1	Tonsil&adenoid dxtic px	Operative
28.2	Tonsillectomy	Operative
28.3	T&A	Operative
28.4	Excision of tonsil tag	Operative
28.5	Excision lingual tonsil	Operative
28.6	Adenoidectomy	Operative
28.7	Hemor control post T&A	Operative
28.9	Other tonsil/adenoid ops	Operative
29.0	Pharyngotomy	Operative
29.1	Pharyngeal dxtic px	Non-Operative
29.11	Pharyngoscopy	Non-Operative
29.2	Exc branchial cleft cyst	Operative
29.3	Exc/destr pharyngeal les	Operative
29.32	PHAR diverticulectomy	Operative
29.4	Plastic op on pharynx	Operative
29.5	Other pharyngeal repair	Operative
29.9	Other pharyngeal ops	Mixed (2, 1)
30.0	Exc/destr les larynx	Operative
30.09	Exc/destr larynx les NEC	Operative
30.1	Hemilaryngectomy	Operative
30.2	Partial laryngectomy NEC	Operative
30.3	Complete laryngectomy	Operative
30.4	Radical laryngectomy	Operative
31.0	Larynx injection	Non-Operative
31.1	Temporary tracheostomy	Non-Operative
31.2	Permanent tracheostomy	Operative
31.29	Other perm tracheostomy	Operative
31.3	Inc larynx/trachea NEC	Operative
31.4	Larynx/trachea dxtic px	Mixed (1, 6)
31.42	Laryngoscopy/tracheoscpy	Non-Operative
31.43	Closed larynx biopsy	Non-Operative
31.5	Loc exc/destr larynx les	Operative
31.6	Repair of larynx	Operative
31.69	Other laryngeal repair	Operative
31.7	Repair of trachea	Operative
31.74	Revision of tracheostomy	Operative
31.9	Other larynx/trachea ops	Mixed (4, 3)
31.99	Tracheal operation NEC	Operative
32.0	Loc exc/destr bronch les	Mixed (1, 1)
32.1	Bronchial excision NEC	Operative
32.2	Loc exc/destr lung les	Mixed (3, 1)
32.28	Endo exc/destr lung les	Non-Operative
32.29	Loc exc lung les NEC	Operative
32.3	Segmental lung resection	Operative
32.4	Lobectomy of lung	Operative
32.5	Complete pneumonectomy	Operative
32.6	RAD dissect thor struct	Operative
32.9	Lung excision NEC	Operative
33.0	Bronchus incision	Operative
33.1	Lung incision	Operative
33.2	Bronchial/lung dxtic px	Mixed (4, 5)
33.21	Bronchoscopy thru stoma	Non-Operative
33.22	Fiber-optic bronchoscopy	Non-Operative
33.23	Bronchoscopy NEC	Non-Operative
33.24	Closed bronchus biopsy	Non-Operative
33.26	Closed lung biopsy	Non-Operative
33.27	Endoscopic lung biopsy	Operative
33.28	Open biopsy of lung	Operative
33.3	Surg collapse of lung	Mixed (2, 3)
33.4	Lung & bronchus repair	Operative
33.5	Lung transplantation	Operative
33.6	Heart-lung transplant	Operative
33.9	Other bronchial lung ops	Mixed (4, 1)
34.0	Inc chest wall & pleura	Mixed (2, 4)
34.01	Chest wall incision	Non-Operative
34.02	Exploratory thoracotomy	Operative
34.04	Insert intercostal cath	Non-Operative
34.09	Pleural incision NEC	Non-Operative
34.1	Mediastinum incision	Operative
34.2	Thorax dxtic procedures	Mixed (6, 3)
34.21	Transpleura thoracoscopy	Operative
34.22	Mediastinoscopy	Operative
34.23	Chest wall biopsy	Non-Operative
34.24	Pleural biopsy	Non-Operative
34.25	Closed mediastinal Bx	Non-Operative
34.26	Open mediastinal biopsy	Operative
34.3	Destr mediastinum les	Operative
34.4	Exc/destr chest wall les	Operative
34.5	Pleurectomy	Operative
34.51	Decortication of lung	Operative
34.59	Pleural excision NEC	Operative
34.6	Pleural scarification	Operative
34.7	Repair of chest wall	Mixed (3, 2)
34.74	Pectus deformity repair	Operative
34.79	Chest wall repair NEC	Operative
34.8	Operations on diaphragm	Operative
34.82	Suture diaphragm lac	Operative
34.9	Other ops on thorax	Mixed (2, 2)
34.91	Thoracentesis	Non-Operative
34.92	Inject into thor cavit	Non-Operative
35.0	Closed heart valvotomy	Operative
35.1	Open heart valvuloplasty	Operative
35.11	Opn aortic valvuloplasty	Operative
35.12	Opn mitral valvuloplasty	Operative
35.2	Heart valve replacement	Operative
35.21	Repl aortic valve-tissue	Operative
35.22	Repl aortic valve NEC	Operative
35.23	Repl mitral valve w tiss	Operative
35.24	Repl mitral valve NEC	Operative
35.3	Tiss adj to hrt valv ops	Operative
35.33	Annuloplasty	Operative
35.4	Septal defect production	Mixed (1, 1)
35.5	Prosth REP heart septa	Operative
35.52	Prosth REP ASD clsd tech	Operative
35.53	Prosth REP VSD	Operative
35.6	Tiss grft REP hrt septa	Operative
35.61	Repair ASD w tiss graft	Operative
35.62	Repair VSD w tiss graft	Operative
35.7	Heart septa repair NEC	Operative
35.71	Repair ASD NEC & NOS	Operative
35.72	Repair VSD NEC & NOS	Operative
35.8	Tot REP cong card anom	Operative
35.81	Tot REP tetralogy Fallot	Operative
35.9	Valves & septa ops NEC	Operative
35.94	Creat conduit atrium-PA	Operative
35.96	PERC valvuloplasty	Operative
36.0	Rmvl cor art obstr/stent	Mixed (5, 3)
36.01	1 PTCA/atherect w/o TL	Operative
36.02	1 PTCA/atherect w TL	Operative
36.05	PTCA/atherect-mult vess	Operative
36.06	Non-drug-elut cor stent	Non-Operative
36.07	Drug-eluting cor stent	Non-Operative

Code	Description	Operative Status
36.1	Hrt revasc bypass anast	Operative
36.11	Ao-cor bypass-1 cor art	Operative
36.12	Ao-cor bypass-2 cor art	Operative
36.13	Ao-cor bypass-3 cor art	Operative
36.14	Ao-cor bypass-4+ cor art	Operative
36.15	1 int mam-cor art bypass	Operative
36.16	2 int mam-cor art bypass	Operative
36.2	Arterial implant revasc	Operative
36.3	Other heart revasc	Operative
36.31	Open transmyo revasc	Operative
36.9	Other heart vessel ops	Operative
37.0	Pericardiocentesis	Non-Operative
37.1	Cardiotomy & pericardiot	Operative
37.12	Pericardiotomy	Operative
37.2	Dxtic px hrt/pericardium	Mixed (1, 8)
37.21	Rt heart cardiac cath	Non-Operative
37.22	Left heart cardiac cath	Non-Operative
37.23	Rt/left heart card cath	Non-Operative
37.25	Cardiac biopsy	Non-Operative
37.26	Card EPS/record studies	Non-Operative
37.3	Pericardiect/exc hrt les	Operative
37.31	Pericardiectomy	Operative
37.32	Heart aneurysm excision	Operative
37.33	Heart les exc/destr NEC	Operative
37.34	Cath ablation heart les	Operative
37.4	REP heart & pericardium	Operative
37.5	Heart transplantation	Operative
37.6	Impl heart assist syst	Operative
37.61	Pulsation balloon impl	Operative
37.7	Cardiac pacer lead op	Mixed (5, 5)
37.71	Insert TV lead-ventricle	Non-Operative
37.72	Insert TV lead-ATR&vent	Non-Operative
37.74	Insert epicardial lead	Operative
37.75	Revision pacemaker lead	Operative
37.76	Repl transvenous lead	Operative
37.78	Insert temp TV pacer	Non-Operative
37.79	Rev pacemaker pocket	Operative
37.8	Cardiac pacemaker dev op	Mixed (5, 3)
37.80	Insert pacemaker dev NOS	Operative
37.81	Insert single chamb dev	Non-Operative
37.82	Insert rate-respon dev	Non-Operative
37.83	Insert dual-chamber dev	Non-Operative
37.85	Repl w 1-chamber device	Operative
37.86	Repl w rate-respon dev	Operative
37.87	Repl w dual-chamb device	Operative
37.89	Rev/rmvl pacemaker dev	Operative
37.9	Hrt/pericardium ops NEC	Mixed (7, 2)
37.94	Impl/repl AICD tot syst	Operative
37.97	Replace AICD lead only	Operative
37.98	Repl AICD generator only	Operative
37.99	Oth ops hrt/pericardium	Operative
38.0	Incision of vessel	Operative
38.03	Upper limb vessel inc	Operative
38.06	Abdominal art incision	Operative
38.08	Lower limb artery inc	Operative
38.1	Endarterectomy	Operative
38.12	Head/nk endarterect NEC	Operative
38.16	Abdominal endarterectomy	Operative
38.18	Lower limb endarterect	Operative
38.2	Dxtic blood vessels px	Mixed (2, 1)
38.21	Blood vessel biopsy	Operative
38.3	Vessel resect w anast	Operative
38.34	Aorta resection w anast	Operative
38.4	Vessel resect w repl	Operative
38.44	Abd aorta resect w repl	Operative
38.45	Thor vess resect w repl	Operative
38.46	Abd artery resect w repl	Operative
38.48	Leg artery resect w repl	Operative
38.5	Lig&strip varicose veins	Operative
38.59	Lower limb VV lig&strip	Operative
38.6	Other vessel excision	Operative
38.63	Up limb vessel exc NEC	Operative
38.68	Low limb artery exc NEC	Operative
38.7	Interruption vena cava	Operative
38.8	Other surg vessel occl	Operative
38.82	Occl head/neck vess NEC	Operative
38.83	Occl upper limb vess NEC	Operative
38.85	Occl thoracic vess NEC	Operative
38.86	Surg occl abd artery NEC	Operative
38.9	Puncture of vessel	Non-Operative
38.91	Arterial catheterization	Non-Operative
38.92	Umbilical vein cath	Non-Operative
38.93	Venous catheter NEC	Non-Operative
38.94	Venous cutdown	Non-Operative
38.95	Venous cath for RD	Non-Operative
38.98	Arterial puncture NEC	Non-Operative
38.99	Venous puncture NEC	Non-Operative
39.0	Systemic to PA shunt	Operative
39.1	Intra-abd venous shunt	Operative
39.2	Other shunt/vasc bypass	Operative
39.21	Caval-PA anastomosis	Operative
39.22	Aorta-scl-carotid bypass	Operative
39.25	Aorta-iliac-femoral byp	Operative
39.27	Arteriovenostomy for RD	Operative
39.29	Vasc shunt & bypass NEC	Operative
39.3	Suture of vessel	Operative
39.31	Suture of artery	Operative
39.32	Suture of vein	Operative
39.4	Vascular px revision	Operative
39.42	Rev AV shunt for RD	Operative
39.43	Rmvl AV shunt for RD	Operative
39.49	Vascular px revision NEC	Operative
39.5	Other vessel repair	Operative
39.50	PTA/atherect oth vessel	Operative
39.51	Clipping of aneurysm	Operative
39.52	Aneurysm repair NEC	Operative
39.53	AV fistula repair	Operative
39.56	REP vess w tiss patch	Operative
39.57	REP vess w synth patch	Operative
39.59	Repair of vessel NEC	Operative
39.6	Open heart auxiliary px	Mixed (1, 5)
39.7	Endovascular vessel REP	Operative
39.71	Endovascular graft-AAA	Operative
39.72	Endov REP HN vessel	Operative
39.79	Endov REP aneurysm NEC	Operative
39.8	Vascular body operations	Operative
39.9	Other vessel operations	Mixed (6, 4)
39.90	Non-drug non-cor stent	Non-Operative
39.93	Insert vess-vess cannula	Operative
39.95	Hemodialysis	Non-Operative
39.98	Hemorrhage control NOS	Operative
40.0	Inc lymphatic structure	Operative

Code	Description	Operative Status
40.1	Lymphatic dxtic px	Operative
40.11	Lymphatic struct biopsy	Operative
40.2	Smp exc lymphatic struct	Operative
40.21	Exc deep cervical node	Operative
40.23	Exc axillary lymph node	Operative
40.24	Exc inguinal lymph node	Operative
40.29	Smp exc lymphatic NEC	Operative
40.3	Regional lymph node exc	Operative
40.4	RAD exc cerv lymph node	Operative
40.41	Unilat RAD neck dissect	Operative
40.5	Oth RAD node dissection	Operative
40.53	RAD exc iliac lymph node	Operative
40.59	RAD exc lymph node NEC	Operative
40.6	Thoracic duct operations	Operative
40.9	Lymphatic struct ops NEC	Operative
41.0	Bone marrow transplant	Operative
41.03	Allo marrow transpl NEC	Operative
41.04	Autlog stem cell transpl	Operative
41.05	Allo stem cell transpl	Operative
41.1	Puncture of spleen	Non-Operative
41.2	Splenotomy	Operative
41.3	Marrow & spleen dxtic px	Mixed (1, 4)
41.31	Bone marrow biopsy	Non-Operative
41.4	Exc/destr splenic tissue	Operative
41.5	Total splenectomy	Operative
41.9	Oth spleen & marrow ops	Mixed (4, 3)
42.0	Esophagotomy	Operative
42.1	Esophagostomy	Operative
42.2	Esophageal dxtic px	Mixed (2, 4)
42.23	Esophagoscopy NEC	Non-Operative
42.24	Closed esophageal biopsy	Non-Operative
42.3	Exc/destr esoph les/tiss	Mixed (3, 1)
42.31	Exc esoph diverticulum	Operative
42.33	Endo exc/destr esoph les	Non-Operative
42.4	Excision of esophagus	Operative
42.41	Partial esophagectomy	Operative
42.42	Total esophagectomy	Operative
42.5	Intrathor esoph anast	Operative
42.6	Antesternal esoph anast	Operative
42.7	Esophagomyotomy	Operative
42.8	Other esophageal repair	Mixed (7, 1)
42.81	Insert perm tube esoph	Non-Operative
42.9	Other esophageal ops	Mixed (1, 2)
42.92	Esophageal dilation	Non-Operative
43.0	Gastrotomy	Operative
43.1	Gastrostomy	Non-Operative
43.11	PEG	Non-Operative
43.19	Gastrostomy NEC	Non-Operative
43.3	Pyloromyotomy	Operative
43.4	Loc exc gastric les	Mixed (2, 1)
43.41	Endo exc gastric les	Non-Operative
43.42	Loc gastric les exc NEC	Operative
43.5	Proximal gastrectomy	Operative
43.6	Distal gastrectomy	Operative
43.7	Part gastrectomy w anast	Operative
43.8	Oth partial gastrectomy	Operative
43.89	Partial gastrectomy NEC	Operative
43.9	Total gastrectomy	Operative
43.99	Total gastrectomy NEC	Operative
44.0	Vagotomy	Operative
44.1	Gastric dxtic px	Mixed (2, 4)

Code	Description	Operative Status
44.13	Gastroscopy NEC	Non-Operative
44.14	Closed gastric biopsy	Non-Operative
44.2	Pyloroplasty	Mixed (2, 1)
44.22	Endo dilation pylorus	Non-Operative
44.29	Other pyloroplasty	Operative
44.3	Gastroenterostomy	Operative
44.31	High gastric bypass	Operative
44.32	PERC gastrojejunostomy	Operative
44.39	Gastroenterostomy NEC	Operative
44.4	Cntrl peptic ulcer hemor	Mixed (3, 3)
44.41	Sut gastric ulcer site	Operative
44.42	Sut duodenal ulcer site	Operative
44.43	Endo cntrl gastric bleed	Non-Operative
44.5	Revision gastric anast	Operative
44.6	Other gastric repair	Mixed (6, 1)
44.61	Suture gastric lac	Operative
44.63	Close stom fistula NEC	Operative
44.66	Creat EG sphinct compet	Operative
44.69	Gastric repair NEC	Operative
44.9	Other stomach operations	Mixed (3, 2)
44.99	Gastric operation NEC	Operative
45.0	Enterotomy	Operative
45.02	Sm intest incision NEC	Operative
45.1	Small intest dxtic px	Mixed (2, 5)
45.13	Sm intest endoscopy NEC	Non-Operative
45.14	Closed small intest Bx	Non-Operative
45.16	EGD w closed biopsy	Non-Operative
45.2	Lg intestine dxtic px	Mixed (2, 7)
45.22	Endo L-intest thru stoma	Non-Operative
45.23	Colonoscopy	Non-Operative
45.24	Flexible sigmoidoscopy	Non-Operative
45.25	Closed lg intest biopsy	Non-Operative
45.3	Loc exc/destr SmB les	Mixed (4, 1)
45.30	Endo exc/destr duod les	Non-Operative
45.31	Loc exc duod les NEC	Operative
45.33	Loc exc S-intest les NEC	Operative
45.4	Loc destr lg intest les	Mixed (2, 2)
45.41	Exc lg intest lesion	Operative
45.42	Endo colon polypectomy	Non-Operative
45.43	Endo destr colon les NEC	Non-Operative
45.5	Intestinal SEG isolation	Operative
45.6	Sm intest excision NEC	Operative
45.61	Mult SEG S-intest resect	Operative
45.62	Part S-intest resect NEC	Operative
45.7	Part lg intest excision	Operative
45.71	Mult SEG L-intest resect	Operative
45.72	Cecectomy	Operative
45.73	Right hemicolectomy	Operative
45.74	Transverse colon resect	Operative
45.75	Left hemicolectomy	Operative
45.76	Sigmoidectomy	Operative
45.79	Part lg intest exc NEC	Operative
45.8	Tot intra-abd colectomy	Operative
45.9	Intestinal anastomosis	Operative
45.91	Sm-to-sm intest anast	Operative
45.93	Sm-lg intest anast NEC	Operative
45.94	Lg-to-lg intest anast	Operative
45.95	Anastomosis to anus	Operative
46.0	Intest exteriorization	Operative
46.01	S-intest exteriorization	Operative
46.03	L-intest exteriorization	Operative

Code	Description	Operative Status
46.1	Colostomy	Mixed (3, 1)
46.10	Colostomy NOS	Operative
46.11	Temporary colostomy	Operative
46.13	Permanent colostomy	Operative
46.2	Ileostomy	Mixed (4, 1)
46.23	Permanent ileostomy NEC	Operative
46.3	Other enterostomy	Non-Operative
46.32	PEJ	Non-Operative
46.39	Enterostomy NEC	Non-Operative
46.4	Intestinal stoma rev	Operative
46.41	Sm intest stoma revision	Operative
46.42	Pericolostomy hernia REP	Operative
46.43	Lg intest stoma rev NEC	Operative
46.5	Intestinal stoma closure	Operative
46.51	Sm intest stoma closure	Operative
46.52	Lg intest stoma closure	Operative
46.6	Fixation of intestine	Operative
46.7	Other intestinal repair	Operative
46.73	Small intest suture NEC	Operative
46.74	Closure SmB fistula NEC	Operative
46.75	Large intestine suture	Operative
46.79	Repair of intestine NEC	Operative
46.8	Bowel dilation & manip	Mixed (3, 1)
46.81	Intra-abd S-intest manip	Operative
46.82	Intra-abd L-intest manip	Operative
46.85	Dilation of intestine	Non-Operative
46.9	Other intestinal ops	Mixed (6, 2)
47.0	Appendectomy	Operative
47.01	Lapscp appendectomy	Operative
47.09	Other appendectomy	Operative
47.1	Incidental appendectomy	Operative
47.11	Lapscp incidental APPY	Operative
47.2	Drain appendiceal absc	Operative
47.9	Other appendiceal ops	Operative
48.0	Proctotomy	Operative
48.1	Proctostomy	Operative
48.2	Rectal/perirect dxtic px	Mixed (2, 5)
48.23	Rig proctosigmoidoscopy	Non-Operative
48.24	Closed rectal biopsy	Non-Operative
48.3	Loc destr rectal lesion	Mixed (1, 5)
48.32	Electrocoag rect les NEC	Non-Operative
48.35	Loc exc rectal les/tiss	Operative
48.36	Endo rectal polypectomy	Non-Operative
48.4	Pull-thru rect resection	Operative
48.49	Pull-thru rect resect	Operative
48.5	Abd-perineal rect resect	Operative
48.6	Other rectal resection	Operative
48.62	Ant rect resect w colost	Operative
48.63	Anterior rect resect NEC	Operative
48.69	Rectal resection NEC	Operative
48.7	Repair of rectum	Operative
48.75	Abdominal proctopexy	Operative
48.76	Proctopexy NEC	Operative
48.8	Perirect tiss inc/exc	Operative
48.81	Perirectal incision	Operative
48.9	Oth rectal/perirect op	Operative
49.0	Perianal tiss inc/exc	Mixed (3, 1)
49.01	Inc perianal abscess	Operative
49.1	Inc/exc of anal fistula	Operative
49.11	Anal fistulotomy	Operative
49.12	Anal fistulectomy	Operative

Code	Description	Operative Status
49.2	Anal & perianal dxtic px	Non-Operative
49.21	Anoscopy	Non-Operative
49.3	Loc destr anal les NEC	Mixed (1, 1)
49.39	Oth loc destr anal les	Operative
49.4	Hemorrhoid procedures	Mixed (4, 4)
49.45	Hemorrhoid ligation	Operative
49.46	Exc of hemorrhoids	Operative
49.5	Anal sphincter division	Operative
49.6	Excision of anus	Operative
49.7	Repair of anus	Operative
49.79	Anal sphincter REP NEC	Operative
49.9	Oth operations on anus	Operative
50.0	Hepatotomy	Operative
50.1	Hepatic dxtic px	Mixed (2, 1)
50.11	Closed liver biopsy	Non-Operative
50.12	Open biopsy of liver	Operative
50.2	Loc exc/destr liver les	Operative
50.22	Partial hepatectomy	Operative
50.29	Hepatic lesion destr NEC	Operative
50.3	Hepatic lobectomy	Operative
50.4	Total hepatectomy	Operative
50.5	Liver transplant	Operative
50.59	Liver transplant NEC	Operative
50.6	Repair of liver	Operative
50.61	Closure of liver lac	Operative
50.9	Other liver operations	Non-Operative
50.91	PERC liver aspiration	Non-Operative
50.94	Hepatic injection NEC	Non-Operative
51.0	GB inc & cholecystostomy	Mixed (3, 1)
51.01	PERC aspiration of GB	Non-Operative
51.03	Cholecystostomy NEC	Operative
51.1	Biliary tract dxtic px	Mixed (2, 5)
51.10	ERCP	Non-Operative
51.11	ERC	Non-Operative
51.14	Clsd BD/sphinct Oddi Bx	Non-Operative
51.2	Cholecystectomy	Operative
51.22	Cholecystectomy NOS	Operative
51.23	Lapscp cholecystectomy	Operative
51.3	Biliary tract anast	Operative
51.32	GB-to-intestine anast	Operative
51.36	Choledochoenterostomy	Operative
51.37	Hepatic duct-GI anast	Operative
51.4	Inc bile duct obstr	Operative
51.43	Insert CBD-hep tube	Operative
51.5	Other bile duct incision	Operative
51.6	Loc exc BD & S of O les	Mixed (4, 1)
51.7	Repair of bile ducts	Operative
51.8	Sphincter of Oddi op NEC	Mixed (4, 5)
51.84	Endo ampulla & BD dilat	Non-Operative
51.85	Endo sphinctot/papillot	Non-Operative
51.87	Endo insert BD stent	Non-Operative
51.88	Endo rmvl biliary stone	Non-Operative
51.9	Other biliary tract ops	Mixed (6, 2)
51.98	PERC op on bil tract NEC	Non-Operative
52.0	Pancreatotomy	Operative
52.01	Drain panc cyst by cath	Operative
52.1	Pancreatic dxtic px	Mixed (2, 3)
52.11	Pancreas aspiration Bx	Non-Operative
52.12	Open pancreatic biopsy	Operative
52.2	Panc/panc duct les destr	Mixed (1, 1)
52.22	Panc duct les destr NEC	Operative

Code	Description	Operative Status
52.3	Pancreatic cyst marsup	Operative
52.4	Int drain panc cyst	Operative
52.5	Partial pancreatectomy	Operative
52.52	Distal pancreatectomy	Operative
52.6	Total pancreatectomy	Operative
52.7	RAD panc/duodenectomy	Operative
52.8	Transplant of pancreas	Mixed (4, 3)
52.9	Other ops on pancreas	Mixed (4, 4)
52.93	Endo insert panc stent	Non-Operative
52.96	Pancreatic anastomosis	Operative
53.0	Unilat IH repair	Operative
53.00	Unilat IH repair NOS	Operative
53.01	Unilat REP direct IH	Operative
53.02	Unilat REP indirect IH	Operative
53.03	Unilat REP DIR IH/graft	Operative
53.04	Unilat indirect IH/graft	Operative
53.05	Unilat REP IH/graft NOS	Operative
53.1	Bilat IH repair	Operative
53.10	Bilat IH repair NOS	Operative
53.12	Bilat indirect IH repair	Operative
53.14	Bilat direct IH REP-grft	Operative
53.15	Bilat indirect IH-graft	Operative
53.16	Direct/indirect IH-graft	Operative
53.17	Bilat IH REP-graft NOS	Operative
53.2	Unilat FH repair	Operative
53.21	Unilat FH REP w graft	Operative
53.29	Unilat FH REP NEC	Operative
53.3	Bilat FH repair	Operative
53.4	Umbilical hernia repair	Operative
53.41	Umb hernia repair-prosth	Operative
53.49	Umb hernia repair NEC	Operative
53.5	REP oth abd wall hernia	Operative
53.51	Incisional hernia repair	Operative
53.59	Abd wall hernia REP NEC	Operative
53.6	REP oth abd hernia-graft	Operative
53.61	Inc hernia repair-prosth	Operative
53.69	Abd hernia REP-grft NEC	Operative
53.7	Abd REP-diaph hernia	Operative
53.8	Repair DH thor appr	Operative
53.80	Repair DH thor appr NOS	Operative
53.9	Other hernia repair	Operative
54.0	Abdominal wall incision	Operative
54.1	Laparotomy	Operative
54.11	Exploratory laparotomy	Operative
54.12	Reopen recent LAP site	Operative
54.19	Laparotomy NEC	Operative
54.2	Abd region dxtic px	Mixed (4, 2)
54.21	Laparoscopy	Operative
54.22	Abd wall or umbilicus Bx	Operative
54.23	Peritoneal biopsy	Operative
54.24	Clsd intra-abd mass Bx	Non-Operative
54.3	Exc/destr abd wall les	Operative
54.4	Exc/destr periton tiss	Operative
54.5	Peritoneal adhesiolysis	Operative
54.51	Lapscp periton ADHESIO	Operative
54.59	Periton adhesiolysis NEC	Operative
54.6	Abd wall/periton suture	Operative
54.61	Reclose postop disrupt	Operative
54.7	Oth abd wall periton REP	Operative
54.71	Repair of gastroschisis	Operative
54.9	Other abd region ops	Mixed (4, 5)

Code	Description	Operative Status
54.91	PERC abd drainage	Non-Operative
54.92	Rmvl FB periton cavity	Operative
54.93	Create cutaneoperit fist	Operative
54.94	Creat peritoneovas shunt	Operative
54.95	Peritoneal incision	Operative
54.98	Peritoneal dialysis	Non-Operative
55.0	Nephrotomy & nephrostomy	Operative
55.01	Nephrotomy	Operative
55.02	Nephrostomy	Operative
55.03	PERC nephrostomy s frag	Operative
55.04	PERC nephrostomy w frag	Operative
55.1	Pyelotomy & pyelostomy	Operative
55.11	Pyelotomy	Operative
55.2	Renal diagnostic px	Mixed (2, 3)
55.23	Closed renal biopsy	Non-Operative
55.24	Open biopsy of kidney	Operative
55.3	Loc exc/destr renal les	Operative
55.39	Loc destr renal les NEC	Operative
55.4	Partial nephrectomy	Operative
55.5	Complete nephrectomy	Operative
55.51	Nephroureterectomy	Operative
55.53	Rejected kid nephrectomy	Operative
55.54	Bilateral nephrectomy	Operative
55.6	Kidney transplant	Operative
55.69	Kidney transplant NEC	Operative
55.7	Nephropexy	Operative
55.8	Other kidney repair	Operative
55.87	Correction of UPJ	Operative
55.9	Other renal operations	Mixed (4, 5)
55.92	PERC renal aspiration	Non-Operative
55.93	Repl nephrostomy tube	Non-Operative
56.0	TU rmvl ureteral obstr	Operative
56.1	Ureteral meatotomy	Operative
56.2	Ureterotomy	Operative
56.3	Ureteral diagnostic px	Mixed (2, 4)
56.31	Ureteroscopy	Non-Operative
56.4	Ureterectomy	Operative
56.41	Partial ureterectomy	Operative
56.5	Cutan uretero-ileostomy	Operative
56.51	Form cutan ileoureterost	Operative
56.6	Ext urin diversion NEC	Operative
56.7	Other ureteral anast	Operative
56.74	Ureteroneocystostomy	Operative
56.8	Repair of ureter	Operative
56.9	Other ureteral operation	Mixed (5, 1)
57.0	TU bladder clearance	Non-Operative
57.1	Cystotomy & cystostomy	Mixed (3, 2)
57.17	Percutaneous cystostomy	Non-Operative
57.18	S/P cystostomy NEC	Operative
57.19	Cystotomy NEC	Operative
57.2	Vesicostomy	Operative
57.3	Bladder diagnostic px	Mixed (3, 2)
57.32	Cystoscopy NEC	Non-Operative
57.33	Closed bladder biopsy	Operative
57.4	TU exc/destr bladder les	Operative
57.49	TU destr bladder les NEC	Operative
57.5	Bladder les destr NEC	Operative
57.59	Oth bladder lesion destr	Operative
57.6	Partial cystectomy	Operative
57.7	Total cystectomy	Operative
57.71	Radical cystectomy	Operative

Code	Description	Operative Status
57.8	Oth urin bladder repair	Operative
57.81	Suture bladder lac	Operative
57.83	Enterovesical fist REP	Operative
57.84	REP oth fistula bladder	Operative
57.87	Urinary bladder reconst	Operative
57.9	Other bladder operations	Mixed (6, 3)
57.91	Bladder sphincterotomy	Operative
57.93	Control bladder hemor	Operative
57.94	Insert indwell urin cath	Non-Operative
57.95	Repl indwell urin cath	Non-Operative
58.0	Urethrotomy	Operative
58.1	Urethral meatotomy	Operative
58.2	Urethral diagnostic px	Non-Operative
58.3	Exc/destr urethral les	Non-Operative
58.39	Urethra les destr NEC	Non-Operative
58.4	Repair of urethra	Operative
58.45	Hypospad/epispadias REP	Operative
58.49	Urethral repair NEC	Operative
58.5	Urethral stricture rel	Operative
58.6	Urethral dilation	Non-Operative
58.9	Other urethral ops	Operative
58.93	Implantation of AUS	Operative
58.99	Periurethral ops NEC	Operative
59.0	Retroperiton dissection	Operative
59.1	Perivesical incision	Operative
59.2	Perirenal dxtic px	Operative
59.3	Urethroves junct plicat	Operative
59.4	Suprapubic sling op	Operative
59.5	Retropubic urethral susp	Operative
59.6	Paraurethral suspension	Operative
59.7	Oth urinary incont REP	Mixed (2, 1)
59.71	Levator musc suspension	Operative
59.79	Urin incont repair NEC	Operative
59.8	Ureteral catheterization	Non-Operative
59.9	Other urinary system ops	Mixed (2, 4)
59.94	Repl cystostomy tube	Non-Operative
60.0	Incision of prostate	Operative
60.1	Pros/sem vesicl dxtic px	Mixed (5, 2)
60.11	Clsd prostatic Bx	Non-Operative
60.2	TU prostatectomy	Operative
60.21	TULIP procedure	Operative
60.29	TU prostatectomy NEC	Operative
60.3	Suprapubic prostatectomy	Operative
60.4	Retropubic prostatectomy	Operative
60.5	Radical prostatectomy	Operative
60.6	Other prostatectomy	Operative
60.62	Perineal prostatectomy	Operative
60.7	Seminal vesicle ops	Mixed (3, 1)
60.8	Periprostatic inc or exc	Operative
60.9	Other prostatic ops	Mixed (6, 2)
60.94	Cntrl postop pros hemor	Operative
61.0	Scrotum & tunica vag I&D	Non-Operative
61.1	Scrotum/tunica dxtic px	Non-Operative
61.2	Excision of hydrocele	Operative
61.3	Scrotal les exc/destr	Non-Operative
61.4	Scrotum & tunica vag REP	Mixed (2, 1)
61.9	Oth scrot/tunica vag ops	Mixed (2, 1)
62.0	Incision of testis	Operative
62.1	Testes dxtic px	Mixed (2, 1)
62.2	Testicular les exc/destr	Operative
62.3	Unilateral orchiectomy	Operative
62.4	Bilateral orchiectomy	Operative
62.41	Rmvl both testes	Operative
62.5	Orchiopexy	Operative
62.6	Testes repair	Operative
62.7	Insert testicular prosth	Operative
62.9	Other testicular ops	Mixed (1, 2)
63.0	Spermatic cord dxtic px	Mixed (1, 1)
63.1	Exc spermatic varicocele	Operative
63.2	Exc epididymis cyst	Operative
63.3	Exc sperm cord les NEC	Operative
63.4	Epididymectomy	Operative
63.5	Sperm cord/epid repair	Mixed (3, 1)
63.6	Vasotomy	Non-Operative
63.7	Vasectomy & vas def lig	Non-Operative
63.8	Vas def & epid repair	Mixed (5, 1)
63.9	Oth sperm cord/epid ops	Mixed (5, 1)
64.0	Circumcision	Operative
64.1	Penile diagnostic px	Mixed (1, 1)
64.2	Loc exc/destr penile les	Operative
64.3	Amputation of penis	Operative
64.4	Penile REP/plastic ops	Operative
64.5	Sex transformation NEC	Operative
64.9	Other male genital ops	Mixed (7, 2)
64.95	Insert/repl non-IPP NOS	Operative
64.96	Rmvl int penile prosth	Operative
64.97	Insert or repl IPP	Operative
64.98	Penile operation NEC	Operative
65.0	Oophorotomy	Operative
65.01	Lapscp oophorotomy	Operative
65.1	Dxtic px on ovaries	Operative
65.2	Loc exc/destr ovary les	Operative
65.25	Lapscp ov les exc NEC	Operative
65.29	Loc exc/destr ov les NEC	Operative
65.3	Unilateral oophorectomy	Operative
65.31	Lapscp unilat oophorect	Operative
65.39	Unilat oophorectomy NEC	Operative
65.4	Unilateral S-O	Operative
65.41	Lapscp unilateral S-O	Operative
65.49	Unilateral S-O NEC	Operative
65.5	Bilateral oophorectomy	Operative
65.51	Rmvl both ovaries NEC	Operative
65.6	Bilat salpingo-oophorect	Operative
65.61	Rmvl both ov & FALL NEC	Operative
65.62	Rmvl rem ov & FALL NEC	Operative
65.63	Lapscp rmvl both ov/FALL	Operative
65.7	Repair of ovary	Operative
65.8	Tubo-ovarian ADHESIO	Operative
65.81	Lapscp ADHESIO ov/FALL	Operative
65.89	ADHESIO ov/FALL tube NEC	Operative
65.9	Other ovarian operations	Operative
65.91	Aspiration of ovary	Operative
66.0	Salpingostomy/salpingot	Operative
66.01	Salpingotomy	Operative
66.02	Salpingostomy	Operative
66.1	Fallopian tube dxtic px	Operative
66.2	Bilat endo occl FALL	Operative
66.22	Bilat endo lig/div FALL	Operative
66.29	Bilat endo occl FALL NEC	Operative
66.3	Oth bilat FALL destr/exc	Operative
66.32	Bilat FALL lig & div NEC	Operative
66.39	Bilat FALL destr NEC	Operative

Code	Description	Operative Status
66.4	Tot unilat salpingectomy	Operative
66.5	Tot bilat salpingectomy	Operative
66.51	Rmvl both FALL tubes	Operative
66.6	Other salpingectomy	Operative
66.61	Exc/destr FALL les	Operative
66.62	Rmvl FALL & tubal preg	Operative
66.69	Partial FALL rmvl NEC	Operative
66.7	Repair of fallopian tube	Operative
66.79	FALL tube repair NEC	Operative
66.8	FALL tube insufflation	Non-Operative
66.9	Other fallopian tube ops	Mixed (7, 1)
67.0	Cervical canal dilation	Non-Operative
67.1	Cervical diagnostic px	Operative
67.12	Cervical biopsy NEC	Operative
67.2	Conization of cervix	Operative
67.3	Exc/destr cerv les NEC	Operative
67.39	Cerv les exc/destr NEC	Operative
67.4	Amputation of cervix	Operative
67.5	Int cervical os repair	Operative
67.59	Int cervical os REP NEC	Operative
67.6	Other repair of cervix	Operative
68.0	Hysterotomy	Operative
68.1	Uter/adnexa dxtic px	Mixed (5, 2)
68.16	Closed uterine biopsy	Operative
68.2	Uterine les exc/destr	Operative
68.23	Endometrial ablation	Operative
68.29	Uter les exc/destr NEC	Operative
68.3	Subtot abd hysterectomy	Operative
68.4	Total abd hysterectomy	Operative
68.5	Vaginal hysterectomy	Operative
68.51	LAVH	Operative
68.59	Vaginal hysterectomy NEC	Operative
68.6	Radical abd hysterectomy	Operative
68.7	Radical vag hysterectomy	Operative
68.8	Pelvic evisceration	Operative
68.9	Hysterectomy NEC & NOS	Operative
69.0	Uterine D&C	Operative
69.01	D&C for term of preg	Operative
69.02	D&C post del or AB	Operative
69.09	D&C NEC	Operative
69.1	Exc/destr uter/supp les	Operative
69.19	Exc uter/supp struct NEC	Operative
69.2	Uterine supp struct REP	Operative
69.3	Paracerv uterine denerv	Operative
69.4	Uterine repair	Operative
69.5	Asp curettage uterus	Mixed (2, 1)
69.51	Asp curettage-preg term	Operative
69.52	Asp curette post del/AB	Operative
69.59	Asp curettage uterus NEC	Non-Operative
69.6	Menstrual extraction	Non-Operative
69.7	Insertion of IUD	Non-Operative
69.9	Other ops uterus/adnexa	Mixed (4, 5)
69.93	Insertion of laminaria	Non-Operative
69.96	Rmvl cervical cerclage	Non-Operative
70.0	Culdocentesis	Non-Operative
70.1	Inc vagina & cul-de-sac	Mixed (3, 1)
70.12	Culdotomy	Operative
70.14	Vaginotomy NEC	Operative
70.2	Vag/cul-de-sac dxtic px	Mixed (3, 2)
70.24	Vaginal biopsy	Operative
70.3	Loc exc/destr vag/cul	Operative
70.33	Exc/destr vaginal lesion	Operative
70.4	Vaginal obliteration	Operative
70.5	Cystocele/rectocele REP	Operative
70.50	REP cystocele/rectocele	Operative
70.51	Cystocele repair	Operative
70.52	Rectocele repair	Operative
70.6	Vaginal constr/reconst	Operative
70.7	Other vaginal repair	Operative
70.71	Suture vagina laceration	Operative
70.73	REP rectovaginal fistula	Operative
70.77	Vaginal susp & fixation	Operative
70.79	Vaginal repair NEC	Operative
70.8	Vaginal vault oblit	Operative
70.9	Oth vag & cul-de-sac ops	Operative
70.92	Cul-de-sac operation NEC	Operative
71.0	Inc vulva & perineum	Operative
71.09	Inc vulva/perineum NEC	Operative
71.1	Vulvar diagnostic px	Operative
71.11	Vulvar biopsy	Operative
71.2	Bartholin's gland ops	Mixed (4, 1)
71.22	Inc Bartholin's gland	Operative
71.3	Loc vulvar/peri exc NEC	Operative
71.4	Operations on clitoris	Operative
71.5	Radical vulvectomy	Operative
71.6	Other vulvectomy	Operative
71.61	Unilateral vulvectomy	Operative
71.7	Vulvar & perineal repair	Operative
71.71	Suture vulvar/peri lac	Operative
71.79	Vulvar/perineum REP NEC	Operative
71.8	Vulvar operations NEC	Operative
71.9	Female genital ops NEC	Operative
72.0	Low forceps operation	Non-Operative
72.1	Low forceps w episiotomy	Non-Operative
72.2	Mid forceps operation	Non-Operative
72.21	Mid forceps w episiotomy	Non-Operative
72.29	Mid forceps op NEC	Non-Operative
72.3	High forceps operation	Non-Operative
72.4	Forceps ROT fetal head	Non-Operative
72.5	Breech extraction	Non-Operative
72.52	Part breech extract NEC	Non-Operative
72.54	Tot breech extract NEC	Non-Operative
72.6	Forceps-aftercoming head	Non-Operative
72.7	Vacuum extraction del	Non-Operative
72.71	VED w episiotomy	Non-Operative
72.79	Vacuum extract del NEC	Non-Operative
72.8	Instrumental del NEC	Non-Operative
72.9	Instrumental del NOS	Non-Operative
73.0	Artificial rupt membrane	Non-Operative
73.01	Induction labor by AROM	Non-Operative
73.09	Artif rupt membranes NEC	Non-Operative
73.1	Surg induction labor NEC	Non-Operative
73.2	Int/comb version/extract	Non-Operative
73.3	Failed forceps	Non-Operative
73.4	Medical induction labor	Non-Operative
73.5	Manually assisted del	Non-Operative
73.51	Manual ROT fetal head	Non-Operative
73.59	Manual assisted del NEC	Non-Operative
73.6	Episiotomy	Non-Operative
73.8	Fetal ops-facilitate del	Non-Operative
73.9	Oth ops assisting del	Mixed (2, 3)
73.91	Ext version-assist del	Non-Operative

Code	Description	Operative Status
74.0	Classical CD	Operative
74.1	Low cervical CD	Operative
74.2	Extraperitoneal CD	Operative
74.3	Rmvl extratubal preg	Operative
74.4	Cesarean section NEC	Operative
74.9	Cesarean section NOS	Operative
74.99	Other CD type NOS	Operative
75.0	Intra-amnio inject-AB	Non-Operative
75.1	Diagnostic amniocentesis	Non-Operative
75.2	Intrauterine transfusion	Non-Operative
75.3	IU ops fetus & amnio NEC	Mixed (1, 7)
75.32	Fetal EKG	Non-Operative
75.34	Fetal monitoring NEC	Non-Operative
75.35	Dxtic px fetus/amnio NEC	Non-Operative
75.37	Amnioinfusion	Non-Operative
75.4	Man rmvl of ret placenta	Non-Operative
75.5	REP current OB lac uter	Operative
75.51	REP current OB lac cerv	Operative
75.6	REP oth current OB lac	Mixed (1, 2)
75.61	REP OB lac blad/urethra	Operative
75.62	REP OB lac rectum/anus	Non-Operative
75.69	REP current OB lac NEC	Non-Operative
75.7	PP manual expl uterus	Non-Operative
75.8	OB tamponade uterus/vag	Non-Operative
75.9	Other obstetrical ops	Mixed (2, 3)
76.0	Facial bone incision	Operative
76.1	Dxtic px facial bone/jt	Operative
76.2	Exc/destr fac bone les	Operative
76.3	Partial facial ostectomy	Operative
76.31	Partial mandibulectomy	Operative
76.4	Facial bone exc/reconst	Operative
76.5	TMJ arthroplasty	Operative
76.6	Other facial bone repair	Operative
76.62	Open osty mand ramus	Operative
76.64	Mand orthognathic op NEC	Operative
76.65	SEG osteoplasty maxilla	Operative
76.66	Tot osteoplasty maxilla	Operative
76.7	Reduction of facial fx	Mixed (6, 4)
76.72	Open red malar/ZMC fx	Operative
76.74	Open red maxillary fx	Operative
76.75	Clsd red mandibular fx	Non-Operative
76.76	Open red mandibular fx	Operative
76.79	Open red facial fx NEC	Operative
76.9	Oth ops facial bone/jt	Mixed (5, 3)
76.97	Rmvl int fix face bone	Operative
77.0	Sequestrectomy	Operative
77.1	Bone inc NEC w/o div	Operative
77.2	Wedge osteotomy	Operative
77.25	Femoral wedge osteotomy	Operative
77.27	Tib & fib wedge osty	Operative
77.3	Other division of bone	Operative
77.35	Femoral division NEC	Operative
77.37	Tibia/fibula div NEC	Operative
77.4	Biopsy of bone	Operative
77.41	Chest cage bone biopsy	Operative
77.42	Humerus biopsy	Operative
77.45	Femoral biopsy	Operative
77.47	Tibia & fibula biopsy	Operative
77.48	Metatarsal/tarsal biopsy	Operative
77.49	Bone biopsy NEC	Operative
77.5	Toe deformity exc/REP	Operative

Code	Description	Operative Status
77.51	Bunionect/STC/osty	Operative
77.6	Loc exc bone lesion	Operative
77.61	Exc chest cage bone les	Operative
77.62	Loc exc humerus lesion	Operative
77.63	Loc exc radius/ulna les	Operative
77.65	Local exc femur lesion	Operative
77.67	Loc exc tibia/fibula les	Operative
77.68	Local exc MT/tarsal les	Operative
77.69	Loc exc bone lesion NEC	Operative
77.7	Exc bone for graft	Operative
77.79	Exc bone for graft NEC	Operative
77.8	Other partial ostectomy	Operative
77.81	Chest cage ostectomy NEC	Operative
77.85	Part ostectomy femur	Operative
77.86	Partial patellectomy	Operative
77.87	Part ostectomy tib/fib	Operative
77.88	Part ostectomy MT/tarsal	Operative
77.89	Partial ostectomy NEC	Operative
77.9	Total ostectomy	Operative
77.91	Tot chest cage ostectomy	Operative
78.0	Bone graft	Operative
78.05	Bone graft to femur	Operative
78.07	Bone graft tibia/fibula	Operative
78.1	Appl ext fixation device	Operative
78.13	Appl ext fix rad/ulna	Operative
78.15	Appl ext fix dev femur	Operative
78.17	Appl ext fix dev tib/fib	Operative
78.2	Limb shortening px	Operative
78.25	Limb short px femur	Operative
78.3	Limb lengthening px	Operative
78.4	Other bone repair	Operative
78.49	Other bone repair NEC	Operative
78.5	Int fix w/o fx reduction	Operative
78.52	Int fix w/o red humerus	Operative
78.55	Int fix w/o red femur	Operative
78.57	Int fix w/o red tib/fib	Operative
78.59	Int fix w/o fx red NEC	Operative
78.6	Rmvl impl dev from bone	Operative
78.62	Rmvl impl dev humerus	Operative
78.63	Rmvl impl dev rad/ulna	Operative
78.65	Rmvl impl dev femur	Operative
78.67	Rmvl impl dev tib & fib	Operative
78.68	Rmvl impl dev MT/tarsal	Operative
78.69	Rmvl impl dev site NEC	Operative
78.7	Osteoclasis	Operative
78.8	Other bone diagnostic px	Operative
78.9	Insert bone growth stim	Operative
79.0	Clsd fx red w/o int fix	Non-Operative
79.01	Clsd fx red humerus	Non-Operative
79.02	Clsd fx red radius/ulna	Non-Operative
79.05	Clsd fx red femur	Non-Operative
79.06	Clsd fx red tibia/fibula	Non-Operative
79.09	Closed fx reduction NEC	Non-Operative
79.1	Clsd fx red w int fix	Operative
79.11	CRIF humerus	Operative
79.12	CRIF radius/ulna	Operative
79.13	CRIF MC/carpals	Operative
79.14	CRIF finger	Operative
79.15	CRIF femur	Operative
79.16	CRIF tibia & fibula	Operative
79.17	CRIF metatarsal/tarsal	Operative

Code	Description	Operative Status
79.2	Open fracture reduction	Operative
79.22	Open red radius/ulna fx	Operative
79.26	Open red tibia/fib fx	Operative
79.3	Op fx reduction int fix	Operative
79.31	ORIF humerus	Operative
79.32	ORIF radius/ulna	Operative
79.33	ORIF carpals/metacarpals	Operative
79.34	ORIF finger	Operative
79.35	ORIF femur	Operative
79.36	ORIF tibia & fibula	Operative
79.37	ORIF metatarsal/tarsal	Operative
79.39	ORIF bone NEC X facial	Operative
79.4	CR sep epiphysis	Operative
79.5	Open red sep epiphysis	Operative
79.56	Op red sep epiph tib/fib	Operative
79.6	Open fx site debridement	Operative
79.62	Debride open fx rad/ulna	Operative
79.64	Debride open fx finger	Operative
79.65	Debride open femur fx	Operative
79.66	Debride opn fx tibia/fib	Operative
79.7	Closed red dislocation	Non-Operative
79.71	Clsd red shoulder disloc	Non-Operative
79.72	Clsd red elbow disloc	Non-Operative
79.75	Clsd red hip disloc	Non-Operative
79.76	Clsd red knee disloc	Non-Operative
79.8	Open red dislocation	Operative
79.85	Open red hip disloc	Operative
79.9	Bone injury op NOS	Operative
80.0	Arthrotomy rmvl prosth	Operative
80.05	Rmvl prosth hip inc	Operative
80.06	Rmvl prosth knee inc	Operative
80.1	Other arthrotomy	Operative
80.11	Arthrotomy NEC shoulder	Operative
80.12	Arthrotomy NEC elbow	Operative
80.14	Arthrotomy NEC hand/fing	Operative
80.15	Arthrotomy NEC hip	Operative
80.16	Arthrotomy NEC knee	Operative
80.17	Arthrotomy NEC ankle	Operative
80.2	Arthroscopy	Operative
80.21	Shoulder arthroscopy	Operative
80.26	Knee arthroscopy	Operative
80.3	Biopsy joint structure	Non-Operative
80.4	Jt capsule/LIG/cart div	Operative
80.46	Knee structure division	Operative
80.5	IV disc exc/destruction	Mixed (3, 1)
80.51	IV disc excision	Operative
80.59	IV disc destruction NEC	Operative
80.6	Exc knee semilunar cart	Operative
80.7	Synovectomy	Operative
80.76	Knee synovectomy	Operative
80.8	Oth exc/destr joint les	Operative
80.81	Exc/destr should les NEC	Operative
80.82	Exc/destr elbow les NEC	Operative
80.84	Exc/destr hand les NEC	Operative
80.85	Exc/destr hip lesion NEC	Operative
80.86	Exc/destr knee les NEC	Operative
80.87	Exc/destr ankle les NEC	Operative
80.9	Other joint excision	Operative
81.0	Spinal fusion	Operative
81.01	Atlas-axis spinal fusion	Operative
81.02	Ant cervical fusion NEC	Operative
81.03	Post cervical fusion NEC	Operative
81.04	Anterior dorsal fusion	Operative
81.05	Posterior dorsal fusion	Operative
81.06	Anterior lumbar fusion	Operative
81.07	Lat trans lumbar fusion	Operative
81.08	Posterior lumbar fusion	Operative
81.1	Foot & ankle arthrodesis	Operative
81.11	Ankle fusion	Operative
81.12	Triple arthrodesis	Operative
81.13	Subtalar fusion	Operative
81.2	Arthrodesis of oth joint	Operative
81.26	Metacarpocarpal fusion	Operative
81.3	Spinal refusion	Operative
81.32	Ant cerv refusion NEC	Operative
81.33	Post cerv refusion NEC	Operative
81.35	Post dorsal refusion	Operative
81.36	Ant lumbar refusion	Operative
81.37	Lat trans lumb refusion	Operative
81.38	Post lumbar refusion	Operative
81.4	Other low limb joint REP	Operative
81.44	Patellar stabilization	Operative
81.45	Cruciate LIG repair NEC	Operative
81.47	Repair of knee NEC	Operative
81.49	Repair of ankle NEC	Operative
81.5	Joint repl lower EXT	Operative
81.51	Total hip replacement	Operative
81.52	Partial hip replacement	Operative
81.53	Hip replacement revision	Operative
81.54	Total knee replacement	Operative
81.55	Knee replacement rev	Operative
81.56	Total ankle replacement	Operative
81.6	Oth spinal procedures	Operative
81.61	360 deg spinal FUS-1 inc	Operative
81.7	Hand/finger arthroplasty	Operative
81.75	Carpal/CMC arthroplasty	Operative
81.8	Should/elb arthroplasty	Operative
81.80	Total shoulder repl	Operative
81.81	Partial shoulder repl	Operative
81.82	Recur should disloc REP	Operative
81.83	Should arthroplasty NEC	Operative
81.84	Total elbow replacement	Operative
81.85	Elbow arthroplasty NEC	Operative
81.9	Other joint structure op	Mixed (7, 2)
81.91	Arthrocentesis	Non-Operative
81.92	Injection into joint	Non-Operative
81.97	Rev joint repl UE	Operative
82.0	Inc hand soft tissue	Mixed (4, 1)
82.01	Expl tendon sheath hand	Operative
82.09	Inc soft tissue hand NEC	Operative
82.1	Div hand musc/tend/fasc	Operative
82.2	Exc les hand soft tissue	Operative
82.3	Oth exc hand soft tissue	Operative
82.4	Suture hand soft tissue	Operative
82.44	Sut flexor tend hand NEC	Operative
82.45	Suture hand tendon NEC	Operative
82.5	Hand musc/tend transpl	Operative
82.6	Reconstruction of thumb	Operative
82.7	Plastic op hnd grft/impl	Operative
82.8	Other plastic ops hand	Operative
82.9	Oth hand soft tissue ops	Mixed (2, 5)
83.0	Inc musc/tend/fasc/bursa	Operative

Code	Description	Operative Status
83.02	Myotomy	Operative
83.03	Bursotomy	Operative
83.09	Soft tissue incision NEC	Operative
83.1	Musc/tend/fasc division	Operative
83.12	Adductor tenotomy of hip	Operative
83.13	Tenotomy NEC	Operative
83.14	Fasciotomy	Operative
83.2	Soft tissue dxtic px	Operative
83.21	Soft tissue biopsy	Operative
83.3	Exc lesion soft tissue	Operative
83.32	Exc muscle lesion	Operative
83.39	Exc les soft tissue NEC	Operative
83.4	Other exc musc/tend/fasc	Operative
83.42	Tenonectomy NEC	Operative
83.44	Fasciectomy NEC	Operative
83.45	Myectomy NEC	Operative
83.49	Soft tissue exc NEC	Operative
83.5	Bursectomy	Operative
83.6	Suture musc/tendon/fasc	Operative
83.61	Tendon sheath suture	Operative
83.63	Rotator cuff repair	Operative
83.64	Suture of tendon NEC	Operative
83.65	Muscle/fasc suture NEC	Operative
83.7	Muscle/tendon reconst	Operative
83.75	Tendon transf/transpl	Operative
83.8	Musc/tend/fasc op NEC	Operative
83.82	Muscle or fascia graft	Operative
83.84	Clubfoot release NEC	Operative
83.85	Change in m/t length NEC	Operative
83.86	Quadricepsplasty	Operative
83.88	Plastic ops tendon NEC	Operative
83.9	Other conn tissue ops	Mixed (4, 5)
83.94	Aspiration of bursa	Non-Operative
83.95	Soft tissue asp NEC	Non-Operative
83.96	Injection into bursa	Non-Operative
84.0	Amputation of upper limb	Operative
84.01	Finger amputation	Operative
84.1	Amputation of lower limb	Operative
84.11	Toe amputation	Operative
84.12	Amputation through foot	Operative
84.15	BK amputation NEC	Operative
84.17	Above knee amputation	Operative
84.2	Extremity reattachment	Operative
84.3	Amputation stump rev	Operative
84.4	Impl or fit prosth limb	Mixed (3, 6)
84.5	Impl oth MS dev & subst	Non-Operative
84.9	Other musculoskeletal op	Operative
85.0	Mastotomy	Non-Operative
85.1	Breast diagnostic px	Mixed (1, 2)
85.11	PERC breast biopsy	Non-Operative
85.12	Open biopsy of breast	Operative
85.2	Exc/destr breast tissue	Operative
85.21	Local exc breast lesion	Operative
85.22	Quadrant resect breast	Operative
85.23	Subtotal mastectomy	Operative
85.3	Red mammoplasty/ectomy	Operative
85.32	Bilat red mammoplasty	Operative
85.4	Mastectomy	Operative
85.41	Unilat simple mastectomy	Operative
85.42	Bilat simple mastectomy	Operative
85.43	Unilat exten simple MAST	Operative
85.44	Bilat exten simple MAST	Operative
85.45	Unilat RAD mastectomy	Operative
85.5	Augmentation mammoplasty	Mixed (3, 2)
85.54	Bilateral breast implant	Operative
85.6	Mastopexy	Operative
85.7	Total breast reconst	Operative
85.8	Other breast repair	Mixed (7, 1)
85.85	Breast muscle flap graft	Operative
85.9	Other breast operations	Mixed (5, 2)
85.91	Aspiration of breast	Non-Operative
85.94	Breast implant removal	Operative
85.96	Rmvl brst tiss expander	Operative
86.0	Incision skin & subcu	Mixed (1, 7)
86.01	Aspiration skin & subcu	Non-Operative
86.03	Incision pilonidal sinus	Non-Operative
86.04	Skin & subcu I&D NEC	Non-Operative
86.05	Inc w rmvl FB skin/subcu	Non-Operative
86.06	Insertion infusion pump	Operative
86.07	VAD insertion	Non-Operative
86.09	Skin/subcu incision NEC	Non-Operative
86.1	Skin & subcu dxtic px	Non-Operative
86.11	Skin & subcu biopsy	Non-Operative
86.2	Exc/destr skin lesion	Mixed (3, 5)
86.21	Excision pilonidal cyst	Operative
86.22	Exc debride WND/infect	Operative
86.23	Nail removal	Non-Operative
86.26	Lig dermal appendage	Non-Operative
86.27	Debridement of nail	Non-Operative
86.28	Nonexc debridement wound	Non-Operative
86.3	Loc exc/destr skin NEC	Non-Operative
86.4	RAD excision skin lesion	Operative
86.5	Skin/subcu suture/close	Non-Operative
86.59	Skin closure NEC	Non-Operative
86.6	Free skin graft	Mixed (8, 1)
86.62	Hand skin graft NEC	Operative
86.63	Fthick skin graft NEC	Operative
86.66	Homograft to skin	Operative
86.67	Dermal regenerative grft	Operative
86.69	Free skin graft NEC	Operative
86.7	Pedicle grafts or flaps	Operative
86.70	Pedicle/flap graft NOS	Operative
86.72	Pedicle graft adv	Operative
86.74	Attach pedicle graft NEC	Operative
86.75	Rev pedicle/flap graft	Operative
86.8	Other skin & subcu REP	Operative
86.82	Facial rhytidectomy	Operative
86.83	Size red plastic op	Operative
86.89	Skin REP & reconst NEC	Operative
86.9	Other skin & subcu ops	Mixed (2, 2)
87.0	Head/neck sft tiss x-ray	Non-Operative
87.02	Brain/skull contr x-ray	Non-Operative
87.03	CAT scan head	Non-Operative
87.1	Other head/neck x-ray	Non-Operative
87.2	X-ray of spine	Non-Operative
87.21	Contrast myelogram	Non-Operative
87.3	Thorax soft tissue x-ray	Non-Operative
87.39	Thor soft tiss x-ray NEC	Non-Operative
87.4	Other x-ray of thorax	Non-Operative
87.41	CAT scan thorax	Non-Operative
87.44	Routine chest x-ray	Non-Operative
87.49	Chest x-ray NEC	Non-Operative

Code	Description	Operative Status
87.5	Biliary tract x-ray	Mixed (1, 4)
87.51	PERC hepat cholangiogram	Non-Operative
87.54	Cholangiogram NEC	Non-Operative
87.6	Oth digestive syst x-ray	Non-Operative
87.61	Barium swallow	Non-Operative
87.62	Upper GI series	Non-Operative
87.64	Lower GI series	Non-Operative
87.7	X-ray of urinary system	Non-Operative
87.71	CAT scan of kidney	Non-Operative
87.73	IV pyelogram	Non-Operative
87.74	Retrograde pyelogram	Non-Operative
87.76	Retro cystourethrogram	Non-Operative
87.77	Cystogram NEC	Non-Operative
87.79	Urinary system x-ray NEC	Non-Operative
87.8	Female genital x-ray	Non-Operative
87.9	Male genital x-ray	Non-Operative
88.0	Abd soft tissue x-ray	Non-Operative
88.01	Abdomen CAT scan	Non-Operative
88.1	Other abdominal x-ray	Non-Operative
88.11	Pelv dye contrast x-ray	Non-Operative
88.19	Abdominal x-ray NEC	Non-Operative
88.2	EXT & pelvis skel x-ray	Non-Operative
88.3	Other x-ray	Non-Operative
88.38	CAT scan NEC	Non-Operative
88.4	Contrast arteriography	Non-Operative
88.41	Cerebral arteriogram	Non-Operative
88.42	Contrast aortogram	Non-Operative
88.43	Pulmonary arteriogram	Non-Operative
88.44	Thor arteriogram NEC	Non-Operative
88.45	Renal arteriogram	Non-Operative
88.47	Abd arteriogram NEC	Non-Operative
88.48	Contrast arteriogram-leg	Non-Operative
88.49	Contrast arteriogram NEC	Non-Operative
88.5	Contrast angiocardiogram	Non-Operative
88.51	VC angiocardiogram	Non-Operative
88.53	Lt heart angiocardiogram	Non-Operative
88.56	Cor arteriogram-2 cath	Non-Operative
88.57	Coronary arteriogram NEC	Non-Operative
88.6	Phlebography	Non-Operative
88.66	Contrast phlebogram-leg	Non-Operative
88.67	Contrast phlebogram NEC	Non-Operative
88.7	Diagnostic ultrasound	Non-Operative
88.71	Head & neck ultrasound	Non-Operative
88.72	Heart ultrasound	Non-Operative
88.73	Thorax ultrasound NEC	Non-Operative
88.74	Digest system ultrasound	Non-Operative
88.75	Urinary syst ultrasound	Non-Operative
88.76	Abd & retroperiton US	Non-Operative
88.77	Periph vasc ultrasound	Non-Operative
88.78	Gravid uterus ultrasound	Non-Operative
88.79	Ultrasound NEC	Non-Operative
88.8	Thermography	Non-Operative
88.9	Other diagnostic imaging	Non-Operative
88.91	Brain & brain stem MRI	Non-Operative
88.92	Chest & myocardium MRI	Non-Operative
88.93	Spinal canal MRI	Non-Operative
88.94	Musculoskeletal MRI	Non-Operative
88.95	Pelvis/pros/bladder MRI	Non-Operative
88.97	MRI site NEC & NOS	Non-Operative
89.0	Dx interview/consul/exam	Non-Operative
89.03	Compr interview/eval	Non-Operative
89.04	Interview & eval NEC	Non-Operative
89.06	Limited consultation	Non-Operative
89.07	Comprehensive consult	Non-Operative
89.08	Consultation NEC	Non-Operative
89.1	Nervous system exams	Non-Operative
89.14	Electroencephalogram	Non-Operative
89.17	Polysomnogram	Non-Operative
89.19	Video/telemetric EEG MON	Non-Operative
89.2	GU system-examination	Non-Operative
89.22	Cystometrogram	Non-Operative
89.26	Gynecologic examination	Non-Operative
89.3	Other examinations	Non-Operative
89.37	Vital capacity	Non-Operative
89.38	Respiratory measure NEC	Non-Operative
89.39	Nonoperative exams NEC	Non-Operative
89.4	Pacer/card stress test	Non-Operative
89.41	Treadmill stress test	Non-Operative
89.44	CV stress test NEC	Non-Operative
89.45	Pacemaker rate check	Non-Operative
89.5	Other cardiac funct test	Non-Operative
89.50	Ambulatory card monitor	Non-Operative
89.51	Rhythm electrocardiogram	Non-Operative
89.52	Electrocardiogram	Non-Operative
89.54	ECG monitoring	Non-Operative
89.59	Nonop card/vasc exam NEC	Non-Operative
89.6	Circulatory monitoring	Non-Operative
89.62	CVP monitoring	Non-Operative
89.64	PA wedge monitoring	Non-Operative
89.65	Arterial bld gas measure	Non-Operative
89.68	Cardiac output MON NEC	Non-Operative
89.7	General physical exam	Non-Operative
89.8	Autopsy	Non-Operative
90.0	Micro exam-nervous syst	Non-Operative
90.1	Micro exam-endocrine	Non-Operative
90.2	Micro exam-eye	Non-Operative
90.3	Micro exam-ENT/larynx	Non-Operative
90.4	Micro exam-lower resp	Non-Operative
90.5	Micro exam-blood	Non-Operative
90.52	Culture-blood	Non-Operative
90.59	Micro exam NEC-blood	Non-Operative
90.6	Micro exam-spleen/marrow	Non-Operative
90.7	Micro exam-lymph system	Non-Operative
90.8	Micro exam-upper GI	Non-Operative
90.9	Micro exam-lower GI	Non-Operative
91.0	Micro exam-bil/pancreas	Non-Operative
91.1	Micro exam-peritoneum	Non-Operative
91.2	Micro exam-upper urinary	Non-Operative
91.3	Micro exam-lower urinary	Non-Operative
91.4	Micro exam-female genit	Non-Operative
91.5	Micro exam-MS/jt fluid	Non-Operative
91.6	Micro exam-integument	Non-Operative
91.7	Micro exam-op wound	Non-Operative
91.8	Micro exam NEC	Non-Operative
91.9	Micro exam NOS	Non-Operative
92.0	Isotope scan & function	Non-Operative
92.02	Liver scan/isotope funct	Non-Operative
92.03	Renal scan/isotope study	Non-Operative
92.04	GI scan & isotope study	Non-Operative
92.05	CV scan/isotope study	Non-Operative
92.1	Other radioisotope scan	Non-Operative
92.14	Bone scan	Non-Operative

Code	Description	Operative Status
92.15	Pulmonary scan	Non-Operative
92.18	Total body scan	Non-Operative
92.19	Scan of site NEC	Non-Operative
92.2	Ther radiology & nu med	Mixed (1, 8)
92.23	Isotope teleradiotherapy	Non-Operative
92.24	Photon teleradiotherapy	Non-Operative
92.26	Partic teleradioTx NEC	Non-Operative
92.27	Radioactive element impl	Operative
92.28	Isotope inject/instill	Non-Operative
92.29	Radiotherapeutic px NEC	Non-Operative
92.3	Stereotactic radiosurg	Non-Operative
92.32	Multi-source photon surg	Non-Operative
93.0	Dxtic physical Tx	Non-Operative
93.01	Functional PT evaluation	Non-Operative
93.08	Electromyography	Non-Operative
93.1	PT exercises	Non-Operative
93.16	Joint mobilization NEC	Non-Operative
93.2	Oth PT MS manipulation	Non-Operative
93.22	Amb & gait training	Non-Operative
93.26	Manual rupt joint adhes	Non-Operative
93.3	Other PT therapeutic px	Non-Operative
93.32	Whirlpool treatment	Non-Operative
93.38	Combined PT NOS	Non-Operative
93.39	Physical therapy NEC	Non-Operative
93.4	Skeletal & oth traction	Non-Operative
93.46	Limb skin traction NEC	Non-Operative
93.5	Oth immob/press/WND attn	Non-Operative
93.51	Plaster jacket appl	Non-Operative
93.53	Cast application NEC	Non-Operative
93.54	Application of splint	Non-Operative
93.56	Pressure dressing appl	Non-Operative
93.57	Appl wound dressing NEC	Non-Operative
93.59	Immob/press/WND attn NEC	Non-Operative
93.6	Osteopathic manipulation	Non-Operative
93.67	OMT NEC	Non-Operative
93.7	Speech/read/blind rehab	Non-Operative
93.75	Speech therapy NEC	Non-Operative
93.8	Other rehab therapy	Non-Operative
93.81	Recreational therapy	Non-Operative
93.83	Occupational therapy	Non-Operative
93.89	Rehabilitation NEC	Non-Operative
93.9	Respiratory therapy	Non-Operative
93.90	CPAP	Non-Operative
93.91	IPPB	Non-Operative
93.93	Nonmech resuscitation	Non-Operative
93.94	Nebulizer therapy	Non-Operative
93.95	Hyperbaric oxygenation	Non-Operative
93.96	Oxygen enrichment NEC	Non-Operative
93.99	Respiratory therapy NEC	Non-Operative
94.0	Psych eval & testing	Non-Operative
94.1	Psych eval/consult	Non-Operative
94.11	Psych mental status	Non-Operative
94.19	Psych interview/eval NEC	Non-Operative
94.2	Psych somatotherapy	Non-Operative
94.22	Lithium therapy	Non-Operative
94.23	Neuroleptic therapy	Non-Operative
94.25	Psych drug therapy NEC	Non-Operative
94.27	Electroshock therapy NEC	Non-Operative
94.29	Psych somatotherapy NEC	Non-Operative
94.3	Individual psychotherapy	Non-Operative
94.35	Crisis intervention	Non-Operative
94.38	Supp verbal psychTx	Non-Operative
94.39	Individual psychTx NEC	Non-Operative
94.4	Oth psychTx/counselling	Non-Operative
94.44	Group therapy NEC	Non-Operative
94.49	Counselling NEC	Non-Operative
94.5	Referral psych rehab	Non-Operative
94.6	Alcohol/drug rehab/detox	Non-Operative
94.61	Alcohol rehabilitation	Non-Operative
94.62	Alcohol detoxification	Non-Operative
94.63	Alcohol rehab/detox	Non-Operative
94.64	Drug rehabilitation	Non-Operative
94.65	Drug detoxification	Non-Operative
94.66	Drug rehab/detox	Non-Operative
94.67	ALC/drug rehabilitation	Non-Operative
94.68	ALC/drug detoxification	Non-Operative
94.69	ALC/drug rehab/detox	Non-Operative
95.0	Gen/subjective eye exam	Mixed (1, 7)
95.1	Form & struct eye exam	Non-Operative
95.2	Objective funct eye test	Non-Operative
95.3	Special vision services	Non-Operative
95.4	Nonop hearing procedure	Non-Operative
95.41	Audiometry	Non-Operative
95.42	Clinical hearing test	Non-Operative
95.43	Audiological evaluation	Non-Operative
95.46	Auditory & vest test NEC	Non-Operative
95.47	Hearing examination NOS	Non-Operative
95.49	Nonop hearing px NEC	Non-Operative
96.0	Nonop GI & resp intub	Non-Operative
96.04	Insert endotracheal tube	Non-Operative
96.05	Resp tract intub NEC	Non-Operative
96.07	Insert gastric tube NEC	Non-Operative
96.08	Insert intestinal tube	Non-Operative
96.09	Insert rectal tube	Non-Operative
96.1	Other nonop insertion	Non-Operative
96.2	Nonop dilation & manip	Non-Operative
96.27	Manual reduction hernia	Non-Operative
96.3	Nonop GI irrig/instill	Non-Operative
96.33	Gastric lavage	Non-Operative
96.35	Gastric gavage	Non-Operative
96.38	Impacted feces removal	Non-Operative
96.39	Transanal enema NEC	Non-Operative
96.4	Digest/GU irrig/instill	Non-Operative
96.48	Indwell cath irrig NEC	Non-Operative
96.49	GU instillation NEC	Non-Operative
96.5	Other nonop irrig/clean	Non-Operative
96.52	Irrigation of ear	Non-Operative
96.56	Bronch/trach lavage NEC	Non-Operative
96.59	Wound irrigation NEC	Non-Operative
96.6	Enteral nutrition	Non-Operative
96.7	Cont mech vent NEC	Non-Operative
96.70	Cont mech vent-time NOS	Non-Operative
96.71	Cont mech vent-<96 hours	Non-Operative
96.72	Cont mech vent->95 hours	Non-Operative
97.0	GI appliance replacement	Non-Operative
97.02	Repl gastrostomy tube	Non-Operative
97.03	Repl small intest tube	Non-Operative
97.05	Repl panc/biliary stent	Non-Operative
97.1	Repl MS appliance	Non-Operative
97.2	Other nonop replacement	Non-Operative
97.23	Repl TRACH tube	Non-Operative
97.3	Rmvl ther dev-head/neck	Non-Operative

Code	Description	Operative Status
97.4	Rmvl thor ther device	Non-Operative
97.49	Rmvl dev from thorax NEC	Non-Operative
97.5	Nonop rmvl GI ther dev	Non-Operative
97.51	Rmvl gastrostomy tube	Non-Operative
97.6	Nonop rmvl urin ther dev	Non-Operative
97.62	Rmvl ureteral drain	Non-Operative
97.7	Rmvl ther dev genit syst	Non-Operative
97.8	Oth nonop rmvl ther dev	Non-Operative
97.89	Rmvl therapeutic dev NEC	Non-Operative
98.0	Rmvl intralum GI FB	Non-Operative
98.02	Rmvl intralum esoph FB	Non-Operative
98.1	Rmvl intralum FB NEC	Non-Operative
98.2	Rmvl oth FB w/o inc	Non-Operative
98.5	ESWL	Non-Operative
98.51	Renal/ureter/blad ESWL	Non-Operative
99.0	Blood transfusion	Non-Operative
99.01	Exchange transfusion	Non-Operative
99.03	Whole blood transfus NEC	Non-Operative
99.04	Packed cell transfusion	Non-Operative
99.05	Platelet transfusion	Non-Operative
99.06	Coag factor transfusion	Non-Operative
99.07	Serum transfusion NEC	Non-Operative
99.09	Transfusion NEC	Non-Operative
99.1	Inject/infuse ther subst	Non-Operative
99.10	Inject thrombolytic	Non-Operative
99.11	Inject Rh immune glob	Non-Operative
99.14	Inject gamma globulin	Non-Operative
99.15	Parenteral nutrition	Non-Operative
99.17	Inject insulin	Non-Operative
99.18	Inject electrolytes	Non-Operative
99.19	Inject anticoagulant	Non-Operative
99.2	Oth inject ther subst	Non-Operative
99.20	Inject platelet inhib	Non-Operative
99.21	Inject antibiotic	Non-Operative
99.22	Inject anti-infect NEC	Non-Operative
99.23	Inject steroid	Non-Operative
99.25	Inject CA chemo agent	Non-Operative
99.28	Inject BRM/antineo agent	Non-Operative
99.29	Inject/infuse NEC	Non-Operative
99.3	Prophyl vacc-bact dis	Non-Operative
99.38	Tetanus toxoid admin	Non-Operative
99.4	Viral immunization	Non-Operative
99.5	Other immunization	Non-Operative
99.52	Influenza vaccination	Non-Operative
99.55	Vaccination NEC	Non-Operative
99.59	Vacc/inoculation NEC	Non-Operative
99.6	Card rhythm conversion	Non-Operative
99.60	CPR NOS	Non-Operative
99.61	Atrial cardioversion	Non-Operative
99.62	Heart countershock NEC	Non-Operative
99.69	Cardiac rhythm conv NEC	Non-Operative
99.7	Ther apheresis/admin NEC	Non-Operative
99.71	Ther plasmapheresis	Non-Operative
99.74	Ther plateletpheresis	Non-Operative
99.8	Misc physical procedures	Non-Operative
99.82	UV light therapy	Non-Operative
99.83	Phototherapy NEC	Non-Operative
99.84	Isolation	Non-Operative
99.88	Ther photopheresis	Non-Operative
99.9	Other misc procedures	Non-Operative
99.99	Misc procedures NEC	Non-Operative:

GLOSSARY

Average Length of Stay: Calculated from the admission and discharge dates by counting the day of admission as the first day; the day of discharge is not included. The average is figured by adding the lengths of stay for each patient and then dividing by the total number of patients. Patients discharged on the day of admission are counted as staying one day in the calculation of average length of stay. Patients with stays over 99 days (>99) are excluded from this calculation.

Distribution Percentiles: A length of stay percentile for a stratified group of patients is determined by arranging the individual patient stays from low to high. Counting up from the lowest stay to the point where one-half of the patients have been counted yields the value of the 50th percentile. Counting one-tenth of the total patients gives the 10th percentile, and so on. The 10th, 25th, 50th, 75th, 90th, 95th, and 99th percentiles of stay are displayed in days. If, for example, the 10th percentile for a group of patients is four, then 10 percent of the patients stayed four days or less. The 50th percentile is the median. Any percentile with a value of 100 days or more is listed as >99. Patients who were hospitalized more than 99 days (>99) are not included in the total patients, average stay, and variance categories. The percentiles, however, do include these patients.

Multiple Diagnoses Patients: Patients are classified in the multiple diagnoses category if they had at least one valid secondary diagnosis in addition to the principal one. The following codes are not considered valid secondary diagnoses for purposes of this classification:

1. Manifestation codes (conditions that evolved from underlying diseases [etiology] and are in italics in ICD-9-CM, Volume 1)
2. Codes V27.0-V27.9 (outcome of delivery)
3. E Codes (external causes of injury and poisoning)

Observed Patients: The number of patients in the stratified group as reported in Solucient's projected inpatient database. Patients with stays longer than 99 days (>99) are not included. This data element does not use the projection factor.

Operated Patients: In the diagnosis tables, operated patients are those who had at least one procedure that is classified by CMS as an operating room procedure. CMS physician panels classify every ICD-9-CM procedure code according to whether the procedure would in most hospitals be performed in the operating room. This classification system differs slightly from that used in Length of Stay publications published previous to 1995, in which patients were categorized as operated if any of their procedures were labeled as Uniform Hospital Discharge Data Set (UHDDS) Class 1. Appendix C contains a list of procedure codes included in this book and their CMS-defined operative status.

Variance: A measure of the spread of the data around the average, the variance shows how much individual patient lengths of stay from the average. The smallest variance is zero, indicating that all lengths of stay are equal. In tables in which there is a large variance and the patient group size is relatively small, the average stay may appear high. This sometimes occurs when one or two patients with long hospitalizations fall into the group.

ALPHABETIC INDEX

This index provides an alphabetical listing by descriptive title for all chapter ICD-9-CM diagnoses and procedures codes included in the book. For ease of use, titles are grouped into major classification chapters (i.e., *Diseases of the Circulatory System*). These classification chapters are listed for your reference below.

ICD-9-CM Classification Chapters

Diagnosis Chapters

Infectious and Parasitic Diseases	Codes 001–139
Neoplasms	Codes 140–239
Endocrine, Nutritional and Metabolic Diseases, and Immunity Disorders	Codes 240–279
Diseases of the Blood and Blood-Forming Organs	Codes 280–289
Mental Disorders	Codes 290–319
Diseases of the Nervous System and Sense Organs	Codes 320–389
Diseases of the Circulatory System	Codes 390–459
Diseases of the Respiratory System	Codes 460–519
Diseases of the Digestive System	Codes 520–579
Diseases of the Genitourinary System	Codes 580–629
Complications of Pregnancy, Childbirth, and the Puerperium	Codes 630–677
Diseases of the Skin and Subcutaneous Tissue	Codes 680–709
Diseases of the Musculoskeletal System and Connective Tissue	Codes 710–739
Congenital Anomalies	Codes 740–759
Certain Conditions Originating in the Perinatal Period	Codes 760–779
Symptoms, Signs, and Ill-Defined Conditions	Codes 780–799
Injury and Poisoning	Codes 800–999
Supplementary Classification of Factors Influencing Health Status and Contact with Health Services	Codes V01–V83

Procedure Chapters

Procedures and Interventions Not Elsewhere Classified	Codes 00
Operations on the Nervous System	Codes 01–05
Operations on the Endocrine System	Codes 06–07
Operations on the Eye	Codes 08–16
Operations on the Ear	Codes 18–20
Operations on the Nose, Mouth, and Pharynx	Codes 21–29
Operations on the Respiratory System	Codes 30–34
Operations on the Cardiovascular System	Codes 35–39
Operations on the Hemic and Lymphatic System	Codes 40–41
Operations on the Digestive System	Codes 42–54
Operations on the Urinary System	Codes 55–59
Operations on the Male Genital Organs	Codes 60–64
Operations on the Female Genital Organs	Codes 65–71
Obstetrical Procedures	Codes 72–75
Operations on the Musculoskeletal System	Codes 76–84
Operations on the Integumentary System	Codes 85–86
Miscellaneous Diagnostic and Therapeutic Procedures	Codes 87–99

Diagnosis Codes

Diagnosis Codes

Code	Description	Page
216	Benign skin neoplasm	118
215	Benign soft tissue neopl	118
226	Benign thyroid neoplasm	125
188	Bladder CA	92
170	Bone & articular cart CA	81
191	Brain CA	97
233	Breast/GU CA in situ	129
234	CA in situ NEC & NOS	130
199	CA site NOS	107
180	Cervix uteri CA	87
153	Colon CA	66
230	Digestive CA in situ	128
150	Esophagus CA	62
190	Eye CA	96
174	Female breast CA	83
235	GI/resp unc behav neopl	130
236	GU unc behav neopl	131
156	Gallbladder & duct CA	72
143	Gum CA	59
228	Hemangioma/lymphangioma	126
201	Hodgkin's disease	109
148	Hypopharynx CA	61
176	Kaposi's sarcoma	87
189	Kidney/urinary CA NEC	95
161	Larynx CA	77
208	Leukemia NOS cell type	114
140	Lip CA	58
214	Lipoma	117
155	Liver & intrahep duct CA	71
204	Lymphoid leukemia	112
200	Lymphosarc/reticulosarc	108
142	Major salivary gland CA	59
175	Male breast CA	86
206	Monocytic leukemia	114
145	Mouth CA NEC & NOS	60
144	Mouth floor CA	60
203	Multiple myeloma et al	111
205	Myeloid leukemia	113
160	Nasal/ME/sinus CA	76
147	Nasopharynx CA	61
146	Oropharynx CA	60
219	Oth benign uterus neopl	121
159	Oth digestive organ CA	76
194	Oth endocrine gland CA	99
202	Oth mal lymph/hist neopl	109
195	Other & ill-defined CA	100
192	Other Nervous system CA	99
184	Other female genital CA	90
149	Other oropharynx CA	62
165	Other resp/intrathor CA	81
198	Other secondary CA	105
173	Other skin CA	83
207	Other specified leukemia	114
183	Ovary/uter adnexa CA NEC	90
157	Pancreas CA	73
187	Penis/male genital CA	92
158	Peritoneum CA	75
181	Placenta CA	89
163	Pleura CA	80
185	Prostate CA	91
154	Rectum & anus CA	70
231	Respiratory CA in situ	128
197	Secondary resp/digest CA	102
232	Skin CA in situ	129
172	Skin malignant melanoma	82
152	Small intestine CA	65
171	Soft tissue CA	82
151	Stomach CA	63
186	Testis CA	91
164	Thymus/heart/mediast CA	80
193	Thyroid CA	99
141	Tongue CA	58
162	Trachea/bronchus/lung CA	78
238	Unc behav neopl NEC&NOS	132
237	Unc neopl endocr/nerv	132
239	Unspecified neoplasm	133
218	Uterine leiomyoma	119
179	Uterus CA NOS	87
182	Uterus body CA	89

ENDOCRINE, NUTRITIONAL, AND METABOLIC DISEASES, AND IMMUNITY DISORDERS (240-279)

Code	Description	Page
270	AA metabolism disorder	158
244	Acquired hypothyroidism	137
255	Adrenal gland disorders	152
267	Ascorbic acid deficiency	157
266	B-complex deficiencies	156
243	Congenital hypothyroidsm	137
250	Diabetes mellitus	139
254	Diseases of thymus gland	152
271	Disord COH & metabolism	158
279	Disord immune mechanism	167
272	Disord lipoid metabol	158
275	Disord mineral metabol	160
276	Fluid/electrolyte disord	161
274	Gout	159
260	Kwashiorkor	154
277	Metabol disord NEC & NOS	164
241	Nontoxic nodular goiter	135
261	Nutritional marasmus	154
278	Obesity & hyperal NEC	166
246	Oth disorders of thyroid	139
259	Oth endocrine disorders	154
269	Oth nutrition deficiency	157
251	Oth pancreatic disorder	149
262	Oth severe malnutrition	155
256	Ovarian dysfunction	153
252	Parathyroid disorder	150
253	Pituitary gland disord	151
273	Plasma prot metabol pbx	159
258	Polyglandular dysfunct	153
263	Prot-cal malnut NEC&NOS	155
240	Simple & NOS goiter	134
257	Testicular dysfunction	153
265	Thiamine & niacin def	156
245	Thyroiditis	138
242	Thyrotoxicosis	136
264	Vitamin A deficiency	156
268	Vitamin D deficiency	157

DISEASES OF THE BLOOD AND BLOOD-FORMING ORGANS (280-289)

Code	Description	Page
283	Acq hemolytic anemia	171
285	Anemia NEC & NOS	173
284	Aplastic anemia	172
286	Coagulation defects	175
282	Hered hemolytic anemia	169
280	Iron deficiency anemias	167
289	Other blood disease	179
281	Other deficiency anemia	168
287	Purpura & oth hemor cond	176
288	WBC disorders	178

MENTAL DISORDERS (290-319)

Code	Description	Page
308	Acute reaction to stress	215
309	Adjustment reaction	216
296	Affective psychoses	194

Diagnosis Codes

DISEASES OF THE NERVOUS SYSTEM AND SENSE ORGANS (320-389)

DISEASES OF THE CIRCULATORY SYSTEM (390-459)

Diagnosis Codes

DISEASE OF THE RESPIRATORY SYSTEM (460-519)

DISEASES OF THE DIGESTIVE SYSTEM (520-579)

DISEASES OF THE GENITOURINARY SYSTEM (580-629)

Diagnosis Codes

Diagnosis Codes

Code	Description	Page
725	Polymyalgia rheumatica	605
714	RA & inflam polyarthrop	585
721	Spondylosis et al	595
CONGENITAL ANOMALIES (740-759)		
740	Anencephalus et al	624
745	Card septal close anomal	626
758	Chromosomal anomalies	635
749	Cleft palate & cleft lip	630
754	Cong MS deformities	633
744	Cong anomal ear/face/nk	626
759	Cong anomalies NEC & NOS	636
757	Cong skin anomalies	635
743	Congenital eye anomaly	626
752	Genital organ anomalies	632
751	Oth anom digestive syst	631
747	Oth cong circ syst anom	628
755	Oth cong limb anomaly	633
742	Oth nerv syst anomalies	625
756	Other MS anomalies	634
746	Other cong anomaly heart	628
750	Other upper GI anomaly	630
748	Respiratory syst anomaly	629
741	Spina bifida	625
753	Urinary system anomalies	632
CERTAIN CONDITIONS ORIGINATING IN THE PERINATAL PERIOD (760-779)		
767	Birth trauma	639
762	Comp plac/cord aff NB	637
772	Fetal/neonatal hemor	642
776	Hematological dis of NB	645
778	Integument/temp cond NB	646
768	Intrauterine asphyxia	639
766	Long gestation/high BWT	638
760	MTL cond aff fetus/NB	636
761	Maternal comp aff NB	636
775	NB endocr/metabol dis	645
773	NB hemoly dis-isoimmun	643
770	Oth NB respiratory cond	640
763	Oth comp del aff NB	637
779	Oth perinatal condition	647
774	Other perinatal jaundice	643
777	Perinatal GI system dis	646
771	Perinatal infection	641
769	Resp distress syndrome	639
765	Short gestation/low BWT	638
764	Slow fetal growth/malnut	637
SYMPTOMS, SIGNS, AND ILL-DEFINED CONDITIONS (780-799)		
793	Abn find-body struct NOS	673
792	Abn find-oth body subst	672
795	Abn hist/immun findings	674
790	Abnormal blood findings	671
794	Abnormal function study	673
791	Abnormal urine findings	672
785	Cardiovascular syst Sx	658
787	GI system symptoms	663
780	General symptoms	647
781	Nervous/MS syst symptoms	651
783	Nutrit/metabol/devel Sx	654
789	Oth abdomen/pelvis Sx	667
799	Oth ill-def morb/mort	675
796	Other abnormal findings	674
786	Resp syst/oth chest Sx	659
797	Senility w/o psychosis	675
782	Skin & integument NEC Sx	653
798	Sudden death cause unkn	675
784	Sx involving head/neck	656
788	Urinary system symptoms	666
INJURY AND POISONING (800-999)		
902	Abd/pelvic vessel injury	757
980	Alcohol toxicity	798
845	Ankle & foot sprain	723
824	Ankle fracture	711
903	Arm blood vessel injury	758
847	Back sprain NEC & NOS	725
904	Blood vessel injury NEC	758
948	Burn by % body surface	777
943	Burn of arm	775
940	Burn of eye & adnexa	774
944	Burn of hand & wrist	775
941	Burn of head/face/neck	774
947	Burn of internal organs	776
945	Burn of leg	776
946	Burn of multiple site	776
942	Burn of trunk	775
949	Burn unspecified	777
814	Carpal fracture	699
851	Cerebral lac/contusion	728
995	Certain adverse eff NEC	804
810	Clavicle fracture	690
999	Comp medical care NEC	823
850	Concussion	726
921	Contusion eye & adnexa	764
920	Contusion head X eye	763
924	Contusion leg & oth site	766
922	Contusion of trunk	764
923	Contusion of upper limb	765
925	Crush inj face/scalp/nk	768
928	Crush injury lower limb	769
926	Crush injury trunk	768
927	Crush injury upper limb	768
839	Dislocation NEC	720
837	Dislocation of ankle	719
834	Dislocation of finger	718
838	Dislocation of foot	720
835	Dislocation of hip	718
836	Dislocation of knee	719
958	Early comp of trauma	780
991	Eff reduced temperature	802
994	Effect ext cause NEC	803
992	Effect of heat/light	803
993	Effects of air pressure	803
990	Effects radiation NOS	802
841	Elbow & forearm sprain	721
832	Elbow dislocation	717
871	Eyeball open wound	743
939	FB in GU tract	773
937	FB in anus & rectum	773
938	FB in digestive syst NOS	773
931	FB in ear	770
930	FB in eye	769
936	FB in intestine & colon	772
935	FB in mouth/esoph/stom	771
932	FB in nose	770
933	FB in pharynx & larynx	770
934	FB in trach/bronch/lung	771
829	Fracture NOS	716
818	Fracture arm mult/NOS	701
820	Fracture neck of femur	701
802	Fracture of face bones	679
809	Fracture of trunk bones	690
826	Fracture phalanges foot	715
816	Fracture phalanges hand	699

Diagnosis Codes

SUPPLEMENTARY CLASSIFICATION OF FACTORS INFLUENCING HEALTH STATUS (V01-V83)

Diagnosis Codes

Procedure Codes

Procedure Codes

Procedure Codes

Procedure Codes

OPERATIONS ON THE URINARY SYSTEM (55-59)

OPERATIONS ON THE MALE GENITAL ORGANS (60-64)

Procedure Codes

Procedure Codes

Procedure Codes